Handbook of
Theories of
Social Psychology

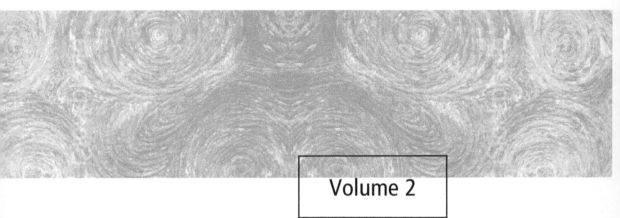

Volume 2

Handbook of
Theories of
Social Psychology

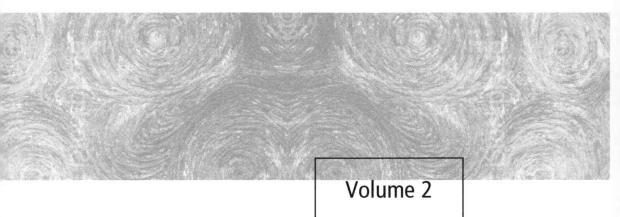

Volume 2

Edited by
Paul A. M. Van Lange,
Arie W. Kruglanski,
and E. Tory Higgins

Los Angeles | London | New Delhi
Singapore | Washington DC

Contents

VOLUME 1

Notes on Editors and Contributors

Jean-Claude Abric is emeritus professor of social psychology at Aix-Marseille University (France) where he directed the Social Psychology Laboratory for 16 years. He initiated one of the major social representation theory frameworks: the "central core theory." Author of many books on social representations, his research interests include group creativity and social communication. His most recent and famous volumes are *Pratiques sociales et représentations* [*Social Practices and Representations*] (PUF, 1994), *Méthodes d'étude des représentations sociales* [*Methods for the Study of Social Representations*] (ERES, 2003), and *Psychologie de la communication, théories et méthodes* [*The Psychology of Communication, Theories and Methods*] (Armand Colin, 1996).

Christopher R. Agnew is professor and head of the department of psychological sciences at Purdue University. He received his PhD in social psychology from the University of North Carolina at Chapel Hill. His research focuses on close, interpersonal relationships. He has published widely, authoring more than 60 articles and chapters. His research has received funding from the National Institutes of Health and the Robert Wood Johnson Foundation. Dr. Agnew serves on the editorial boards for the *Journal of Personality and Social Psychology, Personality and Social Psychology Bulletin,* and *Personal Relationships*. He was the recipient of the Early Career Award from the Relationships Researchers Interest Group of the Society for Personality and Social Psychology and is an elected Fellow of the Association for Psychological Science and the American Psychological Association. He is currently President-Elect of the International Association for Relationship Research.

Ximena B. Arriaga is associate professor of psychological sciences at Purdue University. Her doctoral degree is from the University of North Carolina at Chapel Hill, in social psychology. Her primary areas of research are relationship commitment, uncertainty, and partner aggression. Her research has been funded by the National Institute of Mental Health and contributes to the relationships and intimate partner violence literatures. She has served as an associate editor for *Personal Relationships* and for *Journal of Social and Personal Relationships*, as well as consulting editor for *Journal of Personality and Social Psychology*. In addition, Dr. Arriaga has received several teaching awards.

Roy F. Baumeister is Eppes Eminent Scholar and professor of psychology at the Florida State University. He is the author of over 450 scientific publications, including 27 books, and his works are cited over 1,000 times each year in scientific journals. He seeks to understand the basic, encompassing truths of the human condition, and towards that end his research has covered such topics as self and identity, belongingness and rejection, self-control, evil and violence, sexuality, gender relations, human nature, decision making, how people find meaning in life, consciousness, and free will.

Leonard Berkowitz is currently Vilas Research Professor Emeritus in the Department of Psychology at the University of Wisconsin–Madison. He received his PhD in psychology from the University of Michigan in 1951. He originated the Cognitive Neoassociation Model of aggressive behavior, which was created to help explain instances of aggression that the Frustration-Aggression Hypothesis could not account for. His research includes *American Psychologist* (1990), *Psychological Bulletin* (1989), *Journal of Personality and Social Psychology* (1987), *Psychological Bulletin* (1984). He has also been awarded as APA Distinguished Scientific Award for the Applications of Psychology, SESP Distinguished Scientist Award, and APS James McKeen Cattell Fellow Award.

Marilynn B. Brewer is Professor Emeritus of psychology at the Ohio State University and a visiting professor of psychology at the University of New South Wales in Sydney, Australia. Her primary areas of research are the study of social identity, collective decision making, and intergroup relations and she is the author of numerous research articles and books in this area. Dr. Brewer is past-president of the American Psychological Society and recipient of the 2003 Distinguished Scientist award from the Society of Experimental Social Psychology. In 2004 she was elected as a Fellow of the American Academy of Arts and Sciences and in 2007 she received the Distinguished Scientific Contribution award from the American Psychological Association.

Margaret S. Clark is professor at Yale University and, prior to that, was a professor at Carnegie-Mellon University for many years. She is a social psychologist whose research focuses on relationship processes (with a particular interest in providing and seeking responsiveness, non-contingently, within relationships) and on emotion (with a particular interest in the social functions of emotion). She has edited books on relationships, emotion, pro-social behavior, and methodology in personality and social psychology, served as the President of the *Society of Personality and Social Psychology* and as Chair of the *Society of Experimental Social Psychology* as well as an associate editor of *Psychological Science, Personality and Social Psychology Bulletin, and Emotion.*

Robert B. Cialdini is Regents' Professor Emeritus of psychology and marketing at Arizona State University. His primary research interests involve social influence and persuasion. His book *Influence: Science and Practice* (5th ed., Pearson, 2008) has been published in five editions and 26 languages. His newest coauthored book (with Noah Goldstein and Steve Martin) is *Yes! 50 Scientifically Proven Ways to be Persuasive* (Free Press, 2008).

Morton Deutsch is E.L. Thorndike Professor and Director Emeritus of the International Center for Cooperation and Conflict Resolution (ICCCR) at Teachers College, Columbia University. He studied with Kurt Lewin at MIT's Research Center for Group Dynamics, where he obtained his PhD in 1948. He has been much honored for his pioneering studies in intergroup relations, cooperation-competition, conflict resolution, social conformity, and the social psychology of justice. His books include *Interracial Housing, Research Methods in Social Relations, Preventing World War II: Some Proposals, Theories in Social Psychology, The Resolution of Conflict, Applying Social Psychology, Distributive Justice*, and *The Handbook of Conflict Resolution.*

John F. Dovidio is currently professor of psychology at Yale University. He previously taught at Colgate University and at the University of Connecticut. His research interests are in stereotyping, prejudice, and discrimination; social power and nonverbal communication; and altruism and helping. He has been president of the Society for Personality and Social Psychology, the Society for the Psychological Study of Social Issues, and the Society for Experimental Social Psychology. Dr. Dovidio has been the recipient of several awards, including the Kurt Lewin Award, the Raymond A. Fowler Mentor Award, and the Award for Distinguished Service to Psychological Science. He recently coedited the *Handbook of Prejudice, Stereotyping, and Discrimination* (Sage, 2010) and he is coeditor of the journal, *Social Issues and Policy Review*.

Carol S. Dweck is the Lewis and Virginia Eaton Professor of Psychology at Stanford University. Her research examines the "theories" people use to guide their personal and interpersonal behavior. She is the author of *Self-Theories* (Psychology Press, 1999) and *Mindset* (Random House, 2006) and the coeditor of *Motivation and Self-Regulation Across the Lifespan* (Cambridge University Press, 1998) and the *Handbook of Competence and Motivation* (Guilford Press, 2005). She has been elected to the American Academy of Arts and Sciences and the American Academy of Political and Social Science; and she has recently received the Donald Campbell Award in Social Psychology; the Ann Brown Award in Developmental Psychology; and the Klingenstein Award and the E.L. Thorndike Award in Education. She is using her research to create programs that foster school achievement, self-regulation, and conflict resolution.

Alice H. Eagly is professor of psychology and of management and organizations, James Padilla Chair of arts and sciences, and faculty fellow of the Institute for Policy Research, all at Northwestern University. She is the author, with Shelly Chaiken, of the *Psychology of Attitudes* (Harcourt Brace Jovanovich, 1993) and, with Linda Carli, of *Through the Labyrinth: The Truth About How Women Become Leaders* (Harvard Business School Press, 2007) as well as the coeditor of several volumes. She is the author of numerous articles in *Psychological Bulletin*, *Psychological Review*, *Journal of Personality and Social Psychology*, *Personality and Social Psychology Bulletin*, *Psychology of Women Quarterly*, and other journals. She has received the Distinguished Scientific Contribution Award from the American Psychological Association, the Gold Medal for Life Achievement in the Science of Psychology from the American Psychological Foundation, and other awards. Her current research concerns gender and leadership, the evolution of sex differences and similarities, and the influence of feminism on the science of psychology.

Gerald Echterhoff is professor of social psychology at University of Münster, Germany. Previously he worked as postdoctoral fellow at Columbia University, assistant professor at Bielefeld University, visiting professor at the University of Cologne, and professor of psychology at Jacobs University Bremen, Germany. He received his PhD from New School for Social Research, New York in 2000. His research interests include interpersonal communication, shared reality, social influence on memory, social cognition, and cultural contexts of remembering. In a signature field of investigation, he and his lab group study how communication shapes speakers' own memory and thinking. His research has been published in leading journals such as *Journal of Personality and Social Psychology*, *Journal of Experimental Psychology: General*, *Psychological Science*, *Perspectives on Psychological Science*, and *Social Cognition*.

Naomi Ellemers is professor of social and organizational psychology at the University of Leiden, the Netherlands. Her research includes experimental studies as well as applied work in organizations, and addresses a range of topics in group processes and intergroup relations. She has published extensively on a range of topics such as individual mobility and social change, organizational and team commitment, diversity and innovation, work–family issues, stigmatization and career development. She has coedited books on stereotyping, on social identity theory, and on social identity processes in organizations. She has been active as an associate editor (*British Journal of Social Psychology, Journal of Personality*, and *Social Psychology*) and on the board of national and international scientific organizations, and has received several prestigious grants and awards for her work.

Samuel L. Gaertner is professor of psychology at the University of Delaware. His research interests focus on understanding and reducing prejudice, discrimination, and racism. He has served on the editorial boards of the *Journal of Personality and Social Psychology, Personality and Social Psychology Bulletin*, and *Group Processes and Intergroup Relations*. Professor Gaertner's research, together with John F. Dovidio, has been supported by grants from the Office of Naval Research, the National Institutes of Mental Health and currently, the National Science Foundation. Together with John Dovidio, he shared the Gordon Allport Intergroup Relations Prize in 1985 and 1998, as well as the Kurt Lewin Memorial Award from the Society for the Psychological Study of Social Issues, Division 9 of the American Psychological Association.

Michele J. Gelfand is professor of psychology and distinguished university scholar teacher at the University of Maryland, College Park. She received her PhD in social/organizational psychology from the University of Illinois. Gelfand's work explores cultural influences on conflict, negotiation, justice, and revenge; workplace diversity and discrimination; and theory and methods in cross-cultural psychology. Her work has been published in outlets such as the *Journal of Applied Psychology, Journal of Personality and Social Psychology, Organizational Behavior and Human Decision Processes, Academy of Management Review, Academy of Management Journal*, and the *Annual Review of Psychology*. She is the coeditor of *The Handbook of Negotiation and Culture* (Stanford University Press, 2004) and *The Psychology of Conflict and Conflict Management in Organizations* (Psychology Press, 2008) and is the founding coeditor of the *Advances in Culture and Psychology* and *Frontiers of Culture and Psychology* series.

Christian Guimelli is professor of social psychology at Aix-Marseille University (France) where he manages the "Social Representations" research team of the Social Psychology Laboratory. His areas of research include social representation analysis and methods and the structure and dynamics of social representations. He has published over 70 books, chapters, and journal articles in the field of social representations and is the author of five books including *Structures et transformations des représentations sociales* [*Structure and Transformation of Social Representations*] (Delachaux & Niestlé, 1994), and *La pensée sociale* [*Social Thought*] (PUF, 1999).

S. Alexander Haslam is professor of social and organizational psychology at the University of Exeter. He is former chief editor of the *European Journal of Social Psychology*, and currently on the editorial board of eight international journals. His work with colleagues at Exeter and around the world focuses on the study of social identity in social and organizational contexts. This is represented in his most recent books: *The New Psychology of Leadership: Identity,*

Influence and Power (with Reicher and Platow; Psychology Press, 2011) and *Psychology in Organizations: The Social Identity Approach* (2nd ed., Sage, 2004). He a Fellow of the Canadian Institute of Advanced Research, and a former recipient of EASP's Lewin Medal.

Elaine Hatfield is a professor of psychology at the University of Hawai'i and past-president of the Society for the Scientific Study of Sexuality. In recent years, she has received Distinguished Scientist Awards (for a lifetime of scientific achievement) from the Society of Experimental Social Psychology, the Society for the Scientific Study of Sex, and the University of Hawai'i, and the Alfred Kinsey Award from the Western Region of SSSS. Two of her books have won the American Psychological Association's National Media Award.

E. Tory Higgins is the Stanley Schachter Professor of Psychology, Professor of Business, and Director of the Motivation Science Center at Columbia (where he also received his PhD in 1973). He has received a MERIT Award from the National Institute of Mental Health, the Thomas M. Ostrom Award in Social Cognition, the Donald T. Campbell Award for Outstanding Contributions to Social Psychology (Society of Personality and Social Psychology), and the Lifetime Contribution Award from the International Society for Self and Identity. He has also received the Distinguished Scientist Award from the Society of Experimental Social Psychology, the William James Fellow Award for Distinguished Achievements in Psychological Science (from the American Psychological Society), and the American Psychological Association Award for Distinguished Scientific Contributions. He is a Fellow of the American Academy of Arts and Sciences. He is also a recipient of Columbia's Presidential Award for Outstanding Teaching.

Michael A. Hogg is professor of social psychology at Claremont Graduate University, Los Angeles. He received his PhD from Bristol. He is a Fellow of numerous associations, including the Association for Psychological Science, the Society for Personality and Social Psychology, and the Society for the Psychological Study of Social Issues. He is a Fellow of the Academy of the Social Sciences in Australia, and is the 2010 recipient of the Carol and Ed Diener Award in Social Psychology from the Society for Personality and Social Psychology. Foundation editor, with Dominic Abrams, of Group Processes and Intergroup Relations and a former associate editor of the *Journal of Experimental Social Psychology*, he has published widely on social identity theory, group processes and intergroup relations, and is the author of the Social Identity Theory of Leadership and of Uncertainty-identity Theory.

John T. Jost is professor of social psychology at New York University. His research, which addresses stereotyping, prejudice, political ideology, and system justification theory, has appeared in leading scientific journals and received national and international media attention. He has published over 90 articles and book chapters and four coedited volumes, including *Social and Psychological Bases of Ideology and System Justification* (Oxford University Press, 2009). Jost has received numerous accolades, including the Gordon Allport Intergroup Relations Prize (three times), Erik Erikson Award for Early Career Research Achievement in Political Psychology, International Society for Self and Identity Early Career Award, Society for Personality and Social Psychology Theoretical Innovation Prize, Society of Experimental Social Psychology Career Trajectory Award, and the Morton Deutsch Award for Distinguished Scholarly and Practical Contributions to Social Justice.

Arie W. Kruglanski is a distinguished university professor at the University of Maryland, College Park. He is recipient of the National Institute of Mental Health Research Scientist

Award, the Senior Humboldt Award, the Donald Campbell Award for Oustanding Contributions to Social Psychology from the Society for Personality and Social Psychology, The University of Maryland Regents Award for Scholarship and Creativity, and the Distinguished Scientific Contribution Award from the Society of Experimental Social Psychology, and is recipient of the Regesz Chair at the University of Amsterdam. He was Fellow at the Center for Advanced Studies in the Behavioral Sciences, and is Fellow of the American Psychological Association and the American Psychological Society. He has served as editor of the *Journal of Personality and Social Psychology: Attitudes and Social Cognition*, editor of the *Personality and Social Psychology Bulletin*, and associate editor of the *American Psychologist*. His interests have been in the domains of human judgment and decision making, the motivation-cognition interface, group and intergroup processes, and the psychology of human goals. His work has been dis-seminated in over 200 articles, chapters and books and has been continuously supported by grants from the National Science Foundation, the National Institute of Mental Health, Deutsche Forschungs Gemeineschaft, the Ford Foundation, and the Israeli Academy of Science. He has recently served as member of the National Academy of Science panels on counterterrorism, and educational paradigms in homeland security. Kruglanski is now a co-director of START (National Center for the Study of Terrorism and the Response to Terrorism), at the University of Maryland.

Paul A.M. Van Lange is professor of social psychology and chair of the department of social and organizational psychology at the VU University at Amsterdam, the Netherlands. Most of his research on human cooperation and trust is grounded in interdependence theory, through which he seeks to understand the functions of forgiveness, generosity, empathy, competition, and general beliefs of human nature in various situations. Van Lange has coauthored the *Atlas of Interpersonal Situations* (Cambridge University Press, 2003), edited *Bridging Social Psychology* (Lawrence Erlbaum, 2006), and served as an associate editor for various journals, including the *Journal of Personality and Social Psychology*. He has been a Director of the Kurt Lewin Institute and currently serves as Member and President of the Executive Committee of the Society of Experimental Social Psychology.

Mark R. Leary is professor of psychology and neuroscience at Duke University. He received his PhD in social psychology from the University of Florida and has held positions at Denison University, the University of Texas at Austin, Wake Forest University, and Duke University. His research focuses on social motivation and emotion, particularly the processes by which people think about and evaluate themselves, the effects of self-reflection on emotion and psychologi-cal well-being, and how behavior and emotion are influenced by people's concerns with how they are perceived and evaluated by others. He is a Fellow of the American Psychological Association, the Association for Psychological Science, and the Society for Personality and Social Psychology, and is the 2010 recipient of the Lifetime Career Award from the International Society for Self and Identity. He was the founding editor of the journal, *Self and Identity*, and is currently editor of *Personality and Social Psychology Review*.

Mario Mikulincer is professor of psychology and dean of the New School of Psychology at the Interdisciplinary Center (IDC) Herzliya, Israel. He has published three books and over 250 journal articles and book chapters and serves as a member of the editorial boards of several personality and social psychology journals. Dr. Mikulincer's main research interests are attach-ment theory, terror management theory, personality processes in interpersonal relationships, coping with stress and trauma, grief-related processes and prosocial motives and behavior.

He is a Fellow of the Society for Personality and Social Psychology and the Association for Psychological Sciences. He received the EMET Prize in Social Science for his contribution to psychology and the Berscheid-Hatfield Award for Distinguished Mid-Career Achievement from the International Association for Relationship Research.

Judson R. Mills taught at Syracuse University, University of Missouri, the London School of Economics, and the University of Texas but spent most time as a professor at the University of Maryland. His research interests included attitude formation and change, emotion, mood and affect, communal relationships, and research methodology. He was a student of Leon Festinger at Stanford University and conducted some of the seminal work on cognitive dissonance theory in the late 1950's. He maintained his interest in and research on that theory for several decades and, together with Eddie Harmon-Jones, edited a book on cognitive dissonance in 1999. He was a devoted mentor to social psychologists including Margaret Clark.

Walter Mischel is the Robert Johnston Niven Professor of Humane Letters in Psychology at Columbia University where he has been since 1983, after 21 years as a professor at Stanford University. He received his PhD in clinical psychology from Ohio State in 1956. His monograph *Personality and Assessment* (1968) challenged the traditional trait paradigm in psychology and generated research into the nature and implications of person–situation interactions. His cognitive–affective processing system (*Psychological Review*, 1995), with Yuichi Shoda, provided a model for the analysis of individual differences in interaction with psychological situations, building on empirical findings demonstrating the contextualized expressions of behavioral dispositions. His longitudinal–developmental and experimental studies of the ability to delay gratification identified basic cognitive and attention control mechanisms enabling self-control. He was elected to the National Academy of Sciences in 2004, and to the American Academy of Arts and Sciences in 1991, and is past editor of *Psychological Review*.

Pascal Moliner is professor of social psychology at the University of Montpellier III (France) where he was the director of the Social Psychology Laboratory for many years. His main research areas concern social representations, relationships between social cognition and representations and between images and representations. He is the author or coauthor of many works on these topics: *Images et représentations* [*Images and Social Representations*] (PUG, 1996), *La dynamique des représentations sociales* [*Social Representations Dynamics*] (PUG, 2001), *Les représentations sociales: pratique des études de terrain* [*Social Representations: Practical Studies*] (PUR, 2002), *L'identité en psychologie sociale* [*Social Identity in Social Psychology*] (Armand Colin, 2008), *Représentations sociales et processus sociocognitifs* (*Social Representations and Socio-cognitive Processes*] (PUR, 2009).

Charlan Jeanne Nemeth is a professor in the Department of Psychology, University of California, Berkeley. Her background includes a BA in mathematics from Washington University in St Louis and a PhD in psychology from Cornell University. Her faculty appointments include the University of Chicago, University of Virginia, and University of British Columbia with visiting appointments in Bristol (England), Paris (France), Trento (Italy), and Mannheim (Germany). Her speciality is influence processes, creativity, and small group decision making and her particular emphasis has been on the role of the outsider and of the value of dissenting viewpoints. Her work has been broadly applied, most notably during jury decision making and the managing of innovation in organisational settings. She was the first woman and first social scientist to speak at the Oregon Bar Association, her topic being jury decision making and has given invited addresses at Harvard, MIT, Cornell, Northwestern and Yale Business Schools on entrepreneurs, creativity, and mechanisms for increasing innovation. She was a visiting professor at London Business School from 2005–2009 and is the holder of the prestigious Leverhulme Fellowship.

Felicia Pratto is professor of psychology at the University of Connecticut and has served as a visiting professor in the US, Germany, Italy, Spain, and the Netherlands. She received her PhD from New York University. She has served on the executive board of the Society for Experimental Social Psychology, on editorial boards of several journals, and is currently a vice president of the International Society for Political Psychology. She has authored over 100 articles and chapters concerning power, intergroup relations, discrimination and prejudice, stereotyping, and the social–cognitive processes that contribute to these. Her research has employed a variety of methods, ranging from reaction times to games to surveys to archival analysis and her current research examines the dynamics of power, social change, and intergroup violence.

Richard L. Rapson is professor of history at the University of Hawaii. He received his BA from Amherst and PhD from Columbia. He has written more than a dozen books individually and also has coauthored a number of books with his wife, Dr Elaine Hatfield. A scholarly trilogy, published during the 1990s, included *Love, Sex, and Intimacy: Their Psychology, Biology, and History* (HarperCollins), *Emotional Contagion* (Cambridge University Press), and *Love and Sex: Cross-cultural Perspectives* (Allyn & Bacon).

Patrick Rateau is professor of social psychology at the University of Nîmes (France) and permanent member of the Social Psychology Laboratory at Aix-Marseille University (France). His research interests include social representations theory and methods, social comparison, social memory and environmental social psychology. He authored or coauthored several books, chapters, and journal articles on social representations and social thought. Recently, he has coauthored one book: *Les représentations sociales : pratique des études de terrain* [*Social Representations: Practical Studies*] (PUR, 2002) with Pascal Moliner and Valérie Cohen-Scali, and coedited one volume: *Représentations sociales et processus sociocognitifs*, [*Social Representations and Socio-cognitive Processes*] (PUR, 2009) with Pascal Moliner.

Caryl E. Rusbult (1952–2010) has been a professor of psychology at the University of North Carolina, where she held the J. Ross MacDonald Chair (1997–2003) after which she became professor and chair of the department of social psychology at the VU University at Amsterdam. She adopted an interdependence theoretical approach to the study of close relationships, and developed the investment model of commitment processes to understand relationship maintenance mechanisms, such as accommodation, derogation of alternatives, and personal growth. She coauthored the *Atlas of Interpersonal Situations* (Cambridge University Press, 2003), served as associate editor of *Journal of Personality and Social Psychology*, and received several scientific awards, including the Distinguished Career Award (2008) from the International Association for Relationships Research. Caryl Rusbult passed away in 2010.

Katherine J. Reynolds is an associate professor in the department of psychology at the Australian National University in Canberra, Australia. She has published many papers on the prejudiced personality and prejudice and social conflict more generally. More recently, her research is focused on how and when group memberships (and changes to such groups) come to impact on the individual person (e.g., personality, well-being, self-beliefs). This program of research with its focus on social norms and social influence has expanded into policy areas seeking to affect social and behavioural change (e.g., learning and pro-social behaviour in schools). She is currently an associate editor at Personality and Social Psychology Bulletin and on the editorial board of four other international journals.

Phillip R. Shaver is a distinguished professor of psychology at the University of California, Davis. He has published over 250 scholarly articles and book chapters and coauthored or coedited numerous books including *Measures of Personality and Social Psychological Attitudes* (Academic Press 1991); *Attachment in Adulthood*; *Handbook of Attachment* (2nd ed., Guilford Press, 2008); *Prosocial Motives, Emotions, and Behavior* (APA, 2009); and *Human Aggression and Violence* (APA, 2010). His research focuses on attachment theory, close relationships, emotion, and personality development. He is a member of the editorial boards of several journals and a fellow of the American Psychological Association and the Association for Psychological Science. He served as executive officer of the Society of Experimental Social Psychology and president of the International Association for Relationship Research, from which he received a Distinguished Career Award in 2002 and a Mentoring Award in 2010.

Jim Sidanius is a professor in the departments of psychology and African and African American Studies at the Harvard University. He received his PhD at the University of Stockholm, Sweden, and has taught at several universities in the US and Europe, including the Carnegie Mellon University, the University of Texas at Austin, the New York University, the Princeton University, the University of Stockholm, Sweden, and the University of California, Los Angeles. His primary research interests include the interface between political ideology and cognitive functioning, the political psychology of gender, group conflict, institutional discrimination, and the evolutionary psychology of intergroup prejudice. He has authored and published more than 120 scientific papers, and his most important theoretical contribution to date is the development of social dominance theory, a general model of the development and maintenance of group-based social hierarchy and social oppression. Professor Sidanius' latest books are entitled: *Social Dominance: An Intergroup Theory of Social Hierarchy and Oppression* (Cambridge University Press, 1999), *Racialized Politics: Values, Ideology, and Prejudice in American Public Opinion* (University of Chicago press, 2000), *Key Readings in Political Psychology* (Psychology Press, 2004), and *The Diversity Challenge: Social Identity and Intergroup Relations on the College Campus* (Russell Sage Foundation, 2008). Prof. Sidanius was also the recipient of the 2006 Harold Lasswell Award for "Distinguished Scientific Contribution in the Field of Political Psychology" awarded by the International Society of Political Psychology, and was inducted into the American Academy of Arts and Sciences in 2007.

William B. Swann, Jr. is currently a professor of social-personality psychology at the University of Texas at Austin with appointments in the Psychology Department and School of Business. A doctorate of the University of Minnesota, he studies identity and the self, identity negotiation and, most recently, identity fusion. He has also been elected a Fellow of the American Psychological Association and the American Psychological Society. Once a Fellow at Princeton University as well as the Center for Advanced Study in the Behavioral Sciences, he has received multiple research scientist development awards from the National Institutes of Mental Health. His research has been funded by awards from the National Science Foundation, the National Institutes of Mental Health, and the National Institute for Drug and Alcohol Abuse.

Jojanneke van der Toorn is currently a postdoctoral associate in the department of psychology at Yale University. She holds MA degrees in organizational psychology and cultural anthropology from the VU University, Amsterdam and a PhD from New York University. Her research focuses on processes of legitimation and the social psychological mechanisms implicated in social change and resistance to it. Her work has appeared in *American Sociological Review*, *Journal of Experimental Social Psychology*, and *Social Justice Research*.

Harry C. Triandis is Professor Emeritus of psychology at the University of Illinois. He was born in 1926. His 1958 PhD is from Cornell University in Ithaca, New York.. He received an Honorary Doctorate from the University of Athens, Greece, in 1987. He is the author of *Attitudes and Attitude Change* (Wiley, 1971), *Analysis of Subjective Culture* (Wiley, 1972) *Interpersonal Behavior* (Brooks/Cole, 1977), *Variations in Black and White Perceptions of the Social Environment* (University of Illinois Press, 1976), *Culture and Social Behavior* (McGraw-Hill, 1994) and *Individualism and Collectivism* (Sage, 1995). His most recent (2009) book is *Fooling Ourselves: Self-Deception in Politics, Religion, and Terrorism* (Praeger, 2008) (This book received the William James Award of Div. 1 of the American Psychological Association). He was the general editor of the six-volume *Handbook of Cross-Cultural Psychology* (Allyn & Bacon, 1997), and coeditor (with Dunnette and Hough) of Volume 4 of the *Handbook of Industrial and Organizational Psychology* (Consulting Psychologists Press, 1994).

John C. Turner is an Emeritus Professor in the department of psychology at the Australian National University in Canberra, Australia. His research interests are in social psychology and have covered a number of topics over the years: intergroup relations, prejudice, stereotyping, the nature of the psychological group and group processes, social influence, leadership, power and the self-concept. He has had a longstanding interest in social identity and self-categorization processes since he developed social identity theory with the late Henri Tajfel in the 1970s and originated self-categorization theory in the early 1980s. He was awarded the Henri Tajfel Memorial Medal by the European Association of Experimental Social Psychology in 1999.

Tom R. Tyler is a university professor at New York University. He teaches in the psychology department and the law school. His research explores the dynamics of authority in groups, organizations, and societies. In particular, he examines the role of judgments about the justice or injustice of group procedures in shaping legitimacy, compliance and cooperation. He is the author of several books, including *The social psychology of procedural justice* (1988); *Social justice in a diverse society* (1997); *Cooperation in groups* (2000); *Trust in the law* (2002); and *Why people obey the law* (2006).

Wendy Wood is Provost Professor of psychology and business at the University of Southern California. Her research addresses the evolutionary origins of gender differences in social behavior, along with the ways that gender differences and similarities are constructed in social interactions. She also investigates how habits and attitudes guide behavior, so as to understand how people can best regulate and change aspects of their lifestyles. Her work on these topics appears in *Psychological Bulletin*, *Psychological Review*, and the *Journal of Personality and Social Psychology* and has been supported by grants from the National Science Foundation, National Institutes of Health, the Rockefeller Foundation, and the Radcliffe Institute for Advanced Study. She served as associate editor of *Psychological Review*, *Personality and Social Psychology Review*, *Journal of Personality and Social Psychology*, and *Personality and Social Psychology Bulletin*.

Preface

Ideas make the world go around – especially good ideas and especially in science. Indeed, science is all about ideas and their implementation in empirical research. This is true for the science of social psychology as well. Indisputably, the quintessential carriers of scientific ideas are theories. It is theories that get to the underlying essences of phenomena and trace their implications for myriads of concrete situations. It is theories that pull the strands of seemingly disparate occurrences and tie them into coherent systems guided by common principles. Good theories are not just practical, as Lewin noted; they are essential to the scientific enterprise. It is, therefore, hardly surprising that from its early beginnings social psychological research has been guided by theories of various kinds. Numerous theoretical frameworks have been added by creative thinkers in the course of time. By now, the field of social psychology is rich in theoretical contributions in its many domains of endeavor. Some social psychological theories have been around for a long time, others for little more than a decade. Some have been tested, revised, and extended, while others have remained in their original form and continued to inspire research on the force of their timeless insights. Some theories have intriguingly morphed into other theories, others remained pristinely faithful to their initial version. Some theories have been wonderfully elaborated and articulated. Others have been adumbrated in vague outline, representing work in progress or diamonds in the rough. In this volume, we are interested in all such theories not only because they provide a comprehensive overview of the theories in social psychology, but also because we felt it is important that authors share with the readers the process of theory construction, development, and nurturance that serves such an important function for science. Here is why.

The process of theorizing, and the skills of theory construction, have been shrouded in a cloak of mystery in our field. They are rarely taught in graduate programs in social psychology, nor do they constitute a recognized and trusted tool in the kit of young researchers. A major purpose of the present project was to demystify the process of theorizing and expose its hidden underbelly and intricate entrails. Indeed, chapters by our contributors reveal how serendipity born of personal circumstances often determines the course that one's theory construction would take; how theory development often requires tenacity, persistence, patience, and "blood, sweat and tears." Another purpose of the book was to illustrate how the work of theory construction is indispensable to scientific development, and how important and gratifying it can be to those who manage to stay on the course of constructing and testing their theory.

Our own conviction, stemming from our earlier work, and presented in the introductory chapter, has been that theories should be guided by the regulatory ideas of truth, abstraction, progress, and applicability. This notion served as the basis of a research grant, "Social Psychology: Bridging Theory and Application in Society," (NWO. grant, nr. 400-07-710), awarded by the Netherlands Organization for Scientific Research, which gave the first editor extra time to devote to this Handbook. Because of the immensity of the project and common interest in theory, he invited the second and third editors to join in, and they enthusiastically agreed. After initial discussion, we concurred that this volume should carry a unique mission: illuminating theory construction from the inside out. Accordingly, the instructions we gave to our contributors were explicit and precise. We asked authors not only to give an overview of their theory or model, but also touch on three essential aspects: (1) a personalized history of the theory's beginnings and development over time as recounted by the theoretician; (2) the theory's place in the intellectual space in a given domain (i.e., the contribution it makes to the history of ideas on its topic); and (3) the theory's relevance to real-world concerns (i.e., its potential contribution to solving real-world problems). Inevitably, the various chapters in this volume differed in their primary focus, and in the emphasis accorded to each of these aspects. But overall, these three foci are amply represented across the chapters. Of greatest importance, they tell a fascinating tale documenting the challenges, adversities, and joys that theory construction brings its practitioners, and the rich conceptual endowment that it brings our discipline.

The Editors

26

Self-Control Theory

Walter Mischel

ABSTRACT

The self-control theory my colleagues and I developed evolved slowly over many decades, intended to integrate work on two closely interconnected questions of both my scientific and personal life. From the start of my career I was driven by these two questions, and I felt that the answer to each hinged on the answer to the other. First, given the power of the situation, demonstrated so often by social psychologists, how do individuals manage, at least sometimes, to inhibit and control their impulsive automatic responses to powerful situational pressures, overcoming "stimulus control" with "self-control"? Second, given the great variability one sees in what anyone does and thinks and feels across different situations, what are the consistencies that distinctively characterize individuals over the life course? In this chapter I discuss some of the empirical labors and surprising discoveries, as well as ideas, and the good luck, that ultimately allowed some answers to both these questions that seem – for the moment – to reasonably fit the integrative and still-evolving theory that emerged.

FIRST STEPS

It didn't turn out the way I expected. Half a century ago, I flew on a prop plane out of a cold, slushy, Columbus Ohio January, and landed in sun-drenched, beautiful blue-sky Trinidad, eager to observe and study spirit possession as practiced in the Orisha religion, a blend of African and Catholic beliefs, by a group then known as Shango. The chance to leave Columbus for travel to what then felt like exotic rum and Coca-Cola places on palm-lined beaches outside the tourist routes, still under British colonial rule, was irresistible. It also allowed a break from my graduate training, working towards a clinical psychology PhD at Ohio State from 1953 to 1956. During those years I went repeatedly to Trinidad with my then wife, Frances (now Frances Henry), who was, in the early 1950s, a doctoral student in anthropology. We hoped to find connections between what people do in their daily lives, in which they served the most menial roles at the bottom of their stratified, still-British-colonial society and what they did and became when "possessed" (Mischel and Mischel, 1958). My clinical experiences at Ohio State were already making me worried about the value of projective measures for making decisions in the mental hospital setting. But I was still hopeful about their potential for exploring what goes on at the fantasy level, and thought it was worth a try. Armed with my Rorschach inkblot cards (and a sketch pad), we headed for Trinidad for several summers from 1955 to 1958.

FROM TRINIDAD AND SPIRIT POSSESSION TO DELAY OF GRATIFICATION

A brief anthropology venture

We found Shango practiced in a small village in the southern tip of Trinidad, and befriended its leader, Pa Neezer, who congenially welcomed us to live in one of his little houses as observers to study and understand their ceremonies and practices. The participants in Shango were cooperative and eager to please. This became clear in their responses to my projective tests. Their answers often had more to do with what they thought might interest me (e.g., plots from current American films playing in the next town) than with their inner lives. If the stories they spun had some connections to their inner states, it was beyond me to discern them. They certainly seemed unconnected to what they did in front of my eyes while they were possessed by the spirits that "rode" them during the Shango ceremonies (described in Mischel and Mischel, 1958). I soon put the tests away and started looking at what might be going on around us.

In the Shango ceremonies, stretching over several days and nights, laborers and domestic servants of the British by day became at night possessed by spirits that were a mix of Catholic saints and African gods, and danced in hypnotized trance-like states, with the irresistible drums pounding, and the rum bottles passing. As I found myself struggling to resist hurling myself into the dance I realized that the participant–observer balance was tipping fast, and that while keeping my eyes glued to the scene, I needed to turn my work in other directions.

Small candy now versus big candy later

My transition from resisting the impulse to jump into the dance and instead to invent what decades later the media call the "marshmallow test" took more than a dozen years. It began when I started talking to our neighbors in the village and listened, really listened, as they talked about their lives. The inhabitants in this area of the island were of either African or East Indian background, each group living in its own enclave, on different sides of the same long street. It did not take much listening to hear a recurrent theme in how they characterized each other. The Africans, the East Indians said, were just pleasure-bent, impulsive, eager to have a good time, and live in the moment while never planning or thinking ahead about the future. Reciprocally, the Africans saw their East Indian neighbors as just working for the future and stuffing their money under the mattress without ever enjoying today.

I started to examine these observations in the local schools with young children from both ethnic groups. In their classrooms, I administered a variety of measures that ranged from such demographic descriptors as father's presence–absence in the home, to trust expectations, achievement motivation, diverse indices of social responsibility, and intelligence. At the end of each of these sessions I gave them choices between little treats (a tiny chocolate bar, a small notepad) that they could have immediately or a much bigger, better one that they would get the following week.

Consistent with the stereotypes the two groups had about each other, the black Trinidadian kids generally preferred the immediate rewards and those from East Indian families chose the delayed ones much more often (Mischel, 1961a, 1961b, 1961c). I wondered if the kids who came from homes with absent fathers – then common in the black families in Trinidad, very rare for the other group – might have had fewer experiences with male social agents who kept their promises. If so, those children would have less trust; that is, a lower "expectancy" that the male, and on top of it white, visitor would show up with the promised delayed reward. I had learned about the importance of expectancies from my Ohio State mentor, Julian

Rotter, and was impressed by his social learning theory, and the expectancy construct also was the topic of my doctoral dissertation. So I controlled for the effect of father absence, and was delighted to see that the differences between the ethnic groups disappeared. These findings pointed to the important role that outcome expectancies and beliefs play in goal commitment. People are likely to attempt to exercise self-control (and forego the "bird in the hand") only if they trusted that the delayed larger one ("in the bush") would materialize (Mischel, 1974).

This was the beginning of the studies that identified some of the main determinants of such choice behavior and what later became known as "temporal discounting" – a major topic in current behavioral economics (e.g., Mischel, 1961a, 1961b, 1961c; Mischel and Gilligan, 1964; Mischel and Metzner, 1962; Mischel and Mischel, 1958). These studies showed significant correlations between dominant choice preferences for the immediate rewards and, for example, juvenile delinquency in adolescence, lower social responsibility ratings, less resistance to temptation in experimental situations, lower achievement motivation, and lower intelligence (see Mischel, 1974, for a summary).

Expectancies (trust) and values

Goal commitment does not just depend only on peoples' trust expectations. It is also influenced by the subjective value of the rewards in the situation. Through temporal discounting mechanisms, rewards that are delayed have less value than equivalent rewards that are immediately available (Ainslie, 2001; Loewenstein et al., 2003; Rachlin, 2000). Therefore we expected, and found, that the longer the future rewards were delayed, the less likely it was that children would choose to wait for them (Mischel and Metzner, 1962). Thus, goal commitment in delay of gratification is enhanced with the relative magnitude of the delayed reward and decreases as the required time it takes to attain the reward increases (Mischel, 1966, 1974).

At that point, and consistent with utility theories in economics as well as in psychology, the findings indicated that the choice to wait for a larger but delayed reward is determined largely by an expectancy-value mechanism (discussed in Mischel, 1974; Mischel and Ayduk, 2004). In short, a person must value the delayed reward enough to commit to pursuing it, must believe that they possess the ability to successfully exert self-control should they choose to do so (e.g., Bandura, 1986; Mischel and Staub, 1965), and trust that they will receive the valued delayed reward upon successfully fulfilling their goal. And the delayed rewards must matter to them enough to overcome the temporal discounting effects. Further, we found that these choices could be modified, in either direction, by exposure to high prestige peer models who modeled choice preferences opposite to those of the subject. These changes were still evident several months later when the participants were again tested in a new situation (Bandura and Mischel, 1965).

A WINDOW FOR WATCHING WILLPOWER

Willpower: the scorned fiction of behaviorism

When I initiated my self-control research, behaviorism was the dominant theory, or anti-theory, regnant within American psychological science in the 1950s and early 1960s. Academic psychology was still deep into "positivism" (not to be confused with the current "positive psychology"), well before the cognitive revolution, and dominated by radical behaviorism and Skinner's focus on "stimulus control" and the power of reinforcement. Such concepts as "self-control" and "self" were dismissed as naïve unscientific fictions, and even the word "willpower" was unspeakable in academic circles.

The ridiculed willpower "fiction" became my focus and research agenda as I watched my three closely spaced daughters each morph in the first few years of life, from mostly giggling and gurgling or screaming and sleeping, to becoming people with whom one could have fascinating, thoughtful conversations. Most amazing to me, sometimes they could even sit still for a while to wait for things they wanted that took some time or effort to get. As I tried to make some sense out of what was unfolding in front of me at the kitchen table I mused that in behaviorism as well as in economics the explanatory keys for most human behavior, including what was happening to my children, were rewards. But I did not have a clue about how rewards enable voluntary delay of gratification and "willpower," a term that as a psychologist I even now put into quotes. And trying to understand how that happens became a lifelong obsession.

The decision before entering the restaurant to forego dessert, and the ability to stick to it when the pastry temptations are flashed in front of one's eyes, often are unconnected. The firmest New Year's resolutions easily break before January ends, and the tobacco addict who dumps his cigarettes into the garbage in self-disgust, vowing to quit forever, may be frantically searching for them three hours later. Therefore the question I kept asking myself became: After the choice to delay has been made, the good intention formed and declared at least to oneself, what allows it to be realized? And how does this ability develop in the young child?

The marshmallow test

To go from speculating to empiricism we needed a method to study delay of gratification ability when the young child begins to have it around preschool age. Happily, the newly established Bing Nursery School at Stanford University, with its big one-way glass observation windows, was the ideal laboratory, and as a newly arrived (in 1962)

faculty member I was thrilled to use it. In the next dozen years, my students, notably including Ebbe Ebbesen, Bert Moore, and Antonette Zeiss (but many others also played important parts) and I came up with the preschool "delay of immediate gratification for the sake of delayed but more valued rewards paradigm," in the media later called more simply, albeit incorrectly, *the marshmallow test*.

Typically a preschooler is shown some desired treats; for example, small marshmallows or (more often) little pretzel sticks, or cookies, or tiny plastic toys. The child faces a conflict: wait until the experimenter returns and get two of the desired treats, or ring a bell and the experimenter will come back immediately – but then the child gets only one treat. After the child chooses to wait for the larger outcome, he or she is left alone, waiting while facing both treats, and the measure is the seconds of delay before settling for the one or waiting the full time to get the two (e.g., after 15 minutes). The delay soon becomes difficult and frustration grows quickly. As waiting for the chosen goal drags on, the child becomes increasingly tempted to ring the bell and take the immediately available treat.

This situation has become a prototype for studying the conflict between an immediate smaller temptation and a higher-order but delayed larger goal, the bigger treat that will come later (when the experimenter returns). In this type of situation, my students and I studied hundreds of preschoolers in the Stanford University community, both with experiments and through direct observation, with follow-up studies that are still in progress (e.g., Mischel et al., in press) We began with a series of experiments designed to see how the mental representation of the rewards in the choice situation influence the ability to resist impulsive responding and to continue to wait or work for the chosen delayed but more valuable outcomes, as described in later sections.

The experiments were designed to identify the mental processes that allowed some people to delay gratification while others simply couldn't. I had no reason to expect that seconds of waiting time for a couple of marshmallows or cookies at age four years would predict anything worth knowing about years later. In fact, there was every reason to not expect that since successful attempts to predict long-term consequential life outcomes from psychological tests very early in life were proving to be exceptionally rare (Mischel, 1968). But occasionally I did ask my three daughters, who all had attended the Bing school, how their friends from nursery school were doing as the years passed. Far from systematic follow-up, this was just idle dinnertime conversation, as I asked them: "How's Debbie? How's Sam doing?" By the time the kids were early teenagers I noticed what looked like a possible link between the preschoolers' scores on the "marshmallow test" and the informal judgments about their academic and social progress when I asked my daughter informally to rate their friends on a scale of zero to five. Comparing these ratings with the original data set, a clear correlation was emerging, and I realized I had to do this seriously.

AN UNEXPECTED DIVIDEND: PRESCHOOL DELAY PREDICTS LONG-TERM OUTCOMES

Beginning in 1981, my students and I sent out a questionnaire to the reachable parents, teachers, and academic advisers of preschoolers who had participated in the delay research and who by then were in high school. We asked about all sorts of behaviors and characteristics that might be relevant to impulse control, ranging from their ability to plan and think ahead to their skills and effectiveness in coping with personal and social problems (e.g., how well they got along with their peers). We also requested and obtained their Scholastic Aptitude Test (SAT) scores from the Educational Testing Service. It soon became evident that there were long-term

differences between the preschoolers who were high and low delayers, and we therefore continued to examine them systematically as they developed over many years, and still do so as they reach their mid-forties.

Stumbling into the Bing Longitudinal Study

Participants in the Bing Longitudinal Study come from a sample of more than 300 participants who were enrolled in Stanford University's Bing preschool between 1968 and 1974. Since then, we assessed the ability of these participants to pursue long-term goals in the face of immediate temptation once every decade since the original testing. They now have reached their late thirties and early to mid forties, and information about their life outcomes, such as their occupational, marital, physical health, and mental health status are continuing to become available. The findings have surprised us from the start, and they continue to do so. For example, preschoolers who delayed longer relative to other participants earned much higher SAT scores (on average about 200 points higher) and exhibited better social–cognitive and emotional coping in adolescence (Mischel et al., 1988, 1989; Shoda et al., 1990).

When the high delayers became adults, most continued to have better cognitive–social functioning and better educational and economic life outcomes than their low-delaying peers (e.g., Ayduk et al., 2000; Mischel and Ayduk, 2004; Mischel et al., 1988; Shoda et al., 1990). The high delay individuals also were buffered against the development of diverse mental health problems: they used cocaine/crack less frequently, were less likely to suffer from low self-esteem and self-worth (Ayduk et al., 2000), and had fewer features of borderline personality disorder than matched controls with similar dispositional vulnerability (Ayduk et al., 2008).

To be sure that what we were discovering in these long-term correlates was not restricted to the Bing cohort, we also conducted longitudinal studies with similar measures in a variety of other cohorts and demographic populations. We obtained closely parallel findings with children from the toddler center at Barnard College in New York (e.g., Eigsti et al., 2006; Sethi et al., 2000), and with middle-school children in the South Bronx, New York (e.g., Ayduk et al., 2000; Mischel and Ayduk, 2004), as well as with children and adolescents in a summer residential treatment program for youths at high risk for problems of aggression/externalization and depression/withdrawal (e.g., Mischel and Shoda, 1995; Rodriguez et al., 1989). For example, spontaneous use of self-control strategies in the delay task (e.g., looking away from the rewards, in this case M&M candies, and using self-distraction) predicted reduced verbal and physical aggression as directly observed over six weeks in the summer camp study (e.g., Rodriguez et al., 1989; Wright and Mischel, 1987, 1988).

DECOMPOSING THE ABILITY TO DELAY GRATIFICATION/IMPULSE CONTROL

The fact that the marshmallow test's long-term predictive power turned out to be substantial made me even more eager to understand the cognitive–affective mechanisms that underlie the individual differences in self-control tapped by the test. We did those experiments at Bing in the 1970s, before the longitudinal research was launched, with the hope of finding the mental mechanisms that enable delay of gratification.

Conceptual roots

Initially, I was guided by the idea that delay becomes easier when the desired gratification can be visualized (Mischel et al., 1972). That hypothesis was based on Freud's

(1911/1959) classic idea that delay of gratification becomes possible when the young child creates a mental ("hallucinatory" was Freud's phrase) image of the object of desire (e.g., the mother's breast). In Freud's view, the mental representation of the object allows mental "time binding" and enables the transition from primary process thinking to delay and impulse inhibition (Rapaport, 1967). Using very different language a similar idea came from experiments by researchers working at the behavioral-conditioning level. Their research (e.g., Berlyne, 1960; Estes, 1972) suggested that when animals learn, their approach behavior toward a goal is maintained by "fractional anticipatory goal responses" that cognitively represent the desired rewards. These anticipatory representations sustain the rat's goal pursuit, for example, as it tries to find its way back to the food at the end of a maze in a learning task (Hull, 1931). Again, the prediction was that focusing attention on the delayed rewards should reinforce one's ability to sustain delay gratification in order to fulfill goal pursuit. In the first experiments on delay with four-year-olds we examined these ideas, predicting that waiting would be longer if the rewards were made available for attention during the delay period. The results turned out to be the direct opposite of what we expected.

We got these upsetting results from a series of experiments to explore the role that attention to the rewards plays in self-control (Mischel and Ebbesen, 1970), With that goal, we varied whether or not reward items were available for attention while children were waiting in the delay of gratification paradigm. In one condition, children waited with both the immediately available and the delayed reward exposed in full view. In a second condition both options faced the child, but were concealed from attention by an opaque cover positioned over them. In two other conditions either the delayed reward alone or the immediately available reward alone was exposed during the delay period. On average, children waited more than

11 minutes when none of the rewards were exposed, but waited only a few minutes when any of the rewards – either both rewards, just the delayed reward, or just the immediately available reward – were available to attention. Directly contradicting the predictions coming from both from the psychodynamic and animal learning traditions, the results showed that focusing attention on a desired stimulus decreased the ability to delay gratification.

To try to figure out what might be going on in the heads of the preschoolers as they tried to wait in the marshmallow test, chatting with my daughters and doing some playful but serious mini-experiments with them gave me many hypotheses. And for many hours my students and I simply observed preschool children at the Bing school in their "game room" through the windows of the one-way glass while they were struggling to wait to get the more valuable treat later or rang the bell to get the less valuable one immediately. We saw that the kids who managed to delay were doing anything they could to distract themselves from the rewards and reduce their frustration while continuing to wait; for example, by fidgeting, squirming, hiding their eyes to not see the temptations, kicking the table, playing with their toes and fingers, picking their noses and ears in elaborately imaginative ways, singing little songs they invented ("Oh this is my home in Redwood City"), and so on.

If shifting attention away from the rewards to reduce the temptation is what matters, then distracting children from focusing on the rewards should have the same effect as removing the rewards from view. That's just what was found. In one experiment, for example, we provided children with a distracting toy (a Slinky) to play with while they tried to wait, facing the rewards exposed on the table in front of them (Mischel et al., 1972). In this condition more than half of the children waited the full amount of time until the experimenter returned indicating that the experiment was over (15 minutes). In contrast, none of the children who were left waiting for the exposed rewards without

the distracter toy were able to do so. In another experiment, the same effect of distraction on delay times was found when children were cued to think about fun thoughts while they waited: "While you're waiting, if you want to, you can think of mommy pushing you on a swing at a birthday party." Similar to the Slinky condition, more than half of the children who were cued to distract themselves with fun thoughts waited until the experimenter returned and indicated that the experiment was over (Mischel et al., 1972). Of course not all distracters were equally effective. Unsurprisingly, when the distracting object was not appealing, for example, instructing individuals to think about sad thoughts, then attention was diverted back to the stimulus and delay of gratification was undermined. To effectively keep attention away from the temptations in the situation, attention to the distracter must itself be reinforcing.

Developmental and social–cognitive research points at similar attentional processes in regulating negative affect and behavior. For example, eye-gaze aversion, flexible attention shifting, attention focusing, and resistance to attentional interference are related to reduced impulsivity and anger even in early childhood (Eisenberg et al., 2002; Johnson et al., 1991; Posner et al., 1997). Likewise, social–cognitive research indicates that whereas processes such as emotion-focused rumination maintain and prolong negative affect, self-distraction may be an effective strategy to assuage negative mood (Nolen-Hoeksema, 1991; Rusting and Nolen-Hoeksama, 1998).

Reappraisal processes: from hot to cool

Strategically focusing attention away from a desired stimulus is an effective way of facilitating adaptive self-control in the face of temptation, but that option often is not available or not sustainable. Consider, for example, the dieting pastry chef who has sworn off eating chocolate, yet has to make delectable chocolate cakes for desert each night, creating one potential conflict after another.

In the late 1960s, we began to test systematically how alternative ways of mentally representing the stimulus influence the emotions and behaviors of the children during their self-control efforts. We drew on a distinction that had been made in the research literature between two different aspects or features of a stimulus: its "hot" motivational, consummatory, arousing, action-oriented, or motivating "go" features; and its informational, "cool," cognitive cue or discriminative stimulus "know" functions (Berlyne, 1960; Estes, 1972). Given this distinction, Mischel and Moore (1973) reasoned that when a child thinks about the rewards in front of them as "real," attention is placed on their hot, arousing, consummatory features, which should in turn elicit the motivating effects of the stimulus, making delay of gratification more difficult, and leading quickly to the "go" response: ring the bell, get the treat now. In contrast, we predicted that thinking about the rewards in terms of their cooler, more abstract features should allow the child to focus on the reward without activating consummatory trigger reactions. For example, mentally representing the rewards as pictures emphasizes their cognitive, informational features rather than their consummatory features. Therefore we speculated that this kind of "cool" mental transformation would reduce the conflict between wanting to wait and wanting to ring the bell by shifting attention away from the arousing features of the stimulus and onto their informative meaning (also see Trope and Liberman, 2003).

To test this prediction, Bert Moore and I presented one group of children in the delay of gratification task with slide-presented lifesize pictures of the rewards, formally called "iconic representations." The hypothesis again was that the pictures of the rewards would be relatively more abstract than the actual rewards, and thus the temptation to reach for them should be attenuated. These iconic representations were pitted against the presence of the real rewards themselves during the delay period. As predicted, exposure to the pictures of the images of the rewards significantly increased children's waiting time whereas exposure to the actual rewards decreased delay time (Mischel and Moore, 1973).

In one study, children were faced with actual rewards while they tried to wait, but this time the experimenter cued them in advance to "just pretend" that they were pictures: "Just put a frame around them in your head"(Moore et al., 1976). In a second condition, the children were shown pictures of the rewards but this time asked to think about them as if they were real. The children were able to delay almost 18 minutes when they pretended that the rewards facing them were pictures. In contrast, they were able to wait less than 6 minutes if they pretended that pictures in front of them were real rewards. As one child put it when asked in the postexperimental inquiry how she was able to wait so long: "You can't eat a picture."

In a study with Nancy Baker we identified the types of cognitive reconstrual that facilitate the ability to delay gratification. In this study, we cued children to represent the rewards available in front of them in terms of either their cool informational or hot consummatory features. For example, children in the cool focus condition who were waiting for marshmallows were cued (or "primed" in current terminology) to think of them as "white, puffy clouds." Those waiting for tiny stick pretzels were cued to think of them as "little brown logs." In the hot ideation condition, the instructions cued children to think about the marshmallows as "yummy and chewy" and the pretzels as "salty and crunchy." As expected, when children thought about the rewards in hot terms, they were able to wait only 5 minutes, whereas when they thought about them in cool terms, delay time increased to 13 minutes (Mischel and Baker, 1975).

Summary: hot versus cool focus

In sum, attention to the rewards may either make delay easier or harder, depending on whether the focus on the consummatory (hot, emotional) or nonconsummatory (cool, informational) features of the temptations. A nonconsummatory focus on the rewards can help self-imposed delay even more than comparable distractions; a consummatory focus makes delay exceedingly difficult. How the rewards are represented cognitively in this regard, crucially influences the duration of delay in opposite ways (Mischel et al., 1989). This now seems evident, but 35 years earlier, when behaviorism prevailed and the cognitive revolution was in its infancy, it was startling. For me it was the tipping point, from a focus on external stimulus control to internal self-control and the conditions that enable it as the person interacts with the social world.

The experiments in the late 1960s and early 1970s gradually, step by step, made it clear that the crucial determinant of the young child's ability to delay immediate gratification was not the rewards faced in the situation, as earlier theories had suggested. Instead, and contradicting the expectations both of classic behaviorism and of Freud, what mattered was exactly how they were represented mentally (Mischel, 1974; Mischel et al., 1989). The duration of delay depended on specific types of "hot" or "cool" mental representations, and the precise ways in which attention was deployed during the delay interval (e.g., Mischel and Baker, 1975; Mischel and Moore, 1973; Mischel et al., 1972; Peake et al., 2002). The best news for me was that children could be primed to change the representation from hot to cool, making it much easier for them to exert self-control when needed. If they could be primed by the experimenter in the lab, perhaps they also could learn to activate the needed strategies themselves and to plan to use them in pursuit of their own goals in everyday life.

MAKING SELF-CONTROL AUTOMATIC: PLANS

To exercise self-control effectively when it's needed in vivo in "hot" situations, needed strategies to cool the temptations and maintain adaptive delay behavior have to be activated virtually reflexively. That requires shifting from effortful or "volitional" control to automatic and virtually reflexive activation when they are needed. To explore the mechanisms enabling such a shift, Charlotte Patterson and I examined how different types of plans and rehearsal strategies facilitate preschool children's ability to resist temptation (Mischel and Patterson, 1976; Patterson and Mischel, 1976).

In these experiments preschool children were motivated to work on a long, repetitive task (sticking pegs into holes) in order to get attractive rewards later, and were warned that a "Mister Clown Box" might tempt them to stop working on the task. A temptation-inhibiting plan suggested that they direct attention away from Mister Clown Box; a task-facilitating plan suggested that they direct their attention toward continuing to work on the task. Some children received both plans, another group were given no plans, a third received only the temptation inhibiting plan, and a fourth only the task-facilitating plan. After the self-instructional manipulations, the child was left alone to work while the Clown Box performed a standard routine designed to tempt the child to stop working (e.g., "Please, please come talk to me ... I have big ears and love to have children talk into them and tell me what they think and want." Mister Clown Box, who had a colorfully painted clown face and display windows, exhibited tempting toys placed on a rotating drum in two windows, as he urged the child to "come talk with me and play with my toys." Dependent measures assessed the amount and rate of "work" completed, and the allocation of attention while dealing with the temptations.

The children struggled, often desperately, to resist the temptations, pleading with Mister Clown Box (e.g., "Don't talk to me," "Stop that," "Please don't bother me"). Their spontaneous effective strategies were very similar in intent to the temptation-inhibiting plan suggested by the experimenter, in that both seem designed to suppress the distracting stimuli in the child's environment. The results of this and related studies made clear that the effective plan was the one with specific self-instructions to resist the temptation when it occurred, and that having such plans available and accessible greatly facilitated persistence in goal-directed activity (Mischel and Patterson, 1976; Patterson and Mischel, 1976). The importance of such plans is now fully recognized by Peter Gollwitzer and colleagues in their persuasive and systematic studies showing the value of specific "if–then" implementation plans in the actualization of effective self-control strategies under stressful conditions, and further clarifying the relevant mechanisms (Gollwitzer, 1999).

HOT/COOL SYSTEM INTERACTIONS IN SELF-CONTROL

The important long-term correlates of the marshmallow test, and the clear findings from the experiments that helped identify the ability it tapped, led me to become interested in a more formal way to conceptualize those results. That called for a model of impulse control that could be integrated within the broader Cognitive–Affective Processing System (CAPS) that Yuichi Shoda and I had designed for understanding the expressions of stable individual differences in person-situation interactions (Mischel, 1973; Mischel and Shoda, 1995). With that goal, Janet Metcalfe and I proposed "a two-system framework for understanding the processes that enable–and undermine–self-control or 'willpower' in the execution

of one's intentions, as exemplified in the delay of gratification paradigm" (Metcalfe and Mischel, 1999). We postulated two closely linked systems: a cool cognitive 'know' system, and a hot emotional 'go' system (see also Metcalfe and Jacobs, 1996, 1998).

The hot system is an automatic system that responds reflexively to trigger features in the environment, both positive and negative, and elicits automatic, aversive, fight-and-flight reactions as well as appetitive and sexual approach reactions. It consists of relatively few representations which, when activated by trigger stimuli, elicit virtually reflexive avoidance and approach reactions. The cool system, on the other hand, is conceptualized as a controlled system that is attuned to the informational, cognitive, and spatial aspects of stimuli. It consists of a network of informational, cool nodes that are elaborately interconnected to each other, and generate rational, reflective, and strategic behavior. Whereas the hot system is conceptualized as the basis of emotionality, the cool system is thought to be the basis of self-regulation and self-control.

This hot/cool system idea is of course at least metaphorically related in its historical roots to Freud's conception of the id as characterized by irrational, impulsive urges for immediate wish-fulfillment, and its battles with the rational, logical, executive ego. The difference is that what has been learned from research on this topic over the course of the past century, not least the break-through in methods for imaging activity in the brain, we now can specify more clearly the cognitive and emotional processes, and even the neural process, that underlie these two systems and their interactions to enable effective self-regulation (e.g., Mischel et al., in press).

The regions of neural activity underlying these different systems currently remain a vigorously pursued topic of research (for review see Kross and Ochsner, 2010; also see Lieberman, 2007; Mischel et al., in press; Ochsner and Gross, 2005). Collectively the findings point to the amygdala – a small, almond-shaped region in the forebrain thought to enable fight or flight responses – as critically involved in hot system processing (Gray, 1982, 1987; LeDoux, 2000; Metcalfe and Jacobs, 1996, 1998). This brain structure reacts almost instantly to stimuli that individuals perceive as arousing (Adolphs et al., 1999; LeDoux, 1996, 2000; Phelps et al., 2001; Winston et al., 2002), immediately cueing behavioral, physiological (autonomic), and endocrine responses. The cool system, in contrast, seems to be associated with prefrontal and cingulate systems involved in cognitive control and executive function (e.g., Jackson et al., 2003; Ochsner and Gross, 2005).

The two systems continuously interact with each other, and with the stimuli in the particular context, producing the individual's subjective experiences and behavioral responses (also see Epstein, 1994; Lieberman et al., 2002). Hot representations and cool representations that have the same external referent are directly connected to each other, and link the two systems (Metcalfe and Mischel, 1999; see also Metcalfe and Jacobs, 1996, 1998). Thus hot representations can be evoked by the activation of corresponding cool representations. For example, an abusive man can become enraged by conjuring up a fantasy in which he finds his partner cheating on him. Likewise, hot representations can be cooled through the activation of cool system cognitive processes (e.g., attention switching, reconstrual). Thus the same abusive man can calm himself down by distracting himself or by recognizing that his fantasy is his own self-created fiction. Self-control becomes possible to the extent that cooling strategies are generated by the cognitive cool system to reduce hot system activation. While the particulars are different, the basic mechanisms are no different than those that regulate the child's ability to self-control in the marshmallow test. For the man in the example, the delayed important consequences are preservation of the relationship; for the child in the preschool delay situation, attainment of the two marshmallows.

Effects of stress

The balance of hot/cool system processing is influenced by several factors. The most important determinant of hot/cool system balance in adults tends to be stress. When stress levels are high, the cool system becomes deactivated and the hot system dominates. This makes complex thinking, planning, and remembering virtually impossible, ironically just when it may be most needed. When stress levels jump from low to very high, as in life-threatening emergency conditions, responding tends to be reflexive and automatic. That was probably highly adaptive in earlier evolutionary times: when an animal's life is threatened in the jungle, quick responses driven by innately determined stimuli may be essential. But when humans quarrel angrily at the breakfast table, such automatic reactions undermine rational efforts at constructive self-control.

Developmental level

Age and maturation matter. Early in development young children are primarily under stimulus control, because they have not yet developed the cool system structures needed to regulate hot system processing The hot system develops and dominates early in life, whereas the cool system develops later (by age four) and it becomes increasingly dominant over the developmental course. These developmental differences are consistent with the differential rates of development of the relevant brain areas for these two systems (for reviews see Eisenberger et al., 2004; Rothbart et al., 2004). As the cool system develops, children become increasingly able to generate cooling strategies to regulate impulses (Mischel et al., 1989). These developmental changes also may underlie the greater vulnerability to the effects of stress and traumas early in life.

TOWARDS AN INTEGRATIVE CAPS SELF-CONTROL THEORY

The important and stable long-term differences in self-control tapped by the marshmallow test, and the cognitive–affective mechanisms that underlie those individual differences, coexist with the fact that self-control behavior, like all social behavior, is expressed in highly contextualized if–then situation-specific ways. And that has crucial implications for the integrative CAPS theory of self-control that my colleagues and I developed (e.g., Mischel and Shoda, 1995).

The if–then contextualized expressions of self-control

It is true that, on average, the high delay group in the Bing lifespan study looks very different from the low delay group in follow-ups conducted at roughly ten-year intervals. But when we examine these differences closely, we also see that within each group, and within each individual, there is equally impressive variability. Well-known examples of such variability abound in daily life. Former president Bill Clinton was clearly high in his average overall ability to exert self-control and delay gratification. Without it, he could never have become president of the US, not to mention a Rhodes scholar and a Yale-trained lawyer. Yet, evidence for his systematic failures to exert self-control came in the painful details of his descent towards impeachment (Morrow, 1998).

Less publicized, but even more surprising for many, was the fall of Sol Wachtler, Chief Judge of the State of New York and the Court of Appeals, to incarceration as a felon in federal prison. Judge Wachtler was well known for advocating laws to make marital rape a punishable crime, and he was deeply respected for his landmark decisions on free speech, civil rights, and the right to die. After his mistress left him for another man, however, Judge Wachtler spent 13 months writing obscene letters, making lewd phone calls, and threatening to kidnap her daughter. His descent from the court's bench as the model of jurisprudence and moral wisdom to federal prison testifies that smart people are not necessarily consistently so across different areas of their lives (e.g., Ayduk and Mischel, 2002). As observers of human behavior have long known, even "on average" adaptively controlled lives are not without their surprising failures to exert such control at crucial times.

These everyday observations are supported by extensive research that examined closely the consistency of social behavior as it actually unfolds across diverse situations (e.g., Mischel, 1968, 2004, 2009; Mischel and Peake, 1982a; Mischel and Shoda, 1995). To illustrate, in the Carleton College field study, behavior relevant to conscientiousness in college was observed in vivo over multiple situations and occasions (Mischel and Peake, 1982a, 1982b). Each of the 63 participating college students was observed repeatedly in various situations on campus relevant to their conscientiousness in the college setting. The undergraduates themselves supplied the contexts or situations they considered relevant. Based on this information from pretests, the students' conscientiousness was sampled in diverse situations, such as in the classroom, in the dormitory, or in the library, and these assessments were repeated over multiple occasions in the course of the semester. The directly observed actual consistency correlation in their cross-situational behavior was on average between 0.08 (for single behaviors) to 0.13 for reliable aggregates of the single behaviors within each of the 19 types of conscientiousness sampled. Thus while the correlations were not zero-order, they made clear that an individual may be highly conscientiousness in one type of situation, and much less conscientious than most people in another type of situations, even if both types seem highly similar (Mischel and Peake, 1982a).

Consistent with these findings, and flying in the face of the core assumptions of traditional personality psychology that personality traits are expressed consistently across diverse situations, my monograph, *Personality and Assessment* (1968), called attention to the highly contextualized, situation-specific expressions of individual differences in social behavior. The conscientious man at work may be a scoundrel in his private life; the aggressive child at home may be less aggressive than most when in school; the man exceptionally hostile when rejected in love may be unusually tolerant about criticism of his work; the one who shakes with anxiety in the doctor's office may be a calm mountain climber; the business entrepreneur may take few social risks. And 40 years later a great deal of behavioral evidence continues to support this perspective (e.g., Mischel, 2009; Orom and Cervone, 2009; Van Mechelen, 2009).

But while individual differences are rarely expressed in consistent cross-situational behavior across widely different situations, the new discovery is that consistency is found in distinctive but stable patterns of if–then situation-behavior relations. These patterns of variability form contextualized, psychologically meaningful "personality signatures" (e.g., "she does A when X, but B when Y" that are stable over time). Such behavioral signatures were first revealed in a massive fine-grained observational study of social behavior across multiple repeated situations over time in a summer camp for children and adolescents (Mischel and Shoda, 1995). We found that individuals who were similar in average levels of behavior, for example in their aggression, nevertheless differed predictably and dramatically in the types of situations in which they aggressed; that is in their if–then situation-behavior signatures.

As Figure 26.1 shows, each child showed a distinctive and stable if–then

situation-behavior pattern or "profile" that distinguished him or her characteristically (Shoda et al., 1994). Even when two children are equal in their overall aggressive behavior, for example, the one who regularly becomes aggressive when peers try to play

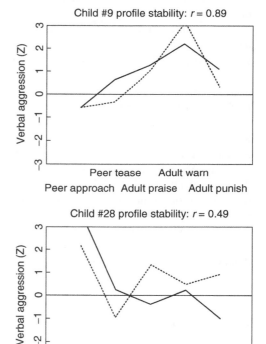

Figure 26.1   Individual if–then situation-behavior signatures for two children. Their aggressive behavior was observed in five different situations many times. Half of the observations are shown as dotted lines; half as solid lines. Profile stability is the correlation between the two sets of observations. (From Shoda, Y., Mischel, W., and Wright, J.C. (1994) Intra-individual stability in the organization and patterning of behavior: Incorporating psychological situations into the idiographic analysis of personality. *Journal of Personality and Social Psychology, 67,* 674–687, fig. 1. © 1994 by the American Psychological Association. Adapted with permission.)

with him is quite different from the one who expresses aggression mostly to adults who try to control him. In short, stable situation-behavior personality signatures, not just stable levels of average overall behavior, characterize individuals, and this is the case for the expressions of conscientiousness and self-control as much as for other individual differences.

These stable signatures of personality have now been extensively documented in various studies of observed behavior as it unfolds over time and across diverse situations (e.g., Andersen and Chen, 2002; Borkenau et al., 2006; Cervone and Shoda, 1999; Fournier et al., 2008; Morf and Rhodewalt, 2001; Moskowitz et al., 1994; Shoda and LeeTiernan 2002; Vansteelandt and Van Mechelen, 1998; Van Mechelen, 2009). Collectively, this work has allowed a new way to conceptualize and assess both the stability and variability of behavior that is produced by the underlying personality system, and has opened a window into the dynamic processes within the system itself (Mischel, 2004).

ways that depend on the person's social and biological history. Other CAUs represent the person's expectancies and beliefs about the self and the world, and about outcomes anticipated for behaviors in different situations. Other CAUs represent affects (feelings, emotions), values, and goals that motivate the person's plans and life projects.

Especially important for understanding self-control patterns are the CAUs representing the individual's repertoire of behavioral competencies. These are the potential behaviors that can be performed, as well as self-control strategies the person uses to regulate his or her behavior, sometimes volitionally but much more often automatically, as described above in the research on delay of gratification. These competencies include cognitive-attention strategies, plans, and scripts for generating diverse types of social behavior necessary for sustained, goal-directed effort in the pursuit of difficult goals whose attainment requires impulse control and delay of gratification (Mischel and Ayduk, 2002, 2004).

Self-control in the Cognitive–Affective Processing System

Yuichi Shoda and I proposed CAPS theory to understand how and why individuals may differ dramatically in their distinctive, stable if–then situation-behavior signatures exhibited by a given individual. CAPS is a complex system of interacting components consisting of cognitive–affective units (CAUs) that mediate between the nominal interpersonal situation the person encounters and the responses generated. Box 26.1 summarizes the types of mediating CAUs hypothesized.

Some mediating CAUs encode and interpret the personal and social perceived situation in terms of the person's categories for the self, other people, and events. Some categories are chronically more accessible than others, thereby biasing social perceptions in

Intraindividual variability in what's too hot to handle

Intuitively, one might expect that a person who is good at self-distraction, or good at abstracting, would be good at these cognitive-attention strategies across situations, and hence there should be extremely broad cross-situational consistency in self-control, particularly since cognitive competencies and skills tend to be broader and more stable than other psychological characteristics (Mischel, 1968). In short, as common sense wisdom also suggests, some people should have more "willpower" than others, no matter what the temptations or hot trigger stimuli. And there indeed are overall aggregate differences: Some people do show overall more self-control than others and these differences are fairly stable over time, as shown in the longitudinal research on the "marshmallow

---

Box 26.1   Types of cognitive–affective units in the personality mediating system

1   *Encodings*: Categories (constructs) for the self, people, events, and situations (external and internal).
2   *Expectancies and Beliefs*: About the social world, about outcomes for behavior in particular situations, about self-efficacy.
3   *Affects*: Feelings, emotions, and affective responses (including physiological reactions).
4   *Goals and Values*: Desirable outcomes and affective states; aversive outcomes and affective states; goals, values, and life projects.
5   *Competencies and Self-regulatory Plans*: Potential behaviors and scripts that one can do, and plans and strategies for organizing action and for affecting outcomes and one's own behavior and internal states.

Note: Based in part on Mischel (1973).

---

test." But as with other characteristics, there is also impressive stable within-person if–then variability: some temptations and trigger stimuli are too hot to handle even for individuals who overall can be very effective in self-control most of the time. Recall again the Clinton example.

To make sense of this requires recognizing that the ease with which an individual can activate cognitive-attention strategies to cool particular hot trigger stimuli depends first of all on how hot that stimulus is for that person within the particular context. What's too hot for Clinton may not be too hot for you, and possibly vice versa. Nevertheless, reasonable consistency within and across particular domains and types of situations also can be identified (e.g., Wright and Mischel, 1987). And individual differences and within-person differences in the subjective salience and valence of different temptations are of course not the only relevant variables. Also at play are such considerations as the expectations for probable consequences that become activated, and the subjective value of those consequences, as well as their ease of activation in the particular situation. Hence no one, including any Gandhi in the world, is immune from moral dilemmas and "now" versus "later" conflicts: even people who are able and willing to cool all sorts of temptations may remain highly vulnerable to

others – from addictive drugs to financial and interpersonal temptations – as even casual observers of the human condition have noted since the biblical loss of paradise.

Architecture of CAPS

The architecture of the overall CAPS system is shown in Figure 26.2. Situations contain a collection of features, some of which are triggered or "turned on" by a particular nominal situation. When stimulated, these input features send "activation" into the mediating CAUs with which they are connected. The amount of activation reaching a given CA mediating unit from an activated input feature depends on importance or "weight" of that input feature's connection to that mediating unit. The aroused CAUs transmit this incoming wave of activation among themselves, ultimately settling into some internal state that will lead some response to be generated in the situation. That response in turn may change the external situation, initiating the next response cycle.

Each person is characterized by his or her own distinctive collection of cognitive–affective units with their own set of connection weights, reflecting how their learning experiences and biological histories have led

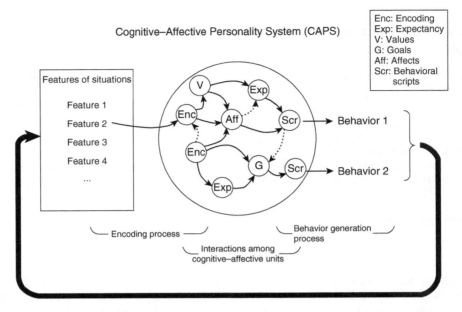

Figure 26.2   The Cognitive–Affective Personality System (CAPS). Situational features activate a given mediating unit which activates specific subsets of other mediating units through a stable network of relations that characterize an individual, generating a characteristic pattern of behavior in response to different situations. The relation may be positive (solid line), which increases the activation, or negative (dashed line), which decreases the activation. (From Mischel, W., and Shoda, Y. (1995). A cognitive–affective system theory of personality: Reconceptualizing situations, dispositions, dynamics, and invariance in personality structure. *Psychological Review, 102*, 246–268. © 1995 by the American Psychological Association. Adapted with permission.)

to particular CAUs and their importance (i.e., connection weightings). The CAUs are organized into distinctive idiographic networks, broadly analogous to neural networks. Whereas each network is unique, individuals can be grouped into types and subtypes. These types may differ both on the basis of similarities in their chronic levels of accessibility (e.g., some readily access anxious expectations for rejection than others; some are more able to delay gratification, to plan effectively, and to control impulses), and on the basis of their organization (interconnections) within the system. The processing system and the situations it generates and encounters interact reciprocally and continuously in a dynamic mutual influence process.

Interaction of self-control ability and dispositional vulnerability: protective dynamics

In the CAPS self-control model, the individual's self-regulatory ability can have important long-term protective effects that buffer against the potential negative effects of various dispositional vulnerabilities. Evidence for such a protective effective was seen in the Bing longitudinal studies discussed above. We identified these processing dynamics in studies of individual differences in the tendency to be highly rejection-sensitive (RS) in interpersonal relationships, guided by the CAPS model. Research on RS indicates that highly rejection-sensitive people in time develop lower self-esteem and become either more aggressive or more depressed, which, in turn, undermines the quality of their lives (Downey and Feldman, 1996). But that sequence is not inevitable. In an adult follow-up of the Bing preschoolers who had participated in the original delay of gratification studies 20 years earlier, preschool delay ability predicted adult resiliency against the potentially destructive effects of RS (Ayduk et al., 2000, Study 1). Specifically, high RS people who were able to delay gratification longer in preschool were buffered in adulthood against low self-esteem and self-worth, were better able to cope with stress, and had greater ego resiliency. High RS people who were unable to delay gratification in preschool had lower academic achievement and more frequent cocaine/crack use than low RS people. In contrast, high RS people who had high preschool delay ability were buffered against such negative outcomes.

In CAPS self-control theory, these findings reflect differences in people's ability to readily (automatically) activate strategies for "cooling" and reducing the "hot thoughts" to which their RS makes them vulnerable. Thereby they can avoid the impulsive reactions (e.g., become enraged, create a fight) to which they are vulnerable. A parallel study, conducted among low-income, urban, minority middle-school children who are at higher demographic risk for maladjustment, replicated these findings with population-appropriate measures (Ayduk et al., 2000, Study 2). Again, among children high in RS, delay of gratification ability was associated with lower aggression against peers, greater interpersonal acceptance, and higher levels of self-worth. Children who were low in delay ability but high in RS exhibited the negative behaviors typical of the RS dynamics. The overall findings support the idea that self-regulatory competencies, and the cooling mechanisms they enable, restrain the negative influence of high RS on the behavior that plays out. The seeds of individual differences in attention control and self-regulation are visible already in the behavior of toddlers in their ability to cool their negative affect during brief separation from the mother. They in turn predict self-regulatory competencies years later, as shown in more adaptive patterns of "cool" attention control when they deal with the challenges of the marshmallow test at age five years (Sethi et al., 2000).

Agency in CAPS

CAPS is not a passive, reactive system: it is agentic and proactive in the sense that it also acts upon itself through a feedback loop, both by generating its own internal situations (e.g., in anticipated and planned events, in fantasy, in self-reflection), and through the behaviors that the system generates in interaction with the social world. Such behaviors (e.g., impulsive reactions, failures to carry out intentions, effective control efforts and goal pursuit) further influence the individual's social–cognitive experiences and evolving social learning history, and modify the subsequent situations encountered and generated. In this view, development of the self-regulatory system is a lifelong process of adaptation both through assimilating new stimuli into the existing CAPS network and by accommodating the network itself in response to novel situations.

PROSPECTS

The questions that motivated my work beginning around the kitchen table talking with my three little daughters 40 years ago have yielded valuable answers, sure to change in the future, but pointing to core cognitive–affective mechanisms that help to demystify "willpower." We are eager to probe ever more deeply into the basic underlying mechanisms that control delay of gratification behavior and impulse control, turning now to the neural and brain level of analysis. Therefore we have formed an interdisciplinary team with cognitive neuroscientists, including B.J. Casey, John Jonides, Ozlem Ayduk, Kevin Ochsner, Edward E. Smith, Yuichi Shoda, and other colleagues to uncover with increasing depth the neural as well as the cognitive, affective, and social–behavioral mechanisms that enable impulse control. Participants in the Bing Longitudinal Study have been invited to the Lucas Center for Imaging at Stanford University but only a few have been scanned to date (Mischel et al., in press). As the participants are reaching middle adulthood, we also are continuing to assess consequential outcomes, including occupational and marital status, economic behavior, social, cognitive, and emotional functioning, as well as mental and physical health and wellbeing. The results we trust will help explain with increasing precision the individual differences in "willpower" revealed in the longitudinal studies, perhaps even extending into the final years of life.

So what?

Not just psychologists, but also economists, policy makers, and educators (as well as the media) have now recognized that the "marshmallow test" taps important long-term individual differences in self-control early in life that predict highly consequential mental and physical health consequences over much of the lifespan, and do so far better than intelligence tests. That kind of long-term predictability for important life outcomes is remarkably rare, if not unique, within psychological science. Most exciting to me, beyond prediction, and of particular social significance, the findings to date help reveal how the mechanisms that underlie willpower can allow people who have difficulty with delay of gratification (including the author) to do so. They can learn strategies to control their attention strategically and to change how the temptations are mentally represented to "cool" their impact. The power of such cognitive reappraisal has been amply demonstrated, at least for short-tem changes in the laboratory. The challenge now is to see

how these strategies can best be taught early in life and maintained virtually automatically for long-term enhancement of self-control ability. The implications for educational and social policy and for therapeutic interventions are potentially enormous, as is now widely recognized even in the media, for example in a *New York Times* editorial column by David Brooks entitled "Marshmallows and Public Policy" (e.g., Brooks, 2006; Gladwell, 2002; Goleman, 2006; Lehrer, 2009).

With the goal of creating educational interventions designed to enhance the psychological skills underlying willpower phenomena, Angela Duckworth and a team of colleagues and I are currently pilot testing such attempts within the schools. The current policies and practices of the American school system, beginning in the early grades, are primarily designed to cultivate knowledge and analytical skills. But it has become evident that such skills are not the only, nor even the most important, competencies essential to successful functioning and flourishing in adulthood. Our science is now poised to identify and enhance with increasing precision the psychological skills and strategies that enable "willpower" in young children so that they can learn to use them to realize their full cognitive and social potential. These skills constitute what Goleman (2006) has labeled the "master aptitude." They promise to be teachable, and with surprisingly simple theory-based core strategies (e.g., Kross et al., 2010; Mischel and Ayduk, 2004). If willpower can be dramatically facilitated by teaching learnable skills and strategies to the young child, the educational policy and therapeutic implications are as evident as they are profound.

REFERENCES

Adolphs, R., Tranel, D., Hamann, S., Young, A.W., Calder, A.J., Phelps, E.A., Anderson, A., Lee, G.P. and Damasio, A.R. (1999) Recognition of facial emotion in nine individuals with bilateral amygdala damage. *Neuropsychologia*, *37*, 1111–1117.

Ainslie, G. (2001) *Breakdown of Will*. Cambridge: Cambridge University Press.

Andersen, S.M. and Chen, S. (2002) The relational self: An interpersonal social–cognitive theory. *Psychological Review*, 109, 619–645.

Ayduk, O., Mendoza-Denton, R., Mischel, W., Downey, G., Peake, P. and Rodriguez, M.L. (2000) Regulating the interpersonal self: Strategic self-regulation for coping with rejection sensitivity. *Journal of Personality and Social Psychology*, 79, 776–792.

Ayduk, O. and Mischel, W. (2002) When smart people behave stupidly: Inconsistencies in social and emotional intelligence. In R.J. Sternberg (ed.), *Why Smart People Can Be So Stupid*, pp. 86–105. New Haven, CT: Yale University Press.

Ayduk, O., Zayas, V., Downey, G., Cole, A.B., Shoda, Y. and Mischel, W. (2008) Rejection sensitivity and executive control: Joint predictors of borderline personality features. *Journal of Research in Personality*, 42, 151–168.

Bandura, A. (1986). *Social Foundations of Thought and Action: A Social Cognitive Theory*. Englewood Cliffs, NJ: Prentice-Hall.

Bandura, A. and Mischel, W. (1965) Modification of self-imposed delay of reward through exposure to live and symbolic models. *Journal of Personality and Social Psychology*, 2, 698–705.

Berlyne, D. (1960) *Conflict, Arousal, and Curiosity*. New York: McGraw Hill.

Borkenau, P., Riemann, R., Spinath, F.M. and Angleitner, A. (2006) Genetic and environmental influences on person situation profiles. *Journal of Personality*, 74, 1451–1479.

Brooks, D. (2006) Marshmallows and public policy. *The New York Times*, 7 May.

Cervone, D. and Shoda, Y. (eds) (1999) *The Coherence of Personality: Social–Cognitive Bases of Consistency, Variability, and Organization*. New York: Guilford Press.

Downey, G. and Feldman, S. (1996) Implications of rejection sensitivity for intimate relationships. *Journal of Personality and Social Psychology*, 70, 1327–1343.

Eigsti, I., Zayas, V., Mischel, W., Shoda, Y., Ayduk, O., Dadlani, M.B., Davidson, M.C., Aber, J.L. and Casey, B.J. (2006) Predicting cognitive control from preschool to late adolescence and young adulthood. *Psychological Science*, 17, 478–484.

Eisenberg, N., Fabes, R.A., Guthrie, I.K. and Reiser, M. (2002) The role of emotionality and regulation in children's social competence and adjustment. In L. Pulkkinen and A. Caspi (eds), *Paths to Successful Development: Personality in the Life Course*, pp. 46–70. New York: Cambridge University Press.

Eisenberger, N., Smith, C.L., Sadovsky, A. and Spinrad, T.L. (2004) Effortful control: reactions with emotion regulation, adjustment, and socialization in childhood. In R.F. Baumeister and K.D. Vohs (eds), *Handbook of Self Regulation*. New York: Guilford Press.

Epstein, S. (1994) Integration of the cognitive and psychodynamic unconscious. *American Psychologist*, 49, 709–724.

Estes, W.K. (1972) Reinforcement in human behavior. *American Scientist*, 60, 723–729.

Fournier, M.A., Moskowitz, D.S. and Zuroff, D.C. (2008) Integrating dispositions, signatures, and the interpersonal domain. *Journal of Personality and Social Psychology*, 94, 531–545; 754–768.

Freud, S. (1959) Formulations regarding the two principles of mental functioning. *Collected Papers, Vol. IV*. New York: Basic Books. (Originally published 1911).

Gladwell, M. (2002) *The Tipping Point: How Little Things Can Make a Big Difference*. New York: Little Brown and Company.

Goleman, D. (2006) *Emotional Intelligence: Why It Can Matter More Than IQ*. New York: Bantam.

Gollwitzer, P.M. (1999) Implementation intentions: Strong effects of simple plans. *American Psychologist*, 54, 493–503.

Gray, J.A. (1982) *The Neuropsychology of Anxiety*. Oxford: Oxford University Press.

Gray, J.A. (1987) *The Psychology of Fear and Stress*, 2nd Edition. New York: McGraw-Hill.

Hull, C.L. (1931) Goal attraction and directing ideas conceived as habit phenomena. *Psychological Review*, 38, 487–506.

Johnson, M.H., Posner, M.I. and Rothbart, M.K. (1991) Components of visual orienting in early infancy: Contingency learning, anticipatory looking, and disengaging. *Journal of Cognitive Neuroscience*, 3, 335–344.

Jackson, D.C., Muller, C.J., Dolski, I., Dalton, K.M., Nitschke, J.B., Urry, H.L., Rosenkranz, M.A., Ryff, D.C., Singer, B.H. and Davidson, R.J. (2003) Now you feel it, now you don't: Frontal brain electrical asymmetry and individual differences in emotion regulation. *Psychological Science*, 14, 612–617.

Kross, E., Mischel, W. and Shoda, Y. (2010) Enabling self-control: A cognitive affective processing system (CAPS) approach to problematic behavior. In J. Maddux and J. Tangney (eds), *Social Psychological Foundations of Clinical Psychology*, pp. 375–394. New York: Guilford.

Kross, E. and Ochsner, K. (2010) Integrating research on self-control across multiple levels of analysis: A social cognitive neuroscience approach.

In R. Hassin, K. Ochsner and Y. Trope. (eds), *From Society to Brain: The New Sciences of Self-Control*, pp. 76–92. New York: Oxford University Press.

LeDoux, J. (1996) *The Emotional Brain*. New York: Touchstone.

LeDoux, J.E. (2000) Emotion circuits in the brain. *Annual Review of Neuroscience*, 23, 155–184.

Lehrer, J. (2009) Don't! The secret of self-control. *The New Yorker*, 18 May.

Lieberman, M.D. (2007) Social cognitive neuroscience: A review of core processes. *Annual Review of Psychology*, 58, 259–89.

Lieberman, M.D., Gaunt, R., Gilbert, D.T. and Trope, Y. (2002). Reflection and reflexion: A social cognitive neuroscience approach to attributional inference. In M. Zanna (ed.), *Advances in Experimental Social Psychology*, 34, 199–249. New York: Academic Press.

Loewenstein, G., Read, D. and Baumeister, R. (eds) (2003) *Time and Decision: Economic and Psychological Perspectives on Intertemporal Choice*. New York: Russell Sage Foundation.

Metcalfe, J. and Jacobs, W.J. (1996) A 'hot/cool-system' view of memory under stress. *PTSD Research Quarterly*, 7, 1–6.

Metcalfe, J. and Jacobs, W.J. (1998) Emotional memory: The effects of stress on 'cool' and 'hot' memory systems. In D.L. Medin (ed.), *The Psychology of Learning and Motivation: Advances in Research and Theory*, 38, 187–222. San Diego: Academic Press.

Metcalfe, J. and Mischel, W. (1999) A hot/cool system analysis of delay of gratification: Dynamics of willpower. *Psychological Review*, 106, 3–19.

Mischel, W. (1961a) Preference for delayed reinforcement and social responsibility. *Journal of Abnormal and Social Psychology*, 62, 1–7.

Mischel, W. (1961b) Delay of gratification, need for achievement and acquiescence in another culture. *Journal of Abnormal and Social Psychology*, 62, 543–552.

Mischel, W. (1961c) Father absence and delay of gratification: Cross-cultural comparisons. *Journal of Abnormal and Social Psychology*, 63, 116–124.

Mischel, W. (1966) Theory and research on the antecedents of self-imposed delay of reward. In B.A. Maher (ed.), *Progress in Experimental Personality Research*, 3, 85–131. New York: Academic Press.

Mischel, W. (1968) *Personality and Assessment*. New Jersey: Erlbaum.

Mischel, W. (1973) Toward a cognitive social learning reconceptualization of personality. *Psychological Review*, 80, 252–283.

Mischel, W. (1974).Processes in delay of gratification. In L. Berkowitz (ed.), *Advances in Experimental Social Psychology*, 7, 249–292. New York: Academic Press.

Mischel, W. (2004) Toward an integrative science of the person. *Annual Review of Psychology*, 55, 1–22.

Mischel, W. (2009) From *Personality and Assessment* (1968) to personality science. *Journal of Research in Personality (Special Issue: Personality and Assessment 40 years later)*, 43, 282–290.

Mischel, W. and Ayduk, O. (2002) Self-regulation in a cognitive-affective personality system: Attentional control in the service of the self. *Self and Identity*, 1, 113–120.

Mischel, W. and Ayduk, O. (2004) Willpower in a cognitive-affective processing system: The dynamics of delay of gratification. In R.F. Baumeister and K.D. Vohs (eds), *Handbook of Self-regulation: Research, Theory, and Applications*, pp. 99–129. New York: Guilford Press.

Mischel, W., Ayduk, O., Berman, M., Casey, B.J., Gotlib, I., Jonides, J., Kross, E., Teslovich, T., Wilson, N., Zayas, V. and Shoda, Y. (in press) 'Willpower' over the life span: decomposing impulse control. *Social and Cognitive Affective Neuroscience (Special Issue on Social and Affective Neuroscience and Neuroeconomics of Aging)*.

Mischel, W. and Baker, N. (1975) Cognitive appraisals and transformations in delay behavior. *Journal of Personality and Social Psychology*, 31, 254–261.

Mischel, W. and Ebbesen, E.B. (1970) Attention in delay of gratification. *Journal of Personality and Social Psychology*, 16, 239–337.

Mischel, W., Ebbesen, E.B. and Zeiss, A.R. (1972) Cognitive and attentional mechanisms in delay of gratification. *Journal of Personality and Social Psychology*, 21, 204–218.

Mischel, W. and Gilligan, C. (1964) Delay of gratification, motivation for the prohibited gratification, and resistance to temptation. *Journal of Abnormal and Social Psychology*, 69, 411–417.

Mischel, W. and Metzner, R. (1962) Preference for delayed reward as a function of age, intelligence, and length of delay interval. *Journal of Abnormal and Social Psychology*, 64, 425–431.

Mischel, W. and Mischel, F. (1958) Psychological aspects of spirit possession: A reinforcement analysis. *American Anthropologist*, 60, 249–260.

Mischel, W. and Moore, B. (1973) Effects of attention to symbolically-presented rewards on self-control. *Journal of Personality and Social Psychology*, 28, 172–179.

Mischel, W. and Patterson, C.J. (1976) Substantive and structural elements of effective plans for self-control. *Journal of Personality and Social Psychology*, *34*, 942–950.

Mischel, W. and Peake, P.K. (1982a) Beyond deja vu in the search for cross-situational consistency. *Psychological Review*, *89*, 730–755.

Mischel, W. and Peake, P. (1982b) In search of consistency: Measure for measure. In M.P. Zanna, E.T. Higgins, and C.P. Herman (eds), *Consistency in Social Behavior: The Ontario Symposium, 2*, 187–207. Hillsdale, NJ: Erlbaum.

Mischel, W. and Shoda, Y. (1995) A cognitive-affective system theory of personality: Reconceptualizing situations, dispositions, dynamics, and invariance in personality structure. *Psychological Review*, *102*, 246–268.

Mischel, W., Shoda, Y. and Peake, P.K. (1988) The nature of adolescent competencies predicted by preschool delay of gratification. *Journal of Personality and Social Psychology*, *54*, 687–699.

Mischel, W., Shoda, Y. and Rodriguez, M.L. (1989) Delay of gratification in children. *Science*, *244*, 933–938.

Mischel, W. and Staub, E. (1965) Effects of expectancy on working and waiting for larger rewards. *Journal of Personality and Social Psychology*, *2*, 625–633.

Moore, B., Mischel, W. and Zeiss, A. (1976) Comparative effects of the reward stimulus and its cognitive representation in voluntary delay. *Journal of Personality and Social Psychology*, *34*, 419–424.

Morf, C.C. and Rhodewalt, F. (2001) Unraveling the paradoxes of narcissism: A dynamic self-regulatory processing model. *Psychological Inquiry*, *12*, 177–196.

Morrow, L. (1998, Feb. 2) The reckless and the stupid: A character of a President eventually determines his destiny. *Time Magazine*.

Moskowitz, D.S., Suh, E.J. and Desaulniers, J. (1994) Situational influences on gender differences in agency and communion. *Journal of Personality and Social Psychology*, *66*, 753–761.

Nolen-Hoeksema, S. (1991) Responses to depression and their effects on the duration of depressive episodes. *Journal of Abnormal Psychology*, *100*, 569–582.

Ochsner, K.N. and Gross, J.J. (2005) The cognitive control of emotion. *Trends in Cognitive Science*, *27*, 26–36.

Ochsner, K.N. and Gross, J.J. (2007) The neural architecture of emotion regulation. In J.J. Gross and R. Buck (eds), *The Handbook of Emotion Regulation*, pp. 87–109. New York: Guilford Press.

Ochsner, K.N. and Gross, J.J. (2008) Cognitive emotion regulation: Insights from social cognitive and affective neuroscience. *Currents Directions in Psychological Science*, *17*, 153–158.

Orom, H. and Cervone, D. (2009) Personality dynamics, meaning, and idiosyncrasy: Identifying cross-situational coherence by assessing personality architecture. *Journal of Research in Personality (Special Issue: Personality and Assessment 40 years later)*, *43*, 228–240.

Patterson, C.J. and Mischel, W. (1976) Effects of temptation-inhibiting and task-facilitating plans on self-control. *Journal of Personality and Social Psychology*, *33*, 209–217.

Peake, P., Hebl, M. and Mischel, W. (2002) Strategic attention deployment in waiting and working situations. *Developmental Psychology*, *38*, 313–326.

Phelps, E.A., O'Connor, K.J., Gatenby, J.C., Gore, J.C., Grillon, C. and Davis, M. (2001) Activation of the left amygdala to a cognitive representation of fear. *Nature Neuroscience*, 4, 437–441.

Posner, M.I., Rothbart, M.K., Gerardi, G. and Thomas-Thrapp, L.J. (1997) Functions of orienting in early infancy. In P. Lang, M. Balaban, and R.F. Simmons (eds), *The Study of Attention: Cognitive Perspectives from Psychophysiology, Reflexology and Neuroscience*, pp. 327–345. Hillsdale, NJ: Erlbaum.

Rachlin, H. (2000) *The Science of Self-control*. Cambridge, MA: Harvard University Press.

Rapaport, D. (1967) *The Collected Papers of David Rapaport*. New York: Basic Books.

Rodriguez, M.L., Mischel, W. and Shoda, Y. (1989) Cognitive person variables in the delay of gratification of older children at-risk. *Journal of Personality and Social Psychology*, *57*, 358–367.

Rothbart, M.K., Ellis, L.K. and Posner, M.I., (2004) Temperament and self-regulation. In R.F. Baumeister and K.D. Vohs (eds), *Handbook of Self-Regulation*. New York: Guilford Press.

Rusting, C.L. and Nolen-Hoeksema, S. (1998) Regulating responses to anger: Effects on rumination and distraction on angry mood. *Journal of Personality and Social Psychology*, *74*, 790–803.

Sethi, A., Mischel, W., Aber, L., Shoda, Y. and Rodriguez, M. (2000) The role of strategic attention deployment in development of self-regulation: Predicting preschoolers' delay of gratification from mother-toddler interactions. *Developmental Psychology*, *36*, 767–777.

Shoda, Y. and LeeTiernan, S.J. (2002) What remains invariant? Finding order within a person's thoughts, feelings, and behaviors across situations. In D. Cervone and W. Mischel (eds), *Advances in Personality Science*, pp. 241–270. New York: Guilford Press.

Shoda, Y., Mischel, W. and Peake, P.K. (1990) Predicting adolescent cognitive and self-regulatory competencies from preschool delay of gratification: Identifying diagnostic conditions. *Developmental Psychology*, *26*, 978–986.

Shoda, Y., Mischel, W. and Wright, J. (1993) The role of situational demands and cognitive competencies in behavior organization and personality coherence. *Journal of Personality and Social Psychology*, *65*, 1023–1035.

Shoda, Y., Mischel, W. and Wright, J.C. (1994) Intra-individual stability in the organization and patterning of behavior: Incorporating psychological situations into the idiographic analysis of personality. *Journal of Personality and Social Psychology*, *67*, 674–687.

Trope, Y. and Liberman, N. (2003) Temporal construal. *Psychological Review*, *110*, 403–421.

Van Mechelen, I. (2009) A royal road to understanding the mechanisms underlying person-in-context behavior. *Journal of Research in Personality (Special Issue: Personality and Assessment 40 years later)*, *43*, 179–186.

Vansteelandt, K. and Van Mechelen, I. (1998) Individual differences in situation–behavior profiles: A triple typology model. *Journal of Personality and Social Psychology*, *75*, 751–765.

Winston, J.S., Strange, B.A., O'Doherty, J. and Dolan, R.J. (2002) Automatic and intentional brain responses during evaluation of trustworthiness of faces. *Nature Neuroscience*, *5*, 277–283.

Wright, J.C. and Mischel, W. (1987) A conditional approach to dispositional constructs: The local predictability of social behavior. *Journal of Personality and Social Psychology*, *53*, 1159–1177.

Wright, J.C. and Mischel, W. (1988) Conditional hedges and the intuitive psychology of traits. *Journal of Personality and Social Psychology*, *55*, 454–469.

Self-Verification Theory

William B. Swann, Jr.

ABSTRACT

Self-verification theory proposes that people prefer others to see them as they see themselves, even if their self-views happen to be negative. For example, those who see themselves as likable want others to see them as such, and people who see themselves as dislikable want others to perceive them that way. Presumably, people seek self-verification because self-verifying evaluations make the world seem coherent and predictable. In addition, self-verifying evaluations smooth social interaction by guiding action and letting people know what to expect from others. People strive for self-verification by gravitating toward interaction partners and settings that seem likely to provide self-confirming evaluations. Moreover, once in relationships, people actively evoke self-confirming reactions from their partners. Finally, people process feedback about themselves in ways that promote the survival of their self-views. In general, self-verification strivings are adaptive and functional, as they foster feelings of coherence, reduce anxiety, improve group functioning, and erode social stereotypes. Nevertheless, for those who possess inappropriately negative self-views, self-verification may thwart positive change and make their life situations harsher than they would be otherwise. In this chapter, I discuss the nature, history, and social implications of self-verification theory and research.

INTRODUCTION

It all started with a seven year old boy named Tommy. I met Tommy while working at a camp for underprivileged children following my sophomore year in college. I still have a vivid memory of our first encounter. It was my first day at the camp, and I was eager to meet the kids. As I approached the camp director's cabin, however, I was alarmed at the sound of some boys fighting. I ran over to find Tommy on the ground, pinned down by two other children who were wailing on him mercilessly. A couple of other adults (counselors, I learned later) and I stepped in to break up the fight. Someone escorted Tommy to the nurse's office to repair the damage, which was minor.

This was the first of my many memorable encounters with Tommy. Unfortunately, these encounters were rarely happy occasions. As the camp director sadly noted, Tommy was a little cloud that hung over "Camp Sunshine," reigning difficulties on almost everyone he encountered. The director then noted that my application indicated that I was a psychology major, which led her to wonder if I might be interested in trying to figure out what was the matter with Tommy. I hesitated before answering. At this point in my life I did not suffer from lack of confidence, but I had enough humility to recognize that there was little hope that I could develop a deep understanding of a character as complex as Tommy, especially in the span of a few months. Nevertheless, I was fascinated by the young boy and his seemingly bizarre behavior. Intrigued, I agreed to spend some time observing Tommy and report back to the director.

Over the next few weeks my fascination with Tommy grew, for I was completely unprepared for what I observed. In his interactions, Tommy seemed hell bent on turning everyone against him: disobeying the counselors, taunting and teasing the other kids, and being generally disruptive. His relationship with "Crazy Louis" was particularly remarkable. Louis earned his "Crazy" label by ruthlessly assaulting the other children on a daily basis. Often his aggressiveness seemed random and unprovoked. All of the children rapidly learned to steer clear of Louis – except for Tommy, that is. Tommy seemed drawn to Louis like a magnet. Louis would oblige by subjecting Tommy to a steady diet of verbal and physical abuse.

And each evening, when I talked to Tommy about his day, he remembered only the negatives – the problems he encountered and the slights that had been directed at him. In contrast, when I mentioned the positive things that had happened he seemed confused, forgetful, and anxious, returning as quickly as possible to his narrative of negativity.

What puzzled me about Tommy was that his activities seemed almost tailored made to sour his relations with others and perpetuate his incredibly negative self-image. When I probed, it seemed like he derived some comfort from the fact that his experiences at the camp were every bit as bad as he expected them to be. Tommy not only seemed convinced that the world hated him; he seemed

reassured when his interactions supported this expectation.

Tommy's pathology became easier to understand after I consulted the case worker who referred Tommy to the camp. She revealed that he had been the target of a steady stream of abuse since he was an infant. Apparently, he had internalized the treatment he received. An incredibly negative identity resulted. It was not surprising to me that Tommy's negative self-views could be traced to terrible experiences with his caregivers. What was surprising was that he seemed to work actively to recreate the negative conditions that generated his negative identity in the first place. Most people would seemingly want to escape an ugly past rather than recreate it. What made Tommy different?

It would take me years before I would get a handle on this question, for as an undergraduate I lacked the sophistication to address it in a meaningful way. My efforts to acquire the training I needed jumpstarted when I gained admission to graduate school in social psychology. From my home in Pennsylvania, I headed north to the University of Minnesota. There I began working with Mark Snyder, an eminent scholar with interests in the self and social interaction. When I arrived I leaned that he was about to launch an exciting new program of research. The topic was the self-fulfilling effects of the expectations of some persons ("perceivers") on the behaviors of their interaction partners ("targets"). This phenomenon seemed to represent the flip side of the activities of Tommy, a "target" whose self-views influenced the behavior of all of the "perceivers" around him. I happily immersed myself in this project, and was later rewarded with three publications (Snyder and Swann, 1978a, 1978b; Swann and Snyder, 1980).

It was not until my final year at Minnesota that Tommy reappeared on my intellectual radar screen. In designing my dissertation, I decided to test the relative power of the expectations of perceivers and the self-views of targets. Guided by my experiences with

Tommy, I expected that targets who had firmly held self-views would repudiate expectations that challenged their self-views, even if their self-views were negative. This was precisely what happened – people with negative self-views elicited more negative reactions than people with positive self-views. Moreover, the tendency for participants to elicit negative self-confirming reactions was particularly strong when they suspected that their interaction partner held positive appraisals of them.

Upon completion of my dissertation, I took a job at the University of Texas at Austin. There, I conducted several follow-ups to my dissertation research with Stephen Read. Those studies were packaged together in two papers that appeared in years to follow (Swann and Read, 1981a, 1981b). The core argument that Steve and I advanced was that people were like Tommy in that they wanted to confirm their self-views. We also suggested that they expressed this preference during each of three successive phases of the interaction sequence. In Study 1, we examined attention. We recruited participants who perceived themselves as either likable or dislikable and told them that another person had likely evaluated them in either a positive or negative manner. The question was how long participants would read a passage that they (erroneously) thought that the evaluator had written about them. Participants who saw themselves as likable spent longer reading the passage when they expected it to be positive. In contrast, those with negative self-views spent longer reading the passage when they expected it to be negative. Study 2, my dissertation study, showed that people behaved in ways that elicited reactions from their interaction partners that confirmed their self-views. Study 3 focused on what participants remembered about evaluations they received. We discovered that participants preferentially recalled self-verifying evaluations. These data offered compelling support for our hypotheses: within each of three distinct phases of social interaction, people sought to verify their self-views.

In a series of follow-up studies, we tested the notion that people seek and value self-verifying evaluations because such evaluations more informative and diagnostic than nonverifying evaluations. Participants in Study 1 preferentially solicited feedback that verified their self-views, whether these self-views were positive or negative. In Study 2, participants spent more money to obtain verifying as compared to nonverifying evaluations. Study 3 revealed that participants perceived self-verifying evaluations to be particularly informative and diagnostic.

Together, the results presented in the Swann and Read papers strongly suggested that Tommy was no anomaly. Rather, there seemed to be a fairly robust tendency for people to prefer self-confirming feedback over nonconfirming feedback. In fact, this preference influenced information seeking, attention, memory, overt behavior, and even perceptions of the diagnosticity of the feedback. These studies provided the empirical foundation on which the theory would rest. The next task was to flesh out the theory and begin to explore its implications. My efforts culminated in the publication of a chapter in which I presented the essential elements of this theory (Swann, 1983).

SELF-VERIFICATION THEORY

The core idea underlying self-verification theory was first articulated by Prescott Lecky (1945). He proposed that chronic self-views give people a strong sense of coherence and they are thus motivated to maintain them. Related ideas resurfaced a few years later in several self-consistency theories (e.g., Aronson, 1968; Festinger, 1957; Secord and Backman, 1965). Nevertheless, the most prominent consistency theorists transformed Lecky's theory in a fundamental way, for the emphasis on experimentation during that era led to the abandonment of Lecky's emphasis on the role of chronic self-views in consistency strivings. Dissonance theory (Aronson, 1968; Festinger, 1957), for example, emphasized the ways in which people found consistency by bringing their transient self-images into accord with their overt behaviors. Self-verification theory (Swann, 1983) reversed this trend by reinstating Lecky's belief that stable self-views organize people's efforts to maximize consistency. Therefore, rather than changing self-views willy nilly to match behavior, self-verification theory holds that people are motivated to maximize the extent to which their experiences confirm and reinforce their self-views.

People's powerful allegiance to stable self-views can be understood by considering how and why they develop self-views in the first place. Theorists have long assumed that people form their self-views by observing how others treat them (e.g., Cooley, 1902; Mead, 1934). As they acquire more and more evidence to support their self-views, people become increasingly certain of them. When certainty increases enough, people begin using their self-views in making predictions about their worlds, guiding behavior, and maintaining a sense of coherence, place, and continuity. In this way, stable self-views not only serve the pragmatic function of guiding behavior, they also serve the epistemic function of affirming people's sense that things are as they should be. Indeed, firmly held self-views form the centerpiece of their knowledge systems. As such, when people strive for self-verification, the viability of that system hangs in the balance. It is thus not surprising that by mid childhood, a preference for evaluations that confirm and stabilize self-views emerges (e.g., Cassidy et al., 2003).

The origins of the self-verification motive can also be understood from an evolutionary perspective. Evolutionary biologists generally agree that humans spent most of their evolutionary history in small hunter-gatherer groups. Self-verification strivings would have been advantageous in such groups. That is, once people used inputs from the social environment to form self-views,

self-verification strivings would have stabilized their identities and behavior, which in turn would make each individual more predictable to other group members (e.g., Goffman, 1959). Mutual predictability would facilitate division of labor, making the group more effective in accomplishing its objectives. Ultimately, the stable self-views fostered by self-verification strivings would bolster survival rates of group members (see Leary and Baumeister's [2000] sociometer theory for another perspective on the utility of accurate self-knowledge for group functioning).

The desire for stable self-views produced by self-verification strivings may also be understood on a neurological level. Of their very nature, self-verifying evaluations will be more predictable and familiar than non-verifying ones. Such stimuli are not only more "perceptually fluent" (more readily processed) than unpredictable and unfamiliar stimuli, they have also been shown to foster positive affect (e.g., Winkielman et al., 2002). The preference for self-verifying evaluations may therefore stem, at least partially, from basic properties of the human brain.

If stable self-views are essential to human functioning, those who are deprived of them should be seriously impaired. This seems to be true. Witness a case study reported by the neurologist Oliver Sacks (1985). Due to chronic alcohol abuse, patient William Thompson suffered from memory loss that was so profound that he forgot who he was. Only able to remember scattered fragments from his past, Thompson lapsed into a state of psychological anarchy. But Thompson did not give up. Instead, he desperately attempted to recover the self that eluded him. For instance, he sometimes developed hypotheses about who he was and then tested these hypotheses on whoever happened to be present. For example, thinking he was a customer at a butcher shop, he approached another patient and tried to identify him: "You must be Hymie, the Kosher butcher next door … But why are there no bloodstains on your coat?" Tragically, Thompson could never remember the results of his latest "test." He was thus doomed to enact such tests repeatedly for the remainder of his life.

Thompson's case not only shows that stable self-views are essential to psychological wellbeing, it also shows how essential such self-views are to guiding action. Plagued by a sense of self that kept disappearing like the Cheshire Cat, Thompson did not know how to act toward people. In a very real sense, his inability to obtain self-verification deprived him of his capacity to have meaningful interactions with the people around him. No wonder, then, that people enact numerous strategies designed to elicit support for their self-views.

How self-verification strivings shape social reality

People may use three distinct processes to create self-verifying social worlds. First, people may construct self-verifying "opportunity structures"; that is, social environments that satisfy their needs (McCall and Simmons, 1966). They may, for example, seek and enter relationships in which they are apt to enjoy confirmation of their self-views (e.g., Swann et al., 1989) and leave relationships in which they fail to receive self-verification (Swann et al., 1994).

A second self-verification strategy involves the systematic communication of self-views to others. For example, people may display "identity cues" – highly visible signs and symbols of who they are. Physical appearances represent a particularly potent class of identity cues. The clothes one wears, for instance, can advertise numerous self-views, including one's political leanings, income level, religious convictions, and so on (e.g., Gosling, 2008; Pratt and Rafaeli, 1997). Even email addresses can communicate identities to others (Chang-Schneider and Swann, 2009).

People may also communicate their identities to others though their actions. Depressed college students, for example, were more likely to solicit unfavorable feedback from their roommates than were nondepressed students (Swann et al., 1992d). Such efforts bore fruit in the form of negative evaluations. That is, the more unfavorable feedback they solicited in the middle of the semester, the more their roommates derogated them and convinced them to make plans to find another roommate at the end of the semester. Furthermore, if people suspect that someone does not perceive them in a manner that befits their self-views, they will redouble their efforts to acquire self-verifying reactions. As noted earlier, in one study, participants who perceived themselves as either likable or dislikable learned that they would be interacting with someone who probably found them likable or dislikable. When participants suspected that their partner saw them either more or less favorably than they perceived themselves, they ramped-up their efforts to elicit self-verifying evaluations (e.g., Brooks et al., 2009; Swann and Hill, 1982; Swann and Read, 1981a, Study 2).

And what if people's efforts to obtain self-verifying evaluations fail? Even then, people may still cling to their self-views through the third strategy of self-verification: "seeing" nonexistent evidence. Self-views may guide at least three stages of information processing: attention, recall, and interpretation. For example, an investigation of selective attention revealed that participants with positive self-views spent longer scrutinizing evaluations they expected to be positive and people with negative self-views spent longer scrutinizing evaluations when they expected them to be negative (Swann and Read, 1981a, Study 1). Participants in a follow-up study displayed signs of selective recall. In particular, participants who perceived themselves positively remembered more positive than negative statements and those who perceived themselves negatively remembered more negative than positive statements. Finally, numerous investigations have shown that people tend to interpret information in ways that reinforce their self-views. Consider evidence that people with low self-esteem perceive their partners' sentiments toward them as being more negative than they actually are (e.g., Murray et al., 2000).

Together, attentional, encoding, retrieval, and interpretational processes may stabilize people's self-views by allowing them to "see" their worlds as offering more confirmation for their self-views than actually exists (for a review, see Swann et al., 2003c). These strategies therefore represent a special case of the tendency for expectancies to channel information processing (e.g., Higgins and Bargh, 1987; Shrauger, 1975).

Interestingly, most investigations of self-verification processes have reported nearly symmetrical preferences of participants with positive and negative self-views. That is, just as participants with positive self-views displayed a preference for positive evaluations, participants with negative self-views displayed a preference for negative evaluations. In the early days of my research on self-verification, I had no idea how controversial this evidence would prove to be. I was soon to discover, however, that most of my colleagues were skeptical of the notion that people with negative self-views preferred negative evaluations. In fact, some of them would not buy a word of it.

The backlash from self-enhancement advocates

In the early 1980s, I noticed a baffling phenomenon. The more evidence for self-verification I published, the more skeptical my critics grew. The full magnitude of the problem, however, did not occur to me until an encounter with the great Stanley Schachter. After I had given a colloquium to the Psychology Department at Columbia (where he was the resident icon), I was excited to see him striding toward me. My excitement morphed into apprehension, however, when I noticed a scowl on his face. This was not just any scowl; it was so menacing that

I instantly became convinced that he was about to take a swing at someone. Worse yet, judging from his trajectory, it seemed likely that that someone would be me. Stopping just short of my nose, he demanded, "So, are you telling me that people with negative self-concepts actually *want* negative evaluations?" I felt trapped. I sensed that if I caved, I would lose face, but if I stood my ground, I would lose my entire head. In the end I persuaded myself that I should hang tough, as my relatively youthful reflexes (he was more than twice my age) and wrestling experience would surely save me from serious injury. So convinced, I answered "At some level, yes" and prepared to duck. He stared at me in disbelief; I defiantly stared back. After what seemed like an eternity (spectators later told me the entire interaction was less than a minute), he announced loudly "I don't believe it" and marched off in a huff.

For a host of reasons, Schachter's reaction was deeply troubling. It was bad enough that one of the world's most eminent social psychologists found my findings unpersuasive. More worrisome was the possibility that his concerns represented the tip of a much more ominous iceberg. Indeed, I would soon realize that for an increasingly vocal group of critics, my findings were not simply counterintuitive; they had been thoroughly discredited more than a decade earlier. The focal point of their concerns was an early study by Aronson and Carlsmith (1962). In this study, the experimenter asked a group of Harvard students to determine if the people pictured in series of photographs suffered from schizophrenia. After each of 100 trials, he delivered either positive or negative feedback to subjects. The crucial group received predominantly negative feedback for the first 80 trials followed by positive feedback on the last 20 trials. Shortly thereafter the experimenter indicated that there had been an oversight and asked subjects to take the final 20 trials of the test again.

Aronson and Carlsmith's (1962) dependent measure was the extent to which subjects modified their responses to the final trials. Surprisingly, those who received unexpectedly positive feedback undermined their good fortune by modifying their responses! Theoretically, 80 trials of negative feedback had caused these participants to develop negative self-conceptions so that the positive feedback on the final trials produced dissonance. They accordingly altered their responses on the last 20 trials to reduce the dissonance created by the unexpectedly positive feedback.

Unfortunately, the results of the Aronson and Carlsmith study proved to be as difficult to replicate as they were provocative, with only 4 of 17 replication attempts succeeding (Dipboye, 1977). This rather dismal track record was enough to convince most people that Aronson and Carlsmith's findings were a fluke. More generally, critics argued that in a fair fight, self-consistency strivings were no match for self-enhancement strivings. This belief remains firmly entrenched among many social psychologists to this day, with most contemporary theorists tending either to subsume self-consistency strivings within a self-enhancement perspective (e.g., Schlenker, 1985; Sedikides and Gregg, 2008; Steele, 1988; Tesser, 1988) or to ignore them altogether.

My critics, noting a superficial similarly between the Aronson and Carlsmith (1962) findings and self-verification effects, dismissed evidence for self-verification. This

was misguided, for it is inappropriate to link the two sets of findings. Most important, if one looks closely at the procedures employed in the two sets of studies, one sees a crucial difference. In the self-verification studies, the experimenters *measured* the self-concepts of participants. This allowed them to tap into people's desire for self-stability and coherence. In contrast, Aronson and Carlsmith sought to *manipulate* self-views (by presenting participants with feedback indicating that they were unable to diagnose schizophrenics). Surely, providing negative feedback to a 20-year-old Harvard student is not likely to convince him that he does not know a crazy person when he sees one. For this reason, such a manipulation may put people in a bad mood, but it will not produce the chronic negative self-views needed to motivate self-verification strivings.

From this perspective, difficulties in replicating the Aronson and Carlsmith findings have no bearing on the replicability of self-verification effects. And, in fact, subsequent research bolstered this conclusion. Indeed, over the next several years, researchers in other labs and my own students replicated the basic self-verification effect (i.e., people with negative self-views preferred and sought negative over positive evaluations) dozens of times (e.g., Hixon and Swann, 1993; Robinson and Smith-Lovin, 1992; Swann et al, 1989, 1990, 1992c, 1992d). Figure 27.1 shows an exemplary set of findings: just as

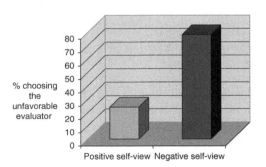

Figure 27.1   Desire to interact with a negative evaluator as a function of self-view. (Adapted from Swann et al. (1992))

people with positive self-views preferred to interact with a positive evaluator, people with negative self-views preferred to interact with someone who evaluated them negatively. Further, people with negative self-views seem to be truly drawn to self-verifying interaction partners rather than simply avoiding nonverifying ones. For example, when given the option of being in a different experiment, people with negative self-views chose to interact with a negative evaluator over participating in another experiment. Similarly, they chose being in a different experiment over interacting with a positive evaluator (Swann et al., 1992c).

Both men and women displayed this propensity, whether or not the self-views were easily changed and whether the self-views were associated with qualities that were specific (intelligence, sociability, dominance) or global (self-esteem, depression). People were particularly likely to seek self-verifying evaluations if their self-views were confidently held (e.g., Pelham and Swann, 1994; Swann and Ely, 1984; Swann et al., 1988) and important (Swann and Pelham, 2002), or extreme (Giesler et al., 1996). Moreover, in recent years researchers have shown that people also strive to verify negative (and positive) self-views associated with group membership. Such strivings emerge for both *collective* self-views (which are identities that characterize the person as well as the typical group member; Chen et al., 2004) and *group identities*, which refer to qualities of typical group members that may or may not characterize individual group members; Gómez et al., in press; Lemay and Ashmore, 2004).

In the face of such converging evidence, most adherents of the assumption that self-enhancement is the prepotent motivator of human behavior eventually relinquished their assertion that self-verification effects were not robust. Instead, they began to assert that the tendency for people with negative self-views to prefer and seek negative evaluations is counter-intuitive and bizarre. To counter such claims, I realized that I needed to show why people seek self-verification.

Why people self-verify

It is obvious why people work to maintain some negative self-views. After all, everyone possesses flaws and weaknesses and it makes perfect sense to develop and maintain negative self-views that correspond to these flaws and weaknesses. For example, people who lack some ability (as in those who are tone-deaf or cannot jump) will have numerous reasons for bringing others to recognize their shortcomings. For instance, when the appraisals of relationship partners square with objective reality, such partners will develop realistic expectations that the person can confirm and thus avoid disappointing the partner.

The adaptiveness of self-verification strivings, however, is much less obvious when people develop globally negative self-views (e.g., "I am worthless") that have no clear objective basis. Active efforts to maintain such negative self-views by, for example, gravitating toward harsh or abusive partners, is surely maladaptive. At the very least, such activities seem to directly contradict the predictions of one of social psychology's most prominent approaches, self-enhancement theory. In fact, one of the greatest challenges to self-verification researchers is understanding how the motive interacts with the self-enhancement motive (e.g., Kwang and Swann, 2009).

Self-enhancement versus self-verification

Self-enhancement theory can be traced back at least as far as Allport (1937). By positing a vital and universal human need to view oneself positively, Allport sowed the seeds for what would develop into a patchwork of loosely related propositions dubbed "self-enhancement theory" (Jones, 1973). Today this theory has received considerable support, including evidence that people are motivated to obtain, maintain, and increase positive self-regard. There are also indications that the desire for self-enhancement is truly fundamental. First, there is the apparent ubiquity of this desire. Whether one examines people's social judgments, attributions, or overt behaviors, there appears to be a widespread tendency for them to favor themselves over others (for a review, see Leary, 2007). Second, traces of a preference for positivity emerge at a tender age. Indeed, within mere weeks of developing the ability to discriminate facial characteristics, five-month-olds attend more to smiling faces than to nonsmiling ones (Shapiro et al., 1987). Similarly, as early as four-and-a-half months of age, children preferentially orient to voices that have the melodic contours of acceptance (Fernald, 1993). Third, among adults, a preference for positive evaluations emerges before other preferences (Swann et al., 1990). In particular, when forced to choose between two evaluators quickly, participants selected the positive evaluator even if they viewed themselves negatively. Only when given time to reflect did participants with negative self-views choose the negative, self-verifying partner.

Yet, as potent as the desire for positivity may be, the results summarized earlier in this chapter indicate that self-verification strivings are quite robust. In fact, contrary to self-enhancement theory, people with negative self-views display a clear tendency to seek and embrace negative rather than positive partners. Furthermore, although the early demonstrations of self-verification strivings were conducted in the laboratory, later field studies showed a parallel pattern that was, in many respects, even more remarkable than the initial studies. The first study in this series was designed to compare how people with positive self-views and negative self-views react to marital partners whose appraisals varied in positivity (Swann et al., 1994). The investigators recruited married couples who were either shopping at a local mall or horseback riding at a ranch in central Texas. The researchers approached potential participants and invited them to complete a series of questionnaires. They began with the

Self-Attributes Questionnaire (SAQ; Pelham and Swann, 1989), a measure that focused on five attributes that most Americans regard as important: intelligence, social skills, physical attractiveness, athletic ability, and artistic ability. Then participants completed it again. This time, however, they rated their spouse. Finally, husbands and wives completed a measure of their commitment to the relationship. While each person completed these questionnaires, his or her spouse completed the same ones. The researchers thus had indices of what everyone thought of themselves, what their spouses thought of them, and how committed they were to the relationship.

How did people react to positive or negative evaluations from their spouses? As shown in Figure 27.2, people with positive self-views responded in the intuitively-obvious way—the more favorable their spouses were, the more committed they were. By contrast, people with negative self-views displayed the opposite reaction; the more favorable their spouses were, the *less* committed they were. Those with moderate self-views were most committed to spouses who appraised them moderately.

Subsequent researchers attempted to replicate this effect (e.g., Cast and Burke, 2002; De La Ronde and Swann, 1998; Murray et al., 2000; Ritts and Stein, 1995; Schafer et al., 1996). Although the strength of the effect varied, each study reported some evidence that people preferred self-verifying spouses, even if their self-views were negative. A meta-analysis revealed that among married persons, the self-verification effect was stronger than the self-enhancement effect (Kwang and Swann, 2010). Moreover, a parallel finding emerged in a study of college student roommates (Swann and Pelham, 2002). Nevertheless, rather than accepting such findings as evidence of a desire for self-verification, advocates of self-enhancement theory refused to give up the fight. Instead, they insisted that what appeared to be self-verification strivings were, ironically, self-enhancement strivings gone awry.

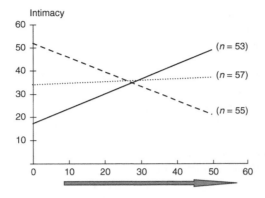

Figure 27.2   Marital intimacy as a function of participants self-views and spouses' appraisals. (Based on Swann et al. (1994))

Are self-verification strivings actually self-enhancement strivings in disguise?

One variation on this argument has been that self-verification effects are driven by a tiny segment of the population who suffer from flawed personalities such as masochism or self-destructive tendencies. From this vantage point, it was the personality flaw rather than the negative self-view that caused people with negative self-views to embrace negative evaluations and evaluators.

One counter to such claims is offered by an interesting aspect of the results of the investigation of married couples described above. Careful inspection of the findings revealed that it was not just persons with negative self-views who eschewed overly positive evaluations, for even people with positive self-views displayed less commitment to spouses whose evaluations were *extremely* favorable (Swann et al., 1994). Thus, the self-verification effect was not restricted to people with negative self-views; anyone who sensed that a spouse appraised them in an overly favorable manner tended to withdraw from the relationship.

Although these data are consistent with a self-verification explanation, they do not explicitly show that it was the *self-views* of

people who thought poorly of themselves that caused them to choose negative evaluators. In search of such evidence, we (Swann et al., 1990) hypothesized that there were differences in the cognitive operations that gave rise to self-enhancement versus self-verification strivings. In principle, self-enhancement strivings seem to require only one step: upon classifying the evaluation, people embrace positive evaluations and reject negative evaluations. In contrast, self-verification strivings logically require at least two steps. After classifying the evaluation, it needed to be compared to the self-view, for only then could the person choose to embrace verifying evaluations and avoid nonverifying ones. With this reasoning in hand, we predicted that depriving people of cognitive resources while they were choosing an interaction partner would interfere with their ability to access their self-concept. As a result, people who might ordinarily self-verify would self-enhance instead (cf. Paulhus and Levitt, 1987).

We tested these ideas by depriving participants of cognitive resources. In one study we did this by having people rehearse a phone number. While they struggled not to forget the phone number, they chose between a positive or negative evaluation. Deprived of the cognitive resources, they needed to compare the evaluation with their self-view; people with negative self-views suddenly behaved like their positive self-view compatriots – they chose positive evaluations over negative ones. When these same participants were later given several moments to access their self-views, however, they chose the negative, self-verifying evaluations. Later studies replicated this effect using other manipulations of resource deprivation, such as having participants choose partners hurriedly (Hixon and Swann, 1993). By showing that it was the ability to access their negative self-views that caused participants to choose negative evaluators, the resource deprivation studies showed that self-views rather than "flawed personalities" underlay self-verification strivings.

Another way of testing the flawed personalities hypothesis was to determine what people were thinking as they chose an interaction partner. To this end, we (Swann et al., 1992b) conducted a "think-aloud" study. People with positive and negative self-views thought out loud into a tape recorder as they chose an evaluator to interact with. As in the earlier studies, people with positive self-views tended to choose the positive evaluator and people with negative self-views tended to choose the negative evaluator. Of greatest relevance here, subsequent analyses of the tape recordings revealed no evidence that masochism or self-destructive tendencies drove the self-verifying choices of participants. To the contrary, participants with negative self-views seemed torn and ambivalent as they chose negative partners. One person with negative self-views, for example, noted that:

> I like the [favorable] evaluation but I am not sure that it is, ah, correct, maybe. It *sounds* good, but [the negative evaluator] … seems to know more about me. So, I'll choose [the negative evaluator].

The think-aloud study also provided direct support for self-verification theory. The remarks of self-verifiers – both those with negative self-views who chose negative partners and those with positive self-views who chose favorable partners – indicated that they preferred partners who made them feel that they knew themselves. Consistent with self-verification theory, they were concerned with the match between the partner's evaluation and what they knew to be true of them:

> Yeah, I think that's pretty close to the way I am. [The negative evaluator] better reflects my own view of myself, from experience.

There was also evidence that pragmatic considerations contributed to self-verification strivings, with self-verifiers voicing a concern with getting along with the evaluators during the forthcoming interaction:

> Since [the negative evaluator] seems to know my position and how I feel sometimes, maybe I'll be able to get along with him.

In short, the results of the think-aloud study indicated that both epistemic and pragmatic considerations motivated participants to choose partners whose evaluations confirmed their self-views. As I will show below, the results of the think-aloud study, together with the marriage partner study, were also useful in addressing the possibility that people sought negative evaluations in a misguided effort to obtain positive evaluations.

Perceptiveness of the evaluator

The distinction between desiring an evaluator who seems perceptive versus one who bolsters one's feelings of coherence parallels the difference between buying a car because it looks sporty versus choosing it because it makes one feel admired. In the think-aloud study, people who mentioned a concern with perceptiveness focused on qualities of the evaluator, such as being "on the ball" or "insightful." In contrast, people who emphasized coherence stressed a concern with feeling that the evaluator made them feel that they knew themselves. Those who mentioned being concerned with the perceptiveness of the evaluator were not the same ones who expressed coherence-related concerns, indicating that the two sets of concerns were independent. In addition, results of the marriage partner study indicated that relationship quality was driven by the extent to which the spouse was self-confirming rather than perceptive. In particular, commitment to relationships correlated with confidence that their spouses' appraisals would make them "feel that they really knew themselves" rather than "confused them." Commitment was not related with estimates of the perceptiveness of spouses, however.

Self-improvement

Another rival explanation was that people with negative self-views choose interaction partners who thought poorly of them because they believed that such partners might give them critical feedback that would help them improve themselves. Participants in the think-aloud study did not mention this possibility, however. The results of the marital partners study also countered this possibility. When asked if they thought their spouse would provide them with information that would enable them to improve themselves, people with negative self-views were decidedly pessimistic, thus arguing against the possibility that this motive drew them into self-verifying relationships.

Perceived similarity

Considerable evidence indicates that people prefer those who have similar values and beliefs. For example, people typically prefer their friends and associates who share their political beliefs, tastes in music, and the like (Byrne, 1971). Given this, it may be that people find self-verifying partners appealing because they suspect that such partners will agree with them on topics and issues that are unrelated to who they are. Contrary to this possibility, participants in the think-aloud study scarcely mentioned the partners' likely attitudes. The results of the marital partner study also provided no evidence that people's affinity for self-verifying partners reflected an effort to align themselves with spouses possessing similar attitudes.

Winning converts

Converting an enemy into a friend is generally difficult, so pulling off such a stunt ought to be especially gratifying. Conceivably, this is what people with negative self-views had on their minds when they chose partners who viewed them negatively. In fact, several participants in the think-aloud study did allude to a desire to win over a partner, as evidenced by comments such as, "I kind of think that [the negative evaluator] is ... the kind of guy or girl I'd like to meet and I would like to show them." Yet, it was only people with *positive* self-views who mentioned this concern; people with negative self-views never brought it up. This stands to reason, as people with negative self-views surely lack confidence that they can readily turn an enemy into a friend.

The marriage partner study provided further ammunition against the "winning converts" hypothesis. If people with negative self-views wished to "convert" a spouse who was initially critical, they should have expressed the most interest in partners whose evaluations of them seemed likely to grow more favorable over the course of the relationship. To the contrary, people with negative self-views tended to commit themselves more to spouses whose evaluations they expected to grow slightly more *negative* over time. Clearly, people with negative self-views choose rejecting interaction partners for very different reasons than people with positive self-views did.

Self-verification versus accuracy

Some critics have asserted that evidence of self-verification processes is unsurprising because people with negative self-views are merely seeking evaluations that confirm actual deficiencies. Let me begin by acknowledging that people with negative self-views undoubtedly possess *some* negative qualities. Tragically, people sometimes develop the conviction that they are flawed when in reality they are not. Support for this idea comes from research in which the researchers examined the feedback-seeking activities of people who were clinically depressed (Giesler et al., 1996). Depressed people regarded negative evaluations to be especially accurate and were more apt to seek them. This finding is significant because there is no evidence that depressed people actually possess chronic deficiencies that would justify their quest for negative feedback. Similarly, it is difficult to imagine a convincing justification for the tendency for people with low self-esteem to feel that they are worthless and undeserving of love. Finally, if depressed persons were truly as deficient as their negative self-views would suggest, one would expect that their negative self-views would remain this way on a more-or-less permanent basis. They do not: once depression clears, the self-views of formerly depressed people bounce back to normal.

Note that I am not suggesting that people have no interest in winning the approval of their relationship partners. Indeed, the self-verification process requires that relationships survive, for there can be no self-verification if there is no relationship. For this reason, people are highly motivated to bring their relationship partners to see them positively on qualities that are essential to the survival of the relationship. Physical attractiveness is one such quality. Not surprisingly, target persons not only want their dating partners to see them as much more attractive than they see themselves, they actually take steps to ensure their partners view them this way (e.g., Swann et al., 2002). Moreover, such steps are effective, for people's partners actually develop appraisals that verify targets' more-attractive-than-usual selves. Apparently, people with negative self-views recognize that for their relationships to remain viable, they must be perceived in a relatively positive manner on relationship-relevant dimensions. We dubbed this phenomenon "strategic self-verification," as people gained verification for strategic selves that differed from their chronic selves.

How can evidence of strategic self-verification be reconciled with the research discussed earlier indicating that people

seek and elicit self-verifying evaluations? Apparently, people with negative self-views prefer and seek negative evaluations regarding characteristics that are low in relationship-relevance (e.g., intelligence, artistic), presumably because verification of such negative qualities will not threaten the viability of the relationship. At the same time, on dimensions that are critical to the relationship, they strive to acquire evaluations that are more positive than those that they typically receive but which verify the self that they have presented to their partners. In this way, targets may receive verification of qualities that are low in relationship relevance as well as verification of circumscribed, highly positive selves that they negotiate with their partner on qualities that are high in relationship relevance (cf. Neff and Karney, 2005).

Interestingly, this evidence for the moderating role of relationship-relevance is consistent with self-verification theory's notion that people strive for convergence between their self-views and the social realities that maintain them. Nevertheless, it is inconsistent with the theory's assumption that people strive to negotiate identities that match their chronic self-views (Swann, 1983). Apparently, people will seek verification of their negative self-views only if doing so does not risk being abandoned, for abandonment would completely cut off the supply of verification (cf. Hardin and Higgins's, 1996, discussion of people's unwillingness to embrace epistemic truth if it undermines the relationship aspect of shared realities). While enacting such relationship-specific selves departs from the assumptions of classical trait and self theory, it is quite consistent with Mischel and Shoda's (1999) notion that people strive for intra-individual consistency and with my suggestion that people strive for circumscribed accuracy (e.g., Gill and Swann, 2004; Swann, 1984). It is also consistent with conceptions of the self in East Asia in which people eschew self-descriptions that emphasize abstract traits in favor of self-views that emphasize responsiveness to social roles and cross-situational flexibility (e.g., Choi and Choi, 2002; Kanagawa et al., 2001; for a discussion, see English et al., 2008).

Returning to the more general point here, our research has uncovered little support for various ironic explanations of self-verification strivings. Instead, it appears that a desire for self-stability and associated feelings of coherence motivates people to strive for self-verification. If self-verification strivings are indeed built into our psychological architecture, one would expect two things. First, self-verification strivings should act as a powerful counterpoint to self-enhancement strivings. A recent meta-analysis supports this possibility, indicating that self-verification strivings trumped self-enhancement strivings on measures of feedback seeking and relationship quality while self-enhancement strivings prevailed only when researchers focused on affective reactions (Kwang and Swann, 2010). Second, researchers should find that self-verification is associated with various personal and social benefits.

THE PERSONAL AND SOCIAL PSYCHOLOGICAL UTILITY OF SELF-VERIFICATION

There is growing evidence that self-verification strivings predict a host of important outcomes. These outcomes occur at several different levels of analysis, including the individual, interpersonal, and societal level of analysis.

Individual outcomes

For the roughly 70 percent of people who have positive self-views (e.g., Diener and Diener, 1995), the case for the personal adaptiveness of self-verification strivings is clear and compelling. Self-verification strivings bring stability to people's lives, rendering their experiences more coherent, orderly, and comprehensible than they would be otherwise. Success in acquiring self-verifying evaluations may bring with it important psychological benefits. For example, insofar as people's partners are self-verifying, their relationships will be more predictable and manageable. Such predictability and manageability may not only enable people to achieve their relationship goals (e.g., raising children, coordinating careers), it may also be psychologically comforting and anxiety reducing.

For people with negative self-views, however, the fruits of self-verification strivings are adaptive in some instances but not in others. In most instances, seeking verification for negative self-views will be adaptive when such views accurately reflect immutable personal limitations (e.g., lack of height). Despite contentions to the contrary (Taylor and Brown, 1988), there is no convincing evidence that self-delusions are adaptive (Kwang and Swann, 2010).

The picture is much cloudier, however, when people develop *inappropriately* negative self-views – that is, self-views that exaggerate or misrepresent their limitations (e.g., believing that one is fat when one is thin, or dull witted when one is bright). On the positive side, eliciting negative but self-verifying evaluations has the virtue of holding anxiety at bay. For example, one set of investigators (Wood et al., 2005) contrasted the reactions of high and low self-esteem participants to success experiences. Whereas high self-esteem persons reacted quite favorably to success, low self-esteem participants reported being anxious and concerned, apparently because they found success to be surprising and unsettling (cf. Lundgren and Schwab, 1977). Similarly, others (Ayduk et al., 2008) observed participants' cardiovascular responses to positive and negative evaluations. When people with negative self-views received positive feedback, they were physiologically "threatened" (distressed and avoidant). In contrast, when they received negative feedback, participants with negative self-views were physiologically "challenged" or "galvanized" (i.e., cardiovascularly aroused but in a manner associated with approach motivation). The opposite pattern emerged for people with positive self-views.

If people with negative self-views are stressed by positive information, over an extended period such information might actually produce debilitation. Empirical support for this possibility comes from several independent investigations. An initial pair of prospective studies (Brown and McGill, 1989) compared the impact of positive life events on the health outcomes of people with low versus high self-esteem. Positive life events (e.g., improvement in living conditions, getting good grades) predicted increases in health among high self-esteem participants but decreases in health among people low in self-esteem. Recent investigations by Shimizu and Pelham (2004) replicated and extended these results while controlling for negative affectivity, thereby undercutting the rival hypothesis that negative affect influenced both self-reported health and reports of symptoms. Remarkably, in all of these studies, positive life events were apparently so unsettling to people with low self-esteem that their physical health suffered.

But if receiving verification for negative self-views may be beneficial in some respects, the costs may outweigh the benefits in cases in which the self-views are more negative than warranted by objective reality. For instance, self-verification strivings may prompt people with negative self-views to gravitate toward partners who mistreat them, undermine their feelings of self-worth, or even abuse them. Once ensconced in such relationships, people may be unable to benefit from therapy because returning home to a self-verifying partner may undo the progress that was made in the therapist's office (Swann and Predmore, 1985). And the workplace may offer little solace, for the feelings of worthlessness that plague people with low self-esteem may make them ambivalent about receiving fair treatment, ambivalence

that may undercut their propensity to insist that they get what they deserve from their employers (Wiesenfeld et al., 2007). Moreover, such tragic outcomes are not limited to global negative self-views. As mentioned above, people who are thin sometimes develop the mistaken impression that they are fat, a perception that gives rise to *anorexia*, a major killer of teenage girls (Hoek, 2006). Clearly, for those who develop erroneous negative self-views, it is important to take steps to disrupt the self-verifying cycles in which they are often trapped (Swann, 1996; Swann et al., 2006). More generally, such instances illustrate how the process of self-verification can sometimes have negative consequences even though it is adaptive for most people most of the time.

Interpersonal outcomes

Earlier, I speculated that during human evolutionary history, self-verification strivings may have increased inclusive fitness by making successful self-verifiers more predictable to other group members. Modern humans may benefit from self-verification strivings for similar reasons. In fact, research indicates that when members of small groups receive self-verification from other group members, their commitment to the group increases and performance improves (Swann et al., 2000, 2004).

Self-verification processes seem to be especially useful in small groups composed of people from diverse backgrounds. That is, out of a fear that they will be misunderstood, members of diverse groups may often refrain from expressing controversial ideas. Self-verification may reduce such fear by convincing them that they *are* understood. For this reason, they may open up to their coworkers. Such openness may, in turn, lead them to express off beat ideas that lead to creative solutions to problems. Performance may benefit (Polzer et al., 2002; Seyle et al., 2009).

Societal outcomes

Self-verification processes are also adaptive for groups and the larger society. Because self-verification processes make people predictable to one another, they may grease the wheels of social interaction. Self-verification processes seem to be especially useful in small groups composed of people from diverse backgrounds. In fact, when group members offer one another self-verification, relatively diverse groups actually outperform relatively nondiverse groups – an instance in which the "value in diversity hypothesis" seems to hold true (e.g., Polzer et al., 2002; Swann et al., 2004).

Self-verification can also help eradicate social stereotypes. In small groups, those who offer other group members self-verification are more apt to individuate them – that is, recognize them as unique individuals rather than as exemplars of social stereotypes (Swann et al., 2003a). Over time, such treatment could influence targets and perceivers alike. Targets who are treated as unique individuals will be encouraged to develop qualities that reflect their idiosyncratic competences and capacities. At the same time, perceivers who individuate other group members will relinquish their social stereotypes (Swann et al., 2003b).

There is also evidence that self-verification strivings may play a role in extreme behaviors. In a recent series of studies, investigators identified a group of people whose personal identities were "fused" with their social identities (Swann et al., 2009). Because the personal and social self are functionally equivalent among such individuals, activating one is tantamount to activating the other. Consistent with this, when we activated a personal self by challenging its validity, people displayed compensatory self-verification strivings. Among fused persons, such compensatory activity took the form of increased willingness to perform extraordinary behaviors, such as dying for the group (see also, Gómez et al., in press; Swann, et al., 2010a, 2010b).

NEW DIRECTIONS

Current research on self-verification is moving in several distinct directions. One approach focuses on tradeoffs between self-verification and other motives such as positivity, particularly in close relationships (e.g., Neff and Karney, 2005). One fascinating issue here is how people create and sustain idiosyncratic social worlds that are disjunctive with the worlds that they have created outside the relationship (Swann et al., 2002). Another emerging theme (e.g., Chen et al., 2004; Gómez et al., 2009) has been on the verification of social identities (i.e., identities associated with the groups people align themselves with, such as Democrat, American, etc.) as compared with personal identities (i.e., self-views referring to personal qualities, such as intelligent, athletic, etc.). A third set of questions have emerged regarding similarities and differences in the way that self-verification strivings unfold in other cultures (English et al., 2008). My take on this issue is that all people desire coherence and predictability but that this desire may express itself differently depending upon the extent to which the culture values selves that are cross-situationally consistent (e.g., Western culture) or relationship specific (e.g., some Asian cultures).

Much of my own recent work has focused on the interplay of self-verification strivings and identity negotiation, the processes whereby people in relationships reach agreements regarding "who is who." Identity negotiation theory (Swann and Bosson, 2008) integrates self-verification theory's emphasis on the activities of targets of social perception with behavioral confirmation theory's (Snyder and Swann, 1978b) emphasis on the activities of perceivers. My recent interest in identity negotiation theory has brought me full circle, as I am once again examining the impact of interpersonal expectancies, as I did as a graduate student. This time around, however, I can exploit the knowledge gained during three decades of research on self-verification processes. At the very least, I feel that I now have some insight into the nature and consequences of the negative identities that Tommy negotiated with his peers and the staff at Camp Sunshine.

ACKNOWLEDGMENTS

I thank Rebecca Caldwell and Tory Higgins for helpful comments on an earlier draft of the article.

REFERENCES

Allport, G.W. (1937) *Personality: A Psychological Interpretation.* New York: Holt.

Aronson, E. (1968) A theory of cognitive dissonance: A current perspective. In L. Berkowitz (ed.), *Advances in Experimental Social Psychology, 4,* 1–34. New York: Academic Press.

Aronson, E. and Carlsmith, J.M. (1962) Performance expectancy as a determinant of actual performance. *Journal of Abnormal and Social Psychology, 65,* 178–182.

Ayduk, O., Gyurak, A., Akinola, M. and Mendes, W.B. (2011) Self-verification processes revealed in implicit and behavioral responses to feedback. Manuscript under review, UC Berkeley.

Brooks, M.L., Mehta, P.H. and Swann, W.B., Jr. (2009) Reclaiming the self: Compensatory self-verification following a deprivation experience. Unpublished manuscript, University of Texas at Austin.

Brown, J.D. and McGill, K.J. (1989) The cost of good fortune: When positive life events produce negative health consequences. *Journal of Personality and Social Psychology, 55,* 1103–1110.

Byrne, D. (1971) *The Attraction Paradigm.* New York: Academic Press.

Cassidy, J., Ziv, Y., Mehta, T.G. and Feeney, B.C. (2003) Feedback seeking in children and adolescents: associations with self-perceptions, representations, and depression. *Child Development, 74,* 612–628.

Cast, A.D. and Burke, P.J. (2002) A theory of self-esteem. *Social Forces, 80,* 1041–1068.

Chang-Schneider, C. and Swann, W.B., Jr. (2009) Wearing self-esteem like a flag: Conveying our high- and low-self-esteem to others. Unpublished manuscript, University of Texas at Austin.

Chen, S., Chen, K.Y. and Shaw, L. (2004) Self-verification motives at the collective level of self-definition. *Journal of Personality and Social Psychology, 86,* 77–94.

Choi, I. and Choi, Y. (2002) Culture and self-concept flexibility. *Personality and Social Psychology Bulletin, 28,* 1508–1517.

Cooley, C.S. (1902) *Human Nature and the Social Order.* New York: Scribner's.

De La Ronde, C. and Swann, W.B., Jr. (1998) Partner verification: Restoring shattered images of our intimates. *Journal of Personality and Social Psychology, 75,* 374–382.

Diener, E. and Diener, M. (1995) Cross-cultural correlates of life satisfaction and self-esteem. *Journal of Personality and Social Psychology, 68,* 653–663.

Dipboye, R.L. (1977) A critical review of Korman's self-consistency theory of work motivation and occupational choice. *Organizational Behavior and Human Performance, 18,* 108–126.

English, T., Chen, S. and Swann, W.B., Jr. (2008) A cross-cultural analysis of self-verification motives. In R. Sorrentino and S. Yamaguchi (eds), *Handbook of Motivation and Cognition Across Cultures,* pp. 119–142, San Diego: Elsevier.

Fernald, A. (1993) Approval and disapproval: Infant responsiveness to verbal affect in familiar and unfamiliar languages. *Child Development, 64,* 657–674.

Festinger, L. (1957) *A Theory of Cognitive Dissonance,* Evanston: Row, Peterson.

Giesler, R.B., Josephs, R.A. and Swann, W.B., Jr. (1996) Self-verification in clinical depression: The desire for negative evaluation. *Journal of Abnormal Psychology, 105,* 358–368.

Gill, M.J. and Swann, W.B., Jr. (2004) On what it means to know someone: A matter of pragmatics. *Journal of Personality and Social Psychology, 86,* 405–418.

Goffman, E. (1959) *The Presentation of Self in Everyday Life.* Garden City, NY: Doubleday–Anchor.

Gómez, Á., Brooks, M.L., Buhrmester, M.D., Vázquez, A., Jetten, J. and Swann, W.B., Jr. (in press) On the nature of identity fusion: Insights into the construct and a new measure. *Journal of Personality and Social Psychology.*

Gómez, Á., Seyle, C., Huici, C. and Swann, W.B., Jr. (2009) Can self-verification strivings fully transcend the self-other barrier? Seeking verification of ingroup identities. *Journal of Personality and Social Psychology, 97,* 1021–1044.

Gosling, S. (2008) *Snoop: What Your Stuff Says About You*. New York: Basic.

Hardin, C.D. and Higgins, E.T. (1996) Shared reality: How social verification makes the subjective objective. In E.T. Higgins and R.M. Sorrentino (eds), *Handbook of Motivation and Cognition: The Interpersonal Context (Vol. 3)*. New York: Guilford Press.

Higgins, E.T. and Bargh, J.A. (1987) Social cognition and social perception. In M.R. Rosenzweig and L.W. Porter (eds), *Annual Review of Psychology, 38*, 369–425. Palo Alto: Annual Reviews.

Hixon, J.G. and Swann, W.B., Jr. (1993) When does introspection bear fruit? Self-reflection, self-insight, and interpersonal choices. *Journal of Personality and Social Psychology, 64*, 35–43.

Hoek, H.W. (2006) Incidence, prevalence and mortality of anorexia nervosa and other eating disorders. *Current Opinion Psychiatry, 19*, 389–94.

Jones, S.C. (1973) Self and interpersonal evaluations: Esteem theories versus consistency theories. *Psychological Bulletin, 79*, 185–199.

Kanagawa, C., Cross, S. and Markus, H. (2001) 'Who am I?' The cultural psychology of the conceptual self. *Personality and Social Psychology Bulletin, 27*, 90–103.

Kwang, T. and Swann, W.B., Jr. (2010) Do people embrace praise even when they feel unworthy? A review of critical tests of self-enhancement versus self-verification. *Personality and Social Psychology Review, 14*, 263–280.

Leary, M.R. (2007) Motivational and emotional aspects of the self. *Annual Review of Psychology, 58*, 317–344.

Leary, M.R. and Baumeister, R.F. (2000) The nature and function of self-esteem: Sociometer theory. In M.P. Zanna (ed.), *Advances in Experimental Social Psychology, 32*, 2–51. San Diego: Academic Press

Lecky, P. (1945) *Self-consistency: A Theory of Personality*. New York: Island Press.

Lemay, E.P. and Ashmore, R.D. (2004) Reactions to perceived categorization by others during the transition to college: Internalizaton of self-verification processes. *Group Processes and Interpersonal Relations*, 173–187.

Lundgren D.C. and Schwab M.R. (1977) Perceived appraisals by others, self-esteem, and anxiety. *Journal of Psychology, 97*, 205–213.

McCall, G.J. and Simmons, J.L. (1966) *Identities and Interactions: An Examination of Human Associations in Everyday Life*. New York: Free Press.

Mead, G.H. (1934) *Mind, Self and Society*. Chicago: University of Chicago Press.

Mischel, W. and Shoda, Y. (1999) Integrating dispositions and processing dynamics within a unified theory of personality: The Cognitive Affective Personality System (CAPS). In L.A. Pervin and O. John (eds), *Handbook of Personality: Theory and Research, 2*, 197–218. New York: Guilford Press.

Murray, S.L., Holmes, J.G., Dolderman, D. and Griffin, D.W. (2000) What the motivated mind sees: Comparing friends' perspectives to married partners' views of each other. *Journal of Experimental Social Psychology, 36*, 600–620.

Neff, L.A. and Karney, B.R. (2005) To know you is to love you: The implications of global adoration and specific accuracy for marital relationships. *Journal of Personality and Social Psychology, 88*, 480–497.

Paulhus, D.L. and Levitt, K. (1987) Desirable responding triggered by affect: Automatic egotism? *Journal of Personality and Social Psychology, 52*, 245–259.

Pelham, B.W. and Swann, W.B., Jr. (1989) From self-conceptions to self-worth: The sources and structure of self-esteem. *Journal of Personality and Social Psychology, 57*, 672–680.

Pelham, B.W. and Swann, W.B., Jr. (1994) The juncture of intrapersonal and interpersonal knowledge: Self-certainty and interpersonal congruence. *Personality and Social Psychology Bulletin, 20*, 349–357.

Polzer, J.T., Milton, L.P. and Swann, W.B., Jr. (2002) Capitalizing on diversity: interpersonal congruence in small work groups. *Administrative Science Quarterly, 47*, 296–324.

Pratt, M.G. and Rafaeli, A. (1997) Organizational dress as a symbol of multilayered social identities. *Academy of Management Journal, 40*, 862–898.

Ritts, V. and Stein, J.R. (1995) Verification and commitment in marital relationships: An exploration of self-verification theory in community college students. *Psychological Reports, 76*, 383–386.

Robinson, D.T. and Smith-Lovin, L. (1992) Selective interaction as a strategy for identity maintenance: An affect control model. *Social Psychology Quarterly, 55*, 12–28.

Sacks, O. (1985) *The Man Who Mistook His Wife for a Hat and Other Clinical Tales*. New York: Simon & Shuster.

Schafer, R.B., Wickrama, K.A.S. and Keith, P.M. (1996) Self-concept disconfirmation, psychological distress, and marital happiness. *Journal of Marriage and the Family, 58*, 167–177.

Schlenker, B.R. (1985) Identity and self-identification. In B.R. Schlenker (ed.), *The Self and Social Life*, pp. 65–99. New York: McGraw-Hill.

Secord, P.F. and Backman, C.W. (1965) An interpersonal approach to personality. In B. Maher (ed.),

Progress in Experimental Personality Research, 2, 91–125. New York: Academic Press.

Sedikides, C. and Gregg, A.P. (2008) Self-enhancement: Food for thought. *Perspectives on Social Psychology, 3,* 102–116.

Seyle, D.C., Athle, D. and Swann, W.B., Jr. (2009) Value in diversity and the self: Verifying self-views promotes group connectedness and performance in diverse groups. Unpublished manuscript, University of Texas at Austin.

Shapiro, B., Eppler, M., Haith, M. and Reis, H. (1987) An event analysis of facial attractiveness and expressiveness. Paper presented at the Society for Research in Child Development, Baltimore, MD.

Shimizu, M. and Pelham, B.W. (2004) The unconscious cost of good fortune: implicit and positive life events, and health. *Health Psychology, 23,* 101–105

Shrauger, J.S. (1975) Responses to evaluation as a function of initial self-perceptions. *Psychological Bulletin, 82,* 581–596.

Snyder, M. and Swann, W.B., Jr. (1978a) Hypothesis testing processes in social interaction. *Journal of Personality and Social Psychology, 36,* 1202–1212.

Snyder, M. and Swann, W.B., Jr. (1978b) Behavioral confirmation in social interaction: From social perception to social reality. *Journal of Experimental Social Psychology, 14,* 148–162.

Steele, C.M. (1988). The psychology of self-affirmation: Sustaining the integrity of the self. In L. Berkowitz (ed.), *Advances in Experimental Social Psychology, Vol. 21,* pp. 261–302. New York: Academic Press.

Swann, W.B., Jr. (1983) Self-verification: Bringing social reality into harmony with the self. In J. Suls and A.G. Greenwald (eds), *Psychological Perspectives on the Self, 2,* 33–66, Hillsdale, NJ: Erlbaum.

Swann, W.B., Jr. (1984) The quest for accuracy in person perception: A matter of pragmatics. *Psychological Review, 91,* 457–477.

Swann, W.B., Jr. (1996) *Self-traps: The Elusive Quest for Higher Self-esteem.* Freeman: New York.

Swann, W.B., Jr. and Bosson, J. (2008) Identity negotiation: A theory of self and social interaction. In O. John, R. Robins, and L. Pervin (eds), *Handbook of Personality Psychology: Theory and Research I,* pp. 448–471. New York: Guilford Press.

Swann, W.B., Jr., Bosson, J.K. and Pelham, B.W. (2002) Different partners, different selves: The verification of circumscribed identities. *Personality and Social Psychology Bulletin, 28,* 1215–1228.

Swann, W.B., Jr., Chang-Schneider, C.S. and McClarty, K.L. (2006) Do people's self-views matter? Self-concept and self-esteem in everyday life. *American Psychologist, 62,* 84–94.

Swann, W.B., Jr., De La Ronde, C. and Hixon, J.G. (1994) Authenticity and positivity strivings in marriage and courtship. *Journal of Personality and Social Psychology, 66,* 857–869.

Swann, W.B., Jr. and Ely, R.J. (1984) A battle of wills: Self-verification versus behavioral confirmation. *Journal of Personality and Social Psychology, 46,* 1287–1302.

Swann, W.B., Jr., Gómez, Á., Seyle, C. and Morales, F. (2009) Identity fusion: The interplay of personal and social identities in extreme group behavior. *Journal of Personality and Social Psychology, 96,* 995–1011.

Swann, W.B., Jr., Gómez, Á., Dovidio, J., Hart, S. and Jetten, J. (2010a) Dying and killing for one's group: Identity fusion moderates responses to intergroup versions of the trolley problem. *Psychological Science,* 21, 1176–1183

Swann, W.B., Jr., Gómez, Á., Huici, C., Morales, F. and Hixon, J.G. (2010b) Identity fusion and self-sacrifice: Arousal as catalyst of pro-group fighting, dying and helping behavior. *Journal of Personality and Social Psychology, 99,* 824–841.

Swann, W.B., Jr. and Hill, C.A. (1982) When our identities are mistaken: Reaffirming self-conceptions through social interaction. *Journal of Personality and Social Psychology,* 43, 59–66.

Swann, W.B., Jr., Hixon, J.G. and De La Ronde, C. (1992a) Embracing the bitter 'truth': Negative self-concepts and marital commitment. *Psychological Science, 3,* 118–121.

Swann, W.B., Jr., Hixon, J.G., Stein-Seroussi, A. and Gilbert, D.T. (1990) The fleeting gleam of praise: Behavioral reactions to self-relevant feedback. *Journal of Personality and Social Psychology, 59,* 17–26.

Swann, W.B., Jr., Kwan, V.S.Y., Polzer, J.T. and Milton, L.P. (2003a) Vanquishing stereotypic perceptions via individuation and self-verification: Waning of gender expectations in small groups. *Social Cognition, 21,* 194–212.

Swann, W.B., Jr., Kwan, V.S.Y., Polzer, J.T. and Milton, L.P. (2003b) Fostering group identification and creativity in diverse groups: The role of individuation and self-verification. *Personality and Social Psychology Bulletin, 29,* 1396–1406.

Swann, W.B., Jr., Milton, L.P. and Polzer, J.T. (2000) Should we create a niche or fall in line? Identity negotiation and small group effectiveness. *Journal of Personality and Social Psychology, 79,* 238–250.

Swann, W.B., Jr. and Pelham, B.W. (2002) Who wants out when the going gets good? Psychological investment and preference for self-verifying college roommates. *Journal of Self and Identity, 1,* 219–233.

Swann, W.B., Jr., Pelham, B.W. and Chidester, T. (1988) Change through paradox: Using self-verification to alter beliefs. *Journal of Personality and Social Psychology, 54,* 268–273.

Swann, W.B., Jr., Pelham, B.W. and Krull, D.S. (1989) Agreeable fancy or disaagreeable truth? Reconciling self-enhancement and self-verification. *Journal of Personality and Social Psychology, 57,* 782–791.

Swann, W.B. Jr., Polzer, J.T., Seyle, C. and Ko, S. (2004) Finding value in diversity: Verification of personal and social self-views in diverse groups. *Academy of Management Review, 29,* 9–27.

Swann, W.B., Jr. and Predmore, S.C. (1985) Intimates as agents of social support: Sources of consolation or despair? *Journal of Personality and Social Psychology, 49,* 1609–1617.

Swann, W.B., Jr. and Read, S.J. (1981a) Self-verification processes: How we sustain our self-conceptions. *Journal of Experimental Social Psychology, 17,* 351–372.

Swann, W.B., Jr. and Read, S.J. (1981b) Acquiring self-knowledge: The search for feedback that fits. *Journal of Personality and Social Psychology, 41,* 1119–1128.

Swann, W.B., Jr., Rentfrow, P.J. and Guinn, J. (2003c) Self-verification: The search for coherence. In M. Leary and J. Tagney, *Handbook of Self and Identity,* pp. 367–383. New York: Guilford Press.

Swann, W.B., Jr. and Snyder, M. (1980) On translating beliefs into action: Theories of ability and their application in an instructional setting. *Journal of Personality and Social Psychology, 38,* 879–888.

Swann, W.B., Jr., Stein-Seroussi, A. and Giesler, B. (1992b) Why people self-verify. *Journal of Personality and Social Psychology, 62,* 392–401.

Swann, W.B., Jr., Wenzlaff, R.M. and Tafarodi, R.W. (1992c) Depression and the search for negative evaluations: More evidence of the role of self-verification strivings. *Journal of Abnormal Psychology, 101,* 314–371.

Swann, W.B., Jr., Wenzlaff, R.M., Krull, D.S. and Pelham, B.W. (1992d) The allure of negative feed-back: Self-verification strivings among depressed persons. *Journal of Abnormal Psychology, 101,* 293–306.

Taylor, S.E. and Brown, J.D. (1988) Illusion and well-being: A social psychological perspective on mental health. *Psychological Bulletin, 103,* 193–210.

Tesser, A. (1988) Toward a self-evaluation maintenance model of social behavior. In L. Berkowitz (ed.), *Advances in Experimental Psychology, Vol. 21: Social Psychological Studies of the Self: Perspectives and Programs,* pp. 181–227. San Diego: Academic Press.

Wiesenfeld, B.M., Swann, W.B., Jr, Brockner, J. and Bartel, C. (2007) Is more fairness always preferred? Self-esteem moderates reactions to procedural justice. *Academy of Management Journal, 50,* 1235–1253.

Winkielman, P., Schwarz, N. and Nowak, A. (2002) Affect and processing dynamics: Perceptual fluency enhances evaluations. In S. Moore and M. Oaksford (eds), *Emotional Cognition: From Brain to Behaviour,* pp. 111–136. Amsterdam: John Benjamins.

Wood, J.V., Heimpel, S.A., Newby-Clark, I. and Ross, M. (2005) Snatching defeat from the jaws of victory: Self-esteem differences in the experience and anticipation of success. *Journal of Personality and Social Psychology, 89,* 764–780.

28

Implicit Theories

Carol S. Dweck

ABSTRACT

My enduring interest has been in the implicit theories, or basic beliefs, that people use to understand their world and to guide their behavior. In my research, I have found that one type of belief about human nature – the belief that fundamental human attributes are fixed traits or that they are malleable qualities that can be developed – has profound consequences for how people function, how they relate to others, and what they achieve. In this chapter, I trace the development of my interest in implicit theories from my beginnings in animal learning during the social awakening of the 1960s and the emerging cognitive revolution. Even then, I rejected the false distinction between basic and applied research, the false separation of affect, cognition, and motivation into different areas of study, and the false boundaries among fields of psychology (e.g., individual differences and social psychology), and I show how this rebellious stance informed and is embodied in my work. I end by showing how implicit theory research is making inroads into closing achievement gaps, promoting intergroup relations and conflict resolution, fostering cultures of productivity, and encouraging health behaviors.

INTRODUCTION

My abiding interest has been in the implicit theories, or basic beliefs, that people use to organize their world and to guide their behavior. I have been most fascinated by the fact that different people can form different basic beliefs. When one speaks of core knowledge about objects, space, time or number, psychologists assume that most people (unless or until they are trained in math or physics) achieve more or less the same kind of understanding. However, when one considers basic beliefs about people and their attributes, different plausible positions are possible.

I have been particularly interested in beliefs with strong motivational properties. It might be interesting from an intellectual standpoint that people can come to different conclusions about the nature of themselves and others, but it becomes even more intriguing if the different conclusions make a difference for the goals people pursue and the outcomes they experience in their lives.

For some years I have studied the consequences of believing either that fundamental human attributes are fixed traits or that they are malleable qualities that can be developed (see Dweck, 1999, 2006). My collaborators and I have built and tested a model of the motivational, cognitive, affective, and behavioral consequences of the different implicit theories – and we have shown that these theories make a difference for people's achievement, relationships, careers, as well as their intergroup attitudes.

PERSONAL NARRATIVE AND INTELLECTUAL HISTORY

I started my research career in a rat lab, studying animal learning, but the call of the cognitive revolution was too great. I had gone to graduate school at Yale to study animal learning, and the work was interesting, especially because I was in on the ground floor of the Wagner–Rescorla theory and because the work combined my interest in motivation and coping (e.g., Dweck and Wagner, 1970). The animal work on learned helplessness was also being conducted at that moment (Seligman, Maier, and Solomon., 1968). It had profound implications for how animals perceived reward contingencies, and how they used these perceptions to cope.

However, attribution theory was emerging and, for me, it held the promise of revealing how *people* interpreted the things that happened to them and how these interpretations guided the way in which they reacted. I could use my training in animal learning – training in parsimonious thinking and economical experimental design – and bring it to bear on the question of how people cope with the events that befall them.

Combining the seminal work on attribution theory (Weiner and Kukla, 1970) with the seminal work on learned helplessness (Seligman et al., 1968), I began to study how children coped with failure. My work revealed that children who attributed their failures to uncontrollable factors (e.g., their own lack of ability) showed a more helpless response to failure than those who attributed their failures to more controllable factors (e.g., their own effort) (Dweck and Reppucci, 1973). This helpless response to failure consisted of negative affect, falling expectancies, less effective strategies, and lower persistence, and did not in any way stem from lower ability.

I also provided evidence of a causal link between attributions and coping reactions through an intervention that changed children's attributions for failure and, in doing so, changed their helpless reactions to failure (Dweck, 1975). In my work, I have sought from the beginning to go back and forth between the lab and the field. The advantages of laboratory work are clear. You have a thrilling degree of control over what happens and how you measure its effects. Yet, you always need field work to tell you whether what you've elegantly controlled and measured bears any resemblance to what happens in the real world to people who are not under your experimental spell.

Graduate school was a fabulous experience. The faculty at Yale made us feel that we could and would change the world, and the cognitive revolution gave us the tools to attempt just that. Coming out of a period of behaviorism, in which the contents of the mind were forbidden territory, it was exhilarating to study beliefs, perceptions, construals, processing strategies, and the like in all their glorious manifestations. The late 1960s were a time of liberation. It was a time that was besotted with the idea of construction and it spawned a generation that rejected the oversimplified, deterministic, one-size-fits all behaviorist theory, as it rejected the one-size-fits all social constraints of the 1950s.

The 1960s and 1970s witnessed the emergence not only of cognitive psychology, but also social cognition in social psychology, cognitive therapy in clinical psychology, and social–cognitive approaches to personality. However, as with any revolution, some of the good things were thrown out with the bad. Cognitions are in the head and much of social psychology remained trapped in the head, giving short shrift to motivation, affect, behavior, and real life. Psychology became so cognitive that the august series *The Nebraska Symposium on Motivation* attempted to drop "motivation" from its title. For me, however, the cognitive revolution meant that I could now address important outcomes with more tools at my disposal. I could now study how cognitive, motivational, and affective processes worked to produce behavior.

I also did not accept the idea that individual differences were not the domain of social psychology, or that social and personality psychology were essentially different fields. Virtually every individual difference I have ever measured, I have also induced experimentally. Both individual-difference measures and the experimental induction of beliefs are ways of understanding what makes people tick, of gaining leverage into the workings of the mind. Moreover, this combination of measurement and experimental induction captures the dynamic way in which people function. People may have strong and lasting beliefs, but they can also be swayed by a powerful situational cue or message.

In truth, I never accepted the idea of disciplinary boundaries within psychology at all. For convenience, psychologists have carved up the person into different parts – the cognitive part, the affective part, the social part, the developing part. This allows us to bring order to academic departments, journals, and organizations. But we should not be deceived into thinking that these boundaries are real. What we are seeking as researchers is an understanding of universal psychological processes and as we achieve this understanding we illuminate all areas of psychology. A commonly expressed fear is that neuroscience, as it burgeons, will reify these boundaries and make psychologists all the more parochial. My secret hope, however, is that neuroscience will do the opposite. The brain will not observe the boundaries psychologists have created, and will show instead how basic processes create commonality among disciplines.

Finally, I did not accept the idea, prevalent at the time, that in order to be scientific a psychological researcher had to avoid applied issues. The 1960s were, above all, a time when people cared about social issues and when unprecedented numbers of people became politically active. Ironically, as this was occurring, much of psychology was becoming increasingly abstract and "irrelevant." Fortunately, Yale was one of the places where modern social psychology was born, as psychologists returned from World War II and tried to capture in their research phenomena like persuasion or obedience to authority, phenomena that had played a role in the war. My mentors, fortunately, valued keeping a foot in the real world and making a difference.

My first job was at the University of Illinois, a wonderful department and, above all, an extraordinarily nurturing one. It is a place where people thrive. With my first graduate students, I took my work to the next level. We showed how the learned helplessness analysis (attribution processes) could shed light on gender differences in motivation and achievement. We demonstrated how girls, through their *better* treatment in grade school, could learn attributions for success and failure that would not serve them well later on when material became more difficult and success more uncertain (Dweck et al., 1978). We also modeled this process experimentally. Later, with Barbara Licht, we showed how girls' differing attributions for setbacks could illuminate their lower representation and achievement in math (Licht and Dweck, 1984). Here, we found the first evidence that the brightest girls might also be the most vulnerable. That is, we found a negative relation between IQ and girls' performance after a setback: the higher a girl's IQ, the less likely she was to master the material after a short period of confusion.

With Therese Goetz, we also showed that the helplessness model applied to social situations, and that we could predict via attributions who would show a helpless versus mastery-oriented response to social setbacks (Goetz and Dweck, 1980). Although many of these processes are easier to study in achievement/problem-solving situations, it has always been important for us to show that our model applies more broadly, and we have done so in every phase of the development of our implicit-theory model.

With Carol Diener, we then fleshed out the helpless versus mastery-oriented responses to failure, monitoring the online moment-to-moment changes in cognition, affect, and behavior as children went from success to failure (Diener and Dweck, 1978). We learned many things from this work. What really hit home was the fact that different children were living in different psychological worlds. First, we saw how some children became excited and energized by difficulty. They were not simply "not helpless," but rather actively welcomed the challenge. Moreover, these were not students who had necessarily done better than others in the initial, success phase. What was also interesting was that, unlike children who showed a helpless response, they did not seem to dwell on their difficulty, the reasons for it, and what it meant about them. In their talk-aloud narrative, they hardly ever even voiced attributions. Instead, they quickly became focused on mastering the new, more difficult problems. Finally, we monitored the exact problem-solving strategies students used and saw the helpless children as a group dissolved into ineffective strategies, while the mastery-oriented children remained highly strategic and taught themselves new ways to solve the problems. One child's self-negating failure was the other child's opportunity to learn. There seemed to be so much more than a simple difference in attribution involved. What else was going on?

An important piece of this puzzle emerged in my collaboration with Elaine Elliott and John Nicholls. In the course of intense discussions of achievement motivation over a period of time, we realized that achievement striving could be motivated by different goals: people could seek to demonstrate their ability (a *performance goal*) and/or to develop their ability (a *learning goal*). Elaine Elliott and I also realized that these different goals could be generating the starkly different helpless versus mastery-oriented responses we had observed in previous research. In research designed to test this hypothesis (Elliott and Dweck, 1988), our hunch was

confirmed. When participants were led to hold strong performance goals and lost confidence in their abilities, we saw the whole helpless pattern of cognition, affect, and behavior emerge. Only when participants given performance goals were able to maintain high confidence in their abilities were they able to hold on and persist in the face of setbacks. In contrast, when participants were led to hold strong learning goals, they displayed a mastery-oriented response to setbacks – interestingly, even when they had low confidence in their ability. When the goal is to learn, one doesn't need to feel that one is already high in ability in order to remain engaged and persistent.

This achievement goal framework has generated a great deal of research, shedding new light on achievement processes and on academic outcomes in the real world. For example, in relatively recent work (Grant and Dweck, 2003), Heidi Grant examined students who were taking a highly challenging premed organic chemistry course, and showed that learning goals predicted the maintenance of intrinsic interest in the face of an initial poor grade, recovery from an initial poor grade, and higher final grades in the course. Performance goals (the desire to show high ability), on the other hand, predicted loss of intrinsic interest after an initial poor grade, a failure to recover from an initial poor grade, and lower final grades in the course. Mediation analyses showed that learning goals predicted higher grades via deeper study strategies (see also Elliot, McGregor, and Gable, 1999) and via motivation-relevant self-regulation (e.g., keeping up interest in the subject matter).

The achievement goal analysis has also been successfully extended to organizational settings, to sports, and to issues in clinical psychology, for example, using chronic goal orientation as a predictor of depression (Dykman, 1998).

As generative as the achievement goal framework seemed to be, for me the picture was not complete. I still wondered why it would be the case that people with equal competence would chronically value and pursue different goals. Why were some people so concerned with proving over and over again how competent they were, whereas others were eagerly looking for challenges and opportunities to learn?

The next eureka moment came in a series of meetings with Mary Bandura. We suddenly realized that the idea of *ability* itself had a very different meaning when one thought about measuring and judging it through performance goals than when one thought about increasing it through learning goals. In the first case, *ability* connotes something deep-seated and permanent, whereas in the second case, *ability* implies something more dynamic and malleable. We then realized that these different conceptions of ability might lie behind differences in people's chronic goal choices. It was this hypothesis – that theories of intelligence would predict people's goal orientation – that was tested and supported in Mary Brandura's dissertation research.

Over the next few years, my students and I began to explore the ramifications of these implicit theories for motivation and behavior. Most memorably, Ellen Leggett and I spent day after day for several years developing the ideas into a broader motivational model, understanding and researching new aspects of the model, and developing implications of the model for personality as a whole (Dweck and Leggett, 1988). Little did I realize that many years later I would still be doing this!

This is not because I am so patient, focused, and systematic. It is because the model, for me, provides a microcosm of human functioning and thus operates on several levels. Aside from the immediate findings are the insights they can give into underlying processes of cognition, affect, and behavior, and, at another level, the insights they can give into the nature of human personality, motivation, and dysfunction. I greatly admire psychologists who have used their more specific research to delve into basic human processes and to reflect on human nature (Mischel and Shoda, 1995; Bandura, 1986).

To best capture what the model has yielded to date, I will leave behind the chronology. Instead, I will describe the body of work (from my own and other laboratories) that has yielded a greater understanding of how implicit theories work, how they develop, how they affect important outcomes, and what role they serve in the larger scheme of human needs. At a more specific level, I will discuss the role they play in stereotyping, interpersonal interactions, group conflict resolution, and clinically relevant psychological processes. However, before doing so, I would like to underscore the importance of the exceptional colleagues I have been so fortunate to have in all the departments I have taught in. The atmosphere of passionate inquiry they fostered provided the perfect context for the development of ideas, and along with that, the development of enthusiastic and dedicated students. Those students, in turn, are the real stars of this research program.

SOME BACKGROUND FACTS ABOUT IMPLICIT THEORIES

What are the entity and incremental theories?

The implicit theories are beliefs about the nature of human attributes. In the case of intelligence or of personality, for example, an *entity theorist* believes that the trait cannot be enhanced, whereas an *incremental theorist* believes that the trait can be developed. Those who hold an incremental theory do not necessarily believe that everyone starts out with the same talent or potential, or that anyone can be anything. They simply believe that everyone has the ability to grow with the proper motivation, opportunity, and instruction.

These are really beliefs about control, not stability. An entity theorist believes that people do not have control over their attributes or the power to change them. However, an entity theorist may believe that intelligence or personality can deteriorate with age. Moreover, an incremental theorist believes that people can change, but not necessarily that most people do change.

Throughout the chapter and throughout much of our research, we proceed as though people who endorse a given theory act consistently in terms of that theory, but the reality is bound to be more dynamic. That is, although the theories are found to be relatively stable across time (e.g., Robins and Pals, 2002), they can also be activated by strong cues or experiences in a situation (Good, Rattan, and Dweck, 2008; Murphy and Dweck, 2010).

Implicit theories are conceptually related to other variables, such as essentialist beliefs (e.g., Bastian and Haslam, 2006), beliefs about group 'entitativity' (e.g., Rydell et al., 2007), or beliefs about genetic determinism (e.g., Keller, 2005). All of these constructs capture the extent to which people or groups are seen as having deep-seated, somewhat immutable natures or structures, and the findings from these different lines of research are consistent with each other (Levy, Chiu, and Hong, 2006). The approach is also related to research on worldviews (e.g., Major et al., 2007; see Plaks, Grant, and Dweck, 2005), which seeks to capture the beliefs people use to organize and predict events in their lives.

Measures and manipulations

We assess implicit theories by asking participants to agree or disagree with a series of statements, half of which present an entity theory and half of which present an incremental theory. In the domain of intelligence, for example, an entity theory item asserts, "You have a certain amount of intelligence, and you can't really do much to change it," whereas an incremental item states, "No matter how much intelligence you have, you can always change it quite a bit." In the domain of personality, an entity theory is tapped by items like, "The kind of person

you are, is something very basic about you and it can't be changed very much," whereas an incremental theory is reflected in items like, "You can change even your most basic qualities." Using these measures, on average, about 40 percent of people endorse an entity theory, 40 percent endorse an incremental theory, and 20 percent do not consistently endorse either theory.

Researchers have also developed domain-specific measures of implicit theories, for example, theories about particular abilities or domains, such as mathematics ability (Good et al., 2008), negotiation skills (Kray and Haselhuhn, 2007), managerial and decision-making skills (Tabernero and Wood, 1999), emotion regulation (Tamir, John, Srivastava, and Gross, 2007), or relationships (e.g., Knee, 1998). Researchers have also developed measures that apply to the self versus others (Dweck, 1999) or to group characteristics rather than individual characteristics (Halperin et al., 2009; Rydell et al., 2007; Tong and Chang, 2008) In each case, the measure asks whether the object in question can be changed/developed or not, and often the more specific and targeted measures have better predictive power (Rydell et al., 2007).

Many researchers have manipulated implicit theories. This has been done by giving instructions that portray the skill or domain in question as inherent and fixed or as learnable (Kray and Haselhuhn, 2007; Martocchio, 1994; Kasimatis, Miller, and Marcussen, 1996), by presenting participants with a "scientific" article to read that portrays the skill or domain as either fixed or malleable (Hong et al., 1999; Chiu et al., 1997b; Kray and Haselhun, 2007), or, in more long-term interventions, by presenting a workshop that teaches the incremental theory (and then comparing the results to control groups that learn potentially useful but theory-irrelevant lessons) (Aronson, Fried, and Good, 2002; Blackwell, Trzesniewski, and Dweck, 2007; Good, Aronson, and Inzlicht, 2003; see also Heslin and Vandewalle, 2008).

Which theory is true?

Both the entity and the incremental theory of intelligence have had their enthusiastic proponents. The entity theory was defended in *The Bell Curve* (Herrnstein and Murray, 1996), while the incremental theory was propounded forcefully by Alfred Binet (1909), the inventor of the IQ test, as well as the research sociologist Benjamin Bloom (1985), paleontologist Steven Gould (1996), and creativity researcher John Hayes (1989). However, although both theories may have some truth, recent research by cognitive psychologists and neuroscientists is suggesting that fundamental aspects of executive function and intelligence can be taught not only in young children (Rueda et al., 2005), but also in college students (Jaeggi et al., 2008). In a study with college students (Jaeggi, et al., 2008), participants who were given training on a demanding working memory task, later scored significantly higher on an unrelated test of fluid intelligence. Fluid intelligence reflects the ability to reason and solve new problems. Moreover, the greater the training, the greater were the gains.

In the domain of personality too, researchers are reporting that even basic traits can show considerable change in adulthood (Roberts et al., 2006). In addition, as I have argued elsewhere, beliefs and belief systems themselves form a central part of personality that can be changed with targeted interventions, leading to widespread effects (Dweck, 2008).

When do implicit theories have the strongest effects?

In general, we find that implicit theories have the greatest effect when people are confronted with challenges or setbacks. For example, in a study of students making the difficult transition to seventh grade (Blackwell et al., 2007), entity and incremental theorists had shown no differences in prior math

achievement in the more nurturing setting of elementary school; however, they showed a clear and continuing divergence in grades in their new, more challenging environment. In a related vein, we found that in a college calculus course or in a pre-med organic chemistry course, entity and incremental students showed diverging grades in these difficult courses as a function of their theories (Good et al., 2008) or their goals (Grant and Dweck, 2003).

Implicit theories also predict how people will judge other people, as I will describe below. People who believe in fixed traits engage in fundamentally different person judgment processes than do people who believe in malleable human qualities. However, experience has taught us that this only holds when people believe they are forming and reporting their personal impressions of people, and not when they think they are performance a cognitive task with a right or wrong answer. When people are treating person information like variables in an equation that they are required to solve, their implicit theories play less of a role.

What psychological functions do implicit theories serve?

Implicit theories are beliefs about what people are made of and, by implication, how they work. As such, they should give people confidence that they can predict and control their social worlds. The work of Jason Plaks and his colleagues (Plaks, Grant, and Dweck, 2005; and Plaks and Stecher, 2007) provides evidence for this idea. They showed that when the predictions derived from people's implicit theories are violated, people experience anxiety and take steps to regain their sense of control. (Interestingly, this means that people will allow researchers to give them a new theory, as is done in experimental inductions or interventions, but they do not want to be left theory-less, that is, without a way of organizing and understanding how things work.)

MEANING SYSTEMS: HOW IMPLICIT THEORIES WORK

Implicit theories create psychological worlds. They operate by recruiting allied goals and beliefs that work together as a "meaning system" (Molden and Dweck, 2006). These psychological worlds are portrayed below.

Goals

First, as I outlined earlier, the two implicit theories orient people toward different goals. Of course, everyone pursues all kinds of goals depending on the situation. Nonetheless, for people holding the entity theory, motivation tends to be organized more around validating their fixed traits via performance goals, whereas for people holding the incremental theory, motivation tends to be organized more around enhancing their malleable traits via learning goals (Beer, 2002; Dweck and Leggett, 1988; Kray and Haselhuhn, 2007; Mangels et al., 2006; Robins and Pals, 2002). Several studies have dramatically shown the lengths that people holding an entity theory of intelligence will go in order to look smart and not look dumb, often at the expense of important learning. For example, Hong et al. (1999) demonstrated that entity theorists express significantly less interest than incremental theorists in a remedial English course even when their English is poor and English proficiency is crucial to their academic success in college.

However, perhaps the most dramatic demonstration of the different goal orientations comes from an ERP (event-related potential) study, in which college students' brain waves were monitored for their patterns of attention as they took a very challenging general information test (Dweck et al., 2004; Mangels et al., 2006). Analysis of the brain-wave data showed that students who held an entity theory of their intelligence entered a strong state of attention to find out, after each question, whether they were right or wrong (satisfying a performance goal), but not to find out what the right answer really was, even when their answer had been wrong. In contrast, students who held an incremental theory of intelligence entered a strong state of attention both to find out whether their answer was correct (since that is also an important part of learning) and then again to find out what the correct answer really was. Indeed, when we later retested students on the questions they had missed (Mangels et al., 2006), these incremental students scored significantly higher on the retest than did those with the entity theory. Thus, different implicit theories appear to consistently engender different goals.

Effort beliefs

According to attribution theory, effort is a controllable factor, and therefore the attribution of outcomes to effort should generate high motivation and resilience and, in general, this seems to be true. However, in the entity theory meaning system, there's a hitch: effort has negative implications for ability (Blackwell et al., 2007; Hong et al., 1999; Dweck and Leggett, 1988; Miele and Molden, 2009) – and ability is what entity theorists care about. In fact, working hard appears to quickly undermine entity theorists' confidence in their abilities. In a recent series of studies, Miele and Molden (2009) showed that any manipulation that gave participants a feeling of exerting effort (even something like small font size in a reading comprehension task) lowered entity theorists', but not incremental theorists', estimates of their ability/performance.

On the other hand, those with an incremental theory believe that high effort is good and necessary for the development of ability, and that even people who are geniuses have to work hard for their discoveries (Blackwell, et al., 2007; Dweck and Leggett, 1988). Their belief, by the way, is receiving increasing support, for example, in the work of Anders Ericsson (Ericsson et al., 1993), who finds that the most successful people in their fields are those who have engaged in the most deliberate practice and not necessarily those who seemed the most talented earlier on.

Incidentally, like the other variables in the meaning system, effort beliefs are not only correlated with implicit theories (e.g., implicit theories and effort beliefs showed a 0.54 correlation in a recent study of 373 adolescents; Blackwell et al., 2007) but also follow on the heel of an implicit theory induction (Hong et al., 1999)

Attributions

Implicit theories predict and generate different attributions for setbacks, with an entity theory orienting people more toward trait and ability attributions and an incremental theory orienting people more toward attributions that focus on effort or motivation. Our model does not argue that attributions are unimportant. Indeed several studies have shown them to be a key pathway from implicit theories to affective and behavioral responses in challenging situations (Blackwell et al., 2007; Hong et al., 1999; Robins and Pals, 2002). However, attributions occur in the context of implicit theories and goals. For example, in a study that tracked students over their college years, Robins and Pals (2002) found that attributions were significantly predicted by implicit theories, both directly and indirectly through goals. In addition, when implicit theories are induced, the allied attributions tend to follow (e.g., Hong et al., 1999).

Helpless and mastery-oriented strategies

The final link in the system, and the one that leads directly to important outcomes, consists of the different strategies that are fostered by the two implicit theories. Whereas the entity theory tends to lead to helpless or defensive strategies, the incremental theory fosters more persistent, strategic, mastery-

oriented strategies. In experimental studies (e.g., Hong et al., 1999; Nussbaum and Dweck, 2008, those taught an entity theory of intelligence more often failed to confront their deficiencies and take steps to remedy them. Nussbaum and Dweck (2008) showed that after failure on a test, college students who were taught an entity theory of intelligence chose to repair their self-esteem, not through learning but through downward social comparison, that is, by looking at the tests of people who had done even worse. Those given an incremental theory overwhelmingly chose to learn by examining the tests of those who had done substantially better than they had. Nussbaum and Dweck also found that engineering students who had been given an entity theory did not choose to take a tutorial on the section of an engineering test on which they had done poorly, whereas those given an incremental theory overwhelmingly did so. In two longitudinal studies (Robins and Pals, 2002; Blackwell et al., 2007), students holding an entity theory were more likely than those holding an entity theory to report responding to academic difficulty with withdrawal of effort or cheating, and less likely to respond with new strategies or renewed effort.

Typically mediated by these strategy differences, the implicit theories have been shown to predict differences in key outcomes, such as grades (Blackwell et al., 2007), IQ test scores (Cury et al., 2008), changes in self-esteem over time (Robins and Pals, 2002), and negotiation success (Kray and Haselhun, 2007). In addition, as will be seen, interventions that teach an incremental theory yield improved outcomes in these and other areas.

SOCIAL INTERACTIONS AND SOCIAL RELATIONSHIPS

Do implicit theories work similarly in other domains, such as interpersonal relationships? Indeed, implicit theories have been found to play a role in intimate relationships (Finkel et al., 2007; Kammrath and Dweck, 2006; Knee, 1998) and peer relationships in both children (Erdley et al., 1997) and adults (Beer, 2002).

Beer (2002), for example, showed that shy people who endorsed an incremental theory about their shyness ("I can change aspects of my shyness if I want to") elected to enter more challenging social situations, were more direct and active versus avoidant in their social interactions, and fared considerably better over the course of a new social interaction than did shy people who endorsed an entity theory about their shyness ("My shyness is something about me that I can't change very much").

In studies of intimate relationships, Ruvolo and Rotondo (1998) and Kammrath and Dweck (2006) measured participants' theories about the malleability of other people's personality ("The kind of person someone is, is something very basic about them and it can't be changed very much"), with the hypothesis that conflicts and setbacks would be more daunting when people believed their partners' flaws were permanent. And in fact, Ruvolo and Rotundo found that incremental theorists were better able to maintain relationship satisfaction even when they were faced with their partners' flaws or weaknesses. Further, Kammrath and Dweck found that following an important conflict, incremental theorists were more likely to give voice to their dissatisfaction in order to solve the problem. And, in several studies involving either romantic partners or peers, incremental theories were found to be more predictive of a tendency toward forgiveness as opposed to revenge (Finkel et al., 2007; Yeager et al., in press). Believing that others can change, it appears, allows people to take steps to influence them and work things out; believing that others cannot change leaves fewer good options: keep silent, leave, or seek payback.

Moreover implicit theories appear to operate in the social domain in similar ways to the intellectual-achievement domain. That is,

people's self-theories are linked to their goals (Beer, 2002; Erdley et al., 1997; Knee, 1998), attributions (Erdley et al., 1997), and mastery-oriented versus helpless responses to threat or setbacks (Beer, 2002; Kammrath and Dweck, 2006).

PERSON PERCEPTION, SOCIAL JUDGMENT, AND STEREOTYPING

It was not long before we began to ask whether implicit theories also affected how people perceived and judged others. If so, we might understand more about the basis of stereotyping and prejudice. This seemed especially interesting to us since it would mean that a belief that on the face of it had little or nothing to do with stereotyping could lay a foundation on which stereotypes thrived.

Ying-yi Hong, C.Y. Chiu, Cynthia Erdley, and I reasoned that the process of person judgment would be quite different for a someone who believes that people are made up of fixed traits than for someone who believes that people are more dynamic and malleable. A belief in fixed traits should lead to a search for fixed traits, a relative neglect of the situation or the target's motivation, and more rigid judgments once they are rendered. This is exactly what we tested.

We found, first of all, that lay dispositionism and the fundamental attribution error were alive and well in entity theorists but were languishing in incremental theorists. For example, we found that entity theorists perceived almost any behavior as indicative of a person's underlying moral character (including such things as making one's bed in the morning) (Chiu et al., 1997b). Interestingly, they did not rate the behaviors themselves as better or worse than incremental theorists; they simply saw different implications for moral character. Entity theorists also more strongly believed that a person who was, say, more friendly or aggressive than another in one situation would also be more friendly or aggressive in a very different situation. Incremental theorists actually believed that the other guy would be the one to be more friendly or aggressive in the new and different situation – the opposite of the fundamental attribution error.

Next, we found that entity theorists were more likely to neglect salient information about the situation (Erdley and Dweck, 1993; Gervey et al., 1999; Molden et al., 2006; Molden et al., 2006) or the target's motivation (Erdley & Dweck, 1993; Chiu, 1994) when making their judgments, but paid heightened attention to trait or trait-consistent information (Molden et al., 2006; Plaks et al., 2001). A similar bias was observed in their explanations for behavior: entity theorists were more likely to generate trait explanations for a target's behavior and less likely to think about psychological processes (e.g., motives, needs, construals) that could have caused the actions (Hong, 1994).

Moreover, even though entity theorists' trait inferences are drawn very rapidly, often from very preliminary information (Butler, 2000; Chiu et al., 1997b), they appear to have great confidence in them. They do not readily revise them in the face of counterinformation (Erdley and Dweck, 1993; Plaks et al., 2001) and they are willing to base decisions on them (Gervey et al., 1999). For example, Gervey et al. showed that entity theorists made strong inferences about moral character based on what the target, a defendant, was wearing on the day of the murder (a black leather jacket versus a business suit) and these judgments paralleled their guilty verdicts – to the point that potentially exonerating evidence had no impact on their decisions. And, believing they have judged a person as good or bad, entity theorists have a stronger tendency to endorse punishment as opposed to education for someone who has transgressed (Gervey et al., 1999; Erdley and Dweck, 1993; Chiu et al., 1997a).

Do these differences in person perception processes apply to the perception of groups and the formation of group stereotypes? Levy et al., (1998) and Levy and Dweck

(1999) set out to explore this question by exposing participants to novel groups. Basically, people were given favorable or unfavorable information about some members of a group (or groups). We found that entity theorists formed stereotypes (global trait judgments of the groups) more readily, perceived greater homogeneity within groups and greater differences between groups, were more likely to generalize group traits to new members about whom they had no information, and had more extreme desire to interact or not interact with a group member based on the group information they had received.

We also found that entity theorists also had more stereotyped views of existing groups (Levy et al., 1998), and that they were more resistant to information that countered a stereotype (Plaks et al., 2001). In other words, as with the perception of individuals, those who held an incremental theory about human attributes made less extreme and more provisional judgments that were open to revision. In fact, Plaks et al. found that incremental theorists were often more attentive to information that countered stereotypes than they were to information that confirmed them. Rydell et al. (2007) extended this work by examining people's theories about the fixed or malleable nature of groups (rather than individuals). Although they replicated past findings by showing that an entity theory about individuals predicted greater stereotyping, they also showed that an entity theory about groups – a more domain-specific measure – was an even better predictor of stereotyping.

For entity theorists there seems to be something "real" about belonging to a group, whether it is a social group, an occupational group, or a group based on race, ethnicity, or gender. For them, group members inevitably share traits. In a striking demonstration of this, Eberhardt et al., (2003) showed people pictures of biracial (morphed African-American and Caucasian) faces, telling them that a given face belonged either to an African-American or a Caucasian individual.

When they were later asked to identify or draw the face, entity theorists chose/drew a face that accorded more with the label than did incremental theorists, who often chose/drew a face that moved farther away from the stereotype.

Yet, believing in fixed traits does not always predict greater stereotyping or prejudice. In very interesting work, Haslam and Levy (2006) showed that believing that gays' sexual preference was inborn and unchangeable predicted *less* prejudice. In this case, people apparently found it more acceptable to think of gays as having inborn tendencies than tendencies that were self-chosen and subject to personal change.

Person theories predict people's actual behavior toward groups as well. In studies of volunteering in the real world, Karafantis and Levy (2004) found that children's implicit person theories were related not only to their attitudes toward homeless children or poor children (e.g., their liking of them, desire to have contact with them, and their perceived similarity to them), but to their efforts on their behalf (volunteering, collecting money for UNICEF) and their enjoyment of those efforts.

Finally et al., (1998) showed that changing implicit theories changed people's tendency to form group stereotypes, along with their attitudes toward group members. Later, I describe a recent study that addressed the question of whether changing implicit theories could change hardened intergroup attitudes and people's desire for reconciliation or compromise. We examined this in the context of the Arab-Israeli conflict, which brings us to our next topic.

SOCIAL ISSUES

Now that we have visited the two different worlds that implicit theories create, let us see whether this knowledge can illuminate social issues, such as longstanding group differences in achievement and intergroup

relations. I will also ask whether implicit theories have a role to play in therapy and in issues of self-regulation and health.

Group differences in achievement

At the heart of American society is a desire for equal outcomes across groups. For this reason, differences between gender, racial, and ethnic groups in academic achievement are cause for great concern. Researchers therefore began to wonder whether implicit theories could shed light on processes that create these group differences and on interventions that can shrink these differences. When a negatively stereotyped person holds an entity theory (or believes that the people evaluating them do), one can see why they might be more vulnerable. In the face of difficulty, they may more readily think, "Maybe they're right. It's fixed and maybe I don't have it."

Thus experimental work has shown that when abilities are portrayed as fixed entities, stereotyped groups tend to show performance deficits on difficult tasks, but when the abilities are portrayed as experience-based or acquirable, those deficits are greatly attenuated or nonexistent. This has been shown for females and math (Dar-Nimrod and Heine, 2006), and for African-Americans in verbal areas (Aronson, 1998). In a similar vein, in a longitudinal study of college women in calculus, Good et al. (2008) found that when women perceived their math environment to portray math as a fixed ability, they were highly susceptible to stereotyping. In the face of stereotyping, they show a marked decrement in their sense that they belonged in math and, as they did, their desire to continue in math declined along with their course grades. However, when women perceived their math environment to be portraying math as an acquirable ability, they were far less susceptible to stereotyping. Even when they reported high levels of stereotyping in their math environment, they were able to maintain a sense that they belonged in math, a desire to continue in math, and high grades in math.

Interestingly, when abilities are portrayed as fixed, the positively stereotyped group, such as men in math, can benefit (Mendoza-Denton et al., 2008). The idea that "it's fixed and I have it" may indeed be motivating in the face of a difficult task. This fits well with findings by Reich and Arkin (2006), who showed that people are quite sensitive to the implicit theories that others hold about them. In this research, when participants were matched with evaluators who held an entity theory of their ability, they reported greater self-doubt when they expected to do poorly but less self-doubt when they expected to do well. Thus, an entity theory may increase the achievement gap both by depressing the confidence, motivation, and performance of the negatively stereotyped groups and by giving a boost to the positively stereotyped group.

Three implicit theory-based intervention studies have been conducted in academic settings, all showing an increase in motivation, grades, and/or achievement test scores for the experimental versus control groups (Aronson et al., 2002; Blackwell et al., 2007; Good et al., 2003). In these studies, middle school or college students in the experimental group learned an incremental theory of intelligence (that the brain forms new connections whenever they learn something new and that this learning makes them smarter over time) and how to apply this to their studies. Students in the control group learned other useful things, such as, in the Blackwell et al. study, a series of important study skills.

In the Aronson et al. (2002) study, African-American college students' grades, enjoyment of academic work, and valuing of academic work increased significantly – even though their perceptions of negative stereotyping in their environment remained high. In the Good et al. (2003) study of adolescents, the gender difference in math performance, which was clear and significant in the control group, was greatly reduced and was not

significant in the experimental groups. A similar pattern was found in a further analysis of the data from the Blackwell et al. (2007) study. Thus, the belief that abilities can be acquired, and messages to that effect from those in one's learning environment, can help students fare better in challenging environments, and this appears to be especially so for targets of negative stereotypes.

Aside from direct interventions about the nature of ability, our research has shown that the type of praise students receive can have a striking effect on their implicit theories. This research was inspired by the self-esteem movement, with its gurus telling parents and educators to praise children's intelligence as lavishly and often as possible. Given our past findings, we thought this was bad advice. Sure enough, our studies (e.g., Mueller and Dweck, 1998) demonstrated that praise for intelligence (as opposed to praise for effort or strategy, i.e., *process* praise) encourages more of an entity theory and performance goals, and, in the face of difficulty, leads to greater decreases in motivation, confidence, and performance. Although this work has not directly addressed achievement gaps, it suggests that in trying to boost the confidence and achievement of underperforming groups, it would not be a good idea to praise their abilities. Rather, it suggests that focusing them on learning and on the processes that lead to success – effort, concentration, persistence, strategies – would be far preferable.

Intergroup relations

Conflict resolution

Because implicit theories appear to have far-reaching effects on attitudes toward other groups (Hong et al., 2004; Levy et al., 1998), they perhaps hold promise of reducing animosity and promoting accord between antagonistic groups. It may be an especially promising approach because changing implicit person theories does not involve directly trying to change people's attitude toward the "enemy," which would almost certainly meet with resistance. Rather it simply involves changing their ideas about people or groups in general. In new work, Halperin et al. (2009) show, first, that Israelis' attitudes towards peace with the Palestinians are predicted by their level of hatred for Palestinians; second, that implicit theories about groups predict Israelis' level of hatred toward Palestinians; and third, that fostering an incremental theory about groups in general both lowered Israelis' hatred of Palestinians and made the Israeli participants more favorable to a peace process. Inducing an incremental theory about groups was accomplished by means of an article that argued that groups do not have an inherent moral or immoral character but rather are incited to aggression by leaders and that when the leaders change so may the group characteristics and behavior. No mention was made of Palestinians or their leaders.

Confronting biased behavior

Biased statements or actions present a good opportunity for educating outgroup members, particularly since such behavior is typically based on stereotypes or misinformation. However, confronting people and attempting to educate them presupposes that they can change. In new work, Rattan and Dweck (2010) show that when faced with biased remarks that included their group, people with incremental person theories were more likely to confront the speaker with the intent of educating him. Entity theorists, although they found the remark equally offensive, were not only less likely to confront the speaker, but also planned to avoid the speaker and people like him in the future. Additionally, we found that when people were led to hold an incremental person theory (by means of a scientific article that espoused and presented evidence for the theory), they were significantly more inclined to confront bias. Although not every situation permits the confronting of bias and although it is not incumbent upon negatively stereotyped individuals to confront bias whenever it arises, holding an incremental person

theory may facilitate the process when it is appropriate or desirable.

Responses to peer bullying

Bullying and school violence have become a serious problems in schools around the world. I include this topic under intergroup relations because the victim of bullying is often a member of an outgroup, whether it is an ethnic or racial outgroup or a peer outgroup (e.g., computer nerds or kids who are physically different). Although the eradication of bullying is a top priority, it is also important to understand why some students respond to bullying with violent retaliation and others do not. Yeager et al. (in press), with sizable samples of high school students from the U.S. and Finland, either asked participants to recall a time when a peer had greatly upset them or gave them a vivid bullying scenario that was written as though it was happening to them. They were asked to choose the actions they would most feel like taking. We found that implicit person theories predicted their preferred responses, with an entity theory consistently predicting festering resentment and the desire for violent, vengeful reactions ("hurting this person," "imagining them getting hurt"). Moreover, an incremental theory intervention lessened students' desire for violent revenge.

Management and business

Now more than ever, business people must be responsive to the constant change that is taking place all around them, must be ready to correct the practices that are no longer working, and must be willing to try new approaches. To do otherwise is to risk stagnation or failure. Several lines of research have shown that implicit theories play a role in these processes. For example, Tabernero and Wood (1999) demonstrated the benefits of an incremental theory of management skills for the performance of individuals and work groups on challenging management tasks, in which new, corrective information was constantly being provided. Kray and Haselhuhn (2007) demonstrated that an implicit theory of negotiation ability predicted (and caused) superior negotiation outcomes, particularly on challenging tasks on which impasses were reached.

In an exciting program of research, Heslin and Vanderwalle (2008) showed that managers who held an entity person theory were less likely than their incremental counterparts (a) to be attuned to changes in employees' performance after an initial good or poor performance was witnessed, remaining stuck in the initial impression; and (b) to mentor their employees, as reported by the employees themselves. Heslin and Vanderwalle then provided workshops that taught an incremental theory to a subset of the managers who had held entity theories. The managers who received this workshop, when tested six weeks later, displayed significantly more sensitivity to changes in an employee's performance than did the managers in the control group, who had gone through a placebo workshop. In addition, they became more willing to provide mentorship and generated higher quality mentoring strategies. In summary, implicit theories have implications for learning, teaching, and productivity in a challenging, changing world.

Clinical psychology, psychotherapy, and health

Because they affect self-regulation processes and interpersonal processes, implicit theories may well contribute to clinical psychology and to psychotherapy. First, research has shown that an entity theory and/or its allied goals (performance goals) play a role in depression (Dykman, 1998), in the loss of self-esteem following setbacks (Niiya et al., 2004), and in the negative impact of self-discrepancies (not matching one's ideal self) (Renaud and McConnell, 2007). There is also evidence that implicit theories about emotion regulation can play a role in emotional and social adjustment during the transition to college, with entity theorists experiencing waning social support and greater depression over time (Tamir et al., 2007).

Holding an entity theory of one's attributes increases defensiveness (Blackwell et al., 2007; Hong et al., 1999; Nussbaum and Dweck, 2008), which is a problem in itself, but can also greatly impede personal change, both within and outside of a therapeutic setting (see Dweck and Elliott-Moskwa, 2009, for a discussion of this). In addition, an incremental theory may predict better adherence to therapy, which inevitably is fraught with challenges and setbacks (see Dweck and Elliott-Moskwa, 2009, for a discussion of the potential role of implicit theories in cognitive behavior therapy). Preliminary evidence is also emerging to suggest that holding an incremental theory may predict better adherence to exercise and dieting in face of setbacks (Burnette, 2007; Kasimatis et al., 1996) This is an important area for future research and may well yield information about adherence to other health-maintaining or change-producing regimes.

Finally, therapists themselves may benefit from an incremental theory. Although most therapists, one hopes, hold the belief that people can change, they may approach very difficult patients (particularly ones who are threatening to their self-image as a competent therapist) with an entity theory. This may help protect the therapist from self-blame, but it may impede the therapeutic process if the therapist is less persistent in seeking strategies that can reach such clients (see Dweck and Elliott-Moskwa, 2009).

CONCLUSION

Research on implicit theories is giving us a portrait of people as dynamic creatures who are highly sensitive to cues in their environment and who are capable of change and growth. Moreover, the research is suggesting ways to promote that change and growth. As such, it is supporting a more incremental view of human abilities, human personality, and perhaps human nature.

When you begin a program of research, you have no idea where it will take you. I have stayed with this program of research because it continues to take me to new places. It remains challenging, it continues to yield provocative findings, and it has drawn me into the real world as people in the fields of education, business, sports, and health have sought to use our research to illuminate their practices. I cannot imagine a career more stimulating or more fulfilling – or one more conducive to personal growth.

REFERENCES

Aronson, J. (1998) The effects of conceiving ability as fixed or improvable on responses to stereotype threat. Unpublished manuscript, University of Texas.

Aronson, J., Fried, C.B. and Good, C. (2002) Reducing the effects of stereotype threat on African American college students by shaping mindsets of intelligence. *Journal of Experimental Social Psychology, 38*, 113–125.

Bandura, A. (1986) *Social Foundations of Thought and Action: A Social Cognitive Theory.* Englewood Cliffs, NJ: Prentice-Hall.

Bastian, B. and Haslam, N. (2006) Psychological essentialism and stereotype endorsement. *Journal of Experimental Social Psychology, 42*, 228–235.

Beer, J.S. (2002) Implicit self-theories of shyness. *Journal of Personality and Social Psychology, 83*, 1009–1024.

Binet, A. (1909) *Les idees modernes sur les enfants* [Modern ideas on children]. Paris: Flamarion. (This edition 1973.)

Blackwell, L., Trzesniewski, K. and Dweck, C.S. (2007) Implicit theories of intelligence predict achievement across an adolescent transition: A longitudinal study and an intervention. *Child Development, 78*, 246–263.

Bloom, B.S. (1985) *Developing Talent in Young People.* New York: Ballentine.

Burnette, J.L. (2007) Implicit theories of weight management: A social cognitive approach to motivation. *Dissertation Abstracts International, 67(7-B)*, 4154.

Butler, R. (2000) Making judgments about ability: The role of implicit theories of ability. *Journal of Personality and Social Psychology, 78*, 965–978.

Chiu, C. (1994) Bases of categorization and person cognition. Unpublished PhD dissertation, Columbia University.

Chiu, C., Dweck, C.S., Tong, J.Y. and Fu, J.H. (1997a) Implicit theories and conceptions of morality. *Journal of Personality and Social Psychology, 73*, 923–940.

Chiu, C., Hong, Y. and Dweck, C.S. (1997b) Lay dispositionism and implicit theories of personality. *Journal of Personality and Social Psychology, 73*, 19–30.

Cury, F., Da Fonseca, D., Zahn, I. and Elliot, A. (2008) Implicit theories and IQ test performance: A sequential mediational analysis. *Journal of Experimental Social Psychology, 44*, 783–791.

Dar-Nimrod, I. and Heine, S.J. (2006) Exposure to scientific theories affects women's math performance. *Science, 314*, 435.

Diener, C.I. and Dweck, C.S. (1978) An analysis of learned helplessness: Continuous changes in performance, strategy and achievement cognitions following failure. *Journal of Personality and Social Psychology, 36*, 451–462.

Dweck, C.S. (1975) The role of expectations and attributions in the alleviation of learned helplessness. *Journal of Personality and Social Psychology, 31*, 674–685.

Dweck, C.S. (1999) *Self-theories: Their Role in Motivation, Personality, and Development.* Philadelphia: Psychology Press.

Dweck, C.S. (2006). *Mindset.* New York: Random House.

Dweck, C.S. (2008) Can personality be changed? The role of beliefs in personality and change. *Current Directions in Psychological Science, 17*, 391–394.

Dweck, C.S., Davidson, W., Nelson, S. and Enna, B. (1978) Sex differences in learned helplessness: (II) The contingencies of evaluative feedback in the classroom and (III) An experimental analysis. *Developmental Psychology, 14*, 268–276.

Dweck, C.S. and Elliott-Moskwa, E. (2009) Self-theories: The roots of defensiveness. In J.E. Maddux and J.P. Tangney (eds), *The Social Psychological Foundations of Clinical Psychology.* New York: Guilford Press.

Dweck, C.S. and Leggett, E.L. (1988) A social-cognitive approach to motivation and personality, *Psychological Review, 95*, 256–273.

Dweck, C.S., Mangels, J. and Good, C. (2004) Motivational effects on attention, cognition, and performance. In D.Y. Dai and R.J. Sternberg (eds),

Motivation, Emotion, and Cognition: Integrated Perspectives on Intellectual Functioning. Mahwah, NJ: Erlbaum.

Dweck, C.S. and Reppucci, N.D. (1973) Learned helplessness and reinforcement responsibility in children. *Journal of Personality and Social Psychology, 25,* 109–116.

Dweck, C.S. and Wagner, A.R. (1970) Situational cues and the correlation between CS and US as determinants of the conditioned emotional response. *Psychonomic Science, 18,* 145–147.

Dykman, B.M. (1998) Integrating cognitive and motivational factors in depression: Initial tests of a goal-oriented approach. *Journal of Personality and Social Psychology, 74,* 139–158.

Eberhardt, J.L., Dasgupta, N. and Banaszynski, T.L. (2003) Believing is seeing: The effects of racial labels and implicit beliefs on face perception. *Personality and Social Psychology Bulletin, 29,* 360–370.

Elliot, A.J., McGregor, H.A. and Gable, S. (1999) Achievement goals, study strategies, and exam performance: A mediational analysis. *Journal of Educational Psychology, 91,* 549–563.

Elliott, E.S. and Dweck, C.S. (1988) Goals: An approach to motivation and achievement. *Journal of Personality and Social Psychology, 54,* 5–12.

Erdley, C., Cain, K., Loomis, C., Dumas-Hines, F. and Dweck, C.S. (1997) The relations among children's social goals, implicit personality theories and response to social failure. *Developmental Psychology, 33,* 263–272.

Erdley, C.S. and Dweck, C.S. (1993) Children's implicit theories as predictors of their social judgments. *Child Development, 64,* 863–878.

Ericsson, K.A., Krampe, R.T. and Tesch-Römer, C. (1993) The role of deliberate practice in the acquisition of expert performance. *Psychological Review, 100,* 363–406.

Finkel, E., Burnette J. and Scissors, L. (2007) Vengefully ever after: Destiny beliefs, state attachment anxiety, and forgiveness. *Journal of Personality and Social Psychology, 92,* 871–886.

Gervey, B., Chiu, C., Hong, Y. and Dweck, C.S. (1999) Differential use of person information in decision-making about guilt vs. innocence: The role of implicit theories. *Personality and Social Psychology Bulletin, 25,* 17–27.

Goetz, T.E. and Dweck, C.S. (1980) Learned helplessness in social situations. *Journal of Personality and Social Psychology, 39,* 246–255.

Good, C., Aronson, J. and Inzlicht, M. (2003) Improving adolescents' standardized test performance: An intervention to reduce the effects of stereotype threat. *Applied Developmental Psychology, 24,* 645–662.

Good, C., Rattan, A. and Dweck, C.S. (2008) Development of the sense of belonging to math survey for adults: A longitudinal study of women in calculus. Unpublished manuscript.

Gould, S.J. (1996) *The Mismeasure of Man.* New York: Norton.

Grant, H. and Dweck, C.S. (2003) Clarifying achievement goals and their impact. *Journal of Personality and Social Psychology, 85,* 541–553.

Halperin, E., Russell, A., Dweck, C.S. and Gross, J. (2009) Emotion regulation in intergroup conflicts: Anger, hatred, implicit theories and prospects for peace. Unpublished manuscript.

Haslam, N. and Levy, S.R. (2006) Essentialist beliefs about homosexuality: Structure and implications for prejudice. *Personality and Social Psychology Bulletin, 32,* 471–485.

Hayes, J.R. (1989) Cognitive processes in creativity. In J. Glover, R. Ronning, and C. Reynolds (eds), *Handbook of Creativity.* New York: Plenum.

Herrnstein, R. and Murray, C. (1996) *The Bell Curve.* New York: Simon & Schuster.

Heslin, P.A. and Vandewalle, D. (2008) Managers' implicit assumptions about personnel. *Current Directions in Psychological Science, 17,* 219–223.

Hong, Y. (1994) Predicting trait versus process inferences: The role of implicit theories. Unpublished PhD dissertation, Columbia University.

Hong, Y., Coleman, J., Chan, G., Wong, R.Y.M., Chiu, C., Hansen, I.G. Lee, S., Tong, Y. and Fu, H. (2004) Predicting intergroup bias: The interactive effects of implicit theory and social identity. *Personality and Social Psychology Bulletin, 30,* 1035–1047.

Hong, Y.Y., Chiu, C., Dweck, C.S., Lin, D. and Wan, W. (1999) Implicit theories, attributions, and coping: A meaning system approach. *Journal of Personality and Social Psychology, 77,* 588–599.

Jaeggi, S.M., Buschkuehl, M., Jonides, J. and Perrig, W.J. (2008) Improving fluid intelligence with training on working memory. *Proceedings of the National Academy of Sciences, 10,* 14931–14936.

Kammrath, L. and Dweck, C.S. (2006) Voicing conflict: Preferred conflict strategies among incremental and entity theorists. *Personality and Social Psychology Bulletin, 32,* 1497–1508.

Karafantis, D.M. and Levy, S.R. (2004) The role of children's lay theories about the malleability of human attributes in beliefs about and volunteering for disadvantaged groups. *Child Development, 75,* 236–250.

Kasimatis, M., Miller, M. and Marcussen, L. (1996) The effects of implicit theories on exercise motivation. *Journal of Research in Personality, 30,* 510–516.

Keller, J. (2005) In genes we trust: The biological component of psychological essentialism and its relationship to mechanisms of motivated social cognition. *Journal of Personality and Social Psychology, 88,* 686–702.

Knee, C.R. (1998) Implicit theories of relationships: Assessment and prediction of romantic relationship initiation, coping, and longevity. *Journal of Personality and Social Psychology, 74,* 360–370.

Kray, L.J. and Haselhuhn, M.P. (2007) Implicit negotiation beliefs and performance: Experimental and longitudinal evidence. *Journal of Personality and Social Psychology, 93,* 49–64.

Levy, S.R., Chiu, C. and Hong, Y. (2006) Lay theories and intergroup relations. *Group Processes and Intergroup Relations, 9,* 5–24.

Levy, S.R. and Dweck, C.S. (1999) Children's static vs. dynamic person conceptions as predictors of their stereotype formation. *Child Development, 70,* 1163–1180.

Levy, S., Stroessner, S. and Dweck, C.S. (1998) Stereotype formation and endorsement: The role of implicit theories. *Journal of Personality and Social Psychology, 74,* 1421–1436.

Licht, B.G. and Dweck, C.S. (1984) Determinants of academic achievement: The interaction of children's achievement orientations with skill area. *Developmental Psychology, 20,* 628–636.

Major, B., Kaiser, C.R., O'Brien, L.T. and McCoy, S.K. (2007) Perceived discrimination as worldview threat or worldview confirmation: Implications for self-esteem. *Journal of Personality and Social Psychology, 92,* 1068–1086.

Mangels, J.A., Butterfield, B., Lamb, J., Good, C.D. and Dweck, C.S. (2006) Why do beliefs about intelligence influence learning success? A social-cognitive-neuroscience model. *Social, Cognitive, and Affective Neuroscience, 1,* 75–86.

Martocchio, J.J. (1994) Effects of conceptions of ability on anxiety, self-efficacy, and learning in training. *Journal of Applied Psychology, 79,* 819–825.

Mendoza-Denton, R., Kahn, K. and Chan, W. (2008) Can fixed views of ability boost performance in the context of favorable stereotypes? *Journal of Experimental Social Psychology, 44,* 1187–1193.

Miele, D.B. and Molden, D.C. (2009) Lay theories of intelligence and the role of processing fluency in perceived comprehension, Unpublished Manuscript, Northwestern University.

Mischel, W. and Shoda, Y. (1995) A cognitive-affective systems theory of personality: Reconceptualizing the invariances in personality and the role of situations. *Psychological Review, 102,* 246–268.

Molden, D.C. and Dweck, C.S. (2006) Finding 'meaning' in psychology: A lay theories approach to self-regulation, social perception, and social development. *American Psychologist, 61,* 192–203.

Molden, D.C., Plaks, J.E. and Dweck, C.S. (2006) 'Meaningful' social inferences: Effects of implicit theories on inferential processes. *Journal of Experimental Social Psychology, 42,* 738–752.

Mueller, C.M. and Dweck, C.S. (1998) Intelligence praise can undermine motivation and performance. *Journal of Personality and Social Psychology, 75,* 33–52.

Murphy, M. and Dweck, C.S. (2010) A culture of genius: How an organization's lay theories shape people's cognition, affect, and behavior. *Personality and Social Psychology Bulletin, 36,* 283–96.

Niiya, Y., Crocker, J. and Bartmess, E.N. (2004) From vulnerability to resilience: Learning orientations buffer contingent self-esteem from failure. *Psychological Science, 15,* 801–805.

Nussbaum, A.D. and Dweck, C.S. (2008) Defensiveness vs. remediation: Self-theories and modes of self-esteem maintenance. *Personality and Social Psychology Bulletin, 34,* 599–612.

Plaks, J., Stroessner, S., Dweck, C.S. and Sherman, J. (2001) Person theories and attention allocation: Preference for stereotypic vs. counterstereotypic information. *Journal of Personality and Social Psychology, 80,* 876–893.

Plaks, J.E, Grant, H. and Dweck, C.S. (2005) Violations of implicit theories and the sense of prediction and control: Implications for motivated person perception. *Journal of Personality and Social Psychology, 88,* 245–262.

Plaks, J.E and Stecher, K. (2007) Unexpected improvement, decline, and stasis: A prediction confidence perspective on achievement success and failure. *Journal of Personality and Social Psychology, 93,* 667–684.

Rattan, A. and Dweck, C.S. (2010) Who confronts prejudice? The role of implicit theories in the motivation to confront prejudice. *Psychological Science, 21,* 952–959.

Reich, D.A. and Arkin, R.M. (2006) Self-doubt, attributions, and the perceived implicit theories of others. *Self and Identity, 5,* 89–109.

Renaud, J.M. and McConnell, A.R. (2007) Wanting to be better but thinking you can't: Implicit theories of personality moderate the impact of self-discrepancies on self-esteem. *Self and Identity*, *6*, 41–50.

Roberts, B.W., Walton, K.E. and Viechtbauer, W. (2006) Patterns of mean-level change in personality traits across the life course: A meta-analysis of longitudinal studies. *Psychological Bulletin*, *132*, 1–25.

Robins, R.W. and Pals, J.L. (2002) Implicit self-theories in the academic domain: Implications for goal orientation, attributions, affect, and self-esteem change. *Self and Identity*, *1*, 313–336.

Rueda, M.R., Rothbart, M.K., McCandliss, B.D., Saccomanno, L. and Posner, M.I. (2005) Training, maturation, and genetic influences on the development of executive attention. *Proceedings of the National Academy of Sciences*, *102*, 14931–14936.

Ruvolo, A.P. and Rotondo, J.L. (1998) Diamonds in the rough: Implicit personality theories and views of partner and self. *Personality and Social Psychology Bulletin*, *24*, 750–758.

Rydell, R.J., Hugenberg, K., Ray, D. and Mackie, D.M. (2007) Implicit theories about groups and stereotyping: The role of group entitativity. *Personality and Social Psychology Bulletin*, *33*, 549–558.

Seligman, M.E.P., Maier, S.F. and Geer, J.H. (1968) Alleviation of learned helplessness in the dog. *Journal of Abnormal Psychology*, *73*, 256–272.

Tabernero, C. and Wood, R.E. (1999) Implicit theories versus the social construal of ability in self-regulation and performance on a complex task. *Organizational Behavior and Human Decision Processes*, *78*, 104–127.

Tamir, M., John, O.P., Srivastava, S. and Gross, J.J. (2007) Implicit theories of emotion: Affective and social outcomes across a major life transition. *Journal of Personality and Social Psychology*, *92*, 731–744.

Tong, E. and Chang, W. (2008) Group entity belief: An individual difference construct based on implicit theories of social identities. *Journal of Personality*, *76*, 707–732.

Weiner, B. and Kukla, A. (1970) An attributional analysis of achievement motivation. *Journal of Personality and Social Psychology*, *15*, 1–20.

Yeager, D.S., Trzesniewski, K.H., Tirri, K., Nokelainen, P. and Dweck, C.S. (in press) Adolescents' implicit theories predict desire for vengeance after peer conflicts: Correlational and experimental evidence. *Developmental Psychology*.

29

Uncertainty-Identity Theory

Michael A. Hogg

ABSTRACT

Uncertainty-identity theory is an account of how feelings of self-uncertainty motivate people to identify with groups in order to reduce their uncertainty. Self-uncertainty can very effectively be reduced by group identification because the process of self-categorization as a group member transforms self-conception so that it is governed by a group prototype that describes and prescribes what one should think, feel, and do, and how others will perceive and interact with you. It also provides consensual validation of self by fellow ingroup members. Group identification can make the world a more predictable place in which people know who they are, what to think, feel, and do, and how the course of interaction with others will play out. However, some groups, specifically high entitativity groups, have properties that make them better than others at reducing uncertainty. Uncertainty-identity theory has direct relevance to an explanation of a range of group phenomena, including social influence, norms, deviance, minority influence, schisms, leadership processes, and extremism and ideological orthodoxy.

INTRODUCTION

Social groups pervade the human experience. Language and symbolic communication, norms and culture, society and governance, commodities and the built environment – all are produced and configured by groups, and regulate and serve groups. Even our closest interpersonal and romantic relationships are shaped and contextualized by group membership. Ethnicity, religion, nation, organization, work team, sports club, family – these are all groups. They differ in size, distribution, distinctiveness, internal structure, longevity, purpose, "group-ness," and of course what they do; but they all share one fundamental characteristic – they provide their members with a sense of who they are, what they should think and do, and how others will perceive and treat them. Groups provide people with a social identity – a shared evaluation and definition of who one is and how one is located in the social world.

This perspective on groups as providers of social identity, and group behavior as a product of social identity processes, has been most fully explored over the past 40 years by social identity theory (Tajfel and Turner, 1979; Turner et al., 1987; also see Abrams and Hogg, 2010; Hogg, 2006; Hogg and Abrams, 1988). In the present chapter, I describe the development, concepts, and social relevance of *uncertainty-identity theory* (Hogg, 2007a), as an account of how social identity processes and phenomena are fundamentally motivated by people's need to reduce uncertainty about themselves. The theory has three basic premises: (1) people are motivated to reduce feelings of uncertainty about or related to themselves; (2) identifying with a group reduces self-uncertainty because the group's attributes are cognitively internalized as a *prototype* that describes and prescribes how one should behave and be treated by others, and one's prototype is consensually validated by fellow group members; and (3) highly entitative groups that are distinctive and clearly defined are most effective at reducing self-uncertainty.

BACKGROUND AND DEVELOPMENT: A PERSONAL NARRATIVE

In the fall of 1978 I arrived at Bristol University to begin my PhD with John Turner. At that time Bristol was the uncontested center for social identity theory – Henri Tajfel was there, Rupert Brown had just left, and Marilynn Brewer was about to arrive for a sabbatical. The 1978 intake of PhD students also included Penny Oakes, Steven Reicher, and Margaret Wetherell. We were all working with John Turner to further develop the social identity concept with a more detailed focus on underlying cognitive mechanisms and on group processes in general. From this came the social identity theory of the group, self-categorization theory (Turner et al., 1987).

My own piece of the puzzle, for my dissertation, was group formation – what is the process through which a group forms or, more precisely, a person identifies with a group? At the time the prevalent social psychological model of group formation was group cohesiveness – interpersonal attraction is the social glue that holds groups together, and group formation is a matter, ultimately, of people developing bonds of attraction to one another. My doctoral research contested this model: distinguishing personal attraction, which has nothing to do with groups,

from social attraction, which has everything to do with groups. Social attraction is the attraction based on categorization of oneself and others as members of the same group – group formation is a matter of self-categorization, not liking (Hogg, 1993).

Of course, the *process* of group formation as self-categorization (the "how") invites the complementary question of what *motivates* people to identify with groups (the "why"). Although my dissertation focused on process, this motivational question interested me right from the start. At that time, the late 1970s, the main motivational dimension of social identity processes was positive intergroup distinctiveness and the pursuit of group-mediated self-esteem (e.g., Tajfel and Turner, 1979) – this aspect of social identity theory was critical as it described the mechanism for social change in intergroup relations. I quickly became involved with Turner in research on self-esteem and social identity.

In the fall of 1981, I became an assistant professor at Bristol and was joined in the fall of 1983 by Dominic Abrams. We had a productive (and very entertaining) 18 months together in Bristol before I headed to Sydney in early 1985 and then Melbourne in 1986, and Abrams headed to Dundee. In addition to planning and subsequently writing our social identity text, *Social Identifications* (Hogg and Abrams, 1988), we decided to clarify the motivational role of self-esteem in social identity processes. Our objective was to unpack and formalize what had already been written and systematize what the data actually showed. We coined the term *self-esteem hypothesis* and differentiated between two corollaries: low self-esteem motivates group identification, and group identification elevates self-esteem. We found that the evidence generally supported the latter but not the former corollary. Published in 1988 (Abrams and Hogg, 1988), this work was heavily cited, and its analysis and conclusions reiterated and supported in numerous subsequent papers by our colleagues.

Abrams and I wrote a number of follow-up chapters, and I can clearly recall sweltering in my study in Brisbane in the subtropical southern summer of 1991/1992, soon after having moved to the University of Queensland, finishing up yet another chapter on the self-esteem hypothesis. I was trying to add a novel twist and increasingly feeling that although positive distinctiveness and self-enhancement were important and might steer the course of group behavior there must be a more fundamental motivation for identifying with groups in the first place. It struck me that groups provide grounding for self-conception and social interaction – they reduce uncertainty about who one is – and that self-categorization is a cognitive process that is ideally suited to self-conceptual uncertainty-reduction. I rather sketchily added this idea to the end of the chapter and sent it to Abrams, telling him to delete it if he thought the idea made no sense. We went back and forth and decided this was actually quite a nice idea; so we retained it as a short three-page section at the end of the chapter and changed the title of the chapter accordingly – it appeared in 1993 (Hogg and Abrams, 1993).

The role of uncertainty as an epistemic motivation for social identity processes and group behaviors became my obsession and a main focus of my research. I gathered graduate students and postdoctoral fellows around me and we conducted empirical studies that all seemed to support the idea that people were more likely to identify with or would identify more strongly with a group if they were uncertain. I was now able to make a full conceptual statement, resting on data, of what at that time I still called the subjective uncertainty-reduction hypothesis – this was first published in preliminary form in 1999 (Hogg and Mullin, 1999) and then more completely in 2000 (Hogg, 2000).

It had struck me that some groups might be structured in ways that were better equipped to reduce uncertainty through group identification – entitativity seemed to fit the bill perfectly as a moderator of the uncertainty-identification relationship. Building on this idea I began to explore what would happen

when uncertainty was subjectively more extreme or enduring – under these circumstances I argued that people would identify very strongly as zealots or true believers and that they would join groups that we would consider extremist, or make existing groups extremist. I had long been interested in how group membership can sometimes become all-enveloping – transforming people into zealous ideologues subscribing to inward-looking orthodoxies, treating dissenters and outsiders intolerantly as less than human, and endorsing and engaging in hurtful or brutal actions. These ideas were first published in 2004 (Hogg, 2004) and more fully in 2005 (Hogg, 2005), and then with an application to autocratic corporate leadership structures in 2007 (Hogg, 2007b).

By now I had been using the term "uncertainty-identity theory" for a number of years and was ready to write a fully integrated and developed theoretical statement, which was published in 2007 (Hogg, 2007a). By mid 2006 when I moved to the Claremont Graduate University in Los Angeles, my interest in uncertainty-identity theory's potential as an explanation of group extremism had become a key focus of my own research and that of my students and collaborators. Building on my social identity theory of leadership (e.g., Hogg and van Knippenberg, 2003) a particular interest has been in the leadership dimension of uncertainty-sponsored extremism, and most recently in the possible role of active minorities and minority influence processes.

BASIC CONCEPTS, PROCESSES, AND PHENOMENA

The core tenet of uncertainty-identity theory is that feelings of uncertainty, particularly about or relating to who one is and how one should behave, motivate uncertainty-reduction, and that the process of self-categorization as a group member reduces self-conceptual uncertainty because it provides a consensually validated group prototype that describes and prescribes who one is and how one should behave.

Uncertainty

Feeling uncertain about one's perceptions, attitudes, feelings, and behaviors has a powerful motivational effect. We strive to reduce such uncertainties so that we feel less uncertain about the world we live in, and thus render it more predictable and our own behavior within it more efficacious. The American pragmatist philosopher John Dewey captures the motivational prominence of uncertainty-reduction rather nicely: "[I]n the absence of actual certainty in the midst of a precarious and hazardous world, men cultivate all sorts of things that would give them the *feeling* of certainty" (Dewey, 1929/2005: 33).

The experience of uncertainty can vary: it can be an exhilarating challenge to be confronted and resolved – it is exciting and makes us feel edgy and alive, and delivers us a sense of satisfaction and mastery when we resolve such uncertainties; or it can be anxiety provoking and stressful, making us feel impotent and unable to predict or control our world and what will happen to us in it. From the perspective of Blascovich's biopsychosocial model of challenge and threat (e.g., Blascovich and Tomaka, 1996) uncertainty can be thought of as a demand; if we believe our resources to deal with the demand are adequate we feel a sense of challenge that sponsors promotive or approach behaviors, if we believe our resources are inadequate we feel a sense of threat that sponsors more protective or avoidant behaviors. In this way people can reduce or regulate their uncertainty through quite different patterns of behavior that reflect a more promotive or more preventative approach (cf. Higgins's, 1998, regulatory focus theory).

The process of resolving uncertainty can be cognitively demanding. So in keeping with the cognitive miser or motivated tactician models of social cognition (e.g., Fiske and Taylor, 1991) we only expend cognitive energy resolving those uncertainties that are important or matter to us in a particular context. One of the key determinants of whether an uncertainty matters enough to warrant resolution is the extent to which self is involved. We are particularly motivated to reduce uncertainty if we feel uncertain about things that reflect on or are relevant to self, or if we are uncertain about self per se; about our identity, who we are, how we relate to others, and how we are socially located. Ultimately, people need to know who they are, how to behave, and what to think; and who others are, how they might behave, and what they might think.

In talking about uncertainty, it is more appropriate to talk about reducing uncertainty than achieving certainty – people cannot feel completely certain but only less uncertain (Pollock, 2003). Absolute certitude is generally viewed as a dangerous delusion that is the province of narcissists, zealots, ideologues, and true believers. People typically work to reduce uncertainty until they are "sufficiently" certain about something to desist from dedicating further cognitive effort to uncertainty reduction – this provides closure, in the gestalt sense (Koffka, 1935), and allows one to move on to dedicate cognitive effort to other things. Hence uncertainty-identity theory is about reducing uncertainty rather than achieving certainty.

However, there is a caveat. The pursuit of uncertainty reduction does not rule out the possibility that individuals or groups sometimes embark on courses of action that may in the short term increase uncertainty. Typically this might happen when an existing state of affairs is marked by glaring contradictions that engender uncertainty. This idea has parallels with the way that formal science progresses – periods of "normal science" where uncertainty is low and small contradictions accumulate but are concealed, punctuated by "scientific revolutions" where contradictions and uncertainties burst to the fore to sponsor a "paradigm shift" and subsequent reduction of uncertainty (Kuhn, 1962). Another example is when a current state of affairs in one's life or the society in which one lives is unbearable and a measured risk must be taken to improve things – change is risky and uncertain and therefore not undertaken lightly (e.g., Jost and Hunyady, 2002).

The idea that uncertainty plays a significant role in motivating human behavior is not new (Fromm, 1947), and there are many social psychological analyses of the causes and consequences of uncertainty (e.g., Kahneman et al., 1982). Because uncertainty-identity theory links self-uncertainty to identity and group processes, the treatments of uncertainty that are most relevant here are those that focus on social comparison processes (e.g., Festinger, 1954; Suls and Wheeler, 2000), uncertainty about or related to self (e.g., Arkin et al., 2010), individual and cultural differences in peoples tolerance and reaction to uncertainty (e.g., Hofstede, 1980; Kruglanski and Webster, 1996; Schwartz, 1992; Sorrentino and Roney, 1999), communication to reduce uncertainty (e.g., Berger, 1987), uncertainty and organizational socialization (e.g., Saks and Ashforth, 1997), and uncertainty-sponsored zealotry and defense of one's world-view (e.g., Kruglanski et al., 2006; McGregor and Marigold, 2003; McGregor et al., 2001; Van den Bos, 2009; Van den Bos et al., 2005). How these ideas relate to uncertainty-identity theory is discussed in detail elsewhere (Hogg, 2007a, 2010a), but the key differences are that (a) social identity and collective self are center-stage, (b) uncertainty is context- not personality-dependent, (c) a social cognitive process transforms uncertainty into group behavior, and (d) it is a motivational account of group phenomena in general not just extremism.

Uncertainty is related to meaning, and some argue that the primary human motive is a search for meaning (e.g., Bartlett, 1932; Maslow, 1987) – people strive to construct a

coherent and meaningful worldview. This idea has been explored recently by Heine et al., (2006) in their meaning maintenance model (cf. Swann's self-verification theory [Swann et al., 2003]): people are meaning-makers driven to establish associative frameworks that (a) tie together elements of the world, (b) tie together elements of themselves, and (c) most importantly bind self to the world. This view of meaning focuses less on meaning than on associative links that one has confidence in and one is certain about, suggesting that reduced uncertainty is critical and may motivationally underpin meaning. From an uncertainty-identity perspective uncertainty reduction is closely linked to meaning-making, however it is the aversive feeling of uncertainty that actually motivates. For example, baseball makes no sense to most Italians and yet they have little motivation to make it meaningful – they are uncertain but do not care as they do not feel it is important to who they are that the game should makes sense to them. For Italians, soccer is an entirely different motivational matter.

Finally, uncertainty takes many forms and has many foci. It can be wide ranging and diffuse; for example, feeling uncertain about one's future, or very specific and focused, for example feeling uncertain about what to wear to a party. Feelings of uncertainty can vary in strength and be transitory or enduring – however, from an uncertainty-identity theory, perspective enduring uncertainty is not primarily a matter of personality but rather a refection of an enduring context that creates uncertainty. As mentioned earlier, uncertainty also varies in the degree to which it reflects on or relates to self-conception in a particular context. Uncertainty about or related to self is likely to have the greatest motivational force because the self is the critical organizing principle, referent point, or integrative framework for perceptions, feelings, and behaviors. It is this self-uncertainty that is most directly implicated in social identity processes.

Self-categorization and group identification

Feelings of uncertainty have different causes and different foci. Uncertainty-identity theory focuses on context-induced feelings of uncertainty that are about self or about things that relate to, reflect on, or matter to self. If a particular context that induces uncertainty endures, for example a long-lasting economic crisis, uncertainty and attempts to reduce or fend off uncertainty may also endure. There may be individual differences in how much uncertainty people feel in a given context and in how people respond to uncertainty; however, this is treated, to use a statistical metaphor, as error variance – it is not the focus of uncertainty-identity theory. This orientation toward personality and individual differences is consistent with the group-focused metatheory that informs social identity theory and uncertainty-identity theory (e.g., Abrams and Hogg, 2004; Turner, 1999; also see Hogg, 2008).

Feelings of uncertainty about or reflecting on self can be resolved in many different ways – for example, one can introspect. However, the crux of uncertainty-identity theory is that group identification, via the process of self-categorization (e.g., Turner et al., 1987), is one of the most powerful and effective ways to reduce self-uncertainty. Human groups are social categories that we cognitively represent as *prototypes* – fuzzy sets of attributes (e.g., perceptions, beliefs, attitudes, values, feelings, behaviors) that define the category and distinguish it from other categories in a specific context. Prototypes describe behaviors; but the prototype of a group we belong to also has prescriptive properties that dictate how we *ought* to behave as a group member.

Prototypes obey the metacontrast principle – they embody attributes that maximize the ratio of intergroup differences to intragroup differences, and thus accentuate perceived differences between and similarities within groups (cf. Tajfel, 1959). This principle ensures that the prototype of a specific group is influenced by what group it is being compared to and for what purpose, and thus that group prototypes are not simply average group attributes but are often ideal group attributes.

When we categorize someone as a member of a specific group we assign the group's prototypical attributes to that person. We view them through the lens of the prototype of that group; seeing them not as unique individuals but as more or less prototypical group members – a process called *depersonalization*. When we categorize others, ingroup or outgroup members, we stereotype them and have expectations of what they think and feel and how they will behave. When we categorize ourselves, self-categorization, exactly the same process occurs – we assign prescriptive ingroup attributes to ourselves, we auto-stereotype, conform to group norms, and transform our self conception.

In this way group identification is very effective at reducing self-related uncertainty. It provides us with a sense of who we are that prescribes what we should think, feel, and do. Because self-categorization is inextricably linked to categorization of others, it also reduces uncertainty about how others, both ingroup and outgroup members, will behave and what course social interaction will take. It also provides consensual validation of our worldview and sense of self, which further reduces uncertainty. Because people in a group tend to share the same prototype of "us" and share the same prototype of "them," our own expectations about the prototype-based behavior of others are usually confirmed, and our fellow group members agree with our perceptions, beliefs, attitudes, and values and approve of how we behave. The discovery that fellow ingroup members do not see the world as we do can be a source of profound uncertainty about what the group stands for and thus about self-conception. I discuss this in the following text.

Clearly, identification can effectively reduce uncertainty and protect one from uncertainty. The implication is that uncertainty reduction motivates group identification – we identify with groups in order to reduce, or protect ourselves from, uncertainty. When people feel uncertain about themselves or things reflecting on self they "join" new groups (e.g., sign up as a member of a community action group), identify with or identify more strongly with existing self-inclusive categories (e.g., one's nation), or identify with or identify more strongly with groups that they already "belong" to (e.g., one's work team).

Uncertainty reduction guides the process responsible for making a social categorization psychologically salient as the basis for self-categorization, group identification, and group behavior. People draw on accessible social categorizations – ones they value, find important, and frequently use to define themselves and perceive others (they are *chronically accessible* in memory), and/or ones that are prominent and self-evident in the immediate situation (they are *situationally accessible*) (e.g., Oakes, 1987; Turner et al., 1994) – gender is often chronically and situationally accessible. People then investigate how well the categorization accounts for similarities and differences among people (*structural/comparative fit* – do the men and women behave differently?) and how well the stereotypical properties of the categorization account for why people behave as they do (*normative fit* – do the men and women behave in accordance with one's gender expectations/stereotypes?).

If the fit of a particular categorization is poor, people cycle through other accessible categorizations until an optimal fit is obtained. This process is primarily fast and automatic because people strive to reduce feelings of uncertainty about self-conception, social interaction, and people's behavior. The very notion that an accessible categorization needs to *fit* implies that it reduces feelings of uncertainty about the social context and our place within it. The categorization with optimal fit

becomes psychologically salient as the basis of self-categorization, group identification, and prototype-based depersonalization. It triggers social identity-related perceptions, cognitions, affect, and behavior.

The uncertainty-identity theory conception of the relation between uncertainty and group identification represents a relatively hydraulic model of group motivation. Uncertainty, however induced, mobilizes one to psychologically identify and is reduced by identification. However, feelings of uncertainty are multiply determined and can be addressed in many different ways. Identification is only one way to address uncertainty, but one that is particularly effective in the case of self-related uncertainties. Feelings of uncertainty can also be fleeting. As soon as one uncertainty is reduced one's mind can be assailed by new uncertainties or we can seek out new ones to resolve.

The most basic prediction that can be made from uncertainty-identity theory is that the more uncertain people are the more likely they are to identify, and to identify more strongly, with a self-inclusive social category. This prediction has been confirmed across a number of minimal group studies in which people identified with relatively minimal groups and engaged in ingroup favoritism and intergroup discrimination only when they were categorized under uncertainty (e.g., Grieve and Hogg, 1999; Mullin and Hogg, 1998; for an overview of this research see Hogg, 2000, 2007a). In these studies uncertainty was manipulated in a variety of ways. For example, participants described what they thought was happening in ambiguous or unambiguous pictures, or they estimated the number of objects displayed in pictures in which there were very few objects or so many objects that they could only make a wild guess.

Other studies showed that uncertainty was a stronger motivation for identification if participants were uncertain about something they felt was important and self-relevant, and if the prototypical properties of the available social category were relevant to the focus of uncertainty. There are also studies showing that uncertainty significantly strengthens identification even when depressed self-esteem as a possible mediator is controlled for (Hogg and Svensson, 2010), and even when people are actually placed in a relatively low status group (Reid and Hogg, 2005).

Entitativity

Are there generic properties of groups that might make some types of groups and associated identities and prototypes better equipped to reduce uncertainty through identification? I have touched on a few of these potential moderators of the uncertainty-identity relationship above, but the most significant is entitativity (Hogg, 2004). Entitativity is that property of a group, resting on clear boundaries, internal homogeneity, social interaction, clear internal structure, common goals, and common fate, which makes a group "groupy" (Campbell, 1958; Hamilton and Sherman, 1996). Groups can vary widely in entitativity from a loose aggregate to a highly distinctive and cohesive unit (e.g., Lickel et al., 2000).

Group identification reduces uncertainty because it provides a clear sense of self that prescribes behavior and renders social interaction predictable. An unclearly structured low entitativity group that has indistinct boundaries, ambiguous membership criteria, limited shared goals, and little agreement on group attributes will do a poor job of reducing or fending off self-related uncertainty. In contrast a clearly structured high entitativity group with sharp boundaries, unambiguous membership criteria, tightly shared goals, and consensus on group attributes will do an excellent job. Identification via self-categorization reduces uncertainty because self is governed by a prototype that prescribes cognition, affect, and behavior. Prototypes that are simple, clear, unambiguous, prescriptive,

focused, and consensual are more effective than those that are vague, ambiguous, unfocused, and dissensual. Clear prototypes, such as the former, are more likely to be grounded in high than low entitativity groups. In addition, people are more likely to anchor the attributes of high entitativity groups in invariant underlying qualities or essences (e.g., Haslam et al., 1998) that provide further interpretative predictability and stability and make the group even better at reducing and fending off uncertainty.

From uncertainty-identity theory the prediction is that although under uncertainty, especially self-uncertainty, people will identify with groups, they will show a strong preference for high entitativity groups. People will seek out highly entitative groups with which to identify or they will work to elevate, subjectively or actually, the entitativity of groups to which they already belong. This idea has support from a number of indirect investigations of uncertainty, entitativity, and group identification (e.g., Castano et al., 2003; Jetten et al., 2000; Pickett and Brewer, 2001; Pickett et al., 2002; Yzerbyt et al., 2000).

Direct tests have provided better and more robust support (Hogg et al., 2007; Sherman et al., 2009). Hogg et al. (2007) conducted two studies in which uncertainty, explicitly about self, was experimentally primed to be high or low, and the perceived entitativity of participants' political party was measured (Study 1) or the perceived entitativity of participants' ad hoc lab group was manipulated (Study 2). Group identification was measured by a multi-item scale. In both cases, participants identified significantly more strongly when they were uncertain and their group was highly entitative. Sherman et al. (2009) conducted a pair of field studies of political party supporters and workers on strike, to provide support for the related idea that self-uncertainty can lead people to perceptually polarize groups in order to accentuate the perceived entitativity of a group they are already members of.

IMPLICATIONS, EXTENSIONS, AND APPLICATIONS

Group identification-based reduction of self-uncertainty has a large array of implications and applications. These implications extend the conceptual reach of the theory to embrace social influence; leadership processes and trust; dissent, deviance, and minority influence; and extremism and ideological orthodoxy.

Self-uncertainty and group influence

As described earlier, one of the ways that social identity reduces self-uncertainty is that it anchors self-conception in a consensual world view – it surrounds one with fellow ingroupers who see the world largely in the same way as you do and who thus provide consensual validation of your perceptions, attitudes, behaviors, and ultimately self-concept. Not surprisingly, discovering that fellow ingroupers do not see the world as you do can be a source of profound self-uncertainty. Indeed, disagreement with fellow ingroups (i.e., normative disagreement) often initiates a process of social influence, *referent informational influence*, through which people urgently seek information to confirm the group's norms and identity in order to know what they are identifying with and therefore what their own identity is (Turner, 1991; Turner et al. 1987; also see Hogg and Smith, 2007; McGarty et al., 1993).

Given how important it is for self-uncertainty management to know what the ingroup prototype/norm is, people can spend substantial time engaged in 'norm talk' – communicating mainly with fellow ingroup members in order to be sure of the groups defining and prescriptive attributes (Hogg and Reid, 2006). Through this normative communication process people tend to look to prototypical ingroup members to provide the most reliable information about ingroup norms. However, outgroups can also be a useful source of normative information. Discovering that you are in disagreement with an outgroup does not produce uncertainty; it is expected and serves to confirm your ingroup identity – they are what you are not. Agreement with an outgroup would, however, be problematic. It would produce self-related uncertainty, causing you to question what your group stands for and whether you really fit in as a member.

Leadership and trust

Within groups, prototypical members are more influential than nonprototypical members and people pay closer attention to the former than the latter as a reliable source of information about group norms and social identity (Hogg, 2010 b). Furthermore, according to the social identity theory of leadership (Hogg, 2001; Hogg and van Knippenberg, 2003) prototypical members tend to occupy leadership positions, and leaders are more effective if they are perceived to be prototypical. The clear implication is that self-uncertainty will cause people to pay even closer attention to their leaders, be more likely to empower them and follow them, and thirst for recognition and validation by them. Under these circumstances people will need to feel they are valued by and can trust their leaders (Lind and Tyler, 1988; Tyler, 1997; Tyler and Lind, 1992), even if such feelings are actually an illusion.

Trust plays an important role here – it is closely associated with predictability and uncertainty. The more we are able to trust someone the more predictable they are and the less uncertain we feel. Trust plays a central role in group, specifically ingroup, life. Ingroups are "bounded communities of mutual trust and obligation" (Brewer, 1999: 433) in which members expect to be able to trust fellow members to do them no harm and to be acting in the best interest of the group. Ingroup members who betray our group-based trust, by leaving the group to pursue their personal interest or by acting in ways that only benefit themselves and are to the detriment of the group as a whole, reduce trust and raise uncertainty and thus invite harsh reactions. This dynamic is particularly pronounced for central members who are prototypical of the group or act as group leaders. Disloyalty and violation of trust on the part of prototypical members is highly disruptive of group equilibrium (e.g., van Vugt and Hart, 2004), and is a particularly potent source of uncertainty about what the group stands for, about one's membership in the group, and ultimately about self.

Because uncertainty can empower leaders it would not be surprising to discover that smart leaders use uncertainty strategically as a resource. Marris's (1996) analysis of the politics of uncertainty supports this idea – certainty is power and the powerful can create uncertainty for the powerless in order to control them. Thus leaders, particularly those who feel the group perceives them to be prototypical and trusts them, can reinstate, maintain or strengthen their authority by engaging in a rhetoric of uncertainty coupled with reassurances that they are able to resolve the uncertainty. This would have the effect of strengthening followers' identification with the group and their support for the leader – a study by Hohman et al. (2010) provides some support for this idea. Furthermore, the media often has examples of national, religious, and corporate leaders doing precisely this – and it is a strategy that can, as I discuss below, produce autocratic or extremist leadership (Hogg, 2007b).

Outsiders: marginal members, deviants, and minorities

Leaders, as we have seen, play a significant role in resolving self-uncertainty because members look to them to define who "we" are – to resolve normative disagreement or ambiguity. However, normative disagreement and ambiguity within a group can produce an array of responses. It undermines the group's entitativity and thus one response is

to disidentify or identify less strongly with the group and identify with other more entitative groups. The tendency for uncertainty to weaken identification with low entitativity groups has been empirically confirmed in a pair of studies of moderate and radical groups by Hogg, Farquharson et al. (2010).

This notion of normative ambiguity, disagreement, or conflict can be taken further by focusing on the source of disagreement. Where disagreement seems to be with the leader's normative example and the leader is trusted and prototypical, then, as we saw above, members' realign themselves with the leader and identify with the group. However, where the leader is less prototypical and/or less trusted, members may initiate or engineer leadership change, or they may simply feel they themselves no longer fit the group and therefore that the group does not anchor their identity, so they weaken their ties, disidentify, and leave the group. Where normative disagreement is with a less prototypical, marginal member who does not occupy a leadership role, little normative uncertainty is evoked, much like encountering disagreement with an outgroup member. On the contrary, normative divergence on the part of nonprototypical members motivates the group to pressure the deviate to conform, but also may invite derogation, marginalization, persecution, and ejection from the group, often orchestrated by the group's leadership (e.g., Hogg et al., 2005; Marques et al., 2001; Marques and Paez, 1994).

Marginal group members who express normative divergence can sometimes avoid derogation and instead play an active role in normative clarification and uncertainty reduction. Specifically this may happen when they do not simply diverge, but rather act as constructive ingroup critics oriented toward clarification and improvement of ingroup normative practices (e.g., Hornsey, 2005). The other way in which normative deviance can impact the group is when those who diverge from normative practices and thus fracture entitativity and potentially raise uncertainty about the group and its identity are themselves a collective or group. This is very common, and more often than not creates a schism around alternative views of what the group stands for (e.g., Sani and Reicher, 1998). This state of affairs creates great uncertainty that usually requires members to identify strongly with one or other faction in order to reduce uncertainty, and of course the original group is usually changed forever.

Another way to view normatively divergent subgroups is as active minorities engaging in minority influence. Indeed, research on minority influence argues that active minorities who maintain their novel alternative position in a consistent manner ultimately change majority views quite radically precisely because they make the majority uncertain about the validity of the majority's position (e.g., Martin and Hewstone, 2008; Moscovici, 1980; Mugny and Pérez, 1991). The uncertainty is resolved by reconfiguring the majority position and identifying strongly with it, a conversion effect associated with social change. Much like it is easier to brush off disagreement with and criticism from outgroup members than fellow ingroupers, outgroup minorities may produce less uncertainty and subsequent normative change than ingroup minorities. This is consistent with the self-categorization theory analysis of minority influence (e.g., David and Turner, 2001) and with Crano's view that ingroup minorities can be more effective because a *leniency contract* is struck in which the majority agrees to be lenient toward the minority and pay attention to its views as long as the minority desists from being "too extreme" (e.g., Crano and Seyranian, 2009).

The discussion in this section is predicated on the idea that group identification effectively reduces self-uncertainty because the group prototype unambiguously defines and prescribes self, and because there is consensual validation of one's social identity. Intragroup disagreement and the existence of normative deviants potentially undermine entitativity and weaken the uncertainty reduction capacity of the group. We explored how different types of normative divergence may sponsor different responses.

A final aspect of this analysis concerns perceived self-prototypicality. What is important here for identity validation and thus uncertainty reduction is feeling that other members of the group believe you are prototypical, and accept and include you as a bone fide member who "fits in." Clearly, if you yourself feel you do not really fit in then the group, however highly entitative it may be, will not very effectively resolve self-uncertainty – you will feel like an imposter, a square peg in a round hole. Indeed poor fit may be a more serious identification and uncertainty management issue in highly entitative than less entitative groups. Even where you yourself feel you fit or that you will work hard to fit, if the group persistently views you as essentially a marginal member, the concomitant lack of acceptance and inclusion leaves you feeling continually uncertain about your membership status. Typically this weakens ties to the group and ultimate leads to disidentification.

Extremism

One of the most far-reaching extensions and implications of uncertainty-identity theory is its analysis of extremism (Hogg, 2004, 2005). There is a substantial literature that documents a relationship between societal uncertainty and various forms of extremism, such as "totalist" groups (Baron et al., 2003), cults (Curtis and Curtis, 1993), genocide (Staub, 1989), terrorism (Moghaddam and Marsella, 2004), fascism (Billig, 1978), ultranationalism (Kosterman and Feshbach, 1989), blind patriotism (Staub, 1997), religious fundamentalism (Altemeyer, 2003; Rowatt and Franklin, 2004), authoritarianism (Doty et al., 1991), ideological thinking (Billig, 1982; Jost and Hunyady, 2002; Jost et al., 2003; Lambert et al., 1999), and fanaticism and being a "true believer"

(Hoffer, 1951) – also see Hogg and Blaylock (in press). Uncertainty-identity theory can describe a process that generates extremism from uncertainty

Extremist groups have closed and carefully policed boundaries, uniform attitudes, values and membership, and inflexible customs. They are rigidly and hierarchically structured with a clearly delineated chain of legitimate influence and command, and substantial intolerance of internal dissent and criticism. Such groups are often ethnocentric, inward looking, and suspicious and disparaging of outsiders. They engage in relatively asocial and overly assertive actions that resemble collective narcissism (cf. Baumeister et al., 1996; Golec de Zavala et al., 2009): grandiosity, self-importance, envy, arrogance, haughtiness, entitlement, exploitativeness, excessive admiration, lack of empathy, fantasies of unlimited success, and feelings of special/unique/high status. In a similar vein, Kruglanski and colleagues describe a constellation of behaviors called "group-centrism," which emerges

[w]hen people care a lot about sharing opinions with others in their group; when they endorse central authority that sets uniform norms and standards; when they suppress dissent, shun diversity, and show in-group favoritism; when they venerate their group's norms and traditions, and display fierce adherence to its views; when above all, they exhibit all these as a package.

Kruglanski et al., 2006: 84

These are "extreme" groups that, even if they have only some of the attributes described above, furnish members with an all-embracing, rigidly defined, exclusive, and highly prescriptive social identity and sense of self.

Not all uncertainty drives people into the arms of totalist groups. Such groups can be uncomfortably constraining as they are often authoritarian and dictate and control every aspect of one's life and identity. However, these groups may seem particularly attractive under conditions of extreme and enduring uncertainty; for example,

widespread societal uncertainty caused by economic collapse, cultural disintegration, civil war, terrorism, and large-scale natural disasters; or more personal uncertainty caused by unemployment, bereavement, divorce, relocation, adolescence, and so forth.

Under these conditions totalist groups do an excellent job of reducing self-uncertainty. They are distinctive with rigid boundaries, often policed by the group, that unequivocally define who is in and who is out – there is no ambiguity or fuzziness about membership. The group's identity is clearly, unambiguously, and relatively simply defined, and often sharply polarized away from other groups. As a member you know exactly who you are and how you should behave and how others will behave. There is strong expectation of homogeneity and consensus that provides powerful social validation of one's identity and worldview, but also encourages a silo mentality in which dissenters and critics are suppressed and vilified. Such groups tend to be insular and inward looking; which provides a comfortably circumscribed world for members, but is also associated with marked ethnocentrism (Brewer and Campbell, 1976), accentuated mistrust and fear of outsiders (Stephan and Stephan, 1985), and a powerful tendency toward essentialism (Haslam et al., 1998) that renders self and social context subjectively stable and immutable.

Orthodoxy prevails (e.g., Deconchy, 1984). There is a single absolute standard of right and wrong in which attitudes, values, and behaviors are tightly woven together into ideological belief systems that are self-contained and explanatory (Larrain, 1979; Thompson, 1990); providing a firm and unassailable platform of certitude. The conjunction of moral absolutism, ideological orthodoxy and ethnocentrism is often a powerful basis for treating outgroup members as less than human – a process of dehumanization that can have terrible consequences (Haslam, 2006; Haslam et al., 2008).

Rigid ideological systems are particularly attractive in a postmodern world of moral and behavioral relativities and "limitless" choice. They resolve what Dunn (1998) has called the postmodern paradox: individual freedom of choice brings with it uncertainty about what to do and who to be and thus a desperate yearning for moral absolutes embedded in groups circumscribed by powerful ideologies. Religion has always provided all-embracing orthodoxies that not only address day-to-day uncertainties but also existential uncertainty – religious identification is such a powerful resolution of self-uncertainty that it can often mutate into zealotry associated, ironically, with intolerance (Hogg, Adelman et al., 2010; McGregor et al., 2008). For example, Lewis (2004), in his analysis of contemporary Islamic fundamentalism, argues that "in a time of intensifying strains, of faltering ideologies, jaded loyalties, and crumbling institutions, an ideology expressed in Islamic terms" (Lewis, 2004: 19) is particularly appealing.

We have already discussed, above, the important role of group leadership in reducing uncertainty, and how leaders can strategically use uncertainty to maintain their position of influence in the group. In extremist groups leadership becomes even more important. These groups are rigidly and consensually structured in terms of relative prototypicality of members, and of course prototype information is supremely important. Ideal conditions exist for prototypical leadership to prevail, and for such leaders to be extremely influential. Ultimately such leaders can become intoxicated by their power and feel isolated from the rank-and-file of the group – they can all too easily become autocratic despots (Hogg, 2007b). History is replete with examples: Adolf Hitler, Idi Amin, Saddam Hussein, Pol Pot, and so forth.

To some extent extremist groups are simply ultraentitative groups, and that is why uncertainty, particularly more extreme uncertainty, can make them attractive and why people identify very strongly with them.

However, the construct of entitativity is primarily a perceptual construct that describes group structure – it does not speak to what a group does, the extent to which a group adopts a moderate or more radical course of action to protect or promote its identity and the welfare of its members. Extremist groups often have a powerful behavioral dimension focused on endorsement of and engagement in radical action.

This action component of a group's identity is likely to become more important to the extent that what the group stands for is self-relevant and viewed as under threat. When people feel their security, prosperity, and lifestyle are threatened, they yearn to identify strongly with a group that can get things done to remove or buffer the threat – a radical extremist group that has a forceful behavioral agenda. Against this background self-uncertainty not only strengthens identification with assertive radical groups, perhaps transforming members into fanatics, zealots, true believers, and ideologues, but also weakens identification with less assertive moderate groups. In this way identification with extreme groups may be a powerful force for social mobilization that transforms attitudes into action (e.g., Hogg and Smith, 2007; Klandermans, 1997; Stürmer and Simon, 2004).

Preliminary support for this idea comes from an experiment by Hogg, Meehan et al. (2010). In the context of a self-relevant threat, uncertainty strengthened students' identification with a radical campus action group and weakened identification with a more moderate group – identification also mediated intentions to engage in behavior on behalf of the group (also see Hogg, Farquharson, et al, 2010). Further support comes from four field studies conducted by Adelman et al. (submitted) in Israel. Palestinian Muslims and Israeli Jews, with stronger, more important, and more central national and religious identities, indicated greater support for violent action under high than low uncertainty.

RELEVANCE AND SOCIAL ENGAGEMENT

Uncertainty-identity theory is not merely an academic account of how feelings of self-uncertainty can motivate group identification. It has far-reaching relevance for understanding and engaging with important social issues. For example, as discussed above, it can help explain the enduring appeal of religious fundamentalism and ideological orthodoxy (Hogg, 2004, 2005; Hogg, Adelman et al., 2010), the conditions under which leadership can become autocratic or despotic (e.g., Hogg, 2007b), why particular groups may marginalize, suppress, and persecute dissenters or critics, and why groups develop an ethnocentric silo mentality that can dehumanize outgroups. It has also been used to explain why western adolescents may identify with extreme adolescent groups that prescribe dangerous behaviors that place their health at risk (Hogg, Siegel and Hohman, in press).

It may also be able to explain why specific individuals resort to terrorism: against a background of identity threat, perceived relative deprivation and uncertain times, elevated self-uncertainty may create a desperate yearning to belong and to do whatever it takes to promote protect and stabilize one's social identity, even engage in extreme violence against innocents if that is thought to be endorsed by the group's leadership. This behavior may also be seen as a way to gain validation of one's identity in the group and to be viewed as a bone fide core member – the oft-witnessed zealotry of neophytes and true believers.

CONCLUSION

In this chapter I have described uncertainty-identity theory (e.g., Hogg, 2000, 2007a) – a personal narrative of its origins and development; a description of its basic concepts, processes, and phenomena; a description of

implications, extensions, and applications; and a short summary of its social relevance. As this is a book on theories, the emphasis has been conceptual, with empirical evidence and issues only briefly referenced as they have been overviewed elsewhere (e.g., Hogg, 2000, 2007a).

Uncertainty-identity theory proposes that self-uncertainty reduction is a key motivation for social identity processes and group and intergroup behaviors. It is a theory that attributes particular forms of group attachment, self-definition, and group structure to people's striving to reduce, via group identification, self-categorization and prototype-based depersonalization, feelings of uncertainty about and related to themselves. The core features of uncertainty-identity theory can be captured by three broad premises.

- *Premise 1.* People are motivated to reduce or avoid feelings of uncertainty about themselves, and about their perceptions, judgments, attitudes, and behaviors that relate to themselves, their interactions with other people, and their place in social context.
- *Premise 2.* Social categorization reduces or protects from uncertainty because it depersonalizes perception to conform to one's ingroup and outgroup prototypes, such that one "knows" how others will behave. Prototypes define and prescribe people's identities and therefore their perceptions, attitudes, feelings, and behaviors, and how they interact with and treat other people, including oneself. Social categorization of self, self-categorization, assigns one an identity with all its associated ingroup prototypical attributes. There is usually substantial agreement within a group on the ingroup prototype and on prototypes of relevant outgroups, further reducing uncertainty through consensual validation of one's behaviors and sense of self.
- *Premise 3.* Prototypes are better at resolving uncertainty to the extent that they are simple, clear, unambiguous, prescriptive, focused, and consensual, as well as coherently integrated, self-contained, and explanatory. These kinds of prototypes circumscribe clear identities and define or are associated with distinctive, well-structured groups that are high in entitativity.

Under uncertainty people identify more strongly with high entitativity groups – they seek them out to join, they create them anew, or they transform existing groups to be more entitative.

These core features are the foundation for a number of elaborations and extensions; for example, relating to social influence and group norms, leadership and trust, and dissent, deviance, and minorities. Perhaps the most significant elaboration and extension is the theory's ability to help explain the emergence of social extremism. Where uncertainty is extreme and enduring the motivation to reduce uncertainty and the quest for high entitativity groups and clear prototypes are strengthened. Under these circumstances people may identify passionately as true believers or zealots, seeking rigidly and hierarchically structured totalist groups with closed boundaries, homogenous and ideological belief structures, inflexible customs, and radical agendas – ethnocentric, insular and somewhat narcissistic groups that suppress dissent, are intolerant of outsiders, and engage in radical actions. These kinds of groups provide all-embracing identities that are powerful buffers against self-uncertainty.

Uncertainty is a pervasive part of life – we get excited and stimulated by it, we get frightened and oppressed by it, and we do what we can to reduce, control, or avoid it. We can never be truly certain so we are always more or less uncertain. In this chapter I have described a theory of how uncertainty may be related to why and how we identify with groups and to the particular types of groups that we identify with, suggesting that extreme uncertainty may encourage zealotry and totalism. In terms of social engagement, it goes without saying that these last are the bane of human existence – at best producing inefficient and oppressive groups; at worst, causing immeasurable human suffering.

REFERENCES

Abrams, D. and Hogg, M.A. (1988) Comments on the motivational status of self-esteem in social identity and intergroup discrimination. *European Journal of Social Psychology*, *18*, 317–334.

Abrams, D. and Hogg, M.A. (2004) Metatheory: Lessons from social identity research. *Personality and Social Psychology Review*, *8*, 98–106.

Abrams, D. and Hogg, M.A. (2010) Social identity and self-categorization. In J.F. Dovidio, M. Hewstone, P. Glick and V.M. Esses (eds), *The SAGE Handbook of Prejudice, Stereotyping, and Discrimination*, pp. 179–193. London: Sage.

Adelman, J.R., Hogg, M.A. and Levin, S. (submitted) Support for political action as a function of religiousness and nationalism under uncertainty: A study of Muslims, Jews, Palestinians and Israelis in Israel. Manuscript submitted for publication.

Altemeyer, B. (2003) Why do religious fundamentalists tend to be prejudiced. *International Journal for the Psychology of Religion*, *13*, 17–28.

Arkin, R.M., Oleson, K.C. and Carroll, P.J. (eds) (2010) *Handbook of the Uncertain Self*. New York: Psychology Press.

Baron, R.S., Crawley, K. and Paulina, D. (2003) Aberrations of power: Leadership in totalist groups. In D. van Knippenberg and M.A. Hogg (eds), *Leadership and Power: Identity Processes in Groups and Organizations*, pp. 169–183. London: Sage.

Bartlett, F.C. (1932) *Remembering*. Cambridge: Cambridge University Press.

Baumeister, R.F., Smart, L. and Boden, J.M. (1996) Relation of threatened egotism to violence and aggression: The dark side of high self-esteem. *Psychological Review*, *103*, 5–33.

Berger, C.R. (1987) Communicating under uncertainty. In M.E. Roloff and G.R. Miller (eds), *Interpersonal Processes: New Directions in Communication Research*, pp. 39–62. Newbury Park, CA: Sage.

Billig, M. (1978) *Fascists: A Social Psychological View of the National Front*. London: Harcourt Brace Jovanovich.

Billig, M. (1982) *Ideology and Social Psychology: Extremism, Moderation and Contradiction*. London: Sage.

Blascovich, J. and Tomaka, J. (1996) The biopsychosocial model of arousal regulation. In M. Zanna (ed.), *Advances in Experimental Social Psychology*, Vol. 28, 1–51. New York: Academic Press.

Brewer, M.B. (1999) The psychology of prejudice: Ingroup love or outgroup hate? *Journal of Social Issues*, *55*, 429–444.

Brewer, M.B. and Campbell, D.T. (1976) *Ethnocentrism and Intergroup Attitudes: East African Evidence*. New York: Sage.

Campbell, D.T. (1958) Common fate, similarity, and other indices of the status of aggregates of persons as social entities. *Behavioral Science, 3*, 14–25.

Castano, E., Yzerbyt, V.Y. and Bourguignon, D. (2003) We are one and I like it: The impact of ingroup entitativity on ingroup identification. *European Journal of Social Psychology, 33*, 735–754.

Crano, W.D. and Seyranian, V. (2009) How minorities prevail: The context/comparison–leniency contract model. *Journal of Social Issues, 65*, 335–363.

Curtis, J.M. and Curtis, M.J. (1993) Factors related to susceptibility and recruitment by cults. *Psychological Reports, 73*, 451–460.

David, B. and Turner, J.C. (2001) Majority and minority influence: A single process self-categorization analysis. In C.K.W. De Dreu and N.K. De Vries (eds), *Group Consensus and Innovation*, pp. 91–121. Oxford: Blackwell.

Deconchy, J.P. (1984) Rationality and social control in orthodox systems. In H. Tajfel, (ed.), *The Social Dimension: European Developments in Social Psychology, 2*, 425–445. Cambridge: Cambridge University Press.

Dewey, J. (1929/2005) *The Quest for Certainty: A Study of the Relation of Knowledge and Action*. Whitefish, MT: Kessinger Publishing.

Doty, R.M., Peterson, B.E. and Winter, D.G. (1991) Threat and authoritarianism in the United States, 1978–1987. *Journal of Personality and Social Psychology, 61*, 629–640.

Dunn, R.G. (1998) *Identity Crises: A Social Critique of Postmodernity*. Minneapolis: University of Minnesota Press.

Festinger, L. (1954) A theory of social comparison processes. *Human Relations, 7*, 117–140.

Fiske, S.T. and Taylor, S.E. (1991) *Social Cognition*, 2nd Edition. New York: McGraw-Hill.

Fromm, E. (1947) *Man for Himself: An Inquiry into the Psychology of Ethics*. New York: Rinehart.

Golec de Zavala, A., Cichocka, A., Eidelson, R. and Jayawickreme, N. (2009) Collective narcissism and its social consequences. *Journal of Personality and Social Psychology, 97*, 1074–1096.

Grieve, P. and Hogg, M.A. (1999) Subjective uncertainty and intergroup discrimination in the minimal group situation. *Personality and Social Psychology Bulletin, 25*, 926–940.

Hamilton, D.L. and Sherman, S.J. (1996) Perceiving persons and groups. *Psychological Review, 103*, 336–355.

Haslam, N. (2006) Dehumanization: An integrative review. *Personality and Social Psychology Review, 10*, 252–264.

Haslam, N., Loughnan, S. and Kashima, Y. (2008) Attributing and denying humanness to others.

European Review of Social Psychology, 19, 55–85.

Haslam, N., Rothschild, L. and Ernst, D. (1998) Essentialist beliefs about social categories. *British Journal of Social Psychology, 39*, 113–127.

Heine, S.J., Proulx, T. and Vohs, K.D. (2006) The meaning maintenance model: On the coherence of social motivations. *Personality and Social Psychology Review, 10*, 88–111.

Higgins, E.T. (1998) Promotion and prevention: Regulatory focus as a motivational principle. In M.P. Zanna (ed.), *Advances in Experimental Social Psychology, 30*, 1–46. New York: Academic Press.

Hoffer, E. (1951) *The True Believer*. New York: Time.

Hofstede, G. (1980) *Culture's Consequences: International Differences in Work-related Values*. Beverly Hills, CA: Sage.

Hogg, M.A. (1993) Group cohesiveness: A critical review and some new directions. *European Review of Social Psychology, 4*, 85–111.

Hogg, M.A. (2000) Subjective uncertainty reduction through self-categorization: A motivational theory of social identity processes. *European Review of Social Psychology, 11*, 223–255.

Hogg, M.A. (2001) A social identity theory of leadership. *Personality and Social Psychology Review, 5*, 184–200.

Hogg, M.A. (2004) Uncertainty and extremism: Identification with high entitativity groups under conditions of uncertainty. In V. Yzerbyt, C.M. Judd and O. Corneille (eds), *The Psychology of Group Perception: Perceived Variability, Entitativity, and Essentialism*, pp. 401–418. New York: Psychology Press.

Hogg, M.A. (2005) Uncertainty, social identity and ideology. In S.R. Thye and E.J. Lawler (eds), *Advances in Group Processes, 22*, 203–230. New York: Elsevier.

Hogg, M.A. (2006) Social identity theory. In P.J. Burke (ed.), *Contemporary Social Psychological Theories*, pp. 111–136. Palo Alto: Stanford University Press.

Hogg, M.A. (2007a) Uncertainty-identity theory. In M.P. Zanna (ed.), *Advances in Experimental Social Psychology, 39*, 69–126. San Diego: Academic Press.

Hogg, M.A. (2007b) Organizational orthodoxy and corporate autocrats: Some nasty consequences of organizational identification in uncertain times. In C.A. Bartel, S. Blader and A. Wrzesniewski (eds), *Identity and the Modern Organization*, pp. 35–59. Mahwah, NJ: Erlbaum.

Hogg, M.A. (2008) Personality, individuality, and social identity. In F. Rhodewalt (ed.), *Personality and Social*

Behavior, pp. 177–196. New York: Psychology Press.

Hogg, M.A. (2010a) Human groups, social categories, and collective self: Social identity and the management of self-uncertainty. In R.M. Arkin, K.C. Oleson, and P.J. Carroll (eds), *Handbook of the Uncertain Self,* pp. 401–420. New York: Psychology Press.

Hogg, M.A. (2010b) Influence and leadership. In S.T. Fiske, D.T. Gilbert and G. Lindzey (eds), *Handbook of Social Psychology,* 5th Edition, *2,* 1166–1207. New York: Wiley.

Hogg, M.A. and Abrams, D. (1988) *Social Identifications: A Social Psychology of Intergroup Relations and Group Processes.* London: Routledge.

Hogg, M.A. and Abrams, D. (1993) Towards a single-process uncertainty-reduction model of social motivation in groups. In M.A. Hogg and D. Abrams, (eds), *Group Motivation: Social Psychological Perspectives,* pp. 173–190. Hemel Hempstead: Harvester Wheatsheaf/New York: Prentice Hall.

Hogg, M.A., Adelman, J.R. and Blagg, R.D. (2010) Religion in the face of uncertainty: An uncertainty-identity theory account of religiousness. *Personality and Social Psychology Review, 14,* 72–83.

Hogg, M.A. and Blaylock, D.L. (eds) (in press) *Extremism and the Psychology of Uncertainty.* Boston: Wiley-Blackwell.

Hogg, M.A., Farquharson, J., Parsons, A. and Svensson, A. (2010) When being moderate is not the answer: Disidentification with moderate groups under uncertainty. Unpublished manuscript, Claremont Graduate University.

Hogg, M.A., Fielding, K.S. and Darley, J. (2005) Fringe dwellers: Processes of deviance and marginalization in groups. In D. Abrams, M.A. Hogg, and J.M. Marques (eds), *The Social Psychology of Inclusion and Exclusion,* pp. 191–210. New York: Psychology Press.

Hogg, M.A., Meehan, C. and Farquharson, J. (2010) The solace of radicalism: Self-uncertainty and group identification in the face of threat. *Journal of Experimental Social Psychology, 46,* 1061–1066.

Hogg, M.A. and Mullin, B.-A. (1999) Joining groups to reduce uncertainty: Subjective uncertainty reduction and group identification. In D. Abrams and M.A. Hogg (eds), *Social Identity and Social Cognition,* pp. 249–279. Oxford: Blackwell.

Hogg, M.A. and Reid, S.A. (2006) Social identity, self-categorization, and the communication of group norms. *Communication Theory, 16,* 7–30.

Hogg, M.A., Sherman, D.K., Dierselhuis, J., Maitner, A.T. and Moffitt, G. (2007) Uncertainty, entitativity,

and group identification. *Journal of Experimental Social Psychology, 43,* 135–142.

Hogg, M.A., Siegel, J.T. and Hohman, Z.P. (in press) Groups can jeopardize your health: Identifying with un-healthy groups to reduce self-uncertainty. *Self and Identity.*

Hogg, M.A. and Smith, J.R. (2007) Attitudes in social context: A social identity perspective. *European Review of Social Psychology, 18,* 89–131.

Hogg, M.A. and Svensson, A. (2010) Uncertainty, self-esteem and group identification. Unpublished manuscript, Claremont Graduate University.

Hogg, M.A. and van Knippenberg, D. (2003) Social identity and leadership processes in groups. In M.P. Zanna (ed.), *Advances in Experimental Social Psychology, Vol. 35,* 1–52. San Diego: Academic Press.

Hohman, Z.P., Hogg, M.A. and Bligh, M.C. (2010) Identity and intergroup leadership: Asymmetrical political and national identification in response to uncertainty. *Self and Identity, 9,* 113–128.

Hornsey, M.J. (2005) Why being right is not enough: Predicting defensiveness in the face of group criticism. *European Review of Social Psychology, 16,* 301–334.

Jetten, J., Hogg, M.A. and Mullin, B.-A. (2000) Ingroup variability and motivation to reduce subjective uncertainty. *Group Dynamics: Theory, Research, and Practice, 4,* 184–198.

Jost, J.T., Glaser, J., Kruglanski, A.W. and Sulloway, F.J. (2003) Political conservatism as motivated social cognition. *Psychological Bulletin, 129,* 339–375.

Jost, J.T. and Hunyady, O. (2002) The psychology of system justification and the palliative function of ideology. *European Review of Social Psychology, 13,* 111–153.

Kahneman, D., Slovic, P. and Tversky, A. (eds) (1982) *Judgment Under Uncertainty: Heuristics and Biases.* New York: Cambridge University Press.

Klandermans, B. (1997) *The Social Psychology of Protest.* Oxford: Blackwell.

Koffka, K. (1935) *Principles of Gestalt Psychology.* New York: Harcourt, Brace and Co.

Kosterman, R. and Feshbach, S. (1989) Towards a measure of patriotic and nationalistic attitudes. *Political Psychology, 10,* 257–274.

Kruglanski, A.W., Pierro, A., Mannetti, L. and De Grada, E. (2006) Groups as epistemic providers: Need for closure and the unfolding of group-centrism. *Psychological Review, 113,* 84–100.

Kruglanski, A.W. and Webster, D.M. (1996) Motivated closing of the mind: 'Seizing' and 'freezing'. *Psychological Review, 103,* 263–283.

Kuhn, T. (1962) *The Structure of Scientific Revolutions*. Chicago, IL: University of Chicago Press.

Lambert, A.J., Burroughs, T. and Nguyen, T. (1999) Perceptions of risk and the buffering hypothesis: The role of just world beliefs and right-wing authoritarianism. *Personality and Social Psychology Bulletin, 25*, 643–656.

Larrain, J. (1979) *The Concept of Ideology*. London: Hutchinson.

Lewis, B. (2004) *The Crisis of Islam: Holy War and Unholy Terror*. London: Phoenix.

Lickel, B., Hamilton, D.L., Wieczorkowska, G., Lewis, A., Sherman, S.J. and Uhles, A.N. (2000) Varieties of groups and the perception of group entitativity. *Journal of Personality and Social Psychology, 78*, 223–246.

Lind, E.A. and Tyler, T.R. (1988) *The Social Psychology of Procedural Justice*. New York: Plenum Press.

Marques, J.M., Abrams, D. and Serôdio, R. (2001) Being better by being right: Subjective group dynamics and derogation of in-group deviants when generic norms are undermined. *Journal of Personality and Social Psychology, 81*, 436–447.

Marques, J.M. and Paez, D. (1994) The 'black sheep effect': Social categorization, rejection of ingroup deviates and perception of group variability. *European Review of Social Psychology, 5*, 37–68.

Marris, P. (1996) *The Politics of Uncertainty: Attachment in Private and Public Life*. London: Routledge.

Martin, R. and Hewstone, M. (2008) Majority versus minority influence, message processing and attitude change: The source-context-elaboration model. In M.P. Zanna (ed.), *Advances in Experimental Social Psychology, 40*, 237–326. San Diego: Elsevier.

Maslow, A.H. (1987) *Motivation and Personality*, 3rd Edition. New York: Harper Collins.

McGarty, C., Turner, J.C., Oakes, P.J. and Haslam, S.A. (1993) The creation of uncertainty in the influence process: The roles of stimulus information and disagreement with similar others. *European Journal of Social Psychology, 23*, 17–38.

McGregor, I., Haji, R., Nash, K.A. and Teper, R. (2008) Religious zeal and the uncertain self. *Basic and Applied Social Psychology, 30*, 183–188.

McGregor, I. and Marigold, D.C. (2003) Defensive zeal and the uncertain self: What makes you so sure? *Journal of Personality and Social Psychology, 85*, 838–852.

McGregor, I., Zanna, M.P., Holmes, J.G. and Spencer, S.J. (2001) Compensatory conviction in the face of personal uncertainty: Going to extremes and being oneself. *Journal of Personality and Social Psychology, 80*, 472–488.

Moghaddam, F.M. and Marsella, A.J. (eds) (2004) *Understanding Terrorism: Psychosocial Roots, Consequences, and Interventions*. Washington, DC: American Psychological Association.

Moscovici, S. (1980) Toward a theory of conversion behavior. In L. Berkowitz (ed.), *Advances in Experimental Social Psychology, 13*, 202–239. New York: Academic Press.

Mugny, G. and Pérez, J. (1991) *The Social Psychology of Minority Influence*. Cambridge: Cambridge University Press.

Mullin, B.-A. and Hogg, M.A. (1998) Dimensions of subjective uncertainty in social identification and minimal intergroup discrimination. *British Journal of Social Psychology, 37*, 345–365.

Oakes, P.J. (1987) The salience of social categories. In J.C. Turner, M.A. Hogg, P.J. Oakes, S.D. Reicher and M.S. Wetherell, (eds), *Rediscovering the Social Group: A Self-categorization Theory*, pp. 117–141. Oxford: Blackwell.

Pickett, C.L. and Brewer, M.B. (2001) Assimilation and differentiation needs as motivational determinants of perceived ingroup and outgroup homogeneity. *Journal of Experimental Social Psychology, 37*, 341–348.

Pickett, C.L., Silver, M.D. and Brewer, M.B. (2002) The impact of assimilation and differentiation needs on perceived group importance and judgments of ingroup size. *Personality and Social Psychology Bulletin, 28*, 546–558.

Pollock, H.N. (2003) *Uncertain Science ... Uncertain World*. Cambridge: Cambridge University Press.

Reid, S.A. and Hogg, M.A. (2005) Uncertainty reduction, self-enhancement, and ingroup identification. *Personality and Social Psychology Bulletin, 31*, 804–817.

Rowatt, W.C. and Franklin, L.M. (2004) Christian orthodoxy, religious fundamentalism, and right-wing authoritarianism as predictors of implicit racial prejudice. *International Journal for the Psychology of Religion, 14*, 125–138.

Saks, A.M. and Ashforth, B.E. (1997) Organizational socialization: Making sense of the past and present as a prologue for the future. *Journal of Vocational Behavior, 51*, 234–279.

Sani, F. and Reicher, S.D. (1998) When consensus fails: An analysis of the schism within the Italian Communist Party (1991). *European Journal of Social Psychology, 28*, 623–45.

Schwartz, S.H. (1992) Universals in the content and structure of values: Theoretical advances and empirical tests in 20 cultures. In M.P. Zanna (ed.),

Advances in Experimental Social Psychology, *25*, 1–65. San Diego: Academic Press.

Sherman, D.K., Hogg, M.A. and Maitner, A.T. (2009) Perceived polarization: Reconciling ingroup and intergroup perceptions under uncertainty. *Group Processes and Intergroup Relations*, *12*, 95–109.

Sorrentino, R.M. and Roney, C.J.R. (1999) *The Uncertain Mind: Individual Differences in Facing the Unknown*. Philadelphia, PA: Psychology Press.

Staub, E. (1989) *The Roots of Evil: The Psychological and Cultural Origins of Genocide and Other Forms of Group Violence*. New York: Cambridge University Press.

Staub, E. (1997) Blind versus constructive patriotism: Moving from embeddedness in the group to critical loyalty and action. In D. Bar-Tal and E. Staub (eds), *Patriotism: In the Lives of Individuals and Nations*, pp. 213–228. Chicago: Nelson-Hall.

Stephan, W.G. and Stephan, C.W. (1985) Intergroup anxiety. *Journal of Social Issues*, *41*, 157–75.

Stürmer, S. and Simon, B. (2004) Collective action: Towards a dual-pathway model. *European Review of Social Psychology*, *15*, 59–99.

Suls, J. and Wheeler, L. (eds) (2000) *Handbook of Social Comparison: Theory and Research*. New York: Kluwer/Plenum.

Swann, W.B. Jr., Rentfrow, P.J. and Guinn, J.S. (2003) Self-verification: The search for coherence. In M.R. Leary and J.P. Tangney (eds), *Handbook of Self and Identity*, pp. 367–383. New York: Guilford Press.

Tajfel, H. (1959) Quantitative judgement in social perception. *British Journal of Psychology*, *50*, 16–29.

Tajfel, H. and Turner, J.C. (1979) An integrative theory of intergroup conflict. In W.G. Austin and S. Worchel (eds), *The Social Psychology of Intergroup Relations*, pp. 33–47. Monterey, CA: Brooks/Cole.

Thompson, J.B. (1990) *Ideology and Modern Culture: Critical Social Theory in the Era of Mass Communication*. Stanford, CA: Stanford University Press.

Turner, J.C. (1991) *Social Influence*. Milton Keynes: Open University Press.

Turner, J.C. (1999) Some current issues in research on social identity and self-categorization theories. In N. Ellemers, R. Spears and B. Doosje (eds), *Social Identity*, pp. 6–34. Oxford: Blackwell.

Turner, J.C., Hogg, M.A., Oakes, P.J., Reicher, S.D. and Wetherell, M.S. (1987) *Rediscovering the Social Group: A Self-categorization Theory*. Oxford: Blackwell.

Turner, J.C., Oakes, P.J., Haslam, S.A. and McGarty, C.A. (1994) Self and collective: Cognition and social context. *Personality and Social Psychology Bulletin*, *20*, 454–463.

Tyler, T.R. (1997) The psychology of legitimacy: A relational perspective on voluntary deference to authorities. *Personality and Social Psychology Review*, *1*, 323–345.

Tyler, T.R. and Lind, E.A. (1992) A relational model of authority in groups. In M.P. Zanna (ed), *Advances in Experimental Social Psychology*, *25*, 115–191. New York: Academic Press.

Van den Bos, K. (2009) Making sense of life: The existential self trying to deal with personal uncertainty. *Psychological Inquiry*, *20*, 197–217.

Van den Bos, K., Poortvliet, P.M., Maas, M., Miedema, J. and Van den Ham, E.-J. (2005) An enquiry concerning the principles of cultural norms and values: The impact of uncertainty and mortality salience on reactions to violations and bolstering of cultural worldviews. *Journal of Experimental Social Psychology*, *41*, 91–113.

Van Vugt, M. and Hart, C.M. (2004) Social identity as social glue: The origins of group loyalty. *Journal of Personality and Social Psychology*, *86*, 585–598.

Yzerbyt, V., Castano, E., Leyens, J.-P. and Paladino, M.-P. (2000) The primacy of the ingroup: The interplay of entitativity and identification. *European Review of Social Psychology*, *11*, 257–295.

30

Optimal Distinctiveness Theory: Its History and Development

Marilynn B. Brewer

ABSTRACT

Optimal distinctiveness theory is a model of the motivations underlying attachment and identification with social groups. The theory posits that humans are characterized by two opposing needs that govern the relationship between the self and membership in social groups. The first is a need for assimilation and inclusion, a desire for belonging that motivates immersion in social groups. The second is a need for differentiation from others that operates in opposition to the need for immersion. As group membership becomes more and more inclusive, the need for inclusion is satisfied but the need for differentiation is activated; conversely, as inclusiveness decreases, the differentiation need is reduced but the need for assimilation is activated. According to the model, the two opposing motives produce an emergent characteristic – the capacity for social identification with distinctive groups that satisfy both needs simultaneously. The theory derived from a general perspective on the evolution of human sociality that recognizes that humans are adapted for group living and that the structural requirements for group cohesion and coordination have shaped social motivational systems at the individual level.

INTRODUCTION

When it comes to the intellectual history of my entire research career, all roads lead to Donald Campbell. When I entered the doctoral program in the Department of Psychology at Northwestern University in 1964, I was nominally admitted to study social psychology. But the social psychology "program" at that time consisted solely of Don Campbell, who was unconvinced that disciplinary boundaries or area labels should constrain intellectual efforts or one's scientific agenda (cf. Campbell, 1969). An intellectual giant, Don Campbell tackled big questions of epistemology, human evolution, and the sociology of science without regard for arbitrary distinctions between philosophy, biology, or the social sciences, and he encouraged his students to do the same. For me, as a recent graduate of a small liberal arts college, working with Don Campbell was a heady experience to say the least.

While I was in graduate school, evolutionary biologist George Williams's influential book *Adaptation and Natural Selection: A Critique of Some Current Evolutionary Thought* (1966) was published, followed a few years later by Edward O. Wilson's *Sociobiology* (1975). These two works became the backdrop for extended discussion and debate between Don and me – a debate that continued until his death in 1996. Convinced by Williams and Wilson that humans, like other organisms, are genetically selfish, Don believed that we had to look to the evolution of social institutions and powerful cultural and religious traditions to understand the social achievements of human beings. These ideas culminated in the text of his presidential address to the American Psychological Association in 1975, where he argued that there is an inherent conflict between the forces of biological evolution (selecting for individual self-interest) and those of social evolution (providing external constraints on selfishness in the interests of group survival). The implications, he suggested, were that psychologists and other social scientists should be wary of challenging moral traditions that have evolved to hold human selfishness in check (Campbell, 1975).

It was on these points that Don and I had our most interesting and challenging disagreements. I just could not accept the idea that the extent of sociality and sustained group living that characterizes human beings could have been maintained solely by external constraints embodied in social institutions, traditions, and practices selected at the group level and operating in opposition to biological selection. (As in all domains, Don nurtured the debate, encouraging me to develop and argue my own position, even though he rarely altered his own.) I expressed my disagreement in print in a short comment on his presidential address (Brewer, 1976; see also Brewer, 1989) where I argued that the profound ambivalence between personal self-gratification and self-sacrifice for collective welfare is not a conflict between internal biological motives and external social constraints but rather an internal biological dualism that reflects human evolutionary history as a social species. My point was that human beings are neither inherently purely selfish nor purely altruistic but instead characterized by a kind of functional antagonism between self-interested and group-interested behavior. Because of the resultant variability in motives underlying human social behavior, I suggested, the distribution of human sociality might best be depicted in terms of a "golden standard deviation" rather than a "golden mean."

Basically, Don and I did not disagree that there is a profound conflict between individual-level self-interest that drives interindividual competition within social groups on the one hand, and the collective level interests that require cooperation and coordination transcending individual self-interest on the other. Where we disagreed was whether the locus of the conflict between selfishness and social cooperation lies in opposing forces of biological and social evolution or in an inherent dualism within our biological nature.

Although Don and I argued these issues sporadically over the years, the concepts of ambivalent sociality and opposing motives were latent influences that shaped some of my interest in social identity and group behavior but were not explicitly developed into more formal theory until 15 years later. It was the occasion of preparing my own presidential address for the Society of Personality and Social Psychology in 1990 that prompted me to formalize the idea of opposing motives in the form of optimal distinctiveness theory (Brewer, 1991). By that time I had become convinced that the product of the tension between human selfishness and human sociality was our capacity for intense identification with nonkin groups and its motivational underpinnings. Reaching that conclusion reflected the convergence of three different lines of research and theory that I had been exposed to in the ensuing 15 years.

THE INTELLECTUAL ANCESTRY OF OPTIMAL DISTINCTIVENESS THEORY

Social identity and ethnocentrism

The first major influence that shaped my future thinking was my exposure to the study of ethnocentrism and ingroup identity during graduate school. At the same time that Don Campbell and I were initiating our debate about the nature of human sociality, we were also involved in an ambitious interdisciplinary project in collaboration with anthropologist Robert LeVine (then at the University of Chicago) to test cross-culturally the universality of ethnocentrism in human societies (see LeVine and Campbell, 1972). The term "ethnocentrism" was coined by William Graham Sumner in his book *Folkways* (1906). The concept was driven by the observation that human social arrangements are universally characterized by differentiation into ingroups and outgroups – the we–they distinctions that demarcate boundaries of loyalty and cooperation among individuals. Attitudes and values are shaped by this ingroup–outgroup distinction in that individuals view all others from the perspective of the ingroup. In Sumner's words, ethnocentrism is

> the view of things in which one's own group is the center of everything, and all others are scaled and rated with reference to it ... Each group nourishes its own pride and vanity, boasts itself superior, exalts its own divinities, and looks with contempt on outsiders. Each group thinks its own folkways the only right ones ... (E)thnocentrism leads a people to exaggerate and intensify everything in their own folkways which is peculiar and which differentiates them from others.
> Sumner, 1906: 12–13

The Cross-Cultural Study of Ethnocentrism (CCSE) project (funded by a grant from the Carnegie Foundation) introduced a novel method of data collection designed to blend ethnographic case study and structured interview techniques. Experienced ethnographers in field sites in Africa, New Guinea, North America, and Asia were commissioned to use their best local informants to obtain information on precolonial ingroup organization and intergroup attitudes, using a structured, open-ended interview format. Back in Evanston, Illinois, I took on the position of graduate research associate for the project, responsible for processing, organizing, and archiving the fieldnotes from each of the project sites as they were submitted by the ethnographers. That experience exposed me to the rich detail of ethnographic accounts of social behavior and provided exotic examples of customs, practices, and beliefs that reveal the enormous range of ways in which groups manage both intragroup and intergroup relationships. It also established in me a fascination with the study of group identity and intergroup attitudes that determined my research career path in social psychology from that point on.

The CCSE project did provide evidence relevant to Sumner's original hypotheses about the nature of ethnocentrism and human societies. Both qualitative and quantitative analyses of the coded interviews and survey responses from respondents in far-flung locations confirmed the robustness of the tendency to differentiate the social environment in terms of ingroup–outgroup distinctions and to value ingroup characteristics over those of other groups (Brewer, 1981, 1986; Brewer and Campbell, 1976). Importantly, the level of ingroup cohesion and loyalty did not appear to be correlated with degree of negativity of attitudes toward outgroups. Our interviews with representatives of non-Western societies revealed a wide range of attitudes toward recognized outgroups, from respect and mutual admiration to relative indifference to outright hostility. As one of our informants put it "[W]e have our ways and they have their ways," and preference for the ingroup ways did not necessarily require intolerance of the outgroup. Thus, it was the experience gained from the CCSE project that first convinced me that ingroup preference and outgroup prejudice are two different constructs, with different origins and different consequences for intergroup behavior (Brewer, 1999, 2001).

Contrary to Sumner's original analysis, I concluded that ingroup formation and attachment had their origins in factors other than intergroup conflict.

Meanwhile back in the laboratory, approximately simultaneous with the data collection phase of the CCSE project, Henri Tajfel's social psychology research group in Bristol, England, was developing a very different paradigm for studying ingroup bias and intergroup discrimination. Experiments with the so-called "minimal intergroup situation" (Tajfel, 1970; Tajfel et al., 1971) provided a powerful demonstration that merely classifying individuals into arbitrary distinct social categories was sufficient to produce ingroup–outgroup discrimination and ingroup favoritism, even in the absence of any interactions with fellow group members or any history of competition or conflict between the groups. Additional experimental research demonstrated just how powerfully mere social categorization can influence thinking, feeling, and behaving toward ingroup members and the ingroup as a whole (Brewer, 1979).

Remarkably, results of the cross-cultural field research and these laboratory studies converged in confirming the power of we–they distinctions to produce differential evaluation, liking, and treatment of other persons depending on whether they are identified as members of the ingroup category or not. The laboratory experiments with the minimal intergroup situation demonstrated that ethnocentric loyalty and bias clearly do not depend on kinship or an extensive history of interpersonal relationships among group members, but can apparently be engaged readily by symbolic manipulations that imply shared attributes or common fate. Further, experiments with the minimal intergroup situation also provided evidence consistent with our CCSE data, that ingroup favoritism is prior to, and not necessarily associated with, outgroup negativity or hostility. What appears to be essential for ingroup attachment is that there be a basis for distinctive identification of who is "us" and who is "them" – a rule of exclusion as well as inclusion. The critical

point drawn from the early experiments with the minimal group paradigm and ingroup favoritism was the evidence that individuals are willing to benefit fellow ingroup members *even in the absence of any direct self-interest or personal gain.*

Accounting for the results of the initial minimal group experiments and subsequent research on ingroup favoritism led to the development of social identity theory (Tajfel, 1981; Tajfel and Turner, 1979) which rests on the assumption that identification and emotional attachment to a social group redefines one's identity from the personal to the group level. Through the processes of self-categorization and group identification, an individual's sense of self and self-interest become inextricably tied to group interests and group welfare. In effect, social identity is a *transformation* of the self that redefines the meaning of self-interest (Brewer, 1991).

I had the opportunity to work with Henri Tajfel and his research group at the University of Bristol for a brief period in 1980, while the theory of social identity was being developed and tested. The remarkable convergence between the qualitative data from our ethnographic field studies, results from survey studies, and findings from laboratory experiments on ingroup bias further convinced me that group identification is an inherent feature of human psychology that serves to regulate and maintain the essential relationship between individuals and their social groups. Social identity provides the constraint on human selfishness that makes cooperation and group existence possible. Understanding the nature of social identity and the motivations that drive and sustain individuals' attachment to their social groups, then, seemed to me a central task of social psychology.

Social dilemmas and collective decision making

The second major influence on my theoretical development came from an interest in the study of social dilemmas early in my academic career. A fundamental feature of group identification is the premise that when a social identity is activated, group interests and welfare supersede individual self-interest. In much of social life, individual self-interest and group interests coincide, so that cooperation and interdependence serve group goals and satisfy individual needs at the same time. If I desire the benefits of winning in a team sport competition, for instance, then cooperating with my fellow team members is clearly the best way for all of us to meet our individual and collective goals. But individual goals and collective interests do not always coincide so perfectly. If my individual interests are enhanced by being the one member of my team that scores the most points, but my team's chances of winning depend on my providing other team members the opportunity to score, working for my personal goal and achieving the group goal are not completely compatible. Whatever the long-term benefits of group living and cooperation may be, they often require mechanisms for overriding individual self-interests in the short-run. When individual self-interest and collective interests are placed in opposition, the innate ambivalences in human nature are revealed.

"Social dilemmas" constitute a special set of interdependence problems in which individual and collective interests are at odds. The dilemma arises whenever individuals acting in their own rational self-interest would engage in behaviors that cumulatively disadvantage everyone. A seminal article by Garret Hardin that appeared in *Science* in 1968 sparked interest in the study of individual decision making in the context of social dilemmas among behavioral economists, political scientists, and sociologists, as well as social psychologists. In his article, Hardin (1968) analyzed the parable of "the tragedy of the commons." The parable describes a situation in which a number of herdsmen graze their herds on a common pasture. Each individual herdsman is aware that it is to his benefit to increase the size of his herd because each animal represents

profit to himself, while the cost of grazing the animal is shared by all the herdsmen. Responding to this incentive structure, each herdsman rationally decides to increase his herd size and, as a result, the commons deteriorates, the carrying capacity of the commons is exceeded, and ultimately leads to the collapse of the commons and the destruction of all of the herds that grazed on it.

Hardin's parable represents a form of social interdependence in which the collective consequence of reasonable self-interested individual choices is disaster. In the modern world, social dilemmas include problems of maintaining scarce collective resources such as water and rainforests, preserving public goods such as parks and public television, and preventing pollution and destruction of the environment. The self-interests of each individual are best served by taking advantage of the benefits of collective resources without contributing to their maintenance, but the cumulative effect of such self-interested actions would be that everyone pays the cost of resource depletion and environmental damage. To the extent that social life is characterized by these types of interdependencies, some mechanisms for balancing individual interests and collective welfare must be achieved.

I was introduced to the study of social dilemmas when I moved to the University of California at Santa Barbara in 1973 and had the opportunity to work with Charles McClintock and David Messick, whose research focused on social exchange and interdependence. For me, the structure of the *n*-person commons dilemma seemed the perfect forum for observing individual behavior when faced with a conflict between personal and collective interests. Together with a team of graduate students, Dave Messick and I developed a laboratory analogue of resource dilemmas (Parker et al., 1983), and Rod Kramer and I set out to explore the role of social identity in individual decision making in this resource dilemma context (Brewer and Kramer, 1986; Kramer and Brewer, 1984).

Results from our own experiments and others indicate that in these choice situations, individuals do not behave consistently selfishly or unselfishly; a great deal depends on the group context in which the decision is made. When a collective social identification is not available, individuals tend to respond to the depletion of a collective resource by increasing their own resource use, at the cost of long-term availability. However, when a symbolic collective identity has been made salient, individuals respond to a resource crisis by dramatically reducing their own resource use (Brewer and Kramer, 1986; Brewer and Schneider, 1990). Further, when a public goods decision is preceded by even a brief period of group discussion, the rate of cooperative choice (when decisions are made individually and anonymously) is almost 100 percent (Caporael et al., 1989). This level of cooperative responding suggests that, under appropriate conditions, group welfare is just as "natural" as self-gratification as a rule for individual decision making. Situational cues, social identity salience, and behavior of others determine which predisposition will dominate on any particular occasion.

Our initial experiments demonstrated that self-sacrificial cooperative behavior in the interest of collective welfare is significantly increased when a salient social identity is shared by the interdependent group. Further experiments set out to determine the psychological mechanisms underlying this cooperative behavior. Willingness to contribute to collective welfare is determined in part by individuals' own social motives and in part by their expectations of what others will do in the dilemma situation. Shared ingroup identity influences both of these factors.

Self-sacrifice on behalf of the collective is wasted unless one has some trust that other members of the collective will also do their share. One function of ingroup formation and ingroup favoritism is providing a solution to the dilemma of social cooperation and trust (Brewer, 1986). Ordinarily, interpersonal trust depends on personal knowledge of other participants, such as a history of interpersonal exchange and future cooperation on an individualized basis. On the other hand, cooperation that is contingent on common membership in a bounded social group bypasses the need for such personalized knowledge or the costs of negotiating reciprocity with individual others. Shared ingroup membership affords a kind of "depersonalized trust" based on group membership (social identity) alone. All that is required for group-based trust and cooperation is (a) the mutual knowledge that oneself and other share a common ingroup membership, and (b) the expectation that the other(s) will act in terms of that group membership in dealings with a fellow group member (and vice versa). In effect, one's own and other's behavior is perceived to be constrained by the requirements of group membership and the desire to retain one's status as an accepted group member. Ingroup trust is the expectation that others will cooperate with me *because* we are members of the same group (Foddy et al., 2008; Kramer and Wei, 1999; Tanis and Postmes, 2005).

Many social dilemmas (e.g., resource dilemmas, public goods contribution dilemmas) involve a decision whether or not to cooperate with the group as whole when one's own cooperative choice does not directly influence the cooperation of others. Under these circumstances, expecting that others will behave cooperatively (i.e., contribute to the public good or restrain consumption of a shared resource) reduces the fear that one's own cooperation will be wasted (i.e., the "sucker's payoff"). However, it does not eliminate the self-interested benefit of noncooperation. If everyone else can be expected to cooperate, then noncooperation takes advantage of the others' contributions to the group welfare and maximizes personal outcomes. Thus, expectations of others' intentions to cooperate are not of themselves sufficient to generate cooperative behavior. Ingroup trust can be exploited, particularly under conditions of anonymity and diffusion of responsibility. Group-based depersonalized trust translates to cooperative behavior only if the individual's own behavior is constrained by the same group norms that underlie his/her expectations of the others' behavior.

The psychological process of group identification, as elaborated in social identity theory, provides a basis for intragroup cooperation that does not necessarily rely on interpersonal trust in fellow group members. When individuals attach their sense of self to their group membership, they see themselves as interchangeable components of a larger social unit (Turner et al., 1987). The consequence of such social identification is not only affective attachment to the group as a whole, but also a shift of motives and values from self-interest to group interest and concern for the welfare of fellow group members. As a result of this redefinition of the self, pursuing the group's interest becomes a direct and natural expression of self-interest, that is, collective and personal interest are interchangeable. When the definition of self changes, the meaning of self-interest and self-serving motivations also changes accordingly. Group identity involves a transformation of goals from the personal to the collective level (De Cremer and Van Vugt, 1999; Kramer and Brewer, 1986).

Goal transformation provides a basis for ingroup cooperation that does not depend directly on expectations that others in the group will reciprocate cooperation. When social identification is strong, then contributing to the group welfare is an end in itself, independent of what benefits ultimately accrue to the self. This is particularly evident when a group as a whole is failing to maintain a shared resource or public good, an indication that others in the group are not contributing sufficiently to group welfare. In the absence of strong, shared identity, indications that others are failing to cooperate is a cue to self-interested behavior that undermines any motive to cooperate. When group identification is strong, however, participants interpret negative group feedback as a signal that their group is in need and as

such they should try harder at achieving their group goals. Consistent with the goal-transformation hypothesis, strong group identifiers exhibit a genuine concern for the group's welfare, and negative group feedback is interpreted as a threat to the group's welfare and a signal that behavioral changes are required, motivating them to cooperate more (Brewer and Schneider, 1990; DeCremer and van Dijk, 2002).

Years of research on how people behave in social dilemma situations both in the laboratory and in real life reinforced my conviction that there are internal psychological constraints on self-interest that are activated by group identification. What remained to be understood was the proximal mechanisms underlying the tie between individuals and their social groups.

Levels of analysis and downward causation

A third influence on the development of optimal distinctiveness theory came from philosophy of science and evolutionary theory, as I was initially introduced to these disciplines by Don Campbell and later through my longstanding collaboration with Linnda Caporael (cf. Brewer and Caporael, 1990, 2006).

One of the problems with accounting for the evolution of self-sacrificial sociality is that the reproductive fitness value of such behaviors could not be modeled at the individual level and instead seemed to require some form of "group selection" mechanism. In its earliest form, group selection was proposed to explain why the size of populations remained within the carrying capacity of their environments (Wynne-Edwards, 1962). Presumably, some members of the population would sacrifice their own reproduction to benefit the group. But by Darwinian logic, genes that caused individuals to lower their fitness by behaving "for the good of the species" would quickly disappear from the population. Thus, gene-based theories of evolution were critical of group-selection ideas (Maynard Smith, 1964; Williams, 1966) and by the early 1970s, Wynne-Edwards and group selection were basically rejected by evolutionary biologists.

More recent developments in evolutionary biology now suggest that the original criticisms of group selection ideas were overstated. With the publication of Leo Buss's book, *The Evolution of Individuality* (1987), scientific consensus began shifting from gene-based selection models of evolution to multilevel evolutionary theories (Maynard Smith and Szathmáry, 1995; Sober and Wilson, 1998). L. Buss (1987) observed that biologists took the notion of the multicellular individual for granted. He argued that multicellularity itself evolved through the consolidation of initially self-replicating units. Evolutionary transitions creating new levels of selection involve both synergies and conflicts between lower and higher levels of organization. Multilevel evolutionary theory provided the needed conceptual frameworks for a new interpretation for the role of group selection in human evolution (Brewer and Caporael, 2006).

Multilevel or hierarchical models of evolution recognize that the concept of "fit" must be conceptualized in terms of embedded structures. Genes, as one level of organization, are adapted to fit the environment of their cellular machinery; cells fit the environment of the individual organism; and individual organisms are adapted to fit the next higher level of organization within which they function. Different levels of social organization and selection provide opportunities for both synergisms and conflicts between levels. In a hierarchical system, adaptive success at one level may need to be curtailed for the sake of success at a higher level in the system. Structural requirements at the higher level of organization constrain competition at lower levels.

This view of adaptation and natural selection provides a new perspective on the concept of group selection as a factor in human evolution (Brewer and Caporael,

2006; Caporael and Brewer, 1995). With coordinated group living as the primary survival strategy of the species, the social group, in effect, provided a buffer between the individual organism and the exigencies of the physical environment. As a consequence, then, the physical environment exercises only indirect selective force on human adaptation, while the requirements of social living constitute the immediate selective environment. The dynamics of multilevel selection resembles what Campbell (1974, 1990) called "downward causation" across system levels. Downward causation operates whenever structural requirements at higher levels of organization determine some aspects of structure and function at lower levels (a kind of reverse reductionism).

Both biological and behavioral scientists today accept the basic premise that human beings are adapted for group living. Even a cursory review of the physical endowments of our species – weak, hairless, extended infancy – makes it clear that we are not suited for survival as lone individuals, or even as small family units. Many of the evolved characteristics that have permitted humans to adapt to a wide range of physical environments, such as omnivorousness and tool making, create dependence on collective knowledge and cooperative information sharing. As a consequence, human beings are characterized by *obligatory interdependence* (Caporael and Brewer, 1995), and our evolutionary history is a story of co-evolution of genetic endowment, social structure, and culture.

If individual humans cannot survive outside of groups, then the structural requirements for sustaining groups create systematic constraints on individual biological and psychological adaptations. Cooperative groups must meet certain structural requirements in order to exist, just as organisms must have certain structural properties in order to be viable. For community-sized groups these organizational imperatives include mobilization and coordination of individual effort, communication, internal differentiation, optimal group size, and boundary definition.

The benefits to individuals of cooperative arrangements cannot be achieved unless prior conditions have been satisfied that make the behavior of other individuals predictable and coordinated. Group survival depends on successful solution to these problems of internal organization and coordination. In other words, the viability of the group becomes a factor in the survival of individuals and their genetic reproduction. The implication of this multilevel perspective on human evolution is that humans will be exquisitely sensitive to the viability of the groups they depend on (or commit themselves to), and that human motivation will be tuned to the requirements of the collective.

Optimal distinctiveness theory: connecting the threads

Optimal distinctiveness theory grew out of these three influences on my thinking about human sociality and group behavior. Social identity and ethnocentric ingroup bias suggested the importance of ingroup differentiation and intergroup distinctiveness in eliciting collective identity and concern for the welfare of others. The role of social identity in resolving social dilemmas defined conditions under which group welfare overrides individual self-interest and reinforced my conviction that a need for group identification is 'built in' to the human motivational system. Finally, the conceptual work on multilevel selection and group living provided an evolutionary framework for understanding that human nature is dualistic, and social motives reflect the tension between the requirements of individual and group survival.

Importantly, the development of optimal distinctiveness theory was in part the product of an exercise in thinking about downward causation from the group to the individual level of analysis. The advantage to early humans of extending social interdependence and cooperation to an ever wider circle of conspecifics comes from the ability to exploit resources across an expanded territory and buffer the effects of temporary depletions or scarcities in any one local environment. But expansion comes at the cost of increased demands on obligatory sharing and regulation of reciprocal cooperation. Both the carrying capacity of physical resources and the capacity for distribution of resources, aid, and information inevitably constrain the potential size of cooperating social networks. Thus, effective social groups cannot be either too small or too large. To function, social collectives must be restricted to some optimal size – sufficiently large and inclusive to realize the advantages of extended cooperation, but sufficiently exclusive to avoid the disadvantages of spreading social interdependence too thin.

Based on this analysis of one structural requirement for group survival, I hypothesized that the conflicting benefits and costs associated with expanding group size would have shaped social motivational systems at the individual level. If humans are adapted to live in groups and depend on group effectiveness for survival, then our motivational systems should be tuned to the requirements of group effectiveness. We should be uncomfortable depending on groups that are too small to provide the benefits of shared resources but also uncomfortable if group resources are distributed too widely. A unidirectional drive for inclusion would not have been adaptive without a counteracting drive for differentiation and exclusion. Opposing motives hold each other in check, with the result that human beings are not comfortable either in isolation or in huge collectives. These social motives at the individual level create a propensity for adhering to social groups that are both bounded and distinctive. As a consequence, groups that are optimal in size are those that will elicit the greatest levels of member loyalty, conformity, and cooperation, and the fit between individual psychology and group structure is better achieved.

In addition to representing the dual nature of human sociality, optimal distinctiveness theory was developed to fill a gap in extant theories of social identity. The original statements of social identity theory (Tajfel, 1981) and the subsequent development of self-categorization theory (Turner et al., 1987) were based heavily on cognitive processes of categorization and perceptual accentuation. This depiction provided an explanation for why and how specific social categorizations and ingroup–outgroup distinctions become salient but it lacks a driver for the process of *identification* with ingroups, particularly for chronic, long-term identification. Although the theory postulated that social identity salience had motivational *consequences* in the form of a striving for positive distinctiveness of the ingroup (Tajfel and Turner, 1979), a motivational component was missing from the theory with respect to antecedents of social identity.

For many social psychologists, the idea that social identification – with all its significant emotional and behavioral concomitants – is based solely on "cold cognition" was intuitively incomplete. Because group identity sometimes entails self-sacrifice in the interests of group welfare and solidarity, understanding why and when individuals are willing to relegate their sense of self to significant group identities requires motivational as well as cognitive analysis. Motivational explanations were also needed to account for why group membership does not always lead to identification and why individuals are more chronically identified with some ingroups rather than others.

OPTIMAL DISTINCTIVENESS: THE BASIC MODEL AND SOME CLARIFICATIONS

Basic premises of the optimal distinctiveness model

If social differentiation and intergroup boundaries are functional for social cooperation,

and social cooperation is essential for human survival, then there should be psychological mechanisms at the individual level that motivate and sustain ingroup identification and differentiation. The optimal distinctiveness model (Brewer, 1991) posits that humans are characterized by two opposing needs that govern the relationship between the self-concept and membership in social groups. The first is a need for assimilation and inclusion, a desire for belonging that motivates immersion in social groups. The second is a need for differentiation from others that operates in opposition to the need for immersion. As group membership becomes more and more inclusive, the need for inclusion is satisfied but the need for differentiation is activated; conversely, as inclusiveness decreases, the differentiation need is reduced but the need for assimilation is activated. These competing drives hold each other in check, assuring that interests at one level are not consistently sacrificed to interests at the other. According to the model, the two opposing motives produce an emergent characteristic – the capacity for social identification with distinctive groups that satisfy both needs simultaneously.

The basic premise of the optimal distinctiveness model is that the two identity needs (inclusion/assimilation and differentiation/distinctiveness) are independent and work in opposition to motivate group identification. More specifically, it is proposed that social identities are selected and activated to the extent that they help to achieve a balance between needs for inclusion and for differentiation in a given social context. Optimal identities are those that satisfy the need for inclusion *within* the ingroup and simultaneously serve the need for differentiation through distinctions *between* the ingroup and outgroups. In the original statement of the theory, I tried to capture the essential ideas in the form of a figure that depicted the opposing drives and the point of equilibrium (Figure 30.1, adapted from Brewer, 1991).

In effect, optimal social identities involve *shared distinctiveness* (Stapel and Marx,

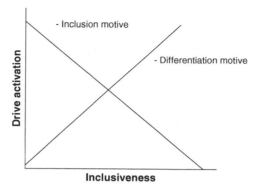

Figure 30.1   The optimal distinctiveness model of group identification (from Brewer, 1991)

2007). Individuals will resist being identified with social categorizations that are either too inclusive or too differentiating but will define themselves in terms of social identities that are optimally distinctive. Equilibrium is maintained by correcting for deviations from optimality. A situation in which a person is overly individuated will excite the need for assimilation, motivating the person to adopt a more inclusive social identity. Conversely, situations that arouse feelings of deindividuation will activate the need for differentiation, resulting in a search for more exclusive or distinct identities.

Evidence for competing social motives comes from empirical demonstrations of efforts to achieve or restore group identification when these needs are deprived. Results of experimental studies have shown that activation of the need for assimilation or the need for differentiation increases the importance of distinctive group memberships (Pickett et al., 2002), that threat to inclusion enhances self-stereotyping on group-characteristic traits (Brewer and Pickett, 1999; Pickett et al., 2002; Spears et al., 1997), and that threat to group distinctiveness motivates overexclusion (Brewer and Pickett, 2002) and intergroup differentiation (Roccas and Schwartz, 1993; Jetten et al., 1998: Hornsey and Hogg, 1999; Jetten et al., 2004). Further, assignment to distinctive minority group

categories engages greater group identification and self-stereotyping than does membership in large, inclusive majority groups (Brewer and Weber, 1994; Leonardelli and Brewer, 2001; Simon and Hamilton, 1994). Thus, there is converging evidence that group attachment is regulated by motives for inclusion and distinctiveness.

Some qualifications and clarifications

Although hypotheses derived from optimal distinctiveness theory have been tested by different researchers in many different contexts, some aspects of the theory are frequently misunderstood. Importantly, the model does *not* postulate that optimal distinctiveness is a property of some groups rather than others and that individuals directly seek identification with such optimal groups. Rather, optimality is an interactive product of current levels of activation of the opposing motives for inclusion and differentiation and group properties that determine its level of inclusiveness and distinctiveness. This leads to three important principles that are essential to understanding optimal distinctiveness.

First, *optimal distinctiveness is context specific*. Context affects both the activation of motives or needs and the relative distinctiveness of specific social categories. Consider, for example, my professional group memberships. In the context of an international psychology conference, categorization as a "psychologist" is far too inclusive, and a subcategory such as "social psychologist" is more likely to be optimally distinctive. On the other hand, in the context of my local community, my identity as a social psychologist is too highly differentiated and instead, categorizing my occupation as an "academic" is optimal. Identifying myself as an academic or a university professor places me in a social group with a significant number of other members of my community who share that occupational status and yet distinguishes us from neighbors who belong to other professions or occupational categories. "Shared distinctiveness" is contextually defined.

Second, *optimal distinctiveness is a dynamic equilibrium*. Even within a given context, optimality is not necessarily fixed because inclusion and differentiation motives are also subject to temporal influences and change over time. When one enters a new group, for example, the awareness of one's marginal status as a newcomer may enhance the need for inclusion relative to the need for differentiation, but as time goes on and inclusion is more secure, differentiation needs become more salient and maintaining group distinctiveness assumes a higher priority. Groups also exhibit dynamic shifts across time in their relative focus on enhancing inclusiveness or reestablishing distinctiveness and exclusiveness.

Finally, *identity motives vary across situation, culture, and individuals*. Asking how "strong" an individual's inclusion motive is like asking how strong is the individual's hunger motivation. Like any need or drive, inclusion and differentiation motives vary as a function of current levels of satiation or deprivation. However, individuals may differ in how sensitive they are to changes in levels of inclusiveness. Just as some individuals start feeling ravenously hungry after an hour or two since they last ate while other individuals don't even notice they haven't eaten all day, so some people will react strongly to a slight loss of inclusiveness (or slight expansion of group boundaries), whereas others will be more tolerant of a range of ingroup inclusiveness. Thus, although the principles incorporated in the optimal distinctiveness model are presumed to be universal, the model can also accommodate individual, situational, and cultural differences in the relative activation of inclusion and differentiation needs and the nature of optimal identities.

Put more formally, the model as depicted in Figure 30.1, has four important parameters: the height (intercept) of the need for differentiation, the height (intercept) of the need for inclusion, the negative slope of the need for inclusion, and the positive slope of the need for differentiation. Of these four, one is presumed to be fixed. The intercept (zero activation) of the need for differentiation is assumed to be at the point of complete individuation (the endpoint of the inclusiveness dimension). All of the other parameters are free to vary; any changes in the intercept or slope of the inclusion drive or the slope of the differentiation drive will alter the point of equilibrium that represents an optimal identity. Thus, the model depicted in Figure 30.1 is just one member of a class of models containing all possible variations in these parameters, and differences across situations, cultures, and individuals can be represented in terms of variation in the slopes of the two drives (which can vary independently). (See Brewer and Roccas, 2001, for a discussion of how cultural differences can be reflected in model parameters and the point of equilibrium.) Again, the overall point is to emphasize that optimal distinctiveness is not a fixed property of groups or of individuals but a consequence of motivational dynamics at both levels.

IMPLICATIONS OF OPTIMAL DISTINCTIVENESS THEORY

Theoretical implications

The theory of optimal distinctiveness (Brewer, 1991) is originally a theory of *collective* social identity. More specifically, it is a model of the opposing motives of inclusion and differentiation that regulate group identification, where a group is defined as a collective unit, or entity, that transcends individual level identities. The concept of opposing motives as a regulatory system, however, has potential broader application than just understanding group identification. I have suggested that analogous opposing needs for separateness and assimilation may also operate at the levels of individual and relational selves to determine optimal identities at those levels as well (Brewer and Gardner, 1996: 91; Brewer and Roccas, 2001, table 1). At the collective level, the conflict is between belonging and inclusion on the one hand, and separation and distinctiveness on the other. At the individual level, the needs are expressed in the opposition between the desire for similarity on the one hand and the need for uniqueness on the other (Snyder and Fromkin, 1980). At the interpersonal (relational) level, the tension is represented by conflicts between the need for autonomy and the need for interdependence and intimacy with specific others. At each level, the person must achieve some optimal balance between these conflicting motives for defining self in relation to others.

Social implications: the upside and the downside of optimal distinctiveness

If social identity motives derive, ultimately, from needs for security and cooperative interdependence, this has important implications for the functions and limits of social identification as a motivator of prosocial behavior. More specifically, the theory predicts that the dynamics of trust and cooperation will be shaped by the need for distinct boundaries between ingroup and outgroups and associated differences between intragroup and intergroup behaviors.

On the positive side, as I have noted, optimal group identities can be thought of as bounded communities of mutual trust and generalized reciprocal cooperation. Mere knowledge that another individual shares a salient group identity is sufficient to engage depersonalized trust, cooperative orientation, and willingness to sacrifice immediate self-interest for collective welfare. The dilemma in all this is that the conditions for ingroup cooperation and trust require group boundaries and clear differentiation between intragroup and intergroup social exchange. The social motives postulated by optimal distinctiveness theory at the individual level create a propensity for adhering to social groups that are both bounded and distinctive. Secure inclusion implies exclusion. The adaptive value of groups lies in interactional norms that facilitate reciprocal exchanges within the group, but are not extended to outsiders. A consequence of ingroup identification and intergroup boundaries is that individuals modify their social behavior depending on whether they are interacting with ingroup or outgroup members.

None of this implies that strong identification with ingroups necessitates conflict with outgroups. Contrary to the notion that ingroup positivity and outgroup derogation are reciprocally related, ingroup love does not imply outgroup hate (Brewer, 1999, 2001). What ingroup favoritism does imply is that positivity and trust extend only to the boundary of the ingroup and not across groups. Thus, intergroup relations are characterized by *lack* of trust, though not necessarily active *distrust*. For example, in our experiments on group-based trust, we find that knowing that a stranger belongs to one's own ingroup elevates trusting choices to near 90 percent (Yuki et al., 2005). With an outgroup stranger, on the other hand, trusting choices drop significantly – but only to around 50 percent, not to zero percent as would be expected if outgroups were assumed to be hostile and malevolent. Instead, exchanges with outgroup members appear to be characterized by uncertainty and lack of trust, rather than by automatic distrust or negativity.

Nonetheless, ingroup positivity and bounded trust are not completely benign. Just as there is a realistic basis for ethnocentric trust of ingroups, differences in norms and sanctions applied to ingroup behavior compared to behavior in interactions with outgroup members provides a realistic basis for outgroup distrust and negative stereotypes. At the same time that groups promote trust and cooperation within, they caution wariness and constraint in intergroup interactions. Psychologically, expectations of cooperation and security promote positive attraction toward other ingroup members and motivate adherence to ingroup norms of appearance and behavior that assure that one will be recognized as a good or legitimate ingroup member. Symbols and behaviors that differentiate the ingroup from local outgroups become particularly important here, to reduce the risk that ingroup benefits will be inadvertently extended to outgroup members, and to ensure that ingroup members will recognize one's own entitlement to receive benefits. Assimilation within and differentiation between groups is thus mutually reinforcing, along with ethnocentric preference for ingroup interactions and institutions. Thus, even in the absence of overt conflict between groups, the differentiation between ingroup and outgroup behavior creates a kind of self-fulfilling prophecy in the realm of intergroup perceptions. As LeVine and Campbell (1972: 173) put it, "[I]f most or all groups are, in fact, ethnocentric, then it becomes an 'accurate' stereotype to accuse an outgroup of some aspect of ethnocentrism."

Combined with the accentuation principle that exaggerates perceived differences between social categories, this leads to a set of "universal stereotypes" to characterize ingroup–outgroup differences. Whereas "we" are trustworthy, peaceful, moral, loyal, and reliable; "they" are clannish, exclusive, and potentially untrustworthy. What is particularly interesting about this pattern of stereotypes is that the same behaviors that are interpreted as reasonable caution on the part of the ingroup in dealings with outgroup members become interpreted as "clannishness" and indicators of mistrust when exhibited by outgroupers toward the ingroup.

Although ingroup favoritism does not necessarily imply outgroup derogation, the motivational dynamics underlying strong ingroup attachment can lay the groundwork for intergroup hostility and conflict. Importantly, the critical function that ingroup distinctiveness holds for both survival of the group and individual psychological security explains why threats to identity can both engender and sustain strong intergroup conflict. Even in the absence of actual physical threat or material conflict of interest, the perception that the boundary between the ingroup and outgroup is being diluted or disrespected can create reactions equivalent to that of a territorial invasion. Bitter and protracted conflict between different religious sects and ethnic subgroups testifies to the role of identity maintenance concerns even between subgroups within the context of a superordinate religion or nation. Especially in the modern world, competition over material resources such as land has as much to do with the identity meaning of those resources as it does actual group survival.

Optimal distinctiveness theory also has implications for when individuals will feel that their ingroup identity and the functions it serves are being threatened. If ingroups provide for both secure inclusion and intergroup differentiation, then anything that undermines either of these needs will activate attempts to restore optimality and enhance intergroup distinctions. The effects of threats to ingroup distinctiveness on hostility toward the threatening outgroup have been well documented (Jetten et al., 2004). But similar effects can be obtained when the individuals' sense of inclusion within the ingroup has been threatened (Pickett and Brewer, 2005). When a member of a group is led to believe that he or she is not a typical group member or is not fully accepted as part of the group, the person should experience distress to the extent that the person relies on that particular group for the satisfaction of belongingness, security, or assimilation needs. Peripheral group members not only need to be concerned with being similar to other ingroup members, but also concerned that they are not confused with the outgroup. This leads to the prediction that marginal ingroup members will be most concerned with maintaining intergroup distance and endorsing negativity toward outgroups.

In sum, then, understanding the origins and nature of ingroup favoritism, and differentiating ingroup attachment from outgroup hostility, may be critical for harnessing the best of human sociality while avoiding the consequences of intergroup hostility.

CONCLUSION

The dilemma that optimal distinctiveness theory poses for the modern world is this: How do we accommodate the need for distinctive ingroup identities that is rooted in our evolutionary past under conditions where interdependence transcends group boundaries at a global level? As a consequence of our evolutionary history, our sense of personal security and certainty are maximized in the context of shared ingroup membership and clear ingroup–outgroup distinctions. The need for social identity and preservation of ingroup distinctiveness has long been recognized as a constraint on the "common ingroup identity" prescription for reducing intergroup discrimination and conflict. Attempts to merge groups or erase social category distinctions threaten optimal identities and limit our

capacity for identification with larger, more inclusive categories.

It was this recognition that led Mummendey and Wenzel (1999) to argue that the question we should be asking is not how we can eliminate intergroup differences but rather under what conditions can intergroup differences be accepted, or even celebrated? The complexity of the modern world does provide us with multiple ways to meet identity needs, with multiple group identities that are optimal within different contexts. In a large and complex society, persons are differentiated or subdivided along many meaningful social dimensions, including gender and sexual orientation, life stage (e.g., student, worker, retiree), economic sector (e.g., technology, service, academics, professional), religion, ethnicity, political ideology, and recreational preferences. Each of these divisions provides a basis for shared identity and group membership that may become an important source of social identification. Further, most of these differentiations are cross-cutting in the sense that individuals may share a common ingroup membership on one dimension but belong to different categories on another dimension. Hence, having multiple group memberships has the potential to reduce the likelihood that one's social world can be reduced to a single ingroup–outgroup distinction. To the extent that we recognize the multiplicity and complexity of our own group identities, we may enhance the capacity for acceptance of intergroup differences and life in a pluralistic social system.

REFERENCES

Brewer, M.B. (1976) Comment on Campbell's 'On the conflicts between biological and social evolution'. *American Psychologist, 31*, 372.

Brewer, M.B. (1979) In-group bias in the minimal intergroup situation: A cognitive motivational analysis. *Psychological Bulletin, 86*, 307–324.

Brewer, M.B. (1981) Ethnocentrism and its role in intergroup trust. In M. Brewer and B. Collins (eds),

Scientific Inquiry in the Social Sciences, pp. 214–231. San Francisco: Jossey-Bass.

Brewer, M.B. (1986) The role of ethnocentrism in intergroup conflict. In W. Austin and S. Worchel and W. Austin (eds), *The Psychology of Intergroup Relations*, pp. 88–102. Chicago: Nelson-Hall.

Brewer, M.B. (1989) Ambivalent sociality: The human condition. *Behavioral and Brain Sciences, 12*, 699.

Brewer, M.B. (1991) The social self: On being the same and different at the same time. *Personality and Social Psychology Bulletin, 17*, 475–482.

Brewer, M.B. (1999) The psychology of prejudice: Ingroup love or outgroup hate? *Journal of Social Issues, 55*, 429–444.

Brewer, M.B. (2001) Ingroup identification and intergroup conflict: When does ingroup love become outgroup hate? In R. Ashmore, L. Jussim, and D. Wilder (eds), *Social Identity, Intergroup Conflict, and Conflict Reduction*. Oxford: Oxford University Press.

Brewer, M.B. and Campbell, D.T. (1976) *Ethnocentrism and Intergroup Attitudes: East African Evidence*. Beverly Hills: Sage.

Brewer, M.B. and Caporael, L.R. (1990) Selfish genes versus selfish people: Sociobiology as origin myth. *Motivation and Emotion, 14*, 237–243.

Brewer, M.B. and Caporael, L.R. (2006) An evolutionary perspective on social identity: Revisiting groups. In M. Schaller, J. Simpson, and D. Kenrick (eds), *Evolution and Social Psychology*, pp. 143–161. New York: Psychology Press.

Brewer, M.B. and Gardner, W. (1996) Who is this 'we'? Levels of collective identity and self representation. *Journal of Personality and Social Psychology, 71*, 83–93.

Brewer, M.B. and Kramer, R.M. (1986) Choice behavior in social dilemmas: Effects of social identity, group size, and decision framing. *Journal of Personality and Social Psychology, 50*, 543–549.

Brewer, M.B. and Pickett, C.L. (1999) Distinctiveness motives as a source of the social self. In T. Tyler, R. Kramer, and O. John (eds), *The Psychology of the Social Self*, pp. 71–87. Mahwah, NJ: Lawrence Erlbaum and Associates.

Brewer, M.B. and Pickett, C.L. (2002) The social self and group identification: Inclusion and distinctiveness motives in interpersonal and collective identities. In J. Forgas and K. Williams (eds), *The Social Self: Cognitive, Interpersonal, and Intergroup Perspectives*, pp. 255–271. Philadelphia: Psychology Press.

Brewer, M.B. and Roccas, S. (2001) Individual values, social identity, and optimal distinctiveness. In C. Sedikides and M. Brewer (eds), *Individual Self, Relational Self, Collective Self*, pp. 219–237. Philadelphia: Psychology Press.

Brewer, M.B. and Schneider, S. (1990) Social identity and social dilemmas: A double-edged sword. In D. Abrams and M. Hoggs (eds), *Social Identity Theory: Constructive and Critical Advances*, pp. 169–184. London: Harvester-Wheatsheaf.

Brewer, M.B. and Weber, J.G. (1994) Self-evaluation effects of interpersonal versus intergroup social comparison. *Journal of Personality and Social Psychology, 66*, 268–275.

Buss, L.W. (1987) *The Evolution of Individuality*. Princeton: Princeton University Press.

Campbell, D.T. (1969) Ethnocentrism of disciplines and the fish-scale model of omniscience. In M. Sherif and C. Sherif (eds), *Interdisciplinary Relationships in the Social Sciences*. Hawthorne, NY: Aldine.

Campbell, D.T. (1974) 'Downward causation' in hierarchically organised biological systems. In F. Ayala and T. Dobzhansky (eds), *Studies in the Philosophy of Biology*, pp. 179–186. London: Macmillan.

Campbell, D.T. (1975) On the conflicts between biological and social evolution and between psychology and moral traditions. *American Psychologist, 30*, 1103–1126.

Campbell, D.T. (1990) Levels of organization, downward causation, and the selection-theory approach to evolutionary epistemology. In G. Greenberg and E. Tobach (eds), *Theories of the Evolution of Knowing*, pp. 1–17. Hillsdale, NJ: Erlbaum.

Caporael, L.R. and Brewer, M.B. (1995) Hierarchical evolutionary theory: There is an alternative, and it's not creationism. *Psychological Inquiry, 6*, 31–34.

Caporael, L.R., Dawes, R.M., Orbell, J.M. and van de Kragt, A. (1989) Selfishness examined: Cooperation in the absence of egoistic incentives. *Behavioral and Brain Sciences, 12*, 683–739.

De Cremer, D. and van Dijk, E. (2002) Reactions to group success and failure as a function of identification level: A test of the goal-transformation hypothesis in social dilemmas. *Journal of Experimental Social Psychology, 38*, 435–442.

De Cremer, D. and Van Vugt, M. (1999) Social identification effects in social dilemmas: A transformation of motives. *European Journal of Social Psychology, 29*, 871–893.

Foddy, M., Platow, M. and Yamagishi, T. (2008) Group-based trust in strangers: The role of stereotypes and group heuristics. Unpublished manuscript.

Hardin, G. (1968) The tragedy of the commons. *Science, 162*, 1243–1248.

Hornsey, M.J. and Hogg, M.A. (1999) Subgroup differentiation as a response to an overly-inclusive group: A test of optimal distinctiveness theory. *European Journal of Social Psychology, 29*, 543–550.

Jetten, J., Spears, R. and Manstead, A.S.R. (1998) Intergroup similarity and group variability: The effects of group distinctiveness on the expression of in-group bias. *Journal of Personality and Social Psychology, 74*, 1481–1492.

Jetten, J., Spears, R. and Postmes, T. (2004) Intergroup distinctiveness and differentiation: A meta-analytic integration. *Journal of Personality and Social Psychology, 86*, 862–879.

Kramer, R.M. and Brewer, M.B. (1984) Effects of group identity on resource utilization in a simulated commons dilemma. *Journal of Personality and Social Psychology, 46*, 1044–1057.

Kramer, R.M. and Brewer, M.B. (1986) Social group identity and the emergence of cooperation in resource conservation dilemmas. In H. Wilke, D. Messick, and C. Rutte (eds), *Psychology of Decisions and Conflict, Vol. 3: Experimental Social Dilemmas*, pp. 205–230. Frankfurt: Verlag Peter Lang.

Kramer, R.M. and Wei, J. (1999) Social uncertainty and the problem of trust in social groups: The social self in doubt. In T.R. Tyler, R.M. Kramer, and O.P. John (eds), *The Psychology of the Social Self*, pp. 145–168. Mahwah, NJ: Lawrence Erlbaum Associates.

Leonardelli, G. and Brewer, M.B. (2001) Minority and majority discrimination: When and why. *Journal of Experimental Social Psychology, 37*, 468–485.

LeVine, R.A. and Campbell, D.T. (1972) *Ethnocentrism: Theories of Conflict, Ethnic Attitudes and Group Behavior*. New York: Wiley.

Maynard Smith, J. (1964) Group selection and kin selection. *Nature, 201*, 1145–1147.

Maynard Smith, J. and Szathmáry, E. (1995) *The Major Transitions in Evolution*. Oxford: W.H. Freeman.

Mummendey, A. and Wenzel, M. (1999) Social discrimination and tolerance in intergroup relations: Reactions to intergroup difference. *Personality and Social Psychology Review, 3*, 158–174.

Parker, R., Lui, L., Messick, D.M., Messick, C., Brewer, M.B., Kramer, R., Samuelson, C. and Wilke, H. (1983) A computer laboratory for studying resource dilemmas. *Behavioral Science, 28*, 298–304.

Pickett, C.L., Bonner, B.L. and Coleman, J.M. (2002) Motivated self-stereotyping: Heightened assimilation and differentiation needs result in increased levels of positive and negative self-stereotyping. *Journal of Personality and Social Psychology, 82*, 543–562.

Pickett, C.L. and Brewer, M.B. (2005) The role of exclusion in maintaining in-group inclusion. In D. Abrams, M. Hogg, and J. Marques (eds), *Social Psychology of Inclusion and Exclusion*, pp. 89–112. New York: Psychology Press.

Pickett, C.L., Silver, M.D. and Brewer, M.B. (2002). The impact of assimilation and differentiation needs on perceived group importance and judgments of group size. *Personality and Social Psychology Bulletin, 28*, 546–558.

Roccas, S. and Schwartz, S. (1993) Effects of intergroup similarity on intergroup relations. *European Journal of Social Psychology, 23*, 581–595.

Simon, B. and Hamilton, D.L. (1994) Social identity and self-stereotyping: The effects of relative group size and group status. *Journal of Personality and Social Psychology, 66*, 699–711.

Snyder, C.R. and Fromkin, H.L. (1980) *Uniqueness: The Human Pursuit of Difference*. New York: Plenum Press.

Sober, E. and Wilson, D.S. (1998) *Unto Others: The Evolution and Psychology of Unselfish Behavior*. Cambridge, MA: Harvard University Press.

Spears, R., Doosje, B. and Ellemers, N. (1997) Self-stereotyping in the face of threats to group status and distinctiveness: The role of group identification. *Personality and Social Psychology Bulletin, 23*, 538–553.

Stapel, D.A. and Marx, D.M. (2007) Distinctiveness is key: How different types of self-other similarity moderate social comparison effects. *Personality and Social Psychology Bulletin, 33*, 437–448.

Sumner, W.G. (1906) *Folkways*. New York: Ginn.

Tajfel, H. (1970) Experiments in intergroup discrimination. *Scientific American, 223*, 96–102.

Tajfel, H. (1981) *Human Groups and Social Categories*. Cambridge: Cambridge University Press.

Tajfel, H., Billig, M., Bundy, R. and Flament, C. (1971) Social categorization and intergroup behaviour. *European Journal of Social Psychology, 1*, 149–178.

Tajfel, H., and Turner. J.C. (1979) An integrative theory of intergroup conflict. In W. Austin and S. Worchel (eds), *Social Psychology of Intergroup Relations,* pp. 33–47. Chicago, Nelson.

Tanis, M. and Postmes, T. (2005) A social identity approach to trust: Interpersonal perception, group membership and trusting behaviour. *European Journal of Social Psychology, 35*, 413–424.

Turner, J.C., Hogg, M., Oakes, P., Reicher, S. and Wetherell, M. (1987) *Rediscovering the Social Group: A Self-categorization Theory.* Oxford: Blackwell.

Willams, G.C. (1966) *Adaptation and Natural Selection: A Critique of Some Current Evolutionary Thought.* Princeton, NJ: Princeton University Press.

Wilson, E.O. (1975) *Sociobiology.* Cambridge, MA: Harvard University Press.

Wynne-Edwards, V.C. (1962) *Animal Dispersion in Relation to Social Behaviour.* London: Oliver and Boyd.

Yuki, M., Maddux, W.W., Brewer, M.B. and Takemura, K. (2005) Cross-cultural differences in relationship- and group-based trust. *Personality and Social Psychology Bulletin, 31*, 48–62.

31

A Cognitive-Neoassociation Theory of Aggression

Leonard Berkowitz

ABSTRACT

The author's cognitive-neoassociation (CNA) analysis of impulsive aggressive reactions can be traced back to the 1939 Dollard et al. frustration – aggression hypothesis, and to its later extensions by Neal Miller, such as his conflict model of hostility displacement. The author's research and writings, starting in the late 1950s, have been generally sympathetic to this perspective. Much of this research initially had to do with the aggression-enhancing influence of situational stimuli, such as weapons and movie violence, but increasingly, starting in the mid 1980s, particular attention was given to the role of negative affect. The author has modified the original frustration – aggression hypothesis by proposing that obstacles to expected goal attainment produce aggressive inclinations only to the extent that these events are experienced as decidedly unpleasant. In spelling out the CNA model, the present chapter maintains that aggression-related stimuli and aversive occurrences tend to activate aggressive reactions automatically and that cognitive processing can then intervene to enhance or weaken the aggressive inclinations. The chapter then concludes by raising a number of important questions still to be resolved.

THEORETICAL FOUNDATION

The theoretical perspective I have employed throughout my research on aggression has a clear starting point: the publication of the monograph *Frustration and Aggression* in 1939 by John Dollard, Leonard Doob, Neal Miller, O. Hobart Mowrer, and Robert Sears, then all at Yale University. Here, in this relatively small book, the authors argued that "aggression is always a consequence of frustration" (1939: 1), and extended this central proposition very broadly to such matters as socialization, adolescent behavior, criminality, and even fascism and communism. This publication drew so much attention throughout psychology at that time that two-thirds of a 1941 issue of the *Psychological Review* was devoted to discussions of this analysis, and these discussion papers were then reprinted in full in the then singularly important *Readings in Social Psychology* published in 1947.[1]

I was so attracted to this conception, when I joined the Psychology Department at the

University of Wisconsin in 1955 and was asked to teach a senior-level course on special topics in psychology, that I devoted most of the semester to research on aggression and centered this coverage on the ideas advanced by the Yale group. My lecture notes then served as the foundation for a successful research grant application to the National Institute of Mental Health and also for an article in the *Psychological Bulletin* (Berkowitz, 1958). A few years later I (Berkowitz, 1963) published a comprehensive survey of the psychological research on aggression, again sympathetic to the perspective employed by Dollard, Miller, and their colleagues and its later modifications and extensions (Miller, 1941, 1948; also see Miller, 1959). But even with all this attention to the frustration – aggression hypothesis in my teaching and literature reviews, my own early research in the 1960s and 1970s did not directly examine the effects of frustrations on subsequent aggression, although I did return to this topic in an edited volume (Berkowitz, 1969) and in a 1989 survey of the pertinent literature (Berkowitz, 1989). My student, Russell Geen (1968), did study the influence of frustrations in his doctoral research. Other problems, such as the displacement of hostility, were then more interesting to me, and I'll say more about this later.

My interest in the Yale group's theoretical perspective does not mean I agreed with this analysis in all respects. Where Dollard and his colleagues (1939) had originally held that every aggressive action "presupposes the existence of frustration" (1939: 1), it seemed obvious to me (e.g., see Berkowitz, 1963, 1989), that aggression can occur at times when there is no barrier to goal attainment, and can have objectives in addition to the target's injury. Many attacks are probably primarily instrumental to the attainment of some nonaggressive goal, and the Dollard et al. (1939) analysis holds only for a limited range of situations.

With this qualification, the Yale writers' theorizing appealed to me for a number of

reasons, most obviously for its sweep and its testability, and not for its central postulate – but also because their thinking was more complex than is commonly realized. These writers did not hold that aggression was the only or even the main response to a thwarting, as Miller (1941) carefully noted. They suggested that an impediment to goal attainment produced instigations to a variety of different actions, of which the instigation to aggression was only one. However, Miller (1941) also said, if the nonaggressive behaviors did not successfully remove the frustration, "the greater is the probability that the instigation to aggression eventually will become dominant so that some responses of aggression actually will occur" (1941: 339).

THEORETICAL CONCEPTIONS DERIVED FROM THE YALE GROUP'S ANALYSES

Automatic and/or cognitively controlled aggressive responses

Yet another reason I liked the Yale group's approach was their implicit conception of the frustration reactions as being automatically evoked. Because of the writers' general adherence to Hullian behavior theory (see Miller, 1959), I assumed they believed the thwarting-produced reactions would occur automatically – with little thought and attention and not guided by any intentions other than the urge to hurt the target. I emphasized this automaticity in my own thinking about many aggressive actions, especially, but not only, those carried out in a fit of rage (e.g., see Berkowitz, 2008). However appealing the Yale group's theorizing was to me, nonetheless, it didn't match the view of aggression widely shared throughout the social sciences. Most analyses of aggression in these disciplines basically think attacks result when the perpetrators decide, not necessarily consciously, that their purposes can be well served by hurting the target. Script theory is a contemporary version of this perspective; it essentially contends that the aggressors, following the cognitive scripts in their minds suggesting what is likely to happen in the presenting situation, choose to assault their target (e.g., Bushman and Anderson, 2001; Huesmann, 1988).

Is the frustration–aggression relationship the result of learning?

It also seemed to me that the Dollard et al. (1939) formulation suggested that the frustration-produced aggressive reactions were, at least to some extent, the result of an innate process, although Miller had stated that he and his colleagues had made no assumptions "as to whether the frustration–aggression relationship is of innate or of learned origin" (1941: 340). Still, many critics caught the implication of a "built-in" basis to the presumed connection between thwartings and aggressive reactions. Maintaining that frustration reactions were learned, they held that frustrations did not necessarily produce an aggressive urge (e.g., Bandura and Walters, 1963). Experiments with infants, however, indicate that quite a few very young children display facial expressions indicative of anger when they are frustrated by the unexpected removal of either a pleasant picture (Lewis, 1993) or a desired toy (Stifter and Grant, 1993), so that it is indeed possible that angry reactions to thwartings are not necessarily always learned.

Hostility displacement

After discussing the relatively indirect forms of aggression that theoretically would occur when direct attacks on the frustrater are inhibited, Dollard and his colleagues (1939) pointed out that the restrained aggressive urge might also be expressed in attacks on persons other than the aggression instigator.

Explicitly adopting Freudian terminology, they referred to this phenomenon as aggression displacement (1939: 41). Social psychology was once quite interested in displaced aggression, as Marcus-Newhall and her colleagues (2000) observed after content analyzing a great many social psychology texts. In recent years, however, according to Marcus-Newhall et al. (2000), displaced aggression has been given little attention by psychological investigators, although, as this survey concluded, it is a "robust" phenomenon. It's worth looking at aggression displacement again since it is very much in accord with my theoretical perspective.

Aggression displacement in hostility toward minorities

In their discussion of the displacement of aggression (e.g., 1939: 41–44), the Yale writers noted that this displacement could also be manifested in hostile attitudes toward minority groups such as "Negroes." The Hovland and Sears (see Dollard et al., 1939: 31) investigation is undoubtedly the best known of their studies on this topic. Because cotton was the main cash crop in the South at that time, these researchers assumed that Southern farmers suffered economic-related frustrations when cotton prices were low. In keeping with their expectation, cotton value in Southern states between 1882 and 1930 was significantly negatively correlated with the number of lynchings of blacks in these states in those years. The farmers' economic hardships apparently had produced aggressive urges which were then displaced onto blacks.

This study was widely discussed in the social sciences in the succeeding decades, sometimes drawing criticism, but also support from more sophisticated statistical analyses (see Green et al., 1998). In what is the most thorough of these follow-up investigations, Green et al. (1998) showed that the cotton price/lynching relationship held only for the time up to the Great Depression, but not afterward. And moreover, on extending their investigation to the effects of economic difficulties on nonlethal hate crimes, Green et al. (1998) found that unemployment rates in New York City in the decade before their study had no relationship to the number of reported hate crimes against homosexuals, Jews, blacks, and Asians during that period. All in all, it could be that when people experience economic frustrations and/or other social stresses, they will openly direct their resulting aggressive urges onto particular minority groups only if they think others important to them, their ingroups, will not disapprove of these assaults. Inhibitions restraining direct attacks against minorities also could have increased substantially in recent decades, dampening overt displays of bigotry. It is even conceivable that minority groups as such no longer possess the decidedly negative stimulus qualities that draw assaults from those disposed to be violent.

Stimulus qualities drawing displaced aggression

Neal Miller's (1948) seminal demonstration of how hostility displacement can be understood in stimulus-response generalization terms can help explain why some available targets are attacked and others are not victimized. Often called a conflict model because it deals with situations in which an aggressor both desires and fears to attack someone openly, Miller's (1948) analysis proposes that how the conflict is resolved depends upon three factors: the strength of this aggressive instigation (often generally termed the approach tendency), the strength of whatever instigations there are at the time to inhibit the open display of direct aggression (the avoidance tendency), and the degree of association between each possible target and the original provocateur. Miller (1948, 1959) also proposed that the avoidance tendency (the inhibitory generalization gradient) frequently mounts more rapidly than does the approach tendency (the instigation to attack generalization gradient) the closer the association between each target and the

provocateur. And so, the model says, thwarted people wanting to assault their frustraters, but who are afraid to do so, will refrain from attacking the provocateurs or perhaps even others who are closely associated with the frustraters, but will instead direct their aggression toward those moderately linked to the source of their disturbance. The possible targets having little or no connection with the provocateur will receive little, if any, aggression.

My reanalysis of Fitz's (1976) experiment documents the applicability of Miller's (1948) model. In this study, angered men who believed they could safely "get even" with the person who had insulted them showed the pattern Miller had predicted: they attacked the provocateur most severely, and another individual associated with him next most intensely, whereas a nonassociated stranger received the lowest level of punishment. And also in accord with the model, the men led to be afraid of the insulter's possible retaliation also exhibited the displaced aggression pattern; here the insulter received relatively little punishment, but the provocateur's friend was punished much more severely (and the stranger was given little punishment).

Various associations linking the available target to the anger instigator

Aggression-eliciting associations can be established in a variety of ways. Hewitt (1974) showed that aggression can be generalized on the basis of the available target's similarity in age to the angering source. Another experiment, conducted by Berkowitz and Knurek (1969), indicated that having the same negative label can also connect the anger instigator to someone else. In this study the participants were provoked by a person having a name they earlier had been conditioned to dislike. When they later interacted with a peer having either the negatively conditioned name or a neutral name, they were harsher in their evaluation of the individual with the unpleasant name than the peer with the neutral name. The hostility generated by the negatively named provocateur had evidently generalized to the person bearing the same unpleasant label.

Dislike for the minority group – a factor in scapegoating?

I have long maintained that we have to consider a minority group's stimulus qualities if we are to explain why some minorities are especially apt to be the targets of displaced aggression. Although theorists have accounted for this selectivity in various ways (see Brewer and Brown, 1998), in my view most of the points they make can be subsumed under one significant general principle: They all provide reasons why the particular group is greatly disliked; that is, has acquired a strongly negative cue value. As a consequence, I suggest, the hostility aroused by other sources can be readily generalized to that particular collection of people.

A number of experiments have reported findings consistent with this proposition. In one of the earliest of these studies (Berkowitz and Holmes, 1960), the female participants were first induced to either dislike or have a neutral attitude toward a peer and then were either insulted or treated in a neutral manner by the experimenter. When all of the women were then given an opportunity to deliver electric shocks to their peer, supposedly as an evaluation of her work on a task, those who had been provoked by the experimenter administered the severest punishment to the person they had earlier learned to dislike. This latter individual's negative cue value apparently had enhanced her ability to draw the hostility engendered by the provocateur.

Another Wisconsin study suggests that people highly disposed to be prejudiced are especially apt to exhibit this hostility generalization to disliked persons. This experiment (Berkowitz, 1959) took advantage of the freedom many Midwestern college students felt at that time to express prejudiced opinions openly. After the female participants had been deliberately derogated by the experimenter, those who had highly anti-Semitic attitudes tended to be the most hostile toward a neutral woman nearby.[2]

THE COGNITIVE-NEOASSOCIATION PERSPECTIVE

In the decades following the studies just cited, my emphasis on the role of situational stimuli automatically eliciting aggressive reactions continued, but I also developed some new conceptions not anticipated by the traditional S-R perspective. One of these is an important revision of the frustration – aggression hypothesis, and another has to do with the interplay of automatic and controlled cognitive processing in the display of aggressive actions.

Why frustrations produce aggressive reactions: the role of negative affect

My 1989 review of the frustration–aggression research (Berkowitz, 1989) offered a possible explanation for why people do not always want to attack someone after they've been thwarted in their attempt to reach a desired goal: they are not sufficiently bothered. Barriers to goal attainment, I proposed (also see Berkowitz, 1983, 1993), produce an instigation to aggression only to the extent that they are decidedly unpleasant.

From this perspective, unexpected or unjustified interferences are more apt to provoke an aggressive reaction than anticipated or legitimate barriers to goal attainment because the former are usually much more unpleasant. And similarly, another person's deliberate attempt to block our goal attainment is more angering than an inadvertent impediment because the former frustration is more disturbing. Furthermore, the factors identified by Dollard and his colleagues as determining the strength of the frustration-produced instigation to aggression, such as the intensity of the drive that cannot be satisfied or the extent to which goal attainment is blocked (Dollard et al., 1939: 28), have this effect because they govern the magnitude of displeasure that is experienced. My formulation also holds that the aggression-instigating effects of frustrations and insults cannot be compared in the abstract, as some psychologists have done. All frustrations are not equally bothersome, and all insults do not generate the same displeasure. In sum, it is not the exact nature of the aversive incident that is important but how intense is the resulting negative affect.

The cognitive-neoassociationistic perspective

My theoretical analysis, which I call a cognitive-neoassociationistic (CNA) model, obviously was influenced to a great extent by the learning theory/associationistic theorizing prominent in psychology before the "cognitive revolution" of the 1960s. But it also was shaped to a large degree by Bower's cognitive-neoassociationism, especially his studies of the effects of mood on memory (e.g., Bower, 1981).

My version of this line of thought holds that both cognitive and automatic, associative processes can function to evoke largely involuntary aggressive reactions. The cognitions in this case can define an event as decidedly unpleasant (although of course, some occurrences are aversive in themselves) and they can also operate to impart an aggressive meaning to situational details. But CNA is primarily concerned with the consequences of aversive stimuli, however this aversiveness originates. Once the strong displeasure is experienced, the model says, there is a sequence of responses. The reactions initially are largely governed by associative processes, with cognitions presumably becoming more important in the later stages. Basically, as can be seen in Figure 31.1, decidedly unpleasant conditions initially tend

to activate, automatically and with relatively little thought, at least two sets of "primitive" inclinations: one to escape from or avoid the aversive stimulation, *and also*, another to attack and even destroy the source of this stimulation. In other words, the aversive state of affairs presumably gives rise to *both* flight *and* fight tendencies. Neither of these inclinations is always dominant. Genetic factors, prior learning, and situational influences all enter to determine the relative strengths of these various reactions.

Also important, both the flight and fight tendencies should be regarded as syndromes, networks of associatively linked physiological, motoric, and cognitive components. The activated flight-associated syndrome is consciously experienced as *fear*, whereas the activated fight-linked syndrome is felt as *annoyance* or *irritation* (at relatively weak levels) or *anger* (at more intense levels). Because the syndromes are associatively linked networks, the activation of any particular syndrome component will also tend to bring the other parts of the network into operation. Thus, more than the formulations resting exclusively on cognitive concepts, this theory can accommodate the research showing that the display of the facial expressions and bodily postures characteristic of a given affective state, such as anger, can generate the feelings typical of this state (see Duclos et al., 1989).

CNA differs from the Anderson's general aggression model (e.g., see Anderson et al., 1995) primarily through its emphasis on these first, relatively automatic and noncognitively mediated reactions to the experienced negative affect. But recognizing the important role cognitions can play, CNA also proposes, as Figure 31.1 shows, that the first fairly primitive reactions can be modified and even substantially altered after the first response tendencies arise. In this second phase any active information processing can bring appraisals, attributions, and the like, into operation, thereby modifying or extinguishing the initial reactions. Thus, people can become angry and assault someone

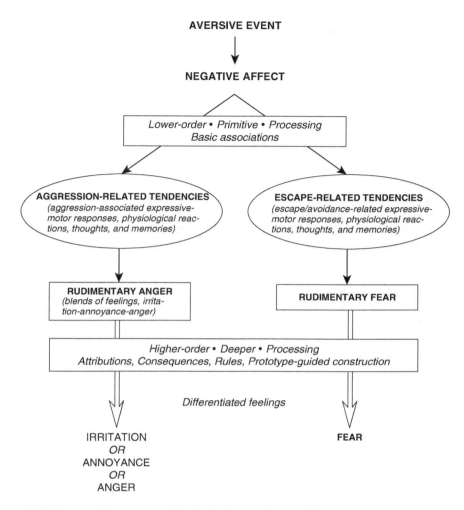

Figure 31.1   The cognitive-neoassociationistic model

impulsively at times without the intervention of the complicated thought processes postulated by appraisal/attribution theorizing. As a matter of fact, I suggest that people exposed to decidedly unpleasant stressful conditions sometimes blame a salient available target for their troubles because of the hostile thoughts and angry feelings that had been generated within them; their attributions might then be the result rather than the cause of their affective reactions (see Quigley and Tedeschi, 1996, and Keltner et al., 1993, for supporting evidence).

Evidence consistent with CNA can be found in the investigations demonstrating that exposure to decidedly unpleasant physical stimuli increases the chances of aggressive behavior (see, among other sources, Berkowitz, 1983, 1993). My thinking here isn't entirely new (e.g., see Baron et al., 1974), but along with Anderson (e.g., Anderson et al., 1995), I have made this a major proposition in my CNA analysis of affective aggression, and contend that negative affect will evoke a number of negative reactions including an instigation to aggression.

Effects of physically unpleasant conditions

Physical pain

Physical pain obviously is almost always aversive and it often instigates aggressive inclinations. On studying patients suffering from frequent bouts of pain, Fernandez and Turk (1995: 165) maintained that anger is a "feature of chronic pain" and that "anger stands out as one of the most salient emotional correlates of pain" (also see Greenwood et al., 2003). Of course, the anger could well contribute to the heightened pain (Fernandez and Turk, 1995; Greenwood et al., 2003), but the pain might also produce anger and aggressive inclinations. Fernandez and Wasan (in press) have recognized this possibility by noting that the suffering persons often develop hostile appraisals of those around them. Couldn't these appraisals be manifestations of the anger and aggressive urges they are experiencing?

Research conducted by Berkowitz et al. (1981) indicates that even relatively moderate pain levels can instigate aggressive impulses. The pain inflicted in these investigations was produced by having half of the female participants immerse a hand in very cold water for about six minutes as they evaluated a partner's solutions to several assigned problems. For the other women the water was at a more comfortable room temperature as they carried out their evaluations. In providing their assessments the participants could give their partner either rewards (nickels) or punishments (unpleasant noise blasts). Cutting across the water temperature variation, half of the women were told any punishment they delivered would actually help the problem solver by motivating her to think better, whereas the remaining women were informed the punishment would hurt their partner.

Those experiencing the moderate pain and who believed they could hurt their partner tended to deliver the most punishments relative to the rewards they provided. Even this mild pain level had evidently heightened their urge to hurt the available target.

Unpleasant atmospheric conditions

Decidedly unpleasant environmental conditions can also increase the proclivity to aggression even though they are not clearly painful. Here is a very brief and limited look at an extensive and controversial literature dealing with the effects of high ambient temperatures (see, for example, Anderson and Anderson, 1996, 1998; Cohn and Rotton, 1997, for more complete discussions).

Social scientists have long noted that, in a number of countries, violent crime rates tend to be higher in their warmer, southern latitudes than in the cooler, northern regions. Anderson and Anderson (1996, 1998) added to these early observations by citing more recent studies showing essentially the same kind of south–north differences. Their own sophisticated analysis of area differences within the US demonstrated that cities having the hottest weather typically had the highest violence rates even when their social and economic characteristics were partialled out (1998: 264–265).

The relatively high homicide rate in the southern US is a good example of such a regional effect on violence. Over the generations, more murders and assaults have been committed in the southern states, controlling for population size, than in the northern parts of the country. Nisbett and Cohen (1996), among others, have attributed this difference primarily to a prevailing *culture of honor* in the South. White males growing up in this area presumably have learned that they must redress a perceived threat to their honor by attacking the offender in order to protect their image as tough and able to protect themselves and their possessions. Although Nisbett and Cohen (1996) provided evidence consistent with their thesis, Anderson and Anderson (1996, 1998) argued that regional temperature is a better predictor of the South's high violence rates than is its "culture of honor." When they analyzed data from 260 standard metropolitan areas in the US for 1980, they concluded that the southerners could have developed and maintained their violence-encouraging attitudes and values largely because of the region's hot weather (1998: 270).

Other research shows that it is important to consider the likelihood and nature of interpersonal encounters when explaining the relationship between temperature and violent offenses. Data obtained by Cohn and Rotton (1997) indicated that the persons exposed to unpleasantly high temperatures might well have an instigation to aggression, but if they are engaged in distracting activities and/or if there is no suitable target nearby and/or if their inhibitions against aggression are fairly strong because of the presence of nearby aggression-restraining people, their urge will not become manifest in open behavior.

The findings from relevant laboratory experiments seem quite inconsistent (see Anderson and Anderson, 1998: 283). The Anderson group's studies repeatedly showed that an unpleasant temperature (cold or hot) produced stronger negative affect, angry feelings, and hostile attitudes and cognitions than did more comfortable ambient temperatures. But these reactions were not always accompanied by strong attacks on an available target. In one of their investigations (see Anderson and Anderson, 1998), as an example, the participants in either an uncomfortably cold or uncomfortably hot room were angrier and had more hostile attitudes than their counterparts exposed to more moderate temperatures – but the former were more aggressive to a partner only the first time they could administer punishment and not on the later occasions. Presumably being aggressively inclined, it may be that they attacked their competitor more or less impulsively at first, but then may have decided it was best to restrain themselves.

Social stresses

A number of social science theorists have proposed that harsh social situations, and especially frustrations, are major contributors to criminal activities. Sociologists and criminologists often speak of these conditions as *social strains* and refer to *strain theories* of crime causation, whereas psychologists

typically employ the term *frustration* much more explicitly. But whatever words are used in these analyses, they highlight the central role of negative affect in antisocial behavior.

An experiment by Passman and Mulhern (1977) is relevant. The mothers in this study worked on an assigned task at the same time that they monitored their child's performance on a puzzle. Those women who were under a high degree of stress as they worked, because their task requirements had been deliberately made confusing, punished their youngsters' mistakes more severely than did their more comfortable counterparts. The stresses encountered in the everyday world can lead to more naturalistic aggression as well. Straus (1980) and his colleagues asked the men and women in their nationally representative US sample to indicate whether they had experienced each of 18 stressful life events – such as "troubles with other people at work," "the death of someone close," "a move to a different neighborhood or town," and "a family member with a health or behavior problem." Whether the respondents were male or female, the greater were the number of stressors they reported experiencing during the past year, the more likely they were also to say they had abused their children. Going further along these lines, other investigations have indicated that the psychological pain felt on being socially rejected can produce aggressive reactions (MacDonald and Leary, 2005) and that the negative affect some people experience at the sight of homosexual activity can prompt aggressive inclinations toward gay men (Parrott et al., 2006).

Automatic elicitation of aggression by situational stimuli

The weapons effect

Many of my investigations since the late 1960s were concerned with the role of environmental stimuli closely associated with aggression generally (e.g., Berkowitz, 1964a).

My experiment demonstrating the "weapons effect" (Berkowitz and LePage, 1967) is a good example. Since guns are connected with aggression generally, I had believed the mere sight of a weapon would increase the aggressive inclinations in people disposed to be aggressive at that time. Hostile ideas would be elicited, and aggression-related motor reactions might even be set into operation, so that the viewers would then lash out at their target, especially if they are ready to attack someone at the time and their restraints against aggression are correspondingly weak.

Although there have been several failures to replicate the original Berkowitz – LePage findings, an impressive number of studies support the existence of such a weapons effect, and moreover, these confirming investigations have been conducted in other countries, including Belgium, Croatia,[3] Italy, and Sweden, as well as the US (see Berkowitz, 1993). I will not here go into a detailed review of this research, but one point is worth emphasizing. According to several experiments conducted by Turner and his associates (see Berkowitz, 1993), the heightened aggression can be displayed even when the research participants are not aware they are taking part in an experiment. In one of these studies, Turner and his colleagues set up a booth at a college-sponsored carnival and invited students to throw sponges at a target person, allowing them to "assault" the target as often as they wished. More sponges were hurled at the target when a rifle was lying nearby than when no weapon was present.

Effects of observed aggression

My associationistic perspective also prompted me to study the effects of seeing aggression on the movie and television screen. Where some proponents of psychoanalytic theorizing had argued that the sight of others fighting would have a cathartic effect, "purging" the viewers' aggressive impulses, I thought the witnessed violence would function as an aggressive cue automatically evoking associated aggression-related ideas and motor impulses.

My early research confirmed this expectation (see Berkowitz, 1964a, 1964b, 1965, 1993). Geen and O'Neal (1969), following the Wisconsin paradigm, added to this evidence. They demonstrated that if people who had seen a violent movie are physiologically greatly aroused by an irrelevant source soon afterward, they become highly punitive in their subsequent judgments of an available target. Very much in accord with Hullian behavior theory (see Miller, 1959), the "irrelevant arousal" had strengthened the movie-induced aggressive reactions.

Perhaps more interestingly, several Wisconsin studies (e.g., Berkowitz, 1965) showed that cognitive processes could also influence how the observers acted after seeing the violent movie. Under some conditions – such as when the depicted assaults were portrayed as justified – the viewers' inhibitions against aggression were reduced, and as a consequence, those who had watched this "legitimate" aggression were apt to retaliate severely against someone nearby who had annoyed them earlier. These results, replicated a number of times, have some disturbing implications. In many, perhaps most, violent movies the "good guy" beats up the "villains," giving them the trashing they supposedly deserve. The hero's aggression is viewed as justified. This is just the kind of depicted aggression that is especially likely to enhance the audience members' willingness to assault the "bad persons" in their own lives, at least for a short time afterward.

This cognitive effect obviously can work together with the viewers' associations in affecting their reactions to movie violence, as one of the Wisconsin studies demonstrates. In this experiment (Berkowitz, 1965), capitalizing on the fact that the university then had a boxing team, each male participant was paired with the experimenter's confederate posing as a student who was either very interested in college boxing or was a speech major. After a brief exchange with the confederate, in which this person either angered the participant by making disparaging remarks or treated him in a neutral manner, the participant was given a short synopsis of the prize-fight scene they would view. In this summary, the prize fight loser in the movie was either said to be a nasty person – so that the beating he received would be regarded as justified – or was depicted in a more favorable light – and the aggression was thus unjustified. And also, as was standard in many Wisconsin experiments, immediately after the prize-fight movie each participant then was given an opportunity to administer electric shocks to the target (i.e., the confederate), supposedly as the participant's evaluation of the confederate's solution to an assigned problem.

The angering target was punished most severely when both associative and cognitive influences operated: when the confederate was linked with the aggression on the screen and the witnessed aggression was made to seem justified. The target's association with the observed violence led him to automatically draw stronger attacks and the viewer's favorable interpretation of the aggressive scene reduced their restraints against acting aggressively.

Automatic and controlled cognitive processing

Because of findings such as these, I now couch my analyses in terms of such notions as *automatic processing* and *controlled cognitive processing,* although I continue to devote more attention to the former, automatic reactions governed primarily by associations. Generally speaking, following Schneider and Shiffrin (1977), automatic processing is fast, effortless, obligatory in that attention to a stimulus is sufficient to trigger associated responses, is unconscious, and can act in parallel with other processes. Controlled processing, on the other hand, requires that attention is clearly focused on particular aspects of the situation, that

effort has to be exerted, and there is an intention. Reductions in cognitive capacity harm controlled processing but not automatic processing.

My 1984 paper (Berkowitz, 1984) on a cognitive-neoassociation analysis of media effects was a harbinger of this change in my terminology. I noted there that situational occurrences, such as witnessed violence, can prime semantically related thoughts, heightening the chances that the viewers will have other aggressive ideas and even aggressive action tendencies. John Bargh and his colleagues (e.g., Bargh and Williams, 2006; Todorov and Bargh, 2002), perhaps the most prominent of the contemporary researchers investigating automatically elicited social behavior, have advanced a very similar formulation, and have demonstrated in a number of clever ways how social acts can be triggered automatically by particular aspects of the surrounding situation (e.g., Chen and Bargh, 1997).

Automatic aggressive reactions to physically unattractive targets

In my earlier discussion of displaced aggression, I proposed that an available target's negative characteristics promote aggressive reactions. Another Wisconsin experiment (Berkowitz and Frodi, 1979; summarized in Berkowitz, 2008), extended this principle to those instances in which the available target had decidedly unattractive physical qualities. In this study, previously annoyed female undergraduates watched a boy, shown on a TV monitor, work on his tasks, and believed their job was to correct his performance over a series of trials. Unbeknownst to the women, they were actually seeing a previously prepared videotape in which the youngster had been made either funny-looking or normal in appearance and, cross-cutting this variation, either stuttered or spoke normally. To enhance the likelihood the participants would respond automatically to what they saw, the women were given another assignment to carry out as they observed the youngster's actions, and were asked to give the child a blast of noise whenever they thought the boy made a mistake.

The boy's physical characteristics clearly influenced the punishment the participants gave him for his mistakes (see Figure 2 in Berkowitz, 2008). Evidently still annoyed by the experimenter's earlier treatment of them and somewhat distracted by their own task, they were harsher to the youngster when he stuttered than when he spoke normally, and also, funny looking rather than normal in appearance. The target's negative character-istics evidently had automatically elicited stronger aggressive reactions.

Cognitions intensifying automatically elicited aggression

Cognitions can intensify or suppress such automatically activated inclinations. These automatic aggressive reactions can be strengthened, for example, when viewers actively think of the witnessed violence they see as "real" – an actual occurrence – and not "fake" or staged. Many of us are especially apt to associate observed aggression with our own life circumstances when this witnessed occurrence seems real (see Berkowitz and Alioto, 1973: 207). We may then become psychologically quite involved in what hap-pens, so that if we're disposed to be assault-ive (and the witnessed aggression appears justified), whatever automatically engen-dered aggressive inclination we have is strengthened.

People are especially likely to associate the behavior they see with themselves when they identify with the actor, that is, when they actively think of themselves as carrying out the witnessed behavior. Yet another Wisconsin experiment (Turner and Berkowitz, 1972) demonstrated that this identification with the observed aggressor can strengthen the angry viewers' own aggressive inclinations. Each male partici-pant was first provoked by his partner's unfa-vorable evaluations of his solutions to an assigned problem, and then three conditions were established before our standard brief fight movie was shown: in one the participant was asked to imagine himself as the fight

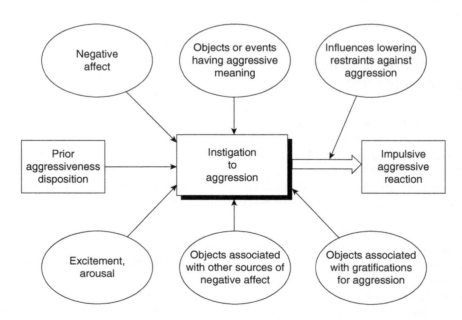

Figure 31.2   Influences affecting the magnitude of an impulsive aggressive reaction

winner (who gave the loser a bad beating in the film), in another condition he was to think of himself as the fight judge, and in the last case the participant was not given any imagination role. After this, the participant judged his partner's solutions to the problems he had been given, delivering electric shocks to that man as his evaluations.

As we had expected, the angry people who had imagined themselves as the fight winner delivered much more severe punishment to the person who had offended them than did any of the other groups. In identifying with the movie character who was pummeling his antagonist, they evidently vicariously engaged in aggression themselves, thereby strengthening their aggressive urge.

Cognitions restraining aggressive reactions

Cognitions can also promote the reduction of aggressive inclinations in a number ways – for example, through bringing about a desirable self-regulation (e.g., see Baumeister and Vohs, 2004). I, here, will confine myself to my own research, and will summarize some investigations demonstrating the involvement of cognitive processes in the self-regulation of automatically evoked aggression.

Much of my research in the last few decades of my academic career was focused on the notion that fairly strong displeasure can give rise to an aggressive urge (see Berkowitz, 1993, 2003). In testing this contention, my colleagues and I made our experimental participants experience negative affect in a wide variety of ways, for instance by asking them to engage in unpleasant and stressful physical activities. And very often, in these early studies, as is quite common in investigations of this kind, we asked the participants to rate their feelings before they were given an opportunity to express their hostility. Much to our surprise, and quite contrary to the "demand characteristics" notion, in some of our initial studies the negative affect led to a *low* level of expressed hostility. It then occurred to me that in rating their feelings the participants could have become highly

aware of their unpleasant affect and hostile tendencies. They might have then regarded these emotional reactions as inappropriate at that time and consequently sought to regulate their expressed reactions.

This interpretation is very similar to the reasoning advanced by Carver and Scheier (1981) in their theorizing about self-awareness and self-regulation. These writers held, in essence, that when people become highly aware of themselves, they also become very conscious of their personal standards pertinent to the kind of situation they are in. If there is a discrepancy between these standards and what they are inclined to do at that moment, they will then attempt to minimize this discrepancy and act in accord with their personal values. Our instructing the students to describe their feelings after the experimental manipulation could have had a similar effect: they might have become very aware of themselves as well as their hostile inclinations. Believing it was improper to be nasty to their experimental partner in the current situation, they presumably then avoided expressing anything very negative about this person.

This evidently happened in an experiment by Berkowitz and Troccoli (1990). Half of the female participants were individually made physically very uncomfortable by requiring them to hold their nondominant arm outward, whereas the other women only rested their arm on the desk before them. Then, while maintaining their arm in the stipulated position, the participants heard a tape recording on which a supposed job applicant talked about herself. When this ended half of the women were asked to think about their feelings at that time, whereas their counterparts were given a distracting word-association task. Finally, about five minutes after they had started, and with the participants still maintaining the specified arm position, all of them evaluated the female job applicant.

Not surprisingly, the women whose attention had been diverted from themselves showed the usual feelings-congruence effect;

those made physically uncomfortable were harsher in their judgments of the applicant than their more comfortable counterparts. By contrast, however, the people who had attended to their negative feelings apparently showed the self-awareness induced self-regulation; the uncomfortable participants actually were kinder to the job applicant than their more comfortable peers.

Yet another of our studies suggests that it is the actions produced by the negative affect that is regulated, not the feeling itself. In this experiment (Berkowitz and Jo, 1992, unpublished) the female participants' feelings were manipulated in such a way that they were unlikely to know the source of whatever affect they experienced. Following the procedure described by Strack et al. (1988), they were asked to hold their mouths in a particular way so that they adopted either a smiling or frowning facial expression. Shortly after this expression was established some of the women rated their feelings and thus became highly aware of their affective state, whereas the other participants were distracted by having them list several word associates. All of the participants then read an autobiographical statement supposedly written by a job applicant, and then, as in the Berkowitz and Troccoli (1990) experiment, evaluated her.

The results obtained here parallel the findings in the previous investigation. Here again, the judgments were congruent with the participants' feelings when their attention had been diverted from themselves; the smiling women assigned fewer bad qualities to the target than did their frowning counterparts. And also, as had been found before, the participants' attention to their feelings led to the feeling-judgment incongruence; the frowning women were less harsh in their judgments than their smiling peers. The active cognitive processing produced by the self-directed attention evidently had caused these latter persons to suppress their display of hostility to the job applicant.

IMPULSIVE AGGRESSION

The results summarized here, together with other research findings, such as those obtained by Bargh and his colleagues (e.g., Bargh and Williams, 2006; Todorov and Bargh, 2002), demonstrate that aggressive verbal and motor actions can be automatically elicited by aggression-related stimuli. I have often (e.g., Berkowitz, 1993, 2003) referred to these attacks as *impulsive* in the sense that they are carried out with little thought in response to situational features, and proceed with little, if any, conscious guidance and attention. Some instances of impulsive aggression are largely the result of overly rapid decision-making, but many impulsive assaults are often primarily a product of factors affecting the disinhibition of situationally induced reactions, with little part played by "higher order" cognitive processes.

Bushman and Anderson (2001) have questioned this contention that many aggressive actions are impulsive attacks automatically activated by relevant situational stimulation rather than because of a decision that had been reached. They maintained, instead, that it is advisable to think of every aggressive action as the product of a decision process greatly affected by the individual's knowledge structures. Nonetheless, in my view, much of the research into individual differences in aggressive behavior support my distinction between impulsive, automatically elicited assaults, and cognitively controlled, chosen attacks. Thus, where Dodge (e.g., Crick and Dodge, 1996), in differentiating between *reactive* and *proactive* aggression, has emphasized the role of information processing in both of these cases (also see Berkowitz, 2008), other investigations (e.g., Raine et al., 2006) have noted that reactive aggressors are often apt to be highly impulsive. For that matter, Barratt (1999), well known for his studies of impulsivity, seemed to prefer the concepts *impulsive* versus *premeditated* aggressive acts instead of Dodge's labels.

Of course, a good many factors can affect the magnitude of an impulsive attack on an available target, and Figure 31.2 lists the influences suggested by my CNA model. Up to now in the present discussion I have dealt mostly with the roles of negative affect and the priming established by objects or events having an aggressive meaning, but here I would like to say a bit more about the weakness of restraints against aggression in impulsivity.

Impulsivity has been operationally defined in a great many different ways (e.g., see Dickman, 1990; White et al., 1994), but according to several investigations, impulsive actions often vary along two underlying dimensions: one dealing mostly with unrestrained acts and the other reflecting an incomplete and inadequate information processing so that overly quick decisions are reached. In the earlier of these studies, Dickman (1990) uncovered two factors that appear to tap these two dimensions. His items (all self-reported) with the highest loadings on Factor 1 included, "I don't like to make decisions quickly, even simple decisions" (disagree), and "I am uncomfortable when I have to make up my mind rapidly," (disagree), suggesting the factor has to do with very hasty decision-making. Factor 2, on the other hand, based on items such as, "I often say and do things without considering the consequences," and "I often get into trouble because I don't think before I act," appears to reflect a tendency to impetuous actions. These two factors had a low but significant positive correlation. Another study (Endicott et al., 2006), in investigating the correlates of self-reported impulsivity, also differentiated between a "nonplanning" impulsiveness and a "motor impulsiveness," with the latter having to do primarily with "inhibitory dyscontrol." Yet another investigation also uncovered these two types of impulsivity. White and Moffitt and their colleagues (1994) factor analyzed the relationships among the 11 different impulsivity measures they employed in their study.

Two correlated but distinct forms of impulsivity were identified. The first of these, termed "behavioral impulsivity," appeared to reflect a lack of behavioral control in that "the variables with the highest loading on this factor were those that tapped disinhibited, undercontrolled behavior." The second factor, labeled "cognitive impulsivity," had more to do with a deficiency in "effortful and planful cognitive performance." Both kinds of impulsivity were associated with delinquency in the White et al. (1998) research, although the data indicated that the relationship between behavioral impulsivity and delinquency was independent of intelligence.

CONCLUSION

The aggressive reactions I and others have seen in the laboratory experiments cited here admittedly have been quite weak. But nevertheless, I argue that the findings obtained in these studies, especially when taken together with more naturalistic investigations, point to a possible explanation of many instances of domestic and even criminal violence. In these assaults (as Figure 31.2 suggests) people disposed to be aggressive, because of their personalities and/or the strong negative affect they were experiencing, could well have impulsively attacked an available target, especially one having (for the aggressor) decidedly negative qualities – without necessarily having consciously decided to do so. Increasing numbers of legal scholars and philosophers now recognize the problems that are raised for legal justice systems by psychological findings such as this. Law codes typically use judgments of an offender's intentions in deciding what punishment he or she should receive for a crime. But what if there was little if any conscious intention? In the case of, say, domestic violence, shouldn't the external influences automatically eliciting aggressive inclinations be considered at least as mitigating circumstances?

One answer, of course, is that people should restrain their aggressive urges, and the threat of punishment could promote this necessary self-regulation. But there are many more, and probably better, ways of getting people to control themselves, as the burgeoning literature on self-regulation (e.g., Baumeister and Vohs, 2004) shows. The previously mentioned experiment by Berkowitz and Troccoli (1990) indicates, for example, along with the Carver and Scheier (1981) analysis, that persons disposed to be assaultive would benefit from both the learning of nonaggressive standards of conduct and the heightening of their self-awareness when they are aggressively inclined. Clearly, further research into the self-regulation of aggressive impulses is highly desirable.

In addition to emphasizing the role of aggression-eliciting situational stimuli, CNA also gives special attention to aversive occurrences generally and decidedly negative affect in particular. Experienced stress is just one variation on this theme. Studies mentioned earlier have documented how people under stress have become assaultive. Combat-induced stress is another example. As a case in point, the New York Times (January 2, 2009) examined the cases of over 120 veterans of the Iraq or Afghanistan wars who were charged with homicide after their return. The reporter concluded that combat trauma and stress "appeared to have set the stage for [many of] the crimes" (p. A12). Interestingly, this article also noted that a number of the accused killers had previously tried to commit suicide, supporting my suggestion (Berkowitz, 1993) that intense depression can also generate an aggressive urge, directed against others as well as to the self. And here too, much more has to be learned. Although I have repeatedly held that strong negative affect generates an aggressive inclination (which may or may not be expressed openly; see Figure 31.1), it is intuitively likely that some kinds of intense unpleasant feelings are more aggression-inducing than other kinds. My guess here is that an agitated displeasure is more apt to have assaultive consequences

than, say, a "flat," listless mood. We don't know, however, whether this is indeed so, or even what just factors produce these different negative feelings.

All in all, then, the CNA model spelled out in this paper is just a preliminary formulation, one that leaves many important questions unanswered. But at least it has the virtue of raising these questions. Hopefully, other investigators will undertake the task of pursuing these problems further.

NOTES

1 These discussions can be found in the Vol. 41(4) issue of *Psychological Review* (1941), and in Newcomb and Hartley (eds) (1947) *Readings in Social Psychology*. New York: Holt.

2 The studies by Pedersen, Miller, and their associates (e.g., Pedersen et al., 2000) into "triggered aggression" are an interesting and important extension of the more usual investigations of displaced aggression just summarized. I had intended to cite some of their experiments in this report, but space limitations unfortunately kept me from doing so.

3 In the Croatian study, as an example, the investigator, Miomir Zuzul (see Berkowitz, 1993), showed that previously frustrated schoolchildren were more aggressive toward their peers in a free play situation after they had been exposed to either real or toy guns than after seeing a neutral object, but primarily if the supervising adult had expressed either a neutral or favorable attitude toward aggression generally.

REFERENCES

Anderson, C. and Anderson, K. (1996) Violent crime rate studies in philosophical context: A destructive testing approach to heat and southern culture of violence effects. *Journal of Personality and Social Psychology*, 70, 740–756.

Anderson, C. and Anderson, K. (1998) Temperature and aggression: Paradox, controversy, and a (fairly) clear picture. In R. Geen and E. Donnerstein (eds), *Human Aggression: Theories, Research, and Implications for Social Policy*, pp. 247–298. San Diego: Academic Press.

Anderson, C., Deuser, W. and DeNeve, K. (1995) Hot temperatures, hostile affect, hostile cognition, and arousal: Tests of a general model of affective aggression. *Personality and Social Psychology Bulletin, 21*, 434–448.

Bandura, A. and Walters, R. (1963) *Social Learning and Personality Development*. New York: Holt, Rinehart and Winston.

Bargh, J. and Williams, E. (2006) The automaticity of social life. *Current Directions in Psychological Science, 15*, 1–4.

Baron, R., Byrne, D. and Griffitt, W. (1974) *Social Psychology*. Boston: Allyn and Bacon.

Barratt, E. (1999) Impulsive and premeditated aggression: A factor analysis of self-reported acts. *Psychiatry Research, 86*, 163–173.

Baumeister, R. and Vohs, K. (2004) *Handbook of Self-regulation*. New York: Guilford Press.

Berkowitz, L. (1958) The expression and reduction of hostility. *Psychological Bulletin, 55*, 257–283.

Berkowitz, L. (1959) Anti-Semitism and the displacement of aggression. *Journal of Abnormal and Social Psychology, 59*, 182–187.

Berkowitz, L. (1963) *Aggression: A Social Psychological Analysis*. New York: McGraw-Hill.

Berkowitz, L. (1964a) Aggressive cues in aggressive behavior and hostility catharsis. *Psychological Review, 71*, 104–122.

Berkowitz, L. (1964b) The effects of observing violence. *Scientific American, 210*, 35–41.

Berkowitz, L. (1965) Some aspects of observed aggression. *Journal of Personality and Social Psychology, 2*, 359–369.

Berkowitz, L. (ed.) (1969) *Roots of Aggression: A Re-examination of the Frustration-aggression Hypothesis*. New York: Atherton Press.

Berkowitz, L. (1983) Aversively stimulated aggression: Some parallels and differences in research with animals and humans. *American Psychologist, 38*, 1135–1144.

Berkowitz, L. (1984) Some effects of thoughts on anti- and prosocial influences of media events: A cognitive-neoassociation analysis. *Psychological Bulletin, 95*, 410–427.

Berkowitz, L. (1989) The frustration-aggression hypothesis: Examination and reformulation. *Psychological Bulletin, 106*, 59–73.

Berkowitz, L. (1993) *Aggression: Its Causes, Consequences, and Control*. New York: McGraw-Hill.

Berkowitz, L. (2003) Affect, aggression, and antisocial behavior. In R. Davidson, K. Scherer and H. Goldsmith (eds), *Handbook of Affective Sciences*, pp. 804–823. Oxford: Oxford University Press.

Berkowitz, L. (2008) On the consideration of automatic as well as controlled psychological

processes in aggression. *Aggressive Behavior, 34*, 117–129.

Berkowitz, L. and Alioto, J. (1973) The meaning of an observed event as a determinant of its aggressive consequences. *Journal of Personality and Social Psychology, 28*, 206–217.

Berkowitz, L., Cochran, S. and Embree, M. (1981) Physical pain and the goal of aversively stimulated aggression. *Journal of Personality and Social Psychology, 40*, 687–700.

Berkowitz, L. and Frodi, A. (1979) Reactions to a child's mistakes as affected by her/his looks and speech. *Social Psychology Quarterly, 42*, 420–425.

Berkowitz, L. and Holmes, D. (1960) A further investigation of hostility generalization to disliked objects. *Journal of Personality, 28*, 427–442.

Berkowitz, L. and Knurek, D. (1969) Label-mediated hostility generalization. *Journal of Personality and Social Psychology, 13*, 200–206.

Berkowitz, L. and LePage, A. (1967) Weapons as aggression-eliciting stimuli. *Journal of Personality and Social Psychology, 7*, 202–207.

Berkowitz, L. and Troccoli, B. (1990) Feelings, direction of attention, and expressed evaluations of others. *Cognition and Emotion, 4*, 305–325.

Bower, G. (1981) Mood and memory. *American Psychologist, 36*, 129–148.

Brewer, M. and Brown, R. (1998) Intergroup relations. In D. Gilbert, S. Fiske, and G. Lindzey (eds) *Handbook of Social Psychology, Vol. 2*, 4th Edition, pp. 554–594. New York: McGraw-Hill.

Bushman, B. and Anderson, C. (2001) Is it time to pull the plug on the hostile versus instrumental aggression dichotomy? *Psychological Review, 108*, 273–279.

Carver, C. and Scheier, M. (1981) *Attention and Self-regulation*. New York: Springer.

Chen, M. and Bargh, J. (1997) Nonconscious behavioral confirmation processes: The self-fulfilling consequences of automatic stereotype activation. *Journal of Experimenal Social Psychology, 33*, 541–560.

Cohn, E. and Rotton, J. (1997) Assault as a function of time and temperature: A moderator-variable time-series analysis. *Journal of Personality and Social Psychology, 72*, 1322–1334.

Crick, N. and Dodge, K. (1996) Social information-processing mechanisms in reactive and proactive aggression. *Child Development, 67*, 993–1002.

Dickman, S. (1990) Functional and dysfunctional impulsivity: Personality and cognitive correlates. *Journal of Personality and Social Psychology, 58*, 95–102.

Dollard, J., Doob, L., Miller, N., Mowrer, O. and Sears, R. (1939) *Frustration and Aggression.* New Haven: Yale University Press.

Duclos, S., Laird, J., Schneider, E., Sexter, M., Stern, L. and Van Lighten, O. (1989) Emotion-specific effects of facial expressions and postures on emotional experience. *Journal of Personality and Social Psychology, 57,* 100–108.

Endicott, P., Ogloff, J. and Bradshaw, J. (2006) *Personality and Individual Differences, 41,* 285–294.

Fernandez, E. and Turk, D. (1995) The scope and significance of anger in the experience of chronic pain. *Pain, 61,* 165–175.

Fernandez, E. and Wasan, A. (in press) The anger of pain sufferers: Attributions to agents and appraisals of wrongdoing. In M. Potegal, G. Stemmler, and C. Spielberger (eds), *Handbook of Anger.* New York: Springer.

Fitz, D. (1976) A renewed look at Miller's conflict theory of aggression displacement. *Journal of Personality and Social Psychology, 33,* 725–732.

Geen, R. (1968) Effects of frustration, attack, and prior training in aggressiveness upon aggressive behavior. *Journal of Personality and Social Psychology, 9,* 316–321.

Geen, R. and O'Neal, E. (1969) Activation of cue-elicited aggression by general arousal. *Journal of Personality and Social Psychology, 11,* 289–292.

Green, D., Glaser, J. and Rich, A. (1998) From lynching to gay bashing: The elusive connection between economic conditions and hate crime. *Journal of Personality and Social Psychology, 75,* 82–92.

Greenwood. K., Thurston, R., Rumble, M., Waters, S. and Keefe, F. (2003) Anger and persistent pain: Current status and future directions. *Pain, 103,* 1–5.

Hewitt, L. (1974) Who will be the target of displaced aggression? In J. De Wit and W. Hartup (eds), *Determinants and Origins of Aggressive Behavior,* pp. 217–223. The Hague: Mouton.

Huesmann, L. (1988) An information processing model for the development of aggression. *Aggressive Behavior, 14,* 13–24.

Keltner, D., Ellsworth, P. and Edwards, K. (1993) Beyond simple pessimism: Effects of sadness and anger on social perception. *Journal of Personality and Social Psychology, 64,* 740–752.

Lewis, M. (1993) The development of anger and rage. In R. Glick and S. Roose (eds), *Rage, Power, and Aggression,* pp. 148–168. New Haven: Yale University Press.

Loew, C. (1967) Acquisition of hostile attitude and its relation to aggressive behavior. *Journal of Personality and Social Psychology, 5,* 335–341.

Marcus-Newhall, A., Pedersen, W., Carlson, M. and Miller, N. (2000) Displaced aggression is alive and well: A meta-analytic review. *Journal of Personality and Social Psychology, 78,* 670–689.

MacDonald, G. and Leary, M. (2005) Why does social exclusion hurt? The relation between social and physical pain. *Psychological Bulletin, 131,* 202–223.

Miller, N. (1941) The frustration-aggression hypothesis. *Psychological Review, 48,* 337–342.

Miller, N. (1948) Theory and experiment relating psychoanalytic displacement to stimulus-response generalization. *Journal of Abnormal and Social Psychology, 43,* 155–178.

Miller, N. (1959). Liberalization of basic S-R concepts: Extensions to conflict behavior, motivation and social learning. In S. Koch (ed.), *Psychology: A Study of a Science, 2,* 196–292. New York: McGraw-Hill.

Nisbett, R. and Cohen, D. (1996) *Culture of Honor: The Psychology of Violence in the South.* Boulder, CO: Westview Press.

Parrott, D., Zeichner, A. and Hoover, R. (2006) Sexual prejudice and anger network activation: Mediating role of negative affect. *Aggressive Behavior, 32,* 7–16.

Passman, R. and Mulhern, R. (1977) Maternal punitiveness as affected by situational stress: An experimental analogue of child abuse. *Journal of Abnormal Psychology, 86,* 565–569.

Pedersen, W., Gonzales, C. and Miller, N. (2000) The moderating effect of trivial triggering provocation on displaced aggression. *Journal of Personality and Social Psychology, 78,* 913–927.

Quigley, B. and Tedeschi, J. (1996) Mediating effects of blame attributions on feelings of anger. *Personality and Social Psychology Bulletin, 22,* 1280–1288.

Raine, A., Dodge, K., Loeber, R., Gatzke-Kopp, L., Lynam, D., Chandra, R., Stouthamer-Loeber, M. and Lie, J. (2006) The reactive-proactive aggression questionnaire: Differential correlates of reactive and proactive aggression in adolescent boys. *Aggressive Behavior, 32,* 159–171.

Schneider, W. and Shiffrin, R. (1977) Controlled and automatic human information processing: I. Detection, search, and attention. *Psychological Review, 84,* 1–66.

Stifter, C. and Grant, W. (1993) Infant responses to frustration: Individual differences in the expression of negative affect. *Journal of Nonverbal Behavior, 17*, 187–204.

Strack. F., Martin, L. and Stepper, S. (1988) Inhibiting and facilitating conditions of the human smile: A nonobtrusive test of the facial feedback hypothesis. *Journal of Personality and Social Psychology, 54*, 768–777.

Straus, M. (1980) Stress and child abuse. In H. Kempe and R. Helfer (eds), *Stress and Child Abuse*, 3rd Edition. Chicago: University of Chicago Press.

Todorov, A. and Bargh, J. (2002) Automatic sources of aggression. *Aggression and Violent Behavior, 7*, 53–68.

Turner, C. and Berkowitz, L. (1972) Identification with film aggressor (covert role taking) and reactions to film violence. *Journal of Personality and Social Psychology, 21*, 256–264.

White, J., Moffitt, T., Caspi, A., Bartusch, D., Needles, D. and Stouthamer-Loeber, M. (1994) Measuring impulsivity and exploring the relationship to delinquency. *Journal of Abnormal Psychology, 103*, 192–205.

PART IV

Interpersonal Level of Analysis

32

Need-to-Belong Theory

Roy F. Baumeister

ABSTRACT

The motivation to form and sustain at least a minimum amount of social connections is one of the most powerful, universal, and influential human drives. It shapes emotion, cognition, and behavior. It explains self-esteem as an internal measure of one's chances of having good relationships. Different ways of satisfying the need to belong can explain gender differences in personality and roles and even reinterpret the history of gender politics, on the assumption that women emphasize close, intimate relationships whereas men are oriented toward larger networks of shallower relationships. Studies of rejection show that thwarting the need to belong produces drastic and sometimes puzzling effects, including increases in aggression and self-destructive acts, and decreases in helpfulness, cooperation, self-control, and intelligent thought. Lab rejection studies produce an emotional numbness that has pointed the way to question the basic functions of emotion and how emotion affects behavior. Culture, which is the ultimate achievement and form of human social life, depends on belongingness, and that observation offers a powerful basis for understanding human nature and many distinctively human traits.

INTRODUCTION

People have a basic need to belong. They are motivated to form and maintain social relationships. This deceptively simple idea was the topic of a review article by Mark Leary and me that kept me busy for several years in the early 1990s, up until its publication (Baumeister and Leary, 1995). It changed my thinking permanently and has formed the basis for much of my subsequent research and theorizing. That article has been cited over a thousand times in the research literature, and so perhaps it has had influence on other people as well.

The idea itself is hardly revolutionary or controversial. Of course people like to be connected to other people, by and large. Yet this simple idea led in many unexpected directions. Its influence on cognition, emotion, and behavior is extensive. Moreover, it raises important basic questions about human nature, culture, gender, emotion, and how the human psyche functions.

HOW THE PROJECT BEGAN

The crucial steps that led Leary and me to write the "need-to-belong" paper were taken in a series of conversations and exchanges in the late 1980s. Inevitably, however, one can look back and point to earlier factors that were relevant. In my own case, this includes a spirit of contrarian inquiry that has been a theme of my life and has contributed to many of my career's biggest problems and failures as well as my best successes and achievements. My (admittedly suspect) autobiographical recollection of the roots of this go back to some point in junior high school, back when I was first assigned to write papers for school. My mother taught high school and pointed out that a teacher who grades a stack of papers on an assigned topic quickly gets bored when one after another says pretty much the same thing, even if that common theme is essentially sound and correct. This occurred long before grade inflation and during the era of heavy tracking, so even in a public school the competition for top grades was intense. I realized that my chances of getting an A would be better if I could say something different from the bulk of other students' papers. I learned to think about a problem not just in terms of question and answer, or problem and solution, but also in terms of what the dominant approach might be overlooking. I wanted my ideas to be not just correct but also unusual.

The same contrarian approach can serve one well in science. If you discern what the prevailing trends and biases are, you can guess what is likely to be missed. I have followed this strategy throughout my career, by habit and now by inclination. It turns out to have risks as well as advantages. When you look where no one else is looking, you find more interesting things more easily than when you hunt in the same hunting grounds that everyone else uses. People think you're creative, because your work is different from the mainstream. But they also value it less (it is, after all, less relevant to what everyone else is working on). It is also much more likely to stray into areas deemed politically incorrect: Political correctness defines what thoughts are not supposed to be considered, and so someone who looks at what others ignore easily strays into danger of being politically incorrect, a danger that is not to be taken lightly.

My university education took place in the 1970s, when psychology was entering into what later became known as the cognitive revolution. Attribution theory was already flourishing in social psychology. The study of attitudes, especially cognitive dissonance, was at its peak as well. Both these approaches had social psychologists thinking heavily about what happens inside the person. As a contrarian, therefore, I attended to what went on between persons. Sure enough, I felt, interpersonal processes were unappreciated and understudied, and so I found a good start there. For example, where others spoke about self-esteem, I focused on self-presentation – not the self's concept of itself, but its concern with how others saw it. Indeed, in the mid 1980s, my first edited book was called *Public Self and Private Self*, in which I asked contributors to reflect on how these inner and outer processes were related.

One of the contributions to that volume was an unusual chapter by Greenberg et al. (1986). I had read some laboratory studies by two of them focusing on how interpersonal events impacted private self-esteem (Greenberg and Pyszczynski, 1985) and invited them on that basis, but instead of writing about that work, they developed a grand theory about human motivation based loosely on some anthropological writings (Becker, 1973). The chapter in my book was in fact the first publication on terror management theory, which has gone on to become quite influential. Based on this early connection, those fellows and I sought each other out at some conferences.

During the 1980s, Bibb Latané held small conferences every summer at a property he owned at Nags Head, North Carolina, on the beach. There was usually one conference on the self, and often the terror management fellows and I all attended. All three of them would be present, and so their work came to constitute a major theme those conferences. They were deliberately controversial.

A central point of their theory was that anxiety was mainly caused by fear of death. (This is the "terror" in the theory's name.)

To be sure, the evidence for terror and anxiety was never strong, and more recent formulations have downplayed the terror aspect, but initially it was central. The core idea was thus highly individualistic: A person knows that he or she is going to die, contemplates mortality, has anxiety as a result, and therefore performs a variety of behaviors to escape from this anxiety. Other people are not directly or necessarily involved in the central drama and theme of life.

One year Leary and I and Dianne Tice were all in attendance and listened to the terror management presentations. We had by now heard them multiple times. We discussed the terror management theory of anxiety. We had various reasons for wondering whether anxiety was really based on death. We did not know what anxiety researchers thought, apart from Freud's early theory that anxiety in men comes from fear of castration, and from his later theory (elaborated by Bowlby and others) that social separation is the root of anxiety.

By now I had a long habit of deliberately considering interpersonal perspectives on things, so the idea of social separation as a theory of what causes anxiety intrigued me. I thought terror nanagement theory could be made much more broadly accurate and appealing if they expanded it to include not just terror of death but also terror of social rejection. I went up to the room where the terror management fellows were staying. Pyszczynski and Solomon were in there, talking about ideas while smoking and drinking in a jovial spirit. I ran the idea by them of expanding their theory to include social exclusion and separation anxiety. They nodded, pondered, and said they liked this idea. They wanted to run it by Greenberg. The next day, however, they told me that Greenberg had vetoed the expansion: death was to be the only source of terror in their theory. I have long wondered how things would have been different had they accepted my overtures, as two of the three of them seemed inclined to do.

Our curiosity piqued and undaunted, Tice and I embarked on a literature review to learn about anxiety. The goal was just to find out what actually causes anxiety. We did find some evidence to support the terror management view: some people do have anxiety over the possibility of injury or death. But by far the biggest stimulus was fear of being rejected and abandoned by others. This evolved into a review article called "Anxiety and social exclusion" (Baumeister and Tice, 1990).

We were not sure where to publish this manuscript. C.R. Snyder had attended some of the Nags Head conferences with us and suggested we publish it in the journal he edited, the *Journal of Social and Clinical Psychology*. He said he would treat it as a target article and get commentaries from various experts. Leary wrote a commentary, as did several others, which turned into quite an intriguing exchange, marred only by an extremely hostile and defensive commentary by the terror management group. Not only were they uninterested in incorporating separation anxiety into their own theory: they rejected the very idea that anxiety could come from fear of social separation.

When this issue was finally published, I thought the episode completed, but in a conversation with Leary the next year he made a crucial comment. He said he thought that our account of anxiety as often stimulated by fear of social exclusion, though largely correct, suffered from not going far enough. He thought the concern over social belongingness versus rejection went beyond just anxiety. His comment was the crucial forward leap that led to the development of our theory.

Assembling the evidence and writing the article on "the need to belong" (Baumeister and Leary, 1995) was a powerful experience. We did not know that this would become the most-cited article that either of us had ever published. We worried at times that we were just trying to prove something that everyone already knows, which is that people are motivated to form social bonds.

Yet the extent of the evidence and the widely varying forms it took continued to surprise us. We kept coming across new find-ings and patterns that showed yet another direction where the need to belong applied. We found echoes of the need to belong in unexpected places. People form social bonds remarkably easily and readily, even just based on having experienced electric shock together in an experiment (Latané et al., 1966). They are irrationally reluctant to let bonds break, even continuing to exchange Christmas cards with people they do not know (Kunz and Woolcott, 1976). Many cog-nitive and emotional patterns are linked with interpersonal connections.

BUILDING THE BASIC THEORY

The core idea of the need to belong is that people have a fundamental, strong, and per-vasive motivation to form and maintain at least a certain minimum number of social relationships. The drawbacks of this idea included its simplicity as well as its lack of novelty. Other theorists had said that people have such a drive to form social bonds. In fact, as reviewers would soon point out, this was not an idea that anyone would vehemently disagree with. Most personality theories had at some point said that people have some sort of drive to affiliate with others.

We had therefore hardly discovered a new motivation. Rather, our contribution was to document the power and extent of this motivation. True, most personality theories had acknowledged such a drive, but it was usually in the background, treated as a rela-tively minor and uninteresting aspect of human nature. Freud, for example, had grad-ually acknowledged separation anxiety as genuine, possibly stemming from the baby's dependency on its mother, but the center-piece motivations in his theory were the sexual and aggressive drives.

The phrase "the need to belong" appealed to Leary and me because it conveyed a greater sense of power and urgency than something

like an "affiliation motive." However, the term "need" itself was potentially problem-atic. Is the need to belong truly a need, or just a want? We had to take a detour to explore metatheory: What makes a drive qualify as a need? Our answers, which were developed in the early part of the article, focused on whether actual harm would come from fail-ing to satisfy the motivation. Not getting something you *need* means more and is worse than not getting something you merely *want*. This does not necessarily predict the strength of the motivation, we realized. Sexual desire may be an extremely strong motivation, especially in some people, but ultimately it is a want rather than a need. No one dies or even gets sick from lack of sex. In fact there does not seem to be any notable harm that stems from not having sex, and some people live long, healthy, happy lives without ever having sex.

Now that we had a theory about what qualifies as a need, we had to face the question of whether our so-called need to belong would actually meet those criteria. Fortunately, the evidence was there. In fact, as we had repeatedly found while reviewing various aspects of the need to belong, the evidence was far stronger and more abundant than we had anticipated. It was not just a matter of a few potential types of harm that could be traced to severe loneliness. Rather, it seemed that the majority of mental and physical illnesses were affected in some way by a lack of social ties. For example, a review of medical research came to the shockingly broad conclusion that mortality rates for *all* major causes of death were higher among people who lacked social bonds than for people who were well connected to other people (Lynch, 1979).

Buoyed by such findings, we felt it justi-fied in asserting that the drive to connect with others was more than a mere desire. What had been up till this point our working title, "the need to belong," became official.

As usual, the paper and its ideas benefited from the journal review process. The review-ers and the journal editor, Robert Sternberg, pressed us to say just exactly what is meant by belongingness. What specifically is needed in the "need to belong"? Is it just a herd instinct, a craving for affiliation, companionship? Leary and I grappled with this, searched for new evidence, and formulated and revised various ideas. We settled on two central aspects of the need to belong. First, the person wants a framework of mutual concern and caring that extends into past and future. Second, the person wants a series of non-negative interactions. Getting either without the other should amount to half a loaf: partly but not wholly satisfactory.

The framework of mutual concern extending into past and future meant that momentary interactions would not be sufficient, no matter how intimate. The need to belong is not satisfied by any amount of social interaction without the bond. The data went along nicely with this. Toll takers on the turnpike may interact with hundreds, possibly thousands of people every day, but these very brief conversations do not satisfy the need to belong. Even prostitutes, who may have a highly intimate ("lovemaking") interaction with several dozen persons a day, do not find these satisfactory, though perhaps they are spared the loneliness of forest rangers and night watchmen (McLeod, 1982). We found evidence that some prostitutes sacrifice the best chances for making the most money in order to cultivate relationships with repeat customers (Symanski, 1980). Meanwhile, though, even without social contact, people do get some benefit from these bonds. Data on long-distance relationships showed that these often have great importance, even when there is no contact for long periods of time (Gerstel and Gross, 1982, 1984). For example, studies of married sailors, especially those in submarines, showed that the sailors and the spouses valued the connection even though six months might go by with no contact at all or at best just an occasional letter (Harrison and Connors, 1984). Thus, a bond without frequent interaction was indeed half a loaf: much more than nothing but far less than fully satisfying.

Meanwhile, what about the interactions? The long-distance relationships data indicated relatedness without interaction was missing something, so the interactions do seem to matter. Here, however, we were faced with some contrary findings that prevented us from simply emphasizing face-to-face contact as a second key. The data were strongly suggestive that when face-to-face contacts are hostile, abusive, or demoralizing, they did not produce good results. We then thought that we should stipulate that people needed the interactions to be positive and pleasant, but reviewers objected, quite reasonably we thought, that many old friends and long-married couples seem to find being together satisfying without a great deal of exuberant positivity. The dual-career couples working apart reported that they wished just to sit and watch television with each other, which is hardly an intimate or emotionally intense experience. These arguments pushed Leary and me to accept, at least tentatively, that interactions could be satisfying without being positive, as long as they were not negative. Hence we settled on the term *non-negative* to describe the sort of actions implicated in the need to belong.

Another challenge raised by the reviews was to make the need-to-belong theory look more like a standard motivational theory, insofar as we were claiming it was a standard motivation. This too presented some difficulties, for we did not have a clear sense of what a standard motivational theory should look like. Indeed, our sense was that motivational metatheory was in shambles (as it still is). Social psychologists have good and clear ideas about what cognitive theories should involve, but there is much less of an accepted paradigm for motivation theories. Still, the point was fair, and we thought we ought to try.

Two hallmarks of motivation, substitution and satiation, seemed sufficiently standard that we thought we ought to see whether they could fit into the need to belong. Substitution was easier to address than satiation. A hungry person needs food, and although the hunger might be stimulated by a picture of a hamburger, the hunger can be satisfied by salami sandwiches or spaghetti instead. Applying this logic to the need to belong, we reasoned that people must desire at least a certain minimum amount of social connection, and to some extent these bonds could substitute for each other. To be sure, they would most like to keep the bonds they have, but if they lose one relationship, having others could cushion the blow and satisfy some of the same need.

Probably romantic relationships offered the most hostile ground for testing the hypothesis of substitution, because people feel (and are encouraged by cultural messages to feel) that each love relationship is unique and irreplaceable. Yet the data on divorce pointed repeatedly in favor of replaceability. When people divorce, their proneness to all manner of dysfunctional behavior and problems goes up, and when they remarry, it goes back down, indicating that at least in terms of the behavioral and health consequences, the second marriage is an effective substitute for the first. Accounts of romantic heartbreak often feature the tragic theme that the lost love cannot be replaced and no one else will ever do, but in general the person finds someone else who is just as good, if not better (Baumeister and Wotman, 1992; Baumeister et al., 1993). Prisoners, who are forcibly removed from their main relationships, typically form new ones within the prison, sometimes amounting to fully elaborated substitute families, which are important and even cherished at the time but are generally abandoned upon release from prison (Burkhart, 1973; Giallombardo, 1966; Toch, 1977).

The idea of motivational satiation was more difficult to find evidence for (either for or against) than substitution. Satiation means that even though you desire something, at some point you get enough of it and do not want or need any more, at least for a while. Studies of university students were useful in this connection, because students are constantly exposed to other people and could in principle interact with all new people every

day, or could form any particular number of stable relationships. They seem mainly to form about four to six main friendships, so that most of their interactions stay within that circle (Wheeler and Nezlek, 1977). Satiation was also suggested in the familiar pattern that when people become deeply involved in an intense relationship, especially a romantic one, they cut back on socializing with friends, as if the one relationship is sufficiently satisfying that they feel less need for the others (e.g., Milardo et al., 1983). In general, we felt we could make a tentative case for satiation, but it was far from solid. The satiation hypothesis of belongingness theory remains relatively untested even today.

CHALLENGES FROM EXISTING THEORIES

As I said, the assumption of a need to belong was not revolutionary. Our contribution was hardly a discovery of a new drive but rather an enhanced recognition of its reach and power. Several important theories had highly relevant positions, however, and we had to deal with these, as a way of placing our work in the appropriate scholarly context.

One of the best-known motivational theories of the twentieth century was Maslow's hierarchy of needs (e.g., Maslow, 1968). He listed five needs, of which the need to belong was half of one. (He combined it with a need for love.) Moreover, it was the middle one. The middle position meant that belongingness needs had to wait until more basic physiological and safety needs were met, though they would take precedence over later ones such as self-actualization and esteem. Putting it in the middle, thought intuitively reasonable, seemed at odds with our argument that it was basic and powerful. Fortunately, most empirical efforts to test Maslow's theory have concluded that his hierarchy is not correct (e.g., Wahba and Bridwell, 1976). People do pursue satisfactions out of the sequence he specified.

This made it easy to accommodate many findings in which people seemingly jeopardize safety and forego basic animal satisfactions in order to cultivate relationships.

The competing ideas of terror management theory have already been noted. Further work from that group of theorists asserted that avoidance of death was the master motive and that all other motivations are either derivative or secondary (Psyzczynski et al., 1997). This challenged our view of the importance and primacy of the need to belong. In their view, the need to belong was at best derivative of the drive to avoid the terrifying thought of death.

We thought there are multiple reasons to give primacy to the need to belong. First, children fear and protest being left alone within the first days of life, but they do not know they will die until quite a few years later. A further and devastating set of findings was reviewed by Leary et al. (1994). They showed that a great many self-presentational behaviors cause risks or harm to health. The implication is that people do things to make a good impression on other people even if these increase one's risk of death. People sunbathe (even after they have already had skin cancer), ride motorcycles without helmets, smoke cigarettes, and do many other things that fit this category. Clearly, the need to belong sometimes empirically takes precedence over fear of death. The need to belong is not derived from fear of death.

We encountered a challenge of a different sort posed by attachment theory, as originally developed by John Bowlby (e.g., 1969, 1973). His views on the basic drive to connect were quite congenial to our ideas about the need to belong. His approach was derived in important ways from Freud's work, and his understanding of anxiety downplayed the Freudian castration scenario in favor of the more plausible ideas about separation anxiety. Did we have anything new to say beyond Bowlby's attachment theories?

There was a fundamental difference, however. True to his Freudian roots, Bowlby saw the child's relationship to the mother as the root cause of much of what came after, including adult relationships. Even adult employment, in his view, involved seeking and building a relationship to one's supervisor to reenact the erstwhile bond to the mother. In contrast, we saw the child's relationship to the mother as simply one (albeit an early and important) manifestation of the need to belong. In our view, then, the adult's need to belong, and the adult's relationships, were continued signs of the same underlying drive, rather than being a consequence of the connection to the mother.

EXTENDING THE THEORY: SELF-ESTEEM AS SOCIOMETER

As we were finalizing the manuscript and dealing with the reviews, we played around with adding a few extensions and implications to broaden the reach of the idea. At one point I slipped in a sentence or two to suggest that there was possibly a link to self-esteem. When Mark sent me back the draft, he had added a bit more, plus some references to a chapter he was going to publish. I did not realize his thinking was far more advanced than mine on this point. He had begun pulling together the basic ideas and some data for what was to become the sociometer theory. But both of us realized that the self-esteem issue was worth more than a short paragraph and could turn into a more substantial treatment – one that could take up possibly too much space in this already long paper. We agreed that we would later write another paper developing the implications for self-esteem.

The follow-up paper, which was mainly Leary's work with a few of my thoughts thrown in, addressed the question of why people care about self-esteem (Leary and Baumeister, 2000). Abundant evidence from decades of research indicated that many thoughts, emotions, and behaviors reflected a basic concern with upholding a favorable image of self. In the 1980s this had made perfect intuitive sense, because people had assumed that high self-esteem produced all manner of beneficial effects. However, the data had gradually failed to support many of those positive assumptions, leaving more and more researchers to wonder why people were so concerned with something (self-esteem) that seemed to have so few pragmatic payoffs (for later review, see Baumeister et al., 2003). One answer was that emotions were tied into self-esteem, and so one might protect self-esteem to prevent unpleasant emotions, but that did not really answer the question: Why were emotional reactions so strongly tied to something that was apparently so useless?

Belongingness offered a powerful context for making sense of self-esteem. Whereas the benefits of self-esteem were dubious and subtle, the benefits of belongingness were clear and strong, as we had found, extending even to life and death. Thus, if self-esteem were tied to belongingness, that would explain why people were so concerned with it.

The link had been established in early studies by Leary et al. (1995). Drops in self-esteem tended to be associated with reductions in belongingness, such as social rejection and the breaking of bonds. Meanwhile, increases in self-esteem were linked to increases in belongingness, such as being accepted for a new relationship or job.

The core idea, then, was that self-esteem served as a sort of mental meter to keep track of belongingness. Humans evolved to be social beings, and so they needed to be connected to each other. Social isolation carried risks to health and wellbeing (plus, obviously, to one's likely success at reproduction), and so the human psyche would benefit from having some sort of alarm go off if the person began to be socially isolated. Conversely, social acceptance would improve one's prospects for survival and reproduction, and so an inner meter that would register social acceptance in a positive manner would be adaptive. Self-esteem could serve these functions by rising and dropping in response to changes in social belongingness.

Editorial feedback on the Leary and Baumeister (2000) sociometer paper pushed us to sharpen the focus. After all, self-esteem was at best imperfectly correlated with number and closeness of interpersonal attachments; should the correlation not approach perfect unity (well, minus error variance), if that were what self-esteem were all about? Moreover, it seemed clear that emotions already reacted strongly to acceptance and rejection, with bad emotions (anxiety, grief, sadness, jealousy) associated with loss of social connection and plenty of positive ones linked to acceptance, so what was the added value of having self-esteem as a sociometer?

Our solution was to link self-esteem to the anticipated long-term probability of belongingness, not one's current status or momentary changes. Emotion was sufficient to react to momentary changes in belongingness. Self-esteem was rather a relatively stable evaluation, not of how many relationships you have, but how eligible you are to have multiple long-term relationships and other social bonds.

One persuasive indication was that the items on self-esteem scales generally measure four things, all of which seemed quite basic to social acceptance versus rejection. First, all self-esteem scales ask whether you are likable and can get along well with others, which is obviously vital to acceptance. Second, they have items to assess perceived competence, which is important for being employed or otherwise being needed by groups that must perform tasks. Third, many (though not all) scales measure (self-rated) physical attractiveness, which again is a strong determinant of whether others like to be with you. Last, some contain some items assessing moral character, which can be translated into being the sort of person who will conform to the rules of the group such as honesty, fairness, trustworthiness, reliability, and reciprocity. Thus, groups and relationships prefer likable, competent, attractive, and morally well-behaved individuals. Self-esteem is based on those same four criteria.

Viewing self-esteem as linked to one's eligibility for, or likelihood of having, good social bonds, rather than counting existing bonds, allowed theoretical room for self-deception. It may be hard for the person with no friends to believe he or she has plenty of friends, but it may be relatively easier to convince oneself that one will soon probably have friends. (The current lack of friends could be dismissed as due to bad luck, special circumstances, or indeed the poor taste of the people around here.) In self-deception, people may concentrate on fooling the meter, as it were: they convince themselves they have traits that will appeal to others without actually having to prove themselves by making these friends.

Another implication is that the focus on eligibility and probability could explain the impostor phenomenon, in which a person might hold low self-esteem despite having multiple friends and other relationships. Such a person might privately fear that, "As soon as they learn what I am really like, they will all desert and abandon me!"

The elaboration of belongingness theory into the sociometer model has implications beyond offering an explanation of self-esteem. Self-esteem is one of the most widely studied constructs in personality, motivation, and self-concept (see Baumeister et al., 2003). To suggest that its primary function involves metering interpersonal relationships and interactions is thus to propose that one of the main intrapsychic structures is driven by interpersonal events.

To me, then, the broadest implication of sociometer theory is this: *inner processes serve interpersonal functions*. In the context of social psychology of recent decades, this is a radical formulation. The prevailing assumption and approach, I believe, treat interpersonal events as a product of intrapsychic ones. That is why so much attention is given to cognition, emotion, and even brain processes: researchers assume that these will offer explanations of what happens between people. I am suggesting that the reverse is more important. What happens between people is of primary importance. What goes on inside them is essentially a set of adaptations to and consequences of the interpersonal events.

The view that inner processes serve interpersonal functions was far from my initial assumptions and theories. But I have been persuaded that it is mostly correct and in powerful, underappreciated ways. If the need to belong is indeed one of the few most basic, powerful, and pervasive motivations, then inner processes and structures may well have evolved and developed to serve it.

EXTENDING THE THEORY: GENDER DIFFERENCES IN BELONGINGNESS

Not long after we published the first paper on the need to belong, I was asked to review a manuscript by Cross and Madson (1997) applying self-construal theory to gender differences. An important cultural difference had been identified by Markus and Kitayama (1991) pertaining to self-construals, which was another term for self-knowledge or self-concepts. As they had stated, Asians tended to think of themselves as interdependent, which meant that their beliefs about themselves focused on how they were related to others, whereas Westerners had more independent self-construals, which meant emphasizing how the individual was different from and stood out from others. Cross and Madson (1997) had proposed that the same distinction could be applied to the differences between men and women in Western culture, namely that men were relatively independent whereas women were more interdependent.

The paper was well documented and well argued, but as I read it I recognized that the thrust of the arguments posed a basic challenge to our theory of the need to belong. In practice, Cross and Madson were suggesting that men did not have the need to belong, or at least not as much as women. Their work was consistent with the newly emerging cultural stereotypes depicting women as more social than men. For example, Gottman (1994) and others have asserted that women are the experts at relationships and that if men want to have good relationships, they should heed the advice and guidance of their female partners, because men do not generally have the skills and knowledge to make relationships succeed as well as women.

Cross and Madson argued, for example, that the difference in self-construals (and the underlying motivation to be social) was evident in gender differences in aggression. In a nutshell, their argument was that women avoid aggression because it could damage a relationship. If you hit or hurt someone, that person might not want to continue a relationship with you. In contrast, they suggested, men have less desire and aptitude for relationships, and so they are willing to be aggressive, undeterred by the possible damage to relationships. The theme that men lack the need to belong (especially combined with the impressive amount of evidence that Cross and Madson had compiled) was thus a fascinating challenge to the generality of the theory of the need to belong.

In general, when I review a paper that challenges my work, I try to give it the benefit of the doubt, to compensate for any negative bias that might come from feeling myself attacked. I thought Cross and Madson had made their case reasonably well even though I disagreed with the conclusion. Hence I recommended publishing the paper. I contacted the editor separately, however, and suggested that from my perspective their findings could be interpreted in a completely different manner. The editor, Nancy Eisenberg, encouraged me to write a comment on their manuscript. Kristin Sommer and I started rereviewing the papers Cross and Madson had cited, as well as searching for further evidence.

The theory we developed to account for the gender differences proposed that there are two different spheres of belongingness, reflecting two different ways of being social (Baumeister and Sommer, 1997). Most psychologists and most laypersons give priority to close, intimate relationships, and

perhaps women were indeed the experts at these. However, it is also possible to be social in larger groups and networks, and there, we thought, men might seem to be more social. Thus, men could be viewed as social beings with a need to belong, indeed as thoroughly and fundamentally as women, just in a different way.

Return, for a moment, to the issue of gender differences in aggression. There was no disputing the basic finding, replicated over and over, that men are generally more aggressive than women. But does this truly reflect a male indifference to intimate relationship? Abundant evidence was emerging that within close relationships, women were just as aggressive as men (for subsequent review article, see Archer, 2000). Thus, women are slightly more likely than men to physically attack a relationship partner or spouse – everything from a slap in the face to assault with a deadly weapon. Women also perpetrate more child abuse than men, though this was difficult to correct statistically for the vastly greater amount of time they spend with children. Still, the view that women refrain from violence for fear of jeopardizing an intimate bond was untenable. The preponderance of male violence was not found in family and love relationships but rather between relative strangers and distant acquaintances. Within large networks, men are much more likely than women to come to blows.

We argued, therefore, that the gender difference in aggression reflected not indifference but concern with social relationships. Women care about close relationships and so they are aggressive there when they feel it necessary, the same as men. But women do not care as much about the relatively distant or casual bonds in large groups and networks, whereas men do, and so mainly men are aggressive in those.

Our motivational argument received a huge boost from converging evidence with helping. Cross and Madson (1997) had recognized the extensive data indicating that men help more than women. This was a challenge to their view of women as the more social beings, and they struggled to reconcile it with their theory. Eventually, they felt it necessary to invoke the feminist clichés that women do not help because they are not socialized to help. But in our response, Sommer and I noted that the evidence of male helpfulness comes mainly from studies with strangers and large groups. Within the family or close relationship, women were plenty helpful, if anything more helpful than men. Thus, the pattern with helping (a major prosocial behavior) was the same as with aggression (a major antisocial behavior): Both men and women do it in close relationships, because both care about these, but mainly men do it in the larger social networks, because men care more about these.

An amusing moment came as Sommer and I were finalizing our manuscript and attended a conference where Leary was also speaking. I gave him the draft of our manuscript and asked him for any thoughts. The next day he told me he had read the first page of the paper, proposing that there are two separate spheres of belongingness, and immediately had the reaction that this was completely wrong ("Oh no!" were his words) and that I was taking our theory in an unfortunate, misguided, and possibly stupid direction. And then, he added, he had read the rest of our paper and become convinced by the mass of evidence that we were right!

The two papers were published together, and the contrasting interpretations stimulated a fair amount of subsequent research. In this case, the evidence has gone in favor of the need-to-belong theory: The social motivations of men extend to large groups and large networks of shallow relationships much more than women, who emphasize more the intimacy of close relationships (e.g., Benenson and Heath, 2006; Gabriel and Gardner, 1999).

The difference in ways of being social, indeed the different requirements of the two spheres of belongingness, can offer a powerful basis for explaining many of the gender differences in personality (see Baumeister, in press). For example, it is widely accepted that women are more emotionally expressive than men. Sharing feelings readily is helpful in close relationships characterized by mutual concern, caring, and support, because the better two people understand each other's feelings, the better they can care for each other. But in a large group, one may have rivals and enemies, and showing all one's feelings can be risky. Likewise, large networks are characterized more than small ones by economic exchange relationships, and a buyer or seller who shows feelings too readily may not be able to get as good a deal as the one who keeps feelings strategically hidden.

Thus, the male pattern of emotional reserve is suited for the large group, whereas the female pattern of emotional expressiveness is more suited to the small group. Similar arguments could be made about many other gender differences, such as agency versus communion, male egotism, emphasis on competence, competitiveness, hierarchy versus egalitarian sentiments, equity versus equality as preferred form of fairness, and rule-based morality versus the so-called "ethic of care" (Baumeister, in press).

Not being primarily interested in gender, I had no idea at the time that these ideas would come back later to lead to substantial further reformulations. But these would depend on a very different line of ideas descended from belongingness theory.

TESTING THE THEORY: EFFECTS OF REJECTION

While finishing up our work on the original review article on the need to belong, I began to wonder about what one might do for laboratory research. It occurred to me that if belongingness were a basic motivation and need, then thwarting it ought to produce a variety of negative, defensive, and/or adaptive reactions. I thought that one might be able to produce strong reactions in the laboratory by manipulating belongingness.

We tried priming the idea of rejection (Sommer and Baumeister, 2002), but this never worked very well, partly because it was not clear whether the priming made people worry about being rejected or made them feel like rejecting someone else. I wanted to try a live interaction study in which people would choose partners and one person might be told that no one from the group had chosen him or her, which seemed like it ought to be enough to evoke unpleasant emotion and maybe some behavioral reactions. But assembling groups and pulling this off seemed like it would be a hassle, and for that or possibly other reasons, I was unable to persuade any of my graduate students or postdoctorates to try it. Hence the idea remained on the back shelf until Jean Twenge came to work with me. Her background was in personality and she did not have strong commitments as to what to do in social psychology, so she was open to trying the rejection manipulations.

We started with a simple hypothesis about aggression. Rejected people would feel upset over being rejected, and this negative affect would translate into higher aggression. Berkowitz (1989) had recently revisited the frustration–aggression theory, one of the pillars of theory in aggression if not social psychology generally, and he concluded that all negative affect (not just frustration) could drive aggression. It was unclear precisely which negative emotions would arise from being rejected in the laboratory – frustration, disappointment, anxiety, sadness, anger, jealousy – but seemingly it should not matter. Aggression should increase regardless of which emotion mediated it.

The findings from this first investigation on rejection and aggression (Twenge et al., 2001) changed the course of my research program in ways that still affect me to this day. Behavioral manipulations and aggression measures often struggle with uncertain impact, small effects hidden by large variance, and other problems. In contrast, we got very large and reliable effects on behavior. The rejected participants were much more aggressive than the various control groups, even toward people other than those who had

rejected them. A parallel study with prosocial behavior yielded equally large effects, though that paper ended up languishing unpublished for the better part of a decade (Twenge et al., 2007) while we ran follow-up studies searching for mediators to satisfy the reviewers. Still, success attracts interest, and soon most of my graduate students wanted to start conducting studies on rejection and social exclusion. New procedures and measures were developed, and the theory about the effects of the rejection began to fill in.

There were two surprising aspects to these findings. One was the utter lack of emotion. We had reasoned that thwarting a powerful motivation such as the need to belong would elicit emotional distress, which in turn would drive the behavioral effects. Over and over, we found large, reliable behavioral effects, but the emotion was absent. We tried all manner of emotion measures. Participants refused to say that they were upset about our rejection measures. If we did get a significant difference between conditions, which was rare, it was because the socially accepted ones were slightly happy and positive, whereas the rejected ones were neutral. And even these differences never mediated the behavior.

The other surprise was why rejected people should be aggressive, especially if they are not carried away by bad feelings. Presumably rejected people should want to find new connections with others. Being aggressive is counterproductive, because people dislike aggressive persons. The optimal, rational, adaptive response to being rejected should seem to be trying to become nicer. Why do they turn aggressive instead? This question too pushed us to do further work.

NEW THEORIZING ABOUT EMOTION

Thus, we began our laboratory studies on the need to belong by assuming that emotion would be a crucial, powerful mediator of the effects of rejection, so that emotion would be the direct cause of behavior. These hypotheses consistently failed to gain support. A recent meta-analysis of nearly 200 studies concluded that rejection conditions generally produce a significant though quite small shift in emotion, away from positive and toward negative – but it typically ends in a neutral state, rather than a negative one (Blackhart et al., in press). In essence, rejected persons in the lab say they feel neither good nor bad. And, again, even those small changes in emotion fail to drive behavior. The fallout from that surprising failure has led to efforts to rethink what emotion is for and how it works.

We wondered whether our failure to find that emotion was the mediator and direct cause of behavior was specific to rejection. Rather painstakingly, we waded through all volumes of the field's premier journal, the *Journal of Personality and Social Psychology*, from 1986 to the present (DeWall et al., 2008). The results were somewhat astonishing. Of 201 studies reporting analyses for mediation of behavior by emotion, only 17 percent reported significant results (at the $p = 0.05$ level). Likewise, of 146 studies analyzing for mediation of judgment by emotion, only 18 percent achieved significance. The field's premier journal is thus relatively full of failed analyses for mediation by emotion. Apparently, somebody – authors, reviewers, or editors, or all three – expects emotion to be the direct and immediate cause of behavior. At least, researchers must disprove the default hypothesis of emotional causation before they can draw any other conclusion.

The idea that emotion is the direct cause of behavior is, we think, deeply rooted in psychological theorizing. As we began to read the literature on emotion, we found repeated evocations of the intuitively compelling theory that fear makes one flee, thereby promoting survival, and so the direct causation of behavior by emotion must have served adaptive purposes.

Yet as one takes a skeptical look at the idea that emotion directly causes behavior, it

becomes untenable, both in terms of inner gaps and inadequacies and in terms of research findings. Relatively few studies show direct effects of emotion on behavior (see, for example, Schwarz and Clore, 1996, 2007, for reviews). Even when emotion does seem to cause behavior, the addition of proper control groups seems to eliminate those effects (Baumeister et al., 2007).

The eventual result was a major reconceptualization of how emotion is linked to behavior (see Baumeister et al., 2007). Instead of direct causation, emotion seems to operate as a feedback system. After the fact, conscious emotion stimulates reflection, consideration, counterfactual replay, and other cognitive processing that can promote learning for the future. In that respect, emotion can contribute to learning and to eventual behavior change, but it is not well suited for directing behavior in the here and now. Indeed, when people do act based on current emotional state, the results are often self-defeating and maladaptive (e.g., Baumeister and Scher, 1988; Leith and Baumeister, 1996).

Even so, the lack of overt emotion in response to rejection manipulations in our studies remained puzzling. A feedback theory as well as intuition would predict that people would have strong emotional reactions to being rejected, even if these did not serve the purpose of driving behavior. Some reviewers began to grumble that we must be doing something wrong if we failed to elicit emotional distress with our manipulations of social exclusion.

A possible answer came based on several other lines of work. Panksepp (1998, 2005) had proposed dating back to the 1970s that when animals began to evolve in the direction of being social, new inner mechanisms were needed to react to social events. Instead of creating wholly new ones, evolution piggybacked the social functions onto the existing structures that registered pleasure and pain. This raised the possibility that social trauma might produce effects resembling physical trauma, including a brief numbness in a state of shock that would allow the animal to finish the battle or complete its escape despite being injured, without being crippled by intense pain. Might social rejection produce the same sort of numbness?

A remarkable article by MacDonald and Leary (2005) reviewed evidence, mostly from the animal literature, on the effects of social exclusion and rejection on physical pain. Sure enough, animals appeared to go numb to physical pain as a result of being excluded by the social group. For example, rat pups ejected from the litter become relatively insensitive to pain.

Intrigued by this possibility, we purchased a device for administering and calibrating physical pain and began to measure how reactions changed when we thwarted the need to belong. To our surprise, pain sensitivity diminished quickly and substantially in response to our laboratory manipulations of rejection. Crucially, and consistent with Panksepp's theory, we found that emotional responses diminished in step with the analgesia.

Apparently, social exclusion causes the body to go numb, both physically and emotionally. The emotional numbness extended even to things bearing no meaningful connection to the rejection, such as predicting one's emotional state as a function of the outcome of next month's big football game, or empathizing with the plight of a fellow student whose leg was broken (DeWall and Baumeister, 2006). Thus, rejected people did not even show the widely replicated patterns of affective forecasting (i.e., predictions of one's own future emotional reactions), in which people overestimate their emotional responses (Wilson and Gilbert, 2003).

Still, it seemed intuitively likely that people would be somewhat upset by being rejected in our studies. Perhaps the shock and numbness response suppressed conscious emotion, but there still ought to be nonconscious reactions. We therefore began to test the effects of exclusion manipulations on implicit measures of emotion. One idea, for example, was that people would react to exclusion by actively suppressing their emotions, so that they would

report no emotion, but their implicit reactions would exhibit considerable distress.

The results of this line of investigation shocked us so much that we ended up replicating them over and over, using different measures and different manipulations (but always getting the same result). Social exclusion did not increase nonconscious distress. It did, however, increase nonconscious positive emotions. Participants who underwent our rejection manipulations showed an increase in the accessibility of affectively positive thoughts and associations. Negative thoughts and associations did not differ between rejection and control conditions (Twenge et al., 2007).

Apparently, when bad things happen, the human psyche copes in the short run by some biochemical response (presumably involving the release of opioids) to create numbness so that the immediate emotional reaction is dampened and forestalled. Meanwhile, the nonconscious mind begins searching for happy thoughts and associations. Thus, when the numbness wears off and the emotion can begin to be felt, it is somewhat reduced by the positive thoughts that have been dragooned in the mean time.

HUMAN NATURE AND CULTURE

The theory about the need to belong led slowly toward a rethinking of human nature itself. The impetus for this was a book that sought to package psychology's message for a broader, interdisciplinary audience. It was dismaying to realize that when scholars in other fields want to use psychology in their work, they still sometimes rely on Freud's system. I thought it would be useful to read through our field's laboratory findings and compile a new, integrated, systematic account of human nature.

The project proceeded piecemeal. I had no overarching ideas of how the human psyche was put together. I organized my search based on questions, not answers. The questions were the ones that I thought scholars in other fields would want to know from psychology: What do people want? How do they think? What do their emotions do? How do people act? How do they interact? And how do they grow up and turn out? I amassed plenty of specific facts and conclusions but the broad, integrative insight I sought eluded me until very late in the project.

A long tradition of psychological and even philosophical theory (through Freud, 1930, and back to the philosopher Rousseau) had emphasized the basic conflicts between individual and society. I had accepted and written about this conflict (Baumeister, 1986a, 1987). Yet the idea of basic hostility between person and society did not square well with the outlines of the human psyche I had documented. Instead, the patterns of wanting, thinking, feeling, and acting seemed designed to facilitate interactions with culture, rather than avoid it or cope with its deficiencies.

This brought me back to the lesson from sociometer theory: *inner processes serve interpersonal functions.* Perhaps the main parts of the human psyche, especially its uniquely human parts, were chiefly designed to enable people to interact with each other. The basic fact of human existence is not conflict but rather cooperation between individual and society.

The statement that humans are social animals had been made by thinkers from Aristotle to Aronson, and the phrase "social animal" has become standard in social psychology. It is true that humans are social animals, but I felt this did not go far enough. There are many social animals. What sets humans apart is the highly advanced form of social life we have developed, specifically culture. And so my organizing principle became the idea that humans are cultural animals (Baumeister, 2005).

Was it plausible? A long tradition has assumed that people evolved physically first and then invented culture. I was suggesting,

instead, that the progressively advancing demands of ever more complex social life may have helped pull physical evolution to develop greater capabilities, indeed the features that make us human. I discovered that other theorists had begun to argue for coevolution of culture and physical capabilities (Boyd and Richerson, 1985).

Meanwhile, ethologists were beginning to argue that rudimentary forms of culture could be observed in multiple other species (De Waal, 2001). If culture existed in other species, then it may have been on the planet before humans did. This brought a crucial implication that no one seemed to have noted. If culture were here before humankind, then culture might easily have been part of the selection environment in which humans evolved. That meant that culture could well have shaped the evolution of human capabilities. Culture could have shaped nature.

A remarkable program of research by Dunbar (1993, 1998) had produced revolutionary ideas about human intelligence. Intelligence has a special place in theories of human nature because humans have named our own species (*Homo sapiens*) after our intelligence. Like most scholars, I had assumed that human intelligence had evolved for solving problems in the physical environment, such as finding food and outsmarting predators. Dunbar tested a variety of such theories and found no support for them. Instead, he found that brain size was linked to the size and complexity of social networks, which he dubbed the "social brain" hypothesis. Although he had not included humans in his studies, the implications are there in spades. Our intelligence was not developed for outsmarting the bears and rabbits, but for understanding each other.

All this cast the need to belong in a new light. To be sure, plenty of animals have a sort of herd instinct that prompts them to be together. They are safer that way. But for humans, social interaction goes beyond a herd instinct. Social interaction (including culture) is humankind's biological strategy.

Humans form relationships, not just intimate bonds but larger social structures with diverse roles, shared information, and even market economies, because these are what have brought the remarkable biological success of our species.

Culture is thus a new way of being social. The human need to belong entails more than just wanting to be near other people. Combined with the improved information processing capacity, it enables people to make culture. And of course the information processing capacity itself is mainly used for dealing with social information also, especially including work and employment.

The cultural animal perspective does put me once again out of step with the prevailing trends in our field, and so I seem condemned to remain a contrarian. These days, the biggest new thrust of research is to explore the brain. I support brain research, but I also think that most psychologists greatly overestimate what is to be learned from it. My impression is that many psychologists believe that studying the brain will reveal the fundamental root causes and ultimate explanations of human behavior. That is why they are willing to suspend research on observing actual behavior in order to focus on brain imaging. They think social behaviors and interactions follow from what happens in the brain.

I think it is the other way around. The brain will gradually be revealed to be a mere switchboard, not the ultimate cause. The ultimate causes lie in social interaction, and the brain evolved as it did in order to facilitate those interactions. The brain is the hardware for inner processes, and inner processes serve interpersonal functions. My prediction is that within a couple decades, after we have mapped out all the various sites and activities in the brain, we will realize that we have not explained social behavior – that in fact we need to take another earnest look at social interaction in order to understand why the brain is the way it is. Relationships are not created by the brain; rather, the brain was created to serve relationships.

MEN, WOMEN, AND CULTURE

Understanding the centrality of culture to human nature pointed the way toward a reconsideration of gender differences. Ultimately, these lines of thought could offer the basis for a sweeping reconceptualization of gender politics, which in recent decades has become dominated by the view that men oppressed women as a main theme of world history.

Earlier I sketched out the theory and evidence about two spheres of belongingness. The core idea was that male and female psyches had slightly different versions of the need to belong, with the women focused primarily on close, intimate relationships and the men orienting more toward larger networks of shallower relationships.

Cultural progress depended on large networks of shallow relationships, because these offer fertile opportunities for sharing information, disseminating innovations, and creating wealth via economic trade (see Baumeister, 2005). Let us assume that prehistoric humans divided their social worlds to some extent into male and female spheres (possibly based on the hunter-gatherer and other task differentiations) and that the separate social worlds took the form favored by most people in them. The women's sphere would be one of close, intimate relationships and pair bonds, whereas the male sphere would develop larger networks of shallower relationships. The male sphere would thus offer a more viable ground than the female sphere for culture to develop.

Hence wealth, knowledge, and power were largely created in the male sphere. This is what accounted for the emergence of gender inequality. It was neither that men had superior talents and abilities, nor that men banded together to conspire to oppress women. (These have been the two main explanations.) It was simply that the male sphere made progress while the women's sphere remained essentially static, because of the different types of social relationships favored by the respective genders. The men's large networks of shallow relationships are not as satisfying or as nurturant as the intimate bonds cultivated by women, but they are conducive to the requirements of cultural progress, such as dissemination of information, competitive innovation, and economic exchange.

I see this line of thought as representing the opportunity for a truce in the so-called battle of the sexes (see Baumeister, 2007, in press). It is not necessary to regard one gender as superior to other, nor to postulate that men and women were fundamentally enemies and rivals, with men becoming oppressors and women victims. Rather, by inclination and social structure, men and women made separate contributions to the group's and indeed the species' welfare. Women provided the vital relationships that enabled the species to reproduce itself and thus to survive, whereas men competed in larger networks and gradually produced most of the advances that made cultural progress. Men and women have been partners more than enemies. Culture advanced not by men banding together against women, but mainly by groups of men competing against other groups of men.

Thus, based on the theory of the need to belong, one can formulate a kinder and gentler account of gender politics. Instead of seeing men as oppressors and women as victims, one can understand the genders as working together. Men's relationships may be less emotionally nurturant and intimately satisfying as female relationships, but they provide alternative advantages. Perhaps the most important of these advantages is that they foster the kinds of interactions and exchanges that make culture possible and enable it to make progress.

APPLICATIONS AND IMPLICATIONS

Although my goal in this and other theories has been to understand people rather than to change the world, there are assorted implications and potential applications.

Most obviously, the findings about the bad effects of rejection indicate the importance of fostering an inclusive society and enabling people to find ways to feel connected with others. Socially excluded people have responded in our laboratory studies with increased aggression, reduced helpfulness, and cooperation with poor self-control, with self-defeating behavior, and with impairments in intellectual performance. Indeed, sociologists have frequently observed that excluded minority groups in many societies exhibit just such socially maladaptive patterns of poor school and intellectual performance, violence and crime, and lack of prosocial activity. Although these behaviors are sometimes regarded as the basis for excluding them, exclusion appears to be a causal factor in exacerbating and even producing those patterns.

Hence one practical implication for societies and organizations is to ensure that all, including those at the bottom, are encouraged to feel accepted and included. It may be tempting for those at the top of the hierarchy to feel that they matter the most, but the destructive responses by those who feel excluded can cause significant costs to all.

Another implication for clinicians and others is that people seem to need at least a minimum number of (perhaps four) close relationships before the need is reasonably satisfied. Simply counting the number of people a person feels close to may be a useful first step in understanding that person's life, world, and prognosis. As to what people are working on in life, those with too few relationships will likely give high priority to finding new bonds, whereas those who are well connected may scarcely give that project another thought. In this modern era of small families, single-person households, and transient relationships, more and more time and energy are likely to be devoted to the task of making social connections.

The new understanding of gender politics also suggests important changes for society. The societal quest to eliminate all gender differences in achievement is likely to remain futile. Assuming that all gender differences stem from male oppression and can be cured by benefiting women is likewise going to lead to disappointment. Meanwhile, society's efforts to change everything for the benefit of women and girls may begin to have harmful effects on boys and men, as is already abundantly evident in American schools. Instead of seeing men and women as basically identical sorts of beings who are political enemies, it may be preferable to regard them as slightly different sorts of creatures who make good partners.

CONCLUSION

The theory of the need to belong has evolved from a simple insight about desiring togetherness into a large complex of interrelated ideas. These address fundamental questions about human nature, culture, gender, emotion, and the relation between inner and interpersonal processes.

The work is far from complete, and further advances seem likely. Some aspects of the basic theory, such as whether people become satiated when they have enough relationships, remain open questions for further work. But given how the theory has developed from relatively unforeseen connections and findings, it seems reckless to predict where it will go next.

Ultimately, it seems vital for psychology to rediscover an appreciation for what happens between people. What happens inside them is important also, but often it happens because of what happens between them. Inner processes serve interpersonal functions. The need to belong is a fundamental and powerful fact about human nature.

REFERENCES

Archer, J. (2000) Sex differences in aggression between heterosexual partners: A meta-analytic review. *Psychological Bulletin, 126*, 697–702.

Baumeister, R.F. (1986a) *Identity: Cultural Change and the Struggle for Self*. New York: Oxford University Press.

Baumeister, R.F. (ed.) (1986b) *Public Self and Private Self*. New York: Springer-Verlag.

Baumeister, R.F. (1987) How the self became a problem: A psychological review of historical research. *Journal of Personality and Social Psychology, 52*, 163–176.

Baumeister, R.F. (2005) *The Cultural Animal: Human Nature, Meaning, and Social Life*. New York: Oxford University Press.

Baumeister, R.F. (2007) Is there anything good about men? Invited address presented to the American Psychological Association, San Francisco, August.

Baumeister, R.F. (2010) *Is There Anything Good About Men? How Cultures Flourish by Exploiting Men*. New York: Oxford University Press.

Baumeister, R.F., Campbell, J.D., Krueger, J.I. and Vohs, K.D. (2003) Does high self-esteem cause better performance interpersonal success, happiness, or healthier lifestyles? *Psychological Science in the Public Interest, 4*, 1–44.

Baumeister, R.F. and Leary, M.R. (1995) The need to belong: Desire for interpersonal attachments as a fundamental human motivation. *Psychological Bulletin, 117*, 497–529.

Baumeister, R.F. and Scher, S.J. (1988) Self-defeating behavior patterns among normal individuals: Review and analysis of common self-destructive tendencies. *Psychological Bulletin, 104*, 3–22.

Baumeister, R.F. and Sommer, K.L. (1997) What do men want? Gender differences and two spheres of belongingness: Comment on Cross and Madson (1997). *Psychological Bulletin, 122*, 38–44.

Baumeister, R.F. and Tice, D.M. (1990) Anxiety and social exclusion. *Journal of Social and Clinical Psychology, 9*, 165–195.

Baumeister, R.F., Vohs, K.D., DeWall, C.N. and Zhang, L. (2007) How emotion shapes behavior: Feedback, anticipation, and reflection, rather than direct causation. *Personality and Social Psychology Review, 11*, 167–203.

Baumeister, R.F. and Wotman, S.R. (1992) *Breaking Hearts: The Two Sides of Unrequited Love*. New York: Guilford Press.

Baumeister, R.F., Wotman, S.R. and Stillwell, A.M. (1993) Unrequited love: On heartbreak, anger, guilt, scriptlessness, and humiliation. *Journal of Personality and Social Psychology, 64*, 377–394.

Becker, E. (1973) *The Denial of Death*. New York: Free Press.

Benenson, J.F. and Heath, A. (2006) Boys withdraw more in one-on-one interactions, whereas girls withdraw more in groups. *Developmental Psychology*, *42*, 272–282.

Berkowitz, L. (1989) Frustration-aggression hypothesis: Examination and reformulation. *Psychological Bulletin*, *106*, 59–73.

Blackhart, G.C., Knowles, M.L., Nelson, B.C. and Baumeister, R.F. (in press) Rejection elicits emotional reactions but neither causes immediate distress nor lowers self-esteem: A meta-analytic review of 192 studies on social exclusion. *Personality and Social Psychology Review*.

Bowlby, J. (1969) *Attachment and Loss. Vol. 1: Attachment*. New York: Basic Books.

Bowlby, J. (1973) *Attachment and Loss. Vol. 2: Separation Anxiety and Anger*. New York: Basic Books.

Boyd, R. and Richerson, P.J. (1985) *Culture and the Evolutionary Process*. Chicago: University of Chicago Press.

Burkhart, K. (1973) *Women in Prison*. Garden City, NY: Doubleday.

Cross, S.E. and Madson, L. (1997) Models of the self: Self-construals and gender. *Psychological Bulletin*, *122*, 5–37.

De Waal, F. (2001) *The Ape and the Sushi Master: Cultural Reflections of a Primatologist*. New York: Basic Books.

DeWall, C.N. and Baumeister, R.F. (2006) Alone but feeling no pain: Effects of social exclusion on physical pain tolerance and pain threshold, affective forecasting, and interpersonal empathy. *Journal of Personality and Social Psychology*, *91*, 1–15.

DeWall, C.N., Baumeister, R.F. and Bushman, B.J. (2008) How frequently does emotion mediate behavior: A survey of articles in the *Journal of Personality and Social Psychology*. Manuscript submitted for publication.

Dunbar, R.I.M. (1993) Coevolution of neocortical size, group size, and language in humans. *Behavioral and Brain Sciences*, *16*, 681–694.

Dunbar, R.I.M. (1998) The social brain hypothesis. *Evolutionary Anthropology*, *6*, 178–190.

Freud, S. (1930) *Civilization and Its Discontents* (J. Riviere, trans.). London: Hogarth Press.

Gabriel, S. and Gardner, W.L. (1999) Are there 'his' and 'her' types of interdependence? The implications of gender differences in collective and relational interdependence for affect, behavior, and cognition. *Journal of Personality and Social Psychology*, *75*, 642–655.

Gerstel, N. and Gross, H. (1982) Commuter marriages: A review. *Marriage and Family Review*, *5*, 71–93.

Gerstel, N. and Gross, H. (1984) *Commuter Marriage: A Study of Work and Family*. New York: Guilford Press.

Giallombardo, R. (1966) *Society of Women: A Study of a Women's Prison*. New York: Wiley.

Gottman, J.M. (1994) *What Predicts Divorce?* Hillsdale, NJ: Erlbaum.

Greenberg, J. and Pyszczynski, T. (1985) Compensatory self-inflation: A response to the threat to self-regard of public failure. *Journal of Personality and Social Psychology*, *49*, 273–280.

Greenberg, J., Pyszczynski, T. and Solomon, S. (1986) The causes and consequences of self-esteem: A terror management theory. In R. Baumeister (ed.), *Public and Private Self*. New York: Springer-Verlag.

Harrison, A.A. and Connors, M.M. (1984) Groups in exotic environments. In L. Berkowitz (ed.), *Advances in Experimental Social Psychology*, *18*, 49–87. New York: Academic Press.

Kunz, P.R. and Woolcott, M. (1976) Season's greetings: From my status to yours. *Social Science Research*, *5*, 269–278.

Latané, B., Eckman, J. and Joy, V. (1966) Shared stress and interpersonal attraction. *Journal of Experimental Social Psychology Supplement*, *1*, 80–94.

Leary, M.R. (1990) Responses to social exclusion: Social anxiety, jealousy, loneliness, depression, and low self-esteem. *Journal of Social and Clinical Psychology*, *9*, 221–229.

Leary, M.R. and Baumeister, R.F. (2000) The nature and function of self-esteem: Sociometer theory. In M. Zanna (ed.), *Advances in Experimental Social Psychology*, *32*, 1–62. San Diego: Academic Press.

Leary, M.R., Tambor, E.S., Terdal, S.K. and Downs, D.L. (1995) Self-esteem as an interpersonal monitor: The sociometer hypothesis. *Journal of Personality and Social Psychology*, *68*, 518–530.

Leary, M.R., Tchividjian, L.R. and Kraxberger, B.E. (1994) Self-presentation can be hazardous to your health: Impression management and health risk. *Health Psychology*, *13*, 461–470.

Leith, K.P. and Baumeister, R.F. (1996) Why do bad moods increase self-defeating behavior? Emotion, risk taking, and self-regulation. *Journal of Personality and Social Psychology*, *71*, 1250–1267.

Lynch, J.J. (1979) *The Broken Heart: The Medical Consequences of Loneliness*. New York: Basic Books.

MacDonald, G. and Leary, M.R. (2005) Why does social exclusion hurt? The relationship between social and physical pain. *Psychological Bulletin*, *131*, 202–223.

Markus, H.R. and Kitayama, S. (1991) Culture and the self: Implications for cognition, emotion, and motivation. *Psychological Review*, *98*, 224–253.

Maslow, A.H. (1968) *Toward a Psychology of Being*. New York: Van Nostrand.

McLeod, E. (1982) *Women Working: Prostitution Today*. London: Croom Helm.

Milardo, R.M., Johnson, M.P. and Huston, T.L. (1983) Developing close relationships: Changing patterns of interaction between pair members and social networks. *Journal of Personality and Social Psychology, 44*, 964–976.

Panksepp, J. (1998) *Affective Neuroscience: The Foundations of Human and Animal Emotions*. New York: Oxford University Press.

Panksepp, J. (2005) Why does separation distress hurt? Comment on MacDonald and Leary (2005). *Psychological Bulletin, 131*, 24–230.

Pyszczynski, T., Greenberg, J. and Solomon, S. (1997) Why do we need what we need? A terror management perspective on the roots of human social motivation. *Psychological Inquiry, 8*, 1–20.

Schwarz, N. and Clore, G.L. (1996) Feelings and phenomenal experiences. In E.T. Higgins and A. Kruglanski (eds), *Social Psychology: Handbook of Basic Principles*, pp. 433–465. New York: Guilford Press.

Schwarz, N. and Clore, G.L. (2007) Feelings and phenomenal experiences. In E.T. Higgins and A. Kruglanski (eds), *Social Psychology: Handbook of Basic Principles*, 2nd Edition. New York: Guilford Press.

Sommer, K.L. and Baumeister, R.F. (2002) Self-evaluation, persistence, and performance following implicit rejection: The role of trait self-esteem. *Personality and Social Psychology Bulletin, 28*, 926–938.

Symanski, R. (1980) Prostitution in Nevada. In E. Muga (ed.), *Studies in Prostitution*, pp. 246–279. Nairobi: Kenya Literature Bureau.

Toch, H. (1977) *Living in Prison: The Ecology of Survival*. New York: Free Press.

Twenge, J.M., Baumeister, R.F., DeWall, C.N., Ciarocco, N.J. and Bartels, J.M. (2007) Social exclusion decreases prosocial behavior. *Journal of Personality and Social Psychology, 92*, 56–66.

Twenge, J.M., Baumeister, R.F., Tice, D.M. and Stucke, T.S. (2001) If you can't join them, beat them: Effects of social exclusion on aggressive behavior. *Journal of Personality and Social Psychology, 81*, 1058–1069.

Wahba, M.A. and Bridwell, L.G. (1976) Maslow reconsidered: A review of research on the need hierarchy theory. *Organizational Behavior and Human Performance, 15*, 212–240.

Wheeler, L. and Nezlek, J. (1977) Sex differences in social participation. *Journal of Personality and Social Psychology, 35*, 742–754.

Wilson, T.D. and Gilbert, D.T. (2003) Affective forecasting. In M.P. Zanna (ed.), *Advances in Experimental Social Psychology, 35*, 345–411. San Diego: Academic Press.

33

Sociometer Theory

Mark R. Leary

ABSTRACT

Sociometer theory proposes that self-esteem is a psychological gauge of the degree to which people perceive that they are relationally valued and socially accepted by other people. In conceptualizing self-esteem as the output of a system that monitors and responds to interpersonal acceptance and rejection, sociometer theory differs from most other explanations of self-esteem in suggesting that people neither need self-esteem nor are motivated to pursue it for its own sake. Rather, according to the theory, when people do things that appear intended to protect or increase their self-esteem, their goal is usually to protect and enhance their relational value and, thus, increase the likelihood of interpersonal acceptance. This chapter reviews previous conceptualizations of self-esteem, examines the development and details of sociometer theory, and reviews research evidence that supports three central predictions of the theory – that acceptance and rejection influence state self-esteem, state self-esteem relates to perceived social acceptance, and trait self-esteem reflects people's perceptions of their general acceptability or relational value. Common objections to sociometer theory are also addressed, along with implications of the theory for clinical and societal interventions.

INTRODUCTION

Self-esteem ranks among the most widely studied constructs in the social and behavioral sciences. More than 30,000 articles and chapters have been published that include the term, "self-esteem," in their title or abstract, and hundreds of thousands more have undoubtedly included some mention of self-esteem. Such a level of scholarly interest suggests that theorists, researchers, and practitioners have regarded self-esteem as an exceptionally important construct, one that helps to explain a great deal of human thought, emotion, and behavior. Fascination with self-esteem has crept into the public mind as well. Not only is self-esteem a frequent topic of popular books and magazine articles, but also most people seem to believe that self-esteem is an essential ingredient in happiness, wellbeing, and success.

Oddly, despite all of the attention, throughout most of the twentieth century, few theorists made an effort to explain why self-esteem is psychologically important, what it actually does, or why it is worthy of so much attention. Sociometer theory was offered in an effort to explain the function of self-esteem and to account for its known relationships with an array of psychological phenomena.

INTELLECTUAL BACKGROUND

Early ideas about self-esteem

Within psychology, self-esteem made its first notable appearance in James' (1890) textbook, *Psychology*. In his chapter on the self, James discussed the feelings that are associated with "self-appreciation" (by which he meant self-evaluation). According to James, the primary causes of people's self-feelings involve their "actual success or failure, and the good or bad actual position one holds in the world" (1890: 182). Yet, he also noted that self-esteem depends not only on people's actual outcomes in life but also on how they judge their outcomes relative to their aspirations. He offered a simple formula suggesting that self-esteem reflects the ratio of one's successes to one's pretensions and observed that people can change their own self-feelings because "such a fraction may be increased as well by diminishing the denominator as by increasing the numerator" (1890: 187). Although James suggested that people wish to feel good rather than bad about themselves, he did not discuss the functions that self-esteem might serve.

Most subsequent writers have followed James' lead, offering ideas about the causes and consequences of self-esteem without entertaining the question of why people have the capacity for self-esteem or what functions it might serve. For example, Rogers (1959) viewed self-esteem as a consequence of the degree to which people receive positive regard from other people. He suggested that people instinctively need both positive regard (e.g., love, affection, attention, nurturance) from other people and positive self-regard (i.e., self-

esteem) in order to become fully functioning. However, because positive regard often depends on behaving in a particular way or being a particular kind of person, people bend themselves in ways that are contrary to their natural inclinations and best interests to obtain it. In the process, self-regard also becomes conditional so that people feel good about themselves only when they meet other people's standards rather than when they actualize their own potentials. Although people who act against their own interests, values, personality, and inclinations probably fare more poorly than those who behave congruently with their inclinations, Rogers and other humanistic theorists did not articulate the role of self-esteem in this process, which can be explained in terms of conformity to social pressures that are incongruent with one's inclinations without invoking the concept of self-esteem at all.

Once the assumption that people need self-esteem became established, theorists began to explain certain behaviors in terms of people's quest for self-esteem. Branden (1969) in particular stressed the role that the basic "need" for self-esteem plays in human behavior. More than most theorists, Branden's view of self-esteem was particularly nonsocial, with the basic "pillars" of self-esteem residing in intrapsychic processes involving self-awareness, integrity, personal responsibility, and being honest with oneself (Branden, 1983).

Functional explanations of self-esteem

Based on the work on Rogers (1959), Branden (1969), and others, the notion that people have a need for self-esteem became a well-entrenched assumption, but few writers addressed the broader question of why people need self-esteem, what it does, or why deficiencies in self-esteem seem to be associated with poor mental health. However, during the 1970s and 1980s, three broad functional perspectives on the nature of self-esteem emerged.

Self-esteem promotes adaptive behavior and psychological wellbeing

The most widely espoused explanation of self-esteem's function suggested that self-esteem promotes psychological wellbeing and success (Bandura, 1977; Greenwald, 1980; Taylor and Brown, 1988). Evidence that self-esteem correlates with happiness and success led many to conclude that self-esteem facilitates positive outcomes. For example, research showed that people with high self-esteem perform better after failure than people with low self-esteem and are also more likely to persevere in the face of obstacles (Perez, 1973; Shrauger and Sorman, 1977). Furthermore, studies showed that trait self-esteem was associated with greater success in academics (Bowles, 1999; Hansford and Hattie, 1982) and social life (Glendinning and Inglis, 1999; LePine and Van Dyne, 1998). Such findings led many to conclude that high self-esteem promotes a variety of positive outcomes and that people seek self-esteem for these benefits. In general, theorists did not explain why self-esteem is related to such outcomes, but at the time the connection seemed indisputable (Taylor and Brown, 1988).

However, this explanation of self-esteem has at least three weaknesses. First, it does not explain why merely feeling good about oneself leads to positive outcomes. Many of these explanations confused self-esteem (valenced feelings about oneself) with self-efficacy (the belief that one is capable of achieving desired outcomes). Although beliefs regarding one's own efficacy promote motivation, perseverance, and positive emotion (Bandura, 1977; Cervone et al., 2006), whether merely feeling good about oneself enhances goal-directed behavior is less clear.

Second, reviews of the literature on the relationship between self-esteem and positive outcomes – including achievement, interpersonal success, adjustment, and social problems – showed that the relationships are far weaker than typically assumed (Baumeister et al., 2003; Mecca et al., 1989). This fact does not dispute that high self-esteem might be associated with beneficial outcomes, but it raises questions regarding whether the function of the self-esteem motive is to facilitate outcomes such as these.

Third, many theorists fell victim to the fallacy of inferring causality from correlation. Virtually all evidence showing that self-esteem is associated with positive outcomes is correlational, yet many writers concluded that self-esteem was the causal factor. Few writers entertained the possibility that self-esteem was caused by positive outcomes, such as academic or social success or that self-esteem, positive emotions, and behavioral effectiveness are coeffects of some other process (Baumeister et al., 2003).

Self-esteem signals dominance or status

A second perspective was proposed in different ways by Tedeschi and Norman (1985) and Barkow (1980) who suggested that self-esteem is an indicator of the degree to which a person has influence or dominance over others. Tedeschi and Norman (1985) suggested that feelings of self-esteem indicate to people that they have influence or power over others and, thus, people seek self-esteem because it is a reinforcer that is associated "with the facilitation of social influence and the attainment of rewards" (1985: 310). Put differently, people seek self-esteem because the behaviors that lead to high self-esteem are associated with having influence over others.

Barkow (1980) rooted a similar explanation in evolutionary ethology. To the extent that being dominant in one's social group would have been associated with greater access to mates and other resources during evolutionary history, the tendency to monitor and increase one's relative social standing would confer fitness benefits. As human beings developed the capacity for self-relevant thought, they may have developed mechanisms for evaluating and enhancing their relative dominance. To the extent that self-esteem is associated with having status and being dominant, people may seek self-esteem not because it has any inherent value but rather because it connotes dominance.

Little research has directly examined the hypothesis that self-esteem monitors dominance, although studies show that dominant people tend to have higher trait self-esteem than less dominant people (Heaven, 1986; Leary et al., 2001; Raskin et al., 1991). Furthermore, two experimental studies that manipulated participants' perceptions of their dominance (by varying the degree to which they believed that other participants wanted them to be group leader) showed that perceived dominance influences state self-esteem. Although the notion that self-esteem is linked to the exercise of status and dominance may have some merit, these explanations do not fully account for all of the factors that influence self-esteem or explain all instances in which people appear to seek to enhance their self-esteem (Leary et al., 2001).

Self-esteem lowers existential anxiety

Terror management theory focuses on the psychological and behavioral tactics that people use to ward off the existential terror that they experience at the prospect of their own death and annihilation (Solomon et al., 1991). According to terror management theory, self-esteem lowers paralyzing terror because death-related anxiety is reduced by the belief that one is a valuable individual in a meaningful universe, and high self-esteem is related to the belief that one is living up to important cultural values (Pyszczynski et al., 2004). Thus, people with high self-esteem feel assured that they will achieve immortality – either literally in terms of going to heaven or being reincarnated, or symbolically in that their impact will remain after they die. In either case, self-esteem buffers them against the anxiety they would otherwise feel.

Like dominance theory, terror management theory moved away from the longstanding assumption that people need self-esteem for its own sake to the idea that people seek self-esteem because it serves an important function. Furthermore, like dominance theory, terror management theory provides a cogent explanation for why self-esteem is linked to

one's social standing in other people's eyes: the anxiety-buffering mechanism is effective only to the extent that people believe that they are a person-of-value according to the standards of their culture.

As a broad theory of the pervasive effects of existential concerns on human behavior, terror management theory has much to recommend it, and a great deal of research has supported its central propositions (Pyszczynski et al., 2004). However, its explanation of self-esteem may have the weakest empirical support. Although self-esteem is associated with anxiety as the theory predicts, this finding can be explained by virtually every other theory of self-esteem as well (Leary, 2004).

Key issues

Each of these perspectives offers insights regarding the nature of self-esteem, but each leaves many unanswered questions, and none addresses all known patterns of findings. Two issues remain particularly problematic. First, most theorists have assumed that self-esteem reflects a private self-evaluation in which people compare themselves with either their personal standards or an idealized sense of self. Yet, research shows that self-esteem is as strongly related to people's beliefs about other people's perceptions and evaluations of them as to their own self-perceptions, if not more so (Leary and Baumeister, 2000). If self-esteem reflects people's private self-evaluations, divorced from interpersonal concerns, then why do others' evaluations affect self-esteem so strongly? If asked, most theorists would either echo Cooley's (1902) notion that people use social feedback to draw inferences about their characteristics or maintain that basing one's self-esteem on others' judgments reflects an unhealthy dependence on other people's opinions (Bednar et al., 1989; Deci and Ryan, 1995; May, 1983; Rogers, 1959).

Second, these perspectives share the view that the motive to enhance and protect one's self-esteem is generally beneficial, even if doing so requires people to hold self-serving illusions about themselves (Taylor and Brown, 1988). However, others have suggested that self-serving biases are maladaptive because misperceiving one's capabilities and goodness sets one up for behavioral miscalculations and maladjustment (Branden, 1969; Colvin and Block, 1994; Robins and Beer, 2001). If we assume that adjustment and success require people to estimate their attributes and abilities reasonably accurately, overestimating one's competence, making excuses, and unfairly blaming other people might be expected to undermine rather than enhance performance and wellbeing (Baumeister et al., 1993; Colvin and Block, 1994; Robins and Beer, 2001). If so, why do people have an inherent need to enhance their self-esteem?

PERSONAL NARRATIVE OF THE DEVELOPMENT OF SOCIOMETER THEORY

The idea for sociometer theory emerged amidst the questions and controversies that swirled around the construct of self-esteem in the early 1990s. Spurred partly by my reading in the emerging field of evolutionary psychology, I began to wonder about the adaptive significance of self-esteem. My starting assumption was that if self-esteem – and the self-esteem motive – were as important as psychologists seemed to think, they must serve some fundamentally important function that goes beyond merely making people feel good (or bad) about themselves. Both dominance theory (Barkow, 1980) and terror management theory (Solomon et al., 1991) had offered such arguments, but neither seemed broadly tenable. On one hand, research suggested that self-esteem was more strongly linked to being liked rather than being dominant, and on the other, I could not understand how evolutionary processes could have created a self-esteem system that lowered an organism's fear of death as terror management theory suggested. I also found it

questionable that the processes identified by terror management theory, which are firmly rooted in culture, could have occurred until the appearance of culture, a mere 40–60,000 years ago (Leary, 2002, 2004).

About this time, I was also becoming interested in the emotional and behavioral effects of interpersonal acceptance and rejection. Much of my earlier research had dealt with people's concerns with how they were perceived and evaluated by others, but in the early 1990s, I began to realize that one fundamental concern underlying people's desire to be evaluated positively was their desire to be accepted and to belong to groups. About this time, I contributed a brief invited response to an article in which Baumeister and Tice (1990) proposed that a great deal of anxiety arises from people's concerns with belonging and acceptance. In my comment (Leary, 1990), I suggested that although Baumeister and Tice were probably correct, many other social emotions – including jealousy, loneliness, and depression – were also reactions to rejection.

Furthermore, in reviewing the literature on the relationship between interpersonal rejection and emotion, I found that social exclusion consistently correlated not only with negative emotions but also with lower self-esteem and that events that evoke negative social emotions also tend to lower self-esteem. In discussing this fact, I proposed the idea that self-esteem may be a

reflection of the individual's assessment of the implications of his or her behavior for social inclusion and exclusion. "State" self-esteem is tied to one's assessment of inclusion in the immediate situation; "trait" self-esteem is a compilation of the individual's history of experienced inclusion and exclusion. (Leary, 1990: 227)

In addition, I suggested that "people behave in ways that maintain self-esteem, not because of a need to preserve self-esteem per se but because such behaviors decrease the likelihood that they will be ignored, avoided, or rejected" and that behaviors that have been conceptualized as efforts to maintain self-esteem – such as approval seeking, self-handicapping, and self-serving attributions – are ways of maintaining or improving social acceptance (Leary, 1990: 227).

These two speculations, which at the time had only indirect empirical support, became the cornerstones of sociometer theory. As my students and I began to work on these ideas, the late Michael Kernis invited me to contribute a chapter to an edited book on self-esteem, and I took that opportunity to lay out the basic ideas of sociometer theory in a venue in which I was less fettered by the lack of empirical evidence than I would be in a peer-reviewed article (Leary and Downs, 1995). About the same time, my students and I published a five-study article that offered the first direct tests of the theory (Leary et al., 1995).

SOCIOMETER THEORY: DETAILS

The central premise of sociometer theory is that self-esteem is a subjective gauge of the degree to which people perceive that they are relationally valued and socially accepted by other people. State self-esteem – people's current feelings about themselves that fluctuate in response to situational events – is conceptualized as a reaction to people's perceptions of the degree to which they are, or are likely to be, valued and accepted by other people in the immediate context or near future. Trait self-esteem – people's average or typical level of self-esteem across situations and time – is conceptualized as a reflection of their sense of the degree to which they are generally valued and accepted by others. Sociometer theory differs from most early explanations of self-esteem in suggesting that self-esteem has no value in its own right and that people neither need self-esteem nor are motivated to pursue it for its own sake. Rather, self-esteem is viewed as the output of a system that monitors and responds to events vis-à-vis interpersonal acceptance and rejection.

Although the evolutionary underpinnings were not a necessary part of the theory, we speculated regarding why human beings might have evolved a system for monitoring their relational value and acceptance. Many biologists, ethologists, and psychologists have suggested that human beings and their hominid ancestors were able to survive only because they lived in cooperative groups (Ainsworth, 1989; Kameda and Tindale, 2006). Without the natural defenses of most terrestrial animals (such as fangs, claws, strength, and the ability to run fast), solitary hominids could not have survived. By living in cooperative groups, however, they could fare reasonably well. Previous theorists had noted that people have a strong motivation toward affiliation and group living, but these sociopetal motives tell only half of the story. To survive and reproduce in nature, people not only must desire other people's company but also must assure that they are accepted rather than rejected by others (Baumeister and Leary, 1995). As a result, natural selection may have favored individuals who attended to the degree to which others accepted them and behaved in ways that led others to value, accept, and support them and refrained from doing things that might lead to rejection and expulsion. Given that social acceptance was literally vital, we hypothesized that a psychological system evolved that monitored and responded to cues indicating that the person may be devalued and rejected by other people.

In our early descriptions of the theory, we described self-esteem as a gauge of the degree to which the person is "being included versus excluded by other people" or an index of their "inclusionary status" (Leary et al., 1995: 519). However, we later began to refer to self-esteem as a marker of one's *relational value* to other people. Relational value refers to the degree to which a person regards his or her relationship with another individual as valuable or important. The higher a person's relational value to other people, the more likely they are to include and support him or her (Leary, 2001). We changed our terminology because concepts such as inclusion/exclusion and acceptance/rejection connoted dichotomous states, whereas people subjectively experience degrees of acceptance and rejection. Furthermore, people may feel rejected even when they have not, strictly speaking, been excluded or rejected. For example, a woman who knows that her husband loves her may nonetheless feel rejected, experience hurt feelings, and show lowered self-esteem if he chooses to watch sports on television rather than to have dinner with her. These reactions occur not because she is excluded or rejected in an objective sense but because, at that moment, she perceives that her relational value is lower than she desires (Leary, 2006).

Thus, according to sociometer theory, the common feature of events that lower self-esteem is that they potentially lower people's relational value to others. From this perspective, failure, rejection, embarrassing situations, negative evaluations, criticism, and being outperformed by other people lower self-esteem not because they damage the person's private self-image (although that may happen as well) but rather because they lower one's relational value and the probability of acceptance. Importantly, people may infer low relational value or acceptance from cues that, in themselves, do not explicitly indicate rejection. For example, being treated unfairly can lead people to feel inadequately valued (Tyler and Lind, 1992) because others typically treat those whose relationships they value fairly. Thus, people respond to injustice as if they were rejected, showing a decrease in self-esteem (Koper et al., 1993; Shroth and Shah, 2000).

The self-esteem motive

People's inclination to behave in ways that maintain, protect, and increase their self-esteem has been well documented (Blaine and Crocker, 1993; Greenwald, 1980; Taylor and Brown, 1988) and, as noted, many psychologists have assumed that such actions arise from a basic need for self-esteem. Sociometer theory disputes the existence of a free-standing need for self-esteem. Rather, according

to the theory, when people do things that appear intended to maintain or raise self-esteem, their goal is usually to protect and enhance their relational value and, thus, increase the likelihood of acceptance (Leary and Baumeister, 2000). The phenomena that have been linked to self-esteem maintenance – such as self-serving attributions, self-handicapping, self-promoting prejudices, and ego-defensive reactions – may reflect efforts to promote acceptance rather than to raise self-esteem per se (Leary, 2006). Granted, such actions may boost self-esteem, but that is because those actions promote one's relational value.

Of course, people sometimes engage in cognitive tactics that help them feel better about themselves even when those tactics do not increase their relational value. However, this observation does not contradict sociometer theory's claim that the fundamental function of the self-esteem system is to monitor and respond to threats to relational value rather than to make people feel good about themselves. Nor does it suggest that people have a 'need' for self-esteem. Rather, people can sometimes think themselves into particular emotional states, using thoughts to bypass age-old monitoring systems.

EVIDENCE

Three types of evidence support the basic propositions of sociometer theory: (1) acceptance and rejection influence state self-esteem in both laboratory experiments and real-world settings, (2) state self-esteem relates strongly to perceived social acceptance, and (3) trait self-esteem reflects people's perceptions of their general acceptability or relational value.

Effects of acceptance and rejection on self-esteem

The central prediction of sociometer theory is that acceptance and rejection influence state self-esteem. Data relevant to this hypothesis has been obtained in lab experiments, studies of naturally occurring rejections, and studies of changes in self-esteem over time.

Experimental evidence

In the first test of this hypothesis (Leary et al., 1995), we wanted to demonstrate that acceptance and rejection affect state self-esteem and also that this effect is due to being rejected rather than merely "left out." Participants came to the laboratory in groups of five and completed self-descriptive questionnaires that were ostensibly shared with the other four participants. After seeing each other's answers, each participant listed the two participants with whom he or she would most like to work on an upcoming task. Participants then received bogus feedback indicating that they had been assigned either to work with the three-person group or to work alone, and that this assignment was based on the preferences of the other members or a random procedure. As hypothesized, the results showed that not being chosen for the group significantly lowered state self-esteem, whereas being excluded for a random reason had no effect. Study 4 of Leary et al. (1995) replicated this finding using feedback from an individual rather than from a group. Participants who were led to believe that another person liked and wanted to interact with them rated themselves more positively than those who thought another person did not like or want to interact with them.

Many other studies have shown that rejection lowers self-esteem using a variety of methods of leading participants to believe that they were rejected, ostracized, ignored, or left out (Buckley et al., 2004; Leary et al., 1998; Nezlek et al., 1997; Smith and Williams, 2004; Snapp and Leary, 2001; Wilcox and Mitchell, 1977; Zadro et al., 2005). Blackhart et al. (2009) conducted a meta-analysis of over 70 experiments that examined the effects of rejection on self-esteem. Although not every study showed the effect, overall, rejection resulted in lower self-esteem than acceptance, with an average effect size of 0.30.

Leary et al. (1998) conducted four experiments that examined how state self-esteem responds over a wider range of feedback than mere acceptance or rejection. As predicted, negative, rejecting feedback consistently lowered self-esteem relative to positive, accepting feedback, but the data also revealed a significant curvilinear pattern. State self-esteem was consistently low when feedback from others was rejecting or neutral, then rose with increasing acceptance until a moderately high level of acceptance was achieved, at which point further increases in acceptance had no further effect. This pattern shows that state self-esteem is most responsive to small variations in relational value when feedback is in the range of neutral to moderately-accepting, possibly because slight changes in relational value have the greatest potential to affect how people are treated by others within this range. Because people are treated differently depending on whether they are slightly, moderately, or highly valued, state self-esteem shows concomitant changes with varying relational value. However, once relational value becomes slightly negative, people are simply ignored or avoided, and greater negativity typically results in no worse outcomes for the rejected person than mildly negative feedback. Likewise, once relational value is relatively high, further increases have little tangible effect, so people's self-esteem does not increase further in the upper range. The patterns suggest that the sociometer distinguishes easily between clearcut rejection and clearcut acceptance but is most sensitive to slight gradations in interpersonal appraisals within the range in which such differences in relational value are most consequential.

Many people maintain that their own self-esteem is immune from the social influences that sociometer theory identifies, asserting that they evaluate themselves solely in accord with their personal standards and are unaffected by other people's judgments. To examine the validity of these claims, Leary et al. (2003a) conducted two experiments that compared the effects of rejection on people who do and do not believe that their self-esteem is affected by other people's evaluations. In both studies, two extreme groups of participants were preselected – one composed of people who strongly and unequivocally maintained that their self-esteem is unaffected by disapproval and rejection, and one composed of people who strongly and unequivocally admitted that their self-esteem is affected by disapproval and rejection. Participants received accepting or rejecting feedback, and their state self-esteem was assessed. Results showed that rejection affected participants' self-esteem equally whether or not they believed that others' evaluations would influence their self-esteem. People who deny that their self-feelings are affected by acceptance and rejection are simply wrong.

The theory predicts that self-esteem is linked to traits that promote relational value and acceptance from other people. Because the characteristics that promote relational value differ across relationships, self-esteem may be attuned to different characteristics in different contexts. Across several studies, Anthony et al. (2007a) showed that self-esteem is generally attuned more strongly to social commodities such as physical attractiveness, popularity, and social skills than to communal qualities such as warmth, kindness, and honesty, possibly because social commodities are more easily observed by other people, and acceptance in many contexts depends more strongly on social commodities than communal qualities. However, in close ongoing relationships and intimate contexts, communal characteristics become more important indicators of people's relational value. Anthony et al. showed that the sociometers of people in romantic relationships are more attuned to their communal qualities than are the sociometers of people who are not in relationships. When social roles emphasize communal qualities for social acceptance, people's self-esteem is more tightly related to their beliefs about their kindness, supportiveness, and honesty.

Correlational evidence

Studies also show that rejection episodes lower self-esteem in people's everyday lives (Leary et al., 1998; Sommer et al., 2001; Williams et al., 1998). In their analyses of real-world cases of ostracism, Williams and his colleagues have repeatedly found that ostracism lowers self-esteem (Williams, 2001; Williams et al., 1998; Williams and Zadro, 2001). Indeed, Williams (2001) suggested that self-esteem is one of four basic needs threatened by ostracism. (In denying the existence of a need for self-esteem, sociometer theory interprets the data differently, suggesting instead that ostracism affects the sociometer and thus self-esteem, but the point remains that ostracism lowers self-esteem.) Similarly, rejecting events that hurt people's feelings also lower their self-esteem, and the magnitude of the change in self-esteem correlates with how rejected people feel (Leary et al., 1998).

In a study of married people, Shackelford (2001) found that self-esteem was inversely related to the degree to which people's spouses engaged in behaviors that inflict costs, such as infidelity, acting in a condescending manner, withholding sex, and derogating their spouse's physical attractiveness. Shackelford interpreted these findings as evidence that self-esteem tracks "spousal cost-infliction," but the results are consistent with sociometer theory. People whose spouses behave in these ways are unlikely to feel sufficiently valued and accepted as marriage partners.

Longitudinal evidence

Four studies have examined the impact of changes in perceived acceptance on self-esteem over time. In a daily diary study of the relationship between people's self-perceived social skills and the quality of their daily interactions, Nezlek (2001) tested 83 participants during two two-week periods separated by two years. Changes in the perceived quality of one's interactions over time predicted changes in self-perceived social skill. If we assume, as Nezlek suggested, that interaction quality (e.g., closeness, responsiveness) is strongly linked to perceived acceptance and that self-ratings of social skill relate strongly to self-esteem, these data suggest that positive, accepting interactions increase people's self-evaluations and self-esteem. In another diary study, Denissen et al. (2008) examined the relationship between ratings of the quantity and quality of people's social interactions and their daily self-esteem. Results showed that the quality (closeness) of people's interactions, but not the quantity of interactions, predicted self-esteem both concurrently and on the subsequent day.

In a more controlled test of the effects of others' regard on self-esteem, Srivastava and Beer (2005) had participants meet four times to work together on tasks and hold group discussions. At the end of each session, measures were taken of self-esteem, perceived regard from the other members, and liking for other members, allowing the researchers to examine the effects of members' evaluations on other participants' self-esteem. Consistent with sociometer theory predictions, both actual liking and perceived regard predicted participants' self-esteem a week later. (Reciprocal effects of self-esteem on later liking were not obtained.)

Murray et al. (2003) examined daily changes in perceived regard, concerns with acceptance, and self-esteem in 154 married or cohabiting couples over a three-week period. Among other findings, they showed that anxiety about acceptance by one's partner predicted decrements in self-esteem on the subsequent day. In brief, dozens of experimental, correlational, and longitudinal studies have provided support for the idea that changes in relational value or acceptance/rejection are associated with systematic changes in state self-esteem.

Concordance between perceived acceptance and self-esteem

A second hypothesis is that people's subjective feelings of acceptance and rejection

should relate to their state self-esteem. As predicted, strong relationships between perceived acceptance and state self-esteem have been obtained.

Leary et al. (1995, Study 2) asked participants to recall a social situation, indicate how included versus excluded they felt in that situation, and rate how they felt about themselves at the time on indices of state self-esteem. Correlations between perceived inclusion/exclusion and state self-esteem were quite high, ranging from –0.68 to –0.92 (depending on which of four types of situations participants were asked to recall). Based on the strength of these findings, Leary et al. concluded that "for all practical purposes, self-feelings were a proxy for perceived exclusion" (1995: 523).

If state self-esteem monitors acceptance-rejection, then the effects of particular events on people's state self-esteem ought to mirror their assumptions about the effects of those events on social acceptance and rejection. To test this idea, Leary et al. (1995; Study 1) had participants imagine performing various behaviors that varied in social desirability (such as *I gave a dollar to a beggar*, *I volunteered to donate blood*, and *I cheated on a final exam*). After imagining each situation, participants rated both how they thought others would react toward them if they performed each behavior (1 = *many other people would reject or avoid me*; 5 = *many other people would accept or include me*) and how they would personally feel about themselves. The two sets of ratings correlated highly and the rank-order of the ratings was nearly identical. As predicted by the theory, people's feelings about themselves mirrored how they thought others would respond to the events vis-à-vis social acceptance and rejection.

Additional evidence linking perceived acceptance or relational value to state self-esteem is provided by some of the experiments described earlier. In many studies that have experimentally led participants to feel accepted or rejected, perceived acceptance-rejection (typically measured as a manipulation check) correlated highly with participants' state self-esteem.

Trait self-esteem

Although sociometer theory focuses primarily on the role of state self-esteem in monitoring and managing people's reactions to events that have implications for their relational value and acceptance, it also speaks to the nature of individual differences in trait self-esteem. In my commentary on the Baumeister and Tice (1990) article discussed earlier, I had suggested that trait self-esteem should relate to the degree to which people generally feel included versus excluded by other people as well as to their personal history of experienced inclusion and exclusion (Leary, 1990). Whereas state self-esteem monitors one's relational value at the moment, trait self-esteem tracks people's general acceptability over time.

Having a global perspective on one's overall relational value is important because how people respond to a particular interpersonal event should be influenced, in part, by their views of their long-term prospects for relationships and group memberships. Elsewhere, I explained the relationship between state and trait with an analogy to the stock market: "Just as a savvy investor must monitor both the current price and long-term prospects for a stock, people must monitor both short-term fluctuations in their relational value (state self-esteem) and their relational value in the long run (trait self-esteem)," (Leary and MacDonald, 2003: 404).

Evidence strongly supports the hypothesis that trait self-esteem reflects people's perceived relational value (for a review, see Leary and MacDonald, 2003). Trait self-esteem correlates highly with people's perceptions of the degree to which they are valued, supported, and accepted by other people (Lakey et al., 1994; Leary et al., 1995, 2001) as well as with the perceived quality of their interactions with other people (Denissen et al., 2008). Along the same lines, people who have higher self-esteem have greater confidence than people with low self-esteem that their romantic partner loves them and regards them favorably (Murray and Holmes, 2000), and people with high self-esteem anticipate greater acceptance from new interaction partners than do lows (Anthony et al., 2007b). In a particularly interesting study that used country as the unit of analysis, data from 31 countries revealed that the average self-esteem of respondents from a particular nation could be predicted by the average quantity and quality of people's interactions with their friends, even after controlling for happiness, neuroticism, individualism, and gross domestic product (Denissen et al., 2008).

In his groundbreaking work on the antecedents of self-esteem, Coopersmith (1967) identified four primary domains from which people derive their self-esteem: significance (social attention, acceptance, and affection), adherence to moral and ethical standards, the ability to influence other people, and competence. Although Coopersmith did not appear to recognize the inherently social nature of these four dimensions or the fact that they are primary determinants of acceptance and rejection by other people, he did observe that people may develop high self-esteem by being successful in just one or two domains, as long as they are approved of by the person's primary reference group, a finding consistent with sociometer theory.

In a more nuanced examination of the relationship between dimensions of self-perceptions and trait self-esteem, MacDonald et al. (2003) showed that people's self-evaluations on particular dimensions predicted trait self-esteem primarily to the degree that people thought those dimensions were important for social approval. Participants completed a measure of trait self-esteem and rated themselves on characteristics such as competence, attractiveness, and sociability, as well as the degree to which they thought people are more approving and accepting of those who are high in each domain and the degree to which people are disapproving and rejecting of those who do not possess these attributes (i.e., those who are incompetent, unattractive, and so on). Consistent with previous research, participants who believed that they possessed more socially desirable characteristics (i.e., characteristics that promote relational value) had higher trait self-esteem. More importantly, for four of the five domains, participants with the highest trait self-esteem were people who both evaluated themselves highly in that domain and also indicated that the domain had implications for acceptance and rejection. For example, self-evaluations of competence, attractiveness, and material wealth predicted trait self-esteem more strongly when participants believed that these domains led to approval, whereas participants who thought great material wealth leads to rejection had lower self-esteem the wealthier they were! Thus, as sociometer theory predicts, believing that one possesses certain desirable characteristics predicts trait self-esteem primarily to the degree that people think that the characteristic leads to acceptance or forestalls rejection. Similar findings show that people whose peer group disdains success show increased self-esteem when they fail (Jones et al., 1990).

SOCIAL AND PSYCHOLOGICAL PROBLEMS

Psychology's interest in self-esteem is based partly on the assumption that low self-esteem is associated with certain emotional, behavioral, and societal problems. The relationship between low self-esteem and dysfunctional behavior is not as strong as many suppose (Baumeister et al., 2003; Mecca et al., 1989), but in general, people with low self-esteem tend to show greater depression, anxiety, alcohol and drug abuse, educational and occupational difficulties, conflicted relationships, and other patterns of problem behaviors than people with higher self-esteem (see Leary and MacDonald, 2003; Leary et al., 1995; Mruk, 1995). Because they have assumed that low self-esteem causes these

kinds of difficulties, many psychologists and social engineers have advocated raising self-esteem as a way to reduce them (Mecca et al., 1989; Mruk, 1995).

From the standpoint of sociometer theory, low self-esteem does not cause these problems, as is typically assumed, but rather is related to dysfunctional behaviors via three general routes. First, being inadequately accepted causes a number of aversive emotions (such as sadness, anger, and loneliness), as well as maladaptive interpersonal behaviors such as defensiveness, aggression, and negative judgments of other people. Not only are people with a history of rejection often depressed, anxious, hostile, and aggressive (Kelly, 2001; Leary et al., 2001, 2003b), but such reactions have also been demonstrated in response to short-term rejections in laboratory experiments (Buckley et al., 2003; Leary et al., 1995; Nezlek et al., 1997; Twenge et al., 2001). As a monitor of relational value, self-esteem decreases with perceived rejection and, thus, correlates with other emotional and behavioral reactions to rejection, but low self-esteem does not *cause* these problems.

Second, feeling inadequately valued typically increases people's desire to be accepted. (Baumeister and Leary, 1995). People usually prefer to build their relational value through socially desirable means such as achievement, being a nice person, or having socially desirable characteristics. However, when people perceive that these routes to acceptance are not available, they may seek acceptance via deviant or antisocial behaviors such as drug use or gang membership. As a result, people who feel inadequately valued and, perhaps, inherently unacceptable (and who thus have lower self-esteem) may join deviant groups in which the standards for acceptance are lower than in socially acceptable groups (Haupt and Leary, 1997). Low self-esteem may correlate with deviant behavior, in part, because deviancy is one route to acceptance for those who feel unaccepted by mainstream groups.

Third, most psychological and interpersonal problems lead other people to devalue and distance themselves from the individual (Corrigan and Penn, 1999), thereby lowering his or her self-esteem. Thus, people who have psychological difficulties or behave in socially unacceptable ways tend to have lower self-esteem. For example, substance abuse, domestic violence, and chronic failure may lead to relational devaluation and, thus, lower self-esteem. In general, low trait self-esteem is more likely to be an effect than a cause of dysfunctional behavior (Baumeister et al., 2003).

In reconceptualizing the relationship between self-esteem and behavior, sociometer theory offers new insights regarding clinical and societal interventions for problems in which low self-esteem is implicated. From the sociometer perspective, low self-esteem is not necessarily a sign of psychological problems and, in fact, may indicate that one's sociometer is functioning properly. People who have low self-esteem because they have been rejected for misdeeds that hurt other people may be quite well adjusted; people shouldn't feel good about themselves when they act in socially undesirable ways. Of course, people are sometimes devalued or rejected for reasons that are not their fault, but even then, the sociometer should naturally respond with lowered self-esteem until it is consciously overridden by a rational analysis of the situation. Helping people to see that low self-esteem does not necessarily indicate that anything is wrong with them may be an important first step in these cases.

From the standpoint of sociometer theory, the therapeutic goal should not be to increase self-esteem (as clinical and social interventions sometimes do; see Bednar et al., 1989; Mecca et al., 1989; Mruk, 1995), because low self-esteem is regarded as a side effect or symptom of low perceived relational value rather as a problem in its own right. Rather, a sociometer-based intervention recognizes that the crux of problems associated with low self-esteem involves concerns with acceptance and rejection. Thus, the first step in any such intervention is to determine whether the problem under consideration arises from

feeling inadequately valued, reflects dysfunctional ways of seeking social acceptance, and/or leads to devaluation and rejection. Then, interventions should focus on addressing the actual source of the problem, which involves low perceived relational value. As it turns out, many clinical psychologists and social engineers inadvertently adopt this approach in that many interventions designed to raise self-esteem rely on programs that promote people's perceptions of their social desirability and relational value (Leary, 1999). But, sociometer theory focuses attention on the real genesis of most problems related to low self-esteem – inadequate relational value.

QUESTIONS AND CRITICISMS

In this concluding section, I examine some recurring questions about sociometer theory.

The inherently interpersonal nature of self-esteem

Perhaps the most common resistance to sociometer theory comes from those who insist that true or healthy self-esteem is, by definition, based solely on adherence to one's own personal standards and should not be affected by other people's evaluations (Deci and Ryan, 1995; May, 1983). This objection is intriguing because it implies that being concerned with other people's impressions and judgments is inherently undesirable, if not maladaptive. Yet, congenial, cooperative, and supportive interpersonal relationships, as well as people's social wellbeing, require that they pay attention to how they are being perceived, evaluated, and accepted by other people. In fact, if people have a need to belong that evolved because it conferred adaptive advantages (Baumeister and Leary, 1995), then we should expect well-functioning people to keep one eye on how other people react to them. Sociometer theory suggests that healthy self-esteem is responsive to the evaluations of other people, at least within bounds.

Far from being a sign of insecurity, manipulation, or vanity, being attuned to other people's reactions – and particularly to the degree to which they are accepting versus rejecting – is essential for personal and social wellbeing. Even though people can be overly concerned with others' reactions in ways that create unnecessary distress or lead them to behave in ways that hurt themselves or others, possessing a mechanism that monitors other people's reactions and affects people's self-relevant feelings when unfavorable interpersonal circumstances are detected is critically beneficial both for the person and for those individuals and groups with whom he or she interacts. In fact, maintaining close relationships and cooperative groups requires that people attend to one another's evaluations, immediately recognize instances in which their own behavior may lead others to devalue their relationship, feel badly when their actions increase social distance, and promote social connections within the relationship or group. This is not to say that people should not behave in ways that might jeopardize their relationship or group when the need arises, but as a rule, the sociometer helps people to maintain the kinds of relationships upon which cooperation and social support is based.

Other sources of self-esteem

A second question is whether factors other than relational value also influence self-esteem. Even if one acknowledges that people feel better about themselves when they are accepted than rejected, one could still argue that other outcomes – such as mastering tasks, professional success, accomplishing difficult goals, or behaving in a morally exemplary manner – also increase self-esteem.

Proponents of sociometer theory concur that such actions influence self-esteem but interpret such patterns as reflecting the effects of excellence, achievement, and moral behavior on relational value and acceptance. People are more likely to be valued and accepted when they are competent, successful, and ethical than when they are not, so any action or outcome that potentially raises or lowers relational value should influence self-esteem. Even if a person's actions or outcomes are not currently known by other people, the sociometer should alert the individual via changes in state self-esteem when private actions or outcomes have potential implications for relational value (Leary and Baumeister, 2000).

Seeking self-esteem

Several writers have misinterpreted sociometer theory to suggest that people should seek self-esteem through social acceptance. Not only have many theorists suggested that healthy self-esteem is decidedly not tied to social approval (Deci and Ryan, 1995; May, 1983), but evidence suggests that trying to build self-esteem by seeking approval and acceptance is associated with negative affect, self-regulatory problems, defensiveness, poor interpersonal relationships, and lower mental and physical health (Crocker and Knight, 2005; Deci and Ryan, 1995; Schimel et al., 2001). Proponents of sociometer theory agree. If self-esteem is merely a gauge, people should not try to influence their self-esteem directly by any means.

Cross-cultural differences

Research showing that Japanese respondents do not engage in the self-enhancing biases that are seen in American and European samples has led some researchers to conclude that people in certain cultures are either indifferent to self-esteem or do not experience self-esteem at all (Heine et al., 1999, 2000, 2001). Sociometer theory offers a different interpretation of such findings. Because the criteria for being relationally valued differ across cultures, people tend to behave in ways that are associated with social acceptance and refrain from behaving in ways that lead to rejection in their culture. Unlike in the US, where maintaining a confident, self-enhancing persona is acceptable, in Japan, self-enhancement does not promote acceptance and, in fact, may result in disapproval and devaluation. As a result, the Japanese are less likely to self-enhance and feel more badly about themselves when they do. Research suggests that behaviors that promote relational value in Japan – self-effacement and deference, for example – result in high self-esteem and that the Japanese "enhance" on communal, self-effacing attributes (Sedikides et al., 2003).

How many sociometers?

We initially assumed that people possess a single sociometer that monitors their relational value across a wide array of relationships and groups. However, based on evolutionary logic, Kirkpatrick and Ellis (2001) suggested that people may possess a number of domain-specific sociometers that monitor relational value in qualitatively different kinds of relationships. They noted that the criteria for acceptance into and rejection from different kinds of relationships – such as family relationships, instrumental coalitions, and mating relationships – differ greatly, as do the means of increasing one's acceptance in each of these kinds of relationships. Given that evolutionary processes would be unlikely to create a single, multipurpose sociometer to manage relational value across all kinds of relationships, human beings may have evolved specific sociometers for dealing with interpersonal problems in different social domains. Kirkpatrick and Ellis also suggested that these sociometers may serve functions in addition to promoting social acceptance, such as facilitating personality development, addressing personal deficiencies, and guiding adaptive relationship choices (Kirkpatrick and Ellis, 2001, 2006).

CONCLUSION

Whatever verdict the field reaches regarding the merits of sociometer theory as an explanation of self-esteem, the ultimate contribution of the sociometer approach may lie as much in the way that it has recast longstanding questions about self-esteem as in the particulars of the theory itself. Sociometer theory has forced researchers to consider the functions of self-esteem and particularly to consider functions of self-esteem that go beyond merely defending the ego or reducing anxiety. It has also helped to focus attention on fundamental social psychological processes involved in how people respond to interpersonal rejection.

In addition, sociometer theory has led many psychologists to question the assumption that people have a motive or need for self-esteem. When examined critically, one finds it difficult to identify precisely what purpose a need to feel good about oneself would serve unless it were associated with important tangible outcomes. Even so, many writers continue to explain various behaviors by invoking the idea that people are trying to protect or enhance their self-esteem. In almost all instances, sociometer theory offers a more parsimonious explanation of the effects of both self-esteem and self-esteem threats in terms of people's efforts to maintain a minimum degree of social acceptance. The idea that people have a need for self-esteem should be retired, and this should be done even if sociometer theory should eventually be found to be lacking as an explanation of self-esteem. Surely, a psychological process that is as pervasive and as related to important outcomes as self-esteem does more than simply make people feel good about themselves.

REFERENCES

Ainsworth, M.S. (1989) Attachments beyond infancy. *American Psychologist*, 44, 709–716.

Anthony, D.B., Holmes, J.G. and Wood, J.V. (2007a) Social acceptance and self-esteem: Tuning the sociometer to interpersonal value. *Journal of Personality and Social Psychology, 92,* 1024–1039.

Anthony, D.B., Wood, J.V. and Holmes, J.G. (2007b) Testing sociometer theory: Self-esteem and the importance of acceptance for social decision-making. *Journal of Experimental Social Psychology, 43,* 425–432.

Bandura, A. (1977) Self-efficacy: Toward a unifying theory of behavioral change. *Psychological Review, 84,* 191–215.

Barkow, J.H. (1980) Prestige and self-esteem: A biosocial interpretation. In D.R. Omark, F. Strayer and D.G. Freedman (eds), *Dominance Relations: An Ethological View of Human Conflict and Social Interaction,* pp. 319–332. New York: Garland STPM.

Baumeister, R.F., Campbell, J.D., Krueger, J.I. and Vohs, K.D. (2003) Does high self-esteem cause better performance, interpersonal success, happiness, or healthier lifestyles? *Psychological Science in the Public Interest, 4,* 1–44.

Baumeister, R.F., Heatheton, T.F. and Tice, D.M. (1993) When ego threats lead to self-regulation failure: Negative consequences of high self-esteem. *Journal of Personality and Social Psychology, 64,* 141–156.

Baumeister, R.F. and Leary, M.R. (1995) The need to belong: Desire for interpersonal attachments as a fundamental human motivation. *Psychological Bulletin, 117,* 497–529.

Baumeister, R.F. and Tice, D.M. (1990) Anxiety and social exclusion. *Journal of Social and Clinical Psychology, 9,* 165–195.

Bednar, R.L., Wells, M.G. and Peterson, S.R. (1989) *Self-esteem: Paradoxes and Innovations in Clinical Theory and Practice.* Washington, DC: American Psychological Association.

Blackhart, G.C., Nelson, B.C., Knowles, M.L. and Baumeister, R.F. (2009) Rejection elicits emotional reactions but neither causes immediate distress nor lowers self-esteem: A meta-analytic review of 192 studies on social exclusion. *Personality and Social Psychology Review, 13,* 269–309.

Blaine, B. and Crocker, J. (1993) Self-esteem and self-serving biases in reactions to positive and negative events: An integrative review. In R.F. Baumeister (ed.), *Self-esteem: The Puzzle of Low Self-Regard,* pp. 55–85. New York: Plenum.

Bowles, T. (1999) Focusing on time orientation to explain adolescent self concept and academic achievement: Part II. Testing a model. *Journal of Applied Health Behaviour, 1,* 1–8.

Branden, N. (1969) *The Psychology of Self-esteem.* New York: Bantam.

Branden, N. (1983) *Honoring the Self.* Los Angeles. Bantam Books.

Buckley, K.E., Winkel, R.E. and Leary, M.R. (2004) Reactions to acceptance and rejection: Effects of level and sequence of relational evaluation. *Journal of Experimental Social Psychology, 40,* 14–28.

Cervone, D., Artistico, D. and Berry, J.M. (2006) Self-efficacy and adult development. In C. Hoare (ed.), *Handbook of Adult Development and Learning,* pp. 169–195. New York: Oxford University Press.

Colvin, C.R. and Block, J. (1994) Do positive illusions foster mental health? An examination of the Taylor and Brown formulation. *Psychological Bulletin, 116,* 3–20.

Cooley, C.H. (1902). *Human Nature and the Social Order.* New York: Scribner.

Coopersmith, S. (1967) *Antecedents of Self-esteem.* San Francisco: Freeman.

Corrigan, P.W. and Penn, D.L. (1999) Lessons from social psychology on discrediting psychiatric stigma. *American Psychologist, 54,* 765–776.

Crocker, J. and Knight, K.M. (2005) Contingencies of self-worth. *Current Directions in Psychological Science, 14,* 200–203.

Deci, E.L. and Ryan, R.M. (1995) Human agency: The basis for true self-esteem. In M.H. Kernis (ed.), *Efficacy, Agency, and Self-esteem,* pp. 31–50. New York: Plenum.

Denissen, J.J.A., Penke, L., Schmitt, D.P. and van Aken, M.A.G. (2008) Self-esteem reactions to social interactions: Evidence for sociometer mechanisms across days, people, and nations. *Journal of Personality and Social Psychology, 95,* 181–196.

Glendinning, A. and Inglis, D. (1999) Smoking behaviour in youth: The problem of low self-esteem? *Journal of Adolescence, 22,* 673–682.

Greenwald, A.G. (1980) The totalitarian ego: Fabrication and revision of personal history. *American Psychologist, 35,* 603–613.

Guay, F., Delisle, M., Fernet, C., Julien, É. and Senécal, C. (2008) Does task-related identified regulation moderate the sociometer effect? A study of performance feedback, perceived inclusion, and state self-esteem. *Social Behavior and Personality, 36,* 239–254.

Hansford, B.C. and Hattie, J.A. (1982) The relationship between self and achievement/performance measures. *Review of Educational Research, 52,* 123–142.

Haupt, A.H. and Leary, M.R. (1997) The appeal of worthless groups: Moderating effects of trait self-esteem. *Group Dynamics: Theory, Research, and Practice, 1,* 124–132.

Heaven, P.C. (1986) Authoritarianism, directiveness, and self-esteem revisited: A cross-cultural analysis. *Personality and Individual Differences, 7*, 225–228.

Heine, S.H., Lehman, D.R., Markus, H.R. and Kitayama, S. (1999) Is there a universal need for positive self-regard? *Psychological Review, 106*, 766–794.

Heine, S.J., Kitayama, S. and Lehman, D.R. (2001) Cultural differences in self-evaluation: Japanese readily accept negative self-relevant information. *Journal of Cross Cultural Psychology, 32*, 434–443.

Heine, S.J., Takata, T. and Lehman, D.R. (2000) Beyond self-presentation: Evidence for self-criticism among Japanese. *Personality and Social Psychology Bulletin, 26*, 71–78

James, W. (1890) *The Principles of Psychology.* New York: Henry Holt.

Jones, E.E., Brenner, K.J. and Knight, J.G. (1990) When failure elevates self-esteem. *Personality and Social Psychology Bulletin, 16*, 200–209.

Kameda, T. and Tindale, R.S. (2006) Groups as adaptive devices: Human docility and group aggregation mechanisms in evolutionary context. In M. Schaller, J.A. Simpson, and D.T. Kenrick (eds), *Evolution and Social Psychology*, pp. 317–341. New York: Psychology Press.

Kelly, K.M. (2001) Individual differences in reactions to rejection. In M.R. Leary (ed.), *Interpersonal Rejection*, pp. 291–315. New York: Oxford University Press.

Kirkpatrick, L.A. and Ellis, B.J. (2001) An evolutionary-psychological approach to self-esteem: multiple domains and multiple functions. In G.J.O. Fletcher and M.S. Clark (eds), *Blackwell Handbook of Social Psychology: Interpersonal Processes*, pp. 411–436. Oxford: Blackwell.

Kirkpatrick, L.A. and Ellis, B.J. (2006) The adaptive functions of self-evaluative psychological mechanisms. In M.H. Kernis (ed.), *Self-esteem: Issues and Answers*, pp. 334–339. New York: Psychology Press.

Koper, G., van Knippenberg, D., Bouhuijs, F., Vermunt, R. and Wilke, H. (1993) Procedural fairness and self-esteem. *European Journal of Social Psychology, 23*, 313–325.

Lakey, B., Tardiff, T.A. and Drew, J.B. (1994) Negative social interactions: Assessment and relations to social support, cognition, and psychological distress. *Journal of Social and Clinical Psychology, 13*, 42–62.

Leary, M.R. (1990) Responses to social exclusion: Social anxiety, jealousy, loneliness, depression, and low self-esteem. *Journal of Social and Clinical Psychology, 9*, 221–229.

Leary, M.R. (1999) The social and psychological importance of self-esteem. In R.M. Kowalski and M.R. Leary (eds), *The Social Psychology of Emotional and Behavioral Problems: Interfaces of Social and Clinical Psychology*, pp. 197–221. Washington, DC: American Psychological Association.

Leary, M.R. (2001) Toward a conceptualization of interpersonal rejection. In M.R. Leary (ed.), *Interpersonal Rejection*, pp. 3–20. New York: Oxford University Press.

Leary, M.R. (2002). The interpersonal basis of self-esteem: Death, devaluation, or deference? In J. Forgas and K.D. Williams (eds), *The Social Self: Cognitive, Interpersonal, and Intergroup Perspectives.* New York: Psychology Press.

Leary, M.R. (2004) The function of self-esteem in terror management theory and sociometer theory: A comment on Pyszczynski, Greenberg, Solomon, Arndt, and Schimel (2004). *Psychological Bulletin, 130*, 478–482.

Leary, M.R. (2005) Varieties of interpersonal rejection. In K.D. Williams, J.P., Forgas, and W. von Hippel (eds), *The Social Outcast,* pp. 35–51. New York: Psychology Press.

Leary, M.R. (2006) Sociometer theory and the pursuit of relational value: Getting to the root of self-esteem. *European Review of Social Psychology, 16*, 75–111.

Leary, M.R. and Baumeister, R.F. (2000) The nature and function of self-esteem: Sociometer theory. In M.P. Zanna (ed.), *Advances in Experimental Social Psychology, 32*, 1–62. San Diego: Academic Press.

Leary, M.R., Cottrell, C.A. and Phillips, M. (2001) Deconfounding the effects of dominance and social acceptance on self-esteem. *Journal of Personality and Social Psychology, 81*, 898–909.

Leary, M.R. and Downs, D.L. (1995) Interpersonal functions of the self-esteem motive: The self-esteem system as a sociometer. In M. Kernis (ed.), *Efficacy, Agency, and Self-esteem*, pp. 123–144. New York: Plenum.

Leary, M.R., Gallagher, B., Fors, E.H., Buttermore, N., Baldwin, E., Lane, K.K. and Mills. A. (2003a) The invalidity of disclaimers about the effects of social feedback on self-esteem. *Personality and Social Psychology Bulletin, 29*, 623–636.

Leary, M.R., Haupt, A., Strausser, K. and Chokel, J. (1998) Calibrating the sociometer: The relationship between interpersonal appraisals and state self-esteem. *Journal of Personality and Social Psychology, 74*, 1290–1299.

Leary, M.R., Kowalski, R.M., Smith, L. and Phillips, S. (2003b) Teasing, rejection, and violence: Case studies of the school shootings. *Aggressive Behavior, 29*, 202–214.

Leary, M.R. and MacDonald, G. (2003) Individual differences in self-esteem: A review and theoretical integration. In M.R. Leary and J.P. Tangney (eds), *Handbook of Self and Identity*, pp. 401–418. New York: Guilford Press.

Leary, M.R., Schreindorfer, L.S. and Haupt, A.L. (1995) The role of low self-esteem in emotional and behavioral problems: Why is low self-esteem dysfunctional? *Journal of Social and Clinical Psychology, 14*, 297–314.

Leary, M.R., Springer, C., Negel, L., Ansell, E. and Evans, K. (1998) The causes, phenomenology, and consequences of hurt feelings. *Journal of Personality and Social Psychology, 74*, 1225–1237.

Leary, M.R., Tambor, E.S., Terdal, S.K. and Downs, D.L. (1995) Self-esteem as an interpersonal monitor: The sociometer hypothesis. *Journal of Personality and Social Psychology, 68*, 518–530.

LePine, J.A. and Van Dyne, L. (1998) Predicting voice behavior in work groups. *Journal of Applied Psychology, 83*, 853–868.

MacDonald, G., Saltzman, J.L. and Leary, M.R. (2003) Social approval and trait self-esteem. *Journal of Research in Personality, 37*, 23–40.

May, R. (1983) *The Discovery of Being*. New York: Norton.

Mecca, A.M., Smelser, N.J. and Vasconcellos, J. (1989) *The Social Importance of Self-esteem*. Berkeley, CA: University of California Press.

Mruk. C. (1995) *Self-esteem: Research, Theory, and Practice*. New York: Springer.

Murray, S.L., Griffin, D.W., Rose, P. and Bellavia, G.M. (2003) Calibrating the sociometer: The relational contingencies of self-esteem. *Journal of Personality and Social Psychology, 85*, 63–84.

Murray, S.L. and Holmes, J.G. (2000) Seeing the self through a partner's eyes: Why self-doubts turn into relationship insecurities. In A. Tesser, R.B. Felson and J.M. Suls (eds), *Psychological Perspectives on Self and Identity*, pp. 173–198. Washington, DC: APA Publications.

Nezlek, J.B. (2001) Causal relationships between perceived social skills and day-to-day social interaction: Extending the sociometer hypothesis. *Journal of Social and Personal Relationships, 18*, 386–403.

Nezlek, J.B., Kowalski, R.M., Leary, M.R., Blevins, T. and Holgate, S. (1997) Personality moderators of reactions to interpersonal rejection: Depression and trait self-esteem. *Personality and Social Psychology Bulletin, 23*, 1235–1244.

Perez, R.C. (1973) The effect of experimentally-induced failure, self-esteem, and sex on cognitive differentiation. *Journal of Abnormal Psychology, 81*, 74–79.

Pyszczynski, T., Greenberg, J., Solomon, S., Arndt, J. and Schimel, J. (2004) Why do people need self-esteem? A theoretical and empirical review. *Psychology Bulletin, 3*, 435–468.

Raskin, R., Novacek, J. and Hogan, R. (1991) Narcissistic self-esteem management. *Journal of Personality and Social Psychology, 60*, 911–918.

Robins, R.W. and Beer, J.S. (2001). Positive illusions about the self: Short-term benefits and long-term costs. *Journal of Personality and Social Psychology, 80*, 340–352.

Rogers, C. (1959) A theory of therapy, personality, and interpersonal relationships, as developed in the client-centered framework. In S. Koch (ed.), *Psychology: A Study of a Science, 3*, 184–256. New York: McGraw-Hill.

Schimel, J., Arndt, J., Pyszczynski, T. and Greenberg, J. (2001) Being accepted for who we are: Evidence that social validation of the intrinsic self reduces general defensiveness. *Journal of Personality and Social Psychology, 80*, 35–52.

Sedikides, C., Gaertner, L. and Toguchi, Y. (2003) Pancultural self-enhancement. *Journal of Personality and Social Psychology, 84*, 60–70.

Shackelford, T.K. (2001) Self-esteem in marriage. *Personality and Individual Differences, 30*, 371–390.

Shraugher, J.S. and Sorman, P.B. (1977) Self-evaluations, initial success and failure, and improvement as determinants of persistence. *Journal of Consulting and Clinical Psychology, 45*, 784–795.

Shroth, H.A. and Shah, P.P. (2000) Procedures: Do we really want to know them? An examination of the effects of procedural justice on self-esteem. *Journal of Applied Psychology, 85*, 462–471.

Smith, A. and Williams, K.D. (2004) R U there? Ostracism by cell phone text messages. *Group Dynamics: Theory, Research, and Practice, 8*, 291–301.

Snapp, C.M. and Leary, M.R. (2001) Hurt feelings among new acquaintances: Moderating effects of interpersonal familiarity. *Journal of Social and Personal Relationships, 18*, 315–326.

Solomon, S., Greenberg, J. and Pyszczynski, T. (1991) A terror management theory of social behavior: The psychological functions of self-esteem and cultural worldviews. In M. Zanna (ed.), *Advances in Experimental Social Psychology, 24*, 91–159. Orlando, FL: Academic Press.

Sommer, K.L., Williams, K.D., Ciarocco, N.J. and Baumeister, R.F. (2001) Explorations into the intrapsychic and interpersonal consequences of social ostracism. *Basic and Applied Social Psychology, 23*, 227–245.

Srivastava, S. and Beer, J.S. (2005) How self-evaluations relate to being liked by others: Integrating sociometer and attachment perspectives. *Journal of Personality and Social Psychology, 89*, 966–977.

Taylor, S.E. and Brown, J.D. (1988) Illusion and well-being: A social psychological perspective on mental health. *Psychological Bulletin, 103*, 193–210.

Tedeschi, J.T. and Norman, N. (1985) Social power, self-presentation, and the self. In B.R. Schlenker (ed.), *The Self and Social Life,* pp. 293–322. New York: McGraw-Hill.

Twenge, J.M., Baumeister, R.F., Tice, D.M. and Stucke, T.S. (2001) If you can't join them, beat them: Effects of social exclusion on aggressive behavior. *Journal of Personality and Social Psychology, 81*, 1058–1069.

Tyler, T.R. and Lind, E.A. (1992) A relational model of authority in groups. In M. Zanna (ed.), *Advances in Experimental Social Psychology, 25*, 115–191. New York: Academic Press.

Wilcox, J. and Mitchell, J. (1977) Effects of group acceptance/rejection of self-esteem levels of individual group members in a task-oriented problem-solving group interaction. *Small Group Behavior, 8*, 169–178.

Williams, K.D. (2001) *Ostracism: The Power of Silence.* New York: Guilford Press.

Williams, K.D., Shore, W.J. and Grahe, J.E. (1998) The silent treatment: Perceptions of its behaviors and associated feelings. *Group Processes and Intergroup Relations, 1*, 117–141.

Williams, K.D. and Zadro, L. (2001) Ostracism: On being ignored, excluded and rejected. In M.R. Leary (ed.), *Interpersonal Rejection,* pp. 21–53. New York: Oxford University Press.

Zadro, L., Williams, K.D. and Richardson, R. (2004) How low can you go? Ostracism by a computer lowers belonging, control, self-esteem and meaningful existence. *Journal of Experimental Social Psychology, 40*, 560–567.

Zadro, L., Williams, K.D. and Richardson, R. (2005) Riding the 'O' train: Comparing the effects of ostracism and verbal dispute on targets and sources. *Group Processes and Intergroup Relations, 8*, 125–143.

34

Attachment Theory

Phillip R. Shaver and Mario Mikulincer

ABSTRACT

In this chapter we recount the origins and development of attachment theory, explain how it has been extended into the domain of adult personality and social psychology, and describe its six major components: (1) the innate attachment behavioral system, (2) attachment-related affect-regulation strategies, (3) internal working models of self and others, (4) attachment patterns or "styles," (5) attachment security viewed as a resilience resource, and (6) dysfunctional aspects of attachment insecurity. We review some of the empirical literature based on these constructs and explain how attachment-related strategies affect such social psychological constructs as self-esteem, affect and affect regulation, mental health, person perception, relationship functioning and satisfaction, prejudice and intergroup hostility, prosocial behavior, leadership, and group functioning. We briefly describe how attachment theory relates to some of the other theories discussed in this handbook and explain how the theory and the research it has generated are currently being, and in the future can be, applied.

INTRODUCTION

In this chapter we explain attachment theory (Bowlby, 1982), its origins, development, and operationalization in studies of human infants and their parents; and our extension of the theory to make it suitable for personality and social psychological studies of adolescents, adults, and their close interpersonal relationships (Mikulincer and Shaver, 2007a; Shaver et al., 1988). The theory deals with close relationships and their psychological foundations and consequences. It integrates insights from psychoanalytic theory; primate ethology; cognitive developmental and social cognitive psychology; theories of stress and coping; and contemporary research on personality development, affect regulation, and relational interdependence.

The chapter begins with an account of the origins of attachment theory during the 1960s and 1970s in the work of John Bowlby and Mary Ainsworth. We then explain how the two of us became involved with extensions of the theory in the 1980s. Next, we describe the theory itself in some detail, placing special emphasis on our version of it, which began in the work of Hazan and Shaver (1987). This version of the theory is designed for and influenced by contemporary social psychologists. We show how attachment security, grounded in responsive, supportive relationships, plays a role in personal and social issues of interest to personality-social psychologists, issues such as self-esteem, person perception, interpersonal behavior, exploration and achievement, and prosocial behavior and intergroup relations. We then consider the darker side of attachment relationships, which includes the defenses and personal and relational difficulties that stem from attachment insecurities. We conclude with a brief discussion of connections between attachment theory and other social psychological theories and a brief consideration of applications of attachment theory and research.

THE ORIGINS OF ATTACHMENT THEORY

Attachment theory was originally proposed by John Bowlby, a British psychoanalyst, and was then strengthened by the theoretical, psychometric, and empirical contributions of Mary Ainsworth, an American developmental psychologist. As explained later in this chapter, Bowlby's theory and Ainsworth's findings were extended into social psychology by Hazan and Shaver (1987), culminating 20 years later in a book-length overview of the theory and the large research literature it has generated (Mikulincer and Shaver, 2007a).

John Bowlby

Bowlby was born in England, in 1907, to economically comfortable and well-educated parents. His father was a physician, and John eventually became one as well – a psychiatrist. While studying to become a child psychiatrist, Bowlby undertook psychoanalytic training with a famous mentor, Melanie Klein, and was psychoanalyzed for several years by Joan Riviere, a close associate of Klein's. From these mentors Bowlby learned about early relationships with caregivers; the tendency of troubled children to deal with painful experiences, especially separations and losses, by defensively excluding them from conscious memory; and the emotions of

anxiety, anger, and sadness. Despite absorbing many of Klein and Riviere's ideas, however, Bowlby rejected their extreme emphasis on fantasies at the expense of reality, and on sexual drives rather than other kinds of relational motives.

Attachment theory also grew out of Bowlby's experiences as a family therapist at the Tavistock Clinic in London, where social and family relationships were considered alongside individual psychodynamics as causes of psychological and social disorders. Bowlby was also influenced by preparing a report for the World Health Organization on children who were homeless following World War II.

As Bowlby's clinical observations and insights accumulated, he became increasingly interested in explaining what, in his first major statement of attachment theory, he called "the child's tie to his mother" (Bowlby, 1958). In formulating the theory, he was especially influenced by Konrad Lorenz's (1952) ideas about "imprinting" in precocial birds and the writings of other ethologists and primatologists, including the primatologist Robert Hinde (1966). These authors, along with Harry Harlow (1959), had begun to show that immature animals' ties to their mothers were not simply due to classical conditioning based on feeding, as learning theorists (and using different language, psychoanalysts) had thought. Instead, Bowlby viewed the human infant's reliance on, and emotional bond with, its mother to be the result of a fundamental instinctual behavioral system that, unlike Freud's sexual libido concept, was viewed as social-relational rather than sexual. Because Bowlby relied so heavily on animal research and on the behavioral-systems construct, he was strongly criticized by other psychoanalysts for being a "behaviorist." He nevertheless continued to view himself as a psychoanalyst and a legitimate heir to Freud, which is how he is largely viewed today.

Bowlby eventually expanded his preliminary articles about core aspects of attachment into three major books, *Attachment and Loss*, Volumes 1, 2, and 3, which are now recognized as landmarks of modern psychology, psychiatry, and social science. The first volume, *Attachment*, was published in 1969 and revised in 1982; the second, *Separation: Anxiety and Anger*, was published in 1973; and the third, *Loss: Sadness and Depression*, was published in 1980. These comprehensive volumes were accompanied in 1979 by a collection of Bowlby's lectures, *The Making and Breaking of Affectional Bonds*, and were supplemented in 1988 by a book, *A Secure Base*, about applying attachment theory and research to psychotherapy. Bowlby died in 1990, having won many professional awards.

Mary Ainsworth

Bowlby's major collaborator, Mary Salter Ainsworth, was born in Ohio in 1913 and received her PhD in developmental psychology from the University of Toronto in 1939, after completing a dissertation on security and dependency that was inspired by her advisor William Blatz's security theory. In her dissertation, "An Evaluation of Adjustment Based on the Concept of Security" (1940), Ainsworth mentioned for the first time what eventually became a central part of attachment theory, the secure-base construct, which emphasized the importance in child–parent attachment relationships of parents' provision of what Ainsworth called a secure base from which to explore the world.

When she moved to London with her anthropologist husband, Ainsworth answered a newspaper ad for a research position with Bowlby, having not known about him or his work beforehand. Part of her job was to analyze films of children's separations from mother. These films convinced her of the value of behavioral observations, which were the centerpiece of her contributions to attachment research. When her husband decided in 1953 to advance his career by undertaking cultural research in Uganda, Ainsworth moved there as well and began an observational study of mothers and infants, whom she visited every two weeks for two hours of observation over a period of several months.

Eventually, after returning to North America and becoming a faculty member at the Johns Hopkins University, in 1967 Ainsworth published a book entitled *Infancy in Uganda: Infant Care and the Growth of Love*.

One of the intellectually and historically significant features of Ainsworth's 1967 book was an appendix that sketched different patterns of infant attachment, which Ainsworth linked empirically with observable aspects of maternal behavior. Although these patterns were not precisely the same as the three attachment types for which Ainsworth later became famous (called secure, anxious, and avoidant in our work; see Ainsworth et al., 1978, for the original details), some definite similarities are evident. The three main patterns of attachment delineated in the 1978 book were based on its 1967 predecessor, but they were greatly refined by intensive studies of middle-class American infants in Baltimore. In these American studies, Ainsworth and her students recorded detailed home observations during infants' first year of life and supplemented them with a new laboratory assessment procedure: the Strange Situation. Ainsworth et al.'s 1978 book explains how to code an infant's behavior with mother in the Strange Situation, and also shows how the three major forms of infant attachment are associated with particular patterns of maternal behavior at home. The measures and ideas advanced in the 1978 book, taken in conjunction with Bowlby's theoretical books on attachment, separation, and loss form the backbone of all subsequent discussions of normative attachment processes and individual differences in attachment behavior. This work provided a foundation for literally thousands of subsequent studies.

OUR EXTENSION OF ATTACHMENT THEORY INTO SOCIAL PSYCHOLOGY

By the time we began to use attachment theory, in the late 1980s it had been extensively tested in studies of child development, and Ainsworth's infant attachment categories were well known. For various reasons, including (we believe) the increasing number of women entering social psychology (Elaine Hatfield and Ellen Berscheid being two prominent and highly influential examples), the increasing divorce rate in the US, and a concern with loneliness in industrialized societies (e.g., Peplau and Perlman, 1982), social psychologists were beginning to concern themselves with the formation, maintenance, and dissolution of close relationships. This concern was manifested in the creation of new professional organizations focused on the study of romantic and marital relationships and in a landmark 1983 book, *Close Relationships*, edited by Harold Kelley, one of the most prominent social psychologists of his (or any other) generation, along with Ellen Berscheid and several others. Suddenly the study of love was not merely professionally acceptable, it was highly visible, even in journals like *Psychological Review* (e.g., Sternberg, 1986).

A problem during that period, at least in our estimation, was the exceptional prominence in social psychology of the attitude construct, which had been central for decades. Its familiarity caused researchers, at first, to consider love to be just another attitude (e.g., Hendrick and Hendrick, 1986). Little consideration was given to the fact that romantic and parental love had existed for millennia (Jankowiak, 1995; Singer, 1987) and that the inherent importance of love and loss could be seen in the lives of nonhuman primates (e.g., Harlow, 1959). These were the days before evolutionary psychology. Moreover, social psychologists were generally unaware that psychoanalysts from Freud to Bowlby had written a great deal about the psychodynamics of filial and romantic love and the relation of romantic love to sexuality. We were unusual among social psychologists in having been deeply interested in psychoanalysis since first encountering it in our undergraduate years.

In our view, anyone who pays close attention to what goes on in people's lives, or who reads romantic novels or poems or studies art or film, realizes that the issues raised by psychoanalysts, beginning with Freud, are crucial: sexual attraction and desire; romantic love and longing; the development of personality in the crucible of family relationships; painful, corrosive emotions such as anger, fear, jealousy, grief, hatred, shame, and remorse, which contribute to intrapsychic conflicts, defenses, and psychopathology; intergroup hostility and war. Given our interests, social psychology at first seemed superficial compared with psychoanalysis. Nevertheless, social psychology's strong point – which was the fatally weak point of psychoanalysis – was the use of experimental methods and creative experimental interventions. Psychoanalytic theorists seemed capable of endlessly inventing hypothetical constructs and invisible mental processes without being constrained by operational definitions, sound psychometrics, or replicable empirical methods. Hence, social psychology was capable of rendering psychodynamic theories testable.

Both of us began our careers as experimental researchers pursuing then-popular topics in social and personality psychology (stress and learned helplessness in Mikulincer's case, self-awareness and fear of success in the case of Shaver), but our interest in psychoanalytic theory never subsided. When we encountered Bowlby's books, we realized that a psychoanalytic thinker could incorporate the full range of scientific perspectives on human behavior, seek empirical evidence for psychoanalytic propositions, and amend or reformulate psychoanalytic theory based on empirical research. Ainsworth's development of the laboratory Strange Situation assessment procedure, which allowed her to systematically classify infants' attachment patterns and relate them to reliable observations of parent–child interactions at home, added to our confidence that extending attachment theory and its research methods into the realm of adolescent and adult love relationships might be possible.

In the mid 1980s, Shaver was studying adolescent and adult loneliness (see, for example, Rubenstein and Shaver, 1982; Shaver and

Hazan, 1984) and noticing both that attachment theory was useful in conceptualizing loneliness (e.g., Weiss, 1973) and that patterns of chronic loneliness were similar in certain respects to the insecure infant attachment patterns identified by Ainsworth and her colleagues (1978). Building on this insight, one of Shaver's doctoral students, Cindy Hazan, wrote a seminar paper suggesting that attachment theory could be used as a framework for studying romantic love – or "romantic attachment," as they called it in their initial article on the topic (Hazan and Shaver, 1987).

That article caught the eye of Mikulincer, who had become interested in attachment theory while studying affect-regulation processes related to learned helplessness, depression, combat stress reactions, and post-traumatic stress disorder in Israel. He noticed similarities between (1) certain forms of helplessness in adulthood and the effects of parental unavailability in infancy; (2) intrusive images and emotions in the case of post-traumatic stress disorder and the anxious attachment pattern described by Ainsworth et al. (1978) and Hazan and Shaver (1987); and (3) avoidant strategies for coping with stress and the avoidant attachment pattern described by these same authors. In 1990, Mikulincer, Florian, and Tolmacz published a study of attachment patterns and conscious and unconscious death anxiety, one of the first studies to use the preliminary self-report measure of adult attachment patterns devised by Hazan and Shaver (1987), and the first to show its ability to illuminate unconscious mental processes.

From then on, both of us continued to pursue the application of attachment theory to the study of adults' emotions, emotion-regulation strategies, and close relationships, noticing that we were both interested in the experimental study of what might be called attachment-related psychodynamics: the kinds of mental processes, including intense needs, powerful emotions and conflicts, and defensive strategies, that had captivated the attention of both Freud and Bowlby. We decided to pool our efforts to craft a more rigorous formulation of adult attachment theory (e.g.,

Mikulincer and Shaver, 2003, 2007a; Shaver and Mikulincer, 2002), clarify and extend our model of the attachment behavioral system, test the model in many different ways, including the use of priming techniques developed by cognitively oriented social psychologists, and incorporate within our theory some of positive psychology's emphasis on personal growth and social virtues (e.g., Gable and Haidt, 2005; Seligman, 2002) and some of organizational psychology's emphasis on leadership and group dynamics (e.g., Davidovitz et al., 2007; Rom and Mikulincer, 2003). Today, adult attachment theory, as summarized in our 2007 book, is one of the leading approaches to research on social relationships, personality processes, and the psychodynamic nature of the human mind. The current form of the theory is summarized in the following section.

ADULT ATTACHMENT THEORY

What we are calling *adult* attachment theory (Mikulincer and Shaver, 2007a) includes six major constructs: (1) the innate attachment behavioral system (Bowlby, 1982; Mikulincer and Shaver, 2006), (2) attachment-related affect-regulation strategies (Main, 1990; Mikulincer et al., 2008), (3) internal working models of self and others (Bowlby, 1982; Mikulincer and Shaver, 2005), (4) attachment patterns or "styles" (Ainsworth et al., 1978; Shaver and Mikulincer, 2009), (5) attachment security viewed as a resilience resource that enhances self-esteem and promotes prosocial emotions and behavior (Bowlby, 1988; Mikulincer and Shaver, 2007b), and (6) dysfunctional aspects of attachment insecurity (Cassidy and Kobak, 1988; Shaver and Mikulincer, 2002). We will discuss each of these constructs in turn.

Behavioral systems

To characterize the motives involved in personal and social development, which Freud had attempted to explain in terms of sexual and aggressive, or life and death, "instincts" or "drives," Bowlby (1982) took from ethology the concept of *behavioral system*s – species-universal, biologically evolved neural programs that organize behavior in ways that increase the likelihood of an animal's survival and reproduction. He viewed these systems as similar to cybernetic control systems, which are not powered by drives.

According to Bowlby (1982), one of the earliest behavioral systems to appear in human development is the *attachment system*, whose biological function is to protect a person (especially during infancy and early childhood) from danger by assuring that he or she maintains proximity to caring and supportive others (whom Bowlby, 1982, called *attachment figures*). In Bowlby's (1982) view, the need to seek out and maintain proximity to attachment figures evolved because of the prolonged dependence of human children on "stronger and wiser" others (often, but not always, the parents), who can defend the children from predators and other dangers while supporting their gradual development of knowledge and skills.

Because human (and other primate) infants seem naturally to look for and gravitate toward *particular* others (those who are familiar and at least sometimes helpful), and to prefer them over alternative caregivers, Bowlby used the terms "affectional bond" and "attachment" for the processes that link one person with another in close relationships. This is the reason he called his theoretical formulation *attachment theory*. Although the attachment system is most important and most evident during the early years of life, Bowlby (1988) claimed that it is active across the lifespan and is most frequently manifested when a person seeks support, affection, or protection from a close relationship partner. This lifespan orientation encouraged developmental and social psychologists (e.g., Main et al., 1985; Shaver et al., 1988) to extend the theory into the domain of adolescent and adult relationships.

During infancy, primary caregivers (usually one or both parents but also grandparents, neighbors, older siblings, daycare workers, and so on) are likely to occupy the role of attachment figure. Ainsworth (1973) reported that infants tend to seek proximity to their primary caregiver when tired or ill, and Heinicke and Westheimer (1966) found that infants tend to be most easily soothed by their primary caregivers. During adolescence and adulthood, other relationship partners often become targets of proximity seeking and emotional support, including close friends and romantic partners. Teachers and supervisors in academic settings or therapists in clinical settings can also serve as real or potential sources of comfort and support. Moreover, groups, institutions, and symbolic personages (e.g., God, the Buddha, or Virgin Mary) can be used mentally as attachment figures. This array of real and symbolic figures, which can vary in importance or centrality, form what Bowlby (1982) called a *hierarchy of attachment figures*.

According to attachment theory, a particular relationship partner is an attachment figure and a relationship is an attachment relationship only to the extent that the relationship partner accomplishes, or is called upon to accomplish, three important functions (e.g., Ainsworth, 1991; Hazan and Shaver, 1994; Hazan and Zeifman, 1994). First, the attachment figure is someone to whom the attached individual seeks proximity in times of stress or need. Moreover, separation from or loss of this person elicits distress, protest, and efforts to achieve reunion (either literally or, in the case of grief, symbolically). Second, the person is viewed as a real or potential "*safe haven*," because he or she provides, or is hoped to provide, comfort, support, protection, and security in times of need. Third, the person is viewed as a "*secure base*," allowing a child or adult to pursue nonattachment goals without undue concerns about safety and to sustain exploration, risk taking, and self-development.

What attachment theory calls *activation of the attachment system* can be seen in the behavior of human infants, who tend to drop whatever they are doing (e.g., playing with interesting toys) and seek comfort and support from an attachment figure if an odd or unexpected noise is heard or a stranger enters the room (Ainsworth et al., 1978). (Bowlby [1982] considered these stimuli, as well as finding oneself in the dark or feeling ill, to be natural clues to danger which have had obvious significance for survival throughout human evolutionary history.) The same kind of attachment-system activation is notable in the minds of adults who are subjected to conscious or unconscious threats. For example, we (Mikulincer et al., 2002) conducted experiments in which we subliminally presented threatening words (e.g., failure, separation) to adults and then assessed indirectly (using reaction times in a word-identification or Stroop color-naming task) which names of relationship partners became more mentally available for processing following the unconscious threat. It turned out that the names of a person's attachment figures became more available following unconscious exposure to threatening words. These words had no effect on the mental availability of names of people, even familiar ones, who were not viewed as attachment figures. That is, attachment figures are not just any relationship partners; they are special people to whom one turns, even unconsciously and automatically, when comfort or support is needed.

According to Bowlby (1982), the natural goal of the attachment system is to increase a person's sense of *security* (which Sroufe and Waters, 1977, called *felt security* to emphasize its emotional qualities) – a sense that the world is a safe place, that one can rely on others for protection, comfort, and support, and that one can confidently explore one's environment and engage in social and nonsocial activities without undue or debilitating fear of damage. This goal is made particularly salient by encounters with actual or symbolic threats or by appraising an attachment figure as not sufficiently available or responsive. In such cases, the attachment system is activated and the individual is

driven to reestablish actual or symbolic proximity to an attachment figure (which attachment researchers call the *primary strategy* of the attachment system; Main, 1990). These bids for proximity persist until the sense of security is restored, at which time the attachment system is deactivated, or downregulated, and the individual can calmly and skillfully return to other activities. That is, the search for protection, support, and security is not only a goal in itself but also an important foundation for attaining non-attachment goals. This makes attachment theory distinct from other social psychological theories that characterize self-esteem, belongingness, cognitive consistency, or social influence or dominance a primary goal. Many of these goals are related to security and insecurity, but we view them as offshoots rather than roots of social motivation.

During infancy, the primary attachment strategy includes tactics such as nonverbal expressions of need (e.g., reaching, crying, pleading) and crawling or toddling toward an attachment figure to increase proximity and safety (Ainsworth et al., 1978). In adulthood, these tactics are expanded to include many other methods of establishing contact (e.g., talking, calling an attachment figure on the telephone, sending an e-mail or text message) as well as ways of calling upon soothing, comforting mental representations of attachment figures or even self-representations associated with these figures (e.g., qualities of oneself modeled on qualities of an attachment figure or feelings associated with being loved and comforted by such figures; Mikulincer and Shaver, 2004). Many studies (reviewed by Mikulincer and Shaver, 2007b) have demonstrated that "priming" a person with conscious or unconscious reminders or representations of attachment figures can increase felt security and thereby alter a person's feelings about objects, situations, and people, reduce hostility to outgroup members, facilitate empathy, compassion, and altruistic helping, and encourage creative forms of exploration.

Bowlby (1988) summarized many of the adaptive benefits of proximity seeking. For example, he viewed successful bids for proximity and the resulting boost in felt security as important to the creation and maintenance of successful, satisfying relationships. Every attachment-related interaction that restores a person's sense of security reaffirms the value of interpersonal closeness and strengthens affectional bonds with the person responsible for boosting one's sense of security. This is how attachment researchers explain many of the effects identified by non-attachment social psychology researchers (e.g., Murray et al., 2006; Reis et al., 2004; Rusbult et al., 1991) as important determinants of relationship stability and quality.

Moreover, successful bids for closeness and emotional support play an important role in helping a person regulate and de-escalate negative emotions such as anger, sadness, anxiety, and demoralization (Bowlby, 1973, 1980). According to attachment theory, successful self-regulation is learned, at first, with the help of attachment figures who accurately perceive one's negative emotions and the situational causes of these emotions and then gently and effectively soothe one's troubled mind and offer useful suggestions for solving problems or reappraising troubling situations. They therefore help a person maintain emotional balance and resilience in the face of stress.

Individual differences in attachment-system functioning

Attachment theory is a general theory of social and emotional development, but it would not have captured the attention of developmental, personality, social, and clinical psychologists if it had been only that. What captured research psychologists' attention were the patterns or styles of attachment emphasized in Bowlby's theory and operationalized in Ainsworth's research on mothers and infants. Most of the research and clinical applications inspired by attachment theory are concerned with those individual differences.

Attachment-figure availability and secondary attachment strategies

Besides its species-universal operating characteristics, the attachment behavioral system includes regulatory parameters than can be influenced by a person's history of interactions with attachment figures. In early infancy, the effects of experience can be conceptualized in terms of simple learning principles. If a particular behavioral strategy (e.g., crying for help, protesting angrily, downregulating distress signals) works with a particular caregiver, it will be reinforced. If a particular strategy results in punishment or caregiver withdrawal, it will become less available in an infant's behavioral repertoire (perhaps by being actively suppressed). The same is true for the young of other mammalian species.

In the case of human children, however, what is learned includes not only automatic behavior patterns but also vivid memories, abstracted assumptions, and expectations about caregivers' reactions and the effectiveness or ineffectiveness of one's own possible behaviors. Because Bowlby and Ainsworth were working during what has been called, in retrospect, the cognitive revolution in psychology, they were sensitive to the role played by memories, cognitive schemas, and other mental representations in regulating the attachment system. In attachment theory, these mental structures and processes are called *internal working models* of self and others (Bowlby, 1982). Over time, a person's working models, which contain both conscious and unconscious elements, become molded by the quality of interactions with attachment figures, thereby "programming" the attachment system to expect and conform to these figures' characteristic behaviors. Through this process, a person learns to adjust his or her attachment system to fit contextual demands and rely on expectations about possible access routes to protection and security. These working models are thought to be the basis of both current individual differences in attachment strategies, or styles, and within-person continuity in the operation of the attachment system over time.

According to Bowlby (1973, 1988), variations in working models, and hence in attachment-system functioning, depend on the availability, sensitivity, and responsiveness of attachment figures in times of need. When one's key relationship partner is available, sensitive, and responsive to one's proximity- and support-seeking efforts, one is likely to experience "felt security" and thus increase one's confidence in proximity seeking as an effective distress-regulation strategy. During such interactions one also acquires procedural knowledge about distress management, which is organized around what attachment researchers (e.g., Mikulincer et al., 2009) have characterized as a *secure-base script*. This script is thought to include the following if–then propositions: "If I encounter an obstacle and/or become distressed, I can approach a significant other for help; he or she is likely to be available and supportive; I will experience relief and comfort as a result of seeking proximity to this person; and I can then return to other activities."

When a primary attachment figure, however, proves not to be available, sensitive, or responsive, felt security is not attained and the distress that initially activated proximity-seeking efforts is compounded by attachment-related doubts and concerns (e.g., Can I trust others in times of need?). These troubling interactions indicate that the primary attachment strategy (seek proximity and support) is failing to accomplish its goal and that alternative strategies should be adopted to cope with current insecurities and distress. Attachment theorists (e.g., Cassidy and Kobak, 1988; Main, 1990) have called these alternative strategies *secondary attachment strategies*, which (based on Ainsworth et al.'s [1978] research) are thought to take two major organized forms: *hyperactivation* and *deactivation* of the attachment behavioral system.

Hyperactivated strategies include what Bowlby (1982) called *protest* reactions to the frustration of attachment needs. Protest often occurs in relationships in which the attachment figure is sometimes unreliably responsive but sometimes not, placing the needy individual on a partial reinforcement schedule that seems to reward persistence in the use of energetic, strident, noisy proximity-seeking strategies, because such attempts sometimes succeed. In such cases, a person does not give up on proximity-seeking and in fact intensifies it in an effort to demand or coerce the attachment figure's attention, love, and support. The main goal of these strategies is to make an unreliable or insufficiently responsive figure provide support and security. This involves exaggerating threat appraisals and overemphasizing indications of attachment-figure unavailability while intensifying demands for attention, care, and love. This strategy can, paradoxically, be viewed as a form of affect regulation, even though it involves upregulation rather than downregulation – the usually taken-for-granted method of effectively regulating emotions (Gross, 1999).

Deactivating strategies, in contrast, are efforts to escape, avoid, or minimize the pain and frustration caused by unavailable, unsympathetic, or unresponsive attachment figures. This kind of response typically occurs in relationships with attachment figures who disapprove of and punish closeness and expressions of need, dependence, and vulnerability (Ainsworth et al., 1978). In such relationships, a needy individual learns to expect better outcomes if proximity-seeking bids are suppressed, the attachment system is deactivated, and threats and dangers are dealt with on one's own. (Bowlby [1982] called this strategy *compulsive self-reliance*.) The primary goal of deactivating strategies is to keep the attachment system quiescent or downregulated to avoid recurring frustration and distress caused by interactions with cold, neglectful, or punishing attachment figures. Such deactivation requires that a person deny attachment needs, avoid intimacy and interdependence in relationships, and distance him- or herself from threats that might cause unwanted and potentially unmanageable activation of attachment-related needs, thoughts, feelings, or behaviors.

Internal working models

As already mentioned, Bowlby (1982) theorized that memories of important social interactions with attachment figures are stored and eventually schematized in an associative memory network. This stored knowledge allows a person to predict the likely course and outcomes of future interactions with an attachment figure and to adjust proximity-seeking bids accordingly. Repeated augmentation and editing of these models generally result in increasingly stable mental representations of self, attachment figures, and relationships. Bowlby (1982) wrote about two major forms of working models: representations of attachment figures' responses and inclinations (*working models of others*) and representations of the self's lovability and efficacy (*working models of self*). Once the attachment system has operated for several years in the context of attachment relationships, it is linked with complex representations of the availability, responsiveness, and sensitivity of these figures as well as representations of the self's ability to elicit a partner's attention and affection when desired.

During infancy and childhood, working models are based on specific interactions, or kinds of interactions, with particular attachment figures. As a result, a child can hold multiple episodic (situation- or person-specific) representations of self and others that differ with respect to an interaction's outcome (especially success or failure at gaining felt security), and with respect to the secondary strategy used to deal with insecurity during that interaction (hyperactivating or deactivating). With experience and in the context of cognitive development, these episodic representations form excitatory and inhibitory associations with each other. For example, experiencing or thinking about an episode of security attainment activates memories of similar security-enhancing episodes and renders memories of attachment

insecurities and worries less accessible. These associations favor the formation of more abstract and generalized attachment representations with a specific partner. Then, through excitatory and inhibitory links with models representing interactions with other attachment figures, even more generic working models are formed to summarize relationships in general. This process of continual model construction, renovation, and integration results, over time, in the creation of a hierarchical associative network that includes episodic memories, relationship-specific models, and generic working models of self and others. Overall et al. (2003) provided statistical evidence for this hierarchical network of attachment working models.

Unfortunately, the theoretical literature on attachment has sometimes made it seem that working models are simple and univocal with respect to important relationship issues. Research evidence suggests, however, in line with Bowlby's (e.g., 1980) original ideas about multiple models, conflicting models, and conscious and unconscious models, that most people can remember and be affected by both security-enhancing interactions with attachment figures and security-reducing interactions (e.g., Baldwin et al., 1996; Mikulincer and Shaver, 2007b). It thus matters a great deal what a particular person is reminded of, or is thinking about, when attachment-related processes and outcomes are assessed. The mental representation of one relationship may differ from the mental representation of another, and focusing on a particular issue (e.g., sexual infidelity) may cause related previous experiences to become temporarily more mentally accessible and psychologically influential than usual.

The notion that everyone has multiple attachment models organized by a hierarchical cognitive network raises questions about which model will be most accessible (i.e., readily activated and used to guide attachment-related expectations, defenses, and behaviors) in a given situation. As with other mental representations, the accessibility of an attachment working model is determined by the amount of experience on which it is based, the number of times it has been applied in the past, the density of its connections with other working models, and the issues made salient in a particular situation (e.g., Shaver et al., 1996). At the relationship-specific level, the model representing the typical interaction with an attachment figure has the highest likelihood of being accessible and guiding subsequent interactions with that person. At the generic level, the model that represents interactions with major attachment figures (e.g., parents and romantic partners) typically becomes the most commonly available representation and has the strongest effect on attachment-related expectations, feelings, and behaviors across relationships and over time.

According to Bowlby (1973), consolidation of a regularly available working model is the most important psychological process accounting for the enduring, long-term effects of attachment interactions during infancy, childhood, and adolescence on attachment-related cognitions and behaviors in adulthood. Given a fairly consistent pattern of interactions with primary caregivers during infancy and childhood, the most representative working models of these interactions become part of a person's implicit procedural knowledge about close relationships, social interactions, and methods of distress regulation; tend to operate automatically and unconsciously; and are resistant to change. Thus, what began as representations of specific interactions with particular primary caregivers during childhood tend to be applied in new situations and relationships, and eventually have an effect on attachment-related experiences, decisions, and actions even in adulthood (Sroufe et al., 2005).

Beyond the pervasive effects of attachment history on the accessibility of working models, attachment theory also emphasizes, as we have mentioned, the importance of contextual factors that influence the availability of particular models or components of models (e.g., Shaver et al., 1996). Recent studies have shown that contextual cues related to the availability and responsiveness of attachment figures, as well as actual or imagined encounters with supportive or unsupportive figures, can affect which working models become active in memory, even if they are incongruent with a person's more general and more typically available working model (e.g., Mikulincer and Shaver, 2007b; Shaver and Mikulincer, 2008). It seems that the generally accessible and more generic models coexist with less typical working models in a person's associative memory network, and the less typical models can be influenced by contextual factors and are important for understanding a person's behavior in a particular situation (Mikulincer and Shaver, 2007b).

Conceptualization and measurement of attachment patterns or styles

According to attachment theory (Bowlby, 1988; Shaver and Hazan, 1993), a particular history of attachment experiences and the resulting consolidation of chronically accessible working models lead to the formation of relatively stable individual differences in *attachment style* – the habitual pattern of expectations, needs, emotions, and behavior in interpersonal interactions and close relationships (Hazan and Shaver, 1987). Depending on how it is measured, attachment style characterizes a person's typical attachment-related mental processes and behaviors in a particular relationship (relationship-specific style) or across relationships (global attachment style).

The concept of attachment patterns or styles was first proposed by Ainsworth (1967) to describe infants' patterns of responses to separations from and reunions with their mother at home and in the laboratory Strange Situation procedure, which was designed to activate an infant's attachment system. Based on this procedure, infants were originally classified into one of three categories: secure, anxious, or avoidant. Main and Solomon (1990) later added a fourth category, *disorganized/disoriented*, characterized by odd, awkward behavior and unusual fluctuations between anxiety and avoidance.

Infants classified as secure in the Strange Situation typically react to separation from mother with observable signs of distress, but recover quickly upon reunion with mother and return to exploring the many interesting toys provided in the Strange Situation test room. They greet their mother with joy and affection, initiate contact with her, and respond positively to being picked up and held (Ainsworth et al., 1978). Avoidant infants' reactions are dramatically different and seem to indicate attachment-system deactivation. These infants express little distress when separated from mother and may actively turn away from or avoid her upon reunion. Anxious infants' reactions are hyperactive; these infants cry and protest angrily during separation and show angry, resistant, hyperaroused reactions (i.e., Bowlby's "protest") upon reunion, making it difficult for them to calm down and return to creative play.

In the 1980s, researchers from different psychological subdisciplines (developmental, clinical, personality, and social) constructed new attachment measures to extend attachment theory into adolescence and adulthood. Based on a developmental and clinical approach, Main and her colleagues (George et al., 1985; Main et al., 1985; see Hesse, 2008, for a review) devised the Adult Attachment Interview (AAI) to study adolescents and adults' mental representations of attachment to their parents during childhood. One of the major findings of this approach to studying adult attachment is that an adult's AAI classification (secure, dismissing, preoccupied, or unresolved) predicts his or her infant child's attachment pattern in the Strange Situation (see van IJzendoorn, 1995, for a review), even if the interview is conducted before the infant was born. In other words, there is good evidence for the intergenerational transmission of attachment patterns, which seems not to be primarily a matter of shared genes (e.g., Vaughn et al., 2008).

In an independent line of research, Hazan and Shaver (1987), who wished to apply Bowlby and Ainsworth's ideas to the study of romantic relationships, developed a self-report measure of adult attachment style. In its original form, the measure consisted of three brief descriptions of constellations of feelings and behaviors in close relationships that were intended to parallel the three infant attachment patterns identified by Ainsworth et al. (1978). College students and community adults were asked to read the three descriptions and place themselves in one of the three attachment categories according to their predominant feelings and behavior in romantic relationships. The three descriptions were as follows:

1 *Secure*: I find it relatively easy to get close to others and am comfortable depending on them and having them depend on me. I don't worry about being abandoned or about someone getting too close to me.
2 *Avoidant*: I am somewhat uncomfortable being close to others; I find it difficult to trust them completely, difficult to allow myself to depend on them. I am nervous when anyone gets too close and often, others want me to be more intimate than I feel comfortable being.
3 *Anxious*: I find that others are reluctant to get as close as I would like. I often worry that my partner doesn't really love me or won't want to stay with me. I want to get very close to my partner and this sometimes scares people away.

Hazan and Shaver's (1987) study was followed by scores of others that used the simple forced-choice self-report measure to examine the interpersonal and intrapersonal correlates of adult attachment style (see reviews by Shaver and Hazan, 1993; Shaver and Mikulincer, 2002). Over time, attachment researchers made methodological and conceptual improvements to the original self-report measure and reached the conclusion that attachment styles are best conceptualized as regions in a two-dimensional space (e.g., Bartholomew and Horowitz, 1991; Brennan et al., 1998). The first dimension, which we call attachment-related *avoidance*, is concerned with discomfort with closeness and with dependence on relationship partners and a preference for emotional distance and self-reliance. Avoidant individuals identified with self-report measures use deactivating attachment and affect-regulation strategies to deal with insecurity and distress. The second dimension, attachment-related *anxiety*, includes a strong desire for closeness and protection, intense worries about one's partner's availability and responsiveness and one's own value to the partner, and the use of hyperactivating strategies for dealing with insecurity and distress. People who score low on both dimensions are said to be secure or to have a secure attachment style.

The two attachment-style dimensions can be measured with the 36-item Experiences in Close Relationships scale (ECR; Brennan et al., 1998), which is reliable in both the internal-consistency and test–retest senses and has high construct, predictive, and discriminant validity (Crowell et al., 2008). Eighteen items tap the avoidance dimension (e.g., "I try to avoid getting too close to my partner," "I prefer not to show a partner how I feel deep down"), and the remaining 18 items tap the anxiety dimension (e.g., "I need a lot of reassurance that I am loved by my partner," "I resent it when my partner spends time away from me"). The two scales were conceptualized as independent and have been found to be empirically uncorrelated or only weakly correlated in most studies. Studies based on self-report measures of adult attachment style, some based on three categories, some on four categories (including two kinds of avoidance, labeled fearful and dismissive), and some on two dimensions, have allowed researchers to document theoretically predictable attachment-style variations in relationship quality, mental health, social adjustment, ways of coping, emotion regulation, self-esteem, interpersonal behavior, and social cognitions (see Mikulincer and Shaver, 2003, 2007a, for reviews).

There is relatively little research on the heritability of the two major forms of attachment insecurity measured with self-report scales (e.g., Crawford et al., 2007; Donnellan et al., 2008) or with the Adult Attachment Interview (Torgersen et al., 2007). The self-report studies provide fairly consistent evidence of genetic influences on attachment anxiety, which is correlated with neuroticism (e.g., Noftle and Shaver, 2006), a personality trait influenced by genes. The evidence for genetic influences on avoidant attachment is less consistent, but Gillath et al. (2008) found that both attachment anxiety and avoidance were associated with particular genetic alleles: anxiety with a polymorphism of the DRD2 dopamine receptor gene and avoidance with a polymorphism of the 5HT2A serotonin receptor gene. This line of research is still in its infancy, but none of the studies published to date suggest that genes are likely to be the most important determinants of attachment style.

ATTACHMENT-FIGURE AVAILABILITY AND THE BROADEN-AND-BUILD CYCLE OF ATTACHMENT SECURITY

Having outlined attachment theory's major constructs and some of the methods and procedures used to operationalize them, we turn to some of the personal, dyadic, and social-system consequences of variations in attachment-system functioning. In the present section of the chapter we are especially interested in beneficial effects of perceived attachment-figure availability and the resulting sense of security on social judgments, self-image, personality development, mental health, and relationship quality. After considering the beneficial effects of security, we will turn to defensive processes related to secondary attachment strategies (anxious hyperactivation and avoidant deactivation) and to the emotional and adjustment difficulties that arise when a person relies on defensive processes.

According to attachment theory, the physical and emotional availability of an actual security provider, or ready access to mental representations of supportive attachment figures, results in a sense of felt security and fosters what we, following Fredrickson (2001), call a *broaden-and-build cycle of attachment security*. This cycle is a cascade of mental and behavioral processes that can be viewed as resources for maintaining emotional stability in times of stress, fostering open and deeply interdependent bonds with others, optimizing personal adjustment, and expanding one's perspectives and capacities. In the long run, repeated experiences of attachment-figure availability have enduring effects on intrapsychic organization and interpersonal behavior. At the intrapsychic level, such experiences can be called upon as resilience resources, sustaining emotional wellbeing and personal adjustment, and resulting in positive working models of self and others that are readily accessible in memory when needed to bolster a person's mood and coping capacity. At the interpersonal level, repeated experiences of attachment-figure availability allow a person to develop the skills and attitudes associated with a secure attachment style, which facilitates the formation and maintenance of warm, satisfying, stable, and harmonious relationships.

The most immediate psychological effect of having reliable, dependable access to an available, sensitive, and responsive attachment figure is effective management of distress and relatively rapid restoration of emotional equanimity following threats and stresses. As a result of good relationships with attachment figures, secure people remain relatively unperturbed in times of stress and experience longer periods of positive affectivity, which contribute to stable mental health. Indeed, several studies have shown that secure attachment is associated positively with measures of wellbeing and negatively with measures of hurt feelings, negative affectivity, depression, and anxiety (for reviews, see Mikulincer and Shaver, 2003, 2007a; Shaver and Mikulincer, 2002, 2009).

Experiences of attachment-figure availability also contribute to the construction of an extensive network of positive mental representations, which plays an important role in maintaining emotional stability and adjustment. One part of this network concerns the appraisal of life's problems as manageable, which helps a person maintain an optimistic and hopeful stance. Relatively secure people can appraise and reappraise stressful events in positive ways and thereby deal more effectively with them. Researchers have consistently found positive correlations between self-reports of attachment security and constructive, optimistic appraisals of stressful events (see Mikulincer and Shaver, 2007a, for an extensive review).

Another set of security-related mental representations concerns other people's intentions and traits. Numerous studies have shown that more securely attached people hold more positive views of human nature, use more positive terms when describing relationship partners, perceive relationship partners as more supportive, have more positive expectations concerning their partners' behavior and tend to explain a partner's hurtful behavior in less negative ways (for reviews, see Mikulincer and Shaver, 2003; Shaver and Mikulincer, 2006).

Interactions with available and sensitive relationship partners reduce worries about being rejected, criticized, or abused. Such interactions confirm that a caring partner is unlikely to betray one's trust, react coldly or abusively to one's expressions of need, or respond unfavorably to bids for closeness and comfort. Numerous studies confirm that secure individuals score higher on measures of self-disclosure, support seeking, intimacy, trust, open communication, prorelational behavior, and relationship satisfaction (for reviews, see Feeney, 2008; and Shaver and Mikulincer, 2006).

Interactions with security-enhancing attachment figures also strengthen a person's authentically positive sense of self-esteem and social value (Mikulincer and Shaver, 2003). That is, secure individuals generally feel safe and protected and perceive themselves as valuable, lovable, and special, thanks to being valued, loved, and regarded as special by caring relationship partners. Research consistently shows that secure individuals have higher self-esteem (e.g., Bartholomew and Horowitz, 1991) and view themselves as more competent and efficacious (e.g., Cooper et al., 1998) than insecure individuals.

A relatively secure person's resources for dealing with stress make it less necessary for them to rely on psychological defenses that distort perception, limit coping flexibility, and generate interpersonal conflict. A secure person can devote mental resources to personal growth that would otherwise have to be devoted to preventive, defensive maneuvers; they can also attend to other people's needs and feelings rather than, or in addition to, their own. Being confident that support is available if needed, a secure person can take calculated risks and accept important challenges that contribute to the broadening of perspectives and skills, which is an important part of personal growth. Indeed, research indicates that attachment security is associated with enhanced curiosity and learning, encourages relaxed exploration of new, unusual information and phenomena, and favors the formation of open and flexible cognitive structures, despite the uncertainty and confusion that a broadening of experience might entail (e.g., Elliot and Reis, 2003).

Attachment security is associated with higher scores on self-report measures of responsiveness to a relationship partner's needs (e.g., Kunce and Shaver, 1994) and with more supportive reactions to a distressed relationship partner (e.g., Simpson et al., 1992). Both dispositional and contextually augmented attachment security have also been associated with heightened compassion for a suffering individual and willingness to relieve the person's distress (e.g., Gillath et al., 2005; Mikulincer et al., 2005).

SECONDARY ATTACHMENT STRATEGIES, EMOTIONAL DIFFICULTIES, AND PSYCHOLOGICAL MALADJUSTMENT

According to attachment theory (Main, 1990; Mikulincer and Shaver, 2003, 2007a; Shaver and Mikulincer, 2002), secondary attachment

strategies (anxious hyperactivation and avoidant deactivation) are defenses against the frustration and pain caused by the unavailability, unreliability, or unresponsiveness of attachment figures in times of need. Although these secondary strategies are initially aimed at achieving a workable relationship with an inconsistently available or consistently distant or unavailable attachment figure, they are maladaptive when used in later relationship situations in which proximity-seeking, psychological intimacy, and collaborative interdependence would be more productive and rewarding. Moreover, these strategies result in the maintenance of distorted or constraining working models and affect-regulation techniques that are likely to interfere with psychological health, personal growth, and social adjustment.

Anxious attachment encourages distress intensification and the arousal of negative memories, expectations, and emotions, which in turn interfere with mental coherence and, in some cases, precipitate episodes of serious psychopathology (Mikulincer and Shaver, 2003). Although avoidant people can maintain a defensive façade of security and imperturbability, they ignore, misinterpret, or misunderstand their own emotions and have difficulty dealing with prolonged, demanding stressors that require active problem confrontation and mobilization of external sources of support (Mikulincer and Shaver, 2003). In addition, although avoidant people are able to consciously suppress or ignore distress, the distress can still be indirectly expressed in somatic symptoms, sleep disturbances, and reduced immunity to diseases. Moreover, avoidant individuals can transform personal distress into feelings of hostility, loneliness, and estrangement from others (Shaver and Hazan, 1993).

Many studies confirm that attachment anxiety is inversely related to wellbeing and positively associated with global distress, depression, anxiety, eating disorders, substance abuse, conduct disorders, and severe personality disorders (see Mikulincer and Shaver, 2007a, for a review). With regard to avoidant attachment, many studies have found no significant associations between avoidant attachment and *self-report measures* of wellbeing and global distress (see Mikulincer and Shaver, 2007a, for a review). However, several studies indicate that avoidant attachment is associated with particular patterns of emotional and behavioral problems, such as a pattern of depression characterized by perfectionism, self-punishment, and self-criticism, somatic complaints; substance abuse and conduct disorders; and schizoid and avoidant personality disorders (see Mikulincer and Shaver, 2007a, for a review). In addition, whereas no consistent association has been found in community samples between avoidant attachment and global distress, studies that focus on highly demanding and stressful events, such as giving birth to a seriously handicapped infant, reveal that avoidance is related to higher levels of distress and poorer long-term outcomes (e.g., Berant et al., 2008).

ATTACHMENT THEORY: RELATION TO OTHER THEORIES AND POTENTIAL APPLICATIONS

Attachment theory interfaces with and has much in common with other theories discussed in this handbook. Attachment theory is, for example, an early evolutionary–psychological theory, having been constructed partly with reference to ethological studies of birds and nonhuman primates. It is closely related to interdependence theories of close relationships, which focus on interpersonal transactions and emphasize the influence of one person's responses on another's person's outcomes. Both attachment and interdependence theories emphasize the importance of trust between relationship partners. Attachment theory is not, however, exclusively relational. It includes the important idea that interactions with attachment figures can be biased by defensive processes related to secondary attachment strategies.

Because of such biases, working models of the self and others do not exclusively reflect the ways in which a person and relationship partners actually behave in a particular interaction. Rather, they are reflections of both actual social encounters and subjective biases resulting from already well-established defensive strategies. Moreover, attachment-system activation in adulthood can occur in the mind without necessarily being expressed directly in behavior, and without necessarily requiring the presence of an actual relationship partner.

Both attachment theory and social-cognition theories (included those discussed in the Cognitive Level of Analysis section of this volume) emphasize the extent to which people subjectively construe person–environment transactions, store representations of typical transactions, and use these representations to understand new transactions and organize action plans. In both theoretical approaches, these mental representations guide and coordinate emotion regulation, self-images, person perception, and cognitions, goals, feelings, and behavior in interpersonal settings. Furthermore, attachment theory conceptualizes working models in the same way that social-cognition theorists conceptualize mental representations: they are stored in an associative memory network, maintain excitatory and inhibitory connections with other representations, have a particular level of accessibility determined by past experiences and other factors, and this accessibility can be heightened in a given situation by relevant contextual cues.

Despite these commonalities, however, it would be a mistake to equate attachment working models with the cognitive structures usually studied in social cognition research. In their review of the nature, content, structure, and functions of attachment working models, Shaver et al. (1996) enumerated four differences between these constructs. As compared to other mental representations, (1) working models also tend to deal with a person's wishes, fears, conflicts, and psychological defenses, and they can be affected by these psychodynamic processes; (2) working models seem to have a larger and more powerful affective component than most social schemas and tend to be shaped more by emotion-regulation processes; (3) working models tend to be construed in more relational terms and to organize representations of the self, others, and social interactions in a highly interdependent fashion; and (4) working models are broader, richer, and more complex structures, and can include tandem or opposite representations of the same person–environment transaction at episodic, semantic, and procedural levels of encoding.

Throughout this chapter we have referred implicitly and explicitly to a wealth of applications of attachment theory and research. In our own research, for example, we have shown that security enhancement, whether accomplished consciously or unconsciously, has a number of laudable prosocial effects: reducing dogmatism, intolerance of ambiguity, and intergroup hostility; increasing empathy, compassion, and altruism; and increasing participation in community activities. Like self-affirmation procedures (Sherman and Cohen, 2006), which are thought to enhance self-integrity and warm feelings toward other people (Crocker et al., 2008), security-priming procedures reduce perceived threats to the self and make it easier to appreciate and assist others. In several studies we have shown the relevance of attachment theory and research to relationship and marital satisfaction, leadership development, group dynamics, and organizational functioning (Mikulincer and Shaver, 2007a). Attachment research from the beginning was intended to be applicable to parenting education and individual psychotherapy. It is now being applied in marital therapy as well.

Stepping back from the details of the theory and the thousands of empirical studies it has inspired, it is clear that every level of social life would be enhanced, and would be less destructive, violent, and depressing, if people were raised by responsive parents, taught by responsive teachers and mentors, living with responsive spouses, and supervised and guided by responsive leaders.

Many new interventions are being created based on attachment research, and so far their track record is very encouraging. In our opinion, attachment theory and research are helping to fulfill the original goal of social psychology, to provide a scientific basis for improving individual and social life.

REFERENCES

Ainsworth, M.D.S. (1940) An evaluation of adjustment based on the concept of security. Unpublished doctoral dissertation, University of Toronto, Ontario, Canada.

Ainsworth, M.D.S. (1967) *Infancy in Uganda: Infant Care and the Growth of Love*. Baltimore, MD: Johns Hopkins University Press.

Ainsworth, M.D.S. (1973) The development of infant-mother attachment. In B.M. Caldwell and H.N. Ricciuti (eds), *Review of Child Development Research*, 3, 1–94. Chicago: University of Chicago Press.

Ainsworth, M.D.S. (1991) Attachment and other affectional bonds across the life cycle. In C.M. Parkes, J. Stevenson-Hinde, and P. Marris (eds), *Attachment Across the Life Cycle*, pp. 33–51. New York: Routledge.

Ainsworth, M.D.S., Blehar, M.C., Waters, E. and Wall, S. (1978) *Patterns of Attachment: Assessed in the Strange Situation and at Home*. Hillsdale, NJ: Erlbaum.

Baldwin, M.W., Keelan, J.P.R., Fehr, B., Enns, V. and Koh Rangarajoo, E. (1996) Social-cognitive conceptualization of attachment working models: Availability and accessibility effects. *Journal of Personality and Social Psychology*, 71, 94–109.

Bartholomew, K. and Horowitz, L.M. (1991) Attachment styles among young adults: A test of a four-category model. *Journal of Personality and Social Psychology*, 61, 226–244.

Berant, E., Mikulincer, M. and Shaver, P.R. (2008) Mothers' attachment style, their mental health, and their children's emotional vulnerabilities: A seven-year study of children with congenital heart disease. *Journal of Personality*, 76, 31–66.

Bowlby, J. (1958) The nature of the child's tie to his mother. *International Journal of Psychoanalysis*, 39, 350–373.

Bowlby, J. (1973) *Attachment and Loss: Vol. 2. Separation: Anxiety and Anger*. New York: Basic Books.

Bowlby, J. (1979) *The Making and Breaking of Affectional Bonds*. London: Tavistock.

Bowlby, J. (1980) *Attachment and Loss: Vol. 3. Sadness and Depression*. New York: Basic Books.

Bowlby, J. (1982) *Attachment and Loss: Vol. 1. Attachment*, 2nd Edition. New York: Basic Books. (Originally published 1969).

Bowlby, J. (1988) *A Secure Base: Clinical Applications of Attachment Theory*. London: Routledge.

Brennan, K.A., Clark, C.L. and Shaver, P.R. (1998) Self-report measurement of adult romantic attachment: An integrative overview. In J.A. Simpson and W.S. Rholes (eds), *Attachment Theory and Close Relationships*, pp. 46–76. New York: Guilford Press.

Cassidy, J. and Kobak, R.R. (1988) Avoidance and its relationship with other defensive processes. In J. Belsky and T. Nezworski (eds), *Clinical Implications of Attachment*, pp. 300–323. Hillsdale, NJ: Erlbaum.

Cooper, M.L., Shaver, P.R. and Collins, N.L. (1998) Attachment styles, emotion regulation, and adjustment in adolescence. *Journal of Personality and Social Psychology, 74*, 1380–1397.

Crawford, T.N., Livesley, W.J., Jang, K.L., Shaver, P.R., Cohen, P. and Ganiban, J. (2007) Insecure attachment and personality disorder: A twin study of adults. *European Journal of Personality, 21*, 191–208.

Crocker, J., Niiya, Y. and Mischkowski, D. (2008) Why does writing about important values reduce defensiveness? Self-affirmation and the role of positive, other-directed feelings. *Psychological Science, 19*, 740–747.

Crowell, J.A., Fraley, R.C. and Shaver, P.R. (2008) Measurement of adult attachment. In J. Cassidy and P.R. Shaver (eds), *Handbook of Attachment: Theory, Research, and Clinical Applications, 2nd Edition*, pp. 599–634. New York: Guilford Press.

Davidovitz, R., Mikulincer, M., Shaver, P.R., Izsak, R. and Popper, M. (2007) Leaders as attachment figures: Leaders' attachment orientations predict leadership-related mental representations and followers' performance and mental health. *Journal of Personality and Social Psychology, 93*, 632–650.

de Wolff, M. and van IJzendoorn, M.H. (1997) Sensitivity and attachment: A meta-analysis on parental antecedents of infant attachment. *Child Development, 68*, 571–591.

Donnellan, M.B., Burt, S.A., Levendosky, A.A. and Klump, K.L. (2008) Genes, personality, and attachment in adults: A multivariate behavioral genetic analysis. *Personality and Social Psychology Bulletin, 34*, 3–16.

Elliot, A.J. and Reis, H.T. (2003) Attachment and exploration in adulthood. *Journal of Personality and Social Psychology, 85*, 317–331.

Feeney, J.A. (2008). Adult romantic attachment and couple relationships. In J. Cassidy and P.R. Shaver (eds), *Handbook of Attachment: Theory, Research, and Clinical Applications, 2nd Edition* pp. 456–481. New York: Guilford Press.

Fredrickson, B.L. (2001) The role of positive emotions in positive psychology: The broaden-and-build theory of positive emotions. *American Psychologist, 56*, 218–226.

Gable, S.L. and Haidt, J. (2005) What (and why) is positive psychology? *Review of General Psychology, 9*, 103–110.

George, C., Kaplan, N. and Main, M. (1985) The Adult Attachment Interview. Unpublished protocol, Department of Psychology, University of California, Berkeley.

Gillath, O., Shaver, P.R., Baek, J. and Chun, D.S. (2008) Genetic correlates of adult attachment style. *Personality and Social Psychology Bulletin, 34*, 1396–1405.

Gillath, O., Shaver, P.R., Mikulincer, M., Nitzberg, R.A., Erez, A. and van IJzendoorn, M.H. (2005) Attachment, caregiving, and volunteering: Placing volunteerism in an attachment-theoretical framework. *Personal Relationships, 12*, 425–446.

Gross, J.J. (1999) Emotion and emotion regulation. In O.P. John and L.A. Pervin (eds), *Handbook of Personality: Theory and Research*, 2nd Edition, pp. 525–552. New York: Guilford Press.

Harlow, H.F. (1959) Love in infant monkeys. *Scientific American, 200*, 68–86.

Hazan, C. and Shaver, P.R. (1987) Romantic love conceptualized as an attachment process. *Journal of Personality and Social Psychology, 52*, 511–524.

Hazan, C. and Shaver, P.R. (1994) Attachment as an organizational framework for research on close relationships. *Psychological Inquiry, 5*, 1–22.

Hazan, C. and Zeifman, D. (1994) Sex and the psychological tether. In K. Bartholomew and D. Perlman (eds), *Advances in Personal Relationships: Attachment Processes in Adulthood, 5*, 151–177. London: Jessica Kingsley.

Heinicke, C. and Westheimer, I. (1966) *Brief Separations*. New York: International Universities Press.

Hendrick, C. and Hendrick, S.S. (1986) A theory and method of love. *Journal of Personality and Social Psychology, 50*, 392–402.

Hesse, E. (2008) The Adult Attachment Interview: Protocol, method of analysis, and empirical studies. In J. Cassidy and P.R. Shaver (eds), *Handbook of Attachment: Theory, Research, and Clinical Applications*, 2nd Edition pp. 552–598. New York: Guilford Press.

Hinde, R. (1966) *Animal Behavior: A Synthesis of Ethology and Comparative Psychology*. New York: McGraw-Hill.

Jankowiak, W.R. (1995) *Romantic Passion*. New York: Columbia University Press.

Kelley H.H., Berscheid, E., Christensen, A., Harvey, J.H., Huston, T.L., Levinger, G., McClintock, E., Peplau, L.A. and Peterson, D.R. (1983) *Close Relationships*. New York: W.H. Freeman.

Kunce, L.J. and Shaver, P.R. (1994) An attachment-theoretical approach to caregiving in romantic relationships. In K. Bartholomew and D. Perlman (eds), *Advances in Personal Relationships*, 5, 205–237. London: Kingsley.

Lorenz, K.Z. (1952) *King Solomon's Ring*. New York: Crowell.

Main, M. (1990) Cross-cultural studies of attachment organization: Recent studies, changing methodologies, and the concept of conditional strategies. *Human Development*, 33, 48–61.

Main, M., Kaplan, N. and Cassidy, J. (1985) Security in infancy, childhood, and adulthood: A move to the level of representation. *Monographs of the Society for Research in Child Development*, 50, 66–104.

Main, M. and Solomon, J. (1990) Procedures for identifying infants as disorganized/disoriented during the Ainsworth strange situation. In M.T. Greenberg, D. Cicchetti, and M. Cummings (eds), *Attachment in the Preschool Years: Theory, Research, and Intervention*, pp. 121–160. Chicago: University of Chicago Press.

Mikulincer, M., Florian, V. and Tolmacz, R. (1990) Attachment styles and fear of personal death: A case study of affect regulation. *Journal of Personality and Social Psychology*, 58, 273–280.

Mikulincer, M., Gillath, O. and Shaver, P.R. (2002) Activation of the attachment system in adulthood: Threat-related primes increase the accessibility of mental representations of attachment figures. *Journal of Personality and Social Psychology*, 83, 881–895.

Mikulincer, M. and Shaver, P.R. (2003) The attachment behavioral system in adulthood: Activation, psychodynamics, and interpersonal processes. In M.P. Zanna (ed.), *Advances in Experimental Social Psychology*, 35, 53–152. New York: Academic Press.

Mikulincer, M. and Shaver, P.R. (2004) Security-based self-representations in adulthood: Contents and processes. In W.S. Rholes and J.A. Simpson (eds), *Adult Attachment: Theory, Research, and Clinical Implications*, pp. 159–195. New York: Guilford Press.

Mikulincer, M. and Shaver, P.R. (2005) Mental representations of attachment security: Theoretical foundation for a positive social psychology. In M.W. Baldwin (ed.), *Interpersonal Cognition*, pp. 233–266. New York: Guilford Press.

Mikulincer, M. and Shaver, P.R. (2006) The behavioral system construct: A useful tool for building an integrative model of the social mind. In P.A.M. Van Lange (ed.), *Bridging Social Psychology: Benefits of Transdisciplinary Approaches*, pp. 279–284. Mahwah, NJ: Erlbaum.

Mikulincer, M. and Shaver, P.R. (2007a) *Attachment in Adulthood: Structure, Dynamics, and Change*. New York: Guilford Press.

Mikulincer, M. and Shaver, P.R. (2007b) Boosting attachment security to promote mental health, prosocial values, and inter-group tolerance. *Psychological Inquiry*, 18, 139–156.

Mikulincer, M., Shaver, P.R., Cassidy, J. and Berant, E. (2008) Attachment-related defensive processes. In J.H. Obegi and E. Berant (eds), *Clinical Applications of Adult Attachment*, pp. 293–327. New York: Guilford Press.

Mikulincer, M., Shaver, P.R., Gillath, O. and Nitzberg, R.A. (2005) Attachment, caregiving, and altruism: Boosting attachment security increases compassion and helping. *Journal of Personality and Social Psychology*, 89, 817–839.

Mikulincer, M., Shaver, P.R., Sapir-Lavid, Y. and Avihou-Kanza, N. (2009) What's inside the minds of securely and insecurely attached people? The secure-base script and its associations with attachment-style dimensions. *Journal of Personality and Social Psychology*, 97, 615–633.

Murray, S.L., Holmes, J.G. and Collins, N.L. (2006) The relational signature of felt security. *Psychological Bulletin*, 132, 641–666.

Noftle, E.E. and Shaver, P.R. (2006) Attachment dimensions and the Big Five personality traits: Associations and comparative ability to predict relationship quality. *Journal of Research in Personality*, 40, 179–208.

Overall, N.C., Fletcher, G.J.O. and Friesen, M.D. (2003) Mapping the intimate relationship mind: Comparisons between three models of attachment representations. *Personality and Social Psychology Bulletin*, 29, 1479–1493.

Peplau, L.A. and Perlman, D. (eds) (1982) *Loneliness: A Sourcebook of Current Theory, Research, and Therapy*. New York: Wiley.

Reis, H.T., Clark, M.S. and Holmes, J.G. (2004) Perceived partner responsiveness as an organizing construct in the study of intimacy and closeness. In D.J. Mashek and A. Aron (eds), *Handbook of Closeness and Intimacy*, pp. 201–225. Mahwah, NJ: Erlbaum.

Rom, E. and Mikulincer, M. (2003) Attachment theory and group processes: The association between attachment style and group-related representations, goals, memories, and functioning. *Journal of Personality and Social Psychology, 84*, 1220–1235.

Rubenstein, C. and Shaver, P.R. (1982) The experience of loneliness. In L.A. Peplau and D. Perlman (eds), *Loneliness: A Sourcebook of Current Theory, Research, and Therapy,* pp. 206–223. New York: Wiley.

Rusbult, C.E., Verette, J., Whitney, G.A., Slovik, L.F. and Lipkus, I. (1991) Accommodation processes in close relationships: Theory and preliminary empirical evidence. *Journal of Personality and Social Psychology, 60*, 53–78.

Seligman, M.E.P. (2002) *Authentic Happiness: Using the New Positive Psychology to Realize Your Potential for Lasting Fulfillment.* New York: Free Press.

Shaver, P.R., Collins, N.L. and Clark, C.L. (1996) Attachment styles and internal working models of self and relationship partners. In G.J.O. Fletcher and J. Fitness (eds), *Knowledge Structures in Close Relationships: A Social Psychological Approach,* pp. 25–61. Mahwah, NJ: Erlbaum.

Shaver, P.R. and Hazan, C. (1984) Incompatibility, loneliness, and limerence. In W. Ickes (ed.), *Compatible and Incompatible Relationships,* pp. 163–184. New York: Springer-Verlag.

Shaver, P.R. and Hazan, C. (1993) Adult romantic attachment: Theory and evidence. In D. Perlman and W. Jones (eds), *Advances in Personal Relationships, 4,* pp. 29–70. London: Jessica Kingsley.

Shaver, P.R., Hazan, C. and Bradshaw, D. (1988) Love as attachment: The integration of three behavioral systems. In R.J. Sternberg and M. Barnes (eds), *The Psychology of Love,* pp. 68–99. New Haven: Yale University Press.

Shaver, P.R. and Mikulincer, M. (2002) Attachment-related psychodynamics. *Attachment and Human Development, 4*, 133–161.

Shaver, P.R. and Mikulincer, M. (2006) Attachment theory, individual psychodynamics, and relationship functioning. In D. Perlman and A. Vangelisti (eds), *Handbook of Personal Relationships,* pp. 251–272. New York: Cambridge University Press.

Shaver, P.R. and Mikulincer, M. (2008) Augmenting the sense of security in romantic, leader-follower, therapeutic, and group relationships: A relational model of psychological change. In J.P. Forgas and J. Fitness (eds), *Social Relationships: Cognitive, Affective, and Motivational Processes,* pp. 55–74. New York: Psychology Press.

Shaver, P.R. and Mikulincer, M. (2009) Attachment theory and attachment styles. In M.R. Leary and R.H. Hoyle (eds), *Handbook of Individual Differences in Social Behavior,* pp. 62–81. New York: Guilford Press.

Sherman, D.K. and Cohen, G.L. (2006) The psychology of self-defense: Self-affirmation theory. In M.P. Zanna (ed.), *Advances in Experimental Social Psychology, 38*, 183–242. San Diego: Academic Press.

Simpson, J.A., Rholes, W.S. and Nelligan, J.S. (1992) Support seeking and support giving within couples in an anxiety-provoking situation: The role of attachment styles. *Journal of Personality and Social Psychology, 62*, 434–446.

Singer, I. (1987) *The Nature of Love: Courtly and Romantic.* Chicago: University of Chicago Press.

Sroufe, L.A., Egeland, B., Carlson, E. and Collins, W.A. (2005) *The Development of the Person: The Minnesota Study of Risk and Adaptation from Birth to Adulthood.* New York: Guilford Press.

Sroufe, L.A. and Waters, E. (1977) Attachment as an organizational construct. *Child Development, 48*, 1184–1199.

Sternberg, R.J. (1986) A triangular theory of love. *Psychological Review, 93*, 119–135.

Torgersen, A.M., Grova, B.K. and Sommerstad, R. (2007) A pilot study of attachment patterns in adult twins. *Attachment and Human Development, 9*, 127–138.

van IJzendoorn, M. (1995) Adult attachment representations, parental responsiveness, and infant attachment: A meta-analysis on the predictive validity of the Adult Attachment Interview. *Psychological Bulletin, 117*, 387–403.

Vaughn, B.E., Bost, K.K. and van IJzendoorn, M.H. (2008) Attachment and temperament: Additive and interactive influences on behavior, affect, and cognition during infancy and childhood. In J. Cassidy and P.R. Shaver (eds), *Handbook of Attachment: Theory, Research, and Clinical Applications,* 2nd Edition, pp. 192–216. New York: Guilford Press.

Weiss, R.S. (1973) *Loneliness: The Experience of Emotional and Social Isolation.* Cambridge, MA: MIT Press.

35

Shared-Reality Theory

Gerald Echterhoff

ABSTRACT

In providing an overview of shared reality theory, the chapter first presents the current formulation of the theory, with a focus on assumptions about critical conditions for the occurrence of shared reality and its underlying psychological processes. The second section provides a selective review of empirical evidence, focusing on interpersonal communication as a main arena for shared reality creation and motivational underpinnings. In the third section, the intellectual history of shared reality theory is outlined. Based on the original contributions by Tory Higgins and his colleagues, the ancestry of the theory is traced to the domain of language and communication, phenomenological approaches in sociology and philosophy, and social influence research. The final section provides illustrations of the applicability of the theory, and a discussion of the theory's utility.

INTRODUCTION

Creating shared views about the world is ubiquitous. For instance, when people meet a new employee at their workplace, they tend to form their impressions of the newcomer jointly with their colleagues, and they feel more confident in their impressions when others agree. People take into account the views of others, especially significant others (see Andersen and Chen, 2002), to appraise experiences and events, and to construct or verify views about various types of issues (Hardin and Higgins, 1996). Social sharing allows us, for example, to evaluate other people or groups; to form general political, moral, or religious convictions; and even to develop and maintain a sense of who we are and what we want (Higgins, 1996b; James, 1890; Sullivan, 1953). The absence of social sharing can have detrimental consequences for people's wellbeing, their feelings of connectedness, and sense of reality. When interaction partners withhold an expected shared reality, such as in the classical conformity studies by Asch (1951), people are left uncertain, uncomfortable, even physically agitated.

Accounts emphasizing the social underpinnings and interpersonal nature of our representations of reality have circulated, in varying shapes and forms, for a long time in the social sciences and psychology (e.g., Asch, 1952; Bar-Tal, 1990, 2000; Cooley, 1964; Festinger, 1950; Heider, 1958; Lewin, 1947; Mead, 1934; Merton and Kitt, 1950; Moscovici, 1981; Newcomb, 1959; Resnick et al., 1991; Rommetveit, 1974; Schachter, 1959; Schütz, 1967; Sherif, 1935, 1936).

Given the long history of these approaches and compared with most theories covered in this handbook, shared reality theory as a distinct theory of social influence on reality construction is relatively young. While the conceptual framework has been developed mainly over the last 20 years (Hardin and Higgins, 1996; Higgins, 1992, 1999), empirical work informed by the theory has been mostly published only within the past five years (for a review, see Echterhoff et al., 2009a).

The theory's concern with the construal of reality conjures up a classical issue that has concerned scholars in philosophy, cognitive psychology, and the neurosciences for many decades. How can people, given the highly constructive and self-contained operation of the human mind, distinguish between what is real and what is mere imagination, dream, or fantasy? Apparently, humans are equipped with cognitive and neural mechanisms, such as comparing predicted and actual sensory input, that tell them whether the output of mental operations and their mental models are sufficiently consistent with external stimulus conditions, that is, whether they are in touch with the real world (e.g., Frith, 2007; Johnson and Raye, 1981). In contrast, shared reality theory focuses on processes that are different from or subsequent to such low-level monitoring of reality. For instance, when members of a work team meet a new colleague, they try to find out what kind of person the newcomer is, whether she is trustworthy, sociable, and open-minded. This allows them to evaluate the newcomer, to predict her actions, and to interact with her purposefully. The relevant question here is not whether the observed events are real, that is, whether the team members trust their perception of the newcomer's appearance and behavior as real (versus imagined). Rather, the question refers to the attributes and qualities of the target entity and the meaning of the observed events; that is, how the team members think about, categorize, judge, and evaluate the newcomer based on their perceptions and observations (see Higgins, in press).

Whereas the cognitive factors of reality construction, like the accessibility of knowledge and its semantic applicability, have been studied extensively and intensively by social psychologists in past decades (see, e.g., Higgins, 1996a, in press), genuinely social factors have typically received less attention. In the example, the experienced reality or truth about the newcomer can result from cognitive processes like the activation and application of pertinent knowledge, but it can also result from sharing impressions about the newcomer between the old team members (Levine and Higgins, 2001). For instance, the team members may create through conversation a shared view as to whether the talkativeness of the newcomer means that she is sociable or cordial (positive traits), rather than conceited or ingratiating (negative traits).

Nowadays, most psychologists would probably accept, or at least not actively dispute, the general notion of a social foundation of mental representations of the world. However, it is less common for psychologists, given the long-standing individual-centered orientation of the discipline, to make this issue the subject of deeper analysis and empirical investigation in its own right. The latter projects represent precisely the agenda of shared reality research. Given the occasional generality and diversity of earlier related theorizing, a key challenge for theory construction was to steer the concept of shared reality toward a greater, adequate level of specificity and carve out its distinctive and unique potential. A challenge for empirical research was to capture the novel theoretical assumptions and hypotheses in experiments that would convince the peer community, and to assess the occurrence – that is, people's experience – of shared reality empirically. The present chapter provides an overview of the results and some of the history of this endeavor.

The first section of this chapter is devoted to the conceptualization of shared reality and assumptions about the critical conditions for the occurrence of shared reality, along with the distinct psychological mechanisms that underlie it. In the second section, I will briefly review empirical evidence supporting the theory, which focuses on shared reality created in interpersonal communication and its motivational underpinnings. In the third section, the intellectual history of shared reality theory is outlined, including the original contributions by Tory Higgins and his colleagues; the ancestry of the theory is traced to the domains of language and communication, phenomenological approaches in sociology and philosophy, and social influence research. The final section provides illustrations of the applicability and utility of the theory.

SHARED REALITY THEORY: CONCEPTUALIZATION AND CRITICAL CONDITIONS

According to the most current proposal (Echterhoff et al., 2009a), shared reality is defined as the product of the motivated process of experiencing with others a commonality of inner states about the world. This conceptualization presumes that four main conditions underlie shared reality. First, the commonality between individuals that is implied by a shared reality refers to their inner states and not just their overt behaviors. Second, shared reality is "about something" – that is, it implies a target referent about which people create a shared reality. Third, shared reality as a product cannot be divorced from the process through which it is attained – in particular, the underlying motives. Fourth, there is no shared reality unless people experience a successful connection to someone else's inner state. These conditions will now be elaborated in turn.

According to the first condition, a shared reality involves a commonality between people's inner states, which include their beliefs, judgments, feelings, or evaluations concerning a target referent. To achieve a shared reality, people cannot simply replicate the observable behavior of others; instead, they

need to obtain a sense of others' inner states about the world. For the occurrence of a shared reality, a correspondence between externally observable states or behaviors is not sufficient – it needs to involve a commonality between inner states (see Brickman, 1978). This claim is supported by the fundamental and well-established role that the perception of others' inner states plays in human development, motivation, and sociality. People know not only that the outcomes for a person (self or other) depend critically on another person's overt responses to that person (e.g., Ostrom, 1984), but also that the other person's responses are mediated by his or her inner states, such as his or her attitudes and beliefs (Higgins, 2005, 2010). Indeed, the discovery of the mediating role of others' inner states in how they respond to the world is a significant step in human development (see Higgins and Pittman, 2008). Once this level of social consciousness is reached, others' inner states begin to play a vital role in human self-regulation (Higgins, 2010).

The achievement of the first condition requires processes that allow people to pick up or infer someone else's inner state. Psychological research suggests a plethora of mechanisms by which this can be accomplished (see, e.g., Higgins and Pittman, 2008; Malle and Hodges, 2005). For instance, people draw on various aspects of others' nonverbal behavior, such as their facial expressions and gestures, to intuit the others' feelings, needs, and intentions. They grasp others' mental states, such as others' beliefs, attitudes, and feelings, drawing on mechanisms like conscious reasoning, unconscious simulation, and theory of mind (e.g., Keysers and Gazzola, 2007); causal theories and schemata (e.g., Heider, 1958; Malle, 1999); or projection of their own inner states (e.g., Keysar and Barr, 2002; Nickerson, 2001). This precondition is a building block of the first condition for shared reality – the perceived sharing of inner states and not just overt behaviors.

The previous argument makes implicit reference to the second condition of shared reality – shared reality is about some target referent. For a shared reality to occur it is not sufficient that people simply exhibit corresponding inner states, such as corresponding heart rates or mood states. If corresponding inner states are not about (i.e., not in reference to) some aspect of the world, then one cannot not speak of a shared reality. This is because *reality* refers to the objects or referents of knowledge – that is, to phenomena that are experienced by actors as being part of the world in the present, as well as in the past and future (such as future desired end-states; Higgins and Pittman, 2008). Thus, shared reality goes beyond simply replicating another person's inner state in that it requires sharing states that are *about* some target referent: for example, about a new colleague at work, about a specific TV program, about a particular politician, or about abstract political or religious issues (see Jost et al., 2007).

Like the first condition, this second condition – that shared reality is *about* some target referent – requires that a critical precondition be met. Specifically, it requires mechanisms that allow people to infer the target referent of their sharing partner's inner state, such as the referent of another person's feeling. Research has identified various mechanisms by which this can be achieved. One basic mechanism is to follow the direction of someone else's eye gaze (e.g., Baron-Cohen, 1995; Tomasello et al., 2005; Tomasello, 2008) to identify the referent of that person's sustained interest or emotional response, such as what it is that she or he fears. Eye-gaze following, together with imputing intentionality to the other person, allows the allocation of shared interest in an object (Baron-Cohen, 1995). Other mechanisms include following someone else's pointing movements or manipulations of objects (Clark, 2003; Tomasello, 2008) and interpreting verbal utterances as referring to an object (Clark, 1996; Clark and Marshall, 1981).

According to the third condition, the occurrence of shared reality depends on the motives that drive the achievement of common inner states. By this view, what needs to be taken into account is the source, or process history, of a commonality of people's inner states. The sheer fact or presence of a commonality is not sufficient. An analogy would be that democracy concerns not only consensus as an outcome or state of agreement but also the processes by which people reach a consensus (see, e.g., Bohman and Rehg, 1997). How a consensus or agreement is reached and whether the right procedures are observed to arrive at a consensus are, in many cases, more important than the product or outcome itself (Mackie and Skelly, 1994). More generally, end states often attain their value from how they were reached and not just from the outcome per se (Higgins, 2006).

What, then, are the motives driving the creation of a shared reality? Two motives have figured prominently in the literature on social motivation in general and on shared reality in particular: epistemic and relational motives (Bar-Tal, 2000; Fiske, 2007; Hardin and Conley, 2001; Hardin and Higgins, 1996; Jost et al., 2007). *Epistemic motives* refer to the need to achieve a valid and reliable understanding of the world (Hardin and Higgins, 1996) and to establish what is real (Higgins, in press). Humans are motivated by what Bartlett (1932) called effort after meaning, a fundamental need to understand the events and circumstances of their lives (e.g., Kagan, 1972), to extend their knowledge continuously (Loewenstein, 1994), and, no less important, to experience themselves as successful in this endeavor (Higgins, in press). Achieving such epistemic goals has various beneficial consequences; for example, a sufficiently accurate understanding of the world allows humans to operate successfully in their environment. It ranges from basic knowledge about how to survive by securing necessary resources and avoid vital risks to sophisticated mental models of how to create and maintain important relationships or to develop one's professional career. The strength of epistemic motives typically increases with uncertainty or ambiguity about a target referent (e.g., Berlyne, 1962; Hogg, 2007).

Consistent with this notion, Festinger (1950) argued that the more ambiguous and difficult to interpret experiences are, the more people seek a social reality provided by appropriate (i.e., sufficiently trustworthy) others (see also Byrne and Clore, 1967; Deutsch and Gerard, 1955; Sherif, 1936). Given that shared reality is about a target referent, it follows that the creation of shared reality always serves, at least to some extent, epistemic motives.

Relational motives induce people to affiliate and feel connected to others. Feeling connected to others has several positive consequences, including emotional wellbeing, a sense of security, and self-esteem (e.g., Baumeister and Leary, 1995; Diener and Seligman, 2002). The desire for connectedness is reflected, for example, in the affiliative tendency that people exhibit when they are confronted with potentially anxiety-arousing situations (Schachter, 1959).

The motivational process that has led to a commonality of inner states is assumed to be critical to whether the commonality is a shared reality. Adopting another person's inner state, for example, could be driven by instrumental goals of securing beneficial social responses or maximizing personal outcomes (see Higgins, 1981; Jones and Thibaut, 1958). Social actors pursue such instrumental goals, for instance, when they ingratiate themselves with others (Jones, 1964) or take the perspective of a competitor to prevail in a social conflict (Epley et al., 2006). In such cases, actors adopt another person's inner state not because they want to achieve a better understanding of a reference target or to establish what is real, but because they hope to attain other, ulterior goals. In such cases, the adopted commonality is not a shared reality.

According to the fourth condition, a shared reality requires that the participating individuals actually experience the sharing – that is, that they experience a commonality with someone else's inner state. Consistent with this view, Bar-Tal (2000) has argued that sharing of beliefs entails more than merely an objective commonality between people

that can be identified by an external observer. Instead, sharing must involve the subjective experience or awareness of a commonality. Even if people are motivated to share inner states with others, they may end up not establishing an experienced commonality. Thus, it is not enough to have taken action to create a commonality with another person's inner state in the service of appropriate (such as relational or epistemic) motives. It is also necessary that one perceive the commonality to have been, in fact, established.

By including the fourth condition that individuals actually experience the sharing, Echterhoff et al. (2009a) emphasized the critical role of the subjective sense of sharing. This aspect can be further elaborated in the context of the first and second condition for shared reality, thus suggesting possible interrelations among the conditions. For the achievement of shared reality, people need to subjectively experience both the commonality of inner states and the referential aboutness of inner states. From this perspective, there can be a shared reality even if both assumptions of sharing are objectively wrong. That is, for Person A to experience a shared reality with Person B, it is not necessary for B to actually have the same inner state as A or for B's inner state to actually refer to the same referent that A has in mind. What is critical is that A believes that B's inner state and the referent of that inner state match A's inner state and referent. Consider, for example, a new member (A) in a research lab who believes that the current members in the lab are arrogant and wants to create a shared reality with another newcomer (B) about these members. For Newcomer A to have a shared reality with B, it is critical that A infer (e.g., by observing that B acts in a tense and uncomfortable manner at a lab meeting) that B has a shared inner state about the current members as referent (i.e., B also believes that they are arrogant). If Newcomer B later makes clear that the current members are her academic idols and that she always feels uncomfortable in encounters with admired people, then A's sense of a shared reality will be eliminated.

The unique contribution of this concept of shared reality can be seen exactly in the formulation of the four critical conditions and its building blocks. This addition to the theory has enhanced the precision, integration, and testability of the theory, and it affords clear distinctions between shared reality and related concepts such as common ground, empathy, perspective-taking, embodied synchrony (see Semin, 2007), and socially distributed knowledge (for a discussion, see Echterhoff et al., 2009a).

EMPIRICAL EVIDENCE SUPPORTING THE THEORY

In the following, I review empirical studies that have examined the creation of shared reality in interpersonal communication, which is arguably the main vehicle for social sharing (Berger and Luckmann, 1966; Higgins, 1992; Higgins and Rholes, 1978). When people are motivated to create a shared reality with others, they often communicate with these others about a target referent. The communication studies presented here are based on the hypothesis that communicating about a target referent can affect communicators' cognitive representations of that target. Studies employing the "saying-is-believing" paradigm have demonstrated such communication effects on subsequent cognition (e.g., Higgins and Rholes, 1978; Higgins et al., 2007; Sedikides, 1990; for reviews see Higgins, 1992, 1999; McCann and Higgins, 1992). In this paradigm, participants are introduced to an ostensible referential communication task (involving a communicator, a target, and an audience) in which they take the role of the communicator. The participants, who are typically students, read an essay about another student (the target person) who supposedly has volunteered to be part of a long-term research project on interpersonal perception. They are told that their task is to describe the target person's behaviors – without mentioning the target's

name – to another volunteer (the audience) who knows the target person. On the basis of their message description, the "audience" volunteer would try to identify the target person as the referent of the message from among a set of several possible targets in the alleged research project.

A short essay consisting of several passages provides the input information about the target person. The behaviors described in each passage are evaluatively ambiguous; they can be interpreted as indicating either a positive or a negative trait with approximately equal likelihood (e.g., "persistent" versus "stubborn" or "independent" versus "aloof"). For example, the behavior described in the following sample passage could be labeled as either "independent" or "aloof": "Other than business engagements, Michael's contacts with people are surprisingly limited. He feels he doesn't really need to rely on anyone." (e.g., Echterhoff et al., 2008). To manipulate the audience's supposed attitude toward the target person, the researchers informed the participants (in an offhand way) that their audience either likes the target (positive audience attitude) or dislikes the target (negative audience attitude). In their subsequent communication, participants typically exhibit audience tuning: They evaluatively tailor, or "tune," their messages to their audience's attitude (i.e., they create evaluatively positive messages for an audience who likes the target and evaluatively negative messages for an audience who dislikes the target).

After a delay (from approximately ten minutes in some studies to several weeks in other studies), researchers test the participants' memory for the original input information. Participants are asked to recall, as accurately as possible, the original essay about the target person in a free, written format. In demonstrations of the saying-is-believing effect, the evaluative tone of the communicators' own recall for the original input information matches the evaluative tone of their previous, audience-tuned message. In other words, communicators' own memory representations of the message topic reflect the audience-tuned view expressed in their message rather than just the original target information. Communicators end up believing and remembering what they said rather than what they originally learned about the target.

After the initial demonstrations of this "saying-is-believing" effect (e.g., Higgins and Rholes, 1978; Higgins and McCann, 1984), a number of studies using other paradigms have shown that people's mental representations of an experience can be profoundly shaped by how they verbally describe the experience to others (e.g., Adaval and Wyer, 2004; Tversky and Marsh, 2000; for reviews, see Chiu et al., 1998; Marsh, 2007). Thus, the influence of verbal communication on subsequent cognition is well established. Also, the saying-is-believing effect in particular has been replicated with several variations in methodology and extended to new areas. For instance, although the effect was originally demonstrated for tuning to the audience's attitude toward the target (Higgins and Rholes, 1978), it has also been found for tuning to the audience's knowledge about the target (Higgins et al., 1982). Also, the effect occurs regardless of whether communicators know their audience's view before or after encoding the input information (Kopietz et al., 2010, Experiment 1). The effect has been extended from situations in which the communication topic is a single individual to situations in which the topic target is a small group (Hausmann et al., 2008). Furthermore, the effect occurs not only with verbal stimulus material as input information about a target, but also with complex visual input material, namely video-filmed behaviors of target persons (Hellmann et al., in press; Kopietz et al., 2009).

Several studies demonstrated that the saying-is-believing effect occurs to the extent that communicators create a shared reality with their audience about the target person, as characterized by the four conditions outlined earlier (e.g., Echterhoff et al., 2005, 2008; Echterhoff et al., 2009b; Hellmann et al., in press; Higgins et al., 2007; Kopietz

et al., 2009; Kopietz et al., 2010). In the studies by Echterhoff, Higgins, and colleagues, for example, communicators' memory representations of the target person (assessed by free recall) were biased by their audience tuning under conditions that support creating a shared reality but not under conditions that undermine creating a shared reality. The creation of a shared reality can fail when any one of the four conditions described earlier fails to be sufficiently satisfied.

The bulk of extant empirical evidence relates to the third condition of shared reality; that is, the motivation underlying creating an interpersonal commonality, and thus this review emphasizes findings relevant to this condition. A discussion of findings regarding the other three conditions can be found in Echterhoff et al. (2009a), who also review evidence that rules out alternative explanations for the saying-is-believing effect such as differential reduction of cognitive dissonance (Festinger, 1957), self-perception (Bem, 1967), and source confusion. What the research shows is that communicators create a shared reality with their audience only when their production of audience-congruent messages is appropriately motivated; that is, the motivation behind the creation of commonality with another person's inner state is critical for a shared reality.

In one set of studies, Echterhoff et al. (2008) directly manipulated the goals underlying audience tuning. It was assumed that, in the standard saying-is-believing conditions (e.g., Higgins and Rholes, 1978), audience tuning serves epistemic motives that are characteristic of shared reality. Specifically, the evaluative ambiguity inherent in the behavioral-input information about the target person should elicit the epistemic motivation to reduce uncertainty. By tuning messages to the audience, communicators construct an audience-congruent representation of the target and thus attain a greater sense of certainty about what the target is like. In the Echterhoff et al. (2008) studies, this standard "shared reality-goal" condition was compared with conditions in which audience tuning served nonshared reality goals. The nonshared reality goals included obtaining monetary incentives for producing an audience-congruent message and entertaining the audience with an exaggerated, caricature-like description of the target person (Echterhoff et al., 2008, Experiments 2a and 2b). Based on the above rationale, it was hypothesized that communicators in the shared reality-goal condition should adopt the audience's inner state during message production to reduce uncertainty about the target person. In contrast, in the nonshared reality-goal conditions communicators should adopt their audience's inner state primarily to attain goals unrelated to the epistemic motivation that is characteristic of shared reality; they pursue alternative, or "ulterior," goals that are not conducive to a shared reality.

As predicted, it was found that communicators in these alternative, nonshared reality-goal conditions tuned their messages even more strongly to their audience's attitude than did communicators in the shared reality-goal condition (for the sake of the incentive or entertainment), but, nonetheless, the audience-tuning memory bias was not found. In contrast, the memory bias was found as usual in the standard shared reality-goal condition. Consistent with shared reality assumptions, additional measures revealed that audience tuning was experienced as being motivated by external demands to a greater extent in the alternative-goal conditions than it was in the shared reality-goal condition. Also, communicators' *epistemic trust* in the audience and in their audience-congruent message was significantly higher in the shared reality-goal condition than in the alternative nonshared reality-goal conditions.

These findings suggest that when people merely want to go along with another person – for instance, to obtain rewards from this person – a shared reality with that person is not produced. When people generate representations corresponding to another person's inner state without being motivated to create a shared view about a target, they do not achieve a shared reality. What matters is not the fact of a commonality with another person per se, but the motivation that produces the commonality.

In another set of studies, the creation of a shared reality was shown to depend on whether communicators were or were not motivated to share inner states with the particular person who was the audience for their message (Echterhoff et al., 2005, Experiment 2; Echterhoff et al., 2008, Experiment 1; Kopietz et al., 2010). Presumably, communicators do not regard just any person to be an appropriate partner with whom to share inner states. As suggested by research on social comparison and group-anchored knowledge (e.g., Festinger, 1950; Kruglanski et al., 2006), individuals regard others who possess certain qualities, such as sufficient similarity and trustworthiness, as more appropriate partners with whom to share reality than others who lack these qualities. Among these qualities, membership in a perceiver's ingroup (versus outgroup) is particularly important.

As suggested by various strands of intergroup research (e.g., Hogg, 2007; Kruglanski et al., 2006; Levine and Higgins, 2001), people should be less motivated to create a shared reality with outgroup members than with ingroup members. Nonetheless, in the standard saying-is-believing paradigm, which involves a referential communication task, communicator participants can still be expected to tune their message to an outgroup audience. However, compared to tuning messages to an ingroup audience, tuning messages to an outgroup audience should be motivated more by task fulfillment and politeness demands than by the desire to achieve a shared reality with the audience for epistemic and relational motives. In the standard saying-is-believing paradigm, shared reality motives are typically induced, but when the audience is an outgroup member alternative, nonshared reality motives should take precedence. Thus, if the motivation behind audience tuning is critical, then communicators tuning messages to an outgroup audience should exhibit little if any audience-congruent recall bias.

These predictions were borne out in studies by Echterhoff, Higgins, and colleagues. Although messages were tuned to both outgroup audience and ingroup audience, communicators talking to an outgroup audience did not incorporate the audience-tuned message into their own memory of the target. They also exhibited lower epistemic trust in their audience's view than did communicators tuning to an ingroup audience (Echterhoff et al., 2005, Experiment 2; Echterhoff et al., 2008, Experiment 1). Furthermore, participants (German students at a German university) who communicated to an audience belonging to a stigmatized outgroup (Turks) reported more often that they made an active effort to adapt their messages to their audience's views than did participants communicating to an ingroup (German) audience (Echterhoff et al., 2008, Experiment 1). These findings suggest that people producing audience-congruent messages merely to comply with external demands (e.g., behaving in a polite or unprejudiced manner; see Dovidio et al., 2002; Richeson and Trawalter, 2005) do not create a shared reality.

While the previous review has focused on the effects of shared reality driven communication on the communicators themselves, these effects are likely to apply to the recipients as well. Support for this notion comes from a recent study by Stukas et al. (2010). These authors found that recipients' beliefs about a target group were biased by messages tuned toward their presumable beliefs, whereas in fact they initially did not know the target group and thus did not hold pre-existing attitudes. Consistent with shared reality theory, the effect on recipients was stronger for those recipients who reported a greater willingness and experience of shared reality with the communicator. Thus, communicators' expectations about recipients' attitudes toward a group can initiate a confirmatory process by which both communicators and recipients come to hold the expected attitudes, thus giving rise to a shared reality created without anyone holding an initial view of that "reality"!

INTELLECTUAL HISTORY OF THE THEORY

The social foundation of basic psychological phenomena has been conceptualized and discussed for a long time in different disciplines, including social psychology (e.g., Asch, 1952; Bar-Tal, 1990; Festinger, 1950; Hardin and Higgins, 1996; Heider, 1958; Levine and Higgins, 2001; Lewin, 1947; Moscovici, 1981; Schachter, 1959; Sherif, 1935, 1936), the general social sciences and sociology (Cooley, 1964; Mead, 1934; Schütz, 1967; Thompson and Fine, 1999), memory and cognition (Graf et al., 2010; Hirst and Echterhoff, 2008; Hirst and Manier, 2002; Marsh, 2010; Smith and Semin, 2004; Weldon, 2001), psycholinguistics (Pickering and Garrod, 2004), organizational behavior (Salas and Fiore, 2004), developmental psychology (Meltzoff and Decety, 2003), evolutionary psychology (Caporael, 2007, 2010; de Waal, 2008), social neuroscience (e.g., Gallese et al., 2004; Iacoboni, 2008, in press), biology (e.g., Dunbar and Shultz, 2007), and philosophy (e.g., Thagard, 1997). While this field spans a wide range of approaches with greatly varying terminology, the development of the distinctive concept of shared reality can be attributed and dated much more specifically. It was originally achieved and literally "nurtured" from its very inception in the 1990s to the present day by Tory Higgins. He, joined over the years by collaborators, both laid the groundwork and continuously developed the theory over the years. Hence, the following brief history is oriented by the publications of Tory Higgins and his colleagues during each phase of the development of shared reality theory.

These contributions – primarily Higgins (1992), Hardin and Higgins (1996), Higgins (1999), Echterhoff et al. (2009a), but to some extent already Higgins (1981) – contain not only the substance of the concept of shared reality but also review the scholarly works that have served as input to the theory. Taken together, the various precursors and sources of inspiration can be organized into three main areas: interpersonal communication and language use, phenomenological approaches in philosophy and sociology, and social influence research. Intermittently, the personal dimension of the theory development is illustrated, including biographical circumstances.

Let me begin with the first and probably most important thread in the theory's lineage. Throughout the development of the theory, a key influence and primary domain for empirical investigation has been interpersonal communication. Higgins' concept of communication as an *interpersonal game* has been the backdrop of the explicit introduction of shared reality theory in a paper published, quite fittingly, in the *Journal of Language and Social Psychology* (Higgins, 1992). It was also the topic of an early chapter, "The 'Communication Game'," that foreshadowed the subsequent, explicit formulations (Higgins, 1981). His theorizing was inspired by pragmatic approaches to language (e.g., Austin, 1962; Grice, 1975; Rommetveit, 1974) and, particularly, Wittgenstein's (1953) characterization of verbal communication as a game. From the perspective of pragmatics, language is a motivated, context-dependent means of interpersonal communication, following (explicit and implicit) rules and assumptions. Motives of communication include conveying information or meaning, creating or maintaining a social relationship, achieving a shared understanding with others, but also influencing others' behavior, maximizing beneficial social responses, and accomplishing a joint task.

In Higgins (1981) and Higgins (1992), communication is characterized, inter alia, as a social action that involves shared and context-dependent expectations and rules concerning the interlocutors' roles and appropriate language, and that requires the mutual consideration of each other's characteristics, specifically their knowledge, attitudes, and intentions. From these and other assumptions about language use in social interaction, Tory Higgins derives several rules of the communication game, including some that are at the heart of empirical work on audience-tuning

effects in the saying-is-believing paradigm. For instance, communicators should say what is relevant, and give neither too much nor too little information (Grice, 1975), and take into account the audience's perspective, knowledge, attitudes, and preferences in their language use. The latter rule gives rise to audience tuning in communicators' message production. As described in the previous section, audience tuning in interpersonal communication has represented the principal arena for empirical demonstrations of shared reality processes in the saying-is-believing paradigm.

One section of the early chapter refers to the "sharing of a social bond" and "social reality" (Higgins, 1981) and contains elements that were elaborated later in the explicit formulations of shared reality theory. In particular, the early chapter foreshadows the key role of goals and motives for the creation of shared reality. The "convergence of opinions and judgments" (Higgins, 1981: 376) – which in the current terminology represents a commonality of inner states – is assumed to depend on whether the interlocutors have "a desire to maintain the social bond and share a common definition of social reality" (Higgins, 1981: 376). These motives translate quite seamlessly into the two main types of motivation, affiliative and epistemic, that are assumed to drive shared reality according to the recent theory formulation (see second section).

In both the 1981 and the 1992 paper, Higgins illustrated the potential and validity of the communication-game approach to a large extent with empirical findings from saying-is-believing and closely related studies. However, the first saying-is-believing publication (Higgins and Rholes, 1978) and empirical follow-up papers were framed quite differently, mostly in information-processing terms based on the nascent social cognition approach, which began to fascinate increasing numbers of social psychologists in the 1970s. It would take almost a decade for Higgins to return to his communication game analysis to account for the saying-is-believing effect.

Ironically, at the time he began the saying-is-believing research, a key interest of Tory Higgins, who had been a joint honors anthropology–sociology student at McGill University in Montreal, was the inter-relation of language, thought, and society, and especially the linguistic relativity hypothesis. The thrust and inspiration of the 1981 chapter, particularly its focus on the pragmatics of language and communication, is chiefly owed to that interest. The irony is that this interest originally emphasized the interpersonal and society-related aspects of the inter-relation, as reflected in the "communication game" label. However, when the saying-is-believing research formally appeared as a published article, it was instead the language-and-thought aspect of the inter-relation that was highlighted. This framing matched the social cognition emphasis during that point in history, not to mention the social cognition emphasis of the editor of the journal in which the first article appeared (Bob Wyer).

The core idea of the linguistic relativity hypothesis is that language provides the essence of human thinking, and that mental representations entertained in our minds are inextricably linguistic. The position has been epitomized by the Sapir–Whorf hypothesis, named after the anthropologist Edward Sapir and his student Benjamin Lee Whorf. In its strong version, this hypothesis states that our experiences with the world are intrinsically linguistic and that cognition is determined by the thinker's language (see Hunt and Agnoli, 1991). Both Sapir (1964) and his student Whorf argued that differences in the structure of speakers' language create differences in cognition: "We dissect nature along the lines laid down by our native languages" (Whorf, 1956: 213). Since the first budding of interest in the 1950s, the hypothesis provoked controversial debates and stimulated a substantial corpus of research, particularly on cognitive differences between speakers belonging to different language communities, such as speakers of Mandarin, English, or Navajo.

Research in this field addresses primarily the extent to which the structural aspects of a language affect the speakers' cognition. By this view, language is predominantly treated as an underlying structure, much in the sense of what Chomsky called linguistic competence. Also, the language-and-thought debate traditionally focused on effects of language at the lexical level, such as whether memory for color stimuli depends on the availability (versus lack) of certain color terms in a language. However, Tory Higgins was interested – as was his dissertation supervisor at Columbia University, Bob Krauss (e.g., Chiu et al., 1998) – identifying effects of the pragmatic usage of language on cognition. According to this idea, which was a major inspiration for the saying-is-believing work, language may influence thought not so much at the structural or lexical level, but at the level of actual language use in motivated, rule-based interpersonal communication. This influence would be due not to the type of language, but concrete instances, or tokens, of verbal communication (Holtgraves and Kashima, 2008). As described above, tuning a message to one's audience's characteristics (attitude, knowledge) is a central phenomenon exemplifying the pragmatic use of language in verbal communication.

The second line of theoretical precursors can be traced to phenomenological approaches in philosophy and sociology. Related to the second condition of shared reality outlined above, philosophers like Husserl (1931) and Brentano (1974), suggested that directedness, or "aboutness," is a general characteristic of human thinking. This understanding is consistent with the social–psychological notion, also emphasized by shared reality theory, that people want to increase their knowledge of the world and hence represent their own and others' behavioral responses as being *about* something (see Heider, 1958). This notion draws attention to the triadic relation implied by many formulations of shared reality theory, specifically the relation between one person experiencing sharing, another person (a "sharing partner") or group of persons with whom the sharing is experienced, and a target referent of the sharing (cf. Tomasello et al., 2005).

As outlined in the second section, shared reality permits a perceiver to experience some target referent in common with another person. There are other cases of social sharing that do not meet this condition. Phenomena such as empathy (de Waal, 2008) and emotional and mood contagion (Neumann and Strack, 2000) do not require that the perceiver share the other person's view about a target referent. The importance of directedness, or aboutness, for shared reality was emphasized first in Higgins (1999). The basis for the inclusion of *aboutness* was a paper published shortly before (Higgins, 1998), in which the importance of aboutness as a general principle of human inference and judgment was emphasized.

The notion that people's *experience* of reality is socially established resonates with earlier conceptualizations in phenomenological sociology, particularly the sociology of knowledge (Berger and Luckmann, 1966; Garfinkel, 1967; Schütz, 1967). For instance, Berger and Luckmann argued that "[t]he reality of everyday life ... presents itself to me as an intersubjective world, a world that I share with others." (1966: 23) Scholars in these fields also understood that social actors "are motivated to create a sense, even an illusory sense, that they share a common universe," so that they might "generate a tacit presumption that there is an external factual order 'out there'" (J.H. Turner, 1987: 19). This emphasis of the motivational underpinnings of a shared world view is compatible with the third condition formulated in shared reality theory, which holds that regarding the commonality of inner states only as an outcome or end product would overlook important psychological underpinnings, specifically the underlying motives and the experience of sharing. Furthermore, the earlier sociologists realized that while people do not have direct access to each others' inner states, they can still "put themselves in each others' place" (Turner, 1987: 18) by means of interpersonal

practices such as exchanging and interpreting signs. Such practices, it was assumed, produce the subjective experience of successfully connecting to others' inner states.

The inspirations in this second ancestry line gained prominence, and were cited more comprehensively, as shared reality theory evolved over time and attracted coauthors. The work of scholars at the interface of sociology and anthropology (e.g., Harold Garfinkel) were cited already in the earlier publications (Higgins, 1981, 1992). However, with the contributions of subsequent close collaborators, to precursor approaches in the humanities, particularly philosophy and sociology, were increasingly acknowledged, for instance in the first comprehensive account of shared reality (Hardin and Higgins, 1996) and other subsequent developments of the theory (Echterhoff et al., 2009a).

Research on social influence represents the third line of intellectual inspiration. Social influence occurs when an individual's responses like behaviors, attitudes, and judgments are shifted to become consistent with the position of one or more others as a result of contact or interaction with these others. A prototypical instance of social influence is persuasion. One possible result of social influence is a commonality of *inner states*, such as attitudes and judgments about something, between at least two people. The close relation between social influence and shared reality is conspicuous in most publications on shared reality (for a direct empirical investigation, see Pinel et al., 2010). The early chapter by Higgins (1981) discussed implications of the communication-game concept for social influence, specifically the role of language use in persuasion. Also, in the first comprehensive exposition of the theory Curtis Hardin and Tory Higgins (1996) discussed how social influence in groups (e.g., Asch, 1951; Deutsch and Gerard, 1955; Festinger, 1950; Latané and Wolf, 1981) can be interpreted through the lens of shared reality theory (also see Levine and Higgins, 2001). In Echterhoff et al. (2009a), a section is devoted to the relation between the concept of shared reality and research on social influence in groups and work teams.

My own involvement in research on shared reality in interpersonal communication was mediated and facilitated to a large extent by my interest in effects of the social and communicative context on memory and remembering (e.g., Echterhoff et al., 2007; Echterhoff and Hirst, 2009; Lindner et al., 2010). It began in the years 2001/2002 when I worked as a postdoctoral researcher with Bob Krauss and Tory at Columbia University. My doctoral dissertation had been supervised by Bill Hirst, an eminent memory researcher at the New School for Social Research who became increasingly interested in the role of the social context for memory processes (e.g., Cuc et al., 2007; Hirst and Manier, 2002). This orientation contributed to the focus on memory, specifically the audience-congruent recall bias, as the main dependent variable in saying-is-believing studies of shared reality, which I embarked on together with Tory Higgins during my postdoc research. Forming one of the rare intersections of personal and global history, I almost gave up completing the first experiment, conducted with the assistance of my doctoral student Stephan Groll, in the immediate aftermath of the shocking events of September 11, 2001, in New York City – we were petrified ourselves, and study participants ceased showing up in the lab.

The studies were initially motivated by the search for a genuinely social, perhaps shared reality, account of the saying-is-believing effect that would go beyond the conclusions of the pioneering studies from around the 1980s (see McCann and Higgins, 1992). Given my own background at the time, the saying-is-believing effect struck me as a type of social influence that differs from "classical" social influence as it affects the source rather than the recipient of communication and represents a subtle, self-produced bias (see Echterhoff and Hirst, 2009). For a long time, memory researchers had paid little attention to genuinely social influences on memory. Conversely, social psychologists

had focused on attitude, judgment, and behavior rather than memory as the object of social influence (see Bless et al., 2001).

APPLICABILITY AND UTILITY OF SHARED REALITY THEORY

Shared reality theory addresses fundamental psychological questions such as how people establish what is real and satisfy basic epistemic needs (see Higgins, in press). Thus, the theory is potentially applicable to various phenomena involving the establishment and experience of reality (for constraints, see the introduction). In a general sense, the goal of creating a shared reality plays a critical role in how communication contributes to the formation and maintenance of people's knowledge. More specifically, the creation of shared reality in social interaction is relevant and applicable to a host of real-life issues, such as persuasion of self and others through political and religious speeches (Vedantam, 2008), belief justification in close relationships and families (Jost et al., 2007; Magee and Hardin, 2010), stereotyping and prejudice (see Huntsinger and Sinclair, 2010; Kashima et al., 2010; Klein et al., 2010; Sinclair et al., 2005a, 2005b), interethnic interaction (Conley et al., 2010), decision-making and performance in work teams (see Salas and Fiore, 2004), the transmission of culture (Echterhoff and Higgins, 2010), and the protection of group identity (Ledgerwood and Liviatan, 2010; Mannetti et al., 2010). Out of these papers, those published in 2010 (except Conley et al., 2010; Echterhoff and Higgins, 2010) are contributions to a special issue on shared reality in the journal *Social Cognition*, for which I served as guest editor (see Echterhoff, 2010).

Testifying to the high political and societal relevance of related approaches, Kashima and colleagues have revealed the role of shared reality in the transmission of cultural stereotypes about various social categories (e.g., men, women, football players) through interpersonal communication (for a review, see Kashima, 2008). For instance, Lyons and Kashima (2003) experimentally manipulated the presence and absence of shared reality about a cultural stereotype to examine the conditions under which the stereotype is transmitted in a serial reproduction chain, which is set up akin to a Chinese whispers game. Stereotype-consistent (versus stereotype-inconsistent) information about a social group was transmitted to a greater extent along the chain when participants were led to believe that their audience shared the stereotypical view of the Jamayans that they had learned. In contrast, no such biased transmission of stereotype-consistent information was found when people believed that their audience did not share the stereotypical view of the Jamayans.

The tendency to create a shared reality with one's interaction partners can also reduce people's stereotypes and thus can have beneficial consequences, as suggested by work by Sinclair, Hardin and colleagues (Sinclair et al., 2005a, 2005b). These researchers found that participants' endorsement of stereotypes of African-Americans, including self-stereotypes, can shift toward the egalitarian (i.e., nonprejudiced) views of an interaction partner, spontaneously achieving an interpersonal shared reality. The studies also elucidated the role of affiliative motivation. Affiliative motivation varied as a function of either a situational induction (the partner's manipulated similarity or likeability) or participants' existing affiliative motivation (assessed by personality scales). Participants' views shifted more toward their interaction partner's ostensible views when the social relationship motive was strong (versus weak).

Regarding the social and motivational dynamics in small groups, Mannetti et al. (2010) demonstrated the role of shared reality as a resource that allows people to ward off threats to a positive social identity. According to their main hypothesis, evaluations of defectors; that is, people who leave their current group to join another group, vary inversely with the threat they pose to other members' sense of shared reality. Consistent with this hypothesis, Mannetti et al. found that group members who have a stronger sense of shared reality within the group experience the defection of a group member as less threatening.

Furthermore, studies using the established saying-is-believing paradigm have applied shared reality theory to applied fields and thus enhanced the ecological validity of the evidence. The research on shared reality in the saying-is-believing paradigm is particularly relevant to the applied domain of eyewitness retellings and memory. In studies by Kopietz et al. (2009) and Hellmann et al. (in press), student participants tuned their retelling of a witnessed incident to their audience's evaluation of the suspects in the incident. In the study by Kopietz et al. (2009) participants' own memories and judgments regarding the incident were more biased toward their audience when they were more motivated to create a shared view with a particular audience (a student with a similar versus a dissimilar academic background). Furthermore, Hellmann et al. (2010, Exp. 2) found that the correlation between message ("saying") and recall ("believing") was significantly higher when participants' experienced a high (versus low) degree of shared reality with their audience.

Applying shared reality theory to the workplace and organizational behavior, Echterhoff et al. (2009b) examined the role of other audience characteristics in the context of personnel assessment. Student communicators described an employee to either an equal-status audience (a student temp) or a higher status audience (a company board member). The higher status audience clearly possessed higher domain-specific expertise, such as professional competence in the assessment of employees. Although audience tuning occurred in both audience-status conditions, the memory bias from audience tuning was found only in the equal-status condition. Apparently, communicators were more willing to share reality with the equal-status audience than with the higher status audience.

An extended measure of trust in the audience, which include epistemic components (e.g., trust in the audience's judgments in general and about other people in particular) and relational components (e.g., readiness to affiliate and be close), was also higher in the equal-status condition and statistically mediated the audience-status effect on memory bias.

These findings show that an audience's domain-specific expertise or status is not sufficient to motivate communicators to create a shared reality with the audience. Rather, the audience's epistemic and relational trustworthiness is more critical. The feelings of general trust and the readiness to connect and affiliate covered by the extended trust measure in Echterhoff et al. (2009b) cannot be reduced to mere expertise. What matters is whether communicators want to make an epistemic and relational connection to the audience.

Regarding its broader utility, shared reality theory draws attention to a potentially important everyday mechanism underlying the construction of culturally shared memories and knowledge – a basic mechanism for constructing social, cultural, and political beliefs (see Hausmann et al., 2008; Jost et al., 2007). Consider community members who trust one another, want to maintain relationships with one another, and are thus prepared and motivated to create a shared reality. When community member A is aware of community member B's view (presumable or actual) regarding some topic (e.g., his or her beliefs or attitudes about something), audience tuning during interpersonal communication is likely to occur. Given that the audience tuning serves a shared reality goal, it will shape communicator A's own later memories and beliefs about the topic in the direction of the audience. Rather than remembering the topic information as originally received, communicator A will remember this information as represented in her or his tuned message. A similar process may then occur when another community member C, being aware of A's communicatively-formed belief, talks about the same topic to member A, and then community member D talks to C, and so on. As a result of continued communication

on the topic, the community members will come to hold increasingly shared beliefs.

This process may occur not only for individuals as topic targets but also for groups as topic targets (see Hausmann et al., 2008; Klein et al., 2008; Lyons and Kashima, 2003), and this could be an important factor in the development of shared stereotypic beliefs about other groups. Creating a shared reality with communication partners, which is ubiquitous in everyday life, can thus create a shared but biased perspective on the world within a community.

ACKNOWLEDGMENTS

The preparation of this chapter was supported by a grant from the German Research Foundation (Deutsche Forschungsgemeinschaft, reference number EC 317/2). I thank Jens Hellmann, Natlija Keck, and Cécile Schain for their help with preparing the chapter for publication.

REFERENCES

Adaval, R. and Wyer, R.S., Jr. (2004) Communicating about a social interaction: Effects on memory for protagonists' statements and nonverbal behaviors. *Journal of Experimental Social Psychology, 40,* 450–465.
Andersen, S.M. and Chen, S. (2002) The relational self: An interpersonal social-cognitive theory. *Psychological Review, 109,* 619–645.
Asch, S.E. (1951) Effects of group pressure upon the modification and distortion of judgments. In H.S. Guetzkow (ed.), *Groups, Leadership and Men,* pp. 177–190. Pittsburgh, PA: Carnegie Press.
Asch, S.E. (1952) *Social Psychology.* Englewood Cliffs, NJ: Prentice Hall.
Austin, J.L. (1962) *How to Do Things with Words.* Oxford: Oxford University Press.
Bar-Tal, D. (1990) *Group Beliefs: A Conception for Analyzing Group Structure, Processes, and Behavior.* New York: Springer-Verlag.
Bar-Tal, D. (2000). *Shared Beliefs in a Society: Social Psychological Analysis.* Thousand Oaks, CA: Sage.

Baron-Cohen, S. (1995) *Mindblindness: An Essay on Autism and Theory of Mind.* Cambridge, MA: MIT Press.

Bartlett, F.C. (1932) *Remembering: A Study in Experimental and Social Psychology.* Cambridge: Cambridge University Press.

Baumeister, R.F. and Leary, M.R. (1995) The need to belong: Desire for interpersonal attachments as a fundamental human motivation. *Psychological Bulletin, 117*, 497–529.

Bem, D.J. (1967) Self perception: An alternative interpretation of cognitive dissonance phenomena. *Psychological Review, 74*, 183–200.

Berger, P.L. and Luckmann, T. (1966) *The Social Construction of Reality: A Treatise in the Sociology of Knowledge.* Garden City, NY: Doubleday.

Berlyne, D.E. (1962) Uncertainty and epistemic curiosity. *British Journal of Psychology, 53*, 27–34.

Bless, H., Strack, F. and Walther, E. (2001) Memory as a target of social influence? Memory distortions as a function of social influence and metacognitive knowledge. In J.P. Forgas and K.D. Williams (eds), *Social Influence: Direct and Indirect processes,* pp. 167–183. Philadelphia: Psychology Press.

Bohman, J.F. and Rehg, W. (eds) (1997) *Deliberative Democracy.* Cambridge, MA: MIT Press.

Brentano, F. (1974) *Psychology from an Empirical Standpoint* (Trans. A. Rancurrello, D. Terrell and L. McAlister). London: Routledge and Kegan. (Originally published 1874).

Brickman, P. (1978) Is it real? In J.H. Harvey, W. Ickes and R.F. Kidd (eds), *New Directions in Attribution Research, 2*, 5–34. Hillsdale, NJ: Erlbaum.

Byrne, D. and Clore, G.L. (1967) Effectance arousal and attraction. *Journal of Personality and Social Psychology, 6*, 1–18.

Caporael, L.R. (2007) Evolutionary theory for social and cultural psychology. In A.W. Kruglanski and E.T. Higgins (eds), *Social Psychology: Handbook of Basic Principles*, 2nd Edition, pp. 3–18. New York: Guilford Press.

Caporael, L.R. (2010) Revolutionary Darwinism: Sociality is the ground. In G. Semin and G. Echterhoff (eds), *Grounding Sociality: Neurons, Minds, and Culture,* pp. 237–259. New York: Psychology Press.

Chiu, C.Y., Krauss, R.M. and Lau, I.Y.M. (1998) Some cognitive consequences of communication. In S.R. Fussell and R. Kreuz (eds), *Social and Cognitive Approaches to Interpersonal Communication,* pp. 259–278. Hillsdale, NJ: Erlbaum.

Clark, H.H. (1996) *Using Language.* New York: Cambridge University Press.

Clark, H.H. (2003) Pointing and placing. In S. Kita (ed.), *Pointing: Where Language, Culture, and Cognition meet,* pp. 243–268. Hillsdale, NJ: Erlbaum.

Clark, H.H. and Marshall, C.E. (1981) Definite reference and mutual knowledge. In A.K. Joshi, B. Webber, and I. Sag (eds), *Elements of Discourse Understanding,* pp. 10–63. Cambridge: Cambridge University Press.

Conley, T.D., Rabinowitz, J.L. and Hardin, C.D. (2010) O.J. Simpson as shared (and unshared) reality: The impact of consensually shared beliefs on interpersonal perceptions and task performance in different- and same-ethnicity dyads. *Journal of Personality and Social Psychology, 99*, 452–466.

Cooley, C.H. (1964) *Human Nature and the Social Order.* New York: Schocken Books. (Originally published 1902.)

Cuc, A., Koppel, J. and Hirst, W. (2007) Silence is not golden: A case for socially shared retrieval-induced forgetting. *Psychological Science, 18*, 727–733.

Deutsch, M. and Gerard, H.B. (1955) A study of normative and informational social influences upon individual judgment. *Journal of Abnormal and Social Psychology, 51*, 629–636.

de Waal, F. (2008) Putting the altruism back into altruism: The evolution of empathy. *Annual Review of Psychology, 59*, 279–300.

Diener, E. and Seligman, M.E.P. (2002) Very happy people. *Psychological Science, 13*, 81–84.

Dovidio, J.F., Gaertner, S.L., Kawakami, K. and Hodson, G. (2002) Why can't we just get along? Interpersonal biases and interracial distrust. *Cultural Diversity and Ethnic Minority Psychology, 8*, 88–102.

Dunbar, R.I.M. and Shultz, S. (2007) Evolution in the social brain. *Science, 317*, 1344–1347.

Echterhoff, G. (2010) Shared reality: Antecedents, processes, and consequences. *Social Cognition, 28*, 273–276.

Echterhoff, G., Groll, S. and Hirst, W. (2007) Tainted truth: Overcorrection for misinformation influence on eyewitness memory. *Social Cognition, 25*, 367–409.

Echterhoff, G. and Higgins, E.T. (2010) How communication shapes memory: Shared reality and implications for culture. In G.R. Semin and G. Echterhoff (eds), *Grounding Sociality: Neurons, Minds, and Culture,* pp. 115–146. New York: Psychology Press.

Echterhoff, G., Higgins, E.T. and Groll, S. (2005) Audience-tuning effects on memory: The role of shared reality. *Journal of Personality and Social Psychology, 89*, 257–276.

Echterhoff, G., Higgins, E.T., Kopietz, R. and Groll, S. (2008) How communication goals determine when audience tuning biases memory. *Journal of Experimental Psychology: General, 137*, 3–21.

Echterhoff, G., Higgins, E.T. and Levine, J.M. (2009a) Shared reality: Experiencing commonality with others' inner states about the world. *Perspectives on Psychological Science, 4*, 496–521.

Echterhoff, G. and Hirst, W. (2009) Social influence on memory. *Social Psychology, 40*, 106–110.

Echterhoff, G., Lang, S., Krämer, N. and Higgins, E.T. (2009b) Audience-tuning effects on communicators' memory: The role of audience status in sharing reality. *Social Psychology, 40*, 150–163.

Epley, N., Caruso, E.M. and Bazerman, M.H. (2006) When perspective-taking increases taking: Reactive egoism in social interaction. *Journal of Personality and Social Psychology, 91*, 872–889.

Festinger, L. (1950) Informal social communication. *Psychological Review, 57*, 271–282.

Festinger, L. (1957) *A Theory of Cognitive Dissonance.* Stanford: Stanford University Press.

Fiske, S.T. (2007) Core social motivations, a historical perspective: Views from the couch, consciousness, classroom, computers, and collectives. In W. Gardner and J.Y. Shah (eds), *Handbook of Motivation Science*, pp. 3–22. New York: Guilford Press.

Frith, C.D. (2007) *Making up the Mind: How the Brain Creates Our Mental World.* Malden, MY: Blackwell.

Gallese, V., Keysers, C. and Rizzolatti, G. (2004) A unifying view of the basis of social cognition. *Trends in Cognitive Sciences, 8*, 396–403.

Garfinkel, H. (1967) *Studies in Ethnomethodology.* Englewood Cliffs, NJ: Prentice-Hall.

Graf, M., Schütz-Bosbach, S. and Prinz, W. (2010) Motor involvement in action and object perception: Similarity and complementarity. In G. Semin and G. Echterhoff (eds), *Grounding Sociality: Neurons, Minds, and Culture*, pp. 27–52. New York: Psychology Press.

Grice, H.P. (1975) Logic and conversation. In P. Cole and J.L. Morgan (eds), *Syntax and Semantics 3: Speech Acts*, pp. 41–58. San Diego: Academic Press.

Hardin, C.D. and Conley, T.D. (2001) A relational approach to cognition: Shared experience and relationship affirmation in social cognition. In G.B. Moskowitz (ed.), *Cognitive Social Psychology: The Princeton Symposium on the Legacy and Future of Social Cognition*, pp. 3–17. Mahwah, NJ: Erlbaum.

Hardin, C.D. and Higgins, E.T. (1996) Shared reality: How social verification makes the subjective objective. In R.M. Sorrentino and E.T. Higgins (eds), *Handbook of Motivation and Cognition: The Interpersonal Context, 3*, 28–84. New York: Guilford Press.

Hausmann, L.R.M., Levine, J.M. and Higgins, E.T. (2008) Communication and group perception: Extending the 'saying is believing' effect. *Group Processes and Intergroup Relations, 11*, 539–554.

Heider, F. (1958) *The Psychology of Interpersonal Relations.* New York: John Wiley.

Hellmann, J.H., Echterhoff, G., Kopietz, R., Niemeier, S. and Memon, A. (in press) Talking about visually perceived events: Communication effects on eyewitness memory. *European Journal of Social Psychology.*

Higgins, E.T. (1981) The 'communication game': Implications for social cognition and persuasion. In E.T. Higgins, C.P. Herman, and M.P. Zanna (eds), *Social Cognition: The Ontario Symposium, 1*, 343–392. Hillsdale, NJ: Erlbaum.

Higgins, E.T. (1992) Achieving 'shared reality' in the communication game: A social action that creates meaning. *Journal of Language and Social Psychology, 11*, 107–131.

Higgins, E.T. (1996a) Knowledge activation: Accessibility, applicability, and salience. In E.T. Higgins and A.W. Kruglanski (eds), *Social Psychology: Handbook of Basic Principles*, pp. 133–168. New York: Guilford Press.

Higgins, E.T. (1996b) Shared reality in the self-system: The social nature of self-regulation. In W. Stroebe and M. Hewstone (eds), *European Review of Social Psychology, 7*, 1–29. Chichester: Wiley.

Higgins, E.T. (1998) The aboutness principle: A pervasive influence on human inference. *Social Cognition, 16*, 173–198.

Higgins, E.T. (1999) 'Saying is believing' effects: When sharing reality about something biases knowledge and evaluations. In L.L. Thompson, J.M. Levine and D.M. Messick (eds), *Shared Cognition in Organizations: The Management of Knowledge*, pp. 33–49. Mahwah, NJ: Erlbaum.

Higgins, E.T. (2005) Humans as applied motivation scientists: Self-consciousness from 'shared reality' and 'becoming'. In H.S. Terrace and J. Metcalfe (eds), *The Missing Link in Cognition: Origins of Self-reflective Consciousness*, pp. 157–173. Oxford: Oxford University Press.

Higgins, E.T. (2006) Value from hedonic experience and engagement. *Psychological Review, 113*, 439–460.

Higgins, E.T. (in press) *Beyond Pleasure and Pain: The New Science of Motivation.* New York: Oxford University Press.

Higgins, E.T. (2010) Sharing inner states: A defining feature of human motivation. In G. Semin and G. Echterhoff (eds), *Grounding Sociality: Neurons, Minds, and Culture*, pp. 149–173. New York: Psychology Press.

Higgins, E.T., Echterhoff, G., Crespillo, R. and Kopietz, R. (2007) Effects of communication on social knowledge: Sharing reality with individual versus group audiences. *Japanese Psychological Research*, *49*, 89–99.

Higgins, E.T. and McCann, C.D. (1984) Social encoding and subsequent attitudes, impressions, and memory: 'Context-driven' and motivational aspects of processing. *Journal of Personality and Social Psychology*, *47*, 26–39.

Higgins, E.T., McCann, C.D. and Fondacaro, R. (1982) The 'communication game': Goal directed encoding and cognitive consequences. *Social Cognition*, *1*, 21–37.

Higgins, E.T. and Pittman, T.S. (2008) Motives of the human animal: Comprehending, managing, and sharing inner states. *Annual Review of Psychology*, *59*, 361–385.

Higgins, E.T. and Rholes, W.S. (1978) 'Saying is believing': Effects of message modification on memory and liking for the person described. *Journal of Experimental Social Psychology*, *14*, 363–378.

Hirst, W. and Echterhoff, G. (2008) Creating shared memories in conversation: Toward a psychology of collective memory. *Social Research*, *75*, 183–216.

Hirst, W. and Manier, D. (2002) The diverse forms of collective memory. In G. Echterhoff and M. Saar (eds), *Kontexte und Kulturen des Erinnerns* [Contexts and cultures of remembering], pp. 37–58. Constance: Universitätsverlag Konstanz.

Hogg, M.A. (2007) Uncertainty-identity theory. In M.P. Zanna (ed.), *Advances in Experimental Social Psychology*, *39*, 69–126. San Diego: Academic Press.

Holtgraves, T.M. and Kashima, Y. (2008) Language, meaning, and social cognition. *Personality and Social Psychology Review*, *12*, 73–94.

Hunt, E. and Agnoli, F. (1991) The Whorfian hypothesis: A cognitive psychology perspective. *Psychological Review*, *98*, 377–389.

Huntsinger, J.R. and Sinclair, S. (2010) When it feels right, go with it: Affective regulation of affiliative social tuning. *Social Cognition*, *28*, 287–302.

Husserl, E. (1931) *Ideas: General Introduction to Pure Phenomenology* (Trans. W.R.B. Gibson). London: George Allen & Unwin. (Originally published 1913.)

Iacoboni, M. (2008) *Mirroring People: The New Science of How We Connect with Others*. New York: Farrar, Straus, and Giroux.

Iacoboni, M. (in press) Mirroring as a key neural mechanism of sociality. In G. Semin and G. Echterhoff (eds), *Grounding Sociality: Neurons, Minds, and Culture*. New York: Psychology Press.

James, W. (1890) *The Principles of Psychology, Vol. 1*. Cambridge, MA: Harvard University Press.

Johnson, M.K. and Raye, C.L. (1981) Reality monitoring. *Psychological Review*, *88*, 67–85.

Jones, E.E. (1964) *Ingratiation: A Social Psychological Analysis*. New York: Appleton-Century-Crofts.

Jones, E.E. and Thibaut, J.W. (1958) Interaction goals as bases of inference in interpersonal perception. In R. Tagiuri and L. Petrullo (eds), *Person Perception and Interpersonal Behavior,* pp. 151–178. Stanford: Stanford University Press.

Jost, J.T., Ledgerwood, A. and Hardin, C.D. (2007) Shared reality, system verification, and the relational basis of ideological beliefs. *Social and Personality Psychology Compass*, *2*, 171–186.

Kagan, J. (1972) Motives and development. *Journal of Personality and Social Psychology*, *22*, 51–66.

Kashima, Y. (2008) A social psychology of cultural dynamics: Examining how cultures are formed, maintained, and transformed. *Social and Personality Psychology Compass*, *2*, 107–120.

Kashima, Y., Kashima E.S., Bain, P., Lyons, A., Tindale, R.S., Robins, G., Vears, C. and Whelan, J. (2010) Communication and essentialism: Grounding the shared reality of a social category. *Social Cognition*, *28*, 306–328.

Keysar, B. and Barr, D.J. (2002) Self anchoring in conversation: Why language users do not do what they 'should'. In T. Gilovich, D.W. Griffin, and D. Kahneman (eds), *Heuristics and Biases: The Psychology of Intuitive Judgment*, pp. 150–166. Cambridge: Cambridge University Press.

Keysers, C. and Gazzola, V. (2007) Integrating simulation and theory of mind: From self to social cognition. *Trends in Cognitive Sciences*, *11*, 194–196.

Klein, O., Clark, A.E. and Lyons, A. (2010) When the social becomes personal: Exploring the role of common ground in stereotype communication. *Social Cognition*, *28*, 329–352.

Klein, O., Tindale, S. and Brauer, M. (2008) The consensualization of stereotypes in small groups. In Y. Kashima, K. Fiedler, and P. Freytag (eds), *Stereotype Dynamics: Language-Based Approaches to the Formation, Maintenance, and Transformation of Stereotypes*, pp. 263–292. New York: Erlbaum.

Kopietz, R., Echterhoff, G., Niemeier, S., Hellmann, J.H. and Memon, A. (2009) Audience-congruent biases in eyewitness memory and judgment: Influences of a co-witness' liking for a suspect. *Social Psychology*, *40*, 138–149.

Kopietz, R., Hellmann, J.H., Higgins, E.T. and Echterhoff, G. (2010) Shared reality effects on memory: Communicating to fulfill epistemic needs. *Social Cognition*, *28*, 353–378.

Kruglanski, A.W., Pierro, A., Mannetti, L. and De Grada, E. (2006) Groups as epistemic providers: Need for closure and the unfolding of group-centrism. *Psychological Review*, *113*, 84–100.

Latané, B. and Wolf, S. (1981) The social impact of majorities and minorities. *Psychological Review, 5,* 438–453.

Ledgerwood, A. and Liviatan, I. (2010) The price of a shared vision: Group identity as goals and the social creation of value. *Social Cognition, 28,* 401–421.

Levine, J.M. and Higgins, E.T. (2001) Shared reality and social influence in groups and organizations. In F. Butera and G. Mugny (eds), *Social Influence in Social Reality: Promoting Individual and Social Change,* pp. 33–52. Seattle: Hogrefe & Huber.

Lewin, K. (1947) Group decision and social change. In T.M. Newcomb and E.L. Hartley (eds), *Readings in Social Psychology,* pp. 330–344. New York: Holt.

Lindner, I., Echterhoff, G., Davidson, P.S.R. and Brand, M. (2010) Observation inflation: Your actions become mine. *Psychological Science, 21,* 1291–1299.

Loewenstein, G. (1994) The psychology of curiosity: A review and reinterpretation. *Psychological Bulletin, 116,* 75–98.

Lyons, A. and Kashima, Y. (2003) How are stereotypes maintained through communication? The influence of stereotype sharedness. *Journal of Personality and Social Psychology, 85,* 989–1005.

Mackie, D.M. and Skelly, J.J. (1994) The social cognition analysis of social influence: Contributions to the understanding of persuasion and conformity. In P. Devine, D. Hamilton, and T. Ostrom (eds), *Social Cognition: Impact on Social Psychology,* pp. 259–289. New York: Academic Press.

Magee, M.W. and Hardin, C.D. (2010) In defense of religion: Shared reality moderates the unconscious threat of evolution. *Social Cognition, 28,* 379–400.

Malle, B.F. (1999) How people explain behavior: A new theoretical framework. *Personality and Social Psychology Review, 3,* 21–43.

Malle, B.F. and Hodges, S.D. (eds) (2005) *Other Minds: How Humans Bridge the Divide Between Self and Other.* New York: Guilford Press.

Mannetti, L., Levine, J.M., Pierro, A. and Kruglanski, A.W. (2010) Group reaction to defection: The impact of shared reality. *Social Cognition, 28,* 447–464.

Marsh, E.J. (2007) Retelling is not the same as recalling: Implications for memory. *Current Directions in Psychological Science, 16,* 16–20.

Marsh, K.L. (2010) Sociality, from an ecological, dynamical perspective. In G. Semin and G. Echterhoff (eds), *Grounding Sociality: Neurons, Minds, and Culture.* pp. 53–81. New York: Psychology Press.

McCann, C.D. and Higgins, E.T. (1992) Personal and contextual factors in communication: A review of the 'communication game'. In G.R. Semin and K. Fiedler (eds), *Language, Interaction and Social Cognition,* pp. 144–171. London: Sage.

Mead, G.H. (1934) *Mind, Self, and Society.* Chicago: University of Chicago Press.

Meltzoff, A.N. and Decety, J. (2003) What imitation tells us about social cognition: A rapprochement between developmental psychology and cognitive neuroscience. *Philosophical Transactions of the Royal Society London, Series B, 358,* 491–500.

Merton, R.K. and Kitt, A. (1950) Contributions to the theory of reference group behavior. In R.K. Merton and P.F. Lazarsfeld (eds), *Continuities in Social Research: Studies in the Scope and Method of 'The American Soldier',* pp. 40–105. Glencoe, IL: Free Press.

Moscovici, S. (1981) On social representations. In J.P. Forgas (ed.), *Social Cognition: Perspectives on Everyday Understanding,* pp. 181–209. London: Academic Press.

Neumann, R. and Strack, F. (2000) 'Mood contagion': The automatic transfer of mood between persons. *Journal of Personality and Social Psychology, 79,* 211–223.

Newcomb, T.M. (1959) Individual systems of orientation. In S. Koch (ed.), *Psychology: A Study of a Science: Formulations of the Person and the Social Context, 3,* 384–422. New York: McGraw-Hill.

Nickerson, R.S. (2001) The projective way of knowing: A useful heuristic that sometimes misleads. *Current Directions in Psychological Science, 10,* 168–172.

Ostrom, T.M. (1984) The sovereignty of social cognition. In R.S. Wyer, Jr. and T.K. Srull (eds), *Handbook of Social Cognition, 1,* 1–38. Hillsdale, NJ: Erlbaum.

Pickering, M.J. and Garrod, S. (2004) Toward a mechanistic psychology of dialogue. *Behavioral and Brain Sciences, 27,* 169–225.

Pinel, E.C., Long, A.E. and Crimin, L.A. (2010) I-sharing and a classic conformity paradigm. *Social Cognition, 28,* 277–289.

Resnick, L.B., Levine, J.M. and Teasley, S.D. (eds) (1991) *Perspectives on Socially Shared Cognition.* Washington, DC: American Psychological Association.

Richeson, J.A. and Trawalter, S. (2005) Why do interracial interactions impair executive function? A resource depletion account. *Journal of Personality and Social Psychology, 88,* 934–947.

Rommetveit, R. (1974) *On Message Structure: A Framework for the Study of Language and Communication.* New York: Wiley.

Salas, E. and Fiore, S.M. (eds) (2004) *Team Cognition: Understanding the Factors That Drive Process* and *Performance*. Washington, DC: American Psychological Association.

Sapir, E. (1964) *Culture, Language, and Personality*. Berkeley, CA: University of California Press. (Originally published 1941.)

Schachter, S. (1959) *The Psychology of Affiliation: Experimental Studies of the Sources of Gregariousness*. Stanford, CA: Stanford University Press.

Schütz, A. (1967) *The Phenomenology of the Social World*. Evanston, IL: Northwestern University Press. (Originally published 1932.)

Sedikides, C. (1990) Efforts of fortuitously activated constructs versus activated communication goals on person impressions. *Journal of Personality and Social Psychology, 58*, 397–408.

Semin, G.R. (2007) Grounding communication: Synchrony. In A.W. Kruglanski and E.T. Higgins (eds), *Social Psychology: Handbook of Basic Principles*, 2nd Edition, pp. 630–649. New York: Guilford Press.

Sherif, M. (1935) A study of some social factors in perception. *Archives of Psychology, 27* (Whole No. 187).

Sherif, M. (1936) *The Psychology of Social Norms*. New York: Harper and Brothers.

Sinclair, S., Huntsinger, J., Skorinko, J. and Hardin, C.D. (2005a) Social tuning of the self: Consequences for the self-evaluations of stereotype targets. *Journal of Personality and Social Psychology, 89*, 160–175.

Sinclair, S., Lowery, B.S., Hardin, C.D. and Colangelo, A. (2005b) Social tuning of automatic racial attitudes: The role of affiliative motivation. *Journal of Personality and Social Psychology, 89*, 583–592.

Smith, E.R. and Semin, G.R. (2004) Socially situated cognition: Cognition in its social context. In M.P. Zanna (ed.), *Advances in Experimental Social Psychology, 36*, 53–115. San Diego: Academic Press.

Stukas, A., Bratanova, B., Kashima, Y., Peters, K. and Beatson, R. (2010) The effect of social tuning and shared reality on recipients' beliefs and impressions. *Social Influence, 5*, 101–117.

Sullivan, H.S. (1953) *The Interpersonal Theory of Psychiatry*. New York: Norton.

Thagard, P. (1997) Collaborative knowledge. *Nous, 31*, 242–261.

Thompson, L. and Fine, G.A. (1999) Socially shared cognition, affect, and behavior: A review and integration. *Personality and Social Psychology Review, 3*, 278–302.

Tomasello, M. (2008) *Origins of Human Communication*. Cambridge, MA: MIT Press.

Tomasello, M., Carpenter, M., Call, J., Behne, T. and Moll, H. (2005) Understanding and sharing intentions: The origins of cultural cognition. *Behavioral and Brain Sciences, 28*, 675–691.

Turner, J.H. (1987) Toward a sociological theory of motivation. *Annual Sociological Review, 52*, 15–27.

Tversky, B. and Marsh, E.J. (2000) Biased retellings of events yield biased memories. *Cognitive Psychology, 40*, 1–38.

Vedantam, S. (2008) For political candidates, saying can become believing. *The Washington Post*, February 25, A03.

Weldon, M.S. (2001) Remembering as a social process. In D.L. Medin (ed.), *The Psychology of Learning and Motivation: Advances in Research and Theory, 40*, 67–120. San Diego: Academic Press.

Whorf, B.L. (1956) *Language Thought, and Reality: Selected Writings of Benjamin Lee Whorf* (John B. Carroll, ed.). Cambridge, MA: MIT Press.

Wittgenstein, L. (1953) *Philosophical Investigations*. New York: Macmillan.

36

Equity Theory in Close Relationships

Elaine Hatfield and Richard L. Rapson

ABSTRACT

Throughout history, people have been concerned with social justice. In the eleventh century, St. Anselm of Canterbury (1998) argued that the will possesses two competing inclinations: an affection for a person's own advantage *and* an affection for justice. The first inclination is stronger, but the second matters, too. Equity theory, too, posits that in personal relationships, two concerns stand out: First, how rewarding are one's societal, family, and work relationships? Second, how fair and equitable are those relationships? According to equity theory, people feel most comfortable when they are getting exactly what they deserve from their relationships – no more and certainly no less. In this paper, we begin by describing the social concerns that sparked our interest in developing a theory of social justice. Then we describe the classic equity paradigm and the research it fostered. We recount the great intellectual debate that arose in the wake of the assertion that even in close, loving relationships, both reward and fairness matter. We end by describing current multicultural and multidisciplinary research that lends a new richness to theories of social justice, and contributes to the theory's usefulness in addressing current social issues.

INTRODUCTION

In the West, the 1960s and 1970s were a time of intellectual and social ferment. There was a great concern with social justice and spirited debate as to what was fair in life, law, marriage, and work. In the US, it was the time of Martin Luther King's historic 1965 civil rights march from Selma to Montgomery. (On "Bloody Sunday," March 7, 1965, 600 civil rights marchers were attacked by state and local police with clubs, dogs, and tear gas.) It was the time of Jane Fonda's 1972 trip to North Vietnam to protest the war. In that same year, women lobbied, marched, petitioned, picketed, and committed acts of civil disobedience in the hopes of persuading the 92nd Congress to pass the Equal Rights Amendment, which guaranteed men and women equal rights under law. (It passed the Senate and the House, but in the end the states failed to ratify it.) It was an era when feminists such as Betty Friedan described the *Feminine Mystique*, Gloria Steinem and her colleagues founded *Ms. Magazine*, and Shulamith Firestone penned *The Dialectic of Sex*. All these feminist leaders argued for women's rights in education, law, and the workplace. On the comic side, Bobby Riggs spewed out chauvinist insults in challenging tennis star Billie Jean King to the "Battle of the Sexes." (King won handily.) Valerie Solanas contributed her mad ravings to the *SCUM Manifesto*. (SCUM = The Society for

Cutting Up Men.) (We assumed Ms. Solanas was a witty satirist until she put her money where her mouth was and shot her pal Andy Warhol.)

PERSONAL NARRATIVE OF EQUITY THEORY'S DEVELOPMENT

Given the times, it is not surprising that many of our friends and colleagues began to hotly debate the nature of social justice and the role that reward and fairness play in men and women's close intimate relationships. Opinions and experiences differed widely. A few older women admitted they were grateful that their husbands allowed them the luxury of working. Thus, they went out of their way to make sure his masculinity was never threatened by their professional commitments – to ensure that their husbands never came home to a tired, disheveled, or cross wife; that the men were never "stuck" with childcare, housework, or yard work. A few of my more spirited younger friends were sick and tired of such inequities and argued that women ought to demand a marriage contract to ensure marital fairness.

Intrigued by all this speculation, Elaine Hatfield, G. William Walster, and Ellen Berscheid (1978) set out to devise a theory as to what men and women perceived to be fair in their daily encounters and the consequences of such perceptions. Ideally, we hoped to devise a theory that would be applicable to all cultures and all historical eras. We believed that a concern with fairness was a cultural universal. We were convinced that during humankind's long evolutionary heritage, a concern with social justice came to be writ in the mind's "architecture" because such values possessed survival value. Such concerns were maintained, we thought, because behaving fairly continued to be a wise and profitable strategy in today's world[1] (For a further discussion of this point, see Hatfield et al., 2008; Tooby and Cosmides, 1992).

Yet, we were also aware that, throughout history, societies have had very different visions as to what constitutes "social justice," "fairness," and "equity." Some dominant views:

- "All men are created equal" (equality).
- "The more you invest in a project, the more profit you deserve to reap" (contemporary American capitalism).
- "To each according to his need" (communism).
- "Winner take all" (dog-eat-dog capitalism).
- It's a man's world (traditional patriarchy. In fifteenth-century England, we knew, the status hierarchy was God, men, farm animals (especially horses), then women and children.

Thus, in crafting equity theory, we attempted to create a model that would allow scholars to take men and women's own social perspectives into account when defining reward and fairness and justice. We came up with this model (Figure 36.1).

Equity theory and research

Equity theory is a straightforward theory. It consists of four propositions:

- *Proposition I:* Men and women are "hardwired" to try to maximize pleasure and minimize pain.
- *Proposition II:* Society, however, has a vested interest in persuading people to behave fairly and equitably. Groups will generally reward members who treat others equitably and punish those who treat others inequitably.
- *Proposition III:* Given societal pressures, people are most comfortable when they perceive that they are getting roughly what they deserve from life and love. If people feel over-benefited, they

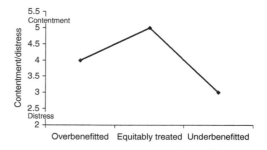

Figure 36.1 The relationship between equity and inequity, and dating and marital satisfaction

may experience pity, guilt, and shame.[2] If they feel under-benefited, they may experience anger, sadness, and resentment.

- *Proposition IV*: People in inequitable relationships will attempt to reduce their distress through a variety of techniques – by restoring psychological equity, actual equity, or leaving the relationship.

Assessing equity

In practice, a relationship's fairness and equity can be reliably and validly assessed with the use of a simple measure – the Global Measure of Equity. Specifically, research participants are asked: "Considering what you put into your dating relationship or marriage, compared to what you get out of it … and what your partner puts in compared to what (s)he gets out of it, how does your dating relationship or marriage 'stack up'"? Respondents are given the following response options:

+3: I am getting a much better deal than my partner.
+2: I am getting a somewhat better deal.
+1: I am getting a slightly better deal.
 0: We are both getting an equally good, or bad, deal.
−1: My partner is getting a slightly better deal.
−2: My partner is getting a somewhat better deal.
−3: My partner is getting a much better deal than I am.

On the basis of their answers, persons can be classified as over-benefited (receiving more than they deserve), equitably treated, or under-benefited (receiving less than they deserve).

Other, more detailed measures of equity exist, of course. Hatfield and her colleagues (2008) asked men and women who were dating, living together, and married to indicate how fair and equitable they considered their relationships to be via a 25-item scale – the Multi-Factor Measure of Equity. The areas of interest included such *personal concerns* as appearance, intelligence, and social grace; *emotional concerns*, such as physical affection and understanding and concern; and *day-to-day concerns*, such as contributing to household expenses and helping around

the house. (See Young and Hatfield, 2009, for information on the reliability and validity of both these measures.)

Regardless of societal definitions or one's own concern with equity, considerations of equity have been found to be important in a wide variety of cultures and relationships – social relationships, romantic and family relationships, friendships, helping relationships, and work relationships.

The importance of equity in close intimate relationships

Social psychologists are well aware that relationships change and deepen over time (Hatfield and Rapson, 1993). In *Intimate Relationships*, for example, Perlman and Duck (1986) argued that relationships go through stages. They charted the initiation, maintenance, problems, repair, and termination of relationships. Equity theorists, too, have been interested in charting the degree to which couples' concerns with reward, fairness, and equity wax and wane during the course of a love affair. Scholars have discovered that how concerned couples are with reward and equity depends on the stage at which their relationship has arrived. When couples are first dating, they participate in a kind of "dating and marriage marketplace," in which considerations of reward, fairness, and equity loom large. Once men and women are deeply committed, however, they become less concerned about day-to-day reward and equity. Should a relationship deteriorate, couples – knowing (perhaps) that they will soon be back on the dating and marriage market – may begin to worry about, "What's in it for me?" and to ask, "Do I deserve better?"

Let us review the research leading to these conclusions.

Beginnings

In fairy tales, Prince Charming often falls in love with the scullery maid. In real life, however, dating couples – whether they are young or old, gay, lesbian, or heterosexual – generally search for "suitable" partners. As Goffman observed: "A proposal of marriage in our society tends to be a way in which a man sums up his social attributes and suggests that hers are not so much better as to preclude a merger" (1952: 456).

Specifically, researchers find:

- Attractive men and women assume that a suitable partner should be more socially desirable – more attractive, intelligent, personable, rich, well adjusted, and kind – than do their less attractive peers.
- Dating couples are more likely to fall in love if they perceive their relationships to be fair and equitable.
- Couples are likely to end up with someone fairly close to themselves in social desirability. They are likely to be matched on the basis of self-esteem, looks, intelligence, education, and mental and physical health (or disability). Evolutionary theorists contend that in the dating marketplace, men are willing to pay a price for good looks, virginity, fidelity, and chastity, while women willingly pay for status, support, and kindness. Market considerations have also been found to affect the amount prostitutes charge for risky sex, the sexual bargains men and women craft in prison, and the like.
- Perceived equity is important in sparking passionate love, sexual attraction, sexual passion, and sexual activity.
- Equitable dating relationships are satisfying and comfortable relationships; inequity is associated with distress, guilt, anger, and anxiety.
- Equitable dating relationships are more stable than are inequitable relationships.

In conclusion, research seems to indicate that in the *early stages* of a dating relationship, considerations of the marketplace prevail. Men and women attempt to attract socially attractive partners and are profoundly concerned with how rewarding, fair, and equitable their budding relationships appear to be. (Additional support for these propositions can be found in Baumeister and Vohs, 2004.)

Flowerings

In *Equity: Theory and Research*, Hatfield and her colleagues (1978) argued that casual dating relationships differ from deeply committed,

loving, intimate relationships in several ways. Specifically:

1 intensity of liking and loving;
2 depth and breadth of information exchange;
3 length of relationship;
4 value of resources exchanged;
5 variety of resources exchanged;
6 interchangeability of resources;
7 the unit of analysis: from "you" and "me" to "we" (1978: 183).

Long married couples, who assume they will be together for a lifetime, are likely to be fairly sanguine about momentary injustices, confident that it will all work out in the end. Also, given the complexity of marital relationships, it may be difficult for married couples to calculate moment-to-moment whether or not their relationships are fair. They may well settle for a rough and ready definition of fairness. ("Yeah, all-in-all, things seem pretty fair to me, I guess.") Love might also affect how people caught up in inequitable relationships go about trying to set momentary inequities right.

Yet, in the end – in even the closest of relationships – fairness and equity do matter. Most intimates assume that good deeds will eventually be rewarded. (Their partners will be grateful. They will love them more. They will wish to reciprocate.) When people are forced to suffer too much, for too long, with no hope of return, they may well begin to resent life's unfairness. The wife of the Alzheimer's patient may begin to ask "Why me?" and to wish she could be released from her terrible burden. Her husband may feel guilty upon contemplating her terrible plight; he, too, may cry, shamefaced: "It's not fair" (Clark and Grote, 1998; Hatfield, et al., 1978, 2008; Markman, 1981).

Scientists have found that most couples – single, living together, or married; affluent or poor; dating for a few weeks or married for 50 years – do care about equity. In all of these groups, degree of reward, fairness, and equity have been found to be linked to passionate and companionate love, sexual satisfaction, marital happiness, contentment, satisfaction, and marital stability (Buunk and van Yperen, 1989; Byers and Wang, 2004; Hatfield et al., 2008; Lawrance and Byers, 1995; Martin, 1985; Schreurs and Buunk, 1996; van Yperen and Buunk, 1990). Couples in equitable relationships are also less likely to risk extramarital affairs than are their peers. They are more confident that their marriages will last, and in fact their relationships *are* longer lasting than those of their peers (Byers and Wang, 2004; Hatfield, et al., 2008; van Ypern and Buunk, 1990).

In one longitudinal study, Pillemer et al. (2008), interviewed a sample of dating and married men and women in Madison, Wisconsin, who ranged in age from 18 to 92; the couples been married between 1 and 53 years. They found that:

- Older women were hesitant to talk about fairness and equity in a marriage. They felt that couples shouldn't think in selfish ways – worrying about whether or not they were getting their fair share.
- The vast majority of older women (85 percent) considered their marriages to be fair and equitable.
- Older women appeared to be less concerned about day-to-day inequities than were dating couples and newlyweds. Nonetheless, even in the best of marriages, most admitted that niggling doubts about fairness did surface now and then. As predicted, those who were over-benefited felt a bit guilty; those who were under-benefited felt far more angry than did their privileged peers.
- Stressful life events – such as the arrival of children, retirement, serious illness, or the awareness of impending death – often brought to awareness long simmering resentments over issues of fairness.

In conclusion, research seems to indicate that although men and women who have been in a close intimate relationship for a long period of time are more tolerant of inequity than are their peers, in the end, they appear to be deeply concerned with how rewarding and equitable their relationships are.

The end of the affair

Hatfield and colleagues (1978) argued that if men and women are unfairly treated for a prolonged period of time, they will begin to wonder: "Does my partner love me? If so, why would he (she) treat me so unfairly?" They begin to ask: "What's in it for me?" and "Am I getting all I deserve in this relationship?" All would agree that when couples are at the point of breakup and divorce, they often become consumed with issues of profit (rewards minus costs) and fairness and equity.

Scholars agree that misery and unfairness are linked. They disagree, however, as to the nature of the causal relationship: Does perceived injustice cause dissatisfaction or is the causal order reversed? Clark (1986) takes the latter view. She argues that in communal relationships, couples do not "keep score"; they simply do not think in terms of reward and equity. Thus, if couples *are* concerned with such issues, it is a sure sign that their marriages are in trouble. Misery, then, is the *cause*, not the consequence of perceived injustice (Grote and Clark, 1998).

In a year-long longitudinal study, van Yperen and Buunk (1990) set out to answer this question. The authors interviewed couples who had been married for various lengths of time. They found that people in inequitable marriages became less satisfied over the course of a year. There was no evidence for the converse. It is possible, of course, that in failing marriages *both* processes are operating. In any case, it is clear that when marriages are faltering, people often become preoccupied with the pain and marital injustices they have endured, and this may well lead to relationship dissolution.

In sum, scientists have explored the impact that degree of reward and perceived fairness have on men and women's marital happiness and stability. It appears that although the concern with fairness may wax and wane during the course of a marriage, such concerns always remain there, just beneath the surface, guiding people's perceptions, happiness, and marital choices. Love is not blind.

IDEAS AND INTELLECTUAL HISTORY OF EQUITY THEORY

Philosophical underpinnings

Philosophers and ethicists have long been interested in the nature of social justice, fairness, and equity. The notion that others should be treated fairly is a ubiquitous one: more than 21 religions endorse some variant of the golden rule: "Do unto others..." Philosophers Thomas Hobbes, John Locke, and Jean-Jacques Rousseau, spoke of the "social contract," Immanuel Kant of the "categorical imperative." John Rawls, a contemporary philosopher, speaks of "the veil of ignorance." All of these concepts ask "What is fair?" and propose that it is generally in a person's best interest to treat others as they deserve – at least most of the time.

Early social exchange theorists

Social psychologists also attempted to understand the nature of social justice. The first modern-day scholars to propose models of social justice and social exchange (in the late 1950 and early 1960s) were sociologists George C. Homans (1958) and Peter Blau (1964) and social psychologists John Thibaut and Harold Kelley (1959). They viewed all social life as involving the exchange of goods, such as approval, esteem, and material goods. All people, they contended, are seeking maximum reward at minimum cost. As a consequence, there tends to be a balance in exchanges. Relying on the economic and behavioristic theories of the day, these scholars attempted to describe the factors that mediate the creation, maintenance, and breakdown of exchange relationships. Later, J. Stacy Adams (1965), an industrial-organizational psychologist, argued that management and labor attempt to maintain equity between the inputs they contribute to their work (such things as time, effort, and sacrifice) and the outcomes they receive from their professions (such things as security, salary, fringe benefits, etc.),

compared with the inputs and outputs of their supervisors, peers, and employees. Relational satisfaction was assumed to depend on how fair or unfair were distributions of rewards.

In the 1960s and 1970s, such social exchange theories were well received – so long as their advocates stuck to trying to predict behavior in academic, legal, or industrial settings. When we suggested that people might also be interested in reward and fairness in the arena of love, however, there was an explosion of indignation.

Early equity theorists and critics

As we observed earlier, equity theory appeared in an era in which traditional views of gender roles, men's and women's liberation, and the rules of love and sex (including innovations such as marriage contracts) were being hotly debated. Thus, it is not surprising that the contention that couples care about "What's in it for me?" and "Am I being treated fairly" sparked a great debate. True, a prominent group of theorists – such as Peter Blau, in *Exchange and Power in Social Life*; Michael McCall, in *Courtship as Social Exchange*; Mirra Komarovsky, in *Blue-Collar Marriage*; Gerald R. Patterson, in *Families*; John Scanzoni, in *Sexual Bargaining*; and Norman W. Storer, in *The Social System of Science* – agreed that in most intimate relationships, people do indeed care about pleasure and pain, fairness, and equity.

Yet, many people found the idea of speculating about the importance of equity in love relationships offensive. They harked back to Erich Fromm's writings. In *The Art of Loving*, Erich Fromm (1956: 3) declared that while flawed "human love relationships [may] follow the same pattern of exchange which governs the commodity and labor market, the truest form of love is unconditional love (love given without any thought of return"). He further observed that while men might be so crass as to act in selfish ways in love relationships, it was in women's nature to love unconditionally – giving without any thought of return. He notes, for example: "Fatherly love is conditional love. Its principle is 'I love you *because* you fulfill my expectations, because you do your duty, because you are like me . . .' Motherly love is by its very nature unconditional" (1956: 35–36).

In the 1970s, a variety of social commentators agreed with Fromm's contention that people, especially women, are generally *not* concerned with reward or fairness in their love relationships – most notably Margaret Clark and Judson Mills (1979), Elizabeth Douvan (1974), and Bernard Murstein (Murstein et al., 1977).

Shortly after the publication of *Equity Theory and Research*, for example, Elaine was invited to give a speech at Yale. At Stanford, Minnesota, and Wisconsin, she was quite used to academic discussions of research. She was stunned when at Yale she received shouts and catcalls from the audience. One fellow, for example, complained that modern-day women were selfish and unfeminine in their concerns about marital fairness. Another shouted that his sainted mother had dedicated her life to him, with nary a thought of reward. "Pleasing the family," he contended, "should be woman's chief joy." Elaine was surprised that in that day and age, academics wouldn't be more aware of the complexities of human experience and of changing gender relationships. Certainly many wives and mothers are altruistic – but even they have moments when they wonder: "How did I get into this?" Certainly, anyone parenting a teenager thinks: "Wait until you have children of your own..." Elaine had just talked to an elderly woman, who had nursed her sick husband for 30 years. After his death, she remarried. At first, she had been joyous, thinking: "Now is my time." When she discovered a few weeks later that her new husband was ill, and she was to be consigned to be a full-time nurse yet again, she couldn't help but cry out: "It isn't fair."

Clark (1986) argued that people participate in two kinds of relationships – communal

relationships and exchange relationships. She observed:

> In communal relationships, often exemplified by friendships and romantic relationships, people feel a special responsibility for one another's welfare. They give benefits in response to the other's needs or to please the other. In exchange relationships, often exemplified by acquaintances and business relationships, people feel no special responsibility for other's welfare. They give benefits with the expectation of receiving comparable benefits in return or in response to benefits previously received (1986: 414).

(Today, a number of theorists would agree with Clark's thesis that if couples are overly concerned with moment-to-moment equity, it is a "tip off" that there is something wrong with their relationships. See, for example, Aron et al., 1991; Sprecher, 1989; Van Lange et al., 1997.)

In a series of studies, Clark studied behavior in communal versus exchange settings. In these prototypic studies, a *communal orientation* was manipulated by introducing college men to an attractive *single* woman who acted as if she were interested in friendship. An *exchange orientation* was manipulated by introducing college men to an attractive *married* woman, who claimed to possess all the friends she desired. Men and women were assigned to work on some puzzles. During the encounter, the young woman asked the young man to assist her with her puzzles, and he complied. She then offered (or did not offer) to reciprocate. Men's feelings for the woman when she immediately offered (did not offer) to assist *him* depended on his orientation. In the communal condition, men preferred women who accepted help without immediately offering to pay them back. In the exchange setting, men preferred the (married) woman who accepted his aid, then offered to reciprocate in kind.

Clark (1986) and Williamson and Clark (1989) concluded that in dating, marital, and family relationships, communal norms prevail: men and women wish to please their partners, to care for and nurture them, and reject such crass considerations as "score-keeping" or a concern with *quid pro quo*. Relationships are complex, however, and a more cynical interpretation of Clark's results is possible. Normally it takes time for people to fall in love and commit themselves to an intimate relationship. In Clark's studies, men and women had just met. When "Prince Charming" assisted the "damsel in distress," there might have been two reasons why he preferred the attractive single women who did not insist on reciprocating in kind: (1) men might have possessed a communal orientation, as Clark believes; or (2) men may offer dinners, theatre tickets, and assistance to a beautiful woman, in hopes that she will willingly repay them with affection, gratitude, a date, or sex. The breathless, "How can I ever repay you?" is a TV cliché. In their heart of hearts, men in Clark's (1986) study may have may have been hoping to participate in an exchange – albeit a complex one.

On the face of it, the Clark perspective seemed diametrically opposed to our own. When one looks closer, however, the two often seem to merge. As they say, "The devil is in the details." Consider the following observations by Clark and her colleagues:

- Men and women prefer physically attractive mates, in part because the attractive are perceived to be more sensitive, kind, and capable of communal relationships than their peers (Clark, 1986).
- People who sacrifice on their partner's behalf, assume that their partners will be grateful, and become more loving and trusting than before, and thus more likely to "be there for *them* when the need arises" (Clark and Grote, 1998; Grote and Clark, 2004).
- Couples may prefer communal relationships, yet when desires and needs conflict, as they inevitably do, in the interests of fairness, men and women often decide to take turns in reaping benefits or suffering costs (Clark and Grote, 1998).
- People may differ in how communally oriented they are. A wife may assume her chivalrous husband is delighted to cater to her needs; her less communally oriented husband may resent what he considers to be her "exploitative" behavior (Mills et al., 2004).
- Some people are cunning and devious. A young medical student may ask his wife to put him

through graduate school, only to divorce her upon graduation. In such cases, his communally oriented wife would naturally feel resentful at the betrayal (Williamson and Clark, 1989).
- When people suspect their mate is not communally oriented – that is, he does not care about their desires and needs – they will begin to mistrust the other, to "keep records," and worry about whether or not they are being fairly treated (Clark and Grote, 1998).

No matter how good a relationship, then, even in Clark's paradigm, it appears that now and then people ask themselves "Am I loved?" "Is my dating relationship or marriage rewarding?" "Is it fair and equitable?" The answers people come up with may well have a profound impact on their feelings about their relationships.

Development and growth of equity theory over the years

In many ways, the changing interests of equity theorists has paralleled changes in social psychology theorizing and research (in general) over the last 25 years (see Berscheid, 1992). Specifically, with the passage of time we became increasingly interested in the cultural, social, and biological forces that shape people's lives; a broadening and deepening of equity theory (to investigate more long-term relationships); and an increased sophistication in social psychological research methods.

Crafting equity theory

First, although from the start we yearned to integrate the insights of Darwinian theory, economic theory, and Hullian and Skinnerian reinforcement theories in crafting equity theory, in fact in those early days we were forced to focus more on nurture than nature. True, in the 1960s and 1970s, some pioneers like Hamilton (1964), Trivers (1971), and Smith (1974) assumed that altruism, as well as aggression, was wired into humankind. Theorists talked about the advantages of "group selection," "kin selection or inclusive fitness," and "reciprocal altruism" (a version of "If you scratch my back, I'll scratch yours"). Nonetheless, the influential theorist was Dawkins (1976), who contended in *The Selfish Gene* that day-to-day people are programmed for savage competition, ruthless exploitation, and deceit. Admittedly, altruistic acts occurred – but alas, such altruism was more apparent than real. Our challenge was, then, to craft a theory that accounted for people's desire for fairness and justice using primarily social constructionist and reinforcement models. Propositions I through IV focused on the social forces that prod people to care about social justice. The evidence for our contentions came, for the most part, from cultural psychology, social psychology, and Industrial-Organizational research.

In a subsequent section, we will discover that Darwinian theory has itself evolved. Today, evolutionary theorists have no trouble accounting for people's desire for fairness and justice. Were we crafting equity theory today, we would be able to argue that people are predisposed both by nature and nurture to care very much indeed about social justice and to provide compelling evidence from a variety of disciplines for that contention.

Broadening and deepening equity theory

In the early 1960s, I (EH) and my colleague Ellen Berscheid were primarily interested in theorizing about a totally neglected area – passionate love affairs. Our interest in this research topic was a natural one. First, we were young and all our friends were personally interested in this topic. Better yet, we were working in an as yet untrodden territory. Anything we discovered was bound to be interesting! Luckily, college students, often in the throes of passionate infatuations, were readily available as research participants.

The critics of equity theory – such as Margaret Clark and the late Judson Mills – were focused primarily on close, intimate, long-term relationships. Their contention that equity processes were likely to operate in a completely different way in deeply intimate settings was an exciting impetus to broaden our theory. It motivated us to try to deal with

people's perceptions of fairness at every stage of the life cycle and to learn more about how equity processes played themselves out in these complex relationships.

The appearance of innovative psychometric and research techniques

Since the 1970s, social psychologists have been hard at work developing a panoply of "user friendly" psychometric techniques for measuring psychological constructs. Technically, equity is defined by a complex formula (Traupmann et al., 1981; Walster, 1975). Respondents' perceptions as to the equitableness of their dating relationships or marriages is computed by entering their estimates of the inputs and outcomes of Persons A and B (I_A, I_B, O_A, and O_B) into the equity formula:[3]

$$\frac{(O_A - I_A)}{(|I_A|)^{KA}} = \frac{(O_B - I_B)}{(|I_B|)^{KB}}$$

Respondents are classified as "over-benefited" if their relative gains exceed those of their partners. They are classified as "equitably treated" if their relative gains equal those of their partners, and as "under-benefited" if their relative gains fall short of those of their partners.

After conducting a great deal of research – and suffering through laborious data entries and complex calculations (which were often done by hand in that era), we abandoned our devilishly complex technique for assessing equity. Our original equity measure required us to ask questions (about inputs and outcomes) that respondents found it difficult to answer, and for the experimenter to record data, and perform calculations that were often difficult to perform – at least without errors! Then one day, it suddenly occurred to us that the best way to find out what we wished to know was to directly ask our respondents! Thus, in the Equity Global Measure (described earlier) we simply asked couples to think about their relationships and tell us how fair and equitable they seemed to be. Possible answers ranged from +3: "I am getting a much better deal than my partner" to –3: " My partner is getting a much better deal than I am."

So obvious – and yet it had taken us a year or two to realize that this was the best way to find out what we wanted to know. (Sort of like the NASCAR builder who suddenly realizes that the horse-and-buggy might not be the best automotive model.) This "time saving" was especially useful when we used the Multi-trait Measure of Equity. Twenty-five questions instead of 100!

Since the early days, social psychologists' repertoire of research techniques has increased markedly. In the 1960s (as today), I (EH) was a specialist in social psychological experiments. Though I still value true experiments, now and then I and my colleagues turn to more complex methodologies – qualitative analyses, cross-sectional and long-term longitudinal studies, interactive paradigms, analyses of papal and church edicts, demographic data, historical and anthropological research, and the like.

The "hardware" of social psychologists has improved, too. Today, scholars can study people's reactions to inequity by utilizing audio-visual recordings, social-psycho-physiological measures, fMRIs, physiological recordings, and a variety of unobtrusive measures. All of these new techniques give us a better understanding of the way concerns with Equity play themselves out in real life settings.

Current research: a multidisciplinary approach

At the present time, some of the most interesting research into the nature of social justice emanates from scholars from four different intellectual traditions: (1) cultural scholars interested in societal definitions as to what is fair and equitable; (2) evolutionary theorists, who argue that a concern for justice arose early in humankind's long prehistory, and speculate about the ways in which this ancient "wiring" might affect contemporary visions of social justice; (3) neuroscientists, who are interested in charting the brain activity associated with perceptions of fairness or unfairness; and (4) primatologists, who speculate about the extent to which primates'

sense of justice is similar or different from that of humankind.

Let us now consider a scattering of research from these four areas, just to give readers a sense of what is going on.

> Is morality relative to culture? I would say that it is – and also that it isn't. Eric Knickerbocker

Equity: cultural considerations

Cultural theorists have long been interested in the impact of culture on perceptions of social justice. Anthropologists like Richard Shweder (1987) and Alan Fiske (2002), for example, surveyed moral concerns across the globe. All people, they argue, possess a sense of fairness; they assume people should reciprocate favors, reward benefactors, and punish cheaters.

Cultural theorists also contend that culture exerts a profound influence on how fairness is defined, how concerned men and women are that their intimate affairs be equitable, and how rewarding and equitable love relationships are likely to be (Amir and Sharon, 1987; Aumer-Ryan et al., 2007; Murphy-Berman and Berman, 2002).

Triandis and his colleagues (1990), for example, argued that in individualistic cultures (such as the US, Britain, Australia, Canada, and the countries of northern and western Europe) people generally focus on personal goals. In such societies, people are concerned with how rewarding (or punishing) their relationships are and how fairly (unfairly) they are treated. Collectivist cultures (such as China, many African and Latin American nations, Greece, southern Italy, and the Pacific Islands), on the other hand, insist that their members subordinate personal goals to those of the group: the family, the clan, or the tribe. It is tradition, duty, and deference to elders that matter. Rosenblatt and Cunningham (1976) claimed that equity is of less importance in collectivist societies: "[regardless of] who has the better life, a man or a woman, they [people of non-US cultures] might argue ... that the lives of men and women are different and not comparable" (cited in Buunk and VanYperen, 1989: 82).

Do cultures differ in how much importance they attach to dating and marital fairness and equity? In a series of studies, Aumer-Ryan and her colleagues (2006) attempted to find out. They interviewed Japanese-American, West Indian, and multicultural internet users, seeking answers to three questions. In different cultures, do men and women: (1) differ in the value they ascribe to equity in dating and marital relationships – some considering it to be crucial, others dismissing "fairness" as of trivial importance; (2) differ in whether they consider their own relationships to be equitable or inequitable; and (3) differ in how satisfied (or upset) when they discover their own relationships have turned out to be strikingly equitable/inequitable?

Aumer-Ryan and her colleagues (2006) found that, in all cultures, people considered reward and equity to be the gold standard of good relationships. Both Westerners and their non-Western counterparts insisted it was "important" or "very important" that a courtship relationship or marriage be equitable.

The authors did observe some fascinating cultural differences, however. People around the world may aspire to social justice, but few were lucky enough to achieve that goal. People in the various cultures differed markedly in how fair and equitable they considered their relationships to be. Men and women from the US claimed to be the most equitably treated. Men and women (especially women) from Jamaica, in the West Indies, felt the least equitably treated. Jamaican women often complained about men treating women as "second class citizens" and about men's lack of commitment to relationships. In describing men's attitudes, one woman quoted a classic Calypso song by Lord Kitchener (1963), and the repeated lyric: "You can always find another wife/but you can never get another mother in your life." Such attitudes, the women claimed, make it very difficult for them to find a relationship that is rewarding, fair, and fulfilling.

In all cultures, men and women reacted much the same way when they felt fairly or badly treated. All were most satisfied when

receiving exactly what they felt they deserved from their relationships – no more (perhaps) but (just as in the West) certainly no less. (For additional research on this topic, see Murphy-Berman and Berman, 2002; Westerman, et al., 2007; Yamaguchi, 1994.)

Cultural psychologists not only give us information as to cultural differences in the way people define social justice. Cultural psychologists and historians also provide a window onto understanding the impact of social change on societal definitions of fairness. Some examples. Historians point out that globalization carries with it profound transformations in men and women's roles and in gender equality (Hatfield and Rapson, 2005). What impact does the movement from a traditional to a modern-day society have on the way men and women define fairness? How contented are men and women facing such changes? Do men tend to cling to the past while women rush into the future? How do men and women attempt to deal with the changes they perceive? Such research may provide new insights into the nature of social justice.

> Is it not reasonable to anticipate that our understanding of the human mind would be aided greatly by knowing the purpose for which it was designed? (George C. Williams)

Equity: the evolution of a cultural universal

In the past 25 years or so, social psychologists have begun to explore the evolutionary underpinnings of social justice. (See, for example, the classic work of Robert Trivers [1972] or Richard Dawkins [1976], on the probable evolution of reciprocal altruism and social exchange.) As Cosmides and Tooby observe:

> It is likely that our ancestors have engaged in social exchange for at least several million years ... Social exchange behavior is both universal and highly elaborated across all human cultures – including hunter-gatherer cultures ... as would be expected if it were an ancient and central part of human life (1992: 164)

Currently, interesting work on social justice from evolutionary perspective is being conducted by scholars such as Rob Boyd (Boyd et al., 2003). They provide strong support for the notion in Proposition II that groups will reward those who treat others fairly and punish those who do not, even at considerable cost to themselves. Later in this chapter, we will discuss some of the evidence from neuroscientists and primatologists relevant to their observations.

Equity: fMRI research

In recent years, neuroscientists have begun to investigate the cognitive factors (and brain processes) that are involved when men and women confront moral dilemmas. These concern such things as the nature of social justice and how a variety of competing moral claims – such as, "What's more important: the claims of friendship or the demands of fairness and equity in a social exchange?" – are resolved. Robertson and her colleagues (2007), for example, presented men and women with several real-life moral dilemmas. Using functional magnetic resonance imaging (fMRI) techniques, they studied people's brain activity as they pondered such dilemmas. The neuroscientists found that sensitivity to moral issues (in general) was associated with activation of the polar medial prefrontal cortex, dorsal posterior cingulated cortex, and posterior superior temporal sulcus (STS). They speculated that moral sensitivity is probably related to people's ability to retrieve autobiographical memories and to take a social perspective. They also assessed whether sensitivity to social concerns as distinguished from impartial justice involved different kinds of neural processing. They found that sensitivity to issues of justice (and social exchange) was associated with greater activation of the left intraparietal sulcus, whereas sensitivity to care issues was associated with greater activation of the ventral posterior cingulate cortex, ventromedial and dorsolateral prefrontal cortex, and the thalamus. These results suggest that different parts of the brain may operate when people ponder their duty to loved ones versus their obligation to be fair and just to all. For addi-

tional neurobiological speculations as to the neural circuits involved in the perception of and reaction to social inequality, see Borg et al. (2006), Raine and Yang (2006), Reis et al. (2007), Watson and Platt (2006), and Witvliet et al. (2008).

Neuroscience is still in its infancy, of course. Many social scientists have sharply criticized the widespread use of fMRI techniques to study the nature of social justice, claiming that currently the fMRI studies track only superficial changes and lack reliability and validity (Cacioppo, et al., 2003; Movshon, 2006; Panksepp, 2007; Wade, cited in Wargo, 2005). Nonetheless, this groundbreaking research has the potential (as it grows ever more sophisticated) to answer age-old questions as to the nature of culture, perceptions of social justice, and the ways in which people react when faced with equitable or inequitable treatment.

Equity: the concern for justice in other species

Today, paleoanthropological evidence supports the view that notions of social justice and equity are extremely ancient. Ravens, for example, have been observed to attack those who violate social norms. Dogs get jealous if their playmates get treats and they do not. Wolves who don't "play fair" are often ostracized – a penalty that may well lead to the wolf's death (Bekoff, 2004; Brosnan, 2006).

Primatologists have amassed considerable evidence that primates and other animals do care about fairness. In a study with brown capuchin (*Cebus apella*) monkeys, Brosnan and de Waal (2003) discovered that female monkeys who were denied the rewards they deserved became furious. They refused to play the game (i.e., refused to exchange tokens for a cucumber) and disdained to eat their prize – holding out for the grapes they deserved. If severely provoked (the other monkey did nothing and still got the highly prized grapes instead of the cucumber) capuchins grew so angry that they began to scream, beat their breasts, and hurl food at the experimenter. Interestingly, in a later study, the authors found that chimpanzees *(Pan troglodytes)* were most upset by injustice in casual relationships. In chimps' close, intimate relationships, injustice caused barely a ripple (Brosnan et al., 2005). There is some evidence that in close groups, chimps will voluntarily set things right. We see, then, that different species, in different settings, may respond differently to injustice. (Some critics have argued that in these experiments there is a confound between "impaired self-interest" and "injustice," since injustice was manipulated by denying the chimps reward. Only subsequent research can determine whether or not these primates can truly be said to be seeking justice.)

In the late 1990s, Ronald Noë and Peter Hammerstein (1994) proposed the notion of "biological markets" – predicting that primates would respond to much the same market forces as men and women do in selecting their mates. Recently, Ronald Gumert (2008) observed 50 longtailed macaques in a reserve in Central Kalimantan, Indonesia. He found that in essence male macaque monkeys pay for sex by grooming the female. "It suggests that sex is a commodity," he observed. And as with other commodities, the value of sex is affected by considerations of supply and demand. Gumert observes:

> A male would spend more time grooming a female if there were fewer females in the vicinity ... And when the female supply is higher, the male spends less time on grooming ... The mating actually becomes cheaper depending on the market (2008: 1)

Potentially, this fascinating animal research may provide some insights into three questions that have intrigued equity researchers:

- When, in primates' long prehistory, did animals begin to feel "guilty" about receiving "too much," as well as feeling outraged when they are "ripped off"? (Brosnan et al., 2005; Brosnan, 2006).
- Are animals more (or less) concerned about fairness in despotic, hierarchical societies than in those that are relatively egalitarian? (Brosnan, 2006).
- Are primates and other animals more (or less) concerned about inequities in close kin relationships than in more distant encounters? (Brosnan et al, 2005).

EQUITY THEORY'S APPLICABILITY TO RELATIONSHIP ISSUES

Essentially, the equity argument goes as follows: People may be motivated by self-interest, but they soon learn that the best way to survive and prosper is by following social rules as to what is fair or unfair. Thus, all in all, men and women will feel most comfortable when they are getting roughly what they deserve from their relationships. This fact has several practical implications:

Mate selection

When pop-psychology authors give advice, they often assume that all their readers are entitled to all of life's riches. Romantics are eager to take such "advice." We once asked one of our clients, who complained that all the good men were taken, what she was looking for in a mate. She quickly scribbled a list of qualities she considered indispensable. Her list comprised more than 200 items! Many of them were contradictory. ("I want an ambitious and successful moneymaker" and "I want someone who will do at least 50 percent of the housecleaning and childcare." This list was presented without a trace of irony. Many people, sad to say, think very much along these lines and are convinced that through the magic of positive thinking, "affirmations," eHarmony.com, and such, they can "have it all" (Rapson, 2008). And, you may ask, why not? To equity theorists, such expectations are wildly impractical. Of course everyone longs for perfection. Unfortunately, the supply of perfection is somewhat limited.

In the musical *Showboat*, a hard working showman, Frank, pleads with a young girl, Ellie, to marry him. Her saucy reply:

> After I have looked around the world for a mate,
> Then, perhaps, I might fall back on you!
> When I am convinced that there is no better fate,
> Then I might decide that you will do.

A harsh way of putting it, but indeed there is more than a grain of truth in her soliloquy.

People do often consider their "market value" when deciding what they will settle for in a mate. In real life, imperfect humans with run-of-the-mill flaws (like all of us) had better resign themselves to the fact that they will have to settle for other humans no better and no worse than themselves.

Saints and sinners

How do couples, caught up in unbalanced relationships, generally handle their feelings of distress? Equity theorists observed that men and women can reduce distress via three techniques:

1 *Restoration of actual equity.* One way individuals can restore equity to an unjust relationship is by voluntarily setting things right, or by urging their partners to do so. Couples do often make considerable effort to balance things out. The husband who has been irritable because of stress at work may try to make amends by taking the family on a holiday when the pressure lets up.
2 *Restoration of psychological equity.* Couples in inequitable relationships can reduce distress in a second way. They can distort reality and convince themselves (and perhaps others as well) that things are perfectly fair just as they are. A variety of studies have documented the imaginative techniques that people use to justify injustice. Some studies find, for example, that harm-doers rationalize the harm they inflict on others by denying they are responsible for the victim's suffering ("I was just following orders"), by insisting that the victim deserved to suffer, or by minimizing the extent to which the victim suffered from their actions. There is even some sparse experimental evidence that, under the right circumstances, victims will justify their own exploitation.
3 *Leave the relationship.* Finally, if couples are unable to restore equity to their intimate relationships, there is a third way they can try to set things right. They can leave the relationship. This does not always mean divorce. A person will sometimes "opt-out" by abandoning their partners emotionally. New mothers, less attracted to their husbands than to their newborns, may insist that their infants sleep between them. This is a most effective strategy for keeping the couple apart. Or couples may spend all their leisure time "drinking with the boys" or "shopping with the girls," ensuring that they will rarely spend time alone together as a twosome. Both partners may

risk their hearts in extramarital affairs. Or, finally, they may simply leave altogether.

The vast literature on how people deal with inequity has practical implications for close relationships. We know, for example, that people come to love those they treat with kindness and to despise those they abuse. Relationships should go best when they are balanced, when both people love one another, sacrifice for one another, and are loved in return.

Yet, even in the best of relationships, people have to be wary if they spot things going awry. If you think about the close relationships of some of your friends, you can probably come up with some examples of people who are emotionally stingy and hence give too little in relationships or who are always willing to give too much. How have these unbalanced affairs have worked out? Here are a couple of examples from our experiences as psychotherapists:

One of our clients was appallingly narcissistic. He was good-looking and had a sort of raffish charm, but he wasn't willing to make *any* compromises. "You compromise once," he said, "and you set a precedent; there's no end to it." In singles bars, women swarmed around him. However, once they started spending time with him, they soon became irritated. At first they could convince themselves that it was "just this once" that they would be stuck in the kitchen preparing a spontaneous dinner for ten of his pals while they watched the Super Bowl. Only this once would he ask her to research and type his reports while he took a nap. But as the days turned into weeks and the "just-this-onces" became a mantra, the rationalizations turned to seething rage. The women felt ripped off. Eventually they left the kitchen and the computer keyboard, and walked away from the relationship. If men and women know deep down that they are taking advantage of their partners, they should be warned that they may be playing a dangerous game. Sometimes people win all the battles only to lose the war. Their partners give in and give in, until finally they have had enough: they get fed up and leave.

Another of our clients was very paternal; he was always attracted to "wounded birds" – beautiful young women who were so troubled and so uneducated that they couldn't make it on their own. He tried to anticipate all their needs and showered them with expensive presents. Any time that trouble threatened, he tried harder and gave yet more. Inevitably, his relationships fell apart. His young girlfriends were grateful; they felt they *should* love him (and were ashamed that they couldn't). But they just didn't. "Where was his self-respect? Why was he so desperate?" "What was wrong with him?" They felt smothered. They couldn't bear to touch him. They had to flee.

Men and women have to be able to set limits. If loving people become aware that their mates are taking them for granted or treating them like doormats, they must have the strength to complain, draw the line, or give up the relationship. Otherwise, the relationship becomes a dangerously inequitable one.

EQUITY THEORY'S APPLICABILITY TO SOCIAL ISSUES

In this chapter, we come full circle. When discussing the origins of equity theory, we spoke of the social ferment of the 1960s and 1970s. Today, 40 years later, in the West, these spirited debates about the nature of social justice have borne fruit. As Rapson (2008) observed, scholars generally agree that the two most significant social transformations of the twentieth and twenty-first centuries are: (1) the globalization of science and technology; and (2) the women's movement.

In the West, we have not yet achieved gender equality, though the approach toward that destination has been rapid in recent decades, particularly in parts of northern Europe. Male supremacy, however, continues to be the rule worldwide. When the United Nations sponsored a trio of human rights conferences in Vienna, Geneva, and Beijing, members of the world community agreed that abuses of women's rights – which include female infanticide, genital mutilation, the sale of brides,

dowry murders, *suttee* or widow burning (in India, widows are still sometimes required to immolate themselves on their husbands' funeral pyres), and discriminatory laws against women's civic, social, and legal equality – are, in fact, abuses of human rights generally. The members also agreed that "culture" and "tradition" can no longer be cited to justify repression of half the world's population, especially since "tradition" has been defined by the powerful men in those societies. Gender equality around the world, including the developed world, is a long way off.

Yet, the winds of modernism are sweeping even into the most well-guarded sanctuaries of the male privilege. A revolution in gender and love relations has begun in China, Japan, Mexico, Latin America, North Africa, Russia, and even in Turkey, Saudi Arabia, and some other Arab nations (see Hatfield and Rapson, 2005, for the research in support of these conclusions). In different societies, these historic changes are moving at different speeds, of course. The women's movement has had a greater impact on men and women's lives in Europe than in the Middle East, in urban than in rural settings, in secular societies than in theistic cultures, and in wealthier than in poorer nations. But the times they are a'- changin' and the changes we have described are of monumental significance.

These epochal historical movements are likely to profoundly transform men and women's perceptions as to what is fair and equitable in love relationships. Historically, women have had little power. This meant that they possessed little freedom to shape their own lives, were forced to resign themselves to minimal expectations, and to be dependent on husbands and sons for most of life's basic needs. But as women gain more social power, they are likely to possess more bargaining power, higher expectations, and be more demanding in the arena of life and love. Given these social changes – as surely as the earth orbits the sun – women's demands for fair and equitable treatment are sure to grow and, consequently, so will men's. We believe that the continued global march towards gender equality will enlarge demands for equity in love relationships and profoundly alter (mostly for the better, we believe) love relationships around the globe.

CONCLUSION

We have traced equity theory from its beginnings to the present day. We reviewed compelling evidence that at all stages in love relationships – from their tentative beginnings, though their flowering, and perhaps to their bitter ending – men and women are concerned with both reward and fairness. We reviewed new multidisciplinary research – cultural, evolutionary, primatological, and neuroscience investigations – which add new depth and richness to our understanding of human nature. We closed by pointing out that the massive social changes that are occurring in our times, suggesting that men and women may well be developing more complex and (especially for women) more fulfilling notions as to what constitutes fair and equitable treatment in love and life.

NOTES

1 As you can see, in developing this theory we were hoping to combine the insights of Darwinian theory, economic theory, and reinforcement theory.

2 And perplexity or disgust when contemplating their partner's weakness.

3 The equity formulas used by previous researchers, from Aristotle to Stacy Adams, only yield meaningful results if A and B's inputs and outcomes are entirely positive or entirely negative. In mixed cases the formulas yield extremely peculiar results. Thus, we proposed an equity computational scheme designed to transcend these limitations. See Walster (1995) for a discussion of the problems and the mathematical solutions. The superscript K simply "scales" equity problems (by multiplying all inputs and outcomes by a positive constant) such that the minimum of $|I_A|$ and $|I_B|$ is greater than or equal to 1.

REFERENCES

Adams, J.S. (1965) Inequity in social exchange. *Advances in Experimental Social Psychology*, 62, 335–343.

Amir, Y. and Sharon, I. (1987) Are social psychological laws cross-culturally valid? *Journal of Cross-Cultural Psychology*, 18, 383–470.

Anselm of Canterbury (1998) Opera omnia. In B. Davies and G. Evans (eds), *Anselem of Canterbury: The Major Works*. New York: Oxford University Press. (Original work 1070–1109 AD).

Aron, A., Aron, E.N., Tudor, M. and Nelson, G. (1991) Close relationships as including other in the self. *Journal of Personality and Social Psychology*, 60, 241–253.

Aumer-Ryan, K., Hatfield, E. and Frey, R. (2007) Equity in romantic relationships: An analysis across self-construal and culture. University of Texas, Austin, Texas.

Baumeister, R.F. and Vohs, K.D. (2004) Sexual economics: Sex as female resource for social exchange in heterosexual interactions. *Personality and Social Psychology Review*, 8, 339–363.

Bekoff, M. (2004) Wild justice, cooperation, and fair play: Minding manners, being nice, and feeling good. In R. Sussman and A. Chapman (eds), *The Origins and Nature of Sociality*, pp. 53–79. Chicago: Aldine.

Bernard, J. (1972) *The Future of Marriage*. New York: World.

Berscheid, E. (1992) A glance back at a quarter century of social psychology. *Journal of Personality and Social Psychology*, 63, 525–533.

Blau, P. (1964) *Exchange and Power in Social Life*. New York: Wiley.

Blau, P. (1986) Exchange and Power in Social Life. New York: Transition Press.

Borg, J.S., Hynes, C., Van Horn, J., Grafton, S. and Sinnott-Armstrong, W. (2006) Consequences, action, and intention as factors in moral judgments: An fMRI investigation. *Journal of Cognitive Neuroscience*, 18, 803–817.

Boyd, R., Gintis, H., Bowles, S. and Richerson, P.J. (2003) The evolution of altruistic punishment. *PNAS*, 100, 3531–3535.

Brosnan, S.F. (2006) At a crossroads of disciplines. *Journal of Social Justice*, 19, 218–227.

Brosnan, S.F., Schiff, H.C. and de Waal, F.B.M. (2005) Tolerance for inequity may increase with social closeness in chimpanzees. *Proceedings of the Royal Society of London, Series B 1560*, 253–258.

Brosnan, S.F. and de Waal, F.B.M. (2003) Monkeys reject unequal pay. *Nature*, 425, 297–299.

Buunk, B.P. and Van Ypern, N.W. (1989) Social comparison, equality, and relationship satisfaction: Gender differences over a ten-year period. *Social Justice Research*, 3, 157–180.

Byers, E.S. and Wang, A. (2004) Understanding sexuality in close relationships from the social exchange perspective. In J.H. Harvey, A. Wenzel, and S. Sprecher (eds), *Handbook of Sexuality in Close Relationships*, pp. 203–234. Mahwah, NJ: Lawrence Erlbaum.

Cacioppo, J.T., Berntson, G.G., Lorig, T.S., Norris, C.J. and Nusbaum, H. (2003) Just because you're imaging the brain doesn't mean you can stop using your head: A primer and set of first principles. *Journal of Personality and Social Psychology, 85*, 650–661.

Clark, M.S. (1986) Evidence for the effectiveness of manipulations of communal and exchange relationships. *Personality and Social Psychology Bulletin, 12*, 414–425.

Clark, M.S. and Grote, N.K. (1998) Why aren't indices of relationship costs always negatively related to indices of relationship quality? *Personality and Social Psychology Review, 2*, 2–17.

Clark, M.S. and Mills, J. (1979) Interpersonal attraction in exchange and communal relationships. *Journal of Personality and Social Psychology, 37*, 12–24.

Cosmides, L. and Tooby, J. (1992) Cognitive adaptations for social exchange. In J.H. Barkow, L. Cosmides, and J. Tooby (eds), *The Adapted Mind*, pp. 161–228. New York: Oxford University Press.

Dawkins, R. (1976) *The Selfish Gene*. Oxford: Oxford University Press.

Douvan, E. (1974) Interpersonal relationships – some questions and observations. Paper presented at the Rausch Conference, Durham, NC, Duke University.

Fiske, A.P. (2002) Moral emotions provide the self-control needed to sustain social relationships. *Self and Identity, 1*, 169–175.

Fromm, E. (1956) *The Art of Loving*. New York: Harper & Row.

Fierstone, S. (1979) *The Dialectic of Sex*. New York: Women's Press.

Friedan, B. (1963) *The Feminine Mystique*. New York: W.W. Norton.

Goffman, E. (1952) On cooling the mark out: Some aspects of adaptation to failure. *Psychiatry, 15*, 451–463.

Grote, N.K. and Clark, M.S. (2004) Distributive justice norms and family work: What is perceived as ideal, what is applied, and what predicts perceived fairness. *Social Justice Research, 11*, 243–269.

Gumert, M. (2008) Macaque monkeys 'pay' for sex. *New Scientist*, January, 1–2.

Hamilton, W.D. (1964) The genetical evolution of social behaviour I and II. *Journal of Theoretical Biology, 7*, 1–32.

Hatfield, E. and Rapson, R.L. (1993) *Love, Sex, and Intimacy: Their Psychology, Biology, and History*. New York: Harper/Collins.

Hatfield, E. and Rapson, R.L. (2005) *Love and Sex: Cross-Cultural Perspectives*. Lanham, MD: University Press of America.

Hatfield, E., Rapson, R.L. and Aumer-Ryan, K. (2007) Equity Theory: Social justice in love relationships. Recent developments. *Social Justice Research*. New York: Springer.

Hatfield, E., Rapson, R.L. and Aumer-Ryan, K. (2008) Social justice in love relationships: Recent developments. *Social Justice Research*.

Hatfield, E., Walster, G.W. and Berscheid, E. (1978) *Equity: Theory and Research*. Boston: Allyn & Bacon.

Homans, G.C. (1958) Social behavior as exchange. *American Journal of Sociology, 63*, 97–606.

Kitchener, L. (1963) Mother and wife [Recorded by The Invaders Steel Band]. On *Air Mail Music: Steel Bands Caraibes* [CD]. Track 12. Boulogne, France: Playasound.

Komarovsky, M. (1964) *Blue-Collar Marriage*. New York: Random House.

Lawrance, K-A. and Byers, E.S. (1995) Sexual satisfaction in long-term heterosexual relationships: The interpersonal exchange model of sexual satisfaction. *Personal Relationships, 2*, 267–285.

Markman, H.J. (1981) Prediction of marital distress: A 5-year follow up. *Journal of Consulting and Clinical Psychology, 49*, 460–762.

Marsella, A.J. (1998) Toward a global psychology: Meeting the needs of a changing world. *American Psychologist, 53*, 1282–1291.

Martin, M.W. (1985) Satisfaction with intimate exchange: Gender-role differences and the impact of equity, equality, and rewards. *Sex Roles, 13*, 597–605.

Mills, J., Clark, M.S., Ford, T.E. and Johnson, M. (2004) Measurement of communal strength. *Personal Relationships, 11*, 213–230.

Movshon, J.A. (2006) Searching for the person in the brain. *The New York Times. Week in Review*, February 5, 1–4.

Murphy-Berman, V. and Berman, J. (2002) Cross-cultural differences in perceptions of distributive justice. *Journal of Cross-Cultural Psychology, 33*, 157–170.

Murstein, B.I., Cerreto, M. and MacDonald, M.G. (1977) A theory and investigation of the effect of exchange-orientation on marriage and friendship. *Journal of Marriage and the Family, 39*, 543–548.

Noë, R. and Hammerstein, P. (1994) Biological markets: supply and demand determine the effect of partner choice in cooperation, mutualism, and mating. *Behavioral Ecology and Sociobiology, 35*, 1–11.

Panksepp, J. (2007) Neurologizing the psychology of affects: How appraisal-based constructivism and basic emotion theory can coexist. *Perspectives on Psychological Science, 2*, 281–312.

Patterson, G. R. (1971) *Families: Applications of Social Learning to Family Life*. Champaign, IL: Research Press.

Perlman, D. and Duck, S. (1986) *Intimate Relationships: Development, Dynamics, and Deterioration*. New York: Sage.

Pillemer, J., Hatfield, E. and Sprecher, S. (2008) The importance of fairness and equity for the marital satisfaction of older women. *Journal of Women and Aging, 20*, 215–230.

Raine, A. and Yang, Y. (2006) Neural foundations to moral reasoning and antisocial behavior. *Social Cognitive and Affective Neuroscience, 1*, 203–213.

Rapson, R.L. (2008) *Magical Thinking and the Decline of America*. Philadelphia: Xlibris.

Reis, D.L., Brackett, M.A., Shamosh, N.A., Kiehl, K.A., Salovey, P. and Gray, J.R. (2007) Emotional intelligence predicts individual differences in social exchange reasoning, *NeuroImage, 35*, 1385–1391.

Robertson, D., Snarey, J., Ousley, O., Harenski, K., Bowman, F.D., Gilkey, R. and Kilts, C. (2007) The neural processing of moral sensitivity to issues of justice and care. *Neuropsychologia*, 755–766.

Rosenblatt, P.C. and Cunningham, M.R. (1976) Sex differences in cross-cultural perspective. In B. Lloyd and J. Archer (eds), *Exploring Sex Differences*, pp. 71–94. London: Academic Press.

Scanzoni, J. (1972) *Sexual Bargaining: Power Politics in the American Marriage*. Englewood Cliffs, NJ: Prentice-Hall.

Schreurs, K.M.G. and Buunk, B.P. (1996) Closeness, autonomy, equity, and relationship satisfaction in lesbian couples. *Psychology of Women Quarterly, 20*, 577–592.

Shweder, R.A. (1987) Culture and moral development. In J. Kagen and S. Lamb (eds), *The Emergence of Morality in Young Children*, pp. 1–88. Chicago: University of Chicago Press.

Smith, M. (1974) *Models in Ecology*. Cambridge: Cambridge University Press.

Sprecher, S. (1989) The effect of exchange orientation on close relationships. *Social Psychology Quarterly, 61*, 220–231.

Storer, N.W. (1966) *The Social System of Science*. New York: Holt, Rinehart, and Winston.

Thibaut, J.W. and Kelley, H.H. (1959) *The Social Psychology of Groups*. New York: John Wiley.

Tooby, J. and Cosmides, L. (1992) The evolutionary and psychological foundations of the social sciences. In J.H. Barkow, L. Cosmides and J. Tooby (eds). *The Adapted Mind: Evolutionary Psychology and the Generation of Culture*, pp. 19–136. New York: Oxford University Press.

Traupmann, J., Peterson, R., Utne, M. and Hatfield, E. (1981) Measuring equity in intimate relations. *Applied Psychological Measurement, 5*, 467–480.

Triandis, H.C., McCusker, C. and Hui, C.H. (1990) Multimethod probes of individualism and collectivism. *Journal of Personality and Social Psychology, 59*, 1006–1020.

Trivers, R.L. (1971) The evolution of reciprocal altruism. *Quarterly Review of Biology, 46*, 35–57.

Trivers, R.L. (1972) The evolution of reciprocal altruism. *Quarterly Review of Biology, 46*, 35–37.

Van Lange, P.A.M., Rusbult, C.E., Drigotas, S.M., Ariaga, X.B., Witcher, B.S. and Cox, C.L. (1997) Willingness to sacrifice in close relationships. *Journal of Personality and Social Psychology, 72*, 1373–1395.

van Yperen, N.W. and Buunk, B.P. (1990) A longitudinal study of equity and satisfaction in intimate relationships. *European Journal of Social Psychology, 20*, 287–309.

Walster, G.W. (1975) Equity formula: A correction. *Representative Research in Social Psychology, 6*, 65–67.

Wargo, E. (2005) With the brain, is seeing believing? *American Psychological Society, 18*, 33.

Watson, K. and Platt, M.L. (2006) Fairness and the neurobiology of social cognition: Commentary on 'Nonhuman species' reactions to inequity and their implications for fairness' by Sarah Brosnan. *Social Justice Research, 19*, 186–193.

Westerman, C.Y.K., Park, H.S. and Lee, H.E. (2007) A test of equity theory in multidimensional friendships: A comparison of the United States and Korea. *Journal of Communication, 57*, 576–598.

Williams, G.C. (1996) *Adaptation and Natural Selection*. Princeton: Princeton University Press.

Williamson, G.M. and Clark, M.S. (1989) The communal/exchange distinction and some implications for understanding justice in families. *Social Justice Research, 3*, 77–103.

Witvliet, C.V.O., Worthington, E.L., Root, L.M., Sato, A.F., Ludwig, T.E. and Exline, J.J. (2008) Retributive justice, restorative justice, and forgiveness; an experimental psychophysiology analysis. *Journal of Experimental Social Psychology, 44*, 10–25.

Yamaguchi, S. (1994) Collectivism among the Japanese: A perspective from the self. In U. Kim, H.C. Triandis and G. Yoon (eds), *Individualism and Collectivism: Theoretical and Methodological Issues*, pp. 175–188. Thousand Oaks: Sage.

Young, D. and Hatfield, E. (2009) Measuring equity in close sexual relationships. In T.D. Fisher, C.M. Davis, W.L. Yaber and S.L. Davis (eds), *Handbook of Sexuality-related Measures: A Compendium*, 3rd Edition. Thousand Oaks, CA: Taylor & Francis.

37

The Investment Model of Commitment Processes

Caryl E. Rusbult,[1] Christopher R. Agnew, and
Ximena B. Arriaga

ABSTRACT

The investment model of commitment processes is rooted in interdependence theory and emerged from the broader scientific zeitgeist of the 1960s and 1970s that sought to understand seemingly irrational persistence in social behavior. The investment model was developed originally to move social psychology beyond focusing only on positive affect in predicting persistence in a close interpersonal relationship. As originally tested, the investment model holds that commitment to a target is influenced by three independent factors: satisfaction level, quality of alternatives, and investment size. Commitment, in turn, is posited to mediate the effects of these three bases of dependence on behavior, including persistence. Commitment is presumed to bring about persistence by influencing a host of relationship maintenance phenomena. The investment model has proven to be remarkably generalizable across a range of commitment targets, including commitment toward both interpersonal (e.g., abusive relationships, friendships) and noninterpersonal (e.g., job, sports participation, support for public policies) targets. Empirical support for the investment model is presented as well as a review of recent applications of the model and a proposed extension of it.

INTRODUCTION

The investment model (Rusbult, 1980, 1983) provides a useful framework for predicting the state of being committed to someone or something, and for understanding the underlying causes of commitment. It was developed to move beyond focusing only on positive affect in predicting persistence in an interpersonal relationship. A major premise of the investment model is that relationships persist not only because of the positive qualities that attract partners to one another (their satisfaction), but also because of the ties that bind partners to each other (their investments) and the absence of a better option beyond the relationship with the current partner (lack of alternatives); all of these factors matter in understanding commitment. Beyond explaining the antecedents of commitment, the investment model has generated a large body of research to account for what differentiates lasting relationships from those that end and on specific cognitive and behavioral maintenance mechanisms that are fueled by commitment. The model also has been applied to predicting commitment to all sorts of other targets, revealing its generalizability beyond close relationships.

ORIGINS OF THE INVESTMENT MODEL

In the summer of 1976, I (CER) took a cross-country road trip from Chapel Hill to Los Angeles. I had just completed my first year of graduate school at the University of North Carolina at Chapel Hill (UNC), and was keen to visit friends and family in LA. On the return leg of the trip my traveling companion brought up an interesting topic: "Tell me why people stick with their partners." I spent the better part of Arizona and New Mexico describing work that seemed relevant – work regarding attitudinal similarity, physical appearance, the gain–loss phenomenon, prat-fall effects, and the like. I gave a good review of the relationships literature as it existed in the mid 1970s. As we crossed the Texas border, however, my traveling companion somewhat sheepishly asked: "Okay, but can you tell me why people stick with their partners?" My companion was correct in his implied assessment of this literature. Although work regarding interpersonal attraction answers some interesting questions – for example, what makes us feel attracted to a partner, and what makes us feel satisfied with a relationship – it does not explain why people sometimes persist in relationships. The issue in this literature was positive affect, not perseverance.

As it turns out, several months earlier I had participated in a seminar on interdependence processes led by John Thibaut at UNC. Interdependence theory, which John developed with Hal Kelley (Thibaut and Kelley, 1959; Kelley and Thibaut, 1978), argues that dependence is a central structural property of relationships and particularly relevant to understanding persistence. We describe dependence in more detail below, but the point here is that there was a compelling theory suggesting that dependence, not satisfaction, drives people to seek further interaction with each other. In the context of ongoing romantic involvements, this meant that relationships persist not only as a function of the positive or negative qualities that derive from a particular partner, but also because being with the partner on the whole is more desirable than not being with the partner.

As described in Rusbult et al. (2006), the investment model was also shaped by the broader scientific zeitgeist in the 1960s and 1970s that sought to explain unjustified persistence. During this period, social scientists from diverse fields sought to understand "irrational persistence" in nonromantic domains. Social science research repeatedly documented commitment-relevant phenomena, such as dedicating more time or effort than desired to a particular activity; increasing commitment to a losing enterprise (i.e., the irrational escalation of commitment; Staw, 1976); being trapped in an escalating conflict (such as in the dollar auction, a bidding game in which a dollar goes to the highest bidder but the second-highest bidder must also pay the highest amount that he or she bid; Shubik, 1971); and the manner in which investments, side bets, and sunk costs may induce perseverance in a line of action (Becker, 1960; Blau, 1967; Brockner et al., 1979; Kiesler, 1971; Schelling, 1956; Teger, 1980; Tropper, 1972; see Rusbult, 1980). Increased scholarly interest in irrational persistence during that time was on par with the broader sociopolitical events, such as the Cold War arms race and US involvement in Vietnam. This is not to say that the investment model, or other models cited here, was directly inspired by such events, but rather that during this era, a fascination with unjustified persistence was "in the air" from a scientific point of view (Rusbult et al., 2006).

INITIAL TESTS OF THE INVESTMENT MODEL

With important personal and scholarly influences as a backdrop, Rusbult completed her dissertation in 1978, in which she developed the investment model. Initial tests of the investment model were published in the early 1980s (Rusbult, 1980, 1983). These early papers included: (1) an experiment in which participants read one vignette of a hypothetical couple varying, in a between-subject design, the costs, alternatives, and investment size to assess the effect of these variables on satisfaction and commitment (Rusbult, 1980, Study 1); (2) a cross-sectional study in which participants completed a survey with respect to their own relationship, assessing the association of costs, rewards, quality of alternatives, and investments with satisfaction and commitment (Rusbult, 1980, Study 2); and (3) a multiwave longitudinal study (12 measurement occasions) in which participants completed a survey about their own relationship, assessing whether changes in satisfaction (costs and rewards), alternatives, and investments predicted subsequent commitment and relationship longevity (Rusbult, 1983).

Together these studies provided strong empirical evidence of several claims that were novel at the time and that launched a shift in relationship research from focusing exclusively on satisfaction to studying commitment processes more generally. The major claim was that satisfaction and commitment are not interchangeable, nor are they equally important in predicting relationship outcomes. Commitment was more strongly related to whether relationships endured than level of satisfaction (Rusbult, 1983). Understanding why some relationships persisted and others ended required understanding commitment, which increased with more rewards or higher satisfaction, with weakening alternatives, and with increasing investments. Whereas having more rewards consistently increased satisfaction, having greater costs associated with a relationship did not necessarily decrease satisfaction. Indeed, costs were not consistently

related to commitment and even increased over time among those whose relationships endured (cf. Clark and Grote, 1998).

These initial tests of the investment model were major contributions to the study of relationships. In addition to providing a more complete and predictive account of enduring relationships, these initial tests accounted for findings that previously could not be explained. One such finding was that individuals left by their partner were very different than those who left their partner: Both decreased in their level of satisfaction, but those "abandoned" continued to invest heavily and had alternatives that declined in quality (Rusbult, 1983). That is, level of satisfaction could not differentiate the distinct processes that characterize "leavers" and the abandoned.

A second finding uniquely explained by the investment model was that rational individuals may persist in a relationship with an abusive partner. Victims of partner abuse experience low satisfaction, which might lead to the prediction that they would leave their partner. Prior to the investment model, it was widely believed that victims experiencing such negative events, and yet remaining with their partner, exhibit irrational, even pathological personal dispositions. In contrast, the investment model underscores structural features of the relationship that account for a victim remaining with an abusive partner: the victim may lack alternatives to the relationship and may have too much invested with that partner, making dissolution too costly. Indeed, Rusbult and Martz (1995) revealed that alternatives and investments were strongly related to whether battered women at a shelter remained committed and returned to their partner, whereas the association of satisfaction was weak or not significant depending on the measure of satisfaction.

More generally, these initial tests of the investment model launched a paradigm shift in the study of relationship processes (see Rusbult et al., 2006, and Agnew, 2009, for descriptions of other commitment models). The shift was from asking why people like each other, to asking how and why people stay together. Research following the development of the investment model identified specific processes by which committed individuals keep their relationship intact. It would be too easy and misguided to say, "They just want to stay together." The model launched an entire area of research on various relationship maintenance phenomena that led to identifying thoughts and behaviors of committed individuals, and explaining the underlying processes that characterize these thoughts and behaviors. At the center of Rusbult's theoretical account of relationship maintenance are the concepts of commitment and dependence, which we describe next.

DEPENDENCE, COMMITMENT, AND RELATIONSHIP MAINTENANCE

Dependence refers to the extent to which an individual "needs" a given relationship, or relies uniquely on that particular relationship for attaining desired outcomes. There are several processes through which individuals become dependent (Rusbult et al., 1998). First, partners become dependent to the extent that they enjoy high satisfaction. Satisfaction level describes the degree to which an individual experiences positive versus negative affect as a result of involvement. Satisfaction level increases to the extent that a relationship gratifies the individual's most important needs, including needs for companionship, security, intimacy, sexuality, and belonging (Rusbult et al., 1998).

Dependence also increases when a person perceives that, on average, the best available alternative to a relationship is less desirable than the current relationship. Conversely, when a person's most important needs could be fulfilled outside of the current relationship – in a specific alternative relationship, by a combination of other involvements (by friends and family members, or on one's own) – a person's dependence on the current relationship diminishes. Interdependence theory

argued that relationships would be more likely to endure when partners want to persist in a given relationship (i.e., satisfaction is high) and perceive they have no choice but to persist because they lack viable options to the relationship (i.e., alternatives are poor).

The investment model extended these claims in several respects. First, satisfaction and alternatives do not fully account for enduring relationships (Rusbult, 1980; Rusbult et al., 1998). If the decision to remain with or leave a partner were based solely on how positive one feels or on how one might anticipate feeling elsewhere, few relationships would endure – a relationship would collapse when positive feelings wane or when an attractive alternative becomes the target of one's attention. Relationships are not static, partners' affections ebb and flow, and many relationships persist in the face of tempting alternatives.

Second, dependence is influenced by high satisfaction, poor alternatives, and a third factor: investment size. Investment size refers to the magnitude and importance of the resources that become attached to a relationship that would be lost or decline in value if the relationship were to end. Partners form deep ties that bind themselves to each other by linking parts of themselves directly to the relationship – for example, investing their time and energy, disclosing personal information that ties their sense of dignity to the partner, sharing their own friends with the partner, and taking on shared possessions or giving things of value to the partner. Partners make such investments in the hope that doing so will create a strong foundation for a lasting future together. Investments increase dependence because the act of investment increases connections to the partner that would be costly to break, in the same way that giving up a part of one's self is costly. As such, investments create a powerful psychological inducement to persist.

Third, the investment model extends prior theory by suggesting that commitment emerges as a consequence of increasing dependence (Rusbult et al., 1998). Dependence is a structural property that describes the additive effects of satisfaction, investments, and (lack of) alternatives. When individuals want to persist (are satisfied), feel "tied into" the relationship or obliged to persist (have high investments), and have no choice but to persist (possess poor alternatives), they find themselves in circumstances objectively characterized as dependence.

As people become increasingly dependent they tend to develop strong commitment. Commitment level is defined as intent to persist in a relationship, including long-term orientation toward the involvement as well as feelings of psychological attachment to it (Arriaga and Agnew, 2001). When partners are satisfied, lack alternatives, and have invested heavily in their relationship, they form a strong intention to stay together, they see themselves as being connected (i.e., developing a strong relational identify and a sense of "we-ness"; Agnew et al., 1998), and adopt an orientation that reflects taking into account how things affect the long-term future of the relationship. As such, the psychological experience of commitment reflects more than the bases of dependence out of which it arises (i.e., high satisfaction, low alternatives, high investment). Commitment is the psychological state that directly influences everyday behavior in relationships and that mediates the effects of satisfaction, alternatives, and investments on behavior.

Having established that strong commitment – not high satisfaction – is the psychological state that characterizes partners in an enduring relationship, Rusbult, her colleagues, and many others have identified a multitude of commitment processes; that is, the many ways in which commitment promotes thoughts, feelings, and actions that, in turn, cause relationships to persist. Relationship maintenance is the upshot of responding to interpersonal situations by acting in the interest of the relationship. Past research has identified several relationship maintenance mechanisms through which highly committed people maintain their relationship.

Highly committed people are inclined to act in ways that promote relationship persistence. Their high commitment is particularly salient when they react to a challenging moment by doing what is best for the relationship. For example, when a partner makes a thoughtless remark or fails to follow through on a promise or acts in some other way that could damage the relationship, high commitment predicts accommodation, namely inhibiting the urge to retaliate and instead respond in ways that promote the relationship (Arriaga and Rusbult, 1998; Kilpatrick et al., 2002; Rusbult et al., 1991). Similarly, highly committed people are more inclined than their less committed counterparts to forego personal preferences for the sake of acting on behalf of the partner's interest (Powell and Van Vugt, 2003; Van Lange et al. 1997a, 1997b); and respond to a partner betrayal by forgiving the partner (Cann and Baucom, 2004; Finkel et al., 2002; McCullough et al., 1998). These relationship maintenance phenomena stem from strong commitment, not necessarily high satisfaction, a fact that would not be commonly accepted were it not for the investment model.

Highly committed people also think about things affecting the relationship differently than less committed people, and these thoughts make a difference in the wellbeing of a relationship. For example, committed people derogate tempting alternatives to shield against them, react to periods of doubt or uncertainty by denying negative qualities of the partner, develop unrealistically positive thoughts about their partner and/or the relationship, and cast others' relationships in a negative light (Agnew et al., 2001; Arriaga, 2002; Arriaga et al., 2007; Johnson and Rusbult, 1989; Lydon et al., 1999; Miller, 1997; Murray and Holmes, 1999; Murray et al., 1996; Rusbult et al., 2000; Simpson et al., 1990). Committed individuals also mentally see themselves in more relational terms – for example, they spontaneously use more plural pronouns – than less committed individuals (Agnew et al., 1998).

Why do committed individuals come to think and act in a prorelationship manner? The interdependence theory distinction between the given situation and the effective situation provides some insight into this process (Kelley & Thibaut, 1978). The *given situation* refers to each partner's immediate, self-centered personal preferences in a specific situation. Within the context of a close relationship, of course, it is clear that people do not always pursue their given preferences. Behavior is often shaped by broader concerns, including long-term goals to promote not only one's own but also one's partner's wellbeing. Movement away from given preferences results from *transformation of motivation*, a process which leads individuals to relinquish their immediate self-interest and act on the basis of broader considerations. The *effective situation* refers to the preferences resulting from the transformation process; effective preferences directly guide behaviors among those who are highly committed to their relationship.

The investment model premise that commitment and dependence are more consequential than satisfaction is the same premise that has guided research on mutual influence in deepening commitment and trust, or "mutual cyclical growth" (Agnew et al., 1998). As one person becomes more committed and acts in ways that reveal responsiveness to the partner and prorelationship tendencies, the partner becomes more comfortable being more dependent on and committed toward the person, which in turn makes the partner more likely to act in ways that reveal responsiveness and prorelationship tendencies, and so the process continues as each individual's commitment and trust in the other's responsiveness grows (Wieselquist et al., 1999). Although research on mutual cyclical growth does not directly examine all investment model components, it rests squarely on the idea that commitment, not satisfaction, brings about actions that will cause a relationship to persist.

Research on mutual cyclical growth underscores the manner in which relationship maintenance phenomena act to increase the partner's commitment. The partner essentially makes an attribution about the person acting in a prorelationship manner, and this attribution (that the person cares) fuels increases in the partner's investments, satisfaction, and commitment. Moreover, when a person acts in a prorelationship manner, such acts make salient to the person that he or she is committed and cares about the relationship unit (Agnew et al., 1998; Wieselquist et al., 1999). As such, relationship maintenance perceptions and acts likely influence couple members' satisfaction, alternatives, and investments and thus "effects" may become "causes." For example, over time, couple members who have personally sacrificed a lot for the partner will likely come to view such sacrifices as increases in their investments).

In short, the investment model has been extraordinarily generative in stimulating an entire research area that explains specifically how and why enduring relationships are maintained, where others end. The investment model triggered a systematic analysis of much of what transpires in ongoing relationships. In the next section, we describe empirical tests assessing the generalizability of the investment model and review ways in which the model has stimulating research on a host of socially relevant topics.

GENERALIZABILITY AND EMPIRICAL ROBUSTNESS OF THE INVESTMENT MODEL

In the years since its initial testing, the investment model has been employed in a range of studies applying the model to participants of diverse ethnicities (Davis and Strube, 1993; Lin and Rusbult, 1995), homosexual and heterosexual partnerships (Duffy and Rusbult, 1986; Kurdek, 1991, 1995), abusive relationships (Choice and Lamke, 1999; Rhatigan and Axsom, 2006; Rusbult and Martz, 1995), socially marginalized relationships (Lehmiller and Agnew, 2006, 2007), and friendships

(Hirofumi, 2003; Lin and Rusbult, 1995; Rusbult, 1980). In all of these studies, satisfaction level, quality of alternatives, and investment size are posited to have additive, main effects on commitment (see Figure 37.1). The model does not suggest that any one of the three predictors will be particularly influential in driving commitment. Rather, it suggests that all three factors may contribute to the prediction of commitment in an additive fashion. Multiple regression analyses have been used most often to test the model.

Although the majority of evidence supporting the investment model comes from studies of interpersonal relationships, the model also has been employed in other, nonrelational contexts (see Le and Agnew, 2003) with nonrelational targets of commitments. For instance, organizational and job commitment (cf. Farrell and Rusbult, 1981; Oliver, 1990) have been predicted in studies based on investment model constructs. In addition, Ping (1993, 1997) adapted the model to describe business interactions, and Lyons and Lowery (1989) have conceptualized commitment to one's residential community using a similar perspective. The investment model has been used successfully to predict patients' commitment to a medical regimen (Putnam et al., 1994), college

students' commitment to their schools (cf. Geyer et al., 1987), and commitment to participating in musical activities (Koslowsky and Kluger, 1986). Finally, the sport commitment model has its roots firmly in the investment model (Raedeke, 1997; Schmidt and Stein, 1991) and has been used to predict commitment of soccer and cricket players to their sports (Carpenter and Coleman, 1998; Carpenter and Scanlan, 1998).

As suggested above, the utility and robustness of the investment model has been demonstrated in numerous studies. A meta-analysis by Le and Agnew (2003) summarizes quantitative data regarding the model's performance, compiling empirical tests conducted through 1999. The meta-analysis included data from 52 studies (including 60 independent samples and over 11,000 participants). Overall, the average correlations between investment model constructs were found to be quite strong. Satisfaction level, quality of alternatives, and investment size each were highly correlated with commitment ($r = 0.68$, -0.48, 0.46 respectively), with the correlation between satisfaction and commitment found to be significantly stronger than the alternatives–commitment and investments–commitment correlations. The absolute magnitudes of the alternatives–commitment and

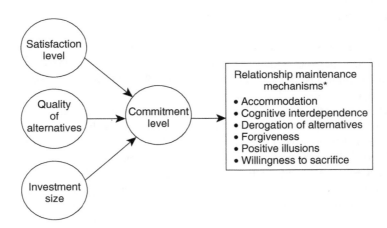

Figure 37.1   The investment model of commitment processes.
* Note that the specific relationship maintenance mechanisms listed here are based on extant empirical findings and that future research may uncover additional mechanisms.

investments–commitment correlations were not significantly different from one another. Satisfaction, alternatives, and investments were also found to be significantly correlated with one another (satisfaction–alternatives $r = -0.44$; satisfaction–investments $r = 0.42$; alternatives–investments $r = -0.25$).

Le and Agnew (2003) also examined the average standardized regression coefficients of commitment regressed simultaneously onto satisfaction, alternatives, and investments, and thus they assessed the relative independent contribution of each variable in predicting commitment. Paralleling the correlational analyses, the meta-analysis revealed that satisfaction was the strongest predictor of commitment (std $\beta = 0.510$), whereas alternatives and investments were of similar absolute magnitude (std $\beta = -0.217$ and 0.240 respectively). In addition, 61 percent of the variance in commitment (95% CI [0.59, 0.63]) was accounted for by satisfaction, alternatives, and investments collectively. Moreover, moderator analyses suggested that the associations between commitment and its theorized bases vary minimally as a function of demographic (e.g., ethnicity) or relational (e.g., duration) factors.

Commitment is held to mediate the effects of satisfaction, alternatives, and investments on consequential behaviors. The meta-analysis also provided support for this supposition. Specifically, the correlation between commitment and later stay-leave behaviors reported by participants (e.g., whether the couple was still together or the worker was still at the job) across 12 studies was found to be 0.47 (95% CI [0.43, 0.50], $N = 1720$).

RECENT APPLICATIONS OF THE INVESTMENT MODEL

Since 1999 (the inclusion year cut-off in the Le and Agnew meta-analysis), dozens of additional studies have been published that test the investment model or aspects of it. Some of these papers confirm the findings from earlier publications on the applicability of the investment model in understanding commitment in various types of relationships, beyond romantic involvements, such as instructors' commitment to student supervision (Peleg-Oren et al., 2007), or parental commitment to their child's pediatrician (Agnew and VanderDrift, 2010).

Recent research also has confirmed findings from earlier publications on the applicability of the investment model in understanding commitment to nonperson targets. For example, the investment model provides predictive value in understanding employees' attitudes toward different job changes (e.g., changing department or relocating to a different office; van Dam, 2005), clients' commitment to their bank (Kastlunger et al., 2008), childcare providers' commitment to the childcare center that employs them (Gable and Hunting, 2001), and customer loyalty to specific brands (Li and Petrick, 2008).

A recent meta-analysis of predictors of nonmarital romantic relationship dissolution also provides additional support for the claim that commitment is a key proximal predictor of stay–leave behavior. Using data collected from nearly 38,000 participants participating in 137 studies over a 33-year period, commitment was found to be a particularly powerful predictor of breakup (Le et al., 2010). Specifically, assuming random effects (Lipsey and Wilson, 2001), the weighted mean effect size (d) for commitment in predicting premarital breakup was found to be -0.832 (95% CI $[-0.934, -0.729]$.

Recently, the investment model has also been applied to understanding public support for government actions regarding foreign policies. Existing public opinion research often focuses on factors such as partisanship to understand where people stand on foreign policy issues (e.g., Zaller, 1994). By contrast, the investment model would predict that people use specific policy performance criteria to determine the value of persisting with the same policy. Agnew and colleagues (Agnew et al., 2007) used the investment model to examine commitment to the "war on terror" waged by the US under President

George W. Bush. They conducted two experiments in which they simultaneously manipulated the three investment model constructs
(a novel aspect of this research). As predicted
by the investment model, participants were
most strongly committed to the war on terror
when satisfaction with reported outcomes of
the war (e.g., reducing threat to the citizens
of the US) and investments in the war (e.g.,
casualties) were described as high and alternatives (e.g., diplomatic solutions) were
described as low. In contrast, participants
were least committed to the war when satisfaction and investments were described as
low and alternatives were described as high.
Similarly, Hoffman et al. (2009) found
significant support for the investment model
in predicting citizen commitment to their
country being a part of both the United
Nations and NATO.

Other researchers have used the investment
model as a springboard for examining related
issues pertinent to commitment. Such papers
have not reported formal tests of the overall
model; rather, they have used it as the basis
for furthering understanding of variables or
processes beyond those specified in the
investment model. For example, in an analysis of how narcissism relates to commitment,
Campbell and Foster (2002) found the association between narcissism and commitment
is negative and largely mediated by perceptions of alternatives. Katz et al. (2006) found
that women involved in sexually coercive
relationships reported greater investment in
their relationship but did not differ from other
women in satisfaction or commitment.
Vaculík and Jedrzejczyková (2009) focused
on describing differences between people
involved in various types of unmarried cohabitation and used investment model variables to
characterize such differences. Taking a social
cognitive approach, Etcheverry and Le (2005)
tested and found support for the notion that
the cognitive accessibility of commitment
moderates the association between self-
reported commitment and relationship persistence, accommodative responses, and
willingness to sacrifice. Finally, in their

examination of safer-sex behavior among
committed gay male partners, Davidovich et
al. (2006) found that low satisfaction with the
relationship was associated with more risky
unprotected anal intercourse, whereas high
commitment to the relationship was associated with greater efforts toward the practice
of safer sex. All of these studies speak to the
generalizability of the investment model
beyond its originally envisioned use.

EXTENDING THE INVESTMENT MODEL

In this last section, we describe a recent
extension to the investment model that
attempts to account for additional variance in
levels of commitment. We begin by focusing
on investments. Goodfriend and Agnew
(2008) have elaborated on the investment
concept, suggesting that the notion of investments should include not only things that
have already been invested, but also any
plans that partners have made, either individually or with the partner, regarding the
relationship. In ending a relationship, one
loses not only those investments that have
been sunken to date but also the possibility of
achieving any future plans with the partner.
Thus, the plans that one forms with a partner
act to keep one's commitment to the partnership alive. One notable aspect of considering
future plans as contributing to current commitment is that such plans do not require that
relationship partners have much of a shared
history together. That is, even partners who
have known one another for a relatively short
period of time may become quite committed
to continuing their relationship, not because
of considerable past sunken costs but because
of a motivation to see cherished future plans
come to fruition. Goodfriend and Agnew
(2008) found that future plans were strongly
predictive of romantic relationship commitment, above and beyond past investments.

Recent research has also examined how
others outside of the dyad might influence a

couple's motivation to continue a relationship. Research has examined the associations between perceptions of a social network's approval or disapproval for a romantic relationship and characteristics of that relationship (Agnew et al., 2001; Arriaga et al., 2004; Bryant and Conger, 1999; Cox et al., 1997; Lehmiller and Agnew, 2006, 2007; Loving, 2006; Parks et al., 1983; Sprecher 1988; Sprecher and Felmlee, 1992). In general, past studies have shown that qualities, structure, and opinions of social network members are associated with the quality and functioning of dyadic relationships embedded in that network.

Research that integrates the investment model with research on social networks has examined the perceived role of social referents: A couple's commitment can be affected by their perceptions of what important others think of their relationship, as well as the couple members' motivation to follow what others think (i.e., the couple members' "subjective norms"; Ajzen and Fishbein, 1980; Fishbein and Ajzen, 1975). Etcheverry and Agnew (2004) found that subjective norms provided additional prediction of relationship commitment, above and beyond the effects of satisfaction, alternatives, and past investments. Moreover, just as behavioral intention mediates the effect of subjective norms on behavior in the theory of reasoned action (Ajzen and Fishbein, 1980), longitudinal analyses indicated that commitment mediated the effect of subjective norms on remaining in a romance approximately 8 months later. Both theoretically and empirically, the subjective norms construct broadens the prediction of relationship commitment beyond the original three predictors of the investment model.

Combining these recent theoretical and empirical advances, Agnew et al. (2008) proposed a new model to account not only for continuity in close relationships but also for possible changes in type of relationship with a given partner (e.g., shifts from romantic involvement to friendship, or vice versa). They proposed the bases of relational commitment model (BORC model), which mirrors the investment model in specifying three predictors of commitment. One predictor combines satisfaction and alternatives by focusing on outcomes relative to standards, harking back to some of the early interdependence writing on outcomes in dyadic interaction (Thibaut and Kelley, 1959). A second predictor is an expanded conceptualization of investments – what they refer to as *valued linkages* – which incorporates recent work on future plans (Goodfriend and Agnew, 2008). A third predictor, subjective norms, incorporates work by Etcheverry and Agnew (2004) showing that couple members' commitment is affected by what important others think about their relationship. Initial tests of the BORC model have yielded supportive findings, with each of the model's specified variables accounting for unique variance in relationship type commitment and the overall model accounting for over three-quarters of the variance in commitment. Of course, the foundation of this model is "standing on the shoulder of giants," benefiting from the decades of accumulated knowledge about commitment processes originally set into motion by the investment model.

CONCLUSION

Most social psychologists are familiar with Kurt Lewin's famous statement, "There is nothing so practical as a good theory" (1951: 169). Lewin would have loved the investment model. The model has provided an extremely practical theoretical framework for understanding and explaining the causes and consequences of commitment. It originated as a model to understand why people remain in romantic relationships. Subsequently, it has been used to examine commitment in all kinds of relationship and to all types of targets. It has also been utilized to examine the specific ways in which commitment brings about persistence, the specific thoughts and actions that differentiate people based on their level of commitment.

There are many ways in which the investment model has had an impact not just on the study of close relationships and the field of social psychology, but also more broadly. First, this model transformed the way scholars in various fields think about commitment. Without the investment model, our understanding of various commitment processes would be diminished – relationship commitment, yes, but also organizational commitment, sports commitment, policy commitment, and so on. Second, the investment model provided a critical new direction in the study of relationships. This new direction comprised a social psychological analysis, vis-à-vis a structural sociological analysis, and it focused on the *ongoing* course of intimate relationships, rather than focusing on their onset alone. Third, by explicitly modeling a psychological process, the investment model advanced a *scientific analysis* of relationships. As we move into the future, we hope and expect that the investment model will continue to advance theory and applications in social psychology and beyond.

NOTES

1 With the exception of the section on origins of the theory, this chapter was prepared following the death of the first author, Caryl Rusbult, our mentor and dear friend.

REFERENCES

Agnew, C.R. (2009) Commitment, theories and typologies. In H.T. Reis and S.K. Sprecher (eds), *Encyclopedia of Human Relationships, 1*, 245–248. Thousand Oaks, CA: Sage.

Agnew, C.R., Arriaga, X.B. and Wilson, J.E. (2008) Committed to what? Using the Bases of Relational Commitment Model to understand continuity and changes in social relationships. In J.P. Forgas and J. Fitness (eds), *Social Relationships: Cognitive, Affective and Motivational Processes*, pp. 147–164. New York: Psychology Press.

Agnew, C.R., Hoffman, A.M., Lehmiller, J.J. and Duncan, N.T. (2007) From the interpersonal to the international: Understanding commitment to the 'War on Terror'. *Personality and Social Psychology Bulletin, 33*, 1559–1571.

Agnew, C.R., Loving, T.J. and Drigotas, S.M. (2001) Substituting the forest for the trees: Social networks and the prediction of romantic relationship state and fate. *Journal of Personality and Social Psychology, 81*, 1042–1057.

Agnew, C.R. and VanderDrift, L.E. (2010) Commitment within the patient-physician relationship: Parental commitment to pediatricians.

Agnew, C.R., Van Lange, P.A.M., Rusbult, C.E. and Langston, C.A. (1998) Cognitive interdependence: Commitment and the mental representation of close relationships. *Journal of Personality and Social Psychology, 74*, 939–954.

Ajzen, I. and Fishbein, M. (1980) *Understanding Attitudes and Predicting Social Behavior*. Englewood Cliffs, NJ: Prentice Hall.

Arriaga, X.B. (2002) Joking violence among highly committed individuals. *Journal of Interpersonal Violence, 17*, 591–610.

Arriaga, X.B. and Agnew, C.R. (2001) Being committed: Affective, cognitive, and conative components of relationship commitment. *Personality and Social Psychology Bulletin, 27*, 1190–1203.

Arriaga, X.B., Goodfriend, W. and Lohmann, A. (2004) Beyond the individual: Concomitants of closeness in the social and physical environment. In D. Mashek and A. Aron (eds), *Handbook on Relationship Closeness*, pp. 287–303. Mahwah, NJ: Erlbaum.

Arriaga, X.B. and Rusbult, C.E. (1998) Standing in my partner's shoes: Partner perspective-taking and reactions to accommodative dilemmas. *Personality and Social Psychology Bulletin, 24*, 927–948.

Arriaga, X.B., Slaughterbeck, E.S., Capezza, N.M. and Hmurovic, J.L. (2007) From bad to worse: Relationship commitment and vulnerability to partner imperfections. *Personal Relationships, 14*, 389–409.

Becker, H.S. (1960) Notes on the concept of commitment. *American Journal of Sociology, 66*, 32–40.

Blau, P.M. (1967) *Exchange and Power in Social Life*. New York: Wiley.

Brockner, J., Shaw, M.C. and Rubin, J.Z. (1979) Factors affecting withdrawal from an escalating conflict: Quitting before it's too late. *Journal of Experimental Social Psychology, 15*, 492–503.

Bryant, C.M. and Conger, R.D. (1999) Marital success and domains of social support in long-term relationships: Does the influence of network members ever end? *Journal of Marriage and the Family, 61*, 437–450.

Campbell, W.K. and Foster, C.A. (2002). Narcissism and commitment in romantic relationships: An investment model analysis. *Personality and Social Psychology Bulletin, 28*, 484–495.

Cann, A. and Baucom, T.R. (2004) Former partners and new rivals as threats to a relationship: Infidelity type, gender, and commitment as factors related to distress and forgiveness. *Personal Relationships, 11*, 305–318.

Carpenter, P.J. and Coleman, R. (1998). A longitudinal test of elite youth cricketers' commitment. *International Journal of Sport Psychology, 29*, 195–210.

Carpenter, P.J. and Scanlan, T.K. (1998) Changes over time in determinants of sport commitment. *Pediatric Exercise Science, 10*, 356–365.

Choice, P. and Lamke, L. (1999) Stay/leave decision-making in abusive dating relationships. *Personal Relationships, 6*, 351–368.

Clark, M.S. and Grote, N.K. (1998) Why aren't indices of relationship costs always negatively related to indices of relationship quality? *Personality and Social Psychology Review, 2*, 2–17.

Cox, C.L., Wexler, M.O., Rusbult, C.E. and Gaines, S.O. Jr. (1997) Prescriptive support and commitment processes in close relationships. *Social Psychology Quarterly, 60*, 79–90.

Davidovich, U., de Wit, J. and Stroebe, W. (2006) Relationship characteristics and risk of HIV Infection: Rusbult's investment model and sexual risk behavior of gay men in steady relationships. *Journal of Applied Social Psychology, 36*, 22–40.

Davis, L. and Strube, M.J. (1993) An assessment of romantic commitment among black and white dating couples. *Journal of Applied Social Psychology, 23*, 212–225.

Duffy, S.M. and Rusbult, C.E. (1986) Satisfaction and commitment in homosexual and heterosexual relationships. *Journal of Homosexuality, 12*, 1–23.

Etcheverry, P.E. and Agnew, C.R. (2004) Subjective norms and the prediction of romantic relationship state and fate. *Personal Relationships, 11*, 409–428.

Etcheverry, P.E. and Le, B. (2005) Thinking about commitment: Accessibility of commitment and prediction of relationship persistence, accommodation, and willingness to sacrifice. *Personal Relationships, 12*, 103–123.

Farrell, D. and Rusbult, C.E. (1981) Exchange variables as predictors of job satisfaction, job commitment, and turnover: The impact of rewards, costs, alternatives, and investments. *Organizational Behavior and Human Performance, 28*, 78–95.

Finkel, E.J., Rusbult, C.E., Kumashiro, M. and Hannon, P.A. (2002) Dealing with betrayal in close relationships: Does commitment promote forgiveness? *Journal of Personality and Social Psychology, 82*, 956–974.

Fishbein, M. and Ajzen, I. (1975) *Belief, Attitude, Intention and Behavior: An Introduction to Theory and Research.* Reading, MA: Addison-Wesley.

Gable, S. and Hunting, M. (2001) Child care providers' organizational commitment: A test of the investment model. *Child and Youth Care Forum, 30*, 265–281.

Geyer, P.D., Brannon, Y.S. and Shearon, R.W. (1987) The prediction of students' satisfaction with community college vocational training. *The Journal of Psychology, 121*, 591–597.

Goodfriend, W. and Agnew, C.R. (2008) Sunken costs and desired plans: Examining different types of investments in close relationships. *Personality and Social Psychology Bulletin, 34*, 1639–1652.

Hirofumi, A. (2003) Closeness and interpersonal outcomes in same-sex friendships: An improvement of the investment model and explanation of closeness. *Japanese Journal of Experimental Social Psychology, 42*, 131–145.

Hoffman, A.M., Agnew, C.R., Lehmiller, J.J. and Duncan, N.T. (2009) Satisfaction, alternatives, investments, and the microfoundations of audience cost models. *International Interactions, 35*, 365–389.

Johnson, D.J. and Rusbult, C.E. (1989) Resisting temptation: Devaluation of alternative partners as a means of maintaining commitment in close relationships. *Journal of Personality and Social Psychology, 57*, 967–980.

Kastlunger, B., Martini, M., Kirchler, E. and Hofmann, E. (2008) Impegno, soddisfazione e fiducia del cliente bancario: Un'analisi empirica a Roma e in Sardegna. *Psicologia Sociale, 3*, 307–324.

Katz, J., Kuffel, S.W. and Brown, F.A. (2006) Leaving a sexually coercive dating partner: A prospective application of the investment model. *Psychology of Women Quarterly, 30*, 267–275.

Kelley, H.H. and Thibaut, J.W. (1978) *Interpersonal Relations: A Theory of Interdependence.* New York: Wiley.

Kiesler, C.A. (1971) *The Psychology of Commitment: Experiments Linking Behavior to Belief.* New York: Academic Press.

Kilpatrick, S.D., Bissonnette, V.L. and Rusbult, C.E. (2002) Empathic accuracy and accommodative behavior among newly married couples. *Personal Relationships, 9*, 369–393.

Koslowsky, M. and Kluger, A. (1986) Commitment to participation in musical activities: An extension and application of the investment model. *Journal of Applied Social Psychology, 16*, 831–844.

Kurdek, L.A. (1991) Correlates of relationship satisfaction in cohabiting gay and lesbian couples: Integration of contextual, investment, and problem-solving models. *Journal of Personality and Social Psychology, 61,* 910–922.

Kurdek, L.A. (1995) Assessing multiple determinants of relationship commitment in cohabiting gay, cohabiting lesbian, dating heterosexual, and married heterosexual couples. *Family Relations, 44,* 261–266.

Le, B. and Agnew, C.R. (2003) Commitment and its theorized determinants: A meta-analysis of the investment model. *Personal Relationships, 10,* 37–57.

Le, B., Dove, N., Agnew, C.R., Korn, M.S. and Mutso, A.A. (2010) Predicting non-marital romantic relationship dissolution: A meta-analytic synthesis. *Personal Relationships, 17,* 377–390.

Lehmiller, J.J. and Agnew, C.R. (2006) Marginalized relationships: The impact of social disapproval on romantic relationship commitment. *Personality and Social Psychology Bulletin, 32,* 40–51.

Lehmiller, J.J. and Agnew, C.R. (2007). Perceived marginalization and the prediction of romantic relationship stability. *Journal of Marriage and Family, 69,* 1036–1049.

Lewin, K. (1951) *Field Theory in Social Science; Selected Theoretical Papers.* In D. Cartwright (ed.). New York: Harper & Row.

Li, X. and Petrick, J.F. (2008) Examining the antecedents of brand loyalty from an investment model perspective. *Journal of Travel Research, 47,* 25–34.

Lin, Y.W. and Rusbult, C.E. (1995) Commitment to dating relationships and cross-sex friendships in America and China. *Journal of Social and Personal Relationships, 12,* 7–26.

Lipsey, M.W. and Wilson, D.B. (2001) *Practical Meta-analysis.* Thousand Oaks, CA: Sage Publications.

Loving, T.J. (2006) Predicting dating relationship fate with insiders' and outsiders' perspectives: Who and what is asked matters. *Personal Relationships, 13,* 349–362.

Lydon, J., Meana, M., Sepinwall, D., Richards, N. and Mayman, S. (1999) The commitment calibration hypothesis: When do people devalue attractive alternatives? *Personality and Social Psychology Bulletin, 25,* 152–161.

Lyons, W.E. and Lowery, D. (1989) Citizen responses to dissatisfaction in urban communities: A partial test of a general model. *Journal of Politics, 51,* 841–868.

McCullough, M.E., Rachal, K.C., Sandage, S.J., Worthington, E.L., Jr., Brown, S.W. and Hight, T.L. (1998) Interpersonal forgiving in close relationships II: Theoretical elaboration and measurement. *Journal of Personality and Social Psychology, 75,* 1586–1603.

Miller, R.S. (1997) Inattentive and contented: Relationships commitment and attention to alternatives. *Journal of Personality and Social Psychology, 73,* 758–766.

Murray, S.L. and Holmes, J.G. (1999) The (mental) ties that bind: Cognitive structures that predict relationship resilience. *Journal of Personality and Social Psychology, 77,* 1228–1244.

Murray, S.L., Holmes, J.G. and Griffin, D.W. (1996) The self-fulfilling nature of positive illusions in romantic relationships: Love is not blind, but prescient. *Journal of Personality and Social Psychology, 71,* 1155–1180.

Oliver, N. (1990) Rewards, investments, alternatives and organizational commitment: Empirical and evidence and theoretical development. *Journal of Occupational Psychology, 63,* 19–31.

Parks, M.R., Stan, C.M. and Eggert, L.L. (1983) Romantic involvement and social network involvement. *Social Psychology Quarterly, 46,* 116–131.

Peleg-Oren, N., Macgowan, M.J. and Even-Zahav, R. (2007) Field instructors' commitment to Student Supervision: Testing the investment model. *Social Work Education, 26,* 684–696.

Ping, R.A., Jr. (1993) The effects of satisfaction and structural constraints on retailer exiting, voice, loyalty, opportunism, and neglect. *Journal of Retailing, 69,* 320–352.

Ping, R.A., Jr. (1997) Voice in business-to-business relationships: Cost-of-exit and demographic antecedents. *Journal of Retailing, 73,* 261–281.

Powell, C. and Van Vugt, M. (2003) Genuine giving or selfish sacrifice?: The role of commitment and cost level upon willingness to sacrifice. *European Journal of Social Psychology, 33,* 403–412.

Putnam, D.E., Finney, J.W., Barkley, P.L. and Bonner, M.J. (1994) Enhancing commitment improves adherence to a medical regimen. *Journal of Consulting and Clinical Psychology, 62,* 191–194.

Raedeke, T.D. (1997) Is athlete burnout more than just stress? A sport commitment perspective. *Journal of Sport and Exercise Psychology, 19,* 396–417.

Rhatigan, D.L. and Axsom, D.K. (2006) Using the investment model to understand battered women's commitment to abusive relationships. *Journal of Family Violence, 21,* 153–162.

Rusbult, C.E. (1980) Commitment and satisfaction in romantic associations: A test of the investment model. *Journal of Experimental Social Psychology, 16,* 172–186.

Rusbult, C.E. (1983) A longitudinal test of the investment model: The development (and deterioration) of satisfaction and commitment in heterosexual involvements. *Journal of Personality and Social Psychology, 45,* 101–117.

Rusbult, C.E., Coolsen, M.K., Kirchner, J.L. and Clarke, J.A. (2006) Commitment. In A.L. Vangelisti and D. Perlman (eds), *The Cambridge Handbook of Personal Relationships,* pp. 615–635. New York: Cambridge University Press.

Rusbult, C.E. and Martz, J.M. (1995) Remaining in an abusive relationship: An investment model analysis of nonvoluntary dependence. *Personality and Social Psychology Bulletin, 21,* 558–571.

Rusbult, C.E., Martz, J.M. and Agnew, C.R. (1998) The investment model scale: Measuring commitment level, satisfaction level, quality of alternatives, and investment size. *Personal Relationships, 5,* 357–391.

Rusbult, C.E., Van Lange, P.A.M., Wildschut, T., Yovetich, N.A. and Verette, J. (2000) Perceived superiority in close relationships: Why it exists and persists. *Journal of Personality and Social Psychology, 79,* 521–545.

Rusbult, C.E., Verette, J., Whitney, G.A., Slovik, L.F. and Lipkus, I. (1991) Accommodation processes in close relationships: Theory and preliminary empirical evidence. *Journal of Personality and Social Psychology, 60,* 53–78.

Schelling, J. (1956) An essay on bargaining. *American Economic Review, 46,* 281–306.

Schmidt, G.W. and Stein, G.L. (1991) Sport commitment: A model integrating enjoyment, dropout, and burnout. *Journal of Sport and Exercise Psychology, 13,* 254–265.

Shubik, M. (1971) The dollar auction game: A paradox in noncooperative behavior and escalation. *Journal of Conflict Resolution, 15,* 109–111.

Simpson, J.A., Gangestad, S.W. and Lerma, M. (1990) Perception of physical attractiveness: Mechanisms involved in the maintenance of romantic relationships. *Journal of Personality and Social Psychology, 59,* 1192–1201.

Sprecher, S. (1988) Investment model, equity, and social support determinants of relationship commitment. *Social Psychology Quarterly, 51,* 318–328.

Sprecher, S. and Felmlee, D. (1992) The influence of parents and friends on the quality and stability of romantic relationships: A three-wave longitudinal investigation. *Journal of Marriage and the Family, 54,* 888–900.

Staw, B.M. (1976) Knee-deep in the big muddy: A study of escalating commitment to a chosen action. *Organization Behavior and Human Performance, 16,* 27–44.

Teger, A.I. (1980) *Too Much Invested to Quit.* New York: Pergamon.

Thibaut, J.W. and Kelley, H.H. (1959) *The Social Psychology of Groups.* New York: Wiley.

Tropper, R. (1972) The consequences of investment in the process of conflict. *Journal of Conflict Resolution, 16,* 97–98.

Vaculík, M. and Jedrzejczyková, V. (2009) Commitment in unmarried cohabitation. *Studia Psychologica, 51,* 101–117.

van Dam, K. (2005) Employee attitudes toward job changes: An application and extension of Rusbult and Farrell's investment model. *Journal of Occupational and Organizational Psychology, 78,* 253–272.

Van Lange, P.A.M., Agnew, C.R., Harnick, F. and Steemers, G.E.M. (1997a) From game theory to real life: How social value orientation affects willingness to sacrifice in ongoing close relationships. *Journal of Personality and Social Psychology, 73,* 1330–1344.

Van Lange, P.A.M., Rusbult, C.E., Drigotas, S.M., Arriaga, X.B., Witcher, B.S. and Cox, C.L. (1997b) Willingness to sacrifice in close relationships. *Journal of Personality and Social Psychology, 72,* 1373–1395.

Wieselquist, J., Rusbult, C.E., Foster, C.A. and Agnew, C.R. (1999) Commitment, pro-relationship behavior, and trust in close relationships. *Journal of Personality and Social Psychology, 77,* 942–966.

Zaller, J. (1994) Strategic politicians, public opinion, and the Gulf crisis. In W.L. Bennett and D.L. Paletz (eds), *Taken by Storm: The Media, Public Opinion, and U.S. Foreign Policy in the Gulf War,* pp. 250–276. Chicago: University of Chicago Press.

38

A Theory of Communal (and Exchange) Relationships

Margaret S. Clark[1] and Judson R. Mills

ABSTRACT

A qualitative distinction between communal and exchange relationships (Clark and Mills, 1979; Mills and Clark, 1982) together with a quantitative dimension to communal relationships (Mills and Clark, 1982; Mills et al., 2004) is described. A review is given of empirical work supporting the theory and its implications for such things as: non-contingent helping; donor and recipient reactions to giving help; emotional expression and reactions to others' emotional expressions; keeping track of contributions and of needs in relationships; and, more broadly, what constitutes healthy and unhealthy intimate and non-intimate relationships. In the process, the theory, details of its development, refinement, and testing as well as challenges to our approach from other researchers are commented upon and placed in historical perspective.

INTRODUCTION

Why, when purchasing a gift for a friend, do we expect price tags to be on items yet, after the purchase, we make sure they been removed? Why did a friend who rented a vacation house and arrived to find no hot water, find it maddening the real estate agent tried to elicit her sympathy by explaining that the owners were experiencing severe personal problems? When we began work on a distinction between communal and exchange relationships in the 1970s, social psychologists did not have ready answers to these questions. Yet the questions were intriguing and we set to work to provide theoretical answers backed with empirical support.

At that time, the now flourishing area of social research on close relationships had yet to emerge. There was work on interpersonal attraction to be sure. There was work on norms governing how people regulated the giving and receiving of benefits and rewards in relationships with equity theory being the most prominent (see, for example, Adams, 1965; Messick and Cook, 1983; Walster et al., 1978). Yet no social psychologist had suggested the possibility that the rules governing behavior might differ by relationship context. It was in that atmosphere that we set forth a qualitative distinction between communal and exchange relationships (Clark and Mills, 1979).

We drew our inspiration from some brief observations made by sociologist Irving Goffman in his book *The Presentation of Self in Everyday Life*. Goffman had noted differences in the nature "social" and "economic" exchange. Social exchange, he said, was compromised by agreement in advance as to what was to be exchanged. Something given in a social exchange "need only be returned if the relationship calls for it; that is when the putative recipient comes to be in need of a favor or when he is ritually stationed for a ceremonial expression of regard." In contrast, in economic exchange, "no amount of mere thanks can presumably satisfy the giver; he must get something of equivalent material value in return." (Goffman, 1961: 275–276). The distinction was made briefly, no experimentation nor indeed any systematic research had been done to document it, and we did not completely agree with Goffman. Yet we thought his comments were important.

A QUALITATIVE DISTINCTION BETWEEN EXCHANGE AND COMMUNAL RELATIONSHIPS

The qualitative distinction we initially drew between exchange and communal relationships dealt with the norms that governed the giving and acceptance of benefits. We defined the term benefit as something one member of a relationship chooses to give to the other that is, in the donor's opinion (and typically in the recipient's and outside observers' as well), of use or value. Benefits take many forms. Services, goods, compliments, provision of information, supporting a person in reaching a goal, and symbols of caring such as cards or flowers, can all be benefits. Importantly, benefits are not the same as rewards. For our purposes the term "reward" refers to all pleasures, satisfactions or gratifications that the recipient might enjoy (Thibaut and Kelley, 1959: 12). For instance, a person might enjoy the reflected glory of being associated

with a famous individual but unless the famous person chose to associate with the person *in order* to confer that reflected glory the enjoyment is a reward, not a benefit. Also, not all benefits constitute rewards. A person may give another person a benefit intending to meet the person's needs or desires but the benefit might *not* be a reward from the recipient's perspective. One of our students once received a bouquet from an admirer. The flowers were a benefit. They had value and the donor intended to give them to the recipient. The recipient generally liked flowers, yet she did not experience receiving *those* flowers as rewarding due to her lack of any desire for a relationship with the donor.[2]

The nature of exchange relationships

In our initial papers (Clark and Mills, 1979; Mills and Clark, 1982; Clark, 1985) we posited that in many relationships members assume that a benefit is given with the expectation of receiving a comparable benefit (or benefits) in return. We chose the term "exchange relationship" as a label for these relationships rather than Goffman's term "economic exchange" because many of the benefits people give and receive do not involve money or things for which a monetary value can easily be calculated. Yet such benefits can still be exchanged, one for another. In these relationships, we said, the receipt of a benefit incurs an obligation (debt) to return a comparable benefit. In such relationships each person is concerned with how much he or she will receive in exchange for benefiting the other and how much is owed for benefits received. (We were using, and still use, the term "exchange" in a narrower sense than some others in the fields of social psychology and sociology.) Exchange relationships are often (but not always) exemplified by relationships that are called, in lay language, business relationships, relationships between acquaintances, and relationships between strangers meeting and interacting for the first time (assuming no desire for a friendship or romantic relationship.)

The nature of communal relationships

Not all relationships follow exchange rules. In some relationships benefits are given in support of the partner's welfare *non-contingently*; that is, benefits are given without the donor or the recipient feeling the recipient has an obligation to repay. This does not rule out the possibility that giving benefits increases the recipient's desire to behave communally toward the donor. It might and often does. Yet it might not. It simply means that the proximal motive for giving benefit is to improve the recipient's welfare and that neither the donor nor the recipient (if both were following a communal norm) feel that benefits come with a price tag, implicit or explicit. The donor may *hope* that the recipient will be similarly responsive to his or her needs as they arise which is likely why Goffman stated that something given in a social exchange, "need only be returned if the relationship calls for it." Yet, *hope* for the recipient having a similar motivation seems more appropriate to us than saying that a benefit "need only be returned when the relationship calls for it" because one can't demand such responsiveness. Moreover, we say *may* hope because there are communal relationships in which abilities to be responsive to one another's welfare differ greatly and, especially in these relationships, donors may not hope for similar responsiveness from the partner. For instance, parents may gladly pay their child's college tuition, yet if one of them decides to return to college they may well *not* hope that the child will strive to pay their tuition even if they must stretch to pay that extra tuition themselves. Ability to provide support matters (a factor that often explains why some communal relationships are asymmetrical in the sense that parties do not feel equal amounts of responsibility for one another's welfare – an aspect of communal relationships that

entails differences in communal strength which is discussed in more detail below). Even when ability does not vary, some communal relationships may be asymmetrical and that may be OK with both sides.

Communal relationships are often exemplified by relationships commonly referred to as friends, family members, romantic partners, and spouses. Yet there are plenty of exceptions to this rule. Early on, when we first said that family relationships often exemplify communal relationships, a colleague responded, "Not my mother! She kept careful track of what relatives gave us for wedding presents and then made sure her gift to their child was exactly comparable." Our sense was that this mother did have a communal relationship with her son but considered her relationships with many other relatives to be exchange in nature.

There is, we believe, an evolutionary basis for the existence of communal relationships. Newborn infants would not survive without someone attending to their needs non-contingently. Kin have likely long supported one another on a non-contingent basis. The very nature of small hunter-gatherer societies was such that there was an unpredictability of who would find food, shelter, and other necessities of life and who would need it. This likely dictated communal sharing and consumption of benefits (cf. Clark, 1984a; Clark and Jordan, 2002; and see Chapter 18, "Twists of Fate" in Kelley et al., 2003). Developmentally, an infant's need for and (one-sided) understanding of a communal norm would seem to emerge prior to his or her need for and understanding of an exchange norm which, in current society, is needed to give and receive benefits from a widening group of nonfamily members and nonfriends (see also Pataki et al., 1994). We once observed a young child at a community pool request a bag of potato chips at a snack bar and happily walk away without paying and without apparent guilt. The attendant called after the child telling him he must pay. Here, we thought, was an example of a child who likely understood communal norms well given that he was given food, unconditionally, by family members, and had some learning left to do when it came to understanding an exchange norm. Historically, the need for exchange in addition to communal relationships likely expanded greatly with the advent of civilization and specialization in skills, which increased differentiation between the skills and goods individuals could supply to one another.

Not all relationships are communal or exchange in nature

Although we have long focused upon communal and exchange relationships, we did not (and do not) believe that all relationships must be communal or exchange in nature. For example, there are also exploitative relationships which fit neither our conceptual definition for communal nor our conceptual definition for exchange relationships. Relationships that seem to be some sort of hybrid of a communal and an exchange relationship also exist. For instance, elementary school teachers are responsible for attending to many aspects of their young students' welfare, especially their need to learn. They do not expect direct repayment from those children nor do the children give much thought (if any) to repayments. But the obligations are circumscribed and the same teacher is paid for these services albeit by the school district or school in exchange for these services and would not provide the services without pay.

Early studies demonstrating the validity of the qualitative distinction

In the 1970s, social psychologists studying interpersonal interactions typically were conducting studies of interactions between strangers. We recall Ellen Berscheid, commenting at the time, that in our zeal to maintain control and to conduct true experiments on social behavior we were all busy studying relationships between people who had never seen one another before and who never expected to see each other in the future. We knew little about interactions in the relationships that matter most to people – those with their friends, family members, and romantic partners. All that has changed rapidly over the last three and a half decades (see, for example, Clark and Lemay, 2010) but to understand our research it is important to understand the context *at the time* the original research was conducted.

Once we had drawn the qualitative distinction, our challenge was to devise a true experimental manipulation of whether our participants would desire a communal or exchange relationship (and would therefore behave differently depending upon experimental condition when interacting with a partner if our postulates were correct). To create desire for a communal relationship a target person had to be interpersonally attractive, the research participant had to be "in the market" for new communal relationships and the target had to be available and interested as well. In the absence of these factors, we thought an exchange relationship would be preferred. We settled on a strategy of bringing two previously unacquainted people together, one of whom was a confederate, the other a true participant. We recruited college students in their early years at a residential college figuring that such students having just been uprooted from family and high school communities were typically "in the market" for new friends and, possibly, a new romantic partner. We selected a physically attractive, relaxed, engaging young woman whom we knew to be popular as our confederate figuring that she would be an appealing potential friend or romantic partner. Then we manipulated *her* availability and seeming interest in a new communal relationship. In our communal condition, we described her as new at the university and eager to form relationships (making her similar to and available to our participants). In our exchange condition, we described her as married and about to be picked up by her husband (making her dissimilar to and unavailable to our participants).

This manipulation worked (see, for instance, Clark and Mills, 1979; Clark, 1986) and was used with minor modification in many of our initial experimental studies.

DO PEOPLE IN (OR DESIRING) COMMUNAL RELATIONSHIPS SHUN BEHAVIORS WHICH SUGGEST THEY OR A POTENTIAL PARTNER MAY BE FOLLOWING AN EXCHANGE NORM?

Our inaugural studies focused on demonstrating that exchange behaviors would occur and be welcomed in our exchange conditions, but would be avoided and reacted to negatively (if they did occur) in our communal conditions. We *had* to start here because, at the time, equity theory was the dominant theory for explaining how people gave and received benefits in relationships. The overall extant assumption was that giving benefits created inequities, resulted in discomfort, and called for repayment (see Walster et al., 1978). We predicted that *only* if an exchange relationship was desired would people positively respond to being repaid for a favor they had given to a target; reactions to such a payment would be negative when a communal relationship was desired. This should occur, we reasoned, because acting in accord with an exchange norm would imply that a communal relationship was not desired.

Our participants were male. They encountered a female target with whom they were led to desire either an exchange or a communal relationship. Each participant and confederate worked on a task. They were allowed to help one another. Tasks were assigned to enable the real participant to finish his task with materials to spare. The experimenter asked if he wished to give materials to the female. All did so and the confederate repaid him or did not with an extra credit point. Finally, under the guise of preparation for another task the male participants indicated their liking of the female confederate.

The results were clear. Repayment increased liking (relative to no repayment) in the exchange conditions; in contrast it reduced liking in the communal conditions. In a second study (Clark and Mills, 1979, Study 2) participants were female and we manipulated desire for a communal or an exchange relationship with a female target. This time participants received help or did not followed by a request to return a comparable benefit or no request. After receiving a benefit, receiving a request for a comparable benefit increased liking in our exchange conditions but decreased liking in our communal conditions. Finally, receiving a request for a benefit in the absence of having received one decreased liking among our exchange condition participants (where it presumably created a debt) but not among our communal condition participants.

These studies and other early studies showing, for instance, that people who are not repaid feel exploited when they desire an exchange relationship but not when they desire a communal one (Clark and Waddell, 1985) and that giving and receiving non-comparable benefits results in a relationship looking more like a friendship than does giving and receiving comparable benefits (Clark, 1981) were greeted with enough interest to be published. Yet they also generated skepticism.

Reviewers and audience members at conferences suggested an alternative explanation: perhaps people in our exchange conditions wanted an *immediate* balancing of accounts whereas participants in our communal conditions still kept track of benefits given and received, but were content to let accounts be balanced across time. This was possible. Yet, we did not "buy" this interpretation for many reasons. It left open many questions: *Why* should there be a difference in time course? Also, even if the projected time courses were different why would someone be liked less in our communal conditions for prompt repayment than for failing to repay? Moreover, in the initial studies reported in Clark and Mills (1979) it seemed unlikely that there was simply more time to "balance the books" in the communal than in the exchange conditions for there was no guarantee that the relationship in the communal conditions would be ongoing. Furthermore, there are plenty of long-term business (exchange) relationships in which bills still must be paid promptly. Why couldn't those debts wait as well? It also seemed impossible to us that people simply could not (even if they wished to) keep track of and balance all the myriad benefits that are given and received over time in intimate relationships. In addition, an exchange rule could not explain such things as, why parents would ever care for a severely handicapped child or why the spouses of many Alzheimers patients continue to care for their partners even after the partners can no longer reciprocate or even recognize them. Finally, and importantly, following an exchange rule simply does not afford the benefit of the unambiguous inferences of being caring (by donors) and of being cared for (by recipients) of benefits. We sensed that these feelings were terribly important in friendships, family relationships, and romantic relationships.

We, of course, could reason all we wished about why we were right. What was needed to convince our critics was evidence that people do not keep track of benefits in all relationships as would be necessary to maintain equity across time. Thus, three studies were conducted to demonstrate this (Clark, 1984a,b). In the first, desire for a communal or an exchange relationship was manipulated; in the second two, we contrasted the behavior of strangers working together with that of friends working together. In each, participants engaged in a task in which they and a partner were working together to find certain number sequences in a large matrix of numbers. For each sequence found the pair earned a monetary reward to be divided afterwards. The partner always started working in either red or black ink. Then it was the participant's turn. Pens of both colors were available. The participant chose one and our dependent measure was whether the participant chose to work with the same color pen (making it unclear, in the end, how many sequences

each person found) or a different color pen (making it absolutely clear who had contributed what). The results of all three studies were clear. Strangers who expected to remain strangers kept track of benefits – the vast majority choosing to use a different color pen; people led to desire a communal relationship or those with an existing communal relationship did not – each time fewer than the 50 percent did so. (This effect also was conceptually replicated by Clark et al., 1989). Indeed, when trying to *form* a communal relationship people seemed to "bend over backwards" not to choose a different color pen choosing one significantly less often than 50 percent of the time.

These results were important. If people who desire or have a communal relationship do not keep track of benefits in the moment they cannot be quietly keeping those inputs in mind across time to make sure the books even out in the end.[3]

DO PEOPLE IN COMMUNAL RELATIONSHIPS FOLLOW A COMMUNAL NORM?

Having established that people led to expect a friendship or romantic relationship (or those having such a relationship) react negatively to and avoid exchange behaviors, we turned to demonstrating that people led to desire communal relationships behave in more communal ways than those led to desire exchange relationships. In one set of studies we showed that people led to desire communal relationships would keep track of a light that indicated that a partner in the next room was experiencing a need (even if they could do nothing about it) whereas those who desired an exchange relationship were less likely to do so (Clark et al., 1986, Study 1; see also Clark et al., 1989). We also demonstrated that attention to needs would take place in exchange relationships *if* the person who could attend to those needs knew that he or she would soon be in the same position as the partner and would want the partner to attend to his or her needs. In that case, repayments might well be needed. Indeed, when roles were to be reversed, attention to needs in our exchange condition rose to levels comparable with those observed in our communal conditions (whether or not role reversals were scheduled). In the communal conditions attention to needs did not vary with the other person's opportunity to repay (Clark et al., 1986, Study 2). Also fitting with findings of attending more to needs when communal relationships are desired or exist, we found and reported evidence of people responding more positively to a partner's expressions of emotion (which are signals of needs or lack thereof) when a communal rather than an exchange relationship is desired (Clark and Taraban, 1991; Yoo et al., 2011, Study 1). We also found that people express more emotion when a communal rather than an exchange relationship is desired (Clark and Finkel, 2005a; Clark et al., 2001). Furthermore, the willingness to express negative emotions prospectively predicts college students forming more relationships over the course of a semester with previously unknown fellow students and with the establishment of more intimacy in the closest of those relationships (Graham et al., 2008). Meanwhile other researchers have reported on links between suppressing emotions and lower social support, less closeness to others, and lower social satisfaction in normatively close relationships (Srivastava et al., 2009), lower rapport in such relationships, poorer communication, and lower chances of relationship formation (Butler et al., 2003).

Of course, levels of helping and responsiveness to another's sad emotion ought to be higher when communal relationships are desired or exist than when exchange relationships are desired or exist and we demonstrated this in a study by Clark et al. (1987, Study 1). People were randomly assigned to desire a communal or exchange relationship by giving them time alone to view an attractive confederate's photo and questionnaire responses that led them to believe that the confederate was either married or single, new to campus, and thinking that doing the study might be a good way to meet people. Participants were then provided an opportunity to voluntarily help a fellow participant by performing a mundane task. Participants in the communal condition helped for longer time periods than did people in the exchange condition. In addition, knowing the other was sad significantly increased time spent helping in the communal but not in the exchange conditions. Other studies revealed that people's moods improve in reaction to having helped a potential partner when communal (but not exchange) relationships are desired (Williamson and Clark, 1989; 1992) and that people feel badly about not helping when communal (but not when exchange) relationships are desired (Williamson et al., 1996). Moreover, people desiring a communal relationship care how much time another spends in picking out a gift *for them*; people desiring an exchange relationship do not (Clark et al., 1998).

ADDING A QUANTITATIVE DIMENSION TO THE THEORY

Whereas we started with a qualitative distinction, early on we added a quantitative dimension to our theory – communal strength (Mills and Clark, 1982) and later we developed a measure of the dimension of communal strength (Mills et al., 2004). Although we considered it necessary to begin by emphasizing the qualitative distinction in order to emphasize the very existence of communal relationships and their distinction from exchange relationships, we knew from the beginning that communal relationships vary in how much responsibility in terms of time, effort, or money a person takes on for another person (what we call communal strength). Clearly, for instance, most people feel more communal responsibility for their children than for their friends and will spent more time, effort, and money to benefit their child than their friends. (Consider, for instance, the fact that many people pay college tuition for their children and almost no one does so for a friend although both relationships are, qualitatively, communal in nature.). Our measure of communal strength (Mills et al., 2004) has been shown to tap a construct distinct from behavioral interdependence as measured by Berscheid et al.'s (1989) Relationship Closeness Inventory and distinct from a measure of liking for the partner. (Consider, for instance, that one may feel considerable communal responsibility for a cranky elderly relative whom one does not like very much or that one can feel considerable liking for an attractive, potential romantic partner whom one has just met but for whom one feels little communal responsibility.) The communal strength scale correlates with Rubin's (1970) Love Scale and has been shown to predict allocation of benefits to peers and diary reports of giving help to and receiving help from friends. (See also Monin et al., 2008, for an additional methodology for measuring communal strength and further evidence that communal strength is not the same construct as liking).

People have very low-strength communal relationships with many other people. For instance, many people if stopped by a stranger and asked the time or for simple directions will provide the requested service to meet almost any requestor's needs without expecting anything in return. They have higher-strength communal relationships with others such as friends and people often have extremely high-strength communal relationships with a single other person or a very select group of people such as children and a spouse or romantic partner. Figure 38.1 depicts one person's set of hierarchically arranged communal relationships. The hierarchy of relationships appears along the x-axis, the degree of felt responsibility appears along the y-axis and the line running through the graph depicts the degree of responsibility felt for various people. The needs of a person high in a communal hierarchy take precedence over equivalent (and sometimes nonequivalent) needs of a person lower in communal strength in the event of a conflict. For instance, a person might forego attending a friend's birthday party in order to be at her own child's birthday party and the friend is very likely to understand and to accept this. Of course, Figure 38.1 depicts just one possible hierarchy. The ordering of people (and of the self) in these implicit hierarchies will vary considerably between persons and cultures.

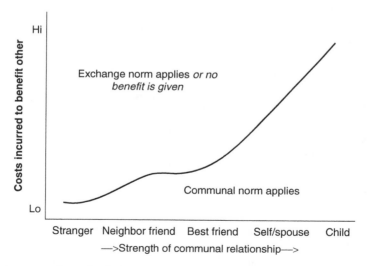

Figure 38.1 Costs one hypothetical person would be willing to incur to benefit a variety of relationship partners

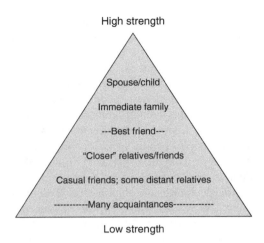

Figure 38.2   One person's hypothetical hierarchy of communal relationship partners

Reis et al. (2004) suggested that people's sets of communal relationships likely fall in a triangular shape as depicted in Figure 38.2 with most people having many low-strength communal relationships, fewer medium-strength communal relationships, and very few very-high-strength communal relationships. There is, after all, a limit on the number of people for whom an individual can assume responsibility. It is also the case that once one has an established network of communal family members, friends and a romantic partner who feel responsibility for one's own welfare, adding more adds little to one's own security.

Note that the "self" is also depicted in Figures 38.1 and 38.2 because people do generally feel a communal responsibility to the self as well as to others. Most people place the "self" high in their hierarchy of communal relationships and consider their responsibility to care for themselves high and to take precedence over their responsibility to many other (but very often not all) other communal partners. For instance, a woman might think that taking care of herself takes clear precedence over taking care of the needs of a casual friend but not over taking care of her child.

Note also that Figure 38.1 implicitly conveys that a person may have both a communal and an exchange relationship with the same relationship partner within different "cost" ranges.

For instance, a person might give a friend advice, a ride, presents, lunch, and include that friend in social events all on a communal basis but sell the friend a car on an exchange basis. More commonly, we believe, benefits are given on a communal basis up to some "cost" threshold and above that they simply are not given or discussed.

Whereas the communal nature of a relationship has a quantitative dimension, exchange norms do not have an equivalent quantitative dimension (Mills and Clark, 1982). If a relationship is exchange in nature, it just is. Benefits given require comparable benefits in return. Repayments may be missed. After all these norms are ideals; violations will occur. For instance, given limited resources and many debts, some people may be forced to choose who to repay and who not to repay. They may do so based on liking, the importance of the exchange relationship to their well-being, the length of the relationship, and/or the demandingness of the person to whom the debt is owed. Yet unpaid debt remains, and with it comes guilt on the debtor's part and annoyance or anger on the grantor's part. There is no parallel in an exchange relationship to a friend's understanding that one could not attend to his need because one's child had a need at the same time. People may try to excuse unpaid debts in exchange relationships by appealing to having other debts but the person who is unpaid will just not understand.

THE DISTINCTION IS NOT ONE OF SHORT- VERSUS LONG-TERM RELATIONSHIPS

From the time we published our first paper on the distinction between exchange versus communal relationships, many people made two assumptions about its basis, neither of which we shared. Daniel Batson raised both in a paper challenging our distinction (Batson, 1993). He actually did us a favor in the sense of pushing us to address in print two issues that others had raised as well (see Clark and

Mills, 1993 for our response). The first assumption he made was that exchange relationships are short-term relationships with each benefit given being quickly repaid, whereas communal relationships are long-term relationships with benefits balancing out across time. As we have already noted in talking about record keeping, this is not the basis for our distinction. Communal and exchange relationships can be either short- or long-term. Some (generally weak) communal relationships are one-time occurrences as in our earlier example of a person telling a stranger the time without expecting anything in return. Other times (as in some emergency situations) one can provide another with larger communal benefits on a short-term basis as once occurred to one of us when the parent of an incoming college student had no money for housing upon bringing her daughter to school and stayed (along with her pets and daughter) in our home for awhile. Other communal relationships, such as many marriages, parent–child relationships, and friendships do last a long time. Responsiveness to needs and desires occurs as those needs and desires arise across time. In symmetrical communal relationships, benefiting may well be roughly equal across time. Yet there are no guarantees and there are also many cases of asymmetrical long-term communal relationships in which benefits may never even out. Perhaps the most common examples are the relationship between parents and children during the younger individuals' childhoods and early adulthood. Of course, if the parents need help as they age it is often given but both parties are unlikely to be distressed (and in fact very likely to be happy) if that need never arises.

THE DISTINCTION IS NOT ONE OF SELFISH VERSUS UNSELFISH RELATIONSHIPS

A second assumption Batson (1993) and others have made is that communal relationships are unselfish in nature and exchange relationships selfish. We do not make that assumption. Once a communal norm is adopted, benefits are given on a non-contingent basis; once an exchange norm is adopted, benefits are given on a contingent basis but *either* selfish or unselfish motives can drive a person to adopt each norm.

Consider a communal norm, for instance. There exist many possible "selfish" reasons for adopting such a norm. One may have just moved to a new community, wish to form new friendships, and act on a communal basis toward potential friends to start a friendship. One may care for a disagreeable, elderly relative on a communal basis because one would feel guilty if one did not or because one fears criticism by others. There also exist unselfish reasons for following a communal norm such as feelings of empathy for one's partner. So too may the drive to communally care for one's offspring compel one to adherence to a communal norm in a manner that seems unselfish to us (though some might consider it selfish in the sense of promoting the survival of one's genes across generations).

The adoption of an exchange norm also may be driven by relatively selfish or relatively unselfish motives. It is likely that most times when a person adopts an exchange norm the motive is selfish. For example, when a person goes to the store to buy a loaf of bread it is because he wants that bread and almost never because he wants to benefit the grocer. When a person forms a car pool it is likely to save time and money for him or herself. Yet people may also adopt an exchange norm for unselfish reasons. It might, for instance, be possible to exploit an employee given a dearth of jobs and to pay the person less than his or her work is worth. If that were done the relationship would not adhere to an exchange norm but would be best characterized as exploitative in nature. In such a situation, unselfish motives (to be moral, to be fair) might drive the decision to follow an exchange norm by paying the person a fair wage. Of course, both selfish and unselfish motives might drive adoption of an exchange (or a communal) relationship.

For instance, currently people advocate buying "fair trade" coffee on an exchange basis seemingly *both* because they want coffee (a selfish motive) and because, although equally good coffee might be purchased at a lower price, they do not wish to exploit coffee workers and instead want to offer them a "fair" trade in exchange terms (a relatively unselfish motive although we know that some might say the buyer gets to feel good about himself and that makes it selfish).

In discussing whether communal relationships are selfish or not, it is also important to point out our assumption that people place themselves in their own hierarchies of communal relationships and that, typically, they place themselves high in those hierarchies. This means that most people do consider taking care of their own needs to take precedence over taking care of most other people's needs even when it may be said that they have communal relationships with those others. It is easy to illustrate this point. People send themselves, not their neighbors or friends, on vacation, but they still can act communally toward those friends.

They may also place certain others at a rank equal to the self in their hierarchies (e.g., a spouse may merit this rank) and some at higher ranks in their hierarchies (e.g., a young, completely dependent child is often "given" such a rank) and make sacrifices for such people and or forgive such people for major wrongdoings. The overall point to be made here, though, is simply that selfishness versus unselfishness is not the defining characteristic of communal relationships.

COMMUNAL RELATIONSHIPS CAN BE SYMMETRICAL OR ASYMMETRICAL

Most communal relationships are symmetrical in the sense that each person assumes about the same level of responsibility for the partner's welfare, as does the partner for him or her. Friendships, romantic relationships, and marriages are examples of relationships that are often both communal in nature and symmetrical in felt responsibility. Yet communal relationships can be asymmetrical as well. A mother generally assumes much greater responsibility for her young child's welfare than vice versa and this pattern often continues right into the child's adulthood. Indeed, one of us recently asked a large class of college students about whether their relationships with their friends and their relationships with their mothers were characterized by feeling "about equal responsibility for one another's welfare," the other feeling "more responsibility for me than I do for her/him," or the self feeling "more responsibility for her/him than s/he does for me." For friends, 84 percent of the students reported feeling equal responsibility, 6 percent said their friend felt more responsibility for them than they did for the friend, and 10 percent said they felt more responsibility for their friend than vice versa. Reports for their mother showed a very different pattern. Only 15 percent said they and their mother felt equal responsibility for one another, 85 percent reported their mother felt more responsibility for them than vice versa, and no student reported that he or she felt more responsibility for his or her mother than she did more the student. Clearly these particular Western, largely affluent, college students tended to have symmetrical communal relationships with their friends and asymmetrical ones with their mothers.

INDIVIDUAL DIFFERENCES IN COMMUNAL AND EXCHANGE ORIENTATION

We believe most variability in communal responsiveness lies between relationships rather than between individuals (Clark and Lemay, 2010). That is, we assume that almost all people have relationships in which they strive to follow a communal norm as well as other relationships in which they make little or no effort to be responsive to partners. That said, differences in people's tendencies

---

Box 38.1   Scales to measure individual differences in communal and in exchange orientation

Communal Orientation Scale

1 It bothers me when other people neglect my needs.
2 When making a decision, I take other people's needs and feelings into account.
3 I'm not especially sensitive to other people's feelings.*
4 I don't consider myself to be a particularly helpful person.*
5 I believe people should go out of their way to be helpful.
6 I don't especially enjoy giving others aid.*
7 I expect people I know to be responsive to my needs and feelings.
8 I often go out of my way to help another person.
9 I believe it's best not to get involved taking care of other people's personal needs.*
10 I'm not the sort of person who often comes to the aid of others.*
11 When I have a need, I turn to others I know for help.
12 When people get emotionally upset, I tend to avoid them.*
13 People should keep their troubles to themselves.*
14 When I have a need that others ignore, I'm hurt.

Items from the Exchange Orientation Scale

1 When I give something to another person, I generally expect something in return.
2 When someone buys me a gift, I try to buy that person as comparable a gift as possible.
3 I don't think people should feel obligated to repay others for favors.*
4 I wouldn't feel exploited if someone failed to repay me for a favor.*
5 I don't bother to keep track of benefits I have given others.*
6 When people receive benefits from others, they ought to repay those others right away.
7 It's best to make sure things are always kept 'even' between two people in a relationship.
8 I usually give gifts only to people who have given me gifts in the past.
9 When someone I know helps me out on a project, I don't feel I have to pay them back.*

*Note: These are two independent scales. Respondents rate each item for each scale on a five-point scale from "extremely uncharacteristic" of them (1) to "extremely characteristic" of them (5). Scores for items followed by an asterisk are reversed prior to calculating a sum indicating the respondent's communal or the respondent's exchange score.

---

to follow communal or exchange norms also exist.

To measure such individual differences, scales of both communal orientation and of exchange orientation have been developed (Clark et al., 1987; Mills and Clark, 1994). These two separate and orthogonal scales appear in Box 38.1. The communal scale has been utilized more extensively than the exchange scale (but note that other researchers, for instance Murstein and his colleagues [1977] and Sprecher [1992], have developed their own methods for measuring exchange orientation and exchange orientation generally has been studied a fair amount).

High scores on communal orientation (using the scale shown in Box 38.1) have been shown

to predict: helping a fellow student in a nonemergency situation (Clark et al., 1987); agreement that support has taken place among friends (Coriell and Cohen, 1995); willingness to express emotion to relationship partners especially when the relationship context calls for so doing (Clark and Finkel, 2005a, 2005b); allocating rewards equally when negotiating a friend, which makes good sense communally assuming equal needs (Thompson and Deharpport, 1998); people giving partners more credit for joint successful performances on a task and blaming them less for failure while attributions to the self remain unaffected by communal orientation (McCall, 1995); greater satisfaction in elderly persons' best friendships (Jones and

---

Box 38.2   The ten-item communal strength measure

1   How far would you be willing to go to visit _____?
2   How happy do you feel when doing something that helps _____?
3   How large a benefit would you be likely to give _____?
4   How large a cost would you incur to meet a need of _____?
5   How readily can you put the needs of ____ out of your thoughts?*
6   How high a priority for you is meeting the needs of ____?
7   How reluctant would you be to sacrifice for ____?*
8   How much would you be willing to give up to benefit____?
9   How far would you go out of your way to do something for ____?
10 How easily could you accept not helping ____?*

Note: The items with asterisks are reversed prior to summing scores. The instructions for this scale are as follows: "As you answer each question, fill in the person's initials in the blank. Circle one answer for each question on the scale from 0 'not at all' to 10 'extremely' before going on to the next question. Your answers will remain confidential."

Vaughan, 1990); and responding to cues of power with greater social responsibility (Chen et al., 2001). Low scores predict: burnout in nurses (Van Yperen et al., 1992) and leaders of self-help groups (Medvene et al., 1997); depression among caregivers of Alzheimer's patients (Williamson and Schulz, 1990); male physical abuse of female partners as well as males' associating with peers who endorse violence against female partners (Williamson and Silverman, 2001); and links between feeling under-benefited and feeling resentful (Thompson et al., 1995). *Matches* on communal orientation have been shown to be linked to better ability to capitalize on mutual opportunities in negotiations (Thompson and Deharpport, 1998). In other words, individual differences in communal orientation can be measured and predict behaviors that one would expect on the basis of following (or failing to follow) a communal norm.

High exchange orientation (using a variety of measures) has been found to predict one's marital satisfaction being tied to considerations of equity and, overall, to lower marital satisfaction, whereas the marital satisfaction of people low in exchange orientation has been shown to be both higher and unrelated to considerations of equity (Buunk and Van Yperen, 1991; see also Murstein et al., 1977) as well as to expectations of becoming

distressed over inequities in a relationship (Sprecher, 1992). High exchange orientation also has been linked to lower compatibility and friendship ratings among roommates and higher anxiety among women in those roommate pairs (Murstein and Azar, 1986).

Many situations clearly call for following one norm or the other and most people, no matter what their overall orientations, adhere to the norm that matches the situation. Yet individual differences in orientation likely do come into play in two types of situations. First, they are likely to come into play in situations lacking strong situational cues regarding how to behave. For instance, Clark et al. (1987, Study 2) found that communal orientation scores predicted how much help a person gave a young research assistant when no manipulation of relationship type had taken place. Second, these individual differences likely influence how easily and with how much equanimity people are able to follow the norm appropriate to a particular situation. That is, we suspect that exchange-oriented individuals likely must exert more effort and more self-consciously follow communal norms in marriage than others. They may also violate a communal norm/appeal to an exchange norm more often than others. In addition, we suspect that communally oriented individuals may have a tougher time sticking to exchange norms when the situation calls for using that norm but evidence of a person being needy exists. For instance, they might find it especially difficult to terminate an employee who needs the job but has not been living up to the (exchange) terms of employment.

Recent work also has begun examining how the individual difference dimensions of attachment-related avoidance and anxiety relate to adherence to communal and to exchange norms. Evidence suggests that higher levels of attachment-related avoidance are linked to: some reluctance to enter situations in which one may (or may not) receive evidence of another's communal interest; slightly greater tendencies to behave in accord with an exchange norm when in situations that are normatively communal in nature; and discomfort in situations in which adherence to a communal norm is occurring or seems to be called for (cf. Bartz and Lydon, 2006, 2008; Beck and Clark, 2009; Clark et al., 2010). Higher levels of attachment related anxiety do not seem to be linked to reluctance to enter communal situations but do seem to be related to ambivalence and discomfort in such situations and more reactivity to behavior suggesting adherence or lack thereof to both communal and exchange norms (Bartz and Lydon, 2006, 2008; Clark et al., 2010).

Four additional theoretical points

Our work on communal relationships has led us to postulate a few criteria for the existence of "high quality" close relationships in addition to being responsive to partner desires and needs and seeking such responsiveness from partners. First, because most peer communal relationships are symmetrical, couple members who implicitly agree on the appropriate strength of their communal relationship and its desired trajectory (Box 38.2) (both in terms of the slope and speed of strengthening the nature of the communal relationship or the sense that the relationship should not be strengthened) ought to feel more satisfied and

comfortable with their relationships than those who do not agree. If one person desires a stronger communal relationship than the other, first person may feel neglected and latter partner may feel smothered.

Second, in connection with people's (usually implicit) hierarchy of communal relationships, we suggest that a couple's or friends' complementarity in communal hierarchies will influence the quality of their relationships with one another. For example, spouses who are in agreement with one another that their newborn's welfare takes precedence over both of their own needs, their obligations to one another come next, and their obligations to their respective families of origin rank third, ought to experience less conflict in their relationship than a couple including a wife who puts her infant first, her parents second and her spouse third while the spouse puts her first (and expects her to do the same for him), his child second, and his own family of origin third (and, expects her to do the same with regard to their child and her family of origin).

Third, we believe that placement of the self within one's hierarchy of communal relationships has important implications for the nature of one's strongest communal relationships and, indeed, to one's ability to have very strong communal relationships. In particular, placing the self high in one's hierarchy but having another person (e.g., a spouse, a child) placed higher in one's hierarchy or at least "tied" with the self may be a requirement for "pulling off" very strong communal relationships. Here is why.

When the self is placed alone at the top of the hierarchy, especially when the self is placed well above everyone else, attending to the self's own needs will always take precedence over attending to others' needs. Compromises and sacrifices will not be made. Forgiveness for transgressions will not take place. Partners will not be able to relax self-defenses knowing that there is someone else to care for them as much or more than they care for themselves.

Finally, we do not suggest that adopting a communal norm is always the best strategy in relationships nor always healthy. Adopting a communal norm when the partner prefers an exchange relationship can be awkward and distressing to both parties. Similarly, acting in accord with a strong communal norm when one's partner desires a weaker communal relationship can produce problems as can mismatches in desires for asymmetrical versus symmetrical communal relationships.

DO PEOPLE REALLY BELIEVE IN AND FOLLOW COMMUNAL NORMS IN THEIR INTIMATE RELATIONSHIPS?

Do people really believe a communal rule is the "right" rule for their friendships, romantic relationships, and family relationship? Do they actually follow this rule in ongoing relationships? After all, one might think, most of the early research was done utilizing relationships between people who were meeting for the first time. Perhaps such people do follow a communal rule to win one another's affections but then drop the rule after commitments have been made. Recently we have been studying ongoing marriages and the results for this research suggest the answer to the first question posed above is yes. People do believe a communal norm is ideal for their marriages and that an exchange norm is decidedly not ideal, and in at least two samples of marriages the vast majority of people report that they and their spouse strive to follow a communal norm. The answer to the second question also appears to be yes (with some caveats). Specifically, both Grote and Clark (1998) and Clark et al. (2010) have found that individuals will rate a communal norm as ideal and an exchange norm as decidedly not ideal for their marriages. Clark et al. (2010) have also shown that, for at least the first two years of marriage, spouses report striving to adhere to such a norm, and that their partners strive to adhere to this norm as well. The caveats are straightforward.

Although members of both samples overwhelmingly reported that both they and their spouse strive to follow communal norms, research also suggests that, especially when they are distressed (Grote and Clark, 2001) or have chronic relationship insecurities (Clark et al., 2010), they may "fall down" on the job and calculate fairness according to an exchange rule.

Of course, it is also the case that the clinical and counseling literature on relationships provides overwhelming evidence that some relationships people normatively desire to be communal in nature (e.g., marriages) may come to be characterized by the antithesis of communal caring. Members may verbally and physically abuse one another, berate and criticize one another, and show contempt for one another. Although we have consistently said that family relationships, romantic relationships and marriages often exemplify communal relationships, at times, we hasten to add, they definitely do not. Adherence to a communal norm, we believe, characterizes well-functioning, healthy, marriages, friendships, and family relationships. Therapists will certainly encounter people in marriages and friendships and family relationships who do not follow communal norms. That ought not to be taken as evidence of a communal norm not applying to intimate relationships or of there being no differences in rules that govern the giving and acceptance of benefits in different relationships. Appeals to an exchange norm may be made in relationships that society calls upon to be communal in nature. When they are made, we suggest, they are signs of trouble. In contrast, when exchange norms are appealed to and followed in, say, a business relationship, they suggest the relationship is a healthy one. A person would not seek counseling because his business partner is keeping track of just who contributes what to the business and just who derives what benefits from the business. If his wife or mother or best friend did the same, it would not be surprising for counseling to be sought.

CONCLUSION

When we set forth our distinction between communal and exchange relationships, we were forging new ground in social psychology. That has all changed dramatically as we pass the thirtieth anniversary of our first communal/exchange paper (Clark and Mills, 1979). Now work on relationships that are, normatively, communal in nature is thriving. Much knowledge has been gained about intra- and interpersonal processes characteristic of well and poorly functioning relationships that society calls for to be communal in nature. We have not attempted a review of the extensive work regarding factors that promote the healthy communal functioning of close relationships and the factors that interfere with such relationships (but see Clark and Lemay, 2010, for a review of such work, much of it done by others; and Clark et al., 2010; Grote and Clark, 2001; Grote et al., 2002, 2004; Lemay and Clark, 2008; Lemay et al., 2007 for theoretical ideas and results from our own laboratory suggesting factors that contribute to and detract from the communal health of a communal relationship.). Rather we have tried to convey a good sense of our original qualitative distinction between communal and exchange relationships, the quantitative concept of the communal strength of relationships, some implications of our theory for relationship functioning and of the empirical research that we, ourselves, have done to test our theoretical ideas.

We conclude by returning to the questions we posed to our readers at the beginning of this chapter. First, why, when purchasing a gift for a friend, do we expect price tags to be on items yet after the purchase make sure they been removed? The answer is that relationships with friends are communal in nature and relationships with storeowners are exchange in nature. Second, why did the friend who rented a vacation house and arrived to find no hot water find it maddening that her real estate agent tried to elicit her sympathy by explaining that the owners were experiencing severe personal problems? It is because

a rental arrangement is exchange in nature and the excuse called upon her to feel communal understanding for the unknown owners with whom she had no relationship at all.

ACKNOWLEDGMENTS

Much of the work reported here was supported by NSF grant BNS 9983417. Opinions, conclusions and recommendations expressed in this paper, however, are those of the authors and do not necessarily reflect the views of the National Science Foundation. I thank Oriana Aragon and Elizabeth Clark-Polner for detailed comments on this chapter.

NOTES

1 After having been invited to prepare this chapter but prior to its completion, Judson R. Mills died. He was my mentor, the inspiration for the original communal/exchange distinction, central to the theoretical ideas expressed here and a co-author on much of the empirical work. In this chapter I have tried to stay true to his thinking. Yet had he lived he would forced me to be conceptually clearer and more precise, added new conceptual ideas, and most certainly debated the new ideas expressed here.

2 In excluding rewards from our theory, we immediately were addressing a more narrow set of issues than equity theorists had dealt with for many equity theorists had included rewards in their calculation of equity (cf. Walster et al., 1978).

3 In saying this it may be helpful to keep in mind that this does not mean that we believe people never violate a communal norm and keep track nor that when people feel their needs have been neglected that they sometimes retrospectively try to calculate "fairness." They do (Grote and Clark, 2001) – often in a very biased manner! It does mean that doing so is a violation of a norm typically followed in communal relationships.

REFERENCES

Adams, J.S. (1965) Inequity in social exchange. *Advances in Experimental Social Psychology, 62,* 335–343.

Bartz, J.A. and Lydon, J.E. (2006) Navigating the interdependence dilemma: Attachment goals and the use of communal norms with potential close others. *Journal of Personality and Social Psychology, 9,* 77–96.

Bartz, J.A. and Lydon, J.E. (2008) Relationship specific attachment, risk regulation, and communal norm adherence in close relationships. *Journal of Experimental Social Psychology, 4,* 655–663.

Batson, C.D. (1993) Communal and exchange relationships: What is the difference? *Personality and Social Psychology Bulletin, 19,* 677–683.

Beck, L.A. and Clark, M.S. (2009) Choosing to enter or avoid diagnostic social situations. *Psychological Science,* 20, 1175–1181.

Berscheid, E., Snyder, M. and Omoto, A. (1989) The relationship closeness inventory: Assessing the closeness of interpersonal relationships. *Journal of Personality and Social Psychology, 57,* 792–807.

Butler, E.A., Egloff, B., Wlhelm, F.H., Smith, N.C., Erickson, E.A. and Gross, J.J. (2003) The social consequences of expressive suppression. *Emotion, 3,* 48–67.

Buunk, B.P. and Van Yperen, N.W. (1991) Referential comparisons, relational comparisons, and exchange orientation: Their relation to marital satisfaction. *Personality and Social Psychology Bulletin, 17,* 709–717.

Chen, S., Lee-Chai, A.Y. and Bargh, J.A. (2001) Relationship orientation as a moderator of the effects of social power. *Journal of Personality and Social Psychology, 80,* 173–187.

Clark, M.S. (1981) Non-comparability of benefits given and received: A cue to the existence of friendship. *Social Psychology Quarterly, 44,* 375–381.

Clark, M.S. (1984a) A distinction between two types of relationships and its implications for development. In J.C. Masters and K. Yarkin-Levin (eds), *Boundary Areas in Social Psychology,* pp. 241–270. New York: Academic Press.

Clark, M.S. (1984b) Record keeping in two types of relationships. *Journal of Personality and Social Psychology, 47,* 549–557.

Clark, M.S. (1985) Implications of relationship type for understanding compatibility. In W. Ickes (ed.), *Compatible and Incompatible Relationships,* pp. 199–140. New York: Springer-Verlag.

Clark, M.S. (1986) Evidence for the effectiveness of manipulations of desire for communal versus exchange relationships. *Personality and Social Psychology Bulletin, 12,* 414–425.

Clark, M.S., Dubash, P. and Mills, J. (1998) Interest in another's consideration of one's needs. *Journal of Experimental Social Psychology, 34,* 246–264.

Clark, M.S. and Finkel, E.J. (2005a) Willingness to express emotion: The impact of relationship type,

communal orientation and their interaction. *Personal Relationships, 12,* 169–180.

Clark, M.S. and Finkel, E.J. (2005b) Does expressing emotion promote well-being? It depends on relationship context. In L.A. Tiedens and C.W. Leach (eds), *The Social Life of Emotions,* pp. 105–126. New York: Cambridge University Press.

Clark, M.S., Fitness, J. and Brissette, I. (2001) Understanding people's perceptions of relationships is crucial to understanding their emotional lives. In G. Fletcher, and M.S. Clark (eds), *Blackwell Handbook of Social Psychology, Vol. 3: Interpersonal Processes,* pp. 253–278. Oxford, UK: Blackwell.

Clark, M.S. and Jordan, S. (2002) Adherence to communal norms: What it means, when it occurs and some thoughts on how it develops. In B. Laursen and W. Graziano (eds), *Justice: New Directions for Childand Adolescent Development,* pp. 3–25. New York: Jossey-Bass.

Clark, M.S. and Lemay, E. (2010) Close Relationships. In S.T. Fiske, D.T. Gilbert and G. Lindsey (eds), *Handbook of Social Psychology,* Vol. 2, 5th Edition., pp. 898–940. Hoboken, NJ: John Wiley & Sons, Inc.

Clark, M.S., Lemay, E.P., Graham, S.M., Pataki, S. and Finkel, E.J. (2010) Ways of giving and receiving benefits in marriage: What's ideal? What happens? Attachment style matters. *Psychological Science, 21,* 944–951.

Clark, M.S. and Mills, J. (1979) Interpersonal attraction in exchange and communal relationships. *Journal of Personality and Social Psychology, 37,* 12–24.

Clark, M.S. and Mills, J. (2001) Behaving in such a way as to maintain and enhance relationship satisfaction. In J.H. Harvey and A.E. Wenzel (eds), *Relationship Maintenance and Enhancement,* pp. 13–26. Mahwah, NJ: Erlbaum.

Clark, M.S., Mills, J. and Corcoran, D. (1989) Keeping track of needs and inputs of friends and strangers. *Personality and Social Psychology Bulletin, 15,* 533–542.

Clark, M.S., Mills, J. and Powell, M. (1986) Keeping track of needs in two types of relationships. *Journal of Personality and Social Psychology, 51,* 333–338.

Clark, M.S, Ouellette, R., Powell, M. and Milberg, S. (1987) Recipient's mood, relationship type, and helping. *Journal of Personality and Social Psychology, 53,* 94–103.

Clark, M.S. and Taraban, C.B. (1991) Reactions to and willingness to express emotion in two types of relationships. *Journal of Experimental Social Psychology, 27,* 324–336.

Clark, M.S. and Waddell, B. (1985) Perceptions of exploitation in communal and exchange relationships. *Journal of Social and Personal Relationships, 2,* 403–418.

Coriell, M. and Cohen, S. (1995) Concordance in the face of a stressful event: When do members of a dyad agree that one person supported the other? *Journal of Personality and Social Psychology, 69,* 289–299.

Goffman, I. (1959) *The Presentation of Self in Everyday Life.* Garden City: Doubleday and Company.

Graham, S.M., Huang, J., Clark, M.S. and Helgeson, V. (2008) The positives of negative emotion: Willingness to express negative emotions promotes relationships. *Personality and Social Psychology Bulletin, 34,* 394–406.

Grote, N.K. and Clark, M.S. (1998) Distributive justice norms and family work: What is perceived as ideal, what is applied, and what predicts perceived fairness? *Social Justice Research, 11,* 243–269.

Grote, N. and Clark, M.S. (2001) Does conflict drive perceptions of unfairness or do perceptions of unfairness drive conflict? *Journal of Personality and Social Psychology, 80,* 281–293; 362 (erratum).

Grote, N.K., Clark, M.S. and Moore, A. (2004) Perceptions of injustice in family work: The role of psychological distress. *Journal of Family Psychology, 18,* 480–492.

Grote, N.K., Naylor, C. and Clark, M.S. (2002) Perceiving the division of family work to be unfair: Do social comparisons, enjoyment, and competence matter? *Journal of Family Psychology, 16,* 510–522.

Jones, D.C. and Vaughan, K. (1990) Close friendships among senior adults. *Psychology and Aging, 3,* 451–457.

Kelley, H.H., Hollmes, J.G., Kerr, N.L., Reis, H.T., Rusbult, C E. and Van Lange, P.A.M. (2003) *An Atlas of Interpersonal Situations.* Cambridge: Cambridge University Press.

Lemay, E.P. and Clark, M.S. (2008) How the head liberates the heart: Projection of communal responsiveness guides relationship promotion. *Journal of Personality and Social Psychology, 94,* 647–671.

Lemay, E.P, Clark, M.S. and Feeney, B. (2007) Projection of responsiveness to needs and the construction of satisfying communal relationships. *Journal of Personality and Social Psychology, 92,* 834–853.

McCall, M. (1995) Orientation, outcome and other-serving attributions. *Basic and Applied Social Psychology, 17,* 49–64.

Medvene, L.I., Volk, F.A. and Meissen, G.J. (1997) Communal orientation and burnout among self-help group leaders. *Journal of Applied Social Psychology, 27,* 262–278.

Messick, D. and Cook, K. (1983) *Equity Theory: Psychological and Sociological Perspectives.* New York: Prager.

Mills, J. and Clark, M.S. (1982) Exchange and communal relationships. In L. Wheeler (ed.), *Review of Personality and Social Psychology,* pp. 121–144. Beverly Hills, CA: Sage.

Mills, J. and Clark, M.S. (1986) Communications that should lead to perceived exploitation in communal and exchange relationships. *Journal of Social and Clinical Psychology, 4,* 225–234.

Mills, J. and Clark, M.S. (1994) Communal and exchange relationships: New research and old controversies. In R. Gilmour and R. Erber (eds), *Theoretical Approaches to Personal Relationships,* pp. 29–42. Hillsdale, NJ: Erlbaum.

Mills, J. and Clark, M.S. (2001) Viewing close romantic relationships as communal relationships: Implications for maintenance and enhancement. In J. Harvey and A. Wenzel (eds), *Close Romantic Relationships: Maintenance and Enhancement,* pp. 13–25. Mahwah, NJ: Lawrence Erlbaum Associates Publishers.

Mills, J., Clark, M.S., Ford, T. and Johnson, M. (2004) Measurement of communal strength. *Personal Relationships, 11,* 213–230.

Monin, J.K., Clark, M.S. and Lemay, E. (2008) Communal responsiveness in relationships with female versus male family members. *Sex Roles, 59,* 176–188.

Murstein, B.I. and Azar, J.A. (1986) The relationship of exchange-orientation to Friendship intensity, roommate compatibility, anxiety, and friendship. *Small Group Research, 17,* 3–17.

Murstein, B.I., Cerreto, M. and MacDonald, M.G. (1977) A theory and investigation of the effect of exchange-orientation on marriage and friendship. *Journal of Marriage and the Family, 39,* 543–548.

Murstein, B.I., Wadlin, R. and Bond, C.F. (1987) The revised exchange-orientation scale. *Small Group Behavior, 18,* 212–223.

Pataki, S., Shapiro, C. and Clark, M.S. (1994) Children's acquisition of appropriate norms for friendships and acquaintances. *Journal of Social and Personal Relationships, 11,* 427–442.

Reis, H., Clark, M.S. and Holmes, J. (2004) Perceived partner responsiveness as an organizing construct in the study of intimacy and closeness. In D. Mashek and A. Aron (eds), *The Handbook of Closeness and Intimacy.* Mahwah, NJ: Lawrence Erlbaum Associates.

Rubin, Z. (1970) Measurement of romantic love. *Journal of Personality and Social Psychology, 16,* 265–273.

Sprecher, S. (1992) How men and women expect to feel and behavior in response to Inequity in close relationships. *Social Psychology Quarterly, 55,* 57–69.

Srivastava, S., Tamir, M., McGonigal, K.M., John, O.P. and Gross, J.J. (2009) The social costs of emotional suppression: A prospective study of the transition to college. *Journal of Personality and Social Psychology, 96,* 883–897.

Thibaut, J.W. and Kelley, H.H. (1959) *The Social Psychology of Groups.* New York: Wiley.

Thompson, L. and Deharpport, T. (1998) Relationships, goal incompatibility, and communal orientation in negotiations. *Basic and Applied Social Psychology, 20,* 33–44.

Thompson, S.C., Medvene, L.J. and Freedman, D. (1995) Caregiving in the close relationships of cardiac patients: Exchange, power, and attributional perspectives on caregiver resentment. *Personal Relationships, 2,* 125–142.

VanYperen, N., Buunk, B.P. and Schaufeli, W.B. (1992) Imbalance, communal orientation, and the burnout syndrome among nurses. *Journal of Applied Social Psychology, 22,* 173–189.

Walster, E., Walster, G.W. and Berscheid, E. (1978) *Equity: Theory and Research.* New York: Allyn & Bacon.

Williamson, G.M. and Clark, M.S. (1989) Providing help and desired relationship type as determinants of changes in moods and self-evaluations. *Journal of Personality and Social Psychology, 56,* 722–734.

Williamson, G.M. and Clark, M.S. (1992) Impact of desired relationship type on affective reactions to choosing and being required to help. *Personality and Social Psychology Bulletin, 18,* 10–18.

Williamson, G.M., Clark, M.S., Pegalis, L. and Behan, A. (1996) Affective consequences of refusing to help in communal and exchange relationships. *Personality and Social Psychology Bulletin, 22,* 34–47.

Williamson, G.M. and Schulz, R. (1990) Communal orientation, quality of prior relationship and distress among caregivers of Alzheimer's patients, *Psychology and Aging, 5,* 502–507.

Williamson, G.M. and Silverman, J.G. (2001) Violence against female partners: Direct and interactive effects of family history, communal orientation and peer-related variables. *Journal of Social and Personal Relationships, 18,* 535–549.

Yoo, S.H., Clark, M.S., Lemay, E.P., Salovey, P. and Monin, J.K. (2011) Responding to partners' expression of anger: The role of communal motivation. *Personality and Social Psychology Bulletin, 37,* 229–241.

39

Interdependence Theory

Paul A. M. Van Lange and Caryl E. Rusbult[1]

ABSTRACT

As one of the classic theories of social psychology, interdependence theory has since its earliest formulation (Thibaut and Kelley, 1959) addressed broad classic themes such as dependence and power, rules and norms, as well as coordination and cooperation. Later, Kelley and Thibaut (1978) provided a more comprehensive statement of the theory which allowed researchers to analyze topics such as attribution and self-presentation, trust and distrust, love and commitment, conflict and communication, and risk and self-regulation. Interdependence theory seeks to capture the essence of social life by advancing a conceptual framework for understanding social interaction. In particular, it identifies the most important characteristics of interpersonal situations via a comprehensive analysis of situation structure, and describes the implications of structure for understanding intrapersonal and interpersonal processes (Kelley et al., 2003). Situation structure matters because it is the interpersonal reality within which motives are activated, toward which cognition is oriented, and around which interaction unfolds. This chapter describes key principles of the theory, and illustrates the utility of an interdependence theoretic analysis via a review of phenomena that we may observe everywhere around us – such as regulatory fit, persistence in the face of dissatisfaction, the basis for understanding generosity, and the ebbs and flows of intergroup relations.

INTRODUCTION

One of the truly classic theories in the social and behavioral sciences is interdependence theory originally developed by John Thibaut and Harold Kelley in 1959. In the 1998 edition of the *Handbook of Social Psychology*, in his chapter on the historic development of social psychology, Ned Jones made the following prediction about interdependence theory: "Given the elegance and profundity of this analysis ... there is good reason that its impact will be durable" (1998: 30). Now, more than a decade later, it is clear that interdependence theory has influenced generations of scientists for more than 50 years. It is especially interesting to see that it has stimulated research in various domains of social psychology, including research focusing on within-person processes such as affect and cognition, as well as between-person processes such as behavior and interaction in dyads and groups. Since Thibaut and Kelley (1959) and Kelley and Thibaut (1978), interdependence theoretical concepts and principles have been used to analyze group dynamics, power and dependence, social comparison, conflict and cooperation, attribution and self-presentation, trust and distrust, emotions, love and commitment, coordination and communication, risk and self-regulation, performance and motivation, social development, and neuroscientific models of social interaction (for recent reviews, see Kelley et al., 2003; Reis, 2008; Rusbult and Van Lange, 2003; Van Lange et al., 2007).

The main focus of interdependence theory is on social interaction, a comprehensive concept that captures the basics of human social life, which helps explain why interdependence theory has been used to understand so many themes for so long. After all, interaction is at the heart of where people live their social lives. Many feelings and emotions are rooted in social interactions, and many beliefs and thoughts are about past or future social interactions. For example, whether a close partner expresses understanding for your bad feelings after you have been mistreated by somebody else is essential for how we feel and think about ourselves, and how we feel and think about the partner – which has strong implications on how we approach a future interaction situation with the partner (and perhaps other people as well). Typically, social interactions exert strong effects in the laboratory, but outside of the lab where interactions often extend over substantial periods of time, social interactions tend to exert even more dramatic effects on us and our relationships. One can indeed go so far as to claim that social interaction colors nearly every phenomenon studied in the social and behavioral sciences, including mental and physical health, personal dispositions, and cognitive and affective experiences (Reis et al., 2000; Rusbult and Van Lange, 2003).

Generally, we argue that the field of psychology would benefit substantially from a social interaction analysis of human psychology, and suggest that interdependence theory can play an important role in this respect. Interdependence theory is one of the few social psychological theories that provide a comprehensive analysis with a strong orientation toward conceptualizing *inter*personal

structure and processes (Kelley and Thibaut, 1978; Kelley et al., 2003; Thibaut and Kelley, 1959). Analogous to contemporary physics – where the relations between particles are as meaningful as the particles themselves – in interdependence theory, *between*-person relations are as meaningful as the individuals themselves (Rusbult and Van Lange, 2003). Indeed, concepts such as coordination, trust, cooperation, communication, commitment can only be understood in terms of social interaction, and many of the needs, motives, and processes that receive considerable attention in contemporary social psychology – such as need-to-belong, uncertainty-management, self-regulation – are often oriented in the service of dealing with the threats and opportunities of social interaction.

In this chapter, we outline the key principles of interdependence theory, provide a historical account of its roots and development over the five decades, and outline some prospects for the future. In doing so, we also provide a narrative of major challenges that the founders of interdependence theory (must have) faced, and those that the next generation, along with Hal Kelley, have faced. It will also become clear that interdependence theory is growing while benefiting from the solid foundation (and more) that the fathers of interdependence theory have provided. We conclude by describing broad implications for various social psychological phenomena and applications in several societal domains.

INTERDEPENDENCE STRUCTURE

Interdependence theory uses two formal tools to represent the outcomes of interaction –matrices and transition lists (Kelley, 1984; Kelley and Thibaut, 1978). The purpose of these formal representations is to precisely specify the character of situation structure – to describe the ways in which people can affect one another's outcomes during the course of interaction. *Interaction* describes two people's (*A* and *B*) needs, thoughts, motives, and behaviors in relation to one another in the context of the specific interdependence situation (*S*) in which their interaction transpires (Kelley et al., 2003). Expressed formally, $I = f(S, A, B)$. To predict what will transpire in an interaction between two persons, we must consider (a) what situation they confront (e.g., are their interests at odds, does one hold greater power?), (b) person *A*'s needs, thoughts, and motives with respect to this interaction (i.e., which traits or values are activated, how does he feel about person *B*?), and (c) person *B*'s needs, thoughts, and motives with respect to this interaction. In the following, we replace persons *A* and *B* with John and Mary, two names that have often been used to illustrate the formal logic of interdependence theory. The model involving the situation and the two persons is sometimes referred to as the SABI model, an acronym for *S*ituation, persons *A* and *B* that collectively account for *I*nteraction (e.g., Holmes, 2002; Kelley et al., 2003; Van Lange et al., 2007; see the principle of structure, and the principle of interaction, Box 39.1).

The precise outcomes of an interaction – the degree to which John and Mary experience it as satisfying – depend on whether the interaction gratifies (versus frustrates) important needs, such as security, belongingness, and exploration (cf. Baumeister and Leary, 1995; Fiske, 2004). Interaction not only yields *concrete outcomes*, or immediate experiences of pleasure versus displeasure, but also *symbolic outcomes*, or experiences that rest on the broader implications of interaction (e.g., Rusbult and Van Lange, 1996). For example, if John and Mary disagree about where to dine yet John suggests Mary's favorite restaurant, Mary not only enjoys the concrete benefits of good food and wine, but also enjoys the symbolic pleasure of perceiving that John is responsive to her needs.

By analyzing how each person's possible behaviors would affect each person's outcomes, we can discern the structure of a situation with respect to degree and type of dependence, examining: (a) *actor control* – the impact of each person's actions on his or her own

outcomes; (b) *partner control* – the impact of each person's actions on the partner's outcomes; and (c) *joint control* – the impact of the partners' joint actions on each person's outcomes. And by examining the across-cell association between outcomes, we can discern *covariation of interests*, or the extent to which the partners' outcomes are correlated. These components define four structural dimensions; two additional dimensions have also been identified more recently (all six are described below; Kelley et al., 2003). Most situations are defined by their properties with respect to two or more dimensions. For example, the *prisoner's dilemma, hero*, and *chicken* situations all involve moderate and mutual dependence along with moderately conflicting interests, but these neighboring situations also differ in the magnitude of actor control, partner control, and joint control, as well as in their implications for interaction.

All conceivable combinations of the six properties define a very large number of patterns. However, we can identify at least 20 to 25 prototypes (Kelley et al., 2003). Everyday situations resemble these abstract patterns, sharing common interpersonal problems and opportunities. For example, the *twists of fate* situation is one wherein each partner, at some point, might unexpectedly find himself or herself in a position of extreme unilateral dependence; this sort of situation is characteristic of health crises and other reversals of fortune. And as another example, the *prisoner's dilemma* is a situation wherein each person's outcomes are more powerfully influenced by the partner's actions than by his or her own actions; this sort of situation is characteristic of interactions involving mutual sacrifice, trading favors, and free-riding. Everyday situations that share the same abstract pattern have parallel implications for motivation, cognition, and interaction.

Importance of interdependence structure

Why should we care about interdependence structure? To begin with, structure in itself

Box 39.1   Overview of basic assumptions of interdependence theory

1 The principle of structure ("the situation")
Understanding interdependence features of a situation are essential to understand psychological process (motives, cognition, and affect), behavior, and social interaction. The features are formalized in a taxonomy of situations, which are degree of dependence, mutuality of dependence, covariation of interest, basis of dependence, temporal structure, and information availability.

2 The principle of transformation (what people make of "the situation")
Interaction situations may be subject to transformations by which individualist consider consequences of own (and other's) behavior in terms of outcomes for self and others and in terms of immediate and future consequences. Transformation is a psychological process that is guided by interaction goals, which may be accompanied and supported by affective, cognitive, and motivational processes.

3 The principle of interaction: SABI: $I = f (A, B, S)$
Interaction is a function of two persons (persons A and B) and (objective properties) of the situation. The situation may activate particular motives, cognitive, and affective experiences in persons A and B, which ultimately through their mutual responses in behavior yield a particular pattern of interaction.

4 The principle of adaptation
Repeated social interaction experiences yield adaptations that are reflected in relatively stable orientations to adopt particular transformations. These adaptations are probabilistic and reflect (a) differences in orientation between people across partners and situations (dispositions), (b) orientations that people adopt to a specific interaction partner (relationship-specific orientations), and (c) rule-based inclinations that are shared by many people within a culture to respond to a particular classes of situation in a specific manner (social norms).

reliably influences behavior. For example, situations with structure resembling the *threat* situation reliably yield demand–withdraw patterns of interaction – demands for change on the part of the lower power actor, met by withdrawal and avoidance on the part of the higher power partner (Holmes and Murray, 1996). And situations with structure resembling the *chicken* situation reliably yield interaction centering on establishing dominance and sustaining one's reputation (Nisbett and Cohen, 1996). In short, the structure of situations often directly shapes behavior above and beyond the specific goals and motives of interacting individuals.

Moreover, specific structural patterns present specific sorts of problems and opportunities, and therefore (a) logically imply the relevance of specific goals and motives, and (b) permit the expression of those goals and motives. The term *affordance* nicely describes what a situation makes possible or may activate (see Table 39.1, which provides an overview

of possible affordances). For example, situations with uncertain information afford misunderstanding, and invite reliance on generalized schemas regarding partners and situations; generalized schemas carry less weight when information is more complete. In short, situation structure matters because it is the interpersonal reality within which motives are activated, toward which cognition is oriented, and around which interaction unfolds.

Dimensions of interdependence structure

Level of dependence describes the degree to which an actor relies on an interaction partner, in that his or her outcomes are influenced by the partner's actions. If Mary can obtain good outcomes irrespective of John's actions (high actor control), she is independent; she is dependent to the extent that John can (a) unilaterally determine her pleasure versus

Table 39.1   The six dimensions of situational structure and their affordances (after Holmes, 2002; and Kelley et al., 2003)

Situation Dimension	Relevant Motives
1 Level of dependence	Comfort versus discomfort with dependence; comfort versus discomfort with independence
2 Mutuality of dependence	Comfort versus discomfort with vulnerability (as dependent)
	Comfort versus discomfort with responsibility (as power holder)
3 Basis of dependence	Dominance (leading) versus submissiveness (following)
	Assertiveness versus passivity
4 Covariation of interests	Prosocial versus self-interested motives (rules for self)
	Trust versus distrust of partner motives (expectations about others)
5 Temporal structure	Dependability versus unreliability
	Loyalty versus disloyalty
6 Information availability	Openness versus need for certainty
	Optimism versus pessimism

displeasure (partner control) or (b) in combination with Mary's actions determine her pleasure versus displeasure (joint control). Increasing dependence tends to cause increased attention to situations and partners, more careful and differentiated cognitive activity, and perseverance in interaction (e.g., Fiske, 1993; Rusbult, 1983). As noted in Table 39.1, dependence affords thoughts and motives centering on comfort versus discomfort with dependence and independence. For example, high dependence situations will activate Mary's trait-based reluctance to rely on others, her discomfort with dependence will strongly shape her behavior, and her discomfort will be particularly evident to others; in low dependence situations, this trait will be less visible and less relevant for her behavior.

Mutuality of dependence describes whether two people are equally dependent upon each other. Nonmutual dependence entails differential power – when Mary is more dependent, John holds greater power. The less dependent partner tends to exert greater control over decisions and resources, whereas the more dependent partner carries the greater burden of interaction costs (sacrifice, accommodation) and is more vulnerable to possible abandonment; threats and coercion are possible (e.g., Attridge et al., 1995; Murray et al., 2006). Interactions with mutual dependence tend to feel "safer" and are more stable and affectively serene (less anxiety, guilt). Situations with nonmutual dependence afford the expression of comfort versus discomfort with another having control over your outcomes (e.g., feelings of vulnerability, for the dependent partner) along with comfort versus discomfort with you having control over other's outcomes (e.g., feelings of responsibility, for the powerful partner; see Table 39.1). For example, unilateral dependence will activate John's insecurity, and his insecurity will powerfully shape his behavior and be highly visible to others; in mutual dependence situations his insecurity will be less visible and less relevant to predicting his behavior.

Basis of dependence describes precisely how partners influence one another's outcomes – the relative importance of partner versus joint control as source of dependence. With partner control, the actor's outcomes rest in the partner's hands, so interaction often involves promises or threats as well as the activation of morality norms ("This is how decent people behave"); common interaction patterns may include unilateral action (when partner control is nonmutual) or tit-for-tat or turn-taking (when partner control is mutual; for example, Clark et al., 1998; Fiske, 1992). In contrast, joint control entails contingency-based coordination of action, such that ability-relevant traits become more important, including intelligence, initiative-taking, and strategic skills; rules of conventional behavior carry more sway than morality norms ("This is the normal way to behave"; for example, Finkel et al., 2006; Turiel, 1983). Basis of dependence affords the expression of dominance versus submissiveness and assertiveness versus passivity, as well as skill such as social intelligence (see Table 39.1).

Covariation of interests describes whether partners' outcomes correspond versus conflict – whether partners' joint activities yield similarly gratifying outcomes for John and Mary. Covariation ranges from perfectly corresponding patterns through mixed motive patterns to perfectly conflicting patterns (zero-sum). Given corresponding interests, interaction is easy – John and Mary simply pursue their own interests, simultaneously producing good outcomes for the other. In contrast, situations with conflicting interests tend to generate negative cognition and emotion (greed, fear) and yield more active and differentiated information-seeking and self-presentation ("Can Mary be trusted?"; for example, Surra and Longstreth, 1990; Van Lange et al., 1997). Situations with conflicting interests afford the expression of cooperation versus competition and trust versus mistrust (see Table 39.1) – in such situations, John may demonstrate his prosocial motives as well as his trust in Mary.

Temporal structure is a fifth important structural dimension – one that captures dynamic and sequential processes. As a result of interaction, some future behaviors, outcomes, or situations may be made available and others may be eliminated. John and Mary may be passively moved from one situation to another or they may be active agents in seeking such movement. *Extended situations* involve a series of steps prior to reaching a goal (e.g., investments leading to a desirable outcome). *Situation selection* describes movement from one situation to another, bringing partners to a situation that differs in terms of behavioral options or outcomes – for example, Mary may seek situations entailing lesser interdependence, or

John may confront the juncture between a present relationship and an alternative relationship by derogating tempting alternatives (e.g., Collins and Feeney, 2004; Miller, 1997). Temporally extended situations afford the expression of self-control, delay of gratification, and the inclination to "stick with it" – dependability versus unreliability, as well as loyalty versus disloyalty (e.g., Mischel, Chapter 26, this volume) (see Table 39.1).

Information availability is the final structural dimension: Do John and Mary possess certain versus uncertain information about: (a) the impact of each person's actions on each person's outcomes; (b) the goals and motives guiding each person's actions; and (c) the opportunities that will be made available versus eliminated as a consequence of their actions? Certain information is critical in novel or risky situations and in interactions with unfamiliar partners. Accordingly, partners engage in a good deal of information exchange during the course of interaction, engaging in attributional activity to understand one another and the situation (e.g., Collins and Miller, 1994). People may also use representations of prior interaction partners to "fill in the informational gaps" in interaction with new partners, or may develop frozen expectations that reliably color their perceptions of situations and partners (e.g., Andersen and Chen, 2002; Holmes, 2002, 2004). For example, people may generally rely on the belief that the most people are (rationally) self-interested, which in turn may help them to fill in the blanks when faced with incomplete information about another person's actions (Vuolevi and Van Lange, 2010). As another example, people with avoidant attachment may perceive a wide range of situations as risky, anticipate that partners are likely to be unresponsive, and readily forecast problematic interactions. Thus, uncertain information affords, among other things, the expression of openness versus the need for certainty, as well as optimism versus pessimism (see Table 39.1).

INTERDEPENDENCE PROCESSES

Recall that interaction ($I = f [S, A, B]$) is shaped not only by interdependence structure (S), but also by partners' needs, thoughts, and motives in relation to one another (A and B) in the context of the situation in which their interaction unfolds (SABI, see Principle of Interaction, Box 39.1). Thus, we must add to our structural analysis a complementary analysis that describes how John and Mary react to the situations they encounter. How do they psychologically transform specific situations, responding on the basis of considerations other than tangible self-interest? What role do mental events and habits play in shaping this process, and how do partners seek to understand and predict one another? And how do people develop relatively stable tendencies to react to specific situations in specific ways?

Transformation process

To describe how situation structure affects motivation, interdependence theory distinguishes between: (a) the *given situation* – preferences based on self-interest (the "virtual structure" of a situation); and (b) the effective situation – preferences based on broader considerations, including concern with the partner's interests, long-term goals, or strategic considerations (Kelley and Thibaut, 1978; Van Lange and Joireman, 2008). Psychological *transformation* describes the shift in motivation from given to effective preferences. People typically behave on the basis of transformed preferences – considerations other than immediate self-interest guide our actions. But people sometimes behave on the basis of given preferences; this is likely in simple situations for which no broader considerations are relevant, when people lack the inclination or wherewithal to take broader considerations into account, and in situations involving time pressure or constrained cognitive capacity.

Transformations are often conceptualized decision rules that a person (often implicitly) adopts during interaction (Kelley et al., 2003; Murray and Holmes, 2009; Van Lange et al., 2007, see the principle of transformation, Box 39.1). People may follow rules that involve sequential or temporal considerations, such as waiting to see how the partner behaves or adopting strategies such as tit-for-tat or turn-taking. Other rules reflect differential concern for one's own and a partner's outcomes, including altruism, or maximizing the partner's outcomes; cooperation, or maximizing combined outcomes; competition, or maximizing the relative difference between one's own and the partner's outcomes; and individualism, or maximizing one's own outcomes irrespective of the partner's outcomes.

Transformation is particularly visible when a given situation structure dictates one type of behavior yet personal traits or values dictate another type of behavior. When people act on the basis of transformed preferences, we are able to discern their personal traits and motives. For example, when Mary helps John with yard work rather than going out with her friends, she communicates concern for his welfare. The transformation process is thus the point at which the "rubber meets the road," or the point at which *intra*personal processes – cognition, affect, and motivation – operate on specific situations in such a manner as to reveal the unique self.

Cognition, affect, and habit

Human intelligence is interpersonal – cognitively and affectively, we are well prepared to construe the world in terms of interdependence (Rusbult and Van Lange, 2003). Mental events are geared toward discerning what a situation is "about," evaluating that structure in terms of one's own needs and motives, perceiving the partner's needs and predicting his or her motives, and forecasting implications for future interactions (e.g., Kelley, 1984). Situation structure partially shapes cognition and affect. For example, the prisoner's dilemma entails a choice between benefiting the partner at low cost to the self versus benefiting the self at substantial cost to the partner. The characteristic blend of fear and greed that is afforded by this situation serves as a rather automatic indicator of the essential opportunities and constraints of this type of situation.

The transformation process is often driven by the cognition and affect that a situation affords. For example, Mary is likely to exhibit self-centered or antisocial transformation when she experiences greedy thoughts and desires ("It'd be nice to take a free ride") or feels fearful about John's motives ("Will he exploit me?"). Cognition and emotion are also shaped by distal causes – by the values, goals, and dispositions that are afforded by the situation. For example, Mary's reaction to situations with conflicting interests will be colored by the value she places on fairness, loyalty, or communal norms (versus greed), as well as by whether she trusts John (or alternatively, fears him). Thus, the mental events that underlie transformation are functionally adapted to situation structure, and take forms that are relevant to that structure.

At the same time, the transformation process does not necessarily rest on extensive mental activity. As a consequence of adaptation to repeatedly encountered patterns, people develop habitual tendencies to react to specific situations in specific ways, such that transformation often transpires with little or no conscious thought (e.g., Rusbult and Van Lange, 1996). For example, following repeated interaction in situations with prisoner's dilemma structure, John and Mary may automatically exhibit mutual cooperation, with little or no cognition or affect. Mediation by mental events is more probable in novel situations with unknown implications, in risky situations with the potential for harm, and in interactions with unfamiliar partners.

Communication, attribution, and self-presentation

During the course of interaction, partners convey their goals, values, and dispositions using both direct and indirect means.

Communication entails self-presentation on the part of one person and attribution on the part of the other. As noted earlier, the material for self-presentation and attribution resides in the disparity between the given and effective situations, in that deviations from self-interested behavior reveal an actor's goals and motives (e.g., Rusbult and Van Lange, 2003). Thus, the ability to communicate self-relevant information is limited by interdependence structure – that is, specific situations afford the display of specific motives. For example, it is difficult for people to convey trustworthiness (or to discern it) in situations with correspondent interests; in such situations, "trustworthy" behavior aligns with "self-interested" behavior.

People engage in *attributional activity* to understand the implications of a partner's actions, seeking to predict future behavior and to explain prior behavior in terms of situation structure versus underlying dispositions. Expectations are not particularly accurate in interactions with new partners, in that they must be based on probabilistic assumptions about how the average person would react in a given situation; in longer-term relationships, expectations can also be based on knowledge of how a partner has behaved across a variety of situations. And *self-presentation* describes people's attempts to communicate their motives and dispositions to one another. Of course, self-presentation may sometimes be geared toward concealing one's true preferences and motives. Moreover, given that people do not always hold complete information about their partners' given outcomes, they may sometimes mistakenly assume that a partner's behavior reflects situation structure rather than psychological transformation. For example, Mary's loyalty or sacrifice may not be visible if John fails to recognize the costs she incurred.

Adaptation

When people initially encounter specific situations, the problems and opportunities inherent in the situation will often be unclear. In such novel situations, Mary may systematically analyze the situation and actively reach a decision about how to behave, or she may simply react on the basis of impulse. Either way, experience is acquired. If her choice yields good outcomes, she will react similarly to future situations with parallel structure; if her choice yields poor outcomes, she will modify her behavior in future situations with parallel structure. *Adaptation* describes the process by which repeated experience in situations with similar structure gives rise to habitual response tendencies that on average yield good outcomes. Adaptations may be embodied in interpersonal dispositions, relationship-specific motives, or social norms (Rusbult and Van Lange, 1996, see the principle of adaptation, Box 39.1).

Interpersonal dispositions are actor-specific inclinations to respond to particular classes of situation in a specific manner across diverse partners (Kelley, 1983). Dispositions emerge because over the course of development, different people experience different histories with different partners, confronting different sorts of interaction opportunities and problems. As a result of adaptation, John and Mary acquire dispositional tendencies to perceive situations and partners in specific ways, and specific sorts of transformations come to guide their behavior. Thus, the "self" is the sum of one's adaptations to previous situations and partners (such adaptations are determined also by needs and motives that are biologically based). For example, if John's mother employed her power in a benevolent manner, gratifying his childhood needs and serving as a secure base from which he could explore, John will have developed trusting and secure expectations about dependence (for a review, see Fraley and Shaver, 2000).

Relationship-specific motives are inclinations to respond to particular classes of situation in a specific manner with a specific partner (Rusbult and Van Lange, 2003). For example, commitment emerges as a result of dependence on a partner, and is strengthened by high satisfaction (John gratifies Mary's most important needs), poor alternatives (Mary's needs could not be gratified independent of her relationship), and high investments (important resources are bound to her relationship). Commitment colors emotional reactions to interaction (feeling affection rather than anger) and gives rise to habits of thought that support sustained involvement (use of plural pronouns; for example, Agnew et al., 1998). In turn, benevolent thoughts encourage prosocial transformation. For example, strong commitment promotes prosocial acts such as sacrifice, accommodation, and forgiveness (e.g., Finkel et al., 2002; Rusbult et al., 1991; Van Lange et al., 1997).

Social norms are rule-based, socially transmitted inclinations to respond to particular classes of situation in a specific manner (Thibaut and Kelley, 1959). For example, most societies develop rules regarding acceptable behavior in specific types of situation; rules of civility and etiquette regulate behavior in such a manner as to yield harmonious interaction. Partners frequently follow agreed-upon rules regarding resource allocation, such as equity, equality, or need (Deutsch, 1975). Such rules may govern a wide range of interactions or may be relationship-specific (e.g., communal norms in close relationships; Clark et al., 1998; Fiske, 1992). Norms not only govern behavior, but also shape cognitive experiences. For example, in interactions guided by communal norms, partners neither monitor nor encode the extent of each person's (short-term) contributions to the other's welfare.

DEVELOPMENT OF INTERDEPENDENCE THEORY: AN INTERPERSONAL ACCOUNT

As noted earlier, the history of interdependence theory is strongly shaped by the long-standing collaboration and friendship between Harold Kelley and John Thibaut. A sketchy summary of the history of interdependence

Table 39.2   Brief historical overview of interdependence theory

1959	Thibaut, J.W. and Kelley, H.H. (1959) *The Social Psychology of Groups.* New York: Wiley	Provides social exchange analysis of interactions and relationships individuals in dyads and small groups.
		Uses games as a conceptual tool and focuses on analysis of dependence, power, rewards, costs, needs, and outcomes in exchange relations.
		Introduces new concepts such as comparison level and comparison level of alternatives (CL and CL-alt) to understand relationship satisfaction and stability.
1978	Kelley, H.H., and Thibaut, J.W. (1978) *Interpersonal Relations: A Theory of Interdependence.* New York: Wiley.	Provides comprehensive analysis of interaction situations in terms of four dimensions, labeled as degree of dependence, mutuality of dependence, correspondence of outcomes, and basis of dependence.
		Introduces transformation from given to effective matrix, thereby formalizing broader interaction goals than immediate self-interest.
		Adopts a functional analysis of transformations, thereby recognizing social learning of transformation rules, and its functional value for particular domains of situation.
2003	Kelley, H.H. et al. (2003) *An Atlas of Interpersonal Situations.* New York: Cambridge University Press	Provides an overview of 21 basic interaction situations, which are analyzed in terms of interdependence features, the psychological processes that they afford, and the interaction processes that they might evoke.
		Extends the taxonomy of situations by two additional dimensions to yield six dimensions, including (a) degree of dependence, (b) mutuality of dependence, (c) basis of dependence, (d) covariation of interest (was formerly referred to as correspondence of outcomes), (e) temporal structure, and (f) information availability.
	At present and in the future:	
		Integrates interdependence theory with principles of evolutionary theory to understand adaptation as a function of the situational structure.
		Extends interdependence theory to neuroscientific models of the social mind.
		Re-extends interdependence theory to group processes and relationships between groups.

theory is provided in Table 39.2. Our narrative is written from the perspective of Harold Kelley, as the authors of this chapter interacted much more with "Hal" (1921–2003) than with John Thibaut (1917–1986), which is why we refer to the former as Hal and the latter as John Thibaut. The collaboration between Thibaut and Kelley started when Hal was invited to write a chapter on "group problem solving" for the *Handbook of Social Psychology*. Hal invited John Thibaut, whom he knew well from the Research Center for Group Dynamics at MIT, to collaborate on writing this chapter. This decision, so he described informally, was one of the very best in his academic career. There was an interpersonal fit from the very beginning, and they wrote a beautiful chapter, inspired by some of the notions put forward by Kurt Lewin, in which they analyzed the interdependence between individuals in their pursuit of group goals. The major themes – interdependence and social interaction – were discussed in a manner that was predictive of their later collaboration, one that lasted for three decades until the death of John Thibaut in 1986. They developed a collaboration that was characterized by many travels between Malibu and Chapel Hill, by deep friendship and tremendous mutual respect, by equality (they were both follower and leader) as well as by similarity *and* complementarity. To magnify the latter (for illustration purposes), the natural distribution of tasks was that Hal focused more strongly on analysis of situations, while John Thibaut focused more strongly on connections with the various literatures inside and outside of psychology. They were also complementary in that Hal's interests focused more on the dyad (later relationships) whereas John's interests' focused more on the (small) group.

They then wrote a book (Thibaut and Kelley, 1959) that was inspired by social exchange theory (in particular, Homans, 1950) and by game theory and decision theory (in particular, a highly influential book by Luce and Raiffa, 1957). Essentially, they analyzed social interactions in dyads and small groups in terms of patterns of social exchange, thereby using games as the conceptual tool – to be able to delineate the patterns of interdependence, such as rewards and costs, and power and dependence. They also introduced new concepts such as comparison level and comparison level for alternatives (CL and CL-alt) to provide a strong conceptual analysis for the differences between satisfaction and dependence. This book was a great success and a must-read for any social psychologist at that (or any) time (see Jones, 1998).

After nearly two decades, Kelley and Thibaut (1978) modestly expressed the belief that their new analysis – an interdependence analysis – might well reach the standards of a theory. While the origins were captured in the 1959 book, interdependence theory was now formally born (Hal and John were careful scientists and they would reserve the label theory only for those kinds of conceptual analysis that would pass stringent tests of scientific rigor – probably defined by Hal and John Thibaut in terms of clear logic and wide

breadth of relevance). In that book, they presented interdependence theory, and it became immediately clear that many years were devoted to very basic theoretical issues.

One decision they faced was whether behavior was primarily based on the given matrix (i.e., on the basis of immediate self-interest) or whether the theory should be extended to include broader considerations. Informed by research during the sixties and seventies, they agreed on the latter and provided a logical framework for a number of fundamental transformations, which they labeled as MaxJoint (enhancement of joint outcomes), MinDiff (minimization of absolute differences in outcomes for self and others), MaxRel (maximization of relative advantage over other's outcomes), and the like. These transformations were also inspired by the work of Messick and McClintock, and many others around the globe, who had already provided empirical evidence for some transformations in their research using experimental games as empirical tools (e.g., Messick and McClintock, 1968). Hal and John also outlined other types of transformation, which emphasize the idea that people respond to contingencies and expected implications of present behavior for the future. Another key difference with the earlier book was that it emphasized the functional value of various transformations. In short, this book contributes logic to the question, What do "people make of situations?" (see also Kelley et al., 2003).

Thus, the classic Kelley and Thibaut interdependence analysis became a comprehensive theory encompassing (a) a formal analysis of the "objective" properties of a situation with the help of a taxonomy of situations, (b) a conceptualization of psychological process in terms of transformations, including motives, cognition, and affect (what do people make of the situation?), and (c) behavior and social interaction – which resulted from both the objective properties of the situation and what both persons made of it. Moreover, they emphasized (d) adaptation and learning, as longer-term orientations that may grow out of experience. Inspired by the work of Messick and McClintock (1968), and their own (Kelley and Stahelski, 1970), they also suggested that people might differ in their "transformational tendencies." These adaptations were later conceptualized in terms of dispositions, relationship-specific motives, and social norms (see Rusbult and Van Lange, 1996).

Over time, numerous people were inspired by the "logic" of interdependence theory – its assumptions, the reasoning, and last but not least, its focus. Logic is one thing, but it appeared to have considerable breadth. And so researchers in areas as diverse as altruism, attribution, coordination, conflict, cooperation, competition, delay of gratification, exchange, investments, fairness, justice, love, power, prosocial behavior, trust, sacrifice, self-presentation, stereotyping, hostility, and aggression in the context of dyads, ongoing relationships (close or not), and groups (small and larger, ongoing or not) either found it exceptionally useful or were inspired by it. Also, researchers studying environmental issues, organizational issues, and political issues have fruitfully used principles from interdependence theory (for a comprehensive review, see Rusbult and Van Lange, 1996, 2003; Van Lange and Joireman, 2008). The list of authors is too long to summarize here, but we wish to note that if we were to list them, it would become clear that interdependence theory had a strong influence in various countries even in the pre-Internet era (most notably, Austria, Australia, Belgium, Canada, France, Germany, Italy, Japan, the Netherlands, New Zealand, Poland, Sweden, the United Kingdom, and the US), and that influence spanned successive generations, so that it is fair to say that it has strong appeal to young-, mid-, and late-career scientists.

To illustrate from the experience of the Atlas project group, John Holmes had worked with John Thibaut and used principles of interdependence theory in his work on trust and conflict (as well as on motivation-management in relationships; Holmes and Rempel, 1989; Murray and Holmes, 2009).

Caryl Rusbult developed the investment model of commitment processes, a framework that was deeply rooted in interdependence theoretic principles, to understand persistence and commitment processes in ongoing relationships (see Rusbult and Van Lange, 2003; Rusbult et al., 2006). Paul Van Lange was intrigued by Kelley and Thibaut's taxonomy of situations ("structure") and transformations (what "persons" make of situations) and found it very useful for his research on social value orientation as well as for understanding the functionality of generosity in social dilemmas (see Van Lange et al., 1997, 2002). Norbert Kerr found an interdependence perspective useful for understanding group-related issues as diverse as motivation and performance, cooperation, and free-riding in social dilemmas (see Baron and Kerr, 2003; Kerr and Tindale, 2004). It was Harry Reis who not only had used interdependence theory in his research on intimacy and responsiveness in relationships (e.g., Reis, 2008; Reis et al., 2000), but also had the vision and skills in getting this group of people together at a joint meeting of the Society of Experimental Social Psychology (SESP) and the European Association of Experimental Social Psychology (EAESP) in Washington in 1995. This resulted in a six-year collaboration and eventually the publication of the *Atlas of Interpersonal Situations* (Kelley et al., 2003).

The group came together at various meetings, often right before or after a major social psychological conference in Europe or the US. There were two meetings that were independent of a conference. First, in 1996, during Caryl's sabbatical at the VU University in Amsterdam, we held a series of eight-hour (nearly nonstop) daily sessions for about seven days. Hal, Caryl Rusbult, and Paul Van Lange discussed aspects of what was later called "temporal structure" and drafted an outline for chapters for the book. But fortunately, those not present later corrected a tendency to embrace complexity rather than parsimony. Second, the other series of meetings was held in 2000 in Boca Raton, Florida, generously sponsored by Bibb Latané. At this series of meetings, we discussed the various drafts of the chapters and reached final consensus over the situations that should – or should not – be included in the book.

The *Atlas* by Kelley et al. (2003) extended Kelley and Thibaut (1978) in very important ways, but perhaps most notably by analyzing 21 situations and by adding two dimensions to the four dimensions of interdependence that Kelley and Thibaut already had previously identified. The added dimensions were (a) temporal structure and (b) information availability. The first copy of the book was published ahead of schedule (thanks to Harry Reis and our publisher, Cambridge University Press) and was given to Hal Kelley about a week or less before he died. Caryl, John, Norb, and Paul saw the first copy at the Society for Personality and Social Psychology (SPSP) meeting in Los Angeles, in February 2003, shortly before a memorial service for Hal at UCLA. Also, Hal suggested earlier that we dedicate the book to the memory of John Thibaut, and that suggestion received strong support, in synchrony, from us all.

As one of us (PvL) edits this chapter, I might be indulged in saying a bit more about the contributions to the development of interdependence theory of my late colleague, collaborator, and dear friend, Caryl Rusbult. Needless to say, Caryl Rusbult was a major contributor to the *Atlas* throughout all six years. As a UCLA undergraduate (where Hal was professor) and UNC (Chapel Hill) graduate student (where John Thibaut was professor) and later faculty member, she developed a strong commitment to interdependence theory. It was only two days before she died (far too young at the age of 57 in January 2010) that she and I re-evaluated the various projects we had worked on together. We decided that the comprehensive review (Rusbult and Van Lange, 1996) and the *Atlas* joint venture (Kelley et al., 2003) were among the highlights of our long-standing collaboration. We truly enjoyed talking about interdependence theory – its logic, the ways in which it needs to be communicated and

extended, and its implications for basic questions about relationship processes (Caryl's passion) and human cooperation (Paul's focus). We also frequently discussed "applications" of interdependence theory by examining why and when an interdependence-theoretical analysis mattered. This is the question that we address next.

APPLICATIONS OF INTERDEPENDENCE THEORY

To comprehend the utility of interdependence concepts it is important to "see them in action" – to perceive the theoretical, empirical, and societal benefits of these concepts in advancing our understanding of specific psychological phenomena. In particular, we suggest that interdependence theory is especially useful for understanding relationship persistence and stability, interpersonal generosity, as well as other broad topics – such as goal pursuits in relationships, and understanding of group processes.

Understanding goal pursuits

Our first example illustrates a simple point: *interdependence matters*. In fact, interdependence shapes many psychological processes that might seem to be thoroughly actor-based and *intra*personal, such as individual goal pursuits. Goals are end states that give direction to behavior, either as overarching life plans or as simple everyday endeavors. Traditional models of goal pursuit have employed *intra*personal explanations, examining individual-level processes such as goal-plan directed behavior, self-regulation, or goal-behavior disparities (e.g., Carver and Scheier, 1998; Mischel, Chapter 26, this volume). The success of goal pursuit has been argued to rest on actor-level variables such as goals, traits, skills, and motivation. A notable approach in this tradition is regulatory focus and regulatory fit theories which suggest that people are more likely to achieve goals when they approach them in a manner that fits their regulatory orientation – when they approach promotion-ideal self-goals of accomplishment in an eager manner and approach prevention-ought self-goals of security in a vigilant manner (Higgins, 1997, 2000, 2011).

An interdependence analysis shares some of these assumptions, but extends them in interesting directions. Indeed, research using diverse empirical techniques has revealed that in ongoing relationships, people enjoy greater movement toward their ideal selves not only when (a) they, themselves, possess strong promotion orientation (actor control), but also when (b) their partners possess strong promotion orientation (partner control) (parallel negative associations are evident for prevention orientation; Righetti and Rusbult, 2007). Indeed, partners with a strong promotion orientation support the actor's movement toward the ideal self because such partners more reliably elicit key components of the actor's ideal-related eagerness. Some empirical support was also obtained for a third form of fit: Above and beyond the above-noted actor and partner effects, there is some evidence for a joint control effect, such that (c) actor–partner commonality in regulatory orientation also influences each person's movement toward the ideal self. Thus, the fact that goal pursuit and attainment are powerfully and reliably influenced by interdependence processes suggests that there is much to recommend in an interdependence theoretic analysis. Interdependence matters.

Understanding persistence

Our second example illustrates the fact that *interdependence structure* matters. Indeed, structure can often help explain otherwise inexplicable phenomena, such as why attitudes do not always satisfactorily predict behavior, or why people sometimes persist in situations that are not particularly satisfying. Traditionally, persistence has been explained by reference to positive affect: people persevere

in specific endeavors because they have positive explicit or implicit attitudes about the endeavor; people persevere in specific jobs or relationships because they feel satisfied with them (e.g., Ajzen, 1991; Greenwald et al., 1998). The affect construct has been operationally defined in terms of satisfaction level, positive attitudes, liking, or attraction.

An important challenge to this "feel good" model of persistence ("So long as it feels good, I'll stick with it") is to be found in situations wherein people persevere despite the existence of negative affect. Clearly, people sometimes persevere even though they hold negative attitudes about behavior-relevant attitude objects; people sometimes stick with jobs or marriages despite feelings of dissatisfaction. Persistence in an abusive relationship is a particularly telling illustration: surely people do not persist because they are delighted with such relationships. Some authors have sought to account for such inexplicable persistence in terms of trait-based explanations – by reference to a victim's low self-esteem or learned helplessness (e.g., Aguilar and Nightingale, 1994; Walker, 2000). Inexplicable persistence is thus assumed to be an actor effect – people persevere because of something peculiar or unhealthy about themselves.

In contrast, an interdependence analysis explains persistence more broadly, by reference to the nature of an actor's dependence. To the extent that people are more dependent upon their jobs or relationships, they are more likely to persist in them; the greater their dependence upon a distal goal, the more likely they are to persist in pursuit of the goal. In relationships, dependence is strengthened by increasing satisfaction (are important needs gratified?), declining alternatives (could important needs be gratified elsewhere?), and increasing investments (are important resources linked to the line of action?; see Rusbult et al., 2006). For example, Mary may persevere in an abusive relationship not necessarily because she has low self-esteem or has acquired a pattern of learned helplessness, but rather, for reasons resting on structural dependence – because she is heavily invested in remaining with her partner (e.g., she is married to John or has young children with him) or has poor alternatives (e.g., she has no driver's license or possesses poor employment opportunities; Rusbult and Martz, 1995).

Why should scientists favor an interdependence-based analysis of persistence? For one thing, positive affect is not particularly reliable – affect ebbs and flows even in the most satisfying jobs and relationships, such that "feeling good" is not sufficient to sustain long-term persistence. In addition, actor-based explanations would appear to be limited in light of clear evidence for dependence-based causes of persistence (e.g., Mary may have invested too much to quit). Moreover, interdependence-based explanations imply unique intervention strategies. For example, if we seek to enhance Mary's freedom to persist versus cease involvement with John, an actor-based explanation might favor psychotherapy geared toward raising self-esteem or eliminating learned helplessness. In contrast, an interdependence-based explanation might inspire interventions designed to reduce (unilateral) dependence – for example, improving the quality of Mary's economic alternatives via driving lessons or job training. Also, in therapy, the focus may not only be on some fluctuation in satisfaction as such, but on the interpersonal causes that might account for it in combination with implications for the future of the relationships. This interdependence-based analysis differs from actor-based approaches, in that they emphasize the actor-and-partner interactions, and what holds them together in the future. For example, sometimes a change (a move) that they initiate and accomplish together may bring about closeness and trust through enhanced interdependence.

Understanding interpersonal generosity

Our third example illustrates how *adaptations* might be influenced by *interdependence structure*. That is, the precise properties of interdependence structure are essential to the basic question of under what circumstances generosity might be functional. Our example concerns the best-known and most thoroughly investigated interdependence situation: the prisoner's dilemma. Traditional analyses of situations with this structure have revealed that people enjoy superior outcomes over the course of long-term interaction when they behave on the basis of *quid pro quo*, or tit-for-tat (Axelrod, 1984; Pruitt, 1998): if an interaction partner cooperates, you should likewise cooperate; if a partner competes, you should compete.

But how effective is tit-for-tat under conditions of suboptimal information availability – for example, when people are aware of how a partner's behavior affects their own outcomes, but are not aware of situational constraints that may have shaped the partner's actions? An interdependence analysis suggests that misunderstanding is often rooted in *noise*, or discrepancies between intended outcomes and actual outcomes for a partner that result from unintended errors (Kollock, 1993). For example, when John fails to receive a response to an email message that he sent to Mary, it may be because of a network breakdown in Mary's workplace rather than to Mary's disregard for his well-being. Noise is ubiquitous in everyday interaction, in that the external world is not error-free (e.g., networks sometimes crash) and people cannot lead error-free lives (e.g., Mary may accidentally delete John's email note in her daily spam purge).

Given that tit-for-tat entails reciprocating a partner's *actual* behavior – and not the partner's *intended* behavior – responding in kind serves to reinforce and exacerbate "accidents." If the accident involves unintended good outcomes, the consequences may be positive. But if the accident entails unintended negative outcomes, the consequences may be more serious. For example, when Mary's actions cause John to suffer poor outcomes, he may respond with tit-for-tat, enacting a behavior that will cause her poor outcomes. In turn – and despite the fact that she did not initially intend to harm John – Mary will react to John's negative behavior with tit-for-tat, causing him to suffer reciprocal poor outcomes. John and Mary will enter into a pattern of negative reciprocity: they can become trapped in an extended echo effect from which they cannot readily exit – an echo effect that tit-for-tat simply reinforces.

Indeed, research reveals that negative noise exerts detrimental effects when people follow a strict reciprocity rule – partners form more negative impressions of one another and both people suffer poorer outcomes (Van Lange et al., 2002). In contrast, a more generous, tit-for-tat-plus-one strategy (giving the partner a bit more than one received from the partner) yields better outcomes – noise does not negatively affect partners' impressions of one another or the outcomes each receives over the course of interaction. Indeed, in the presence of negative noise, a generous strategy yields better outcomes for both people than does tit-for-tat (for more extended evidence, see Klapwijk and Van Lange, 2009). Such findings are reminiscent of the literature regarding interaction in close relationships, where partners have been shown to enjoy better outcomes in conflictual interactions when one or both partners accommodate or forgive (e.g., Karremans and Van Lange, 2008; Rusbult et al., 1991, see also Simpson, 2007).

The societal implications of this interdependence analysis are quite powerful, as they suggest relatively concrete advice for people entering new situations at school, in organizations, and other situations where people interact in dyads and small groups. Under circumstances of imperfect information (which most situations are like) it helps to give people the benefit of the doubt, to reserve judgment, and to add a little generosity to our tendencies to interaction in a tit-for-tat manner. The findings may also be especially relevant to the communication through email, Internet, and other electronic means, as these devices tend to be quite "noisy." But perhaps the use of "smileys" and other devices might just serve the very function

to communicate trust and generosity to cope with noise.

Understanding intergroup relations

Most group phenomena are more complex – often too complex for a comprehensive analysis, which is probably why Thibaut and Kelley often did not go beyond the triad. Nevertheless, the logic provided by interdependence theory has also considerable potential in analyzing intergroup relations.

One important issue is the analysis of intergroup relations. Sometimes groups face high correspondence of outcomes, in that they both (or all) are pursuing the same goal and need each other in that pursuit. For example, neighboring countries help each other in their pursuit of controlling the use of hard drugs. Under such circumstances, groups may actually develop fairly congenial relationships, especially when they hold similar views about the policy for doing so. Sometimes groups face moderate correspondence of outcomes, in the pursuit of some collective goal that is quite costly to each group. For example, countries want to control global warming, but they differ in their interest or views as to how much to contribute. Under such circumstances, groups are faced with social dilemmas (in the intergroup context, a conflict between ingroup interest and common, superordinate interests), and they often exhibit considerably less cooperation than individuals in similar situations (Insko and Schopler, 1998). The primary reasons accounting for that effect are linked to the affordances of the interdependence situation. For example, some degree of conflicting interest challenges trust more (and enhances competitive motivation more) in interactions between groups than between individuals (for a meta-analytic review, see Wildschut et al., 2003). Indeed, there is good deal of evidence that an interdependence approach complements other approaches (such as social identity and self-categorization approaches) in their predictions of intergroup relations.

A strong concern with receiving better outcomes – and not getting worse outcomes – than other groups is often conflicting with good outcomes for the collective (De Dreu, 2010). However, competition can sometimes be a powerful means to cooperation. It takes an interdependence approach to analyze the patterns of interdependence between (a) the individual and their group, (b) the individual and the collective, and (c) the group and the collective (see Bornstein, 1992; Halevy et al., 2008; Wit and Kerr, 2002). For example, a soldier (i.e., the individual) who fights forcefully often serves the group (i.e., his/her country), but not necessarily the world (i.e., the entire collective). In such multilayered social dilemmas, competition can be quite beneficial. When there are two (or more) well-defined groups who comprise the entire collective, then sometimes competition between the groups helps the entire collective. The competition should then deal with something desirable. For example, in the Netherlands, there is a contest between cities aiming for the award "Cleanest City." As another example, two departments at a university may do better (yielding greater research output and enhanced teaching) if the university provides extra resources for only excellent departments. Indeed, organizations often use competition as a means to promote functioning.

Benefits of a taxonomic approach: theoretical development in the future

A unique and exceptionally important contribution of interdependence theory is the advancement of a taxonomy of situations. Indeed, there are very few theories in social psychology that advance a taxonomy of situations, even though social psychology as a field is strongly concerned with situational influence or influences from the social environment (see also Reis, 2008). Also, we believe that "dimensions" of temporal structure and information availability that have been added recently (Kelley et al., 2003) will

prove to be important to several issues in psychological science and beyond.

First, much research and theory in social psychology focuses on processes in an attempt to understand "system-questions," such as how cognition and affect might influence each other, the characterization as a dual-process system, such as the reflective and impulsive systems, hot and cool systems, and so on. We suggest that interdependence theory provides a much-needed taxonomy of situations that may help us understand when (i.e., the situations in which) particular systems might be activated. For example, forms of dependence call for trust, especially when there is some conflict of interest, and perhaps limited time might set into motion a hot system where impulses and gut feelings drive behavior rather than systematic thought (see Hertel et al., 2000). An excellent case in point is the analysis of relationships between "the powerful" and "the powerless" in organizations (Fiske, 1993). Because the latter are strongly dependent on the former, it becomes important to engage in deep, systematical processing for reaching accurate conclusions about the motives and attributes of the powerful. In contrast, the powerful are less dependent on the powerless (and there are often many of the latter), and the powerful are often more shallow, heuristic in forming impressions of the powerless. Accordingly, they are more likely to fall prey to stereotypic information (Fiske, 1993).

Second, a taxonomy of situations is essential to dynamic approaches to social interaction and personality – people do not only respond to situations, they may also actively seek situations, avoid other situations, or shape situations in particular ways (e.g., Snyder and Ickes, 1985). However, it is one thing to recognize that people are not slaves of situational forces – that people select and modify situations in explicit or subtle ways; it is quite another thing to predict the character of situation selection. Interdependence theory provides insight in this respect, in that the dimensions underlying situations should reliably activate and afford specific sorts of goals and motives. For example, sometimes people may avoid situations of dependence – the decision to work on an independent task rather than a joint task. Situation selection is often functional, in that it helps gratify specific needs or promotes long-term outcomes (Mischel and Shoda, 1995; Snyder and Ickes, 1985). But of course, situation selection may also initiate or sustain self-defeating processes. For example, shy children may avoid interaction, which in turn may limit their opportunities for overcoming shyness. The interdependence theory typology of situations can fruitfully be employed to extend predictive specificity in classic psychological domains, including not only the problem of specificity in predicting how traits relate to situation selection, but also specificity in predicting person-by-situation interactions (Kelley et al., 2003). As such, an interdependence theoretic analysis can advance precise predictions about the inextricable link between persons and situations.

Third, a taxonomic approach is essential to basic evolutionary issues. Because evolutionary theory focuses on the question of how common human characteristics interact with the social environment, it is essential to have the theoretical tools to analyze social situations in terms of their key features (e.g., Schaller et al., 2006; Tooby and Cosmides, 2005; Van Vugt, 2006). Interdependence theory shares some assumptions with evolutionary approaches. One such a shared assumption is that people, as individuals, partners, and as members of a group, *adapt* to social situations (Kelley and Thibaut, 1978). At the same time, while evolutionary theory tends to focus on common human characteristics, interdependence theory can make a contribution by specifying key properties of the social situation to which people adapt – such as the dependence, conflicting interest, information availability, and so on. According to interdependence theory, it is plausible that people develop consistent contingencies, which may take the form of "if … then" rules (Mischel and Shoda, 1999; see Murray and Holmes, 2009; Reis, 2008), in their adaptations

to different partners in different social situations. For example, as outlined by Murray and Holmes (2009), if–then rules might reflect the way in which trust is communicated and commitment is built in ongoing relationships – partner's sacrifices might be directly translated into trust. Thus, while evolutionary theory has focused on adaptations, such as coordination and cooperation, interdependence theory provides the conceptual tools for understanding the domains of the situations that afford the expression of the skills and motives relevant to coordination and cooperation. This contribution may be very useful for helping to understand why some cognitions and emotions are closely connected to particular domains of interpersonal situations.

More generally, we suggest that interdependence theory will be exceedingly helpful as a model for understanding when and why particular neurological networks, hormonal responses, or complementary responses might be activated. These biology-based responses will often be adaptive in light of the qualities of both persons and the situation – that is, the SABI model discussed earlier. For example, on the observer's side, responses that are linked to anger are probably best understood when carefully analyzing another person's violation of a norm in situations where people are likely to have somewhat conflicting preferences (e.g., Singer et al., 2006). It is especially striking that people with prosocial orientations tend to react very automatically to a violation of equality (e.g., activation in the amygdala, Haruno and Frith, 2009). Such findings provide neuroscientific evidence in support of the integrative model of social value orientation, which states that prosocial orientation represents not only the tendency to enhance joint outcomes but also the tendency to enhance equality in outcomes (Van Lange, 1999). On the actor's side, feelings of guilt might be evoked in such situations when we ourselves violate such norms (e.g., Pinter et al., 2007). Further, the topic of self-regulation (and affect-regulation and self-control) in the interpersonal domain is of course strongly linked to inhibiting the temptation of self-interest and exercising self-restraint.

CONCLUSION

Social psychology is the field of psychology that is defined most strongly in terms of influences of the situation – specifically, the influence of the social environment on human behavior. Somewhat surprisingly, not much theorizing in social psychology is centered on the analysis of the social environment. By providing a taxonomy of interpersonal situations, interdependence theory has served that role. The addition of new dimensions (information availability and temporal structure) to the well-established ones (dependence, mutuality of dependence, basis of dependence, covariation of interest) should be essential toward understanding the nature and mechanics of (implicit) theories that people bring to bear on situations with limited information (e.g., the hot and cold systems, the degree of processing, the needs and motives involved, as well as the implicit theories by which people make incomplete information complete) as well as the motives and skills that are relevant to time in a general sense (e.g., investment, delay of gratification, consideration for future consequences). A taxonomy of interpersonal situation is essential for theoretical progress.

From a theoretical perspective, it is crucial that we need to know better what a situation "objectively" represents, because only then it is possible to understand what people subjectively make of a situation (construction). Conceptually, the constructs of given situation (objective situation), transformation (meaning analysis), and effective situation (subjective situation) represent the heart of the interdependence theory. It complements much other theorizing in social psychology which tends to focus on the processes relevant to transformation and effective situation preferences. Another reason why a taxonomy is important is that it helps us understand the situations that people might face (in terms of valence, frequency, and intensity), and how these features covary with several factors, such as differences in personality, social class, gender, and age. For example, the frequency with which one faces situations of unilateral dependence on another person might increase from adulthood to old age. A taxonomy of situations also helps us understand the situations that relationship partners and members of small groups are likely to face (or not) – for example, of how they face situation of conflicting interests. As a variation of Lewin's (1952: 169) well-known dictum, one might suggest that "there is nothing as practical as a good taxonomy."

Thus, after more than 50 years since Thibaut and Kelley (1959), interdependence theory comes full circle. It really has helped the field to get a grip on situations that interacting partners face or might face (the given interdependence situation), what they make of it (the transformation process) in terms of cognition and emotion, and how the structure and the processes shape human behavior and social interactions. This also helps to explain why interdependence theory has been well appreciated for over five decades, and why interdependence has been used to understand so many issues – group dynamics, power and dependence, social comparison, conflict and cooperation, attribution and self-presentation, trust and distrust, emotions, love and commitment, coordination and communication, risk and self-regulation, performance and motivation, social development, and neuroscientific models of social interaction. We are looking forward to the theoretical contributions and applications of interdependence theory over the next 50 years.

NOTE

1 Sadly, Caryl Rusbult (1952–2010) passed away on January 27, 2010, some weeks before this chapter was completed. Some of her important contributions to interdependence theory throughout her career are described in this chapter. We thank John

Holmes, Norbert Kerr and Harry Reis for their helpful comments on an earlier draft of this chapter.

REFERENCES

Agnew, C.R., Van Lange, P.A.M., Rusbult, C.E. and Langston, C.A. (1998) Cognitive interdependence: Commitment and the mental representation of close relationships. *Journal of Personality and Social Psychology*, 74, 939–954.

Aguilar, R.J. and Nightingale, N.N. (1994) The impact of specific battering experiences on the self-esteem of abused women. *Journal of Family Violence, 9,* 35–45.

Ajzen, I. (1991) The theory of planned behavior. *Organizational Behavior and Human Decision Processes, 50,* 179–211.

Andersen, S.M. and Chen, S. (2002) The relational self: An interpersonal social-cognitive theory. *Psychological Review, 109,* 619–645.

Attridge, M., Berscheid, E. and Simpson, J.A. (1995) Predicting relationship stability from both partners versus one. *Journal of Personality and Social Psychology, 69,* 254–268.

Axelrod, R. (1984) *The Evolution of Cooperation.* New York: Basic Books.

Baron, R.S. and Kerr, N.L. (2003) *Group Process, Group Decision, Group Action*, 2nd Edition. Buckingham: Open University Press.

Baumeister, R.F. and Leary, M.R. (1995) The need to belong: Desire for interpersonal attachments as a fundamental human motivation. *Psychological Bulletin, 117,* 497–529.

Bornstein, G. (1992) The free rider problem in intergroup conflicts over step-level and continuous public goods. *Journal of Personality and Social Psychology, 62,* 597–606.

Carver, C.S. and Scheier, M.F. (1998) *On the Self-regulation of Behavior.* New York: Cambridge.

Clark, M.S., Dubash, P. and Mills, J. (1998) Interest in another's consideration of one's needs in communal and exchange relationships. *Journal of Experimental Social Psychology, 34,* 246–264.

Collins, N.L. and Feeney, B.C. (2004) Working models of attachment shape perceptions of social support: Evidence from experimental and observational studies. *Journal of Personality and Social Psychology, 87,* 363–383.

Collins, N.L. and Miller, L.C. (1994) Self-disclosure and liking: A meta-analytic review. *Psychological Bulletin, 116,* 457–475.

De Dreu, C.K.W. (2010) Social conflict: The emergence and consequences of struggle and negotiation. In S.T. Fiske, D.T Gilbert and G. Lindzey (eds), *Handbook of Social Psychology, Vol. 2*, 5th Edition, pp. 983–1023. New York: Wiley.

Deutsch, M. (1975) Equity, equality, and need: What determines which value will be used as the basis of distributive justice? *Journal of Social Issues, 31,* 137–149.

Finkel, E.J., Campbell, W.K., Brunnel, A.B., Dalton, A.N., Scarbeck, S.J. and Chartrand, T.L. (2006) High-maintenance interaction: Inefficient social coordination impairs self-reguation. *Journal of Personality and Social Psychology, 91,* 456–475.

Finkel, E.J., Rusbult, C.E., Kumashiro, M. and Hannon, P.A. (2002) Dealing with betrayal in close relationships: Does commitment promote forgiveness? *Journal of Personality and Social Psychology, 82,* 956–974.

Fiske, A.P. (1992) The four elementary forms of sociality: Framework for a unified theory of social relations. *Psychological Review, 99,* 689–723.

Fiske, S.T. (1993) Controlling other people: The impact of power on stereotyping. *American Psychologist, 48,* 621–628.

Fiske, S.T. (2004). *Social Beings: A Core Motives Approach to Social Psychology.* New York: Wiley.

Fraley, R.C. and Shaver, P.R. (2000) Adult romantic attachment: Theoretical developments, emerging controversies, and unanswered questions. *Review of General Psychology, 4,* 132–154.

Greenwald, A.G., McGhee, D.E. and Schwartz, J.L.K. (1998) Measuring individual differences in implicit cognition: The implicit association test. *Journal of Personality and Social Psychology, 74,* 1464–1480.

Halevy, N., Bornstein, G. and Sagiv, L. (2008) 'Ingroup love' and 'Outgroup hate' as motives for individual participation in intergroup conflict: A new game paradigm. *Psychological Science, 19,* 405–411.

Haruno, M. and Frith, C.D. (2009) Activity in the amygdala elicited by unfair divisions predicts social value orientation. *Nature Neuroscience, 13,* 160–161.

Hertel, G., Neuhof, J., Theuer, T. and Kerr, N. (2000) Mood effects on cooperation in small groups: Does positive mood simply lead to more cooperation? *Cognition and Emotion, 14,* 441–472.

Higgins, E.T. (1997) Beyond pleasure and pain. *American Psychologist, 52,* 1280–1300.

Higgins, E.T. (2000) Making a good decision: Value from fit. *American Psychologist, 55,* 1217–1230.

Higgins, E.T. (2011) Regulatory focus theory. In P.A M. Van Lange, A.W. Kruglanksi and E.T. Higgins (eds),

Handbook of Theories of Social Psychology, Vol. 1. London: Sage

Holmes, J.G. (2002) Social relationships: The nature and function of relational schemas. *European Journal of Social Psychology, 30,* 447–495.

Holmes, J.G. (2004) The benefits of abstract functional analysis in theory construction: The case of interdependence theory. *Personality and Social Psychology Review, 8,* 146–155.

Holmes, J.G. and Murray, S.L. (1996) Conflict in close relationships. In E.T. Higgins and A. Kruglanski (eds), *Social Psychology: Handbook of Basic Principles,* pp. 622–654. New York: Guilford Press.

Holmes, J.G. and Rempel, J.K. (1989) Trust in close relationships. In C. Hendrick (ed.), *Review of Personality and Social Psychology, 10,* 187–220. London: Sage.

Homans, G.C. (1950) *The Human Group.* New York: Harcourt, Brace & World.

Insko, C.A. and Schopler, J. (1998) Differential distrust of groups and individuals. In C. Sedikides, J. Schopler and C.A. Insko (eds), *Intergroup Cognition and Intergroup Behavior: Toward a Closer Union,* pp. 75–107. Hillsdale, NJ: Erlbaum.

Jones, E.J. (1998) Major developments in five decades of social psychology. In D. Gilbert, S. Fiske and G. Lindzey (eds), *Handbook of Social Psychology, Vol. 2,* 4th Edition, pp. 3–57. Boston: McGraw-Hill.

Karremans, J.C. and Van Lange, P.A.M. (2008) Forgiveness in personal relationships: Its malleability and powerful consequences. *European Review of Social Psychology, 19,* 202–241.

Kelley, H.H. (1983) The situational origins of human tendencies: A further reason for the formal analysis of structures. *Personality and Social Psychology Bulletin, 9,* 8–30.

Kelley, H.H. (1984) The theoretical description of interdependence by means of transition lists. *Journal of Personality and Social Psychology, 47,* 956–982.

Kelley, H.H., Holmes, J.G., Kerr, N.L., Reis, H.T., Rusbult, C.E. and Van Lange, P.A.M. (2003) *An Atlas of Interpersonal Situations.* New York: Cambridge.

Kelley, H.H. and Stahelski, A.J. (1970) Social interaction basis of cooperators' and competitors' beliefs about others. *Journal of Personality and Social Psychology, 16,* 66–91.

Kelley, H.H. and Thibaut, J.W. (1978) *Interpersonal Relations: A Theory of Interdependence.* New York: Wiley.

Kerr, N.L. and Tindale, R.S. (2004) Small group decision making and performance. *Annual Review of Psychology, 55,* 623–656.

Klapwijk, A. and Van Lange, P.A.M. (2009) Promoting cooperation and trust in 'noisy' situations: The power of generosity. *Journal of Personality and Social Psychology, 96,* 83–103.

Kollock, P. (1993) 'An eye for an eye leaves everyone blind': Cooperation and accounting systems. *American Sociological Review, 58,* 768–786.

Lewin, K. (1952) *Field Theory in Social Sciences: Selected Theoretical Papers.* New York: Harper.

Luce, R.D. and Raiffa, H. (1957) *Games and Decisions: Introduction and Critical Survey.* London: Wiley.

Messick, D.M. and McClintock, C.G. (1968) Motivational bases of choice in experimental games. *Journal of Experimental Social Psychology, 4,* 1–25.

Miller, R.S. (1997) Inattentive and contented: Relationship commitment and attention to alternatives. *Journal of Personality and Social Psychology, 73,* 758–766.

Mischel, W. and Shoda, Y. (1995) A cognitive-affective system theory of personality: Reconceptualizing situations, dispositions, and invariance in personality structure. *Psychological Review, 102,* 246–268.

Murray, S.L. and Holmes, J.G. (2009) The architecture of interdependent minds: A Motivation-management theory of mutual responsiveness. *Psychological Review, 116,* 908–928.

Murray, S.L., Holmes, J.G. and Collins, N.L. (2006) Optimizing assurance: The risk regulation system in relationships. *Psychological Bulletin, 132,* 641–666.

Nisbett, R.E. and Cohen, D. (1996) *Culture of Honor: The Psychology of Violence in the South.* Boulder, CO: Westview.

Pinter, B., Insko, C.A., Wildschut, T., Kirchner, J.L., Montoya, R.M. and Wolf, S.T. (2007) Reduction of the interindividual-intergroup discontinuity: The role of leader accountability and proneness to guilt. *Journal of Personality and Social Psychology, 93,* 250–265.

Pruitt, D. (1998) Social conflict. In D. Gilbert, S. Fiske and G. Lindzey (eds), *Handbook of Social Psychology, Vol. 2,* 4th Edition, pp. 470–503. Boston: McGraw-Hill.

Reis, H.T. (2008) Reinvigorating the concept of situation in social psychology. *Personality and Social Psychology Review, 12,* 311–329.

Reis, H.T., Collins, W.A. and Berscheid, E. (2000) The relationship context of human behavior and development. *Psychological Bulletin, 126,* 844–872.

Righetti, F. and Rusbult, C.E. (2007) Interpersonal regulatory fit: Consequences for goal pursuit. Unpublished manuscript, Vrije Universiteit Amsterdam.

Rusbult, C.E. (1983) A longitudinal test of the investment model: The development (and deterioration) of satisfaction and commitment in heterosexual involvements. *Journal of Personality and Social Psychology*, *45*, 101–117.

Rusbult, C.E., Coolsen, M.K., Kirchner, J.L. and Clarke, J. (2006) Commitment. In A. Vangelisti and D. Perlman (eds), *Handbook of Personal Relationships*, pp. 615–635. New York: Cambridge University Press.

Rusbult, C.E. and Martz, J.M. (1995) Remaining in an abusive relationship: An investment model analysis of nonvoluntary commitment. *Personality and Social Psychology Bulletin*, *21*, 558–571.

Rusbult, C.E. and Van Lange, P.A.M. (1996) Interdependence processes. In E.T. Higgins and A. Kruglanski (eds), *Social Psychology: Handbook of Basic Principles*, pp. 564–596. New York: Guilford Press.

Rusbult, C.E. and Van Lange, P.A.M. (2003) Interdependence, interaction, and relationships. *Annual Review of Psychology*, *54*, 351–375.

Rusbult, C.E., Verette, J., Whitney, G.A., Slovik, L.F. and Lipkus, I. (1991) Accommodation processes in close relationships: Theory and preliminary empirical evidence. *Journal of Personality and Social Psychology*, *60*, 53–78.

Schaller, M., Kenrick, D. and Simpson. J. (eds) (2006) *Evolution and Social Psychology*. New York: Psychology Press.

Simpson, J.A. (2007) Psychological foundations of trust. *Current Directions in Psychological Science*, *16*, 264–268.

Singer, T., Seymour B., O'Doherty J., Klaas E.S., Dolan J.D. and Frith, C. (2006) Empathic neural responses are modulated by the perceived fairness of others. *Nature*, *439*, 466–469.

Snyder, M. and Ickes, W. (1985) Personality and social behavior. In G. Lindzey and E. Aronson (eds), *The Handbook of Social Psychology*, pp. 883–947. New York: Random House.

Surra, C.A. and Longstreth, M. (1990) Similarity of outcomes, interdependence, and conflict in dating relationships. *Journal of Personality and Social Psychology*, *59*, 501–516.

Thibaut, J.W. and Kelley, H.H. (1959) *The Social Psychology of Groups*. New York: Wiley.

Tooby, J. and Cosmides, L. (2005) Conceptual foundations of evolutionary psychology. In D.M. Buss (ed.), *The Handbook of Evolutionary Psychology*, pp. 5–67. Hoboken, NJ: Wiley.

Turiel, E. (1983) *The Development of Social Knowledge: Morality and Convention*. Cambridge: Cambridge University Press.

Van Lange, P.A.M. (1999) The pursuit of joint outcomes and equality in outcomes: An integrative model of social value orientation. *Journal of Personality and Social Psychology*, *77*, 337–349.

Van Lange, P.A.M., De Cremer, D., Van Dijk, E. and Van Vugt, M. (2007) Self-interest and beyond: Basic principles of social interaction. In A.W. Kruglanski and E.T. Higgins (eds), *Social Psychology: Handbook of Basic Principles*, pp. 540–561. New York: Guilford Press.

Van Lange, P.A.M. and Joireman, J.A. (2008) How can we promote behaviour that serves all of us in the future. *Social Issue and Policy Review*, *2*, 127–157.

Van Lange, P.A.M., Otten, W., De Bruin, E.M.N. and Joireman, J.A. (1997) Development of prosocial, individualistic, and competitive orientations: Theory and preliminary evidence. *Journal of Personality and Social Psychology*, *73*, 733–746.

Van Lange, P.A.M., Ouwerkerk, J.W. and Tazelaar, M.J.A. (2002) How to overcome the detrimental effects of noise in social interaction: The benefits of generosity. *Journal of Personality and Social Psychology*, *82*, 768–780.

Van Lange, P.A.M., Rusbult, C.E., Drigotas, S.M., Arriaga, X.B., Witcher, B.S. and Cox, C.L. (1997) Willingness to sacrifice in close relationships. *Journal of Personality and Social Psychology*, *72*, 1373–1395.

Van Vugt, M. (2006) Evolutionary origins of leadership and followership. *Personality and Social Psychology Review*, *10*, 354–372.

Vuolevi, J.H.K. and Van Lange, P.A.M. (2010) Beyond the information given: The power of the belief in self-interest. *European Journal of Social Psychology*, *40*, 26–34.

Walker, L. (2000) *The Battered Woman Syndrome*, 2nd Edition. New York: Springer.

Wildschut, T., Pinter, B., Vevea, J.L., Insko, C.A. and Schopler, J. (2003) Beyond the group mind: A quantitative review of the interindividual-intergroup discontinuity effect. *Psychological Bulletin*, *129*, 698–722.

Wit, A.P. and Kerr, N.L. (2002) 'Me vs. just us vs. us all' Categorization and cooperation in nested social dilemmas. *Journal of Personality and Social Psychology*, *83*, 616–637.

PART V

Group and Cultural Level
of Analysis

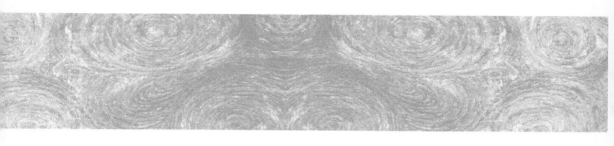

40

A Theory of Cooperation – Competition and Beyond

Morton Deutsch

ABSTRACT

This chapter is concerned with my inter-related theoretical work in the areas of cooperation – competition, conflict resolution, social justice, and social relations. The theory of *cooperation–competition* is a component of the other theories. Thus, the theory of *conflict resolution* is based on this theory and my Crude Law of Social Relations. My work in *social justice* is also based on this theory, the Crude Law, and on my theoretical work dealing with social relations. The work in *social relations* sketches a more generalized approach to the understanding of the bidirectional interaction between social relations and psychological orientations. In a prelude to my theoretical discussion, I consider the personal, social, and professional influences that shaped my work. In the last part, I describe some of the important social effects of this work.

INTRODUCTION

In this chapter, I shall present my inter-related theoretical work on cooperation – competition, conflict resolution, social justice, and social relations. I shall omit a presentation of relevant research since this

has been presented elsewhere. Thus, Johnson and Johnson (2005) in their excellent monograph, New Developments in Social Interdependence Theory, present an extensive summary of relevant research and social practice that relate to this theory. In books related to conflict resolution (Deutsch, 1973; Deutsch et al., 2006) there is considerable discussion of research. Similarly, in Deutsch (1985) and *Social Justice Research* (Vol. 19[1], March 2006) there is presentation of research related to social justice.

This chapter is divided into three parts. The first is concerned with the personal, social, and theoretical influences affecting the development of my theoretical and research work; the second presents my basic theoretical ideas; and the third discusses the social effects of my work.

INFLUENCES ON MY WORK: PERSONAL, SOCIAL, AND THEORETICAL

The choice of areas for social psychological work is affected not only by professional and scientific contacts and readings, but also by personal and familial experiences as well as by broader social and cultural influences. In my case, being Jewish and the youngest child in my family, in my school, and in my neighborhood group exposed me to considerable prejudice[1] and put-downs. These experiences sensitized me to prejudice and led to an identification with underdogs.

At age 15, I entered the City College of New York (CCNY) in 1935 as a premed major with the idea of becoming a psychiatrist, having been intrigued by the writings of Sigmund Freud, some of which I had read before college. I was drawn to psychoanalysis undoubtedly because it appeared to be so relevant to personal issues with which I was struggling, and also because it was so radical (it seemed to be so in the early and mid 1930s). During my adolescence, I was also politically radical and somewhat rebellious toward authority, helping to organize a student strike against terrible food in the Townsend Harris High School lunchroom, and later, a strike against the summer resort owners who were exploiting the college student waiters and bus boys at Camp Copake, of whom I was one.

The 1930s were a turbulent period, internationally as well as domestically. The economic depression; labor unrest; the rise of Nazism and other forms of totalitarianism; the Spanish civil war; the ideas of Marx, Freud, and Einstein; as well as the impending Second World War were shaping the intellectual atmosphere that affected psychology. Several members of the psychology faculty at CCNY were active in creating the Psychologist League, the precursor to the Society for the Psychological Study of Social Issues. Thus, when I became disenchanted with the idea of being a premed student (after dissecting a pig in a biology lab), I was happy to switch to a psychology major: it was a simpatico faculty. Psychology was a part of the Department of Philosophy at CCNY when I started my major in it. Morris Raphael Cohen, the distinguished philosopher of science, was the leading intellectual

figure at CCNY, and his influence permeated the atmosphere. I note that in the lunchroom alcoves at CCNY, I became well versed in Marxist theology and disputation. Students adhering to the First, Second, Third, and Fourth International congregated in different corners of the lunchroom.

My first exposure to Lewin's writings was in two undergraduate courses, taken simultaneously: social psychology, and personality and motivation. In these courses, I read Lewin's *Dynamic Theory of Personality* (1935), *Principles of Topological Psychology* (1936), and "The conceptual representation and measurement of psychological forces" (1938). I and others experienced great intellectual excitement on reading these books more than 60 years ago. These books are permeated by a view of the nature of psychological science different from the traditional. The new view was characterized by Lewin as the *Galilean mode of thought*, which was contrasted with the classic *Aristotelian mode*. In my writings on field theory (Deutsch, 1954), I have characterized in some detail Lewin's approach to psychological theorizing – his metatheory.

Although I was impressed by Lewin's writing, my career aspirations were still focused on becoming a psychoanalytic psychologist as I decided to do graduate work. My undergraduate experiences, in as well as outside the classroom, led me to believe that an integration of psychoanalysis, Marxism, and scientific method, as exemplified by Lewin's work, could be achieved. In the 1930s such influential figures as Wilhelm Reich, Erich Fromm, Max Horkheimer, Theodor Adorno, and Else Frenkel-Brunswik were trying to develop an integration of psychoanalysis and Marxism. Also at this time, some psychoanalytic theorists such as David Rappaport were intrigued by the idea that the research conducted by Lewin and his students on tension systems could be viewed as a form of experimental psychoanalysis.

After obtaining my MA in 1940 in clinical psychology at the University of Pennsylvania, I started a rotating clinical internship at three

New York State institutions: one was for the feebleminded (Letchworth Village), another for delinquent boys (Warwick), and a third for psychotic children as well as adults (Rockland State Hospital). When the attack on Pearl Harbor occurred on December 7, 1941, I was still in my psychology internship. Shortly thereafter, I joined the Air Force. I flew in 30 bombing missions against Germany. During combat, I saw many of our planes as well as German planes shot down, and I also saw massive damage inflicted by our bombs and those of the Royal Air Force on occupied Europe and Germany. Moreover, being stationed in England, I saw the great destruction wreaked by the German air raids and felt common apprehensions while sitting in air-raid shelters during German bombings. Although I had no doubt of the justness of the war against the Nazis, I was appalled by its destructiveness.

After my demobilization, I decided to apply for admission to the doctoral programs at the University of Chicago (where Carl Rogers and L.L. Thurstone were the leading lights), at Yale University (where Donald Marquis was chairman and where Clark Hull was the major attraction), and at MIT (where Kurt Lewin had established a new graduate program and the Research Center for Group Dynamics). As one of the first of the returning soldiers, I had no trouble getting interviews or admissions to all three schools. I was most impressed by Kurt Lewin and his vision of his newly established Research Center and so decided to take my PhD at MIT. I date the start of my career as a social psychologist to my first meeting with Lewin, in which I was enthralled by him and committed myself to studying at his Research Center for Group Dynamics (RCGD).

Lewin assembled a remarkable group of faculty and students to compose the RCGD at MIT. For the faculty, he initially recruited Dorwin Cartwright, Leon Festinger, Ronald Lippitt, and Marian Radke (later Radke-Yarrow). Jack French and Alvin Zander were to join subsequently. The small group of students included Kurt Back, Alex Bavelas, David Emery, Gordon Hearn, Murray Horowitz, David Jenkins, Harold Kelley, Albert Pepitone, Stanley Schachter, Richard Snyder, John Thibaut, Ben Willerman, and myself. These faculty members and students were extraordinarily productive, and they played a pivotal role in developing modern social psychology in its applied as well as its basic aspects.

My career in social psychology has been greatly affected by Kurt Lewin and my experiences at the RCGD. The intellectual atmosphere created by Lewin strongly shaped my dissertation and my value orientation as a social psychologist. Lewin was not only an original, tough-minded theorist and researcher with a profound interest in the philosophy and methodology of science, he was also a tender-hearted psychologist who was deeply involved with developing psychological knowledge that would be relevant to important human concerns (Deutsch, 1992). He provided a scientific role model that I have tried to emulate. Like Lewin, I have wanted my theory and research to be relevant to important social issues, but I also wanted my work to be scientifically rigorous and tough-minded. As a student, I was drawn to both the tough-mindedness of Festinger's work and to the direct social relevance of Lippitt's approach and did not feel the need to identify with one and derogate the other.

My dissertation started off with an interest in issues of war and peace (atomic bombs had been dropped on Hiroshima and Nagasaki shortly before I resumed my graduate studies) and with an image of the possible ways that the nations composing the newly formed United Nations Security Council would interact. The atmosphere at the Center, still persisting after Lewin's premature death, led me to turn this social concern about the risk of nuclear war into a theoretically oriented, experimental investigation of the effects of cooperative and competitive processes. The specific problem that I was first interested in took on a more generalized form. It had been transformed into an attempt to understand the fundamental features of cooperative and competitive relations and the consequences of these different types of interdependencies in a way that would be generally applicable to the relations among individuals, groups, or nations. The problem had become a theoretical one, with the broad scientific goal of attempting to develop insight into a variety of phenomena through several fundamental concepts and basic propositions. The intellectual atmosphere at the Center pushed its students to theory building.

As I reflect back on the intellectual roots of my dissertation, I see it was influenced not only by Lewin's theoretical interest in social interdependence but also by Marxist concerns with two different systems of distributive justice: a cooperative-egalitarian and a competitive-meritocratic one. In addition, the writing of George Herbert Mead (1934) affected my way of thinking about cooperation and its importance to human development. Also, my discussion of the relation between objective social interdependence and perceived social interdependence was much influenced by Koffka's (1935) answer to the question "Why do things look as they do?" Further, my reading of the existing literature on cooperation – competition (Barnard, 1938; Lewin, 1948; Maller, 1929; May and Doob, 1937; G.H. Mead, 1934; M. Mead, 1937) indirectly influenced my work.

THEORY

This part is concerned with my inter-related theoretical work in the areas of cooperation – competition, conflict resolution, social justice, and social relations. The theory of *cooperation–competition* is a component of the other theories. Thus, the theory of *conflict resolution* is based on this theory and my Crude Law of Social Relations. My work in *social justice* is also based on this theory, the Crude Law, and on my theoretical work dealing with social relations. The work in *social relations* sketches a more generalized approach to the understanding of the bidirectional interaction

between social relations and psychological orientations. Social relations are characterized not only by the dimension of cooperation–competition but also by such other dimensions as: equality–inequality; task-oriented versus social–emotional-oriented (*Gemeinschaft* versus *Gesellschaft*); formal versus informal; and degree of importance. Psychological orientations include the following components: cognitive, motivational, moral, and action orientations.

Before discussing this work, let me note that I recognize that my *theories* in social psychology have considerable ambiguity inherent in them and lack the precision of the theories in the natural sciences. For example, in my theoretical and experimental work on cooperation–competition, I discussed the problem of the relation between the "objective" and "perceived" reality of social interdependence; a similar problem confronts all experimental social psychologists.

A theory of cooperation and competition

In my 1949 presentation of my theory of cooperation and competition, I employed the Lewinian terminology related to locomotion in the life space and developed the hypotheses of the theory in a formal, hypotheticodeductive manner. I think the ideas were fine, but the presentation was awkward and the language too idiosyncratic. In more recent presentations, including this one, I have presented the theory in a more accessible, informal manner.

The theory has two basic ideas. One relates to the type of interdependence among goals of the people involved in a given situation. The other pertains to the type of action taken by the people involved. I identify two basic types of goal interdependence: positive (where the goals are linked in such a way that the amount or probability of a person's goal attainment is positively correlated with the amount or probability of another obtaining his goal) and negative (where the goals are linked in such a way that the amount or probability of goal attainment is negatively correlated with the amount or probability of the other's goal attainment). To put it colloquially, if you're positively linked with another, then you sink and swim together; with negative linkage, if the other sinks, you swim, and if the other swims, you sink.

It is well to realize that few situations are "purely" positive or negative. In most situations, people have a mixture of goals so that it is common for some of their goals initially to be positive and some negatively interdependent. In this section, for analytical purposes, I discuss pure situations. In conflict and other mixed situations, the relative strength of the two types of goal interdependence, as well as the parties' general orientation to one another, largely determine the nature of their interaction.

I also characterize two basic types of action by an individual: "effective actions," which improve the actor's chances of obtaining a goal, and "bungling actions," which worsen the actor's chances of obtaining the goal. (For the purpose of simplicity, I use dichotomies for my basic concepts; the dichotomous types of interdependence and the dichotomous types of actions are, I assume, polar ends of continua.) I then combine types of interdependence and types of action to posit how they jointly affect three basic social psychological processes that are discussed later: *substitutability*, *cathexis*, and *inducibility*.

People's goals may be linked for various reasons. Thus, positive interdependence can result from people liking one another; being rewarded in terms of their joint achievement, needing to share a resource or overcome an obstacle together, holding common membership or identification with a group whose fate is important to them, being unable to achieve their task goals unless they divide up the work, being influenced by personality and cultural orientation, being bound together because they are treated this way by a common enemy or an authority, and so on. Similarly, with regard to negative interdependence, it

can result from people disliking one another or from their being rewarded in such a way that the more the other gets of the reward, the less one gets, and so on.

In addition to positive and negative interdependence, it is well to recognize that there can be lack of interdependence, or *independence*, such that the activities and fate of the people involved do not affect one another, directly or indirectly. If they are completely independent of one another, no conflict arises; the existence of a conflict implies some form of interdependence.

One further point: asymmetries may exist with regard to the degree of interdependence in a relationship; suppose that what you do or what happens to you may have a considerable effect on me, but what I do or what happens to me may have little impact on you. I am more dependent on you than you are on me. In the extreme case, you may be completely independent of me and I may be highly dependent on you. As a consequence of this asymmetry, you have greater power and influence in the relationship than I. This power may be general if the asymmetry exists in many situations, or it may be situation-specific if the asymmetry occurs only in a particular situation. A master has general power over a slave, while an auto mechanic repairing my car's electrical system has situation-specific power.

The three concepts mentioned previously – *substitutability*, *cathexis*, and *inducibility* – are vital to understanding the social psychological processes involved in creating the major effects of cooperation and competition. *Substitutability* (how a person's actions can satisfy another person's intentions) is central to the functioning of all social institutions (the family, industry, schools), to the division of labor, and to role specialization. Unless the activities of other people can substitute for yours, you are like a person stranded on a desert island alone: you have to build your own house, find or produce your own food, protect yourself from harmful animals, treat your ailments and illnesses, educate yourself about the nature of your new environment and about how to do all theses tasks, and so on, without the help of others. Being alone, you can neither create children nor have a family. *Substitutability* permits you to accept the activities of others in fulfilling your needs. *Negative substitutability* involves active rejection and effort to counteract the effects of another's activities.

Cathexis refers to the predisposition to respond evaluatively, favorably, or unfavorably to aspects of one's environment or self. Through natural selection, evolution has ensured that all living creatures have the capacity to respond positively to stimuli that are beneficial to them and negatively to those that are harmful. They are attracted to, approach, receive, ingest, like, enhance, and otherwise act positively toward beneficial objects, events, or other creatures; in contrast, they are repelled by harmful objects and circumstances and avoid, eject, attack, dislike, negate, and otherwise act negatively toward them. This inborn tendency to act positively toward the beneficial and negatively toward the harmful is the foundation on which the human potentials for cooperation and love as well as for competition and hate develop. The basic psychological orientation of cooperation implies the positive attitude, "We are for each other," "We benefit one another"; competition, by contrast, implies the negative attitude "We are against one another" and, in its extreme form, "You are out to harm me."

Inducibility refers to the readiness to accept another's influence to do what he or she wants; negative inducibility refers to the readiness to reject or obstruct fulfillment of what the other wants. The complement of *substitutability* is *inducibility*. You are willing to be helpful to another whose actions are helpful to you, but not to someone whose actions are harmful. In fact, you reject any request to help the other engage in harmful actions and, if possible, obstruct or interfere with these actions.

The effects of cooperation and competition

Thus, the theory predicts that if you are in a positive interdependent relationship with someone who bungles, the bungling is not a substitute for effective actions you intended; thus, the bungling is viewed negatively. In fact, when your net-playing tennis partner in a doubles game allows an easy shot to get past him, you have to extend yourself to prevent being harmed by the error. On the other hand, if your relationship is one of negative interdependence, and the other person bungles (as when your tennis opponent double-faults), your opponent's bungle substitutes for an effective action on your part, and it is regarded positively or valued. The reverse is true for effective actions. An opponent's effective actions are not substitutable for yours and are negatively valued; a teammate can induce you to help him or her make an effective action, but you are likely to try to prevent or obstruct a bungling action by your teammate. By contrast, you are willing to help an opponent bungle, but your opponent is not likely to induce you to help him or her make an effective action (which, in effect, harms your chances of obtaining your goal).

The theory of cooperation and competition, then, goes on to make further predictions about different aspects of intrapersonal, interpersonal, intragroup, and intergroup processes from the predictions about substitutability, cathexis, and inducibility. Thus, assuming that the individual actions in a group are more frequently effective than bungling, among the predictions that follow from the theory are that *cooperative relations* (those in which the goals of the parties involved are predominately positive interdependence), as compared with competitive ones, show more of these positive characteristics:

1 *Effective communication is exhibited.* Ideas are verbalized, and group members are attentive to one another, accepting of the ideas of other members, and influenced by them. They have fewer difficulties in communicating with or understanding others.
2 *Friendliness, helpfulness, and lessened obstructiveness* are expressed in the discussions. Members also are more satisfied with the group and its solutions and favorably impressed by the contributions of the other group members.

In addition, members of the cooperative groups rate themselves high in desire to win the respect of their colleagues.

3 The members of each group expect to be treated fairly and feel obliged to treat the others fairly.

4 Attempts to influence one another rely on persuasion and positive inducements.

5 Coordination of *effort, division of labor, orientation to task achievement, orderliness in discussion,* and *high productivity* are manifested in the cooperative groups (if the group task requires effective communication, coordination of effort, division of labor, or sharing of resources).

6 *Feeling of agreement with the ideas of others and a sense of basic similarity in beliefs and values, as well as confidence in one's own ideas and in the value that other members attach to those ideas,* are obtained in the cooperative groups.

7 *Recognizing and respecting the other by being responsive to the other's needs.*

8 *Willingness to enhance the other's power* (e.g., the knowledge, skills, resources) to accomplish the other's goals increases. As the other's capabilities are strengthened, you are strengthened; they are of value to you as well as to the other. Similarly, the other is enhanced from your enhancement and benefits from your growing capabilities and power.

9 *Defining conflicting interests as a mutual problem to be solved by collaborative effort* facilitates recognizing the legitimacy of each other's interests and the necessity to search for a solution responsive to the needs of all. It tends to limit rather than expand the scope of conflicting interests.

In contrast, a *competitive process* has the opposite effects:

1 Communication is impaired as the conflicting parties seek to gain advantage by misleading the other through use of false promises, ingratiation tactics, and disinformation. It is reduced and seen as futile as they recognize that they cannot trust one another's communications to be honest or informative.

2 Obstructiveness and lack of helpfulness lead to mutual negative attitudes and suspicion of one another's intentions. One's perceptions of the other tend to focus on the person's negative qualities and ignore the positive.

3 Fairness to the other is not valued. Each tries to exploit or harm the other to advantage themselves.

4 Attempts to influence the other often involve threat, coercion, or false promises.

5 The parties to the process are unable to divide their work, duplicating one another's efforts such that they become mirror images; if they do divide the work, they feel the need to check what the other is doing continuously.

6 The repeated experience of disagreement and critical rejection of ideas reduce confidence in oneself as well as the other.

7 The conflicting parties seek to enhance their own power and to reduce the power of the other. Any increase in the power of the other is seen as threatening to oneself.

8 The competitive process stimulates the view that the solution of a conflict can be imposed only by one side on the other, which in turn leads to using coercive tactics such as psychological as well as physical threats and violence. It tends to expand the scope of the issues in conflict as each side seeks superiority in power and legitimacy. The conflict becomes a power struggle or a matter of moral principle and is no longer confined to a specific issue at a given time and place. Escalating the conflict increases its motivational significance to the participants and may make a limited defeat less acceptable and more humiliating than a mutual disaster.

Constructive competition

Competition can vary from destructive to constructive; unfair, unregulated competition at the destructive end; fair, regulated competition in between; and constructive competition at the positive end. In constructive competition, the losers as well as the winners gain. Thus, in a tennis match that takes the form of constructive competition, the winner suggests how the loser can improve, offers an opportunity for the loser to learn and practice skills, and makes the match an enjoyable or worthwhile experience for the loser. In constructive competition, winners see to it that losers are better off, or at least not worse off than they were before the competition.

The major difference, for example, between constructive controversy and competitive debate is that in the former, people discuss their differences with the objective of clarifying them and attempting to find a solution that integrates the best thoughts that emerge during the discussion, no matter who articulates them (see Johnson et al., 2006, for a fuller discussion). There is no winner and no loser; both win if during the controversy each party comes to deeper insights and enriched view of the matter that is initially in controversy. Constructive controversy is a process for constructively coping with the inevitable differences that people bring to cooperative interaction because it uses differences in understanding, perspective, knowledge, and worldview as valued resources. By contrast, in competitive contests or debates there is usually a winner and a loser. The party judged to have "the best" – ideas, skills, knowledge, and so on – typically wins, while the other, who is judged to be less good, typically loses. Competition evaluates and ranks people based on their capacity for a particular task, rather than integrating various contributions.

I do not mean to suggest that competition produces no benefits. Competition is part of everyday life. Acquiring the skills necessary to compete effectively can be of considerable value. Moreover, competition in a cooperative, playful context can be fun. It enables one to enact and experience, in a nonserious setting, symbolic emotional dramas relating to victory and defeat, life and death, power and helplessness, dominance and submission; these dramas have deep personal and cultural roots. In addition, competition is a useful social mechanism for selecting those who are more able to perform the activities involved in the competition. Further, when no objective, criterion-referenced basis for measurement of performance exists, the relative performance of students affords a crude yardstick. Nevertheless, serious problems are associated with competition when it does not occur in a cooperative context and if it is not effectively regulated by fair rules (see Deutsch, 1973: 377–388, for a discussion of regulating competition).

Self-destructive tendencies inherent in cooperation

As I have indicated in my writings on cooperation and competition (Deutsch, 1973, 1985), there is a natural tendency for cooperation to break down as a result of the very social psychological processes – *substitutability*, *cathexis*, and *inducibility* – that are central to cooperation. Thus, *substitutability*, which enables the work of one cooperator to replace the work of another so that they don't have to duplicate one another's efforts, leads to specialization of function. Specialization of function, in turn, gives rise to specialized interest and to specialized terminology and language; the likely consequence is a deterioration of group unity as those with special interest compete for scarce resources and communicate in a language that is not fully shared. Similarly, *cathexis* of other group members (the development of personal favorable attitudes and bonds between members) can lead to in-group favoritism, clique formation, nepotism, and so on. Here, the consequences are apt to be a weakening of overall group cohesion as cliques develop, a deterioration of cooperation with other groups as in-group favoritism grows, and a lessening of group effectiveness as a result of nepotism. *Inducibility*, the readiness to be influenced positively by other group members, can lead to excessive conformity with the view of others so that one no longer makes one's own independent, unique contribution to the group. The cooperative process, as a result, may be deprived of the creative contribution that can be made by each of its members, and also, those who suppress their individuality may feel inwardly alienated from themselves and their group despite their outer conformity. In addition, social loafing may occur in which some members shirk their responsibilities to the group and seek to obtain the benefits of group membership without offering the contributions they are able to make to it.

The limitations of the theory of cooperation – competition

My theory deals with pure simple situations of cooperation and competition, in which the interdependent parties each have only one goal and are equally interdependent. Of course, in real life this is rarely the case. In addition, the theory has not the precision and quantitative rigor and strong logical deductibility that ideally a theory should have. There are implicit "common sense" perceptual, cognitive, learning, and cultural assumptions within it that are necessary for its deductions. Like most theories in social psychology, it is not independent of other work on individual and social processes. In addition, my theory only considers the cooperation–competition dimension of social relations. As I have indicated elsewhere (Deutsch 1982, 1985, and in the subsequent section "Social relations and psychological orientations"), social relations differ not only in the cooperation–competition dimension but also in such other dimensions as: equality of power; task orientation versus social–emotional orientation; intimate versus formal; and importance of the relationship. The psychological orientation to a given social relation will be determined by the combined dimensions.

Despite the limitations of my theory, I consider it to be an important one because the dimension of cooperation–competition is one of the central variables of all social relationships whether at the individual, group, or international level. (For a further discussion of the limitations and strengths of the theory see Johnson and Johnson, 2005: 326–342.)

A theory of conflict resolution

After obtaining my PhD in the summer of 1948, I accepted a position at the Research Center for Human Relations (then at the New School) headed by Stuart Cook, which involved developing a comparative study of integrated and segregated interracial housing (Deutsch and Collins 1951). In 1949, the Center moved to New York University (NYU) where I initiated a program of research to develop insight into the conditions that affected the choice to cooperate or to compete. At NYU, I met Howard Raiffa, a scholar much interested in game theory and decision making (Luce and Raiffa, 1957), who introduced me to the prisoner's dilemma when I indicated my research

interests. This led me to initiate research on the prisoner's dilemma and then on other mixed motive situations such as bargaining, negotiation, and conflict where there are typically a mixture of motivations to cooperate and to compete. As a result of doing research with such situations, we reformulated our questions from "What determines the choice to cooperate or compete?" to the conceptually similar but "sexier" "What determines whether a conflict will take a constructive or destructive course?" Our earlier research on the effects of cooperation and competition had indicated that a cooperative process was more likely to lead to constructive conflict resolution and a competitive process to a destructive resolution.

We did much research (Deutsch, 1973) in an attempt to find the answer. The results fell into a pattern I slowly began to grasp. They seemed explainable by an assumption I have immodestly labeled *Deutsch's Crude Law of Social Relations*:

> The characteristic processes and effects elicited by a given type of social relationship also tend to elicit that type of social relationship; and a typical effect tends to induce the other typical effects of the relationship.

Thus, cooperation induces and is induced by perceived similarity in beliefs and attitudes; readiness to be helpful; openness in communication; trusting and friendly attitudes; fair treatment; sensitivity to common interests and de-emphasis of opposed interests; orientation toward enhancing mutual power rather than power differences, and so on. Similarly, competition induces and is induced by use of the tactics of coercion, threat, or deception; attempts to enhance the power differences between oneself and the other; poor communication; minimization of the awareness of similarities in values and increased sensitivity to opposed interests; suspicious and hostile attitudes; unfair treatment; and so on.

In other words, if one has systematic knowledge of the effects of cooperative and competitive processes, one has systematic knowledge of the conditions that typically give rise to such processes and, by extension, to the conditions that affect whether a conflict takes a constructive or destructive course. My early theory of cooperation and competition is a theory of the effects of cooperative and competitive processes. Hence, from the Crude Law of Social Relations, it follows that this theory brings insight into the conditions that give rise to cooperative and competitive processes.

This law is certainly crude. It expresses surface similarities between effects and causes; the basic relationships are genotypical rather than phenotypical. The surface effects of cooperation and competition are due to the underlying type of interdependence (positive or negative) and type of action (effective or bungling), the basic social psychological processes involved in the theory (substitutability, cathexis, and inducibility), and the cultural or social medium and situational context in which these processes are expressed. Thus, how a positive attitude is expressed in an effective, positively interdependent relationship depends on what is appropriate to the cultural or social medium and situational context; presumably one would not seek to express it in a way that is humiliating or embarrassing or likely to be experienced negatively by one's partner.

Similarly, the effectiveness of any typical effect of cooperation of competition as an initiating or inducing condition of a cooperative or competitive process is not due to its phenotype but rather to the inferred genotype of the type of interdependence and types of action. Thus, in most social media and social contexts, perceived similarity in basic values is highly suggestive of the possibility of a positive linkage between oneself and the other. However, we are likely to see ourselves as negatively linked in a context that leads each of us to recognize that similarities in values impel seeking something that is in scarce supply and available for only one of us. Also, it is evident that although threats are mostly perceived in a way that suggests a negative linkage, any threat perceived as intended to compel you to do something that

is good for you or that you feel you should do is apt to be suggestive of a positive linkage.

Although the law is crude, my impression is that it is reasonably accurate; phenotypes often indicate the underlying genotypes. Moreover, it is a synthesizing principle, which integrates and summarizes a wide range of social psychological phenomena. One can integrate much of the literature on the determinants of positive and negative attitudes in terms of the other associated effects of cooperation and competition. Thus, positive attitudes result from perceptions of similarity, open communication, and so on. Similarly, many of the determinants of effective communication can be linked to the other typical effects of cooperation or competition, such as positive attitude and power sharing.

In brief, the *theory of conflict resolution* equates a constructive process of conflict resolution with an effective cooperative problem-solving process in which the conflict is the mutual problem to be resolved cooperatively. It also equates a destructive process of conflict resolution with a competitive process in which the conflicting parties are involved in a competition or struggle to determine who wins and who loses; often, the outcome of the struggle is a loss for both parties. The theory further indicates that a cooperative–constructive process of conflict resolution is fostered by the typical effects of cooperation and a competitive–destructive process by the typical effects of competition. The theory of cooperation and competition outlined in the beginning of this part is a well-verified theory of the effects of cooperation and competition and thus allows insight into what can give rise to a constructive or destructive process.

Limitations and strengths of the theory of conflict resolution

As indicated above, the theory is based upon two key elements: the theory of the effects of cooperation and competition processes and the Crude Law of Social Relations. The limitation and strengths of these two elements lead to the limitations and strengths of the theory of conflict resolution. The main difference between the strengths of the two elements is that the theory of cooperation–competition has generated much supportive research; apart from the research reported in Deutsch (1973, 1985), little research on the Crude Law has yet been done. Both theoretical elements deal with processes central to social psychology and social life.

Recently, two papers have been prepared which present formal models concerned with conflict: "Dynamics of two-actor cooperation – conflict models" (Liebovitch et al., 2008) and "From crude law to precise formalism: identifying the essence of conflict intractability" (Nowak et al., 2008). They are respectively relevant to the two elements of the theory of conflict resolution.

Distributive justice

My theorizing and research in this area has mainly focused on two central questions: What are the effects of different principles of distributive justice? And what leads to preference for one principle or another? My book, *Distributive Justice* (Deutsch, 1985) presents much of the relevant work by my students and myself.

My work on the social psychology of justice was initiated by an invitation from Melvin Lerner, a social psychologist who has made many important contributions to this area. Early in 1972, he invited me to write a paper for a Conference on Injustice in North America (Deutsch, 1974,1985). In preparation for the 1972 conference, I read widely – delving into the literature of the moral and legal philosophers, sociologists, and political scientists, and the relevant work of social psychologists. The more I read, the more dissatisfied I became with the existing literature in social psychology; it seemed too narrowly focused, too parochial, and too unwittingly reflective of the dominant Western ideology. The focus was limited mainly to how subjects in laboratory experiments attempted to restore their psychological equilibrium after experiencing or observing an inequity. There was little research on such topics as the conditions necessary for awakening the sense of injustice, procedural justice, retributive justice, and so on. The emphasis of equity theorists on "proportionality" as the sole canon of distributive justice suggested that they were neglecting other distributive principles, such as "equal share to all" or "to each according to his need," which have been rallying slogans for different political ideologies (Deutsch, 1975). Beyond this, the economic and market orientation of equity theory appeared to reflect, unwittingly, the implicit assumption in much of current Western ideology that economic "rationality" and economic values should pervade all social life and are appropriate in noneconomic social relations (e.g., between lovers, between parent and child).

I note that as I became more involved in this area and started to think about my research – past and present – in the context of "justice," I found myself in the position of the bourgeois gentleman of Moliere's play who was delighted to learn that he had been speaking prose all the time. I was delighted to recognize that my research under other labels could be labeled as "justice" research quite properly. Thus, my early study of the effects of cooperation and competition upon group processes (Deutsch, 1949b) could be considered a study of the consequences of two contrasting distributive values ("rewarding group members equally" or "'rewarding them in terms of their relative rank in their contributions to group performance"). Similarly, our many studies of conflict and bargaining (Deutsch, 1973) are centrally related to the social psychology of justice. They were focused on the important questions: Under what conditions are people with conflicting interests able to work out an agreement (i.e., a system of justice defining what each shall give and receive in the transaction between them) that is stable and mutually satisfying?

In *Distributive Justice*, I concentrated on four distributive principles: *winner-takes-all*, *equity* (proportionality), *equality*, and *need*. I was interested in what effects these principles would have in tasks where interdependent work was neither required nor possible, and in tasks where interdependent work was necessary.

The principles were described as follows:

Winner-takes-all: Under this system, whoever performs the task best in the group wins all the money the group is paid.

Proportionality: Under this system, each person is rewarded in proportion to his or her contribution to the group score. In other words, the person who contributes 50 percent of the group's total output will get 50 percent of the money to be distributed within the group; a person who contributes 10 percent would get 10 percent, and so on.

Equality: Under this system, each person in the group will get an equal share of the money to be distributed within the group.

Need: Under the need distribution system, each group member will be rewarded according to the need expressed on a biographical data sheet. In other words, the person who needs the money most will get proportionately more money; the person who needs the money least will get the least amount of money.

The theory of cooperation and competition and the Crude Law were employed to develop hypotheses about both the effects and the choice of the different principles. With the assumption that our college student subjects were not alienated (from themselves, work, or the experiment) and would work as well as they could, we predicted that there would be no significant differences in the productivity of the subjects when no interdependent work was required or possible. However, we also predicted that the different principles would elicit different attitudes toward the other group members; the more cooperative principles (*equality* and *need*) would elicit more favorable attitudes than the more competitive principles (*winner-takes-all* and *equity*).

In the tasks where interdependent work was necessary, we predicted that the results would be similar to those obtained in the earlier research on cooperation – competition; higher productivity and more favorable attitudes when *cooperative* rather than *competitive*

distributive principles were employed. The results of our various experimental studies (see Deutsch, 1985) were supportive of our hypotheses.

With regard to the choice among the different principles, we employed The Crude Law to make predictions. In my paper, "Interdependence and psychological orientation" (Deutsch 1982, 1985), I developed the idea that different social relations require different psychological orientations (see the section "Social relations and psychological orientations," for further elaboration). Based upon prior research on the effects of cooperation and competition as well as research on the effects of the different distributive justice principles, we characterized two psychological orientations: *solidarity* and *economic*. The *solidarity* orientation is congruent with a relationship that is cooperative, equal, social–emotional, and informal, while the *economic* fits a relationship that is competitive, equal, task-oriented, and formal. A *solidarity* orientation is defined by a sense of positive bonding and positive feelings toward and from the others; more reliance on empathy and intuition in understanding the others; and an awareness of a mutual obligation to be helpful to one another. An *economic* orientation is characterized by detachment, an objective–analytical perspective, a utilitarian self-interest, and expectation that the others have a similar interest.

In Chapter 11 of *Distributive Justice* (Deutch, 1985), some research bearing upon these ideas is presented. The research is supportive, but only a few studies were conducted. I do not consider that the evidence is strong, but I believe that the underlying ideas are. In the following text, I elaborate on some of these ideas.

Social relations and psychological orientation

A number of years ago, I was doing a study of marital couples and I wanted to develop a way of characterizing the nature of the couple relationship. With the help of Myron Wish

(Wish et al., 1976), we developed a method of doing so. In the course of doing so, we identified what we considered to be several of the basic dimensions of social relations: cooperation–competition; power distribution; task-orientated versus social–emotional; formal versus informal; degree of importance. Some of these are similar to those described by other investigators.

In terms of these dimensions, "friends" would be generally considered to be cooperative, of equal power, in a social–emotional, and informal relationship of considerable importance. In contrast, the relationship between a police officer and a thief might be viewed as competitive, unequal power, task-oriented, formal, and of moderate importance.

My next thought was that to act appropriately in a given type of social relation one must have an appropriate psychological orientation to that relationship: one's psychological orientation must "fit" the social relation. For example, my psychological orientation when I am negotiating the price of a car with a used-car salesman will be rather different than when I am playing with my six-year-old grandson. Different types of social relations will induce different types of psychological orientations, and, according to my "Crude Law," different types of psychological orientations will induce different types of social relations.

The nature of psychological orientations

In my current view, a psychological orientation consists of four highly interdependent elements: a cognitive orientation, a motivational orientation, a moral orientation, and an action orientation. In my prior publications (Deutsch 1982, 1985), action orientation was not included.

Cognitive orientations

In recent years, scholars in a number of different disciplines – cognitive psychology, social psychology, sociology, linguistics, anthropology, and artificial intelligence – have utilized such terms as *schema*, *script*, and *frame* to refer to the *structures of expectations* that

help orient the individual cognitively to the situation confronting her. I employ the term *cognitive orientation* as being essentially the same. In the view being presented here, the person's cognitive orientation to his situation is only one aspect of his psychological orientation to a social relationship.

Underlying the concepts of schema, script, and frame is the shared view that people approach their social world actively, with structured expectations about themselves and their social environments that reflect their organized beliefs about different social situations and different people. Our structured expectations make it possible for us to interpret and respond quickly to what is going on in specific situations. If our expectations lead us to inappropriate interpretations and responses, then they are likely to be revised on the basis of our experiences in the situation. Or if the circumstance confronting us is sufficiently malleable, our interpretations and responses to it may help to shape its form.

It is important for the participants in a particular social relationship to know "what's going on here" – to know the actors; the roles they are to perform; and the relations among the different roles, the props and settings, the scenes, and the themes of the social interaction. However, everyday social relations are rarely as completely specified by well-articulated scripts as the social interaction in a play in the traditional theater; ordinary social interactions have more the qualities of improvisational theater in which only the nature of the characters involved in the situation is well-specified and the characters are largely free to develop the detail of the skeletonized script as they interact with one another.

The improvisational nature of most social relations – the fact that given types of social relations occur in widely different contexts and with many different kinds of actors – makes it likely that relatively abstract or generalized cognitive orientations will develop from the different types of social relations. I assume that people are implicit social psychological theorists and, as a result of their experience, have developed cognitive schemas of the different types of social relations, though usually not articulated, that are similar to those articulated by theorists in social psychology and the other social sciences. Undoubtedly, at this early stage of the development of social science theory, the unarticulated conceptions of the average person are apt to be more sophisticated than the articulated ones of the social scientists.

Motivational orientations

Just as different cognitive orientations are associated with the different types of social relations, so also are different motivational orientations. A motivational orientation toward a given social relationship orients one to the possibilities of gratification or frustration of certain types of needs in the given relationship. To the cognitive characterization of the relationship, the motivational orientation adds the personal, subjective features arising from one's situationally relevant motives or need-dispositions.

The motivational orientation gives rise to the cathexis of certain regions of the cognitive landscape, making them positively or negatively valent, and highlights the pathways to and from valent regions. It gives the cognitive map a dynamic character. It predisposes one to certain kinds of fantasies (or nightmares) and to certain kinds of emotions. It orients one to such questions as, "What is to be valued in this relationship?" and "What do I want here and how do I get it?"

Moral orientations[2]

A moral orientation toward a given social relationship direct one to the mutual obligations, rights, and entitlements of the people involved in the given relationship. It adds an "ought," "should," or obligatory quality to a psychological orientation. The moral orientation implies that one experiences one's relationship not only from a personal perspective but also from a social perspective that includes the perspective of the others in the relationship. A moral orientation makes the experience of injustice more than a frustrating, personal experience (Deutsch et al., 1978).

Not only is one personally affected, so are the other participants in the relationship, because its value underpinnings are being undermined. The various participants in a relationship have the mutual obligation to respect and protect the framework of social norms that define what is to be considered as fair or unfair in the interactions and outcomes of the participants. One can expect that the moral orientation, and hence what is considered fair, will differ in different types of social relations.

Action orientation

Action orientations refer to the kinds of behavior which are viewed as appropriate in a given type of social relationship. Different cultures often have different views as to what is appropriate behavior in a given social relationship. Thus, if I felt very pleased with the outcome of my negotiations with the used-car salesman (I got a very good price), it would be inappropriate behavior to express my pleasure by kissing him.

The moral component that exists in all social relations has largely been neglected in social psychological theorizing. I suggest that the *moral orientation*, what is perceived to be just or unjust, will vary in different types of social relations. Let me illustrate the moral component of several different types of social relationships.

Equality–Inequality

There are a number of different moral orientations connected with equality and inequality: other features of the relationship, in addition to the distribution of power within it, will determine the nature of the moral orientation that will be elicited. Thus, in a cooperative, equal relationship one would expect an egalitarian relationship. In a cooperative, unequal relationship, the moral orientation obligates the more powerful person to employ his power in such a way as to benefit the less powerful one, not merely himself. In such a relationship, the less powerful one has the obligation to show appreciation, to defer to, and honor the more powerful person. These obligations may be rather specific and limited if the relationship is task-oriented or they may be diffuse and general if the relationship is a social–emotional one.

In an equal, competitive relationship, one's moral orientation is toward the value of initial equality among the competitors and the subsequent striving to achieve superiority over the others. This orientation favors equal opportunity but not equal outcomes: the competitors start the contest with equal chances to win, but some win and some lose. In an unequal, competitive relationship the moral orientations of the strong and the weak support an exploitative relationship. The strong are likely to adopt the view that the rich and powerful are biologically and hence morally superior; they have achieved their superior positions as a result of natural selection; it would be against nature to interfere with the inequality and suffering of the poor and weak; and it is the manifest destiny of superior people to lead inferior people. In an unequal, competitive relationship, the weak are apt to *identify with the aggressor* (Freud, 1937) and adopt the moral orientation of the more powerful and to feel that their inferior outcomes are deserved. Or, they may feel victimized. If so, they may either develop a revolutionary moral orientation directed toward changing the nature of the existing relationship or they may develop the moral orientation of being a victim. The latter orientation seeks to obtain secondary gratification from being morally superior to the victimizer. "It's better to be sinned against than to sin"; "The meek shall inherit the earth."

Task versus social–emotional relations

The moral orientation in a task-oriented relationship is that of utilitarianism. Its root value is maximization: people should try to get the most out of a situation. Good is viewed as essentially quantitative, as something that can be increased or decreased without limit (Diesing, 1962: 35). A second element in this moral orientation is the means-end schema, in which efficient allocation of means to achieve alternative ends

becomes a salient value. A third element is impartiality in the comparison of means, so that means can be compared on the basis of their merit in achieving given ends rather than on the basis of considerations irrelevant to the means-end relationship. In Parsonian terms, the moral orientation in task-oriented relations is characterized by the values of universalism, affective neutrality, and achievement. In contrast, the moral orientation of social–emotional relations is characterized by the values of particularism, affectivity, and ascription (Diesing, 1962: 90). Obligations to other people in a social–emotional relationship are based on their particular relationship to oneself rather than on general principles: they are strongest when relations are close and weakest when relations are distant. In a task-oriented relation, one strives to detach oneself from the objects of one's actions, to treat them all as equal, separate, interchangeable entities. In a social–emotional relationship, one is the focal point of myriad relationships that one strives to maintain and extend, since action takes place only within relationships (Diesing, 1969: 91). Ascription is the opposite of the achievement value: it means that one's action and obligations toward people spring solely from their relationship to oneself rather than as a response to something they have done.

Some potential research

From the Crude Law, it follows that the causal arrow connecting psychological orientations and types of social relations is bidirectional: a psychological orientation can induce or be induced by a given type of social relation. Here, I would go further and indicate that the cognitive, motivational, and moral components of a psychological orientation can each induce one another – hence, they are likely to be found together – and each of the components can induce or be induced by a given type of social relation. The foregoing assumptions proliferate into a great number of testable, specific hypotheses that would predict a two-way causal arrow between specific modes of thought, and specific types of social relations. Thus, a bureaucratic social situation will tend to induce obsessive–compulsive modes of thought and obsessive–compulsive modes of thought will tend to "bureaucratize" a social relationship. They would also predict that a competitive social relationship will tend to increase the psychological weight or importance of the difference in values between oneself and one's competitors, whereas a cooperative relationship will tend to increase the psychological importance of the similarities in values between oneself and one's fellow cooperators. We would also hypothesize that a tendency to accentuate the difference in values between oneself and others is apt to induce a competitive relationship, whereas a tendency to accentuate the similarities is likely to induce a cooperative relationship. Further, it can be predicted that different principles of distributive justice will be associated with different types of social relations: a fraternal relationship will be connected with the principle of equality, a caring relationship with the principle of need, a hierarchical organization with the principle of equity, and a power struggle with the principle of winner takes all.

Limitations of social relations and psychological orientations

This work, more fully presented in Deutsch (1982, 1985), is a sketch of some important theoretical ideas. It needs much more theoretical development and much more research.

SOCIAL IMPLICATIONS OF MY WORK

I have always considered my contributions to psychology as being theoretical and myself as someone who developed theoretical ideas and did research related to theory. However, my mentor, Kurt Lewin taught his students that 'there is nothing as practical as a good theory'. While I did not anticipate the practical applications of my work, I believe that it has had some important ones. I will describe a few.

First, my dissertation study, a theoretical and experimental study of the effects of cooperation and competition upon group process (Deutsch, 1949a, 1949b) was done in the context of small experimental classes in an undergraduate psychology course I was teaching at MIT. Although the guiding image underlying my study related to issues of war and peace, to whether the then-recently created UN Security Council would function cooperatively or competitively, my experiment involved the creation of cooperative and competitive small classrooms of five students. I published a paper in an education journal on the educational implications of my theory and research. However, it was David W. Johnson – a former doctoral student of mine – who systematically developed these ideas into a pedagogy of cooperative learning and helped many teachers and school systems through the world to adopt this approach to education. It has also been widely applied in industry (see Johnson and Johnson, 2005).

Second, I directed a study on interracial housing (Deutsch and Collins, 1951) which compared the behavioral and attitudinal effects of living in public housing where the white and black residents were integrated (living in the same building) or segregated (living in separate buildings) within the housing project. The integrated housing was in New York City; the segregated housing in Newark. The results of this study played a role in changing the Newark Public Housing from a policy of segregating to integrating the races in their housing projects. I quote from a statement made by the Director of the Newark Housing Projects (from back cover of *Interracial Housing*):

> A new policy ... provides that henceforth all apartments are to be allocated on a basis of need, regardless of race, religion, and color ... In large measure, this change in fundamental policy reflects the impact of the study reported in this book.
> Deutsch and Collins, 1951: back cover

The study not only affected policy in Newark, it played a role in changing policies of the US Public Housing Authority which provided some of the financing for local housing authorities. Additionally, it was a small part of the material that a SPSSI Committee (which included Kenneth Clark, Isadore Chein, and me) prepared for the lawyers who successfully petitioned the US Supreme Court in *Brown* v. *Board of Education* to end racial segregation in publicly supported schools.

Third, my work on conflict resolution, with the help of many former students and many other scholars, helped to stimulate the development of the field of conflict resolution studies. The basic query underlying our theoretical and research work on conflict ("What determines whether a conflict will take a constructive or destructive course?") has direct relevance to conflicts in the real world. I and many of my former students have applied our theoretical work on conflict to such diverse conflicts as marital conflict, intergroup and ethnic conflict, industrial conflict, educational conflict, international conflict, reconciliation after destructive conflict, and so on. The applications have taken various forms; analytical writing, education, workshops with practitioners, mediation, and consultation to the conflicting parties. Such students as Jeffrey Rubin, Roy Lewicki, David Johnson, Michelle Fine, Harvey Hornstein, Madelaine Heilman, Barbara Bunker, Kenneth Kressel, Susan Opotow, Janice Steil, Peter Coleman, Eric Marcus, Ken Sole, Adrienne Asch, and many others have made important, original contributions to the development of practice as well as theory in this area. In addition, the Center that I founded at Teachers College, the International Center for Cooperation and Conflict Resolution (ICCCR), has helped to stimulate the development of conflict resolution and mediation programs in many schools.

For me, one of the applications of my work is an unusually important one. It occurred in Poland where two outstanding psychologists, Janusz Reykowski and Janusz Grzelak, applied some of my ideas during the negotiations between the Communist government and Solidarity which lead to a *peaceful* transfer of

governmental power from the Communist Party to Solidarity in 1989. Reykowski was a leading figure in the Communist Party and Grzelak was a very important influence in the Solidarity movement. Each has indicated that my work influenced him considerably in their approach to the negotiations which facilitated a constructive resolution of the negotiations. In footnote #3, I quote from some remarks made by Professor Reykowski at a Conference in Intractable Conflict held in Poland in the fall of 2006.[3] In footnote #4, I quote from statements made by Professor Grzelak about his role in the negotiations and about my influence in an email sent to Lan Bui-Wrzosinska, and forwarded to me.[4]

The social effects of my work in the areas of cooperation–competition, inter-racial housing, and conflict resolution have been notable. I do not yet have a clear picture of the direct social impact of my work in the area of social justice. Three papers of mine appear to have had a considerable impact on the social psychological study of justice and to have been widely used in classrooms: "Equity, equality, and need" (Deutsch, 1973), "Awakening the sense of injustice" (Deutsch, 1974,1985), and "A framework for thinking about oppression and its change" (Deutsch, 2006).

Let me conclude this section by stating: I did not foresee many of the applications of my theoretical and empirical work. Like throwing a pebble into water, the ripples of one's theoretical work are hard to predict in advance.

CONCLUSION

When I taught a course on theories in social psychology, I suggested to students that there were two types of theorists: *grandiose* and *picayune*. The *grandiose* theorists generalize their ideas widely and freely, the *picayune* keep their generalizations very close to their data. I consider myself to fall into the *grandiose* category. I have generalized my ideas so that they are relevant not only to the

individual as the social interactor but also to
the other types such as groups and nations.
I have done this because I think my ideas
deal with basic social processes. Clearly, my
ideas are not fully baked and they need many
more and different ingredients to deal with
the different types of social actors. It is my
hope that others will finish the baking of
these ideas.

NOTES

1 There was much open antisemitism in the United
States during the 1920s, 1930s, and 1940s, and I
experienced some of it directly during this period.

2 In my view, social psychologists have unduly
neglected the moral aspect of every social relation. In
my study of conflict, I was alerted to how issues of
justice–injustice often played a central role in conflict. This led me to reflect on the difference between
the experiences of unjustice and frustration (Deutsch
et al., 1978) which, in turn, led me to think about the
moral norms in different social relations. Also, during
the 1960s at Columbia, some students flouted the
moral or social norms in an attempt to bring about
social change; for example, by appearing naked in a
classroom. Additionally, the work of Goffman (1959)
was suggestive. By the "moral aspect of every situation," I refer to the social norms which define appropriate and inappropriate behavior and the mutual
obligations which enable the social relation to exist.

3 Professor Reykowski's remarks at the Conference
on Intractable Conflict in Poland, 2006:

Most of the great ideas produced by psychologists
are appreciated for their intellectual value rather
than for their consequences for practical life. There
are, however, some exceptions. For me one such
exception is Morton Deutsch because there are
good reasons to claim that his theories went
beyond academia and have had an impact on
some large scale social processes – that took place
a thousand miles from Morton's home place. In
fact, they took place in Poland in the middle of the
eighties. It was a period of time when Poland ...
was in the state of deep crisis. "Solidarity" – the
massive democratic movement had been crushed
during Martial Law (introduced in Poland in
December 1981) and the country was over-
whelmed by a major political and social conflict ...
As a psychologist, I was especially interested in
analyzing the psychological factors that contributed to the development of the conflict situation
and in possible psychological remedies. That was

why I focused on Morton Deutsch's *The Resolution
of Conflict* (Yale University, 1973) that I received
from him some time ago. And now it seemed to
offer the insight that I needed. The major theses of
the book ... provided excellent conceptual instruments for description of the Polish situation and
were a very good source of ideas for developing
proposals how to deal with it. I wrote an article in
the major, very influential, Polish weekly magazine
(*Polityka*) – widely read by intelligentsia and members of the establishment – presenting Morton's
theory and indicating how it could be applied to
the Polish context. The approach met with an
attack from both sides ...
Unlike earlier time, the attack in the official party
newspaper was not a political death sentence for
its author. To the contrary, I was allowed to
respond to the criticism in the same newspaper
and attacking my opponents I could further
describe the concepts of destructive [and construc-
tive] conflict and their importance for understanding the Polish situation. I have some reasons to
believe that this exchange and my further activities
along this line had some impact on members of the
ruling elite in Poland. A few years later, when the
ruling party came to the conclusion that the policy
of accommodation with Solidarity is a necessary
step for solving the Polish conflict, I was called
upon to help in execution of this policy. The most
important first step of this new policy was the
Round Table negotiations between Government
and Solidarity. As a result of these negotiations the
partially free election took place in Poland and following that the new government held by Tadeusz
Mazowiecki a leading Solidarity figure was introduced. In other words, the starting point for a
series of events that led to dissolution of the so
called Soviet Bloc...
The most important ... [Round Table] was the
political table because there was a place where the
main political changes were formulated and negotiated. I was a co-chair of the political table ...
It is not a place for detailed description of the
negotiation. I would like to conclude that Morton
Deutsch's theory of destructive conflict had not
only an important place in psychological science
but also has some place in the history of social
change in Europe.

4 Quotation from an e-mail by Professor Grzelak:

I was one of the two vice-chairmen of one of the
Round Table workgroups (the chairman was Prof.
Henryk Samsonowicz) – concerning education and
science. I was also asked, as an expert, to participate in the informal, although not secret, talks in
smaller groups. Several of them prepared the most
important decisions. I took part in probably all of
them, mostly as the main negotiator ... Due to the

personal interests in psychology and thanks to 2.5 years spent in the United States, I did know a number of works concerning conflict of interest. Among them most important were those by Kelley, Rapaport and Deutsch. I mentioned the Author whom I owe especially, last. His theoretical (On cooperation and competition, 1949; On the resolution of conflict, 1973; and many more) and empirical works ... helped understand the role of trust, the role of orientation in an interaction, the power of power and the weakness of power, when it is used in conflict management. Theory is the most important but equally important is the "spirit" of the theory. What Morton said and says is filled with respect for people, for their subjectivity, it's a constant search for resolutions both just and satisfying ... My fascination in conflict resolution began with reading Deutsch's works long before the downfall of communism and stayed alive long after the downfall of communism.

REFERENCES

Barnard, C.I. (1938) *The Functions of the Executive*. Cambridge, MA: Harvard University Press.

Deutsch, M. (1949a) A theory of cooperation and competition. *Human Relations, 2*, 129–151.

Deutsch, M. (1949b) An experimental study of the effect of cooperation and competition upon group processes. *Human Relations, 2*, 199–231.

Deutsch, M. (1954) Field theory in social psychology. In G. Lindzey and E. Aronson (eds), *The Handbook of Social Psychology, 1*, 412–487.

Deutsch, M. (1973) *The Resolution of Conflict: Constructive and Destructive Processes*. New Haven, CT: Yale University Press.

Deutsch, M. (1974) Awakening the sense of injustice. In M. Ross and M. Lerner (eds), *The Quest for Justice*, pp. 19–42. Canada: Holt, Reinhart, and Winston.

Deutsch, M. (1975) Equity, equality, and need. *Journal of Social Issues, 31*, 137–149.

Deutsch, M. (1982) Interdependence and psychological orientation. In V. Derlega and J.L. Grzelak (eds), *Cooperation and Helping Behavior*, pp. 16–41. New York: Academic Press.

Deutsch, M. (1985) *Distributive Justice, A Social-psychological Perspective*. New Haven, CT: Yale University Press.

Deutsch, M. (1992) Kurt Lewin: The tough-minded and tender-hearted scientist. *Journal of Social Issues, 48*, 31–43.

Deutsch, M. (2006) A framework for thinking about oppression and its change. *Social Justice Research, 19*, 7–41.

Deutsch, M., Coleman, P.T. and Marcus, E.T. (eds) (2006) *The Handbook of Conflict Resolution: Theory and Practice*, 2nd Edition. San Francisco: Jossey-Bass.

Deutsch, M. and Collins, M.E. (1951) *Interracial Housing: A Psychological Evaluation of a Social Experiment*. Minneapolis: University of Minnesota Press.

Deutsch, M., Steil, J. and Tuchman, B. (1978) An exploratory study of the meanings of injustice and frustration. *Personality and Social Psychology Bulletin, 4*, 393–398.

Diesing, P. (1962) *Reason in Society*. Urbana: University of Illinois Press.

Freud, S. (1937) *The Ego and the Mechanisms of Defense*. London: Hogarth.

Goffman, E. (1959) *The Presentation of Self in Everyday Life*. Garden City, NY: Doubleday Anchor Books.

Johnson, D.W. and Johnson, R.T. (2005) New developments in social interdependence theory. *Psychology Monographs, 131*, 285–360.

Johnson, D.W., Johnson, R.T. and Tjosvold (2006) Constructive controversy: The value of intellectual opposition. In M. Deutsch, P. Coleman and E.C. Marcus (eds), *The Handbook of Conflict Resolution: Theory and Practice*, 2nd Edition. San Francisco: Jossey-Bass.

Koffka, K. (1935) *Principles of Gestalt Psychology*. New York: Harcourt, Brace.

Lewin, K. (1935) *Dynamic Theory of Personality*. New York: McGraw-Hill.

Lewin, K. (1936) *Principles of Topological Psychology*. New York: McGraw-Hill.

Lewin, K. (1938) The conceptual representation and measurement of psychological forces. *Contributions to Psychological Theory, 1* (4).

Lewin, K. (1948) *Resolving Social Conflicts*. New York: Harper and Brothers.

Liebovitch, L.S., Vallacher, R. and Michael, J. (2008). Dynamics of two-actor cooperation-competition models. *Peace and Conflict: Journal of Peace Psychology, 16*, 175–188.

Luce, R.D. and Raiffa, H. (1937) *Games and Decisions*. New York: Wiley.

Maller, J.B. (1929) Cooperation and competition: An experimental study in motivation. *Teachers College Contribution to Education, 384*.

May, M.A. and Doob, L.W. (1937) Cooperation and competition. *Social Science Research Counsel Bulletin, 125*.

Mead, G.H. (1934) *Mind, Self and Society*. Chicago: University of Chicago Press.

Mead, M. (1937) *Cooperation and Competition Among Primitive People*. New York: McGraw-Hill.

Nowak, A., Deutsch, M., Bartowski, W. and Solomon, S. (2008) From Crude Law to precise formulation: Modeling the path to destructiveness in conflict. *Please and Conflict: Journal of Peace Psychology, 16*, 189–210.

Wish, M., Deutsch, M. and Kaplan, S. (1976) Perceived dimensions of interpersonal relations. *Journal of Personality and Social Psychology, 33*, 400–420.

41

The Focus Theory of Normative Conduct

Robert B. Cialdini

ABSTRACT

The focus theory of normative conduct offers a way to make sense of the mixed support in the behavioral sciences for the role of social norms in human behavior. On the basis of the results of subsequent theory-relevant research, it appears that norms do have a considerable impact on behavior, but that the force and form of that impact can only be usefully understood through certain conceptual elements that have not been traditionally or rigorously applied. That is, to predict properly the likelihood of norm-consistent action requires that one must (a) separate two types of norms that at times act antagonistically in a situation – injunctive norms (what most others approve/disapprove) and descriptive norms (what most others do) – and (b) focus individuals' attention principally on the type of norm desired to operate. General support for the theory has emerged via research conducted in a variety of naturally occurring settings (e.g., a parking garage, amusement park, suburban neighborhood, upscale hotel), while employing a variety of communication vehicles (e.g., handbills, park signage, door-hangers, public service announcements), which generated significant change in a variety of environment-relevant activities (e.g., littering, recycling, energy usage, environmental crime).

INTRODUCTION

I was raised in an entirely Italian family, in a predominantly Polish neighborhood, in a historically German city (Milwaukee), in an otherwise rural state. I often ascribe my interest in the social influence process to an early recognition that the groups populating those settings had to be approached somewhat differently in order to obtain their assent, sometimes to the identical request. It also struck me early on that one reason for this complication was that the social norms – the characteristic tendencies and codes of conduct of the groups – differed. Therefore, if I wanted to maximize compliance with a request from a member of one or another of these groups, it would be wise to take into account the dominant norms of that particular unit.

This vague understanding that social norms both vary and make a difference had little impact on my choice of topics to study during graduate training and in the initial stages of my research career; indeed, the chosen topics in those days rarely involved normative issues, and I rarely thought about the social influence process I was studying at the time in normative terms. That began to change, though, when a few of my investigations encountered and even incorporated concepts that could be understood in normative terms: reciprocation, consistency, and social responsibility. I became aware that each of these normative concepts varied (within and between cultures) and made a notable difference in influencing human behavior, as some of my subsequent research has tried to document (Bator and Cialdini, 2006; Cialdini et al., 1995, 1999; Petrova et al., 2007).

However, the major impetus for a *theory* of normative conduct came not from a comfortable state of affairs – the easy fit I could see between social norms and social influence – but from an intriguingly discomforting one: certain thinkers whose judgment in theoretical matters I trusted greatly felt very differently about the usefulness of social norms as an explanatory and predictive concept than did other thinkers whose judgment I trusted just as much. On the one hand were those who saw the concept as central to a proper understanding of human social behavior (e.g., Berkowitz, 1972; Fishbein and Ajzen, 1975; Pepitone, 1976; Triandis, 1977). On the other hand were those who saw little value in the concept, viewing it as vague, overly general, often contradictory, and ill-suited to empirical tests (e.g., Darley and Latané, 1970; Krebs, 1970; Krebs and Miller, 1985; Marini, 1984).

By this time, I was well into my career and had come to recognize that a battle between heavyweights in an important theoretical arena is more than merely interesting or betworthy. It presents an uncommon opportunity for anyone willing to try to settle the argument, an opportunity to do more than just take a side but perhaps to make a genuine contribution by offering a novel way of thinking about the topic that resolves the conflict. With the focus theory of normative conduct and with the invaluable collaboration of excellent coworkers, it has been my hope to make the best of one such recognized opportunity.

EARLY YEARS: PROFITING FROM THE COMPLAINTS

Although I hadn't paid much early attention to the role of social norms in human conduct (or to the controversy surrounding it), I had always counted myself squarely in the camp of its proponents – those who judged that role to be systematic and consequential. But, as I've stated, my view hadn't developed from any close reading of the pertinent literature but, instead, from a set of informal personal observations associated with some accidents of birth. Once I undertook a full and dispassionate assessment of the literature, I had to admit that those who disagreed with my position had a point. In fact, they had a pair of worthy points. The first went as follows: "Well, look, there are social norms that directly contradict one another, such as the norm for minding your own business and the norm for getting involved. So, no matter which behavior occurred, it could be later explained as normative." This struck me as a troublesome matter for a social norms approach, as I had long since recognized that accounts that could explain everything after the fact were probably too vague or circular to explain anything. The second kind of objection to norms-based explanations was different from the first but equally problematic. In this case, critics pointed out that many times in a society people act counternormatively (e.g., declining to provide assistance to a needy other). Therefore, the critics argued, when people do perform normatively (e.g., agreeing to provide assistance), why should we believe it was because of a societal norm? Wasn't that norm also in place within the culture when they behaved counternormatively? Thus, the critics concluded that we would be better advised to attribute either kind of behavior to the action of other factors.

After immersing myself in the relevant research literature and thinking about the issues for a while, it appeared to me that both sides of the debate were right: norms do have a strong and regular impact on behavior, but the force and form of that impact could only be clearly established by making certain theoretical advancements. The first involved a crucial conceptual distinction.

Descriptive versus injunctive norms

In both everyday parlance and academic usage, the term "norm" has two meanings. One meaning refers to what is typically done (i.e., what is *normal*) in a culture or subculture; my coworkers and I have termed these *descriptive norms*. Another meaning refers to what is typically approved/disapproved within a culture or subculture; we have termed these *injunctive norms*. Despite the common label, the two types of norms come from quite different sources of motivation. Descriptive norms (sometimes called the norms of "is") motivate by informing individuals of what is likely to be effective and adaptive action in a situation. As such, they provide a decision-making shortcut and information-processing advantage when one is choosing how to behave in a particular setting. By simply registering what most others are doing there and following suit, one can usually choose efficiently and well (Surowiecki, 2004). In contrast to descriptive norms, which specify what is done, injunctive norms specify what ought to be done. They constitute the moral rules of the group, and they motivate action by promising to provide or withhold a form of social acceptance, which is a potent spur for behavior (Williams, 2007). Hence, whereas descriptive norms inform behavior, injunctive norms enjoin it.

Norm focus

There is substantial evidence that shifting an individual's attention to a specific source of information or motivation will change the individual's responses in ways that are congruent with the features of the now more prominent source (Kallgren and Wood, 1986; Lassiter et al., 2007; Millar and Tesser, 1989; Oyserman and Lee, 2008; Wilson and Gilbert, 2008).

In keeping with such evidence, Deaux and Major (1987) concluded that the occurrence of gender-consistent behavior is frequently determined by situational factors that shift attention to the construct of gender, thereby making it more salient. A similar relationship appears to be obtained in the normative arena. That is, norms motivate and direct action primarily when they are activated (i.e., made salient or otherwise focused upon); thus, persons who are dispositionally or temporarily focused on normative considerations are decidedly more likely to act in norm-consistent ways (Berkowitz, 1972; Kallgren et al., 2000; Miller and Grush, 1986).

An analysis of this sort allows us to retain a belief in the usefulness of normative explanations in the face of the insightful criticisms discussed earlier. That is, it becomes wholly understandable why the dominant norms of a society – that are presumably always in place – may only sometimes predict behavior: they should activate behavior only when *they* have been activated first. Similarly, the simultaneous existence of incompatible social norms is no longer a damaging criticism of normative accounts if we assume that the conflicting norms may coexist within the same society, but that the one that will produce congruent action is the one that is temporarily prominent in consciousness.

Pursuing this last realization further, we can see that it also applies to the distinction between descriptive and injunctive norms. Although it is most frequently the case that what is done and what is approved in a social group are the same, this is often not the case. For instance, even though the majority of people who pass a sidewalk Salvation Army donation kettle might not give a contribution, it is likely that the majority would approve of someone who did. In situations of this kind, with clearly conflicting descriptive and injunctive norms, we would expect that focusing observers on what most people did or on what most people approved would lead to behavior change that is consistent only with whichever has become now the more salient type of norm.

Normative conduct in the field

From the outset, our intention was to test our theoretical model as it applied to individuals' behavioral decisions regarding the environment. We chose environmental action as our primary dependent measure because it allowed us to test our norm focus model on behavior that we felt was of looming practical importance – although at the time we began the work, in the mid 1970s, that view was not widely shared. More recently, things have changed dramatically. For a variety of reasons (e.g., dwindling supplies of non-renewable energy, worrisome climate change data, concern for the welfare of future generations, and a general reverence for nature), numerous organizations have urged citizens toward a proenvironmental stance and away from environmentally wasteful or damaging activities. Plainly, environmental action has proven to be a social issue worthy of study. Nonetheless, when we began the work, our motive was not first and foremost to perform good social service; it was to conduct good social science, which required that we undertake proper tests of our model.

To substantiate the need for the theoretical refinements presented in our norm focus model, two questions needed to be answered: (1) Do behavioral patterns confirm our theorized distinction between descriptive and injunctive norms? And (2) is focus a critical mediator of which type of norm guides behavior? Depending upon how these questions are answered, there is also a third question of the practical implications and applications of our theoretical formulation. To attempt to converge upon the answers to these questions, we began with a set of experiments that examined tendencies to litter in public places. Even though littering is not the worst of environmental sins, it had the advantages of involving a discrete act that was easy to measure and was roundly viewed as counter to existing norms.

We thought it was important to conduct our studies in field settings where littering would occur naturally. Although people will litter in laboratory contexts (e.g., Krauss et al., 1978), the external validity of such studies might be questioned. Given the stormy history surrounding the practical utility of normative explanations, we wanted to maximize our external validity in order to offer suggestions for environmental action programs. Thus, we conducted the bulk of our research in field settings to increase our ability to generalize to real-world situations.

The effects of focusing on descriptive norms

We first turned our attention toward the explication of the effects of focusing on the descriptive norms of a situation. One of the most commonly reported findings from studies of littering is that individuals litter into an already littered environment at a greater rate than they do into an otherwise clean environment. According to our focus theory, this occurs because individuals are to some degree focused on the descriptive norms present in the situation; that is, they can see the amount of litter already there. Of course, our model is not the only one capable of explaining this data pattern. A social learning theorist might say that the effect is due to subjects' imitation of the behavior of those who have been in the environment before them. Consequently, in order to show the utility of our theoretical refinements, we needed to develop a theoretical test that would predict effects for our model that were different from those predicted from the imitation-based alternative account.

Study 1

In one investigation (Cialdini et al., 1990, Experiment 1) that took place in a hospital parking garage, participants were given the opportunity to litter (a handbill they found on their car windshields) either into a previously clean or a fully littered environment after first witnessing a confederate who either dropped trash into the environment or who simply walked through it. By varying the state of the environment (clean versus littered), we sought to manipulate the perceived descriptive norm for littering in the situation. By manipulating whether the confederate dropped trash into the environment, we sought to differentially focus participants' attention on the state of the environment and, consequently, to manipulate the salience of the perceived descriptive norm there (i.e., what most people did).

We had three main predictions. First, we expected that participants would be more likely to litter into an already littered environment than into a clean one. Second, we expected that participants who saw the confederate drop trash into a fully littered environment would be most likely to litter there themselves, because they would have had their attention drawn to evidence of a prolittering descriptive norm – that is, to the fact that people typically litter in that setting. Conversely, we anticipated that participants who saw the confederate drop trash into a clean environment would be least likely to litter there, because they would have had their attention drawn to evidence of an antilittering descriptive norm – that is, to the fact that (except for the confederate) people typically do not litter in that setting. This last expectation distinguished our normative account

from explanations based on simple modeling processes in that we were making the ironic prediction of decreased littering after participants had witnessed a model litter.

As can be seen in Figure 41.1, the data pattern supported our experimental hypotheses. Overall, there was more littering in the littered environment than in the clean environment. In addition, the most littering occurred when participants saw a model drop trash into a littered environment, and, most tellingly, the least littering occurred when participants saw a model drop trash into a clean environment. Counterintuitive findings of this sort call out for replication. Consequently, we conducted a replication and extension of Study 1 in order to detect the hypothesized decrease in littering when subjects were focused on litter in an otherwise clean environment. This second study (Cialdini et al., 1990, Experiment 2) was also designed to determine if the results from Study I were generalizable to other settings and other focus manipulations or whether they were due to some unique characteristics of our previous study.

Study 2

We reasoned that a lone piece of litter would, by its conspicuous nature, draw attention to

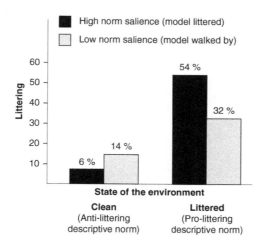

Figure 41.1 Percentage of participants littering as a function of descriptive norm salience and the state of the environment in Study 1

the nearly pristine state of the environment. Thus, we expected subjects' littering would decrease when the amount of litter in the environment increased from zero to one piece because the single piece of litter would serve to focus subjects on the antilittering descriptive norm. As the number of pieces of litter in the environment increased beyond one, however, the perceived descriptive norm would change from antilittering to prolittering. As the descriptive norm changed in this fashion, we expected the littering rate would increase. Thus, we made a counterintuitive prediction that could be best described graphically as a check mark-shaped relationship between amount of existing litter in the environment and the likelihood that subjects would litter into it.

To test these hypotheses, we observed the littering tendencies of adult visitors to an amusement park. At one-minute intervals, the first adult to pass a confederate was given a handbill that read "DON'T MISS TONIGHT'S SHOW." Immediately afterward, upon rounding a comer, subjects were unobtrusively observed by a different experimenter as they walked down a path of approximately 55 meters (60 yards) on which we had placed 0, 1, 2, 4, 8, or 16 clearly visible handbills. All other litter had been removed from the walkway.

A visual inspection of Figure 41.2 reveals a pattern of results that is consistent with our predictions. Indeed, a planned comparison

using trend weights for a check mark function (–2, –4, –1, 1, 2, 4) was significant. Most notable was the finding that littering decreased (from 18 percent to 10 percent) when one piece of litter was added to a litter-free environment.

Interim summary

At this juncture, it appeared to us that one factor that motivated our participants' decisions to litter was the descriptive norm of the situation. That is, under control conditions, they littered more in littered environments (where the descriptive norm favored littering) than they did in clean environments (where the descriptive norm opposed littering). More important, when the saliency of these descriptive norms was increased, our participants tended to litter even more in littered environments and even less in clean environments. From a theoretical perspective, then, focusing people on the appropriate descriptive norm regarding littering increased their norm-consistent behavior regardless of whether the norm favored littering or not littering. With this pattern documented, we turned our focus toward the behavioral influence of injunctive norms.

Effects of focusing on injunctive norms

Recall that, in keeping with the focus theory of normative conduct, our position has been

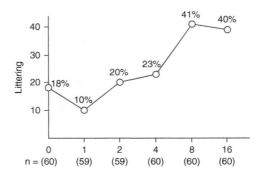

Figure 41.2 Percentage of participants littering as a function of the number of pieces of litter in the environment in Study 2

that norm theorists must be specific about whether they are referring to the descriptive or injunctive norm and which of these, if either, is salient. Up to this point we had only presented supportive evidence in the realm of descriptive norms. A demonstration that focusing on the injunctive norm against littering leads to injunctive norm-consistent behavior (e.g., decreased littering) would be theoretically as well as practically important.

Study 3

To focus people solely on the injunctive norm against littering in a way that was not amenable to alternative explanations, we relied on the effect of cognitive priming (which, by this date in our theory development, had already been established; see Higgins and Bargh, 1987). That is, one concept (e.g., littering) has a greater probability of being activated when attention is drawn to a related concept (e.g., recycling) compared to when attention is drawn to an unrelated concept (e.g., fine arts). Furthermore, many explanations of priming effects invoke the concept of spreading activation, which posits that similar concepts are linked together in memory within a network of nodes and that activation of one concept results in the spreading of the activation along the network to other semantically or conceptually related concepts. If norms are stored in a network format, as was suggested by Harvey and Enzle (1981), then varying the relatedness of activated norms to the target antilittering injunctive norm should result in systematic variations in the activation of the target norm. As the relatedness of the activated norm to the antilittering norm increases, the strength of activation of the target norm should also increase and littering rates should decline.

In selecting which other norms to activate, we considered not only the cognitive similarity between the selected norms and the antilittering norm but also the injunctive normativeness (likelihood that violation of it would meet with disapproval from others) of the selected norms. We based our selections on the results of the following scaling procedure.

A total of 35 possible norms, including the antilittering norm, were presented to two separate classes of upper division psychology students. The first class rated the 35 possibilities as to their normativeness; the second class rated their conceptual similarity to the antilittering norm. Based on these ratings, we selected four norms that were comparable in perceived normativeness to the antilittering norm; however, one was identical to the antilittering norm (refraining from littering), one was rated close to the antilittering norm (recycling), another was rated moderately close to the antilittering norm (turning out lights), and another was rated far from the antilittering norm (voting). We also selected a control issue that was non-normative (the availability of museums).

Our experimental setting was a community library parking lot. We left the extant litter in place (there was a small amount of litter that was equivalent across all conditions). To manipulate focus on the various norms, we tucked flyers with norm-relevant statements under the driver's side windshield wiper of each car while the patrons were in the library. Upon returning to their cars, subjects found handbills on their windshields with one of the following statements that differed in their similarity/closeness to the antilittering norm: "April is Keep Arizona Beautiful Month. Please Do Not Litter." (identical); "April is Preserve Arizona's Natural Resources Month. Please Recycle." (close); "April is Conserve Arizona's Energy Month. Please Turn Off Unnecessary Lights." (moderately close); "April is Arizona's Voter Awareness Month. Please Remember That Your Vote Counts." (far); and "April is Arizona's Fine Arts Month. Please Visit Your Local Art Museum." (control). We unobtrusively recorded littering of these handbills.

As is clearly evidenced in Figure 41.3, a significant linear trend was obtained, as predicted. This trend indicated that as the conceptual distance between the activated norm or concept and the target antilittering norm increased, littering also increased, supporting our contention that it should be possible to

progressively (and significantly) reduce littering by progressively shifting subjects'
focus to the injunctive norm.

MIDDLE YEARS: LOGICAL EXTENSIONS AND PRACTICAL IMPLICATIONS

With bolstered confidence in the validity of
our model's fundamental elements, we began
to think about how those elements could be
employed to reduce more general and more
damaging environmental problems than litter
abatement; for example, how developers of
environmentally oriented public service
announcements might best structure norm-based
messages (Bator and Cialdini, 2000). In addition, we started to test certain logical extensions of the model in settings that would
easily lend themselves to beneficial practical
applications.

For instance, a conceptually and practically important upshot of our formulation
becomes apparent when communicators seek
to persuade an audience to behave in accordance with existing norms. As we've stressed,
for information campaigns to be successful,
their creators must recognize the distinct
power of descriptive and injunctive norms
and must focus the target audience only on
the type of norm that is consistent with the
goal. This is far from always the case. We
recognized that there was an understandable
but misguided tendency of public officials to
try to mobilize action against socially disapproved conduct by depicting it as regrettably
frequent, thereby inadvertently installing a
counterproductive descriptive norm in the
minds of their audiences. To understand the
logic of the error, consider the following
incident that spurred a related experiment.

A graduate student of mine had visited the
Petrified Forest National Park in Arizona
with his fiancée – a woman he described as
the most honest person he'd ever known,
someone who had never borrowed a paper-
clip without returning it. They quickly
encountered a park sign warning visitors
against stealing petrified wood, "OUR
HERITAGE IS BEING VANDALIZED BY

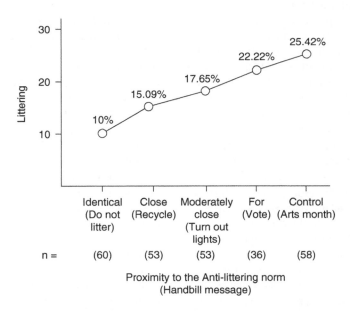

**Figure 41.3 Percentage of participants littering a handbill message as a function of its prox-
imity to the injunctive norm against littering in Study 3**

THE THEFT OF 14 TONS OF WOOD EVERY YEAR." While still reading the sign, he was shocked to hear his fiancée whisper, "We'd better get ours now."

In a team meeting where he related the incident, we wondered what could have spurred this wholly law-abiding young woman to want to become a thief and to deplete a national treasure in the process? After some discussion, we thought it had to do with a mistake that park officials made when creating the sign. They tried to alert visitors to the park's theft problem by telling them that many other visitors were thieves. In so doing, they stimulated the behavior they had hoped to suppress by making it appear the norm.

Although it is understandable that park officials would want to instigate corrective action by describing the dismaying size of the problem, our model warned such a message would be far from optimal. That is, *in situations already characterized by high levels of socially censured conduct*, the distinction between descriptive and injunctive norms offers a clear implication: it is a serious error to focus an audience on the descriptive norm (i.e., what is done there); instead, under such conditions, public service messages should focus the audience on the injunctive norm (i.e., what is approved/disapproved there). Thus, according to an informed normative account, the park signage would have been better designed to focus visitors on the social disapproval (rather than the harmful prevalence) of environmental theft.

Studies

Study 4

To examine this hypothesis – that in a situation characterized by unfortunate levels of socially disapproved conduct, a message that focuses recipients on the injunctive norm will be superior to messages that focus recipients on the descriptive norm – we gained permission from Petrified Forest National Park officials to place secretly marked pieces of

petrified wood along visitor pathways in three park locations. During five consecutive weekends, at the entrance to each path, we displayed signage that emphasized either descriptive or injunctive norms regarding the theft of petrified wood from the park. The descriptive norm sign stated, "Many past visitors have removed petrified wood from the Park, changing the natural state of the Petrified Forest." This wording was accompanied by pictures of three visitors taking wood. In contrast, the injunctive norm sign stated, "Please don't remove the petrified wood from the Park, in order to preserve the natural state of the Petrified Forest." This wording was accompanied by a picture of a lone visitor stealing a piece of wood, with a red circle-and-bar symbol superimposed over his hand. Our measure of message effectiveness was the percentage of marked pieces of wood stolen over the five-week duration of the study. As predicted, the descriptive norm message resulted in significantly more theft than the injunctive norm message, 7.92 percent versus 1.67 percent (Cialdini, 2003).

Should one conclude from these results that highlighting descriptive norms is always likely to be a counterproductive tactic in environmental information campaigns? No. In contrast to situations in which environmentally harmful behavior is prevalent, highlighting descriptive norms should be effective for those action domains in which environmentally *beneficial* behavior is prevalent. For example, if the majority of citizens conserve energy at home, campaign developers would be well advised to include such descriptive normative information in their presentations intended to increase residential energy conservation. Of course, if the majority of citizens also approved of such efforts, the campaign developers would be wise to incorporate this injunctive normative information as well.

Study 5a

Thus, the most effective norm-based persuasive approach under these circumstances would be one that enlisted the conjoint influence of descriptive and injunctive norms.

To examine the impact of an information campaign that combined the influence of injunctive and descriptive norms, my colleagues and I created three public service announcements (PSAs) designed to increase recycling, an activity that was truly both performed and approved by the majority of local residents. Each PSA portrayed a scene in which the majority of depicted individuals engaged in recycling, spoke approvingly of it, and spoke disparagingly of a single individual in the scene who failed to recycle. When, in a field test, these PSAs were played on the local TV and radio stations of four Arizona communities, a 25.35 percent net advantage in recycling tonnage was recorded over a pair of control communities not exposed to the PSAs but whose recycling was also measured during the length of the study.

Although a 25 percent recycling advantage is impressive from a practical standpoint, that study did not allow for confident theoretical conclusions about the causes of the advantage. For instance, it was not possible to determine the extent to which our PSAs may have been effective because of their normative elements. After all, it is conceivable that the PSAs had been successful because they included humorous and informational components unrelated to norms, as both humor and novel information have been shown to increase the persuasiveness of a communication when properly employed. In order to assess whether and to what degree descriptive and injunctive norms – separately and in combination – contribute to message effectiveness, mediational evidence was necessary. To that end, we conducted a study in which college students viewed our three recycling PSAs and rated their impact along several relevant dimensions.

Study 5b

The study (reported in Cialdini, 2003) was designed to determine whether our PSAs had the intended effect of conveying to viewers that recycling was prevalent (descriptive norm) and approved (injunctive norm),

whether these perceived norms influenced viewers' intentions to recycle, and whether the two types of norms operated similarly or differently to affect recycling intentions. This last goal held particular conceptual interest for us. Although considerable research indicates that descriptive and injunctive norms operate independently to affect behavior (Buunk and Bakker, 1995; Okun et al., 2002; Reno et al., 1993), these studies had not examined the mechanisms by which the two types of norms might differ in producing their influence.

Several interesting findings emerged when we examined possible contributors to the effectiveness of the set of PSAs that had been previously successful in stimulating recycling (see Figure 41.4). First, both normative and non-normative factors influenced the intent to recycle. Of course, the finding that non-normative factors (prior attitude, new information, humor) had causal impact in our data is not incompatible with our theoretical position, as we certainly would not claim that normative factors are the only motivators of human responding.

At the same time, it is encouraging from our theoretical perspective that both injunctive and descriptive normative information significantly influenced recycling intentions. That is, as a result of viewing the ads, the more participants came to believe that recycling was (a) approved and (b) prevalent, the more they planned to recycle in the future. It is noteworthy that, despite a strong correlation ($r = 0.79$) between participants' perceptions of the existing prevalence and approval of recycling, these two sources of motivation had independent effects on recycling intentions and appeared to have these effects via differing psychological mechanisms. Information about social approval/disapproval affected recycling intentions by influencing assessments of communication persuasiveness. Information about relative prevalence, on the other hand, influenced intentions directly, without affecting the perceived persuasiveness of the communication. Such results affirm the theoretical distinction between descriptive and injunctive norms.

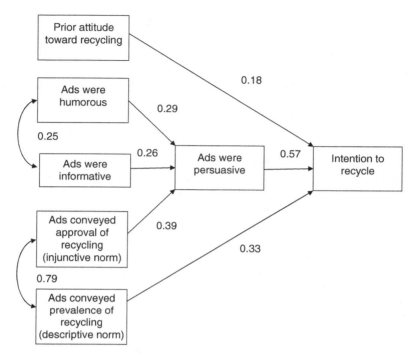

Figure 41.4 Intention to recycle after viewing PSAs. The causal paths (arrows) of the figure depict the impact of participants' attitudes and perceptions on their intentions to recycle in Study 5b. All path coefficients (numbers) are significant at $p < 0.05$

Although what most others do and approve are often highly related, they are conceptually, motivationally, and functionally different. Communicators who fail to recognize these distinctions will imperil their persuasive efforts.

RECENT YEARS: IDENTIFYING DESCRIPTIVE–INJUNCTIVE DIFFERENCES AND A NEW TYPE OF NORM

By this stage of model development, one practical implication of our formulation seemed clear: public service communicators should avoid the tendency to send the normatively muddled message that a targeted activity is socially disapproved but widespread. Norm-based persuasive communications are likely to have their best effects when communicators

align descriptive and injunctive normative messages to work in tandem rather than in competition with one another. Such a line of attack unites the power of two independent sources of normative motivation and can provide a highly successful approach to social influence.

At the same time, certain issues remained to be clarified if we were to advance theory development and the potential impact of norm-based communications. The most prominent concerned the nature of the psychological mechanisms that underlie descriptive and injunctive norms. The results of Study 5 suggested an intriguing difference. Information about social approval/disapproval affected recycling intentions by influencing assessments of communication persuasiveness. Information about relative prevalence, on the other hand, influenced intentions directly, without affecting the perceived persuasiveness of the communication.

Why should that be the case? One possibility is that – in contrast to injunctive norms that are based in an understanding of the moral rules of the society – because descriptive norms are based in perceptions of the raw behavior of others, it becomes relatively easy to accommodate to the norm without much cognitive analysis or awareness. Indeed, organisms with little cognitive capacity are able to do so: birds flock, fish school, and social insects swarm. Hence, we might expect that targets of descriptive norm information would be both significantly affected by it and cognitively unaware of its impact. Evidence in this regard comes from a study of perceived motivations for energy conservation that Wesley Schultz and I conducted recently along with our then-students Jessica Nolan, Noah Goldstein, and Vladas Griskevicius.

Studies

Study 6a

As part of a large-scale survey of residential energy users, we inquired into respondents' views of their reasons for conserving energy at home as well as reports of their actual residential energy-saving activities such as installing energy-efficient appliances and light bulbs, adjusting thermostats, and turning off lights. When respondents were asked to rate the importance to them of several reasons for energy conservation – because it will help save the environments, because it will benefit society, because it will save me money, or because other people are doing it – they rated these motivations in the order just listed, with the actions of others (the descriptive social norm) in a distant last place. However, when we examined the relationship between participants' beliefs in these reasons and their attempts to save energy, we found the reverse: the belief that others were conserving correlated twice as highly with reported energy-saving efforts than did any of the reasons that had been rated as more important personal motivators.

Study 6b

To ensure that our findings weren't the result of the correlational nature of the survey methodology (through a false consensus effect), a follow-up study employed an experimental design. Residents of a mid-size California community received persuasive appeals on door-hangers placed on their doorknobs once a week for four consecutive weeks. The appeals emphasized to residents that energy conservation efforts would (1) help the environment or (2) benefit society or (3) save them money or (4) were common (normative) in their neighborhood. We also included a no-contact control group and a control group that received door-hangers that simply urged energy conservation without providing a specific reason; these controls did not differ from one another in impact on usage. Interviews with participants revealed that those who received the normative appeals rated them as least likely to motivate their conservation behavior and significantly less likely than any of the other appeals. Yet, when we examined actual energy usage (by recording participants' electricity meter readings), the normative appeal proved most helpful, resulting in significantly more conservation than any of the other appeals (Nolan et al., 2008; see Figure 41.5). This illustrates a more specific psychological point than the one articulated masterfully by Nisbett and Wilson (1977) that, in general, people are poor at recognizing why they behave as they do. It asserts that they will be particularly clueless when identifying the similar actions of others as causal antecedents. The upshot of these studies is plain. When it comes to estimating the causes of their conduct, people seem especially blind to the large relative role of others' similar behavior. They don't just fail to get this relative role right; they tend to get it precisely wrong.

The tendency to underestimate the power of descriptive normative information doesn't just apply to the recipients of the information. It applies to potential deliverers of the information as well. This suggests a simple

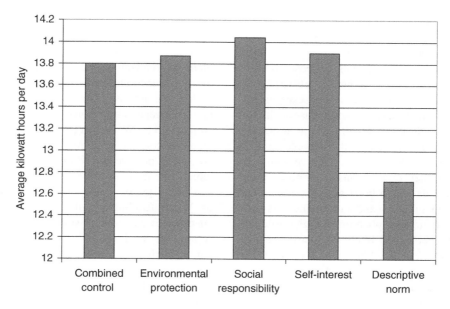

Figure 41.5 Average daily energy consumption as a function of message, controlling for baseline energy usage in Study 6b

way to increase conservation activity – by trumpeting the true levels of conservation that are going unrecognized. However, proenvironmental program developers and communicators frequently fail to do so, relying instead on other forms of motivation than normative information (Nolan et al., 2008).

Study 7

To investigate range of this error of omission, we examined resource conservation choices in upscale hotel rooms, where guests often encounter a card asking them to reuse their towels. As anyone who travels frequently knows this card may urge the action in various ways. Sometimes it requests compliance for the sake of the environment; sometimes it does so for the sake of future generations; and sometimes it exhorts guests to cooperate with the hotel in order to save resources. What the card *never* says, however, is that the great majority (up to 75 percent) of guests do reuse their towels when given the opportunity, even though this percentage is accurate according to data from the Project Planet Corporation that manufactures the cards.

We suspected that the omission was leading to inferior levels of compliance.

To test our suspicion, with the collaboration of the management of an upscale hotel in the Phoenix area, we put one of four different cards in its guestrooms. One of the cards stated "HELP SAVE THE ENVIRONMENT," which was followed by information stressing respect for nature. A different card stated "HELP SAVE RESOURCES FOR FUTURE GENERATIONS," which was followed by information stressing the importance of saving energy for the future. A third type of card stated "PARTNER WITH US TO HELP SAVE THE ENVIRONMENT," which was followed by information urging guests to cooperate with the hotel in preserving the environment. A final type of card stated "JOIN YOUR FELLOW CITIZENS IN HELPING TO SAVE THE ENVIRONMENT," which was followed by information that 75 percent of hotel guests do reuse their towels at some point during their stay when asked to do so. The outcome? Compared with the first three messages, the final (descriptive social norm) message increased towel reuse by an average of 28.4 percent (Goldstein et al., 2007).

We found it instructive that the descriptive normative message was (a) significantly more successful than any of the more traditionally employed appeals, (b) costless to the hotel, (c) entirely honest, yet (d) never employed in any hotel we had ever visited. We think that there is a good reason why this would be the case. Recall that Studies 6a and 6b provided evidence that people tend to dismiss the impact that descriptive norms can have on their own actions. Therefore, it may well be that when hotel energy conservation program creators and communicators consulted their own phenomenologies to determine what would likely be a strong appeal (i.e., what would likely work on them), it didn't occur to them that descriptive norms would be effective. As one form of corrective to this misjudgment, even before submitting a report of our hotel findings to an academic journal, we have published them in an outlet read by hotel managers and executives (Goldstein et al., 2007).

Whose descriptive norms do individuals follow? The emergence of provincial norms

To this point, we have considered when and how individuals adhere to the perceived norms of others, but one central question remains to be addressed: Whose norms are individuals most likely to follow? Social psychologists have long recognized that when making decisions under uncertainty, people tend to follow the norms of others who seem similar to them (Baron et al., 1996; Festinger, 1954; Sherif, 1936). By far the most frequently studied form of similarity has involved common membership in some personally meaningful group or social category such as race, gender, nationality, or ethnicity (Brewer, 2003; Hogg, 2003; Terry and Hogg, 2000). However, another line of research suggests that similarities of a personally meaningful variety – for example, fingerprint type or birthday – are powerful stimulators of compliance with another's requests

(Burger et al., 2004). This latter set of findings made us think that the norms of others who are similar to an observer on a *social identity-irrelevant* dimension might still lead the observer to elevated levels of conformity with those norms. What might that social identity-irrelevant yet powerful dimension of similarity be? We suspected that individuals would follow the behavioral norms of those who share or have shared the environment in which a behavior is to be undertaken.

This suspicion made functional sense to us. When deciding which action to take in a specific environment, it would be adaptive to follow the lead of others who had taken action in that specific environment, even if those individuals were not members of one's meaningful social categories. We labeled the norms of such individuals *provincial norms* to denote simultaneously their local and socially unsophisticated nature. Despite their geographically and interpersonally narrow character, we nonetheless expected provincial norms to be potent directors of conduct because they can be seen to provide highly diagnostic information about wise behavioral choices in the situation at hand.

Study 8

Recall that the descriptive norm used in our hotel study informed guests that similar others – that is, the majority of other guests who had previously stayed at the hotel – had reused their towels at least once during their respective stays. We decided to explore the power of provincial norms by conducting another hotel study in which some occupants saw an appeal communicating the descriptive norm specifically for the guests who had previously stayed in the occupants' hotel rooms (i.e., the provincial norm for reusing towels). Thus, in addition to the standard environmental appeal of our earlier hotel study and the descriptive norm appeal used in that study, participants in a third condition read that "75% of the guests who stayed in this room [room #xxx] participated in our new resource savings program by using their towels more than once."

Consistent with our first hotel study (Study 7), the descriptive norm condition using the hotel's previous guests as the reference group yielded a higher towel reuse rate than did the standard environmental appeal – 18.3 percent higher in this instance. More interesting, however, was the finding that the provincial norm condition using the room's previous occupants as the standard produced an even higher towel reuse rate (32.5 percent) relative to the standard environmental appeal (Goldstein et al., 2008).

It may seem illogical that guests would be more likely to follow the norms of those who previously stayed in their specific room than those who stayed in other rooms throughout the hotel. That is, from a purely rational standpoint, one should not view the previous occupants of one's room in a positive light. After all, these are the same individuals who have reduced the quality of the room and its amenities for the current occupants. In addition, there is no ready reason to believe that the behaviors of those previously occupying one's room are more valid than the behaviors of those previously occupying the room next door. Indeed, because the number of guests previously staying at the hotel constitutes a larger sample than the number of guests previously staying in any one room, the former type of norm should be more instructive than the latter. Yet, the reverse was the case.

Why? It is generally adaptive for one to follow the behavioral norms associated with the particular environment, situation, or circumstances that most closely match one's own environment, situation, or circumstances. Thus, individuals may develop this general tendency into a mental shortcut, which, like other mental shortcuts, can sometimes lead to judgments, decisions, and behaviors not entirely based on logical analysis (Ariely, 2008; Thaler and Sunstein, 2008; Tversky and Kahneman, 1974). The findings from our research suggest that communicators, policymakers, and managers incorporating a descriptive normative component into their persuasive appeals or information campaigns should ensure that the group on which

the norms are based is not just comparable to the intended audience in socially meaningful ways (e.g., age, gender, or ethnicity) but is also comparable in situational and circumstantial ways.

CONCLUSION

The focus theory of normative conduct was launched as a way to make sense of the mixed support at the time for the role of social norms in human behavior. The claim that the concept, as traditionally conceived, possessed great explanatory power had strong proponents and equally strong opponents. From the perspective of the research my colleagues and I have since conducted on the question, it would appear that both camps were right. Norms clearly do have a considerable impact on behavior, but the force and form of that impact can only be usefully understood through certain conceptual elements that had not been traditionally or rigorously applied. That is, to predict properly the likelihood of norm-consistent action requires, first, that one specify the type of norm – descriptive or injunctive – said to be operating. Second, one must take into account the various conditions that would incline individuals to focus attention onto or away from the norm, as it is only when either type of norm is salient that it is likely to direct behavior forcefully. Early research confirmed the importance of both of these conceptual elements in generating norm-consistent conduct.

Because of a desire to advance the theory in both conceptual and practical directions, subsequent research was designed to test certain logical extensions of the model in settings that would easily lend themselves to beneficial practical applications. For example, one implication of the conceptual distinction between injunctive and descriptive norms is that, in a situation characterized by unfortunate levels of socially disapproved conduct, it is a serious error to focus an audience on the descriptive norm (i.e., what is done there); instead, under such conditions, messages should focus the audience on the injunctive norm (i.e., what is approved/disapproved there). A study of signage at the Petrified Forest National Park supported this inference in demonstrating a reduction in theft of petrified wood from an injunctive normative message but an increase in theft from a descriptive normative message. Later work tested a theory-based set of PSA messages and found that descriptive and injunctive components of the messages operated separately and via different psychological processes to increase household recycling intentions and behavior. More recent experiments of signage urging towel reuse in hotel rooms revealed (a) the superiority of norms-based messages to traditional messages and (b) evidence for the special power of provincial norms – descriptive norms of others who have shared precisely the same locale as an observer.

There are several potentially fruitful directions that future research can take. One such direction is the continued exploration of the differences between descriptive and injunctive norms. For instance, because injunctive norms are said to require more cognitive work to operate, they should be less effective than descriptive norms when individuals have recently expended considerable cognitive effort (i.e., are cognitively depleted). Some as yet unpublished evidence supports this expectation: information regarding what most others approved (the injunctive norm) spurred norm-consistent behavior when presented before a strenuous, cognitively depleting activity but not after the activity; in contrast, information regarding what most others did (the descriptive norm) increased norm-consistent behavior whenever it was presented (Jacobson et al., 2009). Another potentially worthwhile program of work would investigate the question of why the norms of similar others lead to norm-consistent conduct. We have suggested that for provincial norms, which engage no sense of meaningful social identification with the similar

others, it is the diagnostic/instructional value of the others' actions that motivates conformity. It is worth asking whether this diagnostic/instructional factor (i.e., the prediction of adaptive outcomes) also leads to conformity with the actions of others' with whom one does share a meaningful social identity. That is, would conformity with the norms of such others (e.g., fellow students at a specific university) occur not because of a sense of identification with those others but because of a sense that their norms are indicative of successful outcomes for anyone like them? Finally, Higgins (pers. comm., May 7, 2009) suggested that descriptive norms may be more associated with the psychological state of assessment, wherein people withhold action until they are confident of the correctness of their views (Higgins et al., 2003), whereas injunctive norms may be more associated with the motivational state of prevention, wherein people are more concerned with avoiding inappropriate conduct (Higgins, 1998). Thus, experimentally inducing either assessment or prevention states may make descriptive or injunctive norms, respectively, more influential. Researchers who wish to pursue these or other implications of the focus theory of normative conduct can be encouraged in this regard because, after all, many others are likely to be doing so.

REFERENCES

Ariely, D. (2008) *Predictably Irrational.* New York: HarperCollins.

Baron, R.S., Vandello and Brunsman, B. (1996) The forgotten variable in conformity research: Impact of task importance on social influence. *Journal of Personality and Social Psychology, 71,* 915–927.

Bator, R.J. and Cialdini, R.B. (2000) The application of persuasion theory to the development of effective pro-environmental public service announcements. *Journal of Social Issues, 56,* 527–541.

Bator, R.J. and Cialdini, R.B. (2006) The nature of consistency motivation: Consistency, aconsistency, and anticonsistency in a dissonance paradigm. *Social Influence, 1,* 208–233.

Berkowitz, L. (1972) Social norms, feelings, and other factors affecting helping and altruism. In L. Berkowitz (ed.), *Advances in Experimental Social Psychology, 6,* 63–108. San Diego: Academic Press.

Brewer, M. (2003) Optimal distinctiveness, social identity, and the self. In M.R. Leary and J.P. Tangney (eds), *Handbook of Self and Identity,* pp. 480–491. New York: Guilford Press.

Burger, J.M., Messian, N., Patel, S., del Prado, A. and Anderson, C. (2004). What a coincidence! The effects of incidental similarity on compliance. *Personality and Social Psychology Bulletin, 30,* 35–43.

Buunk, B.P. and Bakker, A.B. (1995) Extradyadic sex: The role of descriptive and injunctive norms. *Journal of Sex Research, 32,* 313–318.

Cialdini, R.B. (2003) Crafting normative messages to protect the environment. *Current Directions in Psychological Science, 12,* 105–109.

Cialdini, R.B., Reno, R.R. and Kallgren, C.A. (1990) A focus theory of normative conduct: Recycling the concept of norms to reduce littering in public places. *Journal of Personality and Social Psychology, 58,* 1015–1026.

Cialdini, R.B., Trost, M.R. and Newsom, J.T. (1995) Preference for consistency: The development of a valid measure and the discovery of surprising behavioral implications. *Journal of Personality and Social Psychology, 69,* 318–328.

Cialdini, R.B., Wosinska, W., Barrett, D.W., Butner, J. and Gornik-Durose, M. (1999) Compliance with a request in two cultures: The differential influence of social proof and commitment/consistency on collectivists and individualists. *Personality and Social Psychology Bulletin, 25,* 1242–1253.

Darley, J.M. and Latané, B. (1970) Norms and normative behavior: Field studies of social interdependence. In J. Macaulay and L. Berkowitz (eds), *Altruism and Helping Behavior,* pp. 83–102. New York: Academic Press.

Deaux, K. and Major, B. (1987) Putting gender into context: An interactive model of gender-related behavior. *Psychological Review, 94,* 369–389.

Festinger, L. (1954) A theory of social comparison processes. *Human Relations, 7,* 117–140.

Fishbein and Ajzen (1975) *Belief, Attitude, Intention, and Behavior.* Reading, MA: Addison-Wesley.

Goldstein, N.J., Cialdini, R.B. and Griskevicius, V. (2007) Rooms for improvement. *Cornell Hotel and Restaurant Administration Quarterly, 48,* 145–150.

Goldstein, N.J., Cialdini, R.B. and Griskevicius, V. (2008) A room with a viewpoint: Using normative appeals to motivate environmental conservation in a hotel setting. *Journal of Consumer Research, 35,* 472–482.

Harvey, M.D. and Enzle, M.E. (1981) A cognitive model of social norms for understanding the transgression-helping effect. *Journal of Personality and Social Psychology, 41,* 866–875.

Higgins, E.T. (1998) Promotion and prevention: Regulatory focus as a motivational principle. In: M.P. Zanna (ed.), *Advances in Experimental Social Psychology, 30,* 1–46. New York: Academic Press.

Higgins, E.T. and Bargh, J.E. (1987) Social cognition and social perception. *Annual Review of Psychology, 38,* 369–425.

Higgins, E.T., Kruglanski, A.W. and Pierro A. (2003) Regulatory mode: Locomotion and assessment as distinct orientations. In M.P. Zanna (ed.), *Advances in Experimental Social Psychology, 35,* 293–344. New York: Academic Press.

Hogg, M.A. (2003) Social identity. In M.R. Leary and J.P. Tangney (eds), *Handbook of Self and Identity,* pp. 462–479. New York: Guilford Press.

Jacobson, R.P., Mortensen, C.R. and Cialdini, R.B. (2009) The role of self-regulation in normative influence. Poster presented at the Meeting of the Society of Personality and Social Psychology, February, Tampa, FL.

Kallgren, C.A., Reno, R.R. and Cialdini, R.B. (2000) A focus theory of normative conduct: When norms do and do not affect behavior. *Personality and Social Psychology Bulletin, 26,* 1002–1012.

Kallgren, C.A. and Wood, W.W. (1986) Access to attitude-relevant information in memory as a determinant of attitude-behavior consistency. *Journal of Experimental Social Psychology, 22,* 328–338.

Krauss, R.M., Freedman, J.L. and Whitcup, M. (1978) Field and laboratory studies of littering. *Journal of Experimental Social Psychology, 14,* 109–122.

Krebs, D.L. (1970) Altruism: An examination of the concept and a review of the literature. *Psychological Bulletin, 73,* 258–302.

Krebs, D.L. and Miller, D.T. (1985) Altruism and aggression. In G. Lindzey and E. Aronson (eds), *The Handbook of Social Psychology, Vol. 2,* 3rd Edition, pp. 1–71. New York: Random House.

Lassiter, G.D., Diamond, S.S., Schmidt, H.C. and Elek, J.K. (2007) Evaluating videotaped confessions. *Psychological Science, 18,* 224–226.

Marini, M.M. (1984) Age and sequencing norms in the transition to adulthood. *Social Forces, 63,* 229–244.

Millar, M.G. and Tesser, A. (1989) The effects of affective-cognitive consistency and thought on the attitude-behavior relation. *Journal of Experimental Social Psychology, 25,* 189–202.

Miller, L.E. and Grush, J.E. (1986) Individual differences in attitudinal versus normative determination of behavior. *Journal of Experimental and Social Psychology, 22,* 190–202.

Nisbett, R.E. and Wilson, T.D. (1977) Telling more than we can know: Verbal report on mental processes. *Psychological Review, 84,* 231–259.

Nolan, J.M., Schultz, P.W., Cialdini, R.B., Goldstein, N.J. and Griskevicius, V. (2008) Normative social influence is underdetected. *Personality and Social Psychology Bulletin, 34,* 913–923.

Okun, M.A., Karoly, P. and Lutz, R. (2002) Clarifying the contribution of subjective norm to predicting leisure-time exercise. *American Journal of Health Behavior, 26,* 296–305.

Oyserman, D. and Lee, S.W.S. (2008) Does culture influence what and how we think? *Psychological Bulletin, 134,* 311–342.

Pepitone, A. (1976) Toward a normative and comparative biocultural social psychology. *Journal of Personality and Social Psychology, 34,* 641–653.

Petrova, P.K., Cialdini, R.B. and Sills, S.J. (2007) Personal consistency and compliance across cultures. *Journal of Experimental Social Psychology, 43,* 104–111.

Reno, R.R., Cialdini, R.B. and Kallgren, C.A. (1993) The transsituational influence of social norms. *Journal of Personality and Social Psychology, 64,* 104–112.

Sherif, M. (1936) *The Psychology of Social Norms.* New York: Harper.

Suroweicki, J. (2004) *The Wisdom of Crowds.* New York: Doubleday.

Terry, D.J. and Hogg. M.A. (2000) *Attitudes, Behavior, and Social Context: The Role of Norms and Group Membership.* New Jersey: Lawrence Erlbaum Associates.

Thaler, R.H. and Sunstein, C.R. (2008) *Nudge.* New Haven, CT: Yale University Press.

Triandis, H.C. (1977) *Interpersonal Behavior.* Monterey, CA: Brooks/Cole.

Tversky, A. and Kahneman, D. (1974) Judgment under uncertainty: Heuristics and biases. *Science, 185,* 1123–1131.

Williams, K.D. (2007) Ostracism. *Annual Review of Psychology, 58,* 425–452.

Wilson, T.D. and Gilbert, D.T. (2008) Affective forecasting: Knowing what to want. *Current Directions in Psychological Science, 14,* 131–134.

42

System Justification Theory

John T. Jost and Jojanneke van der Toorn

ABSTRACT

According to system justification theory, people are motivated (to varying degrees depending upon situational and dispositional factors) to defend, bolster, and justify prevailing social, economic, and political arrangements (i.e., the status quo). System justification motivation is theorized to manifest itself in a number of different ways (e.g., in terms of stereotyping, ideology, attribution), to occur implicitly (i.e., nonconsciously) as well as explicitly, and to serve underlying epistemic, existential, and relational needs. In this chapter, we trace the historical and intellectual origins of the theory, beginning with a personal narrative of its conceptual and empirical development. We recount major influences and theoretical precursors in philosophy, social theory, and experimental social psychology. We summarize the basic postulates of system justification theory in its current state of development, highlight some illustrative evidence in support of the theory, and discuss a few of its practical consequences.

INTRODUCTION

Most individuals participate in an astonishing number and diversity of relationships, groups, networks, and social systems. Even in solitude, our thoughts, feelings, and actions reflect social norms, expectations, and the ties that bind (Hardin and Higgins, 1996; Moscovici, 1988; Sherif, 1936). But what do we do when these relationships carry within them elements of inequality, exploitation, and injustice? Resistance – if not out-and-out rebellion – would seem to be the most obvious or appropriate response to such situations (Gurr, 1970; Hirschman, 1970; Klandermans, 1997; Reicher, 2004; Turner, 2006), but its occurrence is rarer than most would expect. The infrequency of protest, collective action, and other convincing attempts to reshape social systems to make them more congenial to group interests, including majority group interests, was – throughout the twentieth century – a much-studied, albeit not well understood, phenomenon in philosophy and the social sciences. As we will see in this chapter, authors exemplifying a multiplicity of theoretical traditions have concluded that people, including members of disadvantaged groups, frequently acquiesce in the social order and, in so doing, violate their own objectively defined social interests (Fromm, 1941; Gramsci, 1971; Hochschild, 1981; Jackman, 1994; Kluegel and Smith, 1986; Lane, 1959; MacKinnon, 1989; Mason, 1971; Moore, 1978; Runciman, 1969; Tyler and McGraw, 1986; Zinn, 1968).

However, the acquiescence of those who are disadvantaged by the status quo was not adequately explained or connected to a comprehensive analysis of thought and (in)action in the social and political sphere more generally. More often than not, it was simply attributed to the passive acceptance of "dominant ideology" (e.g., Abercrombie et al., 1990). Almost without exception, scholars failed to consider the possibility that most individuals – and not just those at "the top" – have a psychological interest (or motivation) to uphold the legitimacy of the social system. This is precisely what system justification theory proposes: to varying degrees (based upon dispositional and situational factors), people are motivated (whether consciously or unconsciously) to defend, bolster, and justify aspects of existing social, economic, and political arrangements (Jost and Banaji, 1994; Jost and Hunyady, 2002, 2005; Jost et al., 2004a).

System justification theory has, from its inception, represented a self-conscious attempt to explain why people so frequently adapt themselves to the societal status quo, rather than pushing for change and social betterment, as so many other theories in social science would portend. System justification theory seeks to integrate insights garnered from different philosophical and scientific perspectives on "false consciousness" and political acquiescence and therefore to function as a kind of "umbrella theory" (Jost and Banaji, 1994; Jost and Hunyady, 2002, 2005; Jost et al., 2001). In this chapter, we begin with a fairly personal narrative – consistent with the editorial objectives of this book – of how system justification theory came to be. Second, we review the historical and intellectual origins of the theory, focusing on major influences and theoretical precursors. Third, we summarize the basic tenets (or postulates) of system

justification theory in its current state of development. Fourth and finally, we consider a few of the theory's practical implications, providing a take-home message of sorts.

PERSONAL NARRATIVE OF THE THEORY'S DEVELOPMENT

System justification theory began life as a one-page critical reaction paper and, still in its infancy, grew into a term paper entitled "Salvaging exploitation theories of prejudice: Stereotypes as social justification," submitted by first-year doctoral student John Jost in the spring semester of 1991 for Professor Mahzarin Banaji's seminar on stereotyping and prejudice at Yale University. The term paper opened with two quotations, one from Karl Marx and the other from Gordon Allport:

> The class which has the means of material production at its disposal, has control at the same time over the means of mental production ...
>
> (Marx and Engels, 1846: 64)

> [T]he rationalizing and justifying function of a stereotype exceeds its function as a reflector of group attributes.
>
> (Allport, 1954: 196)

The basic argument of the paper was that

> (a) specific stereotype contents arise because they explain and justify the status quo, especially the exploitation of certain groups of people, (b) they are initially promulgated by those members of society who stand to gain the most advantage by preserving the exploitative system, and (c) they are eventually spread by virtually all members of society, since stereotypes serve the ideological function of explaining social reality in a way which makes it seem natural and just.

From the start, system justification theory represented an attempt to synthesize and unify two distinct theoretical traditions – one coming from philosophy and social theory in the Marxian tradition, which Jost had studied previously, and the other coming from Lewin, Allport, Tajfel, and their scientific heirs in experimental social psychology.

The ideas presented in the paper were enthusiastically received by Professor Banaji and led to several lively discussions during lab meetings, but it was not until the *British Journal of Social Psychology* announced plans for a special issue on the structure and functions of stereotyping that Jost and Banaji resolved to write the first article outlining the basic tenets of a system justification approach to stereotyping and prejudice. The earliest articulations were either ambivalent or agnostic about the notion that members of disadvantaged groups were *motivated* to hold system-justifying stereotypes and ideologies. Rather, processes of persuasion and social learning were largely assumed to account for the apparent acceptance of the status quo on the part of the disadvantaged. Jost and Banaji (1994) ultimately opted for "system justification" over "system rationalization," because the former term seemed less pejorative.

However, the most distinctive aspect of system justification theory, which was not explicitly stated by any of the theory's many influential predecessors (see Figure 42.1), was the possibility that even members of disadvantaged groups would (for psychological and ideological reasons) *want* to believe that the existing social system is good, fair, legitimate, and right. This motivational assumption, which to some extent drew on the philosophical concept of self-deception, was suggested (with some hesitation) by Jost and Banaji (1994), but it was not directly investigated until several years later (e.g., Jost et al., 2010; Kay et al., 2009). Although system justification theory focused initially on stereotyping, prejudice, and intergroup relations, it was later expanded to account for other types of social judgments, including attributions, explanations, and rationalizations for social events; perceptions of fairness, legitimacy, deservingness, and entitlement (concerning the self and others); specific social and political attitudes; and, ultimately, full-fledged ideological belief systems (Jost et al., 2003b, 2004a, 2004b).

Several members of the Yale faculty (especially Mahzarin Banaji, William J. McGuire,

Leonard Doob, and Robert Abelson) encouraged and inspired, either directly or indirectly, the development of system justification theory in its still-fledgling state. Postdoctoral experiences further deepened and broadened Jost's interests in the nature of human attachment to the status quo and the causes of resistance to change. A collaboration with Arie Kruglanski led ultimately to a detailed analysis of political conservatism and its underlying social, cognitive, and motivational underpinnings (Jost et al., 2003b), which provided an empirical basis for Jost and Hunyady (2005) to propose that system-justifying beliefs are appealing in part because they help people to reduce uncertainty and threat. Another postdoctoral collaboration with Brenda Major resulted in an interdisciplinary conference on "The Psychology of Legitimacy" that would eventually take place at Stanford University, where Jost began an assistant professorship in 1997 (see Jost and Major, 2001).

While at Stanford, Jost benefited greatly from interactions with a number of colleagues, but the individual who most advanced the theoretical and empirical development of system justification theory was a doctoral student named Aaron Kay. Their first collaboration, which derived from McGuire and McGuire's (1991) proposal that people engage in "sour grapes" and "sweet lemons" rationalizations, demonstrated that citizens' political preferences were affected by the anticipated status quo; that is, by (manipulated) expectations about which candidate was more likely to win (Kay et al., 2002). Subsequent collaborations addressed the system-justifying potential of complementary stereotypes, such as "poor but happy" and "poor but honest" stereotypes (Jost and Kay, 2005; Kay and Jost, 2003; Kay et al., 2005). Later, as a faculty member at the University of Waterloo, Kay (now at Duke) spearheaded a productive laboratory investigating the aversion to randomness as a motivational antecedent of system-justifying belief systems, including religious ideologies (Kay et al., 2008, 2009).

In 2003 Jost moved to New York University (NYU), where several faculty members were

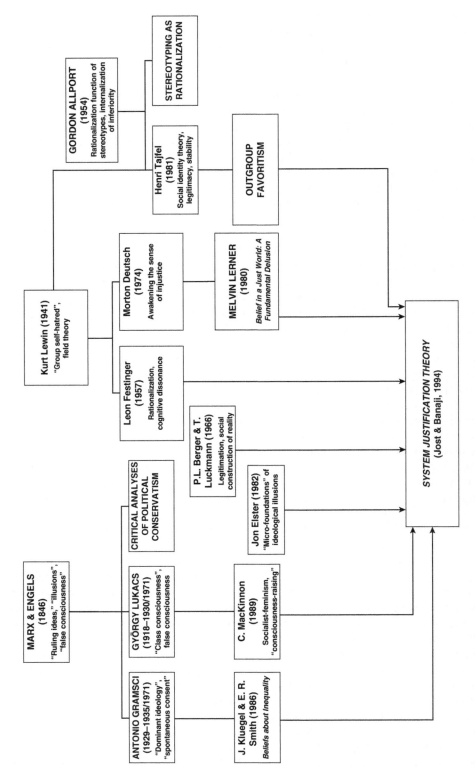

Figure 42.1 System justification theory (Jost and Banaji, 1994)

focused on the possibility that motivation (or goal systems) can operate implicitly, that is, outside of conscious awareness (Bargh et al., 2001). This inspired Jost and his students to adapt experimental paradigms from social cognition to provide direct support for the notion that system justification follows principles of goal pursuit (Jost et al., 2008b, 2010; Ledgerwood et al., in press). Specifically, we postulated the existence of an abstract system-justifying goal or motive that can operate both consciously and unconsciously and that leads people to see the societal status quo as relatively legitimate, fair, desirable, and just – that is, as *better* than if it were not the status quo (see also Kay et al., 2009).

A few other additions to system justification theory are noteworthy. NYU colleague Tom Tyler helped to flesh out (a) the relationship between system justification and other determinants of system legitimacy (e.g., Tyler and Jost, 2007), including procedural fairness and feelings of psychological dependence (van der Toorn et al., 2011), and (b) affective and the relationship between behavioral consequences of system justification, such as the reduction of moral outrage and the withdrawal of support for social change (Wakslak et al., 2007). Furthermore, Jaime Napier (now at Yales) expanded the notion that system justification serves a palliative function to explain why political conservatives are *happier* than liberals (Napier and Jost, 2008). Finally, Jost et al. (2008a) incorporated insights from Hardin and Higgins' (1996) shared reality theory to propose that system justification serves *relational* in addition to epistemic and existential motives (see also Kaiser et al., 2006).

HISTORICAL ORIGINS AND INTELLECTUAL PRECURSORS OF SYSTEM JUSTIFICATION THEORY

There are certain historical and intellectual influences – some within the disciplinary boundaries of social psychology and some without – that played truly major roles in stimulating our thinking about how and why people provide ideological support for the status quo, even when it conflicts with personal or group interests (see also Jost et al., 2004b: 264–269; Jost and Hunyady, 2002: 114–118). These influences are summarized visually (in the form of a hypothetical family tree) in Figure 42.1. The fact that these thinkers have probably never been grouped together before speaks rather strongly in favor of Jorge Luis Borges' (1964) observation that "every writer creates his own precursors." It may well be that the *only* common denominator (other than "social science" in general) to be found in the writings of Marx, Engels, Gramsci, Lukács, Lewin, Allport, Berger and Luckmann, Tajfel, Lerner, Elster, MacKinnon, and the others included in Figure 42.1, is their putative connection to the theoretical construct we have dubbed *system justification*. In fact, we discovered some of these thinkers only *after* the original assumptions of system justification theory had already been laid out; their insights, in other words, were folded into the theory as it developed conceptually as well as empirically.

Approaches to dominant ideology and false consciousness

The concept of system justification is based loosely on the concept of *false consciousness*, which is rooted in the early (humanistic, sociological) work of Karl Marx, especially *The German Ideology* and other works of the 1840s and 1850s (see also Fromm, 1965). In essence, Marx and Engels (1846) argued that ideas favoring dominant groups in society prevail because these groups control the cultural and institutional means by which ideas are spread. The net result, they claimed, is that through the ideological machinations of elites (including philosophers, such as the "young Hegelians"), "men and their circumstances appear upside-down as in a *camera obscura*" (1846: 47); social and political realities, in other words, are systematically inverted and therefore distorted. But it was Engels who actually used the term "false consciousness" in a letter written several years after Marx's death: "Ideology is a process carried out by the so-called thinker with consciousness, but with a false consciousness. The real driving forces that move him remain unknown to him; otherwise it would not be an ideological process" (e.g., see Runciman, 1969).

Marx believed that the working classes would eventually see through the ideological illusions and strive to overthrow the capitalist system. From the perspective of rational self-interest, Marx emphatically assumed that the poor had "nothing to lose but their chains." However, his expectation that the oppressed would recognize and take action against the sources of their oppression may have been overly optimistic (or, from the perspective of the ruling class, pessimistic), considering the various social and psychological obstacles to social change that exist, including denial, rationalization, and other system justification tendencies (see also Crosby et al., 1989; Jost and Banaji, 1994; Major, 1994).

To explain why revolutions against capitalism (and other arguably exploitative systems) did not occur in heavily industrialized nations, later theorists, most notably Gramsci (1971), Lukács (1971/1989), Fromm (1962), Marcuse (1964), Runciman (1969), Cunningham (1987), and MacKinnon (1989), further developed the analysis of dominant ideology, cultural hegemony, and false consciousness. Each of these constructs, but especially the last one, anticipated the subject matter explored by system justification theorists. However, the concept of system justification was intended to ground these sociological constructs in psychological science and to capture the *process* rather than simply the *outcome* (or product) of ideological activity. In Table 42.1 we have summarized the major contributions to the system justification perspective made by various theorists with respect to the study of dominant ideology and false consciousness.

Antonio Gramsci, the Marxian social theorist who was imprisoned unto death in Mussolini's fascist regime in Italy, took seriously Marx's notion that a "popular conviction often has the same energy as a material force." More specifically, Gramsci (1971) sought to understand "the 'spontaneous' consent given by the great masses of the population to the general direction imposed on social life by the dominant fundamental

Table 42.1 Theoretical precursors, part 1: approaches to dominant ideology and false consciousness

Author(s)	Source(s)	Key concepts	Illustrative quotations
Karl Marx and Friedrich Engels	*The German Ideology* (1846)	Ruling ideas, ideology, illusion, palliative function of religion	"The ideas of the ruling class are in every epoch the ruling ideas … The class which has the means of material production at its disposal, has control at the same time over the means of mental production" "If in all ideology men and their circumstances appear upside-down as in a camera obscura, this phenomenon arises just as much from their historical life-process as the inversion of objects on the retina does from their physical life-process" "The people are interested in maintaining the present state of production" "Religion … is the opium of the people" "To call [on the people] to give up their illusions about their condition is to call on them to give up a condition that requires illusions"

Continued

Table 42.1   Cont'd

Author(s)	Source(s)	Key concepts	Illustrative quotations
Antonio Gramsci	*Selections from the Prison Notebooks* (1929–1935)	Dominant ideology, cultural hegemony, "spontaneous consent"	"[The] functions of social hegemony and political government [include]: The 'spontaneous' consent given by the great masses of the population to the general direction imposed on social life by the dominant fundamental group; this consent is 'historically' caused by the prestige (and consequent confidence) which the dominant group enjoys because of its position and function in the world of production" "To the extent that ideologies are historically necessary they have a validity which is 'psychological'; they 'organise' human masses, and create the terrain on which men move, acquire consciousness of their position, struggle, ..." "[A] popular conviction often has the same energy as a material force" "The existing social order is presented as a stable, harmoniously coordinated system, and the great mass of people hesitate and lose heart when they think of what a radical change might bring ... They can only imagine the present being torn to pieces, and fail to perceive the new order which is possible, and which would be better organized, more vital than the old one"
György Lukács	*History and Class Consciousness* (1918–1930)	Class consciousness, reification, false consciousness	"By relating consciousness to the whole of society it becomes possible to infer the thoughts and feelings which men would have in a particular situation if they were able to assess both it and the interests arising from it in their impact on immediate action and on the whole structure of society" "[T]he dialectical method does not permit us simply to proclaim the 'falseness' of this consciousness and to persist in an inflexible confrontation of true and false. On the contrary, it requires us to investigate this 'false consciousness' concretely as an aspect of the historical totality and as a stage in the historical process"
Jon Elster	"Belief, bias and ideology" (1982); *Sour Grapes* (1983)	Micro-foundations of ideological illusions, distortion, rationalization, "analytical Marxism"	"[There is a] tendency of the oppressed and exploited classes in a society to believe in the justice of the social order that oppresses them. This belief, perhaps, is mainly due to distortion, i.e., to such affective mechanisms as rationalization. But there is also an element of illusion, of bias stemming from purely cognitive sources" "The interest of the upper class is better served by the lower classes spontaneously inventing an ideology justifying their inferior status. This ideology, while stemming from the interest of the lower classes in the sense of leading to dissonance reduction, is contrary to their interest because of a tendency to overshoot, resulting in excessive rather than in proper meekness"

Continued

Table 42.1   Cont'd

Author(s)	Source(s)	Key concepts	Illustrative quotations
Jennifer Hochschild	*What's Fair?* (1981)	Why doesn't "the dog bark"?	"[T]he American poor apparently do not support the downward distribution of wealth. The United States does not now have, and seldom ever has had, a political movement among the poor seeking greater economic equality. The fact that such a political movement could succeed constitutionally makes its absence even more startling. Since most of the population have less than an average amount of wealth – the median level of holdings is below the mean – more people would benefit than would lose from downward redistribution. And yet never has the poorer majority of the population, not to speak of the poorest minority, voted itself out of its economic disadvantage"
James R. Kluegel and Eliot R. Smith	*Beliefs about Inequality: Americans' Views of What Is and What Ought to Be* (1986)	Dominant ideology, stratification beliefs, psychological control, emotional benefits	"[C]ertain Marxist theories ... assume working-class people will come to recognize the contradictions between their self-interests and their system justifying beliefs" "[T]he belief in internal control, part of the dominant ideology, is adaptive for an individual's personal life. This belief leads to more positive and less negative emotional experience ... Psychological control – even if not always accompanied by real control of one's important life outcomes – seems to have positive consequences. These consequences in turn may be important in motivating people to maintain a belief in the dominant ideology as a whole"
Sandra L. Bem and Daryl J. Bem	"Case Study of a nonconscious ideology: training the woman to know her place" (1970)	Nonconscious ideology, illusion of equality, complementary stereotyping	"The ideological rationalization that men and women hold complementary but equal positions in society appears to be a fairly recent invention. In earlier times – and in more conservative company today – it was not felt necessary to provide the ideology with an equalitarian veneer" "In 1954 the United States Supreme Court declared that a fraud and hoax lay behind the slogan 'separate but equal.' It is unlikely that any court will ever do the same for the more subtle motto that successfully keeps the woman in her place: 'complementary but equal'"
Catharine A. MacKinnon	*Toward a Feminist Theory of the State* (1989)	Socialist-feminism, sexual objectification, consciousness raising	"Feminist inquiry ... began with a broad unmasking through consciousness raising of the attitudes that legitimate and hide women's status, the daily practices and ideational envelope that contain woman's body" "Gender socialization is the ... process through which women internalize (make their own) a male image of their sexuality as their identity as women, and thus make it real in the world" "Male power is a myth that makes itself true. To raise consciousness is to confront male power in its duality: as at once total on one side and a delusion on the other. In consciousness raising, women learn they have learned that men are everything, women their negation, but the sexes are equal ... [N]o woman escapes the meaning of being a woman within a gendered social system"

group." His analysis stressed the role of social influence and persuasion and distinguished between *active* (spontaneous) and *passive* forms of support for the social system (see also Hochschild, 1981: 260–283). Gramsci also recognized the potentially progressive or revolutionary role of ideology; that is, its ability to "organize" members of disadvantaged groups, to enable them to "acquire consciousness of their position," and to motivate what he (and other Marxists) regarded as a necessary "struggle." At the same time, Gramsci clearly perceived the ideological advantages possessed by those who side with the status quo:

> The existing social order is presented as a stable, harmoniously coordinated system, and the great mass of people hesitate and lose heart when they think of what a radical change might bring ... They can only imagine the present being torn to pieces, and fail to perceive the new order which is possible, and which would be better organized, more vital than the old one.
>
> (Gramsci, 1917, quoted in Fiori, 1970: 106–107)

As far as we know, the first expression of the term "system-justifying beliefs" occurs just once in a book by Kluegel and Smith (1986) entitled *Beliefs about Inequality*, which combines sociological theory in the Gramscian tradition with an analysis of public opinion data. In passing, the authors refer to "certain Marxist theories that assume working-class people will come to recognize the *contradictions between their self-interests and their system-justifying beliefs*" (1986: 15; emphasis added). Kluegel and Smith were also apparently the first to demonstrate empirically that system-justifying beliefs are associated with emotional benefits, including a subjective sense of control, even among poor people. This notion, which is tacit in Marx's provocative claim that religious ideology is the "opium of the masses" (see Turner, 1991) and Lerner's (1980) formulation of the belief in a just world, inspired theoretical and empirical investigations of the *palliative* function of system-justifying beliefs and ideologies (Jost and Hunyady, 2002; Wakslak et al., 2007).

György Lukács, who was sometimes in the good graces of the Communist authorities in Hungary but often not, was in any case better positioned than Gramsci to explore the concept of *false consciousness*. Importantly, Lukács (1971: 59) recognized the necessity of distinguishing between subjective (or perceived) and objective (or actual) class interests:

> By relating consciousness to the whole of society it becomes possible to infer the thoughts and feelings which men would have in a particular situation if they were able to assess both it and the interests arising from it in their impact on immediate action and on the whole structure of society.

Lukács also followed Marx in advocating an empirical, social scientific analysis of ideology and false consciousness, eschewing dogmatic, polemical, and purely speculative philosophical approaches (cf. Jost, 1995; Jost and Jost, 2007).

Elster (1982, 1983) explicitly advocated a scientific approach to Marxian hypotheses about the social functions of ideological beliefs (see also Cunningham, 1987; Runciman, 1969). This was part of a broader movement known as "analytical Marxism" (or, more colloquially, "non-Bullshit" Marxism), which sought to develop and test empirically falsifiable claims derived from Marxian theory on such topics as social class, exploitation, labor, value, and ideology. Here and elsewhere, Elster incorporated the work of social psychologists, including Festinger, Deutsch, Lerner, Abelson, Nisbett, and Ross. In so doing, he advanced several hypotheses that reformulated Marxian ideas in unabashedly psychological terms, including these two statements, which directly influenced the formulation of system justification theory along motivational lines:

> [There is a] tendency of the oppressed and exploited classes in a society to believe in the justice of the social order that oppresses them. This belief, perhaps, is mainly due to distortion, i.e., to such affective mechanisms as rationalization. But there is also an element of illusion, of bias stemming from purely cognitive sources. (Elster, 1982: 131)

> The interest of the upper class is better served by the lower classes spontaneously inventing an ideology justifying their inferior status. This ideology, while stemming from the interest of the lower classes in the sense of leading to dissonance reduction, is contrary to their interest because of a tendency to overshoot, resulting in excessive rather than in proper meekness. (Elster, 1982: 142)

Thus, Elster argued that individuals' "ideological adaptation to their state of submission was endogenous, and not only did not require, but would have been incompatible with, deliberate ideological manipulation by the rulers" (1982: 124).

MacKinnon (1989) shrewdly critiqued Marxism from the perspective of feminism and feminism from the perspective of Marxism. The result was a sophisticated analysis of the social and political significance of "consciousness raising" activity, not only with respect to members of the working class but with respect to members of subjugated groups in general, including women. She argued that "no woman escapes the meaning of being a woman within a gendered social system" and that "male power becomes self-enforcing" to the extent that women internalize sexist norms and standards (1989: 99). MacKinnon's analysis comported with that of Bem and Bem (1970), who pointed out that sexist ideology can operate insidiously at a presumably nonconscious level of awareness (cf. Jost and Kay, 2005).

The notion that people are simultaneously embedded (and therefore psychologically invested) in multiple social systems and institutions, including capitalism, patriarchy, nuclear families, work organizations, and so on, is a crucial insight that inspired the attempt to develop a general theory of system justification. The scientific goal, in other words, is not merely to explain the unique effects of any single system or institution (e.g., capitalism), but rather to identify general mechanisms or processes that play out in a wide variety of social systems (ranging from families to society as a whole) on the thoughts, feelings, and behaviors of individuals and groups (see Jost and Banaji, 1994; Wakslak et al., in press).

In an effort to synthesize various socialist–feminist approaches to the study of dominant ideology and false consciousness, Jost (1995) proposed the following (general) definition of the latter term: "The holding of false or inaccurate beliefs that are contrary to one's own social interest and which thereby contribute to the maintenance of the disadvantaged position of the self or the group" (1995: 400).[1] A literature review suggested the existence of at least six different types of false consciousness beliefs: (1) denial of injustice or exploitation, (2) fatalism about prospects for social change, (3) rationalization of social roles, (4) false attribution of blame, (5) identification with the oppressor, and (6) resistance to social change (Jost, 1995). Many authors, especially those influenced by postmodernist philosophy, have rejected the concept of false consciousness on the grounds that it is difficult (or even impossible) to distinguish between true and false statements in the social and political world. Without conceding this highly skeptical epistemological claim, we recognize that it may be a pragmatic advantage that the concept of system justification sidesteps the issue of whether beliefs and ideologies that sustain social systems are (wholly or partially) true or false. The focus, rather, is on their motivational bases and system-maintaining consequences.

Stereotyping, prejudice, and the internalization of inferiority

From the start, system justification theory reflected an effort to unify the analysis of dominant ideology and false consciousness with social psychological research on stereotyping, prejudice, and the internalization of inferiority. Neither Kurt Lewin (1941) nor Gordon Allport (1954) could be considered Marxists, but both appreciated the deep extent to which hierarchical social systems impinge upon the thoughts, feelings, and behaviors of the individual (see Table 42.2). Lewin, for instance, noted that "self-hatred is a phenomenon which

Table 42.2   Theoretical precursors, part 2: stereotyping, prejudice, and the internalization of inferiority

Author(s)	Source(s)	Key concepts	Illustrative quotations
Kurt Lewin	"Self-hatred among Jews" (1941); "Group decision and social change" (1947)	Group self-hatred, feelings of inferiority, resistance to change, field theory	"Jewish self-hatred is a phenomenon which has its parallel in many underprivileged groups. One of the better known and most extreme cases of self-hatred can be found among American Negroes" "It is recognized in sociology that the members of the lower social strata tend to accept the fashions, values, and ideals of the higher strata" "Self-hatred seems to be a psychopathological phenomenon, and its prevention may seem mainly a task for the psychiatrist. However, modern psychology knows that many psychological phenomena are but an expression of a social situation in which the individual finds himself" "Jewish self-hatred will die out only when actual equality of status with the non-Jew is achieved" "The study of the conditions for change begins appropriately with an analysis of the conditions for 'no change,' that is, for the state of equilibrium"
Gordon Allport	*The Nature of Prejudice* (1954)	Rationalizing function of stereotypes, internalization	"[S]o heavy is the prevailing cultural pressure that members of minority groups sometimes look at themselves through the same lens as other groups" "[In some cases] the victim instead of pretending to agree with his 'betters' actually does agree with them, and sees his own group through their eyes" "[T]he rationalizing and justifying function of a stereotype exceeds its function as a reflector of group attributes" "You and I are not normally aware of the extent to which our behavior is constrained and regulated by such features of the social system"
Norbert Elias	*The Civilizing Process* (1939); *The Established and the Outsiders* (1965, with J. Scotson)	The established, outsiders, group charisma, stigmatization, power superiority and inferiority, social figuration	"Whether they are social cadres, such as feudal lords in relation to villeins, 'whites' in relation to 'blacks,' Gentiles in relation to Jews, Protestants in relation to Catholics and vice versa, men in relation to women (in former days), large and powerful nation-states in relation to others … [or] an old-established working-class group in relation to members of a new working-class settlement in their neighborhood – in all these cases the more powerful groups look upon themselves as the 'better' people, as endowed with a kind of group charisma, with a specific virtue shared by all its members and lacked by the others. What is more, in all these cases the 'superior' people may make the less powerful people themselves feel that they lack virtue – that they are inferior in human terms" "[W]here the power differential is very great, groups in an outsider position measure themselves with the yardstick of their oppressors. In terms of their oppressors' norms they find themselves wanting; they experience themselves as being of lesser worth"

Continued

Table 42.2   Cont'd

Author(s)	Source(s)	Key concepts	Illustrative quotations
Frantz Fanon	*The Wretched of the Earth* (1961)	Colonization, psychology of the oppressed, national consciousness	"The colonialist bourgeoisie is helped in its work of calming down the natives by the inevitable religion. All the saints who have turned the other cheek, who have forgiven trespasses against them, and who have been spat on and insulted without shrinking are studied and held up as examples" "The native is an oppressed person whose permanent dream is to become the persecutor. The symbols of social order – the police, the bugle calls in the barracks, military parades and the waving flags – are at one and the same time inhibitory and stimulating" "A belief in fatality removes all blame from the oppressor; the cause of misfortunes and of poverty is attributed to God: He is Fate. In this way, the individual … bows down before the settler and his lot, and by a kind of interior restabilization acquires a stony calm"
Steven Biko	*I Write What I Like* (1978)	Colonialism, white domination, inferiority complex, "Black Consciousness"	"[T]he most potent weapon in the hands of the oppressor is the mind of the oppressed" "[B]lacks are suffering from inferiority complex – a result of 300 years of deliberate oppression, denigration and derision" "All in all the black man has become a shell, a shadow of man, completely defeated, drowning in his own misery, a slave, an ox bearing the yoke of oppression with sheepish timidity" "'[B]lack consciousness' seeks to show the black people the value of their own standards and outlook. It urges black people to judge themselves according to these standards and not to be fooled by white society who have white-washed themselves and made white standards the yardstick by which even black people judge each other" "We are all oppressed by the same system"
Henri Tajfel	*Human Groups and Social Categories* (1981); "The social identity theory of intergroup behavior" (1986, with J.C. Turner)	Perceived stability and legitimacy of intergroup relations, acceptance of the status quo, absence of "cognitive alternatives"	"[O]utgroup social stereotypes tend to be created and widely diffused in conditions which require: (i) a search for the understanding of complex and usually distressful, large-scale social events; (ii) justification of actions, committed or planned, against outgroups" "Where social-structural differences in the distribution of resources have been institutionalized, legitimized, and justified through a consensually accepted status system (or at least a status system that is sufficiently firm and pervasive to prevent the creation of cognitive alternatives to it), the result has been less and not more ethnocentrism in the different status groups" "[An] important requirement of research on social justice would consist of establishing in detail the links between social myths and the general acceptance of injustice"

has its parallel in many underprivileged groups," including Jews and African Americans. As a field theorist, he clearly saw the problem in contextual, environmental (i.e., system-level) terms, writing that: "Jewish self-hatred will die out only when actual equality of status with the non-Jew is achieved." Allport, too, identified the problem of internalization of inferiority and argued that, above all, stereotypes serve a "rationalizing and justifying function" (see also Eagly and Steffen, 1984; Hoffman and Hurst, 1990; Jost and Banaji, 1994). The German social theorist Norbert Elias distinguished between "established" and "outsider" groups in a wide range of social and cultural contexts and noted that "groups in an outsider position measure themselves with the yardstick of their oppressors" (Elias and Scotson, 1965: 26). Anti-colonial theorists such as Frantz Fanon (1961), Albert Memmi (1968), and Steven Biko (1978) concurred. Biko (1978), for instance, declared in the context of the Apartheid system in South Africa, "The most potent weapon in the hands of the oppressor is the mind of the oppressed."

Tajfel (1981) elaborated a group-based version of Allport's argument that a stereotype's "function is to justify (rationalize) our conduct in relation to that category" (1954: 191). Specifically, he noted that stereotypes justify "actions, committed or planned, against outgroups." Tajfel stopped short of recognizing the *system*-justifying functions of stereotyping and prejudice (as distinct from their *group*-justifying functions), but he did see a correlation between perceptions of the social system and intergroup attitudes:

> Where social–structural differences in the distribution of resources have been institutionalized, legitimized, and justified through a consensually accepted status system (or at least a status system that is sufficiently firm and pervasive to prevent the creation of cognitive alternatives to it), the result has been less and not more ethnocentrism in the different status groups.

Researchers subsequently explored the phenomenon of outgroup favoritism among members of low status or disadvantaged groups (see Hinkle and Brown, 1990), which Jost and Banaji (1994) regarded as a likely manifestation of false consciousness (see also Jost, 1995). System justification theory was developed in order to better understand the social psychological processes whereby social systems are "institutionalized, legitimized, and justified"; that is, the ways in which people who occupy quite different statuses or positions in society nevertheless find reasons to embrace the status quo with an enthusiasm that may seem puzzling in retrospect or when viewed from historical distance.

The tolerance of social injustice

Many social historians, including Chalmers Johnson (1966), Howard Zinn (1968), and Barrington Moore Jr. (1978), have observed that social stability and acceptance of injustice are far more common than protest and rebellion (see Table 42.3). The question is *why*. Whereas sociologists, political scientists, and many laypersons assume that unjust social orders are maintained by force or the threat of force, psychologists since at least the advent of cognitive dissonance theory (Elster, 1982; Festinger, 1957) have understood that people are capable of rationalizing even their own suffering (see also Henry and Saul, 2006; Jost et al., 2003c). Deutsch (1974, 1985) integrated Anna Freud's ideas about "identification with the aggressor" with Lewin's account of "group self-hatred" to explain why it is so difficult to "awaken the sense of injustice." Social justice researchers have often developed psychological theories of why people tolerate injustice and deprivation; processes of denial, rationalization, and social comparison have all been implicated (e.g., Crosby et al., 1989; Major, 1994; Olson and Hafer, 2001). As Major (1994) noted, "One of the more intriguing phenomena of social justice is that people tend to legitimate the status quo, even when it is disadvantageous to the self."

It was Lerner's (1980) account of the "belief in a just world," however, that first postulated

Table 42.3 Theoretical precursors, part 3: the tolerance of social injustice

Author(s)	Source(s)	Key concepts	Illustrative quotations
Chalmers Johnson	*Revolutionary Change* (1966)	Social stability and change, societal equilibrium and disequilibrium	"[P]eople in societies are not inherently mutinous. Society is a form of human interaction that transcends violence, of which one form is revolution. Revolutions are in this sense antisocial, testifying to the existence of extraordinary dissatisfactions … They do not occur randomly, and they need not occur at all. Revolution can be rationally contemplated only in a society that is undergoing radical structural change and that is in need of still further change" "[T]he tragedy of the American race situation was that both Negroes and whites accepted a stable, envalued definition of Negro inferiority – and consequent role assignments – for most of the century after the Civil War... the main body of the Negro population did not support innovations developed by marginal men from their own group"
Howard Zinn	*Disobedience and Democracy* (1968)	"Congealed injustice," law and order, dissent	"Society's tendency is to maintain what has been. Rebellion is only an occasional reaction to suffering in human history; we have infinitely more instances of forbearance to exploitation, and submission to authority, than we have examples of revolt. Measure the number of peasant insurrections against the centuries of serfdom in Europe – the millennia of landlordism in the East; match the number of slave revolts in America with the record of those millions who went through their lifetimes of toil without outward protest. What we should be most concerned about is not some natural tendency toward violent uprising, but rather the inclination of people, faced with an overwhelming environment, to submit to it"
Barrington Moore Jr.	*Injustice: The Social Bases of Obedience and Revolt* (1978)	Suffering, oppression, explanation, justification, "psychological anesthesia"	"People are evidently inclined to grant legitimacy to anything that is or seems inevitable no matter how painful it may be. Otherwise the pain might be intolerable" "The human capacity to withstand suffering and abuse is impressive, tragically so" "[A]t the level of cultural norms and shared perceptions it will be necessary to overcome the illusion that the present state of affairs is just, permanent, and inevitable" "As any oppressed or suffering group seeks to come to terms with its fate, its members, and more especially its leaders and spokesmen, seek an explanation for that fate" "In a stratified society the principles of social inequality, generally systematized by priests, explain and justify the more prevalent and routine forms of suffering"

Continued

Table 42.3   Cont'd

Author(s)	Source(s)	Key concepts	Illustrative quotations
Morton Deutsch	"Awakening the sense of injustice" (1974); *Distributive Justice* (1985)	Tolerance of injustice, identification with the aggressor, group self-hatred	"Although the need to maintain a positive self-regard is common, it is not universal. The victim of injustice, if he views himself favorably, may be outraged by his experience and attempt to undo it; in the process of so doing, he may have to challenge the victimizer. If the victimizer is more powerful than he and has the support of the legal and other institutions of the society, he will realize that it would be dangerous to act on his outrage or even to express it. Under such circumstances, in a process that Anna Freud (1937) labeled 'identification with the aggressor,' the victim may control his dangerous feelings of injustice and outrage by denying them and by internalizing the derogatory attitudes of the victimizer toward himself… Thus, he will become in Lewin's terms (1935) a 'self-hater' who attributes blame for his victimization upon himself or his group"
Melvin Lerner	*The Belief in a Just World: A Fundamental Delusion* (1980)	Belief in a just world, need for control, deservingness, myth, victim-blaming	"People want to and have to believe they live in a just world so that they can go about their daily lives with a sense of trust, hope, and confidence in their future" "As human beings, we judge events in moral terms. People, acts, outcomes are not only evaluated on some dimension of desirability; they are also viewed in terms of their 'appropriateness,' and we want it all to fit together in the appropriate way" "It is virtually a cliché in our culture to consider the poverty-stricken, or even the relatively deprived, as having their own compensating rewards. They are actually happy in their own way – carefree, happy-go-lucky, in touch with and able to enjoy the 'simple pleasures of life'… Some systems of religious belief see virtue in suffering, and assume restitution in later life"
Tom R. Tyler and Kathleen McGraw	"Ideology and the interpretation of personal experience: procedural justice and political quiescence" (1986)	Dominant ideology, cultural socialization, procedural fairness beliefs	"[T]he development of dysfunctional views about procedure is the result of cultural socialization. The disadvantaged accept the dominant American ideology of a 'contest' mobility system. Because they accept this procedure as fair, citizens conclude that the social allocation system is fair and do not examine the distributive consequences of this system: i.e., whether its outcomes actually correspond to distributive justice principles … By accepting societal values, the disadvantaged are led to focus upon aspects of their situation that are ineffective in inducing a sense of injustice and, hence, lead to political quiescence"

Continued

Table 42.3 Cont'd

Author(s)	Source(s)	Key concepts	Illustrative quotations
Brenda Major	"From social inequality to personal entitlement: the role of social comparisons, legitimacy appraisals, and group membership" (1994)	Social comparison biases, depressed entitlement, legitimizing attributions	"Often, people who are objectively disadvantaged report themselves to be just as content and satisfied with their circumstances as are people who are objectively more privileged" "Social comparison biases tend to prevent awareness of disadvantage, and attribution biases tend to legitimize disadvantage" "People typically feel they deserve the same treatment or outcomes that they have received in the past or that others like themselves receive" "[E]ven when members of disadvantaged groups do become aware of their disadvantaged status, they often appraise it as legitimate. As a result, the disadvantaged often come to believe that they are personally entitled to less than do members of more advantaged groups" "One of the more intriguing phenomena of social justice is that people tend to legitimate the status quo, even when it is disadvantageous to the self" "[U]nequal social distributions have a powerful tendency to be legitimated"

a sweeping motivational tendency (a "fundamental delusion") to believe that the social world is orderly, predictable, and above all *just*. Lerner pondered the oft-noted human propensity to imbue social regularities (what "is") with an "ought" quality. He wrote: "People want to and have to believe they live in a just world so that they can go about their daily lives with a sense of trust, hope, and confidence in their future." There are however, significant differences between just world and system justification perspectives (Jost and Hunyady, 2002; Jost et al., 2004b). Most notably, Lerner theorized that the "justice motive" would lead people first to attempt to help innocent victims and to rectify injustice; only when they are *prevented* from doing so did Lerner think that people would engage in denial, rationalization, and victim-blaming strategies to maintain the belief in a just world. System justification theory, by contrast, holds that people are motivated to *exaggerate* the fairness and desirability of social, economic, and political institutions and arrangements; such tendencies are assumed to be *antithetical* to the genuine desire to attain social justice in

practice (Jost and Kay, 2010). According to system justification theory, people may blame victims and defend the status quo even when opportunities to rectify injustice are potentially available and – in a departure from cognitive dissonance theory – even when they bear no personal responsibility for aversive outcomes (see Jost et al., 2003c; Kay et al., 2002).

The institutional legitimation of the social order

Whereas psychologists tend to emphasize the role of individual thoughts, feelings, and behaviors in the perpetuation of the status quo, sociologists (as a general rule) focus on the ways in which the social order accrues legitimacy by fostering social stability through cultural and ideological as well as coercive (i.e., social control) processes (see Table 42.4). For instance, Berger and Luckmann (1966) in *The Social Construction of Reality* noted that "institutions, once formed, have a tendency to persist." To a considerable extent, this is because people

Table 42.4 Theoretical precursors, part 4: the institutional legitimation of the social order

Author(s)	Source(s)	Key concepts	Illustrative quotations
Peter L. Berger and Thomas Luckmann	*The Social Construction of Reality* (1966)	Institutionalization, legitimation, need for cohesion, "taken-for-granted" nature of reality	"[T]he institutional world requires legitimation, that is ways by which it can be 'explained' and justified" "Institutionalization is not, however, an irreversible process, despite the fact that institutions, once formed, have a tendency to persist" "It is possible that this tendency to integrate meanings is based on a psychological need, which may in turn be physiologically grounded (that is, that there maybe a built-in 'need' for cohesion in the psycho-physiological constitution of man" "The legitimation of the institutional order is also faced with the ongoing necessity of keeping chaos at bay"
Jürgen Habermas	*Legitimation Crisis* (1975); *The Theory of Communicative Action* (1987); *The New Conservatism* (1989)	Need for legitimation, justification, system crisis, ideology as "systematically distorted communication"	"In societies organized around a state, a need for legitimation arises that, for structural reasons, could not yet exist in tribal societies" "Social systems adapt inner nature to society with the help of normative structures in which needs are interpreted and actions licensed or made obligatory. The concept of motivation that appears here should not conceal the specific fact that social systems accomplish the integration of inner nature through the medium of norms that have need of justification" "[W]ithin the framework of a legitimate order of authority, the opposition of interests can be kept latent and integrated for a certain time. This is the achievement of legitimating world-views or ideologies" "As soon … as belief in the legitimacy of an existing order vanishes, the latent force embedded in the system of institutions is released"
Pierre Bourdieu	*Outline of a Theory of Practice* (1977)	Legitimating discourses, class habitus, "the established order"	"Once a system of mechanisms has been constituted capable of objectively ensuring the reproduction of the established order of its own motion … the dominant class have only to let the system they dominate take its own course in order to exercise their domination" "[T]he task of legitimating the established order does not fall exclusively to the mechanisms traditionally regarded as belonging to the order of ideology, such as law … The most successful ideological effects are those which have no need of words, and ask no more than complicitous silence" "[T]he ideological use many societies make of the lineage model and, more generally, of genealogical representations, in order to justify and legitimate the established order … would doubtless have become apparent to anthropologists at an earlier date if the theoretical use they themselves make of this theoretical construct had not prevented them from inquiring into the functions of genealogies and genealogists"

Continued

Table 42.4   Cont'd

Author(s)	Source(s)	Key concepts	Illustrative quotations
Vaclav Havel	"The power of the powerless" (1991)	Power, guilt, responsibility, social order	"Position in the power hierarchy determines the degree of responsibility and guilt, but it gives no one unlimited responsibility and guilt, nor does it completely absolve anyone. Thus the conflict between the aims of life and the aims of the system is not a conflict between two socially defined and separate communities; and only a very generalized view (and even that only approximative) permits us to divide society into the rulers and the ruled ... In the post-totalitarian system [the line of conflict] runs de facto through each person, for everyone in his own way is both a victim and a supporter of the system. What we understand by the system is not, therefore, a social order imposed by one group upon another, but rather something which permeates an entire society and is a factor in shaping it"
Mary R. Jackman	The Velvet Glove (1994)	Benevolent paternalism, ideology, coercion, social control	"[G]roups who enjoy the fruits of domination ... work to engage subordinates in a common view of the world that rationalizes the current order. The surest method of social control is to induce subordinates to regulate themselves. To that end, the unmeditated weapon of choice is ideology" "Institutions can legitimize and stabilize inequality by removing compliance from the self-conscious realm ... [T]he advantage of authority over the explicit assertion of power is that the threat remains implicit, submerged beneath an elaborate ideological edifice"

accept "social reality" (the shared assumptions and understandings that are encountered in childhood and afterward) as "taken for granted." Legitimacy, in other words, is the default assumption when people think and speak about the societal status quo. The needs of the individual (e.g., for "cohesion," or epistemic coherence) gratify the needs of the system (for legitimacy) and vice versa.

The philosopher Jürgen Habermas (1975) also addressed the "need for legitimation" of social systems (e.g., the state) and the ways in which "social systems adapt inner [human] nature to society with the help of normative structures." In a semi-Marxian vein, Habermas noted that social systems experience "legitimation crises" and that "value consensus" is attained only when certain social conflicts are sufficiently repressed or kept out of sight.

To the extent that *social integration* is achieved in this manner, value consensus is inherently "ideological" in the classic Marxian sense and requires justification, such as that offered by conservative ideology (Habermas, 1989; see also Jost et al., 2003b).

Bourdieu (1977) was similarly concerned with how relations of dominance and submission in society are sustained over time. In addition to formal mechanisms, such as the law, Bourdieu noted that "[t]he most successful ideological effects are those which ... ask no more than complicitous silence." As suggested also by Berger and Luckmann (1966), among others, it is possible to lend legitimacy to the status quo simply by going along with it; that is, *by appearing not to challenge it* (cf. Jost and Major, 2001). What these various sociological perspectives contribute to system justification theory is the notion that it is remarkably easy for social systems to enjoy legitimacy and stability by winning the apparent (if not always the actual) consent of the majority of the populace. To the extent that people consciously or unconsciously adapt themselves to the systems that affect them, it seems that they cannot help but reinforce those systems.

Vaclav Havel, the first President of the Czech Republic, made a similar set of observations about Communist society in the late twentieth century:

> In the post-totalitarian system [the line of conflict] runs de facto through each person, for everyone in his own way is both a victim and a supporter of the system. What we understand by the system is not, therefore, a social order imposed by one group upon another, but rather something which permeates an entire society and is a factor in shaping it.
> Havel, 1978

Whereas other perspectives in social psychology (especially social identity and social dominance theories) tend to assume that the "social order is imposed by one group upon another," system justification theory takes seriously Havel's (1978) insight that individuals are active (as well as passive) participants in the justification (or legitimation) of the status quo, so that "everyone in his own way is both a victim and a supporter of the system."

Although Mary Jackman (1994) rejects the concept of false consciousness and assumes that social actors (including the disadvantaged) are motivated by self-interest, she astutely accounts the myriad ways in which ideology is used as a "weapon" to insure "social control" by "rationalizing the current order." In analyzing historical cases as diverse as the enslavement of Africans in the Old and New Worlds, and the role of women under patriarchy, Jackman shows how social stability results from a kind of *collaboration* between members of dominant and subordinate groups. She notes that flattering treatment (or "benevolent paternalism") – as exemplified by men's polite but

chauvinistic tendency to place women "on a pedestal" (cf. Bem and Bem, 1970; Glick and Fiske, 2001) – helps to gain compliance. The notion that even flattering stereotypes of disadvantaged group members can be used to justify the status quo by ostensibly compensating for their state of disadvantage and creating an "illusion of equality" was picked up and demonstrated experimentally in later research on system justification theory (Jost and Kay, 2005; Kay and Jost, 2003).

Conservatism, authoritarianism, and social dominance

Writing in 1899, the sociologist Thorstein Veblen sought to understand the sociological and psychological bases of conservative ideology (see also Mannheim, 1925, 1936, and Table 42.5). Specifically, Veblen saw "an instinctive revulsion at any departure from the accepted way of doing and of looking at things – a revulsion common to all men and only to be overcome by stress of circumstances." Half a century later, Adorno et al. (1950) identified conservatism with:

> [A]n attachment, on the surface at least, to 'things as they are,' to the prevailing social organization and ways. Related to the idea that 'what is, is right,' is a tendency to idealize existing authority and to regard the 'American way' as working very well. Social problems tend either to be ignored or to be attributed to extraneous influences rather than to defects intrinsic in the existing social structure. One way of rationalizing chronic problems is to make them 'natural' ... Or, as a prominent ultra-conservative radio commentator observed recently: 'There is nothing wrong with our American system. It is as good as it ever was, but we must do all we can in the New Year to get rid of the charlatans, fakers, and agitators who are responsible for so many problems.' It is clear from the other speeches of this commentator that his 'charlatans' are for the most part leaders of the labor movement or of liberal political groupings – men who, in his eyes, threaten the existing order
> (1950: 153–154)

Adorno and his colleagues associated extremely conservative (or what they termed "pseudo-conservative") outlooks with a propensity to

Table 42.5   Theoretical precursors, part 5: authoritarianism, social dominance, and political ideology

Author(s)	Source(s)	Key concepts	Illustrative quotations
Thorstein Veblen	The Theory of the Leisure Class (1899)	Habit, conservatism, aversion to change	"The opposition of the [wealthy] class to changes in the cultural scheme is instinctive, and does not rest primarily on an interested calculation of material advantages; it is an instinctive revulsion at any departure from the accepted way of doing and of looking at things – a revulsion common to all men and only to be overcome by stress of circumstances. All change in habits of life and of thought is irksome" "Any change in men's views as to what is good and right in human life makes its way but tardily at the best. Especially is this true of any change in the direction of what is called progress"
Theodor W. Adorno, Else Frenkel-Brunswik, Daniel J. Levinson, and R. Nevitt Sanford	The Authoritarian Personality (1950)	Authoritarianism, fascist potential, ethnocentrism, pseudo-conservatism, resistance to social change	"Perhaps the definitive component of conservatism is an attachment, on the surface at least, to 'things as they are,' to the prevailing social organization and ways. Related to the idea that 'what is, is right,' is a tendency to idealize existing authority and to regard the 'American way' as working very well. Social problems tend either to be ignored or to be attributed to extraneous influences rather than to defects intrinsic in the existing social structure. One way of rationalizing chronic problems is to make them 'natural' ... To be 'liberal,' on the other hand, one must be able actively to criticize existing authority. The criticisms may take various forms, ranging from mild reforms (e.g., extension of government controls over business) to complete overthrow of the status quo"
Erich Fromm	Beyond the Chains of Illusion (1962)	Illusion, religious mystification, liberation	"The assumption underlying Marx's 'weapon of truth' is the same as with Freud: that man lives with illusions because these illusions make the misery of real life bearable" "'False consciousness,' that is to say, the distorted picture of reality, weakens man. Being in touch with reality, having an adequate picture of it, makes him stronger"
Robert E. Lane	"The fear of equality" (1959); Political Ideology (1962)	Rationalization, ideology, working class conservatism, "equality of happiness"	"The greater the emphasis in a society upon the availability of 'equal opportunity for all,' the greater the need for members of that society to develop an acceptable rationalization for their own social status" "The greater the strain on a person's self-esteem implied by a relatively low status in an open society, the greater the necessity to explain this status as 'natural' and 'proper' in the social order. Lower status people generally find it less punishing to think of themselves as correctly placed by a just society than to think of themselves as exploited, or victimized by an unjust society" "[I]t is as important to explain why revolutions and radical social movements do not happen as it is to explain why they do"

Continued

Table 42.5   Cont'd

Author(s)	Source(s)	Key concepts	Illustrative quotations
Philip Mason	*Patterns of Dominance* (1971)	Dominance, psychological dependence, the "premise of inequality"	"A social system based on inequality has to provide some degree of psychological satisfaction. Such systems could not otherwise have been so widespread nor have lasted so long" "It is to the rulers' interest that the subjects should think of the rulers as so different from themselves that they can never hope to supplant them, but also as 'their' rulers whom they must defend against outsiders" "The fear of reprisals is not the only force that keeps the slaves, the serfs, the peasants, the workers, subservient … They must somehow be led to believe that the system is part of the order of nature and that things will always be like this" "That so many people for so much of history have accepted treatment manifestly unfair must always be puzzling to an observer from an individualist society"
Jim Sidanius and Felicia Pratto	"Social dominance orientation: a personality variable predicting social and political attitudes" (1994); *Social Dominance* (1999)	Social dominance, hierarchy-enhancing, and hierarchy-attenuating legitimizing myths	"Ideologies that promote or maintain group inequality are the tools that legitimize discrimination. To work smoothly, these ideologies must be widely accepted within a society, appearing as self-apparent truths: hence we call them hierarchy-legitimizing myths": "Despite significant variations in the degree of oppression from one society to another … many societies share the basic social-psychological elements that contribute to inequality: socially shared myths that define 'superior group' and 'inferior group' and that attempt to justify this distinction and the policies that 'should' follow from it" "[W]ithin relatively stable group-based hierarchies, most of the activities of subordinates can be characterized as cooperative rather than subversive to the system of group-based domination"

follow authoritarian, even potentially fascist opinion leaders.

Erich Fromm, like Adorno and Habermas, was a member of the so-called Frankfurt School, which endeavored to merge Marx and Freud, in order to develop a deeper psychological (or psychoanalytic) basis for Marxist social theory. Fromm (1962) saw that both Marx and Freud, in their own ways, were battling against religious and other ideological illusions that kept people from fulfilling their potential. He also suggested in *Escape from Freedom* that most (if not all) human beings possess a fear of personal autonomy that makes them susceptible to authoritarian manipulation (Fromm, 1941). Lane (1959) provided a kindred psychodynamic analysis of working-class conservatives, many of whom were thought to harbor an unconscious "fear of equality." In a statement that foreshadows several key tenets of system justification theory, Lane (1959: 49) wrote:

> The greater the strain on a person's self-esteem implied by a relatively low status in an open society, the greater the necessity to explain this status as 'natural' and 'proper' in the social order. Lower status people generally find it less punishing to think of themselves as correctly placed by a just society than to think of themselves as exploited, or victimized by an unjust society.

Mason (1971) observed that "psychological dependence" often results from relations of domination and subordination. He noted that members of dominant groups frequently persuade subordinates to protect them from both internal and external threats to their hegemony. This is facilitated by fostering a sense of dependence and inevitability among subordinates (see Table 42.5).

Although Jost and Banaji did not learn about social dominance theory until the basic tenets of system justification theory had already been developed, the work of Sidanius and Pratto (1999) served as an inspiration and a foil. Both theoretical perspectives emphasize the ways in which ideologies and other belief systems serve to imbue the existing social order with legitimacy. They also concur in the judgment that "most of the activities of subordinates can be characterized as cooperative rather than subversive to the system of group-based domination." However, system justification theory does not assume, as social dominance theory does, that natural selection pressures have created a strong, potentially insurmountable preference for unequal over equal social relations in human beings. Rather, system justification theory suggests that people are motivated and psychologically equipped to accept and justify a wide range of social systems.

MAJOR POSTULATES OF SYSTEM JUSTIFICATION THEORY AND ILLUSTRATIVE EVIDENCE

System justification theory cheerfully adheres to two basic laws of psychology as described by McGuire: "[F]irst, that basically everybody is the same; and second, that everybody is fundamentally different" (1980: 180). These are the first two postulates of the theory, as summarized in Box 42.1. That is, system justification theory holds first and foremost that people in general are motivated (often unconsciously, i.e., without deliberate awareness or intention) to defend, justify, and bolster aspects of the status quo,

including existing social, economic, and political institutions and arrangements (Postulate I). The general cognitive–motivational process of system justification, in other words, is expected to be largely the same for members of advantaged and disadvantaged groups. Evidence does indicate that people from all walks of life and from many different cultural backgrounds appear to engage in system justification, at least to some extent (e.g., Henry and Hardin, 2006; Henry and Saul, 2006; Jost et al., 2005; Sibley et al., 2007; Ullrich and Cohrs, 2007; Yoshimura and Hardin, 2009). Thus, acceptance and maintenance of the status quo has been observed among the rich and poor, men and women, old and young, heterosexuals and homosexuals, as well as people of diverse national, ethnolinguistic, and racial backgrounds (Glick and Fiske, 2001; Henry and Saul, 2006; Jost and Kay, 2005; Jost et al., 2003c, 2004a; Kay and Jost, 2003; Kilianski and Rudman, 1998; Lau et al., 2008). Members of both advantaged and disadvantaged groups internalize rather than reject existing hierarchies, often favoring the advantaged over the disadvantaged on implicit and sometimes even explicit measures (e.g., Ashburn-Nardo and Johnson, 2008; Ashburn-Nardo et al., 2003; Jost, 2001; Jost et al., 2002, 2004a; Rudman et al., 2002; Uhlmann et al., 2002).

At the same time, the strength of system justification motivation and its expression are expected to vary according to situational (contextual) and dispositional (individual difference) factors (Postulate II). More specifically, system justification motivation is increased when the status quo is perceived to be (a) inevitable or inescapable, or (b) criticized, challenged, or threatened and when (c) the individual feels dependent on or controlled by the system or its representatives (Postulate III). For instance, several experiments reveal that threats to the legitimacy of the social system lead people to increase their use of stereotypes to justify social and economic inequalities and to defend the status quo more vigorously (Jost et al., 2005; Kay et al., 2005). Lau et al. (2008) extended this basic finding to the context of interpersonal attraction, demonstrating that system

Box 42.1 Postulates of system justification theory

I   People in general are motivated (often unconsciously, that is, without deliberate awareness or intention) to defend, justify, and bolster aspects of the status quo, including existing social, economic, and political institutions and arrangements.

II   The strength of system justification motivation and its expression are expected to vary according to situational (contextual) and dispositional (individual difference) factors.

III   System justification motivation is increased when the status quo is perceived to be (a) inevitable or inescapable, or (b) criticized, challenged, or threatened, and when (c) the individual feels dependent on or controlled by the system (or its representatives).

IV   System justification satisfies basic epistemic motives to reduce uncertainty, existential motives to manage threat, and relational motives to coordinate social relationships. Thus, dispositional and situational variability in such needs will affect the strength of system justification motivation.

V   There are several possible means by which the system can be justified, including direct endorsement of certain ideologies, the legitimation of institutions and authorities, denial or minimization of system problems or shortcomings, complementary stereotyping, rationalization, etc.

VI   For members of advantaged groups (or those who are favored by the status quo), system justification is consonant with ego and group justification motives; it is therefore positively associated with self-esteem, ingroup favoritism, and long-term psychological wellbeing.

VII   For members of disadvantaged groups (or those who are disfavored by the status quo), system justification conflicts with ego and group justification motives; it is therefore negatively associated with self-esteem, ingroup favoritism, and long-term psychological wellbeing.

VIII   System justification serves a palliative function; that is, the endorsement of system-justifying beliefs and ideologies is associated in the short term with increased positive affect and decreased negative affect for members of advantaged and disadvantaged groups alike.

IX   Although system justification motivation typically leads people to resist social change (and to perceive it as threatening to the status quo), people are more willing to embrace change when it is perceived as (a) inevitable or extremely likely to occur, and/or (b) congruent with the preservation of at least some aspects of the social system and/or its ideals.

threat leads men to prefer female romantic partners who confirm sexist, system-justifying stereotypes over those who do not. In the U.S., evidence of heightened nationalism, patriotism, and increased support for governmental institutions and authorities (e.g., police, military, Congress, and the President) following the terrorist attacks of September 11, 2001, is consistent with the notion that system threat activates or enhances system justification motivation (Jost et al., 2010; Ullrich and Cohrs, 2007). Similarly, when people feel that restrictive emigration policies prevent them from leaving the country or system or when they otherwise feel extremely dependent upon the current system and its representatives, they exhibit heightened system justification tendencies (e.g., Laurin et al., 2010; van der Toorn et al., 2011).

System justification is thought to satisfy basic *epistemic* needs for consistency, certainty, and meaning; *existential* needs to manage threat and distress; and *relational* needs to coordinate social relationships and achieve shared reality with others (Postulate IV; see Jost et al., 2008a). It follows that dispositional and situational variability in such needs should affect the strength of system justification motivation (Jost and Hunyady, 2005). Consistent with this formulation, a meta-analysis by Jost et al. (2003b) revealed that uncertainty avoidance, intolerance of ambiguity, personal needs for order, structure, and closure, perceptions of a dangerous world, and death anxiety are all positively associated with an affinity for politically conservative, system-justifying (versus liberal, system-challenging) ideologies (see also Jost et al., 2007). Cognitive complexity, openness to new experiences, and the motivation to prolong cognitive closure on the other hand, are negatively associated with political conservatism and other forms of system justification (Carney et al., 2008).

Consistent with a goal systems approach to system justification (Jost et al., 2008b), there are several possible means by which the system can be justified, such as direct endorsement of certain ideologies, the legitimation of institutions and authorities, denial or minimization of system problems or shortcomings, rationalization, and so on (Postulate V). In the context of intergroup relations, system justification needs are frequently satisfied through processes of stereotyping, whereby members of both advantaged and disadvantaged groups accept and perpetuate the existing hierarchy by judging the advantaged to be more competent and industrious (and sometimes better overall) than the disadvantaged (Jost and Hunyady, 2002; Jost et al., 2005; Oldmeadow and Fiske, 2007; Sidanius and Pratto, 1999) and by endorsing complementary stereotypes that create an "illusion of equality" in society (Bem and Bem, 1970; Jost and Kay, 2005; Kay and Jost, 2003).

There are a number of pre-existing *ideologies* or belief systems that people can embrace to bolster the societal status quo (Blasi and Jost, 2006). These include the Protestant work ethic, belief in a just world, meritocratic ideology, fair market ideology, economic system justification, power distance, benevolent sexism, social dominance orientation, right-wing authoritarianism, religious fundamentalism, and political conservatism (Glick and Fiske, 2001; Jost and Burgess, 2000; Jost and Thompson, 2000; Jost et al., 2003a, 2003b; Kaiser and Pratt-Hyatt, 2009; Major, 1994; Oldmeadow and Fiske, 2007; Sibley et al., 2007; Sidanius and Pratto, 1999). What these various belief systems have in common is that they explain social, economic, or political outcomes in a manner that generally maintains the subjective legitimacy of the status quo (Jost and Hunyady, 2005). Because of this feature, their endorsement should satisfy epistemic, existential, and relational needs to a greater extent than belief systems that are openly critical, contemptuous, or challenging of the status quo (e.g., Marxism, feminism, anarchy, and other revolutionary ideologies).[2] The fact that there are so many different types of system-justifying belief systems highlights the fact that such concerns permeate individuals' social relationships, family dynamics, and work lives, as well as their attitudes about society, religion, politics, economics, business, and the law. Research to date suggests that stereotyping, ideological endorsement, and other ways of justifying the system in various domains provide more or less interchangeable means of attaining the system justification goal in practice (Jost et al., 2010; Kay et al., 2005).

Some long-term social psychological consequences of system justification are theorized to be opposite for members of advantaged and disadvantaged groups (Jost and Thompson, 2000). For members of advantaged groups (or those who are favored by the status quo), the perception of being "on top" of society is consonant with the holding of positive attitudes concerning their own group and themselves (Jost et al., 2001, 2002). That is, system justification is consonant with ego and group justification motives; it is positively associated with self-esteem, ingroup favoritism, and psychological wellbeing (Postulate VI). Members of disadvantaged groups (or those who are disfavored by the status quo), however, are faced with a potential conflict between their need to justify the system and competing motives to enhance their own self-esteem and group status. For them, system justification conflicts with ego and group justification motives; it is negatively associated with self-esteem, ingroup favoritism, and long-term psychological wellbeing (Postulate VII). Specifically, the more they justify the system (as well as their own group), the more disadvantaged group members exhibit ambivalence toward the ingroup-outgroup favoritism, and suffer in terms of subjective wellbeing as indexed by levels of self-esteem, neuroticism, depression, and generalized anxiety (Ashburn-Nardo et al., 2003, 2008; Jost and Burgess, 2000; Jost and Thompson, 2000; Jost et al., 2002; O'Brien and Major, 2005).

At the same time, Jost and Hunyady (2002) proposed that system justification can serve a short-term palliative function for members of advantaged and disadvantaged groups alike. That is, the endorsement of system-justifying beliefs and ideologies is associated with increased positive affect, decreased negative affect, and satisfaction with the status quo (Postulate VIII). For instance, the tendency to embrace meritocratic ideology (e.g., believing that economic inequality is legitimate and necessary in capitalist society) is associated with increased life satisfaction and contentment among the poor as well as the rich (Jost et al., 2003c; Kluegel and Smith, 1986). The adoption of system-justifying beliefs and ideologies can reduce feelings of uncertainty, distress, guilt, frustration, helplessness, cognitive dissonance, and moral outrage brought on by social inequality and other potential system deficiencies (e.g., Kay et al., 2008; Wakslak et al., 2007).

Furthermore, the observed gap between liberals and conservatives in terms of self-reported happiness is at least partially explained by the latter's tendency to regard economic inequality as fair and just (Napier and Jost, 2008). It appears that system justification serves the palliative function of increasing positive affect and reducing negative affect for many of its adherents, although once again racial and ethnic minorities may benefit less (Rankin et al., 2009). Nevertheless, the occurrence of system justification is probably better explained by the fact that it helps to satisfy underlying epistemic, existential, and relational needs and not simply because it makes people feel "good" (cf. Elster, 1982).

Most system justification research conducted to date paints a fairly bleak picture with regard to prospects for social change. System justification, like rationalization in general, does seem to help people cope with unwelcome realities (Jost and Hunyady, 2002; Kay et al., 2002), but it also hampers the remediation of injustice and other system-level problems. Studies carried out by Wakslak et al. (2007) demonstrated that because system justification reduces moral outrage, it undermines

the implementation of intentions and actions designed to help the disadvantaged (e.g., support for soup kitchens, job training programs, crisis hotlines, minority outreach, and after-school tutoring programs). Thus, system justification motivation typically leads people to resist social change and to perceive it as threatening to the status quo (Postulate IX).

At the same time, however, research suggests that people are more willing to embrace social change when it is perceived as (a) inevitable or extremely likely to occur, and/or (b) congruent with the preservation of at least some aspects of the social system and/or its ideals. For example, people engage in anticipatory rationalization of a new or emerging regime as soon as its implementation is seen as inevitable, or at least highly probable (Kay et al., 2002). One would expect this process to be facilitated by a rapid transition that replaces the previous regime entirely, thereby avoiding the problem of divided loyalties between current and former systems. Feygina et al. (2010) demonstrated that although system justification tendencies are generally associated with greater denial of global climate change and less commitment to proenvironmental action, it is possible to eliminate the negative effect of system justification on environmentalism by framing proposed changes as "system-sanctioned" (i.e., as patriotic and consistent with protecting the status quo). With the right kind of leadership and message framing, then, it may be possible to harness system justification motivation in a constructive manner so that it enables people to improve upon the status quo rather than reflexively defending against the possibility of change.

PRACTICAL IMPLICATIONS OF SYSTEM JUSTIFICATION THEORY

Robert Lynd (1939) suggested that "the role of the social sciences is to be troublesome, to disconnect the habitual arrangements by which we manage to live along, and to demonstrate the possibility of change in more adequate directions." Conceived of in this way, a primary task of the social scientist is to overcome his or her system-justifying tendencies in order to see society as it really is, so that genuine problems can be recognized and, ultimately, resolved. As Lynd anticipated, "the role of such a constructive troublemaker is scarcely inviting," presumably because it requires confronting and questioning the system-justifying assumptions of others. Indeed, system justification theorists (and, to a much more serious extent, many of the historical predecessors cited in Tables 42.1–42.5) have received more than usual levels of criticism; indeed, if the theory is sound, one would expect defensive, even aggressive reactions to the suggestion that societal arrangements are not as fair or legitimate as most people believe (see also Blasi and Jost, 2006). As Memmi observed, "[P]eople are always accused of exaggeration when they describe injustices to those who do not want to hear about them" (1968: 19). This brings us to an important practical insight of system justification theory, namely that people are wont to ignore, deny, minimize, rationalize, or dismiss criticisms or putative shortcomings of the status quo, even if these – like the problems posed by global climate change – are grounded in scientific evidence.

There are many other practical implications of system justification theory, some of which we have touched on throughout the chapter. These include consequences for intergroup relations involving status or power differences; the pernicious effects of relatively subtle forms of sexism and stereotyping; and the persistence of implicit as well as explicit prejudice. There are also implications of system justification theory for more overtly political behavior, including voting preferences, evaluations of system leaders and representatives, and the psychological advantages conferred by incumbency status and conservative ideology. System justification theory has been used to elucidate the effects of public policies such as restricted immigration (Laurin et al., 2010) and to explain an ever-widening range of consequential outcomes, including religious commitment (Kay et al.,

2008), romantic preferences (Eastwick et al., 2009; Lau et al., 2008), academic performance (Chatard et al., 2008), and willingness to help the disadvantaged (Wakslak et al., 2007). In the spirit of divergent theorizing, one hopes that by applying system justification theory to more and more domains, an increasingly refined set of scientifically and practically significant conclusions will emerge.

CONCLUSION

In this chapter we have traced the historical development of system justification theory, which offers a unique social psychological framework for understanding why so many individuals assume, even in the face of contrary evidence, that the societal status quo is, good, fair, legitimate, desirable, and right. We have identified nine major postulates of the theory and discussed how the theory builds on and extends the work of philosophers, historians, sociologists, psychologists, and political scientists. By positing that system justification is a motivated, goal-directed process for most of the people at least some of the time, we have offered a distinctive psychological perspective that helps to explain, among other things, the perceived legitimacy and stability of social systems and hierarchical arrangements, as well as the relative scarcity of protest and rebellion. Research will continue to identify moderating and mediating variables that help to explain when and why people will reflexively defend, bolster, and maintain the current social system and when they will not. Future work will speak even more directly to the ways in which resistance to change and political acquiescence can be transformed into an open, restless, critical, constructive search for forms of social organization that are better, truer, freer, more sustainable, and just. While these are grand scientific and practical pretensions for a single theory, the ideas have been simmering for at least a century and a half – indeed, since the advent of social science itself.

ACKNOWLEDGMENTS

The authors would like to thank Rick Andrews, Raynee Gutting, Erin Hennes, P.J. Henry, György Hunyady, Lawrence Jost, Aaron Kay, Arie Kruglanski, Alison Ledgerwood, Anesu Mandisodza, Avital Mentovich, Artur Nilsson, Andrew Shipley, Paul van Lange, and Jesse Wynhausen for superb comments on earlier drafts. The writing of this chapter was supported by the National Science Foundation (Award # BCS–0617558).

NOTES

1 In the Marxian tradition, it is possible for members of advantaged groups to hold false beliefs that are *congruent* with self-interest and that still count as instances of false consciousness (e.g., Lukács, 1971). Because it is unclear in these cases, from a social psychological perspective, whether such beliefs are *motivated* by ego, group, or system justification needs, the clearest, least ambiguous cases of false consciousness (and system justification motivation) come from members of disadvantaged groups, who could not simply be motivated by self-interest or group-interest to defend and bolster the societal status quo (Jost, 1995; Jost and Banaji, 1994).

2 To the extent that revolutionaries engage in justification of an anticipated (i.e., utopian) status quo and they are convinced that the transition is inevitable, it is conceivable that revolutionary ideology could satisfy epistemic, existential, and relational motives to some degree (see also Blasi and Jost, 2006). At the same time, it seems self-evident that revolutionary activity itself requires one to embrace uncertainty, danger, and the risk of losing more than a few friends. It follows, that revolutionaries are primarily motivated by other, opposing needs or concerns (e.g., for justice, innovation, group justification, hatred, excitement, etc.).

REFERENCES

Abercrombie, N., Hill, S. and Turner, B. (eds) (1990) *Dominant Ideologies.* London: Unwin Hyman.

Adorno, T.W., Frenkel-Brunswik, E., Levinson, D.J. and Sanford, R.N. (1950) *The Authoritarian Personality.* New York: Harper.

Allport, G. (1954) *The Nature of Prejudice.* Cambridge, MA: Addison-Wesley.

Ashburn-Nardo, L. and Johnson, N. (2008) Implicit outgroup favoritism and intergroup judgment: The moderating role of stereotype context. *Social Justice Research, 21,* 490–508.

Ashburn-Nardo, L., Knowles, M.L. and Monteith, M.J. (2003) Black Americans' implicit racial associations and their implications for intergroup judgment. *Social Cognition, 21,* 61–87.

Bargh, J.A., Gollwitzer, P.M., Lee Chai, A., Barndollar, K. and Trötschel, R. (2001) The automated will: Nonconscious activation and pursuit of behavioral goals. *Journal of Personality and Social Psychology, 81,* 1014–1027.

Bem, S.L. and Bem, D.J. (1970) Case study of a nonconscious ideology: Training the woman to know her place. In D.J. Bem (ed.), *Beliefs, Attitudes, and Human Affairs,* pp. 89–99. Belmont, CA: Brooks/Cole.

Berger, P.L. and Luckmann, T. (1966) *The Social Construction of Reality: A Treatise in the Sociology of Knowledge.* Garden City, NY: Anchor.

Biko, S. (1978) *I Write What I Like.* London: Heinemenn.

Blasi, G. and Jost, J.T. (2006) System justification theory and research: Implications for law, legal advocacy, and social justice. *California Law Review, 94,* 1119–1168.

Borges, J.L. (1964) Kafka and his precursors. In J.L. Borges (ed.), *Other Inquisitions 1937–1952.* Austin: University of Texas Press.

Bourdieu, P. (1977) *Outline of a Theory of Practice* (Edition, 1986) New York: Cambridge University Press.

Carney, D.R., Jost, J.T., Gosling, S.D. and Potter, J. (2008) The secret lives of liberals and conservatives: Personality profiles, interaction styles, and the things they leave behind. *Political Psychology, 29,* 807–840.

Chatard, A., Selimbegovic, L. and Konan, P. (2008) Leftists' and rightists' IQ as a function of stereotype salience. *Journal of Research in Personality, 42,* 602–1606.

Crosby, F.J., Pufall, A., Snyder, R.C., O'Connell, M. and Whalen, P. (1989) The denial of personal disadvantage among you, me, and all the other ostriches. In M. Crawford and M. Gentry (eds), *Gender and Thought: Psychological Perspectives,* pp. 79–99. New York: Springer.

Cunningham, F. (1987) False consciousness. In *Democratic Theory and Socialism,* pp. 236–267. Cambridge: Cambridge University Press.

Deutsch, M. (1974) Awakening the sense of injustice. In M. Lerner, and M. Ross (eds), *The Quest for Justice,* pp. 19–42. New York: Holt.

Deutsch, M. (1985) *Distributive Justice: A Social-psychological Perspective*. New Haven: Yale.

Eagly, A.H. and Steffen, V.J. (1984) Gender stereotypes stem from the distribution of women and men into social roles. *Journal of Personality and Social Psychology*, 46, 735–754.

Eastwick, P.W., Richeson, J.A., Son, D. and Finkel, E.J. (2009) Is love colorblind? Political orientation and interracial romantic desire. *Personality and Social Psychology Bulletin*, 35, 1258–1268.

Elias, N. and Scotson, J.L. (1965) *The Established and the Outsiders: A Sociological Enquiry into Community Problems* (2nd Edition, 1994). London: Sage.

Elster, J. (1982) Belief, bias, and ideology. In M. Hollis and S. Lukes (eds), *Rationality and Relativism*, pp. 123–148. Cambridge, MA: MIT Press.

Elster, J. (1983) *Sour Grapes: Studies in the Subversion of Rationality*. Cambridge: Cambridge University Press.

Fanon, F. (1961) *The Wretched of the Earth* (Edition, 2001). Harmondsworth: Penguin.

Festinger, L. (1957). *A Theory of Cognitive Dissonance*. Stanford, CA: Stanford University Press.

Feygina I., Jost, J.T. and Goldsmith, R. (2010). System justification, the denial of global warming, and the prospect of 'system-sanctioned' change. *Personality and Social Psychology Bulletin*, 36, 326–338.

Fiori, G. (1970). *Antonio Gramsci: Life of a Revolutionary*. London: Verso.

Fromm, E. (1941) *Escape From freedom* (Edition, 1994). New York: Owl.

Fromm, E. (1962) *Beyond the Chains of Illusion: My Encounter with Marx and Freud*. New York: Simon and Schuster.

Fromm, E. (ed.) (1965) *Socialist Humanism: An International Symposium*. Garden City, NY: Doubleday.

Glick, P. and Fiske, S.T. (2001) An ambivalent alliance: Hostile and benevolent sexism as complementary justifications for gender inequality. *American Psychologist*, 56, 109–118.

Gramsci, A. (1971) *Selections from the Prison Notebooks*. New York: International Publishers.

Gurr, T. (1970) *Why Men Rebel*. Princeton, NJ: Princeton University Press.

Habermas, J. (1975) *Legitimation Crisis*. Boston, MA: Beacon.

Habermas, J. (1989) *The New Conservatism: Cultural Criticism and the Historians' Debate*. Cambridge, MA: MIT Press.

Hardin, C.D. and Higgins, E.T. (1996) Shared reality: How social verification makes the subjective reality. In R.M. Sorrentino and E.T. Higgins (eds), *Handbook of Motivation and Cognition*, 3, 28–84. New York: Guilford Press.

Havel, V. (1978) The power of the powerless (abridged). In V. Havel (ed.), *Open Letters* (Edition, 1991), pp. 127–145. London: Faber.

Henry, P.J. and Hardin, C.D. (2006) The contact hypothesis revisited: Status bias in the reduction of implicit prejudice in the United States and Lebanon. *Psychological Science*, 17, 862–868.

Henry P.J. and Saul A. (2006) The development of system justification in the developing world. *Social Justice Research*, 19, 365–378.

Hinkle, S. and Brown, R. (1990) Intergroup comparisons and social identity: Some links and lacunae. In D. Abrams and M.A. Hogg (eds), *Social Identity Theory: Constructive and Critical Advances*, pp. 48–70. London: Harvester.

Hirschman, A.O. (1970) *Exit, Voice, and Loyalty: Responses to Decline in Firms, Organizations, and States*. Cambridge, MA: Harvard University Press.

Hochschild, J.L. (1981) *What's Fair? American Beliefs About Distributive Justice*. Cambridge, MA: Harvard University Press.

Hoffman, C. and Hurst, N. (1990) Gender stereotypes: Perception or rationalization? *Journal of Personality and Social Psychology*, 58, 197–208.

Jackman, M.R. (1994) *The Velvet Glove: Paternalism and Conflict in Gender, Class, and Race Relations*. Berkeley: University of California Press.

Johnson, C. (1966) *Revolutionary Change* (2nd Edition, 1983). Stanford, CA: Stanford.

Jost, J.T. (1995) Negative illusions: Conceptual clarification and psychological evidence concerning false consciousness. *Political Psychology*, 16, 397–424.

Jost, J.T. (2001) Outgroup favoritism and the theory of system justification: An experimental paradigm for investigating the effects of socio-economic success on stereotype content. In G. Moskowitz (ed.), *Cognitive Social Psychology: The Princeton Symposium on the Legacy and Future of Social Cognition*, pp. 89–102. Mahwah, NJ: Erlbaum.

Jost, J.T. and Banaji, M.R. (1994) The role of stereotyping in system-justification and the production of false consciousness. *British Journal of Social Psychology*, 33, 1–27.

Jost, J.T., Banaji, M.R. and Nosek, B.A. (2004a) A decade of system justification theory: Accumulated evidence of conscious and unconscious bolstering of the status quo. *Political Psychology*, 25, 881–919.

Jost, J.T., Blount, S., Pfeffer, J. and Hunyady, G. (2003a) Fair market ideology: Its cognitive-motivational underpinnings. *Research in Organizational Behavior*, *25*, 53–91.

Jost, J.T. and Burgess, D. (2000) Attitudinal ambivalence and the conflict between group and system justification motives in low status groups. *Personality and Social Psychology Bulletin*, *26*, 293–305.

Jost, J.T., Burgess, D. and Mosso, C. (2001) Conflicts of legitimation among self, group, and system: The integrative potential of system justification theory. In J.T. Jost and B. Major (eds), *The Psychology of Legitimacy: Emerging Perspectives on Ideology, Justice, and Intergroup Relations*, pp. 363–388. New York: Cambridge University Press.

Jost, J.T., Fitzsimons, G.M. and Kay, A.C. (2004b) The ideological animal: A system justification view. In J. Greenberg, S.L. Koole, and T. Pyszczynski (eds), *Handbook of Experimental Existential Psychology*, pp. 263–282. New York: Guilford Press.

Jost, J.T., Glaser, J., Kruglanski, A.W. and Sulloway, F. (2003b) Political conservatism as motivated social cognition. *Psychological Bulletin*, *129*, 339–375.

Jost, J.T. and Hunyady, O. (2002) The psychology of system justification and the palliative function of ideology. *European Review of Social Psychology*, *13*, 111–153.

Jost, J.T. and Hunyady, O. (2005) Antecedents and consequences of system-justifying ideologies. *Current Directions in Psychological Science*, *14*, 260–265.

Jost, J.T. and Kay, A.C. (2005) Exposure to benevolent sexism and complementary gender stereotypes: Consequences for specific and diffuse forms of system justification. *Journal of Personality and Social Psychology*, *88*, 498–509.

Jost, J.T. and Kay, A.C. (2010) Social justice: History, theory, and research. In S.T. Fiske, D. Gilbert and G. Lindzey (eds), *Handbook of Social Psychology, Vol. 2* (5th Edition), pp. 1122–1165. New York: Wiley.

Jost, J.T., Kivetz, Y., Rubini, M., Guermandi, G. and Mosso, C. (2005) System-justifying functions of complementary regional and ethnic stereotypes: Cross-national evidence. *Social Justice Research*, *18*, 305–333.

Jost, J.T., Ledgerwood, A. and Hardin, C.D. (2008a) Shared reality, system justification, and the relational basis of ideological beliefs. *Social and Personality Psychology Compass*, *2*, 171–186.

Jost, J.T., Liviatan, I., Van der Toorn, J., Ledgerwood, A., Mandisodza, A. and Nosek, B. (2010) System justification: How do we know it's motivated? In D.R. Bobocel, A.C. Kay, M.P. Zanna, and J.M. Olson (eds), *The Psychology of Justice and Legitimacy: The Ontario Symposium, 11*, 173–203. Hillsdale, NJ: Erlbaum.

Jost, J.T. and Major, B. (eds) (2001) *The Psychology of Legitimacy: Emerging Perspectives on Ideology, Justice, and Intergroup relations*. New York: Cambridge University Press.

Jost, J.T., Napier, J.L., Thorisdottir, H., Gosling, S., Palfai, T.P. and Ostafin, B. (2007) Are needs to manage uncertainty and threat associated with political conservatism or ideological extremity? *Personality and Social Psychology Bulletin*, *33*, 989–1007.

Jost, J.T., Pelham, B.W. and Carvallo, M.R. (2002) Nonconscious forms of system justification: Implicit and behavioral preferences for higher status groups. *Journal of Experimental Social Psychology*, *38*, 586–602.

Jost, J.T., Pelham, B.W., Sheldon, O. and Sullivan, B.N. (2003c) Social inequality and the reduction of ideological dissonance on behalf of the system: Evidence of enhanced system justification among the disadvantaged. *European Journal of Social Psychology*, *33*, 13–36.

Jost, J.T., Pietrzak, J., Liviatan, I., Mandisodza, A.N. and Napier, J.L. (2008b) System justification as conscious and nonconscious goal pursuit. In J. Shah and W. Gardner (eds), *Handbook of Motivation Science*, pp. 591–605. New York: Guilford Press.

Jost, J.T. and Thompson, E.P. (2000) Group-based dominance and opposition to equality as independent predictors of self-esteem, ethnocentrism, and social policy attitudes among African Americans and European Americans. *Journal of Experimental Social Psychology*, *36*, 209–232.

Jost, L.J. and Jost, J.T. (2007) Why Marx left philosophy for social science. *Theory and Psychology*, *17*, 297–322.

Kaiser, C.R., Dyrenforth, P.S. and Hagiwara, N. (2006) Why are attributions to discrimination interpersonally costly? A test of system- and group-justifying motivations. *Personality and Social Psychology Bulletin*, *32*, 1423–1536.

Kaiser, C.R. and Pratt-Hyatt, J.S. (2009) Distributing prejudice unequally: Do whites direct their prejudice toward strongly identified minorities? *Journal of Personality and Social Psychology*, *96*, 432–445.

Kay, A.C., Gaucher, D., Napier, J.L., Callan, M.J. and Laurin, K. (2008) God and the government: Testing a compensatory control mechanism for the support of external systems. *Journal of Personality and Social Psychology*, *95*, 18–35.

Kay, A.C., Gaucher, D., Peach, J.M., Friesen, J., Laurin, K., Zanna, M. and Spencer, S.J. (2009) Inequality, discrimination, and the power of the status quo: Direct evidence for a motivation to view what is as what should be. *Journal of Personality and Social Psychology*, *97*, 421–434.

Kay, A., Jimenez, M.C. and Jost, J.T. (2002) Sour grapes, sweet lemons, and the anticipatory rationalization of the status quo. *Personality and Social Psychology Bulletin*, 28, 1300–1312.

Kay, A.C. and Jost, J.T. (2003) Complementary justice: Effects of 'poor but happy' and 'poor but honest' stereotype exemplars on system justification and implicit activation of the justice motive. *Journal of Personality and Social Psychology*, 85, 823–837.

Kay, A.C., Jost, J.T. and Young, S. (2005) Victim-derogation and victim-enhancement as alternate routes to system justification. *Psychological Science*, 16, 204–246.

Kilianski, S.E. and Rudman, L.A. (1998) Wanting it both ways: Do woman approve of benevolent sexism? *Sex Roles*, 39, 333–352.

Klandermans, B. (1997) *The Social Psychology of Protest*. Oxford: Blackwell.

Kluegel, J.R. and Smith, E.R. (1986) *Beliefs About Inequality: Americans' View of What Is and What Ought to Be*. Hawthorne, NJ: Gruyter.

Lane, R.E. (1959) The fear of equality. *American Political Science Review*, 53, 35–51.

Lau, G.P., Kay, A.C. and Spencer, S.J. (2008) Loving those who justify inequality: The effects of system threat on attraction to women who embody benevolent sexist ideals. *Psychological Science*, 19, 20–21.

Laurin, K., Shepherd, S. and Kay, A.C. (2010) Restricted emigration, system inescapability, and defense of the status quo: System-justifying consequences of restricted exit opportunities. *Psychological Science*, 21, 1075–1082.

Ledgerwood, A., Jost, J.T., Mandisodza, A.N. and Pohl, M. (in press) Working for the system: Motivated defense of meritocratic beliefs. *Social Cognition*.

Lerner, M.J. (1980) *The Belief in a Just World: A Fundamental Delusion*. New York: Plenum Press.

Lewin, K. (1941) Self-hatred among Jews. In K. Lewin (ed.), *Resolving Social Conflicts* (Edition, 1948), pp. 186–200. New York: Harper.

Lukács, G. (1971) Selections from *History and Class Consciousness*. In R.S. Gottlieb (ed.), *An Anthology of Western Marxism: From Lukács and Gramsci to Socialist-Feminism* (Edition, 1989). New York: Oxford University Press.

Lynd, R. (1939) *Knowledge for What?* Princeton, NJ: Princeton University Press.

MacKinnon, C.A. (1989) *Toward a Feminist Theory of the State*. Cambridge, MA: Harvard University Press.

Major, B. (1994) From social inequality to personal entitlement: The role of social comparisons, legitimacy appraisals, and group membership. *Advances in Experimental Social Psychology*, 26, 293–355.

Mannheim, K. (1925) *Conservatism. A Contribution to the Sociology of Knowledge* (Edition, 1986). London: Routledge.

Mannheim, K. (1936) *Ideology and Utopia*. London: Routledge.

Marcuse, H. (1964) *One-dimensional Man: Studies in the Ideology of Advanced Industrial Society*. Boston: Beacon.

Marx, K. and Engels, F. (1846) *The German Ideology* (Edition, 1970; C.J. Arthur, ed.). New York: International Publishers.

Mason, P. (1971) *Patterns of Dominance*. London: Oxford University Press.

McGuire, W.J. (1980) Interview with R.I. Evans (ed.), *The Making of Social Psychology: Discussions with Creative Contributors*, pp. 171–186. New York: Gardner.

McGuire, W.J. and McGuire, C.V. (1991) The content, structure, and operation of thought systems. In R.S. Wyer Jr. and T.K. Srull (eds), *Advances in Social Cognition*, IV, 1–78. Hillsdale, NJ: Erlbaum.

Memmi, A. (1968) *Dominated Man; Notes Towards a Portrait*. New York: Orion.

Moore, B., Jr. (1978) *Injustice: The Social Bases of Obedience and Revolt*. White Plains, NY: Sharpe.

Moscovici, S. (1988) Notes towards a description of social representations. *European Journal of Social Psychology*, 18, 211–250.

Napier, J.L. and Jost, J.T. (2008) Why are conservatives happier than liberals? *Psychological Science*, 19, 565–572.

O'Brien, L.T. and Major, B. (2005) System-justifying beliefs and psychological well-being: The roles of group status and identity. *Personality and Social Psychology Bulletin*, 31, 1718–1729.

Oldmeadow, J. and Fiske, S.T. (2007) System-justifying ideologies moderate status = competence stereotypes: Roles for belief in a just world and social dominance orientation. *European Journal of Social Psychology*, 37, 1135–1148.

Olson, J.M. and Hafer, C.L. (2001) Tolerance of personal deprivation. In J.T. Jost and B. Major (eds), *The Psychology of Legitimacy: Emerging Perspectives on Ideology, Justice, and Intergroup Relations*, pp. 157–175. New York: Cambridge University Press.

Rankin, L.E., Jost, J.T. and Wakslak, C.J. (2009) System justification and the ,meaning of life: Are the existential benefits of ideology distributed unequally across racial groups? *Social Justice Research*, 22, 312–333.

Reicher, S. (2004) The context of social identity: Domination, resistance, and change. *Political Psychology, 20,* 921–945.

Rudman, L.A., Feinberg, J. and Fairchild, K. (2002) Minority members' implicit attitudes: Automatic ingroup bias as a function of group status. *Social Cognition, 20,* 294–320.

Runciman, W. (1969) False consciousness. In W. Runciman (ed.), *Sociology in Its Place,* pp. 212–223. Cambridge: Cambridge University Press.

Sherif, M. (1936) *The Psychology of Social Norms.* Oxford: Harper.

Sibley, C.G., Overall, N.C. and Duckitt, J. (2007) When women become more hostilely sexist toward their gender: The system-justifying effect of benevolent sexism. *Sex Roles, 57,* 743–754.

Sidanius, J. and Pratto, F. (1999) *Social Dominance: An Intergroup Theory of Social Hierarchy and Oppression.* New York: Cambridge University Press.

Tajfel, H. (1981) *Human Groups and Social Categories.* Cambridge, MA: Cambridge Press.

Turner, D. (1991) Religion: Illusions and liberation. In T. Carver (ed.), *The Cambridge Companion to Marx,* pp. 320–337. Cambridge: Cambridge University Press.

Turner, J.C. (2006) Tyranny, freedom and social structure: Escaping our theoretical prisons. *British Journal of Social Psychology, 45,* 41–46.

Tyler, T.R. and Jost, J.T. (2007) Psychology and the law: Reconciling normative and descriptive accounts of social justice and system legitimacy. In A.W. Kruglanski and E.T. Higgins (eds), *Social Psychology: Handbook of Basic Principles* (2nd Edition), pp. 807–825. New York: Guilford Press.

Tyler, T.R. and McGraw, K.M. (1986) Ideology and the interpretation of personal experience: Procedural justice and political quiescence. *Journal of Social Issues, 42,* 115–128.

Uhlmann, E., Dasgupta, N., Elgueta, A., Greenwald, A.G. and Swanson, J. (2002) Subgroup prejudice based on skin color among Hispanics in the United States and Latin America. *Social Cognition, 20,* 198–226.

Ullrich, J. and Cohrs, J.C. (2007) Terrorism salience increases system justification: Experimental evidence. *Social Justice Research, 20,* 117–139.

van der Toorn, J., Tyler, T.R. and Jost, J.T. (2011) More than fair: Outcome dependence, system justification, and the perceived legitimacy of authority figures. *Journal of Experimental Social Psychology, 47,* 127–138.

Veblen, T. (1899) *The Theory of the Leisure Class: An Economic Study of Institutions.* New York: Heubsch.

Wakslak, C.J., Jost, J.T. and Bauer, P. (in press) Spreading rationalization: Increased support for large-scale and small-scale social systems following system threat. *Social Cognition.*

Wakslak, C.J., Jost, J.T., Tyler, T.R. and Chen, E.S. (2007) Moral outrage mediates the dampening effect of system justification on support for redistributive social policies. *Psychological Science, 18,* 267–274.

Yoshimura, K. and Hardin, C.D. (2009) Cognitive salience of subjugation and the ideological justification of U.S. geopolitical dominance in Japan. *Social Justice Research, 22,* 298–311.

Zinn, H. (1968) *Disobedience and Democracy: Nine Fallacies on Law and Order* (Edition, 2002). Cambridge, MA: South End.

43

Justice Theory

Tom R. Tyler

ABSTRACT

Psychological research has repeatedly shown that people are motivated by more than their concern with maximizing gains and minimizing loses. They also want to do what is just, appropriate, and fair. In particular, people's thoughts feelings and actions are shaped by their sense of what is just. Two forms of justice are considered: distributive justice, which involves fair allocations, and procedural justice, the study of fair processes for making decisions. Within each area of justice one concern of psychologists is with research examining whether and when this form of justice influences people's thoughts, feelings, and behaviors. In both areas the study of justice suggests strongly that justice matters. However, while research consistently shows that justice matters, there are several psychological theories concerning why it matters. In particular, some researches emphasize the role of justice in facilitating social exchange, while others focus on the importance of justice for personal and group identities. I argue here that research generally supports an identity-based view of justice.

INTRODUCTION

We live in an historical era in which naïve social theories most often describe human nature as being dominated by people's efforts to pursue personal self-interest, a self-interest broadly defined in terms of material rewards and costs. In contrast to this widely held image, many areas of social psychology show that people have a larger set of motivations that are more strongly linked to values and that include concerns for the well-being of other people and for groups, communities, organizations, and societies (Tyler, in press; Van Lange et al., 2007). This includes studies of empathy, altruism, justice, moral values, and identity. The image of the person that we accept is important because it speaks to the approach we take to a wide variety of social issues. It influences how we motivate people to cooperate, how we enforce rules, and how we address widely varied issues such as social welfare, healthcare, climate change, economic growth, and many others.

Within this set of literatures on social motivations, one of the most well developed and clearly specified set of psychological models concerns the psychology of justice. The first question asked by justice researchers is whether people care about justice. And a core contribution of the psychology of justice has been the demonstration that people's judgments, feelings, and behaviors in social settings are influenced by their views about what is just and fair, views that are distinct from evaluations of personal or group self-interest (Tyler and Smith, 1998). This literature indicates that people are not simply motivated by their assessments of what is beneficial or harmful to them, those they care about, or the groups, organizations, and societies to which they belong. People also make judgments about what is just or unjust, using criterion that reflect justice-based evaluations, and those judgments shape their reactions in social contexts (Tyler, 2000; Tyler and Smith, 1998; Tyler et al., 1997).

The occurrence, strength, and nature of this justice motivation influences how society should address social issues. For example: "What type of appeals are likely to be effective when we seek the redistribution of resources to those less well off?"; "How can we motivate people to care about the well being of future generations so that they conserve energy and work to combat global warming?"; "How do we allocate scarce collective resources when providing aid to different people and companies when trying to stimulate the economy?"; and "How do we manage divisive social issues such as abortion or gay marriage?" In each case, the most effective and viable approach to the issue depends upon our understanding of the psychology of justice.

ARENAS OF JUSTICE RESEARCH

Justice theory argues that people are motivated by concerns about justice. However, within that general framework researchers have studied a variety of types of justice. This chapter will focus on two types of justice: distributive and procedural justice. It will not discuss retributive justice; that is, reactions to rule breaking (see Darley and Pittman, 2003; Vidmar and Miller, 1980). In each of these areas of psychological research

the psychology of justice explores judgments about the principles used to decide what is fair or unfair within social settings. Issues of justice have been important within psychology ever since the World War II era, a period during which there was an explosion of psychology theory and research into the study of social settings and group processes. During the same historical period, psychology also moved beyond psychological models that paid little attention to people's subjective evaluations of the world and the field became more concerned with how people interpreted their social experiences. Concerns about justice emerged once the importance of subjective assessments of social situations became clearly recognized within relative deprivation research (Tyler and Smith, 1998).

Distributive justice

Theories of distributive justice tie comparisons to issues of justice (Walster et al., 1978). They do so by arguing that people compare their outcomes to standards of what is a fair or deserved outcome. In other words, people have a sense of what they are entitled to receive and evaluate their outcomes against this standard. This involves distributive justice – the fairness of the allocation of desirable outcomes across people. People express the greatest satisfaction when they receive a fair distribution, in comparison to receiving more or less in absolute terms but thinking that they are being given "too much" or "too little"; that they will incur material losses to pressure others to distributive resources via principles of justice; and that they will leave situations they view as characterized by the unfair distribution of resources to move to situations where resource distribution is fairer, but in which they receive fewer rewards.

The central premise of distributive justice theories is that people react to what they receive in relation to what they deserve. As noted, there are two potentially unhappy groups: those who receive too little and those who receive too much. As might be expected, those who receive less than they feel they deserve are found to be angry and to engage in a variety of behaviors, ranging from working less to rioting. Justice researchers have studied many instances in which people have received less than they deserve, and have shown that this leads to strong negative emotional reactions and to efforts to seek restitution. Among disadvantaged groups, complex psychological dynamics are unleashed because the disadvantaged often lack the power to compel justice and must therefore find ways to manage their feelings of unfairness.

Interestingly, and less intuitively, those who get too much are also found to be unhappy and to engage in efforts to either restore distributive justice by mechanisms such as working harder or giving resources away, or if those solutions are not practical, by leaving the situation. This latter distributive justice finding is especially important because it suggests that the desire to act fairly can influence the advantaged to take actions on behalf of less well off others.

Of course, while the distributive justice literature argues that people react to deviations from standards of fairness, that argument can be tested only if the standards being used to determine fairness can be determined. Morton Deutsch (1975) has presented three core principles of distributive justice: equity, equality, and need. Equality involves giving everyone similar outcomes, while equity and need differentiate among people either in terms of their productivity or their needs. Deutsch suggests that the use of each principle promotes different social goals: equity leads to productivity, equality to social harmony, and need to social welfare.

Procedural justice

Procedural justice is the study of people's subjective evaluations of the justice of procedures – whether they are fair or unfair, ethical or unethical, and otherwise accord with people's standards of fair processes for social interaction and decision making. Procedural justice

should be distinguished from subjective assessments of distributive justice. In most nontrivial situations some type of process is needed for gathering relevant evidence, deciding upon and implementing decision rules, and managing the interpersonal processes of gaining acceptance for allocations or of resolving conflicts. The area of procedural justice focuses on understanding the fairness of such processes.

Studies in this area show that peoples' choices among allocation procedures are influenced by their evaluations of their relative procedural fairness, as well as by the favorability and fairness of their outcomes; that peoples' satisfaction with and willingness to accept allocations and dispute resolution decisions depends upon the fairness of the procedures used to make them; and that peoples' rule following behavior and cooperation with others are shaped by the procedural fairness of groups, organizations, and societies.

Subjective procedural justice judgments have been the focus of a great deal of research attention by psychologists because they have been found to be a key influence on a wide variety of important group attitudes and behaviors (Lind and Tyler, 1988; Tyler, 2000). Procedural justice has been especially important in studies of decision acceptance and rule following. One reason that people might comply with rules and authorities is that they receive desirable rewards for cooperating and/or fear sanctioning from the group for not cooperating. An alternative reason that people might comply is that they are motivated by their sense of justice to accept what they feel is fair, even if it is not what they want.

A key question is whether justice is effective in resolving conflicts and disagreements when people cannot have everything that they want. To the degree that people defer because allocation decisions are seen as fair, justice is an important factor in creating and maintaining social harmony. Research suggests that social justice can act as a mechanism for resolving social conflicts, and that procedural justice is especially central in such situations.

John Thibaut and Laurens Walker (1975) conducted the first experiments designed to show the impact of procedural justice. Their studies demonstrated that people's assessments of the fairness of third-party decision-making procedures predicted their satisfaction with outcomes. This finding has been widely confirmed in many subsequent laboratory and field studies of procedural justice, studies which show that when third-party decisions are fairly made people are more willing to voluntarily accept them. What is striking is that such procedural justice effects are widely found in studies of real disputes, in real settings, involving actual disputants and are found to have an especially important role in shaping adherence to agreements over time.

Summary

The different aspects of the psychological study of justice outlined are united by the finding that people are very sensitive to issues of justice in their dealings with other people in social settings. In fact, such justice-based judgments are found to be key drivers of a wide variety of reactions, including attitudes, emotions, and behaviors. John Rawls (1971) famously argued that "justice is the first virtue of social institutions" and the findings of psychological research on justice strongly support the parallel suggestion that people view justice as a pivotal evaluation shaping their relationships with one another. Hence, while people might react to their experiences in social settings in terms of personal self-interest, they do not. Instead, they react to their sense of what is just.

Further, when groups, organizations, or societies are seeking to organize themselves, they become centrally preoccupied with issues of justice. The ability of authorities and institutions to be viewed as legitimate and, consequently, to be able to call upon group members for voluntary cooperation is linked to whether they are viewed as just.

The centrality of justice to the organization and functioning of society supports the suggestion that justice must be a key issue when people seek to resolve social problems or manage social conflicts. It is this connection between justice and the dynamics of groups that first led to my own interest in injustice. Anyone who studies political and social processes is soon struck by the centrality of "justice" to people's arguments, irrespective of their particular policy positions. Just as children rapidly learn to argue "that's not fair" societies frame their efforts to make allocations and resolve conflicts around struggles over the meaning of justice.

WHAT TYPE OF JUSTICE MATTERS?

While research on distributive justice has provided evidence that people are most satisfied with fair outcomes in allocation, within group settings distributive justice has been found to be a problematic solution to problems of allocation. Studies indicate that distributive justice judgments are often the product of motivated social cognitions, with people's judgments about what they deserve shaped by the self-interested tendency to exaggerate their contributions to collective products (Messick and Sentis, 1985; Ross and Sicoly, 1979; Thompson and Loewenstein, 1992). As a result, people often cannot be given what they feel they deserve, since their judgments of entitlement do not reflect the views of others about their actual contributions.

For this or other reasons, studies of justice in allocations and dispute resolution indicate that people focus less upon issues of distributive justice than they do upon two other issues: the procedures used to make allocation decisions and their interpersonal treatment within those procedures. These two issues have been collectively referred to as procedural justice. These findings emerge both from studies that look at the weight placed upon these different issues (Tyler and Caine, 1981) and from studies that look at what people talk about when asked to describe situations in which they feel that injustice has occurred (Messick et al., 1985; Mikula et al., 1990). In both of these types of studies the minimal role played by outcome distributions – real or perceived – in experiences of injustice is striking. Hence, in allocations people's focus is found to rest heavily on procedural and interpersonal issues.

Huo (2002) uses a different approach to addressing this issue, but reaches a similar conclusion. She creates a framework in which participants are asked about what should be given to a disliked group. Three issues are considered: monetary resources, procedural protections, and/or treatment with fairness and respect. Her results indicate that when people consider denying members of the disliked group and various things like denial of interpersonal treatment with dignity and respect is considered the most serious denial, while the denial of monetary resources is the least serious. Denial of procedural protections is intermediate. These findings suggest that people view procedural issues as more important than outcomes, with the quality of interpersonal treatment being especially central to the connection between people.

The conclusion of these studies comparing people's focus on different forms of justice is that people are most strongly affected by issues of procedural justice. And within procedural justice both the fairness of decision making and the quality of interpersonal treatment are found to have an influence upon people's reactions. Because it is central to people's concerns in their dealings with others this discussion will focus primarily on issues of procedural justice.

My own interest in procedural justice develops out of a concern with the dynamics of authority in groups, organizations, and societies. Groups respond to problems by creating rules, authorities, and institutions. The success of these organized social entities then becomes a key societal concern. That effectiveness is linked to the ability of those authorities and institutions to gain voluntary acceptance of their policies, rules, and

decisions, a point made long ago by Lewin (Gold, 1999). And, being viewed as legitimate is central to such acceptance (Tyler, 2006a). Studies consistently show that procedural justice shapes the legitimacy of the authorities and institutions with which people deal, and through such attitudes, their willingness to defer to those authorities and institutions. Studies of the legitimacy of authority suggest that people decide how much to defer to authorities and to their decisions primarily by assessing the fairness of their decision-making procedures (Tyler, 2006).

Consequently, using fair decision-making procedures is the key to developing, maintaining, and enhancing the legitimacy of rules and authorities and gaining voluntary deference to social rules. Beyond issues of rule following, studies of procedural justice indicate that it plays an equally important role in motivating commitment to organizations. As a consequence, procedural justice is important in encouraging productivity and extra-role behavior in work organizations (Tyler and Blader, 2000, 2003). Procedural justice is a key antecedent of a wide variety of desirable cooperative behaviors in groups, organizations and societies (see Tyler, in press). Hence, procedural justice is central to any concern with effective group dynamics.

Defining procedural justice

From the beginning models of justice have drawn from broader social psychological models of the relationship between people and groups. The primary model that dominates early social psychology is social exchange (Thibaut and Kelley, 1959). This model argues that people's thoughts, feelings, and behaviors when dealing with others are guided by the desire to obtain material rewards and avoid material costs. This image is central to both theories of distributive justice (e.g., equity theory) and to Thibaut and Walker's control model of procedural justice (Thibaut and

Walker, 1975). However, as research on justice has developed, it has increasingly been guided by a second model: social identity theory (Tajfel and Turner, 1979). This model suggests that people use groups to create and support their identities. More recent models based upon social exchange have also become broader in scope and now recognize social preferences; for example, issues of egalitarianism and altruism (see Kelley and Thibaut, 1978; Kelley et al., 2003; Rusbult and Van Lange, 1996; Van Lange et al., 2007).

My own theoretical development reflects this gradual transition from social exchange perspectives to an emphasis on social identity. That transition reflects the findings of justice research, which are consistently at odds with the predictions of social exchange theories and are more consistent with a social identity framework. My research initial drew upon the social identity framework reflected in Lind and Tyler (1988), and has since involved to include an emphasis on intragroup status dynamics (i.e., respect as well as pride) and a more elaborate understanding of how identity dynamics operate that expands the idea of identity (DeCremer and Tyler, 2005). This shift in the focus of my work comes in response to the findings of studies on justice in real world settings. Tyler and Lind (1992), for example, is based upon field studies conducted among litigants. Litigant concerns were consistently found to be about issues that had very little to do with the gain or loss of resources. They were instead about being treated disrespectfully, about distrust in the motives of authorities and about feeling that those making decisions did not listen to and consider their concerns.

As noted, early work on procedural justice was guided by the influential control model of Thibaut and Walker (1975). Thibaut and Walker centered their procedural justice studies on procedures as mechanisms for settling disputes about the allocation of outcomes. Thibaut and Walker linked their discussions of procedures primarily to issues of decision-making, and in particular to issues of decision making about allocation decisions.

Since their procedural models were rooted in an era where distributive justice dominated, their focus was natural. They also linked people's desire for fair procedures to their desire to achieve equitable outcomes. They proposed that people value procedural justice (i.e., voice or process control) because it facilitates decision-makers' ability to make equitable judgments. In other words, procedures are valued insofar as they affect the outcomes that are associated with them.

Thibaut and Walker (1975) focus upon a narrow set of antecedents of procedural justice, considering only questions of evidence presentation (process control) and outcome control. However, other procedural justice researchers, in particular Leventhal (1980), identify a broader range of antecedents. In a wide-ranging discussion of procedural justice Leventhal identified six core procedural elements: consistency, bias-suppression, accuracy, correctability, representativeness, and ethicality. Of these, representativeness reflects the issues of voice central to Thibaut and Walker's model, while the other elements present a broader set of issues for evaluating procedures.

The exclusive focus on decision making in allocation contexts is no longer true of procedural justice research. Researchers have increasingly moved their attention away from an exclusive focus on the decision-making function of procedures to include more attention to the interpersonal aspects of procedures. Those interpersonal aspects of procedures arise because procedures are settings within which people are involved in a social interaction with one another. This is true irrespective of whether the procedure involves a decision maker.

In social interactions there is considerable variation in the manner in which people treat one another. They can act politely, rudely, respectfully, with hostility, and so on. These aspects of the interpersonal experience of a procedure – which occur in the context of an interaction whose overt purpose is to make a decision to allocate resources or resolve a conflict – may also influence those who are involved. These interpersonal aspects of procedures have been found by recent studies to be so powerful in their impact that some researchers have argued that they might potentially be treated as a separate type of "interactional" justice (Bies and Moag, 1986; Tyler and Bies, 1990). Irrespective of whether the quality of the treatment that people experience via procedures is actually considered a distinct form of justice (see Blader and Tyler, 2003), justice researchers have again followed their findings about what impacts the people they study. This has led them to increasingly turn their research toward exploring interpersonal or interactional aspects of procedures – for example, the quality of one's treatment by others.

Tyler and Lind (1992) drew upon Leventhal to develop the relational model of authority, which explores the role of this broader set of procedural factors in shaping reactions to authorities. They demonstrate that other factors – neutrality, trustworthiness, and status recognition – influence procedural justice judgments and shape reactions to authorities (Tyler, 1988, 1989; 1994; Tyler et al., 1996). Tyler (1994) further demonstrates that procedural justice judgments are distinct from concerns about outcomes and outcome favorability.

Recent discussions of procedural justice recognize four elements of procedures as the primary factors that contribute to judgments about their fairness: opportunities for participation, a neutral forum, trustworthy authorities, and treatment with dignity and respect. Blader and Tyler (2003) refer to the first two elements as involving the quality of decision making, while the latter two elements are concerned with the quality of interpersonal treatment.

The voice effect indicates that people feel more fairly treated if they are allowed to participate in the resolution of their problems or conflicts. People are primarily interested in presenting their perspective and sharing in the discussion of conflicts that affect them, not in controlling decisions about how to handle such conflicts. Instead, people often look to authorities for resolutions. They expect authorities to make final decisions about how

to act based upon the arguments those who are affected by those decisions have presented.

People are also influenced by judgments about neutrality – the honesty, impartiality, and objectivity of the authorities with whom they deal. They believe that authorities should not allow their personal values and biases to enter into their decisions, which should be made based upon rules and facts. Basically, people seek a "level playing field" in which no one is unfairly disadvantaged. If they believe that the authorities are following impartial rules and making factual, objective decisions, they think procedures are fairer.

Another factor shaping people's views about the fairness of a procedure is their assessment of the motives of the third-party authority responsible for resolving the case. People recognize that third parties typically have considerable discretion to implement procedures in varying ways, and they are concerned about the motivation underlying the decisions made by the authority with which they are dealing. Important assessments include whether that person is benevolent and caring, is concerned about their situation and their concerns and needs, considers their arguments, tries to do what is right for them, and tries to be fair.

Studies suggest that people also value having respect shown for their rights and for their status within society. They want their dignity as people and their rights as members of the society to be recognized and acknowledged. Surprisingly, such assessments of respect are largely unrelated to the outcomes they receive. Thus, the importance which people place upon this affirmation of their status is especially relevant to conflict resolution. Unlike the outcomes that determine distributive justice, dignity and respect is something that authorities can give to everyone with whom they deal.

THE INTERPLAY OF JUSTICE AND SELF-INTEREST

The studies of justice outlined make clear that justice can motivate people to behave in ways that are not in accord with their sense of their own personal and group interests. For example, the advantaged may give resources to the disadvantaged. On the other hand, such justice motivations are never absolute. Typically people compromise between the motivation to act justly and the desire to act in their self-interest.

One of the best illustrations of such compromises is found in the literature on ultimatum games (Handgraaf et al., 2004). In the ultimatum game, the proposers make offers about how to divide some set of resources. The responder can either accept or reject this offer. Studies suggest that proposers make, and responders accept, offers somewhere between an equal division and a division favoring the proposer. For example, if ten dollars is to be divided the successful offers fall between zero and five dollars. In other words, both parties compromise between self-interest and fairness, with the proposer giving more than they would be rationally expected to, and the responder accepting less than an equal division. Further, studies show that responders will decline small gains rather than accept "unfairly" low divisions illustrating that people are willing to incur losses to defend principles of fairness.

Of course, there are other ways to deal with conflicts about justice. Early work on distributive justice pointed to the possibility of motivated social cognition, that is, that people might try to restore justice psychologically (Walster et al., 1978). That distributive justice research first developed the distinction between psychological and behavioral responses to wrongdoing. When someone receives too much or provides too little to others, a conflict is created between their behavior and the principles of justice. There are two types of response. One is for outcomes to be reallocated so as to be fair. The victim frequently advocates this response, while the harm doer has mixed feelings – they believe in justice but are also benefiting from the unjust situation. Hence, harmdoers are motivated to psychologically justify the situation, coming to believe that they deserve the outcomes they have. For example, studies of distributive justice show that people who are "overpaid" find ways to justify their payment by increasing their sense of the difficulty of the task, and hence reframing the situation as one in which their pay is reasonable.

The motivation to justify advantage brings harm doers and victims into conflict because the victim wants redistribution while the harm doer seeks to justify their gains. An important function of social authorities is to lend support to victims, or at least avoid social conflict, by supporting the application of objective standards of fairness, which resolves conflicts, and by discouraging psychological justification, which leads to long-term hostility. More generally, there are a variety of social mechanisms through which the advantaged justify their advantage, with the intention of keeping their advantages without the negative emotions that they experience from feeling that they are violating principles of justice (Chen and Tyler, 2001; Wakslak et al., 2007).

Most recently Blader (2007) has demonstrated that such motivational judgments occur when the justice of procedures is ambiguous. Using experimental designs Blader showed that when the nature of a procedure is clear, procedural elements shape perceived procedural justice. However, when procedures themselves were unclear, justice judgments were influenced by identification with the group and outcome favorability. In other words, nonfairness-related judgments became important in making justice judgments primarily when the justice of the situation was unclear.

INSTRUMENTAL VIEWS OF THE PSYCHOLOGY OF JUSTICE

One of the most important questions raised by the finding that justice matters is why people are motivated to act fairly. As I have noted, in theories of distributive justice the answer is traditionally framed in social exchange terms (Thibaut and Kelley, 1959). People are viewed as being concerned with developing effective ways to exchange resources with others, both within particular situations and over time, since such cooperation is generally recognized as being to everyone's advantage. The development of principles of fairness occurs, from this perspective, because it aids in resource exchange.

Shared principles of fairness aid resource exchange because they indicate the distribution of resources which constitutes a reasonable exchange. Having such rules facilitates material exchanges, since there are clear rules for what each person deserves and each exchange does not have to begin with an effort to define reasonable exchange principles. Shared principles also facilitate the occurrence of exchanges since they allow people to alleviate their concerns that they are being disadvantaged in exchanges with others (acting like a "sucker"), or conversely that they are taking advantage of others. People can compare their outcomes to principles of justice to determine if what they are receiving in relationship to others is reasonable and appropriate. As a consequence, everyone can feel both secure and good about themselves during this process.

This argument suggests that having principles of distributive fairness is a precursor to effective cooperation and the ability to develop such shared principles may be a very fundamental aspect of people's social skills that has facilitated the evolution of humans into social beings who live in organized societies and cooperate. Recent research has supported this argument by demonstrating that animals that live in group settings, for example monkeys (Brosnan, 2006) and dogs (Range et al., 2009, recognize and act in accord with principles of distributive fairness. It is particularly striking that the members of both these species share with humans the willingness to forego rewards to defend principles of fairness.

Ironically, however, while these arguments support the idea that justice matters, they diminish the social psychological significance of justice findings because they suggest that people's motivation for caring about justice is their own material self-interest both immediately and over time. Social exchange models, such as that of Rusbult, argue that people in groups have a long-range view of their self-interest, often investing their efforts in groups in anticipation of long-term payoffs (e.g., Rusbult et al., 1991). If the principles of distributive justice are accepted as instruments of coordination in the service of self-interest, they show a sophisticated ability on the part of both people and animals to develop coordinating rules and principles. But they do not suggest that people are motivated by intrinsic justice concerns when they act fairly.

An example of the implications of the social exchange argument is provided by discussions of the scope of justice. While some writers present the motivation to act justly as a core and universal human motivation (Lerner, 1980), others argue that it is bounded or limited in scope. The possibility of a scope of justice has important societal implications, since that scope can shift with events so that both individuals and the members of groups can become included, or excluded, from the scope of other's moral community. Once outside it, people are not longer accorded the presumption of treatment with dignity and respect for rights that group members in good standing assume they will receive (Nagata, 1993; Opotow, 1993).

Deutsch (1985) argues that people do not extend their concern about justice to all living things, or even to all people. Rather their concerns have a clear scope and outside of that scope people do not act in accord with principles of distributive fairness. What defines this scope of justice? To Deutsch it is the domain of productive social exchange relationships. In other words, people follow principles of distributive justice with those with whom they see the potential of beneficial social exchanges, rather than feeling some type of intrinsic justice based motivation to act fairly. And those people or animals that are not viewed as candidates for productive social exchange are not treated with justice.

As has been noted, research has demonstrated that in social settings issues of procedural justice are especially important in shaping people's thoughts, feelings, and behaviors. Does this focus on procedures, rather than outcomes, suggest a need for a shift in our understanding of the psychology of justice away from the model outlined above? The earliest psychological model of procedural justice is the control model presented by Thibaut and Walker (1975) and the control model is based upon the same ideas of social exchange that are presented in earlier discussions of distributive justice. Thibaut and Walker assume that a person's goal when dealing with others is to achieve a distributively fair solution for themselves.

The arguments advanced by Thibaut and Walker in the context of procedural justice are similar to those outlined within the field of distributive justice – justice in the service of obtaining desired outcomes. A similar argument about the development of procedures is found in the work of Thibaut and Faucheux (1965) on the development of rules. Their argument is that rules develop to guide interactions when there is a risk that, without rules, a mutually beneficial exchange relationship will collapse. Hence, procedures/rules develop to facilitate productive resource exchanges.

In the case of procedures, Thibaut and Walker suggest that people prefer to keep control over their decisions, that is, to negotiate with others, and only turn to third-party procedures when necessary to protect productive social exchanges. Even then, people try to retain as much control as possible; for example, preferring mediation to arbitration. This instrumental view of procedures is illustrated in Thibaut and Faucheux's argument that procedures only develop when both parties have countervailing power. People are not viewed as intrinsically motivated to enact fair procedures, any more than they are intrinsically motivated to give others fair outcomes. They do so when they need to have rules or procedures to facilitate productive social exchange. In a situation in which relationships are vulnerable to disruption, people care about issues of justice (Barrett-Howard and Tyler, 1986).

SOCIAL PERSPECTIVES ON THE PSYCHOLOGY OF JUSTICE

Studies have not supported an instrumental view of justice. They support the argument that people want the opportunity to present their arguments to the decision maker, a procedural feature often labeled "voice." However, they have not supported the argument that people link voice to decision control and only value the opportunity to address the decision maker when they believe their arguments are shaping the outcome. Studies indicate that people value voice even when they do not believe that their voice leads to decision control (Lind et al., 1990; Tyler, 1987; Tyler et al., 1985). These studies of voice suggest that having the opportunity for "voice" has interpersonal or "value-expressive" worth that was not linked to any influence over the decisions made (Tyler, 1987).

What factors were driving the influence of voice, even when it clearly could not affect the eventual outcome or decision? If an authority listens to people's arguments the authority is conferring interpersonal respect on that person because they are acknowledging their status in the group and their right as a group member to call upon the group about their needs and concerns. This argument is supported by the finding that people only value voice opportunities if they feel that the authority is "considering" their arguments (Tyler, 1987). This suggests that people focus on whether or not their concerns and needs in the situation are treated respectfully by the decision-maker, who takes them seriously by listening and considering what they have to say, independently of whether or not the course of action the authority recommends reflects their desired course of action.

These findings lead to the group-value model (Lind and Tyler, 1988), which focuses

on the antecedents of judgments of procedural justice. The group-value model argues
that noninstrumental factors influence procedural justice judgments, a prediction
confirmed both by the findings of noninstrumental voice effects already noted (Lind
et al., 1990; Tyler, 1987), and by demonstrations that people care more about a broader
set of issues of procedural justice when dealing with members of their own groups
(Tyler, 1999); issues including how they are
treated, and whether their rights are respected.
These noninstrumental issues are important
because they communicate information to
people about their status within groups; that
is, because they carry an important social
message (Lind and Tyler, 1988). This suggestion led Lind and Tyler to draw upon the
ideas of social identity theory and argue that
people value voice because it shapes their
identity and provides information about their
status in groups.

Of course, it is important to note that like
prior models the group value model also
argues for a scope of justice. In this case that
scope is defined by the range of people or
groups that are relevant to people's definitions
of their status, that is, to the range of their
group. For example, people are less concerned
about justice when they are dealing with outsiders (Smith et al., 1998). Further, those
people who are less concerned about issues of
their status – that is, the quality of their social
connections — are generally less influenced
by information about justice (DeCremer and
Tyler, 2005; Tyler and Lind, 1992). A typical
American, for example, is likely to be relatively indifferent to their status in Japanese
society, so they are unaffected by variations in
treatment by Japanese authorities since that
treatment does not communicate information
about their status in their own group.

Recent studies demonstrate that it is possible to prime people so that they are focused
upon instrumental or relational issues. As
would be predicted, instrumental priming
leads people to focus upon the anticipated
outcomes of third-party decisions, reacting to
what they receive. Relational priming, on the
other hand, leads people to focus upon the
fairness of decision-making procedures
(Stahl et al., 2008).

THE DISTINCTION BETWEEN JUSTICE AND INJUSTICE

Justice theories argue that a variety of types
of reaction follow from justice judgments,
including most importantly behaviors such as
retaliation. Distributive justice research
focuses primarily upon anger and negative
behaviors, that is, upon reactions to
injustice, since this research is rooted in the
literature on relative deprivation, a literature
whose origins lie in efforts to understand and
explain riots and rebellion (Gurr, 1970). This
focus on negative attitudes and behaviors is
reflected in later efforts to understand
distributive influences on pay dissatisfaction,
employee theft, sabotage, turnover, and
resistance to third-party decisions (Tyler and
Smith, 1998).

The relational model also focuses upon
reactions to negative events in the form of
poor outcomes and predicts that procedural
justice will influence reactions to the authorities who deliver them (Tyler, 2006a, 2006b).
Its predominate focus is on decision acceptance. Recent research on procedural justice
has increasingly focused on more prosocial
outcomes, such as how to build trust, encourage responsibility and obligation, generate
intrinsic motivation and creativity, and stimulate voluntary cooperation with others (Tyler
and Blader, 2000). Similarly, there has been
increasing attention to exploring when
justice motivations encourage people to provide resources to the disadvantaged (Montada,
1995). Interestingly, this shift is consistent
with a shift that has been taking place within
psychological research more generally
(Snyder and Lopez, 2002).

This new focus of justice research is
addressed by the group engagement model,
which discusses the antecedents of cooperative behavior in groups, organizations, and

societies (Tyler and Blader, 2000, 2003). The argument of the group engagement model is that justice theories provide a basis for understanding people's general relationship to groups. That includes both people's negative reactions to injustice and the ability of experiencing justice to promote engagement and cooperation. Society, after all, does not just want people not to riot or destroy. It also wants them to be happy, creative, and productive.

How does the group engagement model expand earlier models? First, the objective of the model is to identify and examine the antecedents of attitudes, values, and cooperative behavior in groups. Hence, the group engagement model broadens the focus of justice studies and its predecessor models of justice by positing a general model of the relationship between people and groups. In trying to understand the precursors of people's engagement in their groups, it identifies and examines a much broader set of variables – and dynamics between those variables – than earlier justice models. Rather than focusing simply on what shapes views about justice the model is concerned with the role of justice in social systems.

People have considerable discretion about the degree to which they invest themselves in their groups by working on behalf of the group. To examine this issue, the group engagement model distinguishes between two classes of cooperative behavior: mandatory and discretionary. Mandatory cooperation is behavior that is stipulated by the group, while discretionary cooperation originates with the group member. The model argues that each of these forms of cooperation is differently motivated. Of the two types of cooperative behaviors, mandatory behaviors are more strongly affected by incentives and sanctions, since they are behaviors required by the group and thus the group specifically structures incentives and sanctions to encourage these behaviors. Discretionary behaviors are more strongly under the influence of people's internal motivations (their attitudes and values), since they are behaviors that originate with the individual.

Both attitudes and values are important because they lead people to be internally motivated to engage in and cooperate with the group. To the degree that people are internally motivated, they engage in cooperative behaviors for personal reasons, and they do not need to receive incentives (rewards) or to face the risk of sanctions (punishments) to encourage their group-related behaviors. This benefits groups, which are then free to deploy their assets in other ways that benefit the group.

THE INFLUENCE OF IDENTITY AND RESOURCE MOTIVATIONS ON ENGAGEMENT IN GROUPS

The group engagement model argues that the central reason that people engage themselves in groups is because they use the feedback they receive from those groups to create and maintain their identities. In other words, the group engagement model hypothesizes that of the two types of motivations, it is the development and maintenance of a favorable identity that most strongly influences cooperation. The model predicts that people's willingness to cooperate with their group – especially cooperation that is discretionary in nature – flows from the identity information people receive from the group.

The core argument of the group engagement model is that people want a favorable identity, and use group membership as one source of identity-relevant information. That identity information, in turn, is hypothesized to emanate from evaluations of the justice experienced in the group. This includes judgments of procedural and distributive justice, as well as evaluations of outcome favorability. This suggests that identity evaluations and concerns mediate the relationship between justice judgments and group engagement. This is the *identity mediation hypothesis*.

Why might this be so? Using social identity theory as a framework the model argues that an important function of groups is to provide people with a way of constructing a social identity. It is widely recognized that groups shape people's definitions of themselves and their feelings of wellbeing and self-worth (Hogg and Abrams, 1988; Sedikides and Brewer, 2001). In particular, group memberships shape people's conceptions of their social selves – the aspect of the self that is formed through identification with groups. The groups that people belong to help to define who they are and help people to evaluate their status. Part of this process involves linking views about self-worth and self-esteem to the status of group memberships.

Thus, to some degree people's sense of their own worth is linked to the groups to which they belong. Several new ideas and hypotheses flow from the group engagement model. It predicts that identity judgments will be the primary factors shaping attitudes, values, and cooperative behaviors in groups. Second, it predicts that resource judgments will most strongly influence attitudes, values, and discretionary cooperative behaviors in groups through their indirect influence on identity judgments, rather than directly. Third, it predicts that the primary antecedent

of identity judgments will be judgments about the procedural justice of the group. Fourth, it predicts that status judgments about pride and respect will shape identification with the group. Each of these predictions is reflected in Figure 43.1.

The focus of the group value model of procedural justice; the relational model of authority; and the group value model of engagement is on the psychology of justice – that is, on why justice matters. All three models argue that procedural justice, the form of justice that is central to people's connection to groups, is linked to issues of status and identity. Because of this centrality of issues of identity, this discussion of justice involves attention to identity its role in people's behavior in groups. The group engagement model argues that identity plays an important role in people's relationship to their group. It focuses on what people *get from groups* in the form of acknowledgement and recognition of their identities.

As has been noted, the identity-based model of cooperation can be contrasted to a resource-based model of cooperation. Social psychologists have long recognized that

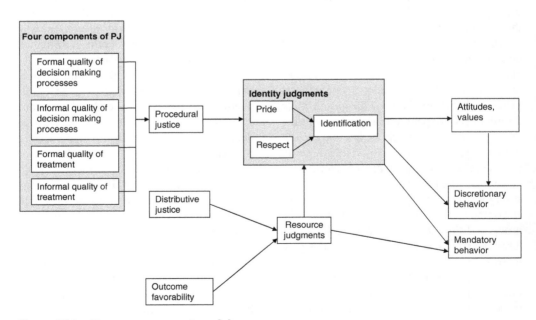

Figure 43.1   Group engagement model

people interact with others to exchange material resources. These material resources can vary widely – from things such as food to money – but regardless they share the characteristic of being material resources that people obtain through their cooperation with others (Thibaut and Kelley, 1959). Guided by social exchange models, many social psychological discussions of people's relationships to groups have argued that this exchange of material resources is the fundamental reason that people engage in groups.

A broadened model of social exchange perspective is the basis of several more recent resource-based models, including the investment model, which focuses on exit and loyalty to groups (Rusbult and Van Lange, 1996) and realistic group conflict theory (Levine and Campbell, 1972). These resource-based perspectives predict that people's level of cooperation with a group will be shaped by the level of the material resources that they receive from that group and/or the sanctioning risks they face within the group. Thus, the willingness to voluntarily cooperate with the group by doing things that help the group flows from assessments of the desirability of the resources that are gained or lost by association with the group. In addition, loyalty to the group will also be shaped by the level of resources people are obtaining, relative to what they might obtain in another group. More recent models of social exchange also recognize that concerns about material gain and loss can be transformed in social interactions to reflect broader social values (see Van Lange et al., 2007) and, in that sense, are similar to the group engagement model in suggesting that nonmaterial issues play an important role in shaping links between people and groups.

The group engagement model proposes that the identity model prevails over the resource model in predicting engagement and cooperation. It argues that resource judgments do not directly shape engagement. This is not to say that the group engagement model argues that resource judgments have no influence on engagement. Instead, the

model hypothesizes that resource judgments indirectly influence most forms of engagement by shaping identity. That is, to some degree, people evaluate their identity and status in a particular group by the level of the resources that they are receiving from that group. To the extent that having more resources in a group leads people to feel better about their status in the group, they will engage themselves more in that group.

The group engagement model argues that this is not the case and that such material rewards primarily influence engagement indirectly, by influencing status. The key argument of the group engagement model is that people's level of cooperation with groups is primarily shaped by the extent to which they identify with those groups. Cooperation is driven, in other words, by the motivation to create and maintain a favorable identity, and that identity flows from justice.

It seems counterintuitive to many people to argue that resources are not the primary factor that directly shapes engagement. Certainly, people can think of many examples from their everyday lives that seem to suggest a resource-based linkage with engagement. The seeming importance of resource concerns is also supported by some research findings. This may reflect evidence of the indirect connection between resource judgments and engagement of the type we have already outlined. If, as the group engagement model argues, resource judgments indirectly influence engagement, then studies that do not measure identity judgments will find a connection between resource judgments and engagement. However, the group engagement model suggests that in a fully specified model, which includes both resource and identity judgments, the spurious connection between resource judgments and engagement will disappear (except for that between resources and mandatory cooperation), while a mediated connection remains.

How does the group matter? The group engagement model also considers how the policies and practices of the group shape identity-based and resource-based judgments. It is this aspect of the group engagement model that directly addresses issues of justice. The group engagement model argues that people are most strongly influenced by one aspect of the policies and practices of their group – the fairness of the group's procedures. This argument builds on the pervasive finding that procedural justice judgments have a strong and widespread influence on people's thoughts, feelings, and behaviors in group contexts (Lind and Tyler, 1988; Tyler and Smith, 1998). In addition, judgments about outcome fairness and outcome favorability both shape identity. Hence, both forms of justice shape identity.

As already noted, it is also possible to conceptualize a relationship between the person and the group that is centered around the exchange of resources. If this were the key motivation that shapes people's engagement in groups, it would be expected that the element of group policies and practices that would most shape their engagement is their estimate of the degree to which the rules and policies of the group provide them with desirable resources. These resource judgments, in turn, influence engagement in the group. In the case of either outcome fairness or outcome favorability, it is the concern over the outcomes that are being received from the group that would be driving engagement in groups. The group engagement model argues that such outcome based judgments influence identity. Hence, people are more likely to identify with groups that deliver desired resources.

Are the hypotheses of the group engagement model valid? Tyler and Blader (2000) tested the model using survey data from employees. Using causal modeling, they tested several of the key hypotheses of the group engagement model and found support for all of them (see Tyler and Blader, 2000: 196). First, they found that identity judgments shaped attitudes, values, and cooperative behaviors. Consistent with the predictions of the model, they found a greater influence of identity judgments on discretionary, as compared to mandatory, behavior. Second, resource judgments are found to influence attitudes, values, and discretionary cooperative behaviors indirectly, through identity judgments, but not directly. Third, procedural justice judgments are found to be the primary antecedent of identity judgments (Tyler and Blader, 2000: 136). Tyler (in press) confirms these findings in both work organizations and communities using panel data, while Blader and Tyler (in press) do so using independently derived indices of cooperative behavior.

A BROADER IDENTITY FRAMEWORK

The underlying argument of the group-value model of procedural justice, the relational model of authority, and the group engagement model of cooperation is that identity plays a central mediating role in shaping people's reaction to groups, organizations and societies. This argument was originally put forward in the context of social identification theories (Hogg and Abrams, 1988). In developing this model identification, the merger of self with the group, was distinguished from pride in the group, which is linked to group status, and respect from the group, which is the consequence of status in the group. This aspect of self, as opposed to the personal self (unique individual traits), or the relational self (the self defined by dyadic relationships) is the collective self and is linked to group memberships (Sedikides and Brewer, 2001). More recently DeCremer and Tyler (2005) have broadened the framework within which identity is studied within the procedural justice literature. In particular, they demonstrate that whenever people link their identities to a group the justice that they experience in the framework of that group has a stronger influence upon their sense of self. This supports the argument that justice is linked to identity and, therefore, justice matters more when identity is more relevant.

CONCLUSION

The findings of justice research are important for several reasons. First, they contribute to the demonstration that people's thoughts, feelings, and behaviors are determined by their internally held values concerning what is just or fair. These values play an important role in making social life possible because they provide a basis for cooperation among people in groups, organizations, and societies. And, as the literature on social justice makes clear, they provide an important confirmation that the social ties between people are central to their actions in social settings. People in social settings do not act simply as self-interested actors, pursuing individual or group gains and losses. Rather their feelings, thoughts and behaviors are shaped by their judgments concerning that is appropriate and fair. The demonstration that people are value-based actors provides a clear demonstration of the centrality of social motivations to people's actions in groups, communities, organizations and societies.

It is not obvious that people's engagement in groups would be the result of procedural justice judgments. People could potentially consider a wide variety of aspects of their relationship to their group when they are evaluating the degree to which they want to engage themselves in a group. One thing that we might expect people to consider is reward level – that is, people might consider their salaries, the number of resources they are given to manage, and/or the size of their office, their car, or their home as key inputs into their judgments about how much to engage themselves in a group. Or, at least, they might consider outcome fairness, as suggested by Thibaut and Walker (1975).

Because an outcome focus is intuitively obvious, the finding that procedural justice is so central to people's thinking is striking. It is especially striking because, of the procedural elements considered, questions of interpersonal treatment consistently emerge as important. In other words, people's focus is upon those aspects of their experience that communicate messages about status, rather than upon those more directly related to issues of decision making. This supports the argument that it is status issues that define people's relationship to groups, and procedural justice that provides information about status.

Overall, the literature on justice contributes to a social vision of the person on several levels: first, because people care about justice, a socially constructed idea, and view it as the core element of social groups; second, because people think of justice in very relational terms; and third, because studies of how justice influences people's behavior suggests that the key connection between people and groups, communities, organizations and societies is rooted in their concerns about self and identity. In all of these ways, people show themselves to be fundamentally social animals, concerned about their relationships with others.

REFERENCES

Barrett-Howard, E. and Tyler, T.R. (1986) Procedural justice as a criterion in allocation decisions. *Journal of Personality and Social Psychology, 50*, 296–304.

Bies, R.J. and Moag, J.S. (1986) Interactional justice. In R.J. Lewicki, B.M. Sheppard, and M.H. Bazerman (eds), *Research on Negotiations in Organizations, 1*, 43–55. Greenwich, CT: JAI.

Blader, S.L. (2007) What determines people's fairness judgments? Identification and outcomes influence procedural fairness evaluations under uncertainty. *Journal of Experimental Social Psychology, 43*, 986–994.

Blader, S.L. and Tyler, T.R. (2003) A four component model of procedural justice. *Personality and Social Psychology Bulletin, 29*, 747–758.

Blader, S.L. and Tyler, T.R. (2009) Testing and extending the group engagement model: Linkages between social identity, procedural justice, economic outcomes and extrarole behavior. *Journal of Applied Psychology. 94*, 445–464.

Brosnan, S.F. (2006) Nonhuman species' reactions to inequity and their implications for fairness. *Social Justice Research, 19*, 153–185.

Chen, E. and Tyler, T.R. (2001) Cloaking power: Legitimizing myths and the psychology of the advantaged. In J.A. Bargh and A.Y. Lee-Chai (eds), *The Use and Abuse of Power*, pp. 241–261. Philadelphia: Psychology Press.

Darley, J.M. and Pittman, T.S. (2003) The psychology of compensation and retributive justice. *Personality and Social Psychology Review, 7*, 324–336.

DeCremer, D. and Tyler, T.R. (2005) Managing group behavior: The interplay between procedural justice, sense of self, and cooperation. *Advances in Experimental Social Psychology, 37*, 151–218.

Deutsch, M. (1975) Equity, equality, and need: What determines which value will be used as the basis for distributive justice? *Journal of Social Issues, 31*, 137–149.

Deutsch, M. (1985) *Distributive Justice*. New Haven: Yale University PRess.

Gold, M. (1999) The Complete Social Scientist: *A Kurt Lewin Reader*. Washington, DC: American Psychological Association.

Gurr, T. (1970) *Why Men Rebel*. Princeton: Princeton University Press.

Handgraaaf, M.J.J., Van Dijk, E., Wilke, H.A.M. and Vermunt, R. (2004) Evaluability of outcomes in ultimatum bargaining. *Organizational Behavior and Human Decision Processes, 95*, 97–106.

Hogg, M.A. and Abrams, D. (1988) *Social Identifications*. London: Routledge.

Huo, Y.J. (2002) Justice and the regulation of social relations: When and why do group members deny claims to social goods? *British Journal of Social Psychology, 41*, 535–562.

Kelley, H.H., Holmes, J.G., Kerr, N.L., Reis, H.T., Rusbult, C.E. and Van Lange, P.A.M. (2003) *An Atlas of Interpersonal Situations*. Cambridge: Cambridge University Press.

Kelley, H.H. and Thibaut, J.W. (1978) *Interpersonal Relations: A Theory of Interdependence*. New York: Wiley.

Lerner, M.J. (1980) *The Belief in a Just World: A Fundamental Delusion*. New York: Plenum.

Leventhal, G.S. (1980) What should be done with equity theory? New approaches to the study of fairness in social relationships. In K. Gergen, M. Greenberg, and R. Willis (eds), *Social Exchange*, pp. 27–55. New York: Plenum.

Levine, R.A. and Campbell, D.T. (1972) *Ethnocentrism: Theories of Conflict, Ethnic Attitudes, and Group Behavior*. New York: Wiley.

Lind, E.A., Kanfer, R. and Earley, C. (1990) Voice, control, and procedural justice. *Journal of Personality and Social Psychology, 59*, 952–959.

Lind, E.A. and Tyler, T.R. (1988) *The Social Psychology of Procedural Justice*. New York: Plenum.

Messick, D.M., Bloom, S., Boldizar, J.P. and Samuelson, C.D. (1985) Why we are fairer than others. *Journal of Experimental Social Psychology, 21*, 389–399.

Messick, D. and Sentis, K. (1985) Estimating social and nonsocial utility functions from ordinal data. *European Journal of Social Psychology, 15*, 389–399.

Mikula, G., Petri, B. and Tanzer, N. (1990) What people regard as unjust. *European Journal of Social Psychology, 22*, 133–149.

Montada, L. (1995) Applying social psychology: The case of redistributions in united Germany. *Social Justice Research, 8*, 73–90.

Nagata, D. (1993) *Legacy of Injustice*. New York: Plenum.

Opotow, S. (1993) Animals and the scope of justice. *Journal of Social Issues, 49*, 71–86.

Range, F., Horn, L., Viranyi, Z. and Huber, L. (2009) The absence of reward induces inequity aversion in dogs. *Proceedings of the National Academy of Science, 106*, 340–345.

Rawls, J. (1971) *A Theory of Justice*. Cambridge: Harvard University Press.

Ross, M. and Sicoly, F. (1979) Egocentric biases in availability and attribution. *Journal of Personality and Social Psychology, 37*, 322–336.

Rusbult, C. and Van Lange, P. (1996) Interdependence processes. In E.T. Higgins and A.W. Kruglanski (eds), *Social Psychology*, pp. 564–596. New York: Guilford Press.

Rusbult, C.E., Verette, J., Whitney, G.A., Slovik, L.F. and Lipkus, I. (1991) Accommodation processes in close relationships: Theory and preliminary empirical evidence. *Journal of Personality and Social Psychology, 60*, 53–78.

Sedikides, C. and Brewer, M.B. (2001) *Individual Self, Relational Self, and Collective Self*. Philadelphia: Psychology Press.

Smith, H.J., Tyler, T.R., Huo, Y.J., Ortiz, D.J. and Lind, E.A. (1998) The self-relevant implications of the group-value model: Group membership, self-worth, and procedural justice. *Journal of Experimental Social Psychology, 34*, 470–493.

Snyder, C.R. and Lopez, S.J. (2002) *Handbook of Positive Psychology*. New York: Oxford University Press.

Stahl, T., Vermunt, R. and Ellemers, N. (2008) For love or money? How activation of relational versus instrumental concerns affects reactions to decision-making procedures. *Journal of Experimental Social Psychology, 44*, 80–94.

Tajfel, H. and Turner, J. (1979) An integrative theory of intergroup conflict. In W.G. Austin and S. Worchel (eds), *The Social Psychology of Intergroup Relations*, pp. 33–47. Monterey, CA: Brooks/Cole.

Thibaut, J. and Faucheux, C. (1965) The development of contractual norms in a bargaining situation under two types of stress. *Journal of Experimental Social Psychology, 1*, 89–102.

Thibaut, J. and Kelley, H.H. (1959) *The Social Psychology of Groups*. New York: Wiley.

Thibaut, J. and Walker, L. (1975) *Procedural Justice*. Hillsdale, NJ: Erlbaum.

Thompson, L. and Loewenstein, G. (1992) Egocentric interpretations of fairness and interpersonal conflict. *Organizational Behavior and Human Decision Processes, 51*, 176–197.

Tyler, T.R. (1987) Conditions leading to value expressive effects in judgments of procedural justice: A test of four models. *Journal of Personality and Social Psychology, 52*, 333–344.

Tyler, T.R. (1988) What is procedural justice?: Criteria used by citizens to assess the fairness of legal procedures. *Law and Society Review, 22*, 103–135.

Tyler, T.R. (1989) The psychology of procedural justice: A test of the group value model. *Journal of Personality and Social Psychology, 57*, 830–838.

Tyler, T.R. (1994) Psychological models of the justice motive. *Journal of Personality and Social Psychology, 67*, 850–863.

Tyler, T.R. (1999) Why people cooperate with organizations: An identity-based perspective. *Research in Organizational Behavior, 21*, 201–246.

Tyler, T.R. (2000) Social justice: Outcome and procedure. *International Journal of Psychology, 35*, 117–125.

Tyler, T.R. (2006) *Why People Obey the Law*. Princeton: Princeton University Press.

Tyler, T.R. and Bies, R. (1990) Interpersonal aspects of procedural justice. In J.S. Carroll (ed.), *Applied Social Psychology in Business Settings*, pp. 77–98. Hillsdale, NJ: Erlbaum.

Tyler, T.R. and Blader, S.L. (2000) *Cooperation in Groups: Procedural Justice, Social Identity, and Behavioral Engagement*. Philadelphia: Psychology Press.

Tyler, T.R. and Blader, S.L. (2003) Procedural justice, social identity, and cooperative behavior. *Personality and Social Psychology Review, 7*, 349–361.

Tyler, T.R., Boeckmann, R., Smith, H.J. and Huo, Y.J. (1997) *Social Justice in a Diverse Society*. Denver, CO: Westview.

Tyler, T.R. and Caine, A. (1981) The role of distributional and procedural fairness in the endorsement of formal leaders. *Journal of Personality and Social Psychology, 41*, 642–655.

Tyler, T.R., Degoey, P. and Smith, H. (1996) Understanding why the justice of group procedures matters: A test of the psychological dynamics of the group-value model. *Journal of Personality and Social Psychology, 70*, 913–930.

Tyler, T.R. and Lind, E.A. (1992) A relational model of authority in groups. *Advances in Experimental Social Psychology, 25*, 115–191.

Tyler, T.R., Rasinski, K. and Spodick, N. (1985) The influence of voice on satisfaction with leaders: Exploring the meaning of process control. *Journal of Personality and Social Psychology, 48*, 72–81.

Tyler, T.R. and Smith, H.J. (1998) Social justice and social movements. In D. Gilbert, S. Fiske and G. Lindzey (eds), *Handbook of Social Psychology, Vol. 2*, 4th Edition, pp.595–629. New York: McGraw-Hill.

Van Lange, P.A.M., De Cremer, D., Van Dijk, E. and Van Vugt, M. (2007) Self-interest and beyond. In A.W. Kruglanski and E.T. Higgins (eds), *Social Psychology: Handbook of Basic Principles*, 2nd Edition. New York: Guilford Press.

Vidmar, N. and Miller, D.T. (1980) The social psychology of punishment. *Law and Society Review, 14*, 565–602.

Wakslak, C.J., Jost, J.T., Tyler, T.R. and Chen, E. (2007) System justification and the alleviation of emotional distress. *Psychological Science, 18*, 267–274.

Walster, E., Walster, G.W. and Berscheid, E. (1978) *Equity: Theory and Research*. Boston: Allyn and Bacon.

44

Minority Influence Theory

Charlan Jeanne Nemeth

ABSTRACT

The study of minority influence began as a reaction to the portrayal of influence as the province of status and numbers and from a realisation that minorities need not just be passive recipients of influence but can actively persuade. From these beginnings, a considerable body of research, including ours, has investigated how minority views prevail. In the decades that followed, we concentrated, not so much on persuasion or attitude change, but rather on the value of minority views for the stimulation of divergent thinking. Dissent, as has been repeatedly documented, 'opens' the mind. People search for information, consider more options and, on balance, make better decisions and are more creative. Dissenters, rather than rogues or obstacles, provide value: they liberate people to say what they believe and they stimulate divergent and creative thought *even when they are wrong*. The implications for group decision making, whether in juries or companies, have been considerable and there is increasing interest in research and in practice for the value of authentic dissent in teams and in creating 'cultures' of innovation.

INTRODUCTION

My lifelong interest has been the study of influence – and in particular, influence by those who hold minority opinions. Initially, we concentrated on how minorities 'win' or persuade others to their position. Stimulated by observations on juries, we recognised the potential value of dissent, not for the truth that it holds or for its ability to persuade, but rather for the thought that it stimulates. Repeatedly we found that dissent stimulates thought that is more enquiring, more divergent and more creative. By contrast, majority views stimulate convergent thinking. People focus on the issue from the perspective of the majority and narrow the range of considerations, often convincing themselves of the majority position.

This work has had influence on the dialogue within social psychology but also on the law as well as corporate cultures in organisations. Dissent has come to be seen as having value and not simply as an 'obstacle'. There is serious consideration of the importance of protecting dissent in juries via procedural rules such as the requirement of unanimity. And, in organisations, the assumptions regarding the value of cohesion and homogeneity have been complicated with a willingness to recognise the importance of diversity and dissent for innovation.

BACKGROUND

As a graduate student in the mid 1960s, I had the good fortune of studying with Henri Tajfel and, through him, meeting Serge Moscovici (in England and France respectively) and, by virtue of their influence, I recommitted to the reasons why I decided to study social psychology. As an undergraduate math major, it was a single lecture on brainwashing that motivated me to pursue graduate studies in social psychology; it was the simple but compelling observation that people are powerful sources of influence. They can educate, inspire and strengthen us or they can diminish and weaken us as human beings. Though graduate school proved to be disappointing with careful, highly choreographed and often single variable studies, it was a 'gap' year in Oxford that renewed my interests. Perhaps it took two Eastern European Jews who went through World War II to teach me that we could and should study the combat between ideas and groups, that there were exemplars of courage and cowardice brought about by social conditions and the influence of others.

It was my time as a visiting professor in Bristol with Henri and in Paris with Serge, the year after my doctorate, that was to have the most influence on my thinking and subsequent professional career. Henri was passionate about categorisation and the importance of ingroups and outgroups. Serge was rethinking the flow of influence.

Social psychology at that time portrayed influence as flowing from the strong to the weak. We learned the value of status, confident styles and numbers. High status individuals (or the perception of higher status) influenced those of lower status (Berger et al., 1977; Hovland et al., 1953). It was the white, tall, wealthy, attractive male who studied at elitist institutions and/or who had position and title who influenced those of us who had few of those attributes or demographics. People who spoke loudly, quickly and with authority exercised influence (Giles et al., 1979). And we certainly learned about the power of majorities. Faced with a disagreeing majority, even one that was wrong, people abdicated information from their own senses and became subject to doubt (Asch, 1956; Kiesler and Kiesler, 1970). The individual or minority of individuals were passive agents. Their only choice seemed to be one of independence or conformity to the majority view.

The power of these elements was true then and it is true now. However, not being in the categories of status nor numbers in psychology (who were predominantly male) nor being particularly loud or authoritative, I can remember feeling relatively powerless in the influence world. Much of the research, including that later embodied in social impact theory (Latané, 1981) conveyed the imagery of a large truck that pummelled people into acquiescence. Perhaps Tajfel and Moscovici and the students who were drawn to them in those days identified with being in a minority and thus found appeal in a conception of an active minority view, but it was also the world in which we found ourselves. During that year, Serge and I spent a lot of time discussing minority views and their power. He would often tell me that American social psychology did not portray the world he saw. The emphasis on winning friends and influencing people, reciprocating favours and continually resolving conflicts was in contrast to the experiences of his generation. Being 1970, it was also in contrast to both his and my then recent experience. He went through the May 1968 uprising which had lasting effects on the university and French society in general.

I, as a brand new assistant professor at the University of Chicago (1968), saw in person a vigorous conflict of ideas about the Vietnam War. The antiwar minority did not conform or remain silently independent. They were vocal, persistent, and aggressive – and there were violent consequences in response. We witnessed the beatings, the 'lessons' taught to faculty who supported those protests but we also saw social change and an evolution of public opinion that was dramatic.

Shortly before, Serge along with Claude Faucheux developed a theory questioning the one-sided conceptualisation of influence (Faucheux and Moscovici, 1967; Moscovici and Faucheux, 1972). Recognising that social change cannot be understood without attention to an initial minority view, they set out to demonstrate that minority views can prevail. As we had all witnessed, individuals and minorities were not simply passive agents who either resisted or conformed to majority judgments; they could in fact exercise influence themselves. Furthermore, behavioural style is important and, in particular, consistency over time is key to exerting influence. Not having the numbers or status to influence at the outset, a member of a minority needed to argue his/her position effectively. It is the orchestration and patterning of verbal and nonverbal behaviour that fosters influence (Moscovici and Nemeth, 1974). And in 1969, an experiment was able to demonstrate just such an effect (Moscovici et al., 1969). That study and its findings have been replicated numerous times and provide, in my judgment, some of the best insights into why and how minorities can prevail. Thus it is worth describing in some detail.

In that study (which is almost a mirror image of a typical conformity experiment), four naïve individuals and two confederates were shown a series of blue slides and were asked to judge the colour and the brightness of those slides. A control group consisting of only naïve individuals had no problem; they repeatedly called the blue slides 'blue'. In the experimental conditions, the two confederates offered a differing view. In the 'consistent' condition, they repeatedly called the blue slides 'green'. In other words, they said 'green' on every trial. In the 'inconsistent' condition, they called the slides 'green' on two-thirds of the trials and called them 'blue' on one-third of the trials.

Most people – and certainly most students in my courses – hypothesise that the inconsistent condition would exert more influence. After all, they are correct on one-third of the trials and, further, they agree with the majority

on those trials and are thus likely to be better liked. The findings were the reverse. In keeping with the theory emphasising the importance of consistency, the findings showed that the consistent minority persuaded the majority to say 'green' on nearly nine per cent of trials whereas the inconsistent minority exerted no influence, not differing statistically from the control group.

Perhaps more importantly, the findings from this study showed that influence was greater at a private or latent level than evident at a public level. After the experimental procedure, individuals were asked to sort a series of blue/green chips into the categories of either 'green' or 'blue'. If you think of the coloured chips you could find in a paint store, you can order the blue/green chips along an actual physical dimension – from 'blue' to 'green'. You can mix up these chips but, at a point along that physical dimension, individuals or a control group call those to the 'blue end' of that point 'blue' and to the 'green end' of that point 'green'. Experimental subjects in the consistent condition shifted that point. They called the chips 'green' when a control group would call them 'blue'. These two findings have stood the test of time.

As I reflect back on conversations in those early years, Serge was very clear about the importance of consistency – and the perils of compromise. He had a rather psychoanalytic view of influence. You had to combat the resistances. There was a war of ideas; there was conflict not easily resolved; and above all, there was clarity, even with exaggeration and omission.

Serge behaved as he theorised and his lessons to me were personal as well as professional. He *always* put my feet to the fire. Whenever I would lapse in the graduate student habit of citing other people to legitimate my point, he would ask what I really believed followed by 'you must write *that*'. He convinced me that consistency and confidence were imperative. Know what you know and speak what you believe. But in those observations, it also became clear that influence involved 'style over time', that there was an orchestration of the verbal and nonverbal ways in which people interacted and persuaded. This stimulated an early study showing that consistency could be maintained without the confrontation of repetition and increasing the conflict, provided that changes in position were due to changes in the stimuli or 'facts' (Nemeth et al., 1974). Above all, we came to recognise that there was a subtlety about influence, a public face that often masked what people really thought.

BEHAVIOURAL STYLE

The early study demonstrating the importance of consistency over time has been repeatedly corroborated and developed (Moscovici and Lage, 1976; Moscovici and Nemeth, 1974; Mugny, 1982; Nemeth et al., 1974, 1990). For the minority to be 'persuasive', they need to be seen as having a position in which they believe. Minimally this means consistency of the position, not necessarily repetition. Mugny has further pointed to the subtlety of consistency by making the distinction between flexibility and rigidity, the former but not the latter being conducive to persuasion. Additionally, numerous studies have confirmed that minority influence is aided by confident behavioural styles; for example, taking the head seat (Moscovici and Lage, 1976; Nemeth and Wachtler, 1974) or even by a perception of confidence which might occur by virtue of simply persisting as a minority voice (Nemeth et al., 1977). This area, in my judgment, is both fascinating and worthy of further development though the subtleties involved in the timing and choreography of behavioural style are challenging for researchers.

THE PRIVATE OR LATENT NATURE OF INFLUENCE

Perhaps the more important development from that early study is the fact that minority views exercise their influence at a private or latent level rather than in public. Even in our early discussions, it was clear to us that influence was deeper and more profound than public adoption of a position. People may not publicly agree with the minority position but they may agree privately, later or in a different form (David and Turner, 2001; Mugny et al., 1995; Nemeth and Wachtler, 1974). It may appear on indirect judgments or be generalised to other subjects (Forgas and Williams, 2001; Maass et al., 1987; Mugny, 1982).

Part of the reason for the 'latent' influence by minorities is that people do not want to publicly move to a minority view since they fear the likely ridicule and rejection, consequences that have been documented since the early work by Schachter (1951).

In one of our own studies (Nemeth and Wachtler, 1974), we saw very clearly how adamantly subjects would resist any public movement to a minority position. The setting was a mock jury involving a personal injury case. The case was hypothetical, but the anger was so evident that subjects were pounding their fists on the table next to the confederate's face (the one who argued a minority position on compensation). The subjects did not move one cent in public. Yet, their judgments shifted dramatically on post-experiment questionnaires both on the case they had discussed and also on new cases with new facts. It was a demonstration of strong resistance against any public agreement with minority views coupled with change at a latent level. That study also made us revise our compensation to include 'combat pay' for the confederate.

Mugny and his colleagues have elaborated the reasons for this reluctance to publicly move to the minority view by invoking considerations of social identity and the desire to belong (Butera and Mugny, 1995, 2001; Mugny et al., 1995). Other considerations have been ingroup and outgroup status. Almost all researchers demonstrate that there is more discomfort and anger (Philips, 2003) when the holder of a minority view is a member of one's ingroup rather than a member of an outgroup. And this discomfort may be one of the reasons why many studies show influence is greater from an ingroup member (Crano, 2000; David and Turner, 1996; Volpato et al., 1990). Discomfort may be a catalyst for further assessment of the message.

Such findings make it clear that it is not easy to maintain a minority viewpoint. Anger and the perceptions of being unintelligent (or worse) are a predictable consequence (Levine, 1989). However, people who persist in a minority view can also be accorded the perceptions of confidence and courage which can be assets in their attempts to influence (Nemeth and Chiles, 1988; Nemeth et al., 1977). This is still an uncharted area of research –why would anyone maintain a dissenting viewpoint given the consequences – but fortunately, it is starting to be investigated (De Dreu et al., 2000; LePine and Van Dyne, 2001).

MOVING TO INFLUENCE AS A STIMULANT TO THOUGHT

Learning that influence may occur at a private or latent level, even if not observable in public, helped us to question the paradigms used to study attitude change. The field conceptualised influence to be attitude change on a Likert scale. If the target moved along that scale to the position of the source, that was influence. Yet, we had increasing evidence that attitudes could change on other dimensions or on other related issues. But convincing researchers to broaden the definition of influence was not as easy as it seemed. Yet, we were convinced that influence was far more subtle and deeper than movement on a Likert scale. It was perhaps a recognition of this possibility plus the fact that dissent had its power at the latent level that was to prime me for the observations that would come to dominate my professional life, and ironically to bring me back to the reasons why I decided to study social psychology.

My own early work on minority influence – the first five years post-PhD – was consumed with understanding when, how, and

why minority views can prevail. A number of us who had studied with Moscovici had become a cohesive and determined minority ourselves and had documented and elaborated the power of the minority to persuade – to 'win'. And we were finding converts to that field of research, initially with a wave of second-generation researchers. However, in 1974, my focus started to shift, much of it owing to an abiding interest in jury deliberations. Jury decisions were often the 'task of choice' in my experimental studies but it started to become a research interest in and of itself while at the University of Virginia.

The Supreme Court had recently ruled that a requirement of non-unanimity in jury decisions did not violate the defendant's constitutional rights (*Apodaca, Cooper, and Madder* v. *Oregon*, 1972; *Johnson* v. *Louisiana*, 1970). Oregon permitted a 10–2 verdict and Messrs Apodaca, Cooper and Madden were convicted by 10–2 or 11–1 verdicts. In Louisiana, crimes subject to hard labour were allowed a 9–3 verdict and Mr Johnson was convicted by such a vote. All of these individuals thus appealed their convictions based on a violation of the Sixth and Fourteenth Amendments. Under 'equal protection of the law', for example, their verdicts would have had to be unanimous had they been tried in another state. The court, however, ruled that their rights had not been violated and essentially argued that the verdicts would have been the same had unanimity been required.

At the time, there was evidence (Kalven and Zeisel, 1966) from real juries that the position held by a majority on the first ballot had a high likelihood (around 90 percent) chance of being the final verdict. Davis and his colleagues (Davis, 1989; Davis et al., 1984) had documented the power of majority views in mock jury decisions; in particular, a two-thirds majority seemed to fit the outcomes quite well. There was little evidence that the verdict differed as a result of a requirement of unanimity. But the issue was larger than that.

In reading the court's decision which, by the way, was rendered by a majority of five justices outvoting a minority of four justices – it was clear that there were broader considerations, those dealing with the *process* (not just the outcome) of decision making, theories about majority and minority influence, and community confidence. For example, the majority justices had a theory that the majority would not outvote a minority until 'reasoned discussion had ceased to have persuasive effect or to serve any other purpose – when a minority, that is, continues to insist upon acquittal without having persuasive reasons in support of its position' (*Johnson* v. *Louisiana*, 1970: 1624). The image of 'obstacle' and rogue dissenter reared its head again. By contrast, the minority opinion of four justices had a different theory and worried that polite and academic conversation might occur once the requisite votes were needed and this was 'no substitute for the earnest and robust argument necessary to reach unanimity' (*Johnson* v. *Louisiana*, 1970: 1647–1648). We decided to study the issue.

We first did an experimental study varying unanimity versus two-thirds majority rule on a first-degree murder case. We studied not only outcome (verdict) but also the process of decision making. In that study, we did a full Bales analysis, coding every comment in terms of who spoke, to whom it was addressed and which of the 12 categories (e.g., 'agreeing', 'giving information', 'asking for opinions') it exemplified. We also collected data on the robustness of the deliberation, on whether the minority was outvoted when the requisite number was reached as well as perceptions of justice and agreement with the verdict, all of which were issues in the court cases.

We then studied the issue in connection with the Law School at the University of Virginia. Third-year law students tried various cases in an actual courtroom with an actual judge and with witnesses. We brought the jury. Each jury of 12 was divided into two groups of six, one under a requirement of unanimity, the other a two-thirds majority. Deliberations were videotaped and analysed as in the experimental study. This way, we hoped for both experimental control and generalisability and fortunately, the findings proved to be in parallel, thus strengthening the findings. We learned that unanimity did not statistically alter the verdict but it did change the process. Under unanimity, deliberations were more robust, more fact oriented and people believed that justice had been better administered (Nemeth, 1977, 1984). However, we learned a great deal more.

Looking in detail at 40-minute deliberations of 60 or so groups, we started to notice something – call it a hunch or an insight. The groups with argumentation and debate, those where dissent was voiced and maintained, seemed to use more information, consider more options and, in our subjective judgment, had higher quality deliberations. That insight led to our first experimental study (Nemeth, 1976; Nemeth and Wachtler, 1983) where findings showed that subjects exposed to a disagreeing minority detected solutions that otherwise would have gone undetected. The task, a hidden figures array, was searched more fully and subjects saw the figure when embedded. They were not guessing; they were actively searching the array and finding 'truth' where it existed. This was in contrast to exposure to a disagreeing majority. In the latter situation, people concentrated on the figures suggested by the majority; they followed them exactly but did not find novel solutions. Such a finding corroborated our 'hunch' about the value of minority views and was presented to the first joint meeting of the American and European Societies of Experimental Social Psychology in Paris 1976.

That presentation had considerable impact. The audience seriously considered the possibility that minority views could influence thought and not just movement in attitude – public or private. I even think it influenced Moscovici's conversion theory (1980) which, while still focusing on attitude change, theorised about the cognitive reasons for majority influence at the public level and minority influence at the private level. The former, he theorised, was a comparison process. The latter was a conversion process where people actively processed the minority's arguments and position.

That first experimental study, conducted in 1973/1974 at Virginia, set the direction for many of our subsequent studies. And the findings provided optimism for raising the quality of thought and decision making. These 'rogues' might educate and stimulate us; they might make us smarter and wiser. It also dovetailed with the insights from that first jury study. Perhaps mostly, the jury work taught me where my interests lie. I didn't really care who won, whether it was the majority or the minority. The possibility that we could construct groups that were wiser and smarter than the sum of the individuals was compelling. And it was in stark contrast to the findings that groups are defective, that they make poor decisions (Janis, 1972). At least they did not always have to do so.

After the initial work in Virginia, we conducted more studies, mostly at Berkeley, continually refining our conception of how majorities and minorities stimulate thought. We already had information that those exposed to a minority view detected solutions that otherwise would have gone undetected (Nemeth, 1976; Nemeth and Wachtler, 1983). In a problem solving setting, those exposed to a minority utilised multiple strategies for problem solving (and performed better) while those exposed to a majority utilised the majority strategy to the detriment of other strategies (Nemeth and Kwan, 1987). There was also evidence of more originality of thought in response to minorities and more conventionality of thought in response to majorities (Nemeth and Kwan, 1985).

This early work convinced us that majorities and minorities stimulated different kinds of thinking and led to a theoretical formulation published in Psychological Review (Nemeth, 1986). Briefly, we hypothesised that majorities stimulate convergent thinking from the perspective posed by the majority. The thinking goes something like this: People exposed to a majority with a differing view are under stress and thus narrow the range of considerations. Further they assume the majority is correct and are motivated to assume that. As such, they focus on the issue or problem from the perspective of that majority in an attempt to understand why they take the position they do (and to find a reason to move to that position). By contrast, people exposed to a minority with a differing view assume the minority is in error. However, with consistency on the part of the minority, people come to reassess the situation and look at the issue anew. They don't assume the minority is correct but they are motivated to consider the issue more carefully since there must be a reason why the minority takes the position it does and, further, is sufficiently confident to maintain it.

Subsequent studies confirmed this set of hypotheses. We had evidence that minorities stimulated a search for information on all sides of the issue while majorities stimulated a search for information that corroborated the majority view (Nemeth and Rogers, 1996). There was better recall of information across categories in response to minority views (Nemeth et al., 1990). We even tested the strength of the theory by predicting when *majorities* might produce better performance. Remember the prediction is that majorities stimulate convergent focused thinking from their perspective.

In one study, we hypothesised that majorities could induce better performance IF it was a task where convergent thinking was useful and the perspective of the majority was appropriate. We chose the Stroop test, one of the few tasks where convergent thinking is useful. People are shown a number of colour words which are printed in an ink of a different colour (e.g., the word red printed in green ink) and are asked to read the colour of *ink* as quickly and accurately as possible. This is a classic test of interference and is quite difficult as one often says the colour word (e.g., red) rather than the colour of ink (e.g., green). Here, if you can convergently focus on ink and not the name, this is adaptive. Conversely, if you convergently focus on name and not the ink, that is particularly maladaptive.

The theory predicts that majorities stimulate convergent thinking from their perspective. The findings showed that when the majority focused on colour of *ink*, individuals were able to perform better on the Stroop test while a majority focus on *name* colour led to reduced performance. When it was a minority, their focus did not matter and performance was in between the two majority conditions (Nemeth et al., 1992). This study was essentially replicated with further evidence that minorities improve flexibility of performance (Peterson and Nemeth, 1996). Such findings gave us additional confidence about the theory since we could shift performance by altering the perspective of the majority and the nature of the task.

RESEARCH STRATEGY

The decision to do very simple problem-solving tasks rather than study the value of dissent in interacting groups was a deliberate one. While the origin of the idea was jury decision making and while our intended application was the role and value of dissent in small groups, we were also aware of the fact that interacting groups are very complex. They are difficult to study and it is difficult to establish cause and effect. Moreover, we wanted to make the point that the thinking, the performance and the decisions were not just different; they *were better*; they were correct. Attitudes are difficult to characterise as better, but if you show that people find correct solutions that otherwise would have gone detected, if you show they take in more information, consider more options and use all available strategies with resulting better performance and more originality, then it becomes easier to argue that groups profit from dissent, from minority views, especially since these effects occur even when those dissenting views are incorrect.

To some extent, this research strategy was also consistent with our theoretical perspective. Serge and I often spoke of the importance of making a clear point and being consistent, not just for personal integrity but also for influence. This was a bit contrary to graduate training where we complicated ideas, added variables and studied contingencies. However, in reflecting back on my early work on this issue, I had both a preference for simple (hopefully elegant) research designs and fundamentally believed that it is clarity, consistency and even simplicity that stimulates thought. The hope was that others would be stimulated to extend the thinking, to correct it, to elaborate on it and to show its boundary conditions, but the guiding theme of the value of dissent for divergent thought and clarity of position would remain. And we would welcome debate, for I was convinced that thought is stimulated by interaction, by discussion and, yes, even argument.

IMPACT AND APPLICATION

Minority influence and social psychology

A good deal of research developed the nature of cognitive activity in the realm of attitude change. Moscovici's (1980) conversion theory, for example, hypothesised quite different cognitive processes in response to a majority versus a minority source. The former created a comparison process where people identified with the majority and tried to 'fit in with their opinions or judgments'. Thus they often adopted the majority position – at least publicly – without scrutiny of the message. The latter created a conversion process – assuming the minority was consistent and confident – whereby people scrutinised the message. They wanted 'to see what the minority saw, to understand what it understood' (Moscovici, 1980: 215). This change, when it occurred, was deeper and longer lasting.

Competing theories arose (Mackie, 1987) which recognised that majorities also induced cognitive activity though, again, it was addressed to processing of the message and attitude change. A natural progression was for them to integrate the majority/minority source issue to the well-established research on peripheral versus central (Petty and Cacioppo, 1981) or systematic versus heuristic (Chaiken, 1980) information processing and attitude change. As a result, we now know much more about such processing and resulting attitude change (see, generally, Hewstone and Martin, 2008; Wood et al., 1994).

What has occasionally concerned me (Nemeth, 2003), however, is that my own work has sometimes been misunderstood and assumed to predict attitude change – and thus included in the dialogue on message processing. Often, cognitive activity is construed as analysing the message of the source while my theory and work deals not so much with processing information as with thinking. Importantly, majorities stimulate people to think about the issue from their perspective. People adopt their framework, utilise their strategies and convince themselves of the truth of that position and way of thinking. Minorities do not just induce thought about their message; they induce thought about the issue. And importantly, they induce thought that is divergent, that considers multiple options only one of which is that suggested by the minority. People open their minds to information, to options, to creative possibilities.

This central idea was developed by a number of creative Italian researchers (Volpato et al., 1990) who demonstrated more original proposals as a result of exposure to minority views and extended the formulation by introducing the ingroup/outgroup nature of this influence. This is a direction further developed by Mugny and his colleagues in their cognitive elaboration model (Mugny and Papastamou, 1980; Mugny and Perez, 1991; Mugny et al., 1995) and, more recently by DeDreu and DeVries (1997) and Philips (2003).

When researchers have tried to integrate this theory into attitude change, it is a bit difficult because our hypothesis regarding divergent thinking doesn't predict what attitude will be adopted. It does suggest, however, that whatever attitude that is, will be better conceived, better understood and probably closer to reality. If you use an intervening variable such as the content and/or direction of thought, you can probably predict attitude change. But long ago, back at the beginning, 'winning' was not the main focus.

Apart from attitude change, there have also been some interesting recent developments related to the minority person's *own* cognitive activity. For example, Levine and Russo (1995) show more divergent thought in preparation for being in a minority position. Others have connected the work to power. For example, there is evidence that those in power focus on a single target while those who are relatively powerless consider multiple sources of information (see Guinote, 2008). These studies have some interesting implications for the cognitive activity of the source and are consistent with hypotheses about differential cognitive activity associated with majority/minority status.

Somewhat ironically, those who have perhaps best understood and utilised our model have been in applied areas. Van Dyne and Saavedra (1996), for example, studied the role of dissent in work groups, finding that groups had improved decision quality when exposed to a minority perspective. They have recently replicated that finding and broadened the work to include value orientations of individualism/collectivism (Goncalo and Staw, 2006; Ng and Van Dyne, 2001). In a study of seven 'Fortune 500' top management teams, Peterson et al. (1998) found evidence that the most successful teams encouraged dissent in private meetings. And, in a study of US hospitals, Dooley and Fryxell (1999) found dissent related to high quality decision making teams.

Perhaps the greatest impact is evident in the applied areas of law and organisational culture. Both areas have a fundamental interest in the quality of decision making and creativity and these practical concerns have spurred an interest in possible mechanisms for achieving that. Dissent has been captured as one such vehicle (De Dreu and De Vries,

1997; Devine et al., 2001; Ford et al., 2008; Van Swol and Seinfeld, 2006).

Juries and justice

In a study of the quality of the Supreme Court's own decisions, Gruenfeld (1995) found that the court's decisions were more integratively complex when there was dissent. In other words, there were more distinctions and integration of varying considerations when there was dissent. Another direct application is in the dialogue on procedural rules protecting dissent such as the requirement of unanimity in juries (Devine et al., 2001). And we were pleased to find the work cited in court cases such as an *amicus curiae* brief in support of considering race and gender in university admissions (*Grutter* v. *Bollinger, James et al.*) where the authors argue for the value of heterogeneity of views. Some of this application, we believe, has come less from published articles than direct persuasion of lawyers and judges – a deliberate strategy on our part.

In the mid 1970s, partly as a consequence of the experimental work on the unanimity issue, there arose an opportunity to study psychology and law for a year at the Battelle Seattle Research Center, courtesy of Gordon Bermant. It was a time to actually learn about the law. We (Bermant et al., 1976) organised a conference and, more importantly, one participant – a judge from Portland, Oregon – agreed to host me for two weeks to study the jury system in Portland. Access to judges, prosecutors, public defenders, almost all files, 'behind closed doors' negotiations and dinner parties that were conducted like seminars, provided invaluable information about how things 'worked' and what issues were legally relevant. It also led to an invited address before the Oregon Bar Association in 1976. The topic for the 1,100 lawyers was, in part, the importance of unanimity for protection of dissenting views.

Some years later (2003), a similar talk before a group of researchers and judges

from Australia and New Zealand led to discussion about the value of dissent as, at that time, both countries were considering 'reform' from unanimity to some form of majority rule in juries. While the promoters of this reform used the words 'rogue' and 'obstacle' to describe the dissenter, our presentation moved the discussion from efficiency to truth, justice and the possible value of dissent.

CORPORATE CULTURES AND VOICE

The application of the dissent research to organisations has a similar trajectory but a broader one. There is now considerable evidence that the model of minority influence (Nemeth, 1986) is robust and well replicated in field settings (Peterson et al., 1998; Van Dyne and Saavadra, 1996). Further, a number of studies demonstrate that dissent increases creativity and better performance, at least under certain circumstances (De Dreu and De Vries, 1997; De Dreu et al., 2000; Ng and Van Dyne, 2001; Van Swol and Seinfeld, 2006). There are also three specific areas where the work has found application in organisations: the devils advocate, brainstorming, and corporate cultures.

The devil's advocate

I had always found it of interest that even when people believed that dissent had value, they still were trying to quash it or to find a mechanism that could have it 'both ways': keep its beneficial properties and yet be more palatable. Many observers, practitioners and researchers have struggled with the implications of dissent, primarily because they fear the frustration, lowered morale and 'slowing down' of the process. They thus often favour mechanisms such as devil's advocate, hoping they can avoid some of the 'downsides' of dissent.

Some research has found the technique to be of value though a number of studies compare it to having no alternatives presented

(Katzenstein, 1996). Janis (1972) himself suggested devil's advocate as an antidote to 'groupthink' on the assumption that it would question the prevailing mode of thought and bring diverse viewpoints to the discussion. After years of working with dissent and thought stimulation, however, we never believed that you could clone the effects that easily. Serious reappraisal of a belief, we thought, required challenge and would be unlikely to occur in a role-playing setting. It was at least worth studying.

In one study (Nemeth et al., 2001b), we compared authentic dissent with devil's advocate in a mock jury decision-making experiment. Groups of four deliberated a personal injury case and decided on appropriate compensation by means of a series of votes and arguments. The position and arguments of the 'minority' remained the same. The only difference was whether or not the person was asked to play the 'devil's advocate' prior to the deliberation. Results showed that 'authentic dissent' (when no such instruction was given) led to more divergent thinking. The subjects generated novel thoughts that were on both sides of the issue. When that person was asked to play a 'devil's advocate', there not only was less thinking on both sides of the issue. There was evidence of 'cognitive bolstering'. Individuals generated thoughts that confirmed their initial position. Thus, we were able to show that not only was devil's advocate not as effective as authentic dissent but, further, it solidified the initial position.

In a second study (Nemeth et al., 2001a), we compared variations of devil's advocate. In the first study, the true position of the 'devil's advocate' was unknown. In the second study, we simply varied whether it was unknown or known and, if known, if it was consistent with the position she advocated or inconsistent with the position she advocated (namely she agreed with the majority). A fourth condition was 'authentic dissent', namely no request to act as a devil's advocate. Surprisingly, the variations of devil's advocate did not matter; they did not differ significantly from one

another. However, as predicted, none achieved the stimulating effect of authentic dissent. In this study, that stimulation took the form of creative solutions to the problem under discussion. Those exposed to authentic dissent generated more creative solutions than did those in any of the devil's advocate conditions. These findings have been replicated by Schultz-Hardt et al. (2002) demonstrating the value of majority/minority viewpoints in the context of information-seeking bias.

This issue of devil's advocate remains controversial as many companies and many researchers still argue for its value. Some well known CEOs have raised doubts about devil's advocate, not because it is ineffective but, rather, for the conflict that it creates. Dave Kelley of IDEO, perhaps the best-known design company in the world and known for its creative culture, argues that devil's advocates are 'naysayers' who can smother a fragile idea. He thus prefers using various nonconfrontational role-playing techniques (Kelley and Littman, 2005). Others, such as Harvard Business School professor, Dorothy Leonard, take our perspective, arguing for authentic dissent (Leonard and Swap, 1999). What becomes important is that there is a dialogue and debate, one we believe is served by clear alternatives and dissenting viewpoints.

Brainstorming

A technique long believed to enhance group creativity is that of brainstorming. This technique (Osborn, 1957), has persisted in practice even though the research shows little evidence of effectiveness. More precisely, brainstorming instructions increase the number of ideas in a group but it is usually less than the total number of ideas generated by the same number of individuals brainstorming alone (Brown and Paulus, 1996).

The instructions for brainstorming are fairly precise:

1 Quantity: come up with as many ideas as you can.

2 Do not criticise others' ideas.
3 Build on others' ideas.
4 Freewheeling is welcome.

The fact that brainstorming instructions do not achieve the level of a 'nominal' group (the sum of ideas made by the same number of individuals brainstorming alone) has led many researchers to focus on the 'losses' generated by groups. The culprits are usually motivational or coordination problems. In particular, Diehl and Stroebe (1987) review the available literature and conclude that one of the biggest problems is production blocking. People can't speak at the same time and, thus, ideas are often lost or not stated as a result. A good deal of work has focused on how to counter these losses – for example, having individuals write down their ideas and then discuss them as a group, using electronic brainstorming and so on. (Brown and Paulus, 1996).

Most of the work assumes that groups are less than the sum of their individuals and the aim is to counter those losses. The work on dissent and cognitive stimulation, however, suggests that groups can be better than the sum of the individuals (Nemeth and Nemeth-Brown, 2003), an orientation compatible with the extensive work done by Paulus and his colleagues (Dugosh et al., 2000; Paulus and Dzindolet, 1993; Paulus and Nijstad, 2003) who recognise that there can be a group synergy, that individuals can stimulate ideas in another. This has spawned research on the usage of computer interaction, facilitators, diversity and group goals, all of which figure in this potential synergy. The one thing that is missing is debate.

Note that, among the four 'rules' of brainstorming, there is the admonition not to criticise each others' ideas. The idea, of course, is that criticism will cause evaluation apprehension: people will be reluctant to express creative ideas; they won't 'free wheel' for fear of evaluation and risk. The dissent model, by contrast, predicts not only cognitive activity but also originality as a result of exposure to opposing views. This is a bit subtle in the brainstorming context.

However, the role of debate and conflict might still be productive.

In a test of this possibility, we conducted a study in both the US and in France (Nemeth et al., 2004). The studies were identical. Individuals were given four instructions. In one condition, it was the four rules as posited by Osborne. In the second condition, there was one exception. The admonition 'not to criticise' was replaced by 'feel free to debate, even criticise'. Most researchers would have predicted that the 'do not criticise' instruction would lead to more ideas than a control group and that the 'debate/criticise' instruction would lead to fewer ideas than a control. In fact, we found the debate instruction led to significantly more ideas than a control, and it was even superior to the 'do not criticise' (though not significantly so). These findings were reflected in both the US and France.

Corporate cultures

Given the interests of business schools on the topic of innovation, the work on dissent was a natural fit. While some learned of the formulation (Nemeth, 1986) in a psychological journal, it was an article directly pertaining to corporate cultures that had the greatest impact (Nemeth, 1977). This article was a direct consequence of an invited address at a conference on Knowledge and the Firm at the Haas School of Business and, much like the legal research, the article required a year to learn about company practices. We came to the conclusion that most organisations try to create cohesion, harmony and alignment with a company vision. They want creativity and innovation but do not embrace the idea of welcoming dissent. In fact, they reward loyalty rather than innovation. And there are many business gurus who are happy to help them achieve the benefits of a 'cult-like' culture (Collins and Porras, 1994).

Given the years of documenting the value of differing views, the potential 'downsides' of morale and cohesion were evident. After all, we and others repeatedly found that majority views stimulate convergent thinking from their perspective. This is useful provided that the majority perspective was the correct or best one. Thus company practices such as recruiting those who 'fit' the organisation, socialising and interaction, and ejecting dissent 'as a virus' – all of which are argued to characterise 'visionary' companies (Collins and Porras, 1994) – seemed relevant for identification, for a sense of belonging and morale but not necessarily for performance and certainly not for innovation. Cults use similar practices (O'Reilly and Chatman, 1996).

From our perspective, the problem seemed to be that such convergence of thought and action is useful to the extent that they are on the *right* page, not just the *same* page. Remember the Stroop study (Nemeth et al., 1992)? The kinds of thoughts stimulated by such practices, we argued, are powerful for implementation of an idea and depend on the value of that idea but they are not conducive to developing or changing an idea, to recognising a changing market or new opportunities. Rather, it is dissent or at least the open airing of competing views that could do this (Nemeth, 1997).

This article, peppered with examples of corporate cultures, was a counter to much of the work arguing for a cult-like culture which, ironically, was often seen as compatible with innovation. As such, this work on the value of dissent (Nemeth, 1997) has become part of the dialogue on the role of dissent, debate, 'voice' and conflict in organisations (Amason, 1996; Ford et al., 2008; Van Dyne et al., 2003). While it would be comforting to think that people are learning to 'welcome' dissent, I suspect that it is more often a stimulant for discussion than taken at face value. The message is still difficult for managers who often want to control when and where innovation occurs. And the recurrent themes of chaos, wasted time and reduced morale still remain.

The issues involved in corporate cultures are complex and varied, ones I knew would require further education on my part, somewhat similar to that required for the

work on the law. That led to a decision to spend another year immersing myself in the issues. I took an unpaid leave of absence in 2005/2006 to teach at the London Business School – another humbling experience of learning. But being a part of the voices for the value of diversity and dissent in the workplace (Detert and Edmondson, 2008; Morrison et al., 2003; Van Dyne et al., 2002) is an opportunity for impact on social issues. It is also an opportunity for complicating my own research, a result whenever one tries to study applied issues.

I learned that it is difficult to balance performance, profitability and innovation. It is difficult to manage creative individuals and the creative process. But it is also difficult to persuade people to speak up and to manage an 'unwanted truth' (Edmondson and Munchus, 2007; Morrison and Milliken, 2000). The problems remain: people fear that speaking up will not serve any purpose save their own branding as a 'nuisance'. No one finds it easy to 'welcome' disagreement.

CONCLUSION

Over the course of these decades studying influence in the laboratory and, more recently, in naturalistic settings, I am convinced of a few things. People are loath to change their minds easily, the attitude change literature notwithstanding. Serge was right. It requires exposure to a differing view, not just in content but in contrast, discussion and debate.

I am also happily convinced that authenticity is important. Most of our work documents the value of authentic dissent. Dissenting for the sake of dissenting is not useful. It is also not useful if it is 'pretend dissent' – for example, if role-played. It is not useful if motivated by considerations other than searching for the truth or the best solutions. But when it is authentic, it stimulates thought, it clarifies and it emboldens.

Finally, it is clear to me that it is still difficult to convince people of the value of diversity and dissent. They accept the principle on the surface – it sounds nice, democratic and tolerant – but, in fact, people get quickly irritated by a dissenting view that persists and fear the lowered morale, the lack of 'harmony' and a loss of control by 'welcoming' dissent. Thus, we continually find attempts to denigrate it or to contain it. People are encouraged to 'role play' their ideas instead of stating them clearly; they are asked to 'fit in', to be on the same page, to not make waves and to be in line with the leader's views or the company vision. They are made to fear repercussions, including being marginalised by gossip or ridicule. I often think that it is our differences that make us interesting as human beings and it is in our differences and our willingness to embrace them that we learn and grow, that at least we *think*.

What I hope is that we start to recognise the courage of minority voices and the value of the open airing of competing views (John Stuart Mill, 1859) and that we achieve some clear understanding of the role of trust that allows the passionate interchange to occur. What I also hope is that we put less emphasis on 'winning', persuading and manipulating others and return to the ways in which interaction clarifies, educates and elevates us.

ACKNOWLEDGEMENTS

This manuscript was supported by the Kauffman Foundation and by the Institute for Industrial Relations at UC Berkeley, support which is gratefully acknowledged. Requests for reprints should be addressed to Professor Charlan Nemeth, Department of Psychology, University of California, Berkeley, CA 94720–1650.

I owe a debt of gratitude to the wonderful graduate students with whom I collaborated at Chicago, Virginia, British Columbia and Berkeley. Special ones who worked with me for years include Jeff Endicott and Joel Wachtler (at Chicago and Virginia), Jack Goncalo, John Rogers, and Keith Brown (at Berkeley). They taught me as much as I taught them. Wonderful other graduate students include: Cindy Chiles, Matt Feinberg, Linda George, Julie Kwan, Ofra Mayseless, Kathy Mosier, Margaret Ormiston, Rhonda Pajak, Randall Peterson, Jeff Sherman and Elaine Wong.

REFERENCES

Amason, A.C. (1996) Distinguishing the effects of functional and dysfunctional conflict on strategic decision making: Resolving a paradox for top management teams. *Academy of Management Journal, 39*, 123–148.

Apodaca, Cooper, and Madder v. Oregon, 406, U.S., 404 (1972).

Asch, S.E. (1956) Studies of independence and conformity: A minority of one against a unanimous majority. *Psychological Monographs, 70*, Whole no. 416.

Berger, J.M., Fisek, M.H., Norman, R.Z. and Zelditch, M. (1977) *Status Characteristics in Social Interactions: An Expectation States Approach.* New York: Elsevier.

Bermant, G., Nemeth, C. and Vidmar, N. (eds) (1976) *Psychology and the Law: Research Frontiers.* Lexington: D.C. Heath and Co.

Brown, V. and Paulus, P.B. (1996) A simple dynamic model of social factors in group brainstorming. *Small Group Research, 27*, 91–114.

Butera, F. and Mugny, G. (1995) Conflict between incompetences and influence of a low-expertise source in hypothesis testing. *European Journal of Social Psychology, 25*, 457–462.

Butera, F. and Mugny, G. (eds) (2001) *Social Influence in Social Reality: Promoting Individual and Social Change.* Ashland: Hogrefe and Huber Publishers.

Chaiken, S. (1980) Heuristic versus systematic information processing and the use of source versus message cues in persuasion. *Journal of Personality and Social Psychology, 39*, 752–766.

Collins, J.C. and Porras, J.I. (1994) *Built to Last: Successful Habits of Visionary Companies.* New York: HarperCollins.

Crano, W.D. (2000) Social influence: effects of leniency on majority and minority-induced focal and indirect attitude change. *Revue Internationale de Psychologie Sociale, 15*, 89–121.

David, B. and Turner, J.C. (1996) Studies in self-categorization and minority conversion: Is being a member of the out-group an advantage? *British Journal of Social Psychology. Special Issue: Minority Influences, 35*, 179–199.

David, B. and Turner, J.C. (2001) Self-categorization principles underlying majority and minority influence. In J.P. Forgas and K.D. Williams (eds), *Social Influence: Direct and Indirect Processes*. Philadelphia: Psychology Press.

Davis, J.H. (1989) Psychology and law: The last 15 years. *Journal of Applied Social Psychology*, *19*, 199–230.

Davis, J.H., Tindale, R.S., Nagao, D.H., Hinsz, V.B. and Robertson, B. (1984) Order effects in multiple decisions by groups: A demonstration with mock juries and trial procedures. *Journal of Personality and Social Psychology*, *44*, 20–33.

De Dreu, C.K.W. and De Vries, N.K. (1997) Minority dissent in organizations. In C.K.W. De Dreu and E. Van de Vliert (eds), *Using Conflict in Organizations*, pp. 72–86. Thousand Oaks: Sage.

De Dreu, C.K.W., De Vries, N.K., Franssen, H. and Altink, W.M.M. (2000) Minority dissent in organizations: Factors influencing willingness to dissent. *Journal of Applied Social Psychology*, *30*, 2451–2466.

Detert, J.R. and Edmondson, A.C. (2008) Silent Saboteurs: How Implicit Theories of Voice Inhibit the Upward Flow of Knowledge in Organizations. *Working Knowledge*, Harvard Business School, December 2008.

Devine, D.J., Clayton, L.D., Dunford, B.B., Seying, R. and Pryce, J. (2001) Jury decision making: 45 years of empirical research on deliberating groups. *Psychology, Public Policy, and Law*, *7*, 622–727.

Diehl, M. and Stroebe, W. (1987) Productivity loss in idea-generating groups: Tracking down the blocking effect: Toward the solution of a riddle. *Journal of Personality and Social Psychology*, *53*, 497–509.

Dooley, R.S. and Fryxell, G.E. (1999) Attaining decision quality and commitment from dissent: The moderating effects of loyalty and competence in strategic decision-making teams. *Academy of Management Journal*, *42*, 389–402.

Dugosh, K.L., Paulus, P.B., Roland, E.J. and Yang, H. (2000) Cognitive stimulation in brainstorming. *Journal of Personality and Social Psychology*, *79*, 722–735.

Edmondson, V.C. and Munchus, G. (2007) Managing the unwanted truth: A framework for dissent strategy. *Journal of Organizational Change Management*, *20*, 747–760.

Faucheux, C. and Moscovici, S. (1967) The style of behavior of a minority and its influence on majority responses. *Bulletin Du C.E.R.P. 16*, 337–361.

Ford, J.D., Ford, L.W. and D'Amelio, A. (2008) Resistance to change: The rest of the story. *Academy of Management Review*, *33*, 362–377.

Forgas, J.P. and Williams, K.D. (eds) (2001) *Social Influence: Direct and Indirect Processes: The Sydney Symposium of Social Psychology*. New York: Psychology Press.

Giles, H., Bourhis, R.Y. and Davies, A. (1979) Prestigous speech styles: The imposed norm and inherent value hypothesis. In W. McCormack and S. Wurm (eds), *Language in Anthropology IV: Language in Many Ways*, pp. 307–348. The Hague: Mouton.

Goncalo, J.A. and Staw, B.M. (2006) Individualism-collectivism and group creativity. *Organizational Behavior and Human Decision Processes*, *100*, 96–109.

Gruenfeld, D.H. (1995) Status, ideology, and integrative complexity on the U.S. Supreme Court: Rethinking the politics of political decision making. *Personality and Social Psychology Bulletin*, *68*, 1013–1022.

Grutter v. Bollinger, James et al., 539 U.S. 306 (2003).

Guinote, A. (2008) Power and affordances: When the situation has more power over powerful than powerless individuals. *Journal of Personality and Social Psychology*, *95*, 237–252.

Hewstone, M. and Martin, R. (2008) Social influence. In M. Hewstone, W. Stroebe and K. Jonas (eds), *Introduction to Social Psychology*, 4th Edition, pp. 216–243. Malden: Blackwell Publishing.

Hovland, C.I., Janis, I.L. and Kelley, H.H. (1953) *Communication and Persuasion: Psychological Studies of Opinion Change*. New Haven: Yale University Press.

Janis, I.L. (1972) *Victims of Groupthink: A Psychological Study of Foreign-Policy Decisions and Fiascos*. Oxford: Houghton Mifflin.

Johnson v. Louisiana, 406 U.S. 356 (1972).

Kalven, H., Jr. and Zeisel, H. (1966) *The American Jury*. Boston: Little, Brown.

Katzenstein, G. (1996) The debate on structured debate: Toward a unified theory. *Organizational Behavior and Human Decision Processes*, *66*, 316–332.

Kelley, T. and Littman, J. (2005) *The Ten Faces of Innovation: IDEO's Strategies for Beating the Devil's Advocate and Driving Creativity Throughout your Organisation*. New York: Currency, Doubleday.

Kiesler, C.A. and Kiesler, S.B. (1970) *Conformity*. New York: Addison Wesley Publishing Company.

Latané, B. (1981) The psychology of social impact. *American Psychologist*, *36*, 343–356.

Leonard, D.A. and Swap, W.C. (1999) *When Sparks Fly: Igniting Creativity in Groups*. Boston: Harvard Business School Press.

LePine, J.A. and Van Dyne, L. (2001) Voice and cooperative behavior as contrasting forms of contextual performance: Evidence of differential relationships with big five personality characteristics and cognitive ability. *Journal of Applied Psychology, 86*, 325–336.

Levine, J.M. (1989) Reaction to opinion deviance in small groups. In P.B. Paulus (ed.), *Psychology of Group Influence*, 2nd Edition, pp. 187–231. Hillsdale: Lawrence Erlbaum Associates.

Levine, J.M. and Russo, E. (1995) Impact of anticipated interaction on information acquisition. *Social Cognition, 13*, 293–317.

Maass, A., West, S.G. and Cialdini, R.B. (1987) Minority influence and conversion. In C. Hendrick (ed.), *Group Processes*, pp. 55–79. Thousand Oaks: Sage.

Mackie, D.M. (1987) Systematic and nonsystematic processing of majority and minority persuasive communications. *Journal of Personality and Social Psychology, 53*, 41–52.

Mill, J.S. (1859) *On Liberty*. New York: Penguin.

Morrison, E.W. and Milliken, F.J. (2000) Organizational silence: A barrier to change and development in a pluralistic world. *Academy of Management Review, 25*, 706–725.

Morrison, E.W., Milliken, F.J., Dyne, L., Ang, S., Botero, I.C. and Bowen, F., (2003) Speaking up, remaining silent: The dynamics of voice and silence in organizations. *Journal of Management Studies, 40*, 1353–1568.

Moscovici, S. (1980) Toward a theory of conversion behavior. In L. Berkowitz (ed.), *Advances in Experimental Social Psychology, Vol. 13*. New York: Academic Press.

Moscovici, S. and Faucheux, C. (1972) Social influence, conforming bias, and the study of active minorities. In L. Berkowitz (ed.), *Advances in Experimental Social Psychology, 6*, 149–202. New York: Academic Press.

Moscovici, S. and Lage, E. (1976) Studies in social influence III: Majority versus minority influence in a group. *European Journal of Social Psychology, 6*, 149–174.

Moscovici, S., Lage, E. and Naffrechoux, M. (1969) Influence of a consistent minority on the responses of a majority in a color perception task. *Sociometry, 32*, 365–380.

Moscovici, S. and Nemeth, C. (1974) *Social Influence: II. Minority Influence*. Oxford: Rand Mcnally.

Mugny, G. (1982) *The Power of Minorities*. London: Academic Press.

Mugny, G., Butera, F., Sanchez-Mazas, M. and Pérez, J.A. (1995) Judgments in conflict: The conflict elaboration theory of social influence. In B. Boothe, R. Hirsig, A. Helminger, B. Meier and R. Volkart (eds), *Perception–Evaluation–Interpretation*, pp. 160–168. Ashland: Hogrefe and Huber Publishers.

Mugny, G. and Papastamou, S. (1980) When rigidity does not fail: Individualization and psychologization as resistances to the diffusion of minority innovations. *European Journal of Social Psychology, 10*, 43–61.

Mugny, G. and Perez, J.A. (1991) *The Social Psychology of Minority Influence*. New York: Cambridge University Press.

Nemeth, C. (1976) A comparison between conformity and minority influence. Paper presented to the International Congress of Psychology, Paris, France.

Nemeth, C. (1977). Interactions between jurors as a function of majority vs. unanimity decision rules. *Journal of Applied Social Psychology, 7*, 38–56.

Nemeth, C., Brown, K. and Rogers, J. (2001a) Devil's advocate versus authentic dissent: Stimulating quantity and quality. *European Journal of Social Psychology, 31*, 707–720.

Nemeth, C. and Chiles, C. (1988) Modeling courage: The role of dissent in fostering independence. *European Journal of Social Psychology, 18*, 275–280.

Nemeth, C., Mayseless, O., Sherman, J. and Brown, Y. (1990) Exposure to dissent and recall of information. *Journal of Personality and Social Psychology, 58*, 429–437.

Nemeth, C., Mosier, K. and Chiles, C. (1992) When convergent thought improves performance: Majority versus minority influence. *Personality and Social Psychology Bulletin, 18*, 139–144.

Nemeth, C. and Rogers, J. (1996) Dissent and the search for information. *British Journal of Social Psychology. Special Issue: Minority Influences, 35*, 67–76.

Nemeth, C., Swedlund, M. and Kanki, B. (1974) Patterning of a minority's responses and their influence on the majority. *European Journal of Social Psychology, 4*, 53–64.

Nemeth, C. and Wachtler, J. (1974) Creating the perceptions of consistency and confidence: A necessary condition for minority influence. *Sociometry, 37*, 529–540.

Nemeth, C., Wachtler, J. and Endicott, J. (1977) Increasing the size of the minority: Some gains and some losses. *European Journal of Social Psychology, 7*, 15–27.

Nemeth, C.J. (1984) Processus de groupe et jurys: Les Etats-Unis et la France. In S. Moscovici (ed.), *Psychologie Sociale*, pp. 229–251. Paris: Presses Universitaires de France.

Nemeth, C.J. (1986) Differential contributions of majority and minority influence. *Psychological Review, 93*, 23–32.

Nemeth, C.J. (1997) Managing innovation: when less is more. *California Management Review, 40*, 59–74.

Nemeth, C.J. (2003) Minority dissent and its 'hidden' benefits. *New Review of Social Psychology, 2,* 21–28.

Nemeth, C.J., Connell, J.B., Rogers, J.D. and Brown, K.S. (2001b) Improving decision making by means of dissent. *Journal of Applied Social Psychology, 31,* 48–58.

Nemeth, C.J. and Kwan, J.L. (1985) Originality of word associations as a function of majority vs minority influence. *Social Psychology Quarterly, 48,* 277–282.

Nemeth, C.J. and Kwan, J.L. (1987) Minority influence, divergent thinking and detection of correct solutions. *Journal of Applied Social Psychology, 17,* 788–799.

Nemeth, C.J. and Nemeth-Brown, B. (2003) Better than individuals? the potential benefits of dissent and diversity for group creativity. In P.B. Paulus and B.A. Nijstad (eds), *Group Creativity: Innovation Through Collaboration,* pp. 63–84. New York: Oxford University Press.

Nemeth, C.J., Personnaz, B., Personnaz, M. and Goncalo, J.A. (2004) The liberating role of conflict in group creativity: A study in two countries. *European Journal of Social Psychology, 34,* 365–374.

Nemeth, C.J. and Wachtler, J. (1983) Creative problem solving as a result of majority vs. minority influence. *European Journal of Social Psychology, 13,* 45–55.

Ng, K.Y. and Van Dyne, L. (2001) Individualism-collectivism as a boundary condition for effectiveness of minority influence in decision making. *Organizational Behavior and Human Decision Processes, 84,* 198–225.

O'Reilly, C.A. and Chatman, J.A. (1996) Culture as social control: Corporations, cults and commitment. *Research in Organizational Behavior, 18,* 157–200.

Osborn, A.F. (1957) *Applied Imagination,* 1st Edition. New York: Scribner.

Paulus, P.B. and Dzindolet, M.T. (1993) Social influence processes in group brainstorming. *Journal of Personality and Social Psychology, 64,* 575–586.

Paulus, P.B. and Nijstad, B.A. (eds) (2003) *Group Creativity: Innovation Through Collaboration.* New York: Oxford University Press.

Peterson, R.S. and Nemeth, C.J. (1996) Focus versus flexibility: majority and minority influence can both improve performance. *Personality and Social Psychology Bulletin, 22,* 14–23.

Peterson, R.S., Owens, P.D., Tetlock, P.E., Fan, E.T. and Martorana, P. (1988) Group dynamics in top management teams: Groupthink, vigilance, and alternative models of organizational failure and success. *Organizational Behavior and Human Decision Processes. Special Issue: Theoretical Perspectives on Groupthink: A Twenty-Fifth Anniversary Appraisal, 73,* 272–305.

Petty, R.E. and Cacioppo, J.T. (1981) *Attitudes and Persuasion – Classic and Contemporary Approaches.* Dubuque: William C. Brown.

Phillips, K. (2003) The effects of categorically based expectations on minority influence: the importance of congruence. *Personality and Social Psychology Bulletin, 29,* 3–12.

Schachter, S. (1951) Deviation, rejection, and communication. *Journal of Abnormal and Social Psychology, 46,* 190–207.

Schulz-Hardt, S., Jochims, M. and Frey, D. (2002) Productive conflict in group decision making: Genuine and contrived dissent as strategies to counteract biased information seeking. *Organizational Behavior and Human Decision Processes, 88,* 563–586.

Van Dyne, L., Ang, S. and Botero, I.C. (2003) Conceptualizing employee silence and employee voice as multidimensional constructs. *Journal of Management Studies. Special Issue: Speaking Up, Remaining Silent: The Dynamics of Voice in Organizations, 40,* 1359–1392.

Van Dyne, L., Jehn, K.A. and Cummings, A. (2002) Differential effects of strain on two forms of work performance: Individual employee sales and creativity. *Journal of Organizational Behavior, 23,* 57–74.

Van Dyne, L. and Saavedra, R. (1996) A naturalistic minority influence experiment: Effects of divergent thinking, conflict and originality in work-groups. *British Journal of Social Psychology. Special Issue: Minority Influences, 35,* 151–167.

Van Swol, L.M. and Seinfeld, E. (2006) Differences between minority, majority, and unanimous group members in the communication of information. *Human Communication Research, 32,* 178–197.

Volpato, C., Maass, A., Mucchi-Faina, A. and Vitti, E. (1990) Minority influence and social categorization. *European Journal of Social Psychology, 20,* 119–132.

Wood, W., Lundgren, S., Ouellette, J.A., Busceme, S. and Blackstone, T. (1994) Minority influence: A meta-analytic review of social influence processes. *Psychological Bulletin, 115,* 323–345.

45

Social Identity Theory

Naomi Ellemers and S. Alexander Haslam

ABSTRACT

Social identity theory is a "grand" theory. Its core premise is that in many social situations people think of themselves and others as *group members*, rather than as unique individuals. The theory argues that social identity underpins intergroup behavior and sees this as qualitatively distinct from interpersonal behavior. It delineates the circumstances under which social identities are likely to become important, so that they become the primary determinant of social perceptions and social behaviors. The theory also specifies different strategies people employ to cope with a devalued social identity. Social identity theory is a truly social psychological theory, in that it focuses on *social context* as the key determinant of self-definition and behavior. People's responses are thus understood in terms of subjective beliefs about different groups and the relations between them, rather than material interdependencies and instrumental concerns, objective individual and group characteristics, or individual difference variables. After its initial formulation as a "theory of intergroup conflict" in the 1970s, the theory has undergone many expansions, refinements, and updates. It has inspired a large body of research, and has been applied to inform the analysis of a range of issues and problems in group dynamics and intergroup relations.

INTRODUCTION

Since it was first proposed in the 1970s, social identity theory (SIT) has been considered one of the major theories in social psychology. It is consistently represented in textbooks and readers, has been used as a theoretical framework in countless empirical investigations, and has informed the analysis of a range of topics in group processes and intergroup relations (for an overview see Haslam et al., 2010a). If this level of representation in the literature indicates the continued relevance of and steady interest in SIT, it also results from the continuous controversy and sometimes heated debate associated with this theoretical approach. Awareness that SIT has enthusiastic supporters as well as strong opponents merits a careful and critical consideration of the value of this theoretical approach. There should be no doubt, however, about the importance of being *informed* about SIT and the work it has inspired, if only to be able to understand ongoing scientific debates, and to allow the reader to place what represents a considerable part of the social psychological literature in an appropriate intellectual context. This chapter aims to provide such information, by describing the origins and further development of SIT and its main applications, as well as providing an overview of the main issues that have emerged as topics of debate over the years.

ORIGINS OF THE THEORY

As was the case with many other social psychologists of his generation, the scientific work of Henri Tajfel – a Jewish survivor of World War II of Polish birth – was inspired by his personal experiences of discrimination and intergroup conflict. In his early writings he explains that he was motivated to understand how people who had been living together as neighbors, colleagues, and friends could come to see each other as dangerous enemies even when there were no rational or objective reasons to do so. However, rather than take a field-study approach (e.g., Sherif, 1967), he sought to understand these issues by using scientific rigor to study groups in the laboratory and by exploring basic social cognitive processes which had been shown to be important in some of his earlier studies on object categorization (Tajfel, 1969).

This resulted in a series of experiments that later became known as the "minimal group studies" (Tajfel et al., 1971). Participants in these studies were informed that they had been assigned to one of two groups on the basis of an irrelevant criterion, or on the basis of chance. They did not know who else was present, they could not see or interact with others, and it was made clear that the choices they made could not affect their own outcomes in any way. Their task was then to allocate points to one member of their own group (not themselves), and one member of the other group. These "minimal" conditions were originally intended to form a baseline or control condition for further studies. As none of the known reasons to differentiate

between a member of one's own group and a member of another group were present, participants were expected to divide the points equally between them.

The historic significance of these studies lay in the observation that even these very minimal conditions proved sufficient to induce ingroup favoritism: the tendency to systematically allocate more points to a member of one's own group than to a member of another group. This effect later became known as the "mere categorization" effect – suggesting that the mere act of categorizing individuals into groups made people think of themselves and others in terms of "us" and "them," and was sufficient to induce them to behave differently towards ingroup and outgroup members.

Importantly, these findings were at odds with the scientific understanding of the time, which was informed largely by realistic conflict theory (RCT). RCT suggests that conflicts between members of different groups arise from competition over scarce resources (Sherif, 1967), but, as noted above, these were conspicuously absent from the minimal group paradigm. The provocative nature of the findings that emerged from the minimal group studies inspired a large body of research that attempted to examine alternative explanations for the mere categorization effect (Diehl, 1990; Rabbie et al., 1989). At the same time, these early findings informed the further development of SIT. After a series of publications in which Tajfel introduced the concept of social identity, and explained how the minimal group studies pointed to the fact that people sometimes behave as group members rather than as individuals (Tajfel, 1974, 1975, 1978a, 1978b, 1978c), he formulated SIT together with his Bristol colleague, John Turner, presenting it as "a theory of intergroup conflict" (Tajfel and Turner, 1979; see also Tajfel, 1982).

BASIC PRINCIPLES

The concept of social identity is defined as "that part of an individual's self-concept which derives from his knowledge of his membership of a social group (or groups) together with the emotional significance attached to that membership" (Tajfel, 1974: 69). The main aim of SIT is to understand and explain how people can come to adopt and behave in terms of such social (rather than personal) identities. When do people think of themselves in terms of "we" instead of "I"? Why is it important to know whether others can be seen as representing "us" or "them"? How does this impact upon our feelings, thoughts, and behaviors? SIT tries to answer these questions, by pointing to the implications of social identity for the perceptions and behaviors of individuals, and examining the way in which this impacts on social relations between individuals and groups.

The basic principles of the theory address three main issues. First, they describe the *psychological processes* that explain how people's social identities are different from their personal identities. Second, they distinguish between different *strategies* people can use to derive a positive social identity. And third, they specify the key *characteristics of the social structure* that determine which of these strategies is most likely to be used in any given case.

Psychological processes

Social categorization is the process through which separate individuals are clustered into groups. Social categorization is seen as a common and functional psychological process that provides a way of responding to complex social situations. Thinking of individuals in terms of a limited number of social categories provides a way of organizing socially relevant information, and helps in the process of both understanding and predicting behavior. When individuals are categorized into the same group, they are thought to share some central group-defining feature, which distinguishes them from others who do not possess this feature (Tajfel, 1978a). For instance, just as different pieces of furniture

in a room can be classified as tables or chairs, so people in a school can be classified as students or teachers. As a result of such classifications, we tend to focus on similarities between individuals within the same category, and see them as interchangeable elements that share some representative common characteristics (e.g., a specific profession, religion, or national citizenship). At the same time, we accentuate differences between individuals who are classified into different categories (e.g., psychologists or economists), as a way of clarifying the meaning of the situation (Tajfel and Wilkes, 1963; Tajfel, 1978a, 1978b, 1978c). Thus, when people are categorized into groups, they come to be seen in terms of characteristic group features that define their social identities (economists use mathematical models), while neglecting individual traits which define their uniqueness (this particular economist interviews people about their emotions).

Social comparison is the process through which characteristic group features are interpreted and valued. Because there is no objective standard that enables us to assess the worth of different groups, we tend to decide whether a group is "good" or "bad" at something, by comparing the characteristics (e.g., traits, attitudes, behaviors) that are seen to define them to the characteristics ascribed to other groups (Tajfel, 1978b, 1978c). Thus, in parallel to interpersonal comparisons that may help determine individual worth (Festinger, 1954), groups and their features can also be evaluated by comparing them with other groups and their defining features (see also Levine and Moreland, 1987). For instance, sociologists may see themselves as relatively more "scientific" than historians, but as less "scientific" than physicists. The constellation of different group traits and how these compare to the traits of most other groups in that context determines the social status or perceived prestige of that group. Where social categorization determines how individuals are classified into groups, social comparisons define the ways in which each group is distinguished from relevant other groups.

Social identification speaks to one key reason why groups of people are different from object categories: the fact that the *self* can also be seen as belonging to a social group (Tajfel, 1974, 1978a, 1978b). That is, just as pieces of furniture can be categorized as chairs or tables, so individuals can be socially categorized as men or women. And just as the comparison between chairs and tables leads to the conclusion that tables are generally larger than chairs, so the comparison between men and women leads to the conclusion that men are generally taller than women. But what makes social categories different from object categories is the process of social identification: the realization that the self is included in some social categories, and excluded from others. It is impossible, for instance, to categorize and compare men and women without realizing that one of these categories includes the self. Thus, when specific features are associated with a social group, or when these features are valued in a certain way, the process of social identification determines how this reflects upon the self. This can either imply that the self is identified with that group and presumably shares its characteristic features, or lead to the conclusion that the self is distinct from that group and its features. Importantly, social identification not only refers to the *cognitive awareness* that one can be included in a particular group, but also incorporates the *emotional significance* of that group membership for the self (Tajfel, 1974, 1978a, 1978b). To the extent that people care about the groups they belong to (i.e., ingroups), they will be motivated to emphasize the distinct identity of those groups, and to uphold, protect, or enhance the value afforded to those groups and their members. On occasion (under conditions specified by the theory – see below), this may occur at the expense of other groups and their members (i.e., outgroups; Tajfel, 1978c).

Identity management strategies

SIT conceives of processes of social categorization, social comparison, and social

identification as ways in which people actively define social reality and their own position relative to others in that reality (Tajfel, 1975, 1978b). The theory explicitly addresses the dynamic nature of social situations (Tajfel, 1974). Because the self is implicated in the group, people are motivated to emphasize and secure the ways in which their group is positively distinct from other groups (Tajfel, 1978c). Those who belong to what are generally seen as privileged groups (e.g., doctors, lawyers) should be motivated to enhance and retain their positive social identity. Clearly, though, many groups in society are devalued (e.g., the unemployed, migrants), and so the question of how members of these groups set about defining themselves positively becomes theoretically very important.

In this regard, a core feature of SIT is that it specifies different strategies that members of low-status social groups can adopt in order to address their situation and try to improve the value of their social identity. This in turn has profound implications for the ways in which members of high-status groups tend to protect and secure the current standing of their group (Tajfel, 1978c; Turner and Brown, 1978).

Individual mobility is an individual-level strategy whereby people may seek to escape, avoid, or deny belonging to a devalued group, and seek instead to be included in (or attempt to "pass" as a member of) a group of higher social standing (Tajfel, 1975). For instance, second-generation migrants may seek to escape their plight by pursuing an education or career that allows them to be seen as a member of a high-status professional group (e.g., as a lawyer) rather than as a member of an ethnic group that has low status in society. Individual mobility thus involves emphasizing how the *individual* self is different from other group members. But even if this helps improve the status of specific group members, and furnishes them with a more positive social identity, individual mobility does not benefit (or even address) the standing of their ingroup as a whole.

Social creativity refers to a process whereby group members seek to redefine the intergroup comparison by representing the ingroup in terms of positive rather than negative characteristics. This can be achieved in at least three ways: first, by focusing on other dimensions of intergroup comparison (e.g., comparing groups in terms of friendliness instead of material wealth); second, by including other groups in the comparison (e.g., as when migrants compare their economic success to those in their country of origin, rather than to others in the host society); and third, by changing the meaning of low-status group membership (e.g., as in the assertion that "black is beautiful"). Again, while this type of strategy is likely to help people cope with their devalued position in society, and may thereby benefit psychological wellbeing, it does not actually address or change the status quo or improve the ingroup's objective outcomes.

Social competition refers to a strategy whereby group members engage in forms of conflict designed to *change* the status quo (in ways that individual and social creativity do not). For instance, workers may seek to improve their work conditions or standard of living through union action, homosexuals may gain marriage or adoption rights due to political pressure, or women may improve their career prospects by pushing for the introduction of equal rights legislation. Social change can be contrasted with individual mobility in the sense that it explicitly addresses the situation of the group as a whole, where individual mobility seeks only to improve the social standing of particular individuals. Social change is also different from social creativity as it focuses on achieving changes to objective or material outcomes, whereas social creativity focuses primarily on a cognitive reinterpretation of the status quo. Importantly too, social competition involves concerted collective action oriented towards the achievement of change. Here groups compete with each other for superiority on a shared value dimension that reflects directly upon their mutual social standing.

Socio-structural characteristics

The final issue that is addressed in SIT concerns the conditions under which people are predicted to pursue these different strategies for social identity maintenance or improvement. Here the theory proposes that the way in which people respond to their group's circumstances depends on perceived characteristics of the prevailing social structure. Obviously, laws and cultural traditions or objective (im)possibilities may pose constraints on which forms of social identity improvement can be realistically achieved. However, the socio-structural characteristics to which SIT refers are explicitly defined as *subjective belief structures* regarding the opportunities ("cognitive alternatives" to the status quo) and valid motives for individual and group status improvement (Tajfel, 1975).

Permeability of group boundaries relates to the subjective belief that it is possible for individuals to act as independent agents within a given social system. Importantly, the main concern here is not whether it is possible to shed central or defining group characteristics, such as one's gender or ethnic origins. In cases as these, a full change of group membership is clearly not feasible. What matters in this context, is whether people feel that *by virtue of these defining group characteristics*, their access to other groups (and the material and psychological outcomes associated with them) is restricted, or whether they believe they can achieve a position in society that reflects their individual merit, regardless of their group membership. If they perceive group boundaries to be permeable they will be more inclined to pursue individual mobility as an attractive and viable strategy. On the other hand, if boundaries are perceived to be impermeable, then individuals are likely to feel more bound to their group. In this case, attempts at status improvement will tend to be pursued at the group level.

Stability of group status refers to the notion that some differences between groups are seen as fluid and as subject to change, while other differences tend to be regarded as more enduring and stable over time. To the extent that groups differ in concrete properties or abilities that are needed to achieve certain outcomes (e.g., physical endurance of male versus female athletes) differences between them are typically seen as inherent and unlikely to change. In many situations, however, people feel that differential group outcomes reflect historic developments (e.g., unequal access to educational opportunities) or are the result of chance occurrences (e.g., differential numerical representation) rather than some essential or inherent difference in group value or deservingness. To the extent that status differences are thought to be stable, individuals with a devalued social identity are less likely to pursue strategies of social change and instead will be inclined to pursue a strategy individual mobility. However, if this is not possible due to impermeable group boundaries, then they should prefer to pursue social creativity strategies.

Legitimacy of current status relations refers to moral convictions that determine the *motivation* to change, where permeability and stability indicate perceived *opportunity* for change. Legitimacy can refer to a number of different aspects of a given social situation. In the first instance, the basis for including individuals in groups can be seen to be illegitimate in being based on incorrect assumptions about group-defining characteristics. This might arise, for instance, if a woman's gender rather than her professional qualifications were used to infer and ascribe her professional identity (e.g., so that she is treated as a secretary rather than as a manager). Status relations between groups can be also seen as illegitimate if important status-defining features (e.g., academic ability, professional competence) are selectively ascribed to some groups (e.g., men) rather than others under conditions where there is no objective indication that this is valid. Finally, the ascription of higher value to certain group characteristics can be seen as illegitimate. This might occur, for example, if the task-oriented leadership behaviors

typically displayed by men are valued more highly than the socio-emotional leadership shown by women. Each of these forms of illegitimacy may motivate people to seek ways to rectify the current state of affairs. Importantly, this is not only the case for those who personally suffer from unjust treatment. Group members who benefit from unearned advantage may also be motivated to correct past injustice and support or sponsor the cause of those suffering from an unfair social system. This is the case, for instance, when senior white men in a company champion measures intended to improve career opportunities for young women or for members of minority ethnic groups.

Core predictions

Building on the above principles, a number of core predictions were subsequently systematized within Tajfel and Turner's (1979) definitive statement of SIT (see also Tajfel and Turner, 1986). These predictions have received empirical support across a range of intergroup contexts and applied settings in studies using a number of different research methodologies (for a recent overview, see Haslam et al., 2010a).

1   To the extent that individuals internalize a group membership as a meaningful aspect of their self-concept, they will strive to make favorable comparisons between this group and relevant outgroups, in order to achieve or maintain a positive social identity.
2   As a result, social categorization can be sufficient to engender intergroup discrimination and intergroup conflict (i.e., in the absence of a conflict of interest over the division of resources or material outcomes, for example, as a result of historical antagonism).
3   The search for positive social identity may take different forms (*individual mobility, social creativity, social competition*), depending on consensual definitions of social reality that pertain to socially shared justifications (*legitimacy of group and individual outcomes*) and perceived *cognitive alternatives* to current status relations (*permeability of group boundaries and stability of status relations*).

THEORETICAL DEVELOPMENTS

After developing different elements of his thinking in the early 1970s (Tajfel, 1974, 1975), Tajfel contributed three chapters to the volume he edited in 1978 to more systematically describe the societal context and psychological mechanisms that inspired SIT (Tajfel, 1978a, 1978b, 1978c). These chapters can be seen to represent the intellectual origins of SIT. The further specification of its basic principles and mechanisms and how these impact on social behavior is laid down in the 1979 chapter (Tajfel and Turner, 1979). As suggested above, because this integrates and systematizes the theory's core ideas, this is typically cited as the definitive source of this theoretical perspective (at the time of writing this chapter has been cited more than 3,000 times). Another comprehensive overview of the central ideas underlying SIT and their implications for intergroup relations was provided by Henri Tajfel, in his 1982 *Annual Review of Psychology* chapter.

Over the years, however, several researchers have reported finding SIT ambiguous or unclear (e.g., Elsbach and Kramer, 1996; Jost and Elsbach, 2001; see also Brown, 2000). This in turn inspired others to clarify theoretical statements in an attempt to redress any misunderstandings, and to clarify exactly which predictions can (and cannot) be derived from the theory (e.g., Ellemers et al., 2003; Haslam and Ellemers, 2005; McGarty, 2001; Turner, 1985, 1999; Turner and Reynolds, 2001). As well as this, a number of researchers and different research groups have been involved in the development and extension of SIT in the process of testing and refining its core ideas.

Indeed, as a result of the large volume of research that it has inspired, various accounts of the theory can be found in the literature. These often emphasize specific aspects of the theory (e.g., the importance of positive distinctiveness) or focus on aspects of the theory relating to a specific concern (e.g., the determinants of collective action). Because of their variety, these developments can easily confuse those interested in learning about SIT, who – seeking an overview that addresses these different issues and connects the large body of recent empirical research to a single underlying framework – find it difficult to identify a core resource. While we would not claim the current contribution to constitute a comprehensive or definitive overview of developments relating to SIT, in the following we aim to summarize the main issues and concerns that have emerged over the years, to help explain how these both derive from and inform SIT.

Testing the core predictions

Early work in the 1970s was mainly concerned with development of the theory. Different researchers tested the validity of the mere categorization effects associated with the minimal group paradigm and the explanation provided to account for these effects. Some of this work addressed questions that were raised concerning the methodology and measures that had been used in the original minimal group studies. This resulted in a series of studies that examined what happens when people are categorized according to different criteria (e.g., shared preferences, similar abilities, random assignment, Billig and Tajfel, 1973; Tajfel and Billig, 1974). It also led a body of research that explored different ways of assessing ingroup favoritism and which looked at the effects of using different outcome allocation methodologies (Bornstein et al., 1983; Turner, 1983).

An important conclusion from these efforts (see Bourhis et al., 1997; Diehl, 1990; Turner, 1999) was that the effects obtained in the minimal group studies could be reliably reproduced when methods specifically excluded the possibility that they arose from (a) material gains and instrumental benefit (as suggested by instrumental or economic approaches to intergroup relations), (b) a conflictual history (as suggested by sociological approaches to intergroup conflict), or (c) personality or a priori individual differences (as suggested by psychodynamic and other personological approaches).

However, one unintended consequence of these initial concerns and the discussions they generated was to evoke an impression that the minimal group studies and the effects they demonstrate constitute the essence of SIT. It is quite common, then, for secondary sources to suggest that the theory revolves around the idea that identification with a social group leads to ingroup bias, so that the ingroup is inevitably favored over any outgroup. Indeed, those who focus on the minimal group studies are often tempted to think that mere categorization is the main process, and that ingroup favoritism is the main outcome with which the theory is concerned. This is incorrect. Instead, the minimal group studies should be seen as an empirical demonstration of the importance of social identities for behavior that served as a catalyst for subsequent theorizing about nature and consequences of those identities. Thus, although the minimal group studies played a critical role in the conception and development of SIT, their significance lies in their historical status as a stimulus for the new way of thinking about the behavior of people in groups that SIT subsequently articulated, not in the fact that they capture the theory's core ideas.

The key problem with thinking that SIT is "all about" mere categorization and ingroup favoritism, is that this characterization (a) fails to recognize that the theory distinguishes between a number of different identity-enhancement strategies (i.e., not only social competition but also individual mobility and social creativity), (b) neglects the fact that the core predictions of SIT refer to specific boundary conditions, and (c) overlooks the moderator variables that are predicted to impact on people's use of particular identity-enhancement strategies. Indeed, other studies that addressed the more complex and dynamic nature of intergroup relations in more messy or real-life situations, were in many ways far better suited to illustrate and test the core predictions made by SIT. These studies

examined evidence for the pursuit of different identity management strategies under specific conditions (e.g., Ellemers, 1993; Lalonde and Silverman, 1994; Reicher and Haslam, 2006). And, in line with SIT's predictions, they found that depending on relevant socio-structural conditions people pursue strategies of either individual mobility, social creativity, or social competition (for overviews see Bettencourt et al., 2001; Brown, 2000).

Interdependence and bias

Following on from early discussion of the minimal group findings, some of the work in the 1980s still sought to compare the effects of realistic conflict and outcome interdependence with those that arose from mere categorization (e.g., Rabbie et al., 1989). In a way, this is an issue that can never be resolved, as this work has convincingly shown that mere categorization effects as well as interdependence and conflict can each in and of themselves promote displays of ingroup favoritism. In another way, though, this demonstration also indicates that this debate *has* been resolved. For the fact that outcome interdependence can promote ingroup favoritism and intensify intergroup conflict does not make it less interesting that (as SIT suggests) mere categorization has similar effects, even in the *absence* of such alternative or additional concerns. Indeed, while the minimal group studies demonstrated that social categorization can be *sufficient* to raise ingroup favoritism, it was never argued that categorization is *necessary* for such effects to emerge. Thus, over the years, it has come to be generally understood that SIT complements realistic conflict theory and that social identity concerns can interact with instrumental concerns. At the same time it is acknowledged that SIT was not intended, and should not be seen, to displace an interest in realistic causes of intergroup conflict (Brown, 2000).

Self-esteem

During the 1990s the emphasis in social identity research shifted from demonstrating the basic phenomenon of intergroup differentiation, to examining *why* people might be motivated to act in ways that reflected a group-level definition of self rather than an individual-level definition. These efforts related to the so-called "self-esteem hypothesis," advanced by Hogg and Abrams. This proposed two corollaries of SIT's core predictions: (a) successful intergroup discrimination should elevate self-esteem, and (b) depressed or threatened self-esteem should promote intergroup discrimination (Abrams and Hogg, 1988; Hogg and Abrams, 1990). Research then examined the role of self-esteem both as a cause and as an effect of positive intergroup differentiation.

Unfortunately, much of this work was plagued by conceptual and methodological imprecisions, leading to empirical studies that generated a range of seemingly inconsistent results (for overviews, see Brown, 2000; Long and Spears, 1997; Turner, 1999). For instance, personal-level or enduring self-esteem measures were used to assess shifts as a result of intergroup differentiation. Arguably, however, the predicted effects should emerge on more situationally defined measures that tap into group-based and collective-level aspects of self-esteem (Crocker and Luhtanen, 1990; Rubin and Hewstone, 1998). In fact, it was noted that individual- and group-level processes may even interact in that those who hold high levels of personal self-esteem should be most inclined to defend and uphold the status of their group when it is devalued by others (Long and Spears, 1997). Furthermore, it was pointed out that the self-esteem hypothesis focuses on intergroup differentiation as the primary response to social identity threat, while failing to acknowledge that alternative (individual-level as well as group-level) strategies may be used to (re)establish a positive social identity (Turner, 1999). Thus, although research efforts only found mixed support for the self-esteem hypothesis, over the years

different scholars noted that both the formulation of these corollaries and the way in which they had been tested were flawed (Long and Spears, 1997; Rubin and Hewstone, 1998; see also Turner, 1999).

The self-esteem hypothesis was also criticized for more metatheoretical reasons. In particular, Turner (1999) voiced a concern that to focus on self-esteem as the critical factor in intergroup differentiation could lead to a misrepresentation of the theory's core ideas. For if positive ingroup differentiation is seen to be driven by self-esteem needs, then this may be taken as implying that, in situations where the individual self is connected to others in a group, intergroup behaviors primarily serve individual-level motives (e.g., associated with outcome interdependence). This emphasis on individual-level instrumental needs and concerns is at odds with the group-level approach that is central to the SIT (and metatheory). Specifically, it goes against the theory's concern to provide a cognitive and psychological account of social perception and behavior that goes beyond individual-level rational choices or cost–benefit analysis.

The lack of evidence for a simple relation between self-esteem and intergroup differentiation also led to the proposal of alternative motives and additional factors that might determine when, how, and why intergroup differentiation is expressed. Reduction of uncertainty about the position of the self in relation to others was proposed as a broader motive that may induce identity enhancement as well as other responses (Hogg and Abrams, 1993; Hogg and Mullin, 1999). Furthermore, researchers demonstrated the force of social reality constraints in determining how and when people express their internal convictions about the worth of their group (see Ellemers et al., 1999a, for an overview).

Importantly, while these developments can be seen as further specifications of SIT and its predictions, they do not really propose novel or contradictory ideas (instead, they essentially flesh out one aspect of the theory's original formulation). That is, the motive of uncertainty reduction is fully consistent with the original idea that people use social categorizations as a basis for imbuing novel situations with meaning. Likewise, the notion that members of consensually devalued groups may refrain from making public claims of ingroup superiority is in line with the original idea that existing power or status differences between groups determine which identity management strategies are likely to prove feasible.

Self-categorization

During the 1980s and early 1990s, Turner and his colleagues (Turner, 1982, 1985; Turner et al., 1987, 1994) set out to elaborate on the cognitive processes that underpin group- rather than individual-level conceptions of self and others. These developments led to the formulation of *self-categorization theory* (SCT). This theory further specifies and extends Tajfel's original proposition that social categorization serves as a basis for understanding and responding meaningfully to complex social situations (Tajfel, 1969). However, SCT focuses more explicitly on the fact that social categorizations can be made at different (nested) levels of inclusiveness or abstraction (e.g., Londoner, UK citizen, European) and that the same individual can be included in multiple categories on the basis of different (cross-cutting) criteria (e.g., as a woman, as a German, as a psychologist). Within SCT, these ideas were formalized in terms of a number of core assumptions and related hypotheses (Turner, 1985). In particular, these asserted that:

1 The self is represented cognitively in terms of self-categories that can be defined at different levels of abstraction. These range from exclusive self-categorization in terms of personal identity (e.g., "I, Christine") to inclusive self-categorization in terms of broad social identities (e.g., "us Dutch").
2 The formation of self-categories is partly a function of the metacontrast between interclass and intraclass differences. This means that people will tend to define themselves in terms of a particular self-category (e.g., as Dutch) to the extent that the differences between members of that category on a given dimension of judgment are perceived to be smaller than the differences between members of that category and others that are salient in a particular context (e.g., Belgians, Germans).
3 Metacontrast also partly determines the internal structure of self-categories and the prototypicality of particular category exemplars. This means that a person's capacity to represent and embody a given social category increases to the extent that the differences between them and other members of that category are smaller than the differences between them and members of other categories that are salient in a particular context.
4 The salience of a particular self-category leads to the accentuation of perceived intraclass similarities and interclass differences. In this way, patterns of assimilation and contrast reflect the relative interchangeability of category exemplars in relation to a currently salient self-categorization.

Additional mechanisms of category accessibility and normative fit were also specified in order to explain and predict which self-categorization is most likely to be used in a given situation (Oakes, 1987; Turner, 1985). In explaining how individuals come to define themselves in terms of one social identity rather than another, SCT thus emphasizes the importance of a range of contextual contexts that elements contexts that serve to make one particular social self-categorization more meaningful than others. The principles it articulates also predict that the same objective group membership will be experienced differently, depending on the groups with which an ingroup is compared and the situation in which these comparisons are made (Haslam and Turner, 1992).

Importantly too, SCT introduced the concept of *depersonalization*, to describe the psychological process through which people come to perceive the self as an interchangeable exemplar of a social category, rather than as a separate individual with unique traits (i.e., so that the self is defined in terms of social identity rather than personal identity; Turner, 1982). Moreover, the theory also specifies the behavioral consequences of depersonalization, arguing that it is this process that makes group behavior possible. In particular, Turner (1982) hypothesized, and early studies confirmed, that depersonalization is a basis for group cohesion, interpersonal attraction, and social cooperation (e.g., Hogg, 1992; Hogg and Turner, 1985). Later work also elaborated upon the implications of self-categorization and depersonalization for processes of stereotyping (Oakes and Turner, 1990; Oakes et al., 1994), social influence (Turner, 1991), and leadership (Turner and Haslam, 2001). More recently still, research has shown that self-categorization processes play a key role in the expression of personal identity (Turner and Onorato, 1999; Turner et al., 2006).

In sum, building upon SIT's original concern with processes of social categorization and its clarification of the importance of social identity for intergroup behavior, SCT provides a more detailed and more general account of the psychological mechanisms that lead individuals to define themselves in terms of particular group memberships and to act in terms of those group memberships. Although they have somewhat different foci and contain a number of quite different hypotheses, SIT and SCT thus share a range of key assumptions, particularly in metatheoretical terms. Accordingly, in recent publications, the two theories are often presented as complementary theoretical frameworks, and treated as component parts of an integrated *social identity approach* or perspective (e.g., Reicher et al., 2010; Turner and Reynolds, 2001).

Conceptualizations and measures

Around the turn of the century it became clear that, as it had evolved, empirical research had incorporated a number of different conceptualizations and measures of social identity as a construct. Accordingly, a number of researchers set out to compare these different conceptualizations and to examine their theoretical and empirical implications. A first source of confusion in this respect was that some researchers used the term "social identity" to refer to the *content* of characteristics typically associated with a particular social group (i.e., social identity *value*), while others used the same term to indicate the extent to which an individual subjectively perceived the self to be *included* in the group (i.e., social identity *strength*). To some extent increased awareness of this potential confusion served to resolve it, as more careful and consistent use of terminology (e.g., positive/negative social identity versus level of social identification) certainly helps to clarify what is meant by any given reference.

Nevertheless, this more specific use of terminology also raised further conceptual questions about the "essence" or "true" definition of social identity (e.g., Kreiner and Ashforth, 2004; Mael and Tetrick, 1992; Van Dick, 2004). Do people's social identities have such profound implications because of the cognitive inclusion of the self in the group, or because of their experience of affective commitment to the group? It is probably no surprise that this question became important, given the many different ways in which researchers had been drawing on social identity and SCTs. This contributed to the view that the (cognitive) process of self-categorization (the focus of SCT) should be seen as distinct from (subjective feelings of) social identification (addressed in SIT).

To some extent this difference in emphasis simply reflects the difference in the two theories' explanatory aims and foci, as indicated above. Importantly, though, a careful reading of the original theoretical formulations reveals that *both* SCT and SIT address the way in which cognitive and affective components of social identity are *connected*, as the cognitive awareness of a certain category membership is a necessary precondition that has to be met before one's group membership can acquire any emotional significance. In line with this point, the original definition quoted above

(Tajfel, 1974) makes it clear that the knowledge and emotional significance of group membership *together* comprise social identity. Nevertheless, because this conceptualization incorporates these different aspects, they can be considered either as separate components or as comprising a single overarching construct. Accordingly, it has been convincingly argued, and shown, that – depending on the issue under concern – it can be useful to focus either on specific components of social identity or to address social identity as a broader multidimensional construct (Ellemers et al., 1999b; Hogg, 1992; Leach et al., 2008; Ouwerkerk et al., 1999).

Treating identification as a multidimensional construct also made it possible to further specify different forms of identity threat that ensue when different identity components are not aligned (Branscombe and Doosje, 2004; Branscombe et al., 1999a; Doosje et al., 1989). For instance, people may experience social identity threat when they feel emotionally involved with a group in which they are not cognitively included, or vice versa. This is likely to happen, for instance, in the process of transitioning to another group during individual mobility, or when internal definitions of self do not correspond to the way in which one is treated by others. Additionally, this work has made it clear that both cognitive and emotional components of identification have to exceed a minimum threshold level before individuals can be expected to respond in terms of their group-based identity. That is, while those who are cognitively included but not emotionally involved in the group may act as group members when individual-level concerns make it attractive for them to do so (e.g., for self-presentational reasons, or for fear of social sanctions), people who are both cognitively included and emotionally involved in the group tend to define the self as group members more consistently across different multiple situations and contexts (Barreto and Ellemers, 2000; Ellemers et al., 2002).

Treating social identity as an important source of behavioral motivation also raised the issue of how it should be conceptualized in relation to other theoretical models of motivation. Over the years, this meant that a number of different questions were raised by researchers from inside and outside the social identity tradition. Should social identity be seen as an individual difference variable indicating chronic levels of altruism or empathy? Does it indicate different psychological needs stemming from early attachment experiences or cultural variations in how we think of individuals and groups (reflecting levels of individualism versus collectivism)? Does it reflect interpersonal or situational variations in a more generic need to belong? Should it primarily be seen as a (stable) cause of intergroup behavior across different contexts, or as a (situational) effect of specific intergroup comparisons?

Empirical studies that addressed these issues generated an abundance of evidence that the effects of social identification are tied to *specific* groups. Hence, group identification does not simply indicate "need to belong," as people prefer to be included and valued by specific groups rather than by groups in general (e.g., Ellemers et al., 2004b). Likewise, the level of identification with the same group tends to change over time and across social contexts (e.g., Doosje et al., 2002). This speaks against a more stable individual difference or cultural difference approach, and is consistent with SIT's core notion that group identification indicates a person's situational inclination to think and act in terms of a group-level self (i.e., as "us" rather than "I"). Indeed, levels of group identification have been shown to develop and change as part of a recursive process (Branscombe et al., 1999b; Schmitt and Branscombe, 2002) in which initial levels of identification determine how people respond to intergroup situations, and this response in turn intensifies or diminishes feelings of identification. Thus, even if researchers have sought to understand this complex process by administering measures of social identification and addressing simple causal relations at specific points of the recursive cycle (i.e., treating identification either as a cause or as an effect of other responses), it is important to bear in mind that identification was originally defined as a dynamic construct and needs always to be understood in these terms.

Intellectual impact of ideas

SIT can be characterized as a "grand theory." It addresses intrapersonal cognitive mechanisms, interpersonal and intergroup behaviors, and social relations, and connects processes occurring at these different levels of analysis to provide a broad theoretical framework that can help understand a range of phenomena. In our review of the theory, we have tried to convey this complex nature of the theory, and have shown how, after its initial formulation, different aspects were further developed and specified. In this sense, then, the theory is not a fixed number of statements, but represents more of a "living" creature to which different theorists and researchers have each added their embellishments, additions, and refinements over the years.

The broad nature of SIT at the same time can be seen both as a strength and as a weakness. On the one hand, the number of references to SIT in empirical studies clearly attests to its explanatory power, and shows that it can be applied to a range of issues. On the other hand, the fact that the theory cannot be distilled into a simple mantra or summarized in a limited number of simple hypotheses that "always work" (without consideration being given to localized context), implies that the broader constellation of ideas is not easy to test or refute. Indeed, the emphasis on dynamic changes and contextual differences, and the realization that different response patterns may emerge depending on specific circumstances, easily evokes the impression that SIT can be used to explain anything and everything – but only after the fact. At the same time, the pressure to reduce to the

theory to a simple message, (e.g., of the form "social identification leads to intergroup discrimination") has contributed to vulgarized textbook summaries that do violence to the theory's core character.

What then is the added value of SIT? We think the answer to this question lies at least in part in this realization that it is different from many other theories in social psychology. Rather than consisting of a limited set of specific predictions, it represents a particular metatheoretical approach, that provides a unique *perspective* on social cognition and social behavior. That is, the general notion that in addition to the personal level of self-definition people may also self-define at the group level (and can switch between these different levels), helps make sense of a range of phenomena that prove hard to explain in terms only of individual-level psychological mechanisms. Accordingly, SIT opens up the possibility of considering whether a group-level approach can help understand a particular phenomenon, and, if this is the case, provides conceptual tools that can usefully inform and structure this type of analysis.

Importantly, this is not to say that each and every issue in social psychology should be addressed as a group-level problem. If only for reasons of theoretical parsimony, more basic or individual-level explanations should be favored when appropriate. Nevertheless, an important driver for the development and application of SIT was an awareness that researchers are generally far more likely to fall into the opposite trap and overlook the appropriateness of group-level analysis. As Turner and Oakes (1997) observe, social psychology (and psychology more generally) has not suffered from an underemphasis on the psychology of the individual, or a shortage of individual-level theories. Thus, if anything, there seems to be a general tendency in social psychology to explain anything and everything from individual-level mechanisms, thereby neglecting the power of the group to inform and motivate social behavior, and excluding the possibility of the group-level self. A key contribution of SIT has been to redress this balance, and provide researchers with analytical options that have otherwise been lacking.

Social issues and applications

Even though the original social categorization studies were very detached and artificial, the theory these gave rise to was focused explicitly on the task of analyzing and explaining social relations in the world at large. When it was developed, SIT brought together insights from a number of intellectual and research traditions, but nevertheless provided an important new perspective and focus on intergroup relations that was genuinely revolutionary. By examining how specific characteristics of social contexts interact with individual cognitive processes, and explaining the origins and consequences of a conceptualization of self at the group level, the theory spells out a number of important ideas about social psychological functioning that have relevance to a host of situations.

In view of Tajfel's original goal of seeking to understand the emergence of conflict in intergroup relations, SIT's original formulations focused closely on social behavior in situations defined by historical between-group differences in power and status. Nevertheless, the prominence of the minimal group studies and SCT's examination of basic cognitive processes makes it easy to overlook the fact that SIT has often been used to examine interactions occurring between members of real social groups. Over the years, then, researchers have used the theory to help them understand tensions between ethnic, religious, or linguistic groups, and to examine and predict responses to migration, changing labor relations, and the development of group motivation. This work both informed and helped develop SIT as researchers examining various group types under different conditions became aware of specific complexities, moderating variables, and boundary conditions that were relevant to the theory's core predictions.

As such work accumulated, it served to validate SIT's core predictions regarding the conditions under which people would pursue particular self-enhancement strategies and experience different forms of identity threat. This support was found across different types of intergroup comparisons and for various sources of group value (Mullen et al., 1992), such as power, status (Sachdev and Bourhis, 1991), or group size (Simon and Brown, 1987). However, the existence of these real and objective differences between groups in social contexts also made it clear that it is not always realistic (or desirable) for group members to strive to make positive intergroup comparisons. When the achievement of positive intergroup comparisons is not feasible or would unduly antagonize an outgroup, group members may seek distinctiveness from other groups (Mummendey and Schreiber, 1983, 1984), especially when the differences between them are ambiguous or ill-defined (Jetten and Spears, 2004; Jetten et al., 2004). For similar reasons, maintenance of current intergroup distinctions may be preferred over attempts to enhance or improve one's social identity (Ellemers et al., 1992; Scheepers and Ellemers, 2005).

While the theory addresses each level of analysis in turn to analyze and understand the psychological mechanisms relevant to individual- and group-level behavior, research has simultaneously considered the effects of intra- and inter-group comparisons. This work has indicated that an awareness of intragroup heterogeneity and individuality does not necessarily exclude the formation of a common group identity (Doosje et al., 1999; Hornsey and Jetten, 2004; Postmes and Jetten, 2006; Rink and Ellemers, 2007; Simon, 1992), and that a positive social identity depends as much on evaluations of the self by others in the group as on evaluations of the group by other groups (Branscombe et al., 2002; Smith et al., 2003; Tyler and Blader, 2000). Finally, the examination of more complex and rich intergroup situations has made it clear that people do not always engage with the intergroup comparisons that others invite them to make, but actively define and carve out their social identity from multiple dimensions (Derks et al., 2007), sources of group value (Leach et al., 2007), and group identities (Spears and Manstead, 1989) available to them in real life.

While all of these insights represent important extensions of social identity theorizing, all remain consistent with the theory's core premises. Moreover, the "grand" nature of SIT and its explicit consideration of social contextual variables in addition to individual-level cognitive processes, makes obvious its relevance to a broad variety of social problems and issues in organizational behavior (see also Ashforth and Mael, 1989; Haslam, 2004; Haslam and Ellemers, 2005; Haslam et al., 2003; Hogg and Terry, 2000). In this vein, most recently, insights from SIT have been used to examine *individual* wellbeing and performance, documenting the implications of people's social identities for the experience of stress, work outcomes, and physical and mental health (e.g., Haslam and Reicher, 2006; Haslam et al., 2009; Scheepers and Ellemers, 2005).

SIT has also proved useful when it comes to understanding *interpersonal* behavioral alignment, for instance when participating in political activities or social protest (Reicher, 1987; Simon and Klandermans, 2001; Wright, 2000). Along related lines, the theory has also been used to analyze and improve *intergroup relations*, for instance by considering interethnic conflict or gender discrimination in terms of social identity concerns (Ellemers et al., 2004c; Ryan and Haslam, 2007).

Intertwined with much of this work, SCT has also been used to further our understanding of important *group dynamics*, particularly those relating to social influence and group polarization (e.g., Levine et al., 2000, 2005; Postmes et al., 2005; Smith et al., 2003; Turner, 1991; Wetherell, 1987). In organizational contexts, this has also led to important insights into processes of leadership (Haslam et al., 2010b; Hogg and Van Knippenberg, 2004; Reicher et al., 2005; Turner and Haslam, 2001), communication

(Postmes, 2003), and work motivation and group performance (Ellemers et al., 2004a).

CONCLUSION

In this chapter we have outlined the core ideas and basic premises of SIT. Supported by a large body of empirical evidence, this theory argues for the importance of distinguishing between social psychological processes at individual, interpersonal, group, and intergroup levels. We have noted that over the years, different accounts or selected ideas have been seen as representing the essence of the theory, resulting in a number of controversies, updates, refinements, and expansions. For some, this may create an impression that theory is overly complex and controversial, and hence not particularly useful as an analytical framework. Against this conclusion, however, it is apparent that SIT has inspired, and been supported by, a large body of important empirical studies and has informed a range of important theoretical developments in social psychology and cognate disciplines. This work makes it clear that the theory provides an analysis of complex social phenomena that can help researchers understand and address a number of important social issues and problems.

Importantly too, because SIT is addressed to the process of *social change*, it also points to the fact that social psychological processes do not simply contribute to the reproduction of the status quo, but also help to bring about change in the world. In this sense too, the theory is progressive and optimistic, rather than conservative and pessimistic. Instead of being reductionist and deterministic, it offers scope for interventions that can help improve individual wellbeing, group interactions, and social relations.

Thus, SIT is more than a metaphor: it provides a different way of thinking about individuals and groups, with an explicit emphasis on the impact of social contextual factors. Even though this makes the theory "grand"

and complex, a careful consideration of its core ideas makes it clear that a relatively limited set of ideas and variables can help understand a range of phenomena across different situations and settings. In order to appreciate this point, there is much to be gained by going back to Tajfel and Turner's original writings (recently reprinted in Postmes and Branscombe, 2010) and enjoying their ideas and lucid explanations first-hand.

REFERENCES

Abrams, D. and Hogg, M.A. (1988) Comments on the motivational status of self-esteem in social identity and intergroup discrimination. *European Journal of Social Psychology*, 18, 317–334.

Ashforth, B. and Mael, F. (1989) Social identity theory and the organization. *Academy of Management Review*, 14, 20–39.

Barreto, M. and Ellemers, N. (2000) You can't always do what you want: Social identity and self-presentational determinants of the choice to work for a low status group. *Personality and Social Psychology Bulletin*, 26, 891–906.

Bettencourt, B.A., Charlton, K., Dorr, N. and Hume, D.L. (2001) Status differences and in-group bias: A meta-analytic examination of the effects of status stability, status legitimacy, and group permeability. *Psychological Bulletin*, 127, 520–542.

Billig, M. and Tajfel, H. (1973) Social categorization and similarity in intergroup behavior. *European Journal of Social Psychology*, 3, 27–52.

Bornstein, G., Crum, L, Wittenbraker, J., Harring, K., Insko, C.A. and Thibaut, J. (1983) On the measurement of social orientations in the minimal group paradigm. *European Journal of Social Psychology*, 13, 321–350.

Bourhis, R.Y., Turner, J.C. and Gagnon, A. (1997) Interdependence, social identity and discrimination. In R. Spears, P.J. Oakes, N. Ellemers and S.A. Haslam (eds), *The Social Psychology of Stereotyping and Group Life*, pp. 273–295. Oxford: Blackwell.

Branscombe, N.R. and Doosje, B. (eds) (2004) *Collective Guilt: International Perspectives*. Cambridge: Cambridge University Press.

Branscombe, N., Ellemers, N., Spears, R. and Doosje, B. (1999a) The context and content of identity threat. In N. Ellemers, R. Spears, and B. Doosje (eds), *Social Identity: Context, Commitment, Content*, pp. 35–58. Oxford: Blackwell.

Branscombe, N.R., Schmitt, M.T. and Harvey, R.D. (1999b) Perceiving pervasive discrimination among African-Americans: Implications for group identification and well-being. *Journal of Personality and Social Psychology*, 77, 135–149.

Branscombe, N., Spears, R., Ellemers, N. and Doosje, B. (2002) Effects of intragroup and intergroup evaluations on group behavior. *Personality and Social Psychology Bulletin*, 28, 744–753.

Brown, R. (2000) Social identity theory: past achievements, current problems and future challenges. *European Journal of Social Psychology*, 30, 745–778.

Crocker, J. and Luhtanen, R. (1990) Collective self-esteem and ingroup bias. *Journal of Personality and Social Psychology*, 58, 60–67.

Derks, B., Van Laar, C. and Ellemers, N. (2007) Social creativity strikes back: Improving low status group members' motivation and performance by valuing ingroup dimensions. *European Journal of Social Psychology*, 37, 470–493.

Diehl, M. (1990) The minimal group paradigm: Theoretical explanations and empirical findings. *European Review of Social Psychology*, 1, 263–292.

Doosje, B., Branscombe, N.R., Spears, R. and Manstead, A.S.R. (1989) Guilty by association: When one's group has a negative history. *Journal of Personality and Social Psychology*, 75, 872–886.

Doosje, B., Spears, R. and Ellemers, N. (2002) Social identity as both cause and effect: The development of group identification in response to anticipated and actual changes in the intergroup status hierarchy. *British Journal of Social Psychology*, 41, 57–76.

Doosje, B., Spears, R., Ellemers, N. and Koomen, W. (1999) Group variability in intergroup relations: The distinctive role of social identity. *European Review of Social Psychology*, 10, 41–74.

Ellemers, N. (1993) The influence of socio-structural variables on identity enhancement strategies. *European Review of Social Psychology*, 4, 27–57.

Ellemers, N., Barreto, M. and Spears, R. (1999a) Commitment and strategic responses to social context. In N. Ellemers, R. Spears, and B. Doosje (eds), *Social Identity: Context, Commitment, Content*, pp. 127–146. Oxford: Blackwell.

Ellemers, N., De Gilder, D. and Haslam, S.A. (2004a) Motivating individuals and groups at work: A social identity perspective on leadership and group performance. *Academy of Management Review*, 29, 459–478.

Ellemers, N., Doosje, B. and Spears, R. (2004b) Sources of respect: The effects of being liked by ingroups and outgroups. *European Journal of Social Psychology, 34,* 155–172.

Ellemers, N., Doosje, E.J., Van Knippenberg, A. and Wilke, H. (1992) Status protection in high status minorities. *European Journal of Social Psychology, 22,* 123–140.

Ellemers, N., Kortekaas, P. and Ouwerkerk, J. (1999b) Self-categorization, commitment to the group and group self-esteem as related but distinct aspects of social identity. *European Journal of Social Psychology, 29,* 371–389.

Ellemers, N., Platow, M., Van Knippenberg, D. and Haslam, A. (2003) Social identity at work: Definitions, debates, and directions. In A. Haslam, D. Van Knippenberg, M. Platow and N. Ellemers (eds), *Social Identity at Work: Developing Theory for Organizational Practice,* pp. 3–28. London: Psychology Press.

Ellemers, N., Spears, R. and Doosje, B. (2002) Self and social identity. *Annual Review of Psychology, 53,* 161–186.

Ellemers, N., Van den Heuvel, H., De Gilder, D., Maass, A. and Bonvini, A. (2004c) The underrepresentation of women in science: Differential commitment or the Queen-bee syndrome? *British Journal of Social Psychology, 43,* 315–338.

Elsbach, K.D. and Kramer, R.D. (1996) Members' responses to organizational identity threats: Encountering and countering the Business Week rankings. *Administrative Science Quarterly, 41,* 442–476.

Festinger, L. (1954) A theory of social comparison processes. *Human Relations, 7,* 117–140.

Haslam, S.A. (2004) *Psychology in Organizations: The Social Identity Approach,* 2nd Edition. London: Sage.

Haslam, S.A. and Ellemers, N. (2005) Social identity in industrial and organizational psychology: Concepts, controversies and contributions. In G.P. Hodgkinson and J.K. Ford (eds), *International Review of Industrial and Organizational Psychology, 20,* 39–118. Chichester: Wiley.

Haslam, S.A., Ellemers, N., Reicher, S., Reynolds, K.J. and Schmitt, M.T. (2010a) The social identity perspective: An assessment of the impact and trajectory of its defining ideas. In T. Postmes and N. Branscombe (eds), *Rediscovering Social Identity: Core Sources.* New York: Psychology Press.

Haslam, S.A., Jetten, J., Postmes, T. and Haslam, C. (2009) Social identity, health and well-being: An emerging agenda for applied psychology. *Applied Psychology: An International Review, 58,* 1–23.

Haslam, S.A. and Reicher, S.D. (2006) Stressing the group: Social identity and the unfolding dynamics of stress. *Journal of Applied Psychology, 91,* 1037–1052.

Haslam, S.A., Reicher, S.D. and Platow, M.J. (2010b) *The New Psychology of Leadership: Identity, Influence and Power.* London: Psychology Press.

Haslam, S.A. and Turner, J.C. (1992) Context-dependent variation in social stereotyping 2: The relationship between frame of reference, self-categorization and accentuation. *European Journal of Social Psychology, 22,* 251–278.

Haslam, S.A., Van Knippenberg, D., Platow, M. and Ellemers, N. (eds) (2003) *Social Identity at Work: Developing Theory for Organizational Practice.* New York: Psychology Press.

Hogg, M.A. (1992) *The Social Psychology of Group Cohesiveness: From Attraction to Social Identity.* Hemel Hempstead: Harvester Wheatsheaf.

Hogg, M.A. and Abrams, D.A. (1990) Social motivation, self-esteeem and social identity. In D. Abrams, and M.A. Hogg (eds), *Social Identity Theory: Constructive and Critical Advances,* pp. 28–74. London: Harvester Wheatsheaf.

Hogg, M.A. and Abrams, D.A. (1993) Towards a single-process uncertainty-reduction model of social motivation in groups. In M.A. Hogg and D. Abrams (eds), *Group Motivation: Social Psychological Perspectives,* pp. 173–190. New York: Harvester Wheatsheaf.

Hogg, M.A. and Mullin, B.A. (1999) Joining groups to reduce uncertainty: Subjective uncertainty reduction and group identification. In D. Abrams and M.A. Hogg (eds), *Social Identity and Social Cognition,* pp. 249–279. Oxford: Blackwell.

Hogg, M.A. and Terry, D.J. (2000) Social identity and self-categorization processes in intergroup contexts. *Academy of Management Review, 25,* 121–140.

Hogg, M.A. and Turner, J.C. (1985) Interpersonal attraction, social identification and psychological group formation. *European Journal of Social Psychology, 15,* 51–66.

Hogg, M.A. and Van Knippenberg, D. (2004) Social identity and leadership processes in groups. *Advances in Experimental Social Psychology, 35,* 1–52.

Hornsey, M.J. and Jetten, J. (2004) The individual within the group: Balancing the need to belong with the need to be different. *Personality and Social Psychology Review, 8,* 248–264.

Jetten, J. and Spears, R. (2004) The divisive potential of differences and similarities: The role of intergroup distinctiveness in intergroup differentiation. *European Review of Social Psychology, 14,* 203–241.

Jetten, J., Spears, R. and Postmes, T. (2004) Intergroup distinctiveness and differentiation: A meta-analytical investigation. *Journal of Personality and Social Psychology, 86*, 862–879.

Jost, J.T. and Elsbach, K.D. (2001) How status and power differences erode personal and social identities at work: A system justification critique of organizational applications of social identity theory. In M.A. Hogg and D.J. Terry (eds), *Social Identity Processes in Organizational Contexts,* pp. 181–196. Philadelphia: Psychology Press.

Kreiner, G.E. and Ashforth, B.E. (2004) Evidence toward an expanded model of organizational identification. *Journal of Organizational Behavior, 25*, 1–27.

Lalonde, R.N. and Silverman, R.A. (1994) Behavioral preferences in response to social injustice: The effects of group permeability and social identity salience. *Journal of Personality and Social Psychology, 66*, 78–85.

Leach, C., Ellemers, N. and Barreto, M. (2007) Group virtue: The importance of morality vs. competence and sociability in the evaluation of in-groups. *Journal of Personality and Social Psychology, 93*, 234–249.

Leach, C.W., Van Zomeren, M., Zebel, S., Vliek, M.L.W., Pennekamp, S.F., Doosje, B., Ouwerkerk, J.W. and Spears, R. (2008) Group-level self-definition and self-investment: A hierarchical (multi-component) model of in-group identification. *Journal of Personality and Social Psychology, 95*, 144–165.

Levine, J.M., Higgins, T.E. and Choi, H.S. (2000) Development of strategic norms in groups. *Organizational Behavior and Human Decision Processes, 82*, 88–101.

Levine, J.M. and Moreland, R.L. (1987) Social comparison and outcome evaluation in group contexts. In J.C. Masters and W.P. Smith (eds), *Social Comparison, Social Justice, and Relative Deprivation: Theoretical, Empirical and Policy Perspectives,* pp. 105–127. Hillsdale, NJ: Lawrence Erlbaum.

Levine, R.M., Prosser, A., Evans, D. and Reicher, S.D. (2005) Identity and emergency intervention: How social group membership and inclusiveness of group boundaries shapes helping behavior. *Personality and Social Psychology Bulletin, 31*, 443–453.

Long, K. and Spears, R. (1997) The self-esteem hypothesis revisited: Differentiation and the disaffected. In R. Spears, P.J. Oakes, N. Ellemers and S.A. Haslam (eds), *The Social Psychology of Stereotyping and Group Life,* pp. 296–317. Oxford: Blackwell.

Mael, F.A. and Tetrick, L.E. (1992. Identifying organizational identification. *Educational and Psychological Measurement, 52*, 813–824.

McGarty, C. (2001) Social identity theory does not maintain that identification produces bias and self-categorization theory does not maintain that salience is identification: Two comments on Mummendey, Klink and Brown. *British Journal of Social Psychology, 40*, 173–176.

Mullen, B., Brown, R.J. and Smith, C. (1992) Ingroup bias as a function of salience, relevance, and status: An integration. *European Journal of Social Psychology, 22*, 103–122.

Mummendey, A. and Schreiber, H.J. (1983) Better or just different? Positive social identity by discrimination against, or by differentiation from outgroups. *European Journal of Social Psychology, 13*, 389–397.

Mummendey, A. and Schreiber, H.J. (1984) 'Different' just means 'better': Some obvious and some hidden pathways to ingroup favoritism. *British Journal of Social Psychology, 23*, 363–368.

Oakes, P.J. (1987) The salience of social categories. In J.C. Turner, M.A. Hogg, P.J. Oakes, S.D. Reicher and M.S. Wetherell (eds), *Rediscovering the Social Group: A Self-categorization Theory,* pp. 117–141. Oxford: Blackwell.

Oakes, P.J., Haslam, S.A. and Turner, J.C. (1994) *Stereotyping and Social Reality.* Oxford: Blackwell.

Oakes, P.J. and Turner, J.C. (1990) Is limited information processing capacity the cause of social stereotyping? *European Review of Social Psychology, 1*, 111–135.

Ouwerkerk, J.W., Ellemers, N. and De Gilder, D. (1999) Group commitment and individual effort in experimental and organizational contexts. In N. Ellemers, R. Spears and B.J. Doosje (eds), *Social Identity: Context, Commitment, Content,* pp. 184–204. Oxford: Blackwell.

Postmes, T. (2003) A social identity approach to communication in organizations. In S.A. Haslam, D. Van Knippenberg, M.J. Platow and N. Ellemers (eds), *Social Identity at Work: Developing Theory for Organizational Practice,* pp. 81–98. New York: Psychology Press.

Postmes, T. and Branscombe, N.R. (2010) *Rediscovering Social Identity: Core Sources.* New York: Psychology Press.

Postmes, T., Haslam, S.A. and Swaab, R. (2005) Social influence in small groups: An interactive model of identity formation. *European Review of Social Psychology, 16*, 1–42.

Postmes, T. and Jetten, J. (eds) (2006) *Individuality and the Group: Advances in Social Identity.* London: Sage.

Rabbie, J.M., Schot, J.C. and Visser, L. (1989) Social identity theory: A conceptual and empirical critique from the perspective of a behavioral interaction model.

European Journal of Social Psychology, *19*, 171–202.

Reicher, S.D. (1987) Crowd behaviour as social action. In J.C. Turner, M.A. Hogg, P.J. Oakes, S.D. Reicher and M.S. Wetherell, *Rediscovering the Social Group: A Self-categorization Theory*, pp. 171–202. Oxford: Blackwell.

Reicher, S.D. and Haslam, S.A. (2006) Rethinking the psychology of tyranny: The BBC Prison Study. *British Journal of Social Psychology*, *45*, 1–40.

Reicher, S.D., Haslam, S.A. and Hopkins, N. (2005) Social identity and the dynamics of leadership: Leaders and followers as collaborative agents in the transformation of social reality. *Leadership Quarterly*, *16*, 547–568.

Reicher, S.D., Spears, R. and Haslam, S.A. (2010) The social identity approach in social psychology. In M.S. Wetherell and C.T. Mohanty (eds), *The Sage Handbook of Identities*. London: Sage.

Rink, F. and Ellemers, N. (2007) Diversity as a source of common identity: Towards a social identity framework for studying the effects of diversity in organizations. *British Journal of Management*, *18*, S17–S27.

Rubin, M. and Hewstone, M. (1998) Social identity theory's self-esteem hypothesis: A review and some suggestions for clarification. *Personality and Social Psychology Review*, *2*, 40–62.

Ryan, M.K. and Haslam, S.A. (2007) The Glass Cliff: Exploring the dynamics surrounding the appointment of women precarious leadership positions. *Academy of Management Review*, *32*, 549–572.

Sachdev, I. and Bourhis, R.Y. (1991) Power and status differentials in minority and majority group relations. *European Journal of Social Psychology*, *21*, 1–24.

Scheepers, D. and Ellemers, N. (2005) When the pressure is up: The assessment of social identity threat in low and high status groups. *Journal of Experimental Social Psychology*, *41*, 192–200.

Schmitt, M.T. and Branscombe, N.R. (2002) The internal and external causal loci of attributions to prejudice. *Personality and Social Psychology Bulletin*, *28*, 620–628.

Sherif, M. (1967) *Group Conflict and Co-operation: Their Social Psychology*. London: Routledge and Kegan Paul.

Simon, B. (1992) The perception of ingroup and outgroup homogeneity: Re-introducing the intergroup context. *European Review of Social Psychology*, *3*, 1–30.

Simon, B. and Brown, R. (1987) Perceived intragroup homogeneity in minority-majority contexts. *Journal of Personality and Social Psychology*, *53*, 703–711.

Simon, B. and Klandermans, B. (2001) Politicized collective identity: A social psychological analysis. *American Psychologist*, *56*, 319–331.

Smith, H.J., Tyler, T.R. and Huo, Y.J. (2003) Interpersonal treatment, social identity, and organizational behavior. In S.A. Haslam, D. van Knippenberg, M. Platnow and N. Ellemers (eds), *Social Identity at Work: Developing Theory for Organizational Practice*, pp. 155–172. London: Psychology Press.

Spears, R. and Manstead, A.S.R. (1989) The social context of stereotyping and differentiation. *European Journal of Social Psychology*, *19*, 101–121.

Tajfel, H. (1969) Cognitive aspects of prejudice. *Journal of Social Issues*, *25*, 79–97.

Tajfel, H. (1974) Social identity and intergroup behaviour. *Social Science Information*, *13*, 65–93.

Tajfel, H. (1975) The exit of social mobility and the voice of social change. *Social Science Information*, *14*, 101–118.

Tajfel, H. (1978a) Interindividual behaviour and intergroup behaviour. In H. Tajfel (ed.), *Differentiation Between Social Groups: Studies in the Social Psychology of Intergroup Relations*, pp. 27–60. London: Academic Press.

Tajfel, H. (1978b) Social categorization, social identity, and social comparison. In H. Tajfel (ed.), *Differentiation Between Social Groups: Studies in the Social Psychology of Intergroup Relations*, pp. 61–76. London: Academic Press.

Tajfel, H. (1978c) The achievement of group differentiation. In H. Tajfel (ed.), *Differentiation Between Social Groups: Studies in the Social Psychology of Intergroup Relations*, pp. 77–98. London: Academic Press.

Tajfel, H. (1982) Social psychology of intergroup relations. *Annual Review of Psychology*, *33*, 1–39.

Tajfel, H. and Billig, M. (1974) Familiarity and categorization in intergroup behavior. *Journal of Experimental Social Psychology*, *10*, 159–170.

Tajfel, H., Billig, M.G., Bundy, R.F. and Flament, C. (1971) Social categorization and intergroup behaviour. *European Journal of Social Psychology*, *1*, 149–177.

Tajfel, H. and Turner, J.C. (1979) An integrative theory of intergroup conflict. In W.G. Austin and S. Worchel (eds), *The Social Psychology of Intergroup Relations*, pp. 33–47. Monterey, CA: Brooks/Cole.

Tajfel, H. and Turner, J.C. (1986) The social identity theory of intergroup behavior. In W.G. Austin, and S. Worchel (eds), *The Social Psychology of Intergroup Relations*, pp. 7–24. Monterey, CA: Brooks/Cole.

Tajfel, H. and Wilkes, A.L. (1963) Classification and quantitative judgement. *British Journal of Psychology*, *54*, 101–114.

Turner, J.C. (1982) Towards a cognitive redefinition of the social group. In H. Tajfel (ed.), *Social Identity and Intergroup Relations*, pp. 15–40. Cambridge: Cambridge University Press.

Turner, J.C. (1983) Some comments on the measurement of social orientations in the minimal group paradigm. *European Journal of Social Psychology, 13*, 351–367.

Turner, J.C. (1985) Social categorization and the self-concept: A social cognitive theory of group behaviour. In E.J. Lawler (ed.), *Advances in Group Processes, 2*, 77–122. Greenwich, CT: JAI Press.

Turner, J.C. (1991) *Social Influence*. Milton Keynes: Open University Press.

Turner, J.C. (1999) Some current issues in research on social identity and self-categorization theories. In N. Ellemers, R. Spears, and B. Doosje (eds), *Social Identity: Context, Commitment, Content*, pp. 6–34. Oxford: Blackwell.

Turner, J.C. and Brown, R.J. (1978) Social status, cognitive alternatives and intergroup relations. In H. Tajfel (ed.), *Differentiation Between Social Groups: Studies in the Social Psychology of Intergroup Relations*, pp. 201–234. London: Academic Press.

Turner, J.C. and Haslam, S.A. (2001) Social identity, organizations and leadership. In M.E. Turner (ed.), *Groups at Work: Advances in Theory and Research*, pp. 25–65. Hillsdale, NJ: Erlbaum.

Turner, J.C., Hogg, M.A., Oakes, P.J., Reicher, S.D. and Wetherell, M.S. (1987) *Rediscovering the Social Group: A Self-categorization Theory*. Oxford: Blackwell.

Turner, J.C. and Oakes, P.J. (1997) The socially structured mind. In C. McGarty and S.A. Haslam (eds), *The Message of Social Psychology: Perspectives on Mind in Society*, pp. 355–373. Malden MA: Blackwell.

Turner, J.C., Oakes, P.J., Haslam, S.A. and McGarty, C.A. (1994) Self and collective: Cognition and social context. *Personality and Social Psychology Bulletin, 20*, 454–463.

Turner, J.C. and Onorato, R. (1999) Social identity, personality and the self-concept: A self-categorization perspective. In T.R. Tyler, R. Kramer and O. John (eds), *The Psychology of the Social Self*. Hillsdale, NJ: Erlbaum.

Turner, J.C. and Reynolds, K.J. (2001) The social identity perspective in intergroup relations: Theories, themes and controversies. In R.J. Brown and S. Gaertner (eds), *Blackwell Handbook of Social Psychology, Vol. 4: Intergroup Processes*, pp. 133–152. Oxford: Blackwell.

Turner, J.C., Reynolds, K.J., Haslam, S.A. and Veenstra, K. (2006) Reconceptualizing personality: Producing individuality through defining the personal self. In T. Postmes and J. Jetten (eds), *Individuality and the Group: Advances in Social Identity*, pp. 11–36. London: Sage.

Tyler, T.R. and Blader, S.L. (2000) *Cooperation in Groups: Procedural Justice, Social Identity, and Behavioral Engagement*. Philadelphia: Psychology Press.

Van Dick, R. (2004) My job is my castle: Identification in organizational contexts. In C.L. Cooper and I.T. Robertson (eds), *International Review of Industrial and Organizational Psychology, 19*, 171–204. Chichester: Wiley.

Wetherell, M.S. (1987) Social identity and group polarization. In J.C. Turner, M.A. Hogg, P.J. Oakes, S.D. Reicher and M.S. Wetherell (eds), *Rediscovering the Social Group: A Self-categorization Theory*, pp. 142–170. Oxford: Blackwell.

Wright, S.C. (2000) Strategic collective action: Social psychology and social change. In R. Brown and S. Gaertner (eds), *Blackwell Handbook of Social Psychology: Intergroup Processes*, pp. 223–256. Oxford: Blackwell.

46

Self-Categorization Theory

John C. Turner and Katherine J. Reynolds

ABSTRACT

The focus of this chapter is self-categorization theory (SCT). SCT is a theory of the nature of the self that recognizes that perceivers are both individuals and group member, explains how and when people will define themselves as individual and group entities and its implications, and examines the impact of this variability in self-perception ('I' to 'we') for understandings of mind and behaviour. As a result, it has generated a range of distinctive subtheories, hypotheses and findings across a range of significant areas in social psychology. This chapter outlines central steps in the theory's development, its unique contribution and the impact of its ideas with specific details provided in the areas of social influence (more recently, leadership and power) and individuality (e.g. personal self, personal self-perception, personal self-beliefs). In the final section, the way SCT can be applied to better understand and solve a range of social issues is highlighted. A specific example is provided of how core SCT ideas are being implemented in secondary schools with the aim of improving school outcomes (e.g. learning, bullying, wellbeing). It is our view that through an understanding of SCT (and related work) it is possible to appreciate the important and distinctive contribution of social psychology to other areas of psychology and cognate fields.

INTRODUCTION

This chapter is focused on self-categorization theory (SCT), its development, distinctive ideas, intellectual contribution and applicability to social issues. Given that the founder of SCT (the first author of this chapter) was a cofounder of social identity theory (SIT) with Henri Tajfel, there is much that these theoretical perspectives co-contribute to understanding and debates in social psychology. To appreciate what is distinctive about SCT it is necessary to some degree to examine aspects of SIT (see also Haslam and Ellemers, Chapter 45, this volume). As far as possible, though, this chapter will focus on SCT, acknowledging where relevant overlaps and common themes. This chapter can only provide an overview of core points. There are other more detailed accounts of the beginnings and contribution of SCT (e.g. Turner, 1987a, 1996; Turner and Oakes, 1989, 1997; Turner and Reynolds, 2010; Turner et al., 1987, 1994).

The proponents of both SIT and SCT are vocal in arguing that social psychology must acknowledge the functional interdependence of mind and society in its theorizing about the nature of mental processes (Turner and Oakes, 1997). People live, work and act in a socially structured system, where there are group-based regularities of perception, cognition and conduct and this reality has psychological consequences. SIT and SCT capture the socially embedded, situated, shared, social, group-located properties of human beings. This view contrasts with other approaches that reduce the working of the mental system to general (individual) psychological properties (e.g. information processing and memory systems) or the asocial (social environment-free) nature of the individual perceiver (e.g. personality, biology).

Building on the work of Lewin, Asch, Sherif and others it is argued that human beings are both individuals and group members, that they have personal and group aspects. Both theories argue that the psychological nature of individuals (e.g. the self, mind, cognition, information processing, memory, behaviour) has to be apprehended within an understanding of groups and membership in society. SIT and SCT define the proper and defining task of social psychology as studying and proposing theories consistent with the interplay between psychological functioning and the socially and/or culturally shared properties of human life (e.g. What does social life tell us about the mind? How does the mind make social interaction and society possible? How is the mind affected by social life?; see Turner and Oakes, 1997 for a more detailed discussion).

Theories in social psychology offer an approximation of reality that can be further investigated, elaborated and refined to provide a consistent explanation of the class of phenomena of interest. Effectiveness and parsimony typically are the dimensions on which theories are assessed. Thinking about SCT in this way the phenomena of interest is to understand, explain and predict how people come to think, feel and act as a psychological group and, importantly, the circumstances when this will occur and its consequences.

Through understanding the cognitive definition of the self, *how* and *when* perceivers define themselves and others as individual and group entities, SCT explains when a group is 'a group'. The theory is at the centre of explaining the way the individual mind makes possible, and is impacted by, the fact that human beings are social animals (Turner and Oakes, 1997). SCT aims to be an effective and parsimonious theory of the self-process which contributes to explaining the functioning of the mind and behaviour.

There is a large body of work that has investigated the workings of the theory and derivations in an immense range of issues in the field (and beyond) including intergroup relations and prejudice, the nature of the group and the psychological basis of group and collective processes, social influence processes such as conformity, group polarization, minority influence, consensualization and leadership, crowd behaviour, social cooperation, group cohesion, social cognition (stereotyping, categorization), collective action and social change, the nature of the self, communication and language, and, latterly, the personal self, individuality and personality processes. In fact, many chapters in this volume engage with fundamental SCT concepts and ideas. It is also the case that implications of this theory extend beyond social psychology to psychology at large (and especially the problem of cognition) and the other social sciences (Haslam et al., 2010; Postmes and Branscombe, 2010; Reynolds et al., 2010). So how did this theory develop, why is it important and what is its impact on a range of social issues? We now turn to explore and explain the theory in more detail starting with the history of its development and then its core aspects and contribution.

SCT: PERSONAL NARRATIVE OF ITS DEVELOPMENT

In this section, the early beginnings of SCT are described. More formally, the development of the contemporary theory broadly can be summarized as involving three main steps (see also Turner and Reynolds, 2010). The first, was the distinction between personal identity and social identity and the hypothesis that it is social identity that is the basis of group behaviour. The second step, which occurred while Turner was at the Institute of Advanced Studies (IAS) at Princeton in 1982–1983, involved both an elaboration of the personal-social identity distinction to levels of self-categorization (e.g., individual, subgroup, superordinate), and the formalization of the theory (Turner, 1985). The third step, conducted mainly in the 1980s and 1990s, involved a systematic program of research on the self-concept and stereotyping. What emerged was a more detailed and integrated understanding of the nature of the self and its implications for the foundation of cognition (Oakes et al., 1994; Turner and Oakes, 1997; Turner and Onorato, 1999; Turner et al., 1994).

Social identity and the psychology of the group

The story of SCT begins in 1971 when John Turner started his PhD under Henri Tajfel's supervision at the University of Bristol in the UK. Like SIT, SCT begins with the minimal group studies published in that year, in the first volume of the *European Journal of Social Psychology*. The minimal group data had shown that social categorization into groups, in isolation from and unconfounded by all the variables normally thought to cause group formation and negative intergroup attitudes (interpersonal interdependence, history of conflict), was sufficient for discrimination. Individuals assigned more of a resource to others who were in the same group as themselves (ingroup) compared to members of a group which did not include them (outgroup). Furthermore, participants acted in ways that maximized the difference in allocations between the two groups even at the expense of allocating maximum resources to

the group to which they belonged. SIT was concerned with explaining why subjects discriminated in the minimal group paradigm. SCT addressed a different question: Why did subjects identify with the minimal groups at all and act in ways that reflected that these group identities mattered to them?

On Turner's arrival at Bristol in September 1971, Tajfel's explanation of the minimal group findings had progressed from there being a 'generic norm' of ingroup favouritism or ethnocentrism (Tajfel, 1972). In a French textbook on social categorization, Tajfel had offered a new explanation of the findings. In this chapter, Tajfel introduces and defines the concept of social identity, outlines that groups provide their members with a positive social identity and that such positivity derives through establishing a valued distinctiveness for their own groups compared with other groups. Turner's first task was to flesh out this social identity and positive ingroup distinctiveness explanation of the minimal group data. He reviewed the role of social categorization in intergroup relations and the findings of the minimal group paradigm, producing a review paper written before the end of 1971. This paper was presented by Turner at the Small Group Meeting of the European Association of Experimental Social Psychology (EAESP) on Intergroup Relations held at Bristol in February 1972. The paper, which was eventually published with additional data in 1975, showed how a systematic account of minimal and other forms of intergroup discrimination and ingroup bias (in terms of a process he called social competition), could be provided using social identity processes and not necessarily conflict of interests (e.g. Sherif, 1967).

The new analysis was summarized by Tajfel as the 'social categorization-social identity-social comparison-positive distinctiveness' sequence (Tajfel, 1974, 1978). The sequence provided a theoretical framework for understanding intergroup behaviour. Social categorizations defined people's place in society and through being internalized into the self, together with their emotional and value significance, provided people with social identities. Through social comparison on dimensions associated subjectively with perceivers' social values these social identities could be evaluated and provide valued positive distinctiveness for one's group (compared with other groups). The motive for positive distinctiveness could lead, under certain conditions, to ingroup favouring intergroup responses. At no time was it argued that ethnocentrism was universal or that social categorization automatically and inevitably produced ingroup bias or favouritism. If this were the case there would be no need for the development of theory to explain when such outcomes were more or less likely to define social relationships (Tajfel and Turner, 1979).

Examination of these processes was an important focus of work during the early to mid seventies at the University of Bristol. During this time, Tajfel proposed a continuum of human behaviour framed at one end by interpersonal behaviour and at the other by intergroup behaviour (Tajfel, 1978). Tajfel referred to the continuum as 'acting in terms of self' versus 'acting in terms of group'. The shift along the continuum is associated with distinct forms of social behaviour. At the interpersonal end, it is expected that there should be variability in behaviour towards ingroup and outgroup members. As the social situation nears the intergroup end, though, attitudes and behaviour become more group-like or uniform.

The continuum was important because it highlighted that group behaviour and social identity were expected only under selected conditions and motivated more work to be done specifying the social psychological conditions that lead to group rather than individual attitudes and actions. Variables such as the permeability, legitimacy and the stability of status differences between groups in a particular social system were identified as shaping whether a situation would be characterized by consensual intergroup or interpersonal behaviour. The continuum also allowed Tajfel and Turner to make a distinction between acting as an individual and acting as a group member while at the same time recognizing that people were capable of both. Work on social categorization could be further developed to specify what this meant psychologically. It was this task that became the focus of SCT.

So while Tajfel and Turner continued their work (with others) on social identity, intergroup relations and social change, that culminated in a series of influential papers (e.g. Tajfel, 1978; Tajfel and Turner, 1979; Turner and Brown, 1978), Turner from 1978 onwards also focused on the psychological processes that underpin movement along the behavioural continuum. At a conference in 1978 at the University of Rennes in France held by the European Laboratory of Social Psychology (LEPS) he presented a paper entitled 'Towards a cognitive redefinition of the social group' which explained ideas on the psychological group (Turner, 1982). Turner developed a causal analysis of the psychological process related to movement along the interpersonal–intergroup continuum. He suggested that an individual's self-concept comprised definitions of self that included both personal identity and social identity. Social identity (self-definition in terms of social category memberships) was explicitly distinguished from personal identity (self-descriptions in terms of personal and idiosyncratic attributes) and situational variations in the self-concept were recognized with the idea that social identity could function at the relative exclusion of personal identity.

Turner proposed a theory of group behaviour in terms of an 'identity mechanism' to explain movement along the interpersonal–intergroup continuum. He hypothesized that as people defined themselves and others as members of the same category, they would self-stereotype in relation to the category and tend to see themselves as more alike in terms of the defining attributes of the category. This process is refered to as depersonalization. It was argued that it is 'the cognitive redefinition of the self – from unique attributes and individual differences to shared social category memberships and associated stereotypes – that mediates group behaviour' (Turner, 1984: 528). It explains how individuals can psychologically be group members and 'reinstates the group as a psychological reality and not merely a convenient label for describing the outcome of interpersonal processes' (Turner, 1984: 535). This identity mechanism transforms the interpersonal–intergroup continuum into a cognitive, social psychological theory of the group (Turner, 1985, Turner et al., 1987; Turner et al., 1994).

Having applied for and received funding in 1978 for the new theory, Turner and his research group (Wetherell, Smith, Reicher, Oakes, Hogg, Colvin in roles as research assistants, PhD students or both) started applying these fundamental ideas in various areas. Initially the focus was social influence (conformity, group polarization, influence within the crowd), psychological group formation and the distinction between personal and group-based attraction (trying to show how group cohesion was a function of social identification rather than interpersonal attraction), and the problem of the salience of social categories.

Levels of self-categorization and formalization of the theory

While Turner was at IAS Princeton (1982–1983) he conceptualized further the categorization processes at work in personal identity and social identity. The focus was on the workings of self-categorization processes and the cognitive grouping of the self as being similar to some class of stimuli in contrast to some other class of stimuli. Ideas by Rosch (e.g. 1978) and others were particularly useful in thinking about processes of class inclusion and levels of inclusiveness. The personal–social identity distinction was reformulated as levels of self-categorization where people can define or categorize themselves at different levels of abstraction; for example, at the interpersonal level (where self is defined as a unique individual relative to others available for comparison), at the

intergroup level (where self is defined as being a group member in contrast to a relevant outgroup), and at the superordinate level (where self is defined as a human being in contrast to other lifeforms). Self-categorizations at levels less inclusive than the individual person are also possible (e.g. intrapersonal comparisons within defining the personal self; for example, Reynolds and Turner, 2006). A central idea is that lower-order self-categories were formed *inter alia* from social comparisons within higher-order ones and higher-order ones were formed *inter alia* on the basis of lower level ones (for more detail see Turner et al., 2006).

As part of the theory's development it was necessary to address the issue of what determines which identity emerges in a given situation (e.g., personal identity or social identity and the specific content of these). It was in Oakes' PhD on the salience of social categories, that Oakes and Turner addressed this issue (Oakes, 1987). Bruner's (1957) analysis of categorization and perception was adapted to correspond to the social domain. Bruner argued that 'all perceptual experience is necessarily the end product of a categorization process' (1957: 124). He held a functional view of categorization where the determinants of cognitive accessibility were a function of contextual factors and the current goals, needs and purposes of the perceiver. He used the formula of 'relative accessibility × fit' to describe the conditions under which a stimulus was captured by a category and given meaning by the perceiver. The aim was to provide the perceiver with the information they needed to make sense of a stimulus and at the point when they needed to know it.

In this SCT work on salience, Oakes and Turner originally defined normative fit as the degree to which perceived similarities and differences between group members correlated with the social meaning of group memberships and in a direction consistent with such meaning of the group identities (e.g. it is expected that men and women differ in relation to independence and dependence and that the pattern of interaction in the given situation between men and women is consist-ent with men being independent and women being dependent; Oakes, 1987). Another aspect of salience was comparative fit. Defining comparative fit also was related to another project where Wetherell and Turner, in Wetherell's PhD, were developing a social identity explanation of group polarization (Wetherell, 1987). While at Princeton, Turner was trying to provide a quantitative principle that would allow some way of explaining why groups would polarize as a function of individuals' pretest views on any issue in any given context. The aim was to predict which person or position would become prototypi-cal (representative, or most defining of the group) and when that prototype would polar-ize or not. Turner succeeded with the devel-opment of the metacontrast principle (Turner, 1985; Turner and Oakes, 1986, 1989).

The principle states that a collection of individuals tend to be categorized as a group to the degree *inter alia* that the perceived dif-ferences between them are less than the per-ceived differences between them and other people (outgroups) in the comparative con-text. As an example, in a given situation men will be categorized as independent and women as dependent when the differences between women and men in relation to this dimension are greater than those amongst the men and amongst the women available for comparison. Furthermore, any specific person or position tends to be seen as more proto-typical of the group as a whole to the degree that the perceived differences between that person and other ingroup members are less than the perceived differences between that person and outgroup members.

Using principles of accessibility (based on Bruner) and fit (comparative and normative) it is possible to explain which of many iden-tities will guide perception and behaviour in any given context. The central insight is that if the meaning given to a situation (including the self) is an outcome of categorization proc-esses that are inherently comparative, then self-categories also are infinitely variable, contextual and relative.

Revisiting the self-concept and stereotyping

A direct implication of the SCT analysis is that a self-category could not be stored as a fixed, cognitive structure in some mental system before it was used waiting to be acti-vated (as Turner along with many others had thought originally). It became clear that basic understandings of the functioning of the cog-nitive system (e.g. memory, perception, information processing, stereotyping) and the self-concept (e.g. core and working self) had to be revisited.

The ideas at this time were facilitated by the work of Tajfel, Bruner and Rosch, but also Medin and Barsalou who argued that categories are expressions of theories and knowledge that explain how things go together ('meaning-making'; for example, Medin and Wattenmaker, 1987) and arguments against concepts as fixed mental models (e.g. Barsalou, 1987; see Oakes et al., 1994; Turner and Reynolds, 2010). Based on SCT it is argued that the variability of self-categories is central to how the perceiver (as an individual and group member) responds in a world that also is variable and dynamic. Which group becomes salient for people, when, and its associated content or meaning, changes as a function of interactions between individuals and groups and the dynamic nature of such interactions. Shifts in self-categorization and the content of group-based judgments of one-self and others (e.g. stereotyping) reveals how self-categories are oriented to reality in which there are both individuals and groups in con-tinuous dynamic interaction.

As an example of this point let us consider a person's stereotypes that men are independ-ent and women are dependent. These stereo-types have to be understood within the broader intergroup relationship between men and women in society and shared understandings of that relationship. At times this intergroup relationship and social comparison as 'males' compared to 'females' will be particularly salient shaping people's social identity and attitudes and behaviours in a given situation.

It is also the case that a fixed stereotype formed and stored as 'women are dependent' and 'men are independent' will not serve the perceiver well in the face of changes in the relationship between men and women in society. To be functional for the perceiver the cognitive process needs to be able to represent new and emerging understandings of intergroup relations and be responsive to social change processes. If this were not the case the cognitive system would be impoverished and not very adaptive to its environment.

Along these lines, research conducted at this time in the theory's evolution demonstrated that stereotypes are not rigid and erroneous but reflect perceptions of group relations from the perceiver's (possibly variable) vantage point. Likewise, one's self-concept (personal and collective) is flexible and responsive to contextual stability and variability. It became clear as expected that different self-categories can become salient (e.g., myself as an individual, woman or Australian) and the content of a particular category can change as a function of the salient comparative context (Australians compared to Americans/Australians compared to Chinese) and ongoing change (e.g., the historically evolving nature of what it means to be Australian).

To summarise this phase of theoretical development, then, it is argued that the self-category is a variable judgment formed on the basis of categorization-in-context. A person brings to a situation relatively enduring knowledge about the self (personal and collective), and this information is used as a psychological resource in a given situation. This knowledge, in interaction with contextual factors, then produces a particular self-categorization and associated attitudes and behaviours. It is also the case that this knowledge (one's perceiver readiness) can be updated as a function of current self-categorizations and the accessibility of certain knowledge (and its meaning) can change as a result of the same processes.

To bring the points highlighted in the above narrative together it is possible to summarize the core theoretical developments in SCT as follows;

1   As with SIT it is argued that humans are not merely individuals and neither are our minds. Individuals, groups and intergroup relations exist. Human beings are both individuals and group members and therefore have both personal identity and social identity. Furthermore, based on SCT the psychological depersonalization of the self in terms of social identity produced 'group behaviour' and emergent group processes (e.g. influence, cooperation, cohesiveness). Conversely, defining oneself in terms of an idiosyncratic personal identity, in terms of individual differences from others and distinctive personal attributes, produces 'individual behaviour'.

2   People can define or categorize themselves at different levels of abstraction. It is possible to define oneself as an individual, as a member of particular groups in contrast to others and as a member of higher-order more inclusive groups. More inclusive self-categories define what is socially negotiated and affirmed as being valued, appropriate and right. At different times in different situations we define the self in different ways and such variation in the relative salience is seen as normal and ever-present.

3   Salience explains the way a particular situation (that includes the self) is categorized and given 'meaning'. The way the situation is categorized and understood by the perceiver will determine both self-perception and behaviour. Salience is a function of an interaction between the perceiver's readiness to use a self-category in a given instance and the fit of that self-category to the apprehended stimulus reality.

These three ideas in combination summarize core aspects of SCT (see Turner, 1987a). We now turn to outline the way these ideas are impacting in two specific areas: social influence, which includes work on leadership and power; and individuality, which includes work on personal identity and personality processes.

SCT: ITS IDEAS AND INTELLECTUAL HISTORY

Given the volume of work that speaks to the intellectual contribution of SCT to the field, in this section the focus will be on out-lining in more detail two areas only: social influence and individuality. Social influence is an area that was a focus for initial work in SCT that has been extended to provide a new analysis of leadership and power (e.g. Turner, 1991; 2005; Turner and Haslam, 2001; Turner et al., 2008). Social influence itself is at the centre of social psychology with many significant theories in the field addressing the scientific study of how people come to influence one another affecting their atti-tudes, affect and actions. A more systematic consideration of personal identity, individu-ality and personality processes is an emerg-ing area of inquiry (over the last 5 years or so) where the scope and relevance of SCT currently is being investigated (e.g. Reynolds and Turner, 2006; Reynolds et al., 2010; Turner et al., 2006). There is also a funda-mental connection and interplay between these two areas. It is argued that it is through social identity processes and associated social influence (from others who are similar and 'like us') that group norms, values and beliefs can come to affect those individuals who define themselves in terms of those groups. This work, then, examines more closely the interplay between the group and the individual person.

SCT and social influence

To engage with the analysis of social influ-ence offered by SCT, it is necessary to recog-nize the way the categorization process is understood within this theory and in particu-lar the workings of the metacontrast princi-ple. To reiterate, all things being equal, a collection of individuals (stimuli) tend to be categorized as a group (cognitively placed into the same class) to the degree that the perceived differences between them are less than the perceived differences between them and other people (outgroups) in the context of interest.

A number of studies have demonstrated how a psychological group emerges using

these principles of categorization (see Haslam and Turner, 1992). Hogg and Turner (1987), for example, showed that when people were organized into mixed-sex groups (men and women) or same-sex groups (men-only or women-only), individuals were more likely to define themselves in terms of gender and to accentuate their similarity to those of the same gender in the mixed-sex settings as opposed to when only men or women were present (see also Oakes et al., 1991).

When people are considered to be in the same class of stimuli ('us' rather than 'them') they are cognitively grouped as similar per-ceivers confronting the same stimulus situa-tion. This similarity leads people to tend to agree; it also creates an expectation that they ought to agree and respond in the same way (in reactions, judgement, attitudes, behav-iour) and motivates people to bring about such agreement. In terms of explaining more specifically how 'others' come to affect one's own attitudes and behaviour, the stages are summarized by Turner (1987b) as follows:

1 Individuals define themselves as members of a distinct social category.
2 They learn or develop the appropriate, expected, desirable behaviours that are correlated with category membership, and differentiate it from other categories (e.g. the stereotypical norm).
3 They assign the norms and attributes of the category to themselves (internalization) through the process of depersonalization and self-stereo-typing.
4 Their behaviour therefore becomes normative as their category membership becomes more salient.

Internalization is critical to the emergent social norms having an impact on one's atti-tudes and behaviour (see also Kelman, 1958, 2006) and is affected by the degree to which individuals consider themselves psychologi-cally to be members of the particular group.

Haslam et al. (1999) provide one demon-stration of aspects of these processes showing that it is precisely through social identity that idiosyncratic views become socially organ-ized and consensual. Participants were asked to reflect on their social category membership as Australians (social identity condition) or to focus on their uniqueness from others (personal identity condition) and completed a checklist identifying words typical of people from Australia before and after a group interaction phase. This manipulation of social identification did result in participants indicating that their national identity was more important to them in the social identity compared with the personal identity condition. There also was evidence that participants defined themselves in terms of the social category membership. In the social identity condition (and especially postinteraction), there was greater consensus on the attributes that defined the category of Australian, as well as the emergence of different content to describe the stereotypical attributes of the category.

Turner (1987b, 1991) also argued that subjective validity, certainty, competence, correctness and so on (e.g. what is considered factual and accurate), is a direct function of similar others in the same stimulus situation being understood to agree with one's own response. It is this point that transformed understandings of informational and normative influence into the one process of referent informational influence (Turner, 1991). Because other ingroup members are viewed as similar to oneself, they become a valid source of information and a testing ground for one's own views on relevant dimensions. Under these conditions, other group members can come to have an impact on one's own thoughts, attitudes and behaviours. It is this process of social influence that is important in explaining how others 'like us' play an important role in shaping the psychology of the person. Both certainty and uncertainty are related to the degree to which 'similar others' are perceived to agree or disagree with one's own response and are an outcome of the workings of the categorization process.

Turner (1987b, 1991) outlines a range of strategies to address situations where there is disagreement with others defined as being 'similar' including (a) changing our views in line with ingroup opinion, (b) attempts to influence other ingroup members to adopt a

different stance through processes of mutual influence, (c) recategorization of ingroup members as being outgroup and (d) clarification of the stimulus situation (i.e. ensuring that reference is being made to the same thing; David and Turner, 1996, 1999; McGarty et al., 1994; Turner, 1991). It is argued that it is only within a shared ingroup framework that differences in perspective (e.g. criticism, new ideas, deviance) can be resolved through discussion, clarification and mutual influence. Through these processes ingroup members can shape each others' norms, values and beliefs in significant ways (re)defining 'who we are' and 'what we do'.

Much of the empirical work on these social influence processes has focused on showing not just that ingroup members are more influential than outgroup members but that the definition of who is included in the ingroup and who is excluded is a dynamic outcome of the workings of the categorization process (Haslam et al., 1992). One example of this point concerns shifts in levels of inclusiveness where hitherto subgroups are recategorised in relation to a higher-order superordinate ingroup along with associated empathy, trust, co-operation, positivity and all the other qualities that follow perceptions of self-other similarity and being 'ingroup'. Who is included in the 'ingroup' and who is excluded can be redefined shifting both the 'meaning' of the group (its defined content and norms) and who has opportunities for influence within the group. Extremists, for example, within a group can gain or lose influence as a function of the outgroup against which the ingroup defines itself (e.g. Haslam and Turner, 1995).

In relation to the social influence process, these ideas have been demonstrated, refined and documented, in particular, in the area of minority and majority influence. In the work of David and Turner (e.g. 1996, 1999), there has been a focus on the SCT principles underlying social influence and engagement with both majority and minority influence (see also Moscovici, 1976; Turner 1991).

In one of the David and Turner studies (1996, Study 1), participants (either proconservationists or prologgers) indicated their attitudes to logging prior to an influence message and immediately after the influence attempt and three weeks after the attempt. Participants were presented with a prologging or proconservation message from the 'Friends of the Timber Industry' or 'Friends of the Forest', respectively. The message was presented as representing the majority or minority position within the timber industry or conservationists. In this way, participants received an influence attempt from an ingroup majority, ingroup minority, outgroup majority or outgroup minority.

The findings revealed that when the source of the message was outgroup irrespective of whether it was majority or minority, participants shifted away from the position advocated by the source – there was not social influence. In the ingroup conditions, participants moved in the direction of the source in both the majority and minority conditions immediately following the influence attempt. In line with Moscovici (1980) the condition that revealed the most long-term shift or change was when the message was attributed to an ingroup minority source. There is additional work showing that as a hitherto outgroup is recategorized as part of a more inclusive ingroup (as a function of the frame of reference shaping the judgements of similarity and difference) it is possible for these members to exert greater influence. The implications of these results for the influence field more broadly are discussed in detail elsewhere (e.g. see David and Turner, 2001; Turner, 1991).

Additional empirical work has investigated the argument that categorization of similarities and differences between stimuli (people) not only leads to the formation of classes (ingroup and outgroup) but defines the relative prototype of the group. There is a hierarchy of relative influence that will follow the hierarchy of members' perceived relative prototypicality: where a specific person (or position) tends to be seen as more prototypical of the group when the perceived differences between the person and other ingroup members is less than the perceived differences between that person and outgroup members. There are direct links between the influence hierarchy and notions of leadership with respect to who will be influential in a group and be able to affect others to willingly engage in certain activities and behaviours. It follows that group members will emerge as leaders (those with the most influence) to the degree that they are perceived as relatively prototypical of the group as a whole (and in ways that fit existing normative expectations with respect to leadership) and that the most prototypical person will tend to be recognized as the leader where such a role is defined.

What has flowed from this analysis of social influence is a fundamentally new understanding of leadership and power (e.g. Haslam et al., 2011; Turner, 2005; Turner and Haslam, 2001; Turner et al., 2008). Leadership within SCT is conceptualized as a group process related to relative influence and power within a group (e.g. Turner and Haslam, 2001; Haslam, 2004). The breakthrough idea is that leadership rests on an individual's ability to be seen as prototypical of a shared social identity and hence will have greater influence as a result of such categorization processes. Influence over other group members becomes possible when leaders are seen as embodying 'who we are' (and in ways that normatively fit expectations of 'our' leaders).

In line with these points, power as the ability to have impact through others also rests on group identity and influence processes (Turner, 2005). It is through social identity processes that leaders are able to get others willingly to exert their will and as such mobilize 'followers' to action to achieve certain 'projects' (including the coercion of those who are not on board). In this SCT analysis group identity and the associated willing support of followers it enables, allows groups to gain the resources they require to achieve their shared goals. These ideas are supported by a range of experimental and field studies which show that ingroup leaders (and those that are more versus less prototypical) have more potential to influence their followers, are perceived as more effective, are trusted more, and are seen as more charismatic (e.g. see Haslam, 2004; Subašic' et al., 2011; van Knippenberg et al., 2004).

People follow leaders because they embody 'us', and define what 'we' think is true and right, and do a better job than the rest of us of expressing what 'we' have in common and what we seek to achieve collectively. There also potentially are individual factors at play, but they exert influence only insofar as they are seen at any time by any given group as representing its identity better than others do. Some leaders are 'identity entrepreneurs' who through engaging in argumentation and political rhetoric seek to maintain their relative prototypicality and their position (e.g. Reicher and Hopkins, 2001). There is also evidence that leaders can attempt to restructure the social context or frame of reference and the definition of the group in ways that make their position more prototypical. Seeking conflict with an outgroup is one such response (e.g. Rabbie and Bekkers, 1978). The same is true when one demonizes, scapegoats and discriminates against a minority (sub)group. Prejudice against a minority can be used to reshape the mainstream identity, put one at the core, and increase one's influence (Turner, 2005; Turner et al., 2008).

Thus understanding leadership as a group process does not deny the capacity of certain leaders to make use of their insights into that process. The point is that leadership is an ability to genuinely influence and it is an outcome of group identity rather than being linked to the preordained life trajectory of any one individual (e.g. Haslam, 2004; Reicher et al., 2005; Turner and Haslam, 2001; Turner, 1991). It is through defining the group identity that leaders are able to position themselves in ways that maximize their influence and impact on 'what we do'. In a more general sense, though, it should be apparent that it is through the construction of definitions of 'who we are' and 'who we are not'

and associated social influence that people's opinion, norms, attitudes and behaviours can become consensualized, coordinated and transformed into collective action.

SCT and individuality

SCT's theoretical analysis of the nature of the self and self-process also has implications for understanding personal identity, individuality and personality processes. The first point is that a key contribution of the SCT is that the social comparative features that define one's social identity in a given context can also be applied to understand one's self-definition as an individual (Haslam et al., 2010; Oakes et al., 1994; Reynolds and Turner, 2006; Turner et al., 2006). A critical idea is that whether impressions, perceptions and judgements of oneself and others are group-based or individuated, depends on the levels of abstraction at which the categorization process operates (which is a function of the goals and motives of the perceiver and the elements of the situation being cognized). Rather than personal identity reflecting the relatively stable and enduring features of an individual, the nature of individuality is forged through categorization and social comparison. This argument means that one's sense of who they are as an individual can vary depending on the social comparative context.

The point to emphasise is that one's values (beliefs, norms, worldviews) are variable and socially mediated and defined by ingroup memberships and relevant social influence processes. Under certain conditions, they also become a referent through which one's distinctiveness from others can be defined and emphasized. The content that is generated to describe personal identity depends on some comparative reference and this can result in different (or the same) self-descriptors being generated depending on the context. In a sense, individual differences can be thought about theoretically in this framework as *relative* individual differences because categorization and 'meaning' involves comparison and contrast (Onorato and Turner, 2004; Turner and Onorato, 1999).

Examining these arguments is complex because the aim is to develop a detailed theoretical analysis of the nature of the self-process (e.g. formation, functioning, consequences, (dis)continuity), but, people bring with them their already defined experiences as individual and group members and often function in relatively stable personal and group contexts. Exploring the mechanisms or processes that might explain self-stability and self-change and its consequences in contexts where for most people there is much stability in their group and personal experiences is a challenge. There is much that can be done, though, to investigate these ideas empirically. A central theme of this work to date is to demonstrate the workings of the categorization process in relation to personal identity processes. Along these lines, Mavor, Reynolds and Skorich (2010) have investigated the impact of having people complete self-ratings in contexts where self and others are evaluated alone (intrapersonal context) or in comparison to each other (interpersonal context). At the group level there is evidence that one's own group is viewed as being more variable and heterogeneous when the group is judged alone (an intragroup context) rather than in comparison to a relevant outgroup (an intergroup context; for example, Haslam et al., 1995). It is also the case that personal self-judgments can vary depending on features of the comparative context (e.g. intrapersonal versus interpersonal). Thus if individuals compare themselves to others (interpersonal) rather than making assessments in isolation (intrapersonal), they are more likely to characterize themselves in a dispositional way. The interpersonal context accentuates the similarities and differences between the person and comparison other, leading to a strong sense of one's self-defining features. In this way, the comparative context has an impact on personal self-categorizations, and such categorizations also can be variable depending on the frame of reference (Guimond et al., 2007).

In addition, there is a growing body of evidence showing the impact social identity processes can have on a range of outcomes often associated more with individual-level characteristics and abilities (cognitive performance, wellbeing, self-reported personality). Work on social identity or stereotype threat shows that when one's social identity is salient and the stereotype of the group on the dimension of interest is negative, this can have an impact on cognitive ability (e.g. intelligence) and performance on dimensions relevant to the meaning or stereotype of the group (Steele and Aronson, 1995). Reicher and Haslam (2006) examined the impact of group processes and social identity on a range of more clinical outcomes (e.g. depression, anxiety, paranoia). Williams et al. (2008) have research findings that show that contamination anxiety (an aspect of obsessive–compulsive disorder) is affected not only by the ethnic social category of the respondent (e.g. African American or European American), but by whether the ethnic identity is salient or not when completing the anxiety measure. Bizumic et al. (2009) show that social identity is significantly related to, and mediated the relationship between, organizational factors and individual psychological wellbeing (e.g. self-esteem, positive affect and job involvement, but also negative aspects such as depression, anxiety, loss of emotional control and aggressive and disruptive behaviour).

More specific investigations also are ongoing in relation to personality and people's self-reported sense of what characterizes and defines them as a person (e.g., self-beliefs, the Big Five). In personality theory and research, there is increasing recognition that one's social roles (e.g. daughter, worker) can impact on self-rated personality (Roberts and Donahue, 1994). The norms, expectations and meanings associated with certain roles can become internalized into the self-concept shaping a person's sense of self. An important element of this process is the impact of social interactions and the function of others' expectations, reactions and appraisals in shaping one's own beliefs about oneself (Roberts and Caspi, 2003).

It is argued that the nexus between one's roles, identity and personality could be a force for continuity through, for example, the selection of environments that are consistent with and affirm one's self view (e.g. Swann and Read, 1981). It is also possible that personality may change through exposure to new roles that provide opportunities to engage in novel behaviours. The new roles could be associated with stages of normal adult development (e.g. parenthood, joining the workforce) or actively sought as people seek to improve, develop and reframe their personhood (e.g. more like their ideal image of themselves). Roberts and Mroczek (2008) argue that the findings that personality traits continue to change across the life course highlights the need for further work on the causes and mechanisms responsible for such change.

Based on the self-categorization theory of social identity and social influence, such life-development change (and broader social changes) may well affect one's group memberships and associated social identities. As different people come to be defined as similar to oneself, they offer new opportunities for social influence and the potential for one's theories, expectations and beliefs about oneself and the world can change. The general point is that these social identity changes may well impact on personhood in significant ways (Reicher and Haslam, 2006; Reynolds et al., 2005; Reynolds and Turner, 2006; Turner et al., 2006).

In one preliminary study related to personality processes, participants complete standard personality measures at one point in time (phase 1) and also again under conditions where their non-Aboriginal Australian versus Aboriginal Australian social identity was made salient (phase 2). Results demonstrated that across time (approximately 8 weeks) there is a high level of consistency in participant-reported Neuroticism. There also was evidence of a significant impact of the social identity manipulation and one's identification as a non-Aboriginal Australian in explaining personality assessed at phase 2. Findings suggested that it was the depression

subscale of the Neuroticism measure (Goldberg IPIP-NEO) that was impacted most strongly as a result of non-Aboriginal identity (Reynolds et al., 2011). It was explained that in this condition, comparisons between non-Aboriginal and Aboriginal Australian may have oriented participants towards collective emotions and stereotypes that are related to what has been a negative intergroup comparison in Australia's history (see Branscombe and Doosje, 2004).

These kinds of studies are designed to investigate the SCT analysis of how self-views or self-beliefs are (re)formed and in ways the recognise social identity processes and group factors. There is evidence that categorization and social comparison affects personal identity and that social identity processes can have an impact on cognitive performance, personality and well-being in ways consistent with theory. Such findings (although preliminary) indicate that group processes may well play a role in (trans) forming personhood in particular ways. There also is more work to be done examining the role one's individuality plays in shaping the nature, functioning and success (or otherwise) of groups. All of these questions flow from the theoretical analysis of the nature of the self offered by SCT.

SCT: ITS APPLICABILITY TO SOCIAL ISSUES

As the above discussions highlight, SCT provides novel and important insights into aspects of psychological function that span intergroup relations to individual functioning. Core theoretical ideas, then, have been applied to a range of areas in psychology many of which can be readily related to current social problems and issues. More specific examples are in the areas of antiracism and prejudice reduction (e.g. Gaertner et al., 1989), the dynamics of social stability and social change (e.g. Spears et al., 2002; Subašić et al., 2008; Turner and Reynolds, 2003; Wright et al., 1990), the relationship between attitudes, social norms and behaviour (e.g. Goldstein et al., 2008 ; Terry and Hogg, 1996), organizational (group) processes such as identification, leadership, negotiation and conflict management, and working effectively with diversity (e.g. Ashforth and Mael, 1989; Haslam, 2004; Haslam et al., 2003; Hogg and Terry, 2000; Rink and Ellemers, 2007) and health and wellbeing related outcomes (e.g. Bizumic et al., 2009; Branscombe et al., 1999; Haslam et al., 2009). There is detailed work in these and other areas that outlines the specific contribution of SCT and the implications of the approach. In the space available, one more recent project will be outlined in detail to give a flavour of the way SCT theoretical ideas (and related work) are being used both to understand and define certain social problems and implement novel solution.

Currently, social psychologists at the Australian National University are involved in a joint project with the local Department of Education concerned with applying core SCT ideas to improving school outcomes such as numeracy and literacy, attendance, challenging behaviour and staff and student wellbeing (Bizumic et al., 2009; Reynolds et al., 2007). Based on the arguments outlined above, as people come to define themselves as group members they should be more willing to internalize the norms and values of the group, act in line with these norms and be influenced by those that are most representative of the group. The aim of the project is to affect core aspects of individual functioning (learning, wellbeing, bullying/aggression) through making changes to the norms, values and beliefs that define the school as a whole (superordinate level) and relationships between groups (conflictual or cooperative) within the school environment (subgroup level). It is argued that to the degree these 'interventions' affect one's psychological connection to the school (school identification) and understandings of what it means to be school members (social identity content) there should be an impact on school outcome measures.

There are a number of strategies that can be implemented to affect social identity processes and to make higher-order identities more salient and thereby unify members in a common purpose and affect intergroup relations within the school setting. It is possible, for example, to (a) clarify the school's (organization's) shared mission and in essence what differentiates the school from others (i.e. what makes us 'us', what are 'our' goals), (b) restructure the way the school functions creating new structures that shape which groups and divisions are likely to become meaningful psychologically (e.g., activities structured by year group are likely to affect the salience of group memberships defined by year groups), and (c) increase the extent to which members participate and are involved in decisions that affect them, which in turn affects their identification with the group, 'ownership' of decisions and willingness (intrinsically) to enact them (Tyler and Blader, 2000).

Building on these points, an initial starting point in applying SCT in schools has been to build a sense of shared mission. Staff, students and interested parents and community members (as subgroups) have been involved in a process where the vision, purpose and ideal behaviours for staff and students within a particular school have been identified (e.g. Haslam et al., 2003). The collated information has been endorsed by the relevant parties and communicated to clarify the norms, values and beliefs that define the school (at school assemblies, in the classroom, on posters displayed around the school). A whole range of school activities and functions are shaped by this sense of 'who we are' (e.g. professional development, codifying shared practices, celebration of achievements, championing individuals who exemplify the school's mission).

In some of the schools, the aim has been to better integrate the school values with the school structure so as to promote more positive cooperative relationships between the subgroups within the school (e.g. junior and senior school, staff and students). At one school, in order to reduce the division amongst staff (across faculties) and amongst staff and students and between year groups of students, a pastoral house care system was introduced, in which other categorizations crossed through being 'house' members (Crisp et al., 2001). Effectively such efforts serve to reduce the fit between certain group memberships and certain attributes and ways of function ing and introduce the possibility of other meaningful identities emerging to shape behaviour (e.g. staff do not just interact within their faculty but also across school planning).

In another school the focus has been on the classroom culture and shifting relationships, from one in which the teacher relies on coercion and extrinsic motivation to manage relationships with students and achieve learning outcomes, to one focused on leadership, influence and building intrinsic motivation (Turner, 2005). It is argued that the ability of one individual (a teacher) to get another party (a student or group of students) to willingly engage in some task or activity is a leadership process. Learning requires, at least in part, a process of social influence to emerge between the teacher and students. In order to achieve this, in the classroom the teacher is encouraged to seek to involve students in decision making about their learning and to reach shared consensus on learning goals and standards. The class is also involved in deciding on the process through which they all will achieve certain learning outcomes. As a result, it is more likely for students to 'own', feel responsible for, and be intrinsically motivated to achieve, certain outcomes and also be more likely to support each other in achieving what is now a shared collective enterprise. Many of these ideas are consistent with initiatives in the educational context (including the quality learning movement) but locating these ideas within a broader theory of psychological functioning provides a more integrated approach and serves to reinforce the importance of certain educational initiatives over others.

The impact of initiatives and interventions such as these are being assessed on a range of school outcomes using a longitudinal design across a time period of up to 4 years. Although the SCT-based interventions are in the early stages of being introduced, initial results are in line with predictions. There is evidence that social (school) identification is significantly related to, and mediates the relationship between, organizational factors and individual psychological wellbeing (Bizumic et al., 2009). Organizational factors include the degree to which staff and student support the goals and objectives of the school, endorsement of school leadership and decision-making processes, the academic emphasis within the school and the fairness and clarity of rules and consistency in their implementation. These factors often form aspects of school climate measures in the educational domain. Measures of wellbeing address positive aspects of personal functioning, such as self-esteem, positive affect and job involvement, but also negative aspects, such as depression, anxiety, loss of emotional control and aggressive and disruptive behaviour (e.g. bullying, attention seeking, victimization, spreading rumours, social exclusion). The covariation of these measures suggests that if changes are made to schools which boost one's sense of psychological connection or belonging to the group, wellbeing and challenging behaviour should also be affected.

This work and the preliminary findings are exciting for a number of reasons. First, they highlight the relevance of social psychology in addressing issues in both clinical and educational contexts (e.g. wellbeing, aggression/bullying in schools). Second, the findings reinforce the need to integrate further the role of social identity processes in understanding the (individual) psychology of the person. Third, the work speaks to the importance of recognizing all aspects of human psychological functioning (personal and social) in addressing social issues and problems. It is argued that there is added value in the definition of issues and the development of solutions that recognize that people are both individuals and group members and target the most appropriate level in relation to the issue at hand.

CONCLUSION

In this chapter, core aspects of SCT have been outlined. This theory is part of a history of ideas in social psychology where there is a rejection that the person and their psychology is bound up with 'basic processes' that somehow sit apart from social experience, interaction and group life. The challenge has been to develop a model of human psychological functioning that engages with the group and society to show both how being social has affected the workings of the human mind (e.g., thoughts, emotions, memory, perception, imagination) and how the workings of the human mind make the social possible. Through a detailed analysis of the basic processes that underlie the psychological group and the cognitive definition of the self, SCT offers a non-reductionist view of the mind which has generated a range of distinctive subtheories, hypotheses and findings across a range of significant areas in social psychology. In this way the theory has demonstrated both its effectiveness and parsimony. This task has not been easy; it has been one that has involved the efforts of many and it is one that is not yet fully completed (Turner and Reynolds, 2010). It is our view that through serious engagement with the nature of the self and self-categorization process as defined in SCT it will be possible to advance social psychology and understanding of human psychology.

ACKNOWLEDGEMENTS

This chapter was supported by funding from the Australian Research Council to both authors, including an Australian Research Fellowship to Dr Reynolds and an Australian Professional Fellowship to Professor Turner. We would like to thank Paul van Lange for his very helpful comments on the draft manuscript.

REFERENCES

Ashforth, B.E. and Mael, F. (1989) Social identity theory and the organization. *Academy of Management Review, 14,* 20–39.

Barsalou, L.W. (1987) The instability of graded structure: Implications for the nature of concepts. In U. Neisser (ed.), *Concepts and Conceptual Development: Ecological and Intellectual Factors in Categorization,* pp. 101–140. Cambridge: Cambridge University Press.

Bizumic, B., Reynolds, K.J., Turner, J.C., Bromhead, D. and Subašić, E. (2009) The role of the group in individual functioning: School identification and the psychological well-being of staff and students. *Applied Psychology: An International Review, 58,* 171–192.

Branscombe, N.R. and Doosje, B. (2004) *Collective Guilt: International Perspectives.* New York: Cambridge University Press.

Branscombe, N.R., Schmitt, M.T. and Harvey, R.D. (1999) Perceiving pervasive discrimination among African-Americans: Implications for group identification and well-being. *Journal of Personality and Social Psychology, 77,* 135–149.

Bruner, J.S. (1957) Going beyond the information given. In J.S. Bruner, E. Brunswik, L. Festinger, F. Heider, K.F. Muenzinger, C.E. Osgood, and D. Rapaport (eds), *Contemporary Approaches to Cognition,* pp. 41–69. Cambridge, MA: Harvard University Press. (Reprinted in Bruner, J.S. [1973]. *Beyond the Information Given* pp. 218–238. New York: Norton).

Crisp, R.J., Hewstone, M. and Rubin, M. (2001) Does multiple categorization reduce intergroup bias? *Personality and Social Psychology Bulletin, 27,* 76–89.

David, B. and Turner, J.C. (1996) Studies in self-categorization and minority conversion: Is being a member of the outgroup an advantage? *British Journal of Social Psychology, 35,* 1–21.

David, B. and Turner, J.C. (1999) Studies in self-categorization and minority conversion: The ingroup minority in intergoup and intragroup social contexts. *British Journal of Social Psychology, 38,* 115–134.

David, B. and Turner, J.C. (2001) Self-categorization principles underlying majority and minority influence. In J.P. Forgas and K.D. Williams (eds), *Social Influence: Direct and Indirect Processes,* pp. 293–313. Philadelphia: Psychology Press.

Gaertner, S.L., Mann, J., Murrell, A. and Dovidio, J.F. (1989) Reducing intergroup bias: The benefits of recategorization. *Journal of Personality and Social Psychology, 57*, 239–249.

Goldstein, N.J., Cialdini, R.B. and Griskevicius, V. (2008) A room with a viewpoint: Using social norms to motivate environmental conservation in hotels. *Journal of Consumer Research, 35*, 472–482.

Guimond, S., Branscombe, N.R., Brunot, S., Buunk, B.P., Chatard, A., Désert, M., Garcia, D.M., Haque, S., Martinot, D. and Yzerbyt, V. (2007) Culture, gender, and the self: Variations and impact of social comparison processes. *Journal of Personality and Social Psychology, 92*, 1118–1134.

Haslam, S.A. (2004) *Psychology in Organizations: The Social Identity Approach*, 2nd Edition. Thousand Oaks, CA: Sage Publications.

Haslam, S.A., Eggins, R.A. and Reynolds, K.J. (2003) The ASPIRe model: Actualizing Social and Personal Identity Resources to enhance organizational outcomes. *Journal of Occupational and Organizational Psychology, 76*, 83–113.

Haslam, S.A., Ellemers, N., Reicher, S., Reynolds, K.J. and Schmitt, M. (2010) The social identity perspective tomorrow. In T. Postmes and N. Branscombe (eds), *Rediscovering Social Identity: Core Sources.* New York: Psychology Press.

Haslam, S.A., Jetten, J., Postmes, T. and Haslam, C. (2009) Social identity, health and well-being: An emerging agenda for applied psychology. *Applied Psychology: An International Review, 58*, 1–23.

Haslam, S.A., Oakes, P.J., Reynolds, K.J. and Turner, J.C. (1999) Social identity salience and the emergence of stereotype consensus. *Personality and Social Psychology Bulletin, 25*, 809–818.

Haslam, S.A., Oakes, P.J., Turner, J.C. and McGarty, C. (1995) Social categorization and group homogeneity: changes in the perceived applicability of stereotype content as a function of comparative context and trait favourableness. *British Journal of Social Psychology, 34*, 139–160.

Haslam, S.A., Ellemers, N., Reicher, S., Reynolds, K.J. and Schmitt, M. (2010) Social identity tomorrow: Opportunities and avenues for advance. In T. Postmes and N. Branscombe (eds). *Rediscovering Social Identity: Core Sources.* pp. 357–379. Psychology Press.

Haslam, S.A., Reicher, S.D. and Platow, M.J. (2011) *The New Psychology of Leadership: Identity, Influence and Power.* London: Psychology Press.

Haslam, S.A. and Turner, J.C. (1992) Context-dependent variation in social stereotyping 2: The relationship between frame of reference, self-categorization and accentuation. *European Journal of Social Psychology, 22*, 251–277.

Haslam, S.A. and Turner, J.C. (1995) Context-dependent variation in social stereotyping 3: Extremism as a self-categorical basis for polarized judgement. *European Journal of Social Psychology, 25*, 341–371.

Haslam, S.A., Turner, J.C., Oakes, P.J., McGarty, C. and Hayes, B.K. (1992) Context-dependent variation in social stereotyping 1: The effects of intergroup relations as mediated by social change and frame of reference, *European Journal of Social Psychology, 22*, 3–20.

Hogg, M.A. and Terry, D.J. (2000) Social identity and self-categorization processes in organizational contexts, *Academy of Management Review, 25*, 121–140.

Hogg, M.A. and Turner, J.C. (1987) Intergroup behavior, self-stereotyping and the salience of social categories. *British Journal of Social Psychology, 26*, 325–340.

Mavor, K.I., Reynolds, K.J. and Skorich, D. (2010) Attributions for one's own behaviour. The role of comparison in explaining dispositional attributions and the actor-observer effect. Unpublished manuscript, The Australian National University.

McGarty, C., Haslam, S.A., Hutchinson, K.J. and Turner, J.C. (1994) The effects of salient group memberships on persuasion. *Small Group Research, 25*, 267–293.

Medin, D.L. and Wattenmaker, W.D. (1987) Category cohesiveness, theories and cognitive archaeology. In U. Neisser (ed.), *Concepts and Conceptual Development, Ecological and Intellectual Factors in Categorization*, pp. 25–62. Cambridge: Cambridge University Press.

Mischel, W. (2004) Towards an integrative science of the person. *Annual Review of Psychology, 55*, 1–22.

Moscovici, S. (1976) *Social Influence and Social Change.* London: Academic Press.

Moscovici, S. (1980) Towards a theory of conversion behaviour. In L. Berkowitz (ed.), *Advances in Experimental Social Psychology, 13*, 209–239. New York: Academic Press.

Oakes, P.J. (1987) The salience of social categories. In J.C. Turner, M.A. Hogg, P.J. Oakes, S.D. Rieche, and M.S. Wetherell, *Rediscovering the Social Group: A Self-Categorization Theory.* pp. 117–141. Oxford: Blackwell.

Oakes, P.J., Haslam, S.A. and Turner, J.C. (1994) *Stereotyping and Social Reality.* Oxford: Blackwell.

Oakes, P.J., Turner, J.C. and Haslam, S.A. (1991) Perceiving people as group members: The role of fit in the salience of social categorizations. *British Journal of Social Psychology, 30*, 125–144.

Onorato, R.S. and Turner, J.C. (2004) Fluidity in the self-concept: The shift from personal to social identity. *European Journal of Social Psychology, 34*, 257–278.

Postmes, T. and Branscombe, N. (2010) Sources of social identity. In T. Postmes and N. Branscombe (eds), *Rediscovering Social Identity: Core Sources.* pp. 1–13. Psychology Press.

Rabbie, J.M. and Bekkers, F. (1978) Threatened leadership and inter-group competition. *European Journal of Social Psychology, 8,* 9–20.

Reicher, S.D. and Haslam, S.A. (2006) Rethinking the psychology of tyranny: The BBC Prison Study. *British Journal of Social Psychology, 45,* 1–40.

Reicher, S.D., Haslam, S.A. and Hopkins, N. (2005) Social identity and the dynamics of leadership: Leaders and followers as collaborative agents in the transformation of social reality. *Leadership Quarterly, 16,* 547–568.

Reicher, S. and Hopkins, N. (2001) *Self and Nation.* London: Sage.

Reynolds, K.J., Bizumic, B., Subašić, E., Melsom, K. and MacGregor, F. (2007) Understanding the school as an intergroup system: Implications for school reform and improving student and staff outcomes. Grant funded by the Australian Research Council and ACT Department of Education and Training. Canberra: The Australian National University.

Reynolds, K.J., Subašić, E., Bizumic, B., Turner, J.C., Branscombe, N. and Mavor, K.I. (2009) Social identity and personality processes: Non-aboriginal Australian identity and neuroticism. Manuscript in submission.

Reynolds, K.J. and Turner, J.C. (2006) Individuality and the prejudiced personality. *European Review of Social Psychology, 17,* 233–270.

Reynolds, K.J., Turner, J.C., Branscombe, N. and Mavor, K.I. (2005) Self-categorization and personal identity: Integrating group and personality processes. Grant funded by the Australian Research Council. Canberra: The Australian National University.

Reynolds, K.J., Turner, J.C., Branscombe, N.R., Mavor, K.I., Bizumic, B. and Subašić, E. (2010) Interactionism in personality and social psychology: An integrated approach to understanding the mind and behaviour. *European Journal of Personality, 24,* 458–482.

Rink, F. and Ellemers, N. (2007) Diversity as a source of common identity: Towards a social identity framework for studying the effects of diversity in organizations. *British Journal of Management, 18,* 19–29.

Roberts, B.W. and Caspi, A. (2003) The cumulative continuity model of personality development: Striking a balance between continuity and change. In U. Staudinger and U. Lindenberger (eds), *Understanding Human Development: Life Span Psychology in Exchange with Other Disciplines,* pp. 183–214. Dodrecht: Kluwer.

Roberts, B.W. and Donahue, E.M. (1994) One personality, multiple selves: Integrating personality and social roles. *Journal of Personality, 62,* 201–218.

Roberts, B.W. and Mroczek, D.K. (2008) Personality trait stability and change. *Current Directions in Psychological Science, 17,* 31–35.

Rosch, E. (1978) Principles of categorization. In E. Rosch and B.B. Lloyd (eds), *Cognition and Categorization.* Hillsdale, NJ: Erlbaum.

Sherif, M. (1967) *Social Interaction Process and Products: Selected Essays.* Chicago: Aldine Publishing.

Spears, R., Jetten, J. and Doosje, B. (2002) The (il)legitimacy of ingroup bias. In J.T. Jost and B. Major (eds), *The Psychology of Legitimacy,* pp. 332–362. UK and US: Cambridge University Press.

Steele, C.M. and Aronson, J. (1995) Stereotype threat and the intellectual test performance of African-Americans. *Journal of Personality and Social Psychology, 69,* 797–811.

Subašić, E., Reynolds, K. J. and Turner, J. C. (2008) The political solidarity model of social change: Dynamics of self-categorization in intergroup power relations. *Personality and Social Psychology Review, 12,* 330–352.

Subašić, E. Reynolds, K.J., Turner, J.C., Veentra, K. and Haslam, S.A. (2011) Leadership, power and the use of surveillance: Implications of shared social identity for leaders' capacity to influence. *Leadership Quarterly.*

Swann, W.B., Jr. and Read, S.J. (1981) Self-verification processes: How we sustain our self-conceptions. *Journal of Experimental Social Psychology, 17,* 351–372.

Tajfel, H. (1972) Social categorization. In S. Moscovici (ed.), *Introduction a la psychologie sociale, Vol. 1.* Paris: Larouse.

Tajfel, H. (1974) Social identity and intergroup behaviour. *Social Science Information, 13,* 66–93.

Tajfel, H. (ed.) (1978) *Differentiation Between Social Groups: Studies in the Social Psychology of Inter group Relations.* London: Academic Press.

Tajfel, H. and Turner, J.C. (1979) An integrative theory of intergroup conflict. In W.G. Austin and S. Worchel (eds), *The Social Psychology of Intergroup Relations,* pp. 33–47. Monterey, CA: Brooks/Cole.

Terry, D.J. and Hogg, M.A. (1996) Group norms and the attitude-behavior relationship: A role for group identification. *Personality and Social Psychology Bulletin, 22,* 776–244.

Turner, J.C. (1975) Social comparison and social identity: Some prospects for intergroup behaviour. *European Journal of Social Psychology, 5,* 5–34.

Turner, J.C. (1978) Social categorization and social discrimination in the minimal group paradigm. In H. Tajfel (ed.), *Differentiation Between Social*

Groups: Studies in the Social Psychology of Intergroup Relations, pp. 27–60. London: Academic Press.

Turner, J.C. (1982) Towards a cognitive redefinition of the social group. In H. Tajfel (ed.), *Social Identity and Intergroup Relations*, pp. 15–40. Cambridge: Cambridge University Press and Paris: Editions de la Maison des Sciences de l'Homme.

Turner, J.C. (1984) Social identification and psychological group formation. In H. Tajfel (ed.), *The Social Dimension: European Developments in Social Psychology*, pp. 518–538. Cambridge: Cambridge University Press.

Turner, J.C. (1985) Social categorization and the self-concept: a social cognitive theory of group behaviour. In E.J. Lawler (ed.), *Advances in Group Processes*, pp. 77–122. Greenwich, CT: JAI Press.

Turner, J.C. (1987a) Introducing the problem: individual and group. *Rediscovering the Social Group: A Self-categorization Theory*, pp. 1–18. Oxford: Blackwell.

Turner, J.C. (1987b) The analysis of social influence. In J.C. Turner, M.A. Hogg, P.J. Oakes, S.D. Riecher and M.S. Wetherell (eds), *Rediscovering the Social Group: A Self-categorization Theory*, pp. 68–88. Oxford: Blackwell.

Turner, J.C. (1991) *Social Influence*. Milton Keynes, England: Open University Press and Pacific Grove, CA.: Brooks/Cole.

Turner, J.C. (1996) Henri Tajfel: An introduction. In W.P. Robinson (ed.), *Social Groups and Identity: Developing the Legacy of Henri Tajfel*, pp. 1–24. Oxford: Butterworth Heinemann.

Turner, J.C. (2005) Explaining the nature of power: A three-process theory. *European Journal of Social Psychology*, 35, 1–22.

Turner, J.C. and Brown, R.J. (1978) Social status, cognitive alternatives and intergroup relations. In H. Tajfel (ed.), *Differentiation Between Social Groups*, pp. 201–234. London: Academic Press.

Turner, J.C. and Haslam, S.A. (2001) Social identity, organizations and leadership. In M.E. Turner (ed.), *Groups at Work: Theory and Research*, pp. 25–65. New Jersey: Lawrence Erlbaum Associates.

Turner, J.C., Hogg, M.A., Oakes, P.J., Reicher, S.D. and Wetherell, M.S. (1987) *Rediscovering the Social Group: A Self-categorization Theory*. Oxford and New York: Basil Blackwell.

Turner, J.C. and Oakes, P.J. (1986) The significance of the social identity concept for social psychology with reference to individualism, interactionism and social influence. *British Journal of Social Psychology*, 25, 237–252.

Turner, J.C. and Oakes, P.J. (1989) Self-categorization theory and social influence. In P.B. Paulus (ed.), *The Psychology of Group Influence*, pp. 233–275. Hillsdale, NJ: Erlbaum.

Turner, J.C. and Oakes, P.J. (1997) The socially structured mind. In C. McGarty and S.A. Haslam (eds), *The Message of Social Psychology*, pp. 355–373. Oxford: Blackwell.

Turner, J.C., Oakes, P.J., Haslam, S.A. and McGarty, C. (1994) Self and collective: Cognition and social context. *Personality and Social Psychology Bulletin*, 20, 454–463.

Turner, J.C. and Onorato, R. (1999) Social identity, personality and the self-concept: A self-categorization perspective. In T.R. Tyler, R. Kramer and O. John (eds), *The Psychology of the Social Self*, pp. 11–46. Mahwah, NJ: Lawrence Erlbaum Associates.

Turner, J.C. and Reynolds, K.J. (2003) Why social dominance theory has been falsified. *British Journal of Social Psychology*, 42, 199–206.

Turner, J.C. and Reynolds, K.J (2010) The story of social identity. In T. Postmes and N. Branscombe (eds), *Rediscovering Social Identity: Core Sources*, pp. 13–32. Psychology Press.

Turner, J.C., Reynolds, K.J., Haslam, S.A. and Veenstra, K. (2006) Reconceptualizing personality: Producing individuality by defining the personal self. In T. Postmes and J. Jetten (eds), *Individuality and the Group: Advances in Social Identity*, pp. 11–36. London: Sage Publications.

Turner, J.C., Reynolds, K.J. and Subašic´, E. (2008) Identity confers power: The new view of leadership in social psychology. In P. 't Hart and J. Uhr (eds), *Public Leadership: Perspectives and Practices*, pp. 52–72. Canberra: ANU E-press.

Tyler, T.R. and Blader, S. (2000) *Cooperation in groups: Procedural justice, social identity, and behavioral engagement*. Philadelphia, PA: Psychology Press.

van Knippenberg, D., van Knippenberg, B., De Cremer, D. and Hogg, M.A. (2004) Leadership, self and identity: A review and research agenda. *The Leadership Quarterly*, 15, 825–856.

Wetherell, M. (1987) Group polarization. In J.C. Turner, M.A. Hogg, P.J. Oakes, S.D. Riecher and M.S. Wetherell, *Rediscovering the Social Group: A Self-categorization Theory*, pp. 142–170. Oxford: Blackwell.

Williams, M.T., Turkheimer, E., Magee, E. and Guterbock, T. (2008) The effects of race and racial priming on self-report of contamination anxiety. *Personality and Individual Differences*, 44, 744–755.

Wright, S.C., Taylor, D.M. and Moghaddam, F.M. (1990) Responding to membership in a disadvantaged group: From acceptance to collective protest. *Journal of Personality and Social Psychology*, 58, 994–1003.

47

Social Dominance Theory

Jim Sidanius and Felicia Pratto

ABSTRACT

This chapter outlines the intellectual and personal influences on the development of social dominance theory (SDT). SDT examines how societies organize themselves as group-based social hierarchies. SDT assumes that processes at different but intersecting levels of social organization, from prejudice to cultural legitimizing ideologies, produce and maintain hierarchical societal structure. The chapter examines the counteracting roles of hierarchy-enhancing and hierarchy-attenuating legitimizing ideologies and social institutions, the intersection between gender and arbitrary set discrimination (i.e., discrimination based on socially constructed group distinctions), the distinction between authoritarianism and social dominance orientation, and emphasizes the critical role of social power (as opposed to social status), and the need to see social dominance as an integrated and dynamic social system.

A BRIEF OVERVIEW OF SOCIAL DOMINANCE THEORY

Stated most simply, social dominance theory (SDT) argues that intergroup oppression, discrimination, and prejudice are the means by which human societies organize themselves as group-based hierarchies, in which members of dominant groups secure a disproportionate share of the good things in life (e.g., powerful roles, good housing, good health), and members of subordinate groups receive a disproportionate share of the bad things in life (e.g., relatively poor housing and poor health). While the severity of group-based inequality varies across different societies and within any given society across time, the fact of group-based social hierarchy appears to be a human universal (e.g., Lenski, 1984). Because SDT attempts to describe the systematic processes that form the dynamic system of societal inequality, its analysis considers the intersection of processes at multiple levels of social organization (see Pratto et al., 2006; Sidanius and Pratto, 1999 for recent reviews).

In a slight modification of Pierre van den Berghe's (1978) taxonomy of social categories, SDT observes that human group-based social hierarchies consist of three distinctly different stratification systems: (1) an *age-system*, in which adults and middle-age people have disproportionate social power over children and younger adults; (2) a *gender* or *patriarchal* system in which men have disproportionate social and political power compared to women; and (3) an *arbitrary-set* system in which socially constructed categories are hierarchically arranged. These arbitrary sets may be constructed to associate power and legitimacy with social categories like "race," caste, ethnicity, nationality, social class, religion, or any other group distinction that human interaction is capable of constructing. As the double-headed arrows in Figure 47.1 are meant to indicate, we argue that group-based hierarchy both affects and is effected by roughly seven processes at three levels of analysis.

At the societal level the degree of group-based social hierarchy is effected by and affects two mutually antagonistic sets of forces: (1) hierarchy-enhancing and hierarchy-attenuating legitimizing ideologies, and (2) hierarchy-enhancing and hierarchy-attenuating social institutions. Hierarchy-enhancing and hierarchy-attenuating ideologies justify the establishment and maintenance of group-based social inequality or its exact opposite, respectively. To the degree that the relative balance of these opposing ideologies remains stable, the degree of social inequality remains stable over time, everything else being equal. Actions of hierarchy-enhancing and hierarchy-attenuating institutions also produce the level of inequality at the societal level. Hierarchy-enhancing social institutions allocate social resources to the advantage of dominant groups and to the disadvantage of subordinate groups, whereas hierarchy-attenuating social institutions have the opposite effect. Examples of hierarchy-enhancing institutions are internal security forces, large segments of the criminal justice system, and most large corporations. Examples of hierarchy-attenuating institutions are human rights and civil rights organizations, charities, and legal aid groups for the poor and the indigent (e.g., Sidanius et al., 1996).

At the intergroup level, we posit two general processes that sustain inequality. First, aspects of unequal intergroup contexts afford prejudicial and discriminatory behavior. Unequal contexts readily dredge up stereotypes and remembered histories of past conflicts, perceived intergroup threat, and belief in separate identities, all of which provoke discrimination and stereotyping (see Pratto, 1999, for a review). Second, members of subordinate groups tend to behave in ways that are less beneficial to themselves and their ingroups than dominant group members do with reference to their ingroups. We call this *behavioral asymmetry*, and it is instantiated in many ways. For example, people in dominant groups follow their doctors' orders and study more than people in subordinate groups (see Sidanius and Pratto, 1999: 227–262). Behavioral asymmetry implies that group-based hierarchies are not solely maintained by the oppressive actions of dominants, but also by agency, albeit constrained agency, on the part of subordinates.

At the person level, the roles, prejudices, social beliefs that contribute to discrimination are coordinated, often in the same directions, so that thousands of aggregated individual acts of cruelty, oppression, and discrimination help sustain group-based hierarchy. Certain values, personality variables,

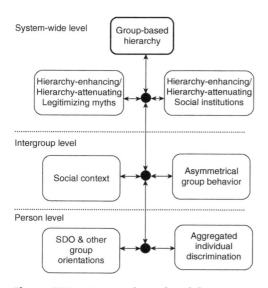

Figure 47.1   An overview of social dominance theory

political ideologies, and temperaments, including openness, conservatism, authoritarianism, and empathy make certain people more or less likely to be prejudiced or to discriminate against subordinates (Akrami and Ekehammar, 2006; Altemeyer, 1998; Pratto et al., 1994; Stephan and Finlay, 1999). In general, an individual's likelihood of performing hierarchy-enhancing or hierarchy-attenuating acts depends on her general desire to support and maintain group-based inequality, a characteristic we call social dominance orientation (SDO).

Thus, at core, there are three basic assumptions underpinning SDT. First, we assume that human social systems are dynamically tenacious. Thus, even as they adapt and change, societies that are group-based dominance hierarchies will tend to continually reorganize themselves, and even other societies, as such. Second, various forms of group-based oppression (e.g., sexism, racism, nationalism, ethnocentrism, classism) should be seen as specific instantiations of group-based social hierarchies. Third, the degree of group-based social hierarchy within any society at any given time will be the net result of the interaction of multileveled hierarchy-enhancing and hierarchy-attenuating forces within that society at any given time. Thus, the ultimate goal of SDT is to understand the multileveled processes which are responsible for the production, maintenance, and reproduction of group-based social hierarchy.

SDT: EARLY ROOTS AND PERSONAL JOURNEYS

Jim's personal narrative

The basic building blocks of SDT were being assembled in my mind since childhood. As a 10-year-old boy growing up in New York City in the mid 1950s I had already become uncomfortably aware that being a "Negro" in America was not an altogether good thing. However, the deadly seriousness of this predicament did not become clear to me until the day I came across a *Jet* magazine article about a young Black man accused of whistling at a White woman in the South. The article described how a group of White men kidnapped this young Black man, castrated him, and poured gasoline onto the open gash where his genitals used to be. This story left a deep impression on me and I reread it over and over again, trying to grasp the meaning of such brutality.

Perhaps my most consciousness-altering confrontation with American racism occurred when I was a 16-year-old high school student. On my way home from school with my Jewish girlfriend and a White male friend, my male friend and I were followed into a public restroom in Highbridge Park by a White policeman, his gun drawn and demanding that we raise our hands and face the restroom wall. Not being aware of having broken any law, I asked the officer why we were being stopped. I was told to shut the fu*k up, and marched off to the 33rd police precinct. Upon arrival I was told to sit down and once again, to "shut the fu*k up!" After some time had passed, I again demanded to know why I was being detained. This resulted in the arresting officer punching me in the face and yelling a string of racial epithets at me. I lost my composure and struck back. Immediately some four or five baton-wielding police officers pounced on me, beat me into near unconsciousness, placed me in overly tight handcuffs, and threw me into a holding cell. I then spent the night in a jail cell at the Brooklyn House of Detention. The next afternoon I was arraigned in criminal court and listened as the arresting officer testified that I was guilty of drunken disorderliness, interfering with traffic, and resisting arrest. Three witnesses disputed these claims (i.e., my girlfriend, my White male friend, and an independent witness to my arrest). After listening to all their testimony, the judge said that he would be lenient with me *this one time*. He then ordered my release, with the admonition that in future, I "show more respect for the law!"

Even though I was released from custody, the message communicated to me was crystal clear. I was arrested, beaten, jailed, and arraigned for multiple acts of insubordination: insubordination for the crime of having a White girlfriend, insubordination for the act of questioning the legitimacy of my arrest, and most critically, insubordination by defending myself against physical attack by the police. By being told to "show more respect for the law," I was clearly being told to keep my place, or else. This critical event led to a visceral understanding of the role the police and other armed authorities play in maintaining generalized submission and acquiescence from Black people in the US. Although this was the last time I was personally subject to police violence, I witnessed this kind of violence across many societies. The direct and vicarious experience of police violence influenced the development of SDT many years later.

Rather than reinforcing my submission to the American racial order, this early experience with the police had the opposite effect. I was transformed from a rather milk-toast liberal into an angry and resentful Black radical. After participating in numerous demonstrations and acts of resistance throughout the 1960s, I had finally had enough of American racism, and left the country in 1970, planning never to return. After traveling to Canada, France, Germany, Denmark, and spending a few months in Algeria hanging out with some members of the Black Panther Party, I made my way to Sweden, where I eventually settled, raised a family, and was awarded a doctoral degree in political psychology.

The early years in Sweden were a revelation. While Swedes treated me with a certain degree of curiosity (at the time many Swedes had never seen a Black person in the flesh), their reactions to me were not laced with that combination of fear and loathing that had become such an intolerable part of my everyday experience with Whites in America.

Although my American origins very often shielded me from various slights and outright discrimination, it soon became clear that a number of other ethnic minorities were serving as targets of discrimination and devaluation (e.g., Finns, Turks, Roma). And so it was within every society I visited or learned anything about. These discrimination targets varied from people of sub-Saharan descent in Algeria, to Arabs from the Maghreb in France, to Turks in Germany and Denmark, to blond haired, blue-eyed Finns in Sweden, and to Roma in every country in Western and Eastern Europe. I also noticed an unsettling similarity in the manner in which the police treated members of these ethnic outgroups across the countries I visited. This treatment varied from a snarling intimidation to outright physical brutality, so reminiscent of my experiences with American police. Not only did I observe a thought-provoking cross-cultural similarity in the nature of police behavior towards ethnic minorities, the content of the stereotypes concerning these groups was also remarkably similar. Across a variety of different societies, the local ethnic subordinates were often described as lazy, conniving, criminal, dangerous, incompetent, and welfare-dependent.

In doing doctoral research in political psychology at the University of Stockholm, I came across a surprising and consistent finding which was to have a major influence on the later development of SDT. Namely, using two large and independent samples of Swedish high school students, my colleague, Bo Ekehammar, and I discovered some noteworthy differences in the sociopolitical attitudes of boys and girls, the strongest of which were the substantially higher levels of xenophobia and racism among boys than girls (see Ekehammar and Sidanius, 1982; Sidanius and Ekehammar, 1980, 1983). These findings were surprising because gender egalitarianism had been a major component of Swedish political culture for half a century. While there was reason to expect attitudinal differences with respect to gendered issues (e.g., abortion rights), there was little reason to expect gender differences with respect to dimensions such as xenophobia and racism. Further, the higher levels of prejudice among boys were not moderated by differences in political ideology (Ekehammar, 1985); they were essentially of the same magnitude among communists as among fascists. Shortly after these findings were published, independent researchers replicated these results in other countries such as Great Britain and South Africa (see Furnham, 1985; Marjoribanks, 1981).

Because of the limited academic opportunities in Sweden, I decided to return to the US in 1983. I was initially comforted by the fact that the America I returned to was substantially less overtly racist than the America I had left behind 13 years earlier. However, it did not take too long for me to realize that beneath the surface of this increased racial inclusiveness, one could still clearly recognize a largely unchanged racial order underlying the bulk of social interactions. Despite the substantial progress achieved by the civil rights movement, it also became clear to me that this movement had failed in its central mission. The hierarchical racial order of American life remained very much as I had left it. The attempt to understand this sameness ensconced within change provided the initial emotional energy for the development of SDT.

Reading the history of reformist and revolutionary social movements, as well as the work of the neoclassical elitism scholars (e.g., Mosca, Pareto, Michels), convinced me that the failure of truly transformational change is the rule rather than the exception. Every attempt to replace group-based hierarchy with truly egalitarian social interaction has failed, without exception. These failures range from attempts at large-scale revolutionary transformation (e.g., the French, Russian, Mexican, Chinese, Vietnamese, Cambodian, and Cuban revolutions and the attempt at introducing economic democracy in Sweden during the mid 1970s), to small-scale attempts at egalitarian communities (e.g., the Oneida, Shaker, Harmonist, and Jassonist Communities of North America). While many of these revolutionary efforts

have succeeded in replacing one group of ruling elites with another, and sometimes even decreasing the overall level of oppression, none have ever succeeded in their original goals of replacing group-based hierarchy with genuine egalitarianism.

While the building blocks of SDT lay scattered across disparate areas of my consciousness by the time I accepted a tenured position as Associate Professor of Psychology at UCLA in 1988, the first and rather underdeveloped form of SDT did not find its way onto paper until the summer of that year. Professor David O. Sears, one of my senior colleagues-to-be at UCLA, gave me a copy of his paper on symbolic racism he was to present at the upcoming meetings of the International Society of Political Psychology, and invited me to present a paper at this panel. I took the opportunity to react to David Sears' symbolic racism thesis. Rather than regard symbolic racism (defined as a combination of anti-Black affect and traditional American values such as self-reliance) as the ultimate source of White opposition to redistributive social policy favoring Blacks (e.g., busing, affirmative action), I argued that symbolic racism is better seen as one among several legitimizing ideologies serving the purpose of justifying the continued domination of Blacks by Whites, and more generally as the attempt of a dominant group to use a legitimizing ideology to maintain supremacy over a subordinate group. My rather incoherent and tedious reaction to Sears' paper was the primitive beginning of what was to grow into SDT (for a more coherent version of this initial argument, see Sidanius et al., 1992). However, the full development of SDT did not take place until I started to have theoretical jam sessions with Marilynn Brewer, a senior colleague, and distinguished intergroup relations specialist, and Felicia Pratto, a brilliant young woman I had first met when she was an undergraduate at Carnegie Mellon University, and with whom I later reconnected when she was a newly minted PhD from the social psychology program at New York University in 1989.

Numerous critical conversations with Marilynn Brewer stimulated me to develop the central idea of the counterbalancing effects of hierarchy-enhancing versus hierarchy-attenuating social forces, while the collaboration with Felicia Pratto led to the conceptualization and initial measurement of the SDO construct, the conceptual and empirical distinctions between arbitrary-set and gender hierarchies, the extension of the person–environment fit perspective onto the psychology of intergroup relations, and several other aspects of SDT as it stands today.

Felicia's personal narrative

My story is not as dramatic as Jim's, but may give a sense of how a person can develop a consciousness of intergroup power, social exclusion, discrimination, legitimizing myths, and social justice.

My family was formed in the foothills of the Rockies by the intermarriages of second-generation Eastern and Southern European immigrants. Although almost no one acknowledges this in the presumption that all Whites are the same in the US, the early twentieth-century immigration produced a great deal of ethnic diversity and multilingualism. My family's story includes the fact that ethnic divides help stabilize power structures. My grandfather, Pete Pratto, born in 1900, became a coal miner for Colorado Fuel and Iron after he gave up being a cowboy and homesteader at age 40. Coal miners from many European countries, Mexico, and Japan lived in company towns, were paid poorly in company scrip, and were worked hard in dangerous conditions. The mining companies housed different ethnic groups in separate areas and did their best to stir up enmity as a way of preventing unionization from taking hold. Several of my grandfather's union activist friends were murdered, and this kind of intimidation and ethnic conflict prevented unions from taking hold for decades longer than they should have

(e.g., Beshoar, 1957). My paternal grandmother, Bertha Bon, was a child at the Ludlow Massacre. Her family, and those of all the other miners on strike, was living in tents in the foothills because they were not allowed to live in company housing while on strike. On Orthodox Easter, 1914, their tents were firebombed and they were shot at by the Colorado state militia, which was working at the beck and call of John D. Rockefeller's Standard Oil. My grandmother told me that she hid behind a kitchen table turned on its side, and the only reason she felt she and her family survived is that a coal train went between where the militia shooters were and the families were cowering, allowing them to escape farther into the hills. With this family history, I could not grow up assuming that poor people are less virtuous than the rich, that hard work inevitably pays, nor that power is usually used for good and justice is always delivered.

In 1969 my family moved from the American West to Greensboro, NC, where my father was offered an academic job as a sociologist. This move from the West, where everyone we knew was a "guy" because everyone had the same social class and was capable and friendly, taught me much about cultural ideologies as not only scripts but masks. We were told to expect "Southern hospitality," but in fact the White neighbor kids yelled "damned Yankees" at my sister Anita and me as we walked home from school. Not much more subtly, my public school fourth-grade teacher, Mrs. Lambert, regularly asked my class to raise their hands and keep them raised if we were Jewish, then if we were Catholic, while she made notes that we never saw. Molly Ivins had a similar awakening about Southern culture when she was asked how a native Texan could grow up to be a progressive. When she had asked her mother about why she couldn't drink out of the "colored" water fountain and her mother said that it was filthy, when Molly could see it was clean, Molly said she realized that if they were lying about race, they were probably lying about everything else too. So I did not feel welcome in North Carolina, but this led me to form great friendships with other "outsiders," like African-Americans, immigrants, and Yankees. Thus, not everybody feels they belong, or is made to feel they belong, everywhere. This basic idea later found a place in SDT.

Attending college in Pittsburgh was refreshing. I enjoyed the mixture of working class and upper class kids from many states in a student culture where everyone could be creative and successful. Carnegie Mellon had its own foibles, but unlike the South, they weren't designed to prevent certain people from serving in certain roles or to keep people on top who were not deserving, except for one problem: sexism.

In 1979 when I started, the student body was 70 percent men, and the science, engineering, and architecture schools had not only higher proportions, but also a very boyish culture. Dr. Goldberg, my wonderful physics section teacher who taught kids from the South and inner cities and got us to pass Physics 1, was the only PhD who taught a section (the others were led by graduate students). I do not know her whole story, but I do know that when I was a physics major, the non PhD instructor gave a full-letter-grade lower grade to every woman in the mechanics lab than he gave to her lab partner. We had thought about insisting on egalitarian relations with men in our personal lives, but not in institutions like schools. Given our instructor's grading and his remarks about "girls" throughout the course, all but one of us women in physics chose to change majors or universities.

I had the fortune to earn my work-study money doing research for several social scientists at Carnegie Mellon, from whom I learned much. Susan T. Fiske, in particular, spent lots of time and effort mentoring me, entertaining my questions, teaching me how to do social psychology experiments, trying to teach my rough sensibilities on how to be a professional. After I graduated, she hired me to help on her research on stereotyping, which enabled me to support myself, grow

up and save more money before graduate school, feel I belonged at Carnegie Mellon, and engage in peace activism. I was deeply vexed by social injustice, and so I thought I should study stereotyping because it was the only domain of social psychology interested in this problem. One afternoon I asked Susan why there were such inequities, such as the fact that I, with a BS, made exactly half as much as my husband-to-be did who had not finished his degree. That was "the market," not really an explanation of why different kinds of work are valued differently. I asked why we have different people doing different kinds of jobs and Susan gave me the then-standard line about cognitive heuristics leading to stereotyping leading to discrimination. But this "how" answer to a "why" question was not satisfactory, and I blurted out, "What about" –searching for the missing concept – "POWER?" I suppose that is when I started to realize that even if scientists mainly answer how and not why questions, they at least should have complete descriptions of the processes. Still, because I was looking to elders about what to research, I did not follow through on my own intuitions until a few years later.

In graduate school at New York University (NYU), I had a ball doing experiments on automatic processing and stereotyping with John Bargh, and the social cognition process-focused atmosphere was very stimulating. But again, some questions remained unanswered. I recall that in some seminars, all the outcome measures correlated with participants' social class, and yet the papers were never trying to explain that relation. Also, during my third year, Trish Devine submitted her dissertation research for publication and made the same stir at NYU as elsewhere. She argued that stereotyping could be traced to more essential, unconscious, and uncontrollable cognitive processes (Devine, 1989). This work was an important lesson to me. This approach was in the air in social psychology – I saw Mahzarin Banaji's students at conferences and they contended that if we could only get at the automatic processes, we could eradicate discrimination (see Blair and Banaji, 1996, as an example of this work). Earlier, Hamilton and Gifford (1976) had shown that negative stereotypes about minority groups could arise simply because of a nonmotivated, nonsocial cognitive process of associating infrequent features (group members and negative behaviors). This work is certainly intellectually elegant and the nonobviousness of the analysis was widely appreciated, including by me. But my read of social psychology at this time was that in erasing the *intention* from stereotyping and discrimination, the discipline also erased the fact that inequality has real *consequences*. Even outside the social cognition domain, our field had shifted from considering the consequences of racism for Black people (Clark and Clark, 1947), to whether focusing on racism would upset White people's self-image (Gaertner and Dovidio, 1986; Katz and Hass, 1988). So the study of racism had moved from being about how justice and equality could be realized by and for Black people, to how White people could be prevented from feeling uncomfortable. At a moment that I could have gone the cognitive–essentialist route in addressing social inequality intellectually, I decided this was just not the right approach. What I felt *was* essential to a theory of social inequality was (1) culture: the systems of meaning and ideologies that pattern behavior and social structure, (2) an overt acknowledgement of power as part of the social context, (3) a focus on consequential outcomes like inequality, and (4) a theoretical analysis that overtly showed how processes at different levels of analysis, from in the person, to intergroup, to society-wide to intersocietal, scaled. For such reasons I was very excited when Jim Sidanius showed me the rough sketch he had made of SDT just after I finished my PhD and was heading to California to join my new (and only) husband. My social cognition training served my work on SDT well because it has systematic methods to substantiate processes and link them together (this is what I tried to do in my pretenure work

on SDT; Pratto, 1999). Through different personal and intellectual routes, Jim and I had come to similar sensibilities about what a real theory was and what had to be included in a theory of inequality.

MAJOR COMPONENTS OF AND INTELLECTUAL INFLUENCES ON SDT

SDT has been influenced by a wide variety of perspectives both inside and outside of social psychology. These influences are all the more varied because of our different training in personality, political history, and social cognition. The most important of these influences have come from:

1 authoritarian personality theory (a psychoanalytic approach to understanding the intersection between child-rearing practices, personality development, political ideology and prejudice; see Adorno et al., 1950);
2 early social identity theory (a psychological theory of intergroup discrimination composed of three basic elements: (a) social categorization, (b) psychological identification, and (c) social comparison and, if possible, the achievement of a positive comparison between an ingroup and an outgroup; see Tajfel and Turner, 1986);
3 Rokeach's two-value theory of political behavior (the notion that political behavior is a joint function of the value one places on both equality and freedom; see Rokeach, 1973);
4 Blumer's (1960) group position theory (the notion that racial prejudice is a result of attempts to establish and maintain favorable positions within a social hierarchy);
5 Marxism (Gramsci, 1971; Marx and Engels, 1846);
6 neoclassical elitism theory (or the notion that social hierarchies are ubiquitous and essentially inevitable; see Michels, 1911; Mosca, 1896; Pareto, 1901);
7 industrial/organizational psychology (Bretz and Judge, 1994); and
8 sociological work on institutional discrimination (Hood and Cordovil, 1992), cultural ideologies (e.g., Sanday, 1981), evolutionary biology (Trivers, 1972), evolutionary psychology (Betzig, 1993; van den Berghe, 1978) and biological anthropology (Dickemann, 1979).

The influence of neo-classical elitism theories and the concept of legitimizing myths

One important idea that we borrowed from classical and neoclassical elitism theories concerns the nature of societal structure. With the decided exception of Marxism, these theories presume that social systems and complex social organizations are inherently hierarchically and oligarchically structured. Thus, what ordinarily passes for democratic rule on the surface is, in actuality, the exercise of control by economic and social elites (e.g., Dahl, 1989). For such reasons, we look not at a society's system of government, but rather its degree of group inequality and the mechanisms responsible for that inequality (e.g., Sidanius and Pratto, 1993).

The second major idea that many of these theories share in common concerns the role of ideas in producing and maintaining group-based inequality. Pareto (1935) argued that there are two major means by which members of dominant groups establish and maintain hegemony, force, and fraud. By force, Pareto simply meant the use or threat of physical force and intimidation. By fraud he referred to the use of consensually shared social ideology functioning to legitimize the dominant position of the powerful over the powerless. Elitism theories and Marxism acknowledge that physical intimidation is an important means by which dominants exploit and control subordinates, but they maintain that, in the long run, it is not the most effective means of social control. A more potent means of sustaining hierarchy is by controlling social legitimacy. Marxists refer to these legitimacy instruments as "ideology" and "false consciousness," Mosca refers them by the term "political formula," Pareto uses the notion of "derivations," and Gramsci invokes the idea of "ideological hegemony." All these assert that elites maintain control over subordinates by controlling what is and what is not considered legitimate discourse, and promoting the idea that the rule of elites is moral, just, necessary, inevitable, and fair. SDT calls these ideological instruments "legitimizing myths."

SDT defines legitimizing myths (LMs) as consensually shared ideologies (including stereotypes, attributions, cosmologies, predominant values or discourses, shared representations, etc.) that organize and justify social relationships. LMs suggest how people and institutions should behave, why things are how they are, and how social value should be distributed. Because they are consensual and closely associated with the structure of their societies, LMs often have the appearance of being true. Consequently, those who reject them take risks and have work to do in explaining how and why they disagree.

Unlike Marxist approaches, including system justification theory (see Jost and Banaji, 1994), SDT does not assume that all such myths are false, nor that they only reinforce social hierarchy (Sidanius and Pratto, 1999). Cultural ideologies can also work against hierarchy. For example, in both our lives, the civil rights and anticolonial movements mobilized Western arguments for equality and liberty (e.g., Klein and Licata, 2003). This aspect of SDT is compatible with much critical theory (e.g., Crenshaw et al., 1996), social representations (e.g., Moscovici, 1988), and discourse analysis (e.g., Chiapello and Fairclough, 2002) in identifying the social and political functions of ideology.

SDO and authoritarianism

Furthermore, SDT argues that the individual's attitudes towards redistributive social ideologies, group-relevant social policies, and social groups themselves, will be strongly determined by how much one favors group-based dominance and social inequality in general. Because we have a concrete measure of SDO (see Pratto et al., 1994), one of the unique features of SDT is that it offers an empirical standard for understanding whether given cultural ideologies legitimize continued hierarchy or increased equality.

If the desire for the establishment and maintenance of group-based social inequality and hierarchy (i.e., SDO) has a positive correlation with support for an ideology, one can regard that ideology as hierarchy-enhancing. If, on the other hand, SDO has a negative correlation with support for an ideology, one can suppose it is hierarchy-attenuating. However, a stronger test is how well an ideology *mediates* SDO and support for policies or practices that influence inequality. For example, Pratto et al. (1998) showed that *noblesse oblige*[1] was negatively correlated with SDO, and mediated between SDO and support for social welfare programs, implying that in that context, *noblesse oblige* was hierarchy-attenuating. In the same study, nationalism was positively correlated with SDO and mediated between SDO and support for the US Gulf War against Iraq.

Although authoritarianism and SDO have both been found to be strong predictors of prejudice and hostility towards a range of groups, the two variables are also both conceptually and empirically distinct. Whereas authoritarianism was conceived from psychoanalytic theorizing as an ego defense against feelings of inadequacy and vulnerability, SDO was not conceived of as psychopathological in any sense, but merely viewed as one orientation for engaging in social life. Furthermore, except where the political system is highly unidimensional (e.g., Duriez et al., 2005), right-wing authoritarianism (RWA), and SDO are only minimally related to each other and both make strong and independent contributions to prejudice against denigrated groups such as gays, foreigners, women, Arabs, Muslims, Blacks, and Jews (e.g., Altemeyer, 1998; McFarland and Adelson, 1996).

Modern conceptualizations of right-wing authoritarianism define it as submission to ingroup authority, the social norms that these authorities endorse, and the propensity to aggress against those who are perceived as violating ingroup norms and traditions (e.g., Altemeyer, 1998). Rather than being about ingroup norms, SDO is primarily about hierarchy between groups. This conceptual distinction between RWA and SDO was recently confirmed in an experiment by Thomsen et al. (2008), who reasoned that RWA and SDO would be differentially associated with hostility against immigrants, depending upon how descriptions of immigrants were framed. High authoritarians were most hostile towards immigrants who were described as refusing to accept ingroup norms and assimilate. In contrast, high dominators were most hostile to those immigrants *who did want to* accept national norms and assimilate; thereby becoming competitors with natives (see Duckitt and Sibley, 2007; Henry et al., 2005 for empirical distinctions between RWA and SDO).

The relation between gender and arbitrary set discrimination

Initially inspired by Jim's early discovery of consistently higher levels of racism and xenophobia among men than among women, and influenced by the biosocial analysis of Laura Betzig (1993), we began to theorize that this syndrome of greater affinity for outgroup hostility, social predation, and group-based dominance among males was most likely grounded in the notion that social dominance had slightly higher fitness-value for males than for females over the course of human evolutionary history. Thus, the "invariance hypothesis" was born, or the notion that, everything else being equal, men will tend to have higher SDO scores than women. There is now very considerable and consistent evidence in support of this hypothesis found in scores of different studies, over dozens of different cultures, and using thousands of respondents (see, for example, Pratto et al., 1997; Sidanius and Pratto, 1999; Sidanius et al., 1994b, 1995, 2000, 2006; see especially the meta-analysis of Lee et al., submitted).

Such gender differences contribute to men obtaining hierarchy-enhancing roles and to women obtaining hierarchy-attenuating roles, due not only to stereotyping, but to self-selection as well (Pratto et al., 1997; Pratto and Espinoza, 2001. These gender differences are not just expressed in attitudes assessed by surveys, or in hierarchy roles, but also in disproportionate acts of violence against outgroups. For example, while women sometimes participate in war, they are very rarely, if ever, the organizers and major protagonists of war (e.g., Keegan, 1993). Similarly, considering US hate crimes as an example of outgroup aggression (i.e., crimes based on arbitrary-set distinctions like race, religion, ethnicity, disability, sexual orientation), men again predominate as perpetrators, both among Whites and Blacks (Bureau of Justice Statistics, 2001).

Another important fact that we have documented concerning gender and arbitrary set discrimination is that even arbitrary set victimhood is gendered. Except for rape and child abuse, extreme violence is primarily targeted against men rather than against women. For example, White males comprised 40 percent of US hate crime victims, while White females were 25 percent of hate crime victims; Black males were 20 percent of hate crime victims, while Black females were 12 percent (Bureau of Justice Statistics, 2001). In a thorough international review of institutional discrimination, we found higher rates of victimhood among subordinate men than among subordinate women in the labor market, the retail and housing markets, the educational system, and the criminal justice system across many nations (see Sidanius and Pratto, 1999, Chapters 5–9). This gender-based asymmetry in discriminatory outcomes is called the *subordinate male target hypothesis* (SMTH; see Sidanius and Pratto, 1999; Sidanius and Veniegas, 2000).

Because this pattern of men being both the more frequent perpetrators and victims of arbitrary-set violence and discrimination is so consistent across nations, we have explored whether evolutionary theory might inform these gender differences. As mentioned above, we have argued that intergroup aggression, which is often both high risk and high gain, suits the fitness strategies of men more than those of women (e.g., Betzig, 1993).

Furthermore, we have recently begun examining this phenomenon by use of the *prepared learning* paradigm. This approach argues that conditioned fear to stimuli which have been dangerous to humans over the course of human evolutionary history (e.g., spiders and snakes) will resist extinction, while conditioned fear responses to stimuli which have not posed a threat across human evolutionary history (e.g., birds and rabbits) will be more readily extinguished (Ohman and Mineka, 2001). Applying this idea to the domain of intergroup relations, Olsson et al. (2005) used men's faces as stimuli and found that conditioned fear of facial pictures of one's racial ingroup readily extinguished, but conditioned fear of facial images of racial outgroups did not. This implies that people are "prepared" to be fearful of members of less familiar outgroups and do not easily stop fearing them.[2] Employing the subordinate male target hypothesis, Navarrete et al. (2009) reasoned that since outgroup males, rather than outgroup females, have posed the most lethal threats over the course of human evolutionary history, conditioned fear of outgroup faces will be most resistant to extinction when these faces are male rather than female. The experimental results were consistent with this hypothesis.

In a further extension of this reasoning, Navarrete et al., (2010) reasoned that whereas men's desire to aggress against outgroups may be motivated by dominance tendencies, women's negative reactions to outgroups may be motivated by fear of sexual coercion and rape. In fact, they found that fear extinction biases against male stimuli were predicted by aggressiveness and SDO among men, but by fear of sexual coercion among women.

These kinds of studies show what SDT has argued from its inception, namely that because some of the psychological differences between men and women are considered to be "prepared" by evolution (e.g., greater affection for the exercise of raw power, violence, and SDO among males), gender can neither be considered as just another form of arbitrary-set inequality, nor is gender only about sexism and irrelevant to arbitrary-set inequality. In this respect, SDT remains different from the many theories of racism that ignore some of the unique characteristics of gender relations, or consider sexism merely a parallel form of racism.[3] Similarly, SDT differs from the many theories of gender that focus only on relations between men and women, and do not recognize how gender intersects with the adult–child and arbitrary set systems, nor how gender influences arbitrary set relations and social structure.[4]

Power, not status

Another important way that social dominance differs from most contemporary theories of intergroup relations is that SDT is centrally concerned with intergroup *power*, not interpersonal power, group status, minority status, intergroup contact, or other structural considerations. The heavy American focus on Black–White US relations and the minority influence school has led many theorists to focus on "minority status" and thus to ignore the examples of apartheid, Israeli treatment of Palestinians, colonization, and sexism, and other cases in which power does not merely come from numbers. Owing to the strong influence of social identity theory, with its motivational engine of positive self-regard (Tajfel and Turner, 1979), of Allport's (1954) view of prejudice as shades of disliking, and of stigma or lack of acceptance (Goffman, 1959), many other theorists have focused on the social status and social evaluation associated with groups (e.g., Fiske et al., 2002). Obviously, these intellectual cousins have made significant contributions to intergroup relations and related processes in their own right, and our initial theorizing was strongly influenced by social identity theory (Tajfel and Turner, 1979), which we admired for linking individual and group psychological processes to social structural variables

(see Sidanius et al., 2004 for an extended discussion). However, theorists before us (e.g., Ng, 1980) showed that power and status are not the same. SDT's most important epistemological assumption is that intergroup power, not which group is liked or respected more, is what matters.

Here it is important to explicate how SDT understands intergroup power. We use terms such as "dominance" and "oppression" to describe some intergroup relations, and this may lead our readers to think we are endorsing a definition of power that social psychologists rejected in the 1950s, namely that power is the ability to get another to act against his or her will, or absolute control. Because of interdependence theory (Thibaut and Kelley, 1959), and the interpersonal interaction model (e.g., Raven, 1986), many social psychologists view power as an aspect of a dyadic relation, wherein the party who can more easily exit the relationship or who exerts more influence has more power. In this view, then, power, is asymmetric interdependence (see Fiske and Berdahl, 2007 for a review). From our perspective, this influence/relational conception of power is not adequate for describing intergroup relations for three reasons.

First, many relations between groups and between group members are simply not interpersonal. There is a good deal of segregation as to where men and women work, where people of different ethnic groups and nations live, worship, and relax, and it is hard to see how not being in interpersonal intergroup contact leads to asymmetric effects for people in more and less powerful groups. What segregation in workplaces, neighborhoods, and service institutions does is to constrain which groups have access to resources, which is properly called power and not status. Another reason that intergroup relations cannot be described simply as aggregated interpersonal power relations is because discrimination is institutionalized (e.g., Feagin and Feagin, 1978). Institutional discrimination reveals that racism and sexism, for example, are not just products of asymmetric discrimination by individuals. There is a group-ness to inter-group relations across a society; for example, when shared categories lead to systematic differential treatment (e.g., Tilly, 1998).

Second, in addition to the kinds of inter-personal influence Raven (e.g., 1986) identified, intergroup relations may not be easily described as if there is only one kind of power. For example, Israel enjoys nation-hood, a functioning society, greater military power, and greater approval by superpowers than the Palestinian people do. On the whole we would have to say that Israel is much more powerful than the Palestinians, who lack first class citizenship and statehood, have an extraordinarily high unemployment rate, receive little social recognition outside the Arab world, and are killed in high numbers by Israelis. But relatively small-scale violence by nonstate actors, like the bombing of the US Marine barracks in Lebanon in 1983, has changed policies of powerful nations (e.g., Pape, 2005). It is pos-sible, then, that certain kinds of actions by less powerful groups, including strikes, boy-cotts, and nonviolent protests, and also cer-tain kinds of violence, can effect change. To understand this we need to acknowledge that power is not uni-typological. In fact, having things that others desire and exerting military might may make relatively rich and powerful countries like the US and Israel vulnerable to attack by people with little money, no stand-ing armies, and no state security. The forms of power that are relevant to intergroup rela-tions extend beyond influence, and elaborat-ing what these are an important agenda for intergroup relations research.

Third, a solely relational view of power does not address two important aspects of power: the extent to which people have voli-tion or agency, and whether they can obtain basic necessities. Both the philosophy and sociology of power consider degree of free-dom or *choice* to be an important aspect of power, a view also held by Lewin (1951). Having power more often enables more choice, whereas survival needs constrain some choices and necessitate others. Wellbeing and

volition may not be absolute dichotomous states, such that one either has or does not have them, but they are also not relative to other people. Unlike relational views of power, SDT's assumptions about power have considered both volition and need.

SDT explicitly allows that both dominants and subordinates can have agency, but has demonstrated that groups in social hierar-chies often have asymmetric outcomes. Rather than viewing power as asymmetric interdependence, though, SDT might be said to be more ontological in focusing on how the wellbeing of people in dominant and sub-ordinate groups differs. For example, four chapters of our book (Sidanius and Pratto, 1999) review institutional discrimination to understand how basic needs like housing, income, education, and healthcare are not enjoyed as much by people in subordinate groups as by people in dominant groups. In addition, from its beginning, SDT has shown that certain basic processes are not symmet-ric for people in more and less powerful groups. For example, SDO is less associated with ingroup identification for people in sub-ordinate groups than for people in dominant groups (Sidanius et al., 1994c), and more generally, the psychological facilitators of dominance do not work as well for members of subordinate groups. Our principle of *behavioral asymmetry* argues that people in subordinate groups do not behave in ways that are as self-serving as people in dominant groups do because of their power situation. Henry (2009), in his low-status compensa-tion theory, may be identifying part of the psychological reason this occurs.

There is another aspect of power that is implicit in SDT, but not in many other social psychological treatments of power. SDT has always acknowledged that societies often have hierarchy-attenuating individuals, cultural ideologies, and even institutions that strive against hierarchy, inequality, and exclu-sion. The fact that these hierarchy-attenuating forces can help the neediest have their needs met, and also effect social change, implies that SDT acknowledges the existence not just of *oppositional* power, but of *transformative* power. As acknowledged in social movements for empowerment (e.g., Ball, 2008) and in philosophy due to feminist theory (Wartenburg, 1990), power can be used to enable people to grow, thrive, develop, and to change relationships, not only for dominance. Indeed, dominance would be fairly easy to maintain were it not for this other kind of power. Given that we have always pointed out the importance of hierarchy-attenuating forces, it would be a mistake to assume that SDT views power only as destructive, coercive, and oppressive.

We view the recognition that social processes and the outcomes they produce are different for people in dominant versus subordinate groups to be an important and growing legacy of SDT. For example, Pratto and Espinoza (2001) tested whether job applicants of different ethnic groups and genders and who were apparently either low or high on SDO would be hired into hierarchy-enhancing or hierarchy-attenuating jobs differentially. The results showed that ethnic group moderated the previous effects found for White applicants, that men and high SDO applicants would be hired into hierarchy-enhancing jobs while women and low SDO applicants would be hired into hierarchy-attenuating jobs disproportionately (Pratto et al., 1997). Pratto and Espinoza (2001) found that Black and Hispanic applicants, regardless of their gender or SDO levels, were placed in hierarchy-attenuating jobs over hierarchy-enhancing jobs, and that only White male applicants were sorted by their SDO level into compatible jobs. In other words, White applicants were individuated and Black and Hispanic applicants were stereotyped more in job placement. To provide a different example, Saguy et al. (2009) showed that intergroup contact is not symmetric for people in low and high power groups. High power group members prefer to talk about what they have in common with low power groups rather than the power differential, and when they do this, low power group members come to expect that power will be addressed, when in fact it won't be. One general heuristic that SDT and other group positions theories suggest is that researchers consider that group power may moderate the processes and outcomes they posit.

Social dominance as a system

Unlike most theories in social psychology, SDT uses not just two (e.g., person–situation) but several levels of analyses. Its range of interest varies from the nature of attitudes and attitude formation at the person level (in its discussion of SDO) and the individual's construal of the social situation, to the asymmetrical behaviors of social groups, to the functions of system-wide social ideologies and the allocative decisions of social institutions (Mitchell and Sidanius, 1995). Furthermore, SDT holds that it is the interactions and intersections of these levels of analysis that account for the maintenance of social hierarchy. For example, research derived from SDT has shown that people in hierarchy-enhancing institutions tend to share the same hierarchy-enhancing legitimizing ideologies as each other (e.g., Sidanius et al., 1994a), and has also shown that performing hierarchy-enhancing roles tends to increase use of such ideologies in the discriminatory behavior of institutions (Michinov et al., 2005; Pratto et al., 1998). These kinds of intersecting processes contribute to the systematic perpetuation of hierarchy.

This example points out that SDT's assumptions that societies are social systems suggests a different kind of theorizing than is common in much of social psychology. Rather than perform critical experiments to rule out alternative explanations for large-scale outcomes like discrimination, or simply chain linear processes back in search of a root cause, SDT assumes that there is both elasticity and tenacity to interlinked social processes. This is why we would expect the contents of legitimizing myths to change over time and to differ from culture to culture, despite the fact that the two functions they perform tend to be found everywhere (e.g., Pratto et al., 2000; Sidanius and Pratto, 1999).

Further, because SDT seeks to account for systematic effects, we have assumed that there are redundant processes in the system of society. For example, we assume that institutional functioning is afforded by good fit between the hierarchy-enhancing or hierarchy-attenuating character of the social institution and the attitudes and behavioral predispositions of the individuals working within these institutions. We have documented evidence for several different processes that contribute to this person–institution fit, including self-selection, hiring and attrition biases, and stereotyping (Pratto et al., 1997; Sidanius et al., 2003; van Laar et al., 1999; see review by Haley and Sidanius, 2005). This redundancy helps to make systems tenacious.

THE APPLICATION OF SDT TO REAL-WORLD ISSUES

One of the strengths of SDT is its broad applicability and ability to make sense of a wide variety of intergroup phenomena and conflicts. We illustrate this wide applicability with respect to three social domains: (1) support for harsh criminal sanctions, (2) understanding the gender gap in social and political attitudes, and (3) understanding support for "terrorism" among Arab and Muslim populations.

Support for the death penalty

The US is among the very few countries in the world, and the only nation among the industrialized "democracies," that still employs the death penalty.[5] Consistent with the expectations of SDT, the evidence shows that the death penalty tends to be disproportionately used against subordinates (e.g., the poor and ethnic minorities), especially when these subordinates have been convicted of capital crimes against dominants (see Sidanius and Pratto, 1999: 214–217).

The standard criminal justice literature suggests that Americans support the death penalty for two major reasons: (1) as a means to deter future criminality, and (2) as a means of retribution or revenge for unacceptable behavior. While we have no reason to doubt the importance of both motives as sources of death penalty support, given the fact that the death penalty is disproportionately used against subordinates rather than dominants, SDT would also expect these attitudes to serve as legitimizing ideologies in the service of continued group-based inequality. If this view is correct, we would also expect to find evidence of a substantial correlation between SDO and death penalty support, and that this relationship should be substantially mediated by both deterrence and retribution beliefs.

Evidence consistent with this view has been found using a large sample of university students and structural equation modeling. Sidanius et al. (2006) not only found that death penalty support is strongly associated with the ideologies of deterrence and retribution, but these ideologies were also found to completely mediate the positive and significant relationship between SDO and death penalty support (see Figure 47.2). Thus, alongside the other functions deterrence and retribution beliefs may serve, there is evidence that one of these functions is continued group-based inequality and dominance within American society.

Exploring the gender gap

Men and women have significantly different social and political attitudes and behaviors. For example, women are more likely to vote for liberal or socialist political parties, are more supportive of social welfare policies, and are less supportive of militaristic and punitive social policies than are men (see Sidanius and Pratto, 1999). The gender difference on SDO discussed earlier helps account for these differences. In extensive analyses of a wide range of social and political attitudes, Sidanius and Pratto (1999: 282–290) found that approximately half of the relationships between gender and these social and political attitudes could be explained in terms of the higher levels of SDO among men.

Support for terrorism

SDT has also been applied to our understanding of support for terrorist violence against the West in general, and support of the 9/11 attack against the World Trade Center (WTC) in particular. There are at least two narratives that can be used to understand popular support for terrorist violence against the West. By far the most well-known narrative is known as the "clash of Civilizations," thesis first proposed by Bernard Lewis (1990), and later popularized by Samuel Huntington (1993). This thesis essentially suggests that Islamic hatred of the West goes beyond mere conflicts of interest and is to be located in the wholesale rejection of Western civilization as such, not only what it does but what it is, and the principles and values that it practices and professes. These are indeed

seen as innately evil, and those who promote or accept them as the "enemies of God" (Lewis, 1990).

In other words, people in other cultures reject the West as being culturally degenerate and even culturally profane.

The second narrative accounts for resentment, not of Western culture, but the politics of Western dominance and hegemony. From our group dominance perspective, support for terrorism against the West can be seen as endorsement of anti- or counterdominance directed at ending the perceived oppression of the Arab and Muslims worlds by the West.

Sidanius et al. (2004) explored the relative plausibilities of these two perspectives using a sample of university students in Beirut, Lebanon. Using structural equation modeling and measures of antidominance and clash-of-civilization attributions for the attack on the WTC, Sidanius and his colleagues found that support for the 9/11 attack on the World Trade Center was strongly related to anti-dominance attributions ($r = 0.32$, $p < 0.05$), while being essentially unrelated to clash-of-civilization attributions ($r = -0.10$, n.s.).

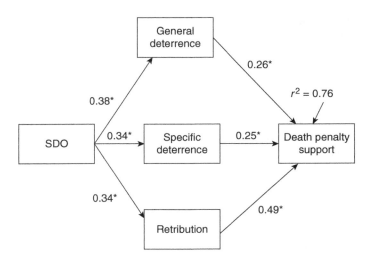

Chi-square = 0.204, df = 1, p = 0.65, RMSEA = 0.00, p(RMSEA < 0.05) = 0.78, AGFI = 0.997

Figure 47.2   Support for the death penalty as a function of belief in general deterrence, specific deterrence, retribution, and social dominance orientation. (From Sidanius et al. (2006))

Furthermore, while a consistent body of evidence shows that support for war and anti-"terrorist" violence in the Middle-East is *positively* associated with SDO among Western populations (Crowson et al., 2006; Heaven et al., 2006; Henry et al., 2005; McFarland, 2005; Sidanius and Liu, 1992), support for "terrorist" violence against the West is *negatively* associated with SDO among Lebanese and Middle-Eastern respondents (Henry et al., 2005). In other words, the more participants supported group-based dominance (and assumedly the present dominance of Israel and the West over Arab lands), the *less* one supported terrorist organizations, and the *less* one supported the attack on the WTC. Thus, rather than being an expression of support for group-based dominance and inequality among Lebanese students, support for terrorist violence against the West appears to be associated with counterdominance motivations. These results illustrate a central but uncommon assumption of SDT, namely that the meaning of actions and psychological states of people in dominant and subordinate groups depend on their group position.

SDT'S CONTRIBUTIONS TO THE INTERGROUP RELATIONS LITERATURE

There are four main areas in which SDT has contributed to the social psychological literature of intergroup relations. First, in contrast to the normative emphasis on factors such as social status, self-esteem, social identity, and individual social cognition and categorization, SDT helped to reintroduce and emphasize the factor of intergroup power in both its hard forms, such as the use of institutionalized and informal physical intimidation and violence, and soft forms such as the control of legitimizing ideologies (see Sidanius and Pratto, 1999; Mitchell and Sidanius, 1995). Consistent with realistic group conflict theory (e.g., Sherif et al., 1961), intergroup behavior is not simply driven by conflicts over social status, social regard, and symbolic rewards, but by conflict over the power to allocate social and economic resources to the benefit of one's own ingroup. We hope this has also refocused the discipline on unequal outcomes.

Second, rather than view prejudice by dominants as the only engine of inequality, SDT also emphasizes the power and agency of subordinates and their allies, for example, in hierarchy-attenuating institutions and in behavioral asymmetry. Whereas stereotyping and prejudice research often assumes only the perspective of dominant groups (e.g., Fiske et al., 2002), and stigma research focuses on the perspective of denigrated groups (e.g., Pinel, 1999), SDT not only considers both perspectives, but also how they relate to one another. This is how SDT can describe the complementarity of the behaviors of groups with different interests while showing how the actions of both sustain group dominance.

Third, although most social psychological approaches to intergroup relations limit their analyses to the intersection between the individual and the social group, SDT's analysis extends our focus from individuals to social context to institutional behavior to cultural ideologies to social structural context and reproductive patterns over historical time.

Fourth and most important, SDT puts the myriad components of intergroup beliefs, values, actions, and structure together to show how they function as a living social system. SDT has not only done this in linking processes at several different levels of social organization together, but by assuming that the stable system of hierarchy has multiple functionally redundant processes that help to stabilize it. This new way of understanding human social life may help social psychologists understand other systematic outcomes as well.

ACKNOWLEDGMENTS

We wish to thank Arnold Ho, Nour Kteily, Jennifer Sheehy-Skeffington, and the editors of this volume for their valuable comments on this chapter.

NOTES

1 Noblesse oblige is defined as the obligations of honorable and generous behavior of those with high rank.

2 However, for a contrary view, see Mallan et al. (2009).

3 Following Kurzban et al. (2001), we also assume that while sex may be a natural category of mind, "race" is not. Rather what we refer to as "race" may be a means of encoding coalitional alliances.

4 For a more comprehensive discussion of these issues, see Sidanius and Pratto (1999: 294–298).

5 The death penalty has been totally abolished in 46 of the 50 European nations. Abolition of the death penalty is also is also a condition for membership in the Council of Europe and its abolition is considered a central value to the European Union.

REFERENCES

Adorno, T.W., Frenkel Brunswik, E., Levinson, D.J. and Sanford, R.N. (1950) *The Authoritarian Personality*. New York: Norton.

Akrami, N. and Ekehammar, B. (2006) Right-wing authoritarianism and social dominance: Their roots in Big Five Personality Factors or Facets. *Journal of Individual Differences, 27*, 117–126.

Allport, G.W. (1954) The nature of prejudice. Menlo Park, CA: Addison-Wesley.

Altemeyer, B. (1998) The other 'authoritarian personality'. In M.P. Zanna (ed.), *Advances in Experimental Social Psychology, 30*, 47–92. San Diego: Academic Press.

Ball, J.B. (2008) A second look at the industrial areas foundation: Lessons for Catholic social thought and ministry. *Horizons, 35*, 271–297.

Beshoar, B.B. (1957) *Out of the Depths: The Story of John R. Lawson, a Labor Leader*. Denver: Colorado Historical Commission and Denver Trades and Labor Assembly.

Betzig, L. (1993) Sex, succession, and stratification in the first six civilizations: How powerful men reproduced, passed power on to their sons, and used power to defend their wealth, women and children. In L. Ellis (ed.), *Social Stratification and Socio*

economic Inequality: A Comparative Biosocial Analysis, pp. 37–74. New York: Praeger.

Blair, I.V. and Banaji, M.R. (1996) Automatic and controlled processing in stereotype priming. *Journal of Personality and Social Psychology, 70*, 1142–1163.

Blumer, H. (1960) Race prejudice as a sense of group position. *Pacific Sociological Review, 1*, 3–5.

Bretz, R.D. and Judge, T.A. (1994) Person-organization fit and the theory of work adjustment: Implications for satisfaction, tenure, and career success. *Journal of Vocational Behavior, 44*, 32–54.

Bureau of Justice Statistics (2001) Hate crimes reported in NIBRS, 1997–1999. Available at: http://www.ojp. usdoj.gov/bjs/pub/pdf/hcrn99.pdf.

Chiapello, E. and Fairclough, N. (2002) Understanding the new management ideology: A transdisciplinary contribution from critical discourse analysis and new sociology of capitalism. *Discourse and Society, 13*, 185–208.

Clark, K.B. and Clark, M.P. (1947) Racial identification and preference in Negro children. In T.M. Newcomb and E.L. Hartley (eds), *Readings in Social Psychology*, pp. 169–178. New York: Holt, Rinehart, and Winston.

Crenshaw, K., Gotanda, N., Peller, G. and Thomas, K. (1996) *Critical Race Theory: The Key Writings That Formed the Movement*. New York: The New Press.

Crowson, H.M., DeBacker, K. and Thomas, S.J. (2006) The role of authoritarianism, perceived threat, and need for closure or structure in predicting post 9/11 attitudes and beliefs. *The Journal of Social Psychology, 146*, 733–750.

Dahl, R.A. (1989) *Democracy and its Critics*. New Haven: Yale University Press.

Devine, P.G. (1989) Stereotypes and prejudice: Their automatic and controlled components. *Journal of Personality and Social Psychology, 56*, 5–18.

Dickemann, M. (1979) Female infanticide, reproductive strategies, and social stratification: A preliminary model. In N.A. Chagnon and W. Irons (eds), *Evolutionary Biology and Human Social Behavior: An Anthropological Perspective*, pp. 321–367. North Scituate, MA: Duxbury Press.

Duckitt, J. and Sibley, C.G. (2007) Right-wing authoritarianism, social dominance orientation and the dimensions of generalized prejudice. *European Journal of Personality, 21*, 113–130.

Duriez, B., Van Hiel, A. and Kossowska, M. (2005) Authoritarianism and social dominance in Western and Eastern Europe: The importance of the sociopolitical context and political interest and involvement. *Political Psychology, 26*, 299–320.

Ekehammar, B. (1985) Sex differences in socio political attitudes revisited. *Educational Studies*, *11*, 3–9.

Ekehammar, B. and Sidanius, J. (1982) Sex differences in socio-political ideology: A replication and extension. *British Journal of Social Psychology*, *21*, 249–257.

Feagin, J.R. and Feagin, C.B. (1978) *Discrimination American Style: Institutional Racism and Sexism.* Englewood Cliffs, Prentice Hall.

Fiske, S.T. and Berdahl, J. (2007) Social power. In A.W. Kruglanski and E.T. Higgins (eds), S*ocial Psychology: Handbook of Basic Principles*, 2nd Edition, pp. 678–692. New York: Guilford Press.

Fiske, S.T., Cuddy, A.J.C., Glick, P. and Xu, J. (2002) A model of (often mixed) stereotype content: Competence and warmth respectively follow from perceived status and competition. *Journal of Personality and Social Psychology*, *82*, 878–902.

Furnham, A. (1985) Adolescents' sociopolitical attitudes: A study of sex and national differences. *Political Psychology*, *6*, 621–636.

Gaertner, S.L. and Dovidio, J.F. (1986) The aversive form of racism. In S.L. Gaertner and J.F. Dovidio (eds), *Prejudice, Discrimination, and Racism: Theory and Research*, pp. 61–89, NY: Academic Press.

Goffman, E. (1959) *The presentation of self in everyday life.* Garden City, NY: Doubleday.

Gramsci, A. (1971). *Selections from the Prison Notebooks.* London: Wishart.

Haley, H. and Sidanius, J. (2005) Person-organization congruence and the maintenance of group-based social hierarchy: A social dominance perspective. *Group Processes & Intergroup Relations*, *8*, 187–203.

Hamilton, D.L. and Gifford, G.K. (1976) Illusory correlation in interpersonal perception: A cognitive basis of stereotype judgments. *Journal of Experiment Social Psychology*, *12*, 392–407.

Heaven, P.C.L., Organ, L., Supavadeeprasit, S. and Leeson, P. (2006) War and prejudice: A study of social values, right-wing authoritarianism, and social dominance orientation. *Personality and Individual Differences*, *40*, 599–608.

Henry, P.J. (2009) Low-status compensation: A theory for understanding the role of status in cultures of honor. *Journal of Personality and Social Psychology*, *97*, 451–466.

Henry, P.J., Sidanius, J., Levin, S. and Pratto, F. (2005) Social dominance orientation, authoritarianism, and support for intergroup violence between the Middle East and America. *Political Psychology*, *26*, 569–583.

Hood, R. and Cordovil, G. (1992) *Race and Sentencing: A Study in the Crown Court. A Report for the Commission for Racial Equality.* Oxford: Clarendon Press.

Huntington, S. (1993) The clash of civilizations. *Foreign Affairs*, *72*, 22–49.

Jost, J.T. and Banaji, M.R. (1994) The role of stereotyping in system-justification and the production of false consciousness. *British Journal of Social Psychology*, *33*, 1–27.

Katz, I. and Hass, R.G. (1988) Racial ambivalence and American value conflict: Correlational and priming studies of dual cognitive structures. *Journal of Personality and Social Psychology*, *55*, 893–905.

Keegan, J. (1993) *The History of Warfare.* New York: Alfred A. Knopf.

Klein, O. and Licata, L. (2003) When group representations serve social change: The speeches of Patrice Lumumba during the Congolese decolonization. *British Journal of Social Psychology*, *42*, 571–593.

Kurzban, R., Tooby, J. and Cosmides, L. (2001) Can race be erased? Coalitional computation and social categorization. *Proceedings of the National Academy of Science*, *98*, 15387–15392.

Lee, I., Pratto, F. and Johnson, B.T. (submitted) Intergroup Consensus/Disagreement in Support of Group-Based Hierarchy: An Examination of Socio-Structural and Psycho-Cultural Factors.

Lenski, G.E. (1984) *Power and Privilege: A Theory of Social Stratification.* Chapel Hill: University of North Carolina Press.

Lewin, K. (1951) Field theory in social science: Selected theoretical papers. (D. Cartwright, ed.). New York: Harpers & Brothers.

Lewis, B. (1990) The roots of Muslim rage: Why so many Muslims deeply resent the West, and why their bitterness will not easily be mollified. *The Atlantic Monthly*, *266*, 47–60.

Mallan, K.M, Sax, J. and Lipp, O.V. (2009) Verbal instructions abolishes fear conditioned to racial out-group faces. *Journal of Experimental Social Psychology*, *45*, 1303–1307.

Marjoribanks, K. (1981) Sex related differences in socio political attitudes: A replication. *Educational Studies*, *7*, 1–6.

Marx, K. and Engels, F. (1846) *The German Ideology*, (1970). New York: International Publishers.

McFarland, S.G. (2005) On the eve of war: Authoritarianism, social dominance, and American students' attitudes toward attacking Iraq. *Personality and Social Psychology Bulletin*, *31*, 360–367.

McFarland, S.G. and Adelson, S. (1996) An omnibus study of personality, values and prejudices. Paper presented at the Annual Convention of the International Society for Political Psychology, Vancouver, British Columbia, July 1996.

Michels, R. (1911) *Political Parties: A Sociological Study of the Oligarchical Tendencies of Modern Democracy*, (1962). New York: Free Press.

Michinov, N., Dambrun, M., Guimond, S. and Meot, A. (2005) Social dominance orientation, prejudice, and discrimination: A new computer method for studying discrimination behavior. *Behavioral Research Methods, 37*, 91–98.

Mitchell, M. and Sidanius, J. (1995) Social hierarchy and executions in the United States: A social dominance perspective. The death penalty: A social dominance perspective. *Political Psychology, 16*, 591–619.

Mosca, G. (1896) *The Ruling Class: Elements of Political Science*, Edition (1939). New York: McGraw-Hill.

Moscovici, S. (1988) Notes toward descriptions of social representations. *European Journal of Social Psychology, 18*, 211–250.

Navarrete, C.D., McDonald, M.M., Molina, L.M. and Sidanius, J. (2010) The psychological architecture of race and gender bias: An outgroup male target hypothesis. *Journal of Personality and Social Psychology, 98*, 933–945.

Navarrete, C.D., Olsson, A., Ho, A.K., Mendes, W.B., Thomsen, L. and Sidanius, J. (2009) Fear extinction to an outgroup face: The role of target gender. *Psychological Science, 20*, 155–158.

Ng, S.H. (1980) *The Social Psychology of Power*. NY: Academic Press.

Ohman, A. and Mineka, S. (2001). Fears, phobias and preparedness: Towards an evolved model of fear and learning. *Psychological Review, 108*, 483–522.

Olsson, A., Ebert, J.P., Banaji, M.R. and Phelps, E.A. (2005) The role of social groups in the persistence of learned fear. *Science, 309*, 785–787.

Pape, R. (2005) *Dying to Win: The Strategic Logic of Suicide Terrorism*. New York: Random House.

Pareto, V. (1901) *The Rise and Fall of the Elites*, (1979). New York: Arno Press.

Pareto, V. (1935) *The Mind and Society: A Treatise on General Sociology*, (1963). New York: Dover.

Pinel, E.C. (1999) Stigma consciousness: The psychological legacy of social stereotypes. *Journal of Personality and Social Psychology, 76*, 114–128.

Pratto, F. (1999) Social dominance theory. In M.P. Zanna (ed.), *Advances in Experimental Social Psychology, 31*, 192–263. New York: Academic Press.

Pratto, F. and Espinoza, P. (2001) Gender, ethnicity and power (2001). *Journal of Social Issues, 57*, 763–780.

Pratto, F., Liu, J.H., Levin, S., Sidanius, J., Shih, M., Bachrach, H. and Hegarty, P. (2000) Social dominance orientation and the legitimization of inequality across cultures. *Journal of Cross-Cultural Psychology, 31*, 369–409.

Pratto, F., Sidanius, J. and Levin, S. (2006) Social dominance theory and the dynamics of intergroup relations: Taking stock and looking forward. *European Review of Social Psychology, 17*, 271–320.

Pratto, F., Sidanius, J., Stallworth, L.M. and Malle, B.F. (1994) Social dominance orientation: A personality variable predicting social and political attitudes. *Journal of Personality and Social Psychology, 67*, 741–763.

Pratto, F., Stallworth, L.M. and Conway-Lanz, S. (1998) Social dominance orientation and the legitimization of policy. *Journal of Applied Social Psychology, 28*, 1853–1875.

Pratto, F., Stallworth, L., Sidanius, J. and Siers, B. (1997) The gender gap in occupational role attainment: A social dominance approach. *Journal of Personality and Social Psychology, 72*, 37–53.

Raven, B.H. (1986) A taxonomy of power in human relations. *Annals of Psychiatry, 16*, 633–636.

Rokeach, M. (1973) *The Nature of Human Values*. New York: Free Press.

Saguy, T., Tasuch,N., Dovidio, J.F. and Pratto, F. (2009) The irony of harmony: intergroup contact can produce false expectations for group equality. *Psychological Science, 20*, 114–121.

Sanday, P. (1981) *Female Power and Male Dominance*. Cambridge: Cambridge University Press.

Sherif, M., Harvey, O.J., White, B.J., Hood, W.R. and Sherif, C. (1961) *Intergroup Conflict and Cooperation: The Robbers' Cave Experiment*. Norman, OK: Institute of Group Relations, University of Oklahoma.

Sidanius, J., Devereux, E. and Pratto, F. (1992) A comparison of symbolic racism theory and social dominance theory: Explanations for Racial Policy Attitudes. *Journal of Social Psychology, 132*, 377–395.

Sidanius, J. and Ekehammar, B. (1980). Sex-related differences in socio-political ideology. *Scandinavian Journal of Psychology, 21*, 17–26.

Sidanius, J. and Ekehammar, B. (1983). Sex, political party preference and higher-order dimensions of socio-political ideology. *Journal of Psychology, 115*, 233–239.

Sidanius, J., Henry, P.J., Pratto, F. and Levin, S. (2004) Arab attributions for the attack on America: The case of Lebanese sub-elites. *Journal of Cross-Cultural Psychology, 35*, 403–416.

Sidanius, J., Levin, S., Liu, J.H. and Pratto, F. (2000) Social dominance orientation and the political psychology of gender: an extension and cross-cultural replication. *European Journal of Social Psychology, 30*, 41–67.

Sidanius, J. and Liu, J. (1992) Racism, support for the Persian Gulf War, and the police beating of Rodney

King: A social dominance perspective. *Journal of Social Psychology, 132*, 685–700.

Sidanius, J., Liu, J., Shaw, J. and Pratto, F. (1994a) Social dominance orientation, hierarchy-attenuators and hierarchy-enhancers: Social dominance theory and the criminal justice system. *Journal of Applied Social Psychology, 24*, 338–366.

Sidanius, J., Mitchell, M., Haley, H. and Navarrete, C.D. (2006) Support for harsh criminal sanctions and criminal justice beliefs: A social dominance perspective. *Social Justice Research, 19*, 433–449.

Sidanius, J. and Pratto, F. (1993) The inevitability of oppression and the dynamics of social dominance. In P. Sniderman and P. Tetlock (eds), *Prejudice, Politics, and the American Dilemma*, pp. 173–211. Stanford: Stanford University Press.

Sidanius, J. and Pratto, F. (1999) *Social Dominance: An Intergroup Theory of Social Hierarchy and Oppression.* Cambridge, MA: Cambridge University Press.

Sidanius, J., Pratto, F. and Bobo, L. (1994b) Social dominance orientation and the political psychology of gender: A case of invariance? *Journal of Personality and Social Psychology, 67*, 998–1011.

Sidanius, J., Pratto, F. and Brief, D. (1995) Group dominance and the political psychology of gender: A cross-cultural comparison. *Political Psychology, 16*, 381–396.

Sidanius, J., Pratto, F. and Rabinowitz, J. (1994c) Gender, ethnic status, ingroup attachment and social dominance orientation. *Journal of Cross-Cultural Psychology, 25*, 194–216.

Sidanius, J., Pratto, F., Sinclair, S. and van Laar, C. (1996) Mother Teresa Meets Genghis Khan: The dialectics of hierarchy-enhancing and hierarchy-attenuating career choices. *Social Justice Research, 9*, 145–170.

Sidanius, J., Sinclair, S. and Pratto, F. (2006) Social dominance orientation, gender and increasing college exposure. *Journal of Applied Social Psychology, 36*, 1640–1653.

Sidanius, J., Van Laar, C., Levin, S. and Sinclair, S. (2003) Social hierarchy maintenance and assortment into social roles: a social dominance perspective. *Group Processes and Intergroup Relations, 6*, 333–352.

Sidanius, J. and Veniegas, R.C. (2000) Gender and race discrimination: The interactive nature of disadvantage. In S. Oskamp (ed.), *Reducing Prejudice and Discrimination the Claremont Symposium on Applied Social Psychology* pp. 47–69. Mahwah, NJ: Lawrence Erlbaum Associates.

Stephan, W.G. and Finlay, K. (1999) The role of empathy in improving intergroup relations. *Journal of Social Issues, 55*, 729–743.

Tajfel, H. and Turner, J.C. (1979). An integrative theory of intergroup conflict. In W.G. Austin and S. Worchel (eds), *The Social Psychology of Intergroup Relations*, pp. 33–47. Monterey, CA: Brooks/Cole.

Tajfel, H. and Turner, J.C. (1986) The social identity theory of intergroup behavior. In S. Worchel and W.G. Austin (eds), *Psychology of Intergroup Relations*, pp. 7–24. Chicago: Nelson-Hall.

Thibaut, J.W. and Kelley, H.H. (1959) *The Social Psychology of Groups.* New York: Wiley.

Thomsen, L., Green, E.G.T. and Sidanius, J. (2008) We will hunt them down: How social dominance orientation and right-wing authoritarianism fuel ethnic persecution of immigrants in fundamentally different ways. *Journal of Experimental Social Psychology, 44*, 1455–1464.

Tilly, C. (1998) *Durable Inequality.* Berkeley, CA: University of California Press.

Trivers, R. (1972) Parental investment and sexual selection. In B. Campbell (ed.), *Sexual Selection and the Descent of Man*, pp. 136–179. New York: Aldine de Gruyter.

van den Berghe, P.L. (1978) *Man in Society: A Biosocial View.* New York: Elsevier North Holland.

van Laar, C., Sidanius, J., Rabinowitz, J. and Sinclair, S. (1999) The three R's of academic achievement: Reading, 'Riting, and Racism. *Personality and Social Psychology Bulletin. 25*, 139–151.

Wartenberg, T.E. (1990). *The Forms of Power: From Domination to Transformation.* Philadelphia: Temple University Press.

48

The Common Ingroup Identity Model

Samuel L. Gaertner and John F. Dovidio

ABSTRACT

This chapter reviews, from both a theoretical and personal perspective, the development of the common ingroup identity model, a social categorization-based perspective for reducing intergroup bias and improving intergroup relations. The model proposes that inducing members of different groups conceive of themselves as belonging to the same, more inclusive entity produces more positive beliefs, feelings, and behaviors toward one another. The chapter demonstrates the metamorphosis of our research interests from identifying a problem, aversive racism, to addressing the issue, the common ingroup identity model. First, we describe our personal journey leading to the development of the common ingroup identity model. Second, we discuss the model's historical intellectual roots and the empirical support for this point of view. Third, we consider how the model can be applied to address actual social problems, including prejudice, discrimination, and racism. The general message that this chapter conveys is that it is not only empirical support that advances theory but also the practical and conceptual challenges to the theory that stimulate conceptual development and new perspectives on enduring social problems.

INTRODUCTION

> We have never been just a collection of individuals or a collection of red states and blue states; we are and always will be the United States of America.
> Barack Obama (Election Eve, November 4, 2008).

This chapter is about the development of the common ingroup identity model (Gaertner and Dovidio, 2000), a social categorization-based perspective for reducing intergroup bias and improving intergroup relations. Fundamentally, this model proposes that if members of different groups (e.g., red states and blue states) would conceive of themselves as belonging to the same more inclusive entity (i.e., the United States, as Barack Obama's quote declares), then they would have more positive beliefs, feelings, and behaviors toward one another. Thus, factors that encourage members of different groups to think in more inclusive ways (e.g., in terms of "we," "us," or "our") can promote more harmonious intergroup relations.

Herein, we describe our personal journey leading to the development of the common ingroup identity model. We identify critical junctures, which are much clearer in hindsight than as we charted our paths, along the route leading to our attraction to this perspective. Then we discuss the model's historical intellectual roots and the empirical support for this point of view. After that, we consider how the model can be applied to address actual social problems, including prejudice, discrimination, and racism, which is where our journey began. We conclude with a discussion of directions that we and others have pursued as the evidence revealed that the theory's initial assumptions, although useful, were incomplete or more complex than we initially presumed and therefore present several problems and challenges for future research.

OUR PERSONAL JOURNEY

We trace the development of the common ingroup identity model back over 30 years. Various seeds of the ideas that formed the basis of the model appeared in our studies of race and helping (e.g., Gaertner and Dovidio, 1977) and prosocial behavior more generally (Piliavin et al., 1981), as well as in our research about identifying and combating subtle racism (Gaertner and Dovidio, 1986). In the concluding chapter of our edited volume, *Prejudice, Discrimination, and Racism*, we wrote, "[T]he research challenge is to discover techniques and strategies that induce members of separate groups to conceive of the aggregate as one entity, and then to examine whether this perception facilitates cooperativeness, acceptance, and personalized interactions" (Gaertner and Dovidio, 1986: 326).

The ideas coalesced into the initial formal presentation of the theoretical framework in 1993 (Gaertner et al., 1993), which was published in the *European Review of Social Psychology*. The most elaborate presentation of the model appeared in the monograph, *Reducing Intergroup Bias: The Common*

Ingroup Identity Model (Gaertner and Dovidio, 2000). In addition, we continue to refine, revise, and update the model (e.g., Dovidio et al., 2008). Consistent with the goals articulated by the editors of this volume, the present account presents our personal story relating to the development of the model and sets its key assumptions into their proper intellectual context.

Our journey is a collaborative one. The common ingroup identity model developed out of a collaborative relationship between the authors that began almost 36 years ago and our early research, together and apart, sowed the seeds for the major theme of the model; namely, the cognitive and motivational processes initiated by the recognition of ingroup membership – that is, "we-ness."

Sam Gaertner, an assistant professor at the University of Delaware and a new PhD from the City University of New York Graduate Center, had been working on the topic of aversive racism, a contemporary and subtle, but insidious, manifestation of racial bias. His work on this topic began with his PhD dissertation that obtained a serendipitous and provocative finding. A study in the dissertation (Gaertner, 1973) involved the willingness of registered Liberal and Conservative Party members in New York City to help a Black or White motorist whose car had broken down on a local highway. Confederates, who were identifiable as Black or White on the basis of their dialects, made telephone calls, claiming to have been dialing their mechanic's number from a public telephone along the highway. The callers explained that they now needed the respondent's help to call a mechanic because they used their last coin for this wrong-number call.

Consistent with previous research using paper and pencil measures of political ideology and racial attitudes (Adorno et al., 1950), Conservative Party members discriminated by helping Black callers less frequently than White callers, whereas Liberal Party members did not discriminate in terms of helping. Surprisingly, however, Liberal Party members discriminated in a different way.

Although Liberals helped Black and White callers equivalently when they knew their assistance was needed, they terminated this encounter more readily for Black than for White callers *prior to* learning fully of the caller's need for *their* help. These latter results were initially puzzling but became more understandable in the context of the notion of aversive racism (Kovel, 1970). This perspective suggested that liberals may be unconsciously biased and engage in subtle rather than blatant discrimination.

In 1973, Jack Dovidio, following the advice of his undergraduate advisors, came to Delaware as a graduate student after earning his BA at Dartmouth. He came with a range of interests, including altruism and nonverbal behavior, but with a primary personal interest in intergroup relations and prejudice. After about two years, our own group-based boundaries as faculty advisor and graduate student disintegrated and *we* became a research team and close personal friends ever since.

As an undergraduate, together with his advisor Bill Morris, Jack investigated the implications of an idea proposed by LeVine and Campbell (1972) that similarity of fate (see also Campbell, 1958) regarding a highly threatening event increases awareness of ingroup identity and the magnification of positive behaviors (e.g., prosocial action) that accompany ingroup membership. In a study by Dovidio and Morris (1975), while the participant and a confederate partner were waiting to participate in either the same or different experiments involving stressful electric shocks or nonstressful word association tasks, the confederate "accidentally" knocked a container of 100 pencils to the floor. The results revealed that prosocial behavior (involving the percentage of participants who helped or the number pencils participants picked up) was highest when participants expected to participate in the same highly stressful experiment than when they were to participate in the same low stress experiment or when they were to participate in different experiments. Dovidio and Morris concluded that "facing stress together

increases the likelihood of positive behaviors such as helping, presumably, by making the ingroup–outgroup distinction more salient and increasing 'we feelings'" (1975: 148).

In 1974, with support from the Office of Naval Research, we began a series of studies to explore predictions derived from the aversive racism framework. The fundamental premise of this research on aversive racism was that many Whites who consciously support egalitarian principles, endorse a liberal political ideology, and believe themselves to be non-prejudiced, also harbor negative attitudes about Blacks and other historically disadvantaged groups. These unconscious negative feelings and beliefs develop as a consequence of normal, almost unavoidable, and frequently functional cognitive, motivational, and social–cultural processes. As a consequence, whereas old-fashioned racists exhibit a direct and overt pattern of discrimination, aversive racists' actions may appear more variable and inconsistent. At times they discriminate (manifesting their negative feelings), and at other times they do not (reflecting their egalitarian beliefs). Specifically, we hypothesized that aversive racists discriminate against Blacks mainly (a) when norms in a situation are weak or ambiguous, so that it is difficult for aversive racists to judge their behavior as inappropriate; or (b) when they can justify or rationalize their negative behavior on the basis of some factor other than race. Thus discrimination occurs without challenging their nonprejudiced self-image. For example, the appropriateness of Liberals terminating their encounter with the Black motorist before learning that *their* help was necessary has no socially prescribed answer. Thus, Liberals discriminated only when their behavior could not be condemned, by others or themselves, as inappropriate.

Over the next decade, we conducted a number of collaborative projects studying race and helping, which not only provided support for the aversive racism framework (Dovidio and Gaertner, 2004; Gaertner and Dovidio, 1986) but also contributed to an emerging literature on bystander intervention. Much of our data were consistent with a general model of emergency intervention introduced by Jane Piliavin and Irving Piliavin (1973). Our convergence of findings and interests led to a collaboration with Jane Piliavin and Russ Clark, resulting in the book, *Emergency Intervention* (Piliavin et al., 1981), which attempted to explain *why* bystanders might intervene into the problems of other people. In this volume, we collectively elaborated and revised the Piliavin and Piliavin model, which proposed that bystander intervention was motivated by a desire to reduce unpleasant arousal elicited by witnessing an emergency while weighing the rewards and costs associated with various alternative actions for reducing this arousal. In the revised *arousal: cost–reward model*, "we-ness" between the bystander and the victim was identified as playing a central role in influencing *both* arousal and the perceptions of costs and rewards of the alternative actions, and thus ultimately was a critical factor in a bystander's responsiveness to an emergency.

In hindsight, we regard the *emergency intervention* project as especially critical in shaping our theoretical perspective and creating a conceptual foundation for the common ingroup identity model. Over the three-year period that we worked on revising the arousal: cost–reward model, our focus became riveted on the value of "we-ness," particularly among virtual strangers, in a context in which one of them needed the assistance of the other. Our interest in the importance of the social connection between individuals expanded our perspective to consider more fully the nature of *intergroup* processes, beyond the intrapsychic processes, such as the ambivalence between the conscious egalitarian values and unconscious bias, we had been focusing on in the study of aversive racism.

INTELLECTUAL CONTEXT OF THE THEORY

Our consideration of the value of "we-ness" in the study of prosocial behavior significantly

altered and widened our perspective on processes underlying racism and on potential ways to combat contemporary forms of racism such as aversive racism. In this section, we describe how changes in the theoretical landscape, influenced by European social psychologists, shaped our perspective, discuss the profound effects of social categorization, and describe the model and present the basic evidence supporting it.

The changing theoretical landscape

As a direct consequence of focusing on "we-ness," we became very interested in the European perspective on the importance of group membership and social identity for influencing intergroup attitudes and the behavior of individuals more generally. Our research on aversive racism and our general perspective on social psychology up until this point had been shaped primarily by North American social psychology, which had a strong emphasis in the individual (Steiner, 1974). The dominant theories of prejudice at that time conceived of bias as an attitude that was shaped by a number of individual-level processes. It was hypothesized to originate from socialization experiences with punitive parents who supported hierarchical relations (Adorno et al., 1950) and personal frustration (Dollard et al., 1939). These theories focused on individuals motivated to satisfy their own individual needs. The social–cognitive movement of the 1970s further implicated intrapersonal processes related to the types of heuristics that people use when thinking about a complex social world, and how these cognitive short-cuts contribute to stereotyping and prejudice (see Fiske and Taylor, 1991).

In contrast to the North American movement in social psychology toward more microlevel mechanisms in prejudice, European social psychology placed more emphasis on prejudice as an intergroup process, involving mechanisms such as collective identity that emphasized the distinct relationships that people have with members of their own group and other groups. European social psychology reflected the influence of Gestalt psychology, in which the focus included the individual but within a dynamic social field in which the individual is an integral part. Similar to the European approach, Sherif et al. (1961), in their classic Robbers Cave studies, emphasized the foundational role of social categorization in demarcating ingroup and outgroup membership and proposed that the functional relations between ingroups and outgroups are critical in determining intergroup attitudes. According to this position, competition between groups produces prejudice and discrimination, whereas intergroup interdependence and cooperative interaction that result in successful outcomes reduce intergroup bias.

In the tradition of European social psychology, social identity theory (Tajfel and Turner, 1979) and self-categorization theory (Turner, 1985) view the distinction between personal identity and social identity as a critical one because of its potential transformational consequences. What struck us as especially intriguing was the notion emerging from this literature that "the attractiveness of an individual is not constant, but varies with ingroup membership" (Turner, 1985: 60). Work in this vein that was particularly influential to us was Brewer's (1979) "cognitive–motivational analysis" of ingroup bias in the minimal intergroup situation. Her qualitative review of research revealed that features that increased the salience of ingroup–outgroup categorization (e.g., competition, similarity) were associated with increased intergroup bias. In particular, Brewer's analysis suggested that increases in intergroup bias were more often due to increased positive regard for ingroup members rather than to the devaluation of outgroup members. Brewer proposed, "Reconceptualizing the process of intergroup differentiation tends to shift the focus of attention from the negative implications of out-group perceptions to the positive consequences of in-group formation" (1979: 322).

According to Brewer, upon group formation, ingroup members are moved closer to and become less differentiated from the self and consequently are accorded more positive beliefs, feelings, and behaviors.

The possibility that intergroup bias could reflect positive orientations toward ingroup members rather than negative orientations toward outgroup members led us to consider the appropriateness of this perspective for understanding aversive racism. Whereas our focus had been primarily on how unconscious negative racial attitudes drive the subtle discrimination we observed, we recognized that discrimination among aversive racists may also be motivated by a tendency to behave in especially positive ways toward Whites. We thought that ingroup favoritism effects might help explain why aversive racists do not report possessing negative racial affect and genuinely regard themselves as nonprejudiced: Their actions may not be based primarily on negative orientations toward Blacks but rather on positive feelings about other ingroup members, Whites (Gaertner et al., 1997). Nevertheless, although positive ingroup regard may not be regarded as prejudice, it is important to recognize that its consequences may often be just as pernicious as anti-outgroup sentiment.

This insight was illuminating when considering ways to combat aversive racism. Over the years, we frequently presented to general as well as to professional audiences alerting them to the existence and dangers of aversive racism. After these presentations, people often asked, if people are unaware of their prejudice, how can we change their attitudes and, more importantly, their behavior toward Blacks? The research on ingroup–outgroup categorization and ingroup favoritism provided an essential clue. If aversive racists could conceive of Blacks and Whites primarily within a common, shared identity (e.g., employees of the same organization, citizens of the same nation) instead of two different racial groups, then the forces of ingroup favoritism could be extended to create more positive orientations toward Blacks.

We were far from being alone in recognizing the potential central role of social categorization in intergroup relations. Allport (1954) in his seminal work, *The Nature of Prejudice*, wrote about the normality and inevitability of social categorization: "The human mind must think with the aid of categories ... Categories are the basis for normal prejudgment. We cannot possibly avoid this process" (1954: 20). In his highly influential article, "Cognitive aspects of prejudice," Tajfel (1969) further emphasized that the cognitive bases of prejudice were not primarily irrational or psychopathological but rather directly related to social categorization and the search for social meaning. With this in mind, it might be easier to understand our attraction to the common ingroup identity model and the potential value of ingroup membership and the recognition of "we-ness" across group lines. Therefore, we began to seek a remedy for aversive racism that reduces indifference and increases the perceptions of connectedness between people across group lines: inducing people to recategorize others as members of a common ingroup.

Social categorization and the benefits to ingroup members

When people or objects are categorized into groups, actual differences between members of the same category tend to be perceptually minimized (Tajfel, 1969) and often ignored in making decisions or forming impressions. Members of the same category seem to be more similar than they actually are, and more similar than they were before they were categorized together. In addition, although members of a social category may be different in some ways from members of other categories, these differences tend to become exaggerated and overgeneralized. Thus, categorization enhances perceptions of similarities within groups and differences between groups, emphasizing social difference and group distinctiveness. For social categorization, this process becomes more ominous because these within- and between-group distortions have a tendency to generalize to additional dimensions (e.g., character traits) beyond those that differentiated the categories originally (Allport, 1954). Furthermore, as the salience of the categorization increases, the magnitude of these distortions also increases (Brewer, 1979).

Upon social categorization of people as members of the ingroup and of outgroups, people favor ingroup members in reward allocations (Tajfel et al., 1971). Upon social categorization, people favor ingroup members, both explicitly and implicitly in evaluations (Otten and Moskowitz, 2000). Cognitively, people retain more information in a more detailed fashion for ingroup members than for outgroup members (Park and Rothbart, 1982), have better memory for information about ways ingroup members are similar and outgroup members are dissimilar to the self (Wilder, 1981). In addition, people are more generous and forgiving in their explanations for the behaviors of ingroup relative to outgroup members. Positive behaviors and successful outcomes are more likely to be attributed to internal, stable characteristics (the personality) of ingroup than outgroup members, whereas negative outcomes are more likely to be ascribed to the personalities of outgroup members than of ingroup members (Pettigrew, 1979). Relatedly, observed behaviors of ingroup and outgroup members are encoded in memory at different levels of abstraction (Maass et al., 1989). Undesirable actions of outgroup members are encoded at more abstract levels that presume intentionality and dispositional origin (e.g., she is hostile) than identical behaviors of ingroup members (e.g., she slapped the girl). Desirable actions of outgroup members, however, are encoded at more concrete levels (e.g., she walked across the street holding the old man's hand) relative to the same behaviors of ingroup members (e.g., she is helpful).

In terms of social relations and behavioral outcomes, people are more cooperative and trustful of ingroup than outgroup members (Voci, 2006), and they exercise more personal restraint when using endangered resources shared with ingroup members than with others (Kramer and Brewer, 1984). Additionally, shared group membership decreases psychological distance from and facilitates arousal of promotive tension or empathy toward ingroup members (Hornstein, 1976). Relatedly, prosocial behavior is offered more readily to ingroup than to outgroup members (Dovidio et al., 1997; Piliavin et al., 1981).

Social categorization is a dynamic process, however, and people possess many different group identities and are capable of focusing on different social categories. By modifying a perceiver's goals, perceptions of past experiences, and/or expectations, there is opportunity to alter the level of category inclusiveness that will be primary or most influential in a given situation. This malleability of the level at which impressions are formed is important because of its implications for altering the way people think about members of ingroups and outgroups, and consequently about the nature of intergroup relations. Attempts to combat these biases can therefore be directed at altering the nature of social categorization.

The common ingroup identity: the theory and initial empirical evidence

The key idea of the common ingroup identity model is that factors that induce members of different groups to recategorize themselves as members of the same more inclusive group can reduce intergroup bias through cognitive and motivational processes involving ingroup favoritism (Gaertner and Dovidio, 2000; Gaertner et al., 1993). Thus, more positive beliefs, feelings, and behaviors, which are usually reserved for ingroup members, are extended or redirected to former outgroup members because of their recategorized ingroup status. Consequently, recategorization dynamically changes the conceptual representations of the different groups from

an "us" versus "them" orientation to a more inclusive, superordinate connection: "we." Allport (1954) also recognized the potential value of perceiving inclusive ingroup membership across group lines when he asked hopefully, "Can a loyalty to [hu]mankind be fashioned before interracial warfare breaks out?"

The common ingroup identity model proposes (see Figure 48.1) that the different types of intergroup interdependence and cognitive, perceptual, linguistic, affective, and environmental factors, which include features specified by Allport's (1954) contact hypothesis (i.e., cooperative intergroup interaction, equal status, egalitarian norms), can either independently or in concert alter individuals' cognitive representations of the aggregate. In addition, common ingroup identity may be achieved by increasing the salience of existing common superordinate memberships (e.g., a team, a school, a company, a nation) or categories (e.g., students; Gómez et al., 2008) or by introducing factors (e.g., common goals or fate; see Gaertner et al., 1999) that are perceived to be shared by the memberships. These cognitive representations as one group, two subgroups within a more inclusive group (i.e., a dual identity), two separate groups, or separate individuals, are proposed to then produce specific cognitive (e.g., accessibility of positive thoughts), affective (e.g., evaluations) and overt behavioral consequences (e.g., self-disclosure and helping)

Once people regard former outgroup members as ingroup members, they are proposed initially to accord them benefits of ingroup status heuristically that, in turn, mediate the relation between a one-group (or dual identity) representation and the ultimate cognitive, affective, and overt behavioral consequences. The benefits awarded heuristically to these new ingroup members include: decreased threat, increased empathy, trust, forgiveness, similarity to the self, increased inclusion of the other in the self, increased willingness to take the other's perspective, and more generous attributional interpretations

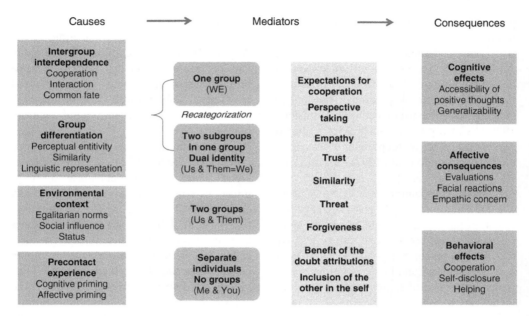

Figure 48.1   The common ingroup identity model

for the other's positive and negative behavior. These benefits are conceived to be the mediating psychological processes that are engaged by the perception of common ingroup identity which ultimately result in more positive cognitive, affective, and behavioral orientations toward these former outgroup members.

We acknowledge that there may be other ways to address the role of social categorization to reduce intergroup bias. In their mutual intergroup differentiation model, Brown and Hewstone (2005) posit that intergroup relations will be harmonious when group identities remain salient but within a context of cooperative intergroup interaction. Alternatively, Wilder (1981) proposed that an effective way to reduce intergroup bias is through decategorization, in which the salience of group boundaries is weakened and people are encouraged to regard one another primarily as distinct individuals. Brewer and Miller (1984; see also Miller, 2002) emphasize the additional value of personalization, in which information about each other's unique qualities is exchanged for reducing bias. We

see these approaches as alternative strategies which over time can often operate in complementary ways with the development of common identity.

One of our first experiments in this area directly explored how both common identity and decategorization can both reduce intergroup bias but in different ways (Gaertner et al., 1989). We compared the consequences of inducing two three-person *ad hoc* laboratory groups of college students to regard themselves as one group, two groups, or separate individuals. To manipulate these representations, we systematically varied a number of elements of the contact situation, including the spatial arrangement of the members (i.e., integrated, segregated or separated seating patterns) and the nature of the interdependence among the participants.

As we predicted, participants in the one-group and separate-individuals conditions reported lower bias (in liking and other evaluative characteristics) of the original ingroup and outgroup members relative to those in the two-groups condition. In addition, and as we hypothesized, participants in the one-group and separate-individuals conditions reduced bias in different ways. In the one-group condition, bias was reduced primarily because evaluations of former outgroup members became more positive; in the separate-individuals condition, evaluations of former ingroup members became less positive. More recently, employing procedures very similar to those used in Gaertner et al. (1989), Guerra et al. (2010), and Rebelo et al. (2004) obtained very similar patterns of findings among 9 and 10-year-old Black and White groups of children in Portugal. The nearly identical patterns of findings across these separate studies conducted with *ad hoc* and racial groups, in different countries, at different times, among people of different age groups, and using different measures illustrate the generalizability of the effects we initially observed.

Encouraged by the findings of our 1989 experiment, which provided initial support for the common ingroup identity model by revealing how recategorization can reduce intergroup bias by increasing the attractiveness of former outgroup members, we thought about what features, beyond the walls of our laboratory, might induce more inclusive group representations among the members of different groups, especially different racial groups. For some time, psychologists have known that the conditions outlined in the contact hypothesis (Allport, 1954; see also Pettigrew, 1998; and Pettigrew and Tropp, 2006), involving cooperative intergroup interaction, equal status between the groups, opportunities for self-revealing interactions, and equalitarian norms endorsed by relevant authority enhance the effect of intergroup contact on reducing intergroup bias. What has been more elusive, however, has been the identification of the psychological processes that are activated by these conditions of contact that mediate their relation to positive intergroup consequences.

It seemed reasonable to us that each of the conditions of contact specified by Allport (1954), which includes the cooperative intergroup interaction component specified in Sherif et al.'s functional model, may share

the capacity to induce more inclusive cognitive representations among the memberships. In turn, these more inclusive representations are proposed to activate the series of psychological processes we specified above. This insight thereby extends Allport's contact hypothesis and Sherif's functional theory by linking their hypotheses to measurable psychological processes.

We directly tested these ideas with regard to the importance of intergroup cooperation in an experiment (Gaertner et al., 1990). This study again brought two three-person laboratory groups together under conditions designed to vary independently the members' representations of the aggregate as one group or two groups (by varying factors such as seating arrangement) and the presence or absence of intergroup cooperative interaction. Supportive of the hypothesis concerning how cooperation reduces bias, among participants induced to feel like two groups, the introduction of cooperative interaction increased their perceptions of one group and also reduced their bias in evaluative ratings, primarily by enhancing evaluations of outgroup members relative to those who did not cooperate during the contact period. Although Sherif et al. (1961) revealed that competition between groups increases intergroup conflict while intergroup cooperation produces intergroup harmony, the current study reveals just how cooperative intergroup interaction, in part, psychologically produces intergroup harmony by influencing the salience of intergroup boundaries. Supportive of the common ingroup identity model, these findings reveal that cooperation between groups changes the members' categorization scheme of the memberships from "us and them" to a more inclusive "we." Although Sherif and Sherif (1969: 286–288) recognized the capacity of intergroup cooperation to facilitate the development of a common superordinate entity, they conceived of this entity more concretely as the development of an emergent, formal organizational system with shared norms and standards, rather than a common identity that exists more ephemerally only in the mind of each member.

The early evidence on the common ingroup identity model was generally strong in support for the model. However, the model was not without critics. For example, with respect to external validity, Hewstone (1996: 351) questioned whether a common ingroup identity can override powerful racial or ethnic categories on "more than a temporary basis." Indeed, our initial support for the model was based primarily on research with groups formed in the laboratory. In the next section we address the issue of the effectiveness of common identity in improving relations between meaningful, enduring groups, and consider the model's potential for addressing social problems.

ADDRESSING SOCIAL PROBLEMS

In this section, we examine research testing the applicability of the common ingroup identity model to relationships between members of groups in meaningful relations in "real-world" contexts and consider related challenges to the framework.

The application of the model to real groups

Since the initial research on the common ingroup identity model, a considerable body of work has demonstrated the applicability of the model to relations between a range of different groups in meaningful naturalistic contexts. Three survey studies across different domains of intergroup life offered converging support for the idea that features specified by the contact hypothesis increase intergroup harmony, in part because they transform members' representations of the memberships from separate groups to one more inclusive group. Participants in these studies included students attending a multiethnic high school (Gaertner et al., 1996), banking executives who had experienced a corporate merger involving a wide variety of banks across the US (Bachman, 1993), and college

students who are members of blended families (Banker and Gaertner, 1998). In general, across these studies the more favorable participants reported the conditions of contact between the groups (e.g., cooperation), the more the school (or company or family) felt like one group. Supportive of the model, the more it felt like one group, the lower the bias in affective reactions in the high school, the less the intergroup anxiety among the banking executives, and the greater the amount of stepfamily harmony. Also, a longitudinal study of stepfamilies found evidence supportive of the direction of causality between the constructs proposed by our model across time (Banker, 2002). Thus, we have found support for the model across a variety of intergroup settings and methodological approaches.

We also obtained experimental evidence of the effects of creating common identity on interracial behavior. One study was a field experiment conducted at the University of Delaware football stadium prior to a game between the University of Delaware and Westchester State University (Nier et al., 2001, Study 2). In this experiment, Black and White students approached fans of the same sex from both universities just before the fans entered the stadium. These fans were asked if they would be willing to be interviewed about their food preferences. Our student interviewers systematically varied whether they were wearing a University of Delaware or Westchester State University hat. By selecting fans who wore similar clothing that identified their university affiliation, we systematically varied whether fans and our interviewers had common or different university identities in a context where we expected these identities to be particularly salient. Although we planned to over-sample Black fans, the sample was still too small to yield any informative findings.

Among White fans, however, sharing common university identity with the Black interviewers significantly increased their compliance (59 percent) relative to when they did not share common identity with the Black interviewer (36 percent). When the interviewers were White, however, there was no significant difference in their levels of compliance as a function of their university identity. They gained equivalent levels of compliance when they shared common university identity with the fan (44 percent) as when they appeared to be affiliated with the rival university (37 percent). These findings offer support for the idea that outgroup members will be treated more favorably when they are perceived to also share a more inclusive, common ingroup affiliation.

In other work, we explored whether a common ingroup identity can affect the fundamental way that Whites think about Blacks during interracial interactions. Within the aversive racism framework, a major motive of Whites in interracial situations is to *avoid wrongdoing*. Supportive of this view, we have found across a variety of different studies that Whites typically do not discriminate against Blacks in situations in which norms for appropriate behaviors are clearly defined. Thus, Whites can, at least under some circumstances, successfully suppress negative beliefs, feelings and behavior toward Blacks when it is obvious that expressing such reactions reflects racial bias. Unfortunately, in view of work on stereotype suppression and rebound, it is possible that once this self-imposed suppression is relaxed, negative beliefs, feelings, and behaviors would be *even more likely* than if they were not suppressed initially.

The common ingroup identity model, because it focuses on redirecting the forces of ingroup favoritism, can potentially change the motivational orientation or intentions of aversive racists from trying to avoid wrongdoing to trying to *do what is right*. Some preliminary evidence from our laboratory suggests the potential promise of a common ingroup identity to alter motivation in just such a positive way (Gaertner and Dovidio, 2000).

In this experiment, White participants who were about to interact with a White or a Black confederate were either asked to try to avoid wrongdoing, instructed to try to behave correctly toward the other person, informed that they were part of the same team with their partner and competing against a team at a rival institution, or were given no instructions. The dependent measure of interest was the relative accessibility of negative thoughts, as assessed by changes in responses on a Stroop color-naming task after the interaction relative to responses on a baseline Stroop task administered before the interaction. A rebound effect would be reflected in greater accessibility (i.e., longer color-naming latencies) of negative relative to positive words on the post-test Stroop task.

We hypothesized that because the primary motivation of aversive racists in interracial interaction is to avoid wrongdoing and thus to suppress negative thoughts and feelings, participants explicitly instructed to avoid wrongdoing and those given no instructions would show relatively strong accessibility of negative thoughts after interacting with a Black confederate. In contrast, we expected participants instructed to behave correctly and those in the "same team" condition (who were hypothesized to adopt a positive orientation on their own) would escape such a rebound effect.

The results revealed that when the confederate was White, the experimental conditions did not affect the accessibility of negative thoughts from one another or from baseline. When the confederate was Black, however, the increased accessibility of negative relative to positive characteristics (from the pre-test to the post-test) in the avoid-wrongdoing and no-instructions conditions was significantly greater than in the do-right and same-team conditions, in which there was an increase in the accessibility of positive relative to negative thoughts. The pattern of these findings suggests that the development of a common ingroup identity can alter motivation in interracial situations from one of suppressing negative thoughts, feelings, and actions to one that is positive, more appetitive and prosocial – and in a way that does not ironically result in further increases in negative thoughts. These findings are particularly encouraging to us because they illustrate the potential of a common ingroup identity for addressing the underlying motivational dynamics of aversive racism, which is where our journey began. Other researchers, however, also have recognized the potential of a common ingroup identity to address a variety of social issues.

Recategorization in terms of a common ingroup identity can promote intergroup forgiveness and trust. For instance, Wohl and Branscombe (2005) showed that increasing the salience of Jewish students' "human identity," in contrast to their "Jewish identity," increased their perceptions of similarity between Jews and Germans, as well as their willingness to forgive Germans for the Holocaust (Study 3) and their willingness to associate with contemporary German students (Study 4). A shared superordinate identity has also been shown to affect responsiveness to others. Kane et al. (2005) found that group members were more accepting of a newcomer's innovation when the newcomer shared a superordinate identity with them than when the newcomer did not, and that the strength of superordinate group identification was positively related to the extent to which group members accepted the innovative solution. Also, people are more responsive to the needs of former outgroup members perceived within a common ingroup identity (Dovidio et al., 1997) across a range of situations, including emergency situations (Levine et al., 2005).

In general, when we present this work people frequently question whether the development of a common ingroup identity is a realistic strategy to change and sustain more tolerant norms and attitudes. Our evaluation study of an elementary school antibias education intervention attempts to address this question.

Houlette et al. (2004) evaluated hypotheses derived from the common ingroup identity model in a quasi field experiment in the context of the Green Circle school-based antibias intervention program, which is designed to combat a range of biases (based on weight and sex, as well as race and ethnicity) among first- and second-grade children. The guiding assumption of the Green Circle

Program, which is practically and theoretically compatible with the common ingroup identity model, is that helping children bring people from different groups conceptually into their own circle of caring and sharing fosters appreciation of their common humanity as well as respect for their differences. In particular, facilitators engage children in a variety of exercises designed to expand the circle, for instance, emphasizing, "All of us belong to one family – the human family." In terms of outcomes, the Green Circle intervention motivated the children to be more inclusive in selecting their most preferred playmate. Specifically, compared with children in the control condition who did not participate in Green Circle activities, those who were part of Green Circle showed significantly greater change in willingness to select other children who were different than themselves in race and in sex as a child that they "would most want to play with." These changes in the most preferred playmate involve a child's greater willingness to cross group boundaries in making friends – a factor that is one of the most potent influences in producing more positive attitudes toward the outgroup as a whole (Pettigrew, 1998).

In terms of future research applying our model to social problems, although racial disparity in health outcomes is a multifaceted problem, we are excited about the opportunity to develop an intervention based upon the common ingroup identity model to provide patients and physicians with a common team identity that has the potential to influence the communication between physician and patient as well as patient trust and adherence to physician recommendations (Penner et al., 2009).

Problems and challenges

Although there is substantial evidence supportive of the usefulness of the common ingroup identity model for reducing intergroup bias and conflict, a number of problems and challenges remain to be addressed.

Conflict at the superordinate level

It is important to recognize that the successful induction of a common ingroup identity does not necessarily eliminate social biases entirely. Upon recategorization, other outgroups, probably at the same level of inclusiveness, are likely to become the focus of "we–they" comparisons intended to maintain or protect the recategorized group's positive distinctiveness. Kessler and Mummendey (2001), for example, found that East Germans who recategorized West Germans and East Germans as Germans became more biased over time toward members of other countries relative to those who continued to use the East–West German categorization scheme. Kessler and Mummendey noted that "recategorization is a 2-edged process: Although it reduces conflict at the subgroup level, it may initiate conflict at the common ingroup level" (2001: 1099). Thus, although recategorization may only redirect bias rather than reduce it completely, this may be desirable when conflict is especially unproductive.

Complementary and reciprocal processes

Although research on the model has generally focused on the immediate impact of creating a common ingroup identity, recategorization may operate in a complementary fashion with other processes over time to reduce intergroup bias in a more general and sustained way (Gaertner and Dovidio, 2000; Hewstone, 1996; Pettigrew, 1998). The more favorable impressions of and orientations toward outgroup members produced by recategorization within a common ingroup identity are not likely to be finely differentiated, at least initially. Rather, these more elaborated, personalized impressions can soon develop within the context of a common identity because the newly formed positivity bias is likely to encourage more open communication and greater self-disclosing interaction (see Dovidio et al., 1997) and friendship (see West et al., 2009) between former outgroup members. Thus, over time a common identity is proposed to encourage personalization of outgroup members (that reduces bias through a decategorization strategy that de-emphasizes group identities altogether; see Miller et al., 1985) and thereby initiates a second route to achieving reduced bias.

Intergroup threat among subgroups

In addition, efforts to induce a common identity can sometimes be met with resistance that can increase bias between members of the original groups. Social identity theory (Tajfel and Turner, 1979) proposes that people are motivated to maintain the positive distinctiveness of their group relative to other groups. When the integrity of one's group identity is threatened, people are motivated to re-establish positive and distinctive group identities and thereby maintain relatively high levels of intergroup bias (Brown and Wade, 1987) or show increased levels of bias (see Jetten et al., 2004 for a review). Consistent with this reasoning, introducing interventions such as emphasizing similarity or overlapping boundaries between the groups (Dovidio et al., 1997) or shared identity (Hornsey and Hogg, 2000) can exacerbate intergroup bias as a way of reaffirming positive distinctiveness. This effect is particularly likely to occur among people who value their original group highly, such as those more highly identified with their original group (Crisp et al., 2006), and when the initiative to form a superordinate identity is perceived to come from an outgroup rather than an ingroup member (Gómez et al., 2008). Additional work, however, suggests that once induced successfully, a common identity can reduce threat among subgroups. Riek et al. (2010) directly manipulated the salience of Democrats' and Republicans' shared identity as Americans and obtained experimental evidence suggesting that common identity increases positive outgroup attitudes by first reducing intergroup threat.

A dual identity

We note that the development of a common ingroup identity does not necessarily require each group to forsake its less inclusive group identity completely (Gaertner et al., 1989).

Social identities are complex, and every individual belongs to multiple groups simultaneously (Brewer, 2000). Thus, depending on their degree of identification with different categories and contextual factors that make particular identities more salient, individuals may activate one or more of these identities simultaneously (Roccas and Brewer, 2002), as well as sequentially (Turner, 1985). As reflected in the "subgroups within one group" (i.e., a dual identity) representation, it is possible for members to conceive of two groups (e.g., science and art majors) as distinct units (thereby establishing "mutual group differentiation") within the context of a superordinate (i.e., university identity) social entity.

When group identities and their associated cultural values are adaptive, or when they are associated with high status or highly visible cues to group membership, it would be undesirable or impossible for people to relinquish these group identities completely or, as perceivers, to be "colorblind." Indeed, demands to forsake these group identities or to adopt a colorblind ideology would likely arouse strong reactance and exacerbate intergroup bias. If, however, people continued to regard themselves as members of different groups, but all playing on the same team, intergroup relations between these "subgroups" would usually become more positive than if members only considered themselves as "separate groups." Although, Allport (1954) observed that "concentric loyalties take time to develop, and often of course they fail completely to do so" (1954: 44–45), when subgroup identities are recognized, valued, and linked positively to the superordinate group identity, a dual identity may be effective for reducing intergroup bias and maintaining harmonious relations between groups. In addition, while it is not likely that a common ingroup identity can replace national, religious, and ethnic bases of categorization for very long, it is encouraging that its effects can be longer lasting, in part because of the reciprocal relation between the different categorization-based strategies (e.g., recategorization and personalization) that can continue to improve relations between the subgroups.

Conceptually, whereas the mutual intergroup differentiation model emphasizes the value of maintaining separate group identities within positive functional relations (i.e., cooperation) between groups, the common ingroup identity model posits that the superordinate identity component of a dual identity can be established in other ways, such as increasing the salience of overarching entities, as well. From the perspective of the common ingroup identity model it is the simultaneous salience of separate and superordinate group identities, not the particular mechanism that achieves this, that is important for intergroup bias. Consistent with this position, there is evidence that the intergroup benefits of a strong superordinate identity can be achieved for both majority and minority group members when the strength of the subordinate identity is also high (Huo et al., 1996). These findings are also conceptually consistent with studies that reveal that interethnic attitudes are more favorable when participants are primed with a multicultural, pluralistic ideology for increasing interethnic harmony that emphasizes the value of a dual identity, relative to an assimilation ideology, which closely parallels a one-group representation (Richeson and Nussbaum, 2004).

Moreover, the benefits of intergroup contact may more easily generalize to additional outgroup members with a dual identity than with the pure one-group representation because the associative link to their original group identity remains intact, as in the mutual intergroup differentiation model. Research by González and Brown (2003, 2006) offers empirical support for this possibility. They found that manipulations designed to emphasize one group or dual identity representations produced equivalently low levels of bias in reward allocations to ingroup and outgroup members who were present in the contact situation. The researchers further investigated generalized bias, involving reward allocations to ingroup and outgroup members who were viewed on videotape. In terms of the relative amount of bias between conditions, generalized bias was somewhat, but not reliably, lower in the dual-identity condition than in the one-group condition. With respect to the extent to which participants within each condition favored their ingroup over the outgroup, there was no significant bias in the dual-identity condition, whereas bias was not fully eliminated in the one-group condition. Thus, a dual identity may offer some advantages over a one-group identity for generalized reductions in bias.

We note, however, that in contrast to the consistently positive relationship between the experience of a common identity (i.e., a one-group representation) and more favorable intergroup orientations, the strength of a dual identity can have divergent effects, associated with either positive or negative intergroup responses. For instance, in the multiethnic high-school study, a dual identity was related to lower bias, whereas in studies of banking executives involved in a merger and of members of blended families, a stronger sense of a dual identity was related to greater bias and conflict (see Gaertner et al., 2001).

One explanation for this latter effect is that when a common identity is made salient for members of different groups, members of one group or both groups may begin to regard their subgroup's characteristics (such as norms, values, and goals) as more prototypical of the common, inclusive category compared with those of the other subgroup (Mummendey and Wenzel, 1999). When this occurs, the outgroup is judged as substandard, deviant, or inferior, leading to greater bias between the subgroups (e.g., Waldzus et al., 2004). This type of group projection that exacerbates bias may be more likely to occur when the superordinate identity represents a dimension directly relevant to the subcategory identities (e.g., Germans for East Germans and West Germans); when the superordinate identity is irrelevant to the subgroup identities, the experience of a dual identity is likely to have more favorable intergroup consequences (Hall and Crisp, 2005; see also Dovidio et al., 2008. Thus, further work is

needed to understand the factors that can moderate the effectiveness of a dual identity for reducing bias and illuminate the mechanisms accounting for these effects.

CONCLUSION

In summary, the evidence reviewed in this chapter reveals consistent support for the key principle of the common ingroup identity model: successfully inducing ingroup and outgroup members to adopt a one-group representation inclusive of both groups, even when earlier group boundaries remain salient, reduces intergroup bias. Furthermore, this fundamental premise has been supported across studies using a variety of methodological approaches with participants of different ages, races and nationalities.

Nevertheless many questions, of both theoretical and practical significance, remain. For example, if recategorization as one group generalizes beyond those participants present (González and Brown, 2003, 2006), what is the mechanism through which this occurs? One explanation is that even when common identity is primary, vestiges of previous different group identities still remain. Thus, functionally, the major difference between the one-group and dual-identity representations may be one of degree – likely relating to the *relative* salience of both the subgroup and the superordinate identities.

Also, it would be important to learn whether it would be beneficial to activate recategorization processes when groups are engaged in direct, potentially mortal, conflict, and if so, how to effectively activate such a representation. Practically, Kelman (1999), whose work has focused on improving Palestinian–Israeli relations to achieve peace in the Middle East, has demonstrated that it is not necessary to create a common ingroup identity among *all* of the people involved in conflict to improve intergroup relations significantly. Kelman's conflict resolution workshops (see Rouhana and Kelman, 1994) bring together 8–16 influential leaders from both sides in interactive, problem-solving exercises. These leaders can potentially create coalitions of peace-minded participants across conflict lines. And the workshops present a model for a new relationship between the parties (1994: 665). Thus even within the context of intense historical and contemporary conflict, it may be possible to be creative and to engineer the development of a common ingroup identity for a subset of group members with significant residual effects for the groups as a whole.

As the Hippocratic Oath proscribes, "Thou shalt do no harm," we need to further identify negative consequences associated with recognition of common identity across group lines as well as factors that might mitigate these effects. For example, Wright (2001) proposed that recognition of common identity may mitigate a lower status group's desire for collective action to address social inequalities. Likewise, Saguy et al. (2009) suggest that commonality-focused contact among disadvantaged groups produced unrealistic expectations of fair and egalitarian treatment which were not forthcoming by members of the advantaged group.

In conclusion, this chapter describes the origins, development, applications, and challenges of the common ingroup identity model from both a theoretical and personal perspective. It reveals the importance of serendipity in scientific research – how unexpected findings can lead to new theoretical opportunities – and shows how different lines of research and professional interests can converge in unforeseeable ways. The chapter demonstrates the metamorphosis of our research interests from identifying a problem, aversive racism, to addressing the issue, the common ingroup identity model. The broader and more fundamental message that our work conveys, however, is that it is not only empirical support that advances theory but also the practical and conceptual challenges to the theory that stimulate conceptual development and new perspectives on age-old problems.

ACKNOWLEDGMENTS

Preparation of this chapter was supported by NSF Grant # BCS–0613218.

REFERENCES

Adorno, T.W., Frenkel-Brunswik, E., Levinson, D.J. and Sanford, R.N. (1950) *The Authoritarian Personality*. New York: Harper.

Allport, G.W. (1954) *The Nature of Prejudice*. Cambridge, MA: Addison-Wesley.

Bachman, B.A. (1993) An intergroup model of organizational mergers. Unpublished PhD dissertation, Department of Psychology, University of Delaware, Newark.

Banker, B.S. (2002) Intergroup conflict and bias reduction in stepfamilies: A longitudinal examination of intergroup relations processes. Unpublished PhD dissertation, Department of Psychology, University of Delaware, Newark.

Banker, B.S. and Gaertner, S.L. (1998) Achieving stepfamily harmony: An intergroup relations approach. *Journal of Family Psychology, 12*, 310–325.

Brewer, M.B. (1979) Ingroup bias in the minimal intergroup situation: A cognitive-motivational analysis. *Psychological Bulletin, 86*, 307–324.

Brewer, M.B. (2000) Reducing prejudice through cross-categorization: Effects of multiple social identities. In S. Oskamp (ed.), *Reducing Prejudice and Discrimination: The Claremont Symposium on Applied Social Psychology*, pp. 165–183. Mahwah, NJ: Erlbaum.

Brewer, M.B. and Miller, N. (1984) Beyond the contact hypothesis: Theoretical perspectives on desegregation. In N. Miller and M.B. Brewer (eds), *Groups in Contact: The Psychology of Desegregation*, pp. 281–302. Orlando: Academic Press.

Brown, R. and Hewstone, M. (2005) An integrative theory of intergroup contact. In M.P. Zanna (ed.), *Advances in Experimental Social Psychology, 37*, 255–343. San Diego: Academic Press.

Brown, R.J. and Wade, G. (1987) Superordinate goals and intergroup behavior: The effect of role ambiguity and status on intergroup attitudes and task performance. *European Journal of Social Psychology, 17*, 131–142.

Campbell, D.T. (1958) Common fate, similarity and other indices of the status of aggregates of persons as social entities. *Behavioral Science, 3*, 14–25.

Crisp, R.J., Walsh, J. and Hewstone, M. (2006) Crossed categorization in common ingroup contexts.

Personality and Social Psychology Bulletin, 32, 1204–1218.

Dollard, J., Doob, L., Miller, N., Mowrer, O.H. and Sears, R.R. (1939) *Frustration and Aggression.* New Haven, CT: Yale University Press.

Dovidio, J.F. and Gaertner, S.L. (2004) Aversive racism. In M.P. Zanna (ed.), *Advances in Experimental Social Psychology, 36,* 1–51. San Diego: Academic Press.

Dovidio, J.F., Gaertner, S.L. and Saguy, T. (2008) Another view of "we": Majority and minority group perspectives on a common ingroup identity. *European Review of Social Psychology, 18,* 296–330.

Dovidio, J.F., Gaertner, S.L., Validzic, A., Matoka, K., Johnson, B. and Frazier, S. (1997) Extending the benefits of re-categorization: Evaluations, self-disclosure and helping. *Journal of Experimental Social Psychology, 33,* 401–420.

Dovidio, J.F. and Morris, W.N. (1975) Effects of stress and commonality of fate on helping behavior. *Journal of Personality and Social Psychology, 31,* 145–149.

Fiske, S.T. and Taylor, S.E. (1991) *Social Cognition,* 2nd Edition. New York: McGraw-Hill.

Gaertner, S.L. (1973) Helping behavior and racial discrimination among liberals and conservatives. *Journal of Personality and Social Psychology, 25,* 335–341.

Gaertner, S.L., Bachman, B.A., Dovidio, J.D. and Banker, B.S. (2001). Corporate mergers and stepfamily marriages: Identity, harmony, and commitment. In M.A. Hogg and D. Terry (eds), *Social Identity in Organizations,* pp. 265–288. Oxford: Blackwell.

Gaertner, S.L. and Dovidio, J.F. (1977) The subtlety of white racism, arousal, and helping behavior. *Journal of Personality and Social Psychology, 35,* 691–707.

Gaertner, S.L. and Dovidio, J.F. (1986) The aversive form of racism. In J.F. Dovidio and S.L. Gaertner (eds), *Prejudice, Discrimination, and Racism,* pp. 61–89. Orlando: Academic Press.

Gaertner, S.L. and Dovidio, J.F. (2000) *Reducing Intergroup Bias: The Common Ingroup Identity Model.* Philadelphia: The Psychology Press.

Gaertner, S.L., Dovidio, J.F., Anastasio, P.A., Bachman, B.A. and Rust, M.C. (1993) The common ingroup identity model: Recategorization and the reduction of intergroup bias. In W. Stroebe and M. Hewstone (eds), *European Review of Social Psychology, 4,* 1–26. New York: John Wiley and Sons.

Gaertner, S.L., Dovidio, J.F., Banker, B.S., Rust, M.C., Nier, J.A. and Ward, C.M. (1997) Does pro-whiteness necessarily mean anti-blackness? In M. Fine, L. Powell, L. Weis, and M. Wong (eds), *Off White,* pp. 167–178. New York: Routledge.

Gaertner, S.L., Dovidio, J.F., Rust, M.C., Nier, J., Banker, B., Ward, C.M., Mottola, G.R. and Houlette, M. (1999) Reducing intergroup bias: Elements of intergroup cooperation. *Journal of Personality and Social Psychology, 76,* 388–402.

Gaertner, S.L., Mann, J.A., Dovidio, J.F., Murrell, A.J. and Pomare, M. (1990) How does cooperation reduce intergroup bias? *Journal of Personality and Social Psychology, 59,* 692–704.

Gaertner, S.L., Mann, J.A., Murrell, A.J. and Dovidio, J.F. (1989) Reduction of intergroup bias: the benefits of recategorization. *Journal of Personality and Social Psychology, 57,* 239–249.

Gaertner, S.L., Rust, M.C., Dovidio, J.F., Bachman, B.A. and Anastasio, P.A. (1996) The Contact Hypothesis: The role of a common ingroup identity on reducing intergroup bias among majority and minority group members. In J.L. Nye and A.M. Brower (eds), *What's Social About Social Cognition?* pp. 230–360. Newbury Park, CA: Sage.

Gómez, A., Dovidio, J.F., Huici, C., Gaertner, S.L. and Cuardrado, I. (2008) The other side of We: When outgroup members express common identity. *Personality and Social Psychology Bulletin, 34,* 1613–1636.

González, R. and Brown, R. (2003) Generalization of positive attitude as a function of subgroup and superordinate group identification in intergroup contact. *European Journal of Social Psychology, 33,* 195–214.

González, R. and Brown, R. (2006) Dual identities and intergroup contact: Group status and size moderate the generalization of positive attitude change. *Journal of Experimental Social Psychology, 42,* 753–767.

Guerra, R., Rebelo, M., Monteiro, M.B., Riek, B.M., Maia, E.W., Gaertner, S.L. and Dovidio, J.F. (2010) How should intergroup contact be structured to reduce bias among majority and minority group children? *Group Processes and Intergroup Relations, 13,* 445–460.

Hall, N.R. and Crisp, R.J. (2005) Considering multiple criteria for social categorization can reduce intergroup bias. *Personality and Social Psychology Bulletin, 31,* 1435–1444.

Hewstone, M. (1996) Contact and categorization: Social psychological interventions to change intergroup relations. In C.N. Macrae, C. Stangor, and M. Hewstone (eds), *Stereotypes and Stereotyping,* pp. 323–368. New York: Guilford Press.

Hornsey, M.J. and Hogg, M.A. (2000) Subgroup relations: A comparison of mutual intergroup differentiation and common ungroup identity models of prejudice reduction. *Personality and Social Psychology Bulletin, 26*, 242–256.

Hornstein, H.A. (1976) *Cruelty and Kindness: A New Look at Aggression and Altruism.* Englewood Cliffs, N.J.: Prentice-Hall.

Houlette, M., Gaertner, S.L., Johnson, K.M., Banker, B.S., Riek, B.M. and Dovidio, J.F. (2004) Developing a more inclusive social identity: An elementary school intervention. *Journal of Social Issues, 60*, 35–56.

Huo, Y.J., Smith, H.J., Tyler, T.R. and Lind, E.A. (1996) Superordinate identification, subgroup identification, and justice concerns: Is separatism the problem; is assimilation the answer? *Psychological Science, 7*, 40–45.

Jetten, J., Spears, R. and Postmes, T. (2004) Intergroup distinctiveness and differentiation: A meta-analytic integration. *Journal of Personality and Social Psychology, 86*, 862–879.

Kane, A.A., Argote, L. and Levine, J.M. (2005) Knowledge transfer between groups via personnel rotation: Effects of social identity and knowledge quality. *Organizational Behavior and Human Decision Processes, 96*, 56–71.

Kelman, H.C. (1999) The interdependence of Israeli and Palestinian national identities: The role of the other in existential conflicts. *Journal of Social Issues, 55*, 581–600.

Kessler, T. and Mummendey, A. (2001) Is there any scapegoat around? Determinants of intergroup conflict at different categorization levels. *Journal of Personality and Social Psychology, 81*, 1090–1102.

Kramer, R.M. and Brewer, M.B. (1984) Effects of group identity on resource utilization in a simulated commons dilemma. *Journal of Personality and Social Psychology, 46*, 1044–1057.

Kovel, J. (1970) *White Racism: A Psychohistory.* New York: Pantheon.

LeVine, R.A. and Campbell, D.T. (1972) *Ethnocentrism: Theories of Conflict, Ethnic Attitudes and Group Behavior.* New York: John Wiley.

Levine, M., Prosser, A., Evans, D. and Reicher, S. (2005) Identity and emergency intervention: How social group membership and inclusiveness of group boundaries shape helping behavior. *Personality and Social Psychology Bulletin, 31*, 443–453.

Maass, A., Salvi, D., Arcuri, L. and Semin, G.R. (1989) Language use in intergroup contexts: The linguistic intergroup bias. *Journal of Personality and Social Psychology, 57*, 981–993.

Miller, N. (2002) Personalization and the promise of Contact Theory. *Journal of Social Issues, 58*, 387–410.

Miller, N., Brewer, M.B. and Edwards, K. (1985) Coopeartive interaction in desegregated settings:

A laboratory analog. *Journal of Social Issues, 41(3)*, 63–75.

Mummendey, A. and Wenzel, M. (1999) Social discrimination and tolerance in intergroup relations: Reactions to intergroup difference. *Personality and Social Psychology Review, 3*, 158–174.

Nier, J.A., Gaertner, S.L., Dovidio, J.F., Banker, B.S. and Ward, C.M. (2001) Changing interracial evaluations and behavior: The effects of a common group identity. *Group Processes and Intergroup Relations, 4*, 299–316.

Otten, S. and Moskowitz, G.B. (2000) Evidence for implicit evaluative in-group bias: Affect-based spontaneous trait inference in a minimal group paradigm. *Journal of Experimental Social Psychology, 36*, 77–89.

Penner, L.A., Dailey, R.K., Markova, T., Porcerelli, H.H. Dovidio, J.F. and Gaertner, S.L. (2009) Using the common group identity model to increase trust and commonality in racially discordant medical interactions. Poster presented at the Annual Meeting of the Society for Personality and Social Psychology, Tampa, FL. (February 7).

Pettigrew, T.F. (1979) The Ultimate Attribution Error: Extending Allport's cognitive analysis of prejudice. *Personality and Social Psychology Bulletin, 5*, 461–476.

Pettigrew, T.F. (1998) Intergroup contact theory. *Annual Review of Psychology, 49*, 65–85.

Pettigrew, T.F. and Tropp, L. (2006) A meta-analytic test of intergroup contact theory. *Journal of Personality and Social Psychology, 90*, 751–783.

Piliavin, J.A., Dovidio, J.F., Gaertner, S.L. and Clark, R.D., III. (1981) *Emergency Intervention.* New York: Academic Press.

Piliavin, J.A. and Piliavin, I.M. (1973) The Good Samaritan: Why *does* he help? Unpublished manuscript, Department of Sociology, University of Wisconsin, Madison.

Rebelo, M., Guerra, R. and Monteiro, M.B. (2004) *Reducing Prejudice: Comparative Effects of Three Theoretical Models.* Paper presented at the 5th Biennial Convention of the Society for the Psychological Study of Social Issues, Washington, DC, (June 27).

Richeson, J.A. and R.J. Nussbaum (2004) The impact of multiculturalism versus color-blindness on racial bias. *Journal of Experimental Social Psychology, 40*, 417–423.

Riek, B.M., Mania, E.W. and Gaertner, S.L. (2006) Intergroup threat and outgroup attitudes: A meta-analytic review. *Personality and Social Psychology Review, 10*, 336–353.

Riek, B.M., Mania, E.W., Gaertner, S.L., Direso, S.A. and Lamoreaux, M.J. (2010) Does a common ingroup identity reduce intergroup threat? *Group Processes and Intergroup Relations, 13,* 403–423.

Roccas, S. and Brewer, M.B (2002) Social identity complexity. *Personality and Social Psychology Review, 6,* 88–106.

Rouhana, N.N. and Kelman, H.C. (1994) Promoting joint thinking in international conflicts: An Israeli-Palestinian continuing workshop. *Journal of Social Issues, 50,* 157–178.

Saguy, T., Tausch, N., Dovidio, J.F. and Pratto, F. (2009) The irony of harmony: Intergroup contact can produce false expectations for equality. *Psychological Science, 20,* 114–121.

Sherif, M., Harvey, O.J., White, B.J., Hood, W.R. and Sherif, C.W. (1961) *Intergroup Conflict and Cooperation: The Robbers Cave Experiment.* Norman, OK: University of Oklahoma Book Exchange.

Sherif, M. and Sherif, C.W. (1969) *Social Psychology.* New York: Harper and Row.

Steiner, I.D. (1974). Whatever happened to the group in social psychology? *Journal of Experimental Social Psychology, 10,* 94–108.

Tajfel, H. (1969). Cognitive aspects of prejudice. *Journal of Social Issues, 25,* 79–97.

Tajfel, H. and Turner, J.C. (1979) An integrative theory of intergroup conflict. In W.G. Austin and S. Worchel (eds), *The Social Psychology of Intergroup Relations,* pp. 33–48. Monterey, CA: Brooks/Cole.

Tajfel, H., Billig, M.G., Bundy, R.F. and Flament, C. (1971) Social categorisation and intergroup behavior. *European Journal of Social Psychology, 1,* 149–177.

Turner, J.C. (1985) Social categorization and the self-concept: A social cognitive theory of group behavior. In E.J. Lawler (ed.), *Advances in Group Processes, 2,* 77–122. Greenwich, CT: JAI Press.

Voci, A. (2006) The link between identification and in-group favouritism: Effects of threat to social identity and trust-related emotions. *British Journal of Social Psychology, 45,* 265–284.

Waldzus, S., Mummendey, A., Wenzel, M. and Boettcher, F. (2004) Of bikers, teachers, and Germans: Groups' diverging views about their proto-typicality. *British Journal of Social Psychology, 43,* 385–400.

West, T.V., Pearson, A.R., Dovidio, J.F., Shelton, N.J. and Trail, T.E. (2009) Strength of superordinate iden-tity and intergroup roommate friendship develop-ment. *Journl of Experimental Social Psychology, 45,* 1266–1272.

Wilder, D.A. (1981) Perceiving persons as a group: Categorization and intergroup relations. In D.L. Hamilton (ed.), *Cognitive Processes in Stereotyping and Intergroup Behavior,* pp. 213–257. Hillsdale, NJ: Erlbaum.

Wohl, M.J.A. and Branscombe, N.R. (2005) Forgiveness and collective guilt assignment to historical perpe-trator groups depend on level of social category inclusiveness. *Journal of Personality and Social Psychology, 88,* 288–303.

Wright, S.C. (2001) Collective action: Social psychology and social change. In R. Brown and, S.L. Gaertner (eds), *Blackwell Handbook of Social Psychology, Vol. 4: Intergroup Processes,* pp. 409–430. Oxford: Blackwell.

49

Social Role Theory

Alice H. Eagly and Wendy Wood

ABSTRACT

What causes sex differences and similarities in behavior? At the core of our account are societal stereotypes about gender. These stereotypes, or gender role beliefs, form as people observe male and female behavior and infer that the sexes possess corresponding dispositions. For example, in industrialized societies, women are more likely to fill caretaking roles in employment and at home. People make the correspondent inference that women are communal, caring individuals. The origins of men's and women's social roles lie primarily in humans' evolved physical sex differences, specifically men's size and strength and women's reproductive activities of gestating and nursing children, which interact with a society's circumstances and culture to make certain activities more efficiently performed by one sex or the other. People carry out gender roles as they enact specific social roles (e.g., parent, employee). Socialization facilitates these sex-typical role performances by enabling men and women to develop appropriate personality traits and skills. Additionally, gender roles influence behavior through a biosocial set of processes: hormonal fluctuations that regulate role performance, self-regulation to gender role standards, and social regulation to others' expectations about women and men. Biology thus works with psychology to facilitate role performance.

SOCIAL ROLE THEORY OF SEX DIFFERENCES AND SIMILARITIES

A profound question about human life is why men and women, and boys and girls, behave differently in many circumstances but similarly in others. There is no one discipline that provides a sovereign, overarching answer, but each discipline favors certain types of causes. For biologists, sex differences reflect gonadal or other sex-differentiated hormones. For sociologists, the differences reflect the position of men and women in broader social hierarchies. For economists, the differences reflect the human capital of women and men. For developmental researchers, they arise from sex-linked temperament and socialization experiences. Evolutionary psychologists usually favor sex-differentiated selection pressures on human ancestors. Our theory begins from a uniquely social psychological vantage point that highlights social roles and interweaves role-related processes with these other perspectives to produce a powerful analysis of sex differences and similarities.

In brief, we argue that sex differences and similarities in behavior reflect *gender role beliefs* that in turn represent people's perceptions of men's and women's *social roles* in the society in which they live. In postindustrial societies, for example, men are more likely than women to be employed, especially in authority positions, and women are more likely than men to fill caretaking roles at home as well as in employment settings. Men and women are differently distributed into social roles because of humans' evolved *physical sex differences* in which men are larger, faster, and have greater upper-body strength, and women gestate and nurse children. Given these physical differences, certain activities are more efficiently accomplished by one sex or the other, depending on a society's circumstances and culture. This task specialization produces an alliance between women and men as they engage in a division of labor. Although these alliances take somewhat different forms across cultures, task specialization furthers the interests of the community as a whole.

Gender role beliefs arise because people observe female and male behavior and infer that the sexes possess corresponding dispositions. Thus, men and women are thought to possess attributes that equip them for sex-typical roles. These attributes are evident in consensually-shared beliefs, or *gender stereotypes*. In daily life, people carry out these gender roles as they enact specific social roles such as parent or employee. Because gender roles seem to reflect innate attributes of the sexes, they appear natural and inevitable. With these beliefs, people construct gender roles that are responsive to cultural and environmental conditions yet appear, for individuals within a society, to be stable, inherent properties of men and women.

To equip men and women for their usual family and employment roles, societies undertake extensive *socialization* to promote personality traits and skills that facilitate role performance. Additionally, gender roles influence behavior through a trio of biological and psychological processes. Biological processes include *hormonal fluctuations* that act as chemical signals that regulate role performance. Psychological processes include individuals' internalization of gender roles as *self standards* against which they regulate their own behavior as well as their experience of other people's *expectations* that provide social regulatory mechanisms. Biology thus works with psychology to facilitate role performance.

The broad scope of our theory enables it to tackle the various causes of female and male behavior that are of interest across the human sciences. But the theory was not developed all in one piece. As we explain, Alice initially developed its core components in the 1980s, drawing largely on work in psychology and sociology. We have since worked together to elaborate the model so that it addresses causation at several levels of analysis. That is, we have placed the theory in a broader *nomological net*, or series of connected theoretical concepts and observable properties that give the constructs particular meaning (Cronbach and Meehl, 1955). By looking upward in the net toward the distal, fundamental causes of sex differences and similarities, we can answer big-picture questions about the evolutionary origins of male and female roles. We also can look downward to understand how men and women enact behavior through proximal psychological and biological processes.

In its scope, our analysis is broader than the more focused theories typical in social and personality psychology, which are suited to explain more fine-grained issues of cognition, affect, and social interaction. Our approach thus explains the ultimate origins of sex differences in behavior. It also shows how the position of women and men in the social structure determines the particular content of the cognitions (i.e., gender role beliefs) that influence female and male behavior. In addition, the theory identifies the psychological and biological processes that act as proximal determinants of sex differences and similarities.

PERSONAL NARRATIVE AND INTELLECTUAL CONTEXT

When Alice began work on the psychology of gender in the late 1970s, social psychologists had paid very little attention to this topic. This fundamental aspect of human life had gone virtually unanalyzed. On those few occasions when social psychologists separated their data according to the sex of their research participants, the differences that sometimes emerged were puzzling and awkward. From a contemporary perspective, this lack of attention to gender is an amazing blind spot in the subdiscipline of psychology most concerned with understanding social life. Yet, the important historical developments in the field were essentially gender blind. Gordon Allport (1954), in his influential book on prejudice, did not consider gender prejudice and instead focused his analytical powers on ethnic and racial prejudice. In Heider's (1958) classic book on social interaction, the terms *sex* and *gender* do not even appear in the index. As social psychologists turned to cognitive consistency theories in the 1960s and to attribution and social cognition in the 1970s, their work still did not broach the topic of gender.

In contrast with the lack of academic attention, the second-wave feminist movement in the 1960s and 1970s (e.g., Friedan, 1963) made gender a major theme of public discourse in the US. The field of social psychology could not remaining on the sidelines of such an engaging conversation. Gender was emerging as a significant political, social, and psychological issue. Nonetheless, there were risks in initiating research in such a neglected area of study. Alice already had attained a tenured university position and established expertise in attitudes, one of social psychology's mainstream research areas. So, hedging her bets and joined by a few other soon-to-be-distinguished scholars (e.g., Bem, 1974; Deaux, 1976), she decided that the potential for contributing to an important set of social and scientific issues outweighed any career risk. In fact, her first major journal article on gender (Eagly, 1978) broke new ground, as confirmed by its winning of two prizes (1976 Gordon Allport Award of Society for the Psychological Study of Social Issues; 1978 Distinguished Publication Award of Association for Women in Psychology). This response was encouraging.

Psychology had produced some significant scholarship on sex and gender in earlier decades, primarily within mental skills testing (Hollingworth, 1916), developmental psychology (Maccoby, 1966), and psychoanalysis (e.g., Horney, 1967). Yet, these perspectives did not incorporate the core message of social psychology – the power of the situation in its interactions with the attributes and processes of individuals. In this void, Alice developed social role theory, which was initially published in a book based on lectures that that she gave at the University of Alberta in 1985 (Eagly, 1987). Wendy Wood was a graduate student with Alice during this period, allowing a productive collaboration on gender to begin.

Core gender role theory

The role concept was crucial to Alice's initial thinking about gender. This reflected her educational background in Harvard and University of Michigan programs that integrated psychological and sociological traditions of social psychology. Alice had studied role theorists in sociology extending back to the writers such as Georg Simmel, George Herbert Mead, Ralph Linton, and Jacob Moreno (see Biddle, 1979) and including then-contemporary writers such as Erving Goffman (1959). As reflected in this tradition, role is a central integrative concept in the social sciences that is important because of the analytical bridge it provides between the individual and the social environment. Role expectations thus exist in the minds of individuals and also are shared with other people, producing the social consensus from which social structure and culture emerge. The role concept thus facilitated a theory of gender that analyzes not only the proximal determinants of male and female behavior but also the more distal influences of culture and social structure that contribute to variability in this behavior.

Within the traditions of role theory, Parsons and Bales (1955) had provided an explicit analysis of female and male roles. These theorists described the division of labor between husbands and wives as a specialization of men in task-oriented (or instrumental) behavior and of women in socioemotional (or expressive) behavior. Allied researchers observed that in mixed-sex groups, men, more than women, specialized in instrumental behaviors related to task accomplishment, and women, more than men, in socioemotional behaviors related to group maintenance and other distinctively social concerns (Strodtbeck and Mann, 1956). Reasoning that role differentiation along these lines is functionally necessary to harmonious social interaction, Parsons and his collaborators viewed these complementary male and female roles as inherent in a smoothly functioning society. As an undergraduate student in one of Parsons' courses, Alice was struck by the power of this analysis, but she also came to realize that it was incomplete. What was missing is an appreciation of the malleability of role structures. Gender roles – that is, expectations for female and male behavior – are not stuck inevitably in the 1950s American form that Parsons and Bales observed. Instead, these expectations change, depending on the typical work and family roles of the sexes. Parsons and Bales had captured a moment in time in a particular cultural context. Change in the work and family roles of men and women follows from the exigencies of the economy, technology, and broader social structure in which these roles are embedded.

Another early catalyst of our theory of gender was a methodological innovation – the late 1970s development of quantitative methods for systematically integrating research findings (e.g., Glass et al., 1981; Rosenthal, 1978). Application of these methods allowed researchers to make more definitive statements concerning female and male behavior. Comparing women and men was an easy application of meta-analytic methods, requiring only a relatively simple two-group, between-subjects comparison. Alice was an early adopter of meta-analysis, initially producing an integration of studies that had compared the influenceability of women and men in conformity and persuasion paradigms (Eagly and Carli, 1981). After Wendy landed her first job at a university without a strong undergraduate research participant pool, a condition that limited her access to participants, she also became impressed with the power of meta-analysis. We each published a number of meta-analytic projects, including ones comparing women and men on aggressive behavior (Eagly and Steffen, 1986), helping behavior (Eagly and Crowley, 1986), group performance (Wood, 1987), and happiness and life satisfaction (Wood et al., 1989).

The sex differences documented in these early meta-analytic investigations required explanation. Although the differences typically were not large when averaged across studies, they were relatively large in some settings, with some interaction partners, and with some forms of the behavior under investigation. Even the average differences were often large enough to be consequential, in view of the substantial cumulative impact that small differences can have if repeatedly enacted over a period of time (Abelson, 1985). Despite being sympathetic to the prevailing view among many psychologists that most sex differences are small, we found the aggregated sex differences and their variability across studies in our meta-analyses to be anything but trivial. Instead, such data posed puzzles to be solved with the aid of relevant theory.

Another input into the beginnings of social role theory was the emergence of psychological research on cultural stereotypes about women and men. Although such work began in the 1950s (McKee and Sherriffs, 1957), it intensified and gained visibility in the 1970s (e.g., Broverman et al., 1972; Spence and Helmreich, 1978). This research identified people's consensual beliefs concerning men and women. Most of these beliefs can be sum-marized in two dimensions, which are often labeled *agentic* and *communal* (Bakan, 1966). Men, more than women, are thought to be agentic – that is, masterful, assertive, com-petitive, and dominant. Women, more than men, are thought to be communal – that is, friendly, unselfish, concerned with others, and emotionally expressive. These qualities are similar to those that Parsons and Bales (1955) had labeled as instrumental and expressive (or task-oriented and socioemotional). As abstract, general beliefs about men and women, these stereotypes constitute gender roles.

Our emerging realization that these stereo-types are neither arbitrary nor essentially inaccurate was buttressed by social psycho-logical research showing that social perceiv-ers usually assume that people's behaviors reflect their intrinsic characteristics. This cog-nitive process of inferring traits from observed behavior is known as *correspondent inference* or *correspondence bias* (Gilbert and Malone, 1995; Ross, 1977). This process is wide-spread (Gawronski, 2003) and largely sponta-neous (Uleman et al., 2008). For example, upon observing an act of kindness, perceivers automatically identify the behavior in trait terms and characterize the actor by the trait that is implied – as a nice, caring person.

Consistent with correspondent inference, we recognized that in various ways the new meta-analytic findings pertaining to male and female behavior matched gender stereotypic findings reflecting people's beliefs about men and women. The behavioral differences thus resembled the beliefs that people hold about differences (Eagly and Wood, 1991). Confirmation of this informal observation followed in research by Swim (1994) and Hall and Carter (1999) that found substantial correlations between participants' beliefs about sex differences and the differences established in meta-analytic reviews. This similarity between gender stereotypes and male and female behavior challenged social psychologists' traditional depiction of stere-otypes as inaccurate portrayals of groups (Allport, 1954).

Our understanding of how gender stereo-typic beliefs can in turn guide behavior was aided by research in psychology and sociol-ogy. Psychological research outlined the power of expectancies to produce behavior that confirms them (e.g., Rosenthal and Rubin, 1978; see review by Olson et al., 1996). That is, stereotypes can act as self-fulfilling proph-ecies. Sociological research featured expecta-tion states theory (Berger et al., 1980), which also linked beliefs about social groups (e.g., sex, race) to the behavior of individual group members. Cecilia Ridgeway, a sociologist working within this tradition and Wendy's colleague for a few years, demonstrated how beliefs about men's greater worth and value, which are based on men's greater access to societal resources and power, produce sex differences in influence in small task-performing groups (Ridgeway, 1981, 1984). These psychological and sociological ideas, although very different in form, provided frameworks to understand how cultural beliefs about gender guide individuals' behav-ior to yield confirmatory evidence of sex dif-ferences in the context of social interaction.

During the years in which we developed our theory, vivid experimental demonstrations of the power of gender roles cumulated in the research literature. For example, Zanna and Pack's (1975) experiment showed that female students shaped their self-presentations to fit the preferences of a highly eligible male inter-action partner. When this man reported pre-ferring women who were traditional (versus nontraditional), these young women presented themselves as conforming to his preferences and furthermore scored worse on a test of intellectual aptitude given that these scores were to be shared with this male partner. In an experiment by Skrypnek and Snyder (1982), task partners negotiated a more traditional division of labor when they believed that their (unseen) partner was of the other sex, regard-less of their partner's actual sex.

Yet another catalyst of social role theory was research showing that people's self-concepts tend to have gender-stereotypic content (e.g., Bem, 1974; Spence and

Helmreich, 1978). Researchers had turned to gender stereotypes to choose items for measuring instruments that assess the ascription of agentic and communal attributes to the self. It thus appeared that, to varying extents, people internalize gender roles as personal gender identities. Wendy later pursued these ideas, evaluating whether gender identities could serve as personal standards for behavior. Her empirical studies showed that, as with other self-regulatory standards (e.g., Carver and Scheier, 1981), men and women regulate their own behavior to correspond to these identities (see Witt and Wood, 2010; Wood et al., 1997).

In summary, Alice built the core concepts of social role theory in the 1980s from a variety of theoretical perspectives and empirical traditions: sociological role theory; research on gender stereotypes; ideas about correspondent inference, behavioral confirmation, and status construction; studies of gender identity and self-regulatory processes; and the methodological innovation of meta-analysis. Indicating the success of this approach, it effectively explained variability in sex differences observed in meta-analyses in the 1980s (Eagly and Crowley, 1986; Eagly and Steffen, 1986; Wood, 1987; Wood et al., 1989). Also, a number of key experimental demonstrations in our own research programs showed the power of these principles to account for variability in perceived and actual sex differences (Eagly and Steffen, 1984; Eagly and Wood, 1982; Eagly et al., 1981; Grossman and Wood, 1993; Wood and Karten, 1986).

The invitation that Alice received to deliver a series of lectures in the fall of 1985 at the University of Alberta included the agreement that the lectures would be turned into a book. The result was a book presenting social role theory along with supportive evidence from meta-analyses and primary research (Eagly, 1987). This invitation was very helpful because the lectures and associated book required a systematic theoretical presentation. This book turned out to be influential as a substantial theoretical statement, as indicated by its 1075 citations recorded in Web of Science and 1906 in Google Scholar.

Biosocial mechanisms

More recently, we enlarged the scope of social role theory to address the origins of the male/female division of labor. A key development in psychology that spurred this growth was the emergence of evolutionary psychology, which provided an essentialist explanation of many sex differences in social behavior (e.g., Buss and Schmitt, 1993). Rather than leave the question of ultimate origins to evolutionary psychology, Wendy and Alice collaborated in challenging its proponents by providing an alternative origin theory that treated female and male behavior as emergent from interacting social and biological causes. This work expanded our theory by considering the distal, evolutionary causes of gender roles.

Our initial foray into the origins question was spurred by Wendy's discussions with her running partner, colleague, and evolutionary psychologist, Jeff Simpson. During their 8-mile Sunday morning runs – which, to Jeff's credit, rarely involved arguments – Wendy was inspired to take up the question of the evolutionary origins of gender roles. At that same time, Alice gave an invited address to the Midwestern Psychological Association that considered the origins of sex differences in social behavior. Eager for some empirical support for our developing ideas about cultural influences on mate preferences, Alice asked David Buss to share data from his wellknown 37 cultures study (Buss, 1989). Alice's 1997 talk featured an initial reanalysis of these data, a small foray that then was considerably enlarged and refined in our subsequent article (Eagly and Wood, 1999).

In reanalyzing the 37 cultures data, we found that in societies with a strong division of labor between male providers and female homemakers (i.e., less gender equality), women were more likely to prefer a mate with resources who could be a good provider, and men were more likely to prefer a mate who was a skilled homemaker and child caretaker. This marital system of a good provider paired with a domestic worker also generated a spousal age difference, given that older men were more likely to have acquired resources, and younger women without resources were more likely to value marriage and older partners with resources. This project thus demonstrated that sex differences in mate preferences, assumed by evolutionary psychologists to stem from sexual selection pressures acting on the human species, reflected the position of women and men in the social structure.

This initial foray into cross-cultural analyses merely whetted our appetite for developing a biosocial evolutionary theory that included as a central component the idea of variability across cultures in men's and women's roles. To expand our analysis and gain additional empirical support, we turned to the anthropological literature on cross-cultural uniformity and variability in female and male behavior. We found rich data and theorizing about the origins of sex differences, much of it compatible with our emerging biosocial perspective. The resulting article presented social role theory as a core set of ideas within the larger biosocial theoretical framework (Wood and Eagly, 2002).

Alice took social role theory in yet another new direction by considering the behavior of men and women in organizational environments, where they act under the influence of specific occupational roles along with gender roles. Although analysis of male and behavior in complex natural settings offers many possibilities, Alice narrowed her focus to consider the conflux of gender roles and managerial roles. A key insight was that for men, managerial (or leader) roles and their own gender role are similar in content but for women, these roles are dissimilar. Female leaders' resulting role incongruity has varied consequences, including prejudice toward them as potential leaders and actual leaders (Eagly and Karau, 2002).

Our most recent collaboration further developed the biosocial roots of gender roles by elaborating the proximal biological and social processes that yield female and male behavior. Wendy spent a year at the Radcliffe Institute for Advanced Study and, listening to

other Institute Fellows talk about their work, she was challenged by the variety of ways that human sciences treat the biology of sex and the sociality and psychology of gender. This experience inspired us to scrutinize the ways in which gender roles influence behavior. Given the growth of science pertaining to the hormonal regulation of female and male behavior (e.g., Archer, 2006; Hines, 2009; Taylor et al., 2000), any theory of the proximal determinants of sex differences that relied only on social psychological mechanisms is incomplete. Therefore, to enhance the biological side of our biosocial framework, we drew on this new science to document how hormones are recruited to facilitate the performance of social roles (Wood and Eagly, 2010).

In summary, the 1980s version of social role theory (Eagly, 1987) has remained intact within a larger biosocial theoretical structure (see Figure 49.1). By reaching upward in the nomological net, we expanded the theory to include the evolutionary origins of the male/female division of labor. By reaching downward, we incorporated the emerging science on the hormonal regulation of social behavior. In addition, the analysis of leadership has provided a model of how the theory could take into account the interaction between gender roles and specific social roles in natural settings. In the next section of this chapter, we offer a summary of the current theory and a brief acknowledgement of some of the relevant empirical literatures.

SOCIAL ROLE THEORY OF SEX DIFFERENCES AND SIMILARITIES: A BIOSOCIAL APPROACH

As indicated by the intellectual history presented in the prior section, our biosocial theory consists of a series of interconnected causes of sex differences and similarities. These causes range from more proximal (or immediate), to more distal (or ultimate). In Figure 49.1, the more distal causes are positioned above the

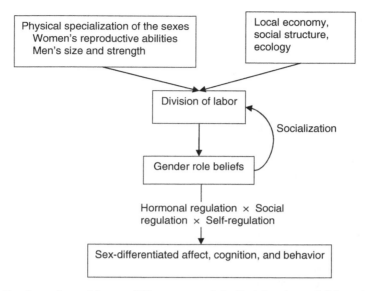

Figure 49.1   Gender roles guide sex differences and similarities through biosocial processes

division of labor, which is the outcome of interaction between the physical specialization of the sexes and local conditions. The division of labor yields gender role beliefs, which then facilitate this division through socialization processes. Gender role beliefs act on behavior through a trio of processes involving regulation by hormonal changes, others' expectations, and self standards. In this section, we begin our presentation of this theory with the ultimate determinants of female and male behavior and move to the more proximal determinants.

Origins of the division of labor

The ultimate origins of male and female behavior derive from evolved physical differences between the sexes, especially women's reproductive activities and men's greater size and strength, as these factors interact with the demands of people's social and economic environment (Wood and Eagly, 2002). This interaction yields constraints whereby one sex performs certain tasks more efficiently than the other sex in a given environment.

Women's reproductive activities of pregnancy and lactation act as powerful constraints because they cede to women the energy-intensive and time-consuming activities of gestating, nursing, and caring for infants (Huber, 2007). These activities make it difficult for women to participate as fully as men in tasks that require speed of locomotion, uninterrupted activity, extended training, or long distance travel away from home. Therefore, in foraging, horticultural, and agricultural societies, women generally participate relatively little in tasks such as hunting large animals, conducting warfare, and plowing. Instead, women favor activities more compatible with childcare (see Murdock and Provost, 1973).

Also, men's greater size and strength equip them to execute tasks that benefit from these qualities, including hunting large animals, plowing, and warfare. Therefore, the division of labor between women and men reflects the specialization of each sex in activities for which they are physically better suited under the circumstances presented by their society. Because these circumstances are variable, the particular activities allocated to women and men differ across cultures (Wood and Eagly, 2002).

In addition to dividing tasks between women and men, societies often, but not always, cede greater power or status to men. In decentralized, nonhierarchical foraging or pastoral societies with limited technology, egalitarian relations between the sexes are common (Hayden et al., 1986; Salzman, 1999). Patriarchy arises when the physical attributes of men and women interact with economic and technological developments to give men the roles that yield decision-making authority (e.g., in warfare) and access to resources (e.g., through intensive agriculture and trade). Under such circumstances, men garner most of the social and economic capital that derives from these activities.

In recent history, both the division of labor and gender hierarchy, especially in industrialized societies, have become weaker. These shifts reflect the declining importance of physical sex differences due to (a) lower birthrates and much less reliance on lactation for feeding infants and young children, and (b) decreased reliance on strength and size as prerequisites for carrying out economically productive activities. These fundamental changes have set in motion far-reaching political, social, and psychological changes that have given women access to a greater range of social roles, including increased access to roles that yield authority and resources.

Despite the less extreme division of labor in contemporary industrialized societies, many sex differences remain. Women perform more domestic work than men and spend fewer hours in paid employment (US Bureau of Labor Statistics, 2008a). Although most women in the US are employed, they have lower wages than men, are concentrated in different occupations, and are rare at the highest levels of corporations and governments (Blau et al., 2006a; US Bureau of Labor Statistics, 2010). This division of activity yields less overall power, status, and resources for women than men (Valian, 1998), thereby retaining some degree of gender hierarchy or patriarchy. In our theory,

these features of social structure – the division of labor and gender hierarchy – are the middle-level causes of sex-differentiated behavior (see Figure 49.1).

Gender roles

Gender roles derive from the specific family and employment roles commonly held by women versus men in a society. Consistent with the correspondent inference principle (Gilbert and Malone, 1995), people infer the traits of men and women from observations of their behavior. Given a homemaker–provider division of labor, people disproportionately observe women and girls engaging in domestic behaviors such as childcare, cooking, and sewing, and men and boys engaging in activities that are marketable in the paid economy. Furthermore, perceivers tend to *essentialize* gender by viewing the different behaviors of the sexes as due to inherent differences in the natures of men and women. Thus, even though the division of labor is tailored to local conditions, it tends to be viewed by the members of a society as inevitable and natural.

The social behaviors that typify the homemaker–provider division of labor differ in their emphasis on communion versus agency (Eagly, 1987; Eagly and Steffen, 1984). Thus, women's accommodation to the domestic role fosters a pattern of interpersonally facilitative and friendly behaviors that can be termed communal. Women's communal activities encompass child-rearing, a responsibility that requires nurturant behaviors. The importance of close relationships to women's nurturing role favors the acquisition of superior relational skills and the ability to communicate nonverbally. In contrast, men's accommodation to the employment role, especially to male-dominated occupations, favors a pattern of relatively assertive behaviors that can be termed agentic (Eagly and Steffen, 1984).

The distribution of the sexes into occupations is another important source of observations of women and men. Given the moderately strong sex segregation of the labor force (Tomaskovic-Devey et al., 2006), perceivers infer the typical qualities of the sexes in part from observations of the type of paid work that they commonly undertake. Research has shown that occupational success is perceived to follow from agentic personal qualities to the extent that occupations are male-dominated and from communal personal qualities to the extent that they are female-dominated (Cejka and Eagly, 1999; Glick, 1991). Also, men have greater access to employment roles yielding higher levels of authority and income, and their adjustment to this aspect of their roles may foster relatively dominant behavior (Ridgeway and Bourg, 2004; Wood and Karten, 1986). Women's lesser access to such roles may favor more supportive behavior (e.g., Conway et al., 1996).

Gender roles are an important part of the culture and social structure of every society. Their power to influence behavior derives from their essential quality, appearing to reflect inherent attributes of women and men and from the related tendency to be relatively consensual and for people to be aware of this consensus (Wood and Eagly, 2010). Because gender roles are shared, people correctly believe that others are likely to react more approvingly to behavior that is consistent rather than inconsistent with these roles. Therefore, the most likely route to a smoothly functioning social interaction is to behave consistently with one's gender role or at least to avoid strongly deviating from it.

In summary, gender roles are emergent from the activities carried out by individuals of each sex in their typical occupational and family roles. To the extent that women more than men occupy roles that are facilitated by predominantly communal behaviors, domestic behaviors, or subordinate behaviors, corresponding attributes become stereotypic of women and part of the female gender role. To the extent that men more than women occupy roles that require predominantly agentic behaviors, resource acquisition behaviors, or dominant behaviors, the corresponding attributes become stereotypic of men and

part of the male gender role. These gender roles, which are an important focus of socialization, begin to be acquired early in childhood and are elaborated throughout childhood and adolescence (e.g., Bussey and Bandura, 1999; Miller et al., 2006).

Gender roles' influence on behavior

How do gender roles influence behavior? As Wood and Eagly (2010) argued, gender roles work through a trio of biosocial mechanisms to influence behavior in role-appropriate directions. These proximal causes of male and female behavior include biological processes involving hormonal changes and sociocultural factors of gender identity and others' stereotypic expectations. These three factors interact to yield both gender differences and similarities.

Influence of hormonal processes

Gender roles and specific social roles guide behavior in part through the activation of hormonal changes, especially in testosterone and oxytocin (Wood and Eagly, 2010). Hormones and related neural structures were shaped in part through ancient selection pressures associated with the basic perceptual, sensory, and motivational processes that humans share with other animals. In the standard interpretation, such inherited biological factors constrain sociocultural influences on men and women. More impressive is the recently emerging evidence that humans activate biological processes to support the sociocultural factors that guide masculine and feminine behaviors within cultures (Wood & Eagly, 2010). As these processes occur, subcortical structures interact with more recently evolved, general-purpose, higher brain functions associated with the neocortex (Panksepp & Panksepp, 2000). Especially important to social interaction are processes located in the medial prefrontal cortex and the ventral anterior cingulate, which allow people to respond flexibly to others' expectations and self-regulate in response to their own identities

(Heatherington, 2011). The evolution of the brain is thus a crucial component of our evolutionary theory, which stresses the importance of higher-level mechanisms for learning and innovation that are centered in the neocortex.

Biological processes include the activation of hormones that support culturally masculine or feminine behaviors. With culturally masculine roles, higher levels of testosterone are associated with dominance behaviors designed to gain or maintain status. In humans, such behaviors frequently entail competition, risk-taking, and aggression that may harm or injure others (Booth et al., 2006). In contrast, with culturally feminine roles, higher levels of oxytocin (as well as reduced cortisol and testosterone) are associated with behaviors that produce parental bonding, nurturance, and intimacy (Campbell, 2008).

Men and women selectively recruit hormones and other neurochemical processes for appropriate roles, in the context of their gender identities and others' expectations for role performance. Testosterone is especially relevant when, due to personal identities and social expectancies, people experience social interactions as dominance contests. Oxytocin is relevant when, due to personal identities and social expectancies, people define social interactions as involving bonding and affiliation with close others. Also important to bonding and affiliation are the neurochemical processes associated with rewards and learning of affiliation, which supplement or even supplant influences of oxytocin.

Influence of gender identities

Gender roles influence people's self-concepts and thereby become *gender identities* – individuals' sense of themselves as female or male. These identities arise because most people accept, or internalize, at least some aspects of cultural meanings associated with their sex (see Wood and Eagly, 2009, 2010).

People differ in the extent to which they incorporate gender roles into their self-concepts. Also, people differ in the aspects of gender roles that they adopt. For example,

women who regard themselves as feminine could be invested in culturally feminine traits such as warmth and niceness or in feminine interests such as sewing or home decoration. People raised in culturally atypical environments may not internalize conventional gender-role norms. Consistent with research showing substantial relationships between sex-differentiated behaviors and self-reported agency and communion (Taylor and Hall, 1982), people who have self-concepts that differ from those that are typical of their sex are less likely to show gender-stereotypic behavior.

Gender identities motivate responding through self-regulatory processes. That is, people use their gender identity as a standard against which to regulate their behavior (Witt and Wood, 2010; Wood et al., 1997). People who have a masculine self-concept involving traits of dominance and assertiveness might regulate their behavior by, for example, seeking opportunities for leadership. Self-regulation proceeds in stages, beginning with *testing* the extent to which current behavior matches self-standards (e.g., Carver and Scheier, 2008). Closer matches produce positive emotions and increased self-esteem, whereas mismatches produce negative emotions and decreased esteem. When signaled by negative feelings, people *operate* on their behavior to bring it more in line with their desired standard. In this way, esteem and emotions constitute feedback about whether adjustments are necessary to meet standards.

Influence of others' expectations

A key assumption of our analysis is that both women and men typically are rewarded by other people for conforming to gender roles and penalized for deviating. Behavior consistent with gender role beliefs garner approval and continued interaction. In contrast, behavior inconsistent with gender roles is often negatively sanctioned and tends to disrupt social interaction. The sanctions for role-inconsistent behavior may be overt (e.g., losing a job) or subtle (e.g., being ignored, receiving disapproving looks).

Research has produced abundant evidence of negative reactions to deviations from gender roles. For example, in a meta-analysis of 61 experiments on evaluations of male and female leaders, Eagly et al. (1992) showed that women who adopted a male-stereotypic assertive and directive leadership style were evaluated more negatively than men who adopted the exact same style, whereas women and men who adopted more democratic and participative styles were evaluated equivalently. In small-group interaction, women who behave in a dominant or extremely competent manner tend to lose likability and influence (Carli, 2001; Shackelford et al., 1996). Women in supervisory roles may be penalized for not attending to others' emotions or for expressing angry emotions (Byron, 2007; Brescoll and Uhlmann, 2008) as well as for performing at extremely well in stereotypically masculine roles (Heilman et al., 2004). In contrast, men may be penalized for behaving passively and unassertively (e.g., Anderson et al., 2001). People thus elicit conformity to gender-role norms by dispensing rewards such as liking and cooperation in return for conformity to these norms and dispensing social punishments such as rejection and neglect in return for nonconformity.

Because people often sanction behavior that is inconsistent with gender roles, these roles have a conservative impact by exacting costs from men and women who deviate from the norm. Given that men and women are aware of these costs, they are not likely to deviate from their gender role unless the behavior produced benefits that would outweigh the costs. Part of these perceived benefits for women, as members of a subordinate group in society, may be having a chance to gain access to rewards and opportunities usually reserved for men.

Behavior influenced by gender roles and specific roles

Gender roles, as shared beliefs about men's and women's attributes, coexist with specific roles defined by factors such as family relationships (e.g., mother, son) and occupation (e.g., secretary, firefighter). In workplace settings, for example, a manager or lawyer occupies a role defined by occupation but is simultaneously a man or women and thus to some extent subjected to the constraints of his or her gender role. Similarly, in a community organization, an individual who has the role of volunteer simultaneously is categorized as a woman or man and is thus perceived in terms of the expectations that are applied to people of that sex.

Because specific roles have direct implications for task performance in many natural settings, they can be more important than gender roles. This conclusion was foreshadowed by experimental demonstrations that stereotypic sex differences can be eliminated by providing information that specifically counters gender-based expectations. For example, Wood and Karten (1986) manipulated perceptions of agency in mixed-sex groups through false feedback that described participants as relatively agentic or not agentic. Controlling agency in this manner eliminated the usual sex differences in interaction style by which men, compared with women, showed more active task behavior and less positive social interactive behavior.

A field study by Moskowitz et al. (1994) used behavioral measures to examine the simultaneous influence of gender roles and organizational roles with a sample of adults who held a wide range of jobs in a variety of organizational settings. Implementing an experience-sampling method, this study found that agentic behavior was controlled by the relative status of the interaction partners, with participants behaving most agentically with a supervisee and least agentically with a boss. Yet, communal behaviors were influenced by the sex of participants, with women behaving more communally, especially in interactions with other women. Similarly, research on physicians demonstrated women's more communal behavior, even in the presence of a constraining occupational role. Female physicians, compared with male physicians, thus engaged in more partnership building with the patient, asked more questions, referenced more emotional and positive concerns, and offered more psychosocial information (e.g., concerning personal habits, impact on family; Roter et al., 2002).

It appears that employment roles provide relatively clear-cut rules about the performance of particular tasks. For example, regardless of whether a physician is male or female, he or she must obtain information about symptoms from a patient, provide a diagnosis, and design treatments to alleviate the patient's symptoms. Within the task rules that regulate physician–patient interactions, there is still room for some variation in behavioral styles. Physicians may behave in a warm, caring manner that focuses on producing a positive relationship or in a less personally responsive style that focuses more exclusively on information exchange and problem solving. The female gender role may foster the caring, communal behavior that has been observed especially in female physicians as well as the participative, team-building style that has been observed especially in female managers (Eagly and Johnson, 1990; Eagly et al., 2003b). Thus, gender roles may have their primary influence on discretionary behaviors that are not required by the occupational role, which may often be behaviors in the communal repertoire. Gender roles are still important even through they become a secondary, background influence in settings in which specific roles are of primary importance.

APPLICATIONS TO SOCIAL ISSUES

Especially since the advent of the second-wave feminist movement, gender equality has been an important societal goal for many people. Yet debates continue about whether equality will come about, even though much social policy has been designed to promote equality. Affirmative action programs facilitating women's entry into nontraditional roles have produced mixed reactions (Heilman and Haynes, 2005). Women entering male-dominated roles contend with cultural incongruity between people's beliefs about what it takes to excel in those roles and stereotypes about the attributes of women (e.g., Eagly and Karau, 2002). As a result, even highly qualified women may be judged to lack the attributes necessary for success. Yet, these beliefs are not inevitable. As women assume nontraditional roles, people may develop new beliefs about women's attributes, given that these beliefs in part reflect role performance.

With respect to changes in men's and women's roles, an important question addressed by our theory is whether men and women differ in their behavior due to intrinsic sex differences built in through evolution or merely due to the social environment. As we have explained, our biosocial theory has a more complex view than these two opposing positions. Sex differences and similarities take a variety of forms, depending on men's and women's roles in society, which in turn reflect the more distal factors of male and female physical attributes, in combination with socioeconomic and cultural conditions. Roles in turn affect behavior through the immediate, proximal causes of hormonal regulation, self-regulation by gender identities, and social regulation by others' sanctions and rewards. It follows that female and male psychology is not fixed but emerges from interactions across multiple biological and sociocultural factors. The varying forms of this interaction depend on the division of labor within a society and the ways in which boys and girls are socialized into sex-typical roles.

The dramatic changes that have occurred in women's roles in recent decades reflect the loosening of biosocial restraints through sharp reductions in birth rates and length of lactation combined with a shift toward an occupational structure that favors brains over brawn. These changes, combined with women's increased education, qualify them for occupations with more status and income. However, this shift has so far produced only partial equality between the sexes.

Men continue to dominate leadership roles, especially at higher levels (e.g., Helfat et al., 2006). Women continue to take responsibility for the majority of childcare and housework (e.g., Bianchi et al., 2006), even when both spouses are employed full-time (US Bureau of Labor Statistics, 2008).

The continuing wage and authority gaps in the workforce can be traced in part to women continuing to fill caretaking roles, especially childcare. Childcare roles that take women out of the labor force or reduce their employment to part-time lessen their training and experience. This reduction of human capital, compounded by job discrimination against mothers (e.g., Correll et al., 2007), lessens women's opportunities to attain jobs that offer high wages and substantial workplace authority (Polachek, 2006).

Social role theory offers a way to understand both stability and change in gender roles and associated behavioral sex differences. The recent social changes involved shifts in the roles of women as they moved into new educational and employment arenas. Thus, we expect to find convergence in those male and female attributes that reflect this masculinizing of women's experiences. A number of findings are consistent with this prediction. For example, women report increasing importance of job attributes such as freedom, challenge, leadership, prestige, and power, thus becoming more similar to men (Konrad et al., 2000). The career plans of female university students have shown corresponding changes (Pryor et al., 2006). Also, meta-analyses found decreases over time in the tendencies of men to engage in riskier behavior than women (Byrnes et al., 1999) and to emerge more than women as leaders in small groups (Eagly and Karau, 1991). Also, women's self-reported agency has increased over time to become more similar to men's agency, whereas the sex difference in communion has been relatively invariant (Twenge, 1997, 2001; although see Lueptow et al., 2001). This increasing gender similarity in traditionally masculine domains is consistent with women's growing labor force participation and lessening concentration on childcare and other domestic activities.

The convergence of the sexes on masculine attributes is sufficiently marked to be apparent to everyday observers of men and women. Diekman and Eagly (2000) showed that people believe that women and men have converged in their personality, cognitive, and physical characteristics during the past 50 years and will continue to converge during the next 50 years. This perceived convergence mainly took the form of women increasing in the qualities typically associated with men. These studies also showed that perceivers function like implicit role theorists by assuming that, because the roles of women and men have become more similar, their attributes converge.

Despite this evidence of social change, men in industrialized nations do not appear to be undergoing transitions in their daily activities comparable to those of women. Men have only modestly increased their contributions to childcare and domestic work (Bianchi et al., 2006) and have yet to enter in large numbers into caring professions and other typically female types of paid employment (Queneau, 2006). Given the logic of social role theory, men's attributes will shift to include more communal qualities to the extent that they enter female-typical roles by performing more family caring activities and holding more communally demanding occupations.

Is it possible for men to adopt more communal roles and develop more caring, warm, emotionally-expressive personalities? A reasoned answer requires knowledge of the biosocial roots of the role structure and the limits it may impose on role flexibility. As we have explained, these roots lay mainly in the ways that male size and strength and female reproductive activities interact with socioeconomic complexity. Contemporary changes in female reproductive activity and the demands of occupations have eased women's inroads into male-dominated professional and managerial occupations and increased their agency. Barriers to men taking on childcare and communally demanding occupations include lower monetary compensation of these occupations (England, 2006), beliefs that men are less well endowed with communal skills (Cejka and Eagly, 1999), and stigma associated with nontraditional roles such as stay-at-home dads (Brescoll and Uhlmann, 2005).

Women undertake childcare more than men in part because of the continuing efficiency of this activity for women. The energetic demands of bearing children and the health benefits of some months of breastfeeding can orient mothers away from continued paid employment and toward infant care. This arrangement is fostered by female socialization and societal beliefs that promote sex-typical role performance. Hormonal processes also may encourage mothers' childcare, as the cascading hormones of pregnancy and lactation support women's tending (Campbell, 2008; Kuzawa et al., 2010; Taylor, 2002). Paternal behavior can also be supported by hormonal processes, as fathers show hormonal accommodation to parenthood similar to that of women (Berg & Wynne-Edwards, 2001; Wynne-Edwards, 2001). New fathers and mothers thus show suppressed testosterone and other hormonal changes, presumably to facilitate caretaking. Caretaking is additionally facilitated in both sexes by neurochemical mechanisms of reward learning that can undergird nurturing of infants and young children (Broad et al., 2006; Depue and Morrone-Strupinsky, 2005). Fathering activities also are fostered by changing norms and attitudes in the US, especially among younger adults, who have become more accepting of men's equal participation in childcare (e.g., Milkie et al., 2002).

In general, change toward gender equality is slowed by societal ideologies and status beliefs that legitimize social inequalities on the basis of sex and other attributes (Ridgeway, 2006; Sidanius and Pratto, 1999). Despite evidence that the pace of change in gender equality has slowed on many attitudinal and behavioral indicators since the second half of the twentieth century (Blau et al., 2006b), women's attitudes and ideologies are more progressive

than men's (e.g., Eagly et al., 2003a), and their political commitments and actions continue to speed social change (e.g., Dodson, 2006; Seguino, 2007). For those committed to gender equality, a challenge for the future is to understand the roots of role asymmetries. Such understanding could facilitate social policy that opens paths for both men and women to occupy a wider range of social roles.

REFERENCES

Abelson, R. (1985) A variance explanation paradox: When a little is a lot. *Psychological Bulletin, 97*, 129–133.
Allport, G.W. (1954) *The Nature of Prejudice.* Cambridge, MA: Perseus Books.
Anderson C., John, O.P., Keltner, D. and Kring, A.M. (2001) Who attains social status? Effects of personality and physical attractiveness in social groups. *Journal of Personality and Social Psychology, 81*, 116–132.
Archer, J. (2006) Testosterone and human aggression: An evaluation of the challenge hypothesis. *Neuroscience and Biobehavioral Reviews, 30*, 319–345.
Bakan, D. (1966) *The Duality of Human Existence: Isolation and Communion in Western Man.* Boston: Beacon Press.
Bem, S.L. (1974) The measurement of psychological androgyny. *Journal of Consulting and Clinical Psychology, 42*, 155–162.
Berg, S.J. and Wynne-Edwards, K.E. (2001) Changes in testosterone, cortisol, and estradiol levels in men becoming fathers. *Mayo Clinic Proceedings, 76*, 582–592.
Berger, J., Rosenholtz, S.J. and Zelditch, M. (1980) Status organizing processes. *Annual Review of Sociology, 6*, 479–508.
Bianchi, S.M., Robinson, J.P. and Milkie, M.A. (2006) *Changing Rhythms of American Family Life.* New York: Russell Sage.
Biddle, B.J. (1979) *Role Theory: Expectancies, Identities, and Behaviors.* New York: Academic Press.
Blau, F.D., Brinton, M.C. and Grusky, D.B. (2006a) The declining significance of gender. In F.D. Blau, M.C. Brinton and D.B. Grusky (eds), *The Declining Significance of Gender?* pp. 215–244. New York: Russell Sage Foundation.
Blau, F.D., Brinton, M.C. and Grusky, D.B. (eds) (2006b). *The Declining Significance of Gender?* New York: Russell Sage Foundation.

Booth, A., Granger, D.A., Mazur, A. and Kivlighan, K.T. (2006) Testosterone and social behavior. *Social Forces*, *85*, 167–191.

Brescoll, V.L. and Uhlmann, E.L. (2005) Attitudes toward traditional and non-traditional parents. *Psychology of Women Quarterly*, *35*, 436–445.

Brescoll, V.L. and Uhlmann, E.L. (2008) Can an angry woman get ahead? Status conferral, gender, and expression of emotion in the workplace. *Psychological Science*, *19*, 268–275.

Broad, K.D., Curley, J.P. and Keverne, E.B. (2006) Mother–infant bonding and the evolution of mammalian social relationships. *Philosophical Transactions of the Royal Society*, *361*, 2199–2214.

Broverman, I.K., Vogel, S.R., Broverman, D.M., Clarkson, F.E. and Rosenkrantz, P.S. (1972) Sex-roles stereotypes: A current appraisal. *Journal of Social Issues*, *28*, 59–78.

Buss, D.M. (1989) Sex differences in human mate preferences: Evolutionary hypotheses tested in 37 cultures. *Behavioral and Brain Sciences*, *12*, 1–49.

Buss, D.M. and Schmitt, D.P. (1993) Sexual strategies theory: An evolutionary perspective on human mating. *Psychological Review*, *100*, 204–232.

Bussey, K. and Bandura, A. (1999) Social cognitive theory of gender development and differentiation. *Psychological Review*, *106*, 676–713.

Byrnes, J.P., Miller, D.C. and Schafer, W.D. (1999) Gender differences in risk taking: A meta-analysis. *Psychological Bulletin*, *125*, 367–383.

Byron, K. (2007) Male and female managers' ability to 'read' emotions: Relationships with supervisor's performance ratings and subordinates' satisfaction ratings. *Journal of Occupational and Organizational Psychology*, *80*, 713–733.

Campbell, A. (2008) Attachment, aggression and affiliation: The role of oxytocin in female social behavior. *Biological Psychology*, *77*, 1–10.

Carli, L.L. (2001) Gender and social influence. *Journal of Social Issues*, *57*, 725–741.

Carver, C.S. and Scheier, M.F. (1981) *Attention and Self-regulation: A Control-theory Approach to Human Behavior*. New York: Springer-Verlag.

Carver, C.S. and Scheier, M.F. (2008) Self-regulatory systems: Action and affect. In J.Y. Shah and W.L. Gardner (eds), *Handbook of Motivation Science*, pp. 308–324. New York: Guilford Press.

Cejka, M.A. and Eagly, A.H. (1999) Gender-stereotypic images of occupations correspond to the sex segregation of employment. *Personality and Social Psychology Bulletin*, *25*, 413–423.

Conway, M., Pizzamiglio, M.T. and Mount, L. (1996) Status, communality, and agency: Implications for stereotypes of gender and other groups. *Journal of Personality and Social Psychology*, *71*, 25–38.

Correll, S.J., Benard, S. and Paik, I. (2007) Getting a job: Is there a motherhood penalty? *American Journal of Sociology*, *112*, 1297–1338.

Cronbach, L. and Meehl, P. (1955) Construct validity in psychological tests. *Psychological Bulletin*, *52*, 281–302.

Deaux, K. (1976) *The Behavior of Women and Men*. Monterey, CA: Brooks/Cole.

Depue, R.A. and Morrone-Strupinsky, J.V. (2005) A neurobehavioral model of affiliative bonding: Implications for conceptualizing a human trait of affiliation. *Behavioral and Brain Sciences*, *28*, 313–395.

Diekman, A.B. and Eagly, A.H. (2000) Stereotypes as dynamic constructs: Women and men of the past, present, and future. *Personality and Social Psychology Bulletin*, *26*, 1171–1188.

Dodson, D.L. (2006) *The Impact of Women in Congress*. New York: Oxford University Press.

Eagly, A.H. (1978) Sex differences in influenceability. *Psychological Bulletin*, *85*, 86–116.

Eagly, A.H. (1987) *Sex Differences in Social Behavior: A Social-role Interpretation*. Hillsdale, NJ: Lawrence Erlbaum.

Eagly, A.H. and Carli, L.L. (1981) Sex of researchers and sex-typed communications as determinants of sex differences in influenceability: A meta-analysis of social influence studies. *Psychological Bulletin*, *90*, 1–20.

Eagly, A.H. and Crowley, M. (1986) Gender and helping behavior: A meta-analytic review of the social psychological literature. *Psychological Bulletin*, *100*, 283–308.

Eagly, A.H., Diekman, A.B., Schneider, M. and Kulesa, P. (2003a) Experimental tests of an attitudinal theory of the gender gap in voting. *Personality and Social Psychology Bulletin*, *29*, 1245–1258.

Eagly, A.H., Johannesen-Schmidt, M.C. and van Engen, M.L. (2003b) Transformational, transactional, and laissez-faire leadership styles: A meta-analysis comparing women and men. *Psychological Bulletin*, *129*, 569–591.

Eagly, A.H. and Johnson, B.T. (1990) Gender and leadership style: A meta-analysis. *Psychological Bulletin*, *108*, 233–256.

Eagly, A.H. and Karau, S.J. (1991) Gender and the emergence of leaders: A meta-analysis. *Journal of Personality and Social Psychology*, *60*, 685–710.

Eagly, A.H. and Karau, S.J. (2002) Role congruity theory of prejudice toward female leaders. *Psychological Review*, *109*, 573–598.

Eagly, A.H., Makhijani, M.G. and Klonsky, B.G. (1992) Gender and the evaluation of leaders: A meta-analysis. *Psychological Bulletin, 111*, 3–22.

Eagly, A.H. and Steffen, V.J. (1984) Gender stereotypes stem from the distribution of women and men into social roles. *Journal of Personality and Social Psychology, 46*, 735–754.

Eagly, A.H. and Steffen, V.J. (1986) Gender and aggressive behavior: A meta-analytic review of the social psychological literature. *Psychological Bulletin, 100*, 309–330.

Eagly, A.H. and Wood, W. (1982) Inferred sex differences in status as a determinant of gender stereotypes about social influence. *Journal of Personality and Social Psychology, 43*, 915–928.

Eagly, A.H. and Wood, W. (1991) Explaining sex differences in social behavior: A meta-analytic perspective. *Personality and Social Psychology Bulletin, 17*, 306–315.

Eagly, A.H. and Wood, W. (1999) The origins of sex differences in human behavior: Evolved dispositions versus social roles. *American Psychologist, 54*, 408–423.

Eagly, A.H., Wood, W. and Fishbaugh, L. (1981) Sex differences in conformity: Surveillance by the group as a determinant of male nonconformity. *Journal of Personality and Social Psychology, 40*, 384–394.

England, P. (2006) Toward gender equality: Progress and bottlenecks. In F.D. Blau, M.C. Brinton, and D.B. Grusky (eds), *The Declining Significance of Gender?* pp. 245–264. New York: Russell Sage Foundation.

Friedan, B. (1963) *The Feminine Mystique*. Harmondsworth: Penguin

Gawronski, B. (2003) On difficult questions and evident answers: Dispositional inference from role-constrained behavior. *Personality and Social Psychology Bulletin, 29*, 1459–1475.

Gilbert, D.T. and Malone, P.S. (1995). The correspondence bias. *Psychological Bulletin, 117*, 21–38.

Glass, A., McGraw, B. and Smith, M. (1981) *Integration of Research Studies: Meta-analysis of Research*. Beverly Hills, CA: Sage.

Glick, P. (1991) Trait-based and sex-based discrimination in occupational prestige, occupational salary, and hiring. *Sex Roles, 25*, 351–378.

Goffman, E. (1959) *The Presentation of Self in Everyday Life*. Garden City, NY: Doubleday Anchor.

Grossman, M. and Wood, W. (1993) Sex differences in intensity of emotional experience: A social role interpretation. *Journal of Personality and Social Psychology, 65*, 1010–1022.

Hall, J.A. and Carter, J.D. (1999) Gender-stereotype accuracy as an individual difference. *Journal of Personality and Social Psychology, 77*, 350–359.

Hayden, B., Deal, M., Cannon, A. and Casey, J. (1986) Ecological determinants of women's status among hunter/gatherers. *Human Evolution, 1*, 449–473.

Heatherington, T.F. (2011) Neuroscience of self and self-regulation. *Annual Review of Psychology, 62*, 363–390. doi: .1146/annurev.psych.121208.131616.

Heider, F. (1958) *The Psychology of Interpersonal Relations*. New York: Wiley.

Heilman, M.E. and Haynes, M.C. (2005) Combating organizational discrimination: Some unintended consequences. In R.L. Dipboye and A. Colella (eds), *Discrimination at Work: The Psychological and Organizational Bases*, pp. 339–362. Mahwah, NJ: Erlbaum.

Heilman, M.E., Wallen, A.S., Fuchs, D. and Tamkins, M.M. (2004) Penalties for success: Reactions to women who succeed at male gender-typed tasks. *Journal of Applied Psychology, 89*, 416–427.

Helfat, C.E., Harris, D. and Wolfson, P.J. (2006) The pipeline to the top: Women and men in the top executive ranks of U.S. corporations. *Academy of Management Perspectives, 20*, 42–64.

Hines, M. (2009) Gonadal hormones and sexual differentiation of human brain and behavior. In (eds), *Hormones, Brain, and Behaviour, Vol. 4*, 2nd Edition, pp. 1869–1909. Oxford: Elsevier.

Hollingworth, L.S. (1916) Sex differences in mental traits. *Psychological Bulletin, 13*, 377–384.

Horney, K. (1967) *Feminine Psychology*. New York: Norton.

Huber, J. (2007) *On the Origins of Gender Inequality*. Boulder, CO: Paradigm Publishers.

Konrad, A.M., Ritchie, J.E., Jr., Lieb, P. and Corrigall, E. (2000).Sex differences and similarities in job attribute preferences: A meta-analysis. *Psychological Bulletin, 126*, 593–641.

Kuzawa, C.W., Gettler, L.T., Huang, Y. and McDade, T.W. (2010) Mothers have lower testosterone than non-mothers: Evidence from the Philippines. *Hormones and Behavior, 57*, 441–447.

Lueptow, L.B., Garovich-Szabo, L. and Lueptow, M.B. (2001) Social change and the persistence of sex-typing: 1974–1997. *Social Forces, 80*, 1–36.

Maccoby, E.E. (1966) Sex differences in intellectual functioning. In E.E. Maccoby (ed.), *The Development of Sex Differences*, pp. 25–55. Stanford, CA: Stanford University Press.

McKee, J.P. and Sherriffs, A.C. (1957) The differential evaluation of males and females. *Journal of Personality, 25*, 356–371.

Milkie, M.A., Bianchi, S.M., Mattingly, M.J. and Robinson, J.P. (2002) Gendered division of childrearing: Ideals realities, and the relationship to parental well-being. *Sex-Roles, 47*, 21–38.

Miller, C.F., Trautner, H.M. and Ruble, D.N. (2006) The role of gender stereotypes in children's preferences and behavior. In L. Balter and C.S. Tamis-LeMonda (eds), *Child Psychology: A Handbook of Contemporary Issues*, 2nd Edition, pp. 293–323. New York: Psychology Press.

Moskowitz, D.S., Suh, E.J. and Desaulniers, J. (1994) Situational influences on gender differences in agency and communion. *Journal of Personality and Social Psychology, 66*, 753–761.

Murdock, G.P. and Provost, C. (1973) Factors in the division of labor by sex: A cross-cultural analysis. *Ethnology, 13*, 203–225.

Olson, J.M., Roese, N.J. and Zanna, M.P. (1996) Expectancies. In E.T. Higgins and A.W. Kruglanski (eds), *Social Psychology: Handbook of Basic Principles*, pp. 211–238. New York: Guilford Press.

Parsons, T. and Bales, R.F. (1955) *Family, Socialization and Interaction Process*. Glencoe, IL: Free Press.

Polachek, S. (2006) How the life-cycle human-capital model explains why the gender wage gap narrowed. In F.D Blau, M.C. Brinton, and D.B. Grusky (eds), *The Declining Significance of Gender?* pp. 102–124. New York: Russell Sage Foundation.

Pryor, J.H., Hurtado, S., Saenz, V.B., Santos, J.L. and Korn, W.S. (2006) The American freshman: Forty year trends. Los Angeles: Higher Education Research Institute, UCLA. Available at: http://www.gseis.ucla.edu/heri/norms06.php, accessed January 27, 2009.

Queneau, H. (2006) Is the long-term reduction in occupational sex segregation still continuing in the United States? *Social Science Journal, 43*, 681–688.

Ridgeway, C.L. (1981) Nonconformity, competence, and influence in groups: A test of two theories. *American Sociological Review, 46*, 333–347.

Ridgeway, C.L. (1984) Dominance, performance and status in groups: A theoretical analysis. *Advances in Group Processes, 1*, 59–93.

Ridgeway, C.L. (2006) Gender as an organizing force in social relations: Implications for the future of inequality, pp. 265–287. In F.D. Blau, M.C. Brinton, and D.B. Grusky (eds), *The Declining Significance of Gender?* pp. 245–264. New York: Russell Sage Foundation.

Ridgeway, C.L. and Bourg, C. (2004) Gender as status: An expectation states theory approach. In A.H. Eagly, A.E. Beall and R.J. Sternberg (eds), *The Psychology of Gender*, 2nd Edition, pp. 217–241. New York: Guilford Press.

Rosenthal, R. (1978) How often are our numbers wrong? *American Psychologist, 33*, 1005–1008.

Rosenthal, R. and Rubin, D.B. (1978) Interpersonal expectancy effects: The first 345 studies. *Behavior and Brain Sciences, 1*, 377–415.

Ross, L. (1977) The intuitive psychologist and his shortcomings. In L. Berkowitz (ed.), *Advances in Experimental Social Psychology, 10*, 173–220. New York: Academic Press.

Roter, D.L., Hall, J.A. and Aoki, Y. (2002) Physician gender effects in medical communication: A meta-analytic review. *Journal of the American Medical Association, 288*, 756–764.

Salzman, P.C. (1999) Is inequality universal? *Current Anthropology, 40*, 31–61.

Seguino, S. (2007) Plus ça change? Evidence on global trends in gender norms and stereotypes. *Feminist Economics, 13*, 1–28.

Shackelford, S., Wood, W. and Worchel, S. (1996) Behavioral styles and the influence of women in mixed-sex groups. *Social Psychology Quarterly, 59*, 284–293.

Sidanius, J. and Pratto, F. (1999) *Social Dominance: An Intergroup Theory of Social Hierarchy and Oppression*. New York: Cambridge University Press.

Skrypnek, B.J. and Snyder, M. (1982) On the self-perpetuating nature of stereotypes about women and men. *Journal of Experimental Social Psychology, 18*, 277–291.

Spence, J.T. and Helmreich, R.L. (1978) *Masculinity and Femininity: Their Psychological Dimensions, Correlates, and Antecedents*. Austin: University of Texas Press.

Strodtbeck, F.L. and Mann, R.D. (1956) Sex role differentiation in jury deliberations. *Sociometry, 19*, 3–11.

Swim, J.K. (1994) Perceived versus meta-analytic effect sizes: An assessment of the accuracy of gender stereotypes. *Journal of Personality and Social Psychology, 66*, 21–36.

Taylor, M.C. and Hall, J.A. (1982) Psychological androgyny: Theories, methods, and conclusions. *Psychological Bulletin, 92*, 347–366.

Taylor, S.E. (2002) *The Tending Instinct: How Nurturing is Essential to Who We Are and How We Live*. New York: Holt.

Taylor, S.E., Klein, L.C., Lewis, B.P., Gruenewald, T.L., Gurung, R.A.R. and Updegraff, J.A. (2000) Biobehavioral responses to stress in females: Tend-and-befriend, not fight-or-flight. *Psychological Review, 107*, 411–429.

Tomaskovic-Devey, D., Zimmer, C., Stainback, K., Robinson, C., Taylor, T. and McTague, T. (2006)

Documenting desegregation: Segregation in American workplaces by race, ethnicity, and sex, 1966–2003. *American Sociological Review, 71*, 565–588.

Twenge, J.M. (1997) Changes in masculine and feminine traits over time: A meta-analysis. *Sex Roles, 36*, 305–325.

Twenge, J.M. (2001) Changes in women's assertiveness in response to status and roles: A cross-temporal meta-analysis, 1931–1993. *Journal of Personality and Social Psychology, 81*, 133–145.

Uleman, J.S., Saribay, S.A. and Gonzalez, C.M. (2008) Spontaneous inferences, implicit impressions, and implicit theories. *Annual Review of Psychology, 59*, 329–360.

US Bureau of Labor Statistics (2008) News – Married parents' use of time, 2003–06. Available at: http://www.bls.gov/news.release/pdf/atus2.pdf, accessed December 10, 2008.

US Bureau of Labor Statistics (2010) Women in the labor force: A databook. Available at: http://www.bls.gov/cps/wlf-databook-2010.pdf, accessed January 11, 2010.

Valian, V. (1998) *Why So Slow? The Advancement of Women.* Cambridge, MA: MIT Press.

Witt, M.G. and Wood, W. (2010) Self-regulation of behavior in everyday life. *Sex Roles, 62*, 635–646. doi: 10.1007/s11199-010-9761-y.

Wood, W. (1987) Meta-analytic review of sex differences in group performance. *Psychological Bulletin, 102*, 53–71.

Wood, W., Christensen, P.N., Hebl, M.R. and Rothgerber, H. (1997) Conformity to sex-typed norms, affect, and the self-concept. *Journal of Personality and Social Psychology, 73*, 523–535.

Wood, W. and Eagly, A.H. (2002) A cross-cultural analysis of the behavior of women and men: Implications for the origins of sex differences. *Psychological Bulletin, 128*, 699–727.

Wood, W. and Eagly, A.H. (2010) Gender. In S. Fiske, D. Gilbert, and G. Lindzey (eds), *Handbook of Social Psychology,* 5th ed., *1*, pp. 629–667. New York: Oxford University Press.

Wood, W. and Eagly, A.H. (2009) Gender identity. In M. Leary and R. Hoyle (eds), *Handbook of Individual Differences,* pp. 109–125. New York: Guilford Press.

Wood, W. and Karten, S.J. (1986) Sex differences in interaction style as a product of perceived sex differences in competence. *Journal of Personality and Social Psychology, 50*, 341–347.

Wood, W., Rhodes, N. and Whelan, M. (1989) Sex differences in positive well-being: A consideration of emotional style and marital status. *Psychological Bulletin, 106*, 249–264.

Wynne-Edwards, K.E. (2001) Hormonal changes in expectant fathers. *Hormones and Behavior, 40*, 139–145.

Zanna, M.P. and Pack, S.J. (1975) On the self-fulfilling nature of apparent sex differences in behavior. *Journal of Experimental Social Psychology, 11*, 583–591.

50

Social Representation Theory

Patrick Rateau, Pascal Moliner, Christian Guimelli, and Jean-Claude Abric

ABSTRACT

As heir to a strong French sociological tradition, the theory of social representations, elaborated by Serge Moscovici in the beginning of the 1960s, has become one of the major theories in social psychology. Mainly European initially, it rapidly brought together a large number of researchers and practitioners worldwide, mainly in the field of social psychology, but also in all other social sciences. These researchers have seen this theory as a flexible conceptual framework that enables us to understand and explain the way individuals and groups elaborate, transform, and communicate their social reality. They have also found in this theory's different developments a vast set of methods and tools, directly applicable to the analysis of a wide range of social issues. Lending itself equally well to qualitative approaches as to experimental applications, studies have multiplied along different lines. Those aiming at making connections between sociorepresentational processes and other processes classically studied in the field of social cognition seem to be the most promising in terms of the theory's future development. This chapter addresses a longstanding tradition of research, covering a period of nearly 100 years of research, from 1893 to 2010.

INTRODUCTION

A common sense theory

In many ways, social psychology is the study of social reality. That is to say that it deals with the explanations to which we automatically have recourse in order to explain and understand the world around us. Indeed, each one of us desires to make sense of events, behaviors, ideas, and exchanges with others and seeks to find around them a certain coherence and stability. Each one of us seeks to explain and understand their environment in order to make it predictable and more controllable. Yet, this environment is made up of innumerable situations and events, and a multiplicity of individuals and groups. Similarly, we are being constantly required, during our everyday interactions, to make decisions, to give our opinion on this or that subject or to explain this or that behavior. In short, we are constantly plunged into an environment where we are bombarded with information and required to deal with it. In order to understand, master, and make sense of this environment we have to simplify it, to make it more predictable and familiar. In others words we have to reconstruct it in our own fashion.

But one cannot help but notice that this process of reconstruction is a constantly repeated process. From our youngest age, school, the family, institutions, and the media, instill in us certain ways of seeing the world and offer us a particular vision of the things around us, presenting us largely with a ready-made construction of the world in which we grow up, the values with which it is invested, the categories which govern it and the principles themselves by which we understand it. Our perception of the environment is next shaped by the groups, the associations, and the clubs that we become part of. It is very largely in our exchanges and our communications with others that our reality of the world around is formed. In the course of our contacts and our multiple involvements with different social groups we ourselves acquire and transmit knowledge, beliefs, and values that allow us to share a common conception of things and of others. In this sense, this reconstruction of reality, this representation of reality, is above all social; that is to say elaborated according to the social characteristics of the individual and shared by a group of other individuals having the same characteristics.

This last point is important. Not all social groups share the same values, the same standards, the same ideologies, or the same concrete experiences. Yet all construct representations that are closely based on these. It follows that social representations bear on the one hand the mark of the social membership of the individuals who adhere to them and give them their identity, and on the other allow these same individuals to distinguish "others," those who do not share the same representations and who appear to them at best as different, at worst as enemies.

To sum up, social representations can be defined as "systems of opinions, knowledge, and beliefs" particular to a culture, a social category, or a group with regard to objects in the social environment. At this introductory stage, it seems unnecessary to go any further. We will simply note at this point that with regard to social representations the distinction between the notions of "opinions," "knowledge," and "beliefs" is unnecessary. Of course opinions are mostly concerned with the field of position taking, knowledge with the field of learning, and experience and beliefs with that of conviction. But our everyday experience shows us that for individuals, there is frequently confusion between these three areas, especially when talking about a socially invested object. To this effect, we observe beliefs that have the status of established truths, or opinions that look peculiarly similar to beliefs, with the result that the lines between what "I think," "I know," and "I believe" often become blurred. As a consequence, the contents of a representation may be indifferently classed as opinions, information, or beliefs, and we may choose that a social representation comes across concretely as a set of "cognitive elements" relative to a social object.

The first characteristic of this set is that of *organization*. This is well and truly a structure, and not just a collection of cognitive elements. This means that the elements that constitute a social representation interact with each other. More exactly, this means that people cooperate in establishing relationships between these diverse elements. Particular opinions are considered equivalent to others, particular beliefs are deemed incompatible with particular information, and so on.

The second specificity of a representation is that of being *shared* by the members of a particular social group. However, the consensuses observed on the elements of a given representation depend at the same time on the homogeneity of the group and on its members' position towards the object, so that the consensual nature of a representation is generally partial, and localized to certain elements of the latter.

The third characteristic of this set resides in its method of construction; it is *collectively produced* through a more global process of communication. Exchange between individuals and exposure to mass communication allow the members of a group to share the elements that will constitute a social representation. This sharing process favors the emergence of a consensus at the same time as conferring social validity on diverse opinions, information, and beliefs.

Finally, the fourth specific role of a social representation concerns its purpose – it is *socially useful*. Firstly, of course, in order to understand the object to which the social representation refers. Representations are above all systems allowing the understanding and interpreting of the social environment. But they also intervene in interactions between groups, particularly when these interactions are engaged in around a social object. Every society, as shown by Adam Smith (1776) and Emile Durkheim (1893), revolves around the division of labor. This division is not only a condition of social cohesion, but also a permanent source of dependency and power relationships within the community. Indeed, it leads to the differentiation of groups, roles, status, professions, castes, and so on. Thus, everyone is interdependent whilst being clear about their separate identity. Complementarity and differentiation are two interdependent operations that are fully active within representations. Furthermore, social representations provide criteria for evaluating the social environment that enable determination, justification, or legitimization of certain behaviors. Taken together, that is how Serge Moscovici (1961) defines the notion of social representation in his first work devoted to the image and the dissemination of the psychoanalytic theory in France in the middle of the twentieth century. Whilst studying the way in which a scientific theory is transformed into a common sense theory, Moscovici traced the first outlines of what would henceforth be called the theory of social representations (SRT), whose success has not wavered since.

The liveliness of the SRT

Some 50 years after its introduction to the field of social psychology, the importance of the SRT is well known; without doubt it is a major theoretical and empirical movement. The reasons for this success are diverse.

Let us start with its interdisciplinary nature. Located in the social and psychological interface, the social representation concept is of interest to all the social sciences. It has found a place in the fields of sociology, anthropology, history, geography, and economy and studies are carried out on its links with ideologies, symbolic systems, and attitudes. But it can also be found in the fields of cognition and linguistics. This multiplicity of relations with other disciplines confers on the SRT a transversal status that mobilizes and connects different fields of research. This interdisciplinary nature constitutes without a doubt one of the most fertile and dynamic contributions made by this field of study.

The second reason is the flexibility of its conceptual framework which has enabled this theory to adapt to various research areas (communication, social practice, intergroup relations, etc.), and to initiate many theoretical and methodological developments. But to these reasons can be added another, more fundamental point from our perspective. As a "socially built and shared knowledge theory" (Jodelet, 1989), the SRT is a theory of social bonding. It gives us an insight on what permanently connects us to the world and to others. It teaches us about how this bond is built. In this sense, one can see here a global theory of the social individual and a possible way for integrating the diverse paradigms and fields of social psychology.

The success of the SRT can be measured in terms of its scientific verve. Indeed, ever since the founding work by Serge Moscovici innumerable works have regularly presented new research developments in the field of social representations. In France, this phenomenon has been particularly marked since the 1980s when publications devoted to this theme appeared approximately every three years. It was also in the 1980s that the theory began its rapid expansion abroad, with the publication and translation into English of many books on the subject (Breakwell and

Canter, 1979; Deaux and Philogène, 2001a, 2001b; Duveen, 2001; Farr and Moscovici, 1984; Moscovici, 1981, 1982, 1984, 1988, 2001a, 2001b; Mugny and Carugati, 1989).

According to the census conducted by Vergès (1996), the SRT, with more than 2000 articles, laid claim to be one of the most famous psychosocial theories, at the same level as cognitive dissonance, which, in its 27 years of existence had had more than 1,000 references (Cooper and Croyle, 1984). In addition, regular international symposiums are dedicated to it (Ravello, 1992; Rio de Janeiro, 1994; Aix-en-Provence, 1996; Mexico, 1998; Montréal, 2000; Stirling, 2002; Guadalajara, 2004; Rome, 2006; Bali, 2008; Tunis, 2010), as are many journals and special editions of journals. Finally, we should mention the creation of an Internet network (Social Representations and Communication Thematic Network) bringing together researchers worldwide (South America, the US, Japan, India, Russia, etc.) and of a European PhD on Communication and Social Representations in 1993. If one can say that a good theory is one that is "talked about," then the sheer quantity of communication around the theory of social representations confers on it the status of a major theory.

Ultimately, the scientific assessment of the SRT may appear to be somewhat flattering. However, it has not always been like this. By examining the historical development of the SRT, we will attempt to show how it progressively found its place in the field of social psychology, the different orientations running through it at present, what connections it has with other major psychosocial paradigms, and finally, in what way it constitutes today an essential theory for analyzing and understanding social problems.

A BRIEF HISTORY OF THE THEORY AND ITS DEVELOPMENTS

After having been the most memorable phenomenon in French social sciences at the beginning of the twentieth century, the notion of collective representations, introduced by the French sociologist Emile Durkheim in 1898, fell into disuse for more than 50 years. It was towards the beginning of the 1960s that Moscovici renewed studies of the concept and aroused the interest of a small group of social psychologists, thus bringing the theory back to life. They saw in it the possibility for tackling their discipline's issues from a new and original angle (Abric, 1976; Codol, 1970; Flament, 1971). The study of knowledge dissemination, of the relationship between thought and communication, and of the genesis of common sense, formed the elements of a new program that has been familiar ever since. But, in between the concept of collective representations and the contemporary researches on social representations, the concept has undergone many a metamorphosis, giving it different forms and colors. It is this history that we shall attempt to retrace here.

From collective representations to social representations

All attempts to reconstitute the past of this concept necessarily begin with sociology. Simmel (1908) was without doubt the first to recognize the connection between the separation of the individual who distances himself from others and the necessity to symbolize these others. He argued that the manner in which we symbolize others shapes reciprocal action and the social circles that they form together. From a different point of view, Weber (1921) saw representations as a reference framework and a channel for action by the individual. He attempts to describe a common knowledge capable of anticipating and prescribing the behavior of individuals.

But the true inventor of this concept is Durkheim (1893, 1895, 1898) insofar as he defines its contours and recognizes its ability to explain various societal phenomena. He defines it as a double separation. First, collective representations are to be distinguished from individual representations. The latter, unique to each individual, are extremely variable, fleeting, short-lived and constitute a steady stream, whereas collective representations are impersonal and untouched by time. Second, individual representations are rooted in the individual consciousness, whereas collective representations are mutually held throughout society. Such representations are thus homogeneous and shared by all members of society. Their function is to preserve what binds them, to prepare and act in a uniform manner. This is why they are collective, why they are handed down over the years from generation to generation, and why they act for individuals as strong cognitive constraints. For Durkheim, the aim is clear: collective thinking has to be studied in itself and for itself. The forms and content of representations have to become a separate domain in order to be able to claim and prove social autonomy. For him, this is social psychology's task, even though it's still in its formative stages and its purpose still seems unclear.

However, during the very beginning of the twentieth century, it was above all sociology, anthropology, and ethnology (Lévi-Strauss, 1962; Lévy-Bruhl, 1922; Linton, 1945; Mauss, 1903) which would use the notion of representations, in a perfectly descriptive manner, to study different collective representations in cultural or ethnic communities. It was not until the 1960s that, following in Durkheim's footsteps, and based on child (Piaget, 1932) and clinical psychology (Freud, 1908, 1922), Serge Moscovici (1961) attempted to elaborate a social psychology of representations. Considering that Durkheim's conceptions left relatively little place for the question of interactions between the individual and the collective, he proposed to replace the term "collective representation" with a more restricted "social representation." In the words of the author, it was to

transfer to modern society a notion that seemed to be reserved to more traditional societies [in response to the] necessity of making representations into a bridge between individual and social spheres, by associating them with the perspective of a changing society. (Moscovici, 1989: 82)

This evolution is marked by two fundamental changes in relation to Durkheimian conceptions.

First, Moscovici considers that representations are not the product of society as a whole, but the products of the social groups who build this society. Second, he focuses on communication processes, considered as explaining the emergence and transmission of social representations. The first point allows the conception of a social mentality which is overdetermined by societal structures and also by the insertion of individuals in these structures, in such a way that different social representations of the same object are seen to exist within a given society. The second change to the representation theory, introduced by Moscovici, permits the conception that through communication – and the influence, normalization and conformity processes that go with it – individual beliefs can be the object of a consensus at the same time as collective beliefs can impose themselves on the individual.

However, the social representation concept would undergo another period of latency before mobilizing the broad stream of research mentioned earlier in this chapter. The theory's true deployment couldn't happen until many epistemological obstacles had been removed, the largest of them all being the behaviorist model, which denied any validity to the consideration of mental processes and their specificity. The decline of behaviorism and the emergence of the "new look" in the 1970s, followed by cognitivism in the 1980s, led to the progressive expansion of the "stimulus-response" (S–R) paradigm. This development meant that internal psychological states, conceived as an active cognitive construction of the environment and dependent on individual and social factors, were recognized as having a creative role in the behavior elaboration process. This is perfectly expressed by Moscovici, when he says that representations determine at the same time stimuli and responses, in other words "that there is no line between the external and internal universes of individuals or a group" (1969: 9).

This overturning of perspectives marked, from the 1980s, the development and improvement of work on social representations. It is also considered, in a diagrammatic sense, that these works were developed along three main lines, each one attempting to develop different facets of the concept. One which examines the regulatory role of social representations on real social interactions, another which studies the impact of social relationships on the elaboration of social representations, and a third which analyses representational dynamics and their structural characteristics, more specifically linked to social conduct. These three lines of development revolve not so much around different points of view as different ways of approaching social representations. This diversity of orientation most probably comes from the fact that Moscovici himself proposed diverse definitions of social representations, all of which are complementary.

There are multiple reasons for this flexibility. First of all, research is not limited by being enclosed within a rigid and narrow theoretical framework. Second, it allows the study of social representations to be situated within the framework of a paradigm, a line of thought and a knowledge structuring tool, rather than within an established and narrow-minded theoretical framework. Finally, the reality of social representations is such that their definition can vary according to the researcher's perspective. We can therefore study them in their emergence and in their role as regulator of social interaction and communications, from the angle of their internal structure or even from that of their links with social relations. We are now going to briefly introduce these three perspectives.

Orientations of the SRT

The sociogenetic model

When he formed his theory, Moscovici (1961) wanted above all to propose a description of the genesis and the development of social representations. According to him, the emergence of a social representation always coincides with the emergence of an unprecedented situation, unknown phenomenon, or unusual event. This new nature of the object implies that information about it is limited, incomplete, or widely spread throughout the different social groups involved with the emergence of this object (what Moscovici called the *dispersion of information*). This new object arouses worry and vigilance or disrupts the normal course of things. It thus motivates intense cognitive activity to understand it, control it, or even defend oneself from it (*inference pressure* phenomenon), and causes a multiplicity of debates and of interpersonal and media communication. As a result of this information, beliefs, hypotheses, or speculations are shared, leading to the emergence of majority positions in different social groups. This emergence is facilitated by the fact that individuals deal with information on the object or the situation selectively, focusing on particular aspects according to their expectations and the orientations of the group (*focalization* phenomenon).

The gradual emergence of a representation occurs spontaneously and is based on three kinds of phenomena: the dispersion of information, focalization and the pressure to make inferences. But these phenomena themselves are developed on the basis of two major processes defined by Moscovici: *objectification* and *anchoring*.

Objectification refers to the way in which a new object, through communication about it, will be rapidly simplified, imaged, and diagrammed. Through the phenomenon of selective construction, different characteristics of the object are taken out of context and sorted according to cultural criteria (all groups do not have an equal access to object relative information), to normative criteria (only what agrees with the group's system of values is retained). The different aspects of the object are thus separated from the field to which they belong to be appropriated by groups who, by projecting them into their own reality, can control them more easily. These selected elements form together what Moscovici calls a *figurative core*, that is to say a coherent visualization that reproduces the object in a concrete and selective manner. By penetrating the social body through communication, by collective generalization, this simplification of the object replaces the objects reality, and is "naturalized." A representation is then created and takes on an "obvious" status. As such, it is an "independent theory" of the object which will serve as a basis for judgments and behavior oriented towards it.

To this effect, Moscovici, while studying the emergence of the representation of psychoanalysis in French society, observed the apparition of a figurative core composed of four parts: the conscious, the unconscious, repression, and complexes. These elements are fully extracted from their original theoretical context. They are also naturalized in the sense that individuals don't consider them as abstract notions but as concrete and observable elements of the psychic apparatus. From there comes the possibility to communicate about psychoanalysis beyond its conceptual framework, to recognize categories of disorders and symptoms (the superiority complex, modesty, the slip, unconscious repression, subconscious acts, etc.) and different categories of people (the complicated, the repressed, the neurotic, etc.).

Anchoring completes the objectification process. It corresponds to the way an object finds its place in a pre-existing individual and group thought system. Depending on an elementary mode of knowledge production based on an analogy principle, the new object is assimilated into forms that are already known and into familiar categories, and so on. At the same time, it will become identified with a network of already present meanings. The hierarchy of values belonging to different groups constitutes a meaning network in which the object will be located and evaluated. The object will thus be interpreted in different ways depending on social groups. Furthermore, this interpretation extends to anything that remotely concerns this object.

Thus, all social groups attach the object to their own meaning networks, guarantors of their identity. In this way a vast set of collective meaning is created around the object. In this way also, the object becomes a mediator and a criteria for relationships between groups. However, and this is an essential point to anchoring, integrating the new object into a pre-existent system of norms and values cannot happen smoothly. An innovative mix results from this contact with the new and the old, due both to the integration of the hitherto unknown object, and to the persistence of the old, the new object reactivating habitual frameworks of thought in order to incorporate it. From this it follows that a social representation always appears as innovative and enduring, changing and unchanging.

On this general theoretical basis of the process of generating social representations has developed a large research field, initiated notably by the work of Denise Jodelet (1989). This stream of research focuses on the descriptive study of social representations as meaning systems that express the relationships that individuals and groups have with their environment. Considering that representations are born essentially through interaction and contact with public discourses, this line of research concentrates firstly on language and speech from two complementary viewpoints. Social representations are approached as being at once fixed *in* language and as functioning themselves *as* language through their symbolic value and the framework they supply for coding and categorizing individuals' environment.

So-called monographic and qualitative approaches to discourse and behavior data collection and analysis (ethnographic techniques, sociological investigations, historical analysis, in-depth interviewing, focus groups, discourse analysis, documentary analysis, verbal association techniques, etc.) constitute the main methodological framework for works carried out in this area (see, for example, Kronberger and Wagner, 2000; Markova, 1997, 2003; Wagner, 1994; Wagner et al., 1999).

The structural model

Based at the same time on Moscovici's objectification process and on Asch's work on social perception (1946), Jean-Claude Abric and Claude Flament proposed an approach known as the "central core theory" (see Abric, 1993, 2001). This approach has massively contributed to clarifying sociocognitive logics underlying the general organization of social representations.

We are reminded that, at the time of his famous observations, Asch showed that amongst the seven character traits suggested to subjects as criteria for evaluating the image of a partner, one of them (warm/cold) played a principal and central role in the process studied, inasmuch as it played a far greater role in determining the perception of the other person than the other traits proposed.

Inspired by these results, Abric proposed transcending the purely genetic framework of the figurative core idea by recognizing its paramount role in all established representations. The basis of the central core theory is to consider that, in the overall picture of cognitive elements which make up a representation, certain elements play a different role to others. These elements, called central elements, form a structure named by Abric the "central core." This internal structure of representations provides two essential functions: (a) a meaning generative function – it is through the central core that other elements in the representational field acquire meaning and specific value for individuals; and (b) an organizational function – it is around the central core that other representational elements are arranged. And it is this same core that determines the relationships that these elements maintain with each other.

Thus, as a cognitive structure providing meaning generative and organizational functions, the core structures in its turn elements that refer to the object of representation. These elements, dependent on the core, are called "peripheral elements."

As proposed by Flament (1989), in reference to the scripts theory (Schank and Abelson,

1977), these peripheral elements allow representations to function as a "decryption" grid of social situations experienced by individuals. If the central core can be understood as the abstract part of the representation, the peripheral system should be understood as its concrete and operational one.

In the end, according to Abric, social representations act as entities, but with two different and complementary components:

1 The central system structures cognitive elements relative to an object and is the fruit of particular historical, symbolic, and social determinisms to which different social groups are subject. It is characterized by two fundamental properties. First, by a great stability, thus assuring the permanence and durability of the representation. In other words, the central system resists any scrutiny, in one way or another, of the representation's general basis. It is, moreover, where consensus on the representation is found, and thus constitutes its collectively shared common basis. It enables each group member to "see things" in approximately the same way, and through it, the group's homogeneity concerning the representation's object is defined. Thanks to the central system, group members can recognize each other, but also differentiate themselves from neighboring groups, and thus, to a great extent, it contributes to social identity.

2 The peripheral system, in tune with every day contingencies, enables a representation to be adapted to various social contexts. Flament assigns to it three essential functions:

   (a) It prescribes behavior and position taking allowing individuals to know what is and is not normal to say or do in a given situation, in view of its purpose.

   (b) It permits personalization of the representation and of the behaviors which are linked to it. Depending on the context, the same representation can lead to different interpersonal opinions within a group. These differences remain compatible with the central system, but correspond to an internal variability of the peripheral system.

   (c) It protects the central core when necessary and acts as a representation's "bumper." In this sense, the transformation of a social representation occurs in most cases through the prior modification of peripheral elements.

From an epistemological point of view, the structural approach marks a major turning point for the theory of social representations. On the one hand, because it provides researchers with a conceptual framework for studying stabilized representations rather than representations in their formative stage. Seen from this perspective, social representations are no longer simple "spheres of opinions," but become structured spheres. In this sense, the study of their structure takes over from that of their content. On the other hand, the structural approach offers a framework for analysis which allows us to identify the interaction between the functioning of the individual and the contexts in which the individual evolves. Finally, because the structural approach offers formalized concepts, it allows the formulation of hypotheses around the sociocognitive adaptation of social actors faced with the evolutions of their environment. And these hypotheses are at the origin of the experimental method in the study of social representations.

The sociodynamic model

Based on the anchoring process defined by Moscovici, Willem Doise (see Clémence, 2001 for an overview) proposed a theoretical model which aimed to reconcile the structural complexity of social representations and their insertion in plural social and ideological contexts.

According to Doise, representations can only be envisaged in the social dynamic which, through communication, places social players in interactive situations. This social dynamic, when elaborated around important issues, arouses specific position taking, in relation to the social integration of individuals. That is to say that positions expressed on a given question depend fundamentally upon peoples' social memberships, which refers back to Moscovici's anchoring process. But Doise adds that these positions depend also on the situations within which they are produced. This double source of variation can generate an apparent multiplicity of position taking even though they arise from common

organizational principles. Indeed, for Doise, all social interactions have symbolic characteristics. They enable people and groups to define themselves in relation to others. They therefore contribute to defining everyone's identity. This is why they have to be organized according to common rules among specific group members. By supplying shared "reference points" serving as a basis for the position taking of individuals and groups, representations constitute common rules. They thus organize the symbolic processes which underlie social interaction.

In other words, this model assigns a double role to representations. They are defined, firstly, as principles that generate position taking. But they are also principles for organizing individual differences. On the one hand, they supply individuals with common reference points. On the other hand, these reference points become issues that individual differences revolve around. If representations allow the object of the debate to be defined, they also organize this debate by suggesting the questions to be asked.

In this conception, there isn't necessarily a consensus regarding opinions expressed by individuals. It is not the points of view which are shared, rather it is the questions which attract conflicting points of view. To sum up, position taking can diverge even when referring to common principles. Let us note finally that the theory of organizational principles gives great importance to intergroup relationships, by trying to show how different social memberships can determine the importance given to different principles. From this perspective, it's to do with studying the anchoring of representations in collective realities.

The sociodynamic approach introduces a new way of thinking of the question of consensus in the SRT. For Moscovici, this consensus resulted from the sharing of certain beliefs within a given group. And this sharing was itself the result of the communication process. Doise considered consensuses more as anchoring points for a social representation. And the convergences or divergences between these anchoring points find their origin in the structuring of existing social relations between groups. Seen from this perspective, the study of social representations needs to make use of multiple approaches that will highlight the links between cognitive elements and also between individuals or groups and cognitive elements (see Doise et al., 1992). So it is a question of establishing principles of homology between the social positions of individuals and their position taking in order to reveal the organizing principles of the representations studied (see Clémence, 2001; Lorenzi-Cioldi and Clémence, 2001; 2010; Spini, 2002).

The expansion of the theory

These three theoretical orientations developed by French and Swiss researchers constituted, and still constitute, the bases on which would develop, notably from the 1980s, a multitude of studies, first from outside of Europe, mainly in Latin America.

Very soon, and mainly under the influence of Robert Farr and Miles Hewstone, the SRT gained a foothold in the UK from which emerged, for example, the work of Gerard Duveen centering on the connection between the individual and the group within the framework of microgenetic socialization processes; that of Sandra Jovchelovitch who proposes the view of social representations as a space between the individual and the society linking objects, the subject, and activities; that of Caroline Howarth centering on the links between the SRT and social identity; or yet again that of Ivana Markova who is developing links between dialogicity and social representations. In Austria, the work of Wolfgang Wagner in particular has demonstrated the role between social interactions and discursive exchanges in the processes of construction of social representations. In Italy, under the impetus of Augusto Palmonari, then of Felice Carrugati, the work of Anna Maria de Rosa led to the establishment and dissemination of the SRT throughout Europe. On the other side of the Atlantic, it was mainly in the countries of Latin America and

South America (particularly Mexico, Brazil, Argentina and Venezuela) that the SRT found, from the 1990s onwards, very fertile ground for expansion. The impact of social, historical, and cultural contexts on the formulation of Latin American scientific issues had a lot to do with this success. Researchers in social psychology have found in it a creative, reflexive and critical way of thinking, suitable for dealing with change and political, economic, and social crises. They participate actively today in the theoretical developments of the SRT by linking it particularly with other psychosocial issues such as, for example, social memory or the processes of social change. We should also mention studies carried out in Portugal, Spain, and Rumania and more recently in Australia, Asia, and Africa, but one chapter does not give us adequate space to do so.

We will point out, on the other hand, that in this international picture, the US is one of the most notable absentees. Despite the remarkable work of Gina Philogene and Serge Moscovici to attempt to integrate the SRT into North American social psychology studies, one cannot but notice that it has not found true ground for development. The reasons for this are many and once again there is not enough space here to draw up a coherent and detailed list. The relative laxity of the initial theoretical arguments and the publication almost exclusively in French of the first developments in the SRT are undoubtedly among the main reasons. But there are also more profound and metatheoretical reasons which have long made SRT and social cognition strangers to each other.

Amongst these reasons, that which appears to us to have the most weight concerns the difference in the types of analysis assigned to research carried out in the two fields. Traditionally, social cognition is mainly interested in the intraindividual processes which underlie social interaction, whereas SRT is historically concerned with interindividual phenomena (Kruglanski, 2001), which affect the consciousness of the individual.

The bridging of the gaps between these two fields of study constitutes without doubt one of the most fascinating scientific issues for the years to come in the field of social psychology. It is also in this direction that a part of our own work lies.

PERSONAL NARRATIVE OF THE THEORY'S DEVELOPMENT

Our personal involvement in social representation research dates back to the mid–1980s. At the time, the theory was beginning to expand rapidly in France and in Europe, but was still the object of much criticism. The theory was reproached mainly for being too flexible in terms of concepts and lacking in terms of methodology. Basically, what new aspects did social representations bring to the notions of opinion and attitude, already solidly anchored in social psychology? To answer this criticism, a team of researchers from the University of Aix en Provence proposed two arguments. For Jean Claude Abric and Claude Flament, who were leading this team, representations had to be conceived as cognitive structures. They were not just spheres of opinions, as advanced by Moscovici, but well and truly structured groups within which some elements had a specific role to play. Moreover, even if this idea wasn't yet clearly formed, Abric and Flament thought that, contrary to attitudes, essentially linked to the *evaluation* of social objects, representations concerned above anything else the *meaning* of those same objects. Basically, the idea was that it is the representation which defines the object of the attitude.

Based on these arguments, it was necessary to propose a theory that would account for both the structure and the dynamics of a social representation. This theory already existed, it had been proposed by Jean-Claude Abric in 1976. It still had to be confirmed and demonstrated that it allowed the stability and the dynamic of representations to be better described. It was in this context that two of us joined the Aix en Provence team as doctoral students. In 1988, two theses were defended. The first showed that within social representations, certain beliefs effectively play a specific role (Moliner, 1988). These beliefs are "non-negotiable," are associated to an object by individuals and are considered by them to as its definition. The second thesis showed that these beliefs also play a role in the dynamics of social representations, particularly when individuals adopt new behavior that contradicts them or makes previous behavior obsolete (Guimelli, 1988). A few years later, a third thesis was defended, this time at the University of Montpellier (Rateau, 1995). In this work, it was shown experimentally that the non-negotiable beliefs structuring representations are themselves hierarchal. These works were our first contributions to social representation research, and apart from their theoretical implications, they also led to the finalization of specific methods dedicated to the study of social representations (Guimelli and Rouquette, 1992; Moliner, 1994; Rouquette and Rateau, 1998). Thus, they all served to answer the criticism of the SRT's first detractors.

But towards the end of the 1990s, new criticism appeared. At this time, it seemed as if social representation research was closing in upon itself, in utter disregard to its obvious links with another up and coming trend; that of social cognition. For us, this criticism had to be taken into consideration, which is why we turned our research towards the systematic exploration of links between social representations and certain sociocognitive processes. All began with research on attitudes (Moliner and Tafani, 1997), followed by social categorization, attribution processes and social comparison processes (Rateau and Moliner, 2009). This work, mostly experimental, shows today that the barrier that some people saw between the social representation field and other areas of social psychology was probably just an illusion that time is beginning to erase. This is in any case our dearest wish as only this bridging of gaps will in the end allow us to fully understand and explain the social problems to which social psychology has the task of replying. It is also partly in this role that the SRT has been most successful as we now going to try and demonstrate.

THE SRT'S APPLICABILITY TO SOCIAL ISSUES

To convince oneself of the SRT's applicability, one could try to list all the research that has adopted it. One would see in this case that numerous societal questions have been approached from this angle, and in fields as varied as health (e.g., Washer and Joffe, 2006), economy (e.g., Kirchler et al., 2003), marketing (e.g., Tafani et al., 2007), environmental psychology (e.g., Leone and Lesales, 2009), or relationships with new technology (e.g., Gal and Berente, 2008). However, apart from the fact that we are unable to make an exhaustive list of all these works in this chapter, it is not certain that such a list would allow the reader to understand why the SRT is used in such a diverse set of questions. From our point of view, the answer to this question depends on three points. The SRT is an adaptable and versatile theory, a common sense psychosocial theory, and is finally a theory that has given rise to the elaboration of varied methodologies.

A flexible and adaptable theory

As we said earlier, one of the most frequent criticisms of SRT concerns the too-great imprecision of its concepts (McKinlay and Potter, 1987; Potter and Litton, 1985). And it is true that upon reading Moscovici's original book, the apparent laxity with which the author presents the elements of his theory can be surprising, starting with the very definition he gives to the notion of social representations. But paradoxically, it is this very flexibility that confers on it its general scope. It is important to remember here that upstream

from the theory, there is a protean phenomenon of which Durkheim had an intuition, and that Moscovici (2001a: 4) summarized with the words: "[T]he idea of social or collective representations is engraved in a societal vision in which coherency and practice are driven by beliefs, knowledge, norms and languages that it produces..." As such, it is a phenomenon that concerns logics of social relations just as much as those of action. And one whose, regulations can operate at different cognitive levels, including that of language. Thus, one understands the danger of attempting to study this kind of phenomena on the basis of concepts that are too narrow. This being the case, it is probably because the SRT's initial concepts are relatively broad that other disciplines, relatively unrelated to psychology, have been able to use them. Let us consider three examples.

The first is supplied by the work of historians who, wanting to transcend simple factual and event historiography, began to be interested by forms of thought and beliefs characteristic of past eras. Thus, they put the notion of "mentality" at the center of their preoccupations. Borrowed from Lévy-Bruhl (1922), this notion referred directly to that of mental representations, in relation to interactions in the social sphere. But it's clear today that the project of a "history of mentalities" comes down to a history of social representations.

The second example that we would like to briefly mention concerns geography. From the introduction of the mental map notion (Downs and Stea, 1977; Gould and White, 1974), and then the idea of a certain subjectivity in relation to space (Tuan, 1975, and finally the premise which recommends taking an interest in the mental processes which contribute to the perception of space, but which will especially lead to space being endowed with meanings and values. From this arises a "geography of representations," which considers representations to be finally determinants of spatial practice (Lussaut, 2007).

Finally, let us mention work carried out in linguistics, and more precisely in language didactics, where the necessity to understand the meanings associated with learning and speaking a given language was noticed. This preoccupation has become central in multilingual situations, because of the identity problems they can give rise to. The notion of "linguistic representation" appeared (Dagenais and Jacquet, 2008), inspired directly by the SRT and designating beliefs relative to languages, their usages, and the groups that use them.

These examples suggest that outside the psychology field, when researchers ask themselves questions about cognitive determinants of behavior, they find in the SRT a conceptual framework that can be adapted to deal with their issues. But this is only possible thanks to the fact that this theory offers a great deal of latitude, which is, from our point of view, one of the reasons of its applicative success in social sciences.

An everyday knowledge theory

Before being a belief or opinion theory, the SRT is first of all a theory of "common sense," in that it accounts for the way in which common sense is formed, how it is structured, and how it combines with the preoccupations and social insertion of the people who use it. From this perspective, the most obvious application of the SRT concerns communication. Indeed, many studies show that different groups can have different representations of the same object. In fact, when these groups interact, whether it be for commercial reasons (a supplier and his clients), educational reasons (teachers versus pupils), or technical reasons (work teams), one can expect that different representations will be a potential source of confusion between groups. Consequently, the study of different existing representations can enable us to take suitable measures in the area of communication. For example, in his study on the representation of a hospital's computer security system, Vaast (2007) observed differences between doctors and nurses. For the doctors, system security meant principally access to data, whereas for

nurses, it meant the protection of patient confidentiality. He concluded by insisting on the fact that the people responsible for the system have to take these differences on board in their personnel training.

Another SRT application is inspired by relations between representations and behavior. Indeed, generally speaking, common sense is what guides most of our every day behavior and interactions. "Our common sense includes a lot of know-how, ways in which to make friends, succeed in life, and avoid crises, eat well, etc. ... It is on the basis of this knowledge that people are mostly aware of their situation or make important decisions..." (Moscovici, 2001b: 11). From this perspective, the study of social representations provides us with elements for understanding the reasons behind decisions or behavior. For example, in a study carried out on 1,005 French drivers, representations of speed were studied (Pianelli et al., 2007). This study showed that different representations coexist. The first one, the larger (44 percent of the population), was organized around the unique notion of "danger." Another one, the smaller (12 percent of the population) was organized around the sole notion of "pleasure." Thus, it was supposed that these two representations determined different driving practices. For those who belonged to the first representation, driving was seen as "careful," whereas the others saw it as "hedonistic." This hypothesis gains a first element of validation when one examines the causal link which the individuals made between speed and the occurrence of road accidents. Sixty-four percent of the "prudent" drivers thought that speed was the main cause of accidents, against only 24 percent of the "hedonists." Moreover, this study showed that there were less members of the first subgroup who admitted to having broken the speed limit than of the second subgroup (52 versus 76 percent on roads, and 47 versus 78 percent on motorways). There were also less people in the first subgroup to have been fined by the Police for speeding (9 versus 19 percent). As in many other studies the relationship between representations and behavior was clearly established. This relationship leads us to expect that action on the first will have an impact on the second. Thus, a third type of application appeared on the horizon, attempting to modify people's behavior. In fact, many studies (Mugny et al., 2000) show that influence procedures can provoke deep changes within social representations. But the few studies to have examined the durability of these changes have led to disappointing results.

However, recently, researchers working on these problems have been exploring a new avenue. It is no longer a question of modifying the contents of social representations, but of using these contents to bring individuals to make a decision. For example, Eyssartier et al. (2007) asked themselves the following question: How can the study of organ donation representations be useful for convincing people to become donors? From there, they identified four central elements and four peripheral elements of this representation. They then elaborated a "foot-in-the-door" technique (Freedman and Fraser, 1966), designed to convince people to sign an organ donor card. It should be remembered that the foot-in-the-door principle consists of asking little (preparatory act) before asking more (final request). Yet, one knows that the importance that individuals grant to the preparatory act is a commitment-increasing factor (Kiesler, 1971, see also Burger, 1999). So the authors considered that a preparatory act referring to a central element of the representation was more important than a preparatory act referring to a peripheral element. Thus, they made the hypothesis that the effects of behavior commitment will be more effective in the first case than in the second. To test this hypothesis, an experimenter introduced himself as a volunteer for the "French Graft Establishment." He only addressed people who were alone walking around a university hall, and asked them to sign a petition (preparatory act). This petition would allegedly be sent to the Ministry of Health, to gain financial aid for a communication campaign on organ donation. The petition's title contained either a slogan using a central element of the representation (i.e., "Organ donation helps others"), or a peripheral element of the representation (i.e., "Organ donation is a civic act"). Whether or not the preparatory act was accepted, the experimenter asked the person to sign an organ donor card (final request). Eight experimental conditions were studied (four "central slogans" and four "peripheral slogans"). The results showed that when the preparatory act concerned a central element of the representation of organ donation, there were significantly more participants who signed an organ donor card (51 percent) than when the preparatory act concerned peripheral elements (34 percent).

A great methodological diversity

Without doubt, the SRT has provoked a remarkable diversity of methodologies because it can be applied to so many problems in various contexts. This methodological preoccupation became tangible from the end of the 1980s, when chapters dedicated to methodological questions were published in collective books on social representations. Later on, from the beginning of the 1990s, entire books were dedicated to methods of studying social representations.

The methodological advances presented in these books concern first of all techniques for collecting social representation content. Based on traditional psychosocial methods (interviewing, focus groups, investigations, etc.), verbal association techniques emerged, aiming to minimize the amount of interpretation to be done by the researcher. To do this, these methods introduce constraints in the associative process, by inviting the subjects to only produce a certain type of answer (only verbs, adjectives or definitions). Furthermore, they invite the people questioned to evaluate their own contributions. For example, using the "Basic Cognitive Schema" technique (Guimelli, 1993, 1998), the participants are asked to say why they gave particular answers, and what inductors they used to do so. Using the Associative Network Method (De Rosa and Kirchler, 2001), the participants evaluate their associative production with help from different criteria supplied by the interviewer (positive or negative connotations, importance, etc.).

Methodological advances can also be found in questionnaire techniques. In contrast once again to more traditional approaches (opinion or attitude questionnaires), authors devise questionnaires that ask people to describe the studied objects in a standardized manner. It is no longer about measuring participants' opinions with regard to an object of representation, but rather highlighting the manner in which this object is described (see, for example, Moliner, 2002), and identifying the structuring elements of these descriptions.

Finally, the development of multivariate techniques, their computerization and their growth in accessibility have driven researchers to detail the specificities of each method compared with the SRT's postulates (see Doise et al., 1992).

Generally, researchers now have a large diversity of methods at their disposal, which helps them tackle a great range of questions in a large array of contexts.

CONCLUSION

By way of conclusion and introduction, we would like to further develop points that we have already mentioned rather allusively, because we think they constitute the basis of an important development in SRT, and more generally, of our knowledge of individual and group psychosocial functioning.

The first point refers to theoretical bridges that it seems possible to establish between the concepts of attitudes and social representation. This issue appears crucial and has already been the object of prolonged theoretical discussions (Billig, 1993; Farr, 1994; Howarth, 2006; Jaspar and Fraser, 1984; Scarbrough,

1990) in the attempt to understand and explain the reasons behind the mutual ignorance these two concepts have of each other. The inventory of these reasons, as interesting as it may be, would take too long to set out here. We prefer to focus on the hypothetical links that some authors have developed.

This is particularly true of Moliner and Tafani (1997) who consider that whatever theoretical definition is referred to, the observable part of attitudes always resides in the affective, behavioral, or cognitive responses that individuals express about an object. Yet, to produce this response, individuals need information about this object. This general idea has also been proposed by Fishbein and Ajzen (1975) and Zanna and Rempel (1988), for whom attitudes are the result of attributes that people associate with an object. In other, more direct words: to express an attitude towards an object, people have to have a representation of it.

This position is also defended by Doise (1989), for whom attitudes find their origin in more general knowledge of their social environment that individuals share. In studying this issue experimentally, Moliner and Tafani (1997) came to the conclusion that attitudes refer above all to evaluation, whereas representations refer above all to meaning. But to be able to evaluate an object, individuals have necessarily to have a meaning for it. In other words, attitudes are an evaluative expression of a shared representation of an object.

Rouquette (1996, 2010) also defends this idea, and recently proposed integrating the concepts of opinion, attitude, social representation and ideology in a global theoretical structure based on two general principles: the growing applicative stability and generality of each of these notions. From this dual viewpoint, Rouquette observes on the one hand that opinions are more volatile than attitudes (whence, for example, the need to do repeated opinion polls to measure fairly rapid fluctuations). On the other hand, he observes that opinions refer to particular objects, groups or individuals, in circumstances that are also particular, whereas attitudes, which are more general, refer to thematic categories involving more than one object. For example, an opinion at a given time about a particular politician stems from the attitude towards politicians in general. In other words, a group's attitudes towards a given object are said to be the definitive source for opinions held about this object.

The same reasoning applies to the attitude/social representation duo. Apart from the first's larger variability than the latter's, it seems to be social representations that provide the basis for an attitude. Echebarria Echabe and Gonzalez Castro (1993) have shown, for example, that attitudes expressed by individuals towards elections are intimately intertwined with their representation of democracy in general.

Moreover, Rouquette proposes considering ideology as providing in its turn the basis for a social representation or a set of social representations. Certainly, ideology needs to be specified, because of its multiple meanings, its comprehensive scope, and its weakness of operationalization. But ideology can be conceived, not as a more or less organized assembly of content that may vary from one society to another, or from a group to its adversary, but as a repertory of general processes, with underlying formalizable qualities, and generic categories that are open to diverse description. It is essentially said to be made of values, norms, beliefs and themata (Moscovici and Vignaux, 2000). This framework obviously needs more development and formalization, but it is without doubt a promising basis for research with the aim of promoting a model of connection between the different conventions of expression of psychosocial functioning.

The second point refers to the links that can be made between the SRT and the processes traditionally studied in the field of social cognition which are the stereotypes, causal attribution or social comparison. Again, these two approaches have been strangers for a long time. The main issue, without doubt, in this mutual ignorance concerns different perceptions of the "social."

Social cognition advocates see social knowledge used by individuals as being the result of an accumulation of individual cognitive processes. Knowledge that is therefore, above all, individual, although shared. As for "social" determinisms, they are more than often limited to "others," thus totally neglecting laws, organizational structures, social relationships, or group history. As regards the advocates of social representation, it has for long time been considered that the processes described by social cognition were highly reductive, studied with the aid of methods that also appeared to be simplistic, and in the end totally incapable of accounting for the historicity and impact of representations in the life of societies and in attitudes. But by wanting too much to account for this impact, studies devoted to social representations have often only led to a compilation of qualitative approaches, with blurred methodological contours, not allowing the restitution or the definition of the cognitive processes invested in their functioning.

However, we think it obvious to consider that the link between social cognition and social representations is twofold. On the one hand, we consider that social cognition processes intervene massively in the elaboration of social representations. It can be expected that the fruit of these processes (categories, stereotypes, causal attributions) are to be found in the contents and the structure of social representations. In other words, even if representations are collective constructions, they are still partially constructed by individuals.

At the same time, one can suppose that the processes studied in the field of social cognition are produced on the basis of representations. Thus, one can expect to observe modulations of these processes, depending on the underlying representations. To categorize, judge or explain one's immediate environment, individuals are thought to rely on, amongst other things, collective beliefs. This reflexive link is what unifies social representations and emotional, identity, attribution, social influence, or social comparison processes: social representations account for these processes, as well as actively participating in their own modes of operation. This idea can be illustrated by three examples.

First, in classic research, intergroup judgments and perceptions are studied through the processes of social categorization and stereotyping. But from the point of view of the SRT, intergroup representations are defined as social representations revolving around groups of people (Lorenzi-Cioldi and Clémence, 2001). Yet, a series of researches show that the central elements of an intergroup representation are the same as the stereotypical elements of the category of people they concern (Moliner and Vidal, 2003); that certain of these central elements play an explanatory role in the behaviors of members of the group in question (Moliner and Gutermann, 2004); and that they intervene to justify or rationalize asymmetric intergroup relations (Moliner et al., 2009).

Second, in the field of research performed on the process of attribution (Heider, 1958), the work of Ross (1977) highlighted the tendency of individuals to prefer dispositional factors (traits, aptitudes, motivation, etc.) to explain the behavior of an actor. On the other hand, we know that in situations of self-presentation, individuals prefer this type of explanation in order to give a good image of themselves, just as they judge more favorably people who prefer this type of explanation (Jellison and Green, 1981). However, in a series of experiments (Moliner, 2000), it was demonstrated that the expression of this preference remains dependent on the representations that the individuals activate in relation to the social situations in which they express themselves. Thus, when one suggests to the participants that the process of attribution to which they are going to submit themselves takes place in an affectively oriented social situation, one notices the disappearance of the systematic preference for dispositional explanations, in favor of the appearance of a self-serving bias (Zuckerman, 1979), or a person-positive bias (Sears, 1983). On the contrary, the systematic preference for dispositional factors is more marked when subjects make attributions in competitive situations with a practical purpose. Thus, the manner in which the subjects interpret the situation in which they find themselves at the moment when they are making the attributions determines the orientation of the process.

Third and finally, in the wide field of social comparison, several works have attested to the existence of a phenomenon of asymmetry in the comparison of the self to others (see Holyoak and Gordon, 1983; Mussweiller, 2001; Srull and Gaellick, 1983). The self and the other are seen as more similar when the other is taken as the point of departure (assimilation effect) and the reverse when it is the self that is taken as a reference point (contrast effect). In a series of recent studies (Chokier and Rateau, 2009; Rateau, submitted), we were able to demonstrate that this general process could be altered by the type of opinion at issue in the comparison and notably by the central or peripheral nature of the latter in structure of the representation of the object involved (in this case the social representation of studies shared by psychology students).

The participants are asked to compare themselves to a peer (either in the order the self–other, or other–self) who, depending on the case, is presented as defending a properipheral opinion, counterperipheral opinion, procentral, or countercentral in relation to studies. With regard to a peripheral opinion, characterized by a significant intragroup heterogeneity, the appearance of the "classic" process of interindividual comparison of the self with another was recorded; that is to say, a contrast effect in the case of a comparison of the self–other order and an assimilation effect in the other–self order, regardless of the valency of the opinion defended by the source. This result illustrates perfectly the flexibility and possibilities for interindividual modulation which traditionally characterizes the peripheral elements of social representations.

With regard to a central opinion, the processes in play are very different. Whatever the order of the comparison, it is noticed that individuals differentiate themselves systematically from a group member who deviates from the central opinion and that they identify with a member who conforms. In other words, the individual seeks here to maintain the cohesiveness of the representation at any cost by systematically stating the "right" opinion in relation to the representation shared by their group of the object. The contrast/assimilation process does not depend here on the meaning of the comparison but only on the position taking displayed by the source, according to whether it contradicts the central opinion or not and ensures the homogeneity and social identity of the group.

This systematic study of the link between social representations and sociocognitive processes represents a desire to unite and mutually enrich both of these research fields. New hypotheses concerning functioning and roles of social representations, as well as sociocognitive processes when they are integrated into representational processes are beginning to appear. Let us wager that they will provide the basis of many studies, and that their theoretical and empirical range will be crucial in the development of our knowledge about the psychosocial functioning of individuals and groups.

ACKNOWLEDGMENTS

The authors would like to sincerely thank Adam Chesterman and Anne Greaves for the translation of this chapter.

REFERENCES

Abric, J.C. (1976) Jeux, conflits et représentations sociales. PhD thesis, Université de Provence, Aix-Marseille.
Abric, J.C. (1993) Central system, peripheral system: their functions and roles in the dynamics of social representation. *Papers on Social Representations, 2,* 75–78.
Abric, J.C. (2001) A structural approach to social representations. In K. Deaux and G. Philogène (eds), *Representations of the Social,* pp. 42–47. Oxford: Blackwell.
Asch, S.E. (1946) Forming impressions of personality. *Journal of Abnormal and Social Psychology, 41,* 258–290.
Billig, M. (1993) Studying the thinking society: Social representations and attitudes. In G.M. Breakwell and D. Canter (eds), *Empirical Approach to Social Representations,* pp. 39–62. New York: Clarendon Press.
Breakwell, G.M. and Canter, D.V. (1979) *Empirical Approach to Social Representations.* Oxford: Clarendon Press.
Burger, J.M. (1999) The foot-in-the-door compliance procedure: A multiple-process analysis and review. *Personality and Social Psychology Review, 3,* 303–325.
Clémence, A. (2001) Social positioning and social representations. In K. Deaux and G. Philogène (eds), *Representations of the Social,* pp. 83–95. Oxford: Blackwell.
Codol, J.P. (1970) Influence de la représentation d'autrui sur l'activité des membres d'un groupe expérimental. *L'Année Psychologique, 70,* 131–150.
Cooper, J. and Croyle, R.T. (1984) Attitudes and attitude change. *Annual Review of Psychology, 35,* 395–426.
Dagenais, D. and Jacquet, M. (2008) Theories of representation in French and English scolarship multilingualism. *International Journal of Multilingualism, 5,* 41–52.
Deaux, K. and Philogène, G. (2001a) *Social Representations: Introductions and Explorations.* New York: Blackwell.
Deaux, K. and Philogène, G. (2001b) *Representations of the Social.* Oxford: Blackwell.
De Rosa, A.S. and Kirchler, E. (2001) Ambiguous images in advertising: An application of the Associative Network Method. In C. Roland-Lévy, E. Kirchler, E. Penz and C. Gray (eds), *Everyday Representations of the Economy,* pp. 49–66. Wien: WUV Universitätsverlag.
Doise, W. (1989) Attitudes et représentations sociales. In D. Jodelet (ed.), *Les Représentations Sociales,* pp. 220–238. Paris: Presses Universitaires de France.
Doise, W., Clémence, A. and Lorenzi-Cioldi, F. (1992) *Représentations Sociales et Analyse de Données.* Grenoble: Presses Universitaires de Grenoble; J. Kaneko, tr. (1993) *The Quantitative Analysis of Social Representations.* Hemel-Hempstead: Harvester Whatsheaf.
Downs, R.M. and Stea, D. (1977) *Maps in Mind: Reflexions on Cognitive Mapping.* New York: Harper and Row.

Durkheim, E. (1893) *La Division du Travail*. Paris: Presses Universitaires de France; G. Simpson, tr. (1947) *The Division of Labor in Society*. New York: The Free Press.

Durkheim, E. (1895) *Les Règles de la Méthode Sociologique*. Paris: Alcan. W.D. Halls, tr. (1982) *The Rules of Sociological Method*. New York: The Free Press.

Durkheim, E. (1898) Représentations individuelles et représentations collectives. *Revue de Métaphysique et de Morale, 6*, 273–302; D.F. Pollock, tr. (1953) Individual and Collective Representations. In E. Durkheim (ed.) *Sociology and Philosophy*, pp. 1–34. London: Cohen and West.

Duveen, G. (2001) Representations, identities, resistance. In K. Deaux and G. Philogene (eds), *Representations of the Social: Bridging Theoretical Tradition*, pp. 257–270. Oxford: Blackwell.

Echebarria Echabe, A. and Gonzalez Castro, J.L. (1993) Social representation of power and democracy, attitudes towards elections and voting behaviour. *International Review of Social Psychology, 6*, 21–46.

Eyssartier, C., Joule, R.V. and Guimelli, C. (2007) Effets comportementaux et cognitifs de l'engagement dans un acte préparatoire activant un élément central vs périphérique de la représentation du don d'organe. *Psychologie Française, 52*, 499–517.

Farr, R.M. (1994) Attitudes, social representations and social attitudes. *Papers on Social Representations, 3*, 33–36.

Farr, R. and Moscovici, S. (1984) *Social Representations*. Cambridge: Cambridge University Press.

Fishbein, M. and Ajzen, I. (1975) *Belief, Attitude, Intention, and Behavior: An Introduction to Theory and Research*. Boston: Addison-Wesley.

Flament, C. (1971) Image des relations amicales dans les groupes hiérarchisés. *L'Année Psychologique, 71*, 117–125.

Flament, C. (1989) Structure et dynamique des représentations sociales. In D. Jodelet (ed.), *Les Représentations Sociales*, pp. 204–219. Paris: Presses Universitaires de France.

Freedman, J.L. and Fraser, S.C. (1966) Compliance without pressure: The foot-in-the-door techniques. *Journal of Personality and Social Psychology, 4*, 195–202.

Freud, S. (1908) *On the Sexual Theories of Children, Vol. 9*. London: Standard Edition.

Freud, S. (1922) *Some Points in a Comparative Study of Organic and Hysterical Crisis, Vol. 1*. London: Hogarth Press.

Gal, U. and Berente, N. (2008) A social representation perspective on informational implementation: rethinking the concept of frames. *Information, Technology and People, 21*, 133–154.

Gould, P. and White, R. (1974) *Mental Maps*. Harmondsworth: Penguin Books.

Guimelli, C. (1988) Agression idéologique, pratiques nouvelles et transformation progressive d'une représentation sociale. PhD thesis, Université de Provence, Aix en Provence.

Guimelli, C. (1993) Locating the central core of social representations: towards a method. *European Journal of Social Psychology, 23*, 555–559.

Guimelli, C. (1998) Differentiation between the central core elements of social representations: normative vs. functional elements. *Swiss Journal of Psychology, 57*, 209–224.

Guimelli, C. and Rouquette, M.L. (1992) Contribution du modèle associatif des Schèmes Cognitifs de Base à l'analyse structurale des représentations sociales. *Bulletin de Psychologie, 405*, 196–202.

Heider, F. (1958) *The Psychology of Interpersonal Relations*. New York: Wiley.

Holyoak, K.J. and Gordon, P.C. (1983) Social reference points. *Journal of Personality and Social Psychology, 44*, 881–887.

Howarth, C. (2006) How social representations of attitudes have informed attitudes theories: the consensual and the reified. *Theory and Psychology, 16*, 691–714.

Jaspar, J. and Fraser, C. (1984) Attitudes and social representations. In R.M. Farr and S. Moscovici (eds), *Social Representations*, pp. 101–123. Cambridge: Cambridge University Press.

Jellison, J. and Green, J. (1981) A self presentation approach to the fundamental attribution error: the norm of internality. *Journal of Personality and Social Psychology, 40*, 643–649.

Jodelet, D. (1989) *Folie et Représentations Sociales*. Paris: Presses Universitaires de France; T. Pownall, tr. (1992) *Madness and Social Representations*. Berkeley: University of California Press.

Kiesler, C.A. (1971) *The Psychology of Commitment. Experiments Linking Behavior to Belief*. New York: Academic Press.

Kirchler, E., Maciejovsky, B. and Schneider, F. (2003) Everyday representations of tax avoidance, tax evasion, and tax flight: Do legal differences matter? *Journal of Economic Psychology, 24*, 535–553.

Kronberger, N. and Wagner, W. (2000) Key words in context: statistical analysis of text features. In M.W. Bauer and G. Gaskell (eds), *Qualitative Researching with Text, Image and Sound. A Practical Handbook*, pp. 299–317. London: Sage.

Kruglanski, A.W. (2001) Social cognition, social representations and the dilemmas of social theory construction. In K. Deaux, and G. Philogène (eds),

Representations of the Social, pp. 242–248. Oxford: Blackwell.

Leone, F. and Lesales, T. (2009) The interest of cartography for a better perception and management of volcanic risk: From scientific to social representations. *Journal of Volcanology and Geothermal Research*, *186*, 186–194.

Lévi-Strauss, C. (1962) *La pensée sauvage*. Paris: Plon; G. Weidenfeld and Nicolson, tr. (1966) *The Savage Mind*. Chicago: University of Chicago Press

Lévy-Bruhl, L. (1922) La mentalité primitive. Paris: Alcan; L.A. Clare, tr. (1978) *Primitive Mentality*. New York: AMS Press.

Linton, R. (1945) *The Cultural Background of Personality*. New York: D. Appleton-Century Co.

Lorenzi-Cioldi, F. and Clémence, A. (2001) Group processes and the construction of social representations. In M.A. Hogg and S. Tindale (eds), *Handbook of Social Psychology: Group Processes*, pp. 311–333. Oxford: Blackwell.

Lorenzi-Cioldi, F. and Clémence, A. (2010) Social representations. In J. Levine and M. Hogg (eds), *Encyclopedia of Group processes and Intergroup Relations*. London: Sage.

Lussaut, M. (2007) *L'homme Spatial. Construction Sociale de l'espace Humain*. Paris: Seuil.

Markova, I. (1997) Language and authenticity. *The Journal for the Theory of Social Behaviour*, *27*, 265–275.

Markova, I. (2003) *Dialogicality and Social Representations. The Dynamics of Mind*. Cambridge: Cambridge University Press.

Mauss, M. (1903) *Représentations Collectives et Diversité des Civilisations*. Paris: Minuit (1974 edition).

McKinlay, A. and Potter, J. (1987) Social representation: A conceptual critique. *Journal for the Theory of Social Behavior*, *17*, 471–487.

Moliner, P. (1988) La représentation sociale comme grille de lecture. PhD thesis, Université de Provence, Aix-en-Provenc.

Moliner, P. (1994) Les méthodes de repérage et d'identification du noyau des représentations sociales. In C. Guimelli (ed.), *Structures et Transformations des Représentations Sociales*, pp. 199–232. Neuchâtel: Delachaux et Niestlé.

Moliner, P. (2000) De la norme d'internalité à la représentation des relations sociales. *Revue Internationale de Psychologie Sociale*, *2*, 7–32.

Moliner, P. (2002) Ambiguous scenario and attribute challenge techniques. Social Representations of 'The Firm' and 'The nurse'. *European Review of Applied Psychology*, *3*, 273–280.

Moliner, P. and Gutermann, M. (2004) Dynamique des descriptions et des explications dans une représentation sociale. *Papers On Social Representations*, *13*, 1–12.

Moliner, P., Lorenzi-Cioldi, F. and Vinet, E. (2009) Utilité sociale des représentations intergroupes de sexe. Domination masculine, contexte professionnel et discrimination positive. *Cahiers Internationaux de Psychologie Sociale*, *83*, 25–44.

Moliner, P. and Tafani, E. (1997) Attitudes and social representations: A theoretical and experimental approach. *European Journal of Social Psychology*, *27*, 687–702.

Moliner, P. and Vidal, J. (2003) Stéréotype de la catégorisation et noyau de la représentation. *Revue Internationale de Psychologie Sociale*, *1*, 157–176.

Moscovici, S. (1961). *La Psychanalyse: Son Image et son Public*. Paris: Presses Universitaires de France (1976 edition); D. Macey, tr. (2008) *Psychoanalysis. Its Image and Its Public*. Cambridge: Polity Press.

Moscovici, S. (1969) Préface. In C. Herzlich, *Santé et Maladie*, pp. 7–12. Paris: Mouton.

Moscovici, S. (1981) On social representations. In J. Forgas (ed.), *Social Cognition: Perspectives on Everyday Understanding*, pp. 181–210. New York: Academic Press.

Moscovici, S. (1982) The coming era of representations. In J.P. Codol and J.P. Leyens (eds), *Cognitive Approaches to Social Behavior*, pp. 115–150. The Hague: M. Nijhoff.

Moscovici, S. (1984) The phenomenon of social representations representations. In R. Farr and S. Moscovici (eds), *Social Representations*, pp. 3–69. Cambridge: Cambridge University Press.

Moscovici, S. (1988) Notes towards a description of social representations. *European Journal of Social Psychology*, *18*(3), 211–250.

Moscovici, S. (1989) Des représentations collectives aux représentations sociales. Eléments pour une histoire. In D. Jodelet (ed.), *Les Représentations Sociales*, pp. 62–86. Paris: Presses Universitaires de France.

Moscovici, S. (2001a) *Social Representations: Explorations in Social Psychology*. Cambridge: Polity Press.

Moscovici, S. (2001b) Why a theory of social representations? In K. Deaux, and G. Philogène (eds), *Representations of the Social*, pp. 8–36. Oxford: Blackwell.

Moscovici, S. and Vignaux, G. (2000) The concept of themata. In S. Moscovici and G. Duveen (eds), *Social Representations. Explorations in Social Psychology*, pp. 156–183. Cambridge: Polity Press.

Mugny, G. and Carugati, F. (1989) *Social Representations of Intelligence*. Cambridge: Cambridge University Press.

Mugny, G., Tafani, E., Falomir, J.M. and Layat, C. (2000) Source credibility, social comparison and social influence. *International Review of Social Psychology*, *13*, 151–175.

Mussweiller, T. (2001) Focus of comparison as a determinant of assimilation versus contrast in social comparison. *Personality and Social Psychology Bulletin*, *27*, 38–47.

Piaget, J. (1932) *Le Jugement Moral Chez l'Enfant*. Paris: Presses Universitaires de France; M. Gabain, tr. (1965) *The Moral Judgment of the Child*. New York: The Free Press.

Pianelli, C., Saad, F. and Abric, J.C. (2007) Social representations and acceptability of LAVIA (French ISA system). *Proceedings of the 14th World Congress and Exhibition on Intelligent Transport Systems and Services*, 8–12 October 2007, Pékin, Paper 4057.

Potter, J. and Litton, I. (1985) Some problems underlying the theory of social representations. *British Journal of Social Psychology*, *24*, 81–90.

Rateau, P. (1995) Structure et fonctionnement du système central des représentations sociales. PhD thesis, Université de Montpellier 3, Montpellier.

Rateau, P. (submitted) Assimilation and contrast to ingroup prime: The moderating effect of central *vs*. peripheral elements of social representations. International Review of Social Psychology.

Rateau, P. and Moliner, P. (2009) *Représentations Sociales et Processus Sociocognitifs*. Rennes: Presses Universitaires de Rennes.

Ross, L. (1977) The intuitive psychologist and his shortcoming: Distortions in the attribution process. In L. Berkowitz (ed.), *Advances in Experimental Social Psychology*, *10*, 173–220. New York: Academic Press.

Rouquette, M.L. (1996) Représentations et idéologie. In J.C. Deschamps and J.L. Beauvois (eds), *Des Attitudes aux Attributions*, pp. 163–173. Grenoble: Presses Universitaires de Grenoble.

Rouquette, M.L. (2010) *La Pensée Sociale*. Toulouse: Erès.

Rouquette, M.L. and Rateau, P. (1998) *Introduction à l'Étude des Représentations Sociales*. Grenoble: Presses Universitaires de Grenoble.

Scarbrough, E. (1990) Attitudes, social representations and ideology. In C. Fraser and G. Gaskell (eds), *The Social Psychological Study of Widespread Beliefs*, pp. 99–117. New York: Clarendon Press.

Schank, R. and Abelson, R. (1977) *Scripts, Plans, Goals and Understanding: An Inquiry into Human Knowledge Structures*. Hillsdale: Erlbaum.

Sears, D.O. (1983) The person-positive bias. *Journal of Personality and Social Psychology*, *44*, 223–250.

Simmel, G. (1908) *Soziologie*. Berlin: Duncker Hamblot; S. Muller and L. Deroche-Gurcel, tr. French (1999) *Sociologie. Etudes sur les Formes de la Socialisation*. Paris: Presses Universitaires de France.

Smith, A. (1776) *An Inquiry into the Nature and Causes of the Wealth of Nations*. London: Strahan & Cadell.

Spini, D. (2002) Multidimensional scaling. A technique for the analysis of the common field of social representations. *European Review of Applied Psychology*, *52*, 231–240.

Srull, T.K. and Gaelick, L. (1983) General principles and individual differences in the self as a habitual reference point: An examination of self-other judgments of similarity. *Social Cognition*, *2*, 108–121.

Tafani, E., Haguel, V. and Menager, A. (2007) From corporate images to social representations: an application to the motor car industry. *Les Cahiers Internationaux de Psychologie Sociale*, *73*, 27–46.

Tuan, Y-F. (1975) Images and mental maps. *Annals of the Association of American Geographers*, *65*, 205–212.

Vaast, E. (2007) Danger is in the eye of the beholders: Social representations of information systems security in healthcare. *Journal of Strategic Information Systems*, *16*, 130–152.

Vergès, P. (1996) Bibliographie des représentations sociales. Third International Conference on Social Representations, Aix-en-Provence, September 27–30.

Wagner, W. (1994) Fields of research and sociogenesis of social representations: a discussion of criteria and diagnostics. *Social Science Information*, *33*, 199–228.

Wagner, W., Duveen, G., Farr, R., Jovchelovitch, S., Lorenzi-Cioldi, F., Markovà, I. and Rose, D. (1999) Theory and method of social representations. *Asian Journal of Social Psychology*, *2*, 95–125.

Washer, P. and Joffe, H. (2006) The 'hospital superbug': Social representations of MRSA. *Social Science and Medicine*, *63*, 2141–2152.

Weber, M. (1921) *Economy and Society*. Berkeley, CA: University of California Press, 1978.

Zanna, M. and Rempel, J. (1988) Attitudes: a new look at an old concept. In D. Bar-tal and A.W. Kruglanski (eds), *The Social Psychology of Knowledge*, pp. 315–334. New York: Cambridge University Press.

Zuckerman, M. (1979) Attribution of success and failure revisited or: The motivational bias is alive and well in attribution theory. *Journal of Personality and Social Psychology*, *47*, 245–287.

51

A Theory of Individualism and Collectivism

Harry C. Triandis and Michele J. Gelfand

ABSTRACT

The evolution of individualism and collectivism theory and research is reviewed. The antecedents of collectivism–individualism can be found in the ecology, family structure, wealth distribution, demography, history, cultural diffusion, and situational conditions. The consequences of collectivism–individualism include differences in attention, attribution, cognition, emotion, motivation, self-definitions, values, language use, and communication, as well as other kinds of social and organizational behavior. Applications of individualism and collectivism include improvements in conflict resolution, health, international relations, and cross-cultural training.

THE EVOLUTION OF INDIVIDUALISM AND COLLECTIVISM THEORY AND RESEARCH

Culture is to society what memory is to individuals (Kluckhohn, 1954). It consists of what "has worked" in the experience of a group of people so it was worth transmitting to peers and descendents. Another definition of culture was provided by anthropologist Redfield (1941): "Culture is shared understandings made manifest in act and artifact." In short, culture is shared behavior and shared human-made aspects of the society. Thus, it includes "practices" (the way things are done here) and "values" (the way things should be done). These older definitions of culture focus on what is outside the person (e.g., do people drive to the right or left). The more recent definitions also stress what is inside the person (e.g., is the self independent or interdependent of in-groups). Almost every aspect of psychological functioning is influenced, to some extent, by culture. Thus, it is best to view culture and psychology as making each other up (Cole, 1996; Shweder, 1990).

Cultures differ in a myriad of ways. By far, the most well-researched dimension of culture to date is *individualism* and *collectivism*.

Within the twentieth century, there has been extensive discussion of the constructs in sociology (e.g., Durkheim, 1933; Parsons, 1949; Riesman et al., 1961), anthropology (Kluckhohn, 1956; Mead, 1967; Redfield, 1956), and psychology (Chinese Culture Connection, 1987; Hofstede, 1980; Schwartz, 1994; Triandis, 1995). Across each of these disciplines, scholars have been concerned with the nature of the relationship between the individual and the group. This theme has also been referred to as *self-emphasis* and *collectivity* (Parsons, 1949), *Gesellschaft* and *Gemeinschaft* (Toennies, 1957), *mechanical* and *organic solidarity* (Durkheim, 1933), *individualism* and *collaterality* (Kluckhohn and Strodtbeck, 1961), *agency* and *community* (Bakan, 1996), *individualism* and *collectivism* (Hofstede, 1980), *autonomy* and *conservation* (Schwartz, 1990), and *independence* and *interdependence* (Markus and Kitayama, 1991). Although there are subtle differences in meanings of these terms, they all relate to a theme which contrasts the extent to which people are autonomous individuals or embedded in their groups (Hofstede, 1980; Schwartz, 1994; Triandis, 1989).

Regardless of their labels, these constructs have been at the cornerstone of theory and research in culture and psychology. In this chapter, we trace the evolution of theory and research on individualism and collectivism, discussing their role first in ancient legal and religious institutions, in later political theory in the nineteenth century, and in empirical work in psychology in the mid and latter twentieth century. Although individualism–collectivism cannot be described as unified theory per se, research over the last four decades has illuminated the defining features of the constructs, their ecological, situational, and dispositional antecedents, and a wide range of consequences that they have for social psychological and organizational phenomena. To be sure, our review in this chapter is necessarily selective, as research in this area is extensive and warrants a volume into itself. After describing the evolution of theory

and research on the constructs, we provide an evaluation of the constructs and discuss practical implications that have been derived from this collective research effort.

HISTORY OF THE INDIVIDUALISM AND COLLECTIVISM CONSTRUCTS: CONTRIBUTIONS FROM LAW, RELIGION, AND PHILOSOPHY

Although individualism and collectivism have been by now well researched in psychology, discussions of the constructs can be found in ancient legal writings, religious texts, and moral–political philosophies. The contrasts between the individualism and collectivism constructs were first found in ancient legal structures in the Middle East in the laws of Hammurabi. In particular, the King of Babylonia (1792–1750 BC) is credited with establishing some of the world's first written laws, wherein universal codes of behaviors supplanted a focus on the rights of individuals. At the time, the codes replaced the more individualistic notion of tit-for-tat retaliation (revenge) with a system of monetary fines that were applied universally. More generally, the code of Hammurabi identified the need for individuals to maintain positive relations with others, lest they face heavy sanctions. The recognition of individuals as being interdependent and having duties and obligations to other group members are defining attributes of the cultural construct that we now call collectivism (Triandis, 1995). Notably, the Code of Hammurabi was not the only legal expression of the collectivist cultural construct in the ancient Middle East. Codes of conduct that centered on creating group standards of behavior were also part of the law of the Hebrews in the book of the Law of Moses (Kagan, 1966), the purpose of which was also to establish standards for individual behavior to protect the group, rather than to allow individual preferences to determine what is right and what is wrong (Durant, 1935).

As cultures later developed, the more individualistic notion of rational principles and individual rights became more prevalent within legal systems. The practice of presenting individual cases before formally appointed judges was prevalent in Athens and in Rome. For example, in the Law of Cincius (204 BC), legal representation was viewed as the most effective way to present the facts of a particular case. Importantly, this system was seen as superior to interpretations of right and wrong based on codes of normative behavior alone, the latter of which was common in earlier centuries and was more akin with collectivism.

The constructs of individualism and collectivism were also manifested in religious institutions throughout the centuries. In the West, concerns with group identity and ingroup–outgroup distinctions, both attributes of collectivism, can be seen in religious philosophies and practices. The ancient Hebrews' religion was based on the strong ethnic identity of the Jews (Durant, 1935), and was predicated on the belief that the group was the "chosen one" of God, as compared with other groups. Other religious groups also viewed their religions as a form of group identity as contrasted to other groups. For example, in the Koran of the Moslems it is stated – "Believers, take neither the Jews nor the Christians for your friends" (Dawood, 1956). Likewise, within the Christian tradition, for individuals to be saved they had to embrace the Christian God as the only one true God and reject other conceptions of god that were found in other religions.

Religions in the East were much more focused on duties and obligations within a hierarchical structure, which is associated with some forms of modern-day collectivism. In India, and in ancient Japan, caste systems were also developed, and group identity was even further reinforced within a legal system that held entire families responsible for individual members' actions (Durant, 1935). These notions of group accountability predated empirical work in psychology which centuries later has indeed shown that East Asians hold many people, particularly groups

and their leaders, accountable for a given action (Chiu and Hong, 1992; Chiu et al., 2000; Menon et al., 1999; Zemba et al., 2006).

Likewise, in China, Confucian philosophy emphasized the importance of group identity, conformity, and long-term relationships. Confucius also stressed the importance of obligations that individuals have within their family, within the nation, and within the world at large. For example, Confucian philosophy dictates that individuals are required to respect their fathers and elder brothers so as to maintain family harmony. This prepared the individual to respect the structures of the state, which was needed to maintain national harmony. Throughout his writings, Confucius emphasized the importance of subjugating personal wants and desires for the greater good of the group (Streep, 1995). This philosophy, while dating back 4,000 years, is still prevalent in much of Eastern Asia today.

The nature of the relationship of the individual to the state was also at the center of much philosophical thought and debate in the late eighteenth century. Conceptions of individualism were associated with liberalism and included the ideas of maximum freedom of the individual, voluntary groups that individuals can join or leave, and equal participation of individuals in group activities (*Encyclopedia Britannica*, 1953, Vol. 12: 256a). As a moral–political philosophy, liberalism placed a great importance on the freedom of individuals to use reason to make personal choices, and to have rights to protect these freedoms (Kim, 1994). Across societies, the importance of the freedom of individuals was also reflected in the American Revolution (all humans are created equal, and pursuit of happiness is their fundamental right) and the French Revolution (liberty, equality, fraternity).

At the same time, other philosophers, most notably Jean Jacques Rousseau, emphasized the importance of the collective over the individual. In the *Social Contract* (1762), Rousseau argued that the individual is only free by submitting to the general will. The general will was conceived as the common core of opinion that remains after private wills cancel each other out. Rousseau argued that the general will, which can be ascertained by majority voting, is "always right and tends to the public advantage" (*Encyclopedia Britannica*, 1953, Vol. 12: 256a).

Later, within the nineteenth century, the French intellectual Alexis de Tocqueville elaborated upon the concept of individualism based on his travels throughout the United States (Bellah et al., 1985). De Tocqueville used the term "individualism" in connection with democracy in American society and contrasted the American social structure with those found in the aristocratic European tradition. Later, political philosophers such as Dewey (1930), Dumont (1986), and Kateb (1992) also discussed ideas related to individualism. Dewey (1930) distinguished what he referred to as "old" individualism, which included the liberation from legal and religious restrictions, from the "new" individualism, which focused on self-cultivation. Dumont (1986) argued that individualism was a consequence of Protestantism (i.e., humans do not have to go to church to communicate with God), political developments (emphasis on equality and liberty), and economic developments (e.g., affluence).

In all, the constructs of individualism and collectivism received much theoretical attention in legal, religious, and philosophical writings for centuries. It wasn't until the 1960s, however, that they began to receive systematic empirical attention in the field of psychology.

INDIVIDUALISM AND COLLECTIVISM: CONTRIBUTIONS FROM PSYCHOLOGISTS ACROSS FOUR DECADES

The development of theory and research on individualism and collectivism in psychology truly represents a collective effort of many psychologists. Rather than being primarily driven by one source of influence, there have been numerous people who have made important contributions. As the ancient Hindu saying dictates, "Truth is one; it has many names"; so too is the case in terms of individualism and collectivism theory and research. In what follows we trace the evolution of theories and research and the serendipity of collaborations and discoveries that have shaped and continue to shape our knowledge of the constructs.

On the origins of individualism– collectivism theory and research: the analysis of subjective culture

Arguably the first empirical evidence for individualism and collectivism in psychology can be traced to a large multination project known as the *Analysis of Subjective Culture* (Triandis, 1972). The concept of culture, at that time, was reflected in the work of three anthropologists: Clyde Kluckhohn (1954), Melvin Herskovits (1955), and Ralph Redfield (1941). Herskovits had defined culture as the human-made part of the environment. The human-made part of the environment consists of *physical* (e.g., tools, bridges, educational systems, religious institutions), as well as *subjective* elements (e.g., beliefs, attitudes, norms, values). Following this lead, in the *Analysis of Subjective Culture*, Triandis (1972) set out to develop a theory and psychological methods to study "subjective culture." At the time, there were no psychological methods available and no overarching framework that examined the psychological underpinnings of culture.

The project that resulted in this publication, like many others described in this book, was the result of serendipitous events. In 1963, the Chief of Naval Operations asked the Office of Naval Research (ONR) to organize and support research so to better prepare Naval officers to manage cultural differences. ONR came to the psychology department of the University of Illinois and asked us if it could undertake this project. Fred Fiedler put together a team that consisted of Charles Osgood, Larry Stolurow, and Harry Triandis. Triandis already had some cross-cultural experience, so it was natural that he was given the job of analyzing "culture" so that it could be converted into computer-supported teaching experiences by Stolurow, and communicated to seamen (Osgood), who would be organized into teams whose leadership would be studied by Fiedler.

Triandis was already familiar with culture-specific (*emic*) and culture-general (*etic*) constructs (Triandis, 1964), so he aimed at developing methods that could include some *etic* elements, so that cultures could be compared, as well as *emic* elements from each culture so that one could understand each culture from the "inside."[1] Many paper-and-pencil methods ware developed which tapped different elements of "subjective culture" including, categorizations, associations, attitudes, beliefs, expectations, and norms, among others. What became clear in the analysis was that *coherent themes* cut across these different elements of subjective culture. The theme of *individualism and collectivism* began to emerge from psychological data for the first time across numerous countries, including the US, Greece, India, and Japan.

Elements of subjective culture

The basic element for the study of culture is *categorization*. What stimuli are treated as equivalent by members of the culture? Members of each culture have unique ways of categorizing experience. For example, who is a member of my ingroup? In some cultures it is those who were born in the same place, or belonged to the same tribe, race, social class, religion, or who were blood relatives. In other cultures it is people who "think like I do." The two categories might overlap, but they are not the same. Thus, there are both *etic* (common elements: my group) and *emic* elements (culture-specific elements: specific groups)

defining this category. Later work (Brewer and Yuki, 2007) distinguished two kinds of definitions of ingroup: a *category-based identity*, such as "I am an American" and a *relationship-based identity*. In all, by studying how people categorize experience we learn much about their culture.

Members of each culture have unique ways of *associating* one category with another. For example, is "socialism" referring to a political party, an ideology, or both? Are "fathers" in this culture assumed to be severe or lenient, with respect to children of different ages? In addition, cultures differ in the kinds of perceived antecedent-consequent relationships that people use (e.g., if you have "hard work" then you have "progress"; if you have "progress" then you have "health"), *attitudes* (e.g., is "socialism" good or bad, would members of the culture support a socialist party?), *beliefs* (e.g., "socialism" results in good health; or results in an impoverished society), *expectations* (e.g., if there is socialism then there is poverty), *ideals* (e.g., widows should not be passionate), *memories* (e.g., I remember the names of each of my cows), *norms* (e.g., members of this society give their seat to old people), *role perceptions* (e.g., the mother–son role is warmer than the father–son role in this culture), *stereotypes* (e.g., lower class people are not intelligent), *tasks* (e.g., to make this tool one has to first get some redwood), *values* (e.g., "security" is very important). Later work by Triandis (1977, 1980) resulted in a model linking *behavioral intentions* (e.g., I intend to do X) and *behavior* (X), which included also *norms* (most people I respect think I should do X), *self-definitions* (e.g., I am the kind of person who does X), *habits* (e.g., I frequently do X), and *facilitating conditions* (e.g., I am highly aroused to do X, I am capable of doing X; the situation calls for me to do X) The theory of reasoned action (Fishbein and Ajzen, 1975) was combined with elements of the 1980 model to form the unified theory of behavior (Fishbein et al., 2001). In addition, some "probes" (Triandis, 1972) into subjective culture were carried out, by studying stereotypes, antecedent-consequent relationships, which also provided clues about the values of each culture, and role perceptions.

Cultural syndromes: interrelated elements of subjective culture

Most importantly, Triandis (1972) examined if the information obtained from each of the "probes" into culture, by the various methods, hangs together. Indeed, a comparison of multiple measures across the US and Greece, showed that the data from each of the methods can be summarized by using certain themes. Specifically, the Greek data indicated much more contrast between behaviors toward the ingroup and outgroup members in Greece than in the US. This turned out to be a major characteristic of collectivist cultures (Triandis, 1995). The traditional Greeks (of the 1960s, when the data were collected) defined their universe in terms of the triumphs of their ingroup over their outgroups, while for Americans this worldview was of little or no importance. In Greece, relationships with authorities and social relations in general reflected the ingroup–outgroup relationships where there is much association and intimacy and low hostility within ingroups whereas in the US, participants express some hostility within ingroups and emotional distance from ingroup members. An ingroup in Greece was defined as a group of individuals about whose welfare a person is concerned, with whom the person is willing to cooperate without demanding equitable returns, and separation from whom leads to anxiety.

Foreshadowing the large literature on culture and self, Triandis (1972) found that Greek self-definition depended on the way ingroup members saw the person, thus individuals' worth was defined by the group. By contrast, American self-definition depended on the way individuals saw themselves. Consistent with the collectivist–individualist contrast, the concept MYSELF was rated (on semantic differential scales) "stronger" by

Americans than by Greeks, but the concept MY RELATIVES was rated stronger by Greeks than by Americans. Greeks also perceived behaviors in *context* to a greater extent than did Americans, an attribute that later proved to be a key characteristic of collectivist cultures. For example, CHEATING was completely unacceptable for the Greeks when the target was an ingroup member, but was perfectly okay if the target was an outgroup member.

Ecocultural framework of dimensions of culture

Another contribution of the *Analysis of Subjective Culture* was that it placed the thematic elements of subjective culture into a larger ecological and historical framework. The theoretical framework that was developed included *distal antecedents* (e.g., climate) and *historical events* (e.g., wars), *proximal antecedents* (e.g., occupations, language used, religion), and *immediate antecedents of action* (which included all the elements listed in the following paragraphs), which result in patterns of action. For example, Greece is cut up into small segments, because of the numerous mountains and islands, and that results in ingroups that are linked to place. The 350-year Ottoman occupation required knowing who could be trusted (i.e., who was ingroup). Furthermore, competition for scarce resources made it difficult to be cooperative with outgroups. The framework offered other ecological antecedents of subjective culture. For example, when resources are abundant there is more individualism. Cultures that are relatively isolated from other cultures, and in which making a living requires people to work together very frequently are likely to be more collectivistic. Climate is also an important factor in shaping subjective culture. For example, self-expression is higher in wealthy countries with harsh climates (cold or hot) than in countries with temperate climates, whereas self-expression is lower in poor countries with harsh climates than in poor countries in temperate climates (Van de Vliert, 2007).

In all, the *Analysis of Subjective Culture* was the first systematic study that illustrated cross-cultural differences in the emphasis on individuals versus groups, and began to trace the ecological and historical correlates of the constructs. As reviewed below, this became a central focus in later work in cross-cultural social psychology.

Development of the individualism–collectivism constructs: the 1980s

At the same time as Triandis was finalizing the *Analysis of Subjective Culture* findings, he happened to meet Geert Hofstede who was also collecting data on the constructs. It was 1971, at the Congress of the International Association of Applied Psychology, in Liege, Belgium, that Hofstede mentioned to Triandis that the dataset existed. Hofstede took Triandis to his office in Brussels and they there discussed the analysis of the dataset. A factor analysis included a factor which Hofstede named *individualism–collectivism* – arguably the first formal use of the terms in psychology. The factor had a strong similarity to the American–Greek dataset of Triandis (1972), and Hofstede (1980) later referred to Triandis (1972) when interpreting his findings.

In 1978, Triandis was asked to review Hofstede's (1980) manuscript. Based on a factor analysis of the sum of all of the responses in each culture, Hofstede named one of the factors individualism versus collectivism, and defined it as follows (1980: 51):

> Individualism pertains to societies in which the ties between individuals are loose; everyone is expected to look after himself or herself and his or her immediate family. Collectivism as its opposite pertains to societies in which people from birth onwards are integrated into strong, cohesive ingroups, which throughout people's lifetime continue to protect them in exchange for unquestioning loyalty.

Triandis enthusiastically endorsed the book and began a research program which examined

the question: How should the collectivism–individualism contrast be defined? In the next decade, a number of studies coming from the University of Illinois sought to elucidate the meaning of the constructs. In the first study, Hui and Triandis (1986) asked a sample of anthropologists and psychologists to provide their insight into the meaning of the concepts. They emphasized the centrality of groups *versus* the centrality of individuals. The next set of studies sought to address the question: How should the constructs be operationalized? The first measurement was provided in Hui's (1988) dissertation which was based on the themes that were identified in Hui and Triandis (1986), and which eventually became the INDCOL measurement of the construct (for later measures developed in this research program, see Triandis and Gelfand, 1998; Triandis et al., 1986, 1988, 1990, 1995, 1998).

Triandis and his students found general consensus, and based on their results, they developed more items to further investigate the constructs. In a series of studies, Triandis et al. (1986) examined the structure of these items at the culture level in nine countries. Their culture-level analysis revealed four factors, two of which were reflective of individualism (*self-reliance with hedonism* and *separation from ingroups*) and two of which were reflective of collectivism (*family integrity* and *interdependence with sociability*). They found Hofstede's (1980) nation scores on individualism and collectivism were only correlated with scores on family integrity (collectivism) ($r = 0.78$). Triandis et al. (1993) extracted multiple universal (i.e., *etic*) and culture-specific (i.e., *emic*) independent dimensions of individualism and collectivism across cultures. Thus, unlike previous analyses, Triandis and colleagues found evidence of the multidimensionality of the constructs at the culture level, while at the same time confirming the overlap of some of the dimensions with Hofstede's (1980) original work.

At the same time that Triandis was validating new measures of individualism and collectivism, Shalom Schwartz and his colleagues (Schwartz, 1992; Schwartz and Bilsky, 1990) were exploring universals in individualism and collectivism values. In a study of the structure of values among over 44,000 teachers and students in 54 countries, Schwartz examined the extent to which people view themselves as autonomous versus embedded in groups, reflecting what they referred to as emphasis on *autonomy versus conservation*.

While work by Triandis and Hofstede was largely "bottom up" (emerging from the data), Schwartz predicted *a priori* the nature of value dimensions, such as autonomy (individualism) and conservation (collectivism), as well as the relations among these values and other values in the circumplex (for other large scale studies of individualism–collectivism see the Chinese Culture Connection, 1987; House et al., 2004; and Smith et al., 1996; for more recent measures, see Fischer et al, 2009; Shteynberg et al., 2009; Zou et al., 2009).

Individualism–collectivism meets social cognition research: the 1990s and beyond

In the late 1980s and early 1990s, two papers had a profound influence on the direction of individualism–collectivism research by connecting theory and empirical work on the constructs with basic social cognition research on the self. In his *Psychological Review* paper "The self and social behavior in differing cultural contexts," Triandis (1989) set forth a theory of how different aspects of the self (private, public, collective) are sampled with different probabilities in different kinds of social environments. It was in this paper that Triandis argued that the more individualistic the culture, the more frequent the sampling of the private self and the less frequent the sampling of the collective self. By contrast, he argued that collectivism, external threat, competition with outgroups, and common fate increase the sampling of the collective self. At much the same time, a seminal paper by Markus and

Kitayama (1991) also advanced key propositions linking the constructs (which they labeled independence and interdependence) to fundamental cultural differences in cognition, emotion, and motivation. The importance of these papers cannot be underestimated, as they, for the first time, situated the study of individualism and collectivism in the mainstream of social psychology. "Basic" findings on the self that were thought to be universal, whether related to self-efficacy, self-enhancement, self-verification, self-actualization, self consciousness, self-control, among others, were challenged and illustrated to be reflective of Western norms and assumptions of individualism (see Markus and Kitayama, 1991).

The influence of the social cognition movement on research on individualism and collectivism can also be seen in other scholars' works. In a landmark study, Trafimow et al. (1991) showed that, as with other constructs that can be primed, asking people to think for a few minutes if they are similar or different from family and friends increases the probability of collectivist or individualist responses. Likewise, Hong et al. (2000) showed that bicultural individuals could be made to have collectivist or individualist mindsets depending on the primes they have received. In a seminal meta-analysis, Oyserman and Wing-sing Lee (2008) illustrated that individualism and collectivism primes have reliable and consistent effects on values, relationality, self-concept, and cognition, across different types of primes and samples. More generally, they showed that the "cognitive tools" that are brought online when collectivism is primed focus on connecting, integrating, and assimilating the figure with the ground and the self with other. By contrast, the "cognitive tools" that are brought online when individualism is primed focus on pulling apart and separating, and contrasting the figure and ground, self and other. Much work by Nisbett and his collaborators (2001) also connected individualism and collectivism research to basic thought processes as discussed below.

DEFINING ATTRIBUTES AND CORRELATES OF INDIVIDUALISM AND COLLECTIVISM

We began this chapter with the roots that individualism and collectivism had in the *Analysis of Subjective culture*. In the decades since this book was published, and through many scholarly efforts, much research has documented key defining attributes of the constructs and its antecedents and consequences, which are reviewed below.

Defining attributes

Research has illuminated a number of defining attributes of individualism and collectivism (Triandis, 1995):

1 In collectivistic cultures, the self is interdependent with some group versus in individualistic cultures, the self is independent of groups (Markus and Kitayama, 1991). For example, when asked to complete 20 sentences that begin with "I am…," in collectivist samples about 35 percent of the responses have "social" content (I am an uncle, I am a member of my fraternity). By contrast, only about 15 percent of the responses from individualist samples have social content. In fact, the mode of social content of 500 Illinois students was zero (Triandis et al., 1990).
2 In collectivist cultures, the goals of the group have priority over individual goals and ingroup and individual goals are usually the same; in individualistic cultures, the goals may be different, and if they are in conflict the individual's goals have priority over the goals of the group (Triandis, 1995).
3 In collectivist cultures, norms, obligations, and duties guide behavior, whereas in individualist cultures attitudes, personal needs, individual rights, and the contracts the individual has established with others are important determinants of behavior (e.g., Davidson et al., 1976).
4 In collectivist cultures, communal relationships (Mills and Clark, 1982) are most frequent, and individuals stays in unpleasant groups or relationships; in individualist cultures individuals tend to leave unsatisfactory relationships (Kim, 1994).

Antecedents of individualism and collectivism

Numerous ecological, institutional, situational, and demographic antecedents of individualism and collectivism have been advanced in the literature. As a general principle, factors that increase the need for people to rely on others and which activate common fate promote collectivism. Factors that allow individuals to separate from others promote individualism.

Ecology

Numerous cross-cultural scholars have posited that cultural differences in individualism and collectivism develop as adaptations to the ecological context (Berry, 1976). Collectivism is generally found in agricultural societies wherein conformity and obedience are crucial for survival, whereas more individualism is found among hunters and in complex (e.g., information) societies than in nomadic or agricultural societies wherein self-reliance and freedom are crucial for survival (Barry et al., 1959). An open frontier (Kitayama et al., 2006) also increases the probability of individualism given that it allows people to separate and live at a distance from other people (Triandis, 1995). Likewise, rural contexts in which there is low mobility and people need to fit into their communities are more collectivistic than urban contexts (Realo et al., 1997). In sum, when the ecology requires connection versus separation, this increases the probability of collectivism versus individualism, respectively.

Family structure

Family structures that promote embeddedness among individuals promote collectivism whereas family structures that allow separation among individuals promote individualism. Individualism is often associated with nuclear family structures, whereas collectivism is associated with extended family structures (Triandis, 1989). In a 16-culture study, Georgas et al. (2001) found that members of individualistic cultures lived farther away from grandparents, aunts/uncles, and cousins and visited them less than members of collectivist cultures. In families with many children and therefore greater interdependence, there is a higher probability of collectivism, whereas in families with only children there is a greater probability of individualism (Falbo, 1992). Individualism at the country level is also significantly related to divorce rates (Lester, 1995).

Distribution of wealth

Wealth affords separation from others and has been associated with higher individualism. Hofstede (1980) found a positive correlation between individualism and wealth, with industrialized wealthy countries scoring higher on individualism than developing countries. Hofstede (1980) later addressed the issue of causality, and argued that an increase in national wealth causes an increase in individualism in a culture, and not vice versa. In this view, individualism is thought to increase as the discretionary capital that is available to people. As people become more affluent, they have more freedom to do their own thing, and accordingly "financial independence leads to social independence" (Triandis, 1994: 165).

Situational conditions

Situations in which common fate and the need for interdependence are made salient (Campbell, 1958) and in which there are crises and threats to the ingroup (McKelvey, 1982) increase the probability of collectivism. The more people are rewarded for group action, the more likely it is that the culture will be collectivist, whereas the more they are rewarded for individual actions the more likely it is that the culture will be individualist (Lillard, 1998). Disjunctive tasks (that can be accomplished by just one member of a group) increase individualism, whereas conjunctive tasks (that require all members of the group to contribute) increase collectivism (Breer and Locke, 1965).

As noted above, subtle situational priming also affects individualism and collectivism.

When the collective self of collectivist participants is primed (by asking people to think of what they have in common with their family and friends, or by exposing participants to words like "we" or "us"; Oyserman and Wing-sing Lee, 2008) participants emit collectivist responses. Collectivist languages, like Chinese or Nepali, can also be used as primes. Samples that are exposed to themes of independence and autonomy in the media are more individualist. For example, exposure to Hollywood–type media increases individualism (McBride, 1998).

Demographics

In general, the lower the status of a group in a social hierarchy, the more likely it is to be collectivistic. Low status requires sharing of resources and the development of values that emphasize security, reliability, and tradition (e.g., Kohn, 1969; Triandis, 2009a). Indeed, research has shown that across many societies, the lower social classes are more collectivist than the upper classes (Kohn, 1969). Schwartz and Smith (1997) also reported that younger and more educated individuals tend to be more individualistic than older and less educated individuals across many societies. In the US, persons of color have scored higher on collectivism (defined as an orientation toward the welfare of one's larger community) and familism (defined as an orientation toward the welfare of one's immediate family) as compared to Caucasians (Gaines et al., 1997; but see Jones, 1997 for a contrasting analysis). With respect to gender, Kashima et al. (1995) found no difference between males and females across five countries on individualism and collectivism. Gender differences, however, were found for a separate construct: relationality (see also Gabriel and Gardner, 1999).

Consequences of individualism and collectivism

Individualism and collectivism have been shown to have wide-ranging consequences for social–psychological phenomena. As a general principle, collectivism promotes cognitions, motivations, emotions, and behaviors all in the service of connecting with one's group, while individualism promotes cognitions, motivations, emotions, and behaviors all in service of pulling apart and separating from others. Below is a summary of a number of important implications of individualism and collectivism (see Gelfand et al., 2004; Kitayama and Cohen, 2007; Triandis, 1995).[2]

Focus of attention
In collectivistic cultures, relationships are the figure, and individuals are in the background; in individualistic cultures, individuals are the figure and groups are in the background.

Attributions
In collectivistic cultures, individuals tend to make external attributions (e.g., norms, roles, group pressure) concerning the determinants of behavior whereas in individualistic cultures, individuals tend to make internal attributions (e.g., attitudes, personality) (Morris and Peng, 1994). In collectivistic cultures, individuals tend to attribute success to the help received from others and failure to a lack of effort. By contrast, in individualistic cultures, individuals tend to attribute success to their own ability and failure to luck or task difficulty.

Self definition
In collectivistic cultures, individuals define the self in context and see the environment as more or less fixed and themselves as changeable, whereas individualists see themselves as more or less stable (invariant attitudes, personality, rights) and the environment as changeable (Chiu et al., 1997; Chiu and Hong, 1999). People in collectivistic cultures generally know more about others than about themselves, whereas people in individualistic cultures generally know more about themselves than about others (Markus and Kitayama, 1991). For collectivists, the self includes the achievements of the group; for individualists, the self includes the achievements of the individual.

Goals
Individuals in collectivistic cultures are motivated by others' choices, whereas individuals in individualistic cultures are motivated when they have a personal choice (Iyengar and Lepper, 1999). Likewise, there is more self-efficacy experienced when working alone in individualistic cultures whereas there is more self-efficacy experienced when working in groups in collectivistic cultures (Earley, 1993). People in collectivistic cultures are also more prevention-focused whereas people in individualistic cultures are more promotion focused (Lalwani et al., 2009; Lee et al., 2000).

Emotions
People in collectivistic cultures tend to have more engaged emotions, such as sympathy, while people in individualistic cultures tend to have more disengaged emotions, such as pride (Kitayama et al., 2007). Collectivists express both good and bad feelings, and tend to be moderate in their expression (Mesquita and Leu, 2007).

Cognitions
The more collectivist the culture the more are individuals likely to use holistic and circular thinking and pay attention to the field, whereas the more individualist the culture the more people are likely to use linear and analytic thinking and pay attention to the object (Nisbett, 2003). People in individualist cultures tend to make more judgments based on explicit rules, while people in collectivist cultures tend to make more judgments based on the family resemblance of the various stimuli (Kitayama et al., 2007). Collectivists also tend to use dialectical thinking and are tolerant of contradiction (Peng and Nisbett, 1999).

Norms
Equality and need are emphasized in the distribution of resources among collectivists, particularly with ingroup members, and equity is emphasized among individualists (Leung, 1997). Norms for behavior are more cooperative among collectivists and more

competitive among individualists (Gelfand and Realo, 1999).

Values
The values of collectivists tend to emphasize family security, social order, respect for tradition, harmony, politeness (Schwartz, 1994). Loyalty to the employer and the country are also important (Engel, 1988). The values of individualists tend to emphasize being curious, broadminded, creative, and having a varied and exciting life (Schwartz, 1994). Independence and self-sufficiency are also important (Engel, 1988).

Calamities
In collectivistic cultures, a major calamity is ostracism; in individualistic cultures, a major calamity is dependence on others (Triandis, 1995).

Ingroups
Collectivists have few ingroups and relationships within them are intense. Individualists have many ingroups, and relations are superficial. In collectivistic cultures, self-sacrifice for ingroup is expected and there is cooperation within ingroups; in individualistic cultures, less willingness for self-sacrifice is expected and debate and confrontation are acceptable in ingroups. In collectivistic cultures, the ingroup is perceived as more homogeneous than outgroups, whereas in individualistic cultures, the ingroup is perceived as more heterogeneous than outgroups. In collectivistic cultures, ingroups are defined by similarity to kinship, tribe, religion, race, language, and village whereas in individualistic cultures, ingroups are defined by similarity in achieved attributes (e.g., profession). When making judgments about the trustworthiness of others, people in collectivistic contexts rely on situational signs (e.g., benevolent interactions with the other) whereas people in individualistic cultures tend to rely on dispositional signs (e.g., ability and integrity) (Branzei et al., 2007).

Social behavior
In collectivistic cultures, behavior is mostly a function of norms and there is a large difference when behavior is toward an ingroup versus an outgroup member. In individualistic cultures, behavior is mostly a function of attitudes and there is less of a distinction between ingroups and outgroups. In the former, people have few skills to enter new groups; in the latter people are skilled in entering and leaving groups. In the former there are communal exchanges and much intimacy. In the latter there are contractual exchanges and less intimacy.

Perceived determinants of social behavior
In collectivistic cultures, ingroup norms, group memberships, context, age, gender, and social relations are especially important determinants of social behavior. In individualistic cultures, beliefs, attitudes, values, and achieved roles are especially important determinants of social behavior.

Language and communication
Language and communication in individualistic cultures is direct and emphasizes the individual whereas it is more indirect and de-emphasizes the individual in collectivistic cultures. For example, pronouns such as "I" and "you" are widely used in individualistic cultures and are frequently dropped in collectivistic cultures (Kashima and Kashima, (1998). In individualistic cultures people use more adjectives which suggests more of a dispositional perspective wherein there is low contextual focus. In collectivist cultures they use more action verbs which suggest more of a contextual and situated focus (Zwier, 1998). The more collectivist the culture the more people are likely to communicate indirectly (paying attention to gestures, body position, tone of voice, and loudness of voice) (Holtgraves, 1997; Triandis, 1994).

Group processes
Individualism is associated with general resistance to teams at the individual and

group level of analysis (Kirkman and Shapiro 2001a, 2001b). Individuals in collectivistic cultures are more likely to perceive groups as "entities" which have agentic qualities and dispositions as compared with individuals in individualistic cultures (e.g., Chiu et al., 2000, Kashima et al., 2005, Morris et al., 2001). Collectivism is associated with greater conformity (Bond and Smith, 1996), cooperation (Cox et al., 1991; Eby and Dobbins, 1997; Wagner, 1995), and more organizational citizenship behaviors (i.e., prosocial behaviors) (Moorman and Blakely, 1995). Schemas for what constitutes "successful" workgroups also vary across cultures. Collectivists perceive that socioemotional behaviors are important for group success, whereas individualists perceive that high task orientation and low socioemotional behaviors are important for group success (Sanchez-Burks et al., 2000). Individuals also hold groups and organizations more accountable for failed actions in collectivistic cultures as compared to individualistic cultures (Chiu and Hong, 1992; Chiu et al., 2000; Menon et al., 1999; Zemba et al., 2006).

Leadership

The attributes that are perceived as important for effective leadership vary across individualistic and collectivistic societies (House et al., 2004). Collectivistic societies and organizations are more likely to endorse charismatic leadership, self-protective leadership (i.e., face-saving leader behaviors), and team-oriented leadership as compared with individualistic societies (Gelfand et al., 2004). Also, leaders' behavior is interpreted differently depending on the culture. For example, "talking behind one's subordinates back" is perceived to be negatively related to considerate leadership in the US, where it is seen as inappropriate to indirectly speak to one's employees. However, such behaviors are positively related to consideration in Japan where face saving and indirect communication are seen as important (Smith et al., 1989).

Conflict and negotiation

Individualism and collectivism affect how individuals perceive and manage conflict. Individualists perceive conflicts to be more about violations of individual rights and autonomy whereas collectivists perceive the same conflicts to be about violations of duties and obligations (Gelfand et al., 2001). Negotiators in individualistic cultures tend to be susceptible to host of competitive biases in negotiations, including self-serving biases (Gelfand et al., 2002), fixed-pie biases (Gelfand and Christakopolou, 1999), and dispositional attribution biases as compared to negotiators in collectivistic cultures (Morris et al., 1999). Negotiators tend to share information directly (e.g., through questions about preferences) in individualistic cultures whereas they tend to share information indirectly (through offer behavior) in collectivistic cultures (e.g., Adair et al., 2001). Situational factors, such as being accountable to constituents (Gelfand and Realo, 1999) or having a high need for closure (Fu et al., 2007, Morris and Fu, 2001) amplify cultural differences in conflict and negotiation.

Additional distinctions: vertical and horizontal dimensions of individualism and collectivism

Triandis (1995) argued that there are many "species" of individualism and collectivism. One such distinction – which was found also in the original *Analysis of Subjective Culture* – is that individualism and collectivism can be both horizontal and vertical. In vertical cultures individuals are motivated to stand out. In horizontal cultures individuals avoid standing out (they try to blend in) (Daun, 1992). Traditional India is vertical, while Australia and Sweden are horizontal. In India individuals seek status, and figuratively they want to stand out, to be "on top of an elephant" parading the streets to the applause of an adoring population. On the other hand, in Australia tall poppies are brought down (Feather, 1994) and in Sweden people avoid standing out (Daun, 1992).

The major value of vertical individualists is achievement. Americans are offended if someone tells them that they are "average" (Weldon, 1984) which suggests considerable vertical individualism. Vertical individualism increases the probability of competition (Triandis, 1995). In vertical individualist cultures people are high in the need for power, achievement, and prestige (Daun, 1992). The major value of horizontal individualists is uniqueness (Triandis and Gelfand, 1998). Horizontal individualism increases the probability that individuals will be motivated by (a) the good, comfortable life, and (b) will seek to be unique without standing out (Inglehart, 1997). The major value of horizontal collectivists is cooperation. The Israeli kibbutz is an example of such a culture. In horizontal collectivist cultures people are high in the need for affiliation, and in modesty (Kurman, 2001, 2003). The major concern of vertical collectivists is to do their duty. Traditional cultures (e.g., Indian village) are high in this tendency. In vertical collectivist cultures people are motivated, more than in other cultures, to conform to authorities (Bond and Smith, 1996). While there are considerable cross-cultural differences on the constructs, it is also important to point out that individuals have all four of the cognitions (Triandis et al., 1998). There is now a literature (e.g., Choiu, 2001; Kurman and Sriram, 2002; Nelson and Shavitt, 2002; Soh and Leong, 2002) that shows that vertical collectivists are quite different from horizontal collectivists and vertical individualists are different from horizontal individualists.

Cultures may emphasize, at particular time periods, a particular syndrome more than the other syndromes. For example, Galtung (1979) divided the history of Europe into three parts: Antiquity up to the fall of the Roman Empire (476 AD), which was dominated by vertical individualism; the Middle Ages, up to the fall of Constantinople in 1453, which was characterized by vertical collectivism; and the modern period, which was characterized by vertical individualism, with the exception of Scandinavian cultures which tend to be higher on horizontal individualism (Triandis, 1995).

Evaluation of individualism and collectivism

Both individualism and collectivism have positive and negative effects on societies and individuals therein. There are data suggesting that divorce, delinquency, drug abuse, heart attacks, and suicide are higher in individualist than in collectivist cultures (Eckersley and Dear, 2002; Triandis et al., 1988). Eckersley, an Australian epidemiologist, argues that individualism is undesirable from the point of view of mental health. Torrey and Miller (2001) reported that the number of insane persons per 1,000 has increased steadily since the beginning of the industrial revolution in England, Ireland, Canada, and the US. The four curves that cover the 1807–1961 period (when insane people were placed in communities in all four countries, so that there is no longer any reliable measurement of this rate) are impressively steep. During this period there have been increases in both affluence (i.e., cultural complexity), and looseness. Thus, theoretically, there has been an increase in individualism. The authors hypothesize that living in cities, changes in diet, alcohol consumption, more toxins in the environment, improved medical care that does not eliminate unfit babies, infectious agents or a combination of these factors might account for the fact that the rates increased seven-fold between 1750 and the present. While there are likely different definitions of mental illness across the world, it is important to consider this work in evaluating the constructs.

On the other hand, subjective wellbeing is higher in individualist than in collectivist cultures (Diener et al., 1995). The US is thirteenth in the world on subjective wellbeing (Tov and Diener, 2007). Japan, which is generally tighter and more collectivist than the United States, scored thirty-fifth. Individualism is also related to high life expectancy, higher satisfaction, and higher scores on the Human Development index (see Gelfand et al., 2004).

The picture is complex and difficult to evaluate. Individualism is a desirable cultural pattern for those who want to achieve, to become distinguished; collectivism is a desirable cultural pattern for those who want to be embedded in social relationships. Longevity is higher in Japan (82) than in most of the West. "Life without disease" averages 74.5 years in Japan, 73.2 in Australia, 73.1 in France, 72.8 in Spain, 72.7 in Italy, 72.5 in Greece, 72.5 in Switzerland, and is only 70.0 in the US (*The Economist*, 2009). It maybe that extreme individualism is not desirable, and a culture that has both collectivist and individualist elements is ideal.

Practical implications of individualism and collectivism

As a major dimension of cultural variation, individualism and collectivism has much practical relevance for managing interdependence in an increasingly "flat" world. The sheer amount of intercultural contact across many areas of life is unprecedented. For example, it is estimated that over 175 million people migrated across national borders each year' and 1 in every 35 people in the world lives in a country different than their birth (Office of the United Nations High Commissioner for Human Rights, 2009). Globalization has dramatically increased contact among people of different cultures, with new mergers, acquisitions, and global ventures happening on a daily basis and millions of expatriates crossing boarders every year. Pressing global concerns, such as preserving the environment, require intercultural collaboration at the international and local levels. And in a world of global threats of conflict and terrorism, understanding cultural differences can arguably be a matter of life or

death. Indeed, in the recent Iraqi Study report, James Baker noted that understanding cultural differences on behavior is of the highest national priority (Baker and Hamilton, 2006).

Within this global context, it is hard to underestimate the importance of the knowledge that has been gleaned from last four decades of individualism and collectivism research. Cross-cultural differences along the individualism and collectivism divide, if not understood and managed, can have disastrous consequences across many domains of life. Within organizational contexts, a lack of understanding of cultural differences can translate into failed mergers and ventures, premature expatriate return and turnover, and organizational conflict. In the US alone, for example, more than 100,000 companies conduct business overseas, and at least one-third of American profits are derived from international business dealings (Erez, 1994); thus, understanding key cultural differences related to individualism and collectivism is a key business imperative.

The need to understand individualism and collectivism to help negotiators negotiate effectively across cultures is also painfully obvious in today's geopolitical scene, where the source of conflict among humankind is thought to be increasingly cultural in nature (Huntington, 1996). Anecdotal examples abound of failed intercultural negotiations, many of which can be linked to basic differences in individualism and collectivism (Gelfand and Realo, 1999; Triandis, 1994). For example, during a summit in 1969, Prime Minister Sato of Japan was told by President Nixon for Japan to exercise export restraint to which he responded, "zensho shimasu" ("I will do my best"). Although Sato really meant "no," Nixon misunderstood this to mean agreement, and when there was no implementation, Nixon denounced Sato as a liar (Cohen, 1997). Without understanding of core elements of individualism and collectivism, such as indirectness versus directness in communication, as reviewed above, intercultural negotiations are seriously compromised.

As another practical example, in the area of health, a failure to understand individualism and collectivism can put patients at serious risk. Much research has relevance of cultural factors to health behaviors such as symptom recognition and help-seeking (e.g., Fabrega, 1994; Kleinman et al., 1978; Zola, 1966). In this respect, doctors' understanding of core cultural differences is critical in the treatment of disease.

With Lewin's famous adage that there is nothing as practical as a good theory in mind, cross-cultural psychologists have been translating the knowledge gained over the last four decades on individualism and collectivism into training programs. As early as the *Analysis of Subjective Culture*, knowledge of individualism and collectivism was developed into "cultural assimilator" training programs, which are books, or computer-based cross-cultural training devices (Fiedler et al., 1971). Assimilators consist of about 100 episodes that reflect a problematic interaction between members of two cultures. For example, an episode might be that an American teacher notices that a Hispanic child does not look at her when she is talking. Under each episode, in the format of a multiple-choice test, are four or five attributions that could explain what is happening in the episode. The trainee is asked to select one of the attributions, and then receives feedback. Some of the attributions are incorrect, and when the trainee selects one of them he/she is asked to try again. When the correct attribution is selected the feedback explains the cultural difference. In the example above the cultural difference is that in the US children are expected to look at a teacher who is talking; but in Latino countries one is "insolent" if one looks directly at a high status person in the eye, and the proper behavior is to respectfully look down.

The attributions are pre-tested with samples from the two cultures, and when members of the host culture select an attribution that is rarely selected by members of the trainee's culture, they begin to understand why the response is not "culturally" accurate.

The effect of this training is that trainees learn to make "*isomorphic attributions*," that is, attributions that are more or less like the attributions that are usually made by members of the host culture in the particular situation. Trainees randomly assigned to a training and a no-training condition show some improvement. The trained feel more comfortable when they are in the host culture.

Early assimilators were developed with a pair of cultures in mind, generally with the aim of training Americans to live in other cultures (e.g., Thailand, Honduras, Japan, Venezuela). For example, the Japanese culture assimilator has 57 incidents that are divided into themes (e.g., hierarchy, face saving behaviors, harmony and emotional control, group-related behaviors, and norm-related behaviors). Typical learnings include such do's and don'ts such as "Students do not wear jewelry to school," "Demeaning oneself is a proper behavior," "Newcomers give small gifts," and "Do not criticize supervisors," among others (Bhawuk, 2001). More recently, however, it has been found that people learn better when the episodes provide feedback organized around cultural syndromes such as individualism and collectivism. By organizing assimilators around elements of individualism–collectivism, trainees are able to move beyond "do's and don'ts" in other cultures – typically superficial attributes – to understand cultural differences through a coherent framework. Bhawuk (2001) outlined such an approach, which includes critical incidents that capture the four defining features of individualism and collectivism reviewed above (Triandis, 1995), including the nature of the self, goal priorities, predictors of behavior, and nature of relationships, along with critical incidents that tap into horizontal and vertical dimensions of the constructs. Importantly, however, although people learn much about another culture through cultural assimilators, they do not change their behavior enough to be really successful in the other culture. Changes in behavior require clinical interventions and behavior shaping. Nonetheless, this application is reported in several handbooks concerned with cross-cultural training (Landis and Bhagat, 1996).

CONCLUSION

Triandis (2009b) discussed the factors used by individuals to construct the way they see the world. Culture is one of them. Much international conflict is due to differences in the subjective cultures of various groups. The future of the planet may depend on further analyses of the subjective cultures around the globe in order to increase understanding, promote wellbeing, and manage our increasing interdependence.

ACKNOWLEDGMENTS

This research is based upon work supported by the US Army Research Laboratory and the US Army Research Office under grant number W911NF-08-1-0144.

NOTES

1 The terms *emic* and *etic* in cross-cultural psychology have been derived from linguistics, where *emic* refers to sounds specific to a particular language and *etic* refers to sounds that are universal to languages.

2 Important caveats, however, are in order. First, a distinction needs to be made between data that use "culture" as the unit of analysis (e.g., Hofstede, 1980), and data that use "individuals" as the unit of analysis. When culture is the unit of analysis the sum or the responses of individuals are entered and the correlation is across cultures. When individuals are the unit of analysis the correlation is within one culture across individuals. Collectivism tends to be the opposite of individualism when culture is the unit of analysis. However, when individuals are the units of analysis, the tendencies toward

individualism and collectivism can be orthogonal to each other (Gelfand et al., 1996). A person can be high in both attributes, or high in one and low on the other attribute. The best way to conceptualize this is to think that both collectivist and individualist cognitions are present in every individual, and the tendencies are elicited by the situation.

REFERENCES

Adair, W.L., Okimura, T. and Brett, J.M. (2001) Negotiation behavior when cultures collide: The United States and Japan. *Journal of Applied Psychology*, 86, 371–385.

Bakan, D. (1996) *The Duality of Human Existence*. Chicago: Rand McNally.

Baker, J.A. and Hamilton, L.H. (2006) *The Iraq Study Group Report: The Way Forward – A New Approach*. US Institute of Peace. New York: Vintage Books.

Barry, H., III, Child, I.L. and Bacon, M.K. (1959) A cross-cultural survey of sex differences in socialization. *Journal of Abnormal and Social Psychology*, 55, 327–332.

Bellah, R.N., Madsen, E., Sulliven, W., Swidler, A. and Tipton, S.M. (1985) *Habits of the Heart: Individualism and Commitment in American Life*. Berkeley: University of California Press.

Berry, J.W. (1976) Sex differences in behavior and cultural complexity. *Indian Journal of Psychology*, 51, 89–97.

Bhawuk, D.P.S. (2001) Evolution of cultural assimilators: Toward theory-based assimilators. *International Journal of Intercultural Relations*, 25, 141–163.

Bond, R. and Smith, P.B. (1996) Culture and conformity: A meta-analysis of studies using Asch's (1952b, 1956) line judgment task. *Psychological Bulletin*, 119, 111–137.

Branzei, O., Vertinsky, I. and Camp, R.D. (2007) Culture contingent signs of trust in emerging relationships. *Organizational Behavior and Human Decision Processes*, 104, 61–82.

Breer, P.E. and Locke, E. (1965) *Task Experience as a Source of Attitudes*. Homewood, IL: Dorsey Press.

Brewer, M.B. and Chen, Y. (2007) Where (and who) are collectives in collectivism: Toward conceptual clarification on individualism and collectivism. *Psychological Review*, 114, 133–151.

Brewer, M.B. and Yuki, M. (2007) Culture and social identity. In S. Kitayama and D. Cohen (eds),

Handbook of Cultural Psychology, pp. 307–322. New York: Guilford Press.

Campbell, D.T. (1958) Common fate, similarity, and other indices of status of aggregates of persons as social entities. *Behavioral Science, 3*, 14–25.

Carneiro, R.L. (1970) Scale analysis, evolutionary sequences, and the ratings of cultures. In R. Naroll and R. Cohen (eds), *A Handbook of Method in Cultural Anthropology*. New York: Columbia University Press.

Carpenter, S. (2000) Effects of cultural tightness and collectivism on self-concept and causal attribution. *Cross-Cultural Research, 34*, 38–56.

Chen, F.F. and West, S.G. (2008) Measuring individualism and collectivism: The importance of considering differential components, reference groups, and measurement invariance. *Journal for Research on Personality, 42*, 259–294.

Chiao, J. and Ambady, N. (2007) Cultural neuroscience: Parsing universality and diversity across levels of analysis. In S. Kitayama and D. Cohen (eds), *The Handbook of Cultural Psychology*, pp. 237–254. New York: Guilford Press.

Chick, G. (1997) Cultural complexity: The concept and its measurement. *Cross-Cultural Research, 31*, 275–307.

Chinese Culture Connection (1987) Chinese values and the search for culture-free dimensions of culture. *Journal of Cross-Cultural Psychology, 18*, 143–164.

Chircov, V.I., Lynch, M. and Niwa, S. (2005) Application of scenario questionnaire of horizontal and vertical individualism and collectivism to the assessment of cultural distance and cultural fit. *International Journal of Intercultural Relations, 29*, 469–490.

Chiu, C., Dweck, C.S., Tong, J.Y. and Fu, J.H. (1997) Implicit theories and concepts of morality. *Journal of Personality and Social Psychology, 73*, 923–940.

Chiu, C. and Hong, Y. (1992) The effect of intentionality and validation of collective responsibility attribution among Hong Kong Chinese. *Journal of Psychology, 126*, 291–300.

Chiu, C. and Hong, Y. (1999) Social identification in a political transition: The role of implicit beliefs. *International Journal of Intercultural Relations, 23*, 297–218.

Chiu, C., Morris, M.W., Hong, Y.Y. and Menon, T. (2000) Motivated cultural cognition: The impact of implicit cultural theories on dispositional attribution varies as a function of need for closure. *Journal of Personal and Social Psychology, 78*, 247–259.

Choiu, J. (2001) Horizontal and vertical individualism and collectivism among college students in the United States, Taiwan, and Argentina. *Journal of Social Psychology, 141*, 667–678.

Cohen, R. (1997) *Negotiating Across Cultures: International Communication in an Interdependent World*. Washington, DC: United States Institute of Peace Press.

Cole, M. (1996) *Cultural Psychology: A Once and Future Discipline*. Cambridge, MA: Harvard University Press.

Cox, T.H., Lobel, S.A. and McLeod, P.L. (1991) Effects of ethics group cultural differences on cooperative and competitive behavior on a group task. *Academy of Management Journal, 34*, 827–847.

Daun, A. (1992) Modern and modest. Mentality and self-stereotypes among Swedes. In A. Sjoegren and L. Janson (eds), *Culture and Management*. Stockholm: Institute of International Business, Series A–7.

Davidson, A.R., Jaccard, J.J., Triandis, H.C., Morales, M.L. and Diaz-Guerrero, R. (1976) Cross-cultural model testing: Toward a solution of the etic emic dilemma. *International Journal of Psychology, 11*, 1–13.

Dawood, N.J. (1956) *The Koran*. New York: Penguin.

Dewey, J. (1930) *Individualism Old and New*. New York: Minton, Balch.

Diener, E., Diener, M. and Diener, C. (1995) Factors predicting the subjective well-being of nations. *Journal of Personality and Social Psychology, 69*, 851–864.

Dumont, L. (1986) *Essays on Individualism*. Chicago: University of Chicago Press.

Durant, W. (1935) *Our Oriental Heritage*. New York: Simon & Schuster.

Durkheim, E. (1933) *The Division of Labor*. Chicago: Free Press.

Earley, C. (1993) East meets West, meets Mideast: Further explorations of collectivistic and individualistic workgroups. *Academy of Management Journal, 36*, 319–348.

Eby, L.T. and Dobbins, G.H. (1997) Collectivistic orientation in teams: An individual and group-level analysis. *Journal of Organizational Behavior, 18*, 275–295.

Eckersley, R. and Dear, K. (2002) Cultural correlates of youth suicide. *Social Science and Medicine, 55*, 1893–1906.

Engel, J.W. (1988) Work values of American and Japanese men. *Journal of Social Behavior and Personality, 3*, 191–200.

Erez, M. (1994) Toward a model of cross-cultural industrial and organizational psychology. In H. Triandis, M. Dunnette and L. Hough (eds), *Handbook of Industrial and Organization Psychology,*

Vol. 4, 2nd Edition, pp. 559–607. Palo Alto, CA: Consulting Psychologists Press.

Fabrega, H. (1994) International systems of diagnosis in psychiatry. *Journal of Nervous and Mental Disease*, *182*, 256–263.

Falbo, T. (1992) Social norms and the one-child family. In F. Boer and J. Dunn (eds), *Children's Sibling Relationship: Developmental and Clinical Issues*, pp. 71–82. Hillsdale, NJ: Erlbaum.

Feather, N.T. (1994) Attitudes toward high achievers and reactions to their fall: Theory and research concerning tall poppies. In M. Zanna (ed.), *Advances in Experimental Social Psychology*, *25*, 1–73. New York: Academic Press.

Fiedler, F.E., Mitchell, T. and Triandis, H.C. (1971) The culture assimilation: An approach to cross-cultural training. *Journal of Applied Psychology*, *55*, 95–102.

Fischer, R., Ferrera, M.C., Redford, P., Harb, C., Glazer S., Chen, B-S. et al. (2009) Individualism and collectivism as descriptive norms: Development of subjective norms approach to culture measurement. *Journal of Cross-Cultural Psychology*, *40*, 187–213.

Fishbein, M. and Ajzen, I. (1975) *Belief, Attitude, Intention, and Behavior: An Introduction to Theory and Research*. Reading, MA: Addison-Wesley.

Fishbein, M., Triandis, H.C., Kanfer, F.H., Becker, M., Middlestadt, S.E. and Eichler, A. (2001) Factors influencing behavior and behavior change. In A. Baum, T.A. Revenson and J.E. Singer (eds), *Handbook of Health Psychology*, pp. 3–18. Mahwah, NJ: Lawrence Erlbaum.

Fu, J.H.-Y., Chiu, C.-Y., Morris, M.W. and Young, M.J. (2007) Spontaneous inferences from cultural cues: Varying responses of cultural insiders and outsiders. *Journal of Cross-Cultural Psychology*, *38*, 58–75.

Gabriel, S. and Gardner, W.L. (1999). Are there 'his' and 'hers' types of interdependence? The implication of gender differences in collective versus relational interdependence for affect, behavior, and cognition. *Journal of Cross-Cultural Psychology*, *28*, 642–655.

Gaines, S.O., Marelich, W.D., Bledsoe, K.L., Steers, W.N., Henderson, M.C., Granrose, C.S. et al. (1997). Links between race/ethnicity and cultural values as mediated by racial/ethnic identity and moderated by gender. *Journal of Personality and Social Psychology*, *72*, 1460–1476.

Galtung, J. (1979) On the last 2,500 years of Western history. In P. Burke (ed.), *New Cambridge Modern History, Comparison Volume*. Cambridge: Cambridge University Press.

Gelfand, M.J., Bhawuk, D.P.S., Nishii, L.H. and Bechtold, D.J. (2004) Individualism and collectivism.

In R.J. House, P.J. Hanges, M. Javidan, P.W. Dorfman and V. Gupta (eds), *Culture, Leadership, and Organizations: The GLOBE Study of 62 Societies*, pp. 437–512. Thousand Oaks, CA: Sage.

Gelfand M.J. and Christakopolou, S. (1999) Culture and negotiator cognition: Judgment accuracy and negotiation processes in individualistic and collectivistic cultures. *Organizational Behavior and Human Decision Processes*, *79*, 248–269.

Gelfand, M.J., Higgins, M. Nishii, L., Raver, J., Dominguez, A., Yamaguchi, S. et al. (2002) Culture and egocentric biases of fairness in conflict and negotiation. *Journal of Applied Psychology*, *87*, 833–845.

Gelfand, M.J., Nishii, L. and Raver, J.L. (2006) On the nature and importance of cultural tightness-looseness, *Journal of Applied Psychology*, *91*, 1225–1244.

Gelfand, M.J., Nishii, L.H., Holcombe, K., Dyer, N., Ohbuchi, K. and Fukumo, N. (2001) Cultural influences on cognitive representation of conflict: Interpretation of conflict episodes in the U.S. and Japan. *Journal of Applied Psychology*, *86*, 1059–1074.

Gelfand, M.J. and Realo, A. (1999) Individualism-collectivism and accountability in intergroup negotiations. *Journal of Applied Psychology*, *84*, 721–736.

Gelfand, M.J., Triandis, H.C. and Chan, D.K.-S. (1996) Individualism versus collectivism or authoritarianism? *European Journal of Social Psychology*, *26*, 397–410.

Georgas, J., Mylonas, K., Bafoiti, T., Poortinga, Y,A, Christakopoulou, S., Kagitcibas, C. et al. (2001) Functional relationships in the nuclear and extended family: A 16-culture study. *International Journal of Psychology*, *36*, 289–300.

Glenn, E. and Glenn, P. (1981) *Man and Mankind: Conflicts and Communication between Cultures*. Norwood, NJ: Ablex.

Harb, C. and Smith, P.B. (2008) Self-construals across cultures: Beyond independence and interdependence. *Journal of Cross-Cultural Psychology*, *39*, 178–197.

Herskovits, M.J. (1955) *Cultural Anthropology*. New York: Knopf.

Hofstede, G. (1980) *Culture's Consequences*. Thousand Oaks, CA: Sage.

Holtgraves, T. (1997) Styles of language use: Individual and cultural variability in conversational indirectness. *Journal of Personality and Social Psychology* *73*, 624–637.

Hong, Y.Y., Morris, M., Chiu, C.-Y. and Benet-Martinez, V. (2000) Multicultural minds: A dynamic constructivist approach to culture and cognition. *American Psychologist, 55,* 709–720.

House, R.J., Hanges, P.J., Javidan, M., Dorfman, P.W. and Gupta, V. (2004) *Culture, Leadership, and Organizations: The GLOBE Study of 62 cultures.* Thousand Oaks, CA: Sage.

Hui, C.H. (1988) Measurement of individualism-collectivism. *Journal of Research on Personality, 22,* 17–36.

Hui, C.H. and Triandis, H.C. (1986) Individualism-collectivism: A study of cross-cultural researchers. *Journal of Cross-Cultural Psychology, 17,* 225–248.

Huntington, S.P. (1996) *The Clash of Civilizations and the Remaking of World Order.* New York: Simon & Schuster.

Inglehart, R. (1997) *Modernization and Post Modernization: Cultural, Economic, and Political Change in 43 Societies.* Princeton, NJ: Princeton University Press.

Inglehart, R. and Baker, W.E. (2000) Modernization, cultural change, and the persistence of traditional values. *American Sociological Review, 65,* 19–51.

Iyengar, S.S. and Lepper, M.R. (1999) Rethinking the value of choice: A cultural perspective on intrinsic motivation. *Journal of Personality and Social Psychology, 76,* 349–366.

Jackson, C.L., Colquitt, J.A., Wesson, M.J. and Zapata-Phelan, C.P. (2006) Psychological collectivism: a measurement validation and linkage to group member performance. *Journal of Applied Psychology, 91,* 884–899.

Kagan, D. (1966) *The Ancient Near East and Greece.* London: Macmillan Group.

Kashima, E.S. and Hardie, E.A. (2000) The development and validation of the Relational, Individual, and Collective Self Aspects (RIC) scale. *Asian Journal of Social Psychology, 3,* 19–48.

Kashima, E.S. and Kashima, Y. (1998) Culture and language: The case of cultural dimensions of personal pronoun use. *Journal of Cross-Cultural Psychology, 29,* 461–486

Kashima, Y., Kashima, E.S., Chiu, C.-Y., Farsides, T., Gelfand, M., Hong, Y.Y. et al. (2005) Culture, essentialism, and agency: Are individuals universally believed to be more real entities than groups? *European Journal of Social Psychology, 35,* 147–169.

Kashima, Y., Yamaguchi, S., Kim, U., Choi, S.C., Gelfand, M.J. and Yuki, M. (1995) Culture, gender and self: A perspective from individualism-collectivism research.. *Journal of Personality and Social Psychology, 59,* 925–937.

Kateb, G. (1992) *The Inner Ocean: Individualism and Democratic Culture.* Ithaca, NY: Cornell University Press.

Kim, U. (1994) Individualism and collectivism: Conceptual clarification and elaboration. In U. Kim, H.C. Triandis, C. Kagitcibasi, S.C. Choi and G. Yoon. (eds), *Individualism and Collectivism Theory, Method, and Application,* pp. 19–40. Thousand Oaks, CA: Sage.

Kirkman, B.L. and Shapiro, D.L. (2001a) The impact of cultural values on job satisfaction and organizational commitment in self-managing work teams: The mediating role of employee resistance. *Academy of Management Journal, 44,* 557–569.

Kirkman, B.L. and Shapiro, D.L. (2001b) The impact of employee cultural values on productivity, cooperation, and empowerment in self-managing work teams. *Journal of Cross-Cultural Psychology, 32,* 597–617.

Kitayama, S. and Cohen, D. (2007) *Handbook of Cultural Psychology.* New York: Guilford Press.

Kitayama, S., Ishii, K., Imada, T., Takemura, K. and Ramaswamy, J. (2006) Voluntary settlement and the spirit of independence: Evidence from Japan's 'Northern frontier.' *Journal of Personality and Social Psychology, 91,* 369–384.

Kleinman, A., Eisenberg, L. and Good, B. (1978) Culture, illness, and care: Clinical lessons from anthropological and cross-cultural research. *Annals of Internal Medicine, 88,* 251–258.

Kluckhohn, C. (1954) Culture and behavior. In G. Lindzey (ed.), *Handbook of Social Psychology, 2,* 921–976. Cambridge, MA: Addison-Wesley.

Kluckhohn, C. (1956) Toward a comparison of value emphasis in different cultures. In L.D. White (ed.), *The State of the Social Sciences,* pp. 116–132. Chicago: University of Chicago Press.

Kluckhohn, F.R. and Strodtbeck, F. (1961) *Variations in Value Orientation.* Evanston, IL: Row, Peterson & Co.

Kohn, M.K. (1969) *Class and Conformity.* Homewood, IL: Dorsey Press.

Kurman, J. (2001) Is self-enhancement related to modesty or to individualism-collectivism? A test with four Israeli groups. *Asian Journal of Social Psychology, 4,* 225–238.

Kurman, J. (2003) Why is self-enhancement low in certain collectivist cultures? *Journal of Cross-Cultural Psychology, 34,* 496–510.

Kurman, J. and Sriram, N. (2002). Interrelationships between vertical and horizontal collectivism, modesty, and self-enhancement. *Journal of Cross-Cultural Psychology, 33,* 71–86.

Lalwani, A.K., Shrum, L.J. and Chiu, C-Y. (2009) Motivated response style: The role of cultural values, regulatory focus, and self-consciousness in socially desirable responding. *Journal of Personality and Social Psychology, 96,* 870–882.

Landis, D. and Bhagat, R.S. (1996) *Handbook of Intercultural Training,* 2nd Edition. Thousand Oaks, CA: Sage.

Lee, A.Y., Aaker, J.L. and Gardner W.L. (2000) The pleasures and pains of distinct self-construals: The role of interdependence in regulatory focus. *Journal of Personality and Social Psychology, 78,* 1122–1134.

Lester, D. (1995) Individualism and divorce. *Psychological Reports, 76,* 258.

Leung, K. (1997) Negotiation and reward allocations across cultures. In P.C. Earley and M. Erez (eds), *New Perspectives on International Industrial and Organizational Psychology,* pp. 640–675. San Francisco, CA: Lexington Press.

Lillard, A. (1998) Ethnopsychologies: Cultural variations in theories of mind. *Psychological Bulletin, 123,* 3–32.

Lomax, A. and Berkowitz, N. (1972) The evolutionary taxonomy of culture. *Science, 177,* 228–239.

Markus, H. and Kitayama, S. (1991) Culture and self: Implications for cognition, emotion, and motivation. *Psychological Review, 98,* 225–253.

McBride, A. (1998) Television, individualism, and social capital. *Political Science and Politics, 31,* 542–555.

McKelvey, B. (1982) *Organizational Systematics: Taxonomy Classification and Evolution.* Los Angeles, CA: University of California Press.

Mead, M. (1967) *Cooperation and Competition Among Primitive Peoples.* Boston: Beacon Press.

Menon, T., Morris, M.W., Chiu, C.-Y. and Hong, Y.Y. (1999) Culture and the construal of agency: Attribution to individual versus group disposition. *Journal of Personal and Social Psychology, 76,* 701–717.

Mesquita, B. and Leu, J. (2007) Cultural psychology of emotion. In S. Kitayama and D. Cohen (eds), *Handbook of Cultural Psychology,* pp. 734–759. New York: Guilford Press.

Miller, J.G. (1984) Culture and the development of everyday social explanation. *Journal of Personality and Social Psychology, 46,* 961–978.

Miller, J.G. (1994) Cultural diversity in the morality of caring: Individually-orientated versus duty-orientated impersonal codes. *Cross-Cultural Research, 28,* 3–39.

Mills, J. and Clark, M.S. (1982) Exchange and communal relationships. In L. Wheeler (ed.), *Review of Personality and Social Psychology, 3,* 121–144.

Moorman, R.H. and Blakely, G.L. (1995) Individualism-collectivism as an individual difference predictor of organizational citizenship behavior. *Journal of Organizational Behavior, 16,* 127–142.

Morris, M.W., Ames, D.R. and Knowles, E. (2001) What we theorize when we theorize that we theorize: Examining the 'implicit theory' constructs from a cross-cultural perspective. In G. Moskowtiz (ed.), *Cognitive Social Psychology,* pp. 143–161. Mahwah, NJ: Lawrence Erlbaun Associates.

Morris, M.W. and Fu, H. (2001) How does culture influence negotiation? Dynamic constructivist analysis. *Social Cognition, 19,* 324–349.

Morris, M.W., Larrick, R.P. and Su, S.K. (1999) Misperceiving negotiation counterparts: When situational determined behaviors are attributed to personality traits. *Journal of Personality and Social Psychology, 77,* 52–67.

Morris, M.W. and Peng, K. (1994) Culture and cause: American and Chinese attributions for social and physical events. *Journal of Personality and Social Psychology, 67,* 949–971.

Murdock, P. and Provost, C. (1973) Measurement of cultural complexity. *Ethnography, 12,* 379–392.

Nelson, M.R. and Shavitt, S. (2002) Horizontal and vertical individualism and achievement values: A multimethod examination of Denmark and the United States. *Journal of Cross-Cultural Psychology, 33,* 439–458.

Nisbett, R. (2003) *The Geography of Thought.* New York: Free Press.

Nisbett, R.E. and Cohen, D. (1996) *Culture of Honor: The Psychology of Violence in the South.* Boulder, CO: Westview Press.

Nisbett, P.E., Peng, K., Choi, I. and Norenzayan, A. (2001) Culture and systems of thought: Holistic vs. analytic cognition. *Psychological Review, 108,* 291–310.

Oyserman, D. and Lee, S.W.S. (2008) Does culture influence what and how we think? Effects of priming individualism and collectivism. *Psychological Bulletin, 134,* 311–342.

Parsons, T. (1949) *Essays in Sociological Theory: Pure and Applied.* New York: Free Press.

Pelto, P.J. (1968) The difference between 'tight' and 'loose' societies. *Transaction,* April, 37–40.

Peng, K. and Nisbett, R.E. (1999) Culture, dialectics and reasoning about contradiction. *American Psychologist, 54,* 741–754.

Realo, A., Allik, J. and Valdi, M. (1997) The hierarchical structure of collectivism. *Journal of Research in Personality*, *31*, 93–116.

Redfield, R. (1941) *The Folk Culture of the Yucatan.* Chicago: University of Chicago Press.

Redfield, R. (1956) *Peasant Society and Culture: An Anthropological Approach to Civilization.* Chicago: University of Chicago Press.

Riesman, D., Glazer, N. and Denney, R. (1961) *The Lonely Crowd: A Study of the Changing American Character.* New Haven, CT: Yale University Press.

Sanchez Burks, J., Nisbett, R.E. and Yabarra, O. (2000) Cultural styles, relational schemas and prejudice against outgroups. *Journal of Personality and Social Psychology*, *79*, 174–189.

Schwartz, S.H. (1992) Universals in the content and structure of value: Theoretical advances and empirical tests in 20 countries. In M. Zanna (ed.), *Advances in Experimental Social Psychology, 25,* 1–66. New York: Academic Press.

Schwartz, S.H. (1994) Beyond individualism and collectivism. New cultural dimensions of values. In U. Kim, H.C Triandis, C. Kagitcibasi, S.C. Choi and G. Yoon (eds), *Individualism and Collectivism: Theory, Method, and Applications*, pp. 85–122. Newbury Park, CA: Sage.

Schwartz, S.H. and Bilsky, W. (1990) Toward a theory of universal structure and content of values: Extension and cross-cultural replications. *Journal of Personality and Social Psychology*, *58*, 878–891.

Shavitt, S. et al. (2011) Horizontal an vertical individualism and collectivism. In M. Gelfand, C. Chiu and Y. Hong (eds), Advances in Culture and Psychology, pp. 309–350. New York: Oxford University Press.

Shteynberg, G., Gelfand, M.J. and Kim, K. (2009) Peering into the 'Magnum Mysterium': The explanatory power of descriptive norms. *Journal of Cross-Cultural Psychology*, *40*, 46–69.

Shweder, R.A. (1990) Cultural psychology – what is it? In J.W. Stigler, R. Shweder and G. Herdt (eds), *Cultural Psychology*, pp. 1–46. Cambridge: Cambridge University Press.

Smith, P.B., Misumi, J., Tayeb, M., Peterson, M. and Bond, M.H. (1989) On the generality of leadership style measures across culture. *Journal of Occupational Psychology*, *62*, 97–100.

Smith, P.B. and Schwartz, S.H. (1997) Values. In J.W. Berry, C. Kagtchibasi, and M.H. Segall (eds), *Handbook of Cross-Cultural Psychology, Vol. 3,* 2nd Edition, pp. 77–119. Boston: Allyn & Bacon.

Soh, S. and Leong, F.T.L. (2002) Validity of vertical and horizontal individualism and collectivism in Singapore. *Journal of Cross-Cultural Psychology*, *33*, 3–15.

Streep, P. (1995) *Confucius: The Wisdom.* Boston: Bullfinch.

Toennies, F. (1957) *Gemeinschaft und Gesellschaft* [Community and society]. New Brunswick, NJ: Transaction Publishing.

Torrey, E.F. and Miller, J. (2001) *The Invisible Plague: The Rise of Mental Illness from 1750 to the Present.* New Brunswick, NJ: Rutgers University Press.

Tov, W. and Diener, E. (2007) Culture and subjective well-being. In S. Kitayama and D. Cohen, (eds), *Handbook of Cultural Psychology*, pp. 691–713. New York: Guilford Press.

Trafimow, D., Triandis, H.C. and Goto, S.G. (1991) Some tests of the distinction between the private and the collective self. *Journal of Personality and Social Psychology*, *60*, 649–655.

Triandis, H.C. (1964) Cultural influences upon cognitive processes. In L. Berkowitz (ed.), *Advances in Experimental Social Psychology*, pp. 1–48. New York: Academic Press.

Triandis, H.C. (1972). *The Analysis of Subjective Culture.* New York: Wiley.

Triandis, H.C. (1977) *Interpersonal Behavior.* Monterey: Brooks/Cole.

Triandis, H.C. (1980) Values, attitudes and interpersonal behavior. In H. Howe and M. Page (eds), *Nebraska Symposium on Motivation, 1979, 27,* 195–260. Lincoln, NE: University of Nebraska Press.

Triandis, H.C. (1989) The self and social behavior in differing cultural context. *Psychological Review*, *96*, 506–520.

Triandis, H.C. (1994) *Culture and Social Behavior.* New York: McGraw-Hill.

Triandis, H.C. (1995) *Individualism and Collectivism.* Boulder, CO: Westview Press.

Triandis, H.C. (2009a) Ecological determinants of cultural variations. In R.W. Wyer, C.-Y. Chiu and Y.Y. Hong (eds), *Understanding Culture: Theory, Research and Applications,* pp. 189–210. New York: Psychology Press.

Triandis, H.C. (2009b) *Fooling Ourselves: Self-deception in Politics, Religion, and Terrorism.* Westport, CT: Praeger.

Triandis, H.C., Bontempo, R., Betancourt, H., Bond, M., Leung, K., Brenes, A. and de Montmollin, G. (1986) The measurement of the etic aspects of individualism and collectivism across cultures. *Australian Journal of Psychology*, *38*, 257–267.

Triandis, H.C., Bontempo, R., Villareal, M.J., Asai, M. and Lucca, N. (1988) Individualism and collectivism: Cross-cultural perspectives on self-ingroup relationships. *Journal of Personality and Social Psychology*, *54*, 323–338.

Triandis, H.C., Chan, D.K.-S., Bhawuk, D.P.S., Iwao, S. and Sinha, J.B.P. (1995) Multimethod probes of allocentrism and idiocentrism. *International Journal of Psychology*, *30*, 461–480.

Triandis, H.C., Chen, X.-P. and Chan, D.K.-S. (1998) Scenarios for the measurement of collectivism and individualism. *Journal of Cross-Cultural Psychology*, *29*, 275–289.

Triandis, H.C. and Gelfand, M.J. (1998) Converging measurement of horizontal and vertical individualism and collectivism. *Journal of Personality and Social Psychology*, *74*, 118–128.

Triandis, H.C., Leung, K., Villareal, M.J. and Clack, F. (1985) Allocentric vs. idiocentric tendencies: Convergent and discriminant validation. *Journal of Research in Personality*, *19*, 395–415.

Triandis, H.C., McCusker, C., Betancourt, H., Iwao, S., Leung, K., Salazar, J.M. et al. (1993) An etic-emic analysis of individualism and collectivism. *Journal of Cross-Cultural Psychology*, *24*, 366–383.

Triandis, H.C., McCusker, C. and Hui, C.H. (1990) Multimethod probes of individualism and collectivism. *Journal of Personality and Social Psychology*, *59*, 1006–1020.

Van de Vliert, E. (2007) Climatoeconomic roots of survival versus self-expression culture. *Journal of Cross-Cultural Psychology*, *38*, 156–172.

Wagner, J.A., III. (1995) Studies of individualism-collectivism: Effects of cooperation in groups. *Academy of Management Journal*, *38*, 152–170.

Weldon, E. (1984) Deindividuation, interpersonal affect, and productivity in laboratory task groups. *Journal of Applied Social Psychology*, *14*, 469–485.

Zemba, Y., Young, M.J. and Morris, M.W. (2006) Blaming leaders for organizational accidents: Proxy logic in collective versus individual-agency cultures. *Organizational Behavior and Human Decision Processes*, *101*, 36–51.

Zola, I.K. (1966) Culture and symptoms: An analysis of patients presenting complaints. *American Sociological Review*, *3*, 615–630.

Zwier, S. (1998) Patterns of language use in individualistic and collectivistic cultures. Unpublished PhD dissertation, Free University of Amsterdam.

Name Index

Subject Index